The Merriam-Webster and

© PAWS

Mini Dictionary

Merriam-Webster, Incorporated
Springfield, Massachusetts, U.S.A.

Contents

Preface

The Merriam-Webster and Garfield Mini Dictionary presents a new approach to dictionary making. It combines the text of a Merriam-Webster dictionary with a collection of Jim Davis's Garfield cartoon strips carefully selected for the ways they illustrate the use of language. This dictionary is designed to meet the day-to-day needs of students with serious information about words combined with the humor and fun of the Garfield comic strips, which help illustrate meanings and usage, make the information more memorable, and make browsing the dictionary more enjoyable than ever.

The heart of this dictionary is the A-Z vocabulary section. Within this section, one finds the core of the English vocabulary; obsolete, rare, and highly technical words and obsolete meanings of common words have been omitted. It is thus a compilation of the most common everyday words and serves as a quick reference for a spelling, meaning, pronunciation, or end-of-line hyphenation point. Every definition in this section is based on examples of actual usage found in the citations in the Merriam-Webster files. In addition, hundreds of entries in this section are illustrated with examples of the word in use in a Garfield cartoon strip specially chosen by Merriam-Webster editors.

The A-Z section is followed by a list of common Abbreviations and other sections that students have found helpful. In addition, following these sections is a special section of Daffy Definitions, illustrating Garfield's distinctive and unconventional approach to defining words.

Just ahead of the A-Z section is a section on Using the Dictionary that should be read carefully by every user of this dictionary. An understanding of the information contained there will add to the satisfaction and pleasure that comes from looking into the pages of this dictionary. A list of the pronunciation symbols used in this dictionary comes just before the beginning of the A-Z section.

The Merriam-Webster and Garfield Mini Dictionary is based on and abridged from the larger *Merriam-Webster and Garfield Dictionary*. The idea for these books was conceived by Jim Davis, and their creation is the result of a collaboration between Jim Davis and Merriam-Webster, a company that has been publishing dictionaries for more than 150 years. Jim Davis and the editors of Merriam-Webster together offer this new book in the firm belief that it will serve well those who want an easy-to-read and fun-to-use reference for everyday English words.

Using the Dictionary

Main entries follow one another in alphabetical order. Centered periods within the entries show points at which a hyphen may be put when the word is broken at the end of a line.

Homographs (words spelled the same but having different meanings) are run in to a single main entry when they are closely related. Second and succeeding homographs are represented by a swung dash: ∼. Homographs of distinctly different origin (as ¹**date** and ²**date**) are given separate entries with preceding raised numerals.

Variant spellings that are quite common appear at the main entry following a comma (as **judg·ment, judge·ment**) and following other boldface entry words, such as inflected forms and run-on entries.

Inflected forms of nouns, verbs, adjectives, and adverbs are shown when they are irregular— as when requiring the dropping of a final *e* or changing a final *y* to *i* before the suffix: (as **waged; wag·ing** at **wage**) or when the form of the base word itself changes: (as **rode . . . ; rid·den** at **ride**)—or when there might be doubt about their spelling: (as *pl* **egos** at **ego**). They are given either in full (as **bet·ter . . . ; best** at **good**) or cut back to a convenient point of division (as **-ut·ed; -ut·ing** at **dis·trib·ute**). Common variants of inflected forms are shown even if they are regular (as **burst** or

burst·ed at **burst**). When the inflected forms of a verb involve no irregularity except the doubling of a final consonant, the double consonant is shown instead of full or cutback inflected forms (as *vb* **-gg-** at **lug**). A variant or inflected form whose alphabetical place is distant from the main entry is entered at its own place with a cross-reference in small capital letters to the main entry (as **hung** *past of* HANG).

Several other kinds of entries are also found in this dictionary. A **run-in entry** is a term related to a main entry that appears within a definition (as **small intestine** at **in·tes·tine**). It is set off by parentheses. Derivative words, made up usually of the main entry and a common word element, such as a suffix, are shown as **undefined run-on entries** following all definitions of a main entry. These are set off by a dash (as **—gar·den·er** at **gar·den**). The meaning of an undefined run-on entry can be inferred from the meaning of the main entry where it appears and that of the added word element, shown elsewhere in the book. A **run-on phrase** is a group of two or more words having the main entry as a major element and having a special meaning of its own (as **in force** at **force** or **look after** at **look**). Run-on phrases are always defined.

Lists of undefined words formed by the addition of a common English prefix to a word entered in the dictionary and having meanings that can be inferred from the meaning of the root word and that of the prefix will be found at entries for the following prefixes: *anti-, bi-, co-, counter-, extra-, hyper-, in-, inter-, mini-, multi-, non-, over-, post-, pre-, re-, self-, sub-, super-, un-,* and *vice-*.

Pronunciation information is either given explicitly or implied for every entry in the dictionary. Pronunciation respellings are placed within reversed slanted lines (as \gē'ämətrē\ at **ge·om·e·try**). Where the pronunciation is not indicated at a particular entry, or is indicated in a cutback form, the full pronunciation is to be inferred from an earlier indicated pronunciation. A full list of the pronunciation symbols used is shown on the page following this section.

The grammatical function of entry words is indicated by an italic **functional label** (as *vb, n,* or *prefix*).

Hyphens that are a fixed part of hyphenated compounds (such as *self-conscious*) are converted to a special "double hyphen" (=) when the compound appears in lightface type and that hyphen comes at the end of a line in this dictionary. This indicates to you that the hyphen is to be retained when the word is not at the end of a line. Fixed hyphens in boldface entry words are shown as short boldface dashes, which are a bit larger than ordinary hyphens. These short dashes or long hyphens in boldface words are retained at the end of a line in this dictionary.

Guide words are used at the top of pages to indicate the range of entries on those pages. In choosing guide words for a page, we select the alphabetically first and last spelled-out boldface words or phrases on that page. This means that any boldface entry—main entry, variant spelling, inflected form, run-in or run-on entry—can be used as a guide word. Please keep this in mind if the word used as a guide word does not happen to be the first or last main entry on the page. The guide words themselves are in alphabetical order throughout the book, so occasionally it has been necessary to modify this rule. When the alphabetically last entry on one page would come later than the alphabetically first entry on the following page, a different word is chosen as guide word. On pages that contain a substantial number of undefined words following a prefix entry, that prefix may be used as the first or last guide word.

All **abbreviations** used in this book are listed, along with a number of other common abbreviations, in a special section immediately following the dictionary proper.

Pronunciation Symbols

ə	banana, collide, abut; raised \ᵊ\ in \ᵊl, ᵊn\ as in battle, cotton; in \lᵊ, mᵊ, rᵊ\ as in French table, prisme, titre	œ	French bœuf, German Hölle
'ə, ˌə	humbug, abut	œ̄	French feu, German Höhle
ər	operation, further	ȯi	toy, sawing
a	map, patch	p	pepper, lip
ā	day, fate	r	rarity
ä	bother, cot, father	s	source, less
à	father as pronounced by those who do not rhyme it with *bother*	sh	shy, mission
aù	now, out	t	tie, attack
b	baby, rib	th	thin, ether
ch	chin, catch	<u>th</u>	then, either
d	did, adder	ü	boot, few \'fyü\
e	set, red	u̇	put, pure \'pyu̇r\
ē	beat, nosebleed, easy	ue	German füllen
f	fifty, cuff	ue̅	French rue, German fühlen
g	go, big	v	vivid, give
h	hat, ahead	w	we, away
hw	whale	y	yard, cue \'kyü\; raised \ʸ\ indicates that a preceding \l\, \n\, or \w\ is modified by the placing of the tongue tip against the lower front teeth, as in French *digne* \dēnʸ\
i	tip, banish		
ī	site, buy		
j	job, edge		
k	kin, cook		
k̲	German ich, Buch	z	zone, raise
l	lily, cool	zh	vision, pleasure
m	murmur, dim	\	slant line used in pairs to mark the beginning and end of a transcription
n	nine, own; raised \ⁿ\ indicates that a preceding vowel or diphthong is pronounced through both nose and mouth, as in French *bon* \bōⁿ\		
		'	mark at the beginning of a syllable that has primary (strongest) stress: \'penmənˌship\
ŋ	sing, singer, finger, ink		
ō	bone, hollow	ˌ	mark at the beginning of a syllable that has secondary (next-strongest) stress: \'penmənˌship\
ȯ	saw, cork		

A

¹a \'ā\ *n, pl* **a's** *or* **as** \'āz\ : 1st letter of the alphabet

²a \ə, 'ā\ *indefinite article* : one or some — used to indicate an unspecified or unidentified individual

aard·vark \'ärd,värk\ *n* : ant-eating African mammal

aback \ə'bak\ *adv* : by surprise

aba·cus \'abəkəs\ *n, pl* **aba·ci** \'abə,sī, -,kē\ *or* **aba·cus·es** : calculating instrument using rows of beads

abaft \ə'baft\ *adv* : toward or at the stern

ab·a·lo·ne \,abə'lōnē\ *n* : large edible shellfish

¹aban·don \ə'bandən\ *vb* : give up without intent to reclaim — **aban·don·ment** *n*

²abandon *n* : thorough yielding to impulses

aban·doned \ə'bandənd\ *adj* : morally unrestrained

abase \ə'bās\ *vb* **abased; abas·ing** : lower in dignity — **abase·ment** *n*

abash \ə'bash\ *vb* : embarrass — **abashment** *n*

abate \ə'bāt\ *vb* **abat·ed; abat·ing** : decrease or lessen

abate·ment \ə'bātmənt\ *n* : tax reduction

ab·at·toir \'abə,twär\ *n* : slaughterhouse

ab·bess \'abəs\ *n* : head of a convent

ab·bey \'abē\ *n, pl* **-beys** : monastery or convent

ab·bot \'abət\ *n* : head of a monastery

ab·bre·vi·ate \ə'brēvē,āt\ *vb* **-at·ed; -at·ing** : shorten — **ab·bre·vi·a·tion** \ə,brēvē'āshən\ *n*

ab·di·cate \'abdi,kāt\ *vb* **-cat·ed; -ca·ting** : renounce — **ab·di·ca·tion** \,abdi'kāshən\ *n*

ab·do·men \'abdəmən, ab'dōmən\ *n* **1** : body area between chest and pelvis **2** : hindmost part of an insect — **ab·dom·i·nal** \ab'dämən²l\ *adj* — **ab·dom·i·nal·ly** *adv*

ab·duct \ab'dəkt\ *vb* : kidnap — **ab·duc·tion** \-'dəkshən\ *n* — **ab·duc·tor** \-tər\ *n*

abed \ə'bed\ *adv or adj* : in bed

ab·er·ra·tion \,abə'rāshən\ *n* : deviation or distortion — **ab·er·rant** \a'berənt\ *adj*

abet \ə'bet\ *vb* **-tt-** : incite or encourage — **abet·tor, abet·ter** \-ər\ *n*

abey·ance \ə'bāəns\ *n* : state of inactivity

ab·hor \əb'hór, ab-\ *vb* **-rr-** : hate — **ab·hor·rence** \-əns\ *n* — **ab·hor·rent** \-ənt\ *adj*

abide \ə'bīd\ *vb* **abode** \-'bōd\ *or* **abid·ed; abid·ing 1** : endure **2** : remain, last, or reside

ab·ject \'ab,jekt, ab'-\ *adj* : low in spirit or hope — **ab·jec·tion** \ab-'jekshən\ *n* — **ab·ject·ly** *adv* — **ab·ject·ness** *n*

ab·jure \ab'júr\ *vb* **1** : renounce **2** : abstain from — **ab·ju·ra·tion** \,abjə'rāshən\ *n*

ablaze \ə'blāz\ *adj or adv* : on fire

able \'ābəl\ *adj* **abler** \-blər\; **ablest** \-bləst\ **1** : having sufficient power, skill, or resources **2** : skilled or efficient — **abil·i·ty** \ə'bilətē\ *n* — **ably** \'āblē\ *adv*

-able, -ible \əbəl\ *adj suffix* **1** : capable of, fit for, or worthy of **2** : tending, given, or liable to

ab·lu·tion \ə'blüshən, a'blü-\ *n* : washing of one's body

ab·ne·gate \'abni,gāt\ *vb* **-gat·ed; -gat·ing 1** : relinquish **2** : renounce — **ab·ne·ga·tion** \,abni'gāshən\ *n*

ab·nor·mal \ab'nórməl\ *adj* : deviating from the normal or average — **ab·nor·mal·i·ty** \,abnər-'mal-ətē, -nór-\ *n* — **ab·nor·mal·ly** *adv*

aboard \ə'bōrd\ *adv* : on, onto, or within a car, ship, or aircraft ~ *prep* : on or within

abode \ə'bōd\ *n* : residence

abol·ish \ə'bälish\ *vb* : do away with — **ab·o·li·tion** \,abə'lishən\ *n*

abom·i·na·ble \ə'bämənəbəl\ *adj* : thoroughly unpleasant or revolting

abom·i·nate \ə'bämə,nāt\ *vb* **-nat·ed; -nat·ing** : hate — **abom·i·na·tion** \ə,bämə'nāshən\ *n*

ab·orig·i·nal \ˌabəˈrijənəl\ *adj* **1** : original **2** : primitive

ab·orig·i·ne \-ˈrijənē\ *n* : original inhabitant

abort \əˈbȯrt\ *vb* : terminate prematurely — **abor·tive** \-ˈbȯrtiv\ *adj*

abor·tion \əˈbȯrshən\ *n* : spontaneous or induced termination of pregnancy

abound \əˈbau̇nd\ *vb* : be plentiful

about \əˈbau̇t\ *adv* : around ~ *prep* **1** : on every side of **2** : on the verge of **3** : having as a subject

above \əˈbəv\ *adv* : in or to a higher place ~ *prep* **1** : in or to a higher place than **2** : more than

above·board *adv or adj* : without deception

abrade \əˈbrād\ *vb* **abrad·ed; abrad·ing** : wear away by rubbing — **abra·sion** \-ˈbrāzhən\ *n*

abra·sive \əˈbrāsiv\ *n* : substance for grinding, smoothing, or polishing — *adj* **1** : tending to abrade **2** : causing irritation — **abra·sive·ly** *adv* — **abra·sive·ness** *n*

abreast \əˈbrest\ *adv or adj* **1** : side by side **2** : up to a standard or level

abridge \əˈbrij\ *vb* **abridged; abridg·ing** : shorten or condense — **abridg·ment, abridge·ment** *n*

abroad \əˈbrȯd\ *adv or adj* **1** : over a wide area **2** : outside one's country

ab·ro·gate \ˈabrəgāt\ *vb* **-gat·ed; -gat·ing** : annul or revoke — **ab·ro·ga·tion** \ˌabrəˈgāshən\ *n*

abrupt \əˈbrəpt\ *adj* **1** : sudden **2** : so quick as to seem rude — **abrupt·ly** *adv*

ab·scess \ˈabˌses\ *n* : collection of pus surrounded by inflamed tissue — **ab·scessed** \-ˌsest\ *adj*

ab·scond \abˈskänd\ *vb* : run away and hide

ab·sent \ˈabsənt\ *adj* : not present ~ **ab·sent** \abˈsent\ *vb* : keep oneself away — **ab·sence** \ˈabsəns\ *n* — **absen·tee** \ˌabsənˈtē\ *n*

ab·sent·mind·ed \ˌabsəntˈmīndəd\ *adj* : unaware of one's surroundings or action — **ab·sent·mind·ed·ly** *adv* — **ab·sent·mind·ed·ness** *n*

ab·so·lute \ˈabsəˌlüt, ˌabsəˈ-\ *adj* **1** : pure **2** : free from restriction **3** : definite — **ab·so·lute·ly** *adv*

ab·so·lu·tion \ˌabsəˈlüshən\ *n* : remission of sins

ab·solve \əbˈzälv, -ˈsälv\ *vb* **-solved; -solv·ing** : set free of the consequences of guilt

ab·sorb \əbˈsȯrb, -ˈzȯrb\ *vb* **1** : suck up or take in as a sponge does **2** : engage (one's attention) — **ab·sor·ben·cy** \-ˈsȯrbənsē, -ˈzȯr-\ *n* — **ab·sor·bent** \-bənt\ *adj or n* — **ab·sorb·ing** *adj* — **ab·sorb·ing·ly** *adv*

ab·sorp·tion \əbˈsȯrpshən, -ˈzȯrp-\ *n* : process of absorbing — **ab·sorp·tive** \-tiv-\ *adj*

ab·stain \əbˈstān\ *vb* : refrain from doing something — **ab·stain·er** *n* — **ab·sten·tion** \-ˈstenchən\ *n* — **ab·sti·nence** \ˈabstənəns\ *n*

ab·ste·mi·ous \abˈstēmēəs\ *adj* : sparing in use of food or drink — **ab·ste·mi·ous·ly** *adv* — **ab·ste·mi·ous·ness** *n*

ab·stract \abˈstrakt, ˈabˌ-\ *adj* **1** : expressing a quality apart from an object **2** : not representing something specific ~ \ˈabˌ-\ *n* : summary ~ \abˈ-, ˈabˌ-\ *vb* **1** : remove or separate **2** : make an abstract of — **ab·stract·ly** *adv* — **ab·stract·ness** *n*

ab·strac·tion \abˈstrakshən\ *n* **1** : act of abstracting **2** : abstract idea or work of art

ab·struse \əbˈstrüs, ab-\ *adj* : hard to understand — **ab·struse·ly** *adv* — **ab·struse·ness** *n*

ab·surd \əbˈsȯrd, -ˈzərd\ *adj* : ridiculous or unreasonable — **ab·sur·di·ty** \-ətē\ *n* — **ab·surd·ly** *adv*

abun·dant \əˈbəndənt\ *adj* : more than enough — **abun·dance** \-dəns\ *n* — **abun·dant·ly** *adv*

◆ **abuse** \əˈbyüz\ *vb* **abused; abus·ing 1** : misuse **2** : mistreat **3** : attack with words ~ \-ˈbyüs\ *n* **1** : corrupt practice **2** : improper use **3** : mistreatment **4** : coarse and insulting speech — **abus·er** *n* — **abu·sive** \-ˈbyüsiv\ *adj* — **abu·sive·ly** *adv* — **abu·sive·ness** *n*

abut \əˈbət\ *vb* **-tt-** : touch along a border — **abut·ter** *n*

abut·ment \əˈbətmənt\ *n* : part of a bridge that supports weight

abys·mal \əˈbizməl\ *adj* **1** : immeasurably deep **2** : wretched — **abys·mal·ly** *adv*

abyss \ə'bis\ *n* : immeasurably deep gulf

-ac \ˌak\ *n suffix* : one affected with

aca·cia \ə'kāshə\ *n* : leguminous tree or shrub

ac·a·dem·ic \ˌakə'demik\ *adj* 1 : relating to schools or colleges 2 : theoretical — **academic** *n* — **ac·a·dem·i·cal·ly** \-iklē\ *adv*

acad·e·my \ə'kadəmē\ *n, pl* **-mies** 1 : private high school 2 : society of scholars or artists

acan·thus \ə'kanthəs\ *n, pl* **acan·thus** 1 : prickly Mediterranean herb 2 : ornament representing acanthus leaves

ac·cede \ak'sēd\ *vb* **-ced·ed; -ced·ing** 1 : become a party to an agreement 2 : express approval 3 : enter upon an office

ac·cel·er·ate \ik'selə,rāt, ak-\ *vb* **-at·ed; -at·ing** 1 : bring about earlier 2 : speed up — **ac·cel·er·a·tion** \-ˌselə'rāshən\ *n*

ac·cel·er·a·tor \ik'selə,rātər, ak-\ *n* : pedal for controlling the speed of a motor vehicle

ac·cent \'ak,sent\ *n* 1 : distinctive manner of pronunciation 2 : prominence given to one syllable of a word 3 : mark (as ´, `, ˆ) over a vowel in writing or printing to indicate pronunciation ~ \'ak,-, ak'-\ *vb* : emphasize — **ac·cen·tu·al** \ak'senchəwəl\ *adj*

ac·cen·tu·ate \ak'senchə,wāt\ *vb* **-at·ed; -at·ing** : stress or show off by a contrast — **ac·cen·tu·a·tion** \-ˌsenchə'wāshən\ *n*

ac·cept \ik'sept, ak-\ *vb* 1 : receive willingly 2 : agree to — **ac·cept·abil·i·ty** \ik,septə'bilətē, ak-\ *n* — **ac·cept·able** \-'septəbəl\ *adj* — **ac·cep·tance** \-'septəns\ *n*

ac·cess \'ak,ses\ *n* : capability or way of approaching — **ac·ces·si-**

bil·i·ty \ik,sesə'bilətē, ak-\ *n* — **ac·ces·si·ble** \-'sesəbəl\ *adj*

ac·ces·sion \ik'seshən, ak-\ *n* 1 : something added 2 : act of taking office

ac·ces·so·ry \ik'sesərē, ak-\ *n, pl* **-ries** 1 : nonessential addition 2 : one guilty of aiding a criminal — **accessory** *adj*

ac·ci·dent \'aksədənt\ *n* 1 : event occurring by chance or unintentionally 2 : chance — **ac·ci·den·tal** \ˌaksə'dent²l\ *adj* — **ac·ci·den·tal·ly** *adv*

ac·claim \ə'klām\ *vb or n* : praise

ac·cla·ma·tion \ˌaklə'māshən\ *n* 1 : eager applause 2 : unanimous vote

ac·cli·mate \'aklə,māt, ə'klīmət\ *vb* **-mat·ed; -mat·ing** : acclimatize — **ac·cli·ma·tion** \ˌaklə'māshən, -ˌklī-\ *n*

ac·cli·ma·tize \ə'klīmə,tīz\ *vb* **-tized; -tiz·ing** : accustom to a new climate or situation — **ac·cli·ma·ti·za·tion** \-ˌklīmətə'zāshən\ *n*

ac·co·lade \'akə,lād\ *n* : expression of praise

ac·com·mo·date \ə'kämə,dāt\ *vb* **-dat·ed; -dat·ing** 1 : adapt 2 : provide with something needed 3 : hold without crowding

ac·com·mo·da·tion \ə,kämə'dāshən\ *n* 1 : quarters — usu. pl. 2 : act of accommodating

ac·com·pa·ny \ə'kəmpənē\ *vb* **-nied; -ny·ing** 1 : go or occur with 2 : play supporting music — **ac·com·pa·ni·ment** \-nəmənt\ *n* — **ac·com·pa·nist** \-nist\ *n*

ac·com·plice \ə'kämpləs, -'kəm-\ *n* : associate in crime

ac·com·plish \ə'kämplish, -'kəm-\ *vb* : do, fulfill, or bring about — **ac·com·plished** *adj* — **ac·com·plish·er** *n* — **ac·com·plish·ment** *n*

ac·cord \ə'kȯrd\ vb 1 : grant 2 : agree ~ n 1 : agreement 2 : willingness to act — **ac·cor·dance** \-'kȯrd°ns\ n — **ac·cor·dant** \-°nt\ adj

ac·cord·ing·ly \ə'kȯrdiŋlē\ adv : consequently

according to prep 1 : in conformity with 2 : as stated by

ac·cor·di·on \ə'kȯrdēən\ n : keyboard instrument with a bellows and reeds ~ adj : folding like an accordion bellows — **ac·cor·di·on·ist** \-nist\ n

ac·cost \ə'kȯst\ vb : approach and speak to esp. aggressively

ac·count \ə'kaúnt\ n 1 : statement of business transactions 2 : credit arrangement with a vendor 3 : report 4 : worth 5 : sum deposited in a bank ~ vb : give an explanation

ac·count·able \ə'kaúntəbəl\ adj : responsible — **ac·count·abil·i·ty** \-ˌkaúntə'bilətē\ n

ac·coun·tant \ə'kaúnt°nt\ n : one skilled in accounting — **ac·coun·tan·cy** \-°nsē\ n

ac·count·ing \ə'kaúntiŋ\ n : financial record keeping

ac·cou·tre, **ac·cou·ter** \ə'kütər\ vb -tred or -tered; -tring or -ter·ing \-'kütəriŋ, -'kütriŋ\ : equip

ac·cou·tre·ment, **ac·cou·ter·ment** \ə'kütrəmənt, -'kütər-\ n 1 : accessory item — usu. pl. 2 : identifying characteristic

ac·cred·it \ə'kredət\ vb 1 : approve officially 2 : attribute — **ac·cred·i·ta·tion** \-ˌkredə'tāshən\ n

ac·crue \ə'krü\ vb -crued; -cru·ing : be added by periodic growth — **ac·cru·al** \-əl\ n

ac·cu·mu·late \ə'kyümyəˌlāt\ vb -lat·ed; -lat·ing : collect or pile up — **ac·cu·mu·la·tion** \-ˌkyümyə'lāshən\ n — **ac·cu·mu·la·tor** \-'kyümyəˌlātər\ n

ac·cu·rate \'akyərət\ adj : free from error — **ac·cu·ra·cy** \-rəsē\ n — **ac·cu·rate·ly** adv — **ac·cu·rate·ness** n

ac·cursed \ə'kərst, -'kərsəd\ **ac·curst** \ə'kərst\ adj 1 : being under a curse 2 : damnable

ac·cuse \ə'kyüz\ vb -cused; -cus·ing : charge with an offense — **ac·cu·sa·tion** \ˌakyə'zāshən\ n — **ac·cus·er** n

ac·cused \ə'kyüzd\ n, pl -cused : defendant in a criminal case

ac·cus·tom \ə'kəstəm\ vb : make familiar through use or experience

ace \'ās\ n : one that excels

acer·bic \ə'sərbik, a-\ adj : sour or biting in temper, mood, or tone

acet·amin·o·phen \əˌsētə'minəfən\ n : pain reliever

ac·e·tate \'asəˌtāt\ n : fabric or plastic derived from acetic acid

ace·tic acid \ə'sētik-\ n : acid found in vinegar

acet·y·lene \ə'set°lən, -°lˌēn\ n : colorless gas used as a fuel in welding

ache \'āk\ vb ached; ach·ing 1 : suffer a dull persistent pain 2 : yearn — **ache** n

achieve \ə'chēv\ vb achieved; achiev·ing : gain by work or effort — **achieve·ment** n — **achiev·er** n

ac·id \'asəd\ adj 1 : sour or biting to the taste 2 : sharp in manner 3 : of or relating to an acid ~ n : sour water-soluble chemical compound that reacts with a base to form a salt — **acid·ic** \ə'sidik\ adj — **acid·i·fy** \ə'sidəˌfī\ vb — **acid·i·ty** \-ətē\ n — **acid·ly** adv

ac·knowl·edge \ik'nälij, ak-\ vb -edged; -edg·ing 1 : admit as true 2 : admit the authority of 3 : express thanks for — **ac·knowl·edg·ment** n

ac·me \'akmē\ n : highest point

ac·ne \'aknē\ n : skin disorder marked esp. by pimples

ac·o·lyte \'akəˌlīt\ n : assistant to a member of clergy in a religious service

acorn \'āˌkȯrn, -kərn\ n : nut of the oak

acous·tic \ə'küstik\ adj : relating to hearing or sound — **acous·ti·cal** \-stikəl\ adj — **acous·ti·cal·ly** \-klē\ adv

acous·tics \ə'küstiks\ n sing or pl 1 : science of sound 2 : qualities in a room that affect how sound is heard

ac·quaint \ə'kwānt\ vb 1 : inform 2 : make familiar

ac·quain·tance \ə'kwānt°ns\ n 1 : personal knowledge 2 : person with whom one is acquainted — **ac·quain·tance·ship** n

ac·qui·esce \ˌakwē'es\ vb -esced; -esc·ing : consent or submit — **ac·qui·es·cence** \-'es°ns\ n — **ac·qui-**

es·cent \-ᵊnt\ *adj* — **ac·qui·es·cent·ly** *adv*

ac·quire \ə'kwīr\ *vb* **-quired; -quir·ing** : gain

ac·qui·si·tion \,akwə'zishən\ *n* : a gaining or something gained — **ac·qui·si·tive** \ə'kwizətiv\ *adj*

ac·quit \ə'kwit\ *vb* **-tt-** 1 : pronounce not guilty 2 : conduct (oneself) usu. well — **ac·quit·tal** \-ᵊl\ *n*

acre \'ākər\ *n* 1 *pl* : lands 2 : 4840 square yards

acre·age \'ākərij\ *n* : area in acres

ac·rid \'akrəd\ *adj* : sharp and biting — **acrid·i·ty** \a'kridətē, ə-\ *n* — **ac·rid·ly** *adv* — **ac·rid·ness** *n*

ac·ri·mo·ny \'akrə,mōnē\ *n, pl* **-nies** : harshness of language or feeling — **ac·ri·mo·ni·ous** \,akrə'mōnēəs\ *adj* — **ac·ri·mo·ni·ous·ly** *adv*

ac·ro·bat \'akrə,bat\ *n* : performer of tumbling feats — **ac·ro·bat·ic** \,akrə'batik\ *adj*

across \ə'krós\ *adv* : to or on the opposite side — *prep* 1 : to or on the opposite side of 2 : on so as to cross

acryl·ic \ə'krilik\ *n* 1 : plastic used for molded parts or in paints 2 : synthetic textile fiber

◆ **act** \'akt\ *n* 1 : thing done 2 : law 3 : main division of a play ~ *vb* 1 : perform in a play 2 : conduct oneself 3 : operate 4 : produce an effect

ac·tion \'akshən\ *n* 1 : legal proceeding 2 : manner or method of performing 3 : activity 4 : thing done over a period of time or in stages 5 : combat 6 : events of a literary plot 7 : operating mechanism

ac·ti·vate \'aktə,vāt\ *vb* **-vat·ed; -vat·ing** : make active or reactive — **ac·ti·va·tion** \,aktə'vāshən\ *n*

ac·tive \'aktiv\ *adj* 1 : causing action or change 2 : lively, vigorous,

or energetic 3 : erupting or likely to erupt 4 : now in operation — **active** *n* — **ac·tive·ly** *adv*

ac·tiv·i·ty \ak'tivətē\ *n, pl* **-ties** 1 : quality or state of being active 2 : what one is actively doing

ac·tor \'aktər\ *n* : one that acts

ac·tress \'aktrəs\ *n* : woman who acts in plays

ac·tu·al \'akchəwəl\ *adj* : really existing — **ac·tu·al·i·ty** \,akchə'walətē\ *n* — **ac·tu·al·iza·tion** \,akchəwələ'zāshən\ *n* — **ac·tu·al·ize** \'akchəwə,līz\ *vb* — **ac·tu·al·ly** *adv*

ac·tu·ary \'akchə,werē\ *n, pl* **-ar·ies** : one who calculates insurance risks and premiums — **ac·tu·ar·i·al** \akchə'werēəl\ *adj*

ac·tu·ate \'akchə,wāt\ *vb* **-at·ed; -at·ing** : put into action — **ac·tu·a·tor** \-,wātər\ *n*

acu·men \ə'kyümən\ *n* : mental keenness

acu·punc·ture \'akyù,pəŋkchər\ *n* : treatment by puncturing the body with needles — **acu·punc·tur·ist** \,akyù'pəŋkchərist\ *n*

acute \ə'kyüt\ *adj* **acut·er; acut·est** 1 : sharp 2 : containing less than 90 degrees 3 : mentally alert 4 : severe — **acute·ly** *adv* — **acute·ness** *n*

ad \'ad\ *n* : advertisement

ad·age \'adij\ *n* : old familiar saying

ad·a·mant \'adəmənt, -,mant\ *adj* : insistent — **ad·a·mant·ly** *adv*

adapt \ə'dapt\ *vb* : adjust to be suitable for a new use or condition — **adapt·abil·i·ty** \ə,daptə'bilətē\ *n* — **adapt·able** *adj* — **ad·ap·ta·tion** \,ad,ap'tāshən, -əp-\ *n* — **adapter** *n* — **adap·tive** \ə'daptiv\ *adj*

add \'ad\ *vb* 1 : join to something else so as to increase in amount 2 : say further 3 : find a sum — **ad·di·tion** \ə'dishən\ *n*

ad·der \'adər\ *n* **1** : poisonous European snake **2** : No. American snake

ad·dict \'adikt\ *n* : one who is psychologically or physiologically dependent (as on a drug) ~ \ə-'dikt\ *vb* : cause to become an addict — **ad·dic·tion** \ə'dikshən\ *n* — **ad·dic·tive** \-'diktiv\ *adj*

ad·di·tion·al \ə'dishənəl\ *adj* : existing as a result of adding — **ad·di·tion·al·ly** *adv*

ad·di·tive \'adətiv\ *n* : substance added to another

ad·dle \'ad³l\ *vb* -dled; -dling : confuse

ad·dress \ə'dres\ *vb* **1** : direct one's remarks to **2** : mark an address on ~ \ə'dres, 'ad,res\ *n* **1** : formal speech **2** : place where a person may be reached or mail may be delivered

ad·duce \ə'düs, -'dyüs\ *vb* -duced; -duc·ing : offer as proof

ad·e·noid \'ad,nóid, -ᵊnóid\ *n* : enlarged tissue near the opening of the nose into the throat — usu. pl. — adenoid, **ad·e·noi·dal** \-əl\ *adj*

adept \ə'dept\ *adj* : highly skilled — **adept·ly** *adv* — **adept·ness** *n*

ad·e·quate \'adikwət\ *adj* : good or plentiful enough — **ad·e·qua·cy** \-kwəsē\ *n* — **ad·e·quate·ly** *adv*

ad·here \ad'hir, əd-\ *vb* -hered; -her·ing **1** : remain loyal **2** : stick fast — **ad·her·ence** \-'hirəns\ *n* — **ad·her·ent** \-ənt\ *adj or n*

ad·he·sion \ad'hēzhən, əd-\ *n* : act or state of adhering

ad·he·sive \-'hēsiv, -ziv\ *adj* : tending to adhere ~ *n* : adhesive substance

adieu \ə'dü, -'dyü\ *n, pl* **adieus** *or* **adieux** \-'düz, -'dyüz\ : farewell

ad·ja·cent \ə'jās³nt\ *adj* : situated near or next

ad·jec·tive \'ajiktiv\ *n* : word that serves as a modifier of a noun — **ad·jec·ti·val** \,ajik'tīvəl\ *adj* — **ad·jec·ti·val·ly** *adv*

ad·join \ə'jóin\ *vb* : be next to

ad·journ \ə'jərn\ *vb* : end a meeting — **ad·journ·ment** *n*

ad·judge \ə'jəj\ *vb* -judged; -judg·ing **1** : think or pronounce to be **2** : award by judicial decision

ad·ju·di·cate \ə'jüdi,kāt\ *vb* -cat·ed; -cat·ing : settle judicially — **ad·ju·di·ca·tion** \ə,jüdi'kāshən\

ad·junct \'aj,əŋkt\ *n* : something joined or added but not essential

ad·just \ə'jəst\ *vb* : fix, adapt, or set right — **ad·just·able** *adj* — **ad·just·er, ad·jus·tor** \-'jəstər\ *n* — **ad·just·ment** \-mənt\ *n*

ad·ju·tant \'ajətənt\ *n* : aide esp. to a commanding officer

ad–lib \'ad'lib\ *vb* -bb- : speak without preparation — **ad–lib** *n or adj*

ad·min·is·ter \əd'minəstər\ *vb* **1** : manage **2** : give out esp. in doses — **ad·min·is·tra·ble** \-strəbəl\ *adj* — **ad·min·is·trant** \-strənt\ *n*

ad·min·is·tra·tion \əd,minə'strāshən, ad-\ *n* **1** : process of managing **2** : persons responsible for managing — **ad·min·is·tra·tive** \əd'minə,strātiv\ *adj* — **ad·min·is·tra·tive·ly** *adv*

ad·min·is·tra·tor \əd'minə,strātər\ *n* : one that manages

ad·mi·ra·ble \'admərəbəl\ *adj* : worthy of admiration — **ad·mi·ra·bly** \-blē\ *adv*

ad·mi·ral \'admərəl\ *n* : commissioned officer in the navy ranking next below a fleet admiral

ad·mire \əd'mīr\ *vb* -mired; -mir·ing : have high regard for — **ad·mi·ra·tion** \,admə'rāshən\ *n* — **ad·mir·er** *n* — **ad·mir·ing·ly** *adv*

ad·mis·si·ble \əd'misəbəl\ *adj* : that can be permitted — **ad·mis·si·bil·i·ty** \-,misə'bilətē\ *n*

ad·mis·sion \əd'mishən\ *n* **1** : act of admitting **2** : admittance or a fee paid for this **3** : acknowledgment of a fact

ad·mit \əd'mit\ *vb* -tt- **1** : allow to enter **2** : permit **3** : recognize as genuine — **ad·mit·ted·ly** *adv*

ad·mit·tance \əd'mit³ns\ *n* : permission to enter

ad·mix·ture \ad'mikschər\ *n* **1** : thing added in mixing **2** : mixture

ad·mon·ish \ad'mänish\ *vb* : rebuke — **ad·mon·ish·ment** \-mənt\ *n* — **ad·mo·ni·tion** \,admə'nishən\ *n* — **ad·mon·i·to·ry** \ad'mänə,tōrē\ *adj*

ado \ə'dü\ *n* **1** : fuss **2** : trouble

ado·be \ə'dōbē\ *n* : sun-dried building brick

ad·o·les·cence \,ad³l'es³ns\ *n* : period of growth between childhood and maturity — **ad·o·les·cent** \-³nt\ *adj or n*

adopt \ə'däpt\ *vb* **1** : take (a child of

other parents) as one's own child 2 : take up and practice as one's own — **adop·tion** \-'däpshən\ *n*

◆ **adore** \ə'dȯr\ *vb* adored; adoring 1 : worship 2 : be extremely fond of — **ador·able** *adj* — **adorably** *adv* — **ad·o·ra·tion** \ˌadə-'rāshən\ *n*

adorn \ə'dȯrn\ *vb* : decorate with ornaments — **adorn·ment** *n*

adrift \ə'drift\ *adv or adj* 1 : afloat without motive power or moorings 2 : without guidance or purpose

adroit \ə'drȯit\ *adj* : dexterous or shrewd — **adroit·ly** *adv* — **adroit·ness** *n*

adult \ə'dəlt, 'ad,əlt\ *adj* : fully developed and mature ~ *n* : grown-up person — **adult·hood** *n*

adul·ter·ate \ə'dəltəˌrāt\ *vb* -ated; -at·ing : make impure by mixture — **adul·ter·a·tion** \-ˌdəltə-'rāshən\ *n*

adul·tery \ə'dəltərē\ *n, pl* -ter·ies : sexual unfaithfulness of a married person — **adul·ter·er** \-tərər\ *n* — **adul·ter·ess** \-tərəs\ *n* — **adul·ter·ous** \-tərəs\ *adj*

ad·vance \əd'vans\ *vb* -vanced; -vancing 1 : bring or move forward 2 : promote 3 : lend ~ *n* 1 : forward movement 2 : improvement 3 : offer ~ *adj* : being ahead of time — **advance·ment** *n*

ad·van·tage \əd'vantij\ *n* 1 : superiority of position 2 : benefit or gain — **ad·van·ta·geous** \ˌad,van'tājəs, -vən-\ *adj* — **ad·van·ta·geous·ly** *adv*

ad·vent \'ad,vent\ *n* 1 *cap* : period before Christmas 2 : a coming into being or use

ad·ven·ti·tious \ˌadvən'tishəs\ *adj* : accidental — **ad·ven·ti·tious·ly** *adv*

ad·ven·ture \əd'venchər\ *n* 1 : risky undertaking 2 : exciting experience — **ad·ven·tur·er** \-chərər\ *n* — **ad·ven·ture·some** \-chərsəm\ *adj* — **ad·ven·tur·ous** \-chərəs\ *adj*

ad·verb \'ad,vərb\ *n* : word that modifies a verb, an adjective, or another adverb — **ad·ver·bi·al** \ad'vərbēəl\ *adj* — **ad·ver·bi·al·ly** *adv*

ad·ver·sary \'advərˌserē\ *n, pl* -sar·ies : enemy or rival — **adversary** *adj*

ad·verse \ad'vərs, 'ad-ˌ\ *adj* : opposing or unfavorable — **ad·verse·ly** *adv*

ad·ver·si·ty \ad'vərsətē\ *n, pl* -ties : hard times

ad·vert \ad'vərt\ *vb* : refer

ad·ver·tise \'advərˌtīz\ *vb* -tised; -tis·ing : call public attention to — **ad·ver·tise·ment** \ˌadvər-'tīzmənt, əd'vərtəzmənt\ *n* — **ad·ver·tis·er** *n*

ad·ver·tis·ing \'advərˌtīziŋ\ *n* : business of preparing advertisements

ad·vice \əd'vīs\ *n* : recommendation with regard to a course of action

ad·vis·able \əd'vīzəbəl\ *adj* : wise or prudent — **ad·vis·abil·i·ty** \-ˌvīzə-'bilətē\ *n*

ad·vise \əd'vīz\ *vb* -vised; -vis·ing : give advice to — **ad·vis·er, ad·vis·or** \-'vīzər\ *n*

ad·vise·ment \əd'vīzmənt\ *n* : careful consideration

ad·vi·so·ry \əd'vīzərē\ *adj* : having power to advise

ad·vo·cate \'advəkət, -ˌkāt\ *n* : one who argues or pleads for a cause or proposal ~ \-ˌkāt\ *vb* -cat·ed; -cat·ing : recommend — **ad·vo·ca·cy** \-vəkəsē\ *n*

adze \'adz\ *n* : tool for shaping wood

ae·gis \'ējəs\ *n* : protection or sponsorship

ae·on \'ēən, 'ē,än\ *n* : indefinitely long time

aer·ate \'ar,āt\ *vb* **-at·ed; -at·ing** : supply or impregnate with air — **aer·a·tion** \,ar'āshən\ *n* — **aer·a·tor** \'ar,ātər\ *n*

ae·ri·al \'arēəl\ *adj* : inhabiting, occurring in, or done in the air ∼ *n* : antenna

ae·rie \'arē, 'irē\ *n* : eagle's nest

aer·o·bic \,ar'ōbik\ *adj* : using or needing oxygen

aer·o·bics \-biks\ *n sing or pl* : exercises that produce a marked increase in respiration and heart rate

aero·dy·nam·ics \,arōdī'namiks\ *n* : science of bodies in motion in a gas — **aero·dy·nam·ic** \-ik\ *adj* — **aero·dy·nam·i·cal·ly** \-iklē\ *adv*

aero·nau·tics \,arə'nótiks\ *n* : science dealing with aircraft — **aero·nau·ti·cal** \-ikəl\ *adj*

aero·sol \'arə,säl, -,sól\ *n* **1** : liquid or solid particles suspended in a gas **2** : substance sprayed as an aerosol

aero·space \'arō,spās\ *n* : earth's atmosphere and the space beyond — **aerospace** *adj*

aes·thet·ic \es'thetik\ *adj* : relating to beauty — **aes·thet·i·cal·ly** \-iklē\ *adv*

aes·thet·ics \-'thetiks\ *n* : branch of philosophy dealing with beauty

afar \ə'fär\ *adv* : from, at, or to a great distance — **afar** *n*

af·fa·ble \'afəbəl\ *adj* : easy to talk to — **af·fa·bil·i·ty** \,afə'bilətē\ *n* — **af·fa·bly** \'afəblē\ *adv*

af·fair \ə'far\ *n* : something that relates to or involves one

¹af·fect \ə'fekt, a-\ *vb* : assume for effect — **af·fec·ta·tion** \,af,ek-'tāshən\ *n*

²affect *vb* : produce an effect on

af·fect·ed \ə'fektəd, a-\ *adj* **1** : pretending to some trait **2** : artificially assumed to impress — **af·fect·ed·ly** *adv*

af·fect·ing \ə'fektiŋ, a-\ *adj* : arousing pity or sorrow — **af·fect·ing·ly** *adv*

◆ **af·fec·tion** \ə'fekshən\ *n* : kind or loving feeling — **af·fec·tion·ate** \-shənət\ *adj* — **af·fec·tion·ate·ly** *adv*

af·fi·da·vit \,afə'dāvət\ *n* : sworn statement

af·fil·i·ate \ə'filē,āt\ *vb* **-at·ed; -at·ing** : become a member or branch — **af·fil·i·ate** \-ēət\ *n* — **af·fil·i·a·tion** \-,filē'āshən\ *n*

af·fin·i·ty \ə'finətē\ *n, pl* **-ties** : close attraction or relationship

af·firm \ə'fərm\ *vb* : assert positively — **af·fir·ma·tion** \,afər-'māshən\ *n*

af·fir·ma·tive \ə'fərmətiv\ *adj* : asserting the truth or existence of something ∼ *n* : statement of affirmation or agreement

af·fix \ə'fiks\ *vb* : attach

af·flict \ə'flikt\ *vb* : cause pain and distress to — **af·flic·tion** \-'flikshən\ *n*

af·flu·ence \'af,lüəns\ *a*'flü-, ə-\ *n* : wealth — **af·flu·ent** \-ənt\ *adj*

af·ford \ə'fórd\ *vb* **1** : manage to bear the cost of **2** : provide

af·fray \ə'frā\ *n* : fight

af·front \ə'frənt\ *vb or n* : insult

af·ghan \'af,gan, -gən\ *n* : crocheted or knitted blanket

afire \ə'fīr\ *adj or adv* : being on fire

aflame \ə'flām\ *adj or adv* : flaming

afloat \ə'flōt\ *adj or adv* : floating

afoot \ə'füt\ *adv or adj* **1** : on foot **2** : in progress

afore·said \ə'fōr,sed\ *adj* : said or named before

afraid \ə'frād, *South also* ə'fred\ *adj* : filled with fear

afresh \ə'fresh\ *adv* : anew

aft \'aft\ *adv* : to or toward the stern or tail

af·ter \'aftər\ *adv* : at a later time ~ *prep* 1 : behind in place or time 2 : in pursuit of ~ *conj* : following the time when ~ *adj* 1 : later 2 : located toward the back

af·ter·life \'aftər,līf\ *n* : existence after death

af·ter·math \-,math\ *n* : results

af·ter·noon \,aftər'nün\ *n* : time between noon and evening

af·ter·thought *n* : later thought

af·ter·ward \'aftərwərd\, **af·ter·wards** \-wərdz\ *adv* : at a later time

◆ **again** \ə'gen, -'gin\ *adv* 1 : once more 2 : on the other hand 3 : in addition

against \ə'genst\ *prep* 1 : directly opposite to 2 : in opposition to 3 : so as to touch or strike

agape \ə'gāp, -'gap\ *adj or adv* : having the mouth open in astonishment

ag·ate \'agət\ *n* : quartz with bands or masses of various colors

age \'āj\ *n* 1 : length of time of life or existence 2 : particular time in life (as majority or the latter part) 3 : quality of being old 4 : long time 5 : period in history ~ *vb* : become old or mature

-age \ij\ *n suffix* 1 : aggregate 2 : action or process 3 : result of 4 : rate of 5 : place of 6 : state or rank 7 : fee

aged *adj* 1 \'ājəd\ : old 2 \'ājd\ : allowed to mature

age·less \'ājləs\ *adj* : eternal

agen·cy \'ājənsē\ *n, pl* **-cies** 1 : one through which something is accomplished 2 : office or function

of an agent 3 : government administrative division

agen·da \ə'jendə\ *n* : list of things to be done

agent \'ājənt\ *n* 1 : means 2 : person acting or doing business for another

ag·gran·dize \ə'gran,dīz, 'agrən-\ *vb* **-dized; -diz·ing** : make great or greater — **ag·gran·dize·ment** \ə-'grandəzmənt, -,dīz-; ,agrən'dīz-\ *n*

ag·gra·vate \'agrə,vāt\ *vb* **-vat·ed; -vat·ing** 1 : make more severe 2 : irritate — **ag·gra·va·tion** \,agrə'vāshən\ *n*

ag·gre·gate \'agrigət\ *adj* : formed into a mass ~ \-,gāt\ *vb* **-gat·ed; -gat·ing** : collect into a mass ~ \-gət\ *n* 1 : mass 2 : whole amount

ag·gres·sion \ə'greshən\ *n* 1 : unprovoked attack 2 : hostile behavior — **ag·gres·sor** \-'gresər\ *n*

ag·gres·sive \ə'gresiv\ *adj* 1 : easily provoked to fight 2 : hard working and enterprising — **ag·gres·sive·ly** *adv* — **ag·gres·sive·ness** *n*

ag·grieve \ə'grēv\ *vb* **-grieved; -griev·ing** 1 : cause grief to 2 : inflict injury on

aghast \ə'gast\ *adj* : struck with amazement or horror

ag·ile \'ajəl\ *adj* : able to move quickly and easily — **agil·i·ty** \ə-'jilətē\ *n*

ag·i·tate \'ajə,tāt\ *vb* **-tat·ed; -tat·ing** 1 : shake or stir back and forth 2 : excite or trouble the mind of 3 : try to arouse public feeling — **ag·i·ta·tion** \,ajə'tāshən\ *n* — **ag·i·ta·tor** \'ajə,tātər\ *n*

ag·nos·tic \ag'nästik, əg-\ *n* : one who doubts the existence of God

ago \ə'gō\ *adj or adv* : earlier than the present

agog \ə'gäg\ *adj* : full of excitement

ag·o·nize \'agə,nīz\ *vb* **-nized; -niz-**

ASLEEP AGAIN, GARFIELD?

DEFINE "AGAIN"

JiM DAViS   10-16

ing : suffer mental agony — **ag·o·niz·ing·ly** *adv*

ag·o·ny \'agənē\ *n, pl* **-nies** : extreme pain or mental distress

agrar·i·an \ə'grerēən\ *adj* : relating to land ownership or farming interests — **agrarian** *n* — **agrar·i·an·ism** *n*

agree \ə'grē\ *vb* **agreed; agreeing 1** : be of the same opinion **2** : express willingness **3** : get along together **4** : be similar **5** : be appropriate, suitable, or healthful

agree·able \-əbəl\ *adj* **1** : pleasing **2** : willing to give approval — **agree·able·ness** *n* — **agree·ably** *adv*

agree·ment \-mənt\ *n* **1** : harmony of opinion or purpose **2** : mutual understanding or arrangement

ag·ri·cul·ture \'agri,kəlchər\ *n* : farming — **ag·ri·cul·tur·al** \,agri'kəlchərəl\ *adj* — **ag·ri·cul·tur·ist** \-rist\, — **ag·ri·cul·tur·al·ist** \-rəlist\ *n*

aground \ə'graúnd\ *adv or adj* : on or onto the bottom or shore

ague \'āgyü\ *n* **1** : fever with recurrent chills and sweating **2** : malaria

ahead \ə'hed\ *adv or adj* **1** : in or toward the front **2** : into or for the future **3** : in a more advantageous position

ahead of *prep* **1** : in front or advance of **2** : in excess of

ahoy \ə'hói\ *interj* — used in hailing

aid \'ād\ *vb* : provide help or support — *n* : help

aide \'ād\ *n* : helper

AIDS \'ādz\ *n* : serious disease of the human immune system

ail \'āl\ *vb* **1** : trouble **2** : be ill

ai·le·ron \'ālə,rän\ *n* : movable part of an airplane wing

ail·ment \'ālmənt\ *n* : bodily disorder

aim \'ām\ *vb* **1** : point or direct (as a weapon) **2** : direct one's efforts ~ *n* **1** : an aiming or the direction of aiming **2** : object or purpose — **aim·less** *adj* — **aim·less·ly** *adv* — **aim·less·ness** *n*

air \'ar\ *n* **1** : mixture of gases surrounding the earth **2** : melody **3** : outward appearance **4** : artificial manner **5** : compressed air **6** : travel by or use of aircraft **7** : medium of transmission of radio waves ~ *vb* **1** : expose to the air **2**

: broadcast — **air·borne** \-,bórn\ *adj*

air–condition *vb* : equip with an apparatus (**air conditioner**) for filtering and cooling the air

air·craft *n, pl* **aircraft** : craft that flies

Aire·dale terrier \'ar,dāl-\ *n* : large terrier with a hard wiry coat

air·field *n* : airport or its landing field

air force *n* : military organization for conducting warfare by air

air·lift *n* : a transporting of esp. emergency supplies by aircraft — **airlift** *vb*

air·line *n* : air transportation system — **air·lin·er** *n*

air·mail *n* : system of transporting mail by airplane — **airmail** *vb*

air·man \-mən\ *n* **1** : aviator **2** : enlisted man in the air force in one of the 3 ranks below sergeant **3** : enlisted man in the air force ranking just below airman first class

airman basic *n* : enlisted man of the lowest rank in the air force

airman first class *n* : enlisted man in the air force ranking just below sergeant

air·plane *n* : fixed-wing aircraft heavier than air

air·port *n* : place for landing aircraft and usu. for receiving passengers

air·ship *n* : powered lighter-than-air aircraft

air·strip *n* : airfield runway

air·tight *adj* : tightly sealed to prevent flow of air

air·waves \'ar,wāvz\ *n pl* : medium of transmission of radio waves

airy \'arē\ *adj* **air·i·er; -est 1** : delicate **2** : breezy

aisle \'īl\ *n* : passage between sections of seats

ajar \ə'jär\ *adj or adv* : partly open

akim·bo \ə'kimbō\ *adj or adv* : having the hand on the hip and the elbow turned outward

akin \ə'kin\ *adj* **1** : related by blood **2** : similar in kind

-al \əl\ *adj suffix* : of, relating to, or characterized by

al·a·bas·ter \'alə,bastər\ *n* : white or translucent mineral

alac·ri·ty \ə'lakrətē\ *n* : cheerful readiness

♦ **alarm** \ə'lärm\ *n* **1** : warning signal or device **2** : fear at sudden danger ~ *vb* **1** : warn **2** : frighten

alas \ə'las\ *interj* — used to express unhappiness, pity, or concern

al·ba·tross \'albə,trós, -,träs\ *n, pl* **-tross** *or* **-tross·es** : large seabird

al·be·it \ól'bēət, al-\ *conj* : even though

al·bi·no \al'bīnō\ *n, pl* **-nos** : person or animal with abnormally white skin — **al·bi·nism** \'albə,nizəm\ *n*

al·bum \'albəm\ *n* **1** : book for displaying a collection (as of photographs) **2** : collection of recordings

al·bu·men \al'byümən\ *n* **1** : white of an egg **2** : albumin

al·bu·min \-mən\ *n* : protein found in blood, milk, egg white, and tissues

al·che·my \'alkəmē\ *n* : medieval chemistry — **al·che·mist** \'alkə-mist\ *n*

al·co·hol \'alkə,hól\ *n* **1** : intoxicating agent in liquor **2** : liquor — **al·co·hol·ic** *adj*

al·co·hol·ic \,alkə'hólik, -'häl-\ *n* : person affected with alcoholism

al·co·hol·ism \'alkə,hól,izəm\ *n* : addiction to alcoholic beverages

al·cove \'al,kōv\ *n* : recess in a room or wall

al·der·man \'óldərmən\ *n* : city official

ale \'āl\ *n* : beerlike beverage — **ale·house** *n*

alert \ə'lərt\ *adj* **1** : watchful **2** : quick to perceive and act ~ *n* : alarm ~ *vb* : warn — **alert·ly** *adv* — **alert·ness** *n*

ale·wife *n* : fish of the herring family

al·fal·fa \al'falfə\ *n* : cloverlike forage plant

al·ga \'algə\ *n, pl* **-gae** \'al,jē\ : any of a group of lower plants that includes seaweed — **al·gal** \-gəl\ *adj*

al·ge·bra \'aljəbrə\ *n* : branch of mathematics — **al·ge·bra·ic** \,aljə'brāik\ *adj* — **al·ge·bra·i·cal·ly** \-'brāəklē\ *adv*

alias \'ālēəs, 'ālyəs\ *adv* : otherwise called ~ *n* : assumed name

al·i·bi \'alə,bī\ *n* **1** : defense of having been elsewhere when a crime was committed **2** : justification ~ *vb* **-bied; -bi·ing** : offer an excuse

alien \'ālēən, 'ālyən\ *adj* : foreign ~ *n* **1** : foreign-born resident **2** : extraterrestrial

alien·ate \'ālēə,nāt, 'ālyə-\ *vb* **-at·ed; -at·ing** : cause to be no longer friendly — **alien·ation** \,ālēə-'nāshən, ,ālyə-\ *n*

alight \ə'līt\ *vb* : dismount

align \ə'līn\ *vb* : bring into line — **align·er** *n* — **align·ment** *n*

alike \ə'līk\ *adj* : identical or very similar ~ *adv* : equally

al·i·men·ta·ry \,alə'mentərē\ *adj* : relating to or functioning in nutrition

al·i·mo·ny \'alə,mōnē\ *n, pl* **-nies** : money paid to a separated or divorced spouse

alive \ə'līv\ *adj* **1** : having life **2** : lively or animated

al·ka·li \'alkə,lī\ *n, pl* **-lies** *or* **-lis** : strong chemical base — **al·ka·line** \-kələn, -,līn\ *adj* — **al·ka·lin·i·ty** \,alkə'linətē\ *n*

all \'ól\ *adj* **1** : the whole of **2** : greatest possible **3** : every one of ~ *adv* **1** : wholly **2** : so much **3** : for each side ~ *pron* **1** : whole number or amount **2** : everything or everyone

Al·lah \'älə, 'al-\ *n* : God of Islam

all–around *adj* : versatile

al·lay \ə'lā\ *vb* **1** : alleviate **2** : calm

al·lege \ə'lej\ *vb* **-leged; -leg·ing** : assert without proof — **al·le·ga·tion**

\ˌali'gāshən\ *n* — **al·leg·ed·ly** \ə-'lejədlē\ *adv*

al·le·giance \ə'lējəns\ *n* : loyalty

al·le·go·ry \'alə,gōrē\ *n, pl* **-ries** : story in which figures and actions are symbols of general truths — **al·le·gor·i·cal** \ˌalə'górikəl\ *adj*

al·le·lu·ia \ˌalə'lüyə\ *interj* : hallelujah

al·ler·gen \'alərjən\ *n* : something that causes allergy — **al·ler·gen·ic** \ˌalər-'jenik\ *adj*

al·ler·gy \'alərjē\ *n, pl* **-gies** : abnormal reaction to a substance — **al·ler·gic** \ə'lərjik\ *adj* — **al·ler·gist** \'alərjist\ *n*

al·le·vi·ate \ə'lēvē,āt\ *vb* **-at·ed; -at·ing** : relieve or lessen — **al·le·vi·a·tion** \ə,lēvē'āshən\ *n*

al·ley \'alē\ *n, pl* **-leys** 1 : place for bowling 2 : narrow passage between buildings

al·li·ance \ə'līəns\ *n* : association

al·li·ga·tor \'alə,gātər\ *n* : large aquatic reptile related to the crocodiles

al·lit·er·a·tion \ə,litə'rāshən\ *n* : repetition of initial sounds of words — **al·lit·er·a·tive** \-'litəˌrātiv\ *adj*

al·lo·cate \'alə,kāt\ *vb* **-cat·ed; -cat·ing** : assign — **al·lo·ca·tion** \ˌalə-'kāshən\ *n*

al·lot \ə'lät\ *vb* **-tt-** : distribute as a share — **al·lot·ment** *n*

al·low \ə'laú\ *vb* 1 : admit or concede 2 : permit — **al·low·able** *adj*

al·low·ance \-əns\ *n* 1 : allotted share 2 : money given regularly for expenses

al·loy \'al,ói\ *n* : metals melted together — **al·loy** \ə'lói\ *vb*

all right *adv or adj* 1 : satisfactorily 2 : yes 3 : certainly

all·spice \'ólspīs\ *n* : berry of a West Indian tree made into a spice

al·lude \ə'lüd\ *vb* **-lud·ed; -lud·ing** : refer indirectly — **al·lu·sion** \-'lüzhən\ *n* — **al·lu·sive** \-'lüsiv\ *adj* — **al·lu·sive·ly** *adv* — **al·lu·sive·ness** *n*

al·lure \ə'lúr\ *vb* **-lured; -lur·ing** : entice ~ *n* : attractive power

al·ly \ə'lī, 'al,ī\ *vb* **-lied; -ly·ing** : enter into an alliance — **al·ly** \'al,ī, ə'lī\ *n*

-al·ly \əlē\ *adv suffix* : -ly

al·ma·nac \'ólmə,nak, 'al-\ *n* : annual information book

al·mighty \ól'mītē\ *adj* : having absolute power

al·mond \'ämənd , 'am-, 'alm-, 'älm-\ *n* : tree with nutlike fruit kernels

al·most \'ól,mōst, ól-'\ *adv* : very nearly

alms \'ämz, 'älmz, 'almz\ *n, pl* **alms** : charitable gift

aloft \ə'lóft\ *adv* : high in the air

alo·ha \ä'lōhä\ *interj* — used to greet or bid farewell

alone \ə'lōn\ *adj* 1 : separated from others 2 : not including anyone or anything else — **alone** *adv*

along \ə'lóŋ\ *prep* 1 : in line with the direction of 2 : at a point on or during ~ *adv* 1 : forward 2 : as a companion 3 : all the time

along·side *adv or prep* : along or by the side

alongside of *prep* : alongside

aloof \ə'lüf\ *adj* : indifferent and reserved — **aloof·ness** *n*

aloud \ə'laúd\ *adv* : so as to be heard

al·paca \al'pakə\ *n* 1 : So. American mammal related to the llama 2 : alpaca wool or cloth made of this

al·pha·bet \'alfə,bet, -bət\ *n* : ordered set of letters of a language — **al·pha·bet·i·cal** \ˌalfə'betikəl\ **al·pha·bet·ic** \-'betik\ *adj* — **al·pha·bet·i·cal·ly** \-klē\ *adv*

al·pha·bet·ize \'alfəbə,tīz\ *vb* **-ized; -iz·ing** : arrange in alphabetical order — **al·pha·bet·iz·er** *n*

al·ready \ól'redē\ *adv* : by a given time

al·so \'ólsō\ *adv* : in addition

al·tar \'óltər\ *n* : structure for rituals

♦ **al·ter** \'óltər\ *vb* : make different — **alter·a·tion** \ˌóltə'rāshən\ *n*

al·ter·ca·tion \ˌóltər'kāshən\ *n* : dispute

al·ter·nate \'óltərnət, 'al-\ *adj* 1 : arranged or succeeding by turns 2 : every other ~ \-,nāt\ *vb* **-nat·ed; -nat·ing** : occur or cause to occur by turns ~ \-nət\ *n* : substitute — **al·ter·nate·ly** *adv* — **al·ter·na·tion** \ˌóltər'nāshən, ˌal-\ *n*

alternating current *n* : electric current that regularly reverses direction

al·ter·na·tive \ól'tərnətiv, al-\ *adj* : offering a choice — **alternative** *n*

al·ter·na·tor \'óltər,nātər, 'al-\ *n* : alternating-current generator

al·though \ól'thō\ *conj* : even though

al·tim·e·ter \al'timətər, 'altə-,mētər\ *n* : instrument for measuring altitude

al·ti·tude \'altə,tüd, -,tyüd\ *n* 1 : distance up from the ground 2 : angular distance above the horizon

al·to \'altō\ *n, pl* **-tos** : lower female choral voice

al·to·geth·er \,óltə'gethər\ *adv* 1 : wholly 2 : on the whole

al·tru·ism \'altru̇,izəm\ *n* : concern for others — **al·tru·ist** \-ist\ *n* — **al·tru·is·tic** \,altru̇'istik\ *adj* — **al·tru·is·ti·cal·ly** \-tiklē\ *adv*

al·um \'aləm\ *n* : crystalline compound containing aluminum

alu·mi·num \ə'lümənəm\ *n* : silver-white malleable ductile light metallic element

alum·na \ə'ləmnə\ *n, pl* **-nae** \-,nē\ : woman graduate

alum·nus \ə'ləmnəs\ *n, pl* **-ni** \-,nī\ : graduate

al·ways \'ólwēz, -wāz\ *adv* 1 : at all times 2 : forever

am *pres 1st sing of* BE

amal·gam \ə'malgəm\ *n* 1 : mercury alloy 2 : mixture

amal·gam·ate \ə'malgə,māt\ *vb* **-at·ed; -at·ing** : unite — **amal·ga·ma·tion** \-,malgə'māshən\ *n*

am·a·ryl·lis \,amə'riləs\ *n* : bulbous herb with clusters of large colored flowers like lilies

amass \ə'mas\ *vb* : gather

am·a·teur \'amə,tər, -,tu̇r, -,tyu̇r, -,chu̇r, -chər\ *n* 1 : person who does something for pleasure rather than for pay 2 : person who is not expert — **am·a·teur·ish** \,amə'tərish, -'tu̇r-, -'tyu̇r-\ *adj* — **ama·teur·ism** \'amə,tər,izəm, -,tu̇r-, -,tyu̇r-, -,chu̇r-, -chər-\ *n*

am·a·to·ry \'amə,tōrē\ *adj* : of or expressing sexual love

amaze \ə'māz\ *vb* **amazed; amaz·ing** : fill with wonder — **amaze·ment** *n* — **amaz·ing·ly** *adv*

am·a·zon \'amə,zän, -zən\ *n* : tall strong woman — **am·a·zo·ni·an** \,amə'zōnēən\ *adj*

am·bas·sa·dor \am'basədər\ *n* : representative esp. of a government — **am·bas·sa·do·ri·al** \-,basə'dōrēəl\ *adj* — **am·bas·sa·dor·ship** *n*

am·ber \'ambər\ *n* : yellowish fossil resin or its color

am·ber·gris \'ambər,gris, -,grēs\ *n* : waxy substance from certain whales used in making perfumes

am·bi·dex·trous \,ambi'dekstrəs\ *adj* : equally skilled with both hands — **am·bi·dex·trous·ly** *adv*

am·bi·ence, am·bi·ance \'ambēəns, 'ämbē,äns\ *n* : pervading atmosphere

am·big·u·ous \am'bigyəwəs\ *adj* : having more than one interpretation — **am·bi·gu·i·ty** \,ambə'gyüətē\ *n*

am·bi·tion \am'bishən\ *n* : eager desire for success or power — **am·bi·tious** \-shəs\ *adj* — **am·bi·tious·ly** *adv*

am·biv·a·lence \am'bivələns\ *n* : simultaneous attraction and repulsion — **am·biv·a·lent** \-lənt\ *adj*

am·ble \'ambəl\ *vb* **-bled; -bling** : go at a leisurely gait — **amble** *n*

am·bu·lance \'ambyələns\ *n* : vehicle for carrying injured or sick persons

am·bu·la·to·ry \'ambyələ,tōrē\ *adj* 1 : relating to or adapted to walking 2 : able to walk about

am·bush \'am,bu̇sh\ *n* : trap by which a surprise attack is made from a place of hiding — **ambush** *vb*

ame·lio·rate \ə'mēlyə₁rāt\ *vb* **-rat-ed; -rat·ing** : make or grow better — **ame·lio·ra·tion** \-₁mēlyə'rāshən\ *n*

amen \'ā'men, ,ä-\ *interj* — used for affirmation esp. at the end of prayers

ame·na·ble \ə'mēnəbəl, -'men-\ *adj* : ready to yield or be influenced

amend \ə'mend\ *vb* **1** : improve **2** : alter in writing

amend·ment \-mənt\ *n* : change made in a formal document (as a law)

amends \ə'mendz\ *n sing or pl* : compensation for injury or loss

ame·ni·ty \ə'menətē, -'mē-\ *n, pl* **-ties 1** : agreeableness **2** *pl* : social conventions **3** : something serving to comfort or accommodate

am·e·thyst \'aməthəst\ *n* : purple gemstone

ami·a·ble \'āmēəbəl\ *adj* : easy to get along with — **ami·a·bil·i·ty** \₁āmēə'bilətē\ *n* — **ami·a·bly** \'āmēəblē\ *adv*

am·i·ca·ble \'amikəbəl\ *adj* : friendly — **am·i·ca·bly** \-blē\ *adv*

amid \ə'mid\, **amidst** \-'midst\ *prep* : in or into the middle of

amino acid \ə'mēnō-\ *n* : nitrogen-containing acid

amiss \ə'mis\ *adv* : in the wrong way ~ *adj* : wrong

am·me·ter \'am₁ētər\ *n* : instrument for measuring electric current

am·mo·nia \ə'mōnyə\ *n* **1** : colorless gaseous compound of nitrogen and hydrogen **2** : solution of ammonia in water

am·mu·ni·tion \₁amyə'nishən\ *n* **1** : projectiles fired from guns **2** : explosive items used in war

am·ne·sia \am'nēzhə\ *n* : sudden loss of memory — **am·ne·si·ac** \-zē₁ak, -zhē-\ **am·ne·sic** \-zik, -sik\ *adj or n*

am·nes·ty \'amnəstē\ *n, pl* **-ties** : a pardon for a group — **amnesty** *vb*

amoe·ba \ə'mēbə\ *n, pl* **-bas** *or* **-bae** \-₁bē\ : tiny one-celled animal that occurs esp. in water — **amoe·bic** \-bik\ *adj*

amok \ə'mək, -'mäk\ *adv* : in a violent or uncontrolled way

among \ə'məŋ\ *prep* **1** : in or through **2** : in the number or class of **3** : in shares to each of

am·o·rous \'amərəs\ *adj* **1** : inclined to love **2** : being in love **3** : indicative of love — **am·o·rous·ly** *adv* — **am·o·rous·ness** *n*

amor·phous \ə'mórfəs\ *adj* : shapeless

am·or·tize \'amər₁tīz, ə'mór-\ *vb* **-tized; -tiz·ing** : get rid of (as a debt) gradually with periodic payments — **amor·ti·za·tion** \₁amərtə'zāshən, ə₁mórt-\ *n*

amount \ə'maúnt\ *vb* **1** : be equivalent **2** : reach a total ~ *n* : total number or quantity

amour \ə'múr, ä-, a-\ *n* **1** : love affair **2** : lover

am·pere \'am₁pir\ *n* : unit of electric current

am·per·sand \'ampər₁sand\ *n* : character & used for the word *and*

am·phib·i·ous \am'fibēəs\ *adj* **1** : able to live both on land and in water **2** : adapted for both land and water — **am·phib·i·an** \-ən\ *n*

am·phi·the·ater \'amfə₁thēətər\ *n* : oval or circular structure with rising tiers of seats around an arena

am·ple \'ampəl\ *adj* **-pler** \-plər\; **-plest** \-pləst\ **1** : large **2** : sufficient — **am·ply** \-plē\ *adv*

am·pli·fy \'amplə₁fī\ *vb* **-fied; -fy·ing** : make louder, stronger, or more thorough — **am·pli·fi·ca·tion** \₁ampləfə'kāshən\ *n* — **am·pli·fi·er** \'amplə₁fīər\ *n*

am·pli·tude \-₁tüd, -₁tyüd\ *n* **1** : fullness **2** : extent of a vibratory movement

♦ **am·pu·tate** \'ampyə₁tāt\ *vb* **-tat-ed; -tat·ing** : cut off (a body part) — **am·pu·ta·tion** \₁ampyə'tāshən\ *n* — **am·pu·tee** \₁ampyə'tē\ *n*

amuck \ə'mək\ *var of* AMOK

am·u·let \'amyələt\ *n* : ornament worn as a charm against evil

amuse \ə'myüz\ *vb* **amused; amus·ing 1** : engage the attention of in an interesting and pleasant way **2** : make laugh — **amuse·ment** *n*

an \ən, 'an\ *indefinite article* : a — used before words beginning with a vowel sound

-an \ən\, **-ian** \ēən\, **-ean** \ēən\ *n suffix* **1** : one that belongs to **2** : one skilled in ~ *adj suffix* **1** : of or belonging to **2** : characteristic of or resembling

anach·ro·nism \ə'nakrə₁nizəm\ *n*

: one that is chronologically out of place — **anach·ro·nis·tic** \ˌə,nak-rə'nistik\ *adj*

an·a·con·da \ˌanə'kändə\ *n* : large So. American snake

ana·gram \'anə,gram\ *n* : word or phrase made by transposing the letters of another word or phrase

anal \'ān°l\ *adj* : relating to the anus

an·al·ge·sic \ˌan°l'jēzik, -sik\ *n* : pain reliever

anal·o·gy \ə'naləjē\ *n, pl* **-gies 1** : similarity between unlike things **2** : example of something similar — **an·a·log·i·cal** \ˌan°l'äjikəl\ *adj* — **an·a·log·i·cal·ly** \-iklē\ *adv* — **anal·o·gous** \ə'naləgəs\ *adj*

anal·y·sis \ə'naləsəs\ *n, pl* **-y·ses** \-ˌsēz\ **1** : examination of a thing to determine its parts **2** : psychoanalysis — **an·a·lyst** \'an°list\ *n* — **an·a·lyt·ic** \ˌan°l'itik\, **an·a·lyt·i·cal** \-ikəl\ *adj* — **an·a·lyt·i·cal·ly** \-iklē\ *adv*

an·a·lyze \'an°l,īz\ *vb* **-lyzed; -lyz·ing** : make an analysis of

an·ar·chism \'anər,kizəm, -,när-\ *n* : theory that all government is undesirable — **an·ar·chist** \-kist\ *n or adj* — **an·ar·chis·tic** \ˌanər-'kistik\ *adj*

an·ar·chy \'anərkē, -,när-\ *n* : lack of government or order — **an·ar·chic** \a'närkik\ *adj* — **an·ar·chi·cal·ly** \-iklē\ *adv*

anath·e·ma \ə'nathəmə\ *n* **1** : solemn curse **2** : person or thing accursed or intensely disliked

anat·o·my \ə'natəmē\ *n, pl* **-mies** : science dealing with the structure of organisms — **an·a·tom·ic** \ˌanə'tämik\ **an·a·tom·i·cal** \-ikəl\ *adj* — **an·a·tom·i·cal·ly** *adv* — **anat·o·mist** \ə'natəmist\ *n*

-ance \əns\ *n suffix* **1** : action or process **2** : quality or state **3** : amount or degree

an·ces·tor \'an,sestər\ *n* : one from whom an individual is descended

an·ces·tress \-trəs\ *n* : female ancestor

an·ces·try \-trē\ *n* **1** : line of descent **2** : ancestors — **an·ces·tral** \an-'sestrəl\ *adj*

an·chor \'aŋkər\ *n* : heavy device that catches in the sea bottom to hold a ship in place ∼ *vb* : hold or become held in place by or as if by an anchor — **an·chor·age** \-kərij\ *n*

an·chor·man \'aŋkər,man\ *n* : news broadcast coordinator

an·cho·vy \'an,chōvē, an'chō-\ *n, pl* **-vies** *or* **-vy** : small herringlike fish

an·cient \'ānshənt\ *adj* **1** : having existed for many years **2** : belonging to times long past — **ancient** *n*

-ancy \ənsē\ *n suffix* : quality or state

and \ənd, 'and\ *conj* — used to indicate connection or addition

and·iron \'an,dīərn\ *n* : one of 2 metal supports for wood in a fireplace

an·drog·y·nous \an'dräjənəs\ *adj* **1** : having characteristics of both male and female **2** : suitable for either sex

an·ec·dote \'anik,dōt\ *n* : brief story — **an·ec·dot·al** \ˌanik'dōt°l\ *adj*

ane·mia \ə'nēmēə\ *n* : blood deficiency — **ane·mic** \ə'nēmik\ *adj*

anem·o·ne \ə'nemənē\ *n* : small herb with showy usu. white flowers

an·es·the·sia \ˌanəs'thēzhə\ *n* : loss of bodily sensation

an·es·thet·ic \ˌanəs'thetik\ *n* : agent that produces anesthesia — **anesthetic** *adj* — **anes·the·tist** \ə-'nesthətist\ *n* — **anes·the·tize** \-thə,tīz\ *vb*

anew \ə'nü, -'nyü\ *adv* : over again

an·gel \'ānjəl\ *n* : spiritual being su-

perior to humans — **an·gel·ic** \an-'jelik\ **an·gel·i·cal** \-ikəl\ *adj* — **an·gel·i·cal·ly** *adv*

an·ger \'aŋgər\ *n* : strong feeling of displeasure ~ *vb* : make angry

an·gi·na \an'jīnə\ *n* : painful disorder of heart muscles — **an·gi·nal** \an'jīnᵊl\ *adj*

¹**an·gle** \'aŋgəl\ *n* **1** : figure formed by the meeting of 2 lines in a point **2** : sharp corner **3** : point of view ~ *vb* -**gled; -gling** : turn or direct at an angle

²**angle** *vb* **an·gled; an·gling** : fish with a hook and line — **an·gler** \-glər\ *n* — **an·gle·worm** *n* — **an·gling** *n*

an·go·ra \aŋ'gōrə, an-\ *n* : yarn or cloth made from the hair of an Angora goat or rabbit

an·gry \'aŋgrē\ *adj* -**gri·er; -est** : feeling or showing anger — **an·gri·ly** \-grəlē\ *adv*

an·guish \'aŋgwish\ *n* : extreme pain or distress of mind — **an·guished** \-gwisht\ *adj*

an·gu·lar \'aŋgyələr\ *adj* **1** : having many or sharp angles **2** : thin and bony — **an·gu·lar·i·ty** \,aŋgyə-'larətē\ *n*

an·i·mal \'anəməl\ *n* **1** : living being capable of feeling and voluntary motion **2** : lower animal as distinguished from humans

an·i·mate \'anəmət\ *adj* : having life ~ \-,māt\ *vb* -**mat·ed; -mat·ing** **1** : give life or vigor to **2** : make appear to move — **an·i·mat·ed** *adj*

an·i·ma·tion \,anə'māshən\ *n* **1** : liveliness **2** : animated cartoon

an·i·mos·i·ty \,anə'mäsətē\ *n, pl* -**ties** : resentment

an·i·mus \'anəməs\ *n* : deep-seated hostility

an·ise \'anəs\ *n* : herb related to the carrot with aromatic seeds (**ani·seed** \-,sēd \) used in flavoring

an·kle \'aŋkəl\ *n* : joint or region between the foot and the leg — **an·kle·bone** *n*

an·nals \'anᵊlz\ *n pl* : chronological record of history — **an·nal·ist** \-ᵊlist\ *n*

an·neal \ə'nēl\ *vb* **1** : make less brittle by heating and then cooling **2** : strengthen or toughen

an·nex \ə'neks, 'an,eks\ *vb* : assume political control over (a territory) ~ \'an,eks, -iks\ *n* : added building — **an·nex·a·tion** \,an,ek-'sāshən\ *n*

an·ni·hi·late \ə'nīə,lāt\ *vb* -**lat·ed; -lat·ing** : destroy — **an·ni·hi·la·tion** \-,nīə'lāshən\ *n*

an·ni·ver·sa·ry \,anə'vərsərē\ *n, pl* -**ries** : annual return of the date of a notable event or its celebration

an·no·tate \'anə,tāt\ *vb* -**tat·ed; -tat·ing** : furnish with notes — **an·no·ta·tion** \,anə'tāshən\ *n* — **an·no·ta·tor** \'anə,tātər\ *n*

an·nounce \ə'nauns\ *vb* -**nounced; -nounc·ing** : make known publicly — **an·nounce·ment** *n* — **an·nounc·er** *n*

an·noy \ə'nói\ *vb* : disturb or irritate — **an·noy·ance** \-əns\ *n* — **an·noy·ing·ly** \-'nóiiŋlē\ *adv*

an·nu·al \'anyəwəl\ *adj* **1** : occurring once a year **2** : living only one year — **annual** *n* — **an·nu·al·ly** *adv*

an·nu·i·ty \ə'nüətē, -'nyü-\ *n, pl* -**ties** : amount payable annually or the right to such a payment

an·nul \ə'nəl\ *vb* -**ll-** : make legally void — **an·nul·ment** *n*

an·ode \'an,ōd\ *n* **1** : positive electrode **2** : negative battery terminal — **an·od·ic** \a'nädik\ *adj*

anoint \ə'nóint\ *vb* : apply oil to as a rite — **anoint·ment** *n*

anom·a·ly \ə'näməlē\ *n, pl* -**lies** : something abnormal or unusual — **anom·a·lous** \ə'nämələs\ *adj*

anon·y·mous \ə'nänəməs\ *adj* : of unknown origin — **an·o·nym·i·ty** \,anə'nimətē\ *n* — **anon·y·mous·ly** *adv*

an·oth·er \ə'nəthər\ *adj* **1** : any or some other **2** : one more ~ *pron* **1** : one more **2** : one different

an·swer \'ansər\ *n* **1** : something spoken or written in reply to a question **2** : solution to a problem ~ *vb* **1** : reply to **2** : be responsible **3** : be adequate — **an·swer·er** *n*

an·swer·able \-rəbəl\ *adj* : responsible

ant \'ant\ *n* : small social insect — **ant·hill** *n*

-ant \ənt\ *n suffix* **1** : one that performs or causes an action **2** : thing that is acted upon — *adj suffix* **1** : performing an action or being in a condition **2** : causing an action or process

an·tag·o·nism \an'tagə,nizəm\ *n*

: active opposition or hostility — **an·tag·o·nist** \-ənist\ *n* — **an·tag·o·nis·tic** \-ˌtagəˈnistik\ *adj*

an·tag·o·nize \anˈtagəˌnīz\ *vb* **-nized; -niz·ing** : cause to be hostile

ant·arc·tic \antˈärktik, -ˈärtik\ *adj* : relating to the region near the south pole

antarctic circle *n* : circle parallel to the equator approximately 23°27' from the south pole

an·te·bel·lum \ˌantiˈbeləm\ *adj* : existing before the U.S. Civil War

an·te·ced·ent \ˌantəˈsēdᵊnt\ *n* : one that comes before — **antecedent** *adj*

an·te·lope \ˈantᵊlˌōp\ *n, pl* **-lope** *or* **-lopes** : deerlike mammal related to the ox

an·ten·na \anˈtenə\ *n, pl* **-nae** \-ˌnē\ *or* **-nas 1** : one of the long slender paired sensory organs on the head of an arthropod **2** *pl* **-nas** : metallic device for sending or receiving radio waves

an·te·ri·or \anˈtirēər\ *adj* : located before in place or time

an·them \ˈanthəm\ *n* : song or hymn of praise or gladness

an·ther \ˈanthər\ *n* : part of a seed plant that contains pollen

an·thol·o·gy \anˈthäləjē\ *n, pl* **-gies** : literary collection

an·thra·cite \ˈanthrəˌsīt\ *n* : hard coal

an·thro·poid \ˈanthrəˌpȯid\ *n* : large ape — **anthropoid** *adj*

an·thro·pol·o·gy \ˌanthrəˈpäləjē\ *n* : science dealing with humans — **an·thro·po·log·i·cal** \-pəˈläjikəl\ *adj* — **an·thro·pol·o·gist** \-ˈpäləjist\ *n*

anti- \ˌantē, -ˌtī\ **ant-, anth-** *prefix* **1** : opposite in kind, position, or action **2** : opposing or hostile toward **3** : defending against **4** : curing or treating

antiabortion
antiacademic
antiadministration
antiaggression
antiaircraft
antialien
antiapartheid
antiaristocratic
antiart

antiauthoritarian
antiauthority
antibacterial
antibias
antiblack
antibourgeois
antiboycott
antibureaucratic
antiburglar

antiburglary
antibusiness
anticancer
anticapitalism
anticapitalist
anti-Catholic
anticensorship
anti-Christian
anti-Christianity
antichurch
anticigarette
anticlerical
anticollision
anticolonial
anticommunism
anticommunist
anticonservation
anticonservationist
anticonsumer
anticonventional
anticorrosion
anticorrosive
anticorruption
anticrime
anticruelty
anticult
anticultural
antidandruff
antidemocratic
antidiscrimination
antidrug
antidumping
antiestablishment
antievolution
antievolutionary
antifamily
antifascism
antifascist
antifatigue
antifemale
antifeminine
antifeminism
antifeminist
antifertility
antiforeign
antiforeigner
antifraud
antigambling
antiglare
antigovernment
antiguerrilla

antigun
antihijack
antihomosexual
antihuman
antihumanism
antihumanistic
antihunting
anti-imperialism
anti-imperialist
anti-inflation
anti-inflationary
anti-institutional
anti-integration
anti-intellectual
anti-intellectualism
antijamming
anti-Jewish
antilabor
antiliberal
antiliberalism
antilitter
antilittering
antilynching
antimale
antimanagement
antimaterialism
antimaterialist
antimicrobial
antimilitarism
antimilitarist
antimilitary
antimiscegenation
antimonopolist
antimonopoly
antimosquito
antinoise
antiobesity
antiobscenity
antipapal
antipersonnel
antipolice
antipollution
antipornographic
antipornography
antipoverty
antiprofiteering
antiprogressive
antiprostitution
antirabies
antiracketeering

antiradical
antirape
antirealism
antirecession
antireform
antireligious
antirevolutionary
antiriot
antiromantic
antitrust
antisegregation
antisex
antisexist
antisexual
antishoplifting
antislavery
antismoking
antismuggling
antismut
antispending
antistrike
antistudent
antisubmarine
antisubversion
antisubversive
antisuicide
antitank
antitax

antitechnological
antitechnology
antiterrorism
antiterrorist
antitheft
antitobacco
antitotalitarian
antitoxin
antitraditional
antitrust
antituberculosis
antitumor
antityphoid
antiulcer
antiunemployment
antiunion
antiuniversity
antiurban
antiviolence
antiviral
antivivisection
antiwar
anti-West
anti-Western
antiwhite
antiwoman

an·ti·bi·ot·ic \ˌantēbīˈätik, -bē-\ *n* : substance that inhibits harmful microorganisms — **antibiotic** *adj*

an·ti·body \ˈantiˌbädē\ *n* : bodily substance that counteracts the effects of a foreign substance or organism

an·tic \ˈantik\ *n* : playful act ~ *adj* : playful

an·tic·i·pate \anˈtisəˌpāt\ *vb* **-pated; -pat·ing 1** : be prepared for **2** : look forward to — **an·tic·i·pa·tion** \-ˌtisə-ˈpāshən\ *n* — **an·tic·i·pa·to·ry** \-ˈtisəpəˌtōrē\ *adj*

an·ti·cli·max \ˌantēˈklīˌmaks\ *n* : something strikingly less important than what has preceded it — **an·ti·cli·mac·tic** \-klīˈmaktik\ *adj*

an·ti·dote \ˈantiˌdōt\ *n* : remedy for poison

an·ti·freeze \ˈantiˌfrēz\ *n* : substance to prevent a liquid from freezing

an·ti·mo·ny \ˈantəˌmōnē\ *n* : brittle white metallic chemical element

an·tip·a·thy \anˈtipəthē\ *n, pl* **-thies** : strong dislike

an·ti·quar·i·an \ˌantəˈkwerēən\ *adj* : relating to antiquities or old books — **antiquarian** *n* — **an·ti·quar·i·an·ism** *n*

an·ti·quary \ˈantəˌkwerē\ *n, pl* **-quar·ies** : one who collects or studies antiquities

an·ti·quat·ed \ˈantəˌkwātəd\ *adj* : out-of-date

an·tique \anˈtēk\ *adj* : very old or out-of-date — **antique** *n*

an·tiq·ui·ty \anˈtikwətē\ *n, pl* **-ties 1** : ancient times **2** *pl* : relics of ancient times

an·ti·sep·tic \ˌantəˈseptik\ *adj* : killing or checking the growth of germs — **antiseptic** *n* — **an·ti·sep·ti·cal·ly** \-tiklē\ *adv*

an·tith·e·sis \anˈtithəsəs\ *n, pl* **-e·ses** \-ˌsēz\ : direct opposite

ant·ler \ˈantlər\ *n* : solid branched horn of a deer — **ant·lered** \-lərd\ *adj*

ant·onym \ˈantəˌnim\ *n* : word of opposite meaning

anus \ˈānəs\ *n* : the rear opening of the alimentary canal

♦ **an·vil** \ˈanvəl\ *n* : heavy iron block on which metal is shaped

anx·i·ety \aŋˈzīətē\ *n, pl* **-eties** : uneasiness usu. over an expected misfortune

anx·ious \ˈaŋkshəs\ *adj* **1** : uneasy **2** : earnestly wishing — **anx·ious·ly** *adv*

any \ˈenē\ *adj* **1** : one chosen at random **2** : of whatever number or quantity ~ *pron* **1** : any one or

ones **2** : any amount ∼ *adv* : to any extent or degree

any·body \-bədē, -ˌbäd-\ *pron* : anyone

any·how \-ˌhaù\ *adv* **1** : in any way **2** : nevertheless

any·more \ˌenē'mōr\ *adv* : at the present time

any·one \-'enēˌwən\ *pron* : any person

any·place *adv* : anywhere

any·thing *pron* : any thing whatever

any·time *adv* : at any time whatever

any·way *adv* : anyhow

any·where *adv* : in or to any place

aor·ta \ā'ōrtə\ *n, pl* **-tas** *or* **-tae** \-ē\ : main artery from the heart — **aor·tic** \ā'ōrtik\ *adj*

apart \ə'pärt\ *adv* **1** : separately in place or time **2** : aside **3** : to pieces

apart·heid \ə'pär,tāt, -,tīt\ *n* : racial segregation

apart·ment \ə'pärtmənt\ *n* : set of usu. rented rooms

ap·a·thy \'apəthē\ *n* : lack of emotion or interest — **ap·a·thet·ic** \ˌapə'thetik\ *adj* — **ap·a·thet·i·cal·ly** \-iklē\ *adv*

ape \'āp\ *n* : large tailless primate ∼ *vb* **aped; ap·ing** : imitate

ap·er·ture \'apər,chùr, -chər\ *n* : opening

apex \'āˌpeks\ *n, pl* **apex·es** *or* **api·ces** \'āpəˌsēz, 'apə-\ : highest point

aphid \'āfid, 'a-\ *n* : small insect that sucks plant juices

aph·o·rism \'afəˌrizəm\ *n* : short saying stating a general truth — **aph·oris·tic** \ˌafə'ristik\ *adj*

aph·ro·di·si·ac \ˌafrə'dēzē,ak, -'diz-\ *n* : substance that excites sexual desire

api·a·rist \'āpēərist\ *n* : beekeeper — **api·ary** \-pē,erē\ *n*

apiece \ə'pēs\ *adv* : for each one

aplen·ty \ə'plentē\ *adj* : plentiful or abundant

aplomb \ə'pläm, -'pləm\ *n* : complete calmness or self-assurance

apoc·a·lypse \ə'päkəˌlips\ *n* : writing prophesying a cataclysm in which evil forces are destroyed — **apoc·alyp·tic** \-ˌpäkə'liptik\ *adj*

apoc·ry·pha \ə'päkrəfə\ *n* : writings of dubious authenticity — **apoc·ry·phal** \-fəl\ *adj*

apol·o·get·ic \əˌpälə'jetik\ *adj* : expressing apology — **apol·o·get·i·cal·ly** \-iklē\ *adv*

apol·o·gize \ə'pälə,jīz\ *vb* **-gized; -giz·ing** : make an apology — **apol·o·gist** \-jist\ *n*

apol·o·gy \ə'päləjē\ *n, pl* **-gies 1** : formal justification **2** : expression of regret for a wrong

ap·o·plexy \'apəˌpleksē\ *n* : sudden loss of consciousness caused by rupture or obstruction of an artery of the brain — **ap·o·plec·tic** \ˌapə'plektik\ *adj*

apos·ta·sy \ə'pästəsē\ *n, pl* **-sies** : abandonment of a former loyalty — **apos·tate** \ə'päs,tāt\ *adj or n*

apos·tle \ə'päsəl\ *n* : disciple or advocate — **apos·tle·ship** *n* — **ap·os·tolic** \ˌapə'stälik\ *adj*

apos·tro·phe \ə'pästrəˌfē\ *n* : punctuation mark ' to indicate the possessive case or the omission of a letter or figure

apoth·e·cary \ə'päthəˌkerē\ *n, pl* **-car·ies** : druggist

ap·pall \ə'pól\ *vb* : fill with horror or dismay

ap·pa·ra·tus \ˌapə'ratəs, -'rāt-\ *n, pl* **-tus·es** *or* **-tus 1** : equipment **2** : complex machine or device

ap·par·el \ə'parəl\ *n* : clothing

ap·par·ent \ə'parənt\ *adj* **1** : visible **2** : obvious **3** : seeming — **ap·par·ent·ly** *adv*

ap·pa·ri·tion \ˌapə'rishən\ *n* : ghost

ap·peal \ə'pēl\ *vb* **1** : try to have a court case reheard **2** : ask earnestly **3** : have an attraction — **appeal** *n*

ap·pear \ə'pir\ *vb* **1** : become visible or evident **2** : come into the presence of someone **3** : seem

ap·pear·ance \ə'pirəns\ *n* **1** : act of appearing **2** : outward aspect

ap·pease \ə'pēz\ *vb* **-peased; -peas·ing** : pacify with concessions — **ap·pease·ment** *n*

ap·pel·late \ə'pelət\ *adj* : having power to review decisions

ap·pend \ə'pend\ *vb* : attach

ap·pend·age \ə'pendij\ *n* : something attached

ap·pen·dec·to·my \ˌapən'dektəmē\ *n, pl* **-mies** : surgical removal of the appendix

ap·pen·di·ci·tis \əˌpendə'sītəs\ *n* : inflammation of the appendix

ap·pen·dix \ə'pendiks\ *n, pl* **-dix·es** *or* **-di·ces** \-də,sēz\ **1** : supplementary matter **2** : narrow closed tube extending from lower right intestine

ap·pe·tite \\'apə₁tīt\\ *n* **1** : natural desire esp. for food **2** : preference

ap·pe·tiz·er \\-₁tīzər\\ *n* : food or drink to stimulate the appetite

ap·pe·tiz·ing \\-ziŋ\\ *adj* : tempting to the appetite — **ap·pe·tiz·ing·ly** *adv*

ap·plaud \\ə'plȯd\\ *vb* : show approval esp. by clapping

ap·plause \\ə'plȯz\\ *n* : a clapping in approval

ap·ple \\'apəl\\ *n* : rounded fruit with firm white flesh

ap·ple·jack \\-₁jak\\ *n* : brandy made from cider

♦ **ap·pli·ance** \\ə'plīəns\\ *n* : household machine or device

ap·pli·ca·ble \\'aplikəbəl, ə'plikə-\\ *adj* : capable of being applied — **ap·pli·ca·bil·i·ty** \\₁aplikə'bilətē, ə-₁plikə-\\ *n*

ap·pli·cant \\'aplikənt\\ *n* : one who applies

ap·pli·ca·tion \\₁aplə'kāshən\\ *n* **1** : act of applying or thing applied **2** : constant attention **3** : request

ap·pli·ca·tor \\'aplə₁kātər\\ *n* : device for applying a substance

ap·pli·qué \\₁aplə'kā\\ *n* : cut-out fabric decoration — **appliqué** *vb*

ap·ply \\ə'plī\\ *vb* **-plied; -ply·ing 1** : place in contact **2** : put to practical use **3** : devote (one's) attention or efforts to something **4** : submit a request **5** : have reference or a connection

ap·point \\ə'pȯint\\ *vb* **1** : set or assign officially **2** : equip or furnish — **ap·poin·tee** \\ə₁pȯin'tē, ₁a-\\ *n*

ap·point·ment \\ə'pȯintmənt\\ *n* **1** : act of appointing **2** : nonelective political job **3** : arrangement for a meeting

ap·por·tion \\ə'pȯrshən\\ *vb* : distrib-

ute proportionately — **ap·por·tion·ment** *n*

ap·po·site \\'apəzət\\ *adj* : suitable — **ap·po·site·ly** *adv* — **ap·po·site·ness** *n*

ap·praise \\ə'prāz\\ *vb* **-praised; -prais·ing** : set value on — **ap·prais·al** \\-'prāzəl\\ *n* — **ap·prais·er** *n*

ap·pre·cia·ble \\ə'prēshəbəl\\ *adj* : considerable — **ap·pre·cia·bly** \\-blē\\ *adv*

ap·pre·ci·ate \\ə'prēshē₁āt\\ *vb* **-at·ed; -at·ing 1** : value justly **2** : be grateful for **3** : increase in value — **ap·pre·cia·tion** \\-₁prēshē'āshən\\ *n*

ap·pre·cia·tive \\ə'prēshətiv, -shē₁āt-\\ *adj* : showing appreciation

ap·pre·hend \\₁apri'hend\\ *vb* **1** : arrest **2** : look forward to in dread **3** : understand — **ap·pre·hen·sion** \\-'henchən\\ *n*

ap·pre·hen·sive \\-'hensiv\\ *adj* : fearful — **ap·pre·hen·sive·ly** *adv* — **ap·pre·hen·sive·ness** *n*

ap·pren·tice \\ə'prentəs\\ *n* : person learning a craft ~ *vb* **-ticed; -tic·ing** : employ or work as an apprentice — **ap·pren·tice·ship** *n*

ap·prise \\ə'prīz\\ *vb* **-prised; -pris·ing** : inform

ap·proach \\ə'prōch\\ *vb* **1** : move nearer or be close to **2** : make initial advances or efforts toward — **approach** *n* — **ap·proach·able** *adj*

ap·pro·ba·tion \\₁aprə'bāshən\\ *n* : approval

ap·pro·pri·ate \\ə'prōprē₁āt\\ *vb* **-at·ed; -at·ing 1** : take possession of **2** : set apart for a particular use ~ \\-prēət\\ *adj* : suitable — **ap·pro·pri·ate·ly** *adv* — **ap·pro·pri·ate·ness** *n* — **ap·pro·pria·tion** \\ə-₁prōprē'āshən\\ *n*

ap·prov·al \\ə'prüvəl\\ *n* : act of approving

ap·prove \ə'prüv\ *vb* **-proved; -prov·ing** : accept as satisfactory

ap·prox·i·mate \ə'präksəmət\ *adj* : nearly correct or exact ~ \-ˌmāt\ *vb* **-mat·ed; -mat·ing** : come near — **ap·prox·i·mate·ly** *adv* — **ap·prox·i·ma·tion** \-ˌpräksə'māshən\ *n*

ap·pur·te·nance \ə'pərtnəns\ *n* : accessory — **ap·pur·te·nant** \-'pərtnənt\ *adj*

apri·cot \'aprəˌkät, 'ā-\ *n* : peachlike fruit

April \'āprəl\ *n* : 4th month of the year having 30 days

◆ **apron** \'āprən\ *n* : protective garment

ap·ro·pos \ˌaprə'pō, 'aprəˌpō\ *adv* : suitably ~ *adj* : being to the point

apropos of *prep* : with regard to

apt \'apt\ *adj* 1 : suitable 2 : likely 3 : quick to learn — **apt·ly** *adv* — **apt·ness** *n*

ap·ti·tude \'aptəˌtüd, -tyüd\ *n* 1 : capacity for learning 2 : natural ability

aqua \'akwə, 'äk-\ *n* : light greenish blue color

aquar·i·um \ə'kwareēəm\ *n, pl* **-i·ums** *or* **-ia** \-ēə\ : glass container for aquatic animals and plants

aquat·ic \ə'kwätik, -'kwat-\ *adj* : of or relating to water — **aquatic** *n*

aq·ue·duct \'akwəˌdəkt\ *n* : conduit for carrying running water

aq·ui·line \'akwəˌlīn, -lən\ *adj* : curved like an eagle's beak

-ar \ər\ *adj suffix* 1 : of, relating to, or being 2 : resembling

ar·a·besque \ˌarə'besk\ *n* : intricate design

ar·a·ble \'arəbəl\ *adj* : fit for crops

ar·bi·ter \'ärbətər\ *n* : final authority

ar·bi·trary \'ärbəˌtrerē\ *adj* 1 : selected at random 2 : autocratic —

ar·bi·trari·ly \ˌärbə'trerəlē\ *adv* — **ar·bi·trari·ness** \'ärbəˌtrer-ēnəs\ *n*

ar·bi·trate \'ärbəˌtrāt\ *vb* **-trat·ed; -trat·ing** : settle a dispute as arbitrator — **ar·bi·tra·tion** \ˌärbə-'trāshən\ *n*

ar·bi·tra·tor \'ärbəˌtrātər\ *n* : one chosen to settle a dispute

ar·bor \'ärbər\ *n* : shelter under branches or vines

ar·bo·re·al \är'bōrēəl\ *adj* : living in trees

arc \'ärk\ *n* 1 : part of a circle 2 : bright sustained electrical discharge ~ *vb* **arced** \'ärkt\; **arc·ing** \'ärkiŋ\ : form an arc

ar·cade \är'kād\ *n* : arched passageway between shops

ar·cane \är'kān\ *adj* : mysterious or secret

¹**arch** \'ärch\ *n* : curved structure spanning an opening ~ *vb* : cover with or form into an arch

²**arch** *adj* 1 : chief — usu. in combination 2 : mischievous — **arch·ly** *adv* — **arch·ness** *n*

ar·chae·ol·o·gy, ar·che·ol·o·gy \ˌärkē'äləjē\ *n* : study of past human life — **ar·chae·o·log·i·cal** \-kēə'läjikəl\ *adj* — **ar·chae·ol·o·gist** \-kē'äləjist\ *n*

ar·cha·ic \är'kāik\ *adj* : belonging to an earlier time — **ar·cha·i·cal·ly** \-iklē\ *adv*

arch·an·gel \'ärkˌānjəl\ *n* : angel of high rank

arch·bish·op \ärch'bishəp\ *n* : chief bishop — **arch·bish·op·ric** \-ə-ˌprik\ *n*

arch·di·o·cese \-'dīəsəs, -ˌsēz, -ˌsēs\ *n* : diocese of an archbishop

ar·chery \'ärchərē\ *n* : shooting with bow and arrows — **ar·cher** \-chər\ *n*

ar·che·type \'ärkiˌtīp\ *n* : original pattern or model

ar·chi·pel·a·go \ˌärkəˈpeləˌgō, ˌärchə-\ *n, pl* **-goes** *or* **-gos** : group of islands

ar·chi·tect \ˈärkəˌtekt\ *n* : building designer

ar·chi·tec·ture \ˈärkəˌtekchər\ *n* **1** : building design **2** : style of building **3** : manner of organizing elements — **ar·chi·tec·tur·al** \ˌärkəˈtekchərəl, -ˈtekshrəl\ *adj* — **ar·chi·tec·tur·al·ly** *adv*

ar·chives \ˈärˌkīvz\ *n pl* : public records or their storage place — **archi·vist** \ˈärkəvist, -ˌkī-\ *n*

arch·way *n* : passageway under an arch

arc·tic \ˈärktik, ˈärt-\ *adj* **1** : relating to the region near the north pole **2** : frigid

arctic circle *n* : circle parallel to the equator approximately 23°27′ from the north pole

-ard \ərd\ *n suffix* : one that is

ar·dent \ˈärd°nt\ *adj* : characterized by warmth of feeling — **ar·dent·ly** *adv*

ar·dor \ˈärdər\ *n* : warmth of feeling

ar·du·ous \ˈärjəwəs\ *adj* : difficult — **ar·du·ous·ly** *adv* — **ar·du·ous·ness** *n*

are *pres 2d sing or pres pl of* BE

ar·ea \ˈareə\ *n* **1** : space for something **2** : amount of surface included **3** : region **4** : range covered by a thing or concept

area code *n* : 3-digit area-identifying telephone number

are·na \əˈrēnə\ *n* **1** : enclosed exhibition area **2** : sphere of activity

ar·gon \ˈärˌgän\ *n* : colorless odorless gaseous chemical element

ar·got \ˈärgət, -ˌgō\ *n* : special language (as of the underworld)

argu·able \ˈärgyəwəbəl\ *adj* : open to dispute

ar·gue \ˈärgyü\ *vb* **-gued; -gu·ing 1** : give reasons for or against something **2** : disagree in words

ar·gu·ment \ˈärgyəmənt\ *n* **1** : reasons given to persuade **2** : dispute with words

ar·gu·men·ta·tive \ˌärgyəˈmentətiv\ *adj* : inclined to argue

ar·gyle \ˈärˌgīl\ *n* : colorful diamond pattern in knitting

aria \ˈäreə\ *n* : opera solo

ar·id \ˈarəd\ *adj* : very dry — **arid·i·ty** \əˈridətē\ *n*

arise \əˈrīz\ *vb* **arose** \-ˈrōz\; **aris·en** \-ˈriz°n\; **aris·ing** \-ˈrīziŋ\ **1** : get up **2** : originate

ar·is·toc·ra·cy \ˌarəˈstäkrəsē\ *n, pl* **-cies** : upper class — **aris·to·crat** \əˈristəˌkrat\ *n* — **aris·to·crat·ic** \əˌristəˈkratik\ *adj*

arith·me·tic \əˈrithməˌtik\ *n* : mathematics that deals with numbers — **ar·ith·met·ic** \ˌarithˈmetik\ **ar·ith·met·i·cal** \-ikəl\ *adj*

ark \ˈärk\ *n* : big boat

¹arm \ˈärm\ *n* **1** : upper limb **2** : branch — **armed** \ˈärmd\ *adj* — **arm·less** *adj*

²arm *vb* : furnish with weapons ~ *n* **1** : weapon **2** : branch of the military forces **3** *pl* : family's heraldic designs

ar·ma·da \ärˈmädə, -ˈmäd-\ *n* : naval fleet

ar·ma·dil·lo \ˌärməˈdilō\ *n, pl* **-los** : burrowing mammal covered with bony plates

ar·ma·ment \ˈärməmənt\ *n* : military arms and equipment

ar·ma·ture \ˈärməˌchur, -chər\ *n* : rotating part of an electric generator or motor

armed forces *n pl* : military

ar·mi·stice \ˈärməstəs\ *n* : truce

ar·mor \ˈärmər\ *n* : protective covering — **ar·mored** \-mərd\ *adj*

ar·mory \ˈärmərē\ *n, pl* **-mor·ies** : factory or storehouse for arms

arm·pit *n* : hollow under the junction of the arm and shoulder

ar·my \ˈärmē\ *n, pl* **-mies 1** : body of men organized for war esp. on land **2** : great number

♦ **aro·ma** \əˈrōmə\ *n* : usu. pleasing odor — **ar·o·mat·ic** \ˌarəˈmatik\ *adj*

around \əˈraund\ *adv* **1** : in or along a circuit **2** : on all sides **3** : near **4** : in an opposite direction ~ *prep* **1** : surrounding **2** : along the circuit of **3** : to or on the other side of **4** : near

arouse \əˈrauz\ *vb* **aroused; arous·ing 1** : awaken from sleep **2** : stir up — **arous·al** \-ˈrauzəl\ *n*

ar·raign \əˈrān\ *vb* **1** : call before a court to answer to an indictment **2** : accuse — **ar·raign·ment** *n*

ar·range \əˈrānj\ *vb* **-ranged; -rang·ing 1** : put in order **2** : settle or agree on **3** : adapt (a musical composition) for voices or instruments — **ar·range·ment** *n* — **ar·rang·er** *n*

ar·ray \ə'rā\ *vb* **1** : arrange in order **2** : dress esp. splendidly ~ *n* **1** : arrangement **2** : rich clothing **3** : imposing group

ar·rears \ə'rirz\ *n pl* : state of being behind in paying debts

ar·rest \ə'rest\ *vb* **1** : stop **2** : take into legal custody — **arrest** *n*

ar·rive \ə'rīv\ *vb* **-rived; -riv·ing 1** : reach a destination, point, or stage **2** : come near in time — **ar·riv·al** \-əl\ *n*

ar·ro·gant \'arəgənt\ *adj* : showing an offensive sense of superiority — **ar·ro·gance** \-gəns\ *n* — **ar·ro·gant·ly** *adv*

ar·ro·gate \-,gāt\ *vb* **-gat·ed; -gat·ing** : to claim without justification

ar·row \'arō\ *n* : slender missile shot from a bow — **ar·row·head** *n*

ar·royo \ə'rȯiȯ, -ə\ *n, pl* **-royos 1** : watercourse **2** : gully

ar·se·nal \'ärsᵊnəl\ *n* **1** : place where arms are made or stored **2** : store

ar·se·nic \'ärsᵊnik\ *n* : solid grayish poisonous chemical element

ar·son \'ärsᵊn\ *n* : willful or malicious burning of property — **ar·son·ist** \-ist\ *n*

art \'ärt\ *n* **1** : skill **2** : branch of learning **3** : creation of things of beauty or works so produced **4** : ingenuity

ar·te·rio·scle·ro·sis \ar,tirēōsklə'rōsəs\ *n* : hardening of the arteries — **ar·te·rio·scle·rot·ic** \-'rätik\ *adj or n*

ar·tery \'ärtərē\ *n, pl* **-ter·ies 1** : tubular vessel carrying blood from the heart **2** : thoroughfare — **ar·te·ri·al** \är'tirēəl\ *adj*

art·ful \-fəl\ *adj* **1** : ingenious **2** : crafty — **art·ful·ly** *adv* — **art·ful·ness** *n*

ar·thri·tis \är'thrītəs\ *n, pl* **-ti·des** \-'thritə,dēz\ : inflammation of the joints — **ar·thrit·ic** \-'thritik\ *adj or n*

ar·thro·pod \'ärthrə,päd\ *n* : invertebrate animal (as an insect or crab) with segmented body and jointed limbs — **arthropod** *adj*

ar·ti·choke \'ärtə,chōk\ *n* : tall thistlelike herb or its edible flower head

ar·ti·cle \'ärtikəl\ *n* **1** : distinct part of a written document **2** : nonfictional published piece of writing **3** : word (as *an, the*) used to limit a noun **4** : item or piece

ar·tic·u·late \är'tikyələt\ *adj* : able to speak effectively ~ \-,lāt\ *vb* **-lated; -lat·ing 1** : utter distinctly **2** : unite by joints — **ar·tic·u·late·ly** *adv* — **ar·tic·u·late·ness** *n* — **ar·tic·u·la·tion** \-,tikyə'lāshən\ *n*

ar·ti·fact \'ärtə,fakt\ *n* : object of esp. prehistoric human workmanship

ar·ti·fice \'ärtəfəs\ *n* **1** : trick or trickery **2** : ingenious device or ingenuity

ar·ti·fi·cial \,ärtə'fishəl\ *adj* **1** : man-made **2** : not genuine — **ar·ti·fi·ci·al·i·ty** \-,fishē'alətē\ *n* — **ar·ti·fi·cial·ly** *adv* — **ar·ti·fi·cial·ness** *n*

ar·til·lery \är'tilərē\ *n, pl* **-ler·ies** : large caliber firearms

ar·ti·san \'ärtəzən, -sən\ *n* : skilled craftsman

art·ist \'ärtist\ *n* : one who creates art — **ar·tis·tic** \är'tistik\ *adj* — **ar·tis·ti·cal·ly** \-iklē\ *adv* — **ar·tis·try** \'ärtəstrē\ *n*

art·less \'ärtləs\ *adj* : sincere or natural — **art·less·ly** *adv* — **art·less·ness** *n*

arty \'ärtē\ *adj* **art·i·er; -est** : pretentiously artistic — **art·i·ly** \'ärtᵊlē\ *adv* — **art·i·ness** *n*

-ary \ˌerē\ *adj suffix* : of, relating to, or connected with

as \əz, ˌaz\ *adv* **1** : to the same degree **2** : for example ~ *conj* **1** : in the same way or degree as **2** : while **3** : because **4** : though ~ *pron* — used after *same* or *such* ~ *prep* : in the capacity of

as·bes·tos \as'bestəs, az-\ *n* : fibrous incombustible mineral

as·cend \ə'send\ *vb* : move upward — **as·cen·sion** \-'senchən\ *n*

as·cen·dan·cy \ə'sendənsē\ *n* : domination

as·cen·dant \ə'sendənt\ *n* : dominant position ~ *adj* **1** : moving upward **2** : dominant

as·cent \ə'sent\ *n* **1** : act of moving upward **2** : degree of upward slope

as·cer·tain \ˌasər'tān\ *vb* : determine — **as·cer·tain·able** *adj*

as·cet·ic \ə'setik\ *adj* : self-denying — **ascetic** *n* — **as·cet·i·cism** \-'setəˌsizəm\ *n*

as·cribe \ə'skrīb\ *vb* -**cribed;** -**crib·ing** : attribute — **as·crib·able** *adj* — **as·crip·tion** \-'skripshən\ *n*

asep·tic \ā'septik\ *adj* : free of disease germs

¹ash \'ash\ *n* : tree related to the olives

²ash *n* : matter left when something is burned — **ash·tray** *n*

ashamed \ə'shāmd\ *adj* : feeling shame — **asham·ed·ly** \-'shāmədlē\ *adv*

ash·en \'ashən\ *adj* : deadly pale

ashore \ə'shōr\ *adv* : on or to the shore

aside \ə'sīd\ *adv* **1** : toward the side **2** : out of the way

aside from *prep* **1** : besides **2** : except for

as·i·nine \'as°nˌīn\ *adj* : foolish — **asi·nin·i·ty** \ˌas°n'inətē\ *n*

ask \'ask\ *vb* **1** : call on for an answer or help **2** : utter (a question or request) **3** : invite

askance \ə'skans\ *adv* **1** : with a side glance **2** : with mistrust

askew \ə'skyū\ *adv or adj* : out of line

asleep \ə'slēp\ *adv or adj* **1** : sleeping **2** : numbed **3** : inactive

as long as *conj* **1** : on condition that **2** : because

as of *prep* : from the time of

as·par·a·gus \ə'sparəgəs\ *n* : tall herb related to the lilies or its edible stalks

as·pect \'asˌpekt\ *n* **1** : way something looks to the eye or mind **2** : phase

as·pen \'aspən\ *n* : poplar

as·per·i·ty \a'sperətē, ə-\ *n, pl* -**ties 1** : roughness **2** : harshness

as·per·sion \ə'spərzhən\ *n* : remark that hurts someone's reputation

as·phalt \'asˌfȯlt\ *n* : dark tarlike substance used in paving

as·phyx·ia \as'fiksēə\ *n* : lack of oxygen causing unconsciousness

as·phyx·i·ate \-sēˌāt\ *vb* -**at·ed;** -**at·ing** : suffocate — **as·phyx·i·a·tion** \-ˌfiksē'āshən\ *n*

as·pi·ra·tion \ˌaspə'rāshən\ *n* : strong desire to achieve a goal

as·pire \ə'spīr\ *vb* -**pired;** -**pir·ing** : have an ambition — **as·pir·ant** \'aspərənt, ə'spīrənt\ *n*

as·pi·rin \'asprən\ *n, pl* **aspirin** or **aspirins** : pain reliever

ass \'as\ *n* **1** : long-eared animal related to the horse **2** : stupid person

as·sail \ə'sāl\ *vb* : attack violently — **as·sail·able** *adj* — **as·sail·ant** *n*

as·sas·si·nate \ə'sas°nˌāt\ *vb* -**nat·ed;** -**nat·ing** : murder esp. for political reasons — **as·sas·sin** \-'sas°n\ *n* — **as·sas·si·na·tion** \-ˌsas°n'āshən\ *n*

as·sault \ə'sȯlt\ *n or vb* : attack

as·say \'asˌā, a'sā\ *n* : analysis (as of an ore) to determine quality or properties — **as·say** \a'sā, 'asˌā\ *vb*

as·sem·ble \ə'sembəl\ *vb* -**bled;** -**bling 1** : collect into one place **2** : fit together the parts of

as·sem·bly \-blē\ *n, pl* -**blies 1** : meeting **2** *cap* : legislative body **3** : a fitting together of parts

as·sem·bly·man \-mən\ *n* : member of a legislative assembly

as·sem·bly·wom·an \-ˌwu̇-mən\ *n* : woman who is a member of a legislative assembly

as·sent \ə'sent\ *vb or n* : consent

as·sert \ə'sərt\ *vb* **1** : declare **2** : defend — **as·ser·tion** \-'sərshən\ *n* — **as·ser·tive** \-'sərtiv\ *adj* — **as·sert·ive·ness** *n*

as·sess \ə'ses\ *vb* **1** : impose (as a tax) **2** : evaluate for taxation — **as·sess·ment** *n* — **as·ses·sor** \-ər\ *n*

as·set \'asˌet\ *n* **1** *pl* : individually

owned property **2** : advantage or resource

as·sid·u·ous \ə'sijəwəs\ *adj* : diligent — **as·si·du·i·ty** \ˌasə'düətē, -'dyü-\ *n* — **as·sid·u·ous·ly** *adv* — **as·sid·u·ous·ness** *n*

as·sign \ə'sīn\ *vb* **1** : transfer to another **2** : appoint to a duty **3** : designate as a task **4** : attribute — **as·sign·able** *adj* — **as·sign·ment** *n*

as·sim·i·late \ə'simə,lāt\ *vb* **-lat·ed; -lat·ing 1** : absorb as nourishment **2** : understand — **as·sim·i·la·tion** \-ˌsimə'lāshən\ *n*

as·sist \ə'sist\ *vb* : help — **assist** *n* — **assis·tance** \-'sistəns\ *n* — **as·sis·tant** \-tənt\ *n*

as·so·ci·ate \ə'sōshē,āt, -sē-\ *vb* **-at·ed; -at·ing 1** : join in companionship or partnership **2** : connect in thought — **as·so·ci·ate** \-shēət, -sēət\ *n* — **as·so·ci·a·tion** \-ˌsōshē'āshən, -sē-\ *n*

as soon as *conj* : when

as·sort·ed \ə'sòrtəd\ *adj* : consisting of various kinds

as·sort·ment \-mənt\ *n* : assorted collection

as·suage \ə'swāj\ *vb* **-suaged; -suag·ing** : ease or satisfy

as·sume \ə'süm\ *vb* **-sumed; -sum·ing 1** : take upon oneself **2** : pretend to have or be **3** : take as true

as·sump·tion \ə'səmpshən\ *n* : something assumed

as·sure \ə'shùr\ *vb* **-sured; -sur·ing 1** : give confidence or conviction to **2** : guarantee — **as·sur·ance** \-əns\ *n*

as·ter \'astər\ *n* : herb with daisylike flowers

as·ter·isk \'astə,risk\ *n* : a character * used as a reference mark or as an indication of omission of words

astern \ə'stərn\ *adv or adj* **1** : behind **2** : at or toward the stern

as·ter·oid \'astə,ròid\ *n* : small planet between Mars and Jupiter

asth·ma \'azmə\ *n* : disorder marked by difficulty in breathing — **asth·mat·ic** \az'matik\ *adj or n*

astig·ma·tism \ə'stigmə,tizəm\ *n* : visual defect — **as·tig·mat·ic** \ˌastig'matik\ *adj*

as to *prep* **1** : concerning **2** : according to

as·ton·ish \ə'stänish\ *vb* : amaze — **as·ton·ish·ing·ly** *adv* — **as·ton·ish·ment** *n*

as·tound \ə'staùnd\ *vb* : fill with confused wonder — **as·tound·ing·ly** *adv*

astrad·dle \ə'stradᵊl\ *adv or prep* : so as to straddle

as·tral \'astrəl\ *adj* : relating to or coming from the stars

astray \ə'strā\ *adv or adj* : off the right path

astride \ə'strīd\ *adv* : with legs apart or one on each side ~ *prep* : with one leg on each side of

as·trin·gent \ə'strinjənt\ *adj* : causing shrinking or puckering of tissues — **as·trin·gen·cy** \-jənsē\ *n* — **astringent** *n*

as·trol·o·gy \ə'sträləjē\ *n* : prediction of events by the stars — **as·trol·o·ger** \-əjər\ *n* — **as·tro·log·i·cal** \ˌastrə-'läjikəl\ *adj*

as·tro·naut \'astrə,nòt\ *n* : space traveler

as·tro·nau·tics \ˌastrə'nòtiks\ *n* : construction and operation of spacecraft — **as·tro·nau·tic** \-ik\ — **as·tro·nau·ti·cal** \-ikəl\ *adj*

as·tro·nom·i·cal \ˌastrə'nämikəl\ *adj* **1** : relating to astronomy **2** : extremely large

as·tron·o·my \ə'stränəmē\ *n, pl* **-mies** : study of the celestial bodies — **as·tron·o·mer** \-əmər\ *n*

as·tute \ə'stüt, -'styüt\ *adj* : shrewd — **as·tute·ly** *adv* — **as·tute·ness** *n*

asun·der \ə'səndər\ *adv or adj* **1** : into separate pieces **2** : separated

asy·lum \ə'sīləm\ *n* **1** : refuge **2** : institution for care esp. of the insane

asym·met·ri·cal \ˌāsə'metrikəl\; **asym·met·ric** \-trik\ *adj* : not symmetrical — **asym·me·try** \ˌā-'simətrē\ *n*

at \ət, 'at\ *prep* **1** — used to indicate a point in time or space **2** — used to indicate a goal **3** — used to indicate condition, means, or manner

at all *adv* : without restriction or under any circumstances

ate *past of* EAT

-ate \ət, ˌāt\ *n suffix* **1** : office or rank **2** : group of persons holding an office or rank ~ *adj suffix* **1** : brought into or being in a state **2** : marked by having

athe·ist \'āthēist\ *n* : one who denies the existence of God — **athe·ism** \-ˌizəm\ *n* — **athe·is·tic** \ˌāthē-'istik\ *adj*

ath·ero·scle·ro·sis \ˌathərōskləˈrō-səs\ *n* : arteriosclerosis with deposition of fatty substances in the arteries — **ath·ero·scle·rot·ic** \-ˈrätik\ *adj*

ath·lete \ˈathˌlēt\ *n* : one trained to compete in athletics

ath·let·ics \athˈletiks\ *n sing or pl* : exercises and games requiring physical skill — **ath·let·ic** \-ik\ *adj*

-a·tion \ˈāshən\ *n suffix* : action or process

-a·tive \ˌātiv, ətiv\ *adj suffix* 1 : of, relating to, or connected with 2 : tending to

atlas \ˈatləs\ *n* : book of maps

at·mo·sphere \ˈatməˌsfir\ *n* 1 : mass of air surrounding the earth 2 : surrounding influence — **at·mo·spher·ic** \ˌatməˈsfirik, -ˈsfer-\ *adj* — **at·mo·spher·i·cal·ly** \-iklē\ *adv*

atoll \ˈaˌtȯl, ˈä-, -ˌtäl\ *n* : ring-shaped coral island

at·om \ˈatəm\ *n* 1 : tiny bit 2 : smallest particle of a chemical element that can exist alone or in combination

atom·ic \əˈtämik\ *adj* 1 : relating to atoms 2 : nuclear

atomic bomb *n* : bomb utilizing the energy released by splitting the atom

at·om·iz·er \ˈatəˌmīzər\ *n* : device for dispersing a liquid as a very fine spray

atone \əˈtōn\ *vb* **atoned; aton·ing** : make amends — **atone·ment** *n*

atop \əˈtäp\ *prep* : on top of ~ *adv or adj* : on, to, or at the top

atri·um \ˈātrēəm\ *n, pl* **atria** \-trēə\ *or* **atriums** 1 : open central room or court 2 : heart chamber that receives blood from the veins

atro·cious \əˈtrōshəs\ *adj* : appalling or abominable — **atro·cious·ly** *adv* — **atro·cious·ness** *n*

atroc·i·ty \əˈträsətē\ *n, pl* **-ties** : savage act

at·ro·phy \ˈatrəfē\ *n, pl* **-phies** : wasting away of a bodily part or tissue — **at·ro·phy** *vb*

at·ro·pine \ˈatrəˌpēn\ *n* : drug used esp. to relieve spasms

at·tach \əˈtach\ *vb* 1 : seize legally 2 : bind by personalities 3 : join — **at·tach·ment** *n*

at·ta·ché \ˌatəˈshā, ˌaˌta-, əˌta-\ *n*

: technical expert on a diplomatic staff

at·tack \əˈtak\ *vb* 1 : try to hurt or destroy with violence or words 2 : set to work on ~ *n* 1 : act of attacking 2 : fit of sickness

at·tain \əˈtān\ *vb* 1 : achieve or accomplish 2 : reach — **at·tain·abil·i·ty** \əˌtānəˈbilətē\ *n* — **at·tain·able** *adj* — **at·tain·ment** *n*

at·tempt \əˈtempt\ *vb* : make an effort toward — **attempt** *n*

at·tend \əˈtend\ *vb* 1 : handle or provide for the care of something 2 : accompany 3 : be present at 4 : pay attention — **at·ten·dance** \-ˈtendəns\ *n* — **at·ten·dant** \-dənt\ *adj or n*

at·ten·tion \əˈtenchən\ *n* 1 : concentration of the mind on something 2 : notice or awareness — **at·ten·tive** \-ˈtentiv\ *adj* — **at·ten·tive·ly** *adv* — **at·ten·tive·ness** *n*

at·ten·u·ate \əˈtenyəˌwāt\ *vb* **-at·ed; -at·ing** 1 : make or become thin 2 : weaken — **at·ten·u·a·tion** \-ˌtenyəˈwāshən\ *n*

at·test \əˈtest\ *vb* : certify or bear witness — **at·tes·ta·tion** \ˌaˌtesˈtāshən\ *n*

at·tic \ˈatik\ *n* : space just below the roof

at·tire \əˈtīr\ *vb* **-tired; -tir·ing** : dress — **attire** *n*

at·ti·tude \ˈatəˌtüd, -ˌtyüd\ *n* 1 : posture or relative position 2 : feeling, opinion, or mood

◆ **at·tor·ney** \əˈtərnē\ *n, pl* **-neys** : legal agent

at·tract \əˈtrakt\ *vb* 1 : draw to oneself 2 : have emotional or aesthetic appeal for — **at·trac·tion** \-ˈtrakshən\ *n* — **at·trac·tive** \-ˈtrak-tiv\ *adj* — **at·trac·tive·ly** *adv* — **at·trac·tive·ness** *n*

at·tri·bute \ˈatrəˌbyüt\ *n* : inherent characteristic ~ \əˈtribyət\ *vb* **-trib·ut·ed; -trib·ut·ing** 1 : regard as having a specific cause or origin 2 : regard as a characteristic — **at·trib·ut·able** *adj* — **at·tri·bu·tion** \ˌatrəˈbyüshən\ *n*

at·tune \əˈtün, -ˈtyün\ *vb* : bring into harmony

au·burn \ˈȯbərn\ *adj* : reddish brown

auc·tion \ˈȯkshən\ *n* : public sale of property to the highest bidder —

auction *vb* — **auc·tion·eer** \ˌȯkshə'nir\ *n*

au·dac·i·ty \ȯ'dasətē\ *n* : boldness or insolence — **au·da·cious** \ȯ'dāshəs\ *adj*

au·di·ble \'ȯdəbəl\ *adj* : capable of being heard — **au·di·bly** \-blē\ *adv*

au·di·ence \'ȯdēəns\ *n* **1** : formal interview **2** : group of listeners or spectators

au·dio \'ȯdē,ō\ *adj* : relating to sound or its reproduction ~ *n* : television sound

au·dio·vi·su·al \ˌȯdēō'vizhəwəl\ *adj* : relating to both hearing and sight

au·dit \'ȯdət\ *vb* : examine financial accounts — **audit** *n* — **au·di·tor** \'ȯdətər\ *n*

au·di·tion \ȯ'dishən\ *n* : tryout performance — **audition** *vb*

au·di·to·ri·um \ˌȯdə'tōrēəm\ *n, pl* **-ri·ums** *or* **-ria** \'-rēa\ : room or building used for public performances

au·di·to·ry \'ȯdə,tōrē\ *adj* : relating to hearing

au·ger \'ȯgər\ *n* : tool for boring

aug·ment \ȯg'ment\ *vb* : enlarge or increase — **aug·men·ta·tion** \ˌȯgmən'tāshən\ *n*

au·gur \'ȯgər\ *n* : prophet ~ *vb* : predict — **au·gu·ry** \'ȯgyərē, -gər-\ *n*

au·gust \ȯ'gəst\ *adj* : majestic

Au·gust \'ȯgəst\ *n* : 8th month of the year having 31 days

auk \'ȯk\ *n* : stocky diving seabird

aunt \'ant, 'änt\ *n* **1** : sister of one's father or mother **2** : wife of one's uncle

au·ra \'ȯrə\ *n* **1** : distinctive atmosphere **2** : luminous radiation

au·ral \'ȯrəl\ *adj* : relating to the ear or to hearing

au·ri·cle \'ȯrikəl\ *n* : atrium or ear-shaped pouch in the atrium of the heart

au·ro·ra bo·re·al·is \ə'rōrə,bōrē-'aləs\ *n* : display of light in the night sky of northern latitudes

aus·pic·es \'ȯspəsəz, -ˌsēz\ *n pl* : patronage and protection

aus·pi·cious \ȯ'spishəs\ *adj* : favorable

aus·tere \ȯ'stir\ *adj* : severe — **aus·tere·ly** *adv* — **aus·ter·i·ty** \ȯ'sterətē\ *n*

au·then·tic \ə'thentik, ȯ-\ *adj* : genuine — **au·then·ti·cal·ly** \-iklē\ *adv* — **au·then·tic·i·ty** \ˌȯ,then-'tisətē\ *n*

au·then·ti·cate \ə'thenti,kāt, ȯ-\ *vb* **-cat·ed; -cat·ing** : prove genuine — **au·then·ti·ca·tion** \-ˌthenti-'kāshən\ *n*

au·thor \'ȯthər\ *n* **1** : writer **2** : creator — **au·thor·ship** *n*

au·thor·i·tar·i·an \ȯ,thärə'terēən, ə-, -ˌthȯr-\ *adj* : marked by blind obedience to authority

au·thor·i·ta·tive \ə'thärə,tātiv, ȯ-, -'thȯr-\ *adj* : being an authority — **au·thor·i·ta·tive·ly** *adv* — **au·thor·i·ta·tive·ness** *n*

au·thor·i·ty \ə'thärətē, ȯ-, -'thȯr-\ *n, pl* **-ties 1** : expert **2** : right, responsibility, or power to influence **3** *pl* : persons in official positions

au·tho·rize \'ȯthə,rīz\ *vb* **-rized; -riz·ing** : permit or give official approval for — **au·tho·ri·za·tion** \ˌȯthərə'zāshən\ *n*

au·to \'ȯtō\ *n, pl* **autos** : automobile

au·to·bi·og·ra·phy \ˌȯtəbī'ägrəfē, -bē-\ *n* : writer's own life story — **au·to·bi·og·ra·pher** \-fər\ *n* — **au·to·bio·graph·i·cal** \-ˌbīə'grafikəl\ *adj*

au·toc·ra·cy \ȯ'täkrəsē\ *n, pl* **-cies** : government by one person having unlimited power — **au·to·crat** \'ȯtə,krat\ *n* — **au·to·crat·ic**

JIM DAVIS 3-11

\,ȯtə'kratik\ *adj* — **au·to·crat·i·cal·ly** \-iklē\ *adv*

au·to·graph \'ȯtə,graf \ *n* : signature ~ *vb* : write one's name on

au·to·mate \'ȯtə,māt\ *vb* **-mat·ed; -mat·ing** : make automatic — **au·to·ma·tion** \,ȯtə'māshən\ *n*

au·to·mat·ic \,ȯtə'matik\ *adj* 1 : involuntary 2 : designed to function without human intervention ~ *n* : automatic device (as a firearm) — **au·to·mat·i·cal·ly** \-iklē\ *adv*

au·tom·a·ton \ȯ'tämətən, -,tän\ *n, pl* **-a·tons** *or* **-a·ta** \-tə, -,tä\ : robot

au·to·mo·bile \,ȯtəmō'bēl, -'mō-,bēl\ *n* : 4-wheeled passenger vehicle with its own power source

au·to·mo·tive \,ȯtə'mōtiv\ *adj* : relating to automobiles

au·ton·o·mous \ȯ'tänəməs\ *adj* : self-governing — **au·ton·o·mous·ly** *adv* — **au·ton·o·my** \-mē\ *n*

au·top·sy \'ȯ,täpsē, 'ȯtəp-\ *n, pl* **-sies** : medical examination of a corpse

au·tumn \'ȯtəm\ *n* : season between summer and winter — **au·tum·nal** \ȯ'təmnəl\ *adj*

aux·il·ia·ry \ȯg'zilyərē, -lərē\ *adj* 1 : being a supplement or reserve 2 : accompanying a main verb form to express person, number, mood, or tense — **auxiliary** *n*

avail \ə'vāl\ *vb* : be of use or make use ~ *n* : use

avail·able \ə'vāləbəl\ *adj* 1 : usable 2 : accessible — **avail·abil·i·ty** \-,vālə-'bilətē\ *n*

av·a·lanche \'avə,lanch\ *n* : mass of sliding or falling snow or rock

av·a·rice \'avərəs\ *n* : greed — **av·a·ri·cious** \,avə'rishəs\ *adj*

avenge \ə'venj\ *vb* **avenged; aveng·ing** : take vengeance for — **aveng·er** *n*

av·e·nue \'avə,nü, -,nyü\ *n* 1 : way of approach 2 : broad street

av·er·age \'avrij\ *adj* 1 : being about midway between extremes 2 : ordinary ~ *vb* 1 : be usually 2 : find the mean of ~ *n* : mean

averse \ə'vərs\ *adj* : feeling dislike or reluctance — **aver·sion** \-'vər-zhən\ *n*

avert \ə'vərt\ *vb* : turn away

avi·ary \'āvē,erē\ *n, pl* **-ar·ies** : place where birds are kept

avi·a·tion \,āvē'āshən, ,av-\ *n* : operation or manufacture of airplanes — **avi·a·tor** \'āvē,ātər, 'av-\ *n*

av·id \'avəd\ *adj* 1 : greedy 2 : enthusiastic — **avid·i·ty** \ə'vidətē, a-\ *n* — **av·id·ly** *adv*

av·o·ca·do \,avə'kädō, ,äv-\ *n, pl* **-dos** : tropical fruit with green pulp

av·o·ca·tion \,avə'kāshən\ *n* : hobby

♦ **avoid** \ə'vȯid\ *vb* 1 : keep away from 2 : prevent the occurrence of 3 : refrain from — **avoid·able** *adj* — **avoid·ance** \-ᵊns\ *n*

av·oir·du·pois \,avərdə'pȯiz\ *n* : system of weight based on the pound of 16 ounces

avow \ə'vau\ *vb* : declare openly — **avow·al** \-'vauəl\ *n*

await \ə'wāt\ *vb* : wait for

awake \ə'wāk\ *vb* **awoke** \-'wōk\; **awok·en** \-'wōkən\ *or* **awaked; awak·ing** : wake up — **awake** *adj*

awak·en \ə'wākən\ *vb* **-ened; -en·ing** : wake up

award \ə'wȯrd\ *vb* : give (something won or deserved) ~ *n* 1 : judgment 2 : prize

aware \ə'war\ *adj* : having realization or consciousness — **aware·ness** *n*

awash \ə'wȯsh, -'wäsh\ *adv or adj* : flooded

away \ə'wā\ *adv* 1 : from this or that place or time 2 : out of the way 3

: in another direction **4** : from one's possession *~ adj* **1** : absent **2** : distant

awe \'ȯ\ *n* : respectful fear or wonder *~ vb* **awed; aw·ing** : fill with awe — **awe·some** \-səm\ *adj* — **awe·struck** *adj*

aw·ful \'ȯfəl\ *adj* **1** : inspiring awe **2** : extremely disagreeable **3** : very great — **aw·ful·ly** *adv*

awhile \ə'hwīl\ *adv* : for a while

awk·ward \'ȯkwərd\ *adj* **1** : clumsy **2** : embarrassing — **awk·ward·ly** *adv* — **awk·ward·ness** *n*

awl \'ȯl\ *n* : hole-making tool

aw·ning \'ȯniŋ\ *n* : window cover

awry \ə'rī\ *adv or adj* : wrong

ax, axe \'aks\ *n* : chopping tool

ax·i·om \'aksēəm\ *n* : generally accepted truth — **ax·i·om·at·ic** \ˌaksēə'matik\ *adj*

ax·is \'aksəs\ *n, pl* **ax·es** \-ˌsēz\ : center of rotation — **ax·i·al** \-sēəl\ *adj* — **ax·i·al·ly** *adv*

ax·le \'aksəl\ *n* : shaft on which a wheel revolves

aye \'ī\ *adv* : yes *~ n* : a vote of yes

aza·lea \ə'zālyə\ *n* : rhododendron with funnel-shaped blossoms

az·i·muth \'azəməth\ *n* : horizontal direction expressed as an angle

azure \'azhər\ *n* : blue of the sky — **azure** *adj*

B

b \'bē\ *n, pl* **b's** *or* **bs** \'bēz\ : 2d letter of the alphabet

bab·ble \'babəl\ *vb* **-bled; -bling** **1** : utter meaningless sounds **2** : talk foolishly or too much — **babble** *n* — **bab·bler** *n*

babe \'bāb\ *n* : baby

ba·bel \'bābəl, 'bab-\ *n* : noisy confusion

ba·boon \ba'bün\ *n* : large Asian or African ape with a doglike muzzle

ba·by \'bābē\ *n, pl* **-bies** : very young child *~ vb* **-bied; -by·ing** : pamper — **baby** *adj* — **ba·by·hood** *n* — **ba·by·ish** *adj*

ba·by–sit *vb* **-sat; -sit·ting** : care for children while parents are away — **baby–sit·ter** *n*

bac·ca·lau·re·ate \ˌbakə'lȯrēət\ *n* : bachelor's degree

bac·cha·na·lia \ˌbakə'nālyə\ *n, pl* **-lia** : drunken orgy — **bac·cha·na·lian** \-yən\ *adj or n*

bach·e·lor \'bachələr\ *n* **1** : holder of lowest 4-year college degree **2** : unmarried man — **bach·e·lor·hood** *n*

ba·cil·lus \bə'siləs\ *n, pl* **-li** \-ˌī\ : rod-shaped bacterium — **bac·il·lary** \'basəˌlerē\ *adj*

back \'bak\ *n* **1** : part of a human or animal body nearest the spine **2** : part opposite the front **3** : player

farthest from the opponent's goal *~ adv* **1** : to or at the back **2** : ago **3** : to or in a former place or state **4** : in reply *~ adj* **1** : located at the back **2** : not paid on time **3** : moving or working backward **4** : not current *~ vb* **1** : support **2** : go or cause to go back **3** : form the back of — **back·ache** *n* — **back·er** *n* — **back·ing** *n* — **back·less** *adj* — **back·rest** *n*

back·bite *vb* **-bit; -bit·ten; -bit·ing** : say spiteful things about someone absent — **back·bit·er** *n*

back·bone *n* **1** : bony column in the back that encloses the spinal cord **2** : firm character

back·drop *n* : painted cloth hung across the rear of a stage

back·fire *n* : loud noise from the wrongly timed explosion of fuel in an engine *~ vb* **1** : make or undergo a backfire **2** : have a result opposite of that intended

back·gam·mon \'bakˌgamən\ *n* : board game

back·ground *n* **1** : scenery behind something **2** : sum of a person's experience or training

back·hand *n* : stroke (as in tennis) made with the back of the hand turned forward — **backhand** *adj or vb* — **back·hand·ed** *adj*

back·lash *n* : adverse reaction

back·log *n* : accumulation of things to be done — **backlog** *vb*

back·pack *n* : camping pack carried on the back ~ *vb* : hike with a backpack — **back·pack·er** *n*

back·slide *vb* **-slid; -slid** *or* **-slid·den** \-ˌslidᵊn\; **-slid·ing** : lapse in morals or religious practice — **back·slid·er** *n*

back·stage *adv or adj* : in or to an area behind a stage

back·up *n* : substitute

back·ward \'bakwərd,\

back·wards *adv* **1** : toward the back **2** : with the back foremost **3** : in a reverse direction **4** : toward an earlier or worse state ~ *adj* **1** : directed, turned, or done backward **2** : retarded in development — **back·ward·ness** *n*

back·woods *n pl* : remote or isolated place

ba·con \'bākən\ *n* : salted and smoked meat from a pig

bac·te·ri·um \bak'tirēəm\ *n, pl* **-ria** \-ēə\ : microscopic plant — **bac·te·ri·al** \-ēəl\ *adj* — **bac·te·ri·o·log·ic** \-ˌtirēə'läjik,\ — **bac·te·ri·o·log·i·cal** \-əl\ *adj* — **bac·te·ri·ol·o·gist** \-ē'äləjist\ *n* — **bac·te·ri·ol·o·gy** \-jē\ *n*

bad \'bad\ *adj* **worse** \'wərs\; **worst** \'wərst\ **1** : not good **2** : naughty **3** : faulty **4** : spoiled — **bad** *n or adv* — **bad·ly** *adv* — **bad·ness** *n*

bade *past of* BID

badge \'baj\ *n* : symbol of status

bad·ger \'bajər\ *n* : burrowing mammal ~ *vb* : harass

bad·min·ton \'bad,mintᵊn\ *n* : tennislike game played with a shuttlecock

baf·fle \'bafəl\ *vb* **-fled; -fling** : perplex ~ *n* : device to alter flow (as of liquid or sound) — **baf·fle·ment** *n*

bag \'bag\ *n* : flexible usu. closable container ~ *vb* **-gg- 1** : bulge out **2** : put in a bag **3** : catch in hunting

bag·a·telle \ˌbagə'tel\ *n* : trifle

ba·gel \'bāgəl\ *n* : hard doughnut-shaped roll

bag·gage \'bagij\ *n* : traveler's bags and belongings

bag·gy \'bagē\ *adj* **-gi·er; -est** : puffed out like a bag — **bag·gi·ly** *adv* — **bag·gi·ness** *n*

bag·pipe *n* : musical instrument

with a bag, a tube with valves, and sounding pipes — often pl.

¹bail \'bāl\ *n* : container for scooping water out of a boat — **bail** *vb* — **bail·er** *n*

²bail *n* **1** : security given to guarantee a prisoner's appearance in court **2** : release secured by bail ~ *vb* : bring about the release of by giving bail

bai·liff \'bāləf\ *n* **1** : British sheriff's aide **2** : minor officer of a U.S. court

bai·li·wick \'bāli,wik\ *n* : one's special field or domain

bail·out \'bā,laút\ *n* : rescue from financial distress

bait \'bāt\ *vb* **1** : harass with dogs usu. for sport **2** : furnish (a hook or trap) with bait ~ *n* : lure esp. for catching animals

bake \'bāk\ *vb* **baked; bak·ing** : cook in dry heat esp. in an oven ~ *n* : party featuring baked food — **bak·er** *n* — **bak·ery** \'bākərē\ *n* — **bake·shop** *n*

bal·ance \'baləns\ *n* **1** : weighing device **2** : counteracting weight, force, or influence **3** : equilibrium **4** : that which remains ~ *vb* **-anced; -anc·ing 1** : compute the balance **2** : equalize **3** : bring into harmony or proportion — **bal·anced** *adj*

bal·co·ny \'balkənē\ *n, pl* **-nies** : platform projecting from a wall

bald \'bóld\ *adj* **1** : lacking a natural or usual covering (as of hair) **2** : plain — **bald·ing** *adj* — **bald·ly** *adv* — **bald·ness** *n*

bal·der·dash \'bóldər,dash\ *n* : nonsense

bale \'bāl\ *n* : large bundle ~ *vb* **baled; bal·ing** : pack in a bale — **bal·er** *n*

bale·ful \'bālfəl\ *adj* **1** : deadly **2** : ominous

balk \'bók\ *n* : hindrance ~ *vb* **1** : thwart **2** : stop short and refuse to go on — **balky** *adj*

¹ball \'ból\ *n* **1** : rounded mass **2** : game played with a ball ~ *vb* : form into a ball

²ball *n* : large formal dance — **ball·room** *n*

bal·lad \'baləd\ *n* **1** : narrative poem **2** : slow romantic song — **bal·lad·eer** \ˌbalə'diər\ *n*

bal·last \'baləst\ *n* : heavy material

to steady a ship or balloon ~ *vb* : provide with ballast

bal·le·ri·na \ˌbaləˈrēnə\ *n* : female ballet dancer

♦ **bal·let** \ˈbaˌlā, baˈlā\ *n* : theatrical dancing

bal·lis·tics \bəˈlistiks\ *n sing or pl* : science of projectile motion — **ballistic** *adj*

bal·loon \bəˈlün\ *n* : inflated bag ~ *vb* 1 : travel in a balloon 2 : swell out — **bal·loon·ist** *n*

bal·lot \ˈbalət\ *n* 1 : paper used to cast a vote 2 : system of voting ~ *vb* : vote

bal·ly·hoo \ˈbalēˌhü\ *n* : publicity — **ballyhoo** *vb*

balm \ˈbäm, ˈbälm\ *n* 1 : fragrant healing or soothing preparation 2 : spicy fragrant herb

balmy \ˈbämē, ˈbälmē\ *adj* **balm·i·er; -est** : gently soothing — **balm·i·ness** *n*

ba·lo·ney \bəˈlōnē\ *n* : nonsense

bal·sa \ˈbolsə\ *n* : very light wood of a tropical tree

bal·sam \-əm\ *n* 1 : aromatic resinous plant substance 2 : balsam-yielding plant — **bal·sam·ic** \bolˈsamik\ *adj*

bal·us·ter \ˈbaləstər\ *n* : upright support for a rail

bal·us·trade \-ˌsträd\ *n* : row of balusters topped by a rail

bam·boo \bamˈbü\ *n* : tall tropical grass with strong hollow stems

bam·boo·zle \bamˈbüzəl\ *vb* **-zled; -zling** : deceive

ban \ˈban\ *vb* **-nn-** : prohibit ~ *n* : legal prohibition

ba·nal \bəˈnäl, -ˈnal; ˈbānᵊl\ *adj* : ordinary and uninteresting — **ba·nal·ity** \bəˈnalətē\ *n*

ba·nana \bəˈnanə\ *n* : elongated fruit of a treelike tropical plant

¹**band** \ˈband\ *n* 1 : something that ties or binds 2 : strip or stripe different (as in color) from nearby matter 3 : range of radio wavelengths ~ *vb* 1 : enclose with a band 2 : unite for a common end — **band·ed** *adj* — **band·er** *n*

²**band** *n* 1 : group 2 : musicians playing together

ban·dage \ˈbandij\ *n* : material used esp. in dressing wounds ~ *vb* : dress or cover with a bandage

ban·dan·na, ban·dana \banˈdanə\ *n* : large colored figured handkerchief

ban·dit \ˈbandət\ *n* : outlaw or robber — **ban·dit·ry** \-dətrē\ *n*

band·stand *n* : stage for band concerts

band·wag·on *n* : candidate, side, or movement gaining support

¹**ban·dy** \ˈbandē\ *vb* **-died; -dy·ing** : exchange in rapid succession

²**bandy** *adj* : curved outward

bane \ˈbān\ *n* 1 : poison 2 : cause of woe — **bane·ful** *adj*

¹**bang** \ˈbaŋ\ *vb* : strike, thrust, or move usu. with a loud noise ~ *n* 1 : blow 2 : sudden loud noise ~ *adv* : directly

²**bang** *n* : fringe of short hair over the forehead —, usu. pl. ~ *vb* : cut in bangs

ban·gle \ˈbaŋgəl\ *n* : bracelet

ban·ish \ˈbanish\ *vb* 1 : force by authority to leave a country 2 : expel — **ban·ish·ment** *n*

ban·is·ter \-əstər\ *n* 1 : baluster 2 : handrail

ban·jo \ˈbanˌjō\ *n, pl* **-jos** : stringed instrument with a drumlike body — **banjo·ist** *n*

¹**bank** \ˈbaŋk\ *n* 1 : piled-up mass 2 : rising ground along a body of water 3 : sideways slope along a curve ~ *vb* 1 : form a bank 2 : cover (as a fire) to keep inactive 3 : incline (an airplane) laterally

²**bank** *n* : tier of objects

³**bank** *n* **1** : money institution **2** : reserve supply ∼ *vb* : conduct business in a bank — **bank·book** *n* — **bank·er** *n* — **bank·ing** *n*

bank·rupt \'baŋ,krəpt\ *n* : one required by law to forfeit assets to pay off debts ∼ *adj* **1** : legally a bankrupt **2** : lacking something essential — **bankrupt** *vb* — **bank·rupt·cy** \-,krəpsē\ *n*

ban·ner \'banər\ *n* : flag ∼ *adj* : excellent

banns \'banz\ *n pl* : announcement in church of a proposed marriage

ban·quet \'baŋkwət\ *n* : ceremonial dinner — **banquet** *vb*

ban·shee \'banshē\ *n* : wailing female spirit that foretells death

ban·tam \'bantəm\ *n* : miniature domestic fowl

ban·ter \'bantər\ *n* : good-natured joking — **banter** *vb*

ban·yan \'banyən\ *n* : large tree that grows new trunks from the limbs

bap·tism \'bap,tizəm\ *n* : Christian rite signifying spiritual cleansing — **bap·tis·mal** \bap'tizməl\ *adj*

bap·tize \bap'tīz, 'bap,tīz\ *vb* -**tized**; -**tiz·ing** : administer baptism to

bar \'bär\ *n* **1** : long narrow object used esp. as a lever, fastening, or support **2** : barrier **3** : body of practicing lawyers **4** : wide stripe **5** : food counter **6** : place where liquor is served **7** : vertical line across the musical staff ∼ *vb* -**rr**- **1** : obstruct with a bar **2** : shut out **3** : prohibit ∼ *prep* : excluding — **barred** *adj* — **bar·room** *n* — **bar·tend·er** *n*

barb \'bärb\ *n* : sharp projection pointing backward — **barbed** *adj*

bar·bar·ian \bär'barēən\ *adj* **1** : relating to people considered backward **2** : not refined — **barbarian** *n*

bar·bar·ic \-'barik\ *adj* : barbarian

bar·ba·rous \'bärbərəs\ *adj* **1** : lacking refinement **2** : mercilessly cruel — **bar·bar·ism** \-bə,rizəm\ *n* — **bar·bar·i·ty** \bär'barətē\ *n* — **bar·ba·rous·ly** *adv*

bar·be·cue \'bärbi,kyü\ *n* : gathering at which barbecued food is served ∼ *vb* -**cued**; -**cu·ing** : cook over hot coals or on a spit often with a highly seasoned sauce

bar·ber \'bärbər\ *n* : one who cuts hair

bar·bi·tu·rate \bär'bichərət\ *n* : sedative or hypnotic drug

bard \'bärd\ *n* : poet

bare \'bar\ *adj* **bar·er**; **bar·est 1** : naked **2** : not concealed **3** : empty **4** : leaving nothing to spare **5** : plain ∼ *vb* **bared**; **bar·ing** : make or lay bare — **bare·foot, bare·foot·ed** *adv or adj* — **bare·hand·ed** *adv or adj* — **bare·head·ed** *adv or adj* — **bare·ly** *adv* — **bare·ness** *n*

bare·back, bare·backed *adv or adj* : without a saddle

bare·faced *adj* : open and esp. brazen

bar·gain \'bärgən\ *n* **1** : agreement **2** : something bought for less than its value ∼ *vb* **1** : negotiate **2** : barter

barge \'bärj\ *n* : broad flat-bottomed boat ∼ *vb* **barged**; **barg·ing** : move rudely or clumsily — **barge·man** *n*

bari·tone \'barə,tōn\ *n* : male voice between bass and tenor

bar·i·um \'barēəm\ *n* : silverwhite metallic chemical element

¹**bark** \'bärk\ *vb* **1** : make the sound of a dog **2** : speak in a loud curt tone ∼ *n* : sound of a barking dog

²**bark** *n* : tough corky outer covering of a woody stem or root ∼ *vb* : remove bark or skin from

³**bark** *n* : sailing ship with a fore=and-aft rear sail

bark·er \'bärkər\ *n* : one who calls out to attract people to a show

bar·ley \'bärlē\ *n* : cereal grass or its seeds

barn \'bärn\ *n* : building for keeping hay or livestock — **barn·yard** *n*

bar·na·cle \'bärnikəl\ *n* : marine crustacean

barn·storm *vb* : tour through rural districts giving performances

ba·rom·e·ter \bə'rämətər\ *n* : instrument for measuring atmospheric pressure — **baro·met·ric** \,barə'metrik\ *adj*

bar·on \'barən\ *n* : British peer — **bar·on·age** \-ij\ *n* — **ba·ro·ni·al** \bə'rōnēəl\ *adj* — **bar·ony** \'barənē\ *n*

bar·on·ess \-ənəs\ *n* **1** : baron's wife **2** : woman holding a baronial title

bar·on·et \-ənət\ *n* : man holding a

rank between a baron and a knight — **bar·on·et·cy** \-sē\ n

ba·roque \bə'rōk, -'räk\ adj : elaborately ornamented

bar·racks \'baraks\ n sing or pl : soldiers' housing

bar·ra·cu·da \,barə'kü̇də\ n, pl -da or -das : large predatory sea fish

bar·rage \bə'räzh, -'räj\ n : heavy artillery fire

bar·rel \'barəl\ n 1 : closed cylindrical container 2 : amount held by a barrel 3 : cylindrical part ~ vb -reled or -relled; -rel·ing or -rel·ling 1 : pack in a barrel 2 : move at high speed — **bar·reled** adj

bar·ren \'barən\ adj 1 : unproductive of life 2 : uninteresting — **bar·ren·ness** n

bar·rette \bä'ret, bə-\ n : clasp for a woman's hair

bar·ri·cade \'barə,kād, ,barə'-\ n : barrier — **barricade** vb

bar·ri·er \'barēər\ n : something that separates or obstructs

bar·ring \'bärīŋ\ prep : omitting

bar·ris·ter \'barəstər\ n : British trial lawyer

bar·row \'barō\ n : wheelbarrow

bar·ter \'bärtər\ vb : trade by exchange of goods — **barter** n

ba·salt \bə'sȯlt, 'bā,-\ n : dark fine-grained igneous rock — **ba·sal·tic** \bə'sȯltik\ adj

¹base \'bās\ n, pl **bas·es** 1 : bottom 2 : fundamental part 3 : beginning point 4 : supply source of a force 5 : compound that reacts with an acid to form a salt ~ vb **based**; **bas·ing** : establish — **base·less** adj

²base adj **bas·er**; **bas·est** 1 : inferior 2 : contemptible — **base·ly** adv — **base·ness** n

base·ball n : game played with a bat and ball by 2 teams

base·ment \-mənt\ n : part of a building below ground level

bash \'bash\ vb : strike violently ~ n : heavy blow

bash·ful \-fəl\ adj : self-conscious — **bash·ful·ness** n

ba·sic \'bāsik\ adj 1 : relating to or forming the base or essence 2 : relating to a chemical base — **ba·si·cal·ly** adv — **ba·sic·i·ty** \bā-'sisətē\ n

ba·sil \'bazəl, 'bās-, 'bāz-\ n : aromatic mint

ba·sil·i·ca \bə'silikə\ n : important church or cathedral

ba·sin \'bās°n\ n 1 : large bowl or pan 2 : region drained by a river

ba·sis \'bāsəs\ n, pl **ba·ses** \-,sēz\ 1 : something that supports 2 : fundamental principle

bask \'bask\ vb : enjoy pleasant warmth

bas·ket \'baskət\ n : woven container — **bas·ket·ful** n

bas·ket·ball n : game played with a ball on a court by 2 teams

bas–re·lief \,bäri'lēf\ n : flat sculpture with slightly raised design

¹bass \'bas\ n, pl **bass** or **bass·es** : spiny-finned sport and food fish

²bass \'bās\ n 1 : deep tone 2 : lowest choral voice

bas·set hound \'basət-\ n : short-legged dog with long ears

bas·si·net \,basə'net\ n : baby's bed

bas·soon \bə'sün, ba-\ n : low-pitched wind instrument

bas·tard \'bastərd\ n 1 : illegitimate child 2 : offensive person ~ adj 1 : illegitimate 2 : inferior — **bas·tard·ize** vb — **bas·tardy** n

¹baste \'bāst\ vb **bast·ed**; **bast·ing** : sew temporarily with long stitches

²baste vb **bast·ed**; **bast·ing** : moisten at intervals while cooking

bas·tion \'baschən\ n : fortified position

¹bat \'bat\ n 1 : stick or club 2 : sharp blow ~ vb -tt- : hit with a bat

²bat n : small flying mammal

³bat vb -tt- : wink or blink

batch \'bach\ n : quantity used or produced at one time

bate \'bāt\ vb **bat·ed**; **bat·ing** : moderate or reduce

bath \'bath, 'båth\ n, pl **baths** \'bathz, 'baths, 'båthz, 'båths\ 1 : a washing of the body 2 : water for washing the body 3 : liquid in which something is immersed 4 : bathroom 5 : large financial loss — **bath·tub** n

bathe \'bāth\ vb **bathed**; **bath·ing** 1 : wash in liquid 2 : flow against so as to wet 3 : shine light over 4 : take a bath or a swim — **bath·er** n

bath·robe n : robe worn around the house

bath·room n : room with a bathtub

or shower and usu. a sink and toilet

ba·tiste \bə'tēst\ *n* : fine sheer fabric

ba·ton \bə'tän\ *n* : musical
conductor's stick

bat·tal·ion \bə'talyən\ *n* : military
unit composed of a headquarters
and two or more companies

bat·ten \'bat³n\ *n* : strip of wood
used to seal or reinforce ~ *vb*
: furnish or fasten with battens

¹**bat·ter** \'batər\ *vb* : beat or damage
with repeated blows

²**batter** *n* : mixture of flour and liquid

³**batter** *n* : player who bats

bat·tery \'batərē\ *n, pl* **-ter·ies 1** : illegal beating of a person **2** : group
of artillery guns **3** : group of electric cells

bat·ting \'batiŋ\ *n* : layers of cotton
or wool for stuffing

bat·tle \'bat³l\ *n* : military fighting
~ *vb* **-tled; -tling** : engage in battle — **battle·field** *n*

bat·tle–ax *n* : long-handled ax formerly used as a weapon

bat·tle·ment \-mənt\ *n* : parapet on
top of a wall

bat·tle·ship *n* : heavily armed warship

bat·ty \'batē\ *adj* **-ti·er; -est** : crazy

bau·ble \'bóbəl\ *n* : trinket

bawdy \'bódē\ *adj* **bawd·i·er; -est**
: obscene or lewd — **bawd·i·ly** *adv*
— **bawd·i·ness** *n*

bawl \'ból\ *vb* : cry loudly ~ *n*
: long loud cry

¹**bay** \'bā\ *adj* : reddish brown ~ *n*
: bay-colored animal

²**bay** *n* : European laurel

³**bay** *n* **1** : compartment **2** : area projecting out from a building and
containing a window (**bay window**)

⁴**bay** *vb* : bark with deep long tones

~ *n* **1** : position of one unable to
escape danger **2** : baying of dogs

⁵**bay** *n* : body of water smaller than a
gulf and nearly surrounded by
land

bay·ber·ry \-,berē\ *n* : shrub bearing small waxy berries

bay·o·net \'bāənət, ,bāə'net\ *n*
: dagger that fits on the end of a rifle ~ *vb* **-net·ed; -net·ing** : stab
with a bayonet

bay·ou \'bīū, -ō\ *n* : creek flowing
through marshy land

ba·zaar \bə'zär\ *n* **1** : market **2** : fair
for charity

ba·zoo·ka \-'zükə\ *n* : weapon that
shoots armor-piercing rockets

BB *n* : small shot pellet

be \'bē\ *vb* **was** \'wəz, 'wäz\; **were**
\'wər\; **been** \'bin\; **be·ing** \'bēiŋ\;
am \əm, 'am\; **is** \'iz, əz\; **are** \ər,
'är\ **1** : equal **2** : exist **3** : occupy a
certain place **4** : occur ~ *verbal
auxiliary* — used to show continuous action or to form the passive
voice

◆ **beach** \'bēch\ *n* : sandy shore of a
sea, lake, or river ~ *vb* : drive
ashore

beach·comb·er \-,kōmər\ *n* : one
who searches the shore for useful
objects

beach·head *n* : shore area held by an
attacking force in an invasion

bea·con \'bēkən\ *n* : guiding or
warning light or signal

bead \'bēd\ *n* : small round body
esp. strung on a thread ~ *vb*
: form into a bead — **bead·ing** *n*
— **beady** *adj*

bea·gle \'bēgəl\ *n* : small short=
legged hound

beak \'bēk\ *n* : bill of a bird —
beaked *adj*

bea·ker \'bēkər\ *n* **1** : large drinking
cup **2** : laboratory vessel

beam \'bēm\ *n* **1** : large long piece of

timber or metal **2** : ray of light **3** : directed radio signals for the guidance of pilots ~ *vb* **1** : send out light **2** : smile **3** : aim a radio broadcast

bean \'bēn\ *n* : edible plant seed borne in pods

¹bear \'bar\ *n, pl* **bears 1** *or pl* **bear** : large heavy mammal with shaggy hair **2** : gruff or sullen person — **bear·ish** *adj*

²bear *vb* **bore** \'bōr\; **borne** \'bōrn\; **bear·ing 1** : carry **2** : give birth to or produce **3** : endure **4** : press **5** : go in an indicated direction — **bear·able** *adj* — **bear·er** *n*

beard \'bird\ *n* **1** : facial hair on a man **2** : tuft like a beard ~ *vb* : confront boldly — **beard·ed** *adj* — **beard·less** *adj*

bear·ing *n* **1** : way of carrying oneself **2** : supporting object or purpose **3** : significance **4** : machine part in which another part turns **5** : direction with respect esp. to compass points

beast \'bēst\ *n* **1** : animal **2** : brutal person — **beast·li·ness** *n* — **beast·ly** *adj*

♦ **beat** \'bēt\ *vb* **beat; beat·en** \'bēt³n\ *or* **beat; beat·ing 1** : strike repeatedly **2** : defeat **3** : act or arrive before **4** : throb ~ *n* **1** : single stroke or pulsation **2** : rhythmic stress in poetry or music ~ *adj* : exhausted — **beat·er** *n*

be·atif·ic \,bēə'tifik\ *adj* : blissful

be·at·i·fy \bē'atə,fī\ *vb* **-fied; -fy·ing** : make happy or blessed — **be·at·i·fi·ca·tion** \-,atəfə'kāshən\ *n*

be·at·i·tude \-'atə,tüd, -,tyüd\ *n* : saying in the Sermon on the Mount (Matthew 5:3-12) beginning "Blessed are"

beau \'bō\ *n, pl* **beaux** \'bōz\ *or* **beaus** : suitor

beau·ty \'byütē\ *n, pl* **-ties** : qualities that please the senses or mind — **beau·te·ous** \-ēəs\ *adj* — **beau·te·ous·ly** *adv* — **beau·ti·fi·ca·tion** \,byütəfə'kāshən\ *n* — **beau·ti·fi·er** \'byütə,fīər\ *n* — **beau·ti·ful** \-ifəl\ *adj* — **beau·ti·ful·ly** *adv* — **beau·ti·fy** \-ə,fī\ *vb*

bea·ver \'bēvər\ *n* : large fur-bearing rodent

be·cause \bi'kȯz, -'kəz\ *conj* : for the reason that

because of *prep* : by reason of

beck \'bek\ *n* : summons

beck·on \'bekən\ *vb* : summon esp. by a nod or gesture

be·come \bi'kəm\ *vb* **-came** \-'kām\; **-come; -com·ing 1** : come to be **2** : be suitable — **be·com·ing** *adj* — **be·com·ing·ly** *adv*

bed \'bed\ *n* **1** : piece of furniture to sleep on **2** : flat or level surface ~ *vb* **-dd-** : put or go to bed — **bed·spread** *n*

bed·bug *n* : wingless bloodsucking insect

bed·clothes *n pl* : bedding

bed·ding *n* **1** : sheets and blankets for a bed **2** : soft material (as hay) for an animal's bed

be·deck \bi'dek\ *vb* : adorn

be·dev·il \-'devəl\ *vb* : harass

bed·lam \'bedləm\ *n* : uproar and confusion

be·drag·gled \bi'dragəld\ *adj* : dirty and disordered

bed·rid·den \'bed,rid³n\ *adj* : kept in bed by illness

bed·rock *n* : solid subsurface rock — **bedrock** *adj*

¹bee \'bē\ *n* **1** : 4-winged honey-producing insect — **bee·hive** *n* — **bee·keep·er** *n* — **bees·wax** *n*

²bee *n* : neighborly work session

beech \'bēch\ *n, pl* **beech·es** *or* **beech** : tree with smooth gray bark and edible nuts (**beech·nuts**) — **beech·en** \-ən\ *adj*

beef \'bēf\ *n, pl* **beefs** \'bēfs\ *or* **beeves** \'bēvz\ : flesh of a steer, cow, or bull — ~ *vb* : strengthen — used with *up* — **beef·steak** *n*

bee·line *n* : straight course

been *past part of* BE

beep \'bēp\ *n* : short usu. high-pitched warning sound — **beep** *vb* — **beep·er** *n*

beer \'bir\ *n* : alcoholic drink brewed from malt and hops — **beery** *adj*

beet \'bēt\ *n* : garden root vegetable

bee·tle \'bētəl\ *n* : 4-winged insect

be·fall \bi'fol\ *vb* **-fell; -fall·en** : happen to

be·fit \bi'fit\ *vb* : be suitable to

be·fore \bi'fōr\ *adv* **1** : in front **2** : earlier ~ *prep* **1** : in front of **2** : earlier than ~ *conj* : earlier than

be·fore·hand *adv or adj* : in advance

be·friend \bi'frend\ *vb* : act as friend to

be·fud·dle \-'fədəl\ *vb* : confuse

beg \'beg\ *vb* **-gg-** : ask earnestly

be·get \bi'get\ *vb* **-got; -got·ten** *or* **-got; -get·ting** : become the father of

beg·gar \'begər\ *n* : one that begs ~ *vb* : make poor — **beg·gar·ly** *adj* — **beg·gary** *n*

be·gin \bi'gin\ *vb* **-gan** \-'gan\; **-gun** \-'gən\; **-gin·ning 1** : start **2** : come into being — **be·gin·ner** *n*

be·gone \bi'gon\ *vb* : go away

be·go·nia \-'gōnyə\ *n* : tropical herb with waxy flowers

be·grudge \-'grəj\ *vb* **1** : concede reluctantly **2** : look upon disapprovingly

be·guile \-'gīl\ *vb* **-guiled; -guil·ing 1** : deceive **2** : amuse

be·half \-'haf, -'häf\ *n* : benefit

be·have \bi'hāv\ *vb* **-haved; -hav·ing** : act in a certain way

be·hav·ior \-'hāvyər\ *n* : way of behaving — **be·hav·ior·al** \-əl\ *adj*

be·head \-'hed\ *vb* : cut off the head of

be·hest \-'hest\ *n* : command

be·hind \bi'hīnd\ *adv* : at the back ~ *prep* **1** : in back of **2** : less than **3** : supporting

be·hold \-'hōld\ *vb* **-held; -hold·ing** : see — **be·hold·er** *n*

be·hold·en \-'hōldən\ *adj* : indebted

be·hoove \-'hüv\ *vb* **-hooved; -hooving** : be necessary for

beige \'bāzh\ *n* : yellowish brown — **beige** *adj*

be·ing \'bēiŋ\ *n* **1** : existence **2** : living thing

be·la·bor \bi'lābər\ *vb* : carry on to absurd lengths

be·lat·ed \-'lātəd\ *adj* : delayed

belch \'belch\ *vb* **1** : expel stomach gas orally **2** : emit forcefully — **belch** *n*

be·lea·guer \bi'lēgər\ *vb* **1** : besiege **2** : harass

bel·fry \'belfrē\ *n, pl* **-fries** : bell tower

be·lie \bi'lī\ *vb* **-lied; -ly·ing 1** : misrepresent **2** : prove false

be·lief \bə'lēf\ *n* **1** : trust **2** : something believed

be·lieve \-'lēv\ *vb* **-lieved; -liev·ing 1** : trust in **2** : accept as true **3** : hold as an opinion — **be·liev·able** *adj* — **be·liev·ably** *adv* — **be·liev·er** *n*

be·lit·tle \bi'litəl\ *vb* **-lit·tled; -lit·tling 1** : disparage **2** : make seem less

bell \'bel\ *n* : hollow metallic device that rings when struck ~ *vb* : provide with a bell

bel·la·don·na \ˌbelə'dänə\ *n* : poisonous herb yielding a drug

belle \'bel\ *n* : beautiful woman

bel·li·cose \'beliˌkōs\ *adj* : pugnacious — **bel·li·cos·i·ty** \ˌbeli'käsətē\ *n*

bel·lig·er·ent \bə'lijərənt\ *adj* **1** : waging war **2** : truculent — **bel·lig·er·ence** \-rəns\ *n* — **bel·lig·er·en·cy** \-rənsē\ *n* — **belligerent** *n*

bel·low \'belō\ *vb* : make a loud deep roar or shout — **bellow** *n*

bel·lows \-ōz, -əz\ *n sing or pl* : device with sides that can be compressed to expel air

bell·weth·er \'bel'wethər, -ˌweth-\ *n* : leader

bel·ly \'belē\ *n, pl* **-lies** : abdomen ~ *vb* **-lied; -ly·ing** : bulge

be·long \bi'loŋ\ *vb* **1** : be suitable **2** : be owned **3** : be a part of

be·long·ings \-iŋz\ *n pl* : possessions

be·loved \bi'ləvəd, -'ləvd\ *adj* : dearly loved — **beloved** *n*

be·low \-'lō\ *adv* : in or to a lower place ~ *prep* : lower than

belt \'belt\ *n* **1** : strip (as of leather) worn about the waist **2** : endless band to impart motion **3** : distinct region ~ *vb* **1** : put a belt around **2** : thrash

be·moan \bi'mōn\ *vb* : lament

be·muse \-'myüz\ *vb* : confuse

bench \'bench\ *n* **1** : long seat **2** : judge's seat **3** : court

bend \'bend\ *vb* **bent** \'bent\; **bending 1** : curve or cause a change of shape in **2** : turn in a certain direction ~ *n* **1** : act of bending **2** : curve

be·neath \bi'nēth\ *adv or prep* : below

bene·dic·tion \,benə'dikshən\ *n* : closing blessing

bene·fac·tor \'benə,faktər\ *n* : one who gives esp. charitable aid

be·nef·i·cence \bə'nefəsəns\ *n* : quality of doing good — **be·nef·i·cent** \-sənt\ *adj*

ben·e·fi·cial \,benə'fishəl\ *adj* : being of benefit — **ben·e·fi·cial·ly** *adv*

ben·e·fi·cia·ry \-'fishē,erē, -'fishərē\ *n, pl* **-ries** : one who receives benefits

ben·e·fit \'benə,fit\ *n* **1** : something that does good **2** : help **3** : fund-raising event — **benefit** *vb*

be·nev·o·lence \bə'nevələns\ *n* **1** : charitable nature **2** : act of kindness — **be·nev·o·lent** \-lənt\ *adj* — **be·nev·o·lent·ly** *adv*

be·night·ed \bi'nītəd\ *adj* : ignorant

be·nign \bi'nīn\ *adj* **1** : gentle or kindly **2** : not malignant — **be·nig·ni·ty** \-'nignətē\ *n*

be·nig·nant \-'nignənt\ *adj* : benign

bent \'bent\ *n* : aptitude or interest

be·numb \bi'nəm\ *vb* : make numb esp. by cold

ben·zene \'ben,zēn\ *n* : colorless flammable liquid

be·queath \bi'kwēth, -'kwēth\ *vb* **1** : give by will **2** : hand down

be·quest \bi'kwest\ *n* : something bequeathed

be·rate \-'rāt\ *vb* : scold harshly

be·reaved \-'rēvd\ *adj* : suffering the death of a loved one ~ *n pl* **bereaved** : one who is bereaved — **be·reave·ment** *n*

be·reft \-'reft\ *adj* : deprived of or lacking something

be·ret \bə'rā\ *n* : round soft visorless cap

beri·beri \,berē'berē\ *n* : thiamine-deficiency disease

berm \'bərm\ *n* : bank of earth

ber·ry \'berē\ *n, pl* **-ries** : small pulpy fruit

ber·serk \bər'ərk, -'zərk\ *adj* : crazed — **berserk** *adv*

berth \'bərth\ *n* **1** : place where a ship is anchored **2** : place to sit or sleep esp. on a ship **3** : job ~ *vb* : to bring or come into a berth

ber·yl \'berəl\ *n* : light-colored silicate mineral

be·seech \bi'sēch\ *vb* **-sought** \-'sot\ *or* **-seeched; -seech·ing** : entreat

be·set \-'set\ *vb* **1** : harass **2** : hem in

be·side \-'sīd\ *prep* **1** : by the side of **2** : besides

be·sides \-'sīdz\ *adv* **1** : in addition **2** : moreover ~ *prep* **1** : other than **2** : in addition to

be·siege \-'sēj\ *vb* : lay siege to — **be·sieg·er** *n*

be·smirch \-'smərch\ *vb* : soil

be·sot \-'sät\ *vb* **-tt-** : become drunk

be·speak \bi'spēk\ *vb* **-spoke; -spoken; -speak·ing 1** : address **2** : indicate

best \'best\ *adj, superlative of* GOOD **1** : excelling all others **2** : most productive **3** : largest ~ *adv superlative of* WELL **1** : in the best way **2** : most ~ *n* : one that is best ~ *vb* : outdo

bes·tial \'beschəl, 'bēs-\ *adj* **1** : relating to beasts **2** : brutish — **bes·ti·al·i·ty** \,beschē'alətē, ,bēs-\ *n*

be·stir \bi'stər\ *vb* : rouse to action

best man *n* : chief male attendant at a wedding

be·stow \bi'stō\ *vb* : give — **be·stow·al** \-əl\ *n*

bet \'bet\ *n* **1** : something risked or pledged on the outcome of a contest **2** : the making of a bet ~ *vb* **bet; bet·ting 1** : risk (as money) on an outcome **2** : make a bet with

be·tide \bi'tīd\ *vb* : happen to

be·to·ken \bi'tōkən\ *vb* : give an indication of

be·tray \bi'trā\ *vb* **1** : seduce **2** : report or reveal to an enemy by treachery **3** : abandon **4** : prove unfaithful to **5** : reveal unintentionally — **be·tray·al** *n* — **be·tray·er** *n*

be·troth \-'träth, -'troth, -'trōth, *or with* th\ *vb* : promise to marry — **be·troth·al** *n* — **be·trothed** *n*

bet·ter \'betər\ *adj, comparative of*

GOOD 1 : more than half **2** : improved in health **3** : of higher quality ~ *adv, comparative of* WELL **1** : in a superior manner **2** : more ~ *n* **1** : one that is better **2** : advantage ~ *vb* **1** : improve **2** : surpass — **bet·ter·ment** \-mənt\ *n*

bet·tor, bet·ter \'betər\ *n* : one who bets

be·tween \bi'twēn\ *prep* **1** — used to show two things considered together **2** : in the space separating **3** — used to indicate a comparison or choice ~ *adv* : in an intervening space or interval

bev·el \'bevəl\ *n* : slant on an edge ~ *vb* **-eled** *or* **-elled; -el·ing** *or* **-el·ling 1** : cut or shape to a bevel **2** : incline

bev·er·age \'bevrij\ *n* : drink

bevy \'bevē\ *n, pl* **bev·ies** : large group

be·wail \bi'wāl\ *vb* : lament

♦ **be·ware** \-'war\ *vb* : be cautious

be·wil·der \-'wildər\ *vb* : confuse — **be·wil·der·ment** *n*

be·witch \-'wich\ *vb* **1** : affect by witchcraft **2** : charm — **be·witch·ment** *n*

be·yond \bē'yänd\ *adv* **1** : farther **2** : besides ~ *prep* **1** : on or to the farther side of **2** : out of the reach of **3** : besides

bi- \'bī, ,bī\ *prefix* **1** : two **2** : coming or occurring every two **3** : twice, doubly, or on both sides

bicolored	bifunctional
biconcave	bimetal
biconcavity	bimetallic
biconvex	binational
biconvexity	biparental
bicultural	bipolar
bidirectional	biracial

bi·an·nu·al \bī'anyəwəl\ *adj* : occurring twice a year — **bi·an·nu·al·ly** *adv*

bi·as \'bīəs\ *n* **1** : line diagonal to the grain of a fabric **2** : prejudice ~ *vb* **-ased** *or* **-assed; -as·ing** *or* **-as·sing** : prejudice

bib \'bib\ *n* : shield tied under the chin to protect the clothes while eating

Bi·ble \'bībəl\ *n* **1** : sacred scriptures of Christians **2** : sacred scriptures of Judaism or of some other religion — **bib·li·cal** \'biblikəl\ *adj*

bib·li·og·ra·phy \,biblē'ägrəfē\ *n, pl* **-phies** : list of writings on a subject or of an author — **bib·li·og·ra·pher** \-fər\ *n* — **bib·li·o·graph·ic** \-lēə- 'grafik\ *adj*

bi·cam·er·al \'bī'kamərəl\ *adj* : having 2 legislative chambers

bi·car·bon·ate \-'kärbə,nāt, -nət\ *n* : acid carbonate

bi·cen·ten·ni·al \,bīsen'tenēəl\ *n* : 200th anniversary — **bicentennial** *adj*

bi·ceps \'bī,seps\ *n* : large muscle of the upper arm

bick·er \'bikər\ *vb or n* : squabble

bi·cus·pid \bī'kəspəd\ *n* : double-pointed tooth

bi·cy·cle \'bī,sikəl\ *n* : 2-wheeled vehicle moved by pedaling ~ *vb* **-cled; -cling** : ride a bicycle — **bi·cy·cler** \-klər\ *n* — **bi·cy·clist** \-list\ *n*

bid \'bid\ *vb* **bade** \'bad, 'bād\ *or* **bid; bid·den** \'bid°n\ *or* **bid; bid·ding 1** : order **2** : invite **3** : express **4** : make a bid ~ *n* **1** : act of bidding **2** : buyer's proposed price — **bid·da·ble** \-əbəl\ *adj* — **bid·der** *n*

bide \'bīd\ *vb* **bode** \'bōd\ *or* **bid·ed; bided; bid·ing 1** : wait **2** : dwell

bi·en·ni·al \bī'enēəl\ *adj* **1** : occurring once in 2 years **2** : lasting 2 years — **biennial** *n* — **bi·en·ni·al·ly** *adv*

bier \'bir\ *n* : stand for a coffin

bifocals \'bī,fōkəlz\ *n pl* : eyeglasses that correct for near and distant vision

big \'big\ *adj* **-gg-** : large in size, amount, or scope — **big·ness** *n*

big·a·my \'bigəmē\ *n* : marrying one person while still married to another — **big·a·mist** \-mist\ *n* — **big·a·mous** \-məs\ *adj*

big·horn *n, pl* **-horn** *or* **-horns** : wild mountain sheep

bight \'bīt\ *n* **1** : loop of a rope **2** : bay

big·ot \'bigət\ *n* : one who is intolerant of others — **big·ot·ed** \-ətəd\ *adj* — **big·ot·ry** \-ətrē\ *n*

◆ **big shot** *n* : important person

big·wig *n* : big shot

bike \'bīk\ *n* : bicycle or motorcycle

bi·ki·ni \bə'kēnē\ *n* : woman's brief 2-piece bathing suit

bi·lat·er·al \bī'latərəl\ *adj* : involving 2 sides — **bi·lat·er·al·ly** *adv*

bile \'bīl\ *n* **1** : greenish liver secretion that aids digestion **2** : bad temper

bi·lin·gual \bī'liŋgwəl\ *adj* : using 2 languages

bil·ious \'bilyəs\ *adj* : irritable — **bil·ious·ness** *n*

bilk \'bilk\ *vb* : cheat

¹bill \'bil\ *n* : jaws of a bird together with their horny covering ∼ *vb* : caress fondly — **billed** *adj*

²bill *n* **1** : draft of a law **2** : list of things to be paid for **3** : printed advertisement **4** : piece of paper money ∼ *vb* : submit a bill or account to

bill·board *n* : surface for displaying advertising bills

bil·let \'bilət\ *n* : soldiers' quarters ∼ *vb* : lodge in a billet

bill·fold *n* : wallet

bil·liards \'bilyərdz\ *n* : game of driving balls into one another or into pockets on a table

bil·lion \'bilyən\ *n, pl* **billions** *or* **billion** : 1000 millions — **billion** *adj* — **bil·lionth** \-yənth\ *adj or n*

bil·low \'bilō\ *n* **1** : great wave **2** : rolling mass ∼ *vb* : swell out — **bil·lowy** \'biləwē\ *adj*

billy goat *n* : male goat

bin \'bin\ *n* : storage box

bi·na·ry \'bīnərē\ *adj* : consisting of 2 things — **binary** *n*

bind \'bīnd\ *vb* **bound** \'baund\; **bind·ing** **1** : tie **2** : obligate **3** : unite into a mass **4** : bandage — **bind·er** *n* — **binding** *n*

binge \'binj\ *n* : spree

bin·go \'biŋgō\ *n, pl* **-gos** : game of covering numbers on a card

bin·oc·u·lar \bī'näkyələr, bə-\ *adj* : of or relating to both eyes ∼ *n* : binocular optical instrument — usu. pl.

bio·chem·is·try \ˌbīō'keməstrē\ *n* : chemistry dealing with organisms — **bio·chemi·cal** *adj or n* — **bio·chem·ist** *n*

bio·de·grad·able \ˌbīōdi'grādəbəl\ *adj* : able to be reduced to harmless products by organisms — **bio·de·grad·abil·i·ty** *n* — **bio·deg·ra·da·tion** *n* — **bio·de·grade** *vb*

bi·og·ra·phy \bī'ägrəfē, bē-\ *n, pl* **-phies** : written history of a person's life — **bi·og·ra·pher** \-fər\ *n* — **bi·o·graph·i·cal** \ˌbīə·'grafikəl\ *adj*

bi·ol·o·gy \bī'äləjē\ *n* : science of living beings and life processes — **bi·o·log·ic** \ˌbīə'läjik\ **bi·o·log·i·cal** \-əl\ *adj* — **bi·ol·o·gist** \bī-'äləjist\ *n*

bio·phys·ics \ˌbīō'fiziks\ *n* : application of physics to biological problems — **bio·phys·i·cal** *adj* — **bio·phys·i·cist** *n*

bi·op·sy \'bī,äpsē\ *n, pl* **-sies** : removal of live bodily tissue for examination

bio·tech·nol·o·gy \ˌbīōtek'näləjē\ *n* : manufacture of products using

techniques involving the manipulation of DNA

bi·par·ti·san \bī'pärtəzən, -sən\ *adj* : involving members of 2 parties

bi·ped \'bī,ped\ *n* : 2-footed animal

birch \'bərch\ *n* : deciduous tree with close-grained wood — **birch, birch·en** \-ən\ *adj*

bird \'bərd\ *n* : warm-blooded egg-laying vertebrate with wings and feathers — **bird·bath** *n* — **bird·house** *n* — **bird·seed** *n*

bird's-eye \'bərdz,ī\ *adj* 1 : seen from above 2 : cursory

birth \'bərth\ *n* 1 : act or fact of being born or of producing young 2 : origin — **birth·day** *n* — **birth·place** *n* — **birth·rate** *n*

birth·mark *n* : unusual blemish on the skin at birth

birth·right *n* : something one is entitled to by birth

bis·cuit \'biskət\ *n* : small bread made with leavening other than yeast

bi·sect \'bī,sekt\ *vb* : divide into 2 parts — **bi·sec·tion** \'bī,sekshən\ *n* — **bi·sec·tor** \-tər\ *n*

bish·op \'bishəp\ *n* : clergy member higher than a priest

bish·op·ric \-shə,prik\ *n* 1 : diocese 2 : office of bishop

bis·muth \'bizməth\ *n* : heavy brittle metallic chemical element

bi·son \'bīs²n, 'bīz-\ *n, pl* **-son** : large shaggy wild ox of central U.S.

bis·tro \'bēstrō, 'bis-\ *n, pl* **-tros** : small restaurant or bar

¹bit \'bit\ *n* 1 : part of a bridle that goes in a horse's mouth 2 : drilling tool

²bit *n* 1 : small piece or quantity 2 : small degree

bitch \'bich\ *n* : female dog ~ *vb* : complain

bite \'bīt\ *vb* **bit** \'bit\; **bit·ten** \'bit²n\; **bit·ing** \'bītiŋ\ 1 : to grip or cut with teeth or jaws 2 : dig in or grab and hold 3 : sting 4 : take bait ~ *n* 1 : act of biting 2 : bit of food 3 : wound made by biting — **bit·ing** *adj*

bit·ter \'bitər\ *adj* 1 : having an acrid lingering taste 2 : intense or severe 3 : extremely harsh or resentful — **bit·ter·ly** *adv* — **bit·ter·ness** *n*

bit·tern \'bitərn\ *n* : small heron

bi·tu·mi·nous coal \bə'tümənəs-,

-'tyü-\ *n* : coal that yields volatile waste matter when heated

bi·valve \'bī,valv\ *n* : animal (as a clam) with a shell of 2 parts — **bivalve** *adj*

biv·ouac \'bivə,wak\ *n* : temporary camp ~ *vb* **-ouacked; -ouack·ing** : camp

bi·zarre \bə'zär\ *adj* : very strange — **bi·zarre·ly** *adv*

blab \'blab\ *vb* **-bb-** : talk too much

black \'blak\ *adj* 1 : of the color black 2 : Negro 3 : soiled 4 : lacking light 5 : wicked or evil 6 : gloomy ~ *n* 1 : black pigment or dye 2 : something black 3 : color of least lightness 4 : person of a dark-skinned race ~ *vb* : blacken — **black·ing** *n* — **black·ish** *adj* — **black·ly** *adv* — **black·ness** *n*

black-and-blue *adj* : darkly discolored from bruising

black·ball \'blak,ból\ *vb* 1 : ostracize 2 : boycott — **blackball** *n*

black·ber·ry \'blak,berē\ *n* : black or purple fruit of a bramble

black·bird *n* : bird of which the male is largely or wholly black

black·board *n* : dark surface for writing on with chalk

black·en \'blakən\ *vb* 1 : make or become black 2 : defame

black·guard \'blagərd, -,ärd\ *n* : scoundrel

black·head *n* : small dark oily mass plugging the outlet of a skin gland

black hole *n* : invisible extremely massive celestial object

black·jack *n* 1 : flexible leather-covered club 2 : card game ~ *vb* : hit with a blackjack

black·list *n* : list of persons to be punished or boycotted — **blacklist** *vb*

black·mail *n* 1 : extortion by threat of exposure 2 : something extorted by blackmail — **blackmail** *vb* — **black·mail·er** *n*

black·out *n* 1 : darkness due to electrical failure 2 : brief fainting spell — **black out** *vb*

black·smith *n* : one who forges iron

black·top *n* : dark tarry material for surfacing roads — **blacktop** *vb*

blad·der \'bladər\ *n* : sac into which urine passes from the kidneys

blade \'blād\ *n* 1 : leaf esp. of grass 2 : something resembling the flat part of a leaf 3 : cutting part of an instrument or tool — **blad·ed** \'blādəd\ *adj*

blame \'blām\ *vb* **blamed; blam·ing 1** : find fault with **2** : hold responsible or responsible for — **blam·able** *adj* — **blame** *n* — **blame·less** *adj* — **blame·less·ly** *adv* — **blame·wor·thi·ness** *n* — **blame·worthy** *adj*

blanch \'blanch\ *vb* : make or become white or pale

bland \'bland\ *adj* **1** : smooth in manner **2** : soothing **3** : tasteless — **bland·ly** *adv* — **bland·ness** *n*

blan·dish·ment \'blandishmənt\ *n* : flattering or coaxing speech or act

blank \'blaŋk\ *adj* **1** : showing or causing a dazed look **2** : lacking expression **3** : empty **4** : free from writing **5** : downright ~ *n* **1** : an empty space **2** : form with spaces to write in **3** : unfinished form (as of a key) **4** : cartridge with no bullet ~ *vb* : cover or close up — **blank·ly** *adv* — **blank·ness** *n*

◆ **blan·ket** \'blaŋkət\ *n* **1** : heavy covering for a bed **2** : covering layer ~ *vb* : cover ~ *adj* : applying to a group

blare \'blar\ *vb* **blared; blar·ing** : make a loud harsh sound — **blare** *n*

blar·ney \'blärnē\ *n* : skillful flattery

bla·sé \blä'zā\ *adj* : indifferent to pleasure or excitement

blas·pheme \blas'fēm\ *vb* **-phemed; -phem·ing** : speak blasphemy — **blas·phem·er** *n*

blas·phe·my \'blasfəmē\ *n, pl* **-mies** : irreverence toward God or anything sacred — **blas·phe·mous** *adj*

blast \'blast\ *n* **1** : violent gust of wind **2** : explosion ~ *vb* : shatter by or as if by explosive — **blast off** *vb* : take off esp. in a rocket

bla·tant \'blāt°nt\ *adj* : offensively showy — **bla·tan·cy** \-°nsē\ *n* — **bla·tant·ly** *adv*

¹**blaze** \'blāz\ *n* **1** : fire **2** : intense direct light **3** : strong display ~ *vb* **blazed; blaz·ing** : burn or shine brightly

²**blaze** *n* **1** : white stripe on an animal's face **2** : trail marker esp. on a tree ~ *vb* **blazed; blaz·ing** : mark with blazes

blaz·er \-ər\ *n* : sports jacket

bleach \'blēch\ *vb* : whiten — **bleach** *n*

bleach·ers \-ərz\ *n sing or pl* : uncovered stand for spectators

bleak \'blēk\ *adj* **1** : desolately barren **2** : lacking cheering qualities — **bleak·ish** *adj* — **bleak·ly** *adv* — **bleak·ness** *n*

blear \'blir\ *adj* : dim with water or tears

bleary \'blirē\ *adj* : dull or dimmed esp. from fatigue

bleat \'blēt\ *n* : cry of a sheep or goat or a sound like it — **bleat** *vb*

bleed \'blēd\ *vb* **bled** \'bled\; **bleed·ing 1** : lose or shed blood **2** : feel distress **3** : flow from a wound **4** : draw fluid from **5** : extort money from — **bleed·er** *n*

blem·ish \'blemish\ *vb* : spoil by a flaw ~ *n* : noticeable flaw

¹**blench** \'blench\ *vb* : flinch

²**blench** *vb* : grow or make pale

blend \'blend\ *vb* **1** : mix thoroughly **2** : combine into an integrated whole — **blend** *n* — **blend·er** *n*

bless \'bles\ *vb* **blessed** \'blest\; **bless·ing 1** : consecrate by religious rite **2** : invoke divine care for **3** : make happy — **bless·ed** \'blesəd\, **blest** \'blest\ *adj* — **bless·ed·ly** \'blesədlē\ *adv* — **bless·ed·ness** \'blesədnəs\ *n* — **bless·ing** *n*

blew *past of* BLOW

blight \'blīt\ *n* **1** : plant disorder

marked by withering or an organism causing it **2** : harmful influence **3** : deteriorated condition ∼ *vb* : affect with or suffer from blight

blimp \'blimp\ *n* : airship holding form by pressure of contained gas

blind \'blīnd\ *adj* **1** : lacking or quite deficient in ability to see **2** : not intelligently controlled **3** : having no way out ∼ *vb* **1** : to make blind **2** : dazzle ∼ *n* **1** : something to conceal or darken **2** : place of concealment — **blind·ly** *adv* — **blindness** *n*

blind·fold *vb* : cover the eyes of — **blindfold** *n*

blink \'bliŋk\ *vb* **1** : wink **2** : shine intermittently ∼ *n* : wink

blink·er *n* : a blinking light

bliss \'blis\ *n* **1** : complete happiness **2** : heaven or paradise — **bliss·ful** *adj* — **bliss·ful·ly** *adv*

blis·ter \'blistər\ *n* **1** : raised area of skin containing watery fluid **2** : raised or swollen spot ∼ *vb* : develop or cause blisters

blithe \'blīth, 'blīth\ *adj* **blith·er**; **blith·est** : cheerful — **blithe·ly** *adv* — **blithe·some** \-əm\ *adj*

blitz \'blits\ *n* **1** : series of air raids **2** : fast intensive campaign — **blitz** *vb*

bliz·zard \'blizərd\ *n* : severe snowstorm

bloat \'blōt\ *vb* : swell

blob \'bläb\ *n* : small lump or drop

bloc \'bläk\ *n* : group working together

block \'bläk\ *n* **1** : solid piece **2** : frame enclosing a pulley **3** : quantity considered together **4** : large building divided into separate units **5** : a city square or the distance along one of its sides **6** : obstruction **7** : interruption of a bodily or mental function ∼ *vb* : obstruct or hinder

block·ade \blä'kād\ *n* : isolation of a place usu. by troops or ships — **block·ade** *vb* — **block·ad·er** *n*

block·head *n* : stupid person

blond, blonde \'bländ\ *adj* **1** : fair in complexion **2** : of a light color — **blond, blonde** *n*

blood \'bləd\ *n* **1** : red liquid that circulates in the heart, arteries, and veins of animals **2** : lifeblood **3** : lineage — **blood·ed** *adj* — **blood·less** *adj* — **blood·stain** *n* — **blood**-

stained *adj* — **blood·suck·er** *n* — **blood·suck·ing** *n* — **bloody** *adj*

blood·cur·dling *adj* : terrifying

blood·hound *n* : large hound with a keen sense of smell

blood·mo·bile \-mō,bēl\ *n* : truck for collecting blood from donors

blood·shed *n* : slaughter

blood·shot *adj* : inflamed to redness

blood·stream *n* : blood in a circulatory system

blood·thirsty *adj* : eager to shed blood — **blood·thirst·i·ly** *adv* — **blood·thirst·i·ness** *n*

bloom \'blüm\ *n* **1** : flower **2** : period of flowering **3** : fresh or healthy look ∼ *vb* **1** : yield flowers **2** : mature — **bloomy** *adj*

bloo·mers \'blümərz\ *n pl* : woman's underwear of short loose trousers

bloop·er \'blüpər\ *n* : public blunder

blos·som \'bläsəm\ *n or vb* : flower

blot \'blät\ *n* : stain **2** : blemish ∼ *vb* **-tt-** **1** : spot **2** : dry with absorbent paper — **blot·ter** *n*

blotch \'bläch\ *n* : large spot — **blotch** *vb* — **blotchy** *adj*

blouse \'blaús, 'blaúz\ *n* : loose garment reaching from the neck to the waist

¹**blow** \'blō\ *vb* **blew** \'blü\; **blown** \'blōn\; **blow·ing** **1** : move forcibly **2** : send forth a current of air **3** : sound **4** : shape by blowing **5** : explode **6** : bungle ∼ *n* **1** : gale **2** : act of blowing — **blow·er** *n* — **blowy** *adj*

²**blow** *n* **1** : forcible stroke **2** *pl* : fighting **3** : calamity

blow·out *n* : bursting of a tire

blow·torch *n* : small torch that uses a blast of air

◆ ¹**blub·ber** \'bləbər\ *n* : fat of whales

²**blubber** *vb* : cry noisily

blud·geon \'bləjən\ *n* : short club ∼ *vb* : hit with a bludgeon

blue \'blü\ *adj* **blu·er**; **blu·est** **1** : of the color blue **2** : melancholy ∼ *n* : color of the clear sky — **blu·ish** \-ish\ *adj*

blue·bell *n* : plant with blue bell-shaped flowers

blue·ber·ry \-,berē\ *n* : edible blue or blackish berry

blue·bird *n* : small bluish songbird

blue·fish *n* : bluish marine food fish

blue jay *n* : American crested jay

blue·print *n* **1** : photographic print in white on blue of a mechanical drawing **2** : plan of action — **blueprint** *vb*

blues \'blüz\ *n pl* **1** : depression **2** : music in a melancholy style

¹**bluff** \'bləf\ *adj* **1** : rising steeply with a broad flat front **2** : frank ~ *n* : cliff

²**bluff** *vb* : deceive by pretense ~ *n* : act of bluffing — **bluff·er** \-ər\ *n*

blu·ing, blue·ing \'blüiŋ\ *n* : laundry preparation to keep fabrics white

blun·der \'bləndər\ *vb* **1** : move clumsily **2** : make a stupid mistake ~ *n* : bad mistake

blun·der·buss \-,bəs\ *n* : obsolete short-barreled firearm

blunt \'blənt\ *adj* **1** : not sharp **2** : tactless ~ *vb* : make dull — **blunt·ly** *adv* — **blunt·ness** *n*

blur \'blər\ *n* **1** : smear **2** : something perceived indistinctly ~ *vb* -**rr**- : cloud or obscure — **blur·ry** \-ē\ *adj*

blurb \'blərb\ *n* : short publicity notice

blurt \'blərt\ *vb* : utter suddenly

blush \'bləsh\ *n* : reddening of the face — **blush** *vb* — **blush·ful** *adj*

blus·ter \'bləstər\ *vb* **1** : blow violently **2** : talk or act with boasts or threats — **blus·ter** *n* — **blus·tery** *adj*

boa \'bōə\ *n* **1** : a large snake (as the **boa con·stric·tor** \-kən'striktər\) that crushes its prey **2** : fluffy scarf

boar \'bōr\ *n* : male swine

board \'bōrd\ *n* **1** : long thin piece of sawed lumber **2** : flat thin sheet esp. for games **3** : daily meals furnished for pay **4** : official body ~ *vb* **1** : go aboard **2** : cover with boards **3** : supply meals to — **board·er** *n*

board·walk *n* : wooden walk along a beach

boast \'bōst\ *vb* : praise oneself or one's possessions — **boast** *n* — **boast·er** *n* — **boast·ful** *adj* — **boast·ful·ly** *adv*

boat \'bōt\ *n* : small vessel for traveling on water — **boat** *vb* — **boat·man** \-mən\ *n*

boat·swain \'bōsªn\ *n* : ship's officer in charge of the hull

¹**bob** \'bäb\ *vb* -**bb**- **1** : move up and down **2** : appear suddenly

²**bob** *n* **1** : float **2** : woman's short haircut ~ *vb* : cut hair in a bob

bob·bin \'bäbən\ *n* : spindle for holding thread

bob·ble \'bäbəl\ *vb* -**bled; -bling** : fumble — **bobble** *n*

bob·cat *n* : small American lynx

bob·o·link \'bäbə,liŋk\ *n* : American songbird

bob·sled \'bäb,sled\ *n* : racing sled — **bobsled** *vb*

bob·white \'bäb'hwīt\ *n* : quail

bock \'bäk\ *n* : dark beer

¹**bode** \'bōd\ *vb* bod·ed; bod·ing : indicate by signs

²**bode** *past of* BIDE

bod·ice \'bädəs\ *n* : close-fitting top of dress

bodi·ly \'bädªlē\ *adj* : relating to the body ~ *adv* **1** : in the flesh **2** : as a whole

body \'bädē\ *n, pl* **bod·ies 1** : the physical whole of an organism **2** : human being **3** : main part **4** : mass of matter **5** : group — **bod·ied** *adj* — **bod·i·less** \-iləs, -ªləs\ *adj* — **body·guard** *n*

bog \'bäg, 'bȯg\ *n* : swamp ~ *vb* -**gg**- : sink in or as if in a bog — **bog·gy** *adj*

bo·gey \'bu̇gē, 'bō-\ *n, pl* -**geys** : someone or something frightening

bog·gle \'bägəl\ vb -gled; -gling : overwhelm with amazement

bo·gus \'bōgəs\ adj : fake

bo·he·mi·an \bō'hēmēən\ n : one living unconventionally — **bohemian** adj

¹**boil** \'bȯil\ n : inflamed swelling

²**boil** vb 1 : heat to a temperature (**boiling point**) at which vapor forms 2 : cook in boiling liquid 3 : be agitated — **boil** n

boil·er \'bȯilər\ n : tank holding hot water or steam

bois·ter·ous \'bȯistərəs\ adj : noisily turbulent — **bois·ter·ous·ly** adv

bold \'bōld\ adj 1 : courageous 2 : insolent 3 : daring — **bold·ly** adv — **bold·ness** n

bo·le·ro \bə'lerō\ n, pl -ros 1 : Spanish dance 2 : short open jacket

boll \'bōl\ n : seed pod

boll weevil n : small grayish weevil that infests the cotton plant

bo·lo·gna \bə'lōnē\ n : large smoked sausage

bol·ster \'bōlstər\ n : long pillow ~ vb -stered; -ster·ing : support

bolt \'bōlt\ n 1 : flash of lightning 2 : sliding bar used to fasten a door 3 : roll of cloth 4 : threaded pin used with a nut — vb 1 : move suddenly 2 : fasten with a bolt 3 : swallow hastily

bomb \'bäm\ n : explosive device ~ vb : attack with bombs — **bombproof** adj

bom·bard \bäm'bärd, bəm-\ vb : attack with or as if with artillery — **bom·bard·ment** n

bom·bar·dier \ˌbämbə'dir\ n : one who releases the bombs from a bomber

bom·bast \'bäm,bast\ n : pretentious language — **bom·bas·tic** \bäm'bastik\ adj

bomb·er n 1 : one that bombs 2 : airplane for dropping bombs

bomb·shell n 1 : bomb 2 : great surprise

bona fide \'bōnə,fīd, 'bän-; ˌbōnə-'fīdē\ adj 1 : made in good faith 2 : genuine

bo·nan·za \bə'nanzə\ n : something yielding a rich return

bon·bon \'bän,bän\ n : piece of candy

bond \'bänd\ n 1 pl : fetters 2 : uniting force 3 : obligation made binding by money 4 : interest-bearing certificate ~ vb 1 : insure 2 : cause to adhere — **bond·hold·er** n

bond·age \'bändij\ n : slavery — **bond·man** \-mən\ n — **bond·wom·an** n

¹**bonds·man** \'bändzmən\ n : slave

²**bondsman** n : surety

bone \'bōn\ n : skeletal material ~ vb **boned; bon·ing** : to free from bones — **bone·less** adj — **bony** \'bōnē\ adj

bon·er \'bōnər\ n : blunder

bon·fire \'bän,fīr\ n : outdoor fire

bo·ni·to \bə'nētō\ n, pl -tos or -to : medium-sized tuna

bon·net \'bänət\ n : hat for a woman or infant

bo·nus \'bōnəs\ n : extra payment

boo \'bü\ n, pl **boos** : shout of disapproval — **boo** vb

boo·by \'bübē\ n, pl -bies : dunce

◆ **book** \'bùk\ n 1 : paper sheets bound into a volume 2 : long literary work or a subdivision of one ~ vb : reserve — **book·case** n — **book·let** \-lət\ n — **book·mark** n — **book·sell·er** n — **book·shelf** n

book·end n : support to hold up a row of books

book·ie \-ē\ n : bookmaker

book·ish \-ish\ adj : fond of books and reading

book·keep·er n : one who keeps

business accounts — **book·keep·ing** *n*

book·mak·er *n* : one who takes bets — **book·mak·ing** *n*

book·worm *n* : one devoted to reading

¹**boom** \'büm\ *n* **1** : long spar to extend the bottom of a sail **2** : beam projecting from the pole of a derrick

²**boom** *vb* **1** : make a deep hollow sound **2** : grow rapidly esp. in value ~ *n* **1** : booming sound **2** : rapid growth

boo·mer·ang \'bümə,raŋ\ *n* : angular club that returns to the thrower

¹**boon** \'bün\ *n* : benefit

²**boon** *adj* : congenial

boon·docks \'bün,däks\ *n pl* : rural area

boor \'bùr\ *n* : rude person — **boor·ish** *adj*

boost \'büst\ *vb* **1** : raise **2** : promote — **boost** *n* — **boost·er** *n*

boot \'büt\ *n* **1** : covering for the foot and leg **2** : kick ~ *vb* : kick

boo·tee, boo·tie \'bütē\ *n* : infant's knitted sock

booth \'büth\ *n, pl* **booths** \'büthz, 'büths\ : small enclosed stall or seating area

boot·leg \'büt,leg\ *vb* : make or sell liquor illegally — **bootleg** *adj or n* — **boot·leg·ger** *n*

boo·ty \'bütē\ *n, pl* **-ties** : plunder

booze \'büz\ *vb* **boozed; booz·ing** : drink liquor to excess ~ *n* : liquor — **booz·er** *n* — **boozy** *adj*

bo·rax \'bōr,aks\ *n* : crystalline compound of boron

bor·der \'bórdər\ *n* **1** : edge **2** : boundary ~ *vb* **1** : put a border on **2** : be close

¹**bore** \'bōr\ *vb* **bored; bor·ing** **1** : pierce **2** : make by piercing ~ *n* : cylindrical hole or its diameter — **bor·er** *n*

²**bore** *past of* BEAR

³**bore** *n* : one that is dull ~ *vb* **bored; bor·ing** : tire with dullness — **bore·dom** \'bōrdəm\ *n*

born \'bórn\ *adj* **1** : brought into life **2** : being such by birth

borne *past part of* BEAR

bo·ron \'bōr,än\ *n* : dark-colored chemical element

bor·ough \'bərō\ *n* : incorporated town or village

bor·row \'bärō\ *vb* **1** : take as a loan **2** : take into use

bo·som \'büzəm, 'bü-\ *n* : breast ~ *adj* : intimate — **bo·somed** *adj*

boss \'bós\ *n* : employer or supervisor ~ *vb* : supervise — **bossy** *adj*

bot·a·ny \'bät°nē\ *n* : plant biology — **bo·tan·i·cal** \bə'tanikəl\ *adj* — **bot·a·nist** \'bät°nist\ *n* — **bot·a·nize** \-°n,īz\ *vb*

botch \'bäch\ *vb* : do clumsily — **botch** *n*

both \'bōth\ *adj or pron* : the one and the other ~ *conj* — used to show each of two is included

both·er \'bäthər\ *vb* **1** : annoy or worry **2** : take the trouble — **bother** *n* — **both·er·some** \-sm\ *adj*

bot·tle \'bät°l\ *n* : container with a narrow neck and no handles ~ *vb* **bot·tled; bot·tling** : put into a bottle

bot·tle·neck *n* : place or cause of congestion

bot·tom \'bätəm\ *n* **1** : supporting surface **2** : lowest part or place — **bottom** *adj* — **bot·tomed** *adj* — **bot·tom·less** *adj*

bot·u·lism \'bächə,lizəm\ *n* : acute food poisoning

bou·doir \'bü,dwär, 'bù-, ,bü-, ,bù'-\ *n* : woman's private room

bough \'baù\ *n* : large tree branch

bought *past of* BUY

bouil·lon \'bü,yän; 'bùl,yän, -yən\ *n* : clear soup

boul·der \'bōldər\ *n* : large rounded rock — **boul·dered** *adj*

bou·le·vard \'bùlə,värd, 'bü-\ *n* : broad thoroughfare

bounce \'baùns\ *vb* **bounced; bounc·ing** **1** : spring back **2** : make bounce — **bounce** *n* — **bouncy** \'baùnsē\ *adj*

¹**bound** \'baùnd\ *adj* : intending to go

²**bound** *n* : limit or boundary ~ *vb* : be a boundary of — **bound·less** *adj* — **bound·less·ness** *n*

³**bound** *adj* **1** : obliged **2** : having a binding **3** : determined **4** : incapable of failing

⁴**bound** *n* : leap ~ *vb* : move by springing

bound·ary \'baùndrē\ *n, pl* **-aries** : line marking extent or separation

boun·ty \'baùntē\ *n, pl* **-ties** **1** : generosity **2** : reward — **boun·te·ous**

\-ēəs\ *adj* — **boun·te·ous·ly** *adv* — **boun·ti·ful** \-ifəl\ *adj* — **boun·ti·ful·ly** *adv*

bou·quet \bō'kā, bü-\ *n* 1 : bunch of flowers 2 : fragrance

bour·bon \'bərbən\ *n* : corn whiskey

bour·geoi·sie \ˌbùrzh,wä'zē\ *n* : middle class of society — **bour·geois** \'bùrzh,wä, bùrzh'wä\ *n or adj*

bout \'baùt\ *n* 1 : contest 2 : outbreak

bou·tique \bü'tēk\ *n* : specialty shop

bo·vine \'bō,vīn, -ˌvēn\ *adj* : relating to cattle — **bovine** *n*

¹bow \'baù\ *vb* 1 : submit 2 : bend the head or body ∼ *n* : act of bowing

²bow \'bō\ *n* 1 : bend or arch 2 : weapon for shooting arrows 3 : knot with loops 4 : rod with stretched horsehairs for playing a stringed instrument ∼ *vb* : curve or bend — **bow·man** \-mən\ *n* — **bow·string** *n*

³bow \'baù\ *n* : forward part of a ship — **bow** *adj*

bow·els \'baùəls\ *n pl* 1 : intestines 2 : inmost parts

bow·er \'baùər\ *n* : arbor

¹bowl \'bōl\ *n* : concave vessel or part — **bowl·ful** \-ˌfùl\ *n*

²bowl *n* : round ball for bowling ∼ *vb* : roll a ball in bowling — **bowl·er** *n*

bowl·ing *n* : game in which balls are rolled to knock down pins

¹box \'bäks\ *n, pl* box *or* box·es : evergreen shrub — **box·wood** \-ˌwùd\ *n*

²box *n* 1 : container usu. with 4 sides and a cover 2 : small compartment ∼ *vb* : put in a box

³box *n* : slap ∼ *vb* 1 : slap 2 : fight with the fists — **box·er** *n* — **box·ing** *n*

box·car *n* : roofed freight car

box office *n* : theater ticket office

boy \'bòi\ *n* : male child — **boy·hood** *n* — **boy·ish** *adj* — **boy·ish·ly** *adv* — **boy·ish·ness** *n*

boy·cott \-ˌkät\ *vb* : refrain from dealing with — **boycott** *n*

boy·friend \'bòi,frend\ *n* 1 : male friend 2 : woman's regular male companion

brace \'brās\ *n* 1 : crank for turning a bit 2 : something that resists

weight or supports 3 : punctuation mark { or } ∼ *vb* **braced; brac·ing** 1 : make taut or steady 2 : invigorate 3 : strengthen

brace·let \'brāslət\ *n* : ornamental band for the wrist or arm

brack·et \'brakət\ *n* 1 : projecting support 2 : punctuation mark [or] 3 : class ∼ *vb* 1 : furnish or fasten with brackets 2 : place within brackets 3 : group

brack·ish \-ish\ *adj* : salty

brad \'brad\ *n* : nail with a small head

brag \'brag\ *vb* **-gg-** : boast — **brag** *n*

brag·gart \'bragərt\ *n* : boaster

braid \'brād\ *vb* : interweave ∼ *n* : something braided

braille \'brāl\ *n* : system of writing for the blind using raised dots

brain \'brān\ *n* 1 : organ of thought and nervous coordination enclosed in the skull 2 : intelligence ∼ *vb* : smash the skull of — **brained** *adj* — **brain·less** *adj* — **brainy** *adj*

braise \'brāz\ *vb* **braised; brais·ing** : cook (meat) slowly in a covered dish

brake \'brāk\ *n* : device for slowing or stopping ∼ *vb* **braked; brak·ing** : slow or stop by a brake

bram·ble \'brambəl\ *n* : prickly shrub

bran \'bran\ *n* : edible cracked grain husks

branch \'branch\ *n* 1 : division of a plant stem 2 : part ∼ *vb* 1 : develop branches 2 : diverge — **branched** *adj*

brand \'brand\ *n* 1 : identifying mark made by burning 2 : stigma 3 : distinctive kind (as of goods from one firm) ∼ *vb* : mark with a brand

bran·dish \'brandish\ *vb* : wave

brand-new *adj* : unused

bran·dy \'brandē\ *n, pl* **-dies** : liquor distilled from wine

brash \'brash\ *adj* 1 : impulsive 2 : aggressively self-assertive

brass \'bras\ *n* 1 : alloy of copper and zinc 2 : brazen self-assurance 3 : high-ranking military officers — **brassy** *adj*

bras·siere \brə'zir\ *n* : woman's undergarment to support the breasts

brat \'brat\ *n* : ill-behaved child — **brat·ti·ness** *n* — **brat·ty** *adj*

bra·va·do \brə'vädō\ *n, pl* **-does** or **-dos** : false bravery

¹**brave** \'brāv\ *adj* **brav·er; brav·est** : showing courage ~ *vb* **braved; brav·ing** : face with courage — **brave·ly** *adv* — **brav·ery** \-ərē\ *n*

²**brave** *n* : American Indian warrior

◆ **bra·vo** \'brävō\ *n, pl* **-vos** : shout of approval

brawl \'brȯl\ *n* : noisy quarrel or violent fight — **brawl** *vb* — **brawl·er** *n*

brawn \'brȯn\ *n* : muscular strength — **brawny** \-ē\ *adj* — **brawn·i·ness** *n*

bray \'brā\ *n* : harsh cry of a donkey — **bray** *vb*

bra·zen \'brāzᵊn\ *adj* 1 : made of brass 2 : bold — **bra·zen·ly** *adv* — **bra·zen·ness** *n*

bra·zier \'brāzhər\ *n* : charcoal grill

breach \'brēch\ *n* 1 : breaking of a law, obligation, or standard 2 : gap ~ *vb* : make a breach in

bread \'bred\ *n* : baked food made of flour ~ *vb* : cover with bread crumbs

breadth \'bredth\ *n* : width

bread·win·ner *n* : wage earner

break \'brāk\ *vb* **broke** \'brōk\; **bro·ken** \'brōkən\; **break·ing** 1 : knock into pieces 2 : transgress 3 : force a way into or out of 4 : exceed 5 : interrupt 6 : fail ~ *n* 1 : act or result of breaking 2 : stroke of good luck — **break·able** *adj* or *n* — **break·age** \'brākij\ *n* — **break·er** *n* — **break in** *vb* 1 : enter by force 2 : interrupt 3 : train — **break out** *vb* 1 : erupt with force 2 : develop a rash

break·down *n* : physical or mental failure — **break down** *vb*

break·fast \'brekfəst\ *n* : first meal of the day — **breakfast** *vb*

breast \'brest\ *n* 1 : milk-producing gland esp. of a woman 2 : front part of the chest

breast·bone *n* : sternum

breath \'breth\ *n* 1 : slight breeze 2 : air breathed in or out — **breath·less** *adj* — **breath·less·ly** *adv* — **breath·less·ness** *n* — **breathy** \'brethē\ *adj*

breathe \'brēth\ *vb* **breathed; breath·ing** 1 : draw air into the lungs and expel it 2 : live 3 : utter

breath·tak·ing *adj* : exciting

breech·es \'brichəz\ *n pl* : trousers ending near the knee

breed \'brēd\ *vb* **bred** \'bred\; **breed·ing** 1 : give birth to 2 : propagate 3 : raise ~ *n* 1 : kind of plant or animal usu. developed by humans 2 : class — **breed·er** *n*

breeze \'brēz\ *n* : light wind ~ *vb* **breezed; breez·ing** : move fast — **breezy** *adj*

breth·ren \'brethrən, -ərn\ *pl of* BROTHER

bre·via·ry \'brēvərē, 'bre-, -vyərē, -vē͑erē\ *n, pl* **-ries** : prayer book used by Roman Catholic priests

brev·i·ty \'brevətē\ *n, pl* **-ties** : shortness or conciseness

brew \'brü\ *vb* : make by fermenting or steeping — **brew** *n* — **brew·er** *n* — **brew·ery** \'brüərē, 'brúrē\ *n*

bri·ar *var of* BRIER

bribe \'brīb\ *vb* **bribed; brib·ing** : corrupt or influence by gifts ~ *n* : something offered or given in bribing — **brib·able** *adj* — **brib·ery** \-ərē\ *n*

bric–a–brac \'brikə,brak\ *n pl* : small ornamental articles

brick \'brik\ *n* : building block of baked clay — **brick** *vb* — **brick·lay·er** *n* — **brick·lay·ing** *n*

bride \'brīd\ *n* : woman just married or about to be married — **brid·al** \-ᵊl\ *adj*

bride·groom *n* : man just married or about to be married

brides·maid *n* : woman who attends a bride at her wedding

¹**bridge** \'brij\ *n* 1 : structure built for passage over a depression or obstacle 2 : upper part of the nose 3 : compartment from which a ship is navigated 4 : artificial replacement for missing teeth ~ *vb* : build a bridge over — **bridge·able** *adj*

²**bridge** *n* : card game for 4 players

bri·dle \'brīd°l\ *n* : headgear to control a horse ~ *vb* **-dled; -dling** 1 : put a bridle on 2 : restrain 3 : show hostility or scorn

brief \'brēf\ *adj* : short or concise ~ *n* : concise summary (as of a legal case) ~ *vb* : give final instructions or essential information to — **brief·ly** *adv* — **brief·ness** *n*

brief·case *n* : case for papers

¹**bri·er** \'brīər\ *n* : thorny plant

²**brier** *n* : heath of southern Europe

¹**brig** \'brig\ *n* : 2-masted ship

²**brig** *n* : jail on a naval ship

bri·gade \brig'ād\ *n* 1 : large military unit 2 : group organized for a special activity

brig·a·dier general \ˌbrigə'dir-\ *n* : officer ranking next below a major general

brig·and \'brigənd\ *n* : bandit — **brig·and·age** \-ij\ *n*

bright \'brīt\ *adj* 1 : radiating or reflecting light 2 : cheerful 3 : intelligent — **bright·en** \-°n\ *vb* — **bright·en·er** \'brīt°nər\ *n* — **bright·ly** *adv* — **bright·ness** *n*

bril·liant \'brilyənt\ *adj* 1 : very bright 2 : splendid 3 : very intelligent — **bril·liance** \-yəns\ *n* — **bril·lian·cy** \-yənsē\ *n* — **bril·liant·ly** *adv*

brim \'brim\ *n* : edge or rim ~ *vb* : be or become full — **brim·less** *adj* — **brimmed** *adj*

brim·ful \-'fúl\ *adj* : full to the brim

brim·stone *n* : sulfur

brin·dled \'brind°ld\ *adj* : gray or tawny with dark streaks or flecks

brine \'brīn\ *n* 1 : salt water 2 : ocean — **brin·i·ness** *n* — **briny** *adj*

bring \'briŋ\ *vb* **brought** \'brȯt\;

bring·ing 1 : cause to come with one 2 : persuade 3 : produce 4 : sell for — **bring·er** *n* — **bring about** *vb* : make happen — **bring up** *vb* 1 : care for and educate 2 : cause to be noticed

brink \'briŋk\ *n* : edge

bri·quette, bri·quet \bri'ket\ *n* : pressed mass (as of charcoal)

brisk \'brisk\ *adj* 1 : lively 2 : invigorating — **brisk·ly** *adv* — **brisk·ness** *n*

bris·ket \'briskət\ *n* : breast or lower chest of a quadruped

bris·tle \'brisəl\ *n* : short stiff hair ~ *vb* **-tled; -tling** 1 : stand erect 2 : show angry defiance 3 : appear as if covered with bristles — **bris·tly** *adj*

brit·tle \'brit°l\ *adj* **-tler; -tlest** : easily broken — **brit·tle·ness** *n*

broach \'brōch\ *n* : pointed tool (as for opening casks) ~ *vb* 1 : pierce (as a cask) to open 2 : introduce for discussion

broad \'brȯd\ *adj* 1 : wide 2 : spacious 3 : clear or open 4 : obvious 5 : tolerant in outlook 6 : widely applicable 7 : dealing with essential points — **broad·en** \-°n\ *vb* — **broad·ly** *adv* — **broad·ness** *n*

broad·cast *n* 1 : transmission by radio waves 2 : radio or television program ~ *vb* **-cast; -cast·ing** 1 : scatter or sow in all directions 2 : make widely known 3 : send out on a broadcast — **broad·cast·er** *n*

broad·cloth *n* : fine cloth

broad·loom *adj* : woven on a wide loom esp. in solid color

broad–mind·ed *adj* : tolerant of varied opinions — **broad–mind·ed·ly** *adv* — **broad–mind·ed·ness** *n*

broad·side *n* 1 : simultaneous firing of all guns on one side of a ship 2 : verbal attack

bro·cade \brō'kād\ *n* : usu. silk fabric with a raised design

broc·co·li \'bräkəlē\ *n* : green vegetable akin to cauliflower

bro·chure \brō'shúr\ *n* : pamphlet

brogue \'brōg\ *n* : Irish accent

broil \'brȯil\ *vb* : cook by radiant heat — **broil** *n*

broil·er *n* 1 : utensil for broiling 2 : chicken fit for broiling

¹**broke** \'brōk\ *past of* BREAK

²**broke** *adj* : out of money

bro·ken \'brōkən\ *adj* : imperfectly spoken — **bro·ken·ly** *adv*

bro·ken-heart·ed \-'härtəd\ *adj* : overcome by grief or despair

bro·ker \'brōkər\ *n* : agent who buys and sells for a fee — **broker** *vb* — **bro·ker·age** \-kərij\ *n*

bro·mine \'brō,mēn\ *n* : deep red liquid corrosive chemical element

bron·chi·tis \brän'kītəs, brän-\ *n* : inflammation of the bronchi

bron·chus \'bräŋkəs\ *n, pl* **-chi** \-,kī, -,kē\ : division of the windpipe leading to a lung — **bron·chi·al** \-kēəl\ *adj*

bronze \'bränz\ *vb* **bronzed; bronz·ing** : make bronze in color ~ *n* 1 : alloy of copper and tin 2 : yellowish brown — **bronzy** \-ē\ *adj*

brooch \'brōch, 'brüch\ *n* : ornamental clasp or pin

brood \'brüd\ *n* : family of young ~ *vb* 1 : sit on eggs to hatch them 2 : ponder ~ *adj* : kept for breeding — **brood·er** *n* — **brood·ing·ly** *adv*

¹**brook** \'brük\ *vb* : tolerate

²**brook** *n* : small stream

broom \'brüm, 'brüm\ *n* 1 : flowering shrub 2 : implement for sweeping — **broom·stick** *n*

broth \'brȯth\ *n, pl* **broths** \'brȯths, 'brȯthz\ : liquid in which meat has been cooked

broth·el \'bräthəl, 'brȯth-\ *n* : house of prostitutes

◆ **broth·er** \'brəthər\ *n, pl* **brothers** *also* **breth·ren** \'brethrən, -ərn\ 1 : male sharing one or both parents with another person 2 : kinsman — **broth·er·hood** *n* — **broth·er·li·ness** *n* — **broth·er·ly** *adj*

broth·er-in-law *n, pl* **brothers-in-law** : brother of one's spouse or husband of one's sister or of one's spouse's sister

brought *past of* BRING

brow \'braú\ *n* 1 : eyebrow 2 : forehead 3 : edge of a steep place

brow·beat *vb* **-beat; -beat·en** *or* **-beat; -beat·ing** : intimidate

brown \'braún\ *adj* 1 : of the color brown 2 : of dark or tanned complexion ~ *n* : a color like that of coffee ~ *vb* : make or become brown — **brown·ish** *adj*

browse \'braúz\ *vb* **browsed; browsing** 1 : graze 2 : look over casually — **brows·er** *n*

bru·in \'brüən\ *n* : bear

bruise \'brüz\ *vb* **bruised; bruising** 1 : make a bruise on 2 : become bruised ~ *n* : surface injury to flesh

brunch \'brənch\ *n* : late breakfast, early lunch, or combination of both

bru·net, bru·nette \brü'net\ *adj* : having dark hair and usu. dark skin — **bru·net, brunette** *n*

brunt \'brənt\ *n* : main impact

¹**brush** \'brəsh\ *n* 1 : small cut branches 2 : coarse shrubby vegetation

²**brush** *n* 1 : bristles set in a handle used esp. for cleaning or painting 2 : light touch ~ *vb* 1 : apply a brush to 2 : remove with or as if with a brush 3 : dismiss in an offhand way 4 : touch lightly — **brush up** *vb* : renew one's skill

³**brush** *n* : skirmish

brush-off *n* : curt dismissal

brusque \'brəsk\ *adj* : curt or blunt in manner — **brusque·ly** *adv*

bru·tal \'brüt°l\ *adj* : like a brute and esp. cruel — **bru·tal·i·ty** \brü'talətē\ *n* — **bru·tal·ize** \'brüt°l,īz\ *vb* — **bru·tal·ly** \-°lē\ *adv*

brute \'brüt\ *adj* 1 : relating to beasts 2 : unreasoning 3 : purely physical ~ *n* 1 : beast 2 : brutal person — **brut·ish** \-ish\ *adj*

bub·ble \'bəbəl\ *vb* **-bled; -bling** : form, rise in, or give off bubbles ∼ *n* : globule of gas in or covered with a liquid — **bub·bly** \-əlē\ *adj*

bu·bo \'bübō, 'byü-\ *n, pl* **buboes** : inflammatory swelling of a lymph gland — **bu·bon·ic** \bü-'bänik, byü-\ *adj*

buc·ca·neer \,bəkə'nir\ *n* : pirate

buck \'bək\ *n, pl* **buck** *or* **bucks 1** : male animal (as a deer) **2** : dollar ∼ *vb* **1** : jerk forward **2** : oppose

buck·et \'bəkət\ *n* : pail — **buck·et·ful** *n*

buck·le \'bəkəl\ *n* **1** : clasp (as on a belt) for two loose ends **2** : bend or fold ∼ *vb* **-led; -ling 1** : fasten with a buckle **2** : apply oneself **3** : bend or crumple

buck·ler \'bəklər\ *n* : shield

buck·shot *n* : coarse lead shot

buck·skin *n* : soft leather (as from the skin of a buck) — **buckskin** *adj*

buck·tooth *n* : large projecting front tooth — **buck–toothed** *adj*

buck·wheat *n* : herb whose seeds are used as a cereal grain or the seeds themselves

bu·col·ic \byü'kälik\ *adj* : pastoral

bud \'bəd\ *n* **1** : undeveloped plant shoot **2** : partly opened flower ∼ *vb* **-dd- 1** : form or put forth buds **2** : be or develop like a bud

Bud·dhism \'bü,dizəm, 'bù-\ *n* : religion of eastern and central Asia — **Bud·dhist** \'büdist, 'bùd-\ *n or adj*

bud·dy \'bədē\ *n, pl* **-dies** : friend

budge \'bəj\ *vb* **budged; budg·ing** : move from a place

bud·get \'bəjət\ *n* **1** : estimate of income and expenses **2** : plan for coordinating income and expenses **3** : money available for a particular use — **budget** *vb or adj* — **bud·get·ary** \-ə,terē\ *adj*

buff \'bəf\ *n* **1** : yellow to orange yellow color **2** : enthusiast ∼ *adj* : of the color buff ∼ *vb* : polish

buf·fa·lo \'bəfə,lō\ *n, pl* **-lo** *or* **-loes** : wild ox (as a bison)

¹buff·er \'bəfər\ *n* : shield or protector

²buffer *n* : one that buffs

¹buf·fet \'bəfət\ *n* : blow or slap ∼ *vb* : hit esp. repeatedly

²buf·fet \,bə'fā, bü-\ *n* **1** : sideboard **2** : meal at which people serve themselves

buf·foon \,bə'fün\ *n* : clown — **buf·foon·ery** \-ərē\ *n*

bug \'bəg\ *n* **1** : small usu. obnoxious crawling creature **2** : 4-winged sucking insect **3** : unexpected imperfection **4** : disease-producing germ **5** : hidden microphone ∼ *vb* **-gg- 1** : pester **2** : conceal a microphone in

bug·a·boo \'bəgə,bü\ *n, pl* **-boos** : bogey

bug·bear *n* : source of dread

bug·gy \'bəgē\ *n, pl* **-gies** : light carriage

bu·gle \'byügəl\ *n* : trumpetlike brass instrument — **bu·gler** \-glər\ *n*

build \'bild\ *vb* **built** \'bilt\; **building 1** : put together **2** : establish **3** : increase ∼ *n* : physique — **build·er** *n*

build·ing \'bildiŋ\ *n* **1** : roofed and walled structure **2** : art or business of constructing buildings

bulb \'bəlb\ *n* **1** : large underground plant bud **2** : rounded or pear-shaped object — **bul·bous** \-əs\ *adj*

bulge \'bəlj\ *n* : swelling projecting part ∼ *vb* **bulged; bulg·ing** : swell out

bulk \'bəlk\ *n* **1** : magnitude **2** : indigestible food material **3** : large mass **4** : major portion ∼ *vb* : cause to swell or bulge — **bulky** \-ē\ *adj*

bulk·head *n* : ship's partition

¹bull \'bùl\ *n* : large adult male animal (as of cattle) ∼ *adj* : male

²bull *n* **1** : papal letter **2** : decree

bull·dog *n* : compact short-haired dog

bull·doze \-,dōz\ *vb* **1** : move or level with a tractor (**bull·doz·er**) having a broad blade **2** : force

bul·let \'bùlət\ *n* : missile to be shot from a gun — **bul·let·proof** *adj*

bul·le·tin \'bùlətən\ *n* **1** : brief public report **2** : periodical

bull·fight *n* : sport of taunting and killing bulls — **bull·fight·er** *n*

bull·frog *n* : large deep-voiced frog

bull·head·ed *adj* : stupidly stubborn

bul·lion \'bùlyən\ *n* : gold or silver esp. in bars

bull·ock \'bùlək\ *n* **1** : young bull **2** : steer

bull's–eye *n, pl* **bull's–eyes** : center of a target

◆ **bul·ly** \'bu̇lē\ *n, pl* **-lies** : one who hurts or intimidates others ~ *vb* **-lied; -ly·ing** : act like a bully toward

bul·rush \'bu̇l,rəsh\ *n* : tall coarse rush or sedge

bul·wark \'bu̇l,wərk, -,wȯrk; 'bəl-,wərk\ *n* **1** : wall-like defense **2** : strong support or protection

bum \'bəm\ *vb* : wander as a tramp **2** : get by begging ~ *n* : idle worthless person ~ *adj* : bad

bum·ble·bee \'bəmbəl,bē\ *n* : large hairy bee

bump \'bəmp\ *vb* : strike or knock forcibly ~ *n* **1** : sudden blow **2** : small bulge or swelling — **bumpy** *adj*

¹**bum·per** \'bəmpər\ *adj* : unusually large

²**bump·er** \'bəmpər\ *n* : shock-absorbing bar at either end of a car

bump·kin \'bəmpkən\ *n* : awkward country person

bun \'bən\ *n* : sweet biscuit or roll

bunch \'bənch\ *n* : group ~ *vb* : form into a group — **bunchy** *adj*

bun·dle \'bənd³l\ *n* **1** : several items bunched together **2** : something wrapped for carrying **3** : large amount ~ *vb* **-dled; -dling** : gather into a bundle

bun·ga·low \'bəngə,lō\ *n* : one-story house

bun·gle \'bəngəl\ *vb* **-gled; -gling** : do badly — **bungle** *n* — **bun·gler** *n*

bun·ion \'bənyən\ *n* : inflamed swelling of the first joint of the big toe

¹**bunk** \'bəngk\ *n* : built-in bed that is often one of a tier ~ *vb* : sleep

²**bunk** *n* : nonsense

bun·ker \-ər\ *n* **1** : storage compartment **2** : protective embankment

bun·kum, bun·combe \'bəngkəm\ *n* : nonsense

bun·ny \'bənē\ *n, pl* **-nies** : rabbit

¹**bun·ting** \'bəntiŋ\ *n* : small finch

²**bunting** *n* : flag material

buoy \'büē, 'bȯi\ *n* : floating marker anchored in water ~ *vb* **1** : keep afloat **2** : raise the spirits of — **buoy·an·cy** \'bȯiənsē, 'büyən-\ *n* — **buoy·ant** \-yənt\ *adj*

bur, burr \'bər\ *n* : rough or prickly covering of a fruit — **bur·ry** *adj*

bur·den \'bərd³n\ *n* **1** : something carried **2** : something oppressive **3** : cargo ~ *vb* : load or oppress — **bur·den·some** \-əm\ *adj*

bur·dock \'bər,däk\ *n* : tall coarse herb with prickly flower heads

bu·reau \'byu̇rō\ *n* **1** : chest of drawers **2** : administrative unit **3** : business office

bu·reau·cra·cy \byu̇'räkrəsē\ *n, pl* **-cies** **1** : body of government officials **2** : unwieldy administrative system — **bu·reau·crat** \'byu̇rə-,krat\ *n* — **bu·reau·crat·ic** \,byu̇rə'kratik\ *adj*

bur·geon \'bərjən\ *vb* : grow

bur·glary \'bərglərē\ *n, pl* **-glar·ies** : forcible entry into a building to steal — **bur·glar** \-glər\ *n* — **bur·glar·ize** \'bərglə,rīz\ *vb*

bur·gle \'bərgəl\ *vb* **-gled; -gling** : commit burglary on or in

Bur·gun·dy \'bərgəndē\ *n, pl* **-dies** : kind of table wine

buri·al \'berēəl\ *n* : act of burying

bur·lap \'bər,lap\ *n* : coarse fabric usu. of jute or hemp

bur·lesque \bər'lesk\ *n* **1** : witty or derisive imitation **2** : broadly humorous variety show ~ *vb* **-lesqued; -lesqu·ing** : mock

bur·ly \'bərlē\ *adj* **-li·er; -est** : strongly and heavily built

burn \\'bərn\ *vb* **burned** \\'bərnd, 'bərnt\ *or* **burnt** \\'bərnt\; **burning 1** : be on fire **2** : feel or look as if on fire **3** : alter or become altered by or as if by fire or heat **4** : cause or make by fire ~ *n* : injury or effect produced by burning — **burn·er** *n*

bur·nish \\'bərnish\ *vb* : polish

burp \\'bərp\ *n or vb* : belch

bur·ro \\'bərō, 'bùr-\ *n, pl* **-os** : small donkey

bur·row \\'bərō\ *n* : hole in the ground made by an animal ~ *vb* : make a burrow — **bur·row·er** *n*

bur·sar \\'bərsər\ *n* : treasurer esp. of a college

bur·si·tis \bər'sītəs\ *n* : inflammation of a sac (**bur·sa** \\'bərsə\) in a joint

burst \\'bərst\ *vb* **burst** *or* **bursted**; **burst·ing 1** : fly apart or into pieces **2** : enter or emerge suddenly ~ *n* : sudden outbreak or effort

◆ **bury** \\'berē\ *vb* **bur·ied**; **bury·ing 1** : deposit in the earth **2** : hide

bus \\'bəs\ *n, pl* **bus·es** *or* **bus·ses** : large motor-driven passenger vehicle ~ *vb* **bused** *or* **bussed**; **bus·ing** *or* **bus·sing** : travel or transport by bus

bus·boy *n* : waiter's helper

bush \\'bùsh\ *n* **1** : shrub **2** : rough uncleared country **3** : a thick tuft or mat — **bushy** *adj*

bush·el \\'bùshəl\ *n* : 4 pecks

bush·ing \\'bùshin\ *n* : metal lining used as a guide or bearing

busi·ness \\'biznəs, -nəz\ *n* **1** : vocation **2** : commercial or industrial enterprise **3** : personal concerns — **busi·ness·man** \-,man\ *n* — **busi·ness·wom·an** \-,wùmən\ *n*

¹**bust** \\'bəst\ *n* **1** : sculpture of the head and upper torso **2** : breasts of a woman

²**bust** *vb* **1** : burst or break **2** : tame ~ *n* **1** : punch **2** : failure

¹**bus·tle** \\'bəsəl\ *vb* **-tled**; **-tling** : move or work briskly ~ *n* : energetic activity

²**bustle** *n* : pad or frame formerly worn under a woman's skirt

busy \\'bizē\ *adj* **busi·er**; **-est 1** : engaged in action **2** : being in use **3** : full of activity ~ *vb* **bus·ied**; **busy·ing** : make or keep busy — **busi·ly** *adv*

busy·body *n* : meddler

but \\'bət\ *conj* **1** : if not for the fact **2** : that **3** : without the certainty that **4** : rather **5** : yet ~ *prep* : other than

butch·er \\'bùchər\ *n* **1** : one who slaughters animals or dresses their flesh **2** : brutal killer **3** : bungler — **butcher** *vb* — **butch·ery** \-ərē\ *n*

but·ler \\'bətlər\ *n* : chief male household servant

¹**butt** \\'bət\ *vb* : strike with a butt ~ *n* : blow with the head or horns

²**butt** *n* **1** : target **2** : victim

³**butt** *vb* : join edge to edge

⁴**butt** *n* : large end or bottom

⁵**butt** *n* : large cask

butte \\'byüt\ *n* : isolated steep hill

but·ter \\'bətər\ *n* : solid edible fat churned from cream ~ *vb* : spread with butter — **but·tery** *adj*

but·ter·cup *n* : yellow-flowered herb

but·ter·fat *n* : natural fat of milk and of butter

but·ter·fly *n* : insect with 4 broad wings

but·ter·milk *n* : liquid remaining after butter is churned

but·ter·nut *n* : edible nut of a tree related to the walnut or this tree

but·ter·scotch \-,skäch\ *n* : candy made from sugar, corn syrup, and water

but·tocks \\'bətəks\\ *n pl* : rear part of the hips

but·ton \\'bət°n\\ *n* **1** : small knob for fastening clothing **2** : buttonlike object ~ *vb* : fasten with buttons

but·ton·hole *n* : hole or slit for a button ~ *vb* : hold in talk

but·tress \\'bətrəs\\ *n* **1** : projecting structure to support a wall **2** : support — **buttress** *vb*

bux·om \\'bəkəm\\ *adj* : full-bosomed

buy \\'bī\\ *vb* **bought** \\'bȯt\\; **buy·ing** : purchase ~ *n* : bargain — **buy·er** *n*

buzz \\'bəz\\ *vb* : make a low humming sound ~ *n* : act or sound of buzzing

buz·zard \\'bəzərd\\ *n* : large bird of prey

buzz·er *n* : signaling device that buzzes

buzz·word \\'bəz₁wərd\\ *n* : word or phrase in vogue

by \\'bī\\ *prep* **1** : near **2** : through **3** : beyond **4** : throughout **5** : no later than ~ *adv* **1** : near **2** : farther

by·gone \\'bī₁gȯn\\ *adj* : past — **bygone** *n*

by·law, bye·law *n* : organization's rule

by–line *n* : writer's name on an article

by·pass *n* : alternate route ~ *vb* : go around

by–prod·uct *n* : product in addition to the main product

by·stand·er *n* : spectator

by·way \\'bī₁wā\\ *n* : side road

by·word *n* : proverb

C

c \\'sē\\ *n, pl* **c's** *or* **cs** \\'sēz\\ : 3d letter of the alphabet

cab \\'kab\\ *n* **1** : light closed horse-drawn carriage **2** : taxicab **3** : compartment for a driver — **cab·bie, cab·by** *n* — **cab·stand** *n*

ca·bal \\kə'bal\\ *n* : group of conspirators

ca·bana \\kə'banə, -nyə\\ *n* : shelter at a beach or pool

cab·a·ret \\₁kabə'rā\\ *n* : nightclub

cab·bage \\'kabij\\ *n* : vegetable with a dense head of leaves

cab·in \\-ən\\ *n* **1** : private room on a ship **2** : small house **3** : airplane compartment

cab·i·net \\'kabnət\\ *n* **1** : display case or cupboard **2** : advisory council of a head of state — **cab·i·net·mak·er** *n* — **cab·i·net·mak·ing** *n* — **cab·i·net·work** *n*

ca·ble \\'kābəl\\ *n* **1** : strong rope, wire, or chain **2** : cablegram **3** : bundle of electrical wires ~ *vb* -**bled; -bling** : send a cablegram to

ca·ble·gram \\-₁gram\\ *n* : message sent by a submarine telegraph cable

ca·boose \\kə'büs\\ *n* : crew car on a train

ca·cao \\kə'kaů, -'kāō\\ *n, pl* **cacaos** : So. American tree whose seeds (**cacao beans**) yield cocoa and chocolate

cache \\'kash\\ *n* **1** : hiding place **2** : something hidden — **cache** *vb*

ca·chet \\ka'shā\\ *n* : prestige or a feature conferring this

cack·le \\'kakəl\\ *vb* -**led; -ling** : make a cry or laugh like the sound of a hen — **cackle** *n* — **cack·ler** *n*

ca·coph·o·ny \\ka'käfənē\\ *n, pl* -**nies** : harsh noise — **ca·coph·o·nous** \\-nəs\\ *adj*

cac·tus \\'kaktəs\\ *n, pl* **cac·ti** \\-₁tī\\ *or* -**tus·es** : drought-resistant flowering plant with scales or prickles

cad \\'kad\\ *n* : ungentlemanly person — **cad·dish** \\-ish\\ *adj* — **cad·dish·ly** *adv* — **cad·dish·ness** *n*

ca·dav·er \\kə'davər\\ *n* : dead body — **ca·dav·er·ous** \\-ərəs\\ *adj*

cad·die, cad·dy \\'kadē\\ *n, pl* -**dies** : golfer's helper — **caddie, caddy** *vb*

cad·dy \\'kadē\\ *n, pl* -**dies** : small tea chest

ca·dence \\'kād°ns\\ *n* : measure of a rhythmical flow — **ca·denced** \\-°nst\\ *adj*

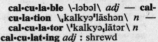

ca·det \kə'det\ *n* : student in a military academy

cadge \'kaj\ *vb* **cadged; cadg·ing** : beg — **cadg·er** *n*

cad·mi·um \'kadmēəm\ *n* : grayish metallic chemical element

cad·re \-rē\ *n* : nucleus of highly trained people

ca·fé \ka'fā, kə-\ *n* : restaurant

caf·e·te·ria \ˌkafə'tirēə\ *n* : self-service restaurant

♦ **caf·feine** \ka'fēn, 'ka,fēn\ *n* : stimulating alkaloid in coffee and tea

cage \'kāj\ *n* : box of wire or bars for confining an animal ~ *vb* **caged; cag·ing** : put or keep in a cage

ca·gey \-ē\ *adj* **-gi·er; -est** : shrewd — **ca·gi·ly** *adv* — **ca·gi·ness** *n*

cais·son \'kā,sän, -sən\ *n* **1** : ammunition carriage **2** : watertight chamber for underwater construction

ca·jole \kə'jōl\ *vb* **-joled; -jol·ing** : persuade or coax — **ca·jol·ery** \-ərē\ *n*

cake \'kāk\ *n* **1** : food of baked or fried usu. sweet batter **2** : compacted mass ~ *vb* **caked; cak·ing** **1** : form into a cake **2** : encrust

cal·a·bash \'kalə,bash\ *n* : gourd

cal·a·mine \'kalə,mīn\ *n* : lotion of oxides of zinc and iron

ca·lam·i·ty \kə'lamətē\ *n, pl* **-ties** : disaster — **ca·lam·i·tous** \-ətəs\ *adj* — **ca·lam·i·tous·ly** *adv* — **ca·lam·i·tous·ness** *n*

cal·ci·fy \'kalsə,fī\ *vb* **-fied; -fy·ing** : harden — **cal·ci·fi·ca·tion** \ˌkalsəfə'kāshən\ *n*

cal·ci·um \'kalsēəm\ *n* : silver-white soft metallic chemical element

cal·cu·late \'kalkyə,lāt\ *vb* **-lated; -lat·ing** **1** : determine by mathematical processes **2** : judge —

cal·cu·la·ble \-ləbəl\ *adj* — **cal·cu·la·tion** \ˌkalkyə'lāshən\ *n* — **cal·cu·la·tor** \'kalkyə,lātər\ *n*

cal·cu·lat·ing *adj* : shrewd

cal·cu·lus \'kalkyələs\ *n, pl* **-li** \-,lī\ : higher mathematics dealing with rates of change

cal·dron *var of* CAULDRON

♦ **cal·en·dar** \'kaləndər\ *n* : list of days, weeks, and months

¹calf \'kaf, 'kàf\ *n, pl* **calves** \'kavz, 'kàvz\ : young cow or related mammal — **calf·skin** *n*

²calf *n, pl* **calves** : back part of the leg below the knee

cal·i·ber, cal·i·bre \'kaləbər\ *n* **1** : diameter of a bullet or shell or of a gun bore **2** : degree of mental or moral excellence

cal·i·brate \'kalə,brāt\ *vb* **-brated; -brat·ing** : adjust precisely — **cal·i·bra·tion** \ˌkalə'brāshən\ *n*

cal·i·co \'kali,kō\ *n, pl* **-coes** *or* **-cos** **1** : printed cotton fabric **2** : animal with fur having patches of different colors

cal·i·pers \'kaləpərz\ *n* : measuring instrument with two adjustable legs

ca·liph \'kāləf, 'kal-\ *n* : title of head of Islam — **ca·liph·ate** \-,āt, -ət\ *n*

cal·is·then·ics \ˌkaləs'theniks\ *n sing or pl* : stretching and jumping exercises — **cal·is·then·ic** *adj*

calk \'kók\ *var of* CAULK

call \'kól\ *vb* **1** : shout **2** : summon **3** : demand **4** : telephone **5** : make a visit **6** : name — **call** *n* — **call·er** *n* — **call down** *vb* : reprimand — **call off** *vb* : cancel

call·ing *n* : vocation

cal·li·ope \kə'līə,pē, 'kalē,ōp\ *n* : musical instrument of steam whistles

cal·lous \'kaləs\ *adj* **1** : thickened and hardened **2** : unfeeling ~ *vb* : make callous — **cal·los·i·ty** \ka-

'läsətē\ *n* — **cal·lous·ly** *adv* — **cal·lous·ness** *n*

cal·low \'kalō\ *adj* : inexperienced or innocent — **cal·low·ness** *n*

cal·lus \'kaləs\ *n* : callous area on skin or bark ∼ *vb* : form a callus

calm \'käm, 'kälm\ *n* 1 : period or condition of peacefulness or still- ness ∼ *adj* : still or tranquil ∼ *vb* : make calm — **calm·ly** *adv* — **calm·ness** *n*

ca·lor·ic \kə'lȯrik\ *adj* : relating to heat or calories

cal·o·rie \'kalərē\ *n* : unit for mea- suring heat and energy value of food

ca·lum·ni·ate \kə'ləmnē͟ˌāt\ *vb* -at- ed; -at·ing : slander — **ca·lum- ni·a·tion** \-ˌləmnē'āshən\ *n*

cal·um·ny \'kaləmnē\ *n, pl* -nies : false and malicious charge — **ca- lum·ni·ous** \kə'ləmnēəs\ *adj*

calve \'kav, 'käv\ *vb* **calved; calv- ing** : give birth to a calf

calves *pl of* CALF

ca·lyp·so \kə'lipsō\ *n, pl* -sos : West Indian style of music

ca·lyx \'kāliks, 'kal-\ *n, pl* -lyx- es *or* -ly·ces \-ləˌsēz\ : sepals of a flower

cam \'kam\ *n* : machine part that slides or rotates irregularly to transmit linear motion

ca·ma·ra·de·rie \ˌkäm'rädərē, ˌkam-, -məˈ-, -'rad-\ *n* : fellowship

cam·bric \'kāmbrik\ *n* : fine thin linen or cotton fabric

came *past of* COME

cam·el \'kaməl\ *n* : large hoofed mammal of desert areas

ca·mel·lia \kə'mēlyə\ *n* : shrub or tree grown for its showy roselike flowers or the flower itself

cam·eo \'kamēˌō\ *n, pl* -eos : gem carved in relief

cam·era \'kamrə\ *n* : box with a lens for taking pictures — **cam·era- man** \-ˌman, -mən\ *n*

cam·ou·flage \'kaməˌfläzh, -ˌfläj\ *vb* : hide by disguising — **camouflage** *n*

camp \'kamp\ *n* 1 : place to stay temporarily esp. in a tent 2 : group living in a camp ∼ *vb* : make or live in a camp — **camp·er** *n* — **camp·ground** *n* — **camp·site** *n*

cam·paign \kam'pān\ *n* : series of military operations or of activities meant to gain a result — **cam- paign** *vb*

cam·pa·ni·le \ˌkampə'nēlē, -'nēl\ *n, pl* -ni·les *or* -ni·li \-'nēlē\ : bell tower

cam·phor \'kamfər\ *n* : gummy vo- latile aromatic compound from an evergreen tree (**cam·phor tree**)

cam·pus \'kampəs\ *n* : grounds and buildings of a college or school

¹**can** \kən, 'kan\ *vb, past* **could** \kəd, 'kud\ *pres sing & pl* **can** 1 : be able to 2 : be permitted to by con- science or feeling 3 : have permis- sion or liberty to

²**can** \'kan\ *n* : metal container ∼ *vb* -**nn**- : preserve by sealing in air- tight cans or jars — **can·ner** *n* — **can·nery** \-ərē\ *n*

ca·nal \kə'nal\ *n* 1 : tubular passage in the body 2 : channel filled with water

can·a·pé \'kanəpē, -ˌpā\ *n* : appetiz- er

ca·nard \kə'närd\ *n* : false report

ca·nary \-'nerē\ *n, pl* -nar·ies : yel- low or greenish finch often kept as a pet

can·cel \'kansəl\ *vb* -celed *or* -celled; -cel·ing *or* -cel·ling 1 : cross out 2 : destroy, neutralize, or match the force or effect of — **cancel** *n* — **can·cel·la·tion** \ˌkansə'lāshən\ *n* — **can·cel·er, can·cel·ler** *n*

can·cer \'kansər\ *n* 1 : malignant tu-

mor that tends to spread **2** : slowly destructive evil — **can·cer·ous** \-sərəs\ *adj* — **can·cer·ous·ly** *adv*

can·de·la·bra \ˌkandə'läbrə, -'läb-\ *n* : candelabrum

can·de·la·brum \-rəm\ *n, pl* **-bra** \-rə\ : ornamental branched candlestick

can·did \'kandəd\ *adj* **1** : frank **2** : unposed — **can·did·ly** *adv* — **can·did·ness** *n*

can·di·date \'kandə،dāt, -dət\ *n* : one who seeks an office or membership — **can·di·da·cy** \-dəsē\ *n*

can·dle \'kand°l\ *n* : tallow or wax molded around a wick and burned to give light — **can·dle·light** *n* — **can·dle·stick** *n*

can·dor \'kandər\ *n* : frankness

can·dy \-dē\ *n, pl* **-dies** : food made from sugar *~ vb* **-died; -dy·ing** : encrust in sugar

cane \'kān\ *n* **1** : slender plant stem **2** : a tall woody grass or reed **3** : stick for walking or beating *~ vb* **caned; can·ing 1** : beat with a cane **2** : weave or make with cane — **can·er** *n*

ca·nine \'kā،nīn\ *adj* : relating to dogs *~ n* **1** : pointed tooth next to the incisors **2** : dog

can·is·ter \'kanəstər\ *n* : cylindrical container

can·ker \'kaŋkər\ *n* : mouth ulcer — **can·ker·ous** \-kərəs\ *adj*

can·na·bis \'kanəbəs\ *n* : preparation derived from hemp

can·ni·bal \'kanəbəl\ *n* : human or animal that eats its own kind — **can·ni·bal·ism** \-bəˌlizəm\ *n* — **can·ni·bal·is·tic** \ˌkanəbə'listik\ *adj*

can·ni·bal·ize \'kanəbəˌlīz\ *vb* **-ized; -iz·ing 1** : take usable parts from **2** : practice cannibalism

can·non \'kanən\ *n, pl* **-nons** *or* **-non**

: large heavy gun — **can·non·ball** *n* — **can·non·eer** \ˌkanə'nir\ *n*

can·non·ade \ˌkanə'nād\ *n* : heavy artillery fire *~ vb* **-ad·ed; -ad·ing** : bombard

can·not \'kan،ät; kə'nät\ : can not — **cannot but** : be bound to

can·ny \'kanē\ *adj* **-ni·er; -est** : shrewd — **can·ni·ly** *adv* — **can·ni·ness** *n*

ca·noe \kə'nü\ *n* : narrow sharp-ended boat propelled by paddles — **canoe** *vb* — **ca·noe·ist** *n*

¹can·on \'kanən\ *n* **1** : regulation governing a church **2** : authoritative list **3** : an accepted principle

²canon *n* : clergy member in a cathedral

ca·non·i·cal \kə'nänikəl\ *adj* **1** : relating to or conforming to a canon **2** : orthodox — **ca·non·i·cal·ly** *adv*

can·on·ize \'kanəˌnīz\ *vb* **-ized** \-ˌnīzd\; **-iz·ing** : recognize as a saint — **can·on·iza·tion** \ˌkanənə'zāshən\ *n*

♦ **can·o·py** \'kanəpē\ *n, pl* **-pies** : overhanging cover — **canopy** *vb*

¹cant \'kant\ *n* **1** : slanting surface **2** : slant *~ vb* **1** : tip up **2** : lean to one side

²cant *vb* : talk hypocritically *~ n* **1** : jargon **2** : insincere talk

can't \'kant, 'kȧnt\ : can not

can·ta·loupe \'kant°l،ōp\ *n* : muskmelon with orange flesh

can·tan·ker·ous \kan'taŋkərəs\ *adj* : hard to deal with — **can·tan·ker·ous·ly** *adv* — **can·tan·ker·ous·ness** *n*

can·ta·ta \kən'tätə\ *n* : choral work

can·teen \kan'tēn\ *n* **1** : place of recreation for service personnel **2** : water container

can·ter \'kantər\ *n* : slow gallop — **can·ter** *vb*

can·ti·cle \'kantikəl\ *n* : liturgical song

can·ti·le·ver \'kant³l¸ēvər, -¸ev-\ *n* : beam or structure supported only at one end

can·to \'kan¸tō\ *n, pl* **-tos** : major division of a long poem

can·tor \'kantər\ *n* : synagogue official who sings liturgical music

can·vas \'kanvəs\ *n* 1 : strong cloth orig. used for making tents and sails 2 : set of sails 3 : oil painting

can·vass \-vəs\ *vb* : solicit votes, orders, or opinions from ~ *n* : act of canvassing — **can·vass·er** *n*

can·yon \'kanyən\ *n* : deep valley with steep sides

cap \'kap\ *n* 1 : covering for the head 2 : top or cover like a cap 3 : upper limit ~ *vb* **-pp-** 1 : provide or protect with a cap 2 : climax — **cap·ful** \-¸ful\ *n*

ca·pa·ble \'kāpəbəl\ *adj* : able to do something — **ca·pa·bil·i·ty** \¸kāpə'bilətē\ *n* — **ca·pa·bly** \'kāpəblē\ *adv*

ca·pa·cious \kə'pāshəs\ *adj* : able to contain much

ca·pac·i·tance \kə'pasətəns\ *n* : ability to store electrical energy

ca·pac·i·tor \-sətər\ *n* : device for storing electrical energy

ca·pac·i·ty \-sətē\ *n, pl* **-ties** 1 : ability to contain 2 : volume 3 : ability 4 : role or job ~ *adj* : equaling maximum capacity

¹**cape** \'kāp\ *n* : point of land jutting out into water

²**cape** *n* : garment that drapes over the shoulders

¹**ca·per** \'kāpər\ *n* : flower bud of a shrub pickled for use as a relish

²**caper** *vb* : leap or prance about ~ *n* 1 : frolicsome leap 2 : escapade

cap·il·lary \'kapə¸lerē\ *adj* 1 : resembling a hair 2 : having a very small bore ~ *n, pl* **-lar·ies** : tiny thin-walled blood vessel

¹**cap·i·tal** \'kapət³l\ *adj* 1 : punishable by death 2 : being in the series A, B, C rather than a, b, c 3 : relating to capital 4 : excellent ~ *n* 1 : capital letter 2 : seat of government 3 : wealth 4 : total face value of a company's stock 5 : investors as a group

²**capital** *n* : top part of a column

cap·i·tal·ism \-¸izəm\ *n* : economic system of private ownership of capital

cap·i·tal·ist \-ist\ *n* 1 : person with capital invested in business 2 : believer in capitalism ~ *adj* 1 : owning capital 2 : practicing, advocating, or marked by capitalism — **cap·i·tal·is·tic** \¸kapət³l'istik\ *adj* — **cap·i·tal·is·ti·cal·ly** \-klē\ *adv*

cap·i·tal·ize \-¸īz\ *vb* **-ized; -iz·ing** 1 : write or print with a capital letter 2 : use as capital 3 : supply capital for 4 : turn something to advantage — **cap·i·tal·iza·tion** \¸kapət³lə'zāshən\ *n*

cap·i·tol \'kapət³l\ *n* : building in which a legislature sits

ca·pit·u·late \kə'pichə¸lāt\ *vb* **-lat·ed; -lat·ing** : surrender — **ca·pit·u·la·tion** \-¸pichə'lāshən\ *n*

ca·pon \'kā¸pän, -pən\ *n* : castrated male chicken

ca·price \kə'prēs\ *n* : whim — **ca·pri·cious** \-'prishəs\ *adj* — **ca·pri·cious·ly** *adv* — **ca·pri·cious·ness** *n*

cap·size \'kap¸sīz, kap'sīz\ *vb* **-sized; -siz·ing** : overturn

cap·stan \'kapstən, -¸stan\ *n* : upright winch

cap·sule \'kapsəl, -¸sül\ *n* 1 : enveloping cover (as for medicine) 2 : small pressurized compartment for astronauts ~ *adj* : very brief or compact — **cap·su·lar** \-sələr\ *adj* — **cap·su·lat·ed** \-sə¸lātəd\ *adj*

cap·tain \'kaptən\ *n* 1 : commander of a body of troops 2 : officer in charge of a ship 3 : commissioned officer in the navy ranking next below a rear admiral or a commodore 4 : commissioned officer (as in the army) ranking next below a major 5 : leader ~ *vb* : be captain of — **cap·tain·cy** *n*

cap·tion \'kapshən\ *n* 1 : title 2 : explanation with an illustration — **caption** *vb*

cap·tious \'kapshəs\ *adj* : tending to find fault — **cap·tious·ly** *adv*

cap·ti·vate \'kaptə¸vāt\ *vb* **-vat·ed; -vat·ing** : attract and charm — **cap·ti·va·tion** \¸kaptə'vāshən\ *n* — **cap·ti·va·tor** \'kaptə¸vātər\ *n*

cap·tive \-tiv\ *adj* 1 : made prisoner 2 : confined or under control — **captive** *n* — **cap·tiv·i·ty** \kap'tivətē\ *n*

cap·tor \'kaptər\ *n* : one that captures

cap·ture \-chər\ *n* : seizure by force or trickery ~ *vb* **-tured; -tur·ing** : take captive

car \'kär\ *n* **1** : vehicle moved on wheels **2** : cage of an elevator

ca·rafe \kə'raf, -'räf\ *n* : decanter

car·a·mel \'karəməl, 'kärməl\ *n* **1** : burnt sugar used for flavoring and coloring **2** : firm chewy candy

¹carat *var of* KARAT

²car·at \'karət\ *n* : unit of weight for precious stones

car·a·van \'karə,van\ *n* : travelers journeying together (as in a line)

car·a·way \'karə,wā\ *n* : aromatic herb with seeds used in seasoning

car·bine \'kär,bēn, -,bīn\ *n* : short-barreled rifle

car·bo·hy·drate \,kärbō'hī,drāt, -drət\ *n* : compound of carbon, hydrogen, and oxygen

car·bon \'kärbən\ *n* **1** : chemical element occurring in nature esp. as diamond and graphite **2** : piece of carbon paper or a copy made with it

¹car·bon·ate \'kärbə,nāt, -nət\ *n* : salt or ester of a carbon-containing acid

²car·bon·ate \-,nāt\ *vb* **-at·ed; -at·ing** : impregnate with carbon dioxide — **car·bon·ation** \,kärbə-'nāshən\ *n*

carbon paper *n* : thin paper coated with a pigment for making copies

car·bun·cle \'kär,bəŋkəl\ *n* : painful inflammation of the skin and underlying tissue

car·bu·re·tor \'kärbə,rātər, -byə-\ *n* : device for mixing fuel and air

car·cass \'kärkəs\ *n* : dead body

car·cin·o·gen \kär'sinəjən\ *n* : agent causing cancer — **car·ci·no·gen·ic** \,kärs²n'ōˌjenik\ *adj*

car·ci·no·ma \,kärs²n'ōmə\ *n, pl* **-mas** *or* **-ma·ta** \-mətə\ : malig-

nant tumor — **car·ci·no·ma·tous** \-mətəs\ *adj*

¹card \'kärd\ *vb* : comb (fibers) before spinning ~ *n* : device for carding fibers — **card·er** *n*

²card *n* **1** : playing card **2** *pl* : game played with playing cards **3** : small flat piece of paper

card·board *n* : stiff material like paper

car·di·ac \'kärdē,ak\ *adj* : relating to the heart

car·di·gan \'kärdigən\ *n* : sweater with an opening in the front

¹car·di·nal \'kärd²nəl\ *n* **1** : official of the Roman Catholic Church **2** : bright red songbird

²cardinal *adj* : of basic importance

cardinal number *n* : number (as 1, 82, 357) used in counting

car·di·ol·o·gy \,kärdē'äləjē\ *n* : study of the heart — **car·di·ol·o·gist** \-jist\ *n*

car·dio·vas·cu·lar \-ō'vaskyələr\ *adj* : relating to the heart and blood vessels

♦ **care** \'ker\ *n* **1** : anxiety **2** : watchful attention **3** : supervision ~ *vb* **cared; car·ing** **1** : feel anxiety or concern **2** : like **3** : provide care — **care·free** *adj* — **care·ful** \-fəl\ *adj* — **care·ful·ly** *adv* — **care·ful·ness** *n* — **care·giv·er** \-,givər\ *n* — **care·less** *adj* — **care·less·ly** *adv* — **care·less·ness** *n*

ca·reen \kə'rēn\ *vb* **1** : sway from side to side **2** : career

ca·reer \kə'rir\ *n* : vocation ~ *vb* : go at top speed

ca·ress \kə'res\ *n* : tender touch ~ *vb* : touch lovingly or tenderly

car·et \'karət\ *n* : mark ^ showing where something is to be inserted

care·tak·er *n* : one in charge for another or temporarily

car·go \'kärgō\ *n, pl* **-goes** *or* **-gos** : transported goods

car·i·bou \'karə‚bü\ *n, pl* **-bou** *or* **-bous** : large No. American deer

car·i·ca·ture \'karikə‚chùr\ *n* : distorted representation for humor or ridicule — **caricature** *vb* — **car·i·ca·tur·ist** \-ist\ *n*

car·ies \'karēz\ *n, pl* **caries** : tooth decay

car·il·lon \'karə‚län\ *n* : set of tuned bells

car·mine \'kärmən, -‚mīn\ *n* : vivid red

car·nage \'kärnij\ *n* : slaughter

car·nal \'kärn³l\ *adj* : sensual — **car·nal·i·ty** \kär'nalətē\ *n* — **car·nal·ly** *adv*

car·na·tion \kär'nāshən\ *n* : showy flower

car·ni·val \'kärnəvəl\ *n* **1** : festival **2** : traveling enterprise offering amusements

car·ni·vore \-‚vȯr\ *n* : flesh-eating animal — **car·niv·o·rous** \kär'nivərəs\ *adj* — **car·niv·o·rous·ly** *adv* — **car·niv·o·rous·ness** *n*

car·ol \'karəl\ *n* : song of joy — **carol** *vb* — **car·ol·er, car·ol·ler** \-ələr\ *n*

car·om \-əm\ *n or vb* : rebound

ca·rouse \kə'raùz\ *vb* **-roused;** **-rous·ing** : drink and be boisterous — **ca·rouse** *n* — **ca·rous·er** *n*

car·ou·sel, car·rou·sel \‚karə-'sel, 'karə‚-\ *n* : merry-go-round

¹carp \'kärp\ *vb* : find fault

²carp *n, pl* **carp** *or* **carps** : freshwater fish

car·pel \'kärpəl\ *n* : modified leaf forming part of the ovary of a flower

car·pen·ter \'kärpəntər\ *n* : one who builds with wood — **carpenter** *vb* — **car·pen·try** \-trē\ *n*

car·pet \'kärpət\ *n* : fabric floor covering ~ *vb* : cover with a carpet — **car·pet·ing** \-iŋ\ *n*

car·port *n* : open-sided automobile shelter

car·riage \'karij\ *n* **1** : conveyance **2** : manner of holding oneself **3** : wheeled vehicle

car·ri·on \'karēən\ *n* : dead and decaying flesh

car·rot \'karət\ *n* : orange root vegetable

car·ry \'karē\ *vb* **-ried; -ry·ing 1** : move while supporting **2** : hold

(oneself) in a specified way **3** : support **4** : keep in stock **5** : reach to a distance **6** : win — **car·ri·er** \-ēər\ *n* — **carry on** *vb* **1** : conduct **2** : behave excitedly — **carry out** *vb* : put into effect

cart \'kärt\ *n* : wheeled vehicle ~ *vb* : carry in a cart — **cart·age** \-ij\ *n* — **cart·er** *n*

car·tel \kär'tel\ *n* : business combination designed to limit competition

car·ti·lage \'kärt³lij\ *n* : elastic skeletal tissue — **car·ti·lag·i·nous** \‚kärt³l'ajənəs\ *adj*

car·tog·ra·phy \kär'tägrəfē\ *n* : making of maps — **car·tog·ra·pher** \-fər\ *n*

car·ton \'kärt³n\ *n* : cardboard box

car·toon \kär'tün\ *n* **1** : humorous drawing **2** : comic strip — **cartoon** *vb* — **car·toon·ist** *n*

car·tridge \'kärtrij\ *n* **1** : tube containing powder and a bullet or shot for a firearm **2** : container of material for insertion into an apparatus

carve \'kärv\ *vb* **carved; carv·ing 1** : cut with care **2** : cut into pieces or slices — **carv·er** *n*

cas·cade \kas'kād\ *n* : small steep waterfall ~ *vb* **-cad·ed; -cad·ing** : fall in a cascade

¹case \'kās\ *n* **1** : particular instance **2** : convincing argument **3** : inflectional form esp. of a noun or pronoun **4** : fact **5** : lawsuit **6** : instance of disease — **in case** : as a precaution — **in case of** : in the event of

²case *n* **1** : box **2** : outer covering ~ *vb* **cased; cas·ing 1** : enclose **2** : inspect

case·ment \-mənt\ *n* : window that opens like a door

cash \'kash\ *n* **1** : ready money **2** : money paid at the time of purchase ~ *vb* : give or get cash for

ca·shew \'kashü, kə'shü\ *n* : tropical American tree or its nut

¹ca·shier \ka'shir\ *vb* : dismiss in disgrace

²cash·ier *n* : person who receives and records payments

cash·mere \'kazh‚mir, 'kash-\ *n* : fine goat's wool or a fabric of this

ca·si·no \kə'sēnō\ *n, pl* **-nos** : place for gambling

cask \'kask\ *n* : barrel-shaped container for liquids

cas·ket \'kaskət\ *n* : coffin

cas·se·role \'kasə,rōl\ *n* : baking dish or the food cooked in this

cas·sette \kə'set, ka-\ *n* : case containing magnetic tape

cas·sock \'kasək\ *n* : long clerical garment

cast \'kast\ *vb* cast; cast·ing 1 : throw 2 : deposit (a ballot) 3 : assign parts in a play 4 : mold ~ *n* 1 : throw 2 : appearance 3 : rigid surgical dressing 4 : actors in a play

cas·ta·nets \,kastə'nets\ *n pl* : shells clicked together in the hand

cast·away \'kastə,wā\ *n* : survivor of a shipwreck — **castaway** *adj*

caste \'kast\ *n* : social class or rank

cast·er \'kastər\ *n* : small wheel on furniture

cas·ti·gate \'kastə,gāt\ *vb* -gat·ed; -gat·ing : chastise severely — **cas·ti·ga·tion** \,kastə'gāshən\ *n* — **cas·ti·ga·tor** \'kastə,gātər\ *n*

cast iron *n* : hard brittle alloy of iron

cas·tle \'kasəl\ *n* : fortified building

cast-off *adj* : thrown away — **cast-off** *n*

cas·trate \'kas,trāt\ *vb* -trat·ed; -trat·ing : remove the testes of — **cas·tra·tion** \ka'strāshən\ *n*

ca·su·al \'kazhəwəl\ *adj* 1 : happening by chance 2 : showing little concern 3 : informal — **ca·su·al·ly** \-ē\ *adv* — **ca·su·al·ness** *n*

ca·su·al·ty \-tē\ *n, pl* -ties 1 : serious or fatal accident 2 : one injured, lost, or destroyed

ca·su·ist·ry \'kazhəwəstrē\ *n, pl* -ries : rationalization — **ca·su·ist** \-wist\ *n*

cat \'kat\ *n* 1 : small domestic mammal 2 : related animal (as a lion) — **cat·like** *adj*

cat·a·clysm \'katə,klizəm\ *n* : violent change — **cat·a·clys·mal** \,katə'klizməl\ **cat·a·clys·mic** \-'klizmik\ *adj*

cat·a·comb \'katə,kōm\ *n* : underground burial place

cat·a·log, cat·a·logue \'kat²l,óg\ *n* 1 : list 2 : book containing a description of items ~ *vb* -loged or -logued; -log·ing or -logu·ing 1 : make a catalog of 2 : enter in a catalog — **cat·a·log·er, cat·a·logu·er** *n*

ca·tal·pa \kə'talpə\ *n* : tree with broad leaves and long pods

ca·tal·y·sis \kə'taləsəs\ *n, pl* -y·ses \-,sēz\ : increase in the rate of chemical reaction caused by a substance (**cat·a·lyst** \'kat²list\) that is itself unchanged — **cat·a·lyt·ic** \,kat²l'itik\ *adj*

cat·a·ma·ran \,katəmə'ran\ *n* : boat with twin hulls

cat·a·mount \'katə,maùnt\ *n* : cougar

cat·a·pult \'katə,pəlt, -,pùlt\ *n* : device for hurling or launching — **catapult** *vb*

cat·a·ract \'katə,rakt\ *n* 1 : large waterfall 2 : cloudiness of the lens of the eye

ca·tarrh \kə'tär\ *n* : inflammation of the nose and throat

ca·tas·tro·phe \kə'tastrə,fē\ *n* 1 : great disaster or misfortune 2 : utter failure — **cat·a·stroph·ic** \,katə'sträfik\ *adj* — **cat·a·stroph·i·cal·ly** \-iklē\ *adv*

cat·bird *n* : American songbird

cat·call *n* : noise of disapproval

♦ **catch** \'kach, 'kech\ *vb* **caught** \'kót\; **catch·ing** 1 : capture esp. after pursuit 2 : trap 3 : detect esp. by surprise 4 : grasp 5 : get entangled 6 : become affected with or by 7 : seize and hold firmly ~ *n* 1 : act of catching 2 : something caught **3** : something that fastens **4** : hidden difficulty — **catch·er** n

catch·ing \-iŋ\ adj : infectious

catch·up \'kechəp, 'kach-; 'katəp\ var of KETCHUP

catch·word n : slogan

catchy \-ē\ adj **catch·i·er; -est** : likely to catch interest

cat·e·chism \'katə,kizəm\ n : set of questions and answers esp. to teach religious doctrine

cat·e·gor·i·cal \,katə'gòrikəl\ adj : absolute — **cat·e·gor·i·cal·ly** \-klē\ adv

cat·e·go·ry \'katə,gōrē\ n, pl **-ries** : group or class — **cat·e·go·ri·za·tion** \,katigərə'zāshən\ n — **cat·e·go·rize** \'katigə,rīz\ vb

ca·ter \'kātər\ vb **1** : provide food for **2** : supply what is wanted — **ca·ter·er** n

cat·er·cor·ner \,katē'kórnər, ,katə-, ,kitē-\; **cat·er·cor·nered** adv or adj : in a diagonal position

cat·er·pil·lar \'katər,pilər\ n : butterfly or moth larva

cat·er·waul \'katər,wól\ vb : make the harsh cry of a cat — **caterwaul** n

cat·fish n : big-headed fish with feelers about the mouth

cat·gut n : tough cord made usu. from sheep intestines

ca·thar·sis \kə'thärsəs\ n, pl **ca·thar·ses** \-,sēz\ : a purging — **ca·thar·tic** \kə'thärtik\ adj

ca·the·dral \-'thēdrəl\ n : principal church of a diocese

cath·e·ter \'kathətər\ n : tube for insertion into a body cavity

cath·ode \'kath,ōd\ n **1** : negative electrode **2** : positive battery terminal — **ca·thod·ic** \ka'thädik\ adj

cath·o·lic \'kathəlik\ adj **1** : universal **2** cap : relating to Roman Catholics

Cath·o·lic n : member of the Roman Catholic Church — **Ca·thol·i·cism** \kə'thälə,sizəm\ n

cat·kin \'katkən\ n : long dense flower cluster

cat·nap n : short light nap — **catnap** vb

cat·nip \-,nip\ n : aromatic mint relished by cats

cat's-paw n, pl **cat's-paws** : person used as if a tool

cat·sup \'kechəp, 'kach-; 'katsəp\ var of KETCHUP

cat·tail n : marsh herb with furry brown spikes

cat·tle \'kat³l\ n pl : domestic bovines — **cat·tle·man** \-mən, -,man\ n

cat·ty \'katē\ adj **-ti·er; -est** : mean or spiteful — **cat·ti·ly** adv — **cat·ti·ness** n

cat·walk n : high narrow walk

Cau·ca·sian \kó'kāzhən\ adj : relating to the white race — **Caucasian** n

cau·cus \'kókəs\ n : political meeting — **caucus** vb

caught past of CATCH

cauldron \'kóldrən\ n : large kettle

cau·li·flow·er \'kóli,flaůər, 'käl-\ n : vegetable having a compact head of usu. white undeveloped flowers

caulk \'kók\ vb : make seams watertight — **caulk** n — **caulk·er** n

caus·al \'kózəl\ adj : relating to or being a cause — **cau·sal·i·ty** \kó'zalətē\ n — **caus·al·ly** \'kózəlē\ adv

cause \'kóz\ n **1** : something that brings about a result **2** : reason **3** : lawsuit **4** : principle or movement to support ∼ vb **caused; caus·ing** : be the cause of — **cau·sa·tion** \kó'zāshən\ n — **causative** \'kózətiv\ adj — **cause·less** adj — **caus·er** n

cause·way n : raised road esp. over water

caus·tic \'kóstik\ adj **1** : corrosive **2** : sharp or biting — **caustic** n

cau·ter·ize \'kótə,rīz\ vb **-ized; -iz·ing** : burn to prevent infection or bleeding — **cau·ter·i·za·tion** \,kótərə'zāshən\ n

cau·tion \'kóshən\ n **1** : warning **2** : care or prudence ∼ vb : warn — **cau·tion·ary** \-shə,nerē\ adj

cau·tious \'kóshəs\ adj : taking caution — **cau·tious·ly** adv — **cau·tious·ness** n

cav·al·cade \,kavəl'kād, 'kavəl,-\ n **1** : procession on horseback **2** : series

cav·a·lier \,kavə'lir\ n : mounted soldier ∼ adj : disdainful or arrogant — **cav·a·lier·ly** adv

cav·al·ry \'kavəlrē\ n, pl **-ries** : troops on horseback or in vehicles — **cav·al·ry·man** \-mən, -,man\ n

THERE ARE MANY WAYS TO MAKE A DIET MORE APPEALING

SOME SAY IT HELPS TO DRESS YOUR FOOD UP

I SAY IT STILL LOOKS LIKE CELERY

© 1987 PAWS, INC.

JIM DAVIS 5-19

cave \'kāv\ *n* : natural underground chamber — **cave in** *vb* : collapse

cav•ern \'kavərn\ *n* : large cave — **cav•ern•ous** *adj* — **cav•ern•ous•ly** *adv*

cav•i•ar, cav•i•are \'kavē₁är, 'käv-\ *n* : salted fish roe

cav•il \'kavəl\ *vb* **-iled** *or* **-illed; -il•ing** *or* **-il•ling** : raise trivial objections — **cavil** *n* — **cav•il•er, cav•il•ler** *n*

cav•i•ty \'kavətē\ *n, pl* **-ties 1** : unfilled place within a mass **2** : decay in a tooth

ca•vort \kə'vȯrt\ *vb* : prance or caper

caw \'kȯ\ *vb* : utter the harsh call of the crow — **caw** *n*

cay•enne pepper \₁kī'en-, ₁kā-\ *n* : ground dried fruits of a hot pepper

CD \₁sē'dē\ *n* : compact disc

cease \'sēs\ *vb* **ceased; ceas•ing** : stop

cease•less \-ləs\ *adj* : continuous

ce•dar \'sēdər\ *n* : cone-bearing tree with fragrant durable wood

cede \'sēd\ *vb* **ced•ed; ced•ing** : surrender — **ced•er** *n*

ceil•ing \'sēliŋ\ *n* **1** : overhead surface of a room **2** : upper limit

cel•e•brate \'selə₁brāt\ *vb* **-brat•ed; -brat•ing 1** : perform with appropriate rites **2** : honor with ceremonies **3** : extol — **cel•e•brant** \-brənt\ *n* — **cel•e•bra•tion** \₁selə'brāshən\ *n* — **cel•e•bra•tor** \'selə₁brātər\ *n*

cel•e•brat•ed \-əd\ *adj* : renowned

ce•leb•ri•ty \sə'lebrətē\ *n, pl* **-ties 1** : renown **2** : well-known person

ce•ler•i•ty \sə'lerətē\ *n* : speed

♦ **cel•ery** \'selərē\ *n, pl* **-er•ies** : herb grown for crisp edible stalks

ce•les•ta \sə'lestə\; **ce•leste** \sə'lest\ *n* : keyboard musical instrument

ce•les•tial \sə'leschəl\ *adj* **1** : relating to the sky **2** : heavenly

cel•i•ba•cy \'seləbəsē\ *n* **1** : state of being unmarried **2** : abstention from sexual intercourse — **cel•i•bate** \'seləbət\ *n or adj*

cell \'sel\ *n* **1** : small room **2** : tiny mass of protoplasm that forms the fundamental unit of living matter **3** : container holding an electrolyte for generating electricity — **celled** *adj*

cel•lar \'selər\ *n* : room or area below ground

cel•lo \'chelō\ *n, pl* **-los** : bass member of the violin family — **cel•list** \-ist\ *n*

cel•lo•phane \'selə₁fān\ *n* : thin transparent cellulose wrapping

cel•lu•lar \'selyələr\ *adj* : relating to or consisting of cells

cel•lu•lose \'selyə₁lōs\ *n* : complex plant carbohydrate

Cel•sius \'selsēəs\ *adj* : relating to a thermometer scale on which the freezing point of water is 0° and the boiling point is 100°

ce•ment \si'ment\ *n* **1** : powdery mixture of clay and limestone that hardens when wetted **2** : binding agent ∼ *vb* : unite or cover with cement — **ce•ment•er** *n*

cem•e•tery \'semə₁terē\ *n, pl* **-ter•ies** : burial ground

cen•ser \'sensər\ *n* : vessel for burning incense

cen•sor \'sensər\ *n* : one with power to suppress anything objectionable (as in printed matter) ∼ *vb* : be a censor of — **cen•so•ri•al** \sen'sōrēəl\ *adj* — **cen•sor•ship** \-₁ship\ *n*

cen•so•ri•ous \sen'sōrēəs\ *adj* : critical — **cen•so•ri•ous•ly** *adv* — **cen•so•ri•ous•ness** *n*

cen•sure \'senchər\ *n* : official reprimand ∼ *vb* **-sured; -sur•ing**

: find blameworthy — **cen·sur·able** *adj*

cen·sus \'sensəs\ *n* : periodic population count — **census** *vb*

cent \'sent\ *n* : monetary unit equal to ¹⁄₁₀₀ of a basic unit of value

cen·taur \'sen,tȯr\ *n* : mythological creature that is half man and half horse

cen·ten·ni·al \sen'tenēəl\ *n* : 100th anniversary — **centennial** *adj*

◆ **cen·ter** \'sentər\ *n* **1** : middle point **2** : point of origin or greatest concentration **3** : region of concentrated population **4** : player near the middle of the team ∼ *vb* **1** : place, fix, or concentrate at or around a center **2** : have a center — **cen·ter·piece** *n*

cen·ti·grade \'sentə,grād, 'sänt-\ *adj* : Celsius

cen·ti·me·ter \'sentə,mētər, 'sänt-\ *n* : ¹⁄₁₀₀ meter

cen·ti·pede \'sentə,pēd\ *n* : long flat many-legged arthropod

cen·tral \'sentrəl\ *adj* **1** : constituting or being near a center **2** : essential or principal — **cen·tral·ly** *adv*

cen·tral·ize \-trə,līz\ *vb* **-ized; -iz·ing** : bring to a central point or under central control — **cen·tral·i·za·tion** \,sentrələ'zāshən\ *n* — **cen·tral·iz·er** *n*

cen·tre *chiefly Brit var of* CENTER

cen·trif·u·gal \sen'trifyəgəl, -'trifigəl\ *adj* : acting in a direction away from a center or axis

cen·tri·fuge \'sentrə,fyüj\ *n* : machine that separates substances by spinning

cen·trip·e·tal \sen'tripətᵊl\ *adj* : acting in a direction toward a center or axis

cen·tu·ri·on \sen'chu̇rēən, -'tu̇r-\ *n* : Roman military officer

cen·tu·ry \'senchərē\ *n, pl* **-ries** : 100 years

ce·ram·ic \sə'ramik\ *n* **1** *pl* : art or process of shaping and hardening articles from clay **2** : product of ceramics — **ceramic** *adj*

ce·re·al \'sirēəl\ *adj* : made of or relating to grain or to the plants that produce it ∼ *n* **1** : grass yielding edible grain **2** : food prepared from a cereal grain

cer·e·bel·lum \,serə'beləm\ *n, pl* **-bel·lums** *or* **-bel·la** \-'belə\ : part of the brain controlling muscular coordination — **cer·e·bel·lar** \-ər\ *adj*

ce·re·bral \sə'rēbrəl, 'serə-\ *adj* **1** : relating to the brain, intellect, or cerebrum **2** : appealing to the intellect

cerebral palsy *n* : disorder caused by brain damage and marked esp. by defective muscle control

cer·e·brate \'serə,brāt\ *vb* **-brat·ed; -brat·ing** : think — **cer·e·bra·tion** \,serə'brāshən\ *n*

ce·re·brum \sə'rēbrəm, 'serə-\ *n, pl* **-brums** *or* **-bra** \-brə\ : part of the brain that contains the higher nervous centers

cer·e·mo·ny \'serə,mōnē\ *n, pl* **-nies** **1** : formal act prescribed by law, ritual, or convention **2** : prescribed procedures — **cer·e·mo·ni·al** \,serə'mōnēəl\ *adj or n* — **cer·e·mo·ni·ous** \-nēəs\ *adj*

ce·rise \sə'rēs\ *n* : moderate red

cer·tain \'sərtᵊn\ *adj* **1** : settled **2** : true **3** : specific but not named **4** : bound **5** : assured ∼ *pron* : certain ones — **cer·tain·ly** *adv* — **cer·tain·ty** \-tē\ *n*

cer·tif·i·cate \sər'tifikət\ *n* : document establishing truth or fulfillment

cer·ti·fy \'sərtə,fī\ *vb* **-fied; -fy·ing** **1** : verify **2** : endorse — **cer·ti·fi-**

able \-ˌfīəbəl\ *adj* — **cer·ti·fi·ably**
\-blē\ *adv* — **cer·ti·fi·ca·tion**
\ˌsərtəfəˈkāshən\ *n* — **cer·ti·fi·er** *n*

cer·ti·tude \ˈsərtəˌtüd, -ˌtyüd\ *n*
: state of being certain

cer·vix \ˈsərviks\ *n, pl* **-vi·ces** \-və-ˌsēz\ *or* **-vix·es** 1 : neck 2 : narrow
end of the uterus — **cer·vi·cal**
\-vikəl\ *adj*

ce·sar·e·an \siˈzarēən\ *n* : surgical
operation to deliver a baby — **ce·sarean** *adj*

ce·si·um \ˈsēzēəm\ *n* : silver-white soft ductile chemical element

ces·sa·tion \seˈsāshən\ *n* : a halting

ces·sion \ˈseshən\ *n* : a yielding

cess·pool \ˈsesˌpül\ *n* : underground
sewage pit

Cha·blis \ˈshabˌlē; shaˈblē\ *n, pl*
Cha·blis \-ˌlēz, -ˈblēz\ : dry white
wine

chafe \ˈchāf\ *vb* **chafed; chaf·ing** 1
: fret 2 : make sore by rubbing

chaff \ˈchaf\ *n* 1 : debris separated
from grain 2 : something worth-less

chaf·ing dish \ˈchāfiŋ-\ *n* : utensil
for cooking at the table

cha·grin \shəˈgrin\ *n* : embarrass-ment or humiliation ∼ *vb* : cause
to feel chagrin

chain \ˈchān\ *n* 1 : flexible series of
connected links 2 *pl* : fetters 3
: linked series ∼ *vb* : bind or con-nect with a chain

◆ **chair** \ˈcher\ *n* 1 : seat with a back
2 : position of authority or dignity
3 : chairman ∼ *vb* : act as chair-man of

chair·man \-mən\ *n* : presiding offi-cer — **chair·man·ship** *n*

chair·wom·an \-ˌwùmən\ *n* : wom-an who acts as a presiding officer

chaise longue \ˈshāzˈlóŋ\ *n, pl*
chaise longues \-ˌlóŋ, -ˈlóŋz\ : long
chair for reclining

cha·let \shaˈlā\ *n* : Swiss mountain
cottage with overhanging roof

chal·ice \ˈchaləs\ *n* : eucharistic cup

chalk \ˈchók\ *n* 1 : soft limestone 2
: chalky material used as a crayon
∼ *vb* : mark with chalk — **chalky**
adj — **chalk up** *vb* 1 : credit 2
: achieve

chalk·board *n* : blackboard

chal·lenge \ˈchalənj\ *vb* **-lenged;**
-leng·ing 1 : dispute 2 : invite or
dare to act or compete — **chal-lenge** *n* — **chal·leng·er** *n*

cham·ber \ˈchāmbər\ *n* 1 : room 2
: enclosed space 3 : legislative
meeting place or body 4 *pl*
: judge's consultation room —
cham·bered *adj*

cham·ber·maid *n* : bedroom maid

chamber music *n* : music by a small
group for a small audience

cha·me·leon \kəˈmēlyən\ *n* : small
lizard whose skin changes color

cham·ois \ˈshamē\ *n, pl* **cham·ois**
\-ē, -ēz\ 1 : goatlike antelope 2
: soft leather

¹**champ** \ˈchamp, ˈchámp\ *vb* : chew
noisily

²**champ** \ˈchamp\ *n* : champion

cham·pagne \shamˈpān\ *n* : spar-kling white wine

cham·pi·on \ˈchampēən\ *n* 1 : advo-cate or defender 2 : winning con-testant ∼ *vb* : protect or fight for

cham·pi·on·ship \-ˌship\ *n* 1 : title of
a champion 2 : contest to pick a
champion

chance \ˈchans\ *n* 1 : unpredictable
element of existence 2 : opportu-nity 3 : probability 4 : risk 5 : raf-fle ticket ∼ *vb* **chanced; chanc-ing** 1 : happen 2 : encounter unex-pectedly 3 : risk — **chance** *adj*

chan·cel \ˈchansəl\ *n* : part of a
church around the altar

chan·cel·lery, **chan·cel·lory**
\ˈchansələrē\ *n, pl* **-ler·ies** *or* **-lor-**

ies 1 : position of a chancellor **2** : chancellor's office

chan·cel·lor \-ələr\ *n* **1** : chief or high state official **2** : head of a university — **chan·cel·lor·ship** *n*

chan·cre \'shaŋkər\ *n* : skin ulcer esp. from syphilis

chancy \'chansē\ *adj* **chanc·i·er; -est** : risky

chan·de·lier \,shandə'lir\ *n* : hanging lighting fixture

chan·dler \'chandlər\ *n* : provisions dealer — **chan·dlery** *n*

change \'chānj\ *vb* **changed; changing 1** : make or become different **2** : exchange **3** : give or receive change for ∼ *n* **1** : a changing **2** : excess from a payment **3** : money in smaller denominations **4** : coins — **change·able** *adj* — **change·less** *adj* — **chang·er** *n*

chan·nel \'chan⁹l\ *n* **1** : deeper part of a waterway **2** : means of passage or communication **3** : strait **4** : broadcast frequency ∼ *vb* **-neled** *or* **-nelled; -nel·ing** *or* **-nel·ling** : make or direct through a channel

chant \'chant\ *vb* : sing or speak in one tone — **chant** *n* — **chant·er** *n*

chan·tey, chan·ty \'shantē, 'chant-\ *n, pl* **-teys** *or* **-ties** : sailors' work song

Cha·nu·kah \'känəkə, 'hän-\ *var of* HANUKKAH

cha·os \'kā,äs\ *n* : complete disorder — **cha·ot·ic** \kā'ätik\ *adj* — **cha·ot·i·cal·ly** \-iklē\ *adv*

¹chap \'chap\ *n* : fellow

²chap *vb* **-pp-** : dry and crack open usu. from wind and cold

cha·pel \'chapəl\ *n* : private or small place of worship

chap·er·on, chap·er·one \'shapə,rōn\ *n* : older person who accompanies young people at a social gathering ∼ *vb* **-oned; -on·ing** : act as chaperon at or for — **chaper·on·age** \-ij\ *n*

chap·lain \'chaplən\ *n* : clergy member in a military unit or a prison — **chap·lain·cy** \-sē\ *n*

chap·ter \'chaptər\ *n* **1** : main book division **2** : branch of a society

char \'chär\ *vb* **-rr- 1** : burn to charcoal **2** : scorch

char·ac·ter \'kariktər\ *n* **1** : letter or graphic mark **2** : trait or distinctive combination of traits **3** : pecu-

liar person **4** : fictional person — **char·ac·ter·i·za·tion** \,kariktərə-'zāshən\ *n* — **char·ac·ter·ize** \'kariktə,rīz\ *vb*

char·ac·ter·is·tic \,kariktə'ristik\ *adj* : typical ∼ *n* : distinguishing quality — **char·ac·ter·is·ti·cal·ly** \-tiklē\ *adv*

cha·rades \shə'rādz\ *n sing or pl* : pantomime guessing game

char·coal \'chär,kōl\ *n* : porous carbon prepared by partial combustion

chard \'chärd\ *n* : leafy vegetable

charge \'chärj\ *vb* **charged; charging 1** : give an electric charge to **2** : impose a task or responsibility on **3** : command **4** : accuse **5** : rush forward in assault **6** : assume a debt for **7** : fix as a price ∼ *n* **1** : excess or deficiency of electrons in a body **2** : tax **3** : responsibility **4** : accusation **5** : cost **6** : attack — **charge·able** *adj*

charg·er \-ər\ *n* : horse ridden in battle

char·i·ot \'chareət\ *n* : ancient 2-wheeled vehicle — **char·i·o·teer** \,chareə'tir\ *n*

cha·ris·ma \kə'rizmə\ *n* : special ability to lead — **char·is·mat·ic** \,karəz'matik\ *adj*

char·i·ty \'charətē\ *n, pl* **-ties 1** : love for mankind **2** : generosity or leniency **3** : alms **4** : institution for relief of the needy — **char·i·ta·ble** \-əbəl\ *adj* — **char·i·ta·ble·ness** *n* — **char·i·ta·bly** \-blē\ *adv*

char·la·tan \'shärlətən\ *n* : impostor

charm \'chärm\ *n* **1** : something with magic power **2** : appealing trait **3** : small ornament ∼ *vb* : fascinate — **charm·er** *n* — **charm·ing** *adj* — **charm·ing·ly** *adv*

char·nel house \'chärn⁹l-\ *n* : place for dead bodies

chart \'chärt\ *n* **1** : map **2** : diagram ∼ *vb* **1** : make a chart of **2** : plan

char·ter \-ər\ *n* **1** : document granting rights **2** : constitution ∼ *vb* **1** : establish by charter **2** : rent — **char·ter·er** *n*

char·treuse \shär'trüz, -'trüs\ *n* : brilliant yellow green

char·wom·an \'chär,wúmən\ *n* : cleaning woman

chary \'charē\ *adj* **chari·er; -est**

: cautious — **char·i·ly** \'charəlē\ *adv*

¹chase \'chās\ *vb* **chased; chas·ing 1** : follow trying to catch **2** : drive away — **chase** *n* — **chas·er** *n*

²chase *vb* **chased; chas·ing** : decorate (metal) by embossing or engraving

chasm \'kazəm\ *n* : gorge

chas·sis \'chasē, 'shasē\ *n, pl* **chas·sis** \-ēz\ : supporting structural frame

chaste \'chāst\ *adj* **chast·er; chast·est 1** : abstaining from all or unlawful sexual relations **2** : modest or decent **3** : severely simple — **chaste·ly** *adv* — **chaste·ness** *n* — **chas·ti·ty** \'chastətē\ *n*

chas·ten \'chās°n\ *vb* : discipline

chas·tise \chas'tīz\ *vb* **-tised; -tis·ing 1** : punish **2** : censure — **chas·tise·ment** \-mənt, 'chastəz-\ *n*

chat \'chat\ *n* : informal talk — **chat** *vb* — **chat·ty** \-ē\ *adj*

châ·teau \sha'tō\ *n, pl* **-teaus** \-'tōz\ *or* **-teaux** \-'tō, -'tōz\ **1** : large country house **2** : French vineyard estate

chat·tel \'chat°l\ *n* : item of tangible property other than real estate

chat·ter \'chatər\ *vb* **1** : utter rapidly succeeding sounds **2** : talk fast or too much — **chatter** *n* — **chat·ter·er** *n*

chat·ter·box *n* : incessant talker

chauf·feur \'shōfər, shō'fər\ *n* : hired car driver ∼ *vb* : work as a chauffeur

chau·vin·ism \'shōvə,nizəm\ *n* : excessive patriotism — **chau·vin·ist** \-vənist\ *n* — **chau·vin·is·tic** \,shōvə'nistik\ *adj*

cheap \'chēp\ *adj* **1** : inexpensive **2** : shoddy — **cheap** *adv* — **cheap·en** \'chēpən\ *vb* — **cheap·ly** *adv* — **cheap·ness** *n*

cheap·skate *n* : stingy person

cheat \'chēt\ *n* **1** : act of deceiving **2** : one that cheats ∼ *vb* **1** : deprive through fraud or deceit **2** : violate rules dishonestly — **cheat·er** *n*

check \'chek\ *n* **1** : sudden stoppage **2** : restraint **3** : test or standard for testing **4** : written order to a bank to pay money **5** : ticket showing ownership **6** : slip showing an amount due **7** : pattern in squares or fabric in such a pattern **8** : mark placed beside an item noted ∼ *vb* **1** : slow down or stop **2** : restrain **3** : compare or correspond with a source or original **4** : inspect or test for condition **5** : mark with a check **6** : leave or accept for safekeeping or shipment **7** : checker — **check in** *vb* : report one's arrival — **check out** *vb* : settle one's account and leave

¹check·er \-ər\ *n* : piece in checkers ∼ *vb* : mark with different colors or into squares

²checker *n* : one that checks

check·er·board \-,bȯrd\ *n* : board of 64 squares of alternate colors

check·ers \'chekərz\ *n* : game for 2 played on a checkerboard

check·mate *vb* : thwart completely — **checkmate** *n*

check·point *n* : place where traffic is checked

check·up *n* : physical examination

ched·dar \'chedər\ *n* : hard smooth cheese

cheek \'chēk\ *n* **1** : fleshy side part of the face **2** : impudence — **cheeked** \'chēkt\ *adj* — **cheeky** *adj*

cheep \'chēp\ *vb* : utter faint shrill sounds — **cheep** *n*

♦ **cheer** \'chir\ *n* **1** : good spirits **2** : food and drink for a feast **3** : shout of applause or encouragement ∼ *vb* **1** : give hope or courage to **2** : make or become glad **3**

: urge on or applaud with shouts — **cheer·er** n — **cheer·ful** \-fəl\ adj — **cheer·ful·ly** adv — **cheer·ful·ness** n — **cheer·lead·er** n — **cheer·less** adj — **cheer·less·ly** adv — **cheer·less·ness** n

cheery \'chirē\ adj **cheer·i·er; -est** : cheerful — **cheer·i·ly** adv — **cheer·i·ness** n

cheese \'chēz\ n : curd of milk usu. pressed and cured — **cheesy** adj

cheese·cloth n : lightweight coarse cotton gauze

chee·tah \'chētə\ n : spotted swift-moving African cat

chef \'shef\ n : chief cook

chem·i·cal \'kemikəl\ adj 1 : relating to chemistry 2 : working or produced by chemicals ~ n : substance obtained by chemistry — **chem·i·cal·ly** \-klē\ adv

che·mise \shə'mēz\ n 1 : woman's one-piece undergarment 2 : loose dress

chem·ist \'kemist\ n 1 : one trained in chemistry 2 Brit : pharmacist

chem·is·try \-istrē\ n, pl **-tries** : science that deals with the composition and properties of substances

che·mo·ther·a·py \ˌkēmō'therəpē, ˌkemō-\ n : use of chemicals in the treatment of disease — **che·mo·ther·a·peu·tic** adj

che·nille \shə'nēl\ n : yarn with protruding pile or fabric of such yarn

cheque \'chek\ chiefly Brit var of CHECK 4

cher·ish \'cherish\ vb : hold dear

cher·ry \'cherē\ n, pl **-ries** : small fleshy fruit of a tree related to the roses or the tree or its wood

cher·ub \'cherəb\ n 1 pl **-u·bim** \-ə-ˌbim, -yə-\ : angel 2 pl **-ubs** : chubby child — **che·ru·bic** \chə'rübik\ adj

chess \'ches\ n : game for 2 played on a checkerboard — **chess·board** n — **chess·man** n

chest \'chest\ n 1 : boxlike container 2 : part of the body enclosed by the ribs and breastbone — **chest·ed** adj

chest·nut \'chesˌnət\ n : nut of a tree related to the beech or the tree

chev·i·ot \'shevēət\ n 1 : heavy rough wool fabric 2 : soft-finished cotton fabric

chev·ron \'shevrən\ n : V-shaped insignia

chew \'chü\ vb : crush or grind with the teeth ~ n : something to chew — **chew·able** adj — **chew·er** n — **chewy** adj

chic \'shēk\ n : smart elegance of dress or manner ~ adj 1 : stylish 2 : currently fashionable

chi·ca·nery \shik'ānərē\ n, pl **-ner·ies** : trickery

chick \'chik\ n : young chicken or bird

chick·a·dee \-ə,dē\ n : small grayish American bird

chick·en \'chikən\ n 1 : common domestic fowl or its flesh used as food 2 : coward

chicken pox n : acute contagious virus disease esp. of children

chi·cle \'chikəl\ n : gum from a tropical evergreen tree

chic·o·ry \'chikərē\ n, pl **-ries** : herb used in salad or its dried ground root used to adulterate coffee

chide \'chīd\ vb **chid** \'chid\ or **chid·ed** \'chīdəd\; **chid** or **chid·den** \'chid°n\ or **chided**; **chid·ing** \'chīdiŋ\ : scold

chief \'chēf\ n : leader ~ adj 1 : highest in rank 2 : most important — **chief·dom** n — **chief·ly** adv

chief·tain \'chēftən\ n : chief

chif·fon \shif'än, 'shifˌ-\ n : sheer fabric

chig·ger \'chigər\ n : bloodsucking mite

chi·gnon \'shēn,yän\ n : knot of hair

chil·blain \'chil,blān\ n : sore or inflamed swelling caused by cold

child \'chīld\ n, pl **chil·dren** \'childrən\ 1 : unborn or recently born person 2 : son or daughter — **child·bear·ing** n or adj — **child·birth** n — **child·hood** n — **child·ish** adj — **child·ish·ly** adv — **child·ish·ness** n — **child·less** adj — **child·less·ness** n — **child·like** adj — **child·proof** \-ˌprüf\ adj

chili, chile, chil·li \'chilē\ n, pl **chil·ies** or **chil·es** or **chil·lies** 1 : hot pepper 2 : spicy stew of ground beef, chilies, and beans

chill \'chil\ vb : make or become cold or chilly ~ adj : moderately cold ~ n 1 : feeling of coldness with shivering 2 : moderate coldness

chilly \-ē\ *adj* **chill·i·er; -est** : noticeably cold — **chill·i·ness** *n*

chime \'chīm\ *n* : set of tuned bells or their sound ∼ *vb* : make bell-like sounds — **chime in** *vb* : break into or join in a conversation

chi·me·ra, chi·mae·ra \kī'mirə, kə-\ *n* 1 : imaginary monster 2 : illusion — **chi·me·ri·cal** \-'merikəl\ *adj*

chim·ney \'chimnē\ *n, pl* **-neys** 1 : passage for smoke 2 : glass tube around a lamp flame

chimp \'chimp, 'shimp\ *n* : chimpanzee

chim·pan·zee \‚chim‚pan'zē, ‚shim-; chim'panzē, shim-\ *n* : small ape

chin \'chin\ *n* : part of the face below the mouth — **chin·less** *adj*

chi·na \'chīnə\ *n* 1 : porcelain ware 2 : domestic pottery

chin·chil·la \chin'chilə\ *n* : small So. American rodent with soft pearl-gray fur or this fur

chink \'chiŋk\ *n* : small crack ∼ *vb* : chinks of

chintz \'chints\ *n* : printed cotton cloth

chip \'chip\ *n* 1 : small thin flat piece cut or broken off 2 : thin crisp morsel of food 3 : counter used in games 4 : flaw where a chip came off 5 : small slice of semiconductor containing electronic circuits ∼ *vb* **-pp-** : cut or break chips from — **chip in** *vb* : contribute

chip·munk \-‚məŋk\ *n* : small striped ground-dwelling rodent

chip·per \-ər\ *adj* : lively and cheerful

chi·rop·o·dy \kə'räpədē, shə-\ *n* : podiatry — **chi·rop·o·dist** \-ədist\ *n*

chi·ro·prac·tic \'kīrə‚praktik\ *n* : system of healing based esp. on manipulation of body structures — **chi·ro·prac·tor** \-tər\ *n*

chirp \'chərp\ *n* : short sharp sound like that of a bird or cricket — **chirp** *vb*

♦ **chis·el** \'chizəl\ *n* : sharp-edged metal tool ∼ *vb* **-eled** *or* **-elled; -el·ing** *or* **-el·ling** 1 : work with a chisel 2 : cheat — **chis·el·er** \-ələr\ *n*

chit \'chit\ *n* : signed voucher for a small debt

chit·chat \-‚chat\ *n* : casual conversation — **chitchat** *vb*

chiv·al·rous \'shivəlrəs\ *adj* 1 : relating to chivalry 2 : honest, courteous, or generous — **chiv·al·rous·ly** *adv* — **chiv·al·rous·ness** *n*

chiv·al·ry \-rē\ *n, pl* **-ries** 1 : system or practices of knighthood 2 : spirit or character of the ideal knight — **chi·val·ric** \shə'valrik\ *adj*

chive \'chīv\ *n* : herb related to the onion

chlo·ride \'klōr‚īd\ *n* : compound of chlorine

chlo·ri·nate \-ə‚nāt\ *vb* **-nat·ed; -nat·ing** : treat or combine with chlorine — **chlo·ri·na·tion** \‚klōrə'nāshən\ *n*

chlo·rine \'klōr‚ēn\ *n* : chemical element that is a heavy strong-smelling greenish yellow irritating gas

chlo·ro·form \'klōrə‚fórm\ *n* : etherlike colorless heavy fluid ∼ *vb* : anesthetize or kill with chloroform

chlo·ro·phyll \'klōrə‚fil\ *n* : green coloring matter of plants

chock \'chäk\ *n* : wedge for blocking the movement of a wheel — **chock** *vb*

chock-full \'chək'fúl, 'chäk-\ *adj* : full to the limit

choc·o·late \'chäkələt, 'chók-\ *n* 1 : ground roasted cacao beans or a beverage made from them 2 : candy made of or with chocolate **3** : dark brown

choice \'chȯis\ *n* **1** : act or power of choosing **2** : one selected **3** : variety offered for selection ~ *adj* **choic·er; choic·est 1** : worthy of being chosen **2** : selected with care **3** : of high quality

choir \'kwīr\ *n* : group of singers esp. in church — **choir·boy** *n* — **choir·mas·ter** *n*

choke \'chōk\ *vb* **choked; chok·ing 1** : hinder breathing **2** : clog or obstruct ~ *n* **1** : a choking or sound of choking **2** : valve for controlling air intake in a gasoline engine

chok·er \-ər\ *n* : tight necklace

cho·ler \'kälər, 'kō-\ *n* : bad temper — **cho·ler·ic** \'kälərik, kə'ler-\ *adj*

chol·era \'kälərə\ *n* : disease marked by severe vomiting and dysentery

cho·les·ter·ol \kə'lestə,rȯl, -,rōl\ *n* : waxy substance in animal tissues

choose \'chüz\ *vb* **chose** \'chōz\; **cho·sen** \'chōz°n\ **choos·ing 1** : select after consideration **2** : decide **3** : prefer — **choos·er** *n*

choosy, choos·ey \'chüzē\ *adj* **choos·i·er; -est** : fussy in making choices

chop \'chäp\ *vb* **-pp- 1** : cut by repeated blows **2** : cut into small pieces ~ *n* **1** : sharp downward blow **2** : small cut of meat often with part of a rib

chop·per \-ər\ *n* **1** : one that chops **2** : helicopter

chop·py \-ē\ *adj* **-pi·er; -est 1** : rough with small waves **2** : jerky or disconnected — **chop·pi·ly** *adv* — **chop·pi·ness** *n*

chops \'chäps\ *n pl* : fleshy covering of the jaws

chop·sticks *n pl* : pair of sticks used in eating in oriental countries

cho·ral \'kȯrəl\ *adj* : relating to or sung by a choir or chorus or in chorus — **cho·ral·ly** *adv*

cho·rale \kə'ral, -'räl\ *n* **1** : hymn tune or harmonization of a traditional melody **2** : chorus or choir

¹chord \'kȯrd\ *n* : harmonious tones sounded together

²chord *n* **1** : cordlike anatomical structure **2** : straight line joining 2 points on a curve

◆ **chore** \'chȯr\ *n* **1** *pl* : daily household or farm work **2** : routine or disagreeable task

cho·re·og·ra·phy \,kȯrē'ägrəfē\ *n, pl* **-phies** : art of composing and arranging dances — **cho·reo·graph** \'kȯrēə,graf\ *vb* — **cho·re·og·ra·pher** \,kȯrē'ägrəfər\ *n* — **cho·reo·graph·ic** \-ēə'grafik\ *adj*

cho·ris·ter \'kȯrəstər\ *n* : choir singer

chor·tle \'chȯrt°l\ *vb* **-tled; -tling** : laugh or chuckle — **chortle** *n*

cho·rus \'kȯrəs\ *n* **1** : group of singers or dancers **2** : part of a song repeated at intervals **3** : composition for a chorus ~ *vb* : sing or utter together

chose *past of* CHOOSE

cho·sen \'chōz°n\ *adj* : favored

¹chow \'chau̇\ *n* : food

²chow *n* : thick-coated muscular dog

chow·der \'chau̇dər\ *n* : thick soup usu. of seafood and milk

chow mein \'chau̇'mān\ *n* : thick stew of shredded vegetables and meat

chris·ten \'kris°n\ *vb* **1** : baptize **2** : name — **chris·ten·ing** *n*

Chris·ten·dom \-dəm\ *n* : areas where Christianity prevails

Chris·tian \'krischən\ *n* : adherent of Christianity ~ *adj* : relating to or professing a belief in Christianity or Jesus Christ — **Chris·tian·ize** \'krischə,nīz\ *vb*

Chris·ti·an·i·ty \ˌkrischē'anətē\ *n* : religion derived from the teachings of Jesus Christ

Christian name *n* : first name

Christ·mas \'krisməs\ *n* : December 25 celebrated as the birthday of Christ

chro·mat·ic \krō'matik\ *adj* 1 : relating to color 2 : proceeding by half steps of the musical scale

chrome \'krōm\ *n* : chromium or something plated with it

chro·mi·um \-ēəm\ *n* : a bluish white metallic element used esp. in alloys

chro·mo·some \'krōmə,sōm, -,zōm\ *n* : part of a cell nucleus that contains the genes — **chro·mo·som·al** \ˌkrōmə'sōməl, -'zō-\ *adj*

chron·ic \'kränik\ *adj* : frequent or persistent — **chron·i·cal·ly** \-iklē\ *adv*

chron·i·cle \'kränikəl\ *n* : history ~ *vb* **-cled; -cling** : record — **chron·i·cler** \-iklər\ *n*

chro·nol·o·gy \krə'näləjē\ *n, pl* **-gies** : list of events in order of their occurrence — **chron·o·log·i·cal** \ˌkrän°l'äjikəl\ *adj* — **chron·o·log·i·cal·ly** \-iklē\ *adv*

chro·nom·e·ter \krə'nämətər\ *n* : very accurate timepiece

chrys·a·lis \'krisələs\ *n, pl* **chrys·al·i·des** \kris'alə,dēz\ *or* **chrys·a·lis·es** : insect pupa enclosed in a shell

chry·san·the·mum \kris'anthəməm\ *n* : plant with showy flowers

chub·by \'chəbē\ *adj* **-bi·er; -est** : fat — **chub·bi·ness** *n*

¹chuck \'chək\ *vb* 1 : tap 2 : toss ~ *n* 1 : light pat under the chin 2 : toss

²chuck *n* 1 : cut of beef 2 : machine part that holds work or another part

chuck·le \'chəkəl\ *vb* **-led; -ling** : laugh quietly — **chuckle** *n*

chug \'chəg\ *n* : sound of a laboring engine ~ *vb* **-gg-** : work or move with chugs

chum \'chəm\ *n* : close friend ~ *vb* **-mm-** : be chums — **chum·my** \-ē\ *adj*

chump \'chəmp\ *n* : fool

chunk \'chəŋk\ *n* 1 : short thick piece 2 : sizable amount

chunky \-ē\ *adj* **chunk·i·er; -est** 1 : stocky 2 : containing chunks

church \'chərch\ *n* 1 : building esp. for Christian public worship 2 : whole body of Christians 3 : denomination 4 : congregation — **church·go·er** *n* — **church·go·ing** *adj or n*

church·yard *n* : cemetery beside a church

churl \'chərl\ *n* : rude ill-bred person — **churl·ish** *adj*

churn \'chərn\ *n* : container in which butter is made ~ *vb* 1 : agitate in a churn 2 : shake violently

chute \'shüt\ *n* : trough or passage

chut·ney \'chətnē\ *n, pl* **-neys** : sweet and sour relish

chutz·pah \'hutspə, 'kut-, -,spä\ *n* : nerve or insolence

ci·ca·da \sə'kädə\ *n* : stout-bodied insect with transparent wings

ci·der \'sīdər\ *n* : apple juice

ci·gar \sig'är\ *n* : roll of leaf tobacco for smoking

cig·a·rette \ˌsigə'ret, 'sigə,ret\ *n* : cut tobacco rolled in paper for smoking

cinch \'sinch\ *n* 1 : strap holding a saddle or pack in place 2 : sure thing — **cinch** *vb*

cin·cho·na \siŋ'kōnə\ *n* : So. American tree that yields quinine

cinc·ture \'siŋkchər\ *n* : belt or sash

cin·der \'sindər\ *n* 1 *pl* : ashes 2 : piece of partly burned wood or coal

cin·e·ma \'sinəmə\ *n* : movies or a movie theater — **cin·e·mat·ic** \ˌsinə'matik\ *adj*

cin·na·mon \'sinəmən\ *n* : spice from an aromatic tree bark

ci·pher \'sīfər\ *n* 1 : zero 2 : code

cir·ca \'sərkə\ *prep* : about

cir·cle \'sərkəl\ *n* 1 : closed symmetrical curve 2 : cycle 3 : group with a common tie ~ *vb* **-cled; -cling** 1 : enclose in a circle 2 : move or revolve around

cir·cuit \'sərkət\ *n* 1 : boundary 2 : regular tour of a territory 3 : complete path of an electric current 4 : group of electronic components

cir·cu·itous \ˌsər'kyüətəs\ *adj* : circular or winding

cir·cuit·ry \'sərkətrē\ *n, pl* **-ries** : arrangement of an electric circuit

cir·cu·lar \'sərkyələr\ *adj* 1 : round 2 : moving in a circle ~ *n* : advertising leaflet — **cir·cu·lar·i·ty** \ˌsərkyə'larətē\ *n*

cir·cu·late \'sərkyəˌlāt\ *vb* **-lat·ed; -lat·ing** : move or cause to move in a circle or from place to place or person to person — **cir·cu·la·tion** \ˌsərkyə'lāshən\ *n* — **cir·cu·la·to·ry** \'sərkyələˌtōrē\ *adj*

cir·cum·cise \'sərkəmˌsīz\ *vb* **-cised; -cis·ing** : cut off the foreskin of — **cir·cum·ci·sion** \ˌsərkəm'sizhən\ *n*

cir·cum·fer·ence \sər'kəmfrəns\ *n* : perimeter of a circle

cir·cum·flex \'sərkəmˌfleks\ *n* : phonetic mark (as ^)

cir·cum·lo·cu·tion \ˌsərkəmlō-'kyüshən\ *n* : excessive use of words

cir·cum·nav·i·gate \ˌsərkəm'navəˌgāt\ *vb* : sail completely around — **cir·cum·nav·i·ga·tion** *n*

cir·cum·scribe \'sərkəmˌskrīb\ *vb* **1** : draw a line around **2** : limit

cir·cum·spect \'sərkəmˌspekt\ *adj* : careful — **cir·cum·spec·tion** \ˌsərkəm'spekshən\ *n*

cir·cum·stance \'sərkəmˌstans\ *n* **1** : fact or event **2** *pl* : surrounding conditions **3** *pl* : financial situation — **cir·cum·stan·tial** \ˌsərkəm'stanchəl\ *adj*

cir·cum·vent \ˌsərkəm'vent\ *vb* : get around esp. by trickery — **cir·cum·ven·tion** \-'venchən\ *n*

♦ **cir·cus** \'sərkəs\ *n* : show with feats of skill, animal acts, and clowns

cir·rho·sis \sə'rōsəs\ *n, pl* **-rho·ses** \-ˌsēz\ : fibrosis of the liver — **cir·rhot·ic** \-'rätik\ *adj or n*

cir·rus \'sirəs\ *n, pl* **-ri** \-ˌī\ : wispy white cloud

cis·tern \'sistərn\ *n* : underground water tank

cit·a·del \'sitədᵊl, -əˌdel\ *n* : fortress

cite \'sīt\ *vb* **cit·ed; cit·ing 1** : summon before a court **2** : quote **3** : refer to esp. in commendation — **ci·ta·tion** \sī'tāshən\ *n*

cit·i·zen \'sitəzən\ *n* : member of a country — **cit·i·zen·ry** \-rē\ *n* — **cit·i·zen·ship** *n*

cit·ron \'sitrən\ *n* : lemonlike fruit

cit·rus \'sitrəs\ *n, pl* **-rus** *or* **-rus·es** : evergreen tree or shrub grown for its fruit (as the orange or lemon)

city \'sitē\ *n, pl* **cit·ies** : place larger or more important than a town

civ·ic \'sivik\ *adj* : relating to citizenship or civil affairs

civ·ics \-iks\ *n* : study of citizenship

civ·il \'sivəl\ *adj* **1** : relating to citizens **2** : polite **3** : relating to or being a lawsuit — **civ·il·ly** *adv*

ci·vil·ian \sə'vilyən\ *n* : person not in a military, police, or fire-fighting force

ci·vil·i·ty \sə'vilətē\ *n, pl* **-ties** : courtesy

civ·i·li·za·tion \ˌsivələ'zāshən\ *n* **1** : high level of cultural development **2** : culture of a time or place

civ·i·lize \'sivəˌlīz\ *vb* **-lized; -liz·ing** : raise from a primitive stage of cultural development — **civ·i·lized** *adj*

civil liberty *n* : freedom from arbitrary governmental interference — usu. pl.

civil rights *n pl* : nonpolitical rights of a citizen

civil service *n* : government service

civil war *n* : war among citizens of one country

clack \'klak\ *vb* : make or cause a clatter — **clack** *n*

clad \'klad\ *adj* : covered

claim \'klām\ *vb* **1** : demand or take as the rightful owner **2** : maintain ~ *n* **1** : demand of right or ownership **2** : declaration **3** : something claimed — **claim·ant** \-ənt\ *n*

clair·voy·ant \klar'vȯiənt\ *adj* : able to perceive things beyond the senses — **clair·voy·ance** \-əns\ *n* — **clairvoy·ant** *n*

clam \'klam\ *n* : bivalve mollusk

clam·ber \'klambər\ *vb* : climb awkwardly

clam·my \'klamē\ *adj* **-mi·er; -est** : being damp, soft, and usu. cool — **clam·mi·ness** *n*

clam·or \-ər\ *n* **1** : uproar **2** : protest — **clamor** *vb* — **clam·or·ous** *adj*

clamp \'klamp\ *n* : device for holding things together — **clamp** *vb*

clan \'klan\ *n* : group of related families — **clan·nish** *adj* — **clan·nish·ness** *n*

clan·des·tine \klan'destən\ *adj* : secret

clang \'klaŋ\ *n* : loud metallic ringing — **clang** *vb*

clan·gor \-ər, -gər\ *n* : jumble of clangs

clank \'klaŋk\ *n* : brief sound of struck metal — **clank** *vb*

clap \'klap\ *vb* **-pp- 1** : strike noisily **2** : applaud ∼ *n* **1** : loud crash **2** : noise made by clapping the hands

clap·board \'klabərd, 'klap-, -,bōrd\ *n* : narrow tapered board used for siding

clap·per \'klapər\ *n* : tongue of a bell

claque \'klak\ *n* **1** : group hired to applaud at a performance **2** : group of sycophants

clar·et \'klarət\ *n* : dry red wine

clar·i·fy \'klarə,fī\ *vb* **-fied; -fy·ing** : make or become clear — **clar·i·fi·ca·tion** \,klarəfə'kāshən\ *n*

clar·i·net \,klarə'net\ *n* : woodwind instrument shaped like a tube — **clar·i·net·ist, clar·i·net·tist** \-ist\ *n*

clar·i·on \'klarēən\ *adj* : loud and clear

clar·i·ty \'klarətē\ *n* : clearness

clash \'klash\ *vb* **1** : make or cause a clash **2** : be in opposition or disharmony ∼ *n* **1** : crashing sound **2** : hostile encounter

clasp \'klasp\ *n* **1** : device for holding things together **2** : embrace or grasp ∼ *vb* **1** : fasten **2** : embrace or grasp

class \'klas\ *n* **1** : group of the same status or nature **2** : social rank **3** : course of instruction **4** : group of students ∼ *vb* : classify — **class·less** *adj* — **class·mate** *n* — **class·room** *n*

clas·sic \'klasik\ *adj* **1** : serving as a standard of excellence **2** : classical ∼ *n* : work of enduring excellence and esp. of ancient Greece or Rome — **clas·si·cal** \-ikəl\ *adj* — **clas·si·cal·ly** \-klē\ *adv* — **clas·si·cism** \'klasə,sizəm\ *n* — **clas·si·cist** \-sist\ *n*

clas·si·fied \'klasə,fīd\ *adj* : restricted for security reasons

clas·si·fy \-,fī\ *vb* **-fied; -fy·ing** : arrange in or assign to classes — **clas·si·fi·ca·tion** \,klasəfə'kāshən\ *n* — **clas·si·fi·er** \'klasə,fīər\ *n*

clat·ter \'klatər\ *n* : rattling sound — **clatter** *vb*

clause \'klȯz\ *n* **1** : separate part of a document **2** : part of a sentence with a subject and predicate

claus·tro·pho·bia \,klȯstrə'fōbēə\ *n* : fear of closed or narrow spaces — **claus·tro·pho·bic** \-bik\ *adj*

clav·i·chord \'klavə,kȯrd\ *n* : early keyboard instrument

clav·i·cle \'klavikəl\ *n* : collarbone

◆ **claw** \'klȯ\ *n* : sharp curved nail or process (as on the toe of an animal) ∼ *vb* : scratch or dig — **clawed** *adj*

clay \\'klā\ *n* : plastic earthy material — **clay·ey** \-ē\ *adj*

clean \\'klēn\ *adj* **1** : free from dirt or disease **2** : pure or honorable **3** : thorough ∼ *vb* : make or become clean — **clean** *adv* — **clean·er** *n* — **clean·ly** \-lē\ *adv* — **clean·ness** *n*

clean·ly \\'klenlē\ *adj* **-li·er; -est** : clean — **clean·li·ness** *n*

cleanse \\'klenz\ *vb* **cleansed; cleans·ing** : make clean — **cleans·er** *n*

clear \\'klir\ *adj* **1** : bright **2** : free from clouds **3** : transparent **4** : easily heard, seen or understood **5** : free from doubt **6** : free from restriction or obstruction ∼ *vb* **1** : make or become clear **2** : go away **3** : free from accusation or blame **4** : explain or settle **5** : net **6** : jump or pass without touching ∼ *n* : clear space or part — **clear** *adv* — **clear·ance** \\'klirəns\ *n*

clear·ing \\'klirіŋ\ *n* : land cleared of wood

clear·ly *adv* **1** : in a clear manner **2** : it is obvious that

cleat \\'klēt\ *n* : projection that strengthens or prevents slipping

cleav·age \\'klēvij\ *n* **1** : a splitting apart **2** : depression between a woman's breasts

¹cleave \\'klēv\ *vb* **cleaved** \\'klēvd\ *or* **clove** \\'klōv\; **cleav·ing** : adhere

²cleave *vb* **cleaved** \\'klēvd\; **cleav·ing** : split apart

cleav·er \\'klēvər\ *n* : heavy chopping knife

clef \\'klef\ *n* : sign on the staff in music to show pitch

cleft \\'kleft\ *n* : crack

clem·ent \\'klemənt\ *adj* **1** : merciful **2** : temperate or mild — **clem·en·cy** \-ənsē\ *n*

clench \\'klench\ *vb* **1** : hold fast **2** : close tightly

cler·gy \\'klərjē\ *n* : body of religious officials — **cler·gy·man** \-jimən\ *n*

cler·ic \\'klerik\ *n* : member of the clergy

cler·i·cal \-ikəl\ *adj* **1** : relating to the clergy **2** : relating to a clerk or office worker

clerk \\'klərk, *Brit* 'klärk\ *n* **1** : official responsible for record-keeping **2** : person doing general office

work **3** : salesperson in a store — **clerk** *vb* — **clerk·ship** *n*

clev·er \\'klevər\ *adj* **1** : resourceful **2** : marked by wit or ingenuity — **clev·er·ly** *adv* — **clev·er·ness** *n*

clew *var of* CLUE

cli·ché \kli'shā\ *n* : trite phrase — **cli·chéd** \-'shād\ *adj*

click \\'klik\ *n* : slight sharp noise ∼ *vb* : make or cause to make a click

cli·ent \\'klīənt\ *n* **1** : person who engages professional services **2** : customer

cli·en·tele \ˌklīən'tel, ˌklē-\ *n* : body of customers

cliff \\'klif\ *n* : high steep face of rock

cli·mate \\'klīmət\ *n* : average weather conditions over a period of years — **cli·mat·ic** \klī'matik\ *adj*

cli·max \\'klīˌmaks\ *n* : the highest point ∼ *vb* : come to a climax — **cli·mac·tic** \klī'maktik\ *adj*

climb \\'klīm\ *vb* **1** : go up or down by use of hands and feet **2** : rise ∼ *n* : a climbing — **climb·er** *n*

clinch \\'klinch\ *vb* **1** : fasten securely **2** : settle **3** : hold fast or firmly — **clinch** *n* — **clinch·er** *n*

cling \\'kliŋ\ *vb* **clung** \\'kləŋ\; **cling·ing 1** : adhere firmly **2** : hold on tightly

clin·ic \\'klinik\ *n* : facility for diagnosis and treatment of outpatients — **clin·i·cal** \-əl\ *adj* — **clin·i·cal·ly** \-klē\ *adv*

clink \\'kliŋk\ *vb* : make a slight metallic sound — **clink** *n*

clin·ker \\'kliŋkər\ *n* : fused stony matter esp. in a furnace

¹clip \\'klip\ *vb* **-pp-** : fasten with a clip ∼ *n* : device to hold things together

²clip *vb* **-pp- 1** : cut or cut off **2** : hit ∼ *n* **1** : clippers **2** : sharp blow **3** : rapid pace

clip·per \\'klipər\ *n* **1** *pl* : implement for clipping **2** : fast sailing ship

clique \\'klēk, 'klik\ *n* : small exclusive group of people

cli·to·ris \\'klitərəs, kli'tòrəs\ *n, pl* **cli·to·ri·des** \-'tòrəˌdēz\ : small organ at the front of the vulva

cloak \\'klōk\ *n* **1** : loose outer garment **2** : something that conceals ∼ *vb* : cover or hide with a cloak

♦ **clob·ber** \'kläbər\ *vb* : hit hard

clock \'kläk\ *n* : timepiece not carried on the person ~ *vb* : record the time of

clock·wise \-,wīz\ *adv or adj* : in the same direction as a clock's hands move

clod \'kläd\ *n* 1 : lump esp. of earth 2 : dull insensitive person

clog \'kläg\ *n* 1 : restraining weight 2 : thick-soled shoe ~ *vb* -gg- 1 : impede with a clog 2 : obstruct passage through 3 : become plugged up

clois·ter \'klòistər\ *n* 1 : monastic establishment 2 : covered passage ~ *vb* : shut away from the world

clone \'klōn\ *n* 1 : offspring produced from a single organism 2 : copy

¹close \'klōz\ *vb* **closed; clos·ing** 1 : shut 2 : cease operation 3 : terminate 4 : bring or come together ~ *n* : conclusion or end

²close \'klōs\ *adj* **clos·er; clos·est** 1 : confining 2 : secretive 3 : strict 4 : stuffy 5 : having little space between items 6 : fitting tightly 7 : near 8 : intimate 9 : accurate 10 : nearly even — **close** *adv* — **close·ly** *adv* — **close·ness** *n*

clos·et \'kläzət, 'klòz-\ *n* : small compartment for household utensils or clothing ~ *vb* : take into a private room for a talk

clo·sure \'klōzhər\ *n* 1 : act of closing 2 : something that closes

clot \'klät\ *n* : dried mass of a liquid — **clot** *vb*

cloth \'klòth\ *n, pl* **cloths** \'klòthz, 'klòths\ 1 : fabric 2 : tablecloth

clothe \'klōth\ *vb* **clothed** *or* **clad** \'klad\; **cloth·ing** : dress

clothes \'klōthz, 'klōz\ *n pl* 1 : clothing 2 : bedclothes

cloth·ier \'klōthyər, -thēər\ *n* : maker or seller of clothing

cloth·ing \'klōthiŋ\ *n* : covering for the human body

cloud \'klaùd\ *n* 1 : visible mass of particles in the air 2 : something that darkens, hides, or threatens ~ *vb* : darken or hide — **cloud·i·ness** *n* — **cloud·less** *adj* — **cloudy** *adj*

cloud·burst *n* : sudden heavy rain

clout \'klaùt\ *n* 1 : blow 2 : influence ~ *vb* : hit forcefully

¹clove \'klōv\ *n* : section of a bulb

²clove *past of* CLEAVE

³clove *n* : dried flower bud of an East Indian tree used as a spice

clo·ver \'klōvər\ *n* : leguminous herb with usu. 3-part leaves

clo·ver·leaf *n, pl* **-leafs** *or* **-leaves** : highway interchange

clown \'klaùn\ *n* : funny costumed entertainer esp. in a circus ~ *vb* : act like a clown — **clown·ish** *adj* — **clown·ish·ly** *adv* — **clown·ish·ness** *n*

cloy \'klòi\ *vb* : disgust with excess — **cloy·ing·ly** \-iŋlē\ *adv*

club \'kləb\ *n* 1 : heavy wooden stick 2 : playing card of a suit marked with a black figure like a clover leaf 3 : group associated for a common purpose ~ *vb* -bb- : hit with a club

club·foot *n* : misshapen foot twisted out of position from birth — **club·foot·ed** \-,fùtəd\ *adj*

cluck \'klək\ *n* : sound made by a hen — **cluck** *vb*

clue \'klü\ *n* : piece of evidence that helps solve a problem ~ *vb* **clued; clue·ing** *or* **clu·ing** : provide with a clue

clump \'kləmp\ *n* 1 : cluster 2 : heavy tramping sound ~ *vb* : tread heavily

clum·sy \'kləmzē\ *adj* **-si·er; -est** 1 : lacking dexterity, nimbleness, or

grace **2** : tactless — **clum·si·ly** *adv*
— **clum·si·ness** *n*

clung *past of* CLING

clunk·er \'kləŋkər\ *n* : old car

clus·ter \'kləstər\ *n* : group ~ *vb*
: grow or gather in a cluster

clutch \'kləch\ *vb* : grasp ~ *n* **1**
: grasping hand or claws **2** : control or power **3** : coupling for two
working parts in machinery

◆ **clut·ter** \'klətər\ *vb* : fill with
things that get in the way — **clut-
ter** *n*

co- *prefix* : with, together, joint, or
jointly

coact	cohostess
coactor	coinvent
coauthor	coinventor
coauthorship	coinvestigator
cocaptain	coleader
cochairman	comanagement
cochampion	comanager
cocomposer	co-organizer
coconspirator	co-own
cocreator	co-owner
codefendant	copartner
codesign	copartnership
codevelop	copresident
codeveloper	coprincipal
codirect	coprisoner
codirector	coproduce
codiscoverer	coproducer
codrive	coproduction
codriver	copromoter
coedit	coproprietor
coeditor	copublish
coexecutor	copublisher
coexist	corecipient
coexistence	coresident
coexistent	cosignatory
cofeature	cosigner
cofinance	cosponsor
cofound	costar
cofounder	cowinner
coheir	coworker
coheiress	cowrite
cohost	

coach \'kōch\ *n* **1** : closed 2-door
4-wheeled carriage **2** : railroad
passenger car **3** : bus **4** : 2d-class
air travel **5** : one who instructs or
trains performers ~ *vb* : instruct
or direct as a coach

co·ag·u·late \kō'agyə.lāt\ *vb* -**lated; -lat·ing** : clot — **co·ag·u·lant**
\-lənt\ *n* — **co·ag·u·la·tion**
\-.agyə'lāshən\ *n*

coal \'kōl\ *n* **1** : ember **2** : black solid
mineral used as fuel — **coal·field**
n

co·alesce \.kōə'les\ *vb* -**alesced;
-alesc·ing** : grow together — **co-
ales·cence** \-'les⁰ns\ *n*

co·ali·tion \-'lishən\ *n* : temporary
alliance

coarse \'kōrs\ *adj* **coars·er; coars-
est 1** : composed of large particles
2 : rough or crude — **coarse·ly**
adv — **coars·en** \-⁰n\ *vb* — **coarse-
ness** *n*

coast \'kōst\ *n* : seashore ~ *vb*
: move without effort — **coast-
al** \-⁰l\ *adj*

coast·er \-ər\ *n* **1** : one that coasts
2 : plate or mat to protect a surface

coast guard *n* : military force that
guards or patrols a coast —
coast·guards·man \'kōst.gärdz-
mən\ *n*

coast·line *n* : shape of a coast

coat \'kōt\ *n* **1** : outer garment for
the upper body **2** : external
growth of fur or feathers **3** : covering layer ~ *vb* : cover with a
coat — **coat·ed** *adj* — **coat·ing** *n*

coax \'kōks\ *vb* : move to action or
achieve by gentle urging or flattery

cob \'käb\ *n* : corncob

co·balt \'kō.bȯlt\ *n* : shiny silver-
white magnetic metallic chemical
element

cob·ble \'käbəl\ *vb* **cob·bled; cob-**

bling : make or put together hastily

cob·bler \'käblər\ *n* 1 : shoemaker 2 : deep-dish fruit pie

cob·ble·stone *n* : small round paving stone

co·bra \'kōbrə\ *n* : venomous snake

cob·web \'käb,web\ *n* : network spun by a spider or a similar filament

co·caine \kō'kān, 'kō,kān\ *n* : drug obtained from the leaves of a So. American shrub (**co·ca** \'kōkə\)

co·chlea \'kōklēə, 'käk-\ *n, pl* **-chleas** *or* **-chle·ae** \-lē,ē, -,ī\ : the usu. spiral part of the inner ear — **coch·le·ar** \-lēər\ *adj*

cock \'käk\ *n* 1 : male fowl 2 : valve or faucet ~ *vb* 1 : draw back the hammer of a firearm 2 : tilt to one side — **cock·fight** *n*

cock·ade \kä'kād\ *n* : badge on a hat

cock·a·too \'käkə,tü\ *n, pl* **-toos** : large Australian crested parrot

cock·eyed \'käk'īd\ *adj* 1 : tilted to one side 2 : slightly crazy

cock·le \'käkəl\ *n* : edible shellfish

cock·pit \'käk,pit\ *n* : place for a pilot, driver, or helmsman

cock·roach *n* : nocturnal insect often infesting houses

cock·tail \'käk,tāl\ *n* 1 : iced drink of liquor and flavorings 2 : appetizer

cocky \'käkē\ *adj* **cock·i·er; -est** : overconfident — **cock·i·ly** \-əlē\ *adv* — **cock·i·ness** *n*

co·coa \'kōkō\ *n* 1 : cacao 2 : powdered chocolate or a drink made from this

♦ **co·co·nut** \'kōkə,nət\ *n* : large nutlike fruit of a tropical palm (**coconut palm**)

co·coon \kə'kün\ *n* : case protecting an insect pupa

cod \'käd\ *n, pl* **cod** : food fish of the No. Atlantic

cod·dle \'käd°l\ *vb* **-dled; -dling** : pamper

code \'kōd\ *n* 1 : system of laws or rules 2 : system of signals

co·deine \'kō,dēn\ *n* : narcotic drug used in cough remedies

cod·ger \'käjər\ *n* : odd fellow

cod·i·cil \'kädəsəl, -,sil\ *n* : postscript to a will

cod·i·fy \'kädə,fī, 'kōd-\ *vb* **-fied; -fy·ing** : arrange systematically — **cod·i·fi·ca·tion** \,kädəfə'kāshən, ,kōd-\ *n*

co·ed \'kō,ed\ *n* : female student in a coeducational institution — **coed** *adj*

co·ed·u·ca·tion \,kō-\ *n* : education of the sexes together — **co·ed·u·ca·tion·al** *adj*

co·ef·fi·cient \,kōə'fishənt\ *n* 1 : number that is a multiplier of another 2 : number that serves as a measure of some property

co·erce \kō'ərs\ *vb* **-erced; -erc·ing** : force — **co·er·cion** \-'ərzhən, -shən\ *n* — **co·er·cive** \-'ərsiv\ *adj*

cof·fee \'kófē\ *n* : drink made from the roasted and ground seeds (**coffee beans**) of a tropical shrub — **cof·fee·house** *n* — **cof·fee·pot** *n*

cof·fer \'kófər\ *n* : box for valuables

cof·fin \-fən\ *n* : box for burial

cog \'käg\ *n* : tooth on the rim of a gear — **cogged** \'kägd\ *adj* — **cog·wheel** *n*

co·gent \'kōjənt\ *adj* : compelling or convincing — **co·gen·cy** \-jənsē\ *n*

cog·i·tate \'käjə,tāt\ *vb* **-tat·ed; -tat·ing** : think over — **cog·i·ta·tion** \,käjə'tāshən\ *n* — **cog·i·ta·tive** \'käjə,tātiv\ *adj*

co·gnac \'kōn,yak\ *n* : French brandy

cog·nate \'käg,nāt\ *adj* : related —
cog·nate *n*

cog·ni·tion \käg'nishən\ *n* : act or
process of knowing — **cog·ni·tive**
\'kägnətiv\ *adj*

cog·ni·zance \'kägnəzəns\ *n* : notice
or awareness — **cog·ni·zant**
\'kägnəzənt\ *adj*

co·hab·it \kō'habət\ *vb* : live together as husband and wife — **co-
hab·i·ta·tion** \-,habə'tāshən\ *n*

co·here \kō'hir\ *vb* **-hered; -her-
ing** : stick together

co·her·ent \-'hirənt\ *adj* 1 : able to
stick together 2 : logically consistent — **co·her·ence** \-əns\ *n* — **co-
her·ent·ly** *adv*

co·he·sion \-'hēzhən\ *n* : a sticking
together — **co·he·sive** \-siv\ *adj*
— **co·he·sive·ly** *adv* — **co·he·sive-
ness** *n*

co·hort \'kō,hȯrt\ *n* 1 : group of soldiers 2 : companion

coif·fure \kwä'fyu̇r\ *n* : hair style

coil \'kȯil\ *vb* : wind in a spiral ~ *n*
: series of loops (as of rope)

coin \'kȯin\ *n* : piece of metal used
as money ~ *vb* 1 : make (a coin)
by stamping 2 : create — **coin-
age** \-ij\ *n* — **coin·er** *n*

co·in·cide \,kōən'sīd, 'kōən,sīd\ *vb*
-cid·ed; -cid·ing 1 : be in the same
place 2 : happen at the same time
3 : be alike — **co·in·ci·dence** \kō-
'insədəns\ *n* — **co·in·ci·dent**
\-ənt\ *adj* — **co·in·ci·den·tal**
\-,insə'dent°l\ *adj*

co·itus \'kōətəs\ *n* : sexual intercourse — **co·ital** \-ət°l\ *adj*

coke \'kōk\ *n* : fuel made by heating
soft coal

co·la \'kōlə\ *n* : carbonated soft
drink

col·an·der \'kələndər, 'käl-\ *n* : per-
forated utensil for draining food

cold \'kōld\ *adj* 1 : having a low or
below normal temperature 2
: lacking warmth of feeling 3 : suffering from lack of warmth ~ *n* 1
: low temperature 2 : minor respi-
ratory illness — **cold·ly** *adv* —
cold·ness *n* — **in cold blood** : with
premeditation

cold–blood·ed *adj* 1 : cruel or mer-
ciless 2 : having a body temperature that varies with the temperature of the environment

cole·slaw \'kōl,slȯ\ *n* : cabbage salad

col·ic \'kälik\ *n* : sharp abdominal
pain — **col·icky** *adj*

col·i·se·um \,kälə'sēəm\ *n* : arena

col·lab·o·rate \kə'labə,rāt\ *vb* **-rat-
ed; -rat·ing** 1 : work jointly with
others 2 : help the enemy — **col-
lab·o·ra·tion** \-,labə'rāshən\ *n* —
col·lab·o·ra·tor \-'labə,rātər\ *n*

col·lapse \kə'laps\ *vb* **-lapsed; -laps-
ing** 1 : fall in 2 : break down physically or mentally 3 : fold down ~
n : breakdown — **col·laps·ible** *adj*

col·lar \'kälər\ *n* : part of a garment
around the neck ~ *vb* 1 : seize by
the collar 2 : grab — **col·lar·less**
adj

col·lar·bone *n* : bone joining the
breastbone and the shoulder
blade

col·lards \'kälərdz\ *n pl* : kale

col·late \kə'lāt; 'käl,āt, 'kōl-\ *vb* **-lat-
ed; -lat·ing** 1 : compare carefully 2
: assemble in order

col·lat·er·al \kə'latərəl\ *adj* 1 : secondary 2 : descended from the
same ancestors but not in the
same line 3 : similar ~ *n* : property used as security for a loan

col·league \'käl,ēg\ *n* : associate

col·lect \kə'lekt\ *vb* 1 : bring, come,
or gather together 2 : receive payment of ~ *adv or adj* : to be paid
for by the receiver — **col·lect·ible,
col·lect·able** *adj* — **col·lec·tion**
\-'lekshən\ *n* — **col·lec·tor**
\-'lektər\ *n*

col·lec·tive \-tiv\ *adj* : denoting or
shared by a group ~ *n* : a cooperative unit — **col·lec·tive·ly** *adv*

col·lege \'kälij\ *n* : institution of
higher learning granting a
bachelor's degree — **col·le·gian**
\kə'lējan\ *n* — **col·le·giate** \kə-
'lējət\ *adj*

col·lide \kə'līd\ *vb* **-lid·ed; -lid-
ing** : strike together — **col·li·sion**
\-'lizhən\ *n*

col·lie \'kälē\ *n* : large long-haired
dog

col·loid \'käl,ȯid\ *n* : tiny particles
in suspension in a fluid — **col-
loi·dal** \kə'lȯid°l\ *adj*

col·lo·qui·al \kə'lōkwēəl\ *adj* : used
in informal conversation — **col-
lo·qui·al·ism** \-ə,lizəm\ *n*

col·lo·quy \'käləkwē\ *n, pl* **-quies**
: formal conversation or confer-
ence

col·lu·sion \kə'lüzhən\ *n* : secret

cooperation for deceit — **col·lu·sive** \-'lüsiv\ *adj*

◆ **co·logne** \kə'lōn\ *n* : perfumed liquid

¹**co·lon** \'kōlən\ *n*, *pl* **colons** *or* **co·la** \-lə\ : lower part of the large intestine — **co·lon·ic** \kō'länik\ *adj*

²**colon** *n*, *pl* **colons** : punctuation mark : used esp. to direct attention to following matter

col·o·nel \'kərn°l\ *n* : commissioned officer (as in the army) ranking next below a brigadier general

col·o·nize \'kälə,nīz\ *vb* **-nized; -nizing** **1** : establish a colony in **2** : settle — **col·o·ni·za·tion** \,kälənə-'zāshən\ *n* — **col·o·niz·er** *n*

col·on·nade \,kälə'nād\ *n* : row of supporting columns

col·o·ny \'kälənē\ *n*, *pl* **-nies** **1** : people who inhabit a new territory or the territory itself **2** : animals of one kind (as bees) living together — **co·lo·nial** \kə'lōnēəl\ *adj or n* — **col·o·nist** \'kälənist\ *n*

col·or \'kələr\ *n* **1** : quality of visible things distinct from shape that results from light reflection **2** *pl* : flag **3** : liveliness ∼ *vb* **1** : give color to **2** : blush — **col·or·fast** *adj* — **col·or·ful** *adj* — **col·or·less** *adj*

col·or–blind *adj* : unable to distinguish colors — **color blindness** *n*

col·ored \'kələrd\ *adj* **1** : having color **2** : of a race other than the white — ∼ *n pl* **colored** *or* **coloreds** : colored person

co·los·sal \kə'läsəl\ *adj* : very large or great

co·los·sus \-səs\ *n*, *pl* **-si** \-'läs,ī\ : something of great size or scope

colt \'kōlt\ *n* : young male horse — **colt·ish** *adj*

col·umn \'käləm\ *n* **1** : vertical section of a printed page **2** : regular feature article (as in a newspaper) **3** : pillar **4** : row (as of soldiers) —

co·lum·nar \kə'ləmnər\ *adj* — **col·um·nist** \'käləmnist\ *n*

co·ma \'kōmə\ *n* : deep prolonged unconsciousness — **co·ma·tose** \-,tōs, 'kämə-\ *adj*

comb \'kōm\ *n* **1** : toothed instrument for arranging the hair **2** : crest on a fowl's head — **comb** *vb* — **combed** \'kōmd\ *adj*

com·bat \kəm'bat, 'käm,bat\ *vb* **-bat·ed** *or* **-bat·ted; -bat·ing** *or* **-bat·ting** : fight — **com·bat** \'käm,bat\ *n* — **com·bat·ant** \kəm-'bat°nt\ *n* — **com·bat·ive** \kəm-'bativ\ *adj*

com·bi·na·tion \,kämbə'nāshən\ *n* **1** : process or result of combining **2** : code for opening a lock

com·bine \kəm'bīn\ *vb* **-bined; -bining** : join together ∼ \'käm,bīn\ *n* **1** : association for business or political advantage **2** : harvesting machine

com·bus·ti·ble \kəm'bəstəbəl\ *adj* : apt to catch fire — **com·bus·ti·bil·i·ty** \-,bəstə'bilətē\ *n* — **combustible** *n*

com·bus·tion \-'bəschən\ *n* : process of burning

come \'kəm\ *vb* **came** \'käm\; **come coming** **1** : move toward or arrive at something **2** : reach a state **3** : originate or exist **4** : amount — **come clean** *vb* : confess — **come into** *vb* : acquire, achieve — **come off** *vb* : succeed — **come to** *vb* : regain consciousness — **come to pass** : happen — **come to terms** : reach an agreement

come·back *n* **1** : retort **2** : return to a former position — **come back** *vb*

co·me·di·an \kə'mēdēən\ *n* **1** : comic actor **2** : funny person **3** : entertainer specializing in comedy

co·me·di·enne \-,mēdē'en\ *n* : a woman who is a comedian

com·e·dy \'kämədē\ *n*, *pl* **-dies** **1** : an

amusing play **2** : humorous entertainment

come·ly \'kəmlē\ *adj* -li·er; -est : attractive — **come·li·ness** *n*

com·et \'kämət\ *n* : small bright celestial body having a tail

com·fort \'kəmfərt\ *n* **1** : consolation **2** : well-being or something that gives it ∼ *vb* **1** : give hope to **2** : console — **com·fort·able** \'kəmftəbəl, 'kəmfərt-\ *adj* — **com·fort·ably** \-blē\ *adv* — **com·fort·less** *adj*

com·fort·er \'kəmfərtər\ *n* **1** : one that comforts **2** : quilt

com·ic \'kämik\ *adj* **1** : relating to comedy **2** : funny ∼ *n* **1** : comedian **2** : sequence of cartoons — **com·i·cal** *adj*

com·ing \'kəmiŋ\ *adj* : next

com·ma \'kämə\ *n* : punctuation mark , used esp. to separate sentence parts

com·mand \kə'mand\ *vb* **1** : order **2** : control ∼ *n* **1** : act of commanding **2** : an order given **3** : mastery **4** : troops under a commander — **com·man·dant** \'kämən,dant, -,dänt\ *n*

com·man·deer \,kämən'dir\ *vb* : seize by force

com·mand·er \kə'mandər\ *n* **1** : officer commanding an army or subdivision of an army **2** : commissioned officer in the navy ranking next below a captain

com·mand·ment \-'mandmənt\ *n* : order

command sergeant major *n* : noncommissioned officer in the army ranking above a first sergeant

com·mem·o·rate \kə'memə,rāt\ *vb* -rat·ed; -rat·ing : celebrate or honor — **com·mem·o·ra·tion** \-,memə'rāshən\ *n* — **com·mem·o·ra·tive** \-'memrətiv, -'memə-,rāt-\ *adj*

com·mence \kə'mens\ *vb* -menced; -menc·ing : start

com·mence·ment \-mənt\ *n* **1** : beginning **2** : graduation ceremony

com·mend \kə'mend\ *vb* **1** : entrust **2** : recommend **3** : praise — **mend·able** \-əbəl\ *adj* — **com·men·da·tion** \,kämən'dāshən, -,en-\ *n*

com·men·su·rate \kə'mensərət, -'mench-\ *adj* : equal in measure or extent

com·ment \'käm,ent\ *n* : statement of opinion or remark — **comment** *vb*

com·men·tary \-ən,terē\ *n, pl* -tar·ies : series of comments

com·men·ta·tor \-ən,tātər\ *n* : one who discusses news

com·merce \'kämərs\ *n* : business

◆ **com·mer·cial** \kə'mərshəl\ *adj* : designed for profit or for mass appeal ∼ *n* : broadcast advertisement — **com·mer·cial·ize** \-,īz\ *vb* — **com·mer·cial·ly** \-ē\ *adv*

com·min·gle \kə'miŋgəl\ *vb* : mix

com·mis·er·ate \kə'mizə,rāt\ *vb* -at·ed; -at·ing : sympathize — **com·mis·er·a·tion** \-,mizə'rāshən\ *n*

com·mis·sary \'kämə,serē\ *n, pl* -sar·ies : store esp. for military personnel

com·mis·sion \kə'mishən\ *n* **1** : order granting power or rank **2** : panel to judge, approve, or act **3** : the doing of an act **4** : agent's fee ∼ *vb* **1** : confer rank or authority to or for **2** : request something be done

com·mis·sion·er \-shənər\ *n* **1** : member of a commission **2** : head of a government department

com·mit \kə'mit\ *vb* -tt- **1** : turn over to someone for safekeeping or confinement **2** : perform or do **3** : pledge — **com·mit·ment** *n*

com·mit·tee \kə'mitē\ *n* : panel that examines or acts on something

com·mo·di·ous \kə'mōdēəs\ *adj* : spacious

com·mod·i·ty \kə'mädətē\ *n, pl* **-ties** : article for sale

com·mo·dore \'kämə,dōr\ *n* **1** : former commissioned officer in the navy ranking next below a rear admiral **2** : officer commanding a group of merchant ships

com·mon \'kämən\ *adj* **1** : public **2** : shared by several **3** : widely known, found, or observed **4** : ordinary ~ *n* : community land — **com·mon·ly** *adv* — **in common** : shared together

com·mon·place \'kämən,plās\ *n* : cliché ~ *adj* : ordinary

common sense *n* : good judgment

com·mon·weal \-,wēl\ *n* : general welfare

com·mon·wealth \-,welth\ *n* : state

com·mo·tion \kə'mōshən\ *n* : disturbance

¹com·mune \kə'myün\ *vb* **-muned; -mun·ing** : communicate intimately

²com·mune \'käm,yün; kə'myün\ *n* : community that shares all ownership and duties — **com·mu·nal** \-ᵊl\ *adj*

com·mu·ni·cate \kə'myünə,kāt\ *vb* **-cat·ed; -cat·ing 1** : make known **2** : transmit **3** : exchange information or opinions — **com·mu·ni·ca·ble** \-'myünikəbəl\ *adj* — **com·mu·ni·ca·tion** \-,myünə'kāshən\ *n* — **com·mu·ni·ca·tive** \-'myüni,kātiv, -kət-\ *adj*

Com·mu·nion \kə'myünyən\ *n* : Christian sacrament of partaking of bread and wine

com·mu·ni·qué \kə'myünə,kā, -,myünə'kā\ *n* : official bulletin

com·mu·nism \'kämyə,nizəm\ *n* **1** : social organization in which goods are held in common **2** *cap* : political doctrine based on revolutionary Marxist socialism — **com·mu·nist** \-nist\ *n or adj, often cap* — **com·mu·nis·tic** \,kämyə'nistik\ *adj, often cap*

com·mu·ni·ty \kə'myünətē\ *n, pl* **-ties** : body of people living in the same place under the same laws

com·mute \kə'myüt\ *vb* **-mut·ed; -mut·ing 1** : reduce (a punishment) **2** : travel back and forth

regularly ~ *n* : trip made in commuting — **com·mu·ta·tion** \,kämyə'tāshən\ *n* — **com·mut·er** *n*

¹com·pact \kəm'pakt, 'käm,pakt\ *adj* **1** : hard **2** : small or brief ~ *vb* : pack together ~ \'käm,pakt\ *n* **1** : cosmetics case **2** : small car — **com·pact·ly** *adv* — **com·pact·ness** *n*

²com·pact \'käm,pakt\ *n* : agreement

compact disc *n* : plastic-coated disc with laser-readable recorded music

com·pan·ion \kəm'panyən\ *n* **1** : close friend **2** : one of a pair — **com·pan·ion·able** *adj* — **com·pan·ion·ship** *n*

com·pa·ny \'kəmpənē\ *n, pl* **-nies 1** : business organization **2** : group of performers **3** : guests **4** : infantry unit

com·par·a·tive \kəm'parətiv\ *adj* **1** : relating to or being an adjective or adverb form that denotes increase **2** : relative — **comparative** *n* — **com·par·a·tive·ly** *adv*

com·pare \kəm'par\ *vb* **-pared; -par·ing 1** : represent as similar **2** : check for likenesses or differences ~ *n* : comparison — **com·pa·ra·ble** \'kämprəbəl\ *adj*

com·par·i·son \kəm'parəsən\ *n* **1** : act of comparing **2** : change in the form and meaning of an adjective or adverb to show different levels of quality, quantity, or relation

com·part·ment \kəm'pärtmənt\ *n* : section or room

com·pass \'kəmpəs, 'käm-\ *n* **1** : scope **2** : device for drawing circles **3** : device for determining direction

com·pas·sion \kəm'pashən\ *n* : pity — **com·pas·sion·ate** \-ənət\ *adj*

com·pat·i·ble \-'patəbəl\ *adj* : harmonious — **com·pat·i·bil·i·ty** \-,patə'bilətē\ *n*

com·pa·tri·ot \kəm'pātrēət, -trē,ät\ *n* : fellow countryman

com·pel \kəm'pel\ *vb* **-ll-** : cause through necessity

com·pen·di·ous \kam'pendēəs\ *adj* **1** : concise and comprehensive **2** : comprehensive

com·pen·di·um \-'pendēəm\ *n, pl* **-di·ums** *or* **-dia** \-dēə\ : summary

com·pen·sate \'kämpən,sāt\ *vb* **-sat-**

ed; -sat·ing 1 : offset or balance 2
: repay — **com·pen·sa·tion**
\ˌkämpənˈsāshən\ n — **com·pensa·to·ry** \kəmˈpensəˌtōrē\ adj

com·pete \kəmˈpēt\ vb -pet·ed; -pet·ing : strive to win — **com·pe·ti·tion** \ˌkämpəˈtishən\ n — **com·pet·i·tive** \kəmˈpetətiv\ adj — **com·pet·i·tive·ness** n — **com·pet·i·tor** \kəmˈpetətər\ n

com·pe·tent \ˈkämpətənt\ adj : capable — **com·pe·tence** \-əns\ n — **com·pe·ten·cy** \-ənsē\ n

com·pile \kəmˈpīl\ vb -piled; -pil·ing : collect or compose from several sources — **com·pi·la·tion** \ˌkämpəˈlāshən\ n — **com·pil·er** \kəmˈpīlər\ n

com·pla·cen·cy \kəmˈplāsᵊnsē\ n : self-satisfaction — **com·pla·cent** \-ᵊnt\ adj

com·plain \kəmˈplān\ vb 1 : express grief, pain, or discontent 2 : make an accusation — **com·plain·ant** n — **com·plain·er** n

com·plaint \-ˈplānt\ n 1 : expression of grief or discontent 2 : ailment 3 : formal accusation

com·ple·ment \ˈkämpləmənt\ n 1 : something that completes 2 : full number or amount — \-ˌment\ vb : complete — **com·ple·men·ta·ry** \ˌkämpləˈmentərē\ adj

com·plete \kəmˈplēt\ adj -plet·er; -est 1 : having all parts 2 : finished 3 : total — vb -plet·ed; -plet·ing 1 : make whole 2 : finish — **com·plete·ly** adv — **com·plete·ness** n — **com·ple·tion** \-ˈplēshən\ n

com·plex \kämˈpleks, kəm-; ˈkämˌpleks\ adj 1 : having many parts 2 : intricate ~ \ˈkämˌpleks\ n : psychological problem — **com·plex·i·ty** \kəmˈplekətē, käm-\ n

com·plex·ion \kəmˈplekshən\ n : hue or appearance of the skin

esp. of the face — **com·plex·ioned** adj

com·pli·cate \ˈkämpləˌkāt\ vb -cat·ed; -cat·ing : make complex or hard to understand — **com·pli·cat·ed** \-əd\ adj — **com·pli·ca·tion** \ˌkämpləˈkāshən\ n

com·plic·i·ty \kəmˈplisətē\ n, pl -ties : participation in guilt

◆ **com·pli·ment** \ˈkämpləmənt\ n 1 : flattering remark 2 pl : greeting ~ \-ˌment\ vb : pay a compliment to

com·pli·men·ta·ry \ˌkämpləˈmentərē\ adj 1 : praising 2 : free

com·ply \kəmˈplī\ vb -plied; -ply·ing : conform or yield — **com·pli·ance** \-əns\ n — **com·pli·ant** \-ənt\ n

com·po·nent \kəmˈpōnənt, ˈkämˌpō-\ n : part of something larger ~ adj : serving as a component

com·port \kəmˈpōrt\ vb 1 : agree 2 : behave — **com·port·ment** \-mənt\ n

com·pose \kəmˈpōz\ vb -posed; -pos·ing 1 : create (as by writing) or put together 2 : calm 3 : set type — **com·pos·er** n — **com·po·si·tion** \ˌkämpəˈzishən\ n

com·pos·ite \kämˈpäzət, kəm-\ adj : made up of diverse parts — **composite** n

com·post \ˈkämˌpōst\ n : decayed organic fertilizing material

com·po·sure \kəmˈpōzhər\ n : calmness

com·pote \ˈkämˌpōt\ n : fruits cooked in syrup

¹**com·pound** \ˈkämˌpaùnd, kəmˈpaùnd\ vb 1 : combine or add 2 : pay (interest) on principal and accrued interest ~ \ˈkämˌpaùnd\ adj : made up of 2 or more parts ~ \ˈkämˌpaùnd\ n : something that is compound

²**com·pound** \'käm,pau̇nd\ *n* : enclosure

com·pre·hend \,kämpri'hend\ *vb* 1 : understand 2 : include — **com·pre·hen·si·ble** \-'hensəbəl\ *adj* — **com·pre·hen·sion** \-'henchən\ *n* — **com·pre·hen·sive** \-siv\ *adj*

com·press \kəm'pres\ *vb* : squeeze together ~ \'käm,pres\ *n* : pad for pressing on a wound — **com·pres·sion** \-'preshən\ *n* — **com·pres·sor** \-'presər\ *n*

compressed air *n* : air under pressure greater than that of the atmosphere

com·prise \kəm'prīz\ *vb* -prised; -pris·ing 1 : contain or cover 2 : be made up of

com·pro·mise \'kämprə,mīz\ *vb* -mised; -mis·ing : settle differences by mutual concessions — **compromise** *n*

comp·trol·ler \kən'trōlər, 'kämp-,trō-\ *n* : financial officer

com·pul·sion \kəm'pəlshən\ *n* 1 : coercion 2 : irresistible impulse — **com·pul·sive** \-siv\ *adj* — **com·pul·so·ry** \-'pəlsərē\ *adj*

com·punc·tion \-'pənkshən\ *n* : remorse

com·pute \-'pyüt\ *vb* -put·ed; -put·ing : calculate — **com·pu·ta·tion** \,kämpyü'tāshən\ *n*

com·put·er \kəm'pyütər\ *n* : electronic data processing machine — **com·put·er·i·za·tion** \-,pyütərə-'zāshən\ *n* — **com·put·er·ize** \-'pyütə,rīz\ *vb*

com·rade \'käm,rad, -rəd\ *n* : companion — **com·rade·ship** *n*

¹**con** \'kän\ *adv* : against ~ *n* : opposing side or person

²**con** *vb* -nn- : swindle

con·cave \kän'kāv, 'kän,kāv\ *adj* : curved like the inside of a sphere — **con·cav·i·ty** \kän'kavətē\ *n*

con·ceal \kən'sēl\ *vb* : hide — **con·ceal·ment** *n*

con·cede \-'sēd\ *vb* -ced·ed; -ced·ing : grant

con·ceit \-'sēt\ *n* : excessively high opinion of oneself — **con·ceit·ed** \-əd\ *adj*

con·ceive \-'sēv\ *vb* -ceived; -ceiv·ing 1 : become pregnant 2 : think of — **con·ceiv·able** \-'sēvəbəl\ *adj* — **con·ceiv·ably** \-blē\ *adv*

con·cen·trate \'känsən,trāt\ *vb* -trat·ed; -trat·ing 1 : gather together 2

: make stronger 3 : fix one's attention ~ *n* : something concentrated — **con·cen·tra·tion** \,känsən-'trāshən\ *n*

con·cen·tric \kən'sentrik\ *adj* : having a common center

con·cept \'kän,sept\ *n* : thought or idea

con·cep·tion \kən'sepshən\ *n* 1 : act of conceiving 2 : idea

con·cern \kən'sərn\ *vb* 1 : relate to 2 : involve ~ *n* 1 : affair 2 : worry 3 : business — **con·cerned** \-'sərnd\ *adj* — **con·cern·ing** \-'sərniŋ\ *prep*

con·cert \'kän,sərt\ *n* 1 : agreement or joint action 2 : public performance of music — **con·cert·ed** \kən'sərtəd\ *adj*

con·cer·ti·na \,känsər'tēnə\ *n* : accordionlike instrument

con·cer·to \kən'chertō\ *n, pl* -ti \-tē\ *or* -tos : orchestral work with solo instruments

con·ces·sion \-'seshən\ *n* 1 : act of conceding 2 : something conceded 3 : right to do business on a property

conch \'käŋk, 'känch\ *n, pl* conchs \'käŋks\ *or* conch·es \'känchəz\ : large spiral-shelled marine mollusk

con·cil·ia·to·ry \kən'silēə,tōrē\ *adj* : mollifying

con·cise \kən'sīs\ *adj* : said in few words — **con·cise·ly** *adv* — **con·cise·ness** *n* — **con·ci·sion** \kən-'sizhən\ *n*

con·clave \'kän,klāv\ *n* : private meeting

con·clude \kən'klüd\ *vb* -clud·ed; -clud·ing 1 : end 2 : decide — **con·clu·sion** \-'klüzhən\ *n* — **con·clu·sive** \-siv\ *adj* — **con·clu·sive·ly** *adv*

con·coct \kən'käkt, kän-\ *vb* : prepare or devise — **con·coc·tion** \-'käkshən\ *n*

con·com·i·tant \-'kämətənt\ *adj* : accompanying — **concomitant** *n*

con·cord \'kän,kȯrd, 'käŋ-\ *n* : agreement

con·cor·dance \kən'kȯrdᵊns\ *n* 1 : agreement 2 : index of words — **con·cor·dant** \-ᵊnt\ *adj*

con·course \'kän,kōrs\ *n* : open space where crowds gather

con·crete \kän'krēt, 'kän,krēt\ *adj* 1 : naming something real 2 : actual or substantial 3 : made of concrete

~ \'kän,krēt, kän'krēt\ *n* : hard building material made of cement, sand, gravel, and water

con·cre·tion \kän'krēshən\ *n* : hard mass

con·cu·bine \'käŋkyu̇,bīn\ *n* : mistress

con·cur \kən'kər\ *vb* **-rr-** : agree — **con·cur·rence** \-'kərəns\ *n*

con·cur·rent \-ənt\ *adj* : happening at the same time

con·cus·sion \kən'kəshən\ *n* **1** : shock **2** : brain injury from a blow

con·demn \-'dem\ *vb* **1** : declare to be wrong, guilty, or unfit for use **2** : sentence — **con·dem·na·tion** \,kän,dem'nāshən\ *n*

con·dense \kən'dens\ *vb* **-densed; -dens·ing 1** : make or become more compact **2** : change from vapor to liquid — **con·den·sa·tion** \,kän,den'sāshən, -dən-\ *n* — **con·dens·er** *n*

con·de·scend \,kändi'send\ *vb* **1** : lower oneself **2** : act haughtily — **con·de·scen·sion** \-'senchən\ *n*

con·di·ment \'kändəmənt\ *n* : pungent seasoning

con·di·tion \kən'dishən\ *n* **1** : necessary situation or stipulation **2** *pl* : state of affairs **3** : state of being ~ *vb* : put into proper condition — **con·di·tion·al** \kən'dishənəl\ *adj* — **con·di·tion·al·ly** \-ē\ *adv*

con·do·lence \kən'dōləns\ *n* : expression of sympathy — usu. pl.

con·do·min·i·um \,kändə'minēəm\ *n, pl* **-ums** : individually owned apartment

con·done \kən'dōn\ *vb* **-doned; -don·ing** : overlook or forgive

con·dor \'kändər, -,dȯr\ *n* : large western American vulture

con·du·cive \kən'düsiv, -'dyü-\ *adj* : tending to help or promote

con·duct \'kän,dəkt\ *n* **1** : management **2** : behavior ~ \kən'dəkt\ *vb* **1** : guide **2** : manage or direct **3** : be a channel for **4** : behave — **con·duc·tion** \-'dəkshən\ *n* — **con·duc·tive** \-'dəktiv\ *adj* — **con·duc·tiv·i·ty** \,kän,dək'tivətē\ *n* — **con·duc·tor** \-'dəktər\ *n*

con·duit \'kän,düət, -,dyü-\ *n* : channel (as for conveying fluid)

cone \'kōn\ *n* **1** : scaly fruit of pine and related trees **2** : solid figure having a circular base and tapering sides

con·fec·tion \kən'fekshən\ *n* : sweet dish or candy — **con·fec·tion·er** \-shənər\ *n*

con·fed·er·a·cy \kən'fedərəsē\ *n, pl* **-cies 1** : league **2** *cap* : 11 southern states that seceded from the U.S. in 1860 and 1861

con·fed·er·ate \-rət\ *adj* **1** : united in a league **2** *cap* : relating to the Confederacy ~ *n* **1** : ally **2** *cap* : adherent of the Confederacy ~ \-'fedə,rāt\ *vb* **-at·ed; -at·ing** : unite — **con·fed·er·a·tion** \-,fedə'rāshən\ *n*

con·fer \kən'fər\ *vb* **-rr-** **1** : give **2** : meet to exchange views — **con·fer·ee** \,känfə'rē\ *n* — **con·fer·ence** \'känfərəns\ *n*

con·fess \kən'fes\ *vb* **1** : acknowledge or disclose one's misdeed, fault, or sin **2** : declare faith in — **con·fes·sion** \-'feshən\ *n* — **con·fes·sion·al** \-'feshənəl\ *n or adj*

con·fes·sor \kən'fesər, 2 *also* 'kän-,fes-\ *n* **1** : one who confesses **2** : priest who hears confessions

con·fet·ti \kən'fetē\ *n* : bits of paper or ribbon thrown in celebration

con·fi·dant \'känfə,dant, -,dänt\ *n* : one to whom secrets are confided

con·fide \kən'fīd\ *vb* **-fid·ed; -fid·ing 1** : share private thoughts **2** : reveal in confidence

con·fi·dence \'känfədəns\ *n* **1** : trust **2** : self-assurance **3** : something confided — **con·fi·dent** \-ənt\ *adj* — **con·fi·den·tial** \,känfə-'denchəl\ *adj* — **con·fi·den·tial·ly** \-ē\ *adv* — **con·fi·dent·ly** *adv*

con·fig·u·ra·tion \kən,figyə'rāshən\ *n* : arrangement

con·fine \kən'fīn\ *vb* **-fined; -fin·ing 1** : restrain or restrict to a limited area **2** : imprison — **con·fine·ment** *n* — **con·fin·er** *n*

confines \'kän,fīnz\ *n pl* : bounds

con·firm \kən'fərm\ *vb* **1** : ratify **2** : verify **3** : admit as a full member of a church or synagogue — **con·fir·ma·tion** \,känfər'māshən\ *n*

con·fis·cate \'känfə,skāt\ *vb* **-cat·ed; -cat·ing** : take by authority — **con·fis·ca·tion** \,känfə'skāshən\ *n* — **con·fis·ca·to·ry** \kən'fiskə-,tōrē\ *adj*

con·fla·gra·tion \ˌkänflə'grāshən\ *n* : great fire

con·flict \'kän,flikt\ *n* **1** : war **2** : clash of ideas ~ \kən'flikt\ *vb* : clash

con·form \kən'förm\ *vb* **1** : make or be like **2** : obey — **con·for·mi·ty** \kən'förmətē\ *n*

con·found \kən'faúnd, kän-\ *vb* : confuse

con·front \kən'frənt\ *vb* : oppose or face — **con·fron·ta·tion** \ˌkänfrən-'tāshən\ *n*

con·fuse \kən'fyüz\ *vb* **-fused; -fus·ing 1** : make mentally uncertain **2** : jumble — **con·fu·sion** \-'fyü-zhən\ *n*

con·fute \-'fyüt\ *vb* **-fut·ed; -fut·ing** : overwhelm by argument

con·geal \kən'jēl\ *vb* **1** : freeze **2** : become thick and solid

con·ge·nial \kən'jēnēəl\ *adj* : kindred or agreeable — **con·ge·ni·al·i·ty** *n*

con·gen·i·tal \kən'jenət³l\ *adj* : existing from birth

con·gest \kən'jest\ *vb* : overcrowd or overfill — **con·ges·tion** \-'jeschən\ *n* — **con·ges·tive** \-'jestiv\ *adj*

con·glom·er·ate \kən'glämərət\ *adj* : made up of diverse parts ~ \-ə-ˌrāt\ *vb* **-at·ed; -at·ing** : form into a mass ~ \-ərət\ *n* : diversified corporation — **con·glom·er·a·tion** \-ˌglämə'rāshən\ *n*

con·grat·u·late \kən'grachə,lāt, -'graj-\ *vb* **-lat·ed; -lat·ing** : express pleasure to for good fortune — **con·grat·u·la·tion** \-ˌgracha-'lāshən, -ˌgraj-\ *n* — **con·grat·u·la·to·ry** \-'grachələ,tōrē'graj-\ *adj*

con·gre·gate \'käŋgri,gāt\ *vb* **-gat·ed; -gat·ing** : assemble

con·gre·ga·tion \ˌkäŋgri'gāshən\ *n* **1** : assembly of people at worship **2** : religious group — **con·gre·ga·tion·al** \-shənəl\ *adj*

con·gress \'käŋgrəs\ *n* : assembly of delegates or of senators and representatives — **con·gres·sio·nal** \kən'greshənəl, kän-\ *adj* — **con·gress·man** \'käŋgrəsmən\ *n* — **con·gress·wom·an** *n*

con·gru·ence \kən'grüəns, 'käŋgrəwəns\ *n* : likeness — **con·gru·ent** \-ənt\ *adj*

con·gru·ity \kən'grüətē, kän-\ *n* : correspondence between things — **con·gru·ous** \'käŋgrəwəs\ *adj*

con·ic \'känik\ *adj* : relating to or like a cone — **con·i·cal** \-ikəl\ *adj*

co·ni·fer \'känəfər, 'kōn-\ *n* : cone-bearing tree — **co·nif·er·ous** \kō-'nifərəs\ *adj*

con·jec·ture \kən'jekchər\ *n or vb* : guess — **con·jec·tur·al** \-əl\ *adj*

con·join \kən'jóin\ *vb* : join together — **con·joint** \-'jóint\ *adj*

con·ju·gal \'känjigəl, kən'jü-\ *adj* : relating to marriage

con·ju·gate \'känjə,gāt\ *vb* **-gat·ed; -gat·ing** : give the inflected forms of (a verb) — **con·ju·ga·tion** \ˌkänjə-'gāshən\ *n*

con·junc·tion \kən'jəŋkshən\ *n* **1** : combination **2** : occurrence at the same time **3** : a word that joins other words together — **con·junc·tive** \-tiv\ *adj*

con·jure \'känjər, 'kən-\ *vb* **-jured; -jur·ing 1** : summon by sorcery **2** : practice sleight of hand **3** : entreat — **con·jur·er, con·ju·ror** \'känjərər, 'kən-\ *n*

con·nect \kə'nekt\ *vb* : join or associate — **con·nect·able** *adj* — **con·nec·tion** \-'nekshən\ *n* — **con·nec·tive** \-tiv\ *n or adj* — **con·nec·tor** *n*

con·nive \kə'nīv\ *vb* **-nived; -niv·ing 1** : pretend ignorance of wrongdoing **2** : cooperate secretly — **con·niv·ance** *n*

♦ **con·nois·seur** \ˌkänə'sər, -'sùr\ *n*
: expert judge esp. of art

con·note \kə'nōt\ *vb* **-not·ed; -not-
ing** : suggest additional meaning
— **con·no·ta·tion** \ˌkänə'tāshən\
n

con·nu·bi·al \kə'nübēəl, -'nyü-\ *adj*
: relating to marriage

con·quer \'käŋkər\ *vb* : defeat or
overcome — **con·quer·or** \-kərər\

con·quest \'kän,kwest, 'käŋ-\ *n* 1
: act of conquering 2 : something
conquered

con·science \'känchəns\ *n* : awareness of right and wrong

con·sci·en·tious \ˌkänchē'enchəs\
adj : honest and hard-working —
con·sci·en·tious·ly *adv*

con·scious \'känchəs\ *adj* 1 : aware
2 : mentally awake or alert 3 : intentional — **con·scious·ly** *adv* —
con·scious·ness *n*

con·script \kən'skript\ *vb* : draft for
military service — **con·script**
\'kän,skript\ *n* — **con·scrip·tion**
\kən'skripshən\ *n*

con·se·crate \'känsə,krāt\ *vb* **-crat-
ed; -crat·ing** 1 : declare sacred 2
: devote to a solemn purpose —
con·se·cra·tion \ˌkänsə'krāshən\ *n*

con·sec·u·tive \kən'sekyətiv\ *adj*
: following in order — **con·sec-
u·tive·ly** *adv*

con·sen·sus \-'sensəs\ *n* 1 : agreement in opinion 2 : collective
opinion

con·sent \-'sent\ *vb* : give permission or approval — **consent** *n*

con·se·quence \'känsə,kwens\ *n* 1
: result or effect 2 : importance —
con·se·quent \-kwənt, -,kwent\
adj — **con·se·quent·ly** *adv*

con·se·quen·tial \ˌkänsə'kwenchəl\
adj : important

con·ser·va·tion \ˌkänsər'vāshən\ *n*
: planned management of natural
resources — **con·ser·va·tion·ist**
\-shənist\ *n*

con·ser·va·tive \kən'sərvətiv\ *adj* 1
: disposed to maintain the status
quo 2 : cautious — **con·ser·va-
tism** \-və,tizəm\ *n* — **conservative**
n — **con·ser·va·tive·ly** *adv*

con·ser·va·to·ry \kən'sərvə,tōrē\ *n*,
pl **-ries** : school for art or music

con·serve \-'sərv\ *vb* **-served; -serv-
ing** : keep from wasting ∼ \'kän-

,sərv\ *n* : candied fruit or fruit
preserves

con·sid·er \kən'sidər\ *vb* 1 : think
about 2 : give thoughtful attention
to 3 : think that — **con·sid·er·ate**
\-'sidərət\ *adj* — **con·sid·er·ation**
\-,sidə'rāshən\ *n*

con·sid·er·able \-'sidərəbəl\ *adj* 1
: significant 2 : noticeably large —
con·sid·er·a·bly \-blē\ *adv*

con·sid·er·ing *prep* : taking notice
of

con·sign \kən'sīn\ *vb* 1 : transfer 2
: send to an agent for sale — **con-
sign·ee** \ˌkänsə'nē, -,sī-; kən,sī-\ *n*
— **con·sign·ment** \kən'sīnmənt\ *n*
— **con·sign·or** \ˌkänsə'nòr, -,sī-;
kən,sī-\ *n*

con·sist \kən'sist\ *vb* 1 : be inherent
— used with *in* 2 : be made up —
used with *of*

con·sis·ten·cy \-'sistənsē\ *n, pl* **-cies**
1 : degree of thickness or firmness
2 : quality of being consistent

con·sis·tent \-tənt\ *adj* : being
steady and regular — **con·sis-
tent·ly** *adv*

¹**con·sole** \kən'sōl\ *vb* **-soled; -sol-
ing** : soothe the grief of — **con-
so·la·tion** \ˌkänsə'lāshən\ *n*

²**con·sole** \'kän,sōl\ *n* : cabinet or
part with controls

con·sol·i·date \kən'sälə,dāt\ *vb*
-dat·ed; -dat·ing : unite or compact — **con·sol·i·da·tion** \-,sälə-
'dāshən\ *n*

con·som·mé \ˌkänsə'mā\ *n* : clear
soup

con·so·nance \'känsənəns\ *n* : agreement or harmony — **con·so·nant**
\-nənt\ *adj* — **con·so·nant·ly** *adv*

con·so·nant \-nənt\ *n* 1 : speech
sound marked by constriction or
closure in the breath channel 2
: letter other than *a, e, i, o,* and *u*
— **con·so·nan·tal** \ˌkänsə'nant³l\
adj

con·sort \'kän,sòrt\ *n* : spouse ∼
\kən'sòrt\ *vb* : keep company

con·spic·u·ous \kən'spikyəwəs\ *adj*
: very noticeable — **con·spic·u-
ous·ly** *adv*

con·spire \kən'spīr\ *vb* **-spired;
-spir·ing** : secretly plan an unlawful act — **con·spir·a·cy** \-'spirəsē\
n — **con·spir·a·tor** \-'spirətər\ *n*
— **con·spir·a·to·ri·al** \-,spirə-
'tōrēəl\ *adj*

con·sta·ble \'känstəbəl, 'kən-\ *n*
: police officer

con·stab·u·lary \kən'stabyə,lerē\ *n*,
pl **-lar·ies** : police force

con·stant \'känstənt\ *adj* **1** : steadfast or faithful **2** : not varying **3**
: continually recurring ∼ *n*
: something unchanging — **con-
stan·cy** \-stənsē\ *n* — **con·stant·
ly** *adv*

con·stel·la·tion \,känstə'lāshən\ *n*
: group of stars

con·ster·na·tion \-stər'nāshən\ *n*
: amazed dismay

con·sti·pa·tion \-stə'pāshən\ *n* : difficulty of defecation — **con·sti·
pate** \'känstə,pāt\ *vb*

con·stit·u·ent \kən'stichəwənt\ *adj*
1 : component **2** : having power to
elect ∼ *n* **1** : component part **2**
: one who may vote for a representative — **con·stit·u·en·cy** \-wənsē\
n

con·sti·tute \'känstə,tüt, -,tyüt\ *vb*
-tut·ed; -tut·ing 1 : establish **2** : be
all or a basic part of

con·sti·tu·tion \,känstə'tüshən,
-'tyü-\ *n* **1** : physical composition
or structure **2** : the basic law of an
organized body or the document
containing it — **con·sti·tu·tion·
al** \-əl\ *adj* — **con·sti·tu·tion·al·
i·ty** \-,tüshə'nalətē, -,tyü-\ *n*

con·strain \kən'strān\ *vb* **1** : compel
2 : confine **3** : restrain — **con-
straint** \-'strānt\ *n*

con·strict \-'strikt\ *vb* : draw or
squeeze together — **con·stric·tion**
\-'strikshən\ *n* — **con·stric·tive**
\-'striktiv\ *adj*

con·struct \kən'strəkt\ *vb* : build or
make — **con·struc·tion** \-'strək-
shən\ *n* — **con·struc·tive** \-tiv\
adj

con·strue \kən'strü\ *vb* **-strued;
-stru·ing** : explain or interpret

con·sul \'känsəl\ *n* **1** : Roman magistrate **2** : government commercial
official in a foreign country —
con·sul·ar \-ələr\ *adj* — **con·sul·
ate** \-lət\ *n*

con·sult \kən'səlt\ *vb* **1** : ask the advice or opinion of **2** : confer —
con·sul·tant \-ənt\ *n* — **con·sul·
ta·tion** \,känsəl'tāshən\ *n*

con·sume \kən'süm\ *vb* **-sumed;
-sum·ing** : eat or use up — **con-
sum·able** *adj* — **con·sum·er** *n*

con·sum·mate \kən'səmət\ *adj*

: complete or perfect ∼ \'känsə-
,māt\ *vb* **-mat·ed; -mat·ing** : make
complete — **con·sum·ma·tion**
\,känsə'māshən\ *n*

con·sump·tion \kən'səmpshən\ *n* **1**
: act of consuming **2** : use of goods
3 : tuberculosis — **con·sump·tive**
\-tiv\ *adj or n*

con·tact \'kän,takt\ *n* **1** : a touching
2 : association or relationship **3**
: connection or communication
∼ *vb* **1** : come or bring into contact **2** : communicate with

con·ta·gion \kən'tājən\ *n* **1** : spread
of disease by contact **2** : disease
spread by contact — **con·ta·gious**
\-jəs\ *adj*

con·tain \-'tān\ *vb* **1** : enclose or include **2** : have or hold within **3** : restrain — **con·tain·er** *n* — **con-
tain·ment** *n*

con·tam·i·nate \kən'tamə,nāt\ *vb*
-nat·ed; -nat·ing : soil or infect by
contact or association — **con-
tam·i·na·tion** \-,tamə'nāshən\ *n*

con·tem·plate \'käntəm,plāt\ *vb*
-plat·ed; -plat·ing : view or consider thoughtfully — **con·tem·
pla·tion** \,käntəm'plāshən\ *n* —
con·tem·pla·tive \kən'templətiv;
'käntəm,plāt-\ *adj*

con·tem·po·ra·ne·ous \kən,tempə-
'rānēəs\ *adj* : contemporary

con·tem·po·rary \-'tempə,rerē\ *adj*
1 : occurring or existing at the
same time **2** : of the same age —
contemporary *n*

con·tempt \kən'tempt\ *n* **1** : feeling
of scorn **2** : state of being despised
3 : disobedience to a court or
legislature — **con·tempt·ible**
\-'temptəbəl\ *adj*

con·temp·tu·ous \-'tempchəwəs\
adj : feeling or expressing contempt — **con·temp·tu·ous·ly** *adv*

con·tend \-'tend\ *vb* **1** : strive
against rivals or difficulties **2** : argue **3** : maintain or claim — **con-
tend·er** *n*

¹con·tent \kən'tent\ *adj* : satisfied ∼
vb : satisfy ∼ *n* : ease of mind —
con·tent·ed *adj* — **con·tent·ed·
ly** *adv* — **con·tent·ed·ness** *n* —
con·tent·ment *n*

²con·tent \'kän,tent\ *n* **1** *pl* : something contained **2** *pl* : subject matter (as of a book) **3** : essential
meaning **4** : proportion contained

con·ten·tion \kən'tenchən\ *n* : state

of contending — **con·ten·tious** \-chəs\ *adj* — **con·ten·tious·ly** *adv*

con·test \kən'test\ *vb* : dispute or challenge ~ \'kän,test\ *n* 1 : struggle 2 : game — **con·test·able** \kən'testəbəl\ *adj* — **con·tes·tant** \-'testənt\ *n*

con·text \'kän,tekst\ *n* : words surrounding a word or phrase

con·tig·u·ous \kən'tigyəwəs\ *adj* : connected to or adjoining — **con·ti·gu·i·ty** \,käntə'gyüətē\ *n*

con·ti·nence \'känt⁰nəns\ *n* : self= restraint — **con·ti·nent** \-ənt\ *adj*

con·ti·nent \'känt⁰nənt\ *n* : great division of land on the globe — **con·ti·nen·tal** \,känt⁰n'ent⁰l\ *adj*

con·tin·gen·cy \kən'tinjənsē\ *n, pl* -cies : possible event

con·tin·gent \-jənt\ *adj* : dependent on something else ~ *n* : a quota from an area or group

con·tin·u·al \kən'tinyəwəl\ *adj* 1 : continuous 2 : steadily recurring — **con·tin·u·al·ly** \-ē\ *adv*

con·tin·ue \kən'tinyü\ *vb* -tin·ued; -tin·u·ing 1 : remain in a place or condition 2 : endure 3 : resume after an intermission 4 : extend — **con·tin·u·ance** \-yəwəns\ *n* — **con·tin·u·ation** \-,tinyə'wāshən\ *n*

con·tin·u·ous \-'tinyəwəs\ *adj* : continuing without interruption — **con·ti·nu·i·ty** \,känt⁰n'üətē, -'yü-\ *n* — **con·tin·u·ous·ly** *adv*

con·tort \kən'tȯrt\ *vb* : twist out of shape — **con·tor·tion** \-'tȯrshən\ *n*

con·tour \'kän,tùr\ *n* 1 : outline 2 *pl* : shape

con·tra·band \'käntrə,band\ *n* : illegal goods

con·tra·cep·tion \,käntrə'sepshən\ *n* : prevention of conception — **con·tra·cep·tive** \-'septiv\ *adj or n*

con·tract \'kän,trakt\ *n* : binding agreement ~ \kən'trakt, *1 usu* 'kän,trakt\ *vb* 1 : establish or undertake by contract 2 : become ill with 3 : make shorter — **con·trac·tion** \kən'trakshən\ *n* — **con·trac·tor** \'kän,traktər, kən'trak-\ *n* — **con·trac·tu·al** \kən'trakchəwəl\ *adj* — **con·trac·tu·al·ly** *adv*

con·tra·dict \,käntrə'dikt\ *vb* : state the contrary of — **con·tra·dic·tion** \-'dikshən\ *n* — **con·tra·dic·to·ry** \-'diktərē\ *adj*

con·tral·to \kən'traltō\ *n, pl* -tos : lowest female singing voice

con·trap·tion \kən'trapshən\ *n* : device or contrivance

con·trary \'kän,trerē; *4 often* kən-'trerē\ *adj* 1 : opposite in character, nature, or position 2 : mutually opposed 3 : unfavorable 4 : uncooperative or stubborn — **con·trari·ly** \-,trerəlē, -'trer-\ *adv* — **con·trari·wise** \-,wīz\ *adv* — **contrary** \'kän,trerē\ *n*

con·trast \'kän,trast\ *n* 1 : unlikeness shown by comparing 2 : unlike color or tone of adjacent parts ~ \kən'trast\ *vb* 1 : show differences 2 : compare so as to show differences

con·tra·vene \,käntrə'vēn\ *vb* -vened; -ven·ing : go or act contrary to

con·trib·ute \kən'tribyət\ *vb* -uted; -ut·ing : give or help along with others — **con·tri·bu·tion** \,käntrə'byüshən\ *n* — **con·trib·u·tor** \kən'tribyətər\ *n* — **con·trib·u·to·ry** \-yə,tōrē\ *adj*

con·trite \'kän,trīt, kən'trīt\ *adj* : repentant — **con·tri·tion** \kən-'trishən\ *n*

con·trive \kən'trīv\ *vb* -trived; -triv·ing 1 : devise or make with ingenuity 2 : bring about — **con·triv·ance** \-'trīvəns\ *n* — **con·triv·er** *n*

con·trol \-'trōl\ *vb* -ll- 1 : exercise power over 2 : dominate or rule ~ *n* 1 : power to direct or regulate 2 : restraint 3 : regulating device — **con·trol·la·ble** *adj* — **con·trol·ler** \-'trōlər, 'kän,-\ *n*

con·tro·ver·sy \'käntrə,vərsē\ *n, pl* -sies : clash of opposing views — **con·tro·ver·sial** \,käntrə'vərshəl, -sēəl\ *adj*

con·tro·vert \'käntrə,vərt, ,käntrə'-\ *vb* : contradict — **con·tro·vert·ible** *adj*

con·tu·ma·cious \,käntə'māshəs, -tyə-\ *adj* : rebellious

con·tu·me·ly \kən'tüməlē, 'käntü-,mēlē, -tyü-\ *n* : rudeness

con·tu·sion \kən'tüzhən, -tyü-\ *n* : bruise — **con·tuse** \-'tüz, -'tyüz\ *vb*

co·nun·drum \kə'nəndrəm\ *n* : riddle

con·va·lesce \,känvə'les\ *vb* -lesced; -lesc·ing : gradually recover health — **con·va·les·cence** \-⁰ns\

n — con·va·les·cent \-ᵊnt\ *adj or n*

con·vec·tion \kən'vekshən\ *n* : circulation in fluids due to warmer portions rising and colder ones sinking — **con·vec·tion·al** \-'vekshənəl\ *adj* — **con·vec·tive** \-'vektiv\ *adj*

con·vene \kən'vēn\ *vb* **-vened; -vening** : assemble or meet

con·ve·nience \-'vēnyəns\ *n* 1 : personal comfort or ease 2 : device that saves work

♦ **con·ve·nient** \-nyənt\ *adj* 1 : suited to one's convenience 2 : near at hand — **con·ve·nient·ly** *adv*

con·vent \'känvənt, -,vent\ *n* : community of nuns

con·ven·tion \kən'venchən\ *n* 1 : agreement esp. between nations 2 : large meeting 3 : body of delegates 4 : accepted usage or way of behaving — **con·ven·tion·al** \-'venchənəl\ *adj* — **con·ven·tion·al·ly** *adv*

con·verge \kən'vərj\ *vb* **-verged; -verg·ing** : approach a single point — **con·ver·gence** \-'vərjəns\ — **con·ver·gent** \-jənt\ *adj*

con·ver·sant \-'vərsᵊnt\ *adj* : having knowledge and experience

con·ver·sa·tion \,känvər'sāshən\ *n* : an informal talking together — **con·ver·sa·tion·al** \-shənəl\ *adj*

¹**con·verse** \kən'vərs\ *vb* **-versed; -vers·ing** : engage in conversation — **con·verse** \'kän,vərs\ *n*

²**con·verse** \kən'vərs, 'kän,vers\ *adj* : opposite — **con·verse** \'kän,vərs\ *n* — **con·verse·ly** *adv*

con·ver·sion \kən'vərzhən\ *n* 1 : change 2 : adoption of religion

con·vert \kən'vərt\ *vb* 1 : turn from one belief or party to another 2 : change ~ \'kän,vərt\ *n* : one who has undergone religious conversion — **con·vert·er, con·ver**-

tor \kən'vərtər\ *n* — **con·vert·ible** *adj*

con·vert·ible \kən'vərtəbəl\ *n* : automobile with a removable top

con·vex \kän'veks, 'kän,-, kən'-\ *adj* : curved or rounded like the outside of a sphere — **con·vex·i·ty** \kən'veksətē, kän-\ *n*

con·vey \kən'vā\ *vb* **-veyed; -vey·ing** : transport or transmit — **con·vey·ance** \-'vāəns\ *n* — **con·vey·or** \-ər\ *n*

con·vict \kən'vikt\ *vb* : find guilty ~ \'kän,vikt\ *n* : person in prison

con·vic·tion \kən'vikshən\ *n* 1 : act of convicting 2 : strong belief

con·vince \-'vins\ *vb* **-vinced; -vinc·ing** : cause to believe — **con·vinc·ing·ly** *adv*

con·viv·ial \-'vivyəl, -'vivēəl\ *adj* : cheerful or festive — **con·viv·i·al·i·ty** \-,vivē'alətē\ *n*

con·voke \kən'vōk\ *vb* **-voked; -vok·ing** : call together to a meeting — **con·vo·ca·tion** \,känvə-'kāshən\ *n*

con·vo·lut·ed \'känvə,lütəd\ *adj* 1 : intricately folded 2 : intricate

con·vo·lu·tion \,känvə'lüshən\ *n* : convoluted structure

con·voy \'kän,vȯi, kən'vȯi\ *vb* : accompany for protection ~ \'kän,vȯi\ *n* : group of vehicles or ships moving together

con·vul·sion \kən'vəlshən\ *n* : violent involuntary muscle contraction — **con·vulse** \-'vəls\ *vb* — **con·vul·sive** \-'vəlsiv\ *adj*

coo \'kü\ *n* : sound of a pigeon — **coo** *vb*

cook \'kük\ *n* : one who prepares food ~ *vb* : prepare food — **cook·book** *n* — **cook·er** *n* — **cook·ery** \-ərē\ *n* — **cook·ware** *n*

cook·ie, cooky \'kükē\ *n, pl* **-ies** : small sweet flat cake

cool \'kül\ *adj* 1 : moderately cold 2

: not excited **3** : unfriendly ∼ *vb* : make or become cool ∼ *n* **1** : cool time or place **2** : composure — **cool·ant** \-ənt\ *n* — **cool·er** *n* — **cool·ly** *adv* — **cool·ness** *n*

coo·lie \'külē\ *n* : unskilled Oriental laborer

coop \'küp, 'kůp\ *n* : enclosure usu. for poultry ∼ *vb* : confine in or as if in a coop

co-op \'kō̧äp\ *n* : cooperative

coo·per \'küpər, 'kůp-\ *n* : barrel maker — **cooper** *vb*

co·op·er·ate \kō'äpə̧rāt\ *vb* : act jointly — **co·op·er·a·tion** \-̧äpə-'rāshən\ *n*

co·op·er·a·tive \kō'äpərətiv, -'äpə-̧rāt-\ *adj* : willing to work with others ∼ *n* : enterprise owned and run by those using its services

co-opt \kō'äpt\ *vb* **1** : elect as a colleague **2** : take over

co·or·di·nate \-'ȯrd°nət\ *adj* : equal esp. in rank ∼ *n* : any of a set of numbers used in specifying the location of a point on a surface or in space ∼ \-°ņāt\ *vb* **-nat·ed; -nat·ing 1** : make or become coordinate **2** : work or act together harmoniously — **co·or·di·nate·ly** *adv* — **co·or·di·na·tion** \-̧ȯrd°n'āshən\ *n* — **co·or·di·na·tor** \-°ņātər\ *n*

coot \'küt\ *n* **1** : dark-colored ducklike bird **2** : harmless simple person

cop \'käp\ *n* : police officer

¹cope \'kōp\ *n* : cloaklike ecclesiastical vestment

²cope *vb* **coped; cop·ing** : deal with difficulties

co·pi·lot \'kō̧pīlət\ *n* : assistant airplane pilot

cop·ing \'kōpiŋ\ *n* : top layer of a wall

co·pi·ous \'kōpēəs\ *adj* : very abundant — **co·pi·ous·ly** *adv* — **co·pi·ous·ness** *n*

cop·per \'käpər\ *n* **1** : malleable reddish metallic chemical element **2** : penny — **cop·pery** *adj*

cop·per·head *n* : largely coppery brown venomous snake

co·pra \'kōprə\ *n* : dried coconut meat

copse \'käps\ *n* : thicket

cop·u·la \'käpyələ\ *n* : verb linking subject and predicate — **cop·u·la·tive** \-̧lātiv\ *adj*

cop·u·late \'käpyə̧lāt\ *vb* **-lat·ed;**

-lat·ing : engage in sexual intercourse — **cop·u·la·tion** \̧käpyə-'lāshən\ *n*

copy \'käpē\ *n, pl* **cop·ies 1** : imitation or reproduction of an original **2** : writing to be set for printing ∼ *vb* **cop·ied; copy·ing 1** : make a copy of **2** : imitate — **copi·er** \-ər\ *n* — **copyist** *n*

copy·right *n* : sole right to a literary or artistic work ∼ *vb* : get a copyright on

co·quette \kō'ket\ *n* : flirt

cor·al \'kȯrəl\ *n* **1** : skeletal material of colonies of tiny sea polyps **2** : deep pink — **coral** *adj*

cord \'kȯrd\ *n* **1** : usu. heavy string **2** : long slender anatomical structure **3** : measure of firewood equal to 128 cu. ft. **4** : small electrical cable ∼ *vb* **1** : tie or furnish with a cord **2** : pile (wood) in cords

cor·dial \'kȯrjəl\ *adj* : warmly welcoming ∼ *n* : liqueur — **cor·di·al·i·ty** \̧kȯrjē'alətē, kȯrd'yal-\ *n* — **cor·dial·ly** \'kȯrjəlē\ *adv*

cor·don \'kȯrd°n\ *n* : encircling line of troops or police — **cordon** *vb*

cor·do·van \'kȯrdəvən\ *n* : soft fine-grained leather

cor·du·roy \'kȯrdə̧rȯi\ *n* **1** : heavy ribbed fabric **2** *pl* : trousers of corduroy

core \'kȯr\ *n* **1** : central part of some fruits **2** : inmost part ∼ *vb* **cored; cor·ing** : take out the core of — **cor·er** *n*

cork \'kȯrk\ *n* **1** : tough elastic bark of a European oak (**cork oak**) **2** : stopper of cork ∼ *vb* : stop up with a cork — **corky** *adj*

cork·screw *n* : device for drawing corks from bottles

cor·mo·rant \'kȯrmərənt, -̧rant\ *n* : dark seabird

¹corn \'kȯrn\ *n* : cereal grass or its seeds ∼ *vb* : cure or preserve in brine — **corn·meal** *n* — **corn·stalk** *n* — **corn·starch** *n*

²corn *n* : local hardening and thickening of skin

corn·cob *n* : axis on which the kernels of Indian corn are arranged

cor·nea \'kȯrnēə\ *n* : transparent part of the coat of the eyeball — **cor·ne·al** *adj*

cor·ner \'kȯrnər\ *n* **1** : point or angle formed by the meeting of lines or sides **2** : place where two streets meet **3** : inescapable position **4** : control of the supply of something ~ *vb* **1** : drive into a corner **2** : get a corner on **3** : turn a corner

cor·ner·stone *n* **1** : stone at a corner of a wall **2** : something basic

cor·net \kȯr'net\ *n* : trumpetlike instrument

cor·nice \'kȯrnəs\ *n* : horizontal wall projection

cor·nu·co·pia \ˌkȯrnə'kōpēə, -nyə-\ *n* : goat's horn filled with fruits and grain emblematic of abundance

co·rol·la \kə'rälə\ *n* : petals of a flower

cor·ol·lary \'kȯrəˌlerē\ *n, pl* **-lar·ies** **1** : logical deduction **2** : consequence or result

co·ro·na \kə'rōnə\ *n* : shining ring around the sun seen during eclipses

cor·o·nary \'kȯrəˌnerē\ *adj* : relating to the heart or its blood vessels ~ *n* **1** : thrombosis of an artery supplying the heart **2** : heart attack

cor·o·na·tion \ˌkȯrə'nāshən\ *n* : crowning of a monarch

cor·o·ner \'kȯrənər\ *n* : public official who investigates causes of suspicious deaths

¹**cor·po·ral** \'kȯrpərəl\ *adj* : bodily

²**corporal** *n* : noncommissioned officer ranking next below a sergeant

cor·po·ra·tion \ˌkȯrpə'rāshən\ *n* : legal creation with the rights and liabilities of a person — **cor·po·rate** \'kȯrpərət\ *adj*

cor·po·re·al \kȯr'pōrēəl\ *adj* : physical or material — **cor·po·re·al·ly** *adv*

corps \'kȯr\ *n, pl* **corps** \'kōrz\ **1** : subdivision of a military force **2** : working group

corpse \'kȯrps\ *n* : dead body

cor·pu·lence \'kȯrpyələns\ *n* : obesity — **cor·pu·lent** \-lənt\ *adj*

cor·pus \'kȯrpəs\ *n, pl* **-po·ra** \-pərə\ **1** : corpse **2** : body of writings

cor·pus·cle \'kȯrˌpəsəl\ *n* : blood cell

cor·ral \kə'ral\ *n* : enclosure for animals — **corral** *vb*

cor·rect \kə'rekt\ *vb* **1** : make right **2** : chastise ~ *adj* **1** : true or factual **2** : conforming to a standard — **cor·rec·tion** \-'rekshən\ *n* —

cor·rec·tive \-'rektiv\ *adj* — **cor·rect·ly** *adv* — **cor·rect·ness** *n*

cor·re·late \'kȯrəˌlāt\ *vb* **-lat·ed; -lat·ing** : show a connection between — **cor·re·late** \-lət, -ˌlāt\ *n* — **cor·re·la·tion** \ˌkȯrə'lāshən\ *n*

cor·rel·a·tive \kə'relətiv\ *adj* : regularly used together — **correlative** *n*

cor·re·spond \ˌkȯrə'spänd\ *vb* **1** : match **2** : communicate by letter — **cor·re·spon·dence** \-'spändəns\ *n* — **cor·re·spond·ing·ly** \-'spändiŋlē\ *adv*

cor·re·spon·dent \-'spändənt\ *n* **1** : person one writes to **2** : reporter

cor·ri·dor \'kȯrədər, -ˌdȯr\ *n* : passageway connecting rooms

cor·rob·o·rate \kə'räbəˌrāt\ *vb* **-rat·ed; -rat·ing** : support with evidence — **cor·rob·o·ra·tion** \-ˌräbə'rāshən\ *n*

cor·rode \kə'rōd\ *vb* **-rod·ed; -rod·ing** : wear away by chemical action — **cor·ro·sion** \-'rōzhən\ *n* — **cor·ro·sive** \-'rōsiv\ *adj or n*

cor·ru·gate \'kȯrəˌgāt\ *vb* **-gat·ed; -gat·ing** : form into ridges and grooves — **cor·ru·gat·ed** *adj* — **cor·ru·ga·tion** \ˌkȯrə'gāshən\ *n*

cor·rupt \kə'rəpt\ *vb* **1** : change from good to bad **2** : bribe ~ *adj* : morally debased — **cor·rupt·ible** *adj* — **cor·rup·tion** \-'rəpshən\ *n*

cor·sage \kȯr'säzh, -'säj\ *n* : bouquet worn by a woman

cor·set \'kȯrsət\ *n* : woman's stiffened undergarment

cor·tege \kȯr'tezh, 'kȯrˌ-\ *n* : funeral procession

cor·tex \'kȯrˌteks\ *n, pl* **-ti·ces** \'kȯrtəˌsēz\ *or* **-tex·es** : outer or covering layer of an organism or part (as the brain) — **cor·ti·cal** \'kȯrtikəl\ *adj*

cor·ti·sone \'kȯrtəˌsōn, -zōn\ *n* : adrenal hormone

cos·met·ic \käz'metik\ *n* : beautifying preparation ~ *adj* : relating to beautifying

cos·mic \'käzmik\ *adj* **1** : relating to the universe **2** : vast or grand

cos·mo·naut \'käzməˌnȯt\ *n* : Soviet or Russian astronaut

cos·mo·pol·i·tan \ˌkäzmə'pälət°n\ *adj* : belonging to all the world — **cosmopolitan** *n*

cos·mos \'käzməs, -ˌmōs, -ˌmäs\ *n* : universe

cos·sack \'käs,ak, -ək\ *n* : Russian czarist cavalryman

cost \'kȯst\ *n* **1** : amount paid for something **2** : loss or penalty ~ *vb* **cost; cost·ing 1** : require so much in payment **2** : cause to pay, suffer, or lose — **cost·li·ness** \-lēnəs\ *n* — **cost·ly** \-lē\ *adj*

cos·tume \'käs,tüm, -,tyüm\ *n* : clothing

co·sy \'kōzē\ *var of* COZY

cot \'kät\ *n* : small bed

cote \'kōt, 'kät\ *n* : small shed or coop

co·te·rie \'kōtə,rē, ,kōtə'-\ *n* : exclusive group of persons

co·til·lion \kō'tilyən\ *n* : formal ball

cot·tage \'kätij\ *n* : small house

cot·ton \'kät³n\ *n* : soft fibrous plant substance or thread or cloth made of it — **cot·ton·seed** *n* — **cot·tony** *adj*

cot·ton·mouth *n* : poisonous snake

couch \'kau̇ch\ *vb* **1** : lie or place on a couch **2** : phrase ~ *n* : bed or sofa

cou·gar \'kügər, -,gär\ *n* : large tawny wild American cat

cough \'kȯf\ *vb* : force air from the lungs with short sharp noises — **cough** *n*

could \'ku̇d\ *past of* CAN

coun·cil \'kau̇nsəl\ *n* **1** : assembly or meeting **2** : body of lawmakers — **coun·cil·lor, coun·cil·or** \-sələr\ *n* — **coun·cil·man** \-mən\ *n* — **coun·cil·wom·an** *n*

coun·sel \'kau̇nsəl\ *n* **1** : advice **2** : deliberation together **3** *pl* -sel : lawyer ~ *vb* -seled *or* -selled; -sel·ing *or* -sel·ling **1** : advise **2** : consult together — **coun·sel·or, coun·sel·lor** \-sələr\ *n*

¹count \'kau̇nt\ *vb* **1** : name or indicate one by one to find the total number **2** : recite numbers in order **3** : rely **4** : be of value or account ~ *n* **1** : act of counting or the total obtained by counting **2** : charge in an indictment — **count·able** *adj*

²count *n* : European nobleman

coun·te·nance \'kau̇nt³nəns\ *n* : face or facial expression ~ *vb* -nanced; -nanc·ing : allow or encourage

¹count·er \'kau̇ntər\ *n* **1** : piece for reckoning or games **2** : surface over which business is transacted

²count·er *n* : one that counts

³coun·ter *vb* : oppose ~ *adv* : in an opposite direction ~ *n* : offsetting force or move ~ *adj* : contrary

counter- *prefix* **1** : contrary or opposite **2** : opposing **3** : retaliatory

counteraccusa-
tion
counteraggres-
sion
counterargue
counterassault
counterattack
counterbid
counterblock-
ade
counterblow
countercam-
paign
countercharge
counterclaim
countercom-
plaint
countercoup
countercriti-
cism
counterdemand
counterdemon-
stration
counterdemon-
strator
countereffort
counterevi-
dence
counterguerril-
la
counterinfla-
tionary
counterinflu-
ence
countermea-
sure
countermove
countermove-
ment
counteroffer

counterpetition
counterploy
counterpower
counterpres-
sure
counterpropa-
ganda
counterpropos-
al
counterprotest
counterques-
tion
counterraid
counterrally
counterreform
counterre-
sponse
counterretalia-
tion
counterrevolu-
tion
counterrevolu-
tionary
counterstrategy
counterstyle
countersue
countersugges-
tion
countersuit
countertenden-
cy
counterterror
counterterror-
ism
counterterror-
ist
counterthreat
counterthrust
countertrend

coun·ter·act *vb* : lessen the force of — **coun·ter·ac·tive** *adj*

coun·ter·bal·ance *n* : balancing influence or weight ~ *vb* : oppose or balance

coun·ter·clock·wise *adv or adj* : opposite to the way a clock's hands move

coun·ter·feit \'kau̇ntər,fit\ *vb* **1** : copy in order to deceive **2** : pretend ~ *adj* : spurious ~ *n*

: fraudulent copy — **coun·ter·feit·er** n

coun·ter·mand \-ˌmand\ vb : supersede with a contrary order

coun·ter·pane \-ˌpān\ n : bedspread

coun·ter·part n : one that is similar or corresponds

coun·ter·point n : music with interwoven melodies

coun·ter·sign n : secret signal ~ vb : add a confirming signature to

count·ess \'kaůntəs\ n : wife or widow of a count or an earl or a woman holding that rank in her own right

count·less \-ləs\ adj : too many to be numbered

coun·try \'kəntrē\ n, pl -tries 1 : nation 2 : rural area — adj : rural — **coun·try·man** \-mən\ n

coun·try·side n : rural area or its people

coun·ty \'kaůntē\ n, pl -ties : local government division esp. of a state

coup \'kü\ n, pl coups \'küz\ 1 : brilliant sudden action or plan 2 : sudden overthrow of a government

coupe \'küp\ n : 2-door automobile with an enclosed body

cou·ple \'kəpəl\ vb -pled; -pling : link together ~ n 1 : pair 2 : two persons closely associated or married

cou·pling \'kəpliŋ\ n : connecting device

cou·pon \'kü,pän, 'kyü-\ n : certificate redeemable for goods or a cash discount

cour·age \'kərij\ n : ability to conquer fear or despair — **cou·ra·geous** \kə'rājəs\ adj

cou·ri·er \'kůrēər, 'kərē-\ n : messenger

course \'kōrs\ n 1 : progress 2 : ground over which something moves 3 : part of a meal served at one time 4 : method of procedure 5 : subject taught in a series of classes ~ vb coursed; cours·ing 1 : hunt with dogs 2 : run speedily — **of course** : as might be expected

court \'kōrt\ n 1 : residence of a sovereign 2 : sovereign and his or her officials and advisers 3 : area enclosed by a building 4 : space marked for playing a game 5 : place where justice is administered ~ vb : woo — **court·house** n — **court·room** n — **court·ship** \-ˌship\ n

cour·te·ous \'kərtēəs\ adj : showing politeness and respect for others — **cour·te·ous·ly** adv

cour·te·san \'kōrtəzən, 'kərt-\ n : prostitute

cour·te·sy \'kərtəsē\ n, pl -sies : courteous behavior

court·ier \'kōrtēər, 'kōrtyər\ n : person in attendance at a royal court

court·ly \'kōrtlē\ adj -li·er; -est : polite or elegant — **court·li·ness** n

court–mar·tial n, pl courts–martial : military trial court — **court–martial** vb

court·yard n : enclosure open to the sky that is attached to a house

◆ **cous·in** \'kəzᵊn\ n : child of one's uncle or aunt

cove \'kōv\ n : sheltered inlet or bay

co·ven \'kəvən\ n : group of witches

cov·e·nant \'kəvənənt\ n : binding agreement — **cov·e·nant** \-nənt, -ˌnant\ vb

cov·er \'kəvər\ vb 1 : place something over or upon 2 : protect or hide 3 : include or deal with ~ n : something that covers — **cov·er·age** \-ərij\ n

cov·er·let \-lət\ n : bedspread

co·vert \'kō,vərt, 'kəvərt\ adj : secret ~ \'kəvərt, 'kō-\ n : thicket that shelters animals cov·et \'kəvət\ vb : desire enviously — cov·et·ous adj

cov·ey \'kəvē\ n, pl -eys 1 : bird with her young 2 : small flock (as of quail)

¹cow \'kaù\ n : large adult female animal (as of cattle) — cow·hide n

²cow vb : intimidate

cow·ard \'kaùərd\ n : one who lacks courage — cow·ard·ice \-əs\ n — cow·ard·ly adv or adj

cow·boy n : a mounted ranch hand who tends cattle

cow·er \'kaùər\ vb : shrink from fear or cold

cow·girl n : woman ranch hand who tends cattle

cowl \'kaùl\ n : monk's hood

cow·lick \'kaù,lik\ n : turned=up tuft of hair that resists control

cow·slip \-,slip\ n : yellow flower

cox·swain \'käkən, -,swän\ n : person who steers a boat

coy \'kói\ adj : shy or pretending shyness

coy·ote \'kī,ōt, kī'ōtē\ n, pl coyotes or coyote : small No. American wolf

coz·en \'kəz³n\ vb : cheat

co·zy \'kōzē\ adj -zi·er; -est : snug

crab \'krab\ n : short broad shellfish with pincers

crab·by \'krabē\ adj -bi·er; -est : cross

¹crack \'krak\ vb 1 : break with a sharp sound 2 : fail in tone 3 : break without completely separating ~ n 1 : sudden sharp noise 2 : witty remark 3 : narrow break 4 : sharp blow 5 : try

²crack adj : extremely proficient

crack·down n : disciplinary action — crack down vb

crack·er \-ər\ n : thin crisp bakery product

crack·le \'krakəl\ vb -led; -ling 1 : make snapping noises 2 : develop fine cracks in a surface — crackle n

crack·pot \'krak,pät\ n : eccentric

crack–up n : crash

cra·dle \'krād³l\ n : baby's bed ~ vb -dled; -dling 1 : place in a cradle 2 : hold securely

craft \'kraft\ n 1 : occupation requiring special skill 2 : craftiness 3 pl usu craft : structure designed to provide transportation 4 pl usu craft : small boat — crafts·man

\'kraftsmən\ n — crafts·man·ship \-,ship\ n

crafty \'kraftē\ adj craft·i·er; -est : sly — craft·i·ness n

crag \'krag\ n : steep cliff — crag·gy \-ē\ adj

cram \'kram\ vb -mm- 1 : eat greedily 2 : pack in tight 3 : study intensely for a test

cramp \'kramp\ n 1 : sudden painful contraction of muscle 2 pl : sharp abdominal pains ~ vb 1 : affect with cramp 2 : restrain

cran·ber·ry \'kran,berē\ n : red acid berry of a trailing plant

crane \'krān\ n 1 : tall wading bird 2 : machine for lifting heavy objects ~ vb craned; cran·ing : stretch one's neck to see

cra·ni·um \'krānēəm\ n, pl -ni·ums or -nia \-nēə\ : skull — cra·ni·al \-əl\ adj

crank \'kraŋk\ n 1 : bent lever turned to operate a machine 2 : eccentric ~ vb : start or operate by turning a crank

cranky \'kraŋkē\ adj crank·i·er; -est : irritable

cran·ny \'kranē\ n, pl -nies : crevice

craps \'kraps\ n : dice game

crash \'krash\ vb 1 : break noisily 2 : fall and hit something with noise and damage ~ n 1 : loud sound 2 : action of crashing 3 : failure

crass \'kras\ adj : crude or unfeeling

crate \'krāt\ n : wooden shipping container — crate vb

cra·ter \'krātər\ n : volcanic depression

cra·vat \krə'vat\ n : necktie

crave \'krāv\ vb craved; crav·ing : long for — crav·ing n

cra·ven \'krāvən\ adj : cowardly — cra·ven n

craw·fish \'krò,fish\ n : crayfish

crawl \'król\ vb 1 : move slowly (as by drawing the body along the ground) 2 : swarm with creeping things ~ n : very slow pace

cray·fish \'krā,fish\ n : lobsterlike freshwater crustacean

cray·on \'krā,än, -ən\ n : stick of chalk or wax used for drawing or coloring — crayon vb

craze \'krāz\ vb crazed; craz·ing : make or become insane ~ n : fad

cra·zy \'krāzē\ adj cra·zi·er; -est 1

: mentally disordered 2 : wildly impractical — **cra·zi·ly** adv — **cra·zi·ness** n

creak \'krēk\ vb or n : squeak — **creaky** adj

cream \'krēm\ n 1 : yellowish fat- rich part of milk 2 : thick smooth sauce, confection, or cosmetic 3 : choicest part ~ vb : beat into creamy consistency — **creamy** adj

cream·ery \-ərē\ n, pl -er·ies : place where butter and cheese are made

crease \'krēs\ n : line made by fold- ing — **crease** vb

cre·ate \krē'āt\ vb -at·ed; -at·ing : bring into being — **cre·ation** \krē'āshən\ n — **cre·ative** \-'ātiv\ adj — **cre·ativ·i·ty** \ˌkrēā'tivətē\ n — **cre·ator** \krē'ātər\ n

crea·ture \'krēchər\ n : lower ani- mal or human being

cre·dence \'krēdⁿs\ n : belief

cre·den·tials \kri'denchəlz\ n : evi- dence of qualifications or author- ity

cred·i·ble \'kredəbəl\ adj : believ- able — **cred·i·bil·i·ty** \ˌkredə- 'bilətē\ n

cred·it \'kredət\ n 1 : balance in a person's favor 2 : time given to pay for goods 3 : belief 4 : esteem 5 : source of honor ~ vb 1 : be- lieve 2 : give credit to

cred·it·able \-əbəl\ adj : worthy of esteem or praise — **cred·it·ably** \-əblē\ adv

cred·i·tor \-ər\ n : person to whom money is owed

cred·u·lous \'krejələs\ adj : easily convinced — **cre·du·li·ty** \kri- 'dülətē, -'dyü-\ n

creed \'krēd\ n : statement of essen- tial beliefs

creek \'krēk, 'krik\ n : small stream

creel \'krēl\ n : basket for carrying fish

creep \'krēp\ vb **crept** \'krept\; **creep·ing** 1 : crawl 2 : grow over a surface like ivy — **creep** n — **creep·er** n

cre·mate \'krē,māt\ vb -mat·ed; -mat·ing : burn up (a corpse) — **cre·ma·tion** \kri'māshən\ n — **cre·ma·to·ry** \'krēmə,tōrē, 'krem-\ n

cre·o·sote \'krēə,sōt\ n : oily wood preservative

crepe, crêpe \'krāp\ n : light crin- kled fabric

cre·scen·do \krə'shendō\ adv or adj : growing louder — **crescendo** n

cres·cent \'kresⁿnt\ n : shape of the moon between new moon and first quarter

crest \'krest\ n 1 : tuft on a bird's head 2 : top of a hill or wave 3 : part of a coat of arms ~ vb : rise to a crest — **crest·ed** \-əd\ adj

crest·fall·en adj : sad

cre·tin \'krētⁿn\ n : stupid person

cre·vasse \kri'vas\ n : deep fissure esp. in a glacier

crev·ice \'krevəs\ n : narrow fissure

crew \'krü\ n : body of workers (as on a ship) — **crew·man** \-mən\ n

crib \'krib\ n 1 : manger 2 : grain storage bin 3 : baby's bed ~ vb -bb- : put in a crib

crib·bage \'kribij\ n : card game scored by moving pegs on a board (**cribbage board**)

crick \'krik\ n : muscle spasm

¹**crick·et** \'krikət\ n : insect noted for the chirping of the male

²**cricket** n : bat and ball game played on a field with wickets

cri·er \'krīər\ n : one who calls out announcements

crime \'krīm\ n : serious violation of law

crim·i·nal \'krimənⁿl\ adj : relating to or being a crime or its punish- ment ~ n : one who commits a crime

crimp \'krimp\ vb : cause to become crinkled, wavy, or bent — **crimp** n

crim·son \'krimzən\ n : deep red — **crimson** adj

cringe \'krinj\ vb **cringed; cring- ing** : shrink in fear

crin·kle \'kriŋkəl\ vb -kled; -kling : wrinkle — **crinkle** n — **crin·kly** \-klē\ adj

crin·o·line \'krinⁿlən\ n 1 : stiff cloth 2 : full stiff skirt or petticoat

crip·ple \'kripəl\ n : disabled person ~ vb -pled; -pling : disable

cri·sis \'krīsəs\ n, pl **cri·ses** \-ˌsēz\ : decisive or critical moment

crisp \'krisp\ adj 1 : easily crumbled 2 : firm and fresh 3 : lively 4 : in- vigorating — **crisp** vb — **crisp- ly** adv — **crisp·ness** n — **crispy** adj

criss·cross \'kris,krós\ n : pattern of crossed lines ~ vb : mark with or follow a crisscross

cri·te·ri·on \krī'tirēən\ *n, pl* **-ria** \-ēə\ : standard

◆ **crit·ic** \'kritik\ *n* : judge of literary or artistic works

crit·i·cal \-ikəl\ *adj* **1** : inclined to criticize **2** : being a crisis **3** : relating to criticism or critics — **crit·i·cal·ly** \-iklē\ *adv*

crit·i·cize \'kritə,sīz\ *vb* **-cized; -cizing** **1** : judge as a critic **2** : find fault — **crit·i·cism** \-ə,sizəm\ *n*

cri·tique \krə'tēk\ *n* : critical estimate

croak \'krōk\ *n* : hoarse harsh cry (as of a frog) — **croak** *vb*

cro·chet \krō'shā\ *n* : needlework done with a hooked needle — **crochet** *vb*

crock \'kräk\ *n* : thick earthenware pot or jar — **crock·ery** \-ərē\ *n*

croc·o·dile \'kräkə,dīl\ *n* : large reptile of tropical waters

cro·cus \'krōkəs\ *n, pl* **-cus·es** : herb with spring flowers

crone \'krōn\ *n* : ugly old woman

cro·ny \'krōnē\ *n, pl* **-nies** : chum

crook \'krúk\ *n* **1** : bent or curved tool or part **2** : thief ~ *vb* : curve sharply

crook·ed \'krúkəd\ *adj* **1** : bent **2** : dishonest — **crook·ed·ness** *n*

croon \'krün\ *vb* : sing softly — **croon·er** *n*

crop \'kräp\ *n* **1** : pouch in the throat of a bird or insect **2** : short riding whip **3** : something that can be harvested ~ *vb* **-pp-** **1** : trim **2** : appear unexpectedly — used with *up*

cro·quet \krō'kā\ *n* : lawn game of driving balls through wickets

cro·quette \-'ket\ *n* : mass of minced food deep-fried

cro·sier \'krōzhər\ *n* : bishop's staff

cross \'krós\ *n* **1** : figure or structure consisting of an upright and a cross piece **2** : interbreeding of unlike strains ~ *vb* **1** : intersect **2** : cancel **3** : go or extend across **4** : interbreed ~ *adj* **1** : going across **2** : contrary **3** : marked by bad temper — **cross·ing** *n* — **crossly** *adv*

cross·bow \-,bō\ *n* : short bow mounted on a rifle stock

cross·breed *vb* **-bred; -breed·ing** : hybridize

cross–ex·am·ine *vb* : question about earlier testimony — **cross–ex·am·i·na·tion** *n*

cross–eyed *adj* : having the eye turned toward the nose

cross–re·fer *vb* : refer to another place (as in a book) — **cross–refer·ence** *n*

cross·roads *n* : place where 2 roads cross

cross section *n* : representative portion

cross·walk *n* : path for pedestrians crossing a street

cross·ways *adv* : crosswise

cross·wise \-,wīz\ *adv* : so as to cross something — **crosswise** *adj*

crotch \'kräch\ *n* : angle formed by the parting of 2 legs or branches

crotch·ety \'krächətē\ *adj* : cranky, ill-natured

crouch \'kraúch\ *vb* : stoop over — **crouch** *n*

croup \'krüp\ *n* : laryngitis of infants

crou·ton \'krü,tän\ *n* : bit of toast

¹crow \'krō\ *n* : large glossy black bird

²crow *vb* **1** : make the loud sound of the cock **2** : gloat ~ *n* : cry of the cock

crow·bar *n* : metal bar used as a pry or lever

crowd \'kraúd\ *vb* : collect or cram together ~ *n* : large number of people

crown \'kraún\ *n* **1** : wreath of hon-

or or victory **2** : royal headdress **3**
: top or highest part ~ *vb* **1** : place
a crown on **2** : honor — **crowned**
\'kraund\ *adj*

cru·cial \'krüshəl\ *adj* : vitally important

cru·ci·ble \'krüsəbəl\ *n* : heat-resisting container

cru·ci·fix \'krüsə,fiks\ *n* : representation of Christ on the cross

cru·ci·fix·ion \,krüsə'fikshən\ *n* : act of crucifying

cru·ci·fy \'krüsə,fī\ *vb* **-fied; -fy·ing 1** : put to death on a cross **2** : persecute

crude \'krüd\ *adj* **crud·er; -est 1** : not refined **2** : lacking grace or elegance ~ *n* : unrefined petroleum — **crude·ly** *adv* — **cru·di·ty** \-ətē\ *n*

cru·el \'krüəl\ *adj* **-el·er** *or* **-el·ler; -el·est** *or* **-el·lest** : causing suffering to others — **cru·el·ly** \-ē\ *adv* — **cru·el·ty** \tē\ *n*

cru·et \'krüət\ *n* : bottle for salad dressings

cruise \'krüz\ *vb* **cruised; cruis·ing 1** : sail to several ports **2** : travel at the most efficient speed — **cruise** *n*

cruis·er \'krüzər\ *n* **1** : warship **2** : police car

crumb \'krəm\ *n* : small fragment

crum·ble \'krəmbəl\ *vb* **-bled; -bling** : break into small pieces — **crum·bly** \-blē\ *adj*

crum·ple \'krəmpəl\ *vb* **-pled; -pling 1** : crush together **2** : collapse

crunch \'krənch\ *vb* : chew or press with a crushing noise ~ *n* : crunching sound — **crunchy** *adj*

cru·sade \krü'sād\ *n* **1** *cap* : medieval Christian expedition to the Holy Land **2** : reform movement — **crusade** *vb* — **cru·sad·er** *n*

crush \'krəsh\ *vb* **1** : squeeze out of shape **2** : grind or pound to bits **3** : suppress ~ *n* **1** : severe crowding **2** : infatuation

crust \'krəst\ *n* **1** : hard outer part of bread or a pie **2** : hard surface layer — **crust·al** *adj* — **crusty** *adj*

crus·ta·cean \,krəs'tāshən\ *n* : aquatic arthropod having a firm shell

crutch \'krəch\ *n* : support for use by the disabled in walking

crux \'krəks, 'krüks\ *n, pl* **crux-**

es **1** : hard problem **2** : crucial point

cry \'krī\ *vb* **cried; cry·ing 1** : call out **2** : weep ~ *n, pl* **cries 1** : shout **2** : fit of weeping **3** : characteristic sound of an animal

crypt \'kript\ *n* : underground chamber

cryp·tic \'kriptik\ *adj* : enigmatic

cryp·tog·ra·phy \krip'tägrəfē\ *n* : coding and decoding of messages — **cryp·tog·ra·pher** \-fər\ *n*

crys·tal \'krist°l\ *n* **1** : transparent quartz **2** : something (as glass) like crystal **3** : body formed by solidification that has a regular repeating atomic arrangement — **crys·tal·line** \-tələn\ *adj*

crys·tal·lize \-tə,līz\ *vb* **-lized; -lizing** : form crystals or a definite shape — **crys·tal·li·za·tion** \,kristələ'zāshən\ *n*

cub \'kəb\ *n* : young animal

cub·by·hole \'kəbē,hōl\ *n* : small confined space

cube \'kyüb\ *n* **1** : solid having 6 equal square sides **2** : product obtained by taking a number 3 times as a factor ~ *vb* **cubed; cub·ing 1** : raise to the 3d power **2** : form into a cube **3** : cut into cubes — **cu·bic** \'kyübik\ *adj*

cu·bi·cle \-bikəl\ *n* : small room

cu·bit \'kyübət\ *n* : ancient unit of length equal to about 18 inches

cuck·old \'kəkəld, 'kük-\ *n* : man whose wife is unfaithful — **cuckold** *vb*

cuck·oo \'kükü, 'kük-\ *n, pl* **-oos** : brown European bird ~ *adj* : silly

cu·cum·ber \'kyü,kəmbər\ *n* : fleshy fruit related to the gourds

cud \'kəd\ *n* : food chewed again by ruminating animals

cud·dle \'kəd°l\ *vb* **-dled; -dling** : lie close

cud·gel \'kəjəl\ *n or vb* : club

¹cue \'kyü\ *n* : signal — **cue** *vb*

²cue *n* : stick used in pool

¹cuff \'kəf\ *n* **1** : part of a sleeve encircling the wrist **2** : folded trouser hem

²cuff *vb or n* : slap

cui·sine \kwi'zēn\ *n* : manner of cooking

cu·li·nary \'kələ,nerē, 'kyülə-\ *adj* : of or relating to cookery

cull \'kəl\ *vb* : select

cul·mi·nate \'kəlmə,nāt\ *vb* **-nat-ed; -nat·ing** : rise to the highest point — **cul·mi·na·tion** \,kəlmə-'nāshən\ *n*

cul·pa·ble \'kəlpəbəl\ *adj* : deserving blame

cul·prit \'kəlprət\ *n* : guilty person

cult \'kəlt\ *n* **1** : religious system **2** : faddish devotion — **cult·ist** *n*

cul·ti·vate \'kəltə,vāt\ *vb* **-vat·ed; -vat·ing 1** : prepare for crops **2** : foster the growth of **3** : refine — **cul·ti·va·tion** \,kəltə'vāshən\ *n*

cul·ture \'kəlchər\ *n* **1** : cultivation **2** : refinement of intellectual and artistic taste **3** : particular form or stage of civilization — **cul·tur·al** \'kəlchərəl\ *adj* — **cul·tured** \'kəlchərd\ *adj*

cul·vert \'kəlvərt\ *n* : drain crossing under a road or railroad

cum·ber·some \'kəmbərsəm\ *adj* : awkward to handle due to bulk

cu·mu·la·tive \'kyümyələtiv, -,lāt-\ *adj* : increasing by additions

cu·mu·lus \'kyümyələs\ *n, pl* **-li** \-,lī, -,lē\ : massive rounded cloud

cun·ning \'kəniŋ\ *adj* **1** : crafty **2** : clever **3** : appealing ~ *n* **1** : skill **2** : craftiness

cup \'kəp\ *n* **1** : small drinking vessel **2** : contents of a cup **3** : a half pint ~ *vb* **-pp-** : shape like a cup — **cup·ful** *n*

cup·board \'kəbərd\ *n* : small storage closet

cup·cake *n* : small cake

cu·pid·i·ty \kyu'pidətē\ *n, pl* **-ties** : excessive desire for money

cu·po·la \'kyüpələ, -,lō\ *n* : small rooftop structure

cur \'kər\ *n* : mongrel dog

cu·rate \'kyurət\ *n* : member of the clergy — **cu·ra·cy** \-əsē\ *n*

cu·ra·tor \kyu'rātər\ *n* : one in charge of a museum or zoo

curb \'kərb\ *n* **1** : restraint **2** : raised edging along a street ~ *vb* : hold back

curd \'kərd\ *n* : coagulated milk

cur·dle \'kərd°l\ *vb* **-dled; -dling 1** : form curds **2** : sour

cure \'kyur\ *n* **1** : recovery from disease **2** : remedy ~ *vb* **cured; cur·ing 1** : restore to health **2** : process for storage or use — **cur·able** *adj*

cur·few \'kər,fyü\ *n* : requirement to be off the streets at a set hour

cu·rio \'kyurē,ō\ *n, pl* **-ri·os** : rare or unusual article

cu·ri·ous \'kyurēəs\ *adj* **1** : eager to learn **2** : strange — **cu·ri·os·i·ty** \,kyurē'äsətē\ *n* — **cu·ri·ous·ness** *n*

curl \'kərl\ *vb* **1** : form into ringlets **2** : curve ~ *n* **1** : ringlet of hair **2** : something with a spiral form — **curl·er** *n* — **curly** *adj*

cur·lew \'kərlü, -lyü\ *n, pl* **-lews** or **-lew** : long-legged brownish bird

curli·cue \'kərli,kyü\ *n* : fanciful curve

cur·rant \'kərənt\ *n* **1** : small seedless raisin **2** : berry of a shrub

cur·ren·cy \'kərənsē\ *n, pl* **-cies 1** : general use or acceptance **2** : money

cur·rent \'kərənt\ *adj* : occurring in or belonging to the present ~ *n* **1** : swiftest part of a stream **2** : flow of electricity

cur·ric·u·lum \kə'rikyələm\ *n, pl* **-la** \-lə\ : course of study

[1]**cur·ry** \'kərē\ *vb* **-ried; -ry·ing** : brush (a horse) with a wire brush (**cur·ry·comb** \-,kōm\) — **curry fa·vor** : seek favor by flattery

[2]**curry** *n, pl* **-ries** : blend of pungent spices or a food seasoned with this

curse \'kərs\ *n* **1** : a calling down of evil or harm upon one **2** : affliction ~ *vb* **cursed; curs·ing 1** : call down injury upon **2** : swear at **3** : afflict

cur·sor \'kərsər\ *n* : indicator on a computer screen

cur·so·ry \'kərsərē\ *adj* : hastily done

curt \'kərt\ *adj* : rudely abrupt — **curt·ly** *adv* — **curt·ness** *n*

cur·tail \kər'tāl\ *vb* : shorten — **cur·tail·ment** *n*

cur·tain \'kərt°n\ *n* : hanging screen that can be drawn back or raised — **curtain** *vb*

curt·sy, curt·sey \'kərtsē\ *n, pl* **-sies** or **-seys** : courteous bow made by bending the knees — **curtsy, curt·sey** *vb*

cur·va·ture \'kərvə,chur\ *n* : amount or state of curving

curve \'kərv\ *vb* **curved; curv·ing** : bend from a straight line or course ~ *n* **1** : a bending without angles **2** : something curved

cush·ion \'kushən\ *n* **1** : soft pillow **2** : something that eases or protects

$\sim vb$ **1** : provide with a cushion **2** : soften the force of

cusp \'kəsp\ *n* : pointed end

cus·pid \'kəspəd\ *n* : a canine tooth

cus·pi·dor \'kəspə₁dȯr\ *n* : spittoon

cus·tard \'kəstərd\ *n* : sweetened cooked mixture of milk and eggs

cus·to·dy \'kəstədē\ *n, pl* -**dies** : immediate care or charge — **cus·to·di·al** \₁kəs'tōdēəl\ *adj* — **cus·to·di·an** \-ēən\ *n*

cus·tom \'kəstəm\ *n* **1** : habitual course of action **2** *pl* : import taxes $\sim adj$: made to personal order — **cus·tom·ar·i·ly** \₁kəstə'merəlē\ *adv* — **cus·tom·ary** \'kəstə₁merē\ *adj* — **custom–built** *adj* — **cus·tom–made** *adj*

cus·tom·er \'kəstəmər\ *n* : buyer

cut \'kət\ *vb* **cut; cut·ting 1** : penetrate or divide with a sharp edge **2** : experience the growth of (a tooth) through the gum **3** : shorten **4** : remove by severing **5** : intersect $\sim n$ **1** : something separated by cutting **2** : reduction — **cut in** *vb* : thrust oneself between others

cu·ta·ne·ous \kyu̇'tānēəs\ *adj* : relating to the skin

cute \'kyüt\ *adj* **cut·er; -est** : pretty

cu·ti·cle \'kyütikəl\ *n* : outer layer (as of skin)

cut·lass \'kətləs\ *n* : short heavy curved sword

cut·lery \-lərē\ *n* : cutting utensils

cut·let \-lət\ *n* : slice of meat

cut·ter \'kətər\ *n* **1** : tool or machine for cutting **2** : small armed motorboat **3** : light sleigh

cut·throat *n* : murderer $\sim adj$: ruthless

-cy \sē\ *n suffix* **1** : action or practice **2** : rank or office **3** : body **4** : state or quality

cy·a·nide \'sīə₁nīd, -nəd\ *n* : poisonous chemical salt

cy·cle \'sīkəl, **4** *also* 'sikəl\ *n* **1** : period of time for a series of repeated events **2** : recurring round of events **3** : long period of time **4** : bicycle or motorcycle $\sim vb$ **-cled; -cling** : ride a cycle — **cy·clic** \'sīklik, 'sik-\ **cy·cli·cal** \-əl\ *adj* — **cy·clist** \'sīklist, 'sik-\ *n*

cy·clone \'sī₁klōn\ *n* : tornado — **cy·clon·ic** \sī'klänik\ *adj*

cy·clo·pe·dia, cy·clo·pae·dia \₁sīklə'pēdēə\ *n* : encyclopedia

cyl·in·der \'siləndər\ *n* **1** : long round body or figure **2** : rotating chamber in a revolver **3** : piston chamber in an engine — **cy·lin·dri·cal** \sə'lindrikəl\ *adj*

♦ **cym·bal** \'simbəl\ *n* : one of 2 concave brass plates clashed together

cyn·ic \'sinik\ *n* : one who attributes all actions to selfish motives — **cyn·i·cal** \-ikəl\ *adj* — **cyn·i·cism** \-ə₁sizəm\ *n*

cy·no·sure \'sīnə₁shu̇r, 'sin-\ *n* : center of attraction

cy·press \'sīprəs\ *n* : evergreen tree related to the pines

cyst \'sist\ *n* : abnormal bodily sac — **cys·tic** \'sistik\ *adj*

czar \'zär\ *n* : ruler of Russia until 1917 — **czar·ist** *n or adj*

D

d \'dē\ *n, pl* **d's** *or* **ds** \'dēz\ : 4th letter of the alphabet

¹dab \'dab\ *n* : gentle touch or stroke ~ *vb* **-bb-** : touch or apply lightly

²dab *n* : small amount

dab·ble \'dabəl\ *vb* **-bled; -bling 1** : splash **2** : work without serious effort — **dab·bler** \-blər\ *n*

dachs·hund \'däks,hůnt\ *n* : small dog with a long body and short legs

dad \'dad\ *n* : father

dad·dy \'dadē\ *n, pl* **-dies** : father

daf·fo·dil \'dafə,dil\ *n* : narcissus with trumpetlike flowers

daft \'daft\ *adj* : foolish — **daft·ness** *n*

dag·ger \'dagər\ *n* : knife for stabbing

dahl·ia \'dalyə, 'däl-\ *n* : tuberous herb with showy flowers

dai·ly \'dālē\ *adj* **1** : occurring, done, or used every day or every weekday **2** : computed in terms of one day ~ *n, pl* **-lies** : daily newspaper — **daily** *adv*

dain·ty \'dāntē\ *n, pl* **-ties** : something delicious ~ *adj* **-ti·er; -est** : delicately pretty — **dain·ti·ly** *adv* — **dain·ti·ness** *n*

dairy \'darē\ *n, pl* **-ies** : farm that produces or company that processes milk — **dairy·maid** *n* — **dairy·man** \-mən, -,man\ *n*

da·is \'dāəs\ *n* : raised platform (as for a speaker)

dai·sy \'dāzē\ *n, pl* **-sies** : tall leafy-stemmed plant bearing showy flowers

dale \'dāl\ *n* : valley

dal·ly \'dalē\ *vb* **-lied; -ly·ing 1** : flirt **2** : dawdle — **dal·li·ance** \-əns\ *n*

dal·ma·tian \dal'māshən\ *n* : large dog having a spotted white coat

¹dam \'dam\ *n* : female parent of a domestic animal

²dam *n* : barrier to hold back water — **dam** *vb*

♦ **dam·age** \'damij\ *n* **1** : loss or harm due to injury **2** *pl* : compensation for loss or injury ~ *vb* **-aged; -ag·ing** : do damage to

dam·ask \'daməsk\ *n* : firm lustrous figured fabric

dame \'dām\ *n* : woman of rank or authority

damn \'dam\ *vb* **1** : condemn to hell **2** : curse — **dam·na·ble** \-nəbəl\ *adj* — **dam·na·tion** \dam'nāshən\ *n* — **damned** *adj*

damp \'damp\ *n* : moisture ~ *vb* **1** : reduce the draft in **2** : restrain **3** : moisten ~ *adj* : moist — **damp·ness** *n*

damp·en \'dampən\ *vb* **1** : diminish in activity or vigor **2** : make or become damp

damp·er \'dampər\ *n* : movable plate to regulate a flue draft

dam·sel \'damzəl\ *n* : young woman

dance \'dans\ *vb* **danced; danc·ing** : move rhythmically to music ~ *n* : act of dancing or a gathering for dancing — **danc·er** *n*

dan·de·li·on \'dand°l,īən\ *n* : common yellow-flowered herb

dan·der \'dandər\ *n* : temper

dan·druff \'dandrəf\ *n* : whitish thin dry scales of skin on the scalp

dan·dy \'dandē\ *n, pl* **-dies 1** : man too concerned with clothes **2** : something excellent ~ *adj* **-di·er; -est** : very good

dan·ger \'dānjər\ *n* **1** : exposure to

BERK!

WAS THERE ANY DAMAGE?

NO. IT LOOKS ALL RIGHT

LYM DAVIS 12-6

injury or evil **2** : something that may cause injury — **dan·ger·ous** \'dānjərəs\ adj

dan·gle \'daŋgəl\ vb **-gled; -gling 1** : hang and swing freely **2** : be left without support or connection **3** : allow or cause to hang **4** : offer as an inducement

dank \'daŋk\ adj : unpleasantly damp

dap·per \'dapər\ adj : neat and stylishly dressed

dap·ple \'dapəl\ vb **-pled; -pling** : mark with colored spots

dare \'dar\ vb **dared; dar·ing 1** : have sufficient courage **2** : urge or provoke to contend — **dare** n — **dar·ing** \'dariŋ\ n or adj

dare·dev·il n : recklessly bold person

dark \'därk\ adj **1** : having little or no light **2** : not light in color **3** : gloomy ~ n : absence of light — **dark·en** \-ən\ vb — **dark·ly** adv — **dark·ness** n

dar·ling \'därliŋ\ n **1** : beloved **2** : favorite ~ adj **1** : dearly loved **2** : very pleasing

darn \'därn\ vb : mend with interlacing stitches — **darn·er** n

◆ **dart** \'därt\ n **1** : small pointed missile **2** pl : game of throwing darts at a target **3** : tapering fold in a garment **4** : quick movement ~ vb : move suddenly or rapidly

dash \'dash\ vb **1** : smash **2** : knock or hurl violently **3** : ruin **4** : perform or finish hastily **5** : move quickly ~ n **1** : sudden burst, splash, or stroke **2** : punctuation mark — **3** : tiny amount **4** : showiness or liveliness **5** : sudden rush **6** : short race **7** : dashboard

dash·board n : instrument panel

dash·ing \'dashiŋ\ adj : dapper and charming

das·tard \'dastərd\ n : one who

sneakingly commits malicious acts

das·tard·ly \-lē\ adj : base or malicious

da·ta \'dātə, 'dat-, 'dät-\ n sing or pl : factual information

da·ta·base \-,bās\ n : data organized for computer search

¹**date** \'dāt\ n : edible fruit of a palm

²**date** n **1** : day, month, or year when something is done or made **2** : historical time period **3** : social engagement or the person one goes out with ~ vb **dat·ed; dat·ing 1** : determine or record the date of **2** : have a date with **3** : originate — **to date** : up to now

dat·ed \-əd\ adj : old-fashioned

da·tum \'dātəm, 'dat-, 'dät-\ n, pl **-ta** \-ə\ or **-tums** : piece of data

daub \'dòb\ vb : smear ~ n : something daubed on — **daub·er** n

daugh·ter \'dòtər\ n : human female offspring

daugh·ter–in–law n, pl **daughters–in–law** : wife of one's son

daunt \'dònt\ vb : lessen the courage of

daunt·less \-ləs\ adj : fearless

dav·en·port \'davən,pȯrt\ n : sofa

daw·dle \'dȯd°l\ vb **-dled; -dling 1** : waste time **2** : loiter

dawn \'dòn\ vb **1** : grow light as the sun rises **2** : begin to appear, develop, or be understood ~ n : first appearance (as of daylight)

day \'dā\ n **1** : period of light between one night and the next **2** : 24 hours **3** : specified date **4** : particular time or age **5** : period of work for a day — **day·light** n — **day·time** n

day·break n : dawn

day·dream n : fantasy of wish fulfillment — **daydream** vb

daylight saving time n : time one hour ahead of standard time

daze \'dāz\ *vb* **dazed; daz·ing 1** : stun by a blow **2** : dazzle — **daze** *n*

daz·zle \'dazəl\ *vb* **-zled; -zling 1** : overpower with light **2** : impress greatly — **dazzle** *n*

DDT \,dē,dē'tē\ *n* : long-lasting insecticide

dea·con \'dēkən\ *n* : subordinate church officer

dea·con·ess \'dēkənəs\ *n* : woman who assists in church ministry

dead \'ded\ *adj* **1** : lifeless **2** : unresponsive or inactive **3** : exhausted **4** : obsolete **5** : precise ~ *n, pl* **dead 1** : one that is dead — usu. with *the* **2** : most lifeless time ~ *adv* **1** : completely **2** : directly — **dead·en** \'dedᵊn\ *vb*

dead·beat *n* : one who will not pay debts

dead end *n* : end of a street with no exit — **dead–end** *adj*

dead heat *n* : tie in a contest

dead·line *n* : time by which something must be finished

dead·lock *n* : struggle that neither side can win — **deadlock** *vb*

dead·ly \'dedlē\ *adj* **-li·er; -est 1** : capable of causing death **2** : very accurate **3** : fatal to spiritual progress **4** : suggestive of death **5** : very great ~ *adv* : extremely — **dead·li·ness** *n*

dead·pan *adj* : expressionless — **dead·pan** *n or vb or adv*

dead·wood *n* : something useless

deaf \'def\ *adj* : unable or unwilling to hear — **deaf·en** \-ən\ *vb* — **deaf·ness** *n*

deaf–mute *n* : deaf person unable to speak

deal \'dēl\ *n* **1** : indefinite quantity **2** : distribution of playing cards **3** : negotiation or agreement **4** : treatment received **5** : bargain ~ *vb* **dealt** \'delt\; **deal·ing** \'dēliŋ\ **1** : distribute playing cards **2** : be concerned with **3** : administer or deliver **4** : take action **5** : sell **6** : reach a state of acceptance — **deal·er** *n* — **deal·ing** *n*

dean \'dēn\ *n* **1** : head of a group of clergy members **2** : university or school administrator **3** : senior member

dear \'dir\ *adj* **1** : highly valued or loved **2** : expensive ~ *n* : loved one — **dear·ly** *adv* — **dear·ness** *n*

dearth \'dərth\ *n* : scarcity

death \'deth\ *n* **1** : end of life **2** : cause of loss of life **3** : state of being dead **4** : destruction or extinction — **death·less** *adj* — **death·ly** *adj or adv*

de·ba·cle \di'bäkəl, -'bakəl\ *n* : disaster or fiasco

de·bar \di'bär\ *vb* : bar from something

de·bark \-'bärk\ *vb* : disembark — **de·bar·ka·tion** \,dē,bär'kāshən\ *n*

de·base \di'bās\ *vb* : disparage — **de·base·ment** *n*

de·bate \-'bāt\ *vb* **-bat·ed; -bat·ing** : discuss a question by argument — **de·bat·able** *adj* — **debate** *n* — **de·bat·er** *n*

de·bauch \-'bȯch\ *vb* : seduce or corrupt — **de·bauch·ery** \-ərē\ *n*

de·bil·i·tate \-'bilə,tāt\ *vb* **-tat·ed; -tat·ing** : make ill or weak

de·bil·i·ty \-'bilətē\ *n, pl* **-ties** : physical weakness

deb·it \'debət\ *n* : account entry of a payment or debt ~ *vb* : record as a debit

deb·o·nair \,debə'nar\ *adj* : suave

de·bris \də'brē, dā-; 'dā,brē\ *n, pl* **-bris** \-'brēz, -,brēz\ : remains of something destroyed

debt \'det\ *n* **1** : sin **2** : something owed **3** : state of owing — **debt·or** \-ər\ *n*

de·bunk \dē'bəŋk\ *vb* : expose as false

de·but \'dā,byü, dā'byü\ *n* **1** : first public appearance **2** : formal entrance into society — **debut** *vb* — **deb·u·tante** \'debyü,tänt\ *n*

de·cade \'dek,ād, -əd; de'kād\ *n* : 10 years

dec·a·dence \'dekədəns, di'kādᵊns\ *n* : deterioration — **dec·a·dent** \-ənt, -ᵊnt\ *adj or n*

de·cal \'dē,kal, di'kal, 'dekal\ *n* : picture or design for transfer from prepared paper

de·camp \di'kamp\ *vb* : depart suddenly

de·cant \di'kant\ *vb* : pour gently

de·cant·er \-ər\ *n* : ornamental bottle

de·cap·i·tate \di'kapə,tāt\ *vb* **-tat·ed; -tat·ing** : behead — **de·cap·i·ta·tion** \-,kapə'tāshən\ *n*

de·cay \di'kā\ *vb* **1** : decline in condition **2** : decompose — **decay** *n*

de·cease \-'sēs\ *n* : death — **decease** *vb*

de·ceit \-'sēt\ *n* **1** : deception **2** : dishonesty — **de·ceit·ful** \-fəl\ *adj* — **de·ceit·ful·ly** *adv* — **de·ceit·ful·ness** *n*

de·ceive \-'sēv\ *vb* **-ceived; -ceiv·ing** : trick or mislead — **de·ceiv·er** *n*

de·cel·er·ate \dē'selə,rāt\ *vb* **-at·ed; -at·ing** : slow down

De·cem·ber \di'sembər\ *n* : 12th month of the year having 31 days

de·cent \'dēs°nt\ *adj* **1** : good, right, or just **2** : clothed **3** : not obscene **4** : fairly good — **de·cen·cy** \-°nsē\ *n* — **de·cent·ly** *adv*

de·cep·tion \di'sepshən\ *n* **1** : act or fact of deceiving **2** : fraud — **de·cep·tive** \-'septiv\ *adj* — **de·cep·tive·ly** *adv* — **de·cep·tive·ness** *n*

de·cide \di'sīd\ *vb* **-cid·ed; -cid·ing** **1** : make a choice or judgment **2** : bring to a conclusion **3** : cause to decide

de·cid·ed *adj* **1** : unquestionable **2** : resolute — **de·cid·ed·ly** *adv*

de·cid·u·ous \di'sijəwəs\ *adj* : having leaves that fall annually

dec·i·mal \'desəməl\ *n* : fraction in which the denominator is a power of 10 expressed by a point (**decimal point**) placed at the left of the numerator — **decimal** *adj*

de·ci·pher \di'sīfər\ *vb* : make out the meaning of — **de·ci·pher·able** *adj*

de·ci·sion \-'sizhən\ *n* **1** : act or result of deciding **2** : determination

de·ci·sive \-'sīsiv\ *adj* **1** : having the power to decide **2** : conclusive **3** : showing determination — **de·ci·sive·ly** *adv* — **de·ci·sive·ness** *n*

deck \'dek\ *n* **1** : floor of a ship **2** : pack of playing cards ～ *vb* **1** : array or dress up **2** : knock down

de·claim \di'klām\ *vb* : speak loudly or impressively — **dec·la·ma·tion** \,deklə'māshən\ *n*

de·clare \di'klar\ *vb* **-clared; -clar·ing** **1** : make known formally **2** : state emphatically — **dec·la·ra·tion** \,deklə'rāshən\ *n* — **de·clar·a·tive** \di'klarətiv\ *adj* — **de·clar·a·to·ry** \di'klarə,tōrē\ *adj* — **de·clar·er** *n*

de·clen·sion \di'klenchən\ *n* : inflectional forms of a noun, pronoun, or adjective

de·cline \di'klīn\ *vb* **-clined; -clin·ing** **1** : turn or slope downward **2** : wane **3** : refuse to accept **4** : inflect ～ *n* **1** : gradual wasting away **2** : change to a lower state or level **3** : a descending slope — **dec·li·na·tion** \,deklə'nāshən\ *n*

de·code \dē'kōd\ *vb* : decipher (a coded message) — **de·cod·er** *n*

de·com·mis·sion \,dēkə'mishən\ *vb* : remove from service

de·com·pose \,dēkəm'pōz\ *vb* **1** : separate into parts **2** : decay — **de·com·po·si·tion** \dē,kämpə'zishən\ *n*

de·con·ges·tant \,dēkən'jestənt\ *n* : agent that relieves congestion

de·cor, dé·cor \dā'kòr, 'dā,kòr\ *n* : room design or decoration

dec·o·rate \'dekə,rāt\ *vb* **-rat·ed; -rat·ing** **1** : add something attractive to **2** : honor with a medal — **dec·o·ra·tion** \,dekə'rāshən\ *n* — **dec·o·ra·tive** \'dekərətiv\ *adj* — **dec·o·ra·tor** \'dekə,rātər\ *n*

de·co·rum \di'kōrəm\ *n* : proper behavior — **dec·o·rous** \'dekərəs, di'kōrəs\ *adj*

◆ **de·coy** \'dē,kòi, di'-\ *n* : something that tempts or draws attention from another ～ *vb* : tempt

de·crease \di'krēs\ *vb* **-creased; -creas·ing** : grow or cause to grow less — **decrease** \'dē,krēs\ *n*

de·cree \di'krē\ *n* : official order — **de·cree** *vb*

de·crep·it \di'krepət\ *adj* : impaired by age

de·cre·scen·do \,dākrə'shendō\ *adv or adj* : with a decrease in volume

de·cry \di'krī\ *vb* : express strong disapproval of

ded·i·cate \'dedi,kāt\ *vb* **-cat·ed; -cat·ing 1** : set apart for a purpose (as honor or worship) **2** : address to someone as a compliment — **ded·i·ca·tion** \,dedi'kāshən\ *n* — **ded·i·ca·to·ry** \'dedikə,tōrē\ *adj*

de·duce \di'düs, -'dyüs\ *vb* **-duced; -duc·ing** : derive by reasoning — **de·duc·ible** *adj*

de·duct \-'dəkt\ *vb* : subtract — **de·duct·ible** *adj*

de·duc·tion \-'dəkshən\ *n* **1** : subtraction **2** : reasoned conclusion — **de·duc·tive** \-'dəktiv\ *adj*

deed \'dēd\ *n* **1** : exploit **2** : document showing ownership ∼ *vb* : convey by deed

deem \'dēm\ *vb* : think

deep \'dēp\ *adj* **1** : extending far or a specified distance down, back, within, or outward **2** : occupied **3** : dark and rich in color **4** : low in tone ∼ *adv* **1** : deeply **2** : far along in time ∼ *n* : deep place — **deep·en** \'dēpən\ *vb* — **deep·ly** *adv*

deep–seat·ed \-'sētəd\ *adj* : firmly established

deer \'dir\ *n, pl* **deer** : ruminant mammal with antlers in the male — **deer·skin** *n*

de·face \di'fās\ *vb* : mar the surface of — **de·face·ment** *n* — **de·fac·er** *n*

de·fame \di'fām\ *vb* **-famed; -fam·ing** : injure the reputation of — **def·a·ma·tion** \,defə'māshən\ *n* — **de·fam·a·to·ry** \di'famə,tōrē\ *adj*

de·fault \di'fȯlt\ *n* : failure in a duty — **default** *vb* — **de·fault·er** *n*

de·feat \di'fēt\ *vb* **1** : frustrate **2** : win victory over ∼ *n* : loss of a battle or contest

def·e·cate \'defi,kāt\ *vb* **-cat·ed; -cat·ing** : discharge feces from the bowels — **def·e·ca·tion** \,defi-'kāshən\ *n*

de·fect \'dē,fekt, di'fekt\ *n* : imperfection ∼ \di'-\ *vb* : desert — **de·fec·tion** \-'fekshən\ *n* — **de·fec·tor** \-'fektər\ *n*

de·fec·tive \di'fektiv\ *adj* : faulty or deficient — **defective** *n*

de·fend \-'fend\ *vb* **1** : protect from danger or harm **2** : take the side of — **de·fend·er** *n*

de·fen·dant \-'fendənt\ *n* : person charged or sued in a court

de·fense \-'fens\ *n* **1** : act of defending **2** : something that defends **3** : party, group, or team that opposes another — **de·fense·less** *adj* — **de·fen·si·ble** *adj* — **de·fen·sive** *adj or n*

¹de·fer \di'fər\ *vb* **-rr-** : postpone — **de·fer·ment** \di'fərmənt\ *n* — **de·fer·ra·ble** \-əbəl\ *adj*

²defer *vb* **-rr-** : yield to the opinion or wishes of another — **def·er·ence** \'defrəns\ *n* — **def·er·en·tial** \,defə'renchəl\ *adj*

de·fi·ance \di'fīəns\ *n* : disposition to resist — **de·fi·ant** \-ənt\ *adj*

de·fi·cient \di'fishənt\ *adj* **1** : lacking something necessary **2** : not up to standard — **de·fi·cien·cy** \-'fishənsē\ *n*

def·i·cit \'defəsət\ *n* : shortage esp. in money

♦ **de·file** \di'fīl\ *vb* **-filed; -fil·ing 1** : make filthy or corrupt **2** : profane or dishonor — **de·file·ment** *n*

de·fine \di'fīn\ *vb* **-fined; -fin·ing 1** : fix or mark the limits of **2** : clarify in outline **3** : set forth the

GUESTS ARE A PAIN

FIRST THEY DEFILE MY WATER DISH...

THEN THEY WANT A TOW

JIM DAVIS 11-5
© 1991 PAWS, INC.

meaning of — **de·fin·able** *adj* — **de·fin·ably** *adv* — **de·fin·er** *n*

def·i·ni·tion \,defə'nishən\ *n*

def·i·nite \'defənət\ *adj* **1** : having distinct limits **2** : clear in meaning, intent, or identity **3** : typically designating an identified or immediately identifiable person or thing — **def·i·nite·ly** *adv*

de·fin·i·tive \di'finətiv\ *adj* **1** : conclusive **2** : authoritative

de·flate \di'flāt\ *vb* **-flat·ed; -flat·ing 1** : release air or gas from **2** : reduce — **de·fla·tion** \-'flāshən\ *n*

de·flect \-'flekt\ *vb* : turn aside — **de·flec·tion** \-'flekshən\ *n*

de·fog \-'fȯg, -'fäg\ *vb* : remove condensed moisture from — **de·fog·ger** *n*

de·fo·li·ate \dē'fōlē,āt\ *vb* **-at·ed; -at·ing** : deprive of leaves esp. prematurely — **de·fo·li·ant** \-lēənt\ *n* — **de·fo·li·a·tion** \-,fōlē'āshən\ *n*

de·form \di'fȯrm\ *vb* **1** : distort **2** : disfigure — **de·for·ma·tion** \dē,fȯr'māshən, ,defər-\ *n* — **de·for·mi·ty** \di'fȯrmətē\ *n*

de·fraud \di'frȯd\ *vb* : cheat

de·fray \-'frā\ *vb* : pay

de·frost \-'frȯst\ *vb* **1** : thaw out **2** : free from ice — **de·frost·er** *n*

deft \'deft\ *adj* : quick and skillful — **deft·ly** *adv* — **deft·ness** *n*

de·funct \di'fəŋkt\ *adj* : dead

de·fy \-'fī\ *vb* **-fied; -fy·ing 1** : challenge **2** : boldly refuse to obey

de·gen·er·ate \di'jenərət\ *adj* : degraded or corrupt ∼ *n* : degenerate person ∼ \-ə,rāt\ *vb* : become degenerate — **de·gen·er·a·cy** \-ərəsē\ *n* — **de·gen·er·a·tion** \-,jenə'rāshən\ *n* — **de·gen·er·a·tive** \-'jenə,rātiv\ *adj*

de·grade \di'grād\ *vb* **1** : reduce from a higher to a lower rank or degree **2** : debase **3** : decompose — **de·grad·able** \-əbəl\ *adj* — **deg·ra·da·tion** \,degrə'dāshən\ *n*

de·gree \di'grē\ *n* **1** : step in a series **2** : extent, intensity, or scope **3** : title given to a college graduate **4** : a 360th part of the circumference of a circle **5** : unit for measuring temperature

de·hy·drate \dē'hī,drāt\ *vb* **1** : remove water from **2** : lose liquid — **de·hy·dra·tion** \,dēhī'drāshən\ *n*

de·i·fy \'dēə,fī, 'dā-\ *vb* **-fied; -fy·ing** : make a god of — **de·i·fi·ca·tion** \,dēəfə'kāshən, ,dā-\ *n*

deign \'dān\ *vb* : condescend

de·i·ty \'dēətē, 'dā-\ *n, pl* **-ties 1** *cap* : God **2** : a god or goddess

de·ject·ed \di'jektəd\ *adj* : sad — **de·jec·tion** \-shən\ *n*

de·lay \di'lā\ *n* : a putting off of something ∼ *vb* **1** : postpone **2** : stop or hinder for a time

de·lec·ta·ble \di'lektəbəl\ *adj* : delicious

del·e·gate \'deligət, -,gāt\ *n* : representative ∼ \-,gāt\ *vb* **-gat·ed; -gat·ing 1** : entrust to another **2** : appoint as one's delegate — **del·e·ga·tion** \,deli'gāshən\ *n*

de·lete \di'lēt\ *vb* **-let·ed; -let·ing** : eliminate something written — **de·le·tion** \-'lēshən\ *n*

del·e·te·ri·ous \,delə'tirēəs\ *adj* : harmful

de·lib·er·ate \di'libərət\ *adj* **1** : determined after careful thought **2** : intentional **3** : not hurried ∼ \-ə,rāt\ *vb* **-at·ed; -at·ing** : consider carefully — **de·lib·er·ate·ly** *adv* — **de·lib·er·ate·ness** *n* — **de·lib·er·a·tion** \-,libə'rāshən\ *n* — **de·lib·er·a·tive** \-'libə,rātiv, -rət-\ *adj*

del·i·ca·cy \'delikəsē\ *n, pl* **-cies 1** : something special and pleasing to eat **2** : fineness **3** : frailty

del·i·cate \'delikət\ *adj* **1** : subtly pleasing to the senses **2** : dainty and charming **3** : sensitive or fragile **4** : requiring fine skill or tact — **del·i·cate·ly** *adv*

del·i·ca·tes·sen \,delikə'tes⁰n\ *n* : store that sells ready-to-eat food

de·li·cious \di'lishəs\ *adj* : very pleasing esp. in taste or aroma — **de·li·cious·ly** *adv* — **de·li·cious·ness** *n*

de·light \di'līt\ *n* **1** : great pleasure **2** : source of great pleasure ∼ *vb* **1** : take great pleasure **2** : satisfy greatly — **de·light·ful** \-fəl\ *adj* — **de·light·ful·ly** *adv*

de·lin·eate \di'linē,āt\ *vb* **-eat·ed; -eat·ing** : sketch or portray — **de·lin·ea·tion** \-,linē'āshən\ *n*

de·lin·quent \-'liŋkwənt\ *n* : delinquent person ∼ *adj* **1** : violating duty or law **2** : overdue in payment — **de·lin·quen·cy** \-kwənsē\ *n*

de·lir·i·um \di'lirēəm\ *n* : mental disturbance — **de·lir·i·ous** \-ēəs\ *adj*

de·liv·er \di'livər\ *vb* **1** : set free **2** : hand over **3** : assist in birth **4** : say or speak **5** : send to an intended destination — **de·liv·er·ance** \-ərəns\ *n* — **de·liv·er·er** *n* — **de·liv·ery** \-ərē\ *n*

dell \'del\ *n* : small secluded valley

del·ta \'deltə\ *n* : triangle of land at the mouth of a river

de·lude \di'lüd\ *vb* **-lud·ed; -lud·ing** : mislead or deceive

del·uge \'delyüj\ *n* **1** : flood **2** : drenching rain ∼ *vb* **-uged; -ug·ing** **1** : flood **2** : overwhelm

de·lu·sion \di'lüzhən\ *n* : false belief

de·luxe \di'lùks, -'ləks, -'lüks\ *adj* : very luxurious or elegant

delve \'delv\ *vb* **delved; delv·ing** **1** : dig **2** : seek information in records

dem·a·gogue, dem·a·gog \'deməˌgäg\ *n* : politician who appeals to emotion and prejudice — **dem·a·gogu·ery** \-ˌgägərē\ *n* — **dem·a·gogy** \-ˌgägē, -ˌgäjē\ *n*

de·mand \di'mand\ *n* **1** : act of demanding **2** : something claimed as due **3** : ability and desire to buy **4** : urgent need ∼ *vb* **1** : ask for with authority **2** : require

de·mar·cate \di'märˌkāt, 'dēˌmär-\ *vb* **-cat·ed; -cat·ing** : mark the limits of — **de·mar·ca·tion** \ˌdēˌmär-'kāshən\ *n*

de·mean \di'mēn\ *vb* : degrade

de·mean·or \-'mēnər\ *n* : behavior

de·ment·ed \-'mentəd\ *adj* : crazy

de·mer·it \-'merət\ *n* : mark given an offender

demi·god \'demiˌgäd\ *n* : mythological being less powerful than a god

de·mise \di'mīz\ *n* **1** : death **2** : loss of status

demi·tasse \'demiˌtas\ *n* : small cup of coffee

de·mo·bi·lize \di'mōbəˌlīz, dē-\ *vb* : disband from military service — **de·mo·bi·li·za·tion** \-ˌmōbələ'zāshən\ *n*

de·moc·ra·cy \di'mäkrəsē\ *n, pl* **-cies** **1** : government in which the supreme power is held by the people **2** : political unit with democratic government

dem·o·crat \'deməˌkrat\ *n* : adherent of democracy

dem·o·crat·ic \ˌdemə'kratik\ *adj* : relating to or favoring democracy — **dem·o·crat·i·cal·ly** \-tiklē\ *adv* — **de·moc·ra·tize** \di'mäkrəˌtīz\ *vb*

de·mol·ish \di'mälish\ *vb* **1** : tear down or smash **2** : put an end to — **de·mo·li·tion** \ˌdemə'lishən, ˌdē-\ *n*

de·mon \'dēmən\ *n* : evil spirit — **de·mon·ic** \di'mänik\ *adj*

dem·on·strate \'demənˌstrāt\ *vb* **-strat·ed; -strat·ing** **1** : show clearly or publicly **2** : prove **3** : explain — **de·mon·stra·ble** \di'mänstrəbəl\ *adj* — **de·mon·stra·bly** \-blē\ *adv* — **dem·on·stra·tion** \ˌdemən'strāshən\ *n* — **de·mon·stra·tive** \di'mänstrətiv\ *adj or n* — **dem·on·stra·tor** \'demənˌstrātər\ *n*

de·mor·al·ize \di'mórəˌlīz\ *vb* : destroy the enthusiasm of

de·mote \di'mōt\ *vb* **-mot·ed; -mot·ing** : reduce to a lower rank — **de·mo·tion** \-'mōshən\ *n*

de·mur \di'mər\ *vb* **-rr-** : object — **de·mur** *n*

de·mure \di'myùr\ *adj* : modest — **de·mure·ly** *adv*

den \'den\ *n* **1** : animal's shelter **2** : hiding place **3** : cozy private little room

de·na·ture \dē'nāchər\ *vb* **-tured; -tur·ing** : make (alcohol) unfit for drinking

♦ **de·ni·al** \di'nīəl\ *n* : rejection of a

request or of the validity of a statement

den·i·grate \'deni‚grāt\ *vb* -grat·ed; -grat·ing : speak ill of

den·im \'denəm\ *n* 1 : durable twilled cotton fabric 2 *pl* : pants of denim

den·i·zen \'denəzən\ *n* : inhabitant

de·nom·i·na·tion \di‚nämə'nāshən\ *n* 1 : religious body 2 : value or size in a series — **de·nom·i·na·tion·al** \-shənəl\ *adj*

de·nom·i·na·tor \-'nämə‚nātər\ *n* : part of a fraction below the line

de·note \di'nōt\ *vb* 1 : mark out plainly 2 : mean — **de·no·ta·tion** \‚dēnō'tāshən\ *n* — **de·no·ta·tive** \'dēnō‚tātiv, di'nōtətiv\ *adj*

de·noue·ment \‚dā‚nü'mäⁿ\ *n* : final outcome (as of a drama)

de·nounce \di'naúns\ *vb* -nounced; -nounc·ing 1 : pronounce blameworthy or evil 2 : inform against

dense \'dens\ *adj* dens·er; -est 1 : thick, compact, or crowded 2 : stupid — **dense·ly** *adv* — **dense·ness** *n* — **den·si·ty** \'densətē\ *n*

dent \'dent\ *n* : small depression — **dent** *vb*

den·tal \'dentᵊl\ *adj* : relating to teeth or dentistry

den·ti·frice \'dentəfrəs\ *n* : preparation for cleaning teeth

den·tin \'dentᵊn\, **den·tine** \'den‚tēn, ‚den'-\ *n* : bonelike component of teeth

den·tist \'dentist\ *n* : one who cares for and replaces teeth — **den·tist·ry** *n*

den·ture \'denchər\ *n* : artificial teeth

de·nude \di'nüd, -'nyüd\ *vb* -nud·ed; -nud·ing : strip of covering

de·nun·ci·a·tion \di‚nənsē'āshən\ *n* : act of denouncing

de·ny \-'nī\ *vb* -nied; -ny·ing 1 : declare untrue 2 : disavow 3 : refuse to grant

de·odor·ant \dē'ōdərənt\ *n* : preparation to prevent unpleasant odors — **de·odor·ize** \-‚rīz\ *vb*

de·part \di'pärt\ *vb* 1 : go away or away from 2 : die — **de·par·ture** \-'pärchər\ *n*

de·part·ment \di'pärtmənt\ *n* 1 : area of responsibility or interest 2 : functional division — **de·part·men·tal** \di‚pärt'mentᵊl, ‚dē-\ *adj*

de·pend \di'pend\ *vb* 1 : rely for

support 2 : be determined by or based on something else — **pend·abil·i·ty** \-‚pendə'bilətē\ *n* — **de·pend·able** *adj* — **de·pen·dence** \di'pendəns\ *n* — **de·pen·den·cy** \-dənsē\ *n* — **de·pen·dent** \-ənt\ *adj or n*

de·pict \di'pikt\ *vb* : show by or as if by a picture — **de·pic·tion** \-'pikshən\ *n*

de·plete \di'plēt\ *vb* -plet·ed; -plet·ing : use up resources of — **de·ple·tion** \-'plēshən\ *n*

de·plore \-'plōr\ *vb* -plored; -plor·ing : regret strongly — **de·plor·able** \-əbəl\ *adj*

de·ploy \-'plói\ *vb* : spread out for battle — **de·ploy·ment** \-mənt\ *n*

de·port \di'pōrt\ *vb* 1 : behave 2 : send out of the country — **de·por·ta·tion** \‚dē‚pōr'tāshən\ *n* — **de·port·ment** \di'pōrtmənt\ *n*

de·pose \-'pōz\ *vb* -posed; -pos·ing 1 : remove (a ruler) from office 2 : testify — **de·po·si·tion** \‚depə-'zishən, ‚dē-\ *n*

de·pos·it \di'päzət\ *vb* -it·ed; -it·ing · : place esp. for safekeeping ~ *n* 1 : state of being deposited 2 : something deposited 3 : act of depositing 4 : natural accumulation — **de·pos·i·tor** \-'päzətər\ *n*

de·pos·i·to·ry \di'päzə‚tōrē\ *n, pl* -ries : place for deposit

de·pot *1 usu* 'depō, *2 usu* 'dēp-\ *n* 1 : place for storage 2 : bus or railroad station

de·prave \di'prāv\ *vb* -praved; -prav·ing : corrupt morally — **de·praved** *adj* — **de·prav·i·ty** \-'pravətē\ *n*

dep·re·cate \'depri‚kāt\ *vb* -cat·ed; -cat·ing 1 : express disapproval of 2 : belittle — **dep·re·ca·tion** \‚depri'kāshən\ *n* — **dep·re·ca·tory** \'deprikə‚tōrē\ *adj*

de·pre·ci·ate \di'prēshē‚āt\ *vb* -at·ed; -at·ing 1 : lessen in value 2 : belittle — **de·pre·ci·a·tion** \-‚prēshē-'āshən\ *n*

dep·re·da·tion \‚deprə'dāshən\ *n* : a laying waste or plundering — **dep·re·date** \'deprə‚dāt\ *vb*

de·press \di'pres\ *vb* 1 : press down 2 : lessen the activity or force of 3 : discourage 4 : decrease the market value of — **de·pres·sant** \-ᵊnt\ *n or adj* — **de·pressed** *adj* — **de-**

pres·sive \-iv\ *adj or n* — **de·pres·sor** \-ər\ *n*

de·pres·sion \di'preshən\ *n* 1 : act of depressing or state of being depressed 2 : depressed place 3 : period of low economic activity

de·prive \-'prīv\ *vb* -**prived**; -**priv·ing** : take or keep something away from — **de·pri·va·tion** \,deprə'vāshən\ *n*

depth \'depth\ *n, pl* **depths** 1 : something that is deep 2 : distance down from a surface 3 : distance from front to back 4 : quality of being deep

dep·u·ta·tion \,depyə'tāshən\ *n* : delegation

dep·u·ty \'depyətē\ *n, pl* -**ties** : person appointed to act for another — **dep·u·tize** \-yə,tīz\ *vb*

de·rail \di'rāl\ *vb* : leave the rails — **de·rail·ment** *n*

de·range \-'rānj\ *vb* -**ranged**; -**rang·ing** 1 : disarrange or upset 2 : make insane — **de·range·ment** *n*

der·by \'dərbē, *Brit* 'där-\ *n, pl* -**bies** 1 : horse race 2 : stiff felt hat with dome-shaped crown

de·reg·u·late \dē'regyù,lāt\ *vb* : remove restrictions on — **de·reg·u·la·tion** \-,regyù'lāshən\ *n*

der·e·lict \'derə,likt\ *adj* 1 : abandoned 2 : negligent ~ *n* 1 : something abandoned 2 : bum — **der·e·lic·tion** \,derə'likshən\ *n*

de·ride \di'rīd\ *vb* -**rid·ed**; -**rid·ing** : make fun of — **de·ri·sion** \-'rizhən\ *n* — **de·ri·sive** \-'rīsiv\ *adj* — **de·ri·sive·ly** *adv* — **de·ri·sive·ness** *n*

de·rive \di'rīv\ *vb* -**rived**; -**riv·ing** 1 : obtain from a source or parent 2 : come from a certain source 3 : infer or deduce — **der·i·va·tion** \,derə'vāshən\ *n* — **de·riv·a·tive** \di'rivətiv\ *adj or n*

der·ma·tol·o·gy \,dərmə'täləjē\ *n* : study of the skin and its disorders — **der·ma·tol·o·gist** \-jist\ *n*

de·rog·a·tive \di'rägətiv\ *adj* : derogatory

de·rog·a·to·ry \di'rägə,tōrē\ *adj* : intended to lower the reputation

der·rick \'derik\ *n* 1 : hoisting apparatus 2 : framework over an oil well

de·scend \di'send\ *vb* 1 : move or climb down 2 : derive 3 : extend downward 4 : appear suddenly (as in an attack) — **de·scen·dant, de·scen·dent** \-ənt\ *adj or n* — **de·scent** \di'sent\ *n*

de·scribe \-'skrīb\ *vb* -**scribed**; -**scrib·ing** : represent in words — **de·scrib·able** *adj* — **de·scrip·tion** \-'skripshən\ *n* — **de·scrip·tive** \-'skriptiv\ *adj*

de·scry \di'skrī\ *vb* -**scried**; -**scry·ing** : catch sight of

des·e·crate \'desi,krāt\ *vb* -**crat·ed**; -**crat·ing** : treat (something sacred) with disrespect — **des·e·cra·tion** \,desi'krāshən\ *n*

de·seg·re·gate \dē'segrə,gāt\ *vb* : eliminate esp. racial segregation in — **de·seg·re·ga·tion** *n*

¹**des·ert** \'dezərt\ *n* : dry barren region — **desert** *adj*

²**de·sert** \di'zərt\ *n* : what one deserves

³**de·sert** \di'zərt\ *vb* : abandon — **desert·er** *n* — **de·ser·tion** \-'zər-shən\ *n*

de·serve \-'zərv\ *vb* -**served**; -**serv·ing** : be worthy of

des·ic·cate \'desi,kāt\ *vb* -**cat·ed**; -**cat·ing** : dehydrate — **des·ic·ca·tion** \,desi'kāshən\ *n*

de·sign \di'zīn\ *vb* 1 : create and work out the details of 2 : make a pattern or sketch of ~ *n* 1 : mental project or plan 2 : purpose 3 : preliminary sketch 4 : underlying arrangement of elements 5 : decorative pattern — **de·sign·er** *n*

des·ig·nate \'dezig,nāt\ *vb* -**nat·ed**; -**nat·ing** 1 : indicate, specify, or name 2 : appoint — **des·ig·na·tion** \,dezig'nāshən\ *n*

de·sire \di'zīr\ *vb* -**sired**; -**sir·ing** 1 : feel desire for 2 : request ~ *n* 1 : strong conscious impulse to have, be, or do something 2 : something desired — **de·sir·abil·i·ty** \-,zīrə'bilətē\ *n* — **de·sir·able** \-'zīrəbəl\ *adj* — **de·sir·able·ness** *n* — **de·sir·ous** \-'zīrəs\ *adj*

de·sist \di'zist, -'sist\ *vb* : stop

desk \'desk\ *n* : table esp. for writing and reading

des·o·late \'desələt, 'dez-\ *adj* 1 : lifeless 2 : disconsolate ~ \-,lāt\ *vb* -**lat·ed**; -**lat·ing** : lay waste — **des·o·la·tion** \,desə'lāshən, ,dez-\ *n*

de·spair \di'spar\ *vb* : lose all hope ~ *n* : loss of hope

des·per·a·do \,despə'rädō, -'rād-\ *n*,

pl **-does** *or* **-dos** : desperate criminal

des·per·ate \'desprət\ *adj* 1 : hopeless 2 : rash 3 : extremely intense — **des·per·ate·ly** *adv* — **des·per·a·tion** \ˌdespəˈrāshən\ *n*

de·spi·ca·ble \diˈspikəbəl, ˈdespik-\ *adj* : deserving scorn

de·spise \diˈspīz\ *vb* **-spised; -spis·ing** : feel contempt for

de·spite \-ˈspīt\ *prep* : in spite of

de·spoil \-ˈspȯil\ *vb* : strip of possessions or value

de·spon·den·cy \-ˈspändənsē\ *n* : dejection — **de·spon·dent** \-dənt\ *adj*

des·pot \'despət, -ˌpät\ *n* : tyrant — **des·pot·ic** \desˈpätik\ *adj* — **des·po·tism** \'despəˌtizəm\ *n*

des·sert \diˈzərt\ *n* : sweet food, fruit, or cheese ending a meal

des·ti·na·tion \ˌdestəˈnāshən\ *n* : place where something or someone is going

des·tine \'destən\ *vb* **-tined; -tin·ing** 1 : designate, assign, or determine in advance 2 : direct

des·ti·ny \'destənē\ *n, pl* **-nies** : that which is to happen in the future

des·ti·tute \'destəˌtüt, -ˌtyüt\ *adj* 1 : lacking something 2 : very poor — **des·ti·tu·tion** \ˌdestəˈtüshən, -ˈtyü-\ *n*

♦ **de·stroy** \diˈstrȯi\ *vb* : kill or put an end to

de·stroy·er \-ˈstrȯiər\ *n* 1 : one that destroys 2 : small speedy warship

de·struc·tion \-ˈstrəkshən\ *n* 1 : action of destroying 2 : ruin — **de·struc·ti·bil·i·ty** \-ˌstrəktəˈbilətē\ *n* — **de·struc·ti·ble** \-ˈstrəktəbəl\ *adj* — **de·struc·tive** \-ˈstrəktiv\ *adj*

des·ul·to·ry \'desəlˌtōrē\ *adj* : aimless

de·tach \diˈtach\ *vb* : separate

de·tached \-ˈtacht\ *adj* 1 : separate 2 : aloof or impartial

de·tach·ment \-ˈtachmənt\ *n* 1 : separation 2 : troops or ships on special service 3 : aloofness 4 : impartiality

de·tail \diˈtāl, ˈdēˌtāl\ *n* : small item or part ～ *vb* : give details of

de·tain \diˈtān\ *vb* 1 : hold in custody 2 : delay

de·tect \diˈtekt\ *vb* : discover — **de·tect·able** *adj* — **de·tec·tion** \-ˈtek-shən\ *n* — **de·tec·tor** \-tər\ *n*

de·tec·tive \-ˈtektiv\ *n* : one who investigates crime

dé·tente \dāˈtänt\ *n* : relaxation of tensions between nations

de·ten·tion \diˈtenchən\ *n* : confinement

de·ter \-ˈtər\ *vb* **-rr-** : discourage or prevent — **de·ter·rence** \-əns\ *n* — **de·ter·rent** \-ənt\ *adj or n*

de·ter·gent \diˈtərjənt\ *n* : cleansing agent

de·te·ri·o·rate \-ˈtirēəˌrāt\ *vb* **-rat·ed; -rat·ing** : make or become worse — **de·te·ri·o·ra·tion** \-ˌtirēəˈrāshən\ *n*

de·ter·mi·na·tion \diˌtərməˈnāshən\ *n* 1 : act of deciding or fixing 2 : firm purpose

de·ter·mine \-ˈtərmən\ *vb* **-mined; -min·ing** 1 : decide on, establish, or settle 2 : find out 3 : bring about as a result

de·test \-ˈtest\ *vb* : hate — **de·test·able** *adj* — **de·tes·ta·tion** \ˌdēˌtesˈtāshən\ *n*

det·o·nate \'detᵊnˌāt\ *vb* **-nat·ed; -nat·ing** : explode — **det·o·na·tion** \ˌdetᵊnˈāshən\ *n* — **det·o·na·tor** \'detᵊnˌātər\ *n*

de·tour \'dēˌtu̇r\ *n* : temporary indirect route — **detour** *vb*

de·tract \diˈtrakt\ *vb* : take away — **de·trac·tion** \-ˈtrakshən\ *n* — **de·trac·tor** \-ˈtraktər\ *n*

det·ri·ment \'detrəmənt\ *n* : damage — **det·ri·men·tal** \ˌdetrə-ˈmentᵊl\ *adj* — **det·ri·men·tal·ly** *adv*

deuce \'düs, 'dyüs\ *n* **1** : 2 in cards or dice **2** : tie in tennis **3** : devil — used as an oath

deut·sche mark \'dòichə-\ *n* : monetary unit of Germany

de·val·ue \dē'val,yü\ *vb* : reduce the value of — **de·val·u·a·tion** *n*

dev·as·tate \'devə,stāt\ *vb* **-tat·ed; -tat·ing** : ruin — **dev·as·ta·tion** \ˌdevə'stāshən\ *n*

de·vel·op \di'veləp\ *vb* **1** : grow, increase, or evolve gradually **2** : cause to grow, increase, or reach full potential — **de·vel·op·er** *n* — **de·vel·op·ment** *n* — **de·vel·op·men·tal** \-ˌveləp'mentᵊl\ *adj*

de·vi·ate \'dēvē,āt\ *vb* **-at·ed; -at·ing** : change esp. from a course or standard — **de·vi·ant** \-vēənt\ *adj or n* — **de·vi·ate** \-vēət, -vē,āt\ *n* — **de·vi·a·tion** \ˌdēvē'āshən\ *n*

de·vice \di'vīs\ *n* **1** : specialized piece of equipment or tool **2** : design

dev·il \'devəl\ *n* **1** : personified supreme spirit of evil **2** : demon **3** : wicked person ~ *vb* **-iled** *or* **-illed; -il·ing** *or* **-il·ling 1** : season highly **2** : pester — **dev·il·ish** \'devəlish\ *adj* — **dev·il·ry** \'devəlrē\, **dev·il·try** \-trē\ *n*

de·vi·ous \'dēvēəs\ *adj* : tricky

de·vise \di'vīz\ *vb* **-vised; -vis·ing 1** : invent **2** : plot **3** : give by will

◆ **de·void** \-'vòid\ *adj* : entirely lacking

de·vote \di'vōt\ *vb* **-vot·ed; -vot·ing** : set apart for a special purpose

de·vot·ed *adj* : faithful

dev·o·tee \ˌdevə'tē, -'tā\ *n* : ardent follower

de·vo·tion \di'vōshən\ *n* **1** : prayer — usu. pl. **2** : loyalty and dedication — **de·vo·tion·al** \-shənəl\ *adj*

de·vour \di'vaûər\ *vb* : consume ravenously — **de·vour·er** *n*

de·vout \-'vaût\ *adj* **1** : devoted to religion **2** : serious — **de·vout·ly** *adv* — **de·vout·ness** *n*

dew \'dü, 'dyü\ *n* : moisture condensed at night — **dew·drop** *n* — **dewy** *adj*

dex·ter·ous \'dekstrəs\ *adj* : skillful with the hands — **dex·ter·i·ty** \dek'sterətē\ *n* — **dex·ter·ous·ly** *adv*

dex·trose \'dek,strōs\ *n* : plant or blood sugar

di·a·be·tes \ˌdīə'bētēz, -'bētəs\ *n* : disorder in which the body has too little insulin and too much sugar — **di·a·bet·ic** \-'betik\ *adj or n*

di·a·bol·ic \-'bälik\, **di·a·bol·i·cal** \-ikəl\ *adj* : fiendish

di·a·crit·ic \-'kritik\ *n* : mark accompanying a letter and indicating a specific sound value — **di·a·crit·i·cal** \-'kritikəl\ *adj*

di·a·dem \'dīə,dem\ *n* : crown

di·ag·no·sis \ˌdīig'nōəs, -əg-\ *n, pl* **-no·ses** \-ˌsēz\ : identifying of a disease from its symptoms — **di·ag·nose** \'dīig,nōs, -əg-\ *vb* — **di·ag·nos·tic** \ˌdīig'nästik, -əg-\ *adj*

di·ag·o·nal \dī'agənəl\ *adj* : extending from one corner to the opposite corner ~ *n* : diagonal line, direction, or arrangement — **di·ag·o·nal·ly** *adv*

di·a·gram \'dīə,gram\ *n* : explanatory drawing or plan ~ *vb* **-gramed** *or* **-grammed; -gram·ing** *or* **-gram·ming** : represent by a diagram — **di·a·gram·mat·ic** \ˌdīəgrə'matik\ *adj*

di·al \'dīəl\ *n* **1** : face of a clock, meter, or gauge **2** : control knob or wheel ~ *vb* **-aled** *or* **-alled; -al-**

ing *or* -al·ling : turn a dial to call, operate, or select

di·a·lect \'dīə,lekt\ *n* : variety of language confined to a region or group

di·a·logue \-,lȯg\ *n* : conversation

di·am·e·ter \dī'amətər\ *n* 1 : straight line through the center of a circle 2 : thickness

di·a·met·ric \,dīə'metrik\, di·a·met·ri·cal \-trikəl\ *adj* : completely opposite — di·a·met·ri·cal·ly \-iklē\ *adv*

di·a·mond \'dīmənd, 'dīə-\ *n* 1 : hard brilliant mineral that consists of crystalline carbon 2 : flat figure having 4 equal sides, 2 acute angles, and 2 obtuse angles 3 : playing card of a suit marked with a red diamond 4 : baseball field

di·a·per \'dīpər\ *n* : baby's garment for receiving bodily wastes ~ *vb* : put a diaper on

di·a·phragm \'dīə,fram\ *n* 1 : sheet of muscle between the chest and abdominal cavity 2 : contraceptive device

di·ar·rhea \,dīə'rēə\ *n* : abnormally watery discharge from bowels

di·a·ry \'dīərē\ *n, pl* -ries : daily record of personal experiences — di·a·rist \'dīərist\ *n*

di·a·tribe \'dīə,trīb\ *n* : biting or abusive denunciation

dice \'dīs\ *n, pl* dice : die or a game played with dice ~ *vb* diced; dic·ing : cut into small cubes

dick·er \'dikər\ *vb* : bargain

dic·tate \'dik,tāt\ *vb* -tat·ed; -tat·ing 1 : speak for a person or a machine to record 2 : command ~ *n* : order — dic·ta·tion \dik'tāshən\ *n*

dic·ta·tor \'dik,tātər\ *n* : person ruling absolutely and often brutally — dic·ta·to·ri·al \,diktətōrēəl\ *adj* — dic·ta·tor·ship \dik'tātər-,ship, 'dik,-\ *n*

dic·tion \'dikshən\ *n* 1 : choice of the best word 2 : precise pronunciation

dic·tio·nary \-shə,nerē\ *n, pl* -nar·ies : reference book of words with information about their meanings

dic·tum \'diktəm\ *n, pl* -ta \-tə\ : authoritative or formal statement

did *past of* DO

di·dac·tic \dī'daktik\ *adj* : intended to teach a moral lesson

¹die \'dī\ *vb* died; dy·ing \'dīiŋ\ 1 : stop living 2 : pass out of existence 3 : stop or subside 4 : long

²die \'dī\ *n* 1 *pl* dice \'dīs\ : small marked cube used in gambling 2 *pl* dies \'dīz\ : form for stamping or cutting

die·sel \'dēzəl, -əl\ *n* : engine in which high compression causes ignition of the fuel

di·et \'dīət\ *n* : food and drink regularly consumed (as by a person) ~ *vb* : eat less or according to certain rules — di·etary \'dīə,terē\ *adj or n* — di·et·er *n*

di·etet·ics \,dīə'tetiks\ *n sing or pl* : science of nutrition — di·etet·ic *adj* — di·eti·tian, di·eti·cian \-'tishən\ *n*

dif·fer \'difər\ *vb* 1 : be unlike 2 : vary 3 : disagree — dif·fer·ence \'difrəns\ *n*

dif·fer·ent \-rənt\ *adj* : not the same — dif·fer·ent·ly *adv*

dif·fer·en·ti·ate \,difə'renchē,āt\ *vb* -at·ed; -at·ing 1 : make or become different 2 : distinguish — dif·fer·en·ti·a·tion \-,renchē'āshən\ *n*

dif·fi·cult \'difikəlt\ *adj* : hard to do, understand, or deal with

dif·fi·cul·ty \-kəltē\ *n, pl* -ties 1 : difficult nature 2 : great effort 3 : something hard to do, understand, or deal with

dif·fi·dent \'difədənt\ *adj* : reserved — dif·fi·dence \-əns\ *n*

dif·fuse \dif'yüs\ *adj* 1 : wordy 2 : not concentrated ~ \-'yüz\ *vb* -fused; -fus·ing : pour out or spread widely — dif·fu·sion \-'yüzhən\ *n*

dig \'dig\ *vb* dug \'dəg\; dig·ging 1 : turn up soil 2 : hollow out or form by removing earth 3 : uncover by turning up earth ~ *n* 1 : thrust 2 : cutting remark — dig in *vb* 1 : establish a defensive position 2 : begin working or eating — dig up *vb* : discover

¹di·gest \'dī,jest\ *n* : body of information in shortened form

²di·gest \dī'jest, də-\ *vb* 1 : think over 2 : convert (food) into a form that can be absorbed 3 : summarize — di·gest·ible *adj* — di·ges·tion \-'jeschən\ *n* — di·ges·tive \-'jestiv\ *adj*

dig·it \'dijət\ *n* 1 : any of the figures

1 to 9 inclusive and usu. the symbol 0 **2** : finger or toe

dig·i·tal \-°l\ *adj* : providing information in numerical digits — **dig·i·tal·ly** *adv*

dig·ni·fy \'dignə,fī\ *vb* **-fied; -fy·ing** : give dignity or attention to

dig·ni·tary \-,terē\ *n, pl* **-taries** : person of high position

dig·ni·ty \'dignətē\ *n, pl* **-ties 1** : quality or state of being worthy or honored **2** : formal reserve (as of manner)

di·gress \dī'gres, də-\ *vb* : wander from the main subject — **di·gres·sion** \-'greshən\ *n*

dike \'dīk\ *n* : earth bank or dam

di·lap·i·dat·ed \də'lapə,dātəd\ *adj* : fallen into partial ruin — **di·lap·i·da·tion** \-,lapə'dāshən\ *n*

di·late \dī'lāt, 'dī,lāt\ *vb* **-lat·ed; -lat·ing** : swell or expand — **dil·a·ta·tion** \dilə'tāshən\ *n* — **di·la·tion** \dī'lāshən\ *n*

dil·a·to·ry \'dilə,tōrē\ *adj* **1** : delaying **2** : tardy or slow

♦ **di·lem·ma** \də'lemə\ *n* **1** : undesirable choice **2** : predicament

dil·et·tante \'dilə,tänt, -,tant; ,dilə-'tänt, -'tant\ *n, pl* **-tantes** *or* **-tan·ti** \-'täntē, -'tantē\ : one who dabbles in a field of interest

dil·i·gent \'diləjənt\ *adj* : attentive and busy — **dil·i·gence** \-jəns\ *n* — **dil·i·gent·ly** *adv*

dill \'dil\ *n* : herb with aromatic leaves and seeds

dil·ly·dal·ly \'dilē,dalē\ *vb* : waste time by delay

di·lute \dī'lüt, də-\ *vb* **-lut·ed; -lut·ing** : lessen the consistency or strength of by mixing with something else ~ *adj* : weak — **di·lu·tion** \-'lüshən\ *n*

dim \'dim\ *adj* **-mm- 1** : not bright or distinct **2** : having no luster **3** : not seeing or understanding clearly —

dim *vb* — **dim·ly** *adv* — **dim·mer** *n* — **dim·ness** *n*

dime \'dīm\ *n* : U.S. coin worth 1/10 dollar

di·men·sion \də'menchən, dī-\ *n* : measurement of extension (as in length, height, or breadth) **2** : extent — **di·men·sion·al** \-'menchə-nəl\ *adj*

di·min·ish \də'minish\ *vb* **1** : make less or cause to appear less **2** : dwindle

di·min·u·tive \də'minyətiv\ *adj* : extremely small

dim·ple \'dimpəl\ *n* : small depression esp. in the cheek or chin

din \'din\ *n* : loud noise

dine \'dīn\ *vb* **dined; din·ing** : eat dinner

din·er \'dīnər\ *n* **1** : person eating dinner **2** : railroad dining car or restaurant resembling one

din·ghy \'diŋē, -gē, -kē\ *n, pl* **-ghies** : small boat

din·gy \'dinjē\ *adj* **-gi·er; -est 1** : dirty **2** : shabby — **din·gi·ness** *n*

din·ner \'dinər\ *n* : main daily meal

di·no·saur \'dīnə,sȯr\ *n* : extinct often huge reptile

dint \'dint\ *n* : force — in the phrase *by dint of*

di·o·cese \'dīəsəs, -,sēz, -,sēs\ *n, pl* **-ces·es** \-əz, 'dīə,sēz\ : territorial jurisdiction of a bishop — **di·oc·e·san** \dī'äsəsən, ,dīə'sēz°n\ *adj or n*

dip \'dip\ *vb* **-pp- 1** : plunge into a liquid **2** : take out with a ladle **3** : lower and quickly raise again **4** : sink or slope downward suddenly ~ *n* **1** : plunge into water for sport **2** : sudden downward movement or incline — **dip·per** *n*

diph·the·ria \dif'thirēə\ *n* : acute contagious disease

diph·thong \'dif,thȯŋ\ *n* : two vowel sounds joined to form one speech sound (as *ou* in *out*)

di·plo·ma \də'plōmə\ *n, pl* **-mas** : record of graduation from a school

di·plo·ma·cy \-məsē\ *n* 1 : business of conducting negotiations between nations 2 : tact — **dip·lo·mat** \'diplə,mat\ *n* — **dip·lo·mat·ic** \,diplə'matik\ *adj*

dire \'dīr\ *adj* **dir·er; -est** 1 : very horrible 2 : extreme

di·rect \də'rekt, dī-\ *vb* 1 : address 2 : cause to move or to follow a certain course 3 : show (someone) the way 4 : regulate the activities or course of 5 : request with authority ~ *adj* 1 : leading to or coming from a point without deviation or interruption 2 : frank — **direct** *adv* — **di·rect·ly** *adv* — **di·rect·ness** *n* — **di·rec·tor** \-tər\ *n*

direct current *n* : electric current flowing in one direction only

di·rec·tion \də'rekshən, dī-\ *n* 1 : supervision 2 : order 3 : course along which something moves — **di·rec·tion·al** \-shənəl\ *adj*

di·rec·tive \-tiv\ *n* : order

di·rec·to·ry \-tərē\ *n, pl* **-ries** : alphabetical list of names and addresses

dirge \'dərj\ *n* : funeral hymn

di·ri·gi·ble \'dirəjəbəl, də'rijə-\ *n* : airship

dirt \'dərt\ *n* 1 : mud, dust, or grime that makes something unclean 2 : soil

dirty \-ē\ *adj* **dirt·i·er; -est** 1 : not clean 2 : unfair 3 : indecent ~ *vb* **dirt·ied; dirty·ing** : make or become dirty — **dirt·i·ness** *n*

dis·able \dis'ābəl\ *vb* **-abled; -abling** : make unable to function — **dis·abil·i·ty** \,disə'bilətē\ *n*

dis·abuse \,disə'byüz\ *vb* : free from error or misconception

dis·ad·van·tage \,disəd'vantij\ *n* : something that hinders success — **dis·ad·van·ta·geous** *adj*

dis·af·fect \,disə'fekt\ *vb* : cause discontent in — **dis·af·fec·tion** *n*

dis·agree \,disə'grē\ *vb* 1 : fail to agree 2 : differ in opinion — **dis·agree·ment** *n*

dis·agree·able \-əbəl\ *adj* : unpleasant

dis·al·low \,disə'laù\ *vb* : refuse to admit or recognize

dis·ap·pear \,disə'pir\ *vb* 1 : pass out of sight 2 : cease to be — **dis·ap·pear·ance** *n*

dis·ap·point \,disə'pòint\ *vb* : fail to fulfill the expectation or hope of — **dis·ap·point·ment** *n*

dis·ap·prove \-ə'prüv\ *vb* 1 : condemn or reject 2 : feel or express dislike or rejection — **dis·ap·prov·al** *n* — **dis·ap·prov·ing·ly** *adv*

dis·arm \dis'ärm\ *vb* 1 : take weapons from 2 : reduce armed forces 3 : make harmless or friendly — **dis·ar·ma·ment** \-'ärməmənt\ *n*

dis·ar·range \,disə'rānj\ *vb* : throw into disorder — **dis·ar·range·ment** *n*

dis·ar·ray \,disə'rā\ *n* : disorder

di·sas·ter \diz'astər, dis-\ *n* : sudden great misfortune — **di·sas·trous** \-'astrəs\ *adj*

dis·avow \,disə'vaù\ *vb* : deny responsibility for — **dis·avow·al** \-'vaùəl\ *n*

dis·band \dis'band\ *vb* : break up the organization of

dis·bar \dis'bär\ *vb* : expel from the legal profession — **dis·bar·ment** *n*

dis·be·lieve \,disbi'lēv\ *vb* : hold not worthy of belief — **dis·be·lief** *n*

dis·burse \dis'bərs\ *vb* **-bursed; -burs·ing** : pay out — **dis·burse·ment** *n*

disc *var of* DISK

dis·card \dis'kärd, 'dis,kärd\ *vb* : get rid of as unwanted — **dis·card** \'dis,kärd\ *n*

dis·cern \dis'ərn, diz-\ *vb* : discover with the eyes or the mind — **dis·cern·ible** *adj* — **dis·cern·ment** *n*

dis·charge \dis'chärj, 'dis,chärj\ *vb* 1 : unload 2 : shoot 3 : set free 4 : dismiss from service 5 : let go or let off 6 : give forth fluid ~ \'dis,-, dis'-\ *n* 1 : act of discharging 2 : a flowing out (as of blood) 3 : dismissal

dis·ci·ple \di'sīpəl\ *n* : one who helps spread another's teachings

dis·ci·pli·nar·i·an \,disəplə'nerēən\ *n* : one who enforces order

♦ **dis·ci·pline** \'disəplən\ *n* 1 : field of study 2 : training that corrects, molds, or perfects 3 : punishment 4 : control gained by obedience or training ~ *vb* **-plined; -plin·ing** 1 : punish 2 : train in self-control — **dis·ci·plin·ary** \'disəplə,nerē\ *adj*

dis·claim \dis'klām\ *vb* : disavow

dis·close \-'klōz\ *vb* : reveal — **dis·clo·sure** \-'klōzhər\ *n*

dis·col·or \dis'kələr\ *vb* : change the color of esp. for the worse — **dis·col·or·ation** \dis,kələ'rāshən\ *n*

dis·com·fit \dis'kəmfət\ *vb* : upset — **dis·com·fi·ture** \dis'kəmfə-,chùr\ *n*

dis·com·fort \dis'kəmfərt\ *n* : uneasiness

dis·con·cert \,diskən'sərt\ *vb* : upset

dis·con·nect \,diskə'nekt\ *vb* : undo the connection of

dis·con·so·late \dis'känsələt\ *adj* : hopelessly sad

dis·con·tent \,diskən'tent\ *n* : uneasiness of mind — **dis·con·tent·ed** *adj*

dis·con·tin·ue \,diskən'tinyü\ *vb* : end — **dis·con·tin·u·ance** *n* — **dis·con·ti·nu·i·ty** \dis,käntə-'nüətē, -'nyü-\ *n* — **dis·con·tin·u·ous** \,diskən'tinyəwəs\ *adj*

dis·cord \'dis,kórd\ *n* : lack of harmony — **dis·cor·dant** \dis-'kórdᵊnt\ *adj* — **dis·cor·dant·ly** *adv*

dis·count \'dis,kaùnt\ *n* : reduction from a regular price ∼ \'dis,-, dis'-\ *vb* 1 : reduce the amount of 2 : disregard — **discount** *adj* — **dis·count·er** *n*

dis·cour·age \dis'kərij\ *vb* -aged; -ag·ing 1 : deprive of courage, confidence, or enthusiasm 2 : dissuade — **dis·cour·age·ment** *n*

dis·course \'dis,kórs\ *n* 1 : conversation 2 : formal treatment of a subject ∼ \dis'-\ *vb* -coursed; -cours·ing : talk at length

dis·cour·te·ous \dis'kərtēəs\ *adj* : lacking courtesy — **dis·cour·te·ous·ly** *adv* — **dis·cour·te·sy** *n*

dis·cov·er \dis'kəvər\ *vb* 1 : make known 2 : obtain the first sight or knowledge of 3 : find out — **dis·cov·er·er** *n* — **dis·cov·ery** \-ərē\ *n*

dis·cred·it \dis'kredət\ *vb* 1 : disbelieve 2 : destroy confidence in ∼ *n* 1 : loss of reputation 2 : disbelief — **dis·cred·it·able** *adj*

dis·creet \dis'krēt\ *adj* : capable of keeping a secret — **dis·creet·ly** *adv*

dis·crep·an·cy \dis'krepənsē\ *n, pl* -cies : difference or disagreement

dis·crete \dis'krēt, 'dis,-\ *adj* : individually distinct

dis·cre·tion \dis'kreshən\ *n* 1 : discreet quality 2 : power of decision or choice — **dis·cre·tion·ary** *adj*

dis·crim·i·nate \dis'krimə,nāt\ *vb* -nat·ed; -nat·ing 1 : distinguish 2 : show favor or disfavor unjustly — **dis·crim·i·na·tion** \-,krimə-'nāshən\ *n* — **dis·crim·i·na·to·ry** \-'krimənə,tōrē\ *adj*

dis·cur·sive \dis'kərsiv\ *adj* : passing from one topic to another — **dis·cur·sive·ly** *adv* — **dis·cur·sive·ness** *n*

dis·cus \'diskəs\ *n, pl* -cus·es : disk hurled for distance in a contest

dis·cuss \dis'kəs\ *vb* : talk about or present — **dis·cus·sion** \-'kəshən\ *n*

dis·dain \dis'dān\ *n* : feeling of contempt ∼ *vb* : look upon or reject with disdain — **dis·dain·ful** \-fəl\ *adj* — **dis·dain·ful·ly** *adv*

dis·ease \di'zēz\ *n* : condition of a body that impairs its functioning — **dis·eased** \-'zēzd\ *adj*

dis·em·bark \,disəm'bärk\ *vb* : get off a ship — **dis·em·bar·ka·tion** \dis,em,bär'kāshən\ *n*

dis·em·bod·ied \,disəm'bädēd\ *adj* : having no substance or reality

dis·en·chant \,disᵊn'chant\ *vb* : to free from illusion — **dis·en·chant·ment** *n*

dis·en·chant·ed \-'chantəd\ *adj* : disappointed

dis·en·gage \-ᵊn'gāj\ *vb* : release — **dis·en·gage·ment** *n*

(SIGH)

(ANYBODY CAN EXERCISE...)

BUT THIS KIND OF LETHARGY TAKES **REAL** DISCIPLINE.

10-18   JIM DAVIS

dis·en·tan·gle \-ᵊn'taŋgəl\ *vb* : free from entanglement

dis·fa·vor \dis'fāvər\ *n* : disapproval

dis·fig·ure \dis'figyər\ *vb* : spoil the appearance of — **dis·fig·ure·ment** *n*

dis·fran·chise \dis'fran,chīz\ *vb* : deprive of the right to vote — **dis·fran·chise·ment** *n*

dis·gorge \dis'górj\ *vb* : spew forth

dis·grace \dis'grās\ *vb* : bring disgrace to ∼ *n* **1** : shame **2** : cause of shame — **dis·grace·ful** \-fəl\ *adj* — **dis·grace·ful·ly** *adv*

dis·grun·tle \dis'grəntᵊl\ *vb* **-tled; -tling** : put in bad humor

dis·guise \dis'gīz\ *vb* **-guised; -guis·ing** : hide the true identity or nature of ∼ *n* : something that conceals

dis·gust \dis'gəst\ *n* : strong aversion ∼ *vb* : provoke disgust in — **dis·gust·ed·ly** *adv* — **dis·gust·ing·ly** *adv*

dish \'dish\ *n* **1** : vessel for serving food or the food it holds **2** : food prepared in a particular way ∼ *vb* : put in a dish — **dish·cloth** *n* — **dish·rag** *n* — **dish·wash·er** *n* — **dish·wa·ter** *n*

dis·har·mo·ny \dis'härmənē\ *n* : lack of harmony — **dis·har·mo·ni·ous** \dishär'mōnēəs\ *adj*

dis·heart·en \dis'härtᵊn\ *vb* : discourage

di·shev·el \di'shevəl\ *vb* **-eled** *or* **-elled; -el·ing** *or* **-el·ling** : throw into disorder — **di·shev·eled, di·shev·elled** *adj*

dis·hon·est \dis'änəst\ *adj* : not honest — **dis·hon·est·ly** *adv* — **dis·hon·es·ty** *n*

dis·hon·or \dis'änər\ *n or vb* : disgrace — **dis·hon·or·able** *adj* — **dis·hon·or·ably** *adv*

dis·il·lu·sion \disə'lüzhən\ *vb* : to free from illusion — **dis·il·lu·sion·ment** *n*

dis·in·cli·na·tion \dis,inklə'nāshən\ *n* : slight aversion — **dis·in·cline** \disᵊn'klīn\ *vb*

dis·in·fect \disᵊn'fekt\ *vb* : destroy disease germs in or on — **dis·in·fec·tant** \-'fektənt\ *adj or n* — **dis·in·fec·tion** \-'fekshən\ *n*

dis·in·gen·u·ous \disᵊn'jenyəwəs\ *adj* : lacking in candor

dis·in·her·it \-ᵊn'herət\ *vb* : prevent from inheriting property

dis·in·te·grate \dis'intə,grāt\ *vb* : break into parts or small bits — **dis·in·te·gra·tion** \dis,intə'grāshən\ *n*

dis·in·ter·est·ed \dis'intərəstəd, -,res-\ *adj* **1** : not interested **2** : not prejudiced — **dis·in·ter·est·ed·ness** *n*

dis·joint·ed \dis'jóintəd\ *adj* **1** : separated at the joint **2** : incoherent

disk \'disk\ *n* : something round and flat

dis·like \dis'līk\ *vb* : regard with dislike ∼ *n* : feeling that something is unpleasant and to be avoided

dis·lo·cate \'dislō,kāt, dis'-\ *vb* : move out of the usual or proper place — **dis·lo·ca·tion** \dislō'kāshən\ *n*

dis·lodge \dis'läj\ *vb* : force out of a place

dis·loy·al \dis'lóiəl\ *adj* : not loyal — **dis·loy·al·ty** *n*

dis·mal \'dizməl\ *adj* : showing or causing gloom — **dis·mal·ly** *adv*

dis·man·tle \dis'mantᵊl\ *vb* **-tled; -tling** : take apart

dis·may \dis'mā\ *vb* **-mayed; -may·ing** : discourage — **dismay** *n*

dis·mem·ber \dis'membər\ *vb* : cut into pieces — **dis·mem·ber·ment** *n*

dis·miss \dis'mis\ *vb* **1** : send away **2** : remove from service **3** : put aside or out of mind — **dis·miss·al** *n*

dis·mount \dis'maúnt\ *vb* **1** : get down from something **2** : take apart

dis·obey \disə'bā\ *vb* : refuse to obey — **dis·obe·di·ence** \-'bēdēəns\ *n* — **dis·obe·di·ent** \-ənt\ *adj*

dis·or·der \dis'órdər\ *n* **1** : lack of order **2** : breach of public order **3** : abnormal state of body or mind — **disorder** *vb* — **dis·or·der·li·ness** *n* — **dis·or·der·ly** *adj*

dis·or·ga·nize \dis'órgə,nīz\ *vb* : throw into disorder — **dis·or·ga·ni·za·tion** *n*

dis·own \dis'ōn\ *vb* : repudiate

dis·par·age \-'parij\ *vb* **-aged; -ag·ing** : say bad things about — **dis·par·age·ment** *n*

dis·pa·rate \dis'parət, 'dispərət\ *adj* : different in quality or character — **dis·par·i·ty** \dis'parətē\ *n*

dis·pas·sion·ate \dis'pashənət\ *adj*

: not influenced by strong feeling
— **dis·pas·sion·ate·ly** adv

dis·patch \dis'pach\ vb 1 : send 2
: kill 3 : attend to rapidly 4 : defeat
~ n 1 : message 2 : news item
from a correspondent 3 : prompt-
ness and efficiency — **dis·patch-
er** n

dis·pel \dis'pel\ vb **-ll-** : clear away

dis·pen·sa·ry \-'pensərē\ n, pl **-ries**
: place where medical or dental
aid is provided

dis·pen·sa·tion \dispən'sāshən\ n 1
: system of principles or rules 2
: exemption from a rule 3 : act of
dispensing

dis·pense \dis'pens\ vb **-pensed;
-pens·ing** 1 : portion out 2 : make
up and give out (remedies) — **dis-
pens·er** n — **dispense with** : do
without

dis·perse \-'pərs\ vb **-persed; -pers-
ing** : scatter — **dis·per·sal**
\-'pərsəl\ n — **dis·per·sion**
\-'perzhən\ n

dis·place \-'plās\ vb 1 : expel or
force to flee from home or native
land 2 : take the place of — **dis-
place·ment** \-mənt\ n

dis·play \-'plā\ vb : present to view
— **display** n

dis·please \-'plēz\ vb : arouse the
dislike of — **dis·plea·sure**
\-'plezhər\ n

dis·port \dis'pōrt\ vb 1 : amuse 2
: frolic

dis·pose \dis'pōz\ vb **-posed; -pos-
ing** 1 : give a tendency to 2 : settle
— **dis·pos·able** \-'pōzəbəl\ adj —
dis·pos·al \-'pōzəl\ n — **dis·pos-
er** n — **dispose of** 1 : determine the
fate, condition, or use of 2 : get rid
of

dis·po·si·tion \dispə'zishən\ n 1
: act or power of disposing of 2
: arrangement 3 : natural attitude

dis·pos·sess \dispə'zes\ vb : deprive
of possession or occupancy — **dis-
pos·ses·sion** \-'zeshən\ n

dis·pro·por·tion \disprə'pōrshən\ n
: lack of proportion — **dis·pro-
por·tion·ate** \-shənət\ adj

dis·prove \dis'prüv\ vb : prove false
— **dis·proof** n

dis·pute \dis'pyüt\ vb **-put·ed; -put-
ing** 1 : argue 2 : deny the truth or
rightness of 3 : struggle against or
over ~ n : debate or quarrel —
dis·put·able \-əbəl, 'dispyət-\ adj

dis·pu·ta·tion \dispyə'tāshən\
n

dis·qual·i·fy \dis'kwälə,fī\ vb
: make ineligible — **dis·qual·i-
fi·ca·tion** n

dis·qui·et \dis'kwīət\ vb : make uneasy or restless ~ n : anxiety

dis·re·gard \disri'gärd\ vb : pay no
attention to ~ n : neglect

dis·re·pair \disri'par\ n : need of
repair

dis·rep·u·ta·ble \dis'repyətəbəl\ adj
: having a bad reputation

dis·re·pute \disri'pyüt\ n : low regard

dis·re·spect \disri'spekt\ n : lack of
respect — **dis·re·spect·ful** adj

dis·robe \dis'rōb\ vb : undress

dis·rupt \dis'rəpt\ vb : throw into
disorder — **dis·rup·tion** \-'rəp-
shən\ n — **dis·rup·tive** \-'rəptiv\
adj

dis·sat·is·fac·tion \dis,satəs'fak-
shən\ n : lack of satisfaction

dis·sat·is·fy \dis'satəs,fī\ vb : fail to
satisfy

dis·sect \di'sekt\ vb : cut into parts
esp. to examine — **dis·sec·tion**
\-'sekshən\ n

dis·sem·ble \di'sembəl\ vb **-bled;
-bling** : disguise feelings or intention — **dis·sem·bler** n

dis·sem·i·nate \di'semə,nāt\ vb
-nat·ed; -nat·ing : spread around
— **dis·sem·i·na·tion** \-,semə-
'nāshən\ n

dis·sen·sion \di'senchən\ n : discord

dis·sent \di'sent\ vb : object or disagree ~ n : difference of opinion
— **dis·sent·er** n — **dis·sen·tient**
\-'senchənt\ adj or n

dis·ser·ta·tion \disər'tāshən\ n
: long written study of a subject

dis·ser·vice \dis'sərvəs\ n : injury

dis·si·dent \'disədənt\ n : one who
differs openly with an establishment — **dis·si·dence** \-əns\ n —
dissident adj

dis·sim·i·lar \di'simələr\ adj : different — **dis·sim·i·lar·i·ty** \di-
,simə'larətē\ n

dis·si·pate \'disə,pāt\ vb **-pat·ed;
-pat·ing** 1 : break up and drive off
2 : squander — **dis·si·pa·tion**
\disə'pāshən\ n

dis·so·ci·ate \dis'ōsē,āt, -shē-\ vb
-at·ed; -at·ing : separate from as-

sociation — **dis·so·ci·a·tion** \dis-ˌōsē'āshən, -shē-\ n

dis·so·lute \'disə,lüt\ adj : loose in morals or conduct

dis·so·lu·tion \ˌdisə'lüshən\ n : act or process of dissolving

dis·solve \di'zälv\ vb 1 : break up or bring to an end 2 : pass or cause to pass into solution

dis·so·nance \'disənəns\ n : discord — **dis·so·nant** \-nənt\ adj

dis·suade \di'swād\ vb -suad·ed; -suad·ing : persuade not to do something — **dis·sua·sion** \-'swāzhən\ n

dis·tance \'distəns\ n 1 : measure of separation in space or time 2 : reserve

dis·tant \-tənt\ adj 1 : separate in space 2 : remote in time, space, or relationship 3 : reserved — **dis·tant·ly** adv

dis·taste \dis'tāst\ n : dislike — **dis·taste·ful** adj

dis·tem·per \dis'tempər\ n : serious virus disease of dogs

dis·tend \dis'tend\ vb : swell out — **dis·ten·sion, dis·ten·tion** \-'tenchən\ n

dis·till \di'stil\ vb : obtain by distillation — **dis·til·late** \'distə,lāt, -lət\ n — **dis·till·er** n — **dis·till·ery** \di'stilərē\ n

dis·til·la·tion \ˌdistə'lāshən\ n : purification of liquid by evaporating then condensing

dis·tinct \dis'tiŋkt\ adj 1 : distinguishable from others 2 : readily discerned — **dis·tinc·tive** \-tiv\ adj — **dis·tinc·tive·ly** adv — **dis·tinc·tive·ness** n — **dis·tinct·ly** adv — **dis·tinct·ness** n

dis·tinc·tion \-'tiŋkshən\ n 1 : act of distinguishing 2 : difference 3 : special recognition

dis·tin·guish \-'tiŋgwish\ vb 1 : perceive as different 2 : set apart 3

: discern 4 : make outstanding — **dis·tin·guish·able** adj — **dis·tin·guished** \-gwisht\ adj

dis·tort \dis'tòrt\ vb : twist out of shape, condition, or true meaning — **dis·tor·tion** \-'tòrshən\ n

dis·tract \di'strakt\ vb : divert the mind or attention of — **dis·trac·tion** \-'strakshən\ n

dis·traught \dis'tròt\ adj : agitated with mental conflict

dis·tress \-'tres\ n 1 : suffering 2 : misfortune 3 : state of danger or great need ~ vb : subject to strain or distress — **dis·tress·ful** adj

dis·trib·ute \-'tribyət\ vb -ut·ed; -ut·ing 1 : divide among many 2 : spread or hand out — **dis·tri·bu·tion** \ˌdistrə'byüshən\ n — **dis·trib·u·tive** \dis'tribyətiv\ adj — **dis·trib·u·tor** \-ər\ n

dis·trict \'dis,trikt\ n : territorial division

dis·trust \dis'trəst\ vb or n : mistrust — **dis·trust·ful** \-fəl\ adj

dis·turb \dis'tərb\ vb 1 : interfere with 2 : destroy the peace, composure, or order of — **dis·tur·bance** \-'tərbəns\ n — **dis·turb·er** n

dis·use \dis'yüs\ n : lack of use

ditch \'dich\ n : trench ~ vb 1 : dig a ditch in 2 : get rid of

dith·er \'dithər\ n : highly nervous or excited state

dit·to \'ditō\ n, pl -tos : more of the same

dit·ty \'ditē\ n, pl -ties : short simple song

di·uret·ic \ˌdīyu'retik\ adj : tending to increase urine flow — **diuretic** n

di·ur·nal \dī'ərn²l\ adj 1 : daily 2 : of or occurring in the daytime

di·van \'dī,van, di'-\ n : couch

♦ **dive** \'dīv\ vb **dived** \'dīvd\ or **dove** \'dōv\; **dived; div·ing** 1 : plunge into water headfirst 2

: submerge **3** : descend quickly ∼
n 1 : act of diving **2** : sharp decline
— **div·er** n

di·verge \də'vərj, dī-\ vb **-verged;**
-verg·ing 1 : move in different directions **2** : differ — **di·ver·gence**
\-'vərjəns\ n — **di·ver·gent** \-jənt\
adj

di·vers \'dīvərz\ adj : various

di·verse \dī'vərs, də-, 'dī,vərs\ adj
: involving different forms — **di·ver·si·fi·ca·tion** \də,vərsəfə'kāshən, dī-\ n — **di·ver·si·fy** \-'vərsə-
,fī\ vb — **di·ver·si·ty** \-sətē\ n

di·vert \də'vərt, dī-\ vb 1 : turn from
a course or purpose **2** : distract **3**
: amuse — **di·ver·sion** \-'vərzhən\
n

di·vest \dī'vest, də-\ vb : strip of
clothing, possessions, or rights

di·vide \də'vīd\ vb **-vid·ed; -vid·ing 1** : separate **2** : distribute
3 : share **4** : subject to mathematical division ∼ n : watershed —
di·vid·er n

div·i·dend \'divə,dend\ n **1** : individual share **2** : bonus **3** : number to
be divided

div·i·na·tion \,divə'nāshən\ n
: practice of trying to foretell future events

di·vine \də'vīn\ adj **-vin·er; -est 1**
: relating to or being God or a god
2 : supremely good ∼ n : clergy
member ∼ vb **-vined; -vin·ing 1**
: infer **2** : prophesy — **di·vine·ly** adv — **di·vin·er** n — **di·vin·i·ty** \də'vinətē\ n

di·vis·i·ble \-'vizəbəl\ adj : capable
of being divided — **di·vis·i·bil·i·ty** \-,vizə'bilətē\ n

di·vi·sion \-'vizhən\ n **1** : distribution **2** : part of a whole **3** : disagreement **4** : process of finding
out how many times one number
is contained in another

di·vi·sive \də'vīsiv, -'vi-, -ziv\ adj
: creating dissension

di·vi·sor \-'vīzər\ n : number by
which a dividend is divided

di·vorce \də'vōrs\ n : legal breaking
up of a marriage — **divorce** vb

di·vor·cée \-,vōr'sā, -'sē\ n : divorced woman

di·vulge \də'vəlj, dī-\ vb **-vulged;**
-vulg·ing : reveal

diz·zy \'dizē\ adj **-zi·er; -est 1** : having a sensation of whirling **2**

: causing or caused by giddiness
— **diz·zi·ly** adv — **diz·zi·ness** n

DNA \,dē,en'ā\ n : compound in
cell nuclei that is the basis of heredity

do \'dü\ vb **did** \'did\; **done** \'dən\
do·ing \'düiŋ\; **does** \'dəz\ **1**
: work to accomplish (an action or
task) **2** : behave **3** : prepare or fix
up **4** : fare **5** : finish **6** : serve the
needs or purpose of **7** — used as
an auxiliary verb — **do away with
1** : get rid of **2** : destroy — **do by**
: deal with — **do·er** \'düər\ n —
do in vb **1** : ruin **2** : kill

doc·ile \'däsəl\ adj : easily managed
— **do·cil·i·ty** \dä'silətē\ n

¹**dock** \'däk\ vb **1** : shorten **2** : reduce

²**dock** n **1** : berth between 2 piers to
receive ships **2** : loading wharf or
platform ∼ vb : bring or come
into dock — **dock·work·er** n

³**dock** n : place in a court for a prisoner

dock·et \'däkət\ n **1** : record of the
proceedings in a legal action **2**
: list of legal causes to be tried —
docket vb

doc·tor \'däktər\ n **1** : person holding one of the highest academic
degrees **2** : one (as a surgeon)
skilled in healing arts ∼ vb **1** : give
medical treatment to **2** : repair or
alter — **doc·tor·al** \-tərəl\ adj

doc·trine \'däktrən\ n : something
taught — **doc·tri·nal** \-trən°l\ adj

doc·u·ment \'däkyəmənt\ n : paper
that furnishes information or legal
proof — **doc·u·ment** \-,ment\ vb
— **doc·u·men·ta·tion** \,däkyəmən-
'tāshən\ n — **doc·u·ment·er** n

doc·u·men·ta·ry \,däkyə'mentərē\
adj **1** : of or relating to documents
2 : giving a factual presentation —
documentary n

dod·der \'dädər\ vb : become feeble
usu. from age

dodge \'däj\ vb **dodged; dodg·ing 1**
: move quickly aside or out of the
way of **2** : evade — **dodge** n

do·do \'dōdō\ n, pl **-does** or **-dos 1**
: heavy flightless extinct bird **2**
: stupid person

doe \'dō\ n, pl **does** or **doe** : adult female deer — **doe·skin** \-,skin\ n

does pres 3d sing of DO

doff \'däf\ vb : remove

dog \'dóg\ n : flesh-eating domestic
mammal ∼ vb **1** : hunt down or

track like a hound **2** : harass — **dog·catch·er** n — **dog·gy** \-ē\ n or *adj* — **dog·house** n

dog–ear \'dȯg,ir\ n : turned-down corner of a page — **dog–ear** *vb* — **dog–eared** \-,ird\ *adj*

dog·ged \'dȯgəd\ *adj* : stubbornly determined

dog·ma \'dȯgmə\ n : tenet or code of tenets

dog·ma·tism \-,tizəm\ n : unwarranted stubbornness of opinion — **dog·ma·tic** \dȯg'matik\ *adj*

dog·wood n : flowering tree

doi·ly \'dȯilē\ n, pl **-lies** : small decorative mat

do·ings \'düiŋz\ n pl : events

dol·drums \'dōldrəmz,'däl-\ n pl : spell of listlessness, despondency, or stagnation

dole \'dōl\ n : distribution esp. of money to the needy or unemployed — **dole out** *vb* : give out esp. in small portions

dole·ful \'dōlfəl\ *adj* : sad — **dole·ful·ly** *adv*

doll \'däll, 'dȯl\ n : small figure of a person used esp. as a child's toy

dol·lar \'dälər\ n : any of various basic monetary units (as in the U.S. and Canada)

dol·ly \'dälē\ n, pl **-lies** : small cart or wheeled platform

dol·phin \'dälfən\ n **1** : sea mammal related to the whales **2** : saltwater food fish

dolt \'dōlt\ n : stupid person — **dolt·ish** *adj*

-dom \dəm\ n *suffix* **1** : office or realm **2** : state or fact of being **3** : those belonging to a group

do·main \dō'mān, də-\ n **1** : territory over which someone reigns **2** : sphere of activity or knowledge

dome \'dōm\ n **1** : large hemispherical roof **2** : roofed stadium

do·mes·tic \də'mestik\ *adj* **1** : relating to the household or family **2** : relating and limited to one's own country **3** : tame — n : household servant — **do·mes·ti·cal·ly** \-tik-lē\ *adv*

do·mes·ti·cate \-ti,kāt\ *vb* **-cat·ed; -cat·ing** : tame — **do·mes·ti·ca·tion** \-,mesti'kāshən\ n

do·mi·cile \'dämə,sīl, 'dō-; 'däm-əsəl\ n : home — **domicile** *vb*

dom·i·nance \'dämənəns\ n : control — **dom·i·nant** \-nənt\ *adj*

dom·i·nate \-,nāt\ *vb* **-nat·ed; -nat·ing** **1** : have control over **2** : rise high above — **dom·i·na·tion** \,dämə'nāshən\ n

dom·i·neer \,dämə'nir\ *vb* : exercise arbitrary control

do·min·ion \də'minyən\ n **1** : supreme authority **2** : governed territory

dom·i·no \'dämə,nō\ n, pl **-noes** or **-nos** : flat rectangular block used as a piece in a game (**dominoes**)

don \'dän\ *vb* **-nn-** : put on (clothes)

do·nate \'dō,nāt\ *vb* **-nat·ed; -nat·ing** : make a gift of — **do·na·tion** \dō'nāshən\ n

¹done \'dən\ *past part of* DO

²done *adj* **1** : finished or ended **2** : cooked sufficiently

don·key \'däŋkē, 'dəŋ-\ n, pl **-keys** : sturdy domestic ass

do·nor \'dōnər\ n : one that gives

doo·dle \'düd⁰l\ *vb* **-dled; -dling** : draw or scribble aimlessly — **doodle** n

doom \'düm\ n **1** : judgment **2** : fate **3** : ruin — **doom** *vb*

door \'dōr\ n : passage for entrance or a movable barrier that can open or close such a passage — **door·jamb** n — **door·knob** n — **door·mat** n — **door·step** n — **door·way** n

dope \'dōp\ **1** : narcotic preparation **2** : stupid person **3** : information $\sim$ *vb* **doped; dop·ing** : drug

dor·mant \'dȯrmənt\ *adj* : not actively growing or functioning — **dor·man·cy** \-mənsē\ n

dor·mer \'dȯrmər\ n : window built upright in a sloping roof

dor·mi·to·ry \'dȯrmə,tōrē\ n, pl **-ries** : residence hall (as at a college)

dor·mouse \'dȯr,maús\ n : squirrellike rodent

dor·sal \'dȯrsəl\ *adj* : relating to or on the back — **dor·sal·ly** *adv*

do·ry \'dōrē\ n, pl **-ries** : flat-bottomed boat

dose \'dōs\ n : quantity (as of medicine) taken at one time $\sim$ *vb* **dosed; dos·ing** : give medicine to — **dos·age** \'dōsij\ n

dot \'dät\ n **1** : small spot **2** : small round mark made with or as if with a pen ~ *vb* **-tt-** : mark with dots

dot·age \'dōtij\ *n* : senility

dote \'dōt\ *vb* **dot·ed; dot·ing 1** : act feebleminded or foolish **2** : be foolishly fond

dou·ble \'dəbəl\ *adj* **1** : consisting of 2 members or parts **2** : being twice as great or as many **3** : folded in two ~ *n* **1** : something twice another **2** : one that resembles another ~ *adv* : doubly ~ *vb* **-bled; -bling 1** : make or become twice as great **2** : fold or bend **3** : clench

dou·ble–cross *vb* : deceive by trickery — **dou·ble–cross·er** *n*

dou·bly \'dəblē\ *adv* : to twice the degree

doubt \'daút\ *vb* **1** : be uncertain about **2** : mistrust **3** : consider unlikely ~ *n* **1** : uncertainty **2** : mistrust **3** : inclination not to believe — **doubt·ful** \-fəl\ *adj* — **doubt·ful·ly** *adv* — **doubt·less** \-ləs\ *adv*

douche \'düsh\ *n* : jet of fluid for cleaning a body part

dough \'dō\ *n* : stiff mixture of flour and liquid — **doughy** \'dōē\ *adj*

dough·nut \-,nət\ *n* : small fried ring-shaped cake

dough·ty \'daútē\ *adj* **-ti·er; -est** : able, strong, or valiant

dour \'daúər, 'dúr\ *adj* **1** : severe **2** : gloomy or sullen — **dour·ly** *adv*

douse \'daús, 'daúz\ *vb* **doused; dous·ing 1** : plunge into or drench with water **2** : extinguish

¹dove \'dəv\ *n* : small wild pigeon

²dove \'dōv\ *past of* DIVE

dove·tail \'dəv,tāl\ *vb* : fit together neatly

dow·a·ger \'daúijər\ *n* **1** : widow with wealth or a title **2** : dignified elderly woman

dowdy \'daúdē\ *adj* **dowd·i·er; -est** : lacking neatness and charm

dow·el \'daúəl\ *n* **1** : peg used for fastening two pieces **2** : wooden rod

dow·er \'daúər\ *n* : property given a widow for life ~ *vb* : supply with a dower

¹down \'daún\ *adv* **1** : toward or in a lower position or state **2** : to a lying or sitting position **3** : as a cash deposit **4** : on paper ~ *adj* **1** : lying on the ground **2** : directed or going downward **3** : being at a low level ~ *prep* : toward the bottom of ~ *vb* **1** : cause to go down **2** : defeat

²down *n* : fluffy feathers

down·cast *adj* **1** : sad **2** : directed down

down·fall *n* : ruin or cause of ruin

down·grade *n* : downward slope ~ *vb* : lower in grade or position

down·heart·ed *adj* : sad

down·pour *n* : heavy rain

down·right *adv* : thoroughly ~ *adj* : absolute or thorough

downs \'daúnz\ *n pl* : rolling treeless uplands

down·size \'daún,sīz\ *vb* : reduce in size

down·stairs *adv* : on or to a lower floor and esp. the main floor — **downstairs** *adj or n*

down–to–earth *adj* : practical

down·town *adv* : to, toward, or in the business center of a town — **downtown** *n or adj*

down·trod·den \'daún,träd°n\ *adj* : suffering oppression

down·ward \'daúnwərd\; **down·wards** \-wərdz\ *adv* : to a lower place or condition — **downward** *adj*

down·wind *adv or adj* : in the direction the wind is blowing

downy \'daúnē\ *adj* **-i·er; -est** : resem·bling or covered with down

dow·ry \'daúrē\ *n, pl* **-ries** : property a woman gives her husband in marriage

dox·ol·o·gy \däk'säləjē\ *n, pl* **-gies** : hymn of praise to God

doze \'dōz\ *vb* **dozed; doz·ing** : sleep lightly — **doze** *n*

doz·en \'dəz°n\ *n, pl* **-ens** *or* **-en** : group of 12 — **doz·enth** \-°nth\ *adj*

drab \'drab\ *adj* **-bb-** : dull — **drab·ly** *adv* — **drab·ness** *n*

dra·co·ni·an \drā'kōnēən, dra-\ *adj, often cap* : harsh, cruel

draft \'draft, 'dráft\ *n* **1** : act of drawing or hauling **2** : act of drinking **3** : amount drunk at once **4** : preliminary outline or rough sketch **5** : selection from a pool or the selection process **6** : order for the payment of money **7** : air current ~ *vb* **1** : select usu. on a compulsory basis **2** : make a preliminary sketch, version, or plan of ~ *adj* : drawn from a container —

draft·ee \draf'tē, dråf-\ n —
drafty \'draftē\ adj
drafts·man \'draftsmən, 'dråft-\ n
: person who draws plans
◆ **drag** \'drag\ n 1 : something
dragged over a surface or through
water 2 : something that hinders
progress or is boring 3 : act or an
instance of dragging ~ vb -gg- 1
: haul 2 : move or work with difficulty 3 : pass slowly 4 : search or
fish with a drag — **drag·ger** n
drag·net \-,net\ n 1 : trawl 2
: planned actions for finding a
criminal
dra·gon \'dragən\ n : fabled winged
serpent
drag·on·fly n : large 4-winged insect
drain \'drān\ vb 1 : draw off or flow
off gradually or completely 2 : exhaust ~ n : means or act of draining — **drain·age** \-ij\ n — **drain-
er** n — **drain·pipe** n
drake \'drāk\ n : male duck
dra·ma \'dråmə, 'dram-\ n 1 : composition for theatrical presentation esp. on a serious subject 2
: series of events involving con-
flicting forces — **dra·mat·ic** \drə-
'matik\ adj — **dra·mat·i·cal·ly**
\-iklē\ adv — **dram·a·tist**
\'dramətist, 'dräm-\ n — **dram-
a·ti·za·tion** \,dramətə'zāshən,
,dräm-\ n — **dra·ma·tize** \'dramə-
,tīz, 'dräm-\ vb
drank past of DRINK
drape \'dråp\ vb **draped; drap-
ing** 1 : cover or adorn with folds of
cloth 2 : cause to hang in flowing
lines or folds ~ n : curtain
drap·ery \'dråpərē\ n, pl **-er·ies**
: decorative fabric hung esp. as a
heavy curtain
dras·tic \'drastik\ adj : extreme or
harsh — **dras·ti·cal·ly** \-tiklē\ adj
draught \'dråft\, **draughty** \'dråftē\
chiefly Brit var of DRAFT, DRAFTY

draw \'drò\ vb **drew** \'drü\; **drawn**
\'dròn\; **draw·ing** 1 : move or
cause to move (as by pulling) 2
: attract or provoke 3 : extract 4
: take or receive (as money) 5
: bend a bow in preparation for
shooting 6 : leave a contest undecided 7 : sketch 8 : write out 9 : deduce ~ n 1 : act, process, or result
of drawing 2 : tie — **draw out**
: cause to speak candidly — **draw
up** 1 : write out 2 : pull oneself
erect 3 : bring or come to a stop
draw·back n : disadvantage
draw·bridge n : bridge that can be
raised
draw·er \'dròr, 'dròər\ n 1 : one that
draws 2 : sliding boxlike compartment 3 pl : underpants
draw·ing \'dròiŋ\ n 1 : occasion of
choosing by lot 2 : act or art of
making a figure, plan, or sketch
with lines 3 : something drawn
drawl \'dròl\ vb : speak slowly —
drawl n
dread \'dred\ vb : feel extreme fear
or reluctance ~ n : great fear ~
adj : causing dread — **dread·ful**
\-fəl\ adj — **dread·ful·ly** adv
◆ **dream** \'drēm\ n 1 : series of
thoughts or visions during sleep 2
: dreamlike vision 3 : something
notable 4 : ideal ~ vb **dreamed**
\'dremt, 'drēmd\ or **dreamt**
\'dremt\; **dream·ing** 1 : have a
dream 2 : imagine — **dream·er** n
— **dream·like** adj — **dreamy** adj
drea·ry \'drirē\ adj **-ri·er; -est** : dismal — **drea·ri·ly** \'drirəlē\ adv
¹**dredge** \'drej\ n : machine for removing earth esp. from under water ~ vb **dredged; dredg·ing** : dig
up or search with a dredge —
dredg·er n
²**dredge** vb **dredged; dredg·ing** : coat
(food) with flour

dregs \'dregz\ *n pl* **1** : sediment **2** : most worthless part

drench \'drench\ *vb* : wet thoroughly

dress \'dres\ *vb* **1** : put clothes on **2** : decorate **3** : prepare (as a carcass) for use **4** : apply dressings, remedies, or fertilizer to ~ *n* **1** : apparel **2** : single garment of bodice and skirt ~ *adj* : suitable for a formal event — **dress·mak·er** *n* — **dress·mak·ing** *n*

dress·er \'dresər\ *n* : bureau with a mirror

dress·ing *n* **1** : act or process of dressing **2** : sauce or a seasoned mixture **3** : material to cover an injury

dressy \'dresē\ *adj* **dress·i·er; -est 1** : showy in dress **2** : stylish

drew *past of* DRAW

drib·ble \'dribəl\ *vb* **-bled; -bling 1** : fall or flow in drops **2** : drool — **dribble** *n*

drier *comparative of* DRY

driest *superlative of* DRY

drift \'drift\ *n* **1** : motion or course of something drifting **2** : mass piled up by wind **3** : general intention or meaning ~ *vb* **1** : float or be driven along (as by a current) **2** : wander without purpose **3** : pile up under force — **drift·er** *n* — **drift·wood** *n*

¹**drill** \'dril\ *vb* **1** : bore with a drill **2** : instruct by repetition ~ *n* **1** : tool for boring holes **2** : regularly practiced exercise — **drill·er** *n*

²**drill** *n* : seed-planting implement

³**drill** *n* : twill-weave cotton fabric

drily *var of* DRYLY

drink \'driŋk\ *vb* **drank** \'draŋk\; **drunk** \'drəŋk\ *or* **drank; drink·ing 1** : swallow liquid **2** : absorb **3** : drink alcoholic beverages esp. to excess ~ *n* **1** : beverage **2** : alcoholic liquor — **drink·able** *adj* — **drink·er** *n*

drip \'drip\ *vb* **-pp-** : fall or let fall in drops ~ *n* **1** : a dripping **2** : sound of falling drops

drive \'drīv\ *vb* **drove** \'drōv\; **driv·en** \'drivən\; **driv·ing 1** : urge or force onward **2** : direct the movement or course of **3** : compel **4** : cause to become **5** : propel forcefully ~ *n* **1** : trip in a vehicle **2** : intensive campaign **3** : aggressive or dynamic quality **4** : basic need — **driv·er** *n*

drive–in *adj* : accommodating patrons in cars — **drive–in** *n*

driv·el \'drivəl\ *vb* **-eled** *or* **-elled; -el·ing** *or* **-el·ling 1** : drool **2** : talk stupidly ~ *n* : nonsense

drive·way *n* : usu. short private road from the street to a house

driz·zle \'drizəl\ *n* : fine misty rain — **drizzle** *vb*

droll \'drōl\ *adj* : humorous or whimsical — **droll·ery** *n* — **drol·ly** *adv*

drom·e·dary \'drämə,derē\ *n, pl* **-dar·ies** : speedy one-humped camel

drone \'drōn\ *n* **1** : male honeybee **2** : deep hum or buzz ~ *vb* **droned; dron·ing** : make a dull monotonous sound

drool \'drül\ *vb* : let liquid run from the mouth

droop \'drüp\ *vb* **1** : hang or incline downward **2** : lose strength or spirit — **droop** *n* — **droopy** \-ē\ *adj*

drop \'dräp\ *n* **1** : quantity of fluid in one spherical mass **2** *pl* : medicine used by drops **3** : decline or fall **4** : distance something drops ~ *vb* **-pp- 1** : fall in drops **2** : let fall **3** : convey **4** : go lower or become less strong or less active — **drop·let** \-lət\ *n* — **drop back** *vb* : move

toward the rear — **drop behind**
: fail to keep up — **drop in** *vb* : pay
an unexpected visit

drop•per *n* : device that dispenses
liquid by drops

drop•sy \'dräpsē\ *n* : edema

dross \'dräs\ *n* : waste matter

drought \'draut\ *n* : long dry spell

¹**drove** \'drōv\ *n* : crowd of moving
people or animals

²**drove** *past of* DRIVE

drown \'draun\ *vb* 1 : suffocate in
water 2 : overpower or become
overpowered

drowse \'drauz\ *vb* **drowsed; drows-
ing** : doze — **drowse** *n*

drowsy \'drauzē\ *adj* **drows•i•er;
-est** : sleepy — **drows•i•ly** *adv* —
drows•i•ness *n*

drub \'drəb\ *vb* **-bb-** : beat severely

drudge \'drəj\ *vb* **drudged; drudg-
ing** : do hard or boring work —
drudge *n* — **drudg•ery** \-ərē\ *n*

drug \'drəg\ *n* 1 : substance used as
or in medicine 2 : narcotic ∼ *vb*
-gg- : affect with drugs — **druggist** \-ist\ *n* — **drug•store** *n*

dru•id \'drüəd\ *n* : ancient Celtic
priest

drum \'drəm\ *n* 1 : musical instrument that is a skin-covered cylinder beaten usu. with sticks 2
: drum-shaped object (as a container) ∼ *vb* **-mm-** 1 : beat a drum
2 : drive, force, or bring about by
steady effort — **drum•beat** *n* —
drum•mer *n*

♦ **drum•stick** *n* 1 : stick for beating
a drum 2 : lower part of a fowl's
leg

drunk \'drəŋk\ *adj* : having the fac-
ulties impaired by alcohol ∼ *n*
: one who is drunk — **drunk•ard**
\'drəŋkərd\ *n* — **drunk•en** \-kən\
adj — **drunk•en•ly** *adv* — **drunk-
en•ness** *n*

dry \'drī\ *adj* **dri•er** \'drīər\; **dri-**
est \'drīəst\ 1 : lacking water or
moisture 2 : thirsty 3 : marked by
the absence of alcoholic beverages 4 : uninteresting 5 : not sweet
∼ *vb* **dried; dry•ing** : make or become dry — **dry•ly** *adv* — **dryness** *n*

dry–clean *vb* : clean (fabrics) chiefly
with solvents other than water —
dry cleaning *n*

dry•er \'drīər\ *n* : device for drying

dry goods *n pl* : textiles, clothing,
and notions

dry ice *n* : solid carbon dioxide

du•al \'düəl, 'dyü-\ *adj* : twofold —
du•al•ism \-ə,lizəm\ *n* — **du•al-
i•ty** \dü'alətē, dyü-\ *n*

dub \'dəb\ *vb* **-bb-** : name

du•bi•ous \'dübēəs, 'dyü-\ *adj* 1 : uncertain 2 : questionable — **du-
bi•ous•ly** *adv* — **du•bi•ous•ness** *n*

du•cal \'dükəl, 'dyü-\ *adj* : relating
to a duke or dukedom

duch•ess \'dəchəs\ *n* 1 : wife of a
duke 2 : woman holding a ducal title

duchy \-ē\ *n, pl* **-ies** : territory of a
duke or duchess

¹**duck** \'dək\ *n* : swimming bird related to the goose and swan ∼ *vb* 1
: thrust or plunge under water 2
: lower the head or body suddenly
3 : evade — **duck•ling** \-liŋ\ *n*

²**duck** *n* : cotton fabric

duct \'dəkt\ *n* : canal for conveying
a fluid — **duct•less** \-ləs\ *adj*

duc•tile \'dəktªl\ *adj* : able to be
drawn out or shaped — **duc•til-
i•ty** \,dək'tilətē\ *n*

dude \'düd, 'dyüd\ *n* 1 : dandy 2
: guy

dud•geon \'dəjən\ *n* : ill humor

due \'dü, 'dyü\ *adj* 1 : owed 2 : appropriate 3 : attributable 4
: scheduled ∼ *n* 1 : something due
2 *pl* : fee ∼ *adv* : directly

du•el \'düəl, 'dyü-\ *n* : combat between 2 persons — **duel** *vb* — **du‧el‧ist** *n*

du‧et \dü'et, dyü-\ *n* : musical composition for 2 performers

due to *prep* : because of

dug *past of* DIG

dug‧out \'dəg,aût\ *n* 1 : boat made by hollowing out a log 2 : shelter made by digging

duke \'dük, 'dyük\ *n* : nobleman of the highest rank — **duke‧dom** *n*

◆ **dull** \'dəl\ *adj* 1 : mentally slow 2 : blunt 3 : not brilliant or interesting — **dull** *vb* — **dul‧lard** \'dələrd\ *n* — **dull‧ness** *n* — **dul‧ly** *adv*

du‧ly \'dülē, 'dyü-\ *adv* : in a due manner or time

dumb \'dəm\ *adj* 1 : mute 2 : stupid — **dumb‧ly** *adv*

dumb‧bell \'dəm,bel\ *n* 1 : short bar with weights on the ends used for exercise 2 : stupid person

dumb‧found, dum‧found \,dəm-'faûnd\ *vb* : amaze

dum‧my \'dəmē\ *n, pl* -**mies** 1 : stupid person 2 : imitative substitute

dump \'dəmp\ *vb* : let fall in a pile ~ *n* : place for dumping something (as refuse) — **in the dumps** : sad

dump‧ling \'dəmpliŋ\ *n* : small mass of boiled or steamed dough

dumpy \'dəmpē\ *adj* **dump‧i‧er; -est** : short and thick in build

¹**dun** \'dən\ *adj* : brownish gray

²**dun** *vb* -**nn**- : hound for payment of a debt

dunce \'dəns\ *n* : stupid person

dune \'dün, 'dyün\ *n* : hill of sand

dung \'dəŋ\ *n* : manure

dun‧ga‧ree \,dəŋgə'rē\ *n* 1 : blue denim 2 *pl* : work clothes made of dungaree

dun‧geon \'dənjən\ *n* : underground prison

dunk \'dəŋk\ *vb* : dip or submerge temporarily in liquid

duo \'düō, 'dyüō\ *n, pl* **du‧os** : pair

du‧o‧de‧num \,düə'dēnəm, ,dyü-; dü- 'ädᵊnəm, dyü-\ *n, pl* -**na** \-'dēnə, -ᵊnə\ *or* -**nums** : part of the small intestine nearest the stomach — **du‧o‧de‧nal** \-'dēnᵊl, -ᵊnəl\ *adj*

dupe \'düp, dyüp\ *n* : one easily deceived or cheated — **dupe** *vb*

du‧plex \'dü,pleks, 'dyü-\ *adj* : double ~ *n* : 2-family house

du‧pli‧cate \'düplikət, 'dyü-\ *adj* 1 : consisting of 2 identical items 2 : being just like another ~ *n* : exact copy ~ \-,kāt\ *vb* -**cat‧ed; -cat‧ing** 1 : make an exact copy of 2 : repeat or equal — **du‧pli‧ca‧tion** \,düpli'kāshən, ,dyü-\ *n* — **du‧pli‧ca‧tor** \'düpli,kātər, dyü-\ *n*

du‧plic‧i‧ty \dù'plisətē, ,dyü-\ *n, pl* -**ties** : deception

du‧ra‧ble \'dùrəbəl, 'dyùr-\ *adj* : lasting a long time — **du‧ra‧bil‧i‧ty** \,dùrə'bilətē, ,dyùr-\ *n*

du‧ra‧tion \dù'rāshən, dyù-\ *n* : length of time something lasts

du‧ress \dù'res, dyù-\ *n* : coercion

dur‧ing \'dùriŋ, 'dyùr-\ *prep* 1 : throughout 2 : at some point in

dusk \'dəsk\ *n* : twilight — **dusky** *adj*

dust \'dəst\ *n* : powdered matter ~ *vb* 1 : remove dust from 2 : sprinkle with fine particles — **dust‧er** *n* — **dust‧pan** *n* — **dusty** *adj*

du‧ty \'dütē, 'dyü-\ *n, pl* -**ties** 1 : action required by one's occupation or position 2 : moral or legal obligation 3 : tax — **du‧te‧ous** \-əs\ *adj* — **du‧ti‧able** \-əbəl\ *adj* — **du‧ti‧ful** \'dütifəl, 'dyü-\ *adj*

dwarf \'dwôrf\ *n, pl* **dwarfs** \'dwôrfs\ *or* **dwarves** \'dwôrvz\ : one that is much below normal size ~ *vb* 1 : stunt 2 : cause to seem smaller — **dwarf‧ish** *adj*

dwell \'dwel\ *vb* **dwelt** \'dwelt\ *or* **dwelled** \'dweld, 'dwelt\; **dwell·ing 1** : reside **2** : keep the attention directed — **dwell·er** *n* — **dwell·ing** *n*

dwin·dle \'dwind°l\ *vb* **-dled; -dling** : become steadily less

dye \'dī\ *n* : coloring material ~ *vb* **dyed; dye·ing** : give a new color to

dying *pres part of* DIE

dyke *var of* DIKE

dy·nam·ic \dī'namik\ *adj* **1** : relating to physical force producing motion **2** : energetic or forceful

dy·na·mite \'dīnə,mīt\ *n* : explosive made of nitroglycerin — **dyna·mite** *vb*

dy·na·mo \-,mō\ *n, pl* **-mos** : electrical generator

dy·nas·ty \'dīnəstē, -,nas-\ *n, pl* **-ties** : succession of rulers of the same family — **dy·nas·tic** \dī'nastik\ *adj*

dys·en·tery \'dis°n,terē\ *n, pl* **-ter·ies** : disease marked by diarrhea

dys·lex·ia \dis'leksēə\ *n* : disturbance of the ability to read — **dys·lex·ic** \-sik\ *adj*

dys·pep·sia \-'pepshə, -sēə\ *n* : indigestion — **dys·pep·tic** \-'peptik\ *adj or n*

dys·tro·phy \'distrəfē\ *n, pl* **-phies** : disorder involving nervous and muscular tissue

E

e \'ē\ *n, pl* **e's** *or* **es** \'ēz\ : 5th letter of the alphabet

each \'ēch\ *adj* : being one of the class named ~ *pron* : every individual one — *adv* : apiece

ea·ger \'ēgər\ *adj* : enthusiastic or anxious — **ea·ger·ly** *adv* — **ea·ger·ness** *n*

ea·gle \'ēgəl\ *n* : large bird of prey

-ean — see -AN

¹**ear** \'ir\ *n* : organ of hearing or the outer part of this — **ear·ache** *n* — **eared** *adj* — **ear·lobe** \-,lōb\ *n*

²**ear** *n* : fruiting head of a cereal

ear·drum *n* : thin membrane that receives and transmits sound waves in the ear

earl \'ərl\ *n* : British nobleman — **earl·dom** \-dəm\ *n*

ear·ly \'ərlē\ *adj* **-li·er; -est 1** : relating to or occurring near the beginning or before the usual time **2** : ancient — **early** *adv*

ear·mark *vb* : designate for a specific purpose

earn \'ərn\ *vb* **1** : receive as a return for service **2** : deserve

ear·nest \'ərnəst\ *n* : serious state of mind — **earnest** *adj* — **ear·nest·ly** *adv* — **ear·nest·ness** *n*

earn·ings \'ərniŋz\ *n pl* : something earned

ear·phone *n* : device that reproduces sound and is worn over or in the ear

ear·ring *n* : earlobe ornament

ear·shot *n* : range of hearing

earth \'ərth\ *n* **1** : soil or land **2** : planet inhabited by man — **earth·li·ness** *n* — **earth·ly** *adj* — **earth·ward** \-wərd\ *adv*

earth·en \'ərthən\ *adj* : made of earth or baked clay — **earth·en·ware** \-,war\ *n*

earth·quake *n* : shaking or trembling of the earth

earth·worm *n* : long segmented worm

earthy \'ərthē\ *adj* **earth·i·er; -est 1** : relating to or consisting of earth **2** : practical **3** : coarse — **earth·i·ness** *n*

ease \'ēz\ *n* **1** : comfort **2** : naturalness of manner **3** : freedom from difficulty ~ *vb* **eased; eas·ing 1** : relieve from distress **2** : lessen the tension of **3** : make easier

ea·sel \'ēzəl\ *n* : frame to hold a painter's canvas

east \'ēst\ *adv* : to or toward the east ~ *adj* : situated toward or at or coming from the east ~ *n* **1** : direction of sunrise **2** *cap* : regions to the east — **east·er·ly** \'ēstərlē\ *adv or adj* — **east·ward** *adv or adj* — **east·wards** *adv*

Eas·ter \'ēstər\ *n* : church feast celebrating Christ's resurrection

east·ern \'ēstərn\ *adj* 1 *cap* : relating to a region designated East 2 : lying toward or coming from the east — **East·ern·er** *n*

easy \'ēzē\ *adj* **eas·i·er;** **-est** 1 : marked by ease 2 : lenient — **eas·i·ly** \'ēzəlē\ *adv* — **eas·i·ness** \-ēnəs\ *n*

easy·go·ing *adj* : relaxed and casual

eat \'ēt\ *vb* **ate** \'āt\; **eat·en** \'ētᵊn\; **eat·ing** 1 : take in as food 2 : use up or corrode — **eat·able** *adj or n* — **eat·er** *n*

eaves \'ēvz\ *n pl* : overhanging edge of a roof

eaves·drop *vb* : listen secretly — **eaves·drop·per** *n*

ebb \'eb\ *n* 1 : outward flow of the tide 2 : decline ~ *vb* 1 : recede from the flood state 2 : wane

eb·o·ny \'ebənē\ *n, pl* **-nies** : hard heavy wood of tropical trees ~ *adj* 1 : made of ebony 2 : black

ebul·lient \i'bu̇lyənt, -'bəl-\ *adj* : exuberant — **ebul·lience** \-yəns\ *n*

♦ **ec·cen·tric** \ik'sentrik\ *adj* 1 : odd in behavior 2 : being off center — **eccentric** *n* — **ec·cen·tri·cal·ly** \-triklē\ *adv* — **ec·cen·tric·i·ty** \ˌek₁sen'trisətē\ *n*

ec·cle·si·as·tic \ikˌlēzē'astik\ *n* : clergyman

ec·cle·si·as·ti·cal \-tikəl\; **ecclesiastic** *adj* : relating to a church — **ec·cle·si·as·ti·cal·ly** \-tiklē\ *adv*

ech·e·lon \'eshəˌlän\ *n* 1 : steplike arrangement 2 : level of authority

echo \'ekō\ *n, pl* **ech·oes** : repetition of a sound caused by a reflection of the sound waves — **echo** *vb*

éclair \ā'klar\ *n* : custard-filled pastry

eclec·tic \e'klektik, i-\ *adj* : drawing or drawn from varied sources

eclipse \i'klips\ *n* : total or partial obscuring of one celestial body by another — **eclipse** *vb*

ecol·o·gy \i'käləjē, e-\ *n, pl* **-gies** : science concerned with the interaction of organisms and their environment — **eco·log·i·cal** \ˌēkə-'läjikəl, ˌek-\ *adj* — **eco·log·i·cal·ly** *adv* — **ecol·o·gist** \i'käləjist, e-\ *n*

eco·nom·ic \ˌekə'nämik, ˌēkə-\ *adj* : relating to the producing and the buying and selling of goods and services

eco·nom·ics \-'nämiks\ *n* : branch of knowledge dealing with goods and services — **econ·o·mist** \i'känəmist\ *n*

econ·o·mize \i'känəˌmīz\ *vb* **-mized;** **-miz·ing** : be thrifty — **econ·o·miz·er** *n*

econ·o·my \-əmē\ *n, pl* **-mies** 1 : thrifty use of resources 2 : economic system — **eco·nom·i·cal** \ˌekə'nämikəl, ˌēkə-\ *adj* — **eco·nom·i·cal·ly** *adv* — **economy** *adj*

ecru \'ekrü, 'äkrü\ *n* : beige

ec·sta·sy \'ekstəsē\ *n, pl* **-sies** : extreme emotional excitement — **ec·stat·ic** \ek'statik, ik-\ *adj* — **ec·stat·i·cal·ly** \-iklē\ *adv*

ec·u·men·i·cal \ˌekyə'menikəl\ *adj* : promoting worldwide Christian unity

ec·ze·ma \ig'zēmə, 'egzəmə, 'ekə-\ *n* : itching skin inflammation

¹-ed \d *after a vowel or* b, g, j, l, m, n, ŋ, r, th, v, z, zh; əd, id *after* d, t; t *after other sounds*\ *vb suffix or adj suffix* 1 — used to form the past participle of regular verbs 2 : having or having the characteristics of

²-ed *vb suffix* — used to form the past tense of regular verbs

ed·dy \'edē\ *n, pl* **-dies** : whirlpool — **eddy** *vb*

ede·ma \i'dēmə\ n : abnormal accumulation of fluid in the body tissues — edem·a·tous \-'demətəs\ adj

Eden \'ēd³n\ n : paradise

edge \'ej\ n 1 : cutting side of a blade 2 : line where something begins or ends ~ vb edged; edg·ing 1 : give or form an edge 2 : move gradually 3 : narrowly defeat — edg·er n

edge·wise \-ˌwīz\ adv : sideways

edgy \'ejē\ adj edg·i·er; -est : nervous — edg·i·ness n

ed·i·ble \'edəbəl\ adj : fit or safe to be eaten — ed·i·bil·i·ty \ˌedə-'bilətē\ n — edible n

edict \'ē,dikt\ n : order or decree

ed·i·fi·ca·tion \ˌedəfə'kāshən\ n : instruction or information — ed·i·fy \'edə,fī\ vb

ed·i·fice \'edəfəs\ n : large building

ed·it \'edət\ vb 1 : revise and prepare for publication 2 : delete — ed·i·tor \-ər\ n — ed·i·tor·ship n

edi·tion \i'dishən\ n 1 : form in which a text is published 2 : total number published at one time

ed·i·to·ri·al \ˌedə'tōrēəl\ adj 1 : relating to an editor or editing 2 : expressing opinion ~ n : article (as in a newspaper) expressing the views of an editor — ed·i·to·ri·al·ize \-ēə,līz\ vb — ed·i·to·ri·al·ly adv

ed·u·cate \'ejə,kāt\ vb -cat·ed; -cat·ing 1 : give instruction to 2 : develop mentally and morally 3 : provide with information — ed·u·ca·ble \'ejəkəbəl\ adj — ed·u·ca·tion \ˌejə'kāshən\ n — ed·u·ca·tion·al \-shənəl\ adj — ed·u·ca·tor \-ər\ n

eel \'ēl\ n : snakelike fish

ee·rie \'irē\ adj -ri·er; -est : weird — ee·ri·ly \'irəlē\ adv

ef·face \i'fās, e-\ vb -faced; -fac-ing : obliterate by rubbing out — ef·face·ment n

ef·fect \i'fekt\ n 1 : result 2 : meaning 3 : influence 4 pl : goods or possessions ~ vb : cause to happen — in effect : in substance

♦ ef·fec·tive \i'fektiv\ adj 1 : producing a strong or desired effect 2 : being in operation — ef·fec·tive·ly adv — ef·fec·tive·ness n

ef·fec·tu·al \i'fekchəwəl\ adj : producing an intended effect — ef·fec·tu·al·ly adv — ef·fec·tu·al·ness n

ef·fem·i·nate \ə'femənət\ adj : unsuitably womanish — ef·fem·i·na·cy \-nəsē\ n

ef·fer·vesce \ˌefər'ves\ vb -vesced; -vesc·ing 1 : bubble and hiss as gas escapes 2 : show exhilaration — ef·fer·ves·cence \-'ves³ns\ n — ef·fer·ves·cent \-³nt\ adj — ef·fer·ves·cent·ly adv

ef·fete \e'fēt\ adj 1 : worn out 2 : weak or decadent 3 : effeminate

ef·fi·ca·cious \ˌefə'kāshəs\ adj : effective — ef·fi·ca·cy \'efikəsē\ n

ef·fi·cient \i'fishənt\ adj : working well with little waste — ef·fi·cien·cy \-ənsē\ n — ef·fi·cient·ly adv

ef·fi·gy \'efəjē\ n, pl -gies : usu. crude image of a person

ef·flu·ent \'e,flüənt, e'flü-\ n : something that flows out — effluent adj

ef·fort \'efərt\ n 1 : a putting forth of strength 2 : use of resources toward a goal 3 : product of effort — ef·fort·less adj — ef·fort·less·ly adv

ef·fron·tery \i'frəntərē\ n, pl -ter·ies : insolence

ef·fu·sion \i'fyüzhən, e-\ n : a gushing forth — ef·fu·sive \-'fyüsiv\ adj — ef·fu·sive·ly adv

¹egg \'eg, 'āg\ vb : urge to action

²egg n 1 : rounded usu. hard-shelled reproductive body esp. of birds

and reptiles from which the young hatches **2** : ovum — **egg·shell** n

egg·nog \-₁näg\ n : rich drink of eggs and cream

egg·plant n : edible purplish fruit of a plant related to the potato

ego \'ēgō\ n, pl **egos** : self-esteem

ego·cen·tric \₁ēgō'sentrik\ adj : self-centered

ego·tism \'ēgə₁tizəm\ n : exaggerated sense of self-importance — **ego·tist** \-tist\ n — **ego·tis·tic** \₁ēgə'tistik\ **ego·tis·ti·cal** \-tikəl\ adj — **ego·tis·ti·cal·ly** adv

egre·gious \i'grējəs\ adj : notably bad — **egre·gious·ly** adv

egress \'ē₁gres\ n : a way out

egret \'ēgrət, i'gret, 'egrət\ n : long-plumed heron

ei·der·down \'īdər₁daûn\ n : soft down obtained from a northern sea duck (**eider**)

eight \'āt\ n **1** : one more than 7 **2** : 8th in a set or series **3** : something having 8 units — **eight** adj or pron — **eighth** \'ātth\ adj or adv or n

eigh·teen \āt'tēn\ n : one more than 17 — **eighteen** adj or pron — **eigh·teenth** \-'tēnth\ adj or n

eighty \'ātē\ n, pl **eight·ies** : 8 times 10 — **eight·i·eth** \'ātēəth\ adj or n — **eighty** adj or pron

ei·ther \'ēthər, 'ī-\ adj **1** : both **2** : being the one or the other of two ~ pron : one of two or more ~ conj : one or the other

ejac·u·late \i'jakyə₁lāt\ vb **-lat·ed; -lat·ing 1** : say suddenly **2** : eject a fluid (as semen) — **ejac·u·la·tion** \-₁jakyə'lāshən\ n

eject \i'jekt\ vb : drive or throw out — **ejec·tion** \-'jekshən\ n

eke \'ēk\ vb **eked; ek·ing** : barely gain with effort — usu. with out

elab·o·rate \i'labərət\ adj **1** : planned in detail **2** : complex and ornate ~ \-₁rāt\ vb **-rat·ed; -rat·ing** : work out in detail — **elab·o·rate·ly** adv — **elab·o·rate·ness** n — **elab·o·ra·tion** \-₁labə'rāshən\ n

elapse \i'laps\ vb **elapsed; elaps·ing** : slip by

elas·tic \i'lastik\ adj **1** : springy **2** : flexible ~ n **1** : elastic material **2** : rubber band — **elas·tic·i·ty** \-₁las'tisətē, ₁ē₁las-\ n

elate \i'lāt\ vb **elat·ed; elat·ing** : fill with joy — **ela·tion** \-'lāshən\ n

el·bow \'el₁bō\ n **1** : joint of the arm **2** : elbow-shaped bend or joint ~ vb : push aside with the elbow

el·der \'eldər\ adj : older ~ n **1** : one who is older **2** : church officer

el·der·ber·ry \'eldər₁berē\ n : edible black or red fruit or a tree or shrub bearing these

el·der·ly \'eldərlē\ adj : past middle age

el·dest \'eldəst\ adj : oldest

elect \i'lekt\ adj : elected but not yet in office ~ n **elect** pl : exclusive group ~ vb : choose esp. by vote — **elec·tion** \i'lekshən\ n — **elec·tive** \i'lektiv\ n or adj — **elec·tor** \i'lektər\ n — **elec·tor·al** \-tərəl\ adj

elec·tor·ate \i'lektərət\ n : body of persons entitled to vote

elec·tric \i'lektrik\ adj **1** or **elec·tri·cal** \-trikəl\ : relating to or run by electricity **2** : thrilling — **elec·tri·cal·ly** adv

elec·tri·cian \i₁lek'trishən\ n : person who installs or repairs electrical equipment

elec·tric·i·ty \-'trisətē\ n, pl **-ties 1** : fundamental form of energy occurring naturally (as in lightning) or produced artificially **2** : electric current

elec·tri·fy \i'lektrə₁fī\ vb **-fied; -fy·ing 1** : charge with electricity **2** : equip for use of electric power **3** : thrill — **elec·tri·fi·ca·tion** \-₁lektrəfə'kāshən\ n

elec·tro·car·dio·gram \i₁lektrō-'kärdēə₁gram\ n : tracing made by an electrocardiograph

elec·tro·car·dio·graph \-₁graf\ n : instrument for monitoring heart function

elec·tro·cute \i'lektrə₁kyüt\ vb **-cut·ed; -cut·ing** : kill by an electric shock — **elec·tro·cu·tion** \-₁lektrə'kyüshən\ n

elec·trode \i'lek₁trōd\ n : conductor at a nonmetallic part of a circuit

elec·trol·y·sis \i₁lek'träləsəs\ n **1** : production of chemical changes by passage of an electric current through a substance **2** : destruction of hair roots with an electric current — **elec·tro·lyt·ic** \-trə-'litik\ adj

elec·tro·lyte \i'lektrə₁līt\ n : nonmetallic electric conductor

elec·tro·mag·net \i₁lektrō'magnət\ *n* : magnet made using electric current

elec·tro·mag·ne·tism \-nə₁tizəm\ *n* : natural force responsible for interactions between charged particles — **elec·tro·mag·net·ic** \-mag'netik\ *adj* — **elec·tro·mag·net·i·cal·ly** \-iklē\ *adv*

elec·tron \i'lek₁trän\ *n* : negatively charged particle within the atom

elec·tron·ic \i₁lek'tränik\ *adj* : relating to electrons or electronics — **elec·tron·i·cal·ly** \-iklē\ *adv*

elec·tron·ics \-iks\ *n* : physics of electrons and their use esp. in devices

elec·tro·plate \i'lektrə₁plāt\ *vb* : coat (as with metal) by electrolysis

el·e·gance \'eligəns\ *n* : refined gracefulness — **el·e·gant** \-gənt\ *adj* — **el·e·gant·ly** *adv*

el·e·gy \'eləjē\ *n, pl* **-gies** : poem expressing grief for one who is dead — **ele·gi·ac** \₁elə'jīək, -₁ak\ *adj*

el·e·ment \'eləmənt\ *n* **1** *pl* : weather conditions **2** : natural environment **3** : constituent part **4** *pl* : simplest principles **5** : substance that has atoms of only one kind — **el·e·men·tal** \₁elə'ment⁹l\ *adj*

el·e·men·ta·ry \₁elə'mentrē\ *adj* **1** : simple **2** : relating to the basic subjects of education

el·e·phant \'eləfənt\ *n* : huge mammal with a trunk and 2 ivory tusks

el·e·vate \'elə₁vāt\ *vb* **-vat·ed; -vat·ing 1** : lift up **2** : exalt

el·e·va·tion \₁elə'vāshən\ *n* : height or a high place

el·e·va·tor \'elə₁vātər\ *n* **1** : cage or platform for raising or lowering something **2** : grain storehouse

elev·en \i'levən\ *n* **1** : one more than 10 **2** : 11th in a set or series **3** : something having 11 units — **eleven** *adj or pron* — **elev·enth** \-ənth\ *adj or n*

elf \'elf\ *n, pl* **elves** \'elvz\ : mischievous fairy — **elf·in** \'elfən\ *adj* — **elf·ish** \'elfish\ *adj*

elic·it \i'lisət\ *vb* : draw forth

el·i·gi·ble \'eləjəbəl\ *adj* : qualified to participate or to be chosen — **el·i·gi·bil·i·ty** \₁eləjə'bilətē\ *n* — **eligible** *n*

elim·i·nate \i'limə₁nāt\ *vb* **-nat-** ed; **-nat·ing** : get rid of — **elim·i·na·tion** \i₁limə'nāshən\ *n*

elite \ā'lēt\ *n* : choice or select group

elix·ir \i'likər\ *n* : medicinal solution

elk \'elk\ *n* : large deer

el·lipse \i'lips, e-\ *n* : oval

el·lip·sis \-'lipsəs\ *n, pl* **-lip·ses** \-₁sēz\ **1** : omission of a word **2** : marks (as . . .) to show omission

el·lip·ti·cal \-'tikəl\; **el·lip·tic** \-'tik\ *adj* **1** : relating to or shaped like an ellipse **2** : relating to or marked by ellipsis

elm \'elm\ *n* : tall shade tree

el·o·cu·tion \₁elə'kyüshən\ *n* : art of public speaking

elon·gate \i'lȯŋ₁gāt\ *vb* **-gat·ed; -gat·ing** : make or grow longer — **elon·ga·tion** \₁ē₁lȯŋ'gāshən\ *n*

elope \i'lōp\ *vb* **eloped; elop·ing** : run away esp. to be married — **elope·ment** *n* — **elop·er** *n*

el·o·quent \'eləkwənt\ *adj* : forceful and persuasive in speech — **el·o·quence** \-kwəns\ *n* — **el·o·quent·ly** *adv*

else \'els\ *adv* **1** : in a different way, time, or place **2** : otherwise ~ *adj* **1** : other **2** : more

else·where *adv* : in or to another place

elu·ci·date \i'lüsə₁dāt\ *vb* **-dat·ed; -dat·ing** : explain — **elu·ci·da·tion** \i₁lüsə'dāshən\ *n*

elude \ē'lüd\ *vb* **elud·ed; elud·ing** : evade — **elu·sive** \ē'lüsiv\ *adj* — **elu·sive·ly** *adv* — **elu·sive·ness** *n*

elves *pl of* ELF

ema·ci·ate \i'māshē₁āt\ *vb* **-at·ed; -at·ing** : become or make very thin — **ema·ci·a·tion** \i₁māsē-'āshən, -shē-\ *n*

em·a·nate \'emə₁nāt\ *vb* **-nat·ed; -nat·ing** : come forth — **em·a·na·tion** \₁emə'nāshən\ *n*

eman·ci·pate \i'mansə₁pāt\ *vb* **-pat-** ed; **-pat·ing** : set free — **eman·ci·pa·tion** \i₁mansə'pāshən\ *n* — **eman·ci·pa·tor** \i'mansə₁pātər\ *n*

emas·cu·late \i'maskyə₁lāt\ *vb* **-lat-** ed; **-lat·ing 1** : castrate **2** : weaken — **emas·cu·la·tion** \i₁maskyə-'lāshən\ *n*

em·balm \im'bäm, -'bälm\ *vb* : preserve (a corpse) — **em·balm·er** *n*

em·bank·ment \im'baŋkmənt\ *n* : protective barrier of earth

em·bar·go \im'bärgō\ *n, pl* **-goes**
: ban on trade — **embargo** *vb*

em·bark \-'bärk\ *vb* **1** : go on board
a ship or airplane **2** : make a start
— **em·bar·ka·tion** \ˌembˌbär'kā-
shən\ *n*

em·bar·rass \im'barəs\ *vb* : cause
distress and self-consciousness —
em·bar·rass·ment *n*

em·bas·sy \'embəsē\ *n, pl* **-sies** : residence and offices of an ambassa-
dor

em·bed \im'bed\ *vb* **-dd-** : fix firmly

em·bel·lish \-'belish\ *vb* : decorate
— **em·bel·lish·ment** *n*

em·ber \'embər\ *n* : smoldering
fragment from a fire

em·bez·zle \im'bezəl\ *vb* **-zled;
-zling** : steal (money) by falsifying
records — **em·bez·zle·ment** *n* —
em·bez·zler \-ələr\ *n*

em·bit·ter \im'bitər\ *vb* : make bitter

em·bla·zon \-'blāzᵊn\ *vb* : display
conspicuously

em·blem \'embləm\ *n* : symbol —
em·blem·at·ic \ˌemblə'matik\ *adj*

em·body \im'bädē\ *vb* **-bod·ied;
-body·ing** : give definite form or
expression to — **em·bodi·ment**
\-'bädimənt\ *n*

em·boss \-'bäs, -'bȯs\ *vb* : ornament
with raised work

em·brace \-'brās\ *vb* **-braced; -brac-
ing 1** : clasp in the arms **2** : wel-
come **3** : include — **embrace** *n*

em·broi·der \-'brȯidər\ *vb* : ornament with or do needlework —
em·broi·dery \-ərē\ *n*

em·broil \im'brȯil\ *vb* : involve in
conflict or difficulties

em·bryo \'embrē͟ˌō\ *n* : living being
in its earliest stages of development — **em·bry·on·ic** \ˌembrē-
'änik\ *adj*

emend \ē'mend\ *vb* : correct —
emen·da·tion \ˌēˌmen'dāshən\ *n*

em·er·ald \'emrəld, 'emə-\ *n* : green
gem ∼ *adj* : bright green

emerge \i'mərj\ *vb* **emerged;
emerg·ing** : rise, come forth, or
appear — **emer·gence** \-'mər-
jəns\ *n* — **emer·gent** \-jənt\
adj

emer·gen·cy \i'mərjənsē\ *n, pl* **-cies**
: condition requiring prompt action

em·ery \'emərē\ *n, pl* **-er·ies** : dark

granular mineral used for grinding

emet·ic \i'metik\ *n* : agent that induces vomiting — **emetic** *adj*

em·i·grate \'eməˌgrāt\ *vb* **-grat-
ed; -grat·ing** : leave a country to
settle elsewhere — **em·i·grant**
\-igrənt\ *n* — **em·i·gra·tion** \ˌemə-
'grāshən\ *n*

em·i·nence \'emənəns\ *n* **1** : prominence or superiority **2** : person of
high rank

em·i·nent \-nənt\ *adj* : prominent
— **em·i·nent·ly** *adv*

em·is·sary \'eməˌserē\ *n, pl* **-sar-
ies** : agent

emis·sion \ē'mishən\ *n* : substance
discharged into the air

emit \ē'mit\ *vb* **-tt-** : give off or out

emol·u·ment \i'mälyəmənt\ *n* : sal-
ary or fee

emote \i'mōt\ *vb* **emot·ed; emot-
ing** : express emotion

emo·tion \i'mōshən\ *n* : intense
feeling — **emo·tion·al** \-shənəl\
adj — **emo·tion·al·ly** *adv*

em·per·or \'empərər\ *n* : ruler of an
empire

em·pha·sis \'emfəsəs\ *n, pl* **-pha-
ses** \-ˌsēz\ : stress

em·pha·size \-ˌsīz\ *vb* **-sized; -siz-
ing** : stress

em·phat·ic \im'fatik, em-\ *adj* : uttered with emphasis — **em·phat-
i·cal·ly** \-iklē\ *adv*

em·pire \'emˌpīr\ *n* : large state or a
group of states

em·pir·i·cal \im'pirikəl\ *adj* : based
on observation — **em·pir·i·cal-
ly** \-iklē\ *adv*

em·ploy \im'plȯi\ *vb* **1** : use **2** : occupy ∼ *n* : paid occupation —
em·ploy·ee, em·ploye \imˌplȯi'ē,
-'plȯiˌē\ *n* — **em·ploy·er** *n* — **em-
ploy·ment** \-mənt\ *n*

em·pow·er \im'paůər\ *vb* : give
power to — **em·pow·er·ment** *n*

em·press \'emprəs\ *n* **1** : wife of an
emperor **2** : woman emperor

emp·ty \'emptē\ *adj* **1** : containing
nothing **2** : not occupied **3** : lacking value, sense, or purpose ∼ *vb*
-tied; -ty·ing : make or become
empty — **emp·ti·ness** \-tēnəs\ *n*

emu \'ēmyü\ *n* : Australian bird related to the ostrich

em·u·late \'emyəˌlāt\ *vb* **-lat·ed;
-lat·ing** : try to equal or excel —
em·u·la·tion \ˌemyə'lāshən\ *n*

emul·si·fy \i'məlsə,fī\ *vb* **-fied; -fy-ing** : convert into an emulsion — **emul·si·fi·ca·tion** \i,məlsəfə'kā-shən\ *n* — **emul·si·fi·er** \-'məlsə,fīər\ *n*

emul·sion \i'məlshən\ *n* **1** : mixture of mutually insoluble liquids **2** : light-sensitive coating on photographic film

-en \ən,ᵊn\ *vb suffix* **1** : become or cause to be **2** : cause or come to have

en·able \in'ābəl\ *vb* **-abled; -abling** : give power, capacity, or ability to

en·act \in'akt\ *vb* **1** : make into law **2** : act out — **en·act·ment** *n*

enam·el \in'aməl\ *n* **1** : glasslike substance used to coat metal or pottery **2** : hard outer layer of a tooth **3** : glossy paint — **enamel** *vb*

en·am·or \in'amər\ *vb* : excite with love

en·camp \in'kamp\ *vb* : make camp — **en·camp·ment** *n*

en·case \in'kās\ *vb* : enclose in or as if in a case

-ence \əns,ᵊns\ *n suffix* **1** : action or process **2** : quality or state

en·ceph·a·li·tis \in,sefə'lītəs\ *n, pl* **-lit·i·des** \-'litə,dēz\ : inflammation of the brain

en·chant \in'chant\ *vb* **1** : bewitch **2** : fascinate — **en·chant·er** *n* — **en·chant·ment** *n* — **en·chant·ress** \-'chantrəs\ *n*

en·cir·cle \in'sərkəl\ *vb* : surround

en·close \in'klōz\ *vb* **1** : shut up or surround **2** : include — **en·clo·sure** \in'klōzhər\ *n*

en·co·mi·um \en'kōmēəm\ *n, pl* **-mi·ums** *or* **-mia** \-mēə\ : high praise

en·com·pass \in'kəmpəs, -'käm-\ *vb* : surround or include

◆ **en·core** \'än,kōr\ *n* : further performance

en·coun·ter \in'kaùntər\ *vb* **1** : fight **2** : meet unexpectedly — **encounter** *n*

en·cour·age \in'kərij\ *vb* **-aged; -ag-ing** **1** : inspire with courage and hope **2** : foster — **en·cour·age·ment** *n*

en·croach \in'krōch\ *vb* : enter upon another's property or rights — **en·croach·ment** *n*

en·crust \in'krəst\ *vb* : form a crust on

en·cum·ber \in'kəmbər\ *vb* : burden — **en·cum·brance** \-brəns\ *n*

-en·cy \ənsē,ᵊn-\ *n suffix* : -ence

en·cyc·li·cal \in'siklikəl, en-\ *n* : papal letter to bishops

en·cy·clo·pe·dia \in,sīklə'pēdēə\ *n* : reference work on many subjects — **en·cy·clo·pe·dic** \-'pēdik\ *adj*

end \'end\ *n* **1** : point at which something stops or no longer exists **2** : cessation **3** : purpose ~ *vb* **1** : stop or finish **2** : be at the end of — **end·ed** *adj* — **end·less** *adj* — **end·less·ly** *adv*

en·dan·ger \in'dānjər\ *vb* : bring into danger

en·dear \in'dir\ *vb* : make dear — **en·dear·ment** \-mənt\ *n*

en·deav·or \in'devər\ *vb or n* : attempt

end·ing \'endiŋ\ *n* : end

en·dive \'en,dīv\ *n* : salad plant

en·do·crine \'endəkrən, -,krīn, -,krēn\ *adj* : producing secretions distributed by the bloodstream

en·dorse \in'dórs\ *vb* **-dorsed; -dors·ing** **1** : sign one's name to **2** : approve — **en·dorse·ment** *n*

en·dow \in'daù\ *vb* **1** : furnish with funds **2** : furnish naturally — **en·dow·ment** *n*

en·dure \in'dùr, -'dyùr\ *vb* **-dured; -dur·ing** **1** : last **2** : suffer patiently **3** : tolerate — **en·dur·able** *adj* — **en·dur·ance** \-əns\ *n*

en·e·ma \'enəmə\ *n* : injection of liquid into the rectum

en·e·my \-mē\ *n, pl* **-mies** : one that attacks or tries to harm another

en·er·get·ic \enər'jetik\ *adj* : full of energy or activity — **en·er·get·i·cal·ly** \-iklē\ *adv*

en·er·gize \'enər,jīz\ *vb* **-gized; -giz·ing** : give energy to

en·er·gy \'enərjē\ *n, pl* **-gies** 1 : capacity for action 2 : vigorous action 3 : capacity for doing work

en·er·vate \'enər,vāt\ *vb* **-vat·ed; -vat·ing** : make weak or listless — **en·er·va·tion** \enər'vāshən\ *n*

en·fold \in'fōld\ *vb* : surround or embrace

en·force \-'fōrs\ *vb* 1 : compel 2 : carry out — **en·force·able** \-əbəl\ *adj* — **en·force·ment** *n*

en·fran·chise \-'fran,chīz\ *vb* **-chised; -chis·ing** : grant voting rights to — **en·fran·chise·ment** \-,chīzmənt, -chəz-\ *n*

en·gage \in'gāj\ *vb* **-gaged; -gag·ing** 1 : participate or cause to participate 2 : bring or come into working contact 3 : bind by a pledge to marry 4 : hire 5 : bring or enter into conflict — **en·gage·ment** \-mənt\ *n*

en·gag·ing *adj* : attractive

en·gen·der \in'jendər\ *vb* **-dered; -der·ing** : create

en·gine \'enjən\ *n* 1 : machine that converts energy into mechanical motion 2 : locomotive

en·gi·neer \enjə'nir\ *n* 1 : one trained in engineering 2 : engine operator ~ *vb* : lay out or manage as an engineer

en·gi·neer·ing \-iŋ\ *n* : practical application of science and mathematics

en·grave \in'grāv\ *vb* **-graved; -grav·ing** : cut into a surface — **en·grav·er** *n* — **en·grav·ing** *n*

en·gross \-'grōs\ *vb* : occupy fully

en·gulf \-'gəlf\ *vb* : swallow up

en·hance \-'hans\ *vb* **-hanced; -hanc·ing** : improve in value — **en·hance·ment** *n*

enig·ma \i'nigmə\ *n* : puzzle or mystery — **enig·mat·ic** \enig'matik, ,ē-\ *adj* — **enig·mat·i·cal·ly** *adv*

en·join \in'jóin\ *vb* 1 : command 2 : forbid

♦ **en·joy** \-'jói\ *vb* : take pleasure in — **en·joy·able** *adj* — **en·joy·ment** *n*

en·large \-'lärj\ *vb* **-larged; -larg·ing** : make or grow larger — **en·large·ment** *n* — **en·larg·er** *n*

en·light·en \-'līt°n\ *vb* : give knowledge or spiritual insight to — **en·light·en·ment** *n*

en·list \-'list\ *vb* 1 : join the armed forces 2 : get the aid of — **en·list·ee** \-,lis'tē\ *n* — **en·list·ment** \-'listmənt\ *n*

en·liv·en \in'līvən\ *vb* : give life or spirit to

en·mi·ty \'enmətē\ *n, pl* **-ties** : mutual hatred

en·no·ble \in'ōbəl\ *vb* **-bled; -bling** : make noble

en·nui \,än'wē\ *n* : boredom

enor·mi·ty \i'nórmətē\ *n, pl* **-ties** 1 : great wickedness 2 : huge size

enor·mous \i'nórməs\ *adj* : great in size, number, or degree — **enor·mous·ly** *adv* — **enor·mous·ness** *n*

enough \i'nəf\ *adj* : adequate ~ *adv* 1 : in an adequate manner 2 : in a tolerable degree ~ *pron* : adequate number, quantity, or amount

en·quire \in'kwīr\; **en·qui·ry** \'in-,kwīrē, in'-; 'inkwərē, 'in-\ *var of* INQUIRE, INQUIRY

en·rage \in'rāj\ *vb* : fill with rage

en·rich \-'rich\ *vb* : make rich — **en·rich·ment** *n*

en·roll, en·rol \-'rōl\ *vb* **-rolled;**

-roll·ing 1 : enter on a list **2** : become enrolled — **en·roll·ment** n

en route \än'rüt, en-, in-\ adv or adj : on or along the way

en·sconce \in'skäns\ vb **-sconced; -sconc·ing** : settle snugly

en·sem·ble \än'sämbəl\ n **1** : small group **2** : complete costume

en·shrine \in'shrīn\ vb **1** : put in a shrine **2** : cherish

en·sign \'ensən, 1 also 'en₁sīn\ n **1** : flag **2** : lowest ranking commissioned officer in the navy

en·slave \in'slāv\ vb : make a slave of — **en·slave·ment** n

en·snare \-'snar\ vb : trap

en·sue \-'sü\ vb **-sued; -su·ing** : follow as a consequence

en·sure \-'shu̇r\ vb **-sured; -sur·ing** : guarantee

en·tail \-'tāl\ vb : involve as a necessary result

en·tan·gle \-'taŋgəl\ vb : tangle — **en·tan·gle·ment** n

en·ter \'entər\ vb **1** : go or come in or into **2** : start **3** : set down (as in a list)

en·ter·prise \'entər₁prīz\ n **1** : an undertaking **2** : business organization **3** : initiative

en·ter·pris·ing \-₁prīziŋ\ adj : showing initiative

en·ter·tain \₁entər'tān\ vb **1** : treat or receive as a guest **2** : hold in mind **3** : amuse — **en·ter·tain·er** n — **en·ter·tain·ment** n

en·thrall, en·thral \in'throl\ vb **-thralled; -thrall·ing** : hold spellbound

en·thu·si·asm \-'thüzē₁azəm, -'thyü-\ n : strong excitement of feeling or its cause — **en·thu·si·ast** \-₁ast, -əst\ n — **en·thu·si·as·tic** \-₁thüzē'astik, -₁thyü-\ adj — **en·thu·si·as·ti·cal·ly** \-tiklē\ adv

en·tice \-'tīs\ vb **-ticed; -tic·ing** : tempt — **en·tice·ment** n

en·tire \in'tīr\ adj : complete or whole — **en·tire·ly** adv — **en·tire·ty** \-'tīrətē, -'tīrtē\ n

en·ti·tle \-'tīt⁵l\ vb **-tled; -tling 1** : name **2** : give a right to

en·ti·ty \'entətē\ n, pl **-ties** : something with separate existence

en·to·mol·o·gy \₁entə'mäləjē\ n : study of insects — **en·to·mo·log·i·cal** \-mə'läjikəl\ adj — **en·to·mol·o·gist** \-'mäləjist\ n

en·tou·rage \₁äntu̇'räzh\ n : retinue

en·trails \'entrəlz, -₁trālz\ n pl : intestines

¹en·trance \'entrəns\ n **1** : act of entering **2** : means or place of entering — **en·trant** \'entrənt\ n

²en·trance \in'trans\ vb **-tranced; -tranc·ing** : fascinate or delight

en·trap \in'trap\ vb : trap — **en·trap·ment** n

en·treat \-'trēt\ vb : ask urgently — **en·treaty** \-'trētē\ n

en·trée, en·tree \'än₁trā\ n : principal dish of the meal

en·trench \in'trench\ vb : establish in a strong position — **en·trench·ment** n

en·tre·pre·neur \₁äntrəprə'nər\ n : organizer or promoter of an enterprise

en·trust \in'trəst\ vb : commit to another with confidence

en·try \'entrē\ n, pl **-tries 1** : entrance **2** : an entering in a record or an item so entered

en·twine \in'twīn\ vb : twine together or around

enu·mer·ate \i'nümə₁rāt, -'nyü-\ vb **-at·ed; -at·ing 1** : count **2** : list — **enu·mer·a·tion** \i₁nümə'rāshən, -₁nyü-\ n

enun·ci·ate \ē'nənsē₁āt\ vb **-at·ed; -at·ing 1** : announce **2** : pronounce — **enun·ci·a·tion** \-₁nənsē'āshən\ n

en·vel·op \in'veləp\ vb : surround — **en·vel·op·ment** n

en·ve·lope \'envə₁lōp, 'än-\ n : paper container for a letter

en·vi·ron·ment \in'vīrənmənt\ n : surroundings — **en·vi·ron·men·tal** \-₁vīrən'ment⁵l\ adj

en·vi·ron·men·tal·ist \-⁹list\ n : person concerned about the environment

en·vi·rons \in'vīrənz\ n pl : vicinity

en·vis·age \in'vizij\ vb **-aged; -ag·ing** : have a mental picture of

en·vi·sion \-'vizhən\ vb : picture to oneself

en·voy \'en₁vȯi, 'än-\ n : diplomat

en·vy \'envē\ n **1** : resentful awareness of another's advantage **2** : object of envy ~ vb **-vied; -vy·ing** : feel envy toward or on account of — **en·vi·able** \-vēəbəl\ adj — **en·vi·ous** \-vēəs\ adj — **en·vi·ous·ly** adv

en·zyme \'en₁zīm\ n : biological catalyst

eon \'ēən, ē₁än\ var of AEON

ep·au·let \\ˌepə'let\ *n* : shoulder ornament on a uniform

ephem·er·al \i'femərəl\ *adj* : short-lived

ep·ic \'epik\ *n* : long poem about a hero — **epic** *adj*

ep·i·cure \'epiˌkyu̇r\ *n* : person with fastidious taste esp. in food and wine — **ep·i·cu·re·an** \ˌepikyu̇-'rēən, -'kyu̇rē-\ *n or adj*

ep·i·dem·ic \ˌepə'demik\ *adj* : affecting many persons at one time — **epidemic** *n*

epi·der·mis \ˌepə'dərməs\ *n* : outer layer of skin

ep·i·gram \'epəˌgram\ *n* : short witty poem or saying — **ep·i·gram·mat·ic** \ˌepəgrə'matik\ *adj*

ep·i·lep·sy \'epəˌlepsē\ *n, pl* **-sies** : nervous disorder marked by convulsive attacks — **ep·i·lep·tic** \ˌepə'leptik\ *adj or n*

epis·co·pal \i'piskəpəl\ *adj* : governed by bishops

ep·i·sode \'epəˌsōd, -ˌzōd\ *n* : occurrence — **ep·i·sod·ic** \ˌepə'sädik, -'zäd-\ *adj*

epis·tle \i'pisəl\ *n* : letter

ep·i·taph \'epəˌtaf\ *n* : inscription in memory of a dead person

ep·i·thet \'epəˌthet, -thət\ *n* : characterizing often abusive word or phrase

epit·o·me \i'pitəmē\ *n* **1** : summary **2** : ideal example — **epit·o·mize** \-ˌmīz\ *vb*

ep·och \'epək, 'epˌäk\ *n* : extended period — **ep·och·al** \'epəkəl, 'epˌäkəl\ *adj*

ep·oxy \'epˌäksē, ep'äksē\ *n* : synthetic resin used esp. in adhesives ~ *vb* **-ox·ied** *or* **-oxyed; -oxy·ing** : glue with epoxy

equa·ble \'ekwəbəl, 'ēkwə-\ *adj* : free from unpleasant extremes — **eq·ua·bil·i·ty** \ˌekwə'bilətē, ˌē-\ *n* — **eq·ua·bly** \-blē\ *adv*

equal \'ēkwəl\ *adj* : of the same quantity, value, quality, number, or status as another ~ *n* : one that is equal ~ *vb* **equaled** *or* **equalled; equal·ing** *or* **equal·ling** : be or become equal to — **equal·i·ty** \i'kwälətē\ *n* — **equal·ize** \'ēkwə-ˌlīz\ *vb* — **equal·ly** \'ēkwəlē\ *adv*

equa·nim·i·ty \ˌēkwə'nimətē, ˌek-\ *n, pl* **-ties** : calmness

equate \i'kwāt\ *vb* **equat·ed; equat·ing** : treat or regard as equal

equa·tion \i'kwāzhən, -shən\ *n* : mathematical statement that two things are equal

equa·tor \i'kwātər\ *n* : imaginary circle that separates the northern and southern hemispheres — **equa·to·ri·al** \ˌēkwə'tōrēəl, ˌek-\ *adj*

eques·tri·an \i'kwestrēən\ *adj* : relating to horseback riding ~ *n* : horseback rider

equi·lat·er·al \ˌēkwə'latərəl\ *adj* : having equal sides

equi·lib·ri·um \-'librēəm\ *n, pl* **-ri·ums** *or* **-ria** \-rēə\ : state of balance

equine \'ēˌkwīn, 'ek\ *adj* : relating to the horse — **equine** *n*

equi·nox \'ēkwəˌnäks, 'ek-\ *n* : time when day and night are everywhere of equal length

equip \i'kwip\ *vb* **-pp-** : furnish with needed resources — **equip·ment** \-mənt\ *n*

eq·ui·ta·ble \'ekwətəbəl\ *adj* : fair

eq·ui·ty \'ekwətē\ *n, pl* **-ties 1** : justice **2** : value of a property less debt

equiv·a·lent \i'kwivələnt\ *adj* : equal — **equiv·a·lence** \-ləns\ *n* — **equivalent** *n*

equiv·o·cal \i'kwivəkəl\ *adj* : ambiguous or uncertain

equiv·o·cate \i'kwivəˌkāt\ *vb* **-cat·ed; -cat·ing 1** : use misleading language **2** : avoid answering definitely — **equiv·o·ca·tion** \-ˌkwivə-'kāshən\ *n*

¹-er \ər\ *adj suffix or adv suffix* — used to form the comparative degree of adjectives and adverbs and esp. those of one or two syllables

²-er \ər\; **-ier** \ēər, yər\; **-yer** \yər\ *n suffix* **1** : one that is associated with **2** : one that performs or is the object of an action **3** : one that is

era \'irə, 'erə, 'ērə\ *n* : period of time associated with something

erad·i·cate \i'radəˌkāt\ *vb* **-cat·ed; -cat·ing** : do away with

erase \i'rās\ *vb* **erased; eras·ing** : rub or scratch out — **eras·er** *n* — **era·sure** \i'rāshər\ *n*

ere \'er\ *prep or conj* : before

erect \i'rekt\ *adj* : not leaning or lying down ~ *vb* **1** : build **2** : bring to an upright position — **erec·tion** \i'rekshən\ *n*

er·mine \'ərmən\ *n* : weasel with white winter fur or its fur

erode \i'rōd\ *vb* **erod·ed; erod·ing** : wear away gradually

ero·sion \i'rōzhən\ *n* : process of eroding

erot·ic \i'rätik\ *adj* : sexually arousing — **erot·i·cal·ly** \-iklē\ *adv* — **erot·i·cism** \i'rätə,sizəm\ *n*

err \'er, 'ər\ *vb* : be or do wrong

er·rand \'erənd\ *n* : short trip taken to do something often for another

er·rant \-ənt\ *adj* **1** : traveling about **2** : going astray

er·rat·ic \ir'atik\ *adj* **1** : eccentric **2** : inconsistent — **er·rat·i·cal·ly** \-iklē\ *adv*

er·ro·ne·ous \ir'ōnēəs, e'rō-\ *adj* : wrong — **er·ro·ne·ous·ly** *adv*

er·ror \'erər\ *n* **1** : something that is not accurate **2** : state of being wrong

er·satz \'er,säts\ *adj* : phony

erst·while \'ərst,hwīl\ *adv* : in the past ~ *adj* : former

er·u·di·tion \,erə'dishən, ,eryə-\ *n* : great learning — **er·u·dite** \'erə-,dīt, 'eryə-\ *adj*

erupt \i'rəpt\ *vb* : burst forth esp. suddenly and violently — **erup·tion** \i'rəpshən\ *n* — **erup·tive** \-tiv\ *adj*

-ery \ərē\ *n suffix* **1** : character or condition **2** : practice **3** : place of doing

¹-es \əz, iz *after* s, z, sh, ch; z *after* v or a vowel\ *n pl suffix* — used to form the plural of some nouns

²-es *vb suffix* — used to form the 3d person singular present of some verbs

es·ca·late \'eskə,lāt\ *vb* **-lat·ed; -lat·ing** : become quickly larger or greater — **es·ca·la·tion** \,eskə-'lāshən\ *n*

es·ca·la·tor \'eskə,lātər\ *n* : moving stairs

es·ca·pade \'eskə,pād\ *n* : mischievous adventure

es·cape \is'kāp\ *vb* **-caped; -cap·ing** : get away or get away from ~ *n* **1** : flight from or avoidance of something unpleasant **2** : leakage **3** : means of escape ~ *adj* : providing means of escape — **es·cap·ee** \is,kā'pē, -es-\ *n*

es·ca·role \'eskə,rōl\ *n* : salad green

es·carp·ment \is'kärpmənt\ *n* : cliff

es·chew \is'chü\ *vb* : shun

es·cort \'es,kórt\ *n* : one accompa-

nying another — **es·cort** \is'kórt, es-\ *vb*

es·crow \'es,krō\ *n* : deposit to be delivered upon fulfillment of a condition

esoph·a·gus \i'säfəgəs\ *n, pl* **-gi** \-,gī, -,jī\ : muscular tube connecting the mouth and stomach

es·o·ter·ic \,esə'terik\ *adj* : mysterious or secret

es·pe·cial·ly \is'peshəlē\ *adv* : particularly or notably

es·pi·o·nage \'espēə,näzh, -nij\ *n* : practice of spying

es·pous·al \is'pauzəl\ *n* **1** : betrothal **2** : wedding **3** : a taking up as a supporter — **es·pouse** \-'pauz\ *vb*

espres·so \e'spresō\ *n, pl* **-sos** : strong steam-brewed coffee

es·py \is'pī\ *vb* **-pied; -py·ing** : catch sight of

es·quire \'es,kwīr\ *n* — used as a title of courtesy

-ess \əs, ,es\ *n suffix* : female

es·say \'es,ā\ *n* : literary composition ~ *vb* \e'sā, 'es,ā\ : attempt — **es·say·ist** \'es,āist\ *n*

es·sence \'es°ns\ *n* **1** : fundamental nature or quality **2** : extract **3** : perfume

es·sen·tial \i'senchəl\ *adj* : basic or necessary — **essential** *n* — **es·sen·tial·ly** *adv*

-est \əst, ist\ *adj suffix or adv suffix* — used to form the superlative degree of adjectives and adverbs and esp. those of 1 or 2 syllables

es·tab·lish \is'tablish\ *vb* **1** : bring into existence **2** : put on a firm basis **3** : cause to be recognized

es·tab·lish·ment \-mənt\ *n* **1** : business or a place of business **2** : an establishing or being established **3** : controlling group

es·tate \is'tāt\ *n* **1** : one's possessions **2** : large piece of land with a house

es·teem \is'tēm\ *n or vb* : regard

es·ter \'estər\ *n* : organic chemical compound

esthetic *var of* AESTHETIC

es·ti·ma·ble \'estəməbəl\ *adj* : worthy of esteem

es·ti·mate \'estə,māt\ *vb* **-mat·ed; -mat·ing** : judge the approximate value, size, or cost ~ \-mət\ *n* **1** : rough or approximate calculation **2** : statement of the cost of a job — **es·ti·ma·tion** \,estə-

'mashən\ *n* — es·ti·ma·tor \'estə-ˌmātər\ *n*

es·trange \is'trānj\ *vb* **-tranged; -trang·ing** : make hostile — **es·trange·ment** *n*

es·tro·gen \'estrəjən\ *n* : hormone that produces female characteristics

es·tu·ary \'eschəˌwerē\ *n, pl* **-ar·ies** : arm of the sea at a river's mouth

et cet·era \et'setərə, -'setrə\ : and others esp. of the same kind

etch \'ech\ *vb* : produce by corroding parts of a surface with acid — **etch·er** *n* — **etch·ing** *n*

eter·nal \i'tərnᵊl\ *adj* : lasting forever — **eter·nal·ly** *adv*

eter·ni·ty \-nətē\ *n, pl* **-ties** : infinite duration

eth·ane \'ethˌān\ *n* : gaseous hydrocarbon

eth·a·nol \'ethəˌnȯl, -ˌnōl\ *n* : alcohol

ether \'ēthər\ *n* : light flammable liquid used as an anesthetic

ethe·re·al \i'thirēəl\ *adj* **1** : celestial **2** : exceptionally delicate

eth·i·cal \'ethikəl\ *adj* **1** : relating to ethics **2** : honorable — **eth·i·cal·ly** *adv*

eth·ics \-iks\ *n sing or pl* **1** : study of good and evil and moral duty **2** : moral principles or practice

eth·nic \'ethnik\ *adj* : relating to races or groups of people with common customs ∼ *n* : member of a minority ethnic group

eth·nol·o·gy \eth'näləjē\ *n* : study of the races of human beings — **eth·no·log·i·cal** \ˌethnə'läjikəl\ *adj* — **eth·nol·o·gist** \eth'näləjist\ *n*

◆ **et·i·quette** \'etikət, -ˌket\ *n* : good manners

et·y·mol·o·gy \ˌetə'mäləjē\ *n, pl* **-gies 1** : history of a word **2** : study of etymologies — **et·y·mo·log·i-**

cal \-mə'läjikəl\ *adj* — **et·y·mol·o·gist** \-'mäləjist\ *n*

eu·ca·lyp·tus \ˌyükə'liptəs\ *n, pl* **-ti** \-ˌtī\ *or* **-tus·es** : Australian evergreen tree

Eu·cha·rist \'yükərəst\ *n* : Communion — **eu·cha·ris·tic** \ˌyükə-'ristik\ *adj*

eu·lo·gy \'yüləjē\ *n, pl* **-gies** : speech in praise — **eu·lo·gis·tic** \ˌyülə-'jistik\ *adj* — **eu·lo·gize** \'yülə-ˌjīz\ *vb*

eu·nuch \'yünək\ *n* : castrated man

eu·phe·mism \'yüfəˌmizəm\ *n* : substitution of a pleasant expression for an unpleasant or offensive one — **eu·phe·mis·tic** \ˌyüfə'mistik\ *adj*

eu·pho·ni·ous \yu'fōnēəs\ *adj* : pleasing to the ear — **eu·pho·ny** \'yüfənē\ *n*

eu·pho·ria \yu'fōrēə\ *n* : elation — **eu·phor·ic** \-'fȯrik\ *adj*

eu·tha·na·sia \ˌyüthə'nāzhə, -zhēə\ *n* : mercy killing

evac·u·ate \i'vakyəˌwāt\ *vb* **-at·ed; -at·ing 1** : discharge wastes from the body **2** : remove or withdraw from — **evac·u·a·tion** \iˌvakyə'wāshən\ *n*

evade \i'vād\ *vb* **evad·ed; evad·ing** : manage to avoid

eval·u·ate \i'valyəˌwāt\ *vb* **-at·ed; -at·ing** : appraise — **eval·u·a·tion** \iˌvalyə'wāshən\ *n*

evan·gel·i·cal \ˌēˌvan'jelikəl, ˌevən-\ *adj* : relating to the Christian gospel

evan·ge·lism \i'vanjəˌlizəm\ *n* : the winning or revival of personal commitments to Christ — **evan·ge·list** \i'vanjəlist\ *n* — **evan·ge·lis·tic** \iˌvanjə'listik\ *adj*

evap·o·rate \i'vapəˌrāt\ *vb* **-rat·ed; -rat·ing 1** : pass off in or convert into vapor **2** : disappear quickly — **evap·o·ra·tion** \iˌvapə-**

MY UNCLE ED WAS BIG ON ETIQUETTE

"NEVER BELCH OUT LOUD" HE ALWAYS SAID

THEN ONE DAY HE BLEW OUT AN EYEBALL

GARFIELD

'rāshən\ *n* — **evap·ora·tor** \i'vapəˌrātər\ *n*

eva·sion \i'vāzhən\ *n* : act or instance of evading — **eva·sive** \i'vāsiv\ *adj* — **eva·sive·ness** *n*

eve \'ēv\ *n* : evening

even \'ēvən\ *adj* 1 : smooth 2 : equal or fair 3 : fully revenged 4 : divisible by 2 ~ *adv* 1 : already 2 — used for emphasis ~ *vb* : make or become even — **even·ly** *adv* — **even·ness** *n*

eve·ning \'ēvniŋ\ *n* : early part of the night

event \i'vent\ *n* 1 : occurrence 2 : noteworthy happening 3 : eventuality — **event·ful** *adj*

even·tu·al \i'venchəwəl\ *adj* : later — **even·tu·al·ly** *adv*

even·tu·al·i·ty \iˌvenchə'walətē\ *n*, *pl* **-ties** : possible occurrence or outcome

ev·er \'evər\ *adv* 1 : always 2 : at any time 3 : in any case

ev·er·green *adj* : having foliage that remains green — **evergreen** *n*

ev·er·last·ing \ˌevər'lastiŋ\ *adj* : lasting forever

ev·ery \'evrē\ *adj* 1 : being each one of a group 2 : all possible

ev·ery·body \'evriˌbädē, -bəd-\ *pron* : every person

ev·ery·day *adj* : ordinary

ev·ery·one \-ˌwən\ *pron* : every person

ev·ery·thing *pron* : all that exists

ev·ery·where *adv* : in every place or part

evict \i'vikt\ *vb* : force (a person) to move from a property — **evic·tion** \i'vikshən\ *n*

ev·i·dence \'evədəns\ *n* 1 : outward sign 2 : proof or testimony

ev·i·dent \-ənt\ *adj* : clear or obvious — **ev·i·dent·ly** \-ədəntlē, -əˌdent-\ *adv*

evil \'ēvəl\ *adj* **evil·er** *or* **evil·ler**; **evil·est** *or* **evil·lest** : wicked ~ *n* 1 : sin 2 : source of sorrow or distress — **evil·do·er** \ˌēvəl'düər\ *n* — **evil·ly** *adv*

evince \i'vins\ *vb* **evinced; evinc·ing** : show

evis·cer·ate \i'visəˌrāt\ *vb* **-at·ed; -at·ing** : remove the viscera of — **evis·cer·a·tion** \iˌvisə'rāshən\ *n*

evoke \i'vōk\ *vb* **evoked; evok·ing** : call forth or up — **evo·ca-**

tion \ˌēvō'kāshən, ˌevə-\ *n* — **evoc·a·tive** \i'väkətiv\ *adj*

evo·lu·tion \ˌevə'lüshən\ *n* : process of change by degrees — **evo·lu·tion·ary** \-shəˌnerē\ *adj*

evolve \i'välv\ *vb* **evolved; evolv·ing** : develop or change by degrees

ewe \'yü\ *n* : female sheep

ew·er \'yüər\ *n* : water pitcher

ex·act \ig'zakt\ *vb* : compel to furnish ~ *adj* : precisely correct — **ex·act·ing** *adj* — **ex·ac·tion** \-'zakshən\ *n* — **ex·ac·ti·tude** \-'zaktəˌtüd, -ˌtyüd\ *n* — **ex·act·ly** *adv* — **ex·act·ness** *n*

ex·ag·ger·ate \ig'zajəˌrāt\ *vb* **-at·ed; -at·ing** : say more than is true — **ex·ag·ger·at·ed·ly** *adv* — **ex·ag·ger·a·tion** \-ˌzajə'rāshən\ *n* — **ex·ag·ger·a·tor** \-'zajərātər\ *n*

ex·alt \ig'zolt\ *vb* : glorify — **ex·al·ta·tion** \ˌegˌzol'tāshən, ˌekˌsol-\ *n*

ex·am \ig'zam\ *n* : examination

ex·am·ine \-ən\ *vb* **-ined; -in·ing** 1 : inspect closely 2 : test by questioning — **ex·am·i·na·tion** \-ˌzamə'nāshən\ *n*

ex·am·ple \ig'zampəl\ *n* 1 : representative sample 2 : model 3 : problem to be solved for teaching purposes

ex·as·per·ate \ig'zaspəˌrāt\ *vb* **-at·ed; -at·ing** : thoroughly annoy — **ex·as·per·a·tion** \-ˌzaspə'rāshən\ *n*

ex·ca·vate \'ekskəˌvāt\ *vb* **-vat·ed; -vat·ing** : dig or hollow out — **ex·ca·va·tion** \ˌekskə'vāshən\ *n* — **ex·ca·va·tor** \'ekskəˌvātər\ *n*

ex·ceed \ik'sēd\ *vb* 1 : go or be beyond the limit of 2 : do better than

ex·ceed·ing·ly *adv* : extremely

ex·cel \ik'sel\ *vb* **-ll-** : do extremely well or far better than

ex·cel·lence \'eksələns\ *n* : quality of being excellent

ex·cel·len·cy \-lənsē\ *n*, *pl* **-cies** — used as a title of honor

ex·cel·lent \'eksələnt\ *adj* : very good — **ex·cel·lent·ly** *adv*

ex·cept \ik'sept\ *vb* : omit ~ *prep* : excluding ~ *conj* : but — **ex·cep·tion** \-'sepshən\ *n*

ex·cep·tion·al \-'sepshənəl\ *adj* : superior — **ex·cep·tion·al·ly** *adv*

ex·cerpt \'ekˌsərpt, 'egˌzərpt\ *n* : brief passage ~ \ek'-, eg'-, 'ekˌ-, 'egˌ-\ *vb* : select an excerpt

ex·cess \ik'ses, 'ekˌses\ *n* : amount left over — **excess** *adj* — **ex·ces-**

sive \ik'sesiv\ *adj* — **ex·ces·sive·ly** *adv*

ex·change \iks'chānj, 'eks,chānj\ *n* 1 : the giving or taking of one thing in return for another 2 : marketplace esp. for securities ~ *vb* -changed; -chang·ing : transfer in return for some equivalent — **ex·change·able** \iks'chānjəbəl\ *adj*

¹**ex·cise** \'ek,sīz, -,sīs\ *n* : tax
²**ex·cise** \ik'sīz\ *vb* -cised; -cis·ing : cut out — **ex·ci·sion** \-'sizhən\ *n*

ex·cite \ik'sīt\ *vb* -cit·ed; -cit·ing 1 : stir up 2 : kindle the emotions of — **ex·cit·abil·i·ty** \-,sītə'bilətē\ *n* — **ex·cit·able** \-'sītəbəl\ *adj* — **ex·ci·ta·tion** \,ek,sī'tāshən, -ə-\ *n* — **ex·cit·ed·ly** *adv* — **ex·cite·ment** \ik'sītmənt\ *n*

ex·claim \iks'klām\ *vb* : cry out esp. in delight — **ex·cla·ma·tion** \,eksklə'māshən\ *n* — **ex·clam·a·to·ry** \iks'klamə,tōrē\ *adj*

exclamation point *n* : punctuation mark ! used esp. after an interjection or exclamation

ex·clude \iks'klüd\ *vb* -clud·ed; -clud·ing : leave out — **ex·clu·sion** \-'klüzhən\ *n*

ex·clu·sive \-'klüsiv\ *adj* 1 : reserved for particular persons 2 : stylish 3 : sole — **exclusive** *n* — **ex·clu·sive·ly** *adv* — **ex·clu·sive·ness** *n*

ex·com·mu·ni·cate \,ekskə'myünə,kāt\ *vb* : expel from a church — **ex·com·mu·ni·ca·tion** \-,myünə-'kāshən\ *n*

ex·cre·ment \'ekskrəmənt\ *n* : bodily waste — **ex·cre·men·tal** \,ekskrə'mentᵊl\ *adj*

ex·crete \ik'skrēt\ *vb* -cret·ed; -cret·ing : eliminate wastes from the body — **ex·cre·tion** \-'skrēshən\ *n* — **ex·cre·to·ry** \'ekskrə,tōrē\ *adj*

ex·cru·ci·at·ing \ik'skrüshē,ātiŋ\ *adj* : intensely painful — **ex·cru·ci·at·ing·ly** *adv*

ex·cul·pate \'ekskəl,pāt\ *vb* -pat·ed; -pat·ing : clear from alleged fault

ex·cur·sion \ik'skərzhən\ *n* : pleasure trip

ex·cuse \ik'skyüz\ *vb* -cused; -cus·ing 1 : pardon 2 : release from an obligation 3 : justify ~ \-'skyüs\ *n* 1 : justification 2 : apology

ex·e·cute \'eksi,kyüt\ *vb* -cut·ed; -cut·ing 1 : carry out fully 2 : enforce 3 : put to death — **ex·e·cu·tion** \,eksi'kyüshən\ *n* — **ex·e·cu·tion·er** \-shənər\ *n*

ex·ec·u·tive \ig'zekyətiv\ *adj* : relating to the carrying out of decisions, plans, or laws ~ *n* 1 : branch of government with executive duties 2 : administrator

ex·ec·u·tor \-yətər\ *n* : person named in a will to execute it

ex·ec·u·trix \ig'zekyə,triks\ *n, pl* **ex·ec·u·tri·ces** \-,zekyə'trī-,sēz\ *or* **ex·ec·u·trix·es** : woman executor

ex·em·pla·ry \ig'zemplərē\ *adj* : so commendable as to serve as a model

ex·em·pli·fy \-plə,fī\ *vb* -fied; -fy·ing : serve as an example of — **ex·em·pli·fi·ca·tion** \-,zempləfə'kā-shən\ *n*

ex·empt \ig'zempt\ *adj* : being free from some liability ~ *vb* : make exempt — **ex·emp·tion** \-'zemp-shən\ *n*

ex·er·cise \'eksər,sīz\ *n* 1 : a putting into action 2 : exertion to develop endurance or a skill 3 *pl* : public ceremony ~ *vb* -cised; -cis·ing 1 : exert 2 : engage in exercise — **ex·er·cis·er** *n*

ex·ert \ig'zərt\ *vb* : put into action — **ex·er·tion** \-'zərshən\ *n*

ex·hale \eks'hāl\ *vb* -haled; -hal·ing : breathe out — **ex·ha·la·tion** \eksho'lāshən\ *n*

♦ **ex·haust** \ig'zòst\ *vb* 1 : draw out

or develop completely **2** : use up **3** : tire or wear out ~ *n* : waste steam or gas from an engine or a system for removing it — **ex·haus·tion** \-ˈzöschən\ *n* — **ex·haus·tive** \-ˈzöstiv\ *adj*

ex·hib·it \igˈzibət\ *vb* : display esp. publicly ~ *n* **1** : act of exhibiting **2** : something exhibited — **ex·hi·bi·tion** \ˌeksəˈbishən\ *n* — **ex·hib·i·tor** \igˈzibətər\ *n*

ex·hil·a·rate \igˈziləˌrāt\ *vb* **-rat·ed; -rat·ing** : thrill — **ex·hil·a·ra·tion** \-ˌzilə̇ˈrāshən\ *n*

ex·hort \-ˈzȯrt\ *vb* : urge earnestly — **ex·hor·ta·tion** \ˌeksˌȯrˈtāshən, ˌegz-, -ər-\ *n*

ex·hume \igzˈüm, -ˈyüm; iksˈyüm, -ˈhyüm\ *vb* **-humed; -hum·ing** : dig up (a buried corpse) — **ex·hu·ma·tion** \ˌeksyüˈmāshən, -hyü-; ˌegzü-, -zyü-\ *n*

ex·i·gen·cies \ˈeksəjənsēz, igˈzijən-\ *n pl* : requirements (as of a situation)

ex·ile \ˈegˌzīl, ˈekˌsīl\ *n* **1** : banishment **2** : person banished from his or her country — **exile** *vb*

ex·ist \igˈzist\ *vb* **1** : have real or actual being **2** : live — **ex·is·tence** \-əns\ *n* — **ex·is·tent** \-ənt\ *adj*

ex·it \ˈegzət, ˈeksət\ *n* **1** : departure **2** : way out of an enclosed space **3** : way off an expressway — **exit** *vb*

ex·o·dus \ˈeksədəs\ *n* : mass departure

ex·on·er·ate \igˈzänəˌrāt\ *vb* **-at·ed; -at·ing** : free from blame — **ex·on·er·a·tion** \-ˌzänəˈrāshən\ *n*

ex·or·bi·tant \igˈzȯrbətənt\ *adj* : exceeding what is usual or proper

ex·or·cise \ˈekˌsȯrˌsīz, -ər-\ *vb* **-cised; -cis·ing** : drive out (as an evil spirit) — **ex·or·cism** \-ˌsizəm\ *n* — **ex·or·cist** \-ˌsist\ *n*

ex·ot·ic \igˈzätik\ *adj* : foreign or strange — **exotic** *n* — **ex·ot·i·cal·ly** \-iklē\ *adv*

ex·pand \ikˈspand\ *vb* : enlarge

ex·panse \-ˈspans\ *n* : very large area

ex·pan·sion \-ˈspanchən\ *n* **1** : act or process of expanding **2** : expanded part

ex·pan·sive \-ˈspansiv\ *adj* **1** : tending to expand **2** : warmly benevolent **3** : of large extent — **ex·pan·sive·ly** *adv* — **ex·pan·sive·ness** *n*

ex·pa·tri·ate \ekˈspātrēˌāt, -ət\ *n* : exile — **expatriate** \-ˌāt\ *adj or vb*

ex·pect \ikˈspekt\ *vb* **1** : look forward to **2** : consider probable or one's due — **ex·pec·tan·cy** \-ənsē\ *n* — **ex·pec·tant** \-ənt\ *adj* — **ex·pec·tant·ly** *adv* — **ex·pec·ta·tion** \ˌek̩spekˈtāshən\ *n*

ex·pe·di·ent \ikˈspēdēənt\ *adj* : convenient or advantageous rather than right or just ~ *n* : convenient often makeshift means to an end

ex·pe·dite \ˈekspəˌdīt\ *vb* **-dit·ed; -dit·ing** : carry out or handle promptly — **ex·pe·dit·er** *n*

ex·pe·di·tion \ˌekspəˈdishən\ *n* : long journey for work or research or the people making this

ex·pe·di·tious \-əs\ *adj* : prompt and efficient

ex·pel \ikˈspel\ *vb* **-ll-** : force out

ex·pend \-ˈspend\ *vb* **1** : pay out **2** : use up — **ex·pend·able** *adj*

ex·pen·di·ture \-ˈspendichər, -də-ˌchu̇r\ *n* : act of using or spending

ex·pense \ikˈspens\ *n* : cost — **ex·pen·sive** \-ˈspensiv\ *adj* — **ex·pen·sive·ly** *adv*

ex·pe·ri·ence \ikˈspirēəns\ *n* **1** : a participating in or living through an event **2** : an event that affects one **3** : knowledge from doing ~ *vb* **-enced; -enc·ing** : undergo

ex·per·i·ment \ikˈsperəmənt\ *n* : test to discover something ~ *vb* : make experiments — **ex·per·i·men·tal** \-ˌsperəˈmentᵊl\ *adj* — **ex·per·i·men·ta·tion** \-mənˈtāshən\ *n* — **ex·per·i·men·ter** \-ˈsperə-ˌmentər\ *n*

ex·pert \ˈekˌspərt\ *adj* : thoroughly skilled ~ *n* : person with special skill — **ex·pert·ly** *adv* — **ex·pert·ness** *n*

ex·per·tise \ˌekspərˈtēz\ *n* : skill

ex·pi·ate \ˈekspēˌāt\ *vb* : make amends for — **ex·pi·a·tion** \ˌekspēˈāshən\ *n*

ex·pire \ikˈspīr, ek-\ *vb* **-pired; -pir·ing** **1** : breathe out **2** : die **3** : end — **ex·pi·ra·tion** \ˌekspəˈrāshən\ *n*

ex·plain \ikˈsplān\ *vb* **1** : make clear **2** : give the reason for — **ex·plain·able** \-əbəl\ *adj* — **ex·pla·na·tion** \ˌekspləˈnāshən\ *n* — **ex·plan·a·to·ry** \ikˈsplanəˌtōrē\ *adj*

ex·ple·tive \ˈeksplətiv\ *n* : usu. profane exclamation

ex·pli·ca·ble \ekˈsplikəbəl, ˈeksplik-\ *adj* : capable of being explained

ex·plic·it \ik'splisət\ *adj* : absolutely clear or precise — **ex·plic·it·ly** *adv* — **ex·plic·it·ness** *n*

ex·plode \ik'splōd\ *vb* **-plod·ed; -plod·ing** 1 : discredit 2 : burst or cause to burst violently 3 : increase rapidly

ex·ploit \'ek,sploit\ *n* : heroic act ~ \ik'sploit\ *vb* 1 : utilize 2 : use unfairly — **ex·ploi·ta·tion** \,ek,sploi-'tāshən\ *n*

ex·plore \ik'splōr\ *vb* **-plored; -plor·ing** : examine or range over thoroughly — **ex·plo·ra·tion** \,eksplə-'rāshən\ *n* — **ex·plor·a·to·ry** \ik-'splōrə,tōrē\ *adj* — **ex·plor·er** *n*

ex·plo·sion \ik'splōzhən\ *n* : process or instance of exploding

ex·plo·sive \-siv\ *adj* 1 : able to cause explosion 2 : likely to explode — **explosive** *n* — **ex·plo·sive·ly** *adv*

ex·po·nent \ik'spōnənt, 'ek,spō-\ *n* 1 : mathematical symbol showing how many times a number is to be repeated as a factor 2 : advocate — **ex·po·nen·tial** \,ekspə'nen-chəl\ *adj* — **ex·po·nen·tial·ly** *adv*

ex·port \ek'spōrt, 'ek,spōrt\ *vb* : send to foreign countries — **export** \'ek,-\ *n* — **ex·por·ta·tion** \,ek,spōr'tāshən\ *n* — **ex·port·er** \ek'spōrtər, 'ek,spōrt-\ *n*

ex·pose \ik'spōz\ *vb* **-posed; -pos·ing** 1 : deprive of shelter or protection 2 : subject (film) to light 3 : make known — **ex·po·sure** \-'spōzhər\ *n*

ex·po·sé, ex·po·se \,ekspō'zā\ *n* : exposure of something discreditable

ex·po·si·tion \,ekspə'zishən\ *n* : public exhibition

ex·pound \ik'spaúnd\ *vb* : set forth or explain in detail

¹ex·press \-'spres\ *adj* 1 : clear 2 : specific 3 : traveling at high speed with few stops — **express** *adv or n* — **ex·press·ly** *adv*

²express *vb* 1 : make known in words or appearance 2 : press out (as juice)

ex·pres·sion \-'spreshən\ *n* 1 : utterance 2 : mathematical symbol 3 : significant word or phrase 4 : look on one's face — **ex·pres·sion·less** *adj* — **ex·pres·sive**

\-'spresiv\ *adj* — **ex·pres·sive·ness** *n*

ex·press·way \ik'spres,wā\ *n* : high-speed divided highway with limited access

ex·pul·sion \ik'spəlshən\ *n* : an expelling or being expelled

ex·pur·gate \'ekspər,gāt\ *vb* **-gat·ed; -gat·ing** : censor — **ex·pur·ga·tion** \,ekspər'gāshən\ *n*

ex·qui·site \ek'skwizət, 'ekskwiz-\ *adj* 1 : flawlessly beautiful and delicate 2 : keenly discriminating

ex·tant \'ekstənt, ek'stant\ *adj* : existing

ex·tem·po·ra·ne·ous \ek,stempə-'rānēəs\ *adj* : impromptu — **ex·tem·po·ra·ne·ous·ly** *adv*

ex·tend \ik'stend\ *vb* 1 : stretch forth or out 2 : prolong 3 : enlarge — **ex·tend·able** \-'stendəbəl\ *adj*

ex·ten·sion \-'stenchən\ *n* 1 : an extending or being extended 2 : additional part 3 : extra telephone line

ex·ten·sive \-'stensiv\ *adj* : of considerable extent — **ex·ten·sive·ly** *adv*

ex·tent \-'stent\ *n* : range, space, or degree to which something extends

ex·ten·u·ate \ik'stenyə,wāt\ *vb* **-at·ed; -at·ing** : lessen the seriousness of — **ex·ten·u·a·tion** \-,stenyə-'wāshən\ *n*

ex·te·ri·or \ek'stirēər\ *adj* : external ~ *n* : external part or surface

ex·ter·mi·nate \ik'stərmə,nāt\ *vb* **-nat·ed; -nat·ing** : destroy utterly — **ex·ter·mi·na·tion** \-,stərmə-'nāshən\ *n* — **ex·ter·mi·na·tor** \-'stərmə,nātər\ *n*

ex·ter·nal \ek'stərnªl\ *adj* : relating to or on the outside — **ex·ter·nal·ly** *adv*

ex·tinct \ik'stiŋkt\ *adj* : no longer existing — **ex·tinc·tion** \-'stiŋk-shən\ *n*

ex·tin·guish \-'stiŋgwish\ *vb* : cause to stop burning — **ex·tin·guish·able** *adj* — **ex·tin·guish·er** *n*

ex·tir·pate \'ekstər,pāt\ *vb* **-pat·ed; -pat·ing** : destroy

ex·tol \ik'stōl\ *vb* **-ll-** : praise highly

ex·tort \-'stórt\ *vb* : obtain by force or improper pressure — **ex·tor·tion** \-'stórshən\ *n* — **ex·tor·tion·er** *n* — **ex·tor·tion·ist** *n*

ex·tra \'ekstrə\ *adj* **1** : additional **2** : superior — **extra** *n or adv*

extra- *prefix* : outside or beyond

ex·tract \ik'strakt\ *vb* **1** : pull out forcibly **2** : withdraw (as a juice) ~ \'ek₁-\ *n* **1** : excerpt **2** : product (as a juice) obtained by extracting — **ex·tract·able** *adj* — **ex·trac·tion** \ik'strakshən\ *n* — **ex·trac·tor** \-tər\ *n*

ex·tra·cur·ric·u·lar \₁ekstrəkə-'rikyələr\ *adj* : lying outside the regular curriculum

ex·tra·dite \'ekstrə₁dīt\ *vb* **-dit·ed; -dit·ing** : bring or deliver a suspect to a different jurisdiction for trial — **ex·tra·di·tion** \₁ekstrə-'dishən\ *n*

ex·tra·mar·i·tal \₁ekstrə'marət°l\ *adj* : relating to sexual relations of a married person outside of the marriage

ex·tra·ne·ous \ek'strānēəs\ *adj* : not essential or relevant — **ex·tra·ne·ous·ly** *adv*

ex·traor·di·nary \ik'strórd°n₁erē, ₁ekstrə'órd-\ *adj* : notably unusual or exceptional — **ex·traor·di·nari·ly** \ik₁strórd°n'erəlē, ₁ekstrə-₁órd-\ *adv*

ex·tra·sen·so·ry \₁ekstrə'sensərē\ *adj* : outside the ordinary senses

ex·tra·ter·res·tri·al \₁ekstrətə-'restrēəl\ *n* : one existing or coming from outside the earth ~ *adj* : relating to an extraterrestrial

ex·trav·a·gant \ik'stravigənt\ *adj* : wildly excessive, lavish, or costly — **ex·trav·a·gance** \-gəns\ *n* — **ex·trav·a·gant·ly** *adv*

ex·trav·a·gan·za \-₁stravə'ganzə\ *n* : spectacular event

ex·tra·ve·hic·u·lar \₁ekstrəvē-'hikyələr\ *adj* : occurring outside a spacecraft

ex·treme \ik'strēm\ *adj* **1** : very great or intense **2** : very severe **3** : not moderate **4** : most remote ~ *n* **1** : extreme state **2** : something located at one end or the other of a range — **ex·treme·ly** *adv*

ex·trem·i·ty \-'stremətē\ *n, pl* **-ties 1**

: most remote part **2** : human hand or foot **3** : extreme degree or state (as of need)

ex·tri·cate \'ekstrə₁kāt\ *vb* **-cat·ed; -cat·ing** : set or get free from an entanglement or difficulty — **ex·tri·ca·ble** \ik'strikəbəl, ek-; 'ekstrik-\ *adj* — **ex·tri·ca·tion** \₁ekstrə'kāshən\ *n*

ex·tro·vert \'ekstrə₁vərt\ *n* : gregarious person — **ex·tro·ver·sion** \₁ekstrə'vərzhən\ *n* — **ex·tro·vert·ed** \'ekstrə₁vərtəd\ *adj*

ex·trude \ik'strüd\ *vb* **-trud·ed; -trud·ing** : to force or push out

ex·u·ber·ant \ig'zübərənt\ *adj* : joyously unrestrained — **ex·u·ber·ance** \-rəns\ *n* — **ex·u·ber·ant·ly** *adv*

ex·ude \ig'züd\ *vb* **-ud·ed; -ud·ing 1** : discharge slowly through pores **2** : display conspicuously

ex·ult \ig'zəlt\ *vb* : rejoice — **ex·ul·tant** \-'zəlt°nt\ *adj* — **ex·ul·tant·ly** *adv* — **ex·ul·ta·tion** \₁ek-səl'tāshən, ₁egzəl-\ *n*

-ey — see -Y

eye \'ī\ *n* **1** : organ of sight consisting of a globular structure (**eye·ball**) in a socket of the skull with thin movable covers (**eye·lids**) bordered with hairs (**eye·lash·es**) **2** : vision **3** : judgment **4** : something suggesting an eye ~ *vb* **eyed; eye·ing** *or* **ey·ing** : look at — **eye·brow** \-₁braủ\ *n* — **eyed** \'īd\ *adj* — **eye·strain** *n*

eye·drop·per *n* : dropper

eye·glass·es *n pl* : glasses

eye·let \'īlət\ *n* : hole (as in cloth) for a lacing or rope

eye·open·er *n* : something startling — **eye·open·ing** *adj*

eye·piece *n* : lens at the eye end of an optical instrument

eye·sight *n* : sight

eye·sore *n* : unpleasant sight

eye·tooth *n* : upper canine tooth

eye·wit·ness *n* : person who actually sees something happen

ey·rie \'īrē, *or like* AERIE\ *var of* AERIE

F

f \ˈef\ *n, pl* **f's** *or* **fs** \ˈefs\ : 6th letter of the alphabet

fa·ble \ˈfābəl\ *n* **1** : legendary story **2** : story that teaches a lesson — **fa·bled** \-bəld\ *adj*

fab·ric \ˈfabrik\ *n* **1** : structure **2** : material made usu. by weaving or knitting fibers

fab·ri·cate \ˈfabri,kāt\ *vb* **-cat·ed; -cat·ing 1** : construct **2** : invent — **fab·ri·ca·tion** \,fabri'kāshən\ *n*

fab·u·lous \ˈfabyələs\ *adj* **1** : like, told in, or based on fable **2** : incredible or marvelous — **fab·u·lous·ly** *adv*

fa·cade \fə'säd\ *n* **1** : principal face of a building **2** : false or superficial appearance

face \ˈfās\ *n* **1** : front or principal surface (as of the head) **2** : presence **3** : facial expression **4** : grimace **5** : outward appearance ~ *vb* **faced; fac·ing 1** : challenge or resist firmly or brazenly **2** : cover with different material **3** : sit or stand with the face toward **4** : have the front oriented toward — **faced** \ˈfāst\ *adj* — **face·less** *adj* — **fa·cial** \ˈfāshəl\ *adj or n*

face·down *adv* : with the face downward

face-lift \ˈfās,lift\ *n* **1** : cosmetic surgery on the face **2** : modernization

fac·et \ˈfasət\ *n* **1** : surface of a cut gem **2** : phase — **fac·et·ed** *adj*

fa·ce·tious \fə'sēshəs\ *adj* : jocular — **fa·ce·tious·ly** *adv* — **fa·ce·tious·ness** *n*

fac·ile \ˈfasəl\ *adj* **1** : easy **2** : fluent

fa·cil·i·tate \fə'silə,tāt\ *vb* **-tat·ed; -tat·ing** : make easier

fa·cil·i·ty \fə'silətē\ *n, pl* **-ties 1** : ease in doing or using **2** : something built or installed to serve a purpose or facilitate an activity

fac·ing \ˈfāsin\ *n* : lining or covering or material for this

fac·sim·i·le \fak'siməlē\ *n* : exact copy

fact \ˈfakt\ *n* **1** : act or action **2** : something that exists or is real **3** : piece of information — **fac·tu·al** \ˈfakchəwəl\ *adj* — **fac·tu·al·ly** *adv*

fac·tion \ˈfakshən\ *n* : part of a larger group — **fac·tion·al·ism** \-shənə,lizəm\ *n*

fac·tious \ˈfakshəs\ *adj* : causing discord

fac·ti·tious \fak'tishəs\ *adj* : artificial

fac·tor \ˈfaktər\ *n* **1** : something that has an effect **2** : gene **3** : number used in multiplying

fac·to·ry \ˈfaktərē\ *n, pl* **-ries** : place for manufacturing

fac·to·tum \fak'tōtəm\ *n* : person (as a servant) with varied duties

fac·ul·ty \ˈfakəltē\ *n, pl* **-ties 1** : ability to act **2** : power of the mind or body **3** : body of teachers or department of instruction

fad \ˈfad\ *n* : briefly popular practice or interest — **fad·dish** *adj* — **fad·dist** *n*

fade \ˈfād\ *vb* **fad·ed; fad·ing 1** : wither **2** : lose or cause to lose freshness or brilliance **3** : grow dim **4** : vanish

fag \ˈfag\ *vb* **-gg- 1** : drudge **2** : tire or exhaust

fag·ot, fag·got \ˈfagət\ *n* : bundle of twigs

Fahr·en·heit \ˈfarən,hīt\ *adj* : relating to a thermometer scale with the boiling point at 212 degrees and the freezing point at 32 degrees

fail \ˈfāl\ *vb* **1** : decline in health **2** : die away **3** : stop functioning **4** : be unsuccessful **5** : become bankrupt **6** : disappoint **7** : neglect ~ *n* : act of failing

fail·ing *n* : slight defect in character or conduct ~ *prep* : in the absence or lack of

faille \ˈfīl\ *n* : closely woven ribbed fabric

fail·ure \ˈfālyər\ *n* **1** : absence of expected action or performance **2** : bankruptcy **3** : deficiency **4** : one that has failed

faint \ˈfānt\ *adj* **1** : cowardly or spiritless **2** : weak and dizzy **3** : lacking vigor **4** : indistinct ~ *vb* : lose

consciousness ∼ n : act or condition of fainting — **faint·heart·ed** adj — **faint·ly** adv — **faint·ness** n

¹fair \'far\ adj 1 : pleasing in appearance 2 : not stormy or cloudy 3 : just or honest 4 : conforming with the rules 5 : open to legitimate pursuit or attack 6 : light in color 7 : adequate — **fair·ness** n

²fair adv, chiefly Brit : FAIRLY

³fair n : exhibition for judging or selling — **fair·ground** n

fair·ly \'farlē\ adv 1 : in a manner of speaking 2 : without bias 3 : somewhat

fairy \'farē\ n, pl **fair·ies** : usu. small imaginary being — **fairy tale** n

fairy·land \-,land\ n 1 : land of fairies 2 : beautiful or charming place

faith \'fāth\ n, pl **faiths** \'fāths, 'fāthz\ 1 : allegiance 2 : belief and trust in God 3 : confidence 4 : system of religious beliefs — **faith·ful** \-fəl\ adj — **faith·ful·ly** adv — **faith·ful·ness** n — **faith·less** adj — **faith·less·ly** adv — **faith·less·ness** n

fake \'fāk\ vb **faked**; **fak·ing** 1 : falsify 2 : counterfeit ∼ n : copy, fraud, or impostor ∼ adj : not genuine — **fak·er** n

fa·kir \fə'kir\ n : wandering beggar of India

fal·con \'falkən, 'fȯl-\ n : small long-winged hawk used esp. for hunting — **fal·con·ry** \-rē\ n

fall \'fȯl\ vb **fell** \'fel\; **fall·en** \'fȯlən\; **fall·ing** 1 : go down by gravity 2 : hang freely 3 : go lower 4 : be defeated or ruined 5 : commit a sin 6 : happen at a certain time 7 : become gradually ∼ n 1 : act of falling 2 : autumn 3 : downfall 4 pl : waterfall 5 : distance something falls

fal·la·cy \'faləsē\ n, pl **-cies** 1 : false

idea 2 : false reasoning — **fal·la·cious** \fə'lāshəs\ adj

fal·li·ble \'faləbəl\ adj : capable of making a mistake — **fal·li·bly** \-blē\ adv

fall·out n 1 : radioactive particles from a nuclear explosion 2 : secondary effects

fal·low \'falō\ adj 1 : plowed but not planted 2 : dormant — **fallow** n or vb

false \'fȯls\ adj **fals·er**; **fals·est** 1 : not genuine, true, faithful, or permanent 2 : misleading — **false·ly** adv — **false·ness** n — **fal·si·fi·ca·tion** \,fȯlsəfə'kāshən\ n — **fal·si·fy** \'fȯlsə,fī\ vb — **fal·si·ty** \'fȯlsətē\ n

false·hood \'fȯls,hu̇d\ n : lie

fal·set·to \fȯl'setō\ n, pl **-tos** : artificially high singing voice

fal·ter \'fȯltər\ vb **-tered**; **-ter·ing** 1 : move unsteadily 2 : hesitate — **fal·ter·ing·ly** adv

fame \'fām\ n : public reputation — **famed** \'fāmd\ adj

fa·mil·ial \fə'milyəl\ adj : relating to a family

¹fa·mil·iar \fə'milyər\ n 1 : companion 2 : guardian spirit

²familiar adj 1 : closely acquainted 2 : forward 3 : frequently seen or experienced — **fa·mil·iar·i·ty** \fə,mil'yarətē, -,milē'yar-\ n — **fa·mil·iar·ize** \fə'milyə,rīz\ vb — **fa·mil·iar·ly** adv

fam·i·ly \'famlē\ n, pl **-lies** 1 : persons of common ancestry 2 : group living together 3 : parents and children 4 : group of related individuals

fam·ine \'famən\ n : extreme scarcity of food

fam·ish \'famish\ vb : starve

♦ **fa·mous** \'fāməs\ adj : widely known or celebrated

fa·mous·ly adv : very well

¹**fan** \\'fan\ *n* : device for producing a current of air ~ *vb* -**nn**- 1 : move air with a fan 2 : direct a current of air upon 3 : stir to activity

²**fan** *n* : enthusiastic follower or admirer

fa·nat·ic \fə'natik\; **fa·nat·i·cal** \-ikəl\ *adj* : excessively enthusiastic or devoted — **fanatic** *n* — **fa·nat·i·cism** \-'natə₃sizəm\ *n*

fan·ci·er \'fansēər\ *n* : one devoted to raising a particular plant or animal

fan·cy \'fansē\ *n, pl* -**cies** 1 : liking 2 : whim 3 : imagination ~ *vb* -**cied**; -**cy·ing** 1 : like 2 : imagine ~ *adj* -**cier**; -**est** 1 : not plain 2 : of superior quality — **fan·ci·ful** \-sifəl\ *adj* — **fan·ci·ful·ly** \-fəlē\ *adv* — **fan·ci·ly** *adv*

fan·dan·go \fan'daŋgō\ *n, pl* -**gos** : lively Spanish dance

fan·fare \'fan₃far\ *n* 1 : a sounding of trumpets 2 : showy display

fang \'faŋ\ *n* : long sharp tooth

fan·light *n* : semicircular window

fan·ta·sia \fan'tāzhə, -zēə; ₃fantə-'zēə\ *n* : music written to fancy rather than to form

fan·tas·tic \fan'tastik\ *adj* 1 : imaginary or unrealistic 2 : exceedingly or unbelievably great — **fan·tas·ti·cal·ly** \-tiklē\ *adv*

fan·ta·sy \'fantəsē\ *n* 1 : imagination 2 : product (as a daydream) of the imagination 3 : fantasia — **fan·ta·size** \'fantə₃sīz\ *vb*

far \\'fär\ *adv* **far·ther** \-thər\ *or* **further** \'fər-\; **far·thest** *or* **fur·thest** \-thəst\ 1 : at or to a distance 2 : much 3 : to a degree 4 : to an advanced point or extent ~ *adj* **farther** *or* **further**; **far·thest** *or* **furthest** 1 : remote 2 : long 3 : being more distant

far·away *adj* : distant

farce \'färs\ *n* 1 : satirical comedy with an improbable plot 2 : ridiculous display — **far·ci·cal** \-sikəl\ *adj*

¹**fare** \'far\ *vb* **fared**; **far·ing** : get along

²**fare** *n* 1 : price of transportation 2 : range of food

fare·well \far'wel\ *n* 1 : wish of welfare at parting 2 : departure — **farewell** *adj*

far–fetched \'fär'fecht\ *adj* : improbable

fa·ri·na \fə'rēnə\ *n* : fine meal made from cereal grains

farm \'färm\ *n* : place where something is raised for food ~ *vb* 1 : use (land) as a farm 2 : raise plants or animals for food — **farm·er** *n* — **farm·hand** \-₃hand\ *n* — **farm·house** *n* — **farm·ing** *n* — **farm·land** \-₃land\ *n* — **farm·yard** *n*

far–off *adj* : remote in time or space

far·ri·er \'farēər\ *n* : blacksmith who shoes horses

far·row \'farō\ *vb* : give birth to a litter of pigs — **farrow** *n*

far·sight·ed *adj* 1 : better able to see distant things than near 2 : judicious or shrewd — **far·sight·ed·ness** *n*

far·ther \'färthər\ *adv* 1 : at or to a greater distance or more advanced point 2 : to a greater degree or extent ~ *adj* : more distant

far·ther·most *adj* : most distant

far·thest \'färthəst\ *adj* : most distant ~ *adv* 1 : to or at the greatest distance 2 : to the most advanced point 3 : by the greatest extent

fas·ci·cle \'fasikəl\ *n* 1 : small bundle 2 : division of a book published in parts — **fas·ci·cled** \-kəld\ *adj*

fas·ci·nate \'fas°n₃āt\ *vb* -**nat·ed**; -**nat·ing** : transfix and hold spellbound — **fas·ci·na·tion** \₃fas°n-'āshən\ *n*

fas·cism \'fash₃izəm\ *n* : dictatorship that exalts nation and race — **fas·cist** \-ist\ *n or adj* — **fas·cis·tic** \fa'shistik\ *adj*

fash·ion \'fashən\ *n* 1 : manner 2 : prevailing custom or style ~ *vb* : form or construct — **fash·ion·able** \-ənəbəl\ *adj* — **fash·ion·ably** \-blē\ *adv*

¹**fast** \'fast\ *adj* 1 : firmly fixed, bound, or shut 2 : faithful 3 : moving or acting quickly 4 : indicating ahead of the correct time 5 : deep and undisturbed 6 : permanently dyed 7 : wild or promiscuous ~ *adv* 1 : so as to be secure or bound 2 : soundly or deeply 3 : swiftly

²**fast** *vb* : abstain from food or eat sparingly ~ *n* : act or time of fasting

fas·ten \'fas°n\ *vb* : attach esp. by

pinning or tying — **fas·ten·er** *n* — **fas·ten·ing** *n*

fas·tid·i·ous \fas'tidēəs\ *adj* : hard to please — **fas·tid·i·ous·ly** *adv* — **fas·tid·i·ous·ness** *n*

fat \'fat\ *adj* **-tt- 1** : having much fat **2** : thick ~ *n* : animal tissue rich in greasy or oily matter — **fat·ness** *n* — **fat·ten** \'fat°n\ *vb* — **fat·ty** *adj or n*

fa·tal \'fāt°l\ *adj* : causing death or ruin — **fa·tal·i·ty** \fā'talətē, fə-\ *n* — **fa·tal·ly** *adv*

fa·tal·ism \'fāt°l,izəm\ *n* : belief that fate determines events — **fa·tal·ist** \-ist\ *n* — **fa·tal·is·tic** \,fāt°l'istik\ *adj* — **fa·tal·is·ti·cal·ly** \-tiklē\ *adv*

fate \'fāt\ *n* **1** : principle, cause, or will held to determine events **2** : end or outcome — **fat·ed** *adj* — **fate·ful** \-fəl\ *adj* — **fate·ful·ly** *adv*

fa·ther \'fäthər, 'fȧth-\ *n* **1** : male parent **2** *cap* : God **3** : originator — **father** *vb* — **fa·ther·hood** \-,hùd\ *n* — **fa·ther·land** \-,land\ *n* — **fa·ther·less** *adj* — **fa·ther·ly** *adj*

father–in–law *n, pl* **fa·thers–in–law** : father of one's spouse

fath·om \'fathəm\ *n* : nautical unit of length equal to 6 feet ~ *vb* : understand — **fath·om·able** *adj* — **fath·om·less** *adj*

fa·tigue \fə'tēg\ *n* **1** : weariness from labor or use **2** : tendency to break under repeated stress ~ *vb* **-tigued; -tigu·ing** : tire out

fat·u·ous \'fachəwəs\ *adj* : foolish or stupid — **fat·u·ous·ly** *adv* — **fat·u·ous·ness** *n*

fau·cet \'fòsət, 'fäs-\ *n* : fixture for drawing off a liquid

fault \'fòlt\ *n* **1** : weakness in character **2** : something wrong or imperfect **3** : responsibility for something wrong **4** : fracture in the earth's crust ~ *vb* : find fault in or with — **fault·find·er** *n* — **fault·find·ing** *n* — **fault·i·ly** \'fòltəlē\ *adv* — **fault·less** *adj* — **fault·less·ly** *adv* — **faulty** *adj*

fau·na \'fònə\ *n* : animals or animal life esp. of a region — **fau·nal** \-°l\ *adj*

faux pas \'fō'pä\ *n, pl* **faux pas** *same or* -'päz\ : social blunder

fa·vor \'fāvər\ *n* **1** : approval **2** : par-

tiality **3** : act of kindness ~ *vb* : regard or treat with favor — **fa·vor·able** \'fāvərəbəl\ *adj* — **fa·vor·ably** \-blē\ *adv*

fa·vor·ite \'fāvərət\ *n* : one favored — **favorite** *adj* — **fa·vor·it·ism** \-,izəm\ *n*

¹**fawn** \'fòn\ *vb* : seek favor by groveling

²**fawn** *n* : young deer

faze \'fāz\ *vb* **fazed; faz·ing** : disturb the composure of

fear \'fir\ *n* : unpleasant emotion caused by expectation or awareness of danger ~ *vb* : be afraid of — **fear·ful** \-fəl\ *adj* — **fear·ful·ly** *adv* — **fear·less** *adj* — **fear·less·ly** *adv* — **fear·less·ness** *n* — **fear·some** \-səm\ *adj*

fea·si·ble \'fēzəbəl\ *adj* : capable of being done — **fea·si·bil·i·ty** \,fēzə'bilətē\ *n* — **fea·si·bly** \'fēzəblē\ *adv*

feast \'fēst\ *n* **1** : large or fancy meal **2** : religious festival ~ *vb* : eat plentifully

feat \'fēt\ *n* : notable deed

feath·er \'fethər\ *n* : one of the light horny outgrowths that form the external covering of a bird's body — **feather** *vb* — **feath·ered** \-ərd\ *adj* — **feath·er·less** *adj* — **feath·ery** *adj*

fea·ture \'fēchər\ *n* **1** : shape or appearance of the face **2** : part of the face **3** : prominent characteristic **4** : special attraction ~ *vb* : give prominence to — **fea·ture·less** *adj*

Feb·ru·ary \'febyə,werē, 'febə-, 'febrə-\ *n* : 2d month of the year having 28 and in leap years 29 days

fe·ces \'fē,sēz\ *n pl* : intestinal body waste — **fe·cal** \-kəl\ *adj*

feck·less \'fekləs\ *adj* : irresponsible

fe·cund \'fekənd, 'fē-\ *adj* : prolific — **fe·cun·di·ty** \fi'kəndətē, fe-\ *n*

fed·er·al \'fedrəl, -dərəl\ *adj* : of or constituting a government with power distributed between a central authority and constituent units — **fed·er·al·ism** \-rə,lizəm\ *n* — **fed·er·al·ist** \-list\ *n or adj* — **fed·er·al·ly** *adv*

fed·er·ate \'fedə,rāt\ *vb* **-at·ed; -at·ing** : join in a federation

fed·er·a·tion \,fedə'rāshən\ *n* : union of organizations

fe·do·ra \fi'dōrə\ *n* : soft felt hat

fed up *adj* : out of patience

fee \'fē\ *n* : fixed charge

fee·ble \'fēbəl\ *adj* **-bler; -blest** : weak or ineffective — **fee·ble·mind·ed** \,fēbəl'mīndəd\ *adj* — **fee·ble·mind·ed·ness** *n* — **fee·ble·ness** *n* — **fee·bly** \-blē\ *adv*

feed \'fēd\ *vb* **fed** \'fed\; **feed·ing 1** : give food to **2** : eat **3** : furnish ~ *n* : food for livestock — **feed·er** *n*

feel \'fēl\ *vb* **felt** \'felt\; **feel·ing 1** : perceive or examine through physical contact **2** : think or believe **3** : be conscious of **4** : seem **5** : have sympathy ~ *n* **1** : sense of touch **2** : quality of a thing imparted through touch — **feel·er** *n*

feel·ing \'fēliŋ\ *n* **1** : sense of touch **2** : state of mind **3** *pl* : sensibilities **4** : opinion

feet *pl of* FOOT

feign \'fān\ *vb* : pretend

feint \'fānt\ *n* : mock attack intended to distract attention — **feint** *vb*

fe·lic·i·tate \fi'lisə,tāt\ *vb* **-tat·ed; -tat·ing** : congratulate — **fe·lic·i·ta·tion** \-,lisə'tāshən\ *n*

fe·lic·i·tous \fi'lisətəs\ *adj* : aptly expressed — **fe·lic·i·tous·ly** *adv*

fe·lic·i·ty \-'lisətē\ *n, pl* **-ties 1** : great happiness **2** : pleasing faculty esp. in art or language

fe·line \'fē,līn\ *adj* : relating to cats — **feline** *n*

¹fell \'fel\ *vb* : cut or knock down

²fell *past of* FALL

fel·low \'felō\ *n* **1** : companion or associate **2** : man or boy — **fel·low·ship** \-,ship\ *n*

fel·low·man \,felō'man\ *n* : kindred human being

fel·on \'felən\ *n* : one who has committed a felony

fel·o·ny \'felənē\ *n, pl* **-nies** : serious crime — **fe·lo·ni·ous** \fə'lōnēəs\ *adj*

¹felt \'felt\ *n* : cloth made of pressed wool and fur

²felt *past of* FEEL

fe·male \'fē,māl\ *adj* : relating to or being the sex that bears young — **female** *n*

fem·i·nine \'femənən\ *adj* : relating to the female sex — **fem·i·nin·i·ty** \,femə'ninətē\ *n*

fem·i·nism \'femə,nizəm\ *n* : organized activity on behalf of women's rights — **fem·i·nist** \-nist\ *n or adj*

fe·mur \'fēmər\ *n, pl* **fe·murs** or **fem·o·ra** \'femərə\ : long bone of the thigh — **fem·o·ral** \'femərəl\ *adj*

◆ **fence** \'fens\ *n* : enclosing barrier esp. of wood or wire ~ *vb* **fenced; fenc·ing 1** : enclose with a fence **2** : practice fencing — **fenc·er** *n*

fenc·ing \'fensiŋ\ *n* **1** : combat with swords for sport **2** : material for building fences

fend \'fend\ *vb* : ward off

fend·er \'fendər\ *n* : guard over an automobile wheel

fen·nel \'fenᵊl\ *n* : herb related to the carrot

fer·ment \fər'ment\ *vb* : cause or undergo fermentation ~ \'fər,ment\ *n* : agitation

fer·men·ta·tion \,fərmən'tāshən, -,men-\ *n* : chemical decomposition of an organic substance in the absence of oxygen

fern \'fərn\ *n* : flowerless seedless green plant

fe·ro·cious \fə'rōshəs\ *adj* : fierce or savage — **fe·ro·cious·ly** *adv* — **fe·ro·cious·ness** *n* — **fe·roc·i·ty** \-'räsətē\ *n*

fer·ret \'ferət\ *n* : white European polecat ~ *vb* : find out by searching

fer·ric \'ferik\, **fer·rous** \'ferəs\

adj : relating to or containing iron

fer·rule \'ferəl\ *n* : metal band or ring

fer·ry \'ferē\ *vb* **-ried; -ry·ing** : carry by boat over water ~ *n, pl* **-ries** : boat used in ferrying — **fer·ry·boat** *n*

fer·tile \'fərtʰl\ *adj* 1 : producing plentifully 2 : capable of developing or reproducing — **fer·til·i·ty** \fərʰtilətē\ *n*

fer·til·ize \'fərtʰl,īz\ *vb* **-ized; -iz·ing** : make fertile — **fer·til·iza·tion** \,fərtʰlə'zāshən\ *n* — **fer·til·iz·er** *n*

fer·vid \'fərvəd\ *adj* : ardent or zealous — **fer·vid·ly** *adv*

fer·vor \'fərvər\ *n* : passion — **fer·ven·cy** \-vənsē\ *n* — **fer·vent** \-vənt\ *adj* — **fer·vent·ly** *adv*

fes·ter \'festər\ *vb* 1 : form pus 2 : become more bitter or malignant

fes·ti·val \'festəvəl\ *n* : time of celebration

fes·tive \-tiv\ *adj* : joyous or happy — **fes·tive·ly** *adv* — **fes·tiv·i·ty** \fes'tivətē\ *n*

fes·toon \fes'tün\ *n* : decorative chain or strip hanging in a curve — **festoon** *vb*

fe·tal \'fētʰl\ *adj* : of, relating to, or being a fetus

fetch \'fech\ *vb* 1 : go or come after and bring or take back 2 : sell for

fetch·ing \'fechiŋ\ *adj* : attractive — **fetch·ing·ly** *adv*

fête \'fāt, 'fet\ *n* : lavish party ~ *vb* **fêt·ed; fêt·ing** : honor or commemorate with a fête

fet·id \'fetəd\ *adj* : having an offensive smell

fe·tish \'fetish\ *n* 1 : object believed to have magical powers 2 : object of unreasoning devotion or concern

fet·lock \'fet,läk\ *n* : projection on the back of a horse's leg above the hoof

fet·ter \'fetər\ *n* : chain or shackle for the feet — **fetter** *vb*

fet·tle \'fetʰl\ *n* : state of fitness

fe·tus \'fētəs\ *n* : vertebrate not yet born or hatched

feud \'fyüd\ *n* : prolonged quarrel — **feud** *vb*

feu·dal \'fyüdʰl\ *adj* : of or relating to feudalism

feu·dal·ism \-,izəm\ *n* : medieval

political order in which land is granted in return for service — **feu·dal·is·tic** \,fyüdʰl'istik\ *adj*

fe·ver \'fēvər\ *n* 1 : abnormal rise in body temperature 2 : state of heightened emotion — **fe·ver·ish** *adj* — **fe·ver·ish·ly** *adv*

few \'fyü\ *pron* : not many ~ *adj* : some but not many — often with *a* ~ *n* : small number — often with *a*

few·er \-ər\ *pron* : smaller number of things

fez \'fez\ *n, pl* **fez·zes** : round flat-crowned hat

fi·an·cé \,fē,än'sā\ *n* : man one is engaged to

fi·an·cée \,fē,än'sā\ *n* : woman one is engaged to

fi·as·co \fē'askō\ *n, pl* **-coes** : ridiculous failure

fi·at \'fēət, -,at, -,ät; 'fīət, -,at\ *n* : decree

fib \'fib\ *n* : trivial lie — **fib** *vb* — **fib·ber** *n*

fi·ber, fi·bre \'fībər\ *n* 1 : threadlike substance or structure (as a muscle cell or fine root) 2 : indigestible material in food 3 : element that gives texture or substance — **fi·brous** \-brəs\ *adj*

fi·ber·board *n* : construction material made of compressed fibers

fi·ber·glass *n* : glass in fibrous form in various products (as insulation)

fi·bril·la·tion \,fibrə'lāshən, ,fīb-\ *n* : rapid irregular contractions of heart muscle — **fib·ril·late** \'fibrə,lāt, 'fīb-\ *vb*

fib·u·la \'fibyələ\ *n, pl* **-lae** \-lē, -lī\ *or* **-las** : outer of the two leg bones below the knee — **fib·u·lar** \-lər\ *adj*

fick·le \'fikəl\ *adj* : unpredictably changeable — **fick·le·ness** *n*

fic·tion \'fikshən\ *n* : a made-up story or literature consisting of these — **fic·tion·al** \-shənəl\ *adj*

fic·ti·tious \fik'tishəs\ *adj* : made up or pretended

fid·dle \'fidʰl\ *n* : violin ~ *vb* **-dled; -dling** 1 : play on the fiddle 2 : move the hands restlessly — **fid·dler** \'fidlər, -ʰlər\ *n*

fid·dle·sticks *n* : nonsense — used as an interjection

fi·del·i·ty \fə'delətē, fī-\ *n, pl* **-ties** 1 : quality or state of being faithful 2 : quality of reproduction

fid·get \\'fijət\\ *n* **1** *pl* : restlessness **2** : one that fidgets ~ *vb* : move restlessly — **fid·gety** *adj*

fi·du·cia·ry \\fə'düshē͵erē, -'dyü-, -shərē\\ *adj* : held or holding in trust — **fiduciary** *n*

field \\'fēld\\ *n* **1** : open country **2** : cleared land **3** : land yielding some special product **4** : sphere of activity **5** : area for sports **6** : region or space in which a given effect (as magnetism) exists ~ *vb* : put into the field — **field** *adj* — **field·er** *n*

fiend \\'fēnd\\ *n* **1** : devil **2** : extremely wicked person — **fiend·ish** *adj* — **fiend·ish·ly** *adv*

fierce \\'firs\\ *adj* **fierc·er; -est 1** : violently hostile or aggressive **2** : intense **3** : menacing looking — **fierce·ly** *adv* — **fierce·ness** *n*

fi·ery \\'fīərē\\ *adj* **fi·er·i·er; -est 1** : burning **2** : hot or passionate — **fi·eri·ness** \\'fīərēnəs\\ *n*

fi·es·ta \\fē'estə\\ *n* : festival

fife \\'fīf\\ *n* : small flute

fif·teen \\fif'tēn\\ *n* : one more than 14 — **fifteen** *adj or pron* — **fif·teenth** \\-'tēnth\\ *adj or n*

fifth \\'fifth\\ *n* **1** : one that is number 5 in a countable series **2** : one of 5 equal parts of something — **fifth** *adj or adv*

fif·ty \\'fiftē\\ *n, pl* **-ties** : 5 times 10 — **fif·ti·eth** \\-tēəth\\ *adj or n* — **fifty** *adj or pron*

fif·ty–fif·ty *adv or adj* : shared equally

fig \\'fig\\ *n* : pear-shaped edible fruit

♦ **fight** \\'fīt\\ *vb* **fought** \\'fȯt\\; **fighting 1** : contend against another in battle **2** : box **3** : struggle ~ *n* **1** : hostile encounter **2** : boxing match **3** : verbal disagreement — **fight·er** *n*

fig·ment \\'figmənt\\ *n* : something imagined or made up

fig·u·ra·tive \\'figyərətiv, -gə-\\ *adj* : metaphorical — **fig·u·ra·tive·ly** *adv*

fig·ure \\'figyər, -gər\\ *n* **1** : symbol representing a number **2** *pl* : arithmetical calculations **3** : price **4** : shape or outline **5** : illustration **6** : pattern or design **7** : prominent person ~ *vb* **-ured; -ur·ing 1** : be important **2** : calculate — **fig·ured** *adj*

fig·u·rine \\͵figyə'rēn\\ *n* : small statue

fil·a·ment \\'filəmənt\\ *n* : fine thread or threadlike part — **fil·a·men·tous** \\͵filə'mentəs\\ *adj*

fil·bert \\'filbərt\\ *n* : edible nut of a European hazel

filch \\'filch\\ *vb* : steal furtively

¹file \\'fīl\\ *n* : tool for smoothing or sharpening ~ *vb* **filed; fil·ing** : rub or smooth with a file

²file *vb* **filed; fil·ing 1** : arrange in order **2** : enter or record officially ~ *n* : device for keeping papers in order

³file *n* : row of persons or things one behind the other ~ *vb* **filed; fil·ing** : march in file

fil·ial \\'filēəl, 'filyəl\\ *adj* : relating to a son or daughter

fil·i·bus·ter \\'filə͵bəstər\\ *n* : long speeches to delay a legislative vote — **filibuster** *vb* — **fil·i·bus·ter·er** *n*

fil·i·gree \\'filə͵grē\\ *n* : ornamental designs of fine wire — **fil·i·greed** \\-͵grēd\\ *adj*

fill \\'fil\\ *vb* **1** : make or become full **2** : stop up **3** : feed **4** : satisfy **5** : occupy fully **6** : spread through ~ *n* **1** : full supply **2** : material for filling — **fill·er** *n* — **fill in** *vb* **1** : provide information to or for **2** : substitute

fil·let \\'filət, fi'lā, 'fil͵ā\\ *n* : piece of

boneless meat or fish ~ *vb* : cut into fillets

fill·ing *n* : material used to fill something

fil·ly \'filē\ *n, pl* **-lies** : young female horse

film \'film\ *n* **1** : thin skin or membrane **2** : thin coating or layer **3** : strip of material used in taking pictures **4** : movie ~ *vb* : make a movie of — **filmy** *adj*

film·strip *n* : strip of film with photographs for still projection

fil·ter \'filtər\ *n* **1** : device for separating matter from a fluid **2** : device (as on a camera lens) that absorbs light ~ *vb* **1** : pass through a filter **2** : remove by means of a filter — **fil·ter·able** *adj* — **fil·tra·tion** \fil'trāshən\ *n*

filth \'filth\ *n* : repulsive dirt or refuse — **filth·i·ness** *n* — **filthy** \'filthē\ *adj*

fin \'fin\ *n* **1** : thin external process controlling movement in an aquatic animal **2** : fin-shaped part (as on an airplane) **3** : flipper — **finned** \'find\ *adj*

fi·na·gle \fə'nāgəl\ *vb* **-gled; -gling** : get by clever or tricky means — **fi·na·gler** *n*

fi·nal \'fīnᵊl\ *adj* **1** : not to be changed **2** : ultimate **3** : coming at the end — **final** *n* — **fi·nal·ist** \'fīnᵊlist\ *n* — **fi·nal·i·ty** \fī'nalətē, fə-\ *n* — **fi·nal·ize** \-,īz\ *vb* — **fi·nal·ly** *adv*

fi·na·le \fə'nalē, fi'näl-\ *n* : last or climactic part

fi·nance \fə'nans, 'fī,nans\ *n* **1** *pl* : money resources **2** : management of money affairs ~ *vb* **-nanced; -nanc·ing 1** : raise funds for **2** : give necessary funds to **3** : sell on credit

fi·nan·cial \fə'nanchəl, fī-\ *adj* : relating to finance — **fi·nan·cial·ly** *adv*

fi·nan·cier \,finən'sir, ,fī,nan-\ *n* : person who invests large sums of money

finch \'finch\ *n* : songbird (as a sparrow or linnet) with a strong bill

find \'fīnd\ *vb* **found** \'faůnd\; **finding 1** : discover or encounter **2** : obtain by effort **3** : experience or feel **4** : gain or regain the use of **5** : decide on (a verdict) ~ *n* **1** : act or instance of finding **2** : something found — **find·er** *n* — **finding** *n* — **find out** *vb* : learn, discover, or verify something

fine \'fīn\ *n* : money paid as a penalty ~ *vb* **fined; fin·ing** : impose a fine on ~ *adj* **fin·er; -est 1** : free from impurity **2** : small or thin **3** : not coarse **4** : superior in quality or appearance ~ *adv* : finely — **fine·ly** *adv* — **fine·ness** *n*

fin·ery \'fīnərē\ *n, pl* **-er·ies** : showy clothing and jewels

fi·nesse \fə'nes\ *n* **1** : delicate skill **2** : craftiness — **finesse** *vb*

fin·ger \'fiŋgər\ *n* **1** : one of the 5 divisions at the end of the hand and esp. one other than the thumb **2** : something like a finger **3** : part of a glove for a finger ~ *vb* **1** : touch with the fingers **2** : identify as if by pointing — **fin·gered** *adj* — **fin·ger·nail** *n* — **fin·ger·tip** *n*

fin·ger·ling \-gərliŋ\ *n* : small fish

fin·ger·print *n* : impression of the pattern of marks on the tip of a finger — **fingerprint** *vb*

◆ **fin·icky** \'finikē\ *adj* : excessively particular in taste or standards

fin·ish \'finish\ *vb* **1** : come or bring to an end **2** : use or dispose of entirely **3** : put a final coat or surface on ~ *n* **1** : end **2** : final treatment given a surface — **fin·ish·er** *n*

fi·nite \'fī,nīt\ *adj* : having definite limits

fink \'fiŋk\ *n* : contemptible person

fiord *var of* FJORD

fir \'fər\ *n* : erect evergreen tree or its wood

fire \'fīr\ *n* 1 : light or heat and esp. the flame of something burning 2 : destructive burning (as of a house) 3 : enthusiasm 4 : the shooting of weapons ~ *vb* **fired**; **fir·ing** 1 : kindle 2 : stir up or enliven 3 : dismiss from employment 4 : shoot 5 : bake — **fire·bomb** *n or vb* — **fire·fight·er** *n* — **fire·less** *adj* — **fire·proof** *adj or vb* — **fire·wood** *n*

fire·arm *n* : weapon (as a rifle) that works by an explosion of gunpowder

fire·ball *n* 1 : ball of fire 2 : brilliant meteor

fire·boat *n* : boat equipped for fighting fire

fire·box *n* 1 : chamber (as of a furnace) that contains a fire 2 : fire-alarm box

fire·break *n* : cleared land for checking a forest fire

fire·bug *n* : person who deliberately sets destructive fires

fire·crack·er *n* : small firework that makes noise

fire·fly *n* : night-flying beetle that produces a soft light

fire·man \'fīrmən\ *n* 1 : person trained to put out fires 2 : stoker

fire·place *n* : opening made in a chimney to hold an open fire

fire·plug *n* : hydrant

fire·side *n* 1 : place near the fire or hearth 2 : home ~ *adj* : having an informal quality

fire·trap *n* : place apt to catch on fire

fire·work *n* : device that explodes to produce noise or a display of light

¹firm \'fərm\ *adj* 1 : securely fixed in place 2 : strong or vigorous 3 : not subject to change 4 : resolute ~ *vb* : make or become firm — **firm·ly** *adv* — **firm·ness** *n*

²firm *n* : business enterprise

fir·ma·ment \'fərməmənt\ *n* : sky

first \'fərst\ *adj* 1 : being number one 2 : foremost ~ *adv* 1 : before any other 2 : for the first time ~ *n* 1 : number one 2 : one that is first — **first class** *n* — **first–class**

adj or adv — **first·ly** *adv* — **first–rate** *adj or adv*

first aid *n* : emergency care

first lieutenant *n* : commissioned officer ranking next below a captain

first sergeant *n* 1 : noncommissioned officer serving as the chief assistant to the commander of a military unit 2 : rank in the army below a command sergeant major and in the marine corps below a sergeant major

firth \'fərth\ *n* : estuary

fis·cal \'fiskəl\ *adj* : relating to money — **fis·cal·ly** *adv*

fish \'fish\ *n, pl* **fish** *or* **fish·es** : water animal with fins, gills, and usu. scales ~ *vb* 1 : try to catch fish 2 : grope — **fish·er** *n* — **fish·hook** *n* — **fish·ing** *n*

fish·er·man \-mən\ *n* : one who fishes

fish·ery \'fishərē\ *n, pl* **-er·ies** : fishing business or a place for this

fishy \'fishē\ *adj* **fish·i·er**; **-est** 1 : relating to or like fish 2 : questionable

fis·sion \'fishən, 'fizh-\ *n* : splitting of an atomic nucleus — **fis·sion·able** \-ənəbəl\ *adj*

fis·sure \'fishər\ *n* : crack

fist \'fist\ *n* : hand doubled up — **fist·ed** \'fistəd\ *adj* — **fist·ful** \-,fůl\ *n*

fist·i·cuffs \'fisti,kəfs\ *n pl* : fist fight

¹fit \'fit\ *n* : sudden attack of illness or emotion

²fit *adj* **-tt-** 1 : suitable 2 : qualified 3 : sound in body ~ *vb* **-tt-** 1 : be suitable to 2 : insert or adjust correctly 3 : make room for 4 : supply or equip 5 : belong ~ *n* : state of fitting or being fitted — **fit·ly** *adv* — **fit·ness** *n* — **fit·ter** *n*

fit·ful \'fitfəl\ *adj* : restless — **fit·ful·ly** *adv*

fit·ting *adj* : suitable ~ *n* : a small part

five \'fīv\ *n* 1 : one more than 4 2 : 5th in a set or series 3 : something having 5 units — **five** *adj or pron*

fix \'fiks\ *vb* 1 : attach 2 : establish 3 : make right 4 : prepare 5 : improperly influence ~ *n* 1 : predicament 2 : determination of location — **fix·er** *n*

fix·a·tion \fik'sāshən\ *n* : obsessive attachment — **fix·ate** \'fik,sāt\ *vb*

fixed \'fikst\ *adj* 1 : stationary 2 : settled — **fixed·ly** \'fiksədlē\ *adv* — **fixed·ness** \-nəs\ *n*

♦ **fix·ture** \'fikschər\ *n* : permanent part of something

fizz \'fiz\ *vb* : make a hissing sound ~ *n* : effervescence

fiz·zle \'fizəl\ *vb* **-zled; -zling** 1 : fizz 2 : fail ~ *n* : failure

fjord \fē'ord\ *n* : inlet of the sea between cliffs

flab \'flab\ *n* : flabby flesh

flab·ber·gast \'flabər,gast\ *vb* : astound

flab·by \'flabē\ *adj* **-bi·er; -est** : not firm — **flab·bi·ness** *n*

flac·cid \'flaksəd, 'flasəd\ *adj* : not firm

¹**flag** \'flag\ *n* : flat stone

²**flag** *n* 1 : fabric that is a symbol (as of a country) 2 : something used to signal ~ *vb* **-gg-** : signal with a flag — **flag·pole** *n* — **flag·staff** *n*

³**flag** *vb* **-gg-** : lose strength or spirit

flag·el·late \'flajə,lāt\ *vb* **-lat·ed; -lat·ing** : whip — **flag·el·la·tion** \,flajə'lāshən\ *n*

flag·on \'flagən\ *n* : container for liquids

fla·grant \'flāgrənt\ *adj* : conspicuously bad — **fla·grant·ly** *adv*

flag·ship *n* : ship carrying a commander

flag·stone *n* : flag

flail \'flāl\ *n* : tool for threshing grain ~ *vb* : beat with or as if with a flail

flair \'flar\ *n* : natural aptitude

flak \'flak\ *n, pl* **flak** 1 : antiaircraft fire 2 : criticism

flake \'flāk\ *n* : small flat piece ~ *vb* **flaked; flak·ing** : separate or form into flakes

flam·boy·ant \flam'boiənt\ *adj* : showy — **flam·boy·ance** \-əns\ *n* — **flam·boy·ant·ly** *adv*

flame \'flām\ *n* 1 : glowing part of a fire 2 : state of combustion 3 : burning passion — **flame** *vb* — **flam·ing** *adj*

fla·min·go \flə'miŋgō\ *n, pl* **-gos** : long-legged long-necked tropical water bird

flam·ma·ble \'flaməbəl\ *adj* : easily ignited

flange \'flanj\ *n* : rim

flank \'flaŋk\ *n* : side of something ~ *vb* 1 : attack or go around the side of 2 : be at the side of

flan·nel \'flan⁰l\ *n* : soft napped fabric

flap \'flap\ *n* 1 : slap 2 : something flat that hangs loose ~ *vb* **-pp-** 1 : move (wings) up and down 2 : swing back and forth noisily

flap·jack \-,jak\ *n* : pancake

flare \'flar\ *vb* **flared; flar·ing** : become suddenly bright or excited ~ *n* : blaze of light

flash \'flash\ *vb* 1 : give off a sudden flame or burst of light 2 : appear or pass suddenly ~ *n* 1 : sudden burst of light or inspiration 2 : instant ~ *adj* : coming suddenly

flash·light *n* : small battery-operated light

flashy \'flashē\ *adj* **flash·i·er; -est** : showy — **flash·i·ly** *adv* — **flash·i·ness** *n*

flask \'flask\ *n* : flattened bottle

flat \'flat\ *adj* **-tt-** 1 : smooth 2 : broad and thin 3 : definite 4 : uninteresting 5 : deflated 6 : below the true pitch ~ *n* 1 : level surface of land 2 : flat note in music 3 : apartment 4 : deflated tire ~ *adv* **-tt-** 1 : exactly 2 : below the true pitch ~ *vb* **-tt-** : make flat — **flat·ly** *adv* — **flat·ness** *n* — **flat·ten** \-⁰n\ *vb*

flat·car *n* : railroad car without sides

flat·fish *n* : flattened fish with both eyes on the upper side

flat·foot *n, pl* **flat·feet** : foot condition in which the arch is flattened — **flat–foot·ed** *adj*

flat–out *adj* **1** : being maximum effort or speed **2** : downright

flat·ter \'flatər\ *vb* **1** : praise insincerely **2** : judge or represent too favorably — **flat·ter·er** *n* — **flat·tery** \'flatərē\ *n*

flat·u·lent \'flachələnt\ *adj* : full of gas — **flat·u·lence** \-ləns\ *n*

flat·ware *n* : eating utensils

flaunt \'flȯnt\ *vb* : display ostentatiously — **flaunt** *n*

fla·vor \'flāvər\ *n* **1** : quality that affects the sense of taste **2** : something that adds flavor ~ *vb* : give flavor to — **fla·vor·ful** *adj* — **fla·vor·ing** *n* — **fla·vor·less** *adj*

flaw \'flȯ\ *n* : fault — **flaw·less** *adj* — **flaw·less·ly** *adv* — **flaw·less·ness** *n*

flax \'flaks\ *n* : plant from which linen is made

flax·en \'flaksən\ *adj* : made of or like flax

flay \'flā\ *vb* **1** : strip off the skin of **2** : criticize harshly

flea \'flē\ *n* : leaping bloodsucking insect

fleck \'flek\ *vb or n* : streak or spot

fledg·ling \'flejliŋ\ *n* : young bird

flee \'flē\ *vb* **fled** \'fled\; **flee·ing** : run away

fleece \'flēs\ *n* : sheep's wool ~ *vb* **fleeced; fleec·ing 1** : shear **2** : get money from dishonestly — **fleecy** *adj*

¹fleet \'flēt\ *vb* : pass rapidly ~ *adj* : swift — **fleet·ing** *adj* — **fleet·ness** *n*

²fleet *n* : group of ships

fleet admiral *n* : commissioned officer of the highest rank in the navy

flesh \'flesh\ *n* **1** : soft parts of an animal's body **2** : soft plant tissue (as fruit pulp) — **fleshed** \'flesht\ *adj* — **fleshy** *adj* — **flesh out** *vb* : make fuller

flesh·ly \'fleshlē\ *adj* : sensual

flew *past of* FLY

flex \'fleks\ *vb* : bend

flex·i·ble \'fleksəbəl\ *adj* **1** : capable of being flexed **2** : adaptable —

flex·i·bil·i·ty \ˌfleksə'bilətē\ *n* — **flex·i·bly** \-əblē\ *adv*

flick \'flik\ *n* : light jerky stroke ~ *vb* **1** : strike lightly **2** : flutter

flick·er \'flikər\ *vb* **1** : waver **2** : burn unsteadily ~ *n* **1** : sudden movement **2** : wavering light

fli·er \'flīər\ *n* **1** : aviator **2** : advertising circular

¹flight \'flīt\ *n* **1** : act or instance of flying **2** : ability to fly **3** : a passing through air or space **4** : series of stairs — **flight·less** *adj*

²flight *n* : act or instance of running away

flighty \-ē\ *adj* **flight·i·er; -est** : capricious or silly — **flight·i·ness** *n*

flim·flam \'flimˌflam\ *n* : trickery

flim·sy \-zē\ *adj* **-si·er; -est 1** : not strong or well made **2** : not believable — **flim·si·ly** *adv* — **flim·si·ness** *n*

flinch \'flinch\ *vb* : shrink from pain

fling \'fliŋ\ *vb* **flung** \'fləŋ\; **fling·ing 1** : move brusquely **2** : throw ~ *n* **1** : act or instance of flinging **2** : attempt **3** : period of self=indulgence

flint \'flint\ *n* : hard quartz that gives off sparks when struck with steel — **flinty** *adj*

flip \'flip\ *vb* **-pp- 1** : cause to turn over quickly or many times **2** : move with a quick push ~ *adj* : insolent — **flip** *n*

flip·pant \'flipənt\ *adj* : not serious enough — **flip·pan·cy** \-ənsē\ *n*

flip·per \'flipər\ *n* : paddlelike limb (as of a seal) for swimming

flirt \'flərt\ *vb* **1** : be playfully romantic **2** : show casual interest ~ *n* : one who flirts — **flir·ta·tion** \ˌflər'tāshən\ *n* — **flir·ta·tious** \-shəs\ *adj*

flit \'flit\ *vb* **-tt-** : dart

float \'flōt\ *n* **1** : something that floats **2** : vehicle carrying an exhibit ~ *vb* **1** : rest on or in a fluid without sinking **2** : wander **3** : finance by issuing stock or bonds — **float·er** *n*

flock \'fläk\ *n* : group of animals (as birds) or people ~ *vb* : gather or move as a group

floe \'flō\ *n* : mass of floating ice

flog \'fläg\ *vb* **-gg-** : beat with a rod or whip — **flog·ger** *n*

flood \'fləd\ *n* **1** : great flow of water over the land **2** : overwhelming

volume ~ *vb* : cover or fill esp.
with water — **flood·wa·ter** *n*

floor \'flōr\ *n* **1** : bottom of a room
on which one stands **2** : story of a
building **3** : lower limit ~ *vb* **1**
: furnish with a floor **2** : knock
down **3** : amaze — **floor·board** *n*
— **floor·ing** \-iŋ\ *n*

floo·zy, floo·zie \'flüzē\ *n, pl* -**zies**
: promiscuous young woman

flop \'fläp\ *vb* -**pp**- **1** : flap **2** : slump
heavily **3** : fail — **flop** *n*

flop·py \'fläpē\ *adj* -**pi·er; -est** : soft
and flexible

flo·ra \'flōrə\ *n* : plants or plant life
of a region

flo·ral \'flōrəl\ *adj* : relating to
flowers

flor·id \'flórəd\ *adj* **1** : very flowery
in style **2** : reddish

flo·rist \'flórist\ *n* : flower dealer

floss \'fläs\ *n* **1** : soft thread for embroidery **2** : thread used to clean
between teeth — **floss** *vb*

flo·ta·tion \flō'tāshən\ *n* : process
or instance of floating

flo·til·la \flō'tilə\ *n* : small fleet

flot·sam \'flätsəm\ *n* : floating
wreckage

¹flounce \'flaúns\ *vb* **flounced;
flounc·ing** : move with exaggerated jerky motions — **flounce** *n*

²flounce *n* : fabric border or wide
ruffle

¹floun·der \'flaúndər\ *n, pl* **flounder**
or **flounders** : flatfish

²flounder *vb* **1** : struggle for footing **2**
: proceed clumsily

flour \'flaúər\ *n* : finely ground
meal ~ *vb* : coat with flour —
floury *adj*

flour·ish \'flərish\ *vb* **1** : thrive **2**
: wave threateningly ~ *n* **1** : em-
bellishment **2** : fanfare **3** : wave **4**
: showiness of action

flout \'flaút\ *vb* : treat with disdain

flow \'flō\ *vb* **1** : move in a stream **2**
: proceed smoothly and readily ~
n : uninterrupted stream

flow·er \'flaúər\ *n* **1** : showy plant
shoot that bears seeds **2** : state of
flourishing ~ *vb* **1** : produce flowers **2** : flourish — **flow·ered** *adj* —
flow·er·i·ness *n* — **flow·er·less**
adj — **flow·er·pot** *n* — **flow·ery**
\-ē\ *adj*

flown *past part of* FLY

flu \'flü\ *n* **1** : influenza **2** : minor virus ailment

flub \'fləb\ *vb* -**bb**- : bungle — **flub** *n*

fluc·tu·ate \'fləkchə,wāt\ *vb* -**at-
ed; -at·ing** : change rapidly esp. up
and down — **fluc·tu·a·tion**
\,fləkchə'wāshən\ *n*

flue \'flü\ *n* : smoke duct

flu·ent \'flüənt\ *adj* : speaking with
ease — **flu·en·cy** \-ənsē\ *n* — **flu-
ent·ly** *adv*

fluff \'fləf\ *n* **1** : something soft and
light **2** : blunder ~ *vb* **1** : make
fluffy **2** : make a mistake — **fluffy**
\-ē\ *adj*

flu·id \'flüəd\ *adj* : flowing ~ *n*
: substance that can flow — **flu-
id·i·ty** \flü'idətē\ *n* — **flu·id·ly**
adv

fluid ounce *n* : unit of liquid measure equal to ¹⁄₁₆ pint

fluke \'flük\ *n* : stroke of luck

flume \'flüm\ *n* : channel for water

flung *past of* FLING

flunk \'fləŋk\ *vb* : fail in school
work

flun·ky, flun·key \'fləŋkē\ *n, pl*
-**kies** *or* -**keys** : lackey

flu·o·res·cence \,flúr'es°ns, ,flór-\ *n*
: emission of light after initial absorption — **flu·o·resce** \-'es\ *vb* —
flu·o·res·cent \-'es°nt\ *adj*

flu·o·ri·date \'flórə,dāt, 'flúr-\ *vb*
-**dat·ed; -dat·ing** : add fluoride to
— **flu·o·ri·da·tion** \,flórə'dāshən,
,flúr-\ *n*

flu·o·ride \'flór,īd, 'flúr-\ *n* : compound of fluorine

flu·o·rine \'flúr,ēn, -ən\ *n* : toxic
gaseous chemical element

flu·o·ro·car·bon \,flórō'kärbən,
,flúr-\ *n* : compound containing
fluorine and carbon

flu·o·ro·scope \'flúrə,skōp\ *n* : instrument for internal examination
— **flu·o·ro·scop·ic** \,flúrə'skäpik\
adj — **flu·o·ros·co·py** \,flúr-
'äskəpē\ *n*

flur·ry \'flərē\ *n, pl* -**ries 1** : light
snowfall **2** : bustle **3** : brief burst
of activity — **flurry** *vb*

¹flush \'fləsh\ *vb* : cause (a bird) to
fly from cover

²flush *n* **1** : sudden flow (as of water)
2 : surge of emotion **3** : blush ~
vb **1** : blush **2** : wash out with a
rush of liquid ~ *adj* **1** : filled to
overflowing **2** : of a reddish
healthy color **3** : smooth or level **4**
: abutting — **flush** *adv*

³flush *n* : cards of the same suit

flus·ter \'fləstər\ *vb* : upset — **fluster** *n*

flute \'flüt\ *n* 1 : pipelike musical instrument 2 : groove — **flut·ed** *adj* — **flut·ing** *n* — **flut·ist** \-ist\ *n*

flut·ter \'flətər\ *vb* 1 : flap the wings rapidly 2 : move with quick wavering or flapping motions 3 : behave in an agitated manner ~ *n* 1 : a fluttering 2 : state of confusion — **flut·tery** \-ərē\ *adj*

flux \'fləks\ *n* : state of continuous change

¹**fly** \'flī\ *vb* **flew** \'flü\; **flown** \'flōn\; **fly·ing** 1 : move through the air with wings 2 : float or soar 3 : flee 4 : move or pass swiftly 5 : operate an airplane

²**fly** *n, pl* **flies** : garment closure

◆ ³**fly** *n, pl* **flies** : winged insect

fly·er *var of* FLIER

fly·pa·per *n* : sticky paper for catching flies

fly·speck *n* 1 : speck of fly dung 2 : something tiny

fly·wheel *n* : rotating wheel that regulates the speed of machinery

foal \'fōl\ *n* : young horse — **foal** *vb*

foam \'fōm\ *n* 1 : mass of bubbles on top of a liquid 2 : material of cellular form ~ *vb* : form foam — **foamy** *adj*

fob \'fäb\ *n* : short chain for a pocket watch

fo'·c'sle *var of* FORECASTLE

fo·cus \'fōkəs\ *n, pl* **-ci** \-ˌsī\ 1 : point at which reflected or refracted rays meet 2 : adjustment (as of eyeglasses) for clear vision 3 : central point ~ *vb* : bring to a focus — **fo·cal** \-kəl\ *adj* — **fo·cal·ly** *adv*

fod·der \'fädər\ *n* : food for livestock

foe \'fō\ *n* : enemy

fog \'fȯg, 'fäg\ *n* 1 : fine particles of water suspended near the ground 2 : mental confusion ~ *vb* **-gg-** : obscure or be obscured with fog — **fog·gy** *adj*

fog·horn *n* : warning horn sounded in a fog

fo·gy \'fōgē\ *n, pl* **-gies** : person with old-fashioned ideas

foi·ble \'fȯibəl\ *n* : minor character fault

¹**foil** \'fȯil\ *vb* : defeat ~ *n* : light fencing sword

²**foil** *n* 1 : thin sheet of metal 2 : one that sets off another by contrast

foist \'fȯist\ *vb* : force another to accept

¹**fold** \'fōld\ *n* 1 : enclosure for sheep 2 : group with a common interest

²**fold** *vb* 1 : lay one part over another 2 : embrace ~ *n* : part folded

fold·er \'fōldər\ *n* 1 : one that folds 2 : circular 3 : folded cover or envelope for papers

fol·de·rol \'fäldəˌräl\ *n* : nonsense

fo·liage \'fōlēij, -lij\ *n* : plant leaves

fo·lio \'fōlēˌō\ *n, pl* **-li·os** : sheet of paper folded once

folk \'fōk\ *n, pl* **folk** *or* **folks** 1 : people in general 2 **folks** *pl* : one's family ~ *adj* : relating to the common people

folk·lore *n* : customs and traditions of a people — **folk·lor·ist** *n*

folksy \'fōksē\ *adj* **folks·i·er; -est** : friendly and informal

fol·li·cle \'fälikəl\ *n* : small anatomical cavity or gland

fol·low \'fälō\ *vb* 1 : go or come after 2 : pursue 3 : obey 4 : proceed along 5 : keep one's attention fixed on 6 : result from — **follow·er** *n*

fol·low·ing \'fäləwiŋ\ *adj* : next ~ *n* : group of followers ~ *prep* : after

fol·ly \'fälē\ *n, pl* **-lies** : foolishness

fo·ment \fō'ment\ *vb* : incite

◆ **fond** \'fänd\ *adj* 1 : strongly attracted 2 : affectionate 3 : dear — **fond·ly** *adv* — **fond·ness** *n*

fon·dle \'fänd°l\ *vb* **-dled; -dling** : touch lovingly

fon·due \fän'dü, -'dyü\ *n* : preparation of melted cheese

font \'fänt\ *n* 1 : baptismal basin 2 : fountain

food \'füd\ *n* : material eaten to sustain life

fool \'fül\ *n* 1 : stupid person 2 : jester ∼ *vb* 1 : waste time 2 : meddle 3 : deceive — **fool·ery** \'fülərē\ *n* — **fool·ish** \'fülish\ *adj* — **fool·ish·ly** *adv* — **fool·ish·ness** *n* — **fool·proof** *adj*

fool·har·dy \'fül,härdē\ *adj* : rash — **fool·har·di·ness** *n*

foot \'fút\ *n, pl* **feet** \'fēt\ 1 : end part of a leg 2 : unit of length equal to ⅓ yard 3 : unit of verse meter 4 : bottom — **foot·age** \-ij\ *n* — **foot·ed** *adj* — **foot·path** *n* — **foot·print** *n* — **foot·race** *n* — **foot·rest** *n* — **foot·wear** *n*

foot·ball *n* : ball game played by 2 teams on a rectangular field

foot·bridge *n* : bridge for pedestrians

foot·hill *n* : hill at the foot of higher hills

foot·hold *n* : support for the feet

foot·ing *n* 1 : foothold 2 : basis

foot·lights *n pl* : stage lights along the floor

foot·lock·er *n* : small trunk

foot·loose *adj* : having no ties

foot·man \'fútmən\ *n* : male servant

foot·note *n* : note at the bottom of a page

foot·step *n* 1 : step 2 : distance covered by a step 3 : footprint

foot·stool *n* : stool to support the feet

foot·work *n* : skillful movement of the feet (as in boxing)

fop \'fäp\ *n* : dandy — **fop·pery** \-ərē\ *n* — **fop·pish** *adj*

for \'fór\ *prep* 1 — used to show preparation or purpose 2 : because of 3 — used to show a recipient 4 : in support of 5 : so as to support or help cure 6 : so as to be equal to 7 : concerning 8 : through the period of ∼ *conj* : because

for·age \'fórij\ *n* : food for animals ∼ *vb* **-aged; -ag·ing** 1 : hunt food 2 : search for provisions

for·ay \'fór,ā\ *n or vb* : raid

¹**for·bear** \fór'bar\ *vb* **-bore** \-'bōr\; **-borne** \-'bōrn\; **-bear·ing** 1 : refrain from 2 : be patient — **for·bear·ance** \-'barəns\ *n*

²**forbear** *var of* FOREBEAR

for·bid \fər'bid\ *vb* **-bade** \-'bad, -'bād\ *or* **-bad** \-'bad\; **-bid·den** \-'bid°n\; **-bid·ding** 1 : prohibit 2 : order not to do something

for·bid·ding *adj* : tending to discourage

force \'fórs\ *n* 1 : exceptional strength or energy 2 : military strength 3 : body (as of persons) available for a purpose 4 : violence 5 : influence (as a push or pull) that causes motion ∼ *vb* forced; forc·ing 1 : compel 2 : gain against resistance 3 : break open — **force·ful** \-fəl\ *adj* — **force·ful·ly** *adv* — **in force** 1 : in great numbers 2 : valid

for·ceps \'fórsəps\ *n, pl* **forceps** : surgical instrument for grasping objects

forc·ible \'fórsəbəl\ *adj* 1 : done by force 2 : showing force — **forc·i·bly** \-blē\ *adv*

ford \'fórd\ *n* : place to wade across a stream ∼ *vb* : wade across

fore \'fōr\ *adv* : in or toward the front ∼ *adj* : being or coming before in time, place, or order ∼ *n* : front

fore–and–aft *adj* : lengthwise

fore•arm \'fōr₁ärm\ *n* : part of the arm between the elbow and the wrist

fore•bear \'fōr₁bar\ *n* : ancestor

fore•bod•ing \fōr'bōdiŋ\ *n* : premonition of disaster — **fore•bod•ing** *adj*

fore•cast \'fōr₁kast\ *vb* -**cast**; -**casting** : predict — **forecast** *n* — **forecast•er** *n*

fore•cas•tle \'fōksəl\ *n* : forward part of a ship

fore•close \fōr'klōz\ *vb* : take legal measures to terminate a mortgage — **fore•clo•sure** \-'klōzhər\ *n*

fore•fa•ther \'fōr₁fäthər\ *n* : ancestor

fore•fin•ger \'fōr₁fiŋgər\ *n* : finger next to the thumb

fore•foot \'fōr₁fut\ *n* : front foot of a quadruped

fore•front \'fōr₁frənt\ *n* : foremost position or place

¹**fore•go** \fōr'gō\ *vb* -**went**; -**gone**; -**go•ing** : precede

²**forego** *var of* FORGO

fore•go•ing *adj* : preceding

fore•gone *adj* : determined in advance

fore•ground \'fōr₁graund\ *n* : part of a scene nearest the viewer

fore•hand \'fōr₁hand\ *n* : stroke (as in tennis) made with the palm of the hand turned forward — **forehand** *adj*

fore•head \'fōrəd, 'fōr₁hed\ *n* : part of the face above the eyes

for•eign \'fōrən\ *adj* 1 : situated outside a place or country and esp. one's own country 2 : belonging to a different place or country 3 : not pertinent 4 : related to or dealing with other nations — **for•eign•er** \-ər\ *n*

fore•know \fōr'nō\ *vb* -**knew**; -**known**; -**know•ing** : know beforehand — **fore•knowl•edge** *n*

fore•leg \'fōr₁leg\ *n* : front leg

fore•lock \'fōr₁läk\ *n* : front lock of hair

fore•man \'fōrmən\ *n* 1 : spokesman of a jury 2 : workman in charge

fore•most \'fōr₁mōst\ *adj* : first in time, place, or order — **foremost** *adv*

fore•noon \'fōr₁nün\ *n* : morning

fo•ren•sic \fə'rensik\ *adj* : relating to courts or public speaking or debate

fo•ren•sics \-siks\ *n pl* : art or study of speaking or debating

fore•or•dain \₁fōrór'dān\ *vb* : decree beforehand

fore•quar•ter \'fōr₁kwórtər\ *n* : front half on one side of the body of a quadruped

fore•run•ner \'fōr₁rənər\ *n* : one that goes before

fore•see \fōr'sē\ *vb* -**saw**; -**seen**; -**see•ing** : see or realize beforehand — **fore•see•able** *adj*

fore•shad•ow \fōr₁shadō\ *vb* : hint or suggest beforehand

fore•sight \'fōr₁sīt\ *n* : care or provision for the future — **fore•sight•ed** *adj* — **fore•sight•ed•ness** *n*

for•est \'fórəst\ *n* : large thick growth of trees and underbrush — **for•est•ed** \'fórəstəd\ *adj* — **for•est•er** \-əstər\ *n* — **for•est•land** \-₁land\ *n* — **for•est•ry** \-əstrē\ *n*

fore•stall \fōr'stól, fòr-\ *vb* : prevent by acting in advance

foreswear *var of* FORSWEAR

fore•taste \'fōr₁tāst\ *n* : advance indication or notion ~ *vb* : anticipate

fore•tell \fōr'tel\ *vb* -**told**; -**tell•ing** : predict

fore•thought \'fōr₁thót\ *n* : foresight

for•ev•er \fōr'evər\ *adv* 1 : for a limitless time 2 : always

for•ev•er•more \-₁evər'mōr\ *adv* : forever

fore•warn \fōr'wórn\ *vb* : warn beforehand

fore•word \'fōrwərd\ *n* : preface

for•feit \'fórfət\ *n* : something forfeited ~ *vb* : lose or lose the right to by an error or crime — **for•fei•ture** \-fə₁chùr\ *n*

¹**forge** \'fōrj\ *n* : smithy ~ *vb* **forged**; **forg•ing** 1 : form (metal) by heating and hammering 2 : imitate falsely esp. to defraud — **forg•er** *n* — **forg•ery** \-ərē\ *n*

²**forge** *vb* **forged**; **forg•ing** : move ahead steadily

for•get \fər'get\ *vb* -**got** \-'gät\; -**got•ten** \-'gät°n\ *or* -**got**; -**get•ting** 1 : be unable to think of or recall 2 : fail to think of at the proper time — **for•get•ta•ble** *adj* — **for•get•ful** \-fəl\ *adj* — **for•get•ful•ly** *adv*

forget–me–not \n : small herb with blue or white flowers

for·give \fər'giv\ vb **-gave** \-'gāv\; **-giv·en** \-'givən\; **-giv·ing** : pardon — **for·giv·able** adj — **for·give·ness** n

for·giv·ing adj 1 : able to forgive 2 : allowing room for error or weakness

for·go, fore·go \fōr'gō\ vb **-went**; **-gone**; **-go·ing** : do without

fork \'fȯrk\ n 1 : implement with prongs for lifting, holding, or digging 2 : forked part 3 : a dividing into branches or a place where something branches ~ vb 1 : divide into branches 2 : move with a fork — **forked** \'fȯrkt, 'fȯrkəd\ adj

◆ **fork·lift** n : machine for lifting with steel fingers

for·lorn \fər'lȯrn\ adj 1 : deserted 2 : wretched — **for·lorn·ly** adv

form \'fȯrm\ n 1 : shape 2 : set way of doing or saying something 3 : document with blanks to be filled in 4 : manner of performing with respect to what is expected 5 : mold 6 : kind or variety 7 : one of the ways in which a word is changed to show difference in use ~ vb 1 : give form or shape to 2 : train 3 : develop 4 : constitute — **for·ma·tive** \'fȯrmətiv\ adj — **form·less** \-ləs\ adj

for·mal \'fȯrməl\ adj : following established custom ~ n : formal social event — **for·mal·i·ty** \fȯr'malətē\ n — **for·mal·ize** \'fȯrmə‚līz\ vb — **for·mal·ly** adv

form·al·de·hyde \fȯr'maldə‚hīd\ n : colorless pungent gas used as a preservative and disinfectant

for·mat \'fȯr‚mat\ n : general style or arrangement of something — **format** vb

for·ma·tion \fȯr'māshən\ n 1 : a giving form to something 2 : something formed 3 : arrangement

for·mer \'fȯrmər\ adj : coming before in time — **for·mer·ly** adv

for·mi·da·ble \'fȯrmədəbəl, fȯr'mid-\ adj 1 : causing fear or dread 2 : very difficult — **for·mi·da·bly** \-blē\ adv

for·mu·la \'fȯrmyələ\ n, pl **-las** or **-lae** \-‚lē, -‚lī\ 1 : set form of words for ceremonial use 2 : recipe 3 : milk mixture for a baby 4 : group of symbols or figures briefly expressing information 5 : set form or method

for·mu·late \-‚lāt\ vb **-lat·ed**; **-lat·ing** : design, devise — **for·mu·la·tion** \‚fȯrmyə'lāshən\ n

for·ni·ca·tion \‚fȯrnə'kāshən\ n : illicit sexual intercourse — **for·ni·cate** \'fȯrnə‚kāt\ vb — **for·ni·ca·tor** \-‚kātər\ n

for·sake \fər'sāk\ vb **-sook** \-'sùk\; **-sak·en** \-'sākən\; **-sak·ing** : renounce completely

for·swear \fȯr'swar\ vb **-swore**; **-sworn**; **-swear·ing** 1 : renounce under oath 2 : perjure

for·syth·ia \fər'sithēə\ n : shrub grown for its yellow flowers

fort \'fȯrt\ n 1 : fortified place 2 : permanent army post

forte \'fȯrt, 'fȯr‚tā\ n : something at which a person excels

forth \'fȯrth\ adv : forward

forth·com·ing adj 1 : coming or available soon 2 : open and direct

forth·right adj : direct — **forth·right·ly** adv — **forth·right·ness** n

forth·with adv : immediately

for·ti·fy \'fȯrtə‚fī\ vb **-fied**; **-fy·ing** : make strong — **for·ti·fi·ca·tion** \‚fȯrtəfə'kāshən\ n

for·ti·tude \'fȯrtə‚tüd, -‚tyüd\ n : ability to endure

fort·night \'fȯrt‚nīt\ n : 2 weeks — **fort·night·ly** adj or adv

for·tress \'fórtrəs\ *n* : strong fort

for·tu·itous \fór'tüətəs, -'tyü-\ *adj* : accidental

for·tu·nate \'fórchənət\ *adj* 1 : coming by good luck 2 : lucky — **for·tu·nate·ly** *adv*

for·tune \'fórchən\ *n* 1 : prosperity attained partly through luck 2 : good or bad luck 3 : destiny 4 : wealth

for·tune–tell·er \-,telər\ *n* : one who foretells a person's future — **for·tune–tell·ing** \-iŋ\ *n or adj*

for·ty \'fórtē\ *n, pl* **forties** : 4 times 10 — **for·ti·eth** \-ēəth\ *adj or n* — **forty** *adj or pron*

fo·rum \'fórəm\ *n, pl* **-rums** 1 : Roman marketplace 2 : medium for open discussion

for·ward \'fórwərd\ *adj* 1 : being near or at or belonging to the front 2 : brash ~ *adv* : toward what is in front ~ *n* : player near the front of his team ~ *vb* 1 : help onward 2 : send on — **for·ward·er** \-wərdər\ *n* — **for·ward·ness** *n*

for·wards \'fórwərdz\ *adv* : forward

fos·sil \'fäsəl\ *n* : preserved trace of an ancient plant or animal ~ *adj* : being or originating from a fossil — **fos·sil·ize** *vb*

fos·ter \'fóstər\ *adj* : being, having, or relating to substitute parents ~ *vb* : help to grow or develop

fought *past of* FIGHT

foul \'faúl\ *adj* 1 : offensive 2 : clogged with dirt 3 : abusive 4 : wet and stormy 5 : unfair ~ *n* : a breaking of the rules in a game ~ *adv* : foully ~ *vb* 1 : make or become foul or filthy 2 : tangle — **foul·ly** *adv* — **foul–mouthed** \-'maúthd, -'maútht\ *adj* — **foul·ness** *n*

fou·lard \fú'lärd\ *n* : lightweight silk

foul–up *n* : error or state of confusion — **foul up** *vb* : bungle

¹**found** \'faúnd\ *past of* FIND

²**found** *vb* : establish — **found·er** *n*

foun·da·tion \faún'dāshən\ *n* 1 : act of founding 2 : basis for something 3 : endowed institution 4 : supporting structure — **foun·da·tion·al** \-shənəl\ *adj*

foun·der \'faúndər\ *vb* : sink

found·ling \'faúndliŋ\ *n* : abandoned infant that is found

found·ry \'faúndrē\ *n, pl* **-dries** : place where metal is cast

fount \'faúnt\ *n* : fountain

foun·tain \'faúnt³n\ *n* 1 : spring of water 2 : source 3 : artificial jet of water

four \'fōr\ *n* 1 : one more than 3 2 : 4th in a set or series 3 : something having 4 units — **four** *adj or pron*

four·fold *adj* : quadruple — **four·fold** *adv*

four·score *adj* : 80

four·some \'fōrsəm\ *n* : group of 4

four·teen \fōr'tēn\ *n* : one more than 13 — **fourteen** *adj or pron* — **four·teenth** \-'tēnth\ *adj or n*

fourth \'fōrth\ *n* 1 : one that is 4th 2 : one of 4 equal parts of something — **fourth** *adj or adv*

fowl \'faúl\ *n, pl* **fowl** *or* **fowls** 1 : bird 2 : chicken

fox \'fäks\ *n, pl* **fox·es** 1 : small mammal related to wolves 2 : clever person ~ *vb* : trick — **foxy** \'fäksē\ *adj*

fox·glove *n* : flowering plant that provides digitalis

fox·hole \'fäks,hōl\ *n* : pit for protection against enemy fire

foy·er \'fóiər, 'fói,yā\ *n* : entrance hallway

fra·cas \'frākəs, 'frak-\ *n, pl* **-cas·es** \-əsəz\ : brawl

frac·tion \'frakshən\ *n* 1 : number indicating one or more equal parts of a whole 2 : portion — **frac·tion·al** \-shənəl\ *adj* — **frac·tion·al·ly** *adv*

frac·tious \'frakshəs\ *adj* : hard to control

frac·ture \'frakchər\ *n* : a breaking of something — **fracture** *vb*

frag·ile \'frajəl, -,īl\ *adj* : easily broken — **fra·gil·i·ty** \frə'jilətē\ *n*

frag·ment \'fragmənt\ *n* : part broken off ~ \-,ment\ *vb* : break into parts — **frag·men·tary** \'fragmən,terē\ *adj* — **frag·men·ta·tion** \,fragmən'tāshən, -,men-\ *n*

fra·grant \'frāgrənt\ *adj* : sweet=smelling — **fra·grance** \-grəns\ *n* — **fra·grant·ly** *adv*

frail \'frāl\ *adj* : weak or delicate — **frail·ty** \-tē\ *n*

frame \'frām\ *vb* **framed; fram·ing** 1 : plan 2 : formulate 3 : construct or arrange 4 : enclose in a frame 5 : make appear guilty ~ *n*

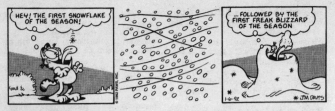

1 : makeup of the body 2 : supporting or enclosing structure 3 : state or disposition (as of mind) — **frame·work** *n*

franc \'fraŋk\ *n* : monetary unit (as of France)

fran·chise \'fran,chīz\ *n* 1 : special privilege 2 : the right to vote — **fran·chi·see** \,fran,chī'zē, -chə-\ *n*

fran·gi·ble \'franjəbəl\ *adj* : breakable — **fran·gi·bil·i·ty** \,franjə-'bilətē\ *n*

¹**frank** \'fraŋk\ *adj* : direct and sincere — **frank·ly** *adv* — **frank·ness** *n*

²**frank** *vb* : mark (mail) with a sign showing it can be mailed free ~ *n* : sign on franked mail

frank·furt·er \'fraŋkfərtər, -,fərt-\; **frank·furt** \-fərt\ *n* : cooked sausage

frank·in·cense \'fraŋkən,sens\ *n* : incense resin

fran·tic \'frantik\ *adj* : wildly excited — **fran·ti·cal·ly** \-iklē\ *adv*

fra·ter·nal \frə'tərnᵊl\ *adj* 1 : brotherly 2 : of a fraternity — **fra·ter·nal·ly** *adv*

fra·ter·ni·ty \frə'tərnətē\ *n, pl* -**ties** : men's student social group

frat·er·nize \'fratər,nīz\ *vb* -**nized**; -**niz·ing** 1 : mingle as friends 2 : associate with members of a hostile group — **frat·er·ni·za·tion** \,fratərnə'zāshən\ *n*

frat·ri·cide \'fratrə,sīd\ *n* : killing of a sibling — **frat·ri·cid·al** \,fratrə-'sīdᵊl\ *adj*

fraud \'frȯd\ *n* : trickery — **fraud·u·lent** \'frȯjələnt\ *adj* — **fraud·u·lent·ly** *adv*

fraught \'frȯt\ *adj* : full of or accompanied by something specified

¹**fray** \'frā\ *n* : fight

²**fray** *vb* 1 : wear by rubbing 2 : separate the threads of 3 : irritate

fraz·zle \'frazəl\ *vb* -**zled**; -**zling** : wear out ~ *n* : exhaustion

♦ **freak** \'frēk\ *n* 1 : something abnormal or unusual 2 : enthusiast — **freak·ish** *adj* — **freak out** *vb* 1 : experience nightmarish hallucinations from drugs 2 : distress or become distressed

freck·le \'frekəl\ *n* : brown spot on the skin — **freckle** *vb*

free \'frē\ *adj* **fre·er**; **fre·est** 1 : having liberty or independence 2 : not taxed 3 : given without charge 4 : voluntary 5 : not in use 6 : not fastened ~ *adv* : without charge ~ *vb* **freed**; **free·ing** : set free — **free** *adv* — **free·born** *adj* — **free·dom** \'frēdəm\ *n* — **free·ly** *adv*

free·boo·ter \-,bütər\ *n* : pirate

free-for-all *n* : fight with no rules

free·load *vb* : live off another's generosity — **free·load·er** *n*

free·stand·ing *adj* : standing without support

free·way \'frē,wā\ *n* : expressway

free will *n* : independent power to choose — **free·will** *adj*

freeze \'frēz\ *vb* **froze** \'frōz\; **fro·zen** \'frōzᵊn\; **freez·ing** 1 : harden into ice 2 : become chilled 3 : damage by frost 4 : stick fast 5 : become motionless 6 : fix at one stage or level ~ *n* 1 : very cold weather 2 : state of being frozen — **freez·er** *n*

freeze–dry *vb* : preserve by freezing then drying — **freeze–dried** *adj*

freight \'frāt\ *n* 1 : carrying of goods or payment for this 2 : shipped goods ~ *vb* : load or ship goods — **freigh·ter** *n*

french fry *vb* : fry in deep fat — **french fry** *n*

fre·net·ic \fri'netik\ *adj* : frantic — **fre·net·i·cal·ly** \-iklē\ *adv*

fren·zy \'frenzē\ *n, pl* -**zies** : violent agitation — **fren·zied** \-zēd\ *adj*

fre·quen·cy \'frēkwənsē\ *n, pl* **-cies 1** : frequent or regular occurrence **2** : number of cycles or sound waves per second

fre·quent \'frēkwənt\ *adj* : happening often ~ \frē'kwent, 'frē-kwənt\ *vb* : go to habitually — **fre·quent·er** *n* — **fre·quent·ly** *adv*

fres·co \'freskō\ *n, pl* **-coes** : painting on fresh plaster

fresh \'fresh\ *adj* **1** : not salt **2** : pure **3** : not preserved **4** : not stale **5** : like new **6** : insolent — **fres·hen** \-ən\ *vb* — **fresh·ly** *adv* — **fresh·ness** *n*

fresh·et \-ət\ *n* : overflowing stream

fresh·man \-mən\ *n* : first-year student

fresh·wa·ter *n* : water that is not salty

fret \'fret\ *vb* **-tt- 1** : worry or become irritated **2** : fray **3** : agitate ~ *n* **1** : worn spot **2** : irritation — **fret·ful** \-fəl\ *adj* — **fret·ful·ly** *adv* — **fret·ful·ness** *n*

fri·a·ble \'frīəbəl\ *adj* : easily pulverized

fri·ar \'frīər\ *n* : member of a religious order

fri·ary \-ē\ *n, pl* **-ar·ies** : monastery of friars

fric·as·see \'frikə‚sē, ‚frikə'-\ *n* : meat stewed in a gravy ~ *vb* **-seed; -see·ing** : stew in gravy

fric·tion \'frikshən\ *n* **1** : a rubbing between 2 surfaces **2** : clash of opinions — **fric·tion·al** *adj*

Fri·day \'frīdā\ *n* : 6th day of the week

friend \'frend\ *n* : person one likes — **friend·less** \-ləs\ *adj* — **friend·li·ness** \-lēnəs\ *n* — **friend·ly** *adj* — **friend·ship** \-‚ship\ *n*

frieze \'frēz\ *n* : ornamental band around a room

frig·ate \'frigət\ *n* : warship smaller than a destroyer

fright \'frīt\ *n* : sudden fear — **frigh·ten** \-ᵊn\ *vb* — **fright·ful** \-fəl\ *adj* — **fright·ful·ly** *adv* — **fright·ful·ness** *n*

frig·id \'frijəd\ *adj* : intensely cold — **fri·gid·i·ty** \frij'idətē\ *n*

frill \'fril\ *n* **1** : ruffle **2** : pleasing but nonessential addition — **frilly** *adj*

fringe \'frinj\ *n* **1** : ornamental border of short hanging threads or strips **2** : edge — **fringe** *vb*

frisk \'frisk\ *vb* **1** : leap about **2** : search (a person) esp. for weapons

frisky \'friskē\ *adj* **frisk·i·er; -est** : playful — **frisk·i·ly** *adv* — **frisk·i·ness** *n*

¹frit·ter \'fritər\ *n* : fried batter containing fruit or meat

²fritter *vb* : waste little by little

friv·o·lous \'frivələs\ *adj* : not important or serious — **fri·vol·i·ty** \friv'älətē\ *n* — **friv·o·lous·ly** *adv*

frizz \'friz\ *vb* : curl tightly — **frizz** *n* — **frizzy** *adj*

fro \'frō\ *adv* : away

frock \'fräk\ *n* **1** : loose outer garment **2** : dress

frog \'frog, 'fräg\ *n* **1** : leaping amphibian **2** : hoarseness **3** : ornamental braid fastener **4** : small holder for flowers

frog·man \-‚man, -mən\ *n* : underwater swimmer

frol·ic \'frälik\ *vb* **-icked; -ick·ing** : romp ~ *n* : fun — **frol·ic·some** \-səm\ *adj*

from \'frəm, 'främ\ *prep* — used to show a starting point

frond \'fränd\ *n* : fern or palm leaf

front \'frənt\ *n* **1** : face **2** : behavior **3** : main side of a building **4** : forward part **5** : boundary between air masses ~ *vb* **1** : have the main side adjacent to something **2** : serve as a front — **fron·tal** \-ᵊl\ *adj*

front·age \'frəntij\ *n* : length of boundary line on a street

fron·tier \‚frən'tir\ *n* : outer edge of settled territory — **fron·tiers·man** \-'tirzmən\ *n*

fron·tis·piece \'frəntə‚spēs\ *n* : illustration facing a title page

frost \'frost\ *n* **1** : freezing temperature **2** : ice crystals on a surface ~ *vb* **1** : cover with frost **2** : put icing on (a cake) — **frosty** *adj*

frost·bite \-‚bīt\ *n* : partial freezing of part of the body — **frost·bit·ten** \-‚bitᵊn\ *adj*

frost·ing *n* : icing

froth \'froth\ *n, pl* **froths** \'froths, 'frothz\ : bubbles on a liquid — **frothy** *adj*

fro·ward \'frōwərd\ *adj* : willful

frown \'fraun\ *vb or n* : scowl

frow·sy, frow·zy \'frauzē\ *adj* **-si·er or -zi·er; -est** : untidy

froze *past of* FREEZE

frozen *past part of* FREEZE

fru·gal \'frügəl\ *adj* : thrifty — **fru·gal·i·ty** \frü'galətē\ *n* — **fru·gal·ly** *adv*

fruit \'früt\ *n* 1 : usu. edible and sweet part of a seed plant 2 : result ~ *vb* : bear fruit — **fruit·cake** *n* — **fruit·ed** \-əd\ *adj* — **fruit·ful** *adj* — **fruit·ful·ness** *n* — **fruit·less** *adj* — **fruit·less·ly** *adv* — **fruity** *adj*

fru·ition \frü'ishən\ *n* : completion

frumpy \'frəmpē\ *adj* **frump·i·er; -est** : dowdy

frus·trate \'frəs.trāt\ *vb* **-trat·ed; -trat·ing** 1 : block 2 : cause to fail — **frus·trat·ing·ly** *adv* — **frus·tra·tion** \frəs'trāshən\ *n*

¹fry \'frī\ *vb* **fried; fry·ing** 1 : cook esp. with fat or oil 2 : be cooked by frying ~ *n, pl* **fries** 1 : something fried 2 : social gathering with fried food

²fry *n, pl* **fry** : recently hatched fish

fud·dle \'fəd²l\ *vb* **-dled; -dling** : muddle

fud·dy-dud·dy \'fədē.dədē\ *n, pl* **-dies** : one who is old-fashioned or unimaginative

fudge \'fəj\ *vb* **fudged; fudg·ing** : cheat or exaggerate ~ *n* : creamy candy

fu·el \'fyüəl\ *n* : material burned to produce heat or power ~ *vb* **-eled** *or* **-elled; -el·ing** *or* **-el·ling** : provide with or take in fuel

fu·gi·tive \'fyüjətiv\ *adj* 1 : running away or trying to escape 2 : not lasting — **fugitive** *n*

-ful \'fəl\ *adj suffix* 1 : full of 2 : having the qualities of 3 : -able ~ *n suffix* : quantity that fills

ful·crum \'fúlkrəm, 'fəl-\ *n, pl* **-crums** *or* **-cra** \-krə\ : support on which a lever turns

ful·fill, ful·fil \fúl'fil\ *vb* **-filled; -fill·ing** 1 : perform 2 : satisfy — **ful·fill·ment** *n*

¹full \'fúl\ *adj* 1 : filled 2 : complete 3 : rounded 4 : having an abundance of something ~ *adv* : entirely ~ *n* : utmost degree — **full·ness** *n* — **ful·ly** *adv*

²full *vb* : shrink and thicken woolen cloth — **full·er** *n*

full-fledged \'fúl'flejd\ *adj* : fully developed

ful·some \'fúlsəm\ *adj* : copious verging on excessive

fum·ble \'fəmbəl\ *vb* **-bled; -bling** : fail to hold something properly — **fumble** *n*

fume \'fyüm\ *n* : irritating gas ~ *vb* **fumed; fum·ing** 1 : give off fumes 2 : show annoyance

fu·mi·gate \'fyümə.gāt\ *vb* **-gat·ed; -gat·ing** : treat with pest-killing fumes — **fu·mi·gant** \'fyümigənt\ *n* — **fu·mi·ga·tion** \.fyümə'gāshən\ *n*

◆ **fun** \'fən\ *n* 1 : something providing amusement or enjoyment 2 : enjoyment ~ *adj* : full of fun

func·tion \'fəŋkshən\ *n* 1 : special purpose 2 : formal ceremony or social affair ~ *vb* : have or carry on a function — **func·tion·al** \-shənəl\ *adj* — **func·tion·al·ly** *adv*

func·tion·ary \-shə.nerē\ *n, pl* **-ar·ies** : official

fund \'fənd\ *n* 1 : store 2 : sum of money intended for a special purpose 3 *pl* : available money ~ *vb* : provide funds for

fun·da·men·tal \.fəndə'mentªl\ *adj* 1 : basic 2 : of central importance or necessity — **fundamental** *n* — **fun·da·men·tal·ly** *adv*

fu·ner·al \'fyünərəl\ *n* : ceremony for a dead person — **funeral** *adj* — **fu·ne·re·al** \fyü'nirēəl\ *adj*

fun·gi·cide \'fənjə.sīd, 'fəngə-\ *n* : agent that kills fungi — **fun·gi·cid·al** \.fənjə'sīdªl, .fəngə-\ *adj*

fun·gus \'fəŋgəs\ *n, pl* **fun·gi** \'fən,jī, 'fəŋ,gī\ : lower plant that lacks chlorophyll — **fun·gal** \'fəŋgəl\ *adj* — **fun·gous** \-gəs\ *adj*

funk \'fəŋk\ *n* 1 : state of depression

funky \'fəŋkē\ *adj* **funk·i·er; -est** : unconventional and unsophisticated

fun·nel \'fən³l\ *n* 1 : cone-shaped utensil with a tube for directing the flow of a liquid 2 : ship's smokestack ~ *vb* **-neled; -nel·ing** : move to a central point or into a central channel

fun·nies \'fənēz\ *n pl* : section of comic strips

fun·ny \'fənē\ *adj* **-ni·er; -est** 1 : amusing 2 : strange

fur \'fər\ *n* 1 : hairy coat of a mammal 2 : article of clothing made with fur — **fur** *adj* — **furred** \'fərd\ *adj* — **fur·ry** \-ē\ *adj*

fur·bish \'fərbish\ *vb* : make lustrous or new looking

fu·ri·ous \'fyurēəs\ *adj* : fierce or angry — **fu·ri·ous·ly** *adv*

fur·long \'fər,lȯŋ\ *n* : a unit of distance equal to 220 yards

fur·lough \'fərlō\ *n* : authorized absence from duty — **furlough** *vb*

fur·nace \'fərnəs\ *n* : enclosed structure in which heat is produced

fur·nish \'fərnish\ *vb* 1 : provide with what is needed 2 : make available for use

fur·nish·ings \-iŋs\ *n pl* 1 : articles or accessories of dress 2 : furniture

fur·ni·ture \'fərnichər\ *n* : movable articles for a room

fu·ror \'fyur,ȯr\ *n* 1 : anger 2 : sensational craze

fur·ri·er \'fərēər\ *n* : dealer in furs

fur·row \'fərō\ *n* 1 : trench made by a plow 2 : wrinkle or groove — **furrow** *vb*

fur·ther \'fərthər\ *adv* 1 : at or to a more advanced point 2 : more ~ *adj* : additional ~ *vb* : promote — **fur·ther·ance** \-ərəns\ *n*

fur·ther·more \'fərthər,mōr\ *adv* : in addition

fur·ther·most \-,mōst\ *adj* : most distant

fur·thest \'fərthəst\ *adv or adj* : farthest

fur·tive \'fərtiv\ *adj* : slyly or secretly done — **fur·tive·ly** *adv* — **fur·tive·ness** *n*

fu·ry \'fyurē\ *n, pl* **-ries** 1 : intense rage 2 : violence

¹fuse \'fyüz\ *n* 1 : cord lighted to transmit fire to an explosive 2 *usu* **fuze** : device for exploding a charge ~ *or* **fuze** *vb* **fused** *or* **fuzed; fus·ing** *or* **fuz·ing** : equip with a fuse

²fuse *vb* **fused; fus·ing** 1 : melt and run together 2 : unite ~ *n* : electrical safety device — **fus·ible** *adj*

fu·se·lage \'fyüsə,läzh, -zə-\ *n* : main body of an aircraft

fu·sil·lade \'fyüsə,läd, -,lād, ,fyüsə'-, -zə-\ *n* : volley of fire

fu·sion \'fyüzhən\ *n* 1 : process of merging by melting 2 : union of atomic nuclei

fuss \'fəs\ *n* 1 : needless bustle or excitement 2 : show of attention 3 : objection or protest ~ *vb* : make a fuss

fuss·bud·get \-,bəjət\ *n* : one who fusses or is fussy about trifles

fussy \'fəsē\ *adj* **fuss·i·er; -est** 1 : irritable 2 : paying very close attention to details — **fuss·i·ly** *adv* — **fuss·i·ness** *n*

fu·tile \'fyüt³l, 'fyü,tīl\ *adj* : useless or vain — **fu·til·i·ty** \fyü'tilətē\ *n*

fu·ture \'fyüchər\ *adj* : coming after the present ~ *n* 1 : time yet to come 2 : what will happen — **fu·tur·is·tic** \,fyüchə'ristik\ *adj*

fuze *var of* FUSE

fuzz \'fəz\ *n* : fine particles or fluff

fuzzy \-ē\ *adj* **fuzz·i·er; -est** 1 : covered with or like fuzz 2 : indistinct — **fuzz·i·ness** *n*

-fy \,fī\ *vb suffix* : make — **-fi·er** \,fīər\ *n suffix*

G

g \'jē\ *n, pl* **g's** *or* **gs** \'jēz\ **1** : 7th letter of the alphabet **2** : unit of gravitational force

gab \'gab\ *vb* **-bb-** : chatter — **gab** *n* — **gab·by** \'gabē\ *adj*

gab·ar·dine \'gabər,dēn\ *n* : durable twilled fabric

ga·ble \'gābəl\ *n* : triangular part of the end of a building — **ga·bled** \-bəld\ *adj*

gad \'gad\ *vb* **-dd-** : roam about — **gad·der** *n*

gad·fly *n* : persistently critical person

gad·get \'gajət\ *n* : device — **gad·get·ry** \'gajətrē\ *n*

gaff \'gaf\ *n* : metal hook for lifting fish — **gaff** *vb*

gaffe \'gaf\ *n* : social blunder

gag \'gag\ *vb* **-gg- 1** : prevent from speaking or crying out by stopping up the mouth **2** : retch or cause to retch ~ *n* **1** : something that stops up the mouth **2** : laugh-provoking remark or act

gage *var of* GAUGE

gag·gle \'gagəl\ *n* : flock of geese

gai·ety \'gāətē\ *n, pl* **-eties** : high spirits

gai·ly \'gālē\ *adv* : in a gay manner

♦ **gain** \'gān\ *n* **1** : profit **2** : obtaining of profit or possessions **3** : increase ~ *vb* **1** : get possession of **2** : win **3** : arrive at **4** : increase or increase in **5** : profit — **gain·er** *n* — **gain·ful** *adj* — **gain·ful·ly** *adv*

gain·say \gān'sā\ *vb* **-said** \-'sād, -'sed\; **-say·ing**; **-says** \-'sāz, -'sez\ : deny or dispute — **gain·say·er** *n*

gait \'gāt\ *n* : manner of walking or running — **gait·ed** *adj*

gal \'gal\ *n* : girl

ga·la \'gālə, 'galə, 'gälə\ *n* : festive celebration — **gala** *adj*

gal·axy \'galəksē\ *n, pl* **-ax·ies** : very large group of stars — **ga·lac·tic** \gə'laktik\ *adj*

gale \'gāl\ *n* **1** : strong wind **2** : outburst

¹gall \'gȯl\ *n* **1** : bile **2** : insolence

²gall *n* **1** : skin sore caused by chafing **2** : swelling of plant tissue caused by parasites ~ *vb* **1** : chafe **2** : irritate or vex

gal·lant \gə'lant, -'länt; 'galənt\ *n* : man very attentive to women ~ \'galənt; gə'lant, -'länt\ *adj* **1** : splendid **2** : brave **3** : polite and attentive to women — **gal·lant·ly** *adv* — **gal·lant·ry** \'galəntrē\ *n*

gall·blad·der *n* : pouch attached to the liver in which bile is stored

gal·le·on \'galyən\ *n* : large sailing ship formerly used esp. by the Spanish

gal·lery \'galərē\ *n, pl* **-ler·ies 1** : outdoor balcony **2** : long narrow passage or hall **3** : room or building for exhibiting art **4** : spectators — **gal·ler·ied** \-rēd\ *adj*

gal·ley \'galē\ *n, pl* **-leys 1** : old ship propelled esp. by oars **2** : kitchen of a ship or airplane

gal·li·um \'galēəm\ *n* : bluish white metallic chemical element

gal·li·vant \'galə,vant\ *vb* : travel or roam about for pleasure

gal·lon \'galən\ *n* : unit of liquid measure equal to 4 quarts

gal·lop \'galəp\ *n* : fast 3-beat gait of a horse — **gallop** *vb* — **gal·lop·er** *n*

gal·lows \'galōz\ *n, pl* **-lows** *or*

-lows·es : upright frame for hanging criminals

gall·stone *n* : abnormal concretion in the gallbladder or bile passages

ga·lore \gə'lōr\ *adj* : in abundance

ga·losh \gə'läsh\ *n* : overshoe — usu. pl.

gal·va·nize \'galvə,nīz\ *vb* **-nized; -niz·ing 1** : shock into action **2** : coat (iron or steel) with zinc — **gal·va·ni·za·tion** \,galvənə'zāshən\ *n* — **gal·va·niz·er** *n*

gam·bit \'gambit\ *n* **1** : opening tactic in chess **2** : stratagem

gam·ble \'gambəl\ *vb* **-bled; -bling 1** : play a game for stakes **2** : bet **3** : take a chance ~ *n* : risky undertaking — **gam·bler** \-blər\ *n*

gam·bol \'gambəl\ *vb* **-boled** *or* **-bolled; -bol·ing** *or* **-bol·ling** : skip about in play — **gambol** *n*

game \'gām\ *n* **1** : playing activity **2** : competition according to rules **3** : animals hunted for sport or food ~ *vb* **gamed; gam·ing** : gamble ~ *adj* **1** : plucky **2** : lame — **game·ly** *adv* — **game·ness** *n*

game·cock *n* : fighting cock

game·keep·er *n* : person in charge of game animals or birds

gam·ete \gə'mēt, 'gam,ēt\ *n* : mature germ cell — **ga·met·ic** \gə-'metik\ *adj*

ga·mine \ga'mēn\ *n* : charming tomboy

gam·ut \'gamət\ *n* : entire range or series

gamy *or* **gam·ey** \'gāmē\ *adj* **gam·i·er; -est** : having the flavor of game esp. when slightly tainted — **gam·i·ness** *n*

¹gan·der \'gandər\ *n* : male goose

²gander *n* : glance

gang \'gaŋ\ *n* **1** : group of persons working together **2** : group of criminals ~ *vb* : attack in a gang — with *up*

gan·gling \'gaŋgliŋ\ *adj* : lanky

gan·gli·on \'gaŋglēən\ *n, pl* **-glia** \-glēə\ : mass of nerve cells

gang·plank *n* : platform used in boarding or leaving a ship

gan·grene \'gaŋ,grēn, gaŋ'-; 'gaŋ-, gaŋ-\ *n* : local death of body tissue — **gangrene** *vb* — **gan·gre·nous** \'gaŋgrənəs\ *adj*

gang·ster \'gaŋstər\ *n* : member of criminal gang

gang·way \-,wā\ *n* : passage in or out

gan·net \'ganət\ *n* : large fish-eating marine bird

gan·try \'gantrē\ *n, pl* **-tries** : frame structure supported over or around something

gap \'gap\ *n* **1** : break in a barrier **2** : mountain pass **3** : empty space

gape \'gāp\ *vb* **gaped; gap·ing 1** : open widely **2** : stare with mouth open — **gape** *n*

ga·rage \gə'räzh, -'räj\ *n* : shelter or repair shop for automobiles ~ *vb* **-raged; -rag·ing** : put or keep in a garage

garb \'gärb\ *n* : clothing ~ *vb* : dress

gar·bage \'gärbij\ *n* **1** : food waste **2** : trash — **gar·bage·man** *n*

gar·ble \'gärbəl\ *vb* **-bled; -bling** : distort the meaning of

gar·den \'gärd°n\ *n* **1** : plot for growing fruits, flowers, or vegetables **2** : public recreation area ~ *vb* : work in a garden — **gar·den·er** \'gärd°nər\ *n*

gar·de·nia \gär'dēnyə\ *n* : tree or shrub with fragrant white or yellow flowers or the flower

gar·gan·tuan \gär'ganchəwən\ *adj* : having tremendous size or volume

gar·gle \'gärgəl\ *vb* **-gled; -gling** : rinse the throat with liquid — **gargle** *n*

gar·goyle \'gär,gòil\ *n* : waterspout in the form of a grotesque human or animal

gar·ish \'garish\ *adj* : offensively bright or gaudy

gar·land \'gärlənd\ *n* : wreath ~ *vb* : form into or deck with a garland

gar·lic \'gärlik\ *n* : herb with pungent bulbs used in cooking — **gar·licky** \-likē\ *adj*

gar·ment \'gärmənt\ *n* : article of clothing

gar·ner \'gärnər\ *vb* : acquire by effort

gar·net \'gärnət\ *n* : deep red mineral

gar·nish \'gärnish\ *vb* : add decoration to (as food) — **garnish** *n*

gar·nish·ee \,gärnə'shē\ *vb* **-eed; -ee·ing** : take (as a debtor's wages) by legal authority

gar·nish·ment \'gärnishmənt\ *n*

: attachment of property to satisfy a creditor

gar·ret \'garət\ *n* : attic

gar·ri·son \'garəsən\ *n* : military post or the troops stationed there — **garrison** *vb*

gar·ru·lous \'garələs\ *adj* : talkative — **gar·ru·li·ty** \gə'rülətē\ *n* — **gar·ru·lous·ly** *adv* — **gar·ru·lous·ness** *n*

gar·ter \'gärtər\ *n* : band to hold up a stocking or sock

gas \'gas\ *n, pl* **gas·es** 1 : fluid (as hydrogen or air) that tends to expand indefinitely 2 : gasoline ~ *vb* **gassed; gas·sing** 1 : treat with gas 2 : fill with gasoline — **gas·eous** \'gasēəs, 'gashəs\ *adj*

gash \'gash\ *n* : deep long cut — **gash** *vb*

gas·ket \'gaskət\ *n* : material or a part used to seal a joint

gas·light *n* : light of burning illuminating gas

gas·o·line \'gasə,lēn, ,gasə'-\ *n* : flammable liquid from petroleum

gasp \'gasp\ *vb* 1 : catch the breath audibly 2 : breathe laboriously — **gasp** *n*

gas·tric \'gastrik\ *adj* : relating to or located near the stomach

gas·tron·o·my \gas'tränəmē\ *n* : art of good eating — **gas·tro·nom·ic** \,gastrə'nämik\ *adj*

gate \'gāt\ *n* : an opening for passage in a wall or fence — **gate·keep·er** *n* — **gate·post** *n*

gate·way *n* : way in or out

gath·er \'gathər\ *vb* 1 : bring or come together 2 : harvest 3 : pick up little by little 4 : deduce — **gath·er·er** *n* — **gath·er·ing** *n*

gauche \'gōsh\ *adj* : crude or tactless

gaudy \'gȯdē\ *adj* **gaud·i·er; -est** : tastelessly showy — **gaud·i·ly** \'gȯd°lē\ *adv* — **gaud·i·ness** *n*

gauge \'gāj\ *n* : instrument for measuring ~ *vb* **gauged; gaug·ing** : measure

gaunt \'gȯnt\ *adj* : thin or emaciated — **gaunt·ness** *n*

¹**gaunt·let** \-lət\ *n* 1 : protective glove 2 : challenge to combat

²**gauntlet** *n* : ordeal

gauze \'gȯz\ *n* : thin often transparent fabric — **gauzy** *adj*

gave *past of* GIVE

gav·el \'gavəl\ *n* : mallet of a presiding officer, auctioneer, or judge

gawk \'gȯk\ *vb* : stare stupidly

gawky \-ē\ *adj* **gawk·i·er; -est** : clumsy

gay \'gā\ *adj* 1 : merry 2 : bright and lively 3 : homosexual — **gay** *n*

gaze \'gāz\ *vb* **gazed; gaz·ing** : fix the eyes in a steady intent look — **gaze** *n* — **gaz·er** *n*

ga·zelle \gə'zel\ *n* : small swift antelope

ga·zette \-'zet\ *n* : newspaper

gaz·et·teer \,gazə'tir\ *n* : geographical dictionary

gear \'gir\ *n* 1 : clothing 2 : equipment 3 : toothed wheel — **gear** *vb*

gear·shift *n* : mechanism by which automobile gears are shifted

geek \'gēk\ *n* : socially inept person

geese *pl of* GOOSE

gei·sha \'gāshə, 'gē-\ *n, pl* **-sha** *or* **-shas** : Japanese girl or woman trained to entertain men

gel·a·tin \'jelət°n\ *n* : sticky substance obtained from animal tissues by boiling — **ge·lat·i·nous** \jə'lat°nəs\ *adj*

geld \'geld\ *vb* : castrate

geld·ing \-iŋ\ *n* : castrated horse

gem \'jem\ *n* : cut and polished valuable stone — **gem·stone** *n*

gen·der \'jendər\ *n* 1 : sex 2 : division of a class of words (as nouns) that determines agreement of other words

gene \'jēn\ *n* : segment of DNA that controls inheritance of a trait

ge·ne·al·o·gy \,jēnē'äləjē, ,jen-, -'al-\ *n, pl* **-gies** : study of family pedigrees — **ge·ne·a·log·i·cal** \-ēə'läjikəl\ *adj* — **ge·ne·a·log·i·cal·ly** *adv* — **ge·ne·al·o·gist** \-ē-'äləjist, -'al-\ *n*

genera *pl of* GENUS

gen·er·al \'jenrəl, 'jenə-\ *adj* 1 : relating to the whole 2 : applicable to all of a group 3 : common or widespread ~ *n* 1 : something that involves or is applicable to the whole 2 : commissioned officer in the army, air force, or marine corps ranking above a lieutenant general — **gen·er·al·ly** *adv* — **in general** : for the most part

gen·er·al·i·ty \,jenə'ralətē\ *n, pl* **-ties** : general statement

gen·er·al·ize \'jenrə,līz, 'jenə-\ *vb* **-ized; -iz·ing** : reach a general conclusion esp. on the basis of particular instances — **gen·er·al·iza·tion** \ˌjenrələ'zāshən, ˌjenə-\ n

general of the air force : commissioned officer of the highest rank in the air force

general of the army : commissioned officer of the highest rank in the army

gen·er·ate \'jenəˌrāt\ vb -at·ed; -at·ing : create or produce

♦ **gen·er·a·tion** \ˌjenə'rāshən\ n 1 : living beings constituting a single step in a line of descent 2 : production — **gen·er·a·tive** \'jenəˌrātiv, -rət-\ adj

gen·er·a·tor \'jenəˌrātər\ n 1 : one that generates 2 : machine that turns mechanical into electrical energy

ge·ner·ic \jə'nerik\ adj 1 : general 2 : not protected by a trademark 3 : relating to a genus — **generic** n

gen·er·ous \'jenərəs\ adj : freely giving or sharing — **gen·er·os·i·ty** \ˌjenə'räsətē\ n — **gen·er·ous·ly** adv — **gen·er·ous·ness** n

ge·net·ics \jə'netiks\ n : biology dealing with heredity and variation — **ge·net·ic** \-ik\ adj — **ge·net·i·cal·ly** adv — **ge·net·i·cist** \-'netəsist\ n

ge·nial \'jēnēəl\ adj : cheerful — **ge·nial·i·ty** \ˌjēnē'alətē\ n — **ge·nial·ly** adv

ge·nie \'jēnē\ n : supernatural spirit that often takes human form

gen·i·tal \'jenətᵊl\ adj : concerned with reproduction — **gen·i·tal·ly** \-təlē\ adv

gen·i·ta·lia \ˌjenə'tālyə\ n pl : external genital organs

gen·i·tals \'jenətᵊlz\ n pl : genitalia

ge·nius \'jēnyəs\ n 1 : single strongly marked capacity 2 : extraordinary intellectual power or a person having such power

geno·cide \'jenəˌsīd\ n : systematic destruction of a racial or cultural group

genre \'zhänrə, 'zhäⁿrə\ n : category esp. of literary composition

gen·teel \jen'tēl\ adj : polite or refined

gen·tile \'jenˌtīl\ n : person who is not Jewish — **gentile** adj

gen·til·i·ty \jen'tilətē\ n, pl -ties 1 : good birth and family 2 : good manners

gen·tle \'jentᵊl\ adj -tler; -tlest 1 : of a family of high social station 2 : not harsh, stern, or violent 3 : soft or delicate ~ vb -tled; -tling : make gentle — **gen·tle·ness** n — **gen·tly** adv

gen·tle·man \-mən\ n : man of good family or manners — **gen·tle·man·ly** adv

gen·tle·wom·an \-ˌwùmən\ n : woman of good family or breeding

gen·try \'jentrē\ n, pl -tries : people of good birth or breeding

gen·u·flect \'jenyəˌflekt\ vb : bend the knee in worship — **gen·u·flec·tion** \ˌjenyə'flekshən\ n

gen·u·ine \'jenyəwən\ adj : being the same in fact as in appearance — **gen·u·ine·ly** adv — **gen·u·ine·ness** n

ge·nus \'jēnəs\ n, pl **gen·era** \'jenərə\ : category of biological classification

ge·ode \'jēˌōd\ n : stone having a mineral-lined cavity

geo·de·sic \ˌjēə'desik, -'dēs-\ adj : made of a framework of linked polygons

ge·og·ra·phy \jē'ägrəfē\ n 1 : study of the earth and its climate, products, and inhabitants 2 : natural features of a region — **ge·og·ra·pher** \-fər\ n — **geo·graph·ic** \ˌjēə'grafik\ **geo·graph·i·cal**

\-ikəl\ *adj* — **geo·graph·i·cal·ly** *adv*

ge·ol·o·gy \jē'äləjē\ *n* : study of the history of the earth and its life esp. as recorded in rocks — **geo·log·ic** \jēə'läjik\ **geo·log·i·cal** \-ikəl\ *adj* — **geo·log·i·cal·ly** *adv* — **ge·ol·o·gist** \jē'äləjist\ *n*

ge·om·e·try \jē'ämətrē\ *n, pl* **-tries** : mathematics of the relations, properties, and measurements of solids, surfaces, lines, and angles — **geo·met·ric** \jēə'metrik\ **geo·met·ri·cal** \-rikəl\ *adj*

geo·ther·mal \jēō'thərməl\ *adj* : relating to or derived from the heat of the earth's interior

ge·ra·ni·um \jə'rānēəm\ *n* : garden plant with clusters of white, pink, or scarlet flowers

ger·bil \'jərbəl\ *n* : burrowing desert rodent

ge·ri·at·ric \jerē'atrik\ *adj* 1 : relating to aging or the aged 2 : old

ge·ri·at·rics \-triks\ *n* : medicine dealing with the aged and aging

germ \'jərm\ *n* 1 : microorganism 2 : source or rudiment

ger·mane \jər'mān\ *adj* : relevant

ger·ma·ni·um \-'mānēəm\ *n* : grayish white hard chemical element

ger·mi·cide \'jərmə,sīd\ *n* : agent that destroys germs — **ger·mi·cid·al** \jərmə'sīd°l\ *adj*

ger·mi·nate \'jərmə,nāt\ *vb* **-nated; -nat·ing** : begin to develop — **ger·mi·na·tion** \jərmə'nāshən\ *n*

ger·ry·man·der \'jerē'mandər, 'jerē,-, gerē'-, 'gerē,-\ *vb* : divide into election districts so as to give one political party an advantage — **gerrymander** *n*

ger·und \'jerənd\ *n* : word having the characteristics of both verb and noun

ge·sta·po \gə'stäpō\ *n, pl* **-pos** : secret police

ges·ta·tion \je'stāshən\ *n* : pregnancy or incubation — **ges·tate** \'jes,tāt\ *vb*

ges·ture \'jeschər\ *n* 1 : movement of the body or limbs that expresses something 2 : something said or done for its effect on the attitudes of others — **ges·tur·al** \-chərəl\ *adj* — **gesture** *vb*

ge·sund·heit \gə'zunt,hīt\ *interj* — used to wish good health to one who has just sneezed

get \'get\ *vb* **got** \'gät\; **got** *or* **gotten** \'gät°n\; **get·ting** 1 : gain or be in possession of 2 : succeed in coming or going 3 : cause to come or go or to be in a certain condition or position 4 : become 5 : be subjected to 6 : understand 7 : be obliged — **get along** *vb* 1 : get by 2 : be on friendly terms — **get by** *vb* : meet one's needs

get·away \'getə,wā\ *n* 1 : escape 2 : a starting or getting under way

gey·ser \'gīzər\ *n* : spring that intermittently shoots up hot water and steam

ghast·ly \'gastlē\ *adj* **-li·er; -est** : horrible or shocking

gher·kin \'gərkən\ *n* : small pickle

ghet·to \'getō\ *n, pl* **-tos** *or* **-toes** : part of a city in which members of a minority group live

ghost \'gōst\ *n* : disembodied soul — **ghost·ly** *adv*

ghost·write *vb* **-wrote; -writ·ten** : write for and in the name of another — **ghost·writ·er** *n*

ghoul \'gül\ *n* : legendary evil being that feeds on corpses — **ghoul·ish** *adj*

GI \jē'ī\ *n, pl* **GI's** *or* **GIs** : member of the U.S. armed forces

gi·ant \'jīənt\ *n* 1 : huge legendary being 2 : something very large or very powerful — **giant** *adj*

gib·ber \'jibər\ *vb* **-bered; -ber·ing** : speak rapidly and foolishly

♦ **gib·ber·ish** \'jibərish\ *n* : unintelligible speech or language

gib·bon \'gibən\ *n* : manlike ape

gibe \'jīb\ *vb* **gibed; gib·ing** : jeer at — **gibe** *n*

gib·lets \'jibləts\ *n pl* : edible fowl viscera

gid·dy \'gidē\ *adj* **-di·er; -est** 1 : silly 2 : dizzy — **gid·di·ness** *n*

gift \'gift\ *n* 1 : something given 2 : talent — **gift·ed** *adj*

gi·gan·tic \jī'gantik\ *adj* : very big

gig·gle \'gigəl\ *vb* **-gled; -gling** : laugh in a silly manner — **giggle** *n* — **gig·gly** \-əlē\ *adj*

gig·o·lo \'jigə,lō\ *n, pl* **-los** : man living on the earnings of a woman

Gi·la monster \'hēlə-\ *n* : large venomous lizard

gild \'gild\ *vb* **gild·ed** \'gildəd\ *or* **gilt** \'gilt\; **gild·ing** : cover with or as if with gold

gill \'gil\ *n* : organ of a fish for obtaining oxygen from water

gilt \'gilt\ *adj* : gold-colored ~ *n* : gold or goldlike substance on the surface of an object

gim·bal \'gimbəl, 'jim-\ *n* : device that allows something to incline freely

gim·let \'gimlət\ *n* : small tool for boring holes

gim·mick \'gimik\ *n* : new and ingenious scheme, feature, or device — **gim·mick·ry** *n* — **gim·micky** \-ikē\ *adj*

gimpy \'gimpē\ *adj* : lame

¹**gin** \'jin\ *n* : machine to separate seeds from cotton — **gin** *vb*

²**gin** *n* : clear liquor flavored with juniper berries

gin·ger \'jinjər\ *n* : pungent aromatic spice from a tropical plant — **gin·ger·bread** *n*

gin·ger·ly *adj* : very cautious or careful — **gingerly** *adv*

ging·ham \'giŋəm\ *n* : cotton clothing fabric

gin·gi·vi·tis \,jinjə'vītəs\ *n* : inflammation of the gums

gink·go \'giŋkō\ *n, pl* **-goes** *or* **-gos** : tree of eastern China

gin·seng \'jin,siŋ, -,seŋ, -saŋ\ *n* : aromatic root of a Chinese herb

gi·raffe \jə'raf\ *n* : African mammal with a very long neck

gird \'gərd\ *vb* **gird·ed** \'gərdəd\ *or* **girt** \'gərt\; **gird·ing** 1 : encircle or fasten with or as if with a belt 2 : prepare

gird·er \'gərdər\ *n* : horizontal supporting beam

gir·dle \'gərdºl\ *n* : woman's supporting undergarment ~ *vb* : surround

girl \'gərl\ *n* 1 : female child 2 : young woman 3 : sweetheart — **girl·hood** \-,hùd\ *n* — **girl·ish** *adj*

girl·friend *n* : frequent or regular female companion of a boy or man

girth \'gərth\ *n* : measure around something

gist \'jist\ *n* : main point or part

give \'giv\ *vb* **gave** \'gāv\; **giv·en** \'givən\; **giv·ing** 1 : put into the possession or keeping of another 2 : pay 3 : perform 4 : contribute or donate 5 : produce 6 : utter 7 : yield to force, strain, or pressure ~ *n* : capacity or tendency to yield to force or strain — **give in** *vb* : surrender — **give out** *vb* : become used up or exhausted — **give up** *vb* 1 : let out of one's control 2 : cease from trying, doing, or hoping

give·away *n* 1 : unintentional betrayal 2 : something given free

giv·en \'givən\ *adj* 1 : prone or disposed 2 : having been specified

giz·zard \'gizərd\ *n* : muscular usu. horny-lined enlargement following the crop of a bird

gla·cial \'glāshəl\ *adj* 1 : relating to glaciers 2 : very slow — **gla·cial·ly** *adv*

gla·cier \'glāshər\ *n* : large body of ice moving slowly

glad \'glad\ *adj* **-dd-** 1 : experiencing or causing pleasure, joy, or delight 2 : very willing — **glad·den** \-ºn\ *vb* — **glad·ly** *adv* — **glad·ness** *n*

glade \'glād\ *n* : grassy open space in a forest

glad·i·a·tor \'gladē,ātər\ *n* : one who fought to the death for the entertainment of ancient Romans — **glad·i·a·to·ri·al** \,gladēə'tōr-ēəl\ *adj*

glad·i·o·lus \,gladē'ōləs\ *n, pl* **-li** \-lē, -,lī\ : plant related to the irises

glam·our, glam·or \'glamər\ *n* : romantic or exciting attractiveness — **glam·or·ize** \-ə,rīz\ *vb* — **glam·or·ous** \-ərəs\ *adj*

glance \'glans\ *vb* **glanced; glanc·ing** 1 : strike and fly off to one side

2 : give a quick look ∼ *n* : quick look

gland \'gland\ *n* : group of cells that secretes a substance — **glan·du·lar** \'glanjələr\ *adj*

glans \'glanz\ *n, pl* **glan·des** \'glan-ˌdēz\ : conical vascular body forming the end of the penis or clitoris

◆ **glare** \'glar\ *vb* **glared; glar·ing 1** : shine with a harsh dazzling light **2** : stare angrily ∼ *n* **1** : harsh dazzling light **2** : angry stare

glar·ing \'glariŋ\ *adj* : painfully obvious — **glar·ing·ly** *adv*

glass \'glas\ *n* **1** : hard usu. transparent material made by melting sand and other materials **2** : something made of glass **3** *pl* : lenses used to correct defects of vision — **glass** *adj* — **glass·ful** \-ˌfúl\ *n* — **glass·ware** \-ˌwar\ *n* — **glassy** *adj*

glass·blow·ing *n* : art of shaping a mass of molten glass by blowing air into it — **glass·blow·er** *n*

glau·co·ma \glaù'kōmə, glò-\ *n* : state of increased pressure within the eyeball

glaze \'glāz\ *vb* **glazed; glaz·ing 1** : furnish with glass **2** : apply glaze to ∼ *n* : glassy surface or coating

gla·zier \'glāzhər\ *n* : one who sets glass in window frames

gleam \'glēm\ *n* **1** : transient or partly obscured light **2** : faint trace ∼ *vb* : send out gleams

glean \'glēn\ *vb* : collect little by little — **glean·able** *adj* — **glean·er** *n*

glee \'glē\ *n* : joy — **glee·ful** *adj*

glen \'glen\ *n* : narrow hidden valley

glib \'glib\ *adj* **-bb-** : speaking or spoken with ease — **glib·ly** *adv*

glide \'glīd\ *vb* **glid·ed; glid·ing** : move or descend smoothly and effortlessly — **glide** *n*

glid·er \'glīdər\ *n* **1** : winged aircraft

having no engine **2** : swinging porch seat

glim·mer \'glimər\ *vb* : shine faintly or unsteadily ∼ *n* **1** : faint light **2** : small amount

glimpse \'glimps\ *vb* **glimpsed; glimps·ing** : take a brief look at — **glimpse** *n*

glint \'glint\ *vb* : gleam or sparkle — **glint** *n*

glis·ten \'glis°n\ *vb* : shine or sparkle by reflection — **glisten** *n*

glit·ter \'glitər\ *vb* : shine with brilliant or metallic luster ∼ *n* : small glittering ornaments — **glit·tery** *adj*

gloat \'glōt\ *vb* : think of something with triumphant delight

glob \'gläb\ *n* : large rounded lump

glob·al \'glōbəl\ *adj* : worldwide — **glob·al·ly** *adv*

globe \'glōb\ *n* **1** : sphere **2** : the earth or a model of it

glob·u·lar \'gläbyələr\ *adj* **1** : round **2** : made up of globules

glob·ule \'gläbyül\ *n* : tiny ball

glock·en·spiel \'gläkənˌshpēl\ *n* : portable musical instrument consisting of tuned metal bars

gloom \'glüm\ *n* **1** : darkness **2** : sadness — **gloom·i·ly** *adv* — **gloom·i·ness** *n* — **gloomy** *adj*

glop \'gläp\ *n* : messy mass or mixture

glo·ri·fy \'glōrəˌfī\ *vb* **-fied; -fy·ing 1** : make to seem glorious **2** : worship — **glo·ri·fi·ca·tion** \ˌglōrəfə'kāshən\ *n*

glo·ry \'glōrē\ *n, pl* **-ries 1** : praise or honor offered in worship **2** : cause for praise or renown **3** : magnificence **4** : heavenly bliss ∼ *vb* **-ried; -ry·ing** : rejoice proudly — **glo·ri·ous** \'glōrēəs\ *adj* — **glo·ri·ous·ly** *adv*

¹gloss \'gläs, 'glòs\ *n* : luster — **gloss·i·ly** \-əlē\ *adv* — **gloss·i·ness**

\-ēnəs\ *n* — **glossy** \-ē-\ *adj* —
gloss over *vb* **1** : mask the true nature of **2** : deal with only superficially

²**gloss** *n* : brief explanation or translation ~ *vb* : translate or explain

glos·sa·ry \'gläsərē, 'glòs-\ *n, pl* **-ries** : dictionary — **glos·sar·i·al** \glä-'sareəl, glò-\ *adj*

glove \'gləv\ *n* : hand covering with sections for each finger

glow \'glō\ *vb* **1** : shine with or as if with intense heat **2** : show exuberance ~ *n* : brightness or warmth of color or feeling

glow·er \'glau̇ər\ *vb* : stare angrily — **glower** *n*

glow·worm *n* : insect or insect larva that emits light

glu·cose \'glü,kōs\ *n* : sugar found esp. in blood, plant sap, and fruits

♦ **glue** \'glü\ *n* : substance used for sticking things together — **glue** *vb* — **glu·ey** \'glüē\ *adj*

glum \'gləm\ *adj* **-mm- 1** : sullen **2** : dismal

glut \'glət\ *vb* **-tt- :** fill to excess — **glut** *n*

glu·ten \'glüt°n\ *n* : gluey protein substance in flour

glu·ti·nous \'glüt°nəs\ *adj* : sticky

glut·ton \'glət°n\ *n* : one who eats to excess — **glut·ton·ous** \'glət°nəs\ *adj* — **glut·tony** \'glət°nē\ *n*

gnarled \'närld\ *adj* **1** : knotty **2** : gloomy or sullen

gnash \'nash\ *vb* : grind (as teeth) together

gnat \'nat\ *n* : small biting fly

gnaw \'nò\ *vb* : bite or chew on — **gnaw·er** *n*

gnome \'nōm\ *n* : dwarf of folklore — **gnom·ish** *adj*

gnu \'nü, 'nyü\ *n, pl* **gnu** *or* **gnus** : large African antelope

go \'gō\ *vb* **went** \'went\; **gone** \'gòn, 'gän\; **go·ing** \'gȯiŋ\; **goes** \'gōz\ **1**
: move, proceed, run, or pass **2** : leave **3** : extend or lead **4** : sell or amount — with *for* **5** : happen **6** — used in present participle to show intent or imminent action **7** : become **8** : fit or harmonize **9** : belong ~ *n pl* **goes 1** : act or manner of going **2** : vigor **3** : attempt — **go back on** : betray — **go by the board** : be discarded — **go for** : favor — **go off** : explode — **go one better** : outdo — **go over 1** : examine **2** : study — **go to town** : be very successful — **on the go** : constantly active

goad \'gōd\ *n* : something that urges — **goad** *vb*

goal \'gōl\ *n* **1** : mark to reach in a race **2** : purpose **3** : object in a game through which a ball is propelled

goal·ie \'gōlē\ *n* : player who defends the goal

goal·keep·er *n* : goalie

goat \'gōt\ *n* : horned ruminant mammal related to the sheep — **goat·skin** *n*

goa·tee \gō'tē\ *n* : small pointed beard

gob \'gäb\ *n* : lump

¹**gob·ble** \'gäbəl\ *vb* **-bled; -bling** : eat greedily

²**gobble** *vb* **-bled; -bling** : make the noise of a turkey (**gobbler**)

gob·ble·dy·gook \'gäbəldē,gu̇k, -'gu̇k\ *n* : nonsense

gob·let \'gäblət\ *n* : large stemmed drinking glass

gob·lin \'gäblən\ *n* : ugly mischievous sprite

god \'gäd, 'gòd\ *n* **1** *cap* : supreme being **2** : being with supernatural powers — **god·like** *adj* — **god·ly** *adj*

god·child *n* : person one sponsors at baptism — **god·daugh·ter** *n* — **god·son** *n*

god·dess \'gädəs, 'gód-\ n : female god

god·less \-ləs\ adj : not believing in God — god·less·ness n

god·par·ent n : sponsor at baptism — god·fa·ther n — god·moth·er n

god·send \-,send\ n : something needed that comes unexpectedly

goes pres 3d sing of GO

go–get·ter \'gō,getər\ n : enterprising person — go–get·ting \-iŋ\ adj or n

gog·gle \'gägəl\ vb -gled; -gling : stare wide-eyed

gog·gles \-əlz\ n pl : protective glasses

go·ings–on \,gōiŋz'ón, -'än\ n pl : events

goi·ter \'góitər\ n : abnormally enlarged thyroid gland

gold \'gōld\ n : malleable yellow metallic chemical element — gold·smith \-,smith\ n

gold·brick \-,brik\ n : person who shirks duty — goldbrick vb

gold·en \'gōldən\ adj 1 : made of, containing, or relating to gold 2 : having the color of gold 3 : precious or favorable

gold·en·rod \'gōldən,räd\ n : herb having tall stalks with tiny yellow flowers

gold·finch \'gōld,finch\ n : yellow American finch

gold·fish \-,fish\ n : small usu. orange or golden carp

golf \'gälf, 'gólf\ n : game played by hitting a small ball (golf ball) with clubs (golf clubs) into holes placed in a field (golf course) — golf vb — golf·er n

go·nad \'gō,nad\ n : sex gland

gon·do·la \'gändələ (usual for 1), gän'dō-\ n 1 : long narrow boat used on the canals of Venice 2 : car suspended from a cable

gon·do·lier \,gändə'lir\ n : person who propels a gondola

gone \'gòn\ adj 1 : past 2 : involved

gon·er \'gònər\ n : hopeless case

gong \'gäŋ, 'gòŋ\ n : metallic disk that makes a deep sound when struck

gon·or·rhea \,gänə'rēə\ n : bacterial inflammatory venereal disease of the genital tract — gon·or·rhe·al \-'rēəl\ adj

goo \'gü\ n : thick or sticky substance — goo·ey \-ē\ adj

good \'gùd\ adj bet·ter \'betər\; best \'best\ 1 : satisfactory 2 : salutary 3 : considerable 4 : desirable 5 : well-behaved, kind, or virtuous ∼ n 1 : something good 2 : benefit 3 pl : personal property 4 pl : wares ∼ adv : well — good–heart·ed \-'härtəd\ adj — good–look·ing adj — good–na·tured adj — good·ness n — good–tem·pered \-'tempərd\ adj — for good : forever

good–bye, good–by \gùd'bī\ n : parting remark

good–for–noth·ing n : idle worthless person

Good Friday n : Friday before Easter observed as the anniversary of the crucifixion of Christ

good·ly adj -li·er; -est : considerable

good·will n 1 : good intention 2 : kindly feeling

goody \'gùdē\ n, pl good·ies : something that is good esp. to eat

goody–goody adj : affectedly or annoyingly sweet or self-righteous — goody–goody n

♦ goof \'güf\ vb 1 : blunder 2 : waste time — usu. with off or around — goof n — goof–off n

goofy \'güfē\ adj goof·i·er; -est : crazy — goof·i·ness n

goose \'güs\ n, pl geese \'gēs\ : large bird with webbed feet

goose·ber·ry \'güs₁berē, 'güz-\ *n* : berry of a shrub related to the currant

goose bumps *n pl* : roughening of the skin caused by fear, excitement, or cold

goose·flesh *n* : goose bumps

goose pimples *n pl* : goose bumps

go·pher \'gōfər\ *n* : burrowing rodent

¹**gore** \'gōr\ *n* : blood

²**gore** *vb* **gored; gor·ing** : pierce or wound with a horn or tusk

¹**gorge** \'górj\ *n* : narrow ravine

²**gorge** *vb* **gorged; gorg·ing** : eat greedily

gor·geous \'górjəs\ *adj* : supremely beautiful

go·ril·la \gə'rilə\ *n* : African manlike ape

gory \'gōrē\ *adj* **gor·i·er; -est** : bloody

gos·hawk \'gäs₁hók\ *n* : long-tailed hawk with short rounded wings

gos·ling \'gäzliŋ, 'góz-\ *n* : young goose

gos·pel \'gäspəl\ *n* **1** : teachings of Christ and the apostles **2** : something accepted as infallible truth — **gospel** *adj*

gos·sa·mer \'gäsəmər, gäz-\ *n* **1** : film of cobweb **2** : light filmy substance

gos·sip \'gäsəp\ *n* **1** : person who reveals personal information **2** : rumor or report of an intimate nature ∼ *vb* : spread gossip — **gos·sipy** \-ē\ *adj*

got *past of* GET

Goth·ic \'gäthik\ *adj* : relating to a medieval style of architecture

gotten *past part of* GET

gouge \'gaúj\ *n* **1** : rounded chisel **2** : cavity or groove scooped out ∼ *vb* **gouged; goug·ing 1** : cut or scratch a groove in **2** : overcharge

gou·lash \'gü₁läsh, -₁lash\ *n* : beef stew with vegetables and paprika

gourd \'gōrd, 'gùrd\ *n* **1** : any of a group of vines including the cucumber, squash, and melon **2** : inedible hard-shelled fruit of a gourd

gour·mand \'gùr₁mänd\ *n* : person who loves good food and drink

gour·met \'gùr₁mā, gùr'mā\ *n* : connoisseur of food and drink

gout \'gaút\ *n* : disease marked by painful inflammation and swelling of the joints — **gouty** *adj*

gov·ern \'gəvərn\ *vb* **1** : control and direct policy in **2** : guide or influence strongly **3** : restrain — **gov·ern·ment** \-ərmənt\ *n* — **gov·ern·men·tal** \₁gəvər'ment°l\ *adj*

gov·ern·ess \'gəvərnəs\ *n* : female teacher in a private home

gov·er·nor \'gəvənər, 'gəvər-\ *n* **1** : head of a political unit **2** : automatic speed-control device — **gov·er·nor·ship** *n*

gown \'gaún\ *n* **1** : loose flowing outer garment **2** : woman's formal evening dress — **gown** *vb*

grab \'grab\ *vb* **-bb-** : take by sudden grasp — **grab** *n*

grace \'grās\ *n* **1** : unmerited divine assistance **2** : short prayer before or after a meal **3** : respite **4** : ease of movement or bearing ∼ *vb* **graced; grac·ing 1** : honor **2** : adorn — **graceful** \-fəl\ *adj* — **grace·ful·ly** *adv* — **grace·ful·ness** *n* — **grace·less** *adj*

gra·cious \'grāshəs\ *adj* : marked by kindness and courtesy or charm and taste — **gra·cious·ly** *adv* — **gra·cious·ness** *n*

grack·le \'grakəl\ *n* : American blackbird

gra·da·tion \grā'dāshən, grə-\ *n* : step, degree, or stage in a series

grade \'grād\ *n* **1** : stage in a series, order, or ranking **2** : division of school representing one year's work **3** : mark of accomplishment in school **4** : degree of slope ∼ *vb* **grad·ed; grad·ing 1** : arrange in grades **2** : make level or evenly sloping **3** : give a grade to — **grad·er** *n*

grade school *n* : school including the first 4 or 8 grades

gra·di·ent \'grādēənt\ *n* : slope

grad·u·al \'grajəwəl\ *adj* : going by steps or degrees — **grad·u·al·ly** *adv*

grad·u·ate \'grajəwət\ *n* : holder of a diploma ∼ *adj* : of or relating to studies beyond the bachelor's degree ∼ \-ə₁wāt\ *vb* **-at·ed; -at·ing 1** : grant or receive a diploma **2** : mark with degrees of measurement — **grad·u·a·tion** \₁grajə'wāshən\ *n*

graf·fi·to \gra'fētō, grə-\ *n, pl* **-ti** \-ē\ : inscription on a wall

graft \'graft\ *vb* : join one thing to another so that they grow together — *n* 1 : grafted plant 2 : the getting of money dishonestly or the money so gained — **graft·er** *n*

grain \'grān\ *n* 1 : seeds or fruits of cereal grasses 2 : small hard particle 3 : arrangement of fibers in wood — **grained** \'grānd\ *adj* — **grainy** *adj*

gram \'gram\ *n* : metric unit of weight equal to 1/1000 kilogram

gram·mar \'gramər\ *n* : study of words and their functions and relations in the sentence — **gram·mar·i·an** \grə'mareən\ *n* — **gram·mat·i·cal** \-'matikəl\ *adj* — **gram·mat·i·cal·ly** *adv*

grammar school *n* : grade school

gra·na·ry \'grānərē, 'gran-\ *n, pl* **-ries** : storehouse for grain

♦ **grand** \'grand\ *adj* 1 : large or striking in size or scope 2 : fine and imposing 3 : very good — **grand·ly** *adv* — **grand·ness** *n*

grand·child \-,chīld\ *n* : child of one's son or daughter — **grand·daugh·ter** *n* — **grand·son** *n*

gran·deur \'granjər\ *n* : quality or state of being grand

gran·dil·o·quence \gran'diləkwəns\ *n* : pompous speaking — **gran·dil·o·quent** \-kwənt\ *adj*

gran·di·ose \'grandē,ōs, ,grandē'-\ *adj* 1 : impressive 2 : affectedly splendid — **gran·di·ose·ly** *adv*

grand·par·ent \'grand,parənt\ *n* : parent of one's father or mother — **grand·fa·ther** \-,fäthər, -,fäth-\ *n* — **grand·moth·er** \-,məthər\ *n*

grand·stand \-,stand\ *n* : usu. roofed stand for spectators

grange \'grānj\ *n* : farmers association

gran·ite \'granət\ *n* : hard igneous rock

grant \'grant\ *vb* 1 : consent to 2 : give 3 : admit as true ~ *n* 1 : act of granting 2 : something granted — **grant·ee** \grant'ē\ *n* — **grant·er** \'grantər\ *n* — **grant·or** \-ər, -,ȯr\ *n*

gran·u·late \'granyə,lāt\ *vb* **-lat·ed; -lat·ing** : form into grains or crystals — **gran·u·la·tion** \,granyə'lāshən\ *n*

gran·ule \'granyül\ *n* : small particle — **gran·u·lar** \-yələr\ *adj* — **gran·u·lar·i·ty** \,granyə'larətē\ *n*

grape \'grāp\ *n* : smooth juicy edible berry of a woody vine (**grape·vine**)

grape·fruit *n* : large edible yellow-skinned citrus fruit

graph \'graf\ *n* : diagram that shows relationships between things — **graph** *vb*

graph·ic \'grafik\ *adj* 1 : vividly described 2 : relating to the arts (**graphic arts**) of representation and printing on flat surfaces ~ *n* 1 : picture used for illustration 2 *pl* : computer screen display — **graph·i·cal·ly** \-iklē\ *adv*

graph·ite \'graf,īt\ *n* : soft carbon used for lead pencils and lubricants

grap·nel \'grapnəl\ *n* : small anchor with several claws

grap·ple \'grapəl\ *vb* **-pled; -pling** 1 : seize or hold with or as if with a hooked implement 2 : wrestle

grasp \'grasp\ *vb* 1 : take or seize firmly 2 : understand ~ *n* 1 : one's hold or control 2 : one's reach 3 : comprehension

grass \'gras\ *n* : plant with jointed stem and narrow leaves — **grassy** *adj*

grass·hop·per \-,häpər\ *n* : leaping plant-eating insect

grass·land *n* : land covered with grasses

¹**grate** \'grāt\ *n* 1 : grating 2 : frame of iron bars to hold burning fuel

²**grate** *vb* **grat·ed; -ing** 1 : pulverize by rubbing against something rough 2 : irritate — **grat·er** *n* — **grat·ing·ly** *adv*

grate·ful \'grātfəl\ *adj* : thankful or appreciative — **grate·ful·ly** *adv* — **grate·ful·ness** *n*

grat·i·fy \'gratə,fī\ *vb* **-fied; -fy·ing** : give pleasure to — **grat·i·fi·ca·tion** \,gratəfə'kāshən\ *n*

grat·ing \'grātiŋ\ *n* : framework with bars across it

gra·tis \'gratəs, 'grāt-\ *adv or adj* : free

grat·i·tude \'gratə,tüd, -,tyüd\ *n* : state of being grateful

gra·tu·itous \grə'tüətəs, -'tyü-\ *adj* 1 : free 2 : uncalled-for

gra·tu·ity \-ətē\ *n, pl* **-ities** : tip

¹**grave** \'grāv\ *n* : place of burial — **grave·stone** *n* — **grave·yard** *n*

²**grave** *adj* **grav·er; grav·est** 1 : threatening great harm or danger 2 : solemn — **grave·ly** *adv* — **grave·ness** *n*

grav·el \'gravəl\ *n* : loose rounded fragments of rock — **grav·el·ly** *adj*

grav·i·tate \'gravə,tāt\ *vb* **-tat·ed; -tat·ing** : move toward something

grav·i·ta·tion \,gravə'tāshən\ *n* : natural force of attraction that tends to draw bodies together — **grav·i·ta·tion·al** \-shənəl\ *adj* — **grav·i·ta·tion·al·ly** *adv*

grav·i·ty \'gravətē\ *n, pl* **-ties** 1 : serious importance 2 : gravitation

gra·vy \'grāvē\ *n, pl* **-vies** : sauce made from thickened juices of cooked meat

gray \'grā\ *adj* 1 : of the color gray 2 : having gray hair ∼ *n* : neutral color between black and white ∼ *vb* : make or become gray — **gray·ish** \-ish\ *adj* — **gray·ness** *n*

¹**graze** \'grāz\ *vb* **grazed; graz·ing** : feed on herbage or pasture — **graz·er** *n*

²**graze** *vb* **grazed; graz·ing** : touch lightly in passing

grease \'grēs\ *n* : thick oily material or fat ∼ \'grēs, 'grēz\ *vb* **greased; greas·ing** : smear or lubricate with grease — **greasy** \'grēsē, -zē\ *adj*

great \'grāt\ *adj* 1 : large in size or number 2 : larger than usual — **great·ly** *adv* — **great·ness** *n*

grebe \'grēb\ *n* : diving bird related to the loon

greed \'grēd\ *n* : selfish desire beyond reason — **greed·i·ly** \-'lē\ *adv* — **greed·i·ness** \-ēnəs\ *n* — **greedy** \'grēdē\ *adj*

green \'grēn\ *adj* 1 : of the color green 2 : unripe 3 : inexperienced ∼ *vb* : become green ∼ *n* 1 : color between blue and yellow 2 *pl* : leafy parts of plants — **green·ish** *adj* — **green·ness** *n*

green·ery \'grēnərē\ *n, pl* **-er·ies** : green foliage or plants

green·horn *n* : inexperienced person

green·house *n* : glass structure for the growing of plants

greet \'grēt\ *vb* 1 : address with expressions of kind wishes 2 : react to — **greet·er** *n*

greet·ing *n* 1 : friendly address on meeting 2 *pl* : best wishes

gre·gar·i·ous \gri'garēəs\ *adj* : social or companionable — **gre·gar·i·ous·ly** *adv* — **gre·gar·i·ous·ness** *n*

grem·lin \'gremlən\ *n* : small mischievous gnome

gre·nade \grə'nād\ *n* : small missile filled with explosive or chemicals

grew *past of* GROW

grey *var of* GRAY

grey·hound \'grā,haùnd\ *n* : tall slender dog noted for speed

grid \'grid\ *n* 1 : grating 2 : evenly spaced horizontal and vertical lines (as on a map)

grid·dle \'grid²l\ *n* : flat metal surface for cooking

grid·iron \'grid,īərn\ *n* 1 : grate for broiling 2 : football field

grief \'grēf\ *n* 1 : emotional suffering caused by or as if by bereavement 2 : disaster

griev·ance \'grēvəns\ *n* : complaint

grieve \'grēv\ *vb* **grieved; griev·ing** : feel or cause to feel grief or sorrow

griev·ous \'grēvəs\ *adj* 1 : oppressive 2 : causing grief or sorrow — **griev·ous·ly** *adv*

grill \'gril\ *vb* 1 : cook on a grill 2 : question intensely ∼ *n* 1 : griddle 2 : informal restaurant

grille, grill \'gril\ *n* : grating forming a barrier or screen — **grill·work** *n* grim \'grim\ adj -mm- 1 : harsh and forbidding in appearance 2 : relentless — grim·ly adv — grim·ness n

gri·mace \'griməs, grim'ās\ n : facial expression of disgust — grimace vb

grime \'grīm\ n : embedded or accumulated dirt — grimy adj

grin \'grin\ vb -nn- : smile so as to show the teeth — grin n

grind \'grīnd\ vb ground \'graùnd\; grind·ing 1 : reduce to powder 2 : wear down or sharpen by friction 3 : operate or produce by turning a crank ∼ n : monotonous labor or routine — grind·er n — grind·stone \'grīn,stōn\ n

grip \'grip\ vb -pp- : seize or hold firmly ∼ n 1 : grasp 2 : control 3 : device for holding

gripe \'grīp\ vb griped; grip·ing 1 : cause pains in the bowels 2 : complain — gripe n

grippe \'grip\ n : influenza

gris·ly \'grizlē\ adj -li·er; -est : horrible or gruesome

grist \'grist\ n : grain to be ground or already ground — grist·mill n

gris·tle \'grisəl\ n : cartilage — gristly \-lē\ adj

grit \'grit\ n 1 : hard sharp granule 2 : material composed of granules 3 : unyielding courage ∼ vb -tt- : press with a grating noise — grit·ty adj

grits \'grits\ n pl : coarsely ground hulled grain

griz·zled \'grizəld\ adj : streaked with gray

groan \'grōn\ vb 1 : moan 2 : creak under a strain — groan n

gro·cer \'grōsər\ n : food dealer — gro·cery \'grōsrē, 'grōsh-, -ərē\ n

grog \'gräg\ n : rum diluted with water

grog·gy \-ē\ adj -gi·er; -est : dazed and unsteady on the feet — grog·gi·ly adv — grog·gi·ness n

groin \'gròin\ n : juncture of the lower abdomen and inner thigh

grom·met \'grämət, 'grəm-\ n : eyelet

groom \'grüm, 'grùm\ n 1 : one who cares for horses 2 : bridegroom ∼ vb 1 : clean and care for (as a horse) 2 : make neat or attractive 3 : prepare

groove \'grüv\ n 1 : long narrow channel 2 : fixed routine — groove vb

grope \'grōp\ vb groped; grop·ing : search for by feeling

gros·beak \'grōs,bēk\ n : finch with large conical bill

¹gross \'grōs\ adj 1 : glaringly noticeable 2 : bulky 3 : consisting of an overall total exclusive of deductions 4 : vulgar ∼ n : the whole before any deductions ∼ vb : earn as a total — gross·ly adv — gross·ness n

²gross n, pl gross : 12 dozen

gro·tesque \grō'tesk\ adj 1 : absurdly distorted or repulsive 2 : ridiculous — gro·tesque·ly adv

grot·to \'grätō\ n, pl -toes : cave

grouch \'graùch\ n : complaining person — grouch vb — grouchy adj

¹ground \'graùnd\ n 1 : bottom of a body of water 2 pl : sediment 3 : basis for something 4 : surface of the earth 5 : conductor that makes electrical connection with the earth or a framework ∼ vb 1 : force or bring down to the ground 2 : give basic knowledge to 3 : connect with an electrical ground — ground·less adj

²ground past of GRIND

ground·hog n : woodchuck

ground·wa·ter n : underground water

ground·work n : foundation

group \'grüp\ n : number of associated individuals ∼ vb : gather or collect into groups

grou·per \'grüpər\ n : large fish of warm seas

grouse \'graùs\ n, pl grouse or grouses : ground-dwelling game bird

grout \'graùt\ n : mortar for filling cracks — grout vb

grove \'grōv\ n : small group of trees

grov·el \'grävəl, 'grəv-\ vb -eled or -elled; -el·ing or -el·ling : abase oneself

grow \'grō\ vb grew \'grü\; grown \'grōn\; grow·ing 1 : come into existence and develop to maturity 2 : be able to grow 3 : advance or increase 4 : become 5 : cultivate — grow·er n

growl \'graùl\ vb : utter a deep threatening sound — growl n

grown-up \'grōn₁əp\ n : adult — **grown-up** adj

growth \'grōth\ n 1 : stage in growing 2 : process of growing 3 : result of something growing

grub \'grəb\ vb **-bb- 1** : root out by digging 2 : search about ~ n 1 : thick wormlike larva 2 : food

grub-by \'grəbē\ adj **-bi-er; -est** : dirty — **grub-bi-ness** n

grub-stake n : supplies for a prospector

grudge \'grəj\ vb **grudged; grudging** : be reluctant to give ~ n : feeling of ill will

gru-el \'grüəl\ n : thin porridge

gru-el-ing, gru-el-ling \-əliŋ\ adj : requiring extreme effort

grue-some \'grüsəm\ adj : horribly repulsive

gruff \'grəf\ adj : rough in speech or manner — **gruff-ly** adv

grum-ble \'grəmbəl\ vb **-bled; -bling** : mutter in discontent — **grumbler** \-blər\ n

grumpy \-pē\ adj **grump-i-er; -est** : cross — **grump-i-ly** adv — **grump-i-ness** n

grun-ion \'grənyən\ n : fish of the California coast

grunt \'grənt\ n : deep guttural sound — **grunt** vb

gua-no \'gwänō\ n : excrement of seabirds used as fertilizer

guar-an-tee \₁garən'tē\ n 1 : assurance of the fulfillment of a condition 2 : something given or held as a security ~ vb **-teed; -tee-ing 1** : promise to be responsible for 2 : state with certainty — **guar-an-tor** \₁garən'tor\ n

guar-an-ty \'garəntē\ n, pl **-ties 1** : promise to answer for another's failure to pay a debt 2 : guarantee 3 : pledge ~ vb **-tied; -ty-ing** : guarantee

guard \'gärd\ n 1 : defensive position 2 : act of protecting 3 : an individual or group that guards against danger 4 : protective or safety device ~ vb 1 : protect or watch over 2 : take precautions — **guard-house** n — **guard-room** n

guard-ian \'gärdēən\ n : one who has responsibility for the care of the person or property of another — **guard-ian-ship** n

gua-va \'gwävə\ n : shrubby tropical tree or its mildly acid fruit

gu-ber-na-to-ri-al \₁gübənə'tōrēəl, ₁gyü-\ adj : relating to a governor

guer-ril-la, gue-ril-la \gə'rilə\ n : soldier engaged in small-scale harassing tactics

guess \'ges\ vb 1 : form an opinion from little evidence 2 : state correctly solely by chance 3 : think or believe — **guess** n

guest \'gest\ n 1 : person to whom hospitality (as of a house) is extended 2 : patron of a commercial establishment (as a hotel) 3 : person not a regular cast member who appears on a program

guf-faw \gə'fó, 'gəf₁ó\ n : loud burst of laughter — **guf-faw** \gə'fó\ vb

guide \'gīd\ n 1 : one that leads or gives direction to another 2 : device on a machine to direct motion ~ vb **guid-ed; guid-ing 1** : show the way to 2 : direct — **guid-able** adj — **guid-ance** \'gīdⁿns\ n — **guide-book** n

guide-line \-₁līn\ n : summary of procedures regarding policy or conduct

guild \'gild\ n : association

guile \'gīl\ n : craftiness — **guile-ful** adj — **guile-less** adj — **guile-less-ness** n

guil-lo-tine \'gilə₁tēn; ₁gēyə'tēn, 'gēyə₁-\ n : machine for beheading persons — **guillotine** vb

♦ **guilt** \'gilt\ n 1 : fact of having

committed an offense **2** : feeling of responsibility for offenses — **guilt·i·ly** adv — **guilt·i·ness** n — **guilty** \'giltē\ adj

guin·ea \'ginē\ n **1** : old gold coin of United Kingdom **2** : 21 shillings

guinea pig n : small So. American rodent

guise \'gīz\ n : external appearance

gui·tar \gə'tär, gi-\ n : 6-stringed musical instrument played by plucking

gulch \'gəlch\ n : ravine

gulf \'gəlf\ n **1** : extension of an ocean or a sea into the land **2** : wide gap

¹**gull** \'gəl\ n : seabird with webbed feet

²**gull** vb : make a dupe of ~ n : dupe — **gull·ible** adj

gul·let \'gələt\ n : throat

gul·ly \'gəlē\ n, pl **-lies** : trench worn by running water

gulp \'gəlp\ vb : swallow hurriedly or greedily — **gulp** n

¹**gum** \'gəm\ n : tissue along the jaw at the base of the teeth

²**gum** n **1** : sticky plant substance **2** : gum usu. of sweetened chicle prepared for chewing — **gum·my** adj

gum·bo \'gəmbō\ n : thick soup

gum·drop n : gumlike candy

gump·tion \'gəmpshən\ n : initiative

gun \'gən\ n **1** : cannon **2** : portable firearm **3** : discharge of a gun **4** : something like a gun ~ vb **-nn-** : hunt with a gun — **gun·fight** n — **gun·fight·er** n — **gun·fire** n — **gunman** \-mən\ n — **gun·pow·der** n — **gun·shot** n — **gun·smith** n

gun·boat n : small armed ship

gun·ner \'gənər\ n : person who uses a gun

gun·nery sergeant \'gənərē-\ n : noncommissioned officer in the marine corps ranking next below a first sergeant

gun·ny·sack \'gənē,sak\ n : burlap sack

gun·sling·er \'gən,sliŋər\ n : skilled gunman in the old West

gun·wale \'gən³l\ n : upper edge of a boat's side

gup·py \'gəpē\ n, pl **-pies** : tiny tropical fish

gur·gle \'gərgəl\ vb **-gled; -gling** : make a sound like that of a flowing and gently splashing liquid — **gurgle** n

gu·ru \'gü,rü\ n, pl **-rus 1** : personal religious teacher in Hinduism **2** : expert

gush \'gəsh\ vb : pour forth violently or enthusiastically — **gush·er** \'gəshər\ n

gushy \-ē\ adj **gush·i·er; -est** : effusively sentimental

gust \'gəst\ n **1** : sudden brief rush of wind **2** : sudden outburst — **gust** vb — **gusty** adj

gus·ta·to·ry \'gəstə,tōrē\ adj : relating to the sense of taste

gus·to \'gəstō\ n : zest

gut \'gət\ n **1** pl : intestines **2** : digestive canal **3** pl : courage ~ vb **-tt-** : eviscerate

gut·ter \'gətər\ n : channel for carrying off rainwater

gut·tur·al \'gətərəl\ adj : sounded in the throat — **guttural** n

¹**guy** \'gī\ n : rope, chain, or rod attached to something to steady it — **guy** vb

²**guy** n : person

guz·zle \'gəzəl\ vb **-zled; -zling** : drink greedily

gym \'jim\ n : gymnasium

gym·na·si·um \jim'nāzēəm, -zhəm\ n, pl **-si·ums** or **-sia** \-zēə, -zhə\ : place for indoor sports

gym·nas·tics \jim'nastiks\ n : physical exercises performed in a gymnasium — **gym·nast** \'jim,nast\ n — **gym·nas·tic** adj

gy·ne·col·o·gy \,gīnə'käləjē, ,jin-\ n : branch of medicine dealing with the diseases of women — **gy·ne·co·log·ic** \-ikə'läjik\, **gy·ne·co·log·i·cal** \-ikəl\ adj — **gy·ne·col·o·gist** \-ə'käləjist\ n

gyp \'jip\ n **1** : cheat **2** : trickery — **gyp** vb

gyp·sum \'jipsəm\ n : calcium-containing mineral

gy·rate \'jī,rāt\ vb **-rat·ed; -rat·ing** : revolve around a center — **gy·ra·tion** \jī'rāshən\ n

gy·ro·scope \'jīro,skōp\ n : wheel mounted to spin rapidly about an axis that is free to turn in various directions

H

h \'āch\ *n, pl* **h's** *or* **hs** \'āchəz\ : 8th letter of the alphabet

hab·er·dash·er \'habər,dashər\ *n* : men's clothier — **hab·er·dash·ery** \-ərē\ *n*

hab·it \'habət\ *n* **1** : monk's or nun's clothing **2** : usual behavior **3** : addiction — **hab·it–form·ing** *adj*

hab·it·able \-əbəl\ *adj* : capable of being lived in

hab·i·tat \'habə,tat\ *n* : place where a plant or animal naturally occurs

hab·i·ta·tion \,habə'tāshən\ *n* **1** : occupancy **2** : dwelling place

ha·bit·u·al \hə'bichəwəl\ *adj* **1** : commonly practiced or observed **2** : doing, practicing, or acting by habit — **ha·bit·u·al·ly** *adv* — **ha·bit·u·al·ness** *n*

ha·bit·u·ate \hə'bichə,wāt\ *vb* **-at·ed; -at·ing** : accustom

ha·ci·en·da \,häsē'endə\ *n* : ranch house

¹hack \'hak\ *vb* **1** : cut with repeated irregular blows **2** : cough in a short dry manner **3** : manage successfully — **hack** *n* — **hack·er** *n*

²hack *n* **1** : horse or vehicle for hire **2** : saddle horse **3** : writer for hire — **hack** *adj* — **hack·man** \-mən\ *n*

hack·le \'hakəl\ *n* **1** : long feather on the neck or back of a bird **2** *pl* : hairs that can be erected **3** *pl* : temper

hack·ney \-nē\ *n, pl* **-neys 1** : horse for riding or driving **2** : carriage for hire

hack·neyed \-nēd\ *adj* : trite

hack·saw *n* : saw for metal

had *past of* HAVE

had·dock \'hadək\ *n, pl* **haddock** : Atlantic food fish

Ha·des \'hādēz\ *n* **1** : mythological abode of the dead **2** *often not cap* : hell

haft \'haft\ *n* : handle of a weapon or tool

hag \'hag\ *n* **1** : witch **2** : ugly old woman

hag·gard \'hagərd\ *adj* : worn or emaciated — **hag·gard·ly** *adv*

hag·gle \'hagəl\ *vb* **-gled; -gling** : argue in bargaining — **hag·gler** *n*

¹hail \'hāl\ *n* **1** : precipitation in small lumps of ice **2** : something like a rain of hail ~ *vb* : rain hail — **hail·stone** *n* — **hail·storm** *n*

²hail *vb* **1** : greet or salute **2** : summon ~ *n* : expression of greeting or praise — often used as an interjection

◆ **hair** \'har\ *n* : threadlike growth from the skin — **hair·brush** *n* — **hair·cut** *n* — **hair·dress·er** *n* — **haired** *adj* — **hair·i·ness** *n* — **hair·less** *adj* — **hair·pin** *n* — **hair·style** *n* — **hair·styl·ing** *n* — **hair·styl·ist** *n* — **hairy** *adj*

hair·breadth \-,bredth\; **hairs·breadth** \'harz-\ *n* : tiny distance or margin

hair·do \-,dü\ *n, pl* **-dos** : style of wearing hair

hair·line *n* **1** : thin line **2** : outline of the hair on the head

hair·piece *n* : toupee

hair–rais·ing *adj* : causing terror or astonishment

hake \'hāk\ *n* : marine food fish

hal·cy·on \'halsēən\ *adj* : prosperous or most pleasant

¹hale \'hāl\ *adj* : healthy or robust

²hale *vb* **haled; hal·ing 1** : haul **2** : compel to go

half \'haf, 'håf \ *n, pl* **halves** \'havz, 'håvz\ : either of 2 equal parts ~ *adj* **1** : being a half or nearly a half **2** : partial — **half** *adv*

half brother *n* : brother related through one parent only

half-heart-ed \-'härtəd\ *adj* : without enthusiasm — **half-heart-ed-ly** *adv* — **half-heart-ed-ness** *n*

half-life *n* : time for half of something to undergo a process

half sister *n* : sister related through one parent only

half-way *adj* : midway between 2 points — **half-way** *adv*

half-wit \-,wit*n* : foolish person — **half-wit-ted** \-,witəd\ *adj*

hal-i-but \'haləbət\ *n, pl* **halibut** : large edible marine flatfish

hal-i-to-sis \,halə'tōsəs\ *n* : bad breath

hall \'hól\ *n* **1** : large public or college or university building **2** : lobby **3** : auditorium

hal-le-lu-jah \,halə'lüyə\ *interj* : used to express praise, joy, or thanks

hall-mark \'hól,märk\ *n* : distinguishing characteristic

hal-low \'halō\ *vb* : consecrate — **hal-lowed** \-ōd, -əwəd\ *adj*

Hal-low-een \,halə'wēn, ,häl-\ *n* : evening of October 31 observed esp. by children in merrymaking and masquerading

hal-lu-ci-na-tion \hə,lüs°n'āshən\ *n* : perception of objects that are not real — **hal-lu-ci-nate** \ha'lüs°n,āt\ *vb* — **hal-lu-ci-na-to-ry** \-'lüs°nə-,tōrē\ *adj*

hal-lu-ci-no-gen \hə'lüs°nəjən\ *n* : substance that induces hallucinations — **hal-lu-ci-no-gen-ic** \-,lüs°nə'jenik\ *adj*

hall-way *n* : entrance hall

ha-lo \'hālō\ *n, pl* **-los** *or* **-loes** : circle of light appearing to surround a shining body

¹**halt** \'hólt\ *adj* : lame

²**halt** *vb* : stop or cause to stop — **halt** *n*

hal-ter \'hóltər\ *n* **1** : rope or strap for leading or tying an animal **2** : brief blouse held up by straps ~ *vb* : catch (an animal) with a halter

halt-ing \'hóltiŋ\ *adj* : uncertain — **halt-ing-ly** *adv*

halve \'hav, 'håv\ *vb* **halved; halv-**

ing 1 : divide into halves **2** : reduce to half

halves *pl of* HALF

ham \'ham\ *n* **1** : thigh — usu. pl. **2** : cut esp. of pork from the thigh **3** : showy actor **4** : amateur radio operator ~ *vb* **-mm-** : overplay a part — **ham** *adj*

ham-burg-er \'ham,bərgər\; **ham-burg** \-,bərg\ *n* : ground beef or a sandwich made with this

ham-let \'hamlət\ *n* : small village

ham-mer \'hamər\ *n* **1** : hand tool for pounding **2** : gun part whose striking explodes the charge ~ *vb* : beat, drive, or shape with a hammer — **hammer out** *vb* : produce with effort

ham-mer-head *n* **1** : striking part of a hammer **2** : shark with a hammerlike head

ham-mock \'hamək\ *n* : swinging bed hung by cords at each end

¹**ham-per** \'hampər\ *vb* : impede

²**hamper** *n* : large covered basket

ham-ster \'hamstər\ *n* : stocky shorttailed rodent

ham-string \'ham,striŋ\ *vb* **-strung** \-,strəŋ\; **-string-ing** \-,striŋiŋ\ **1** : cripple by cutting the leg tendons **2** : make ineffective or powerless

hand \'hand\ *n* **1** : end of a front limb adapted for grasping **2** : side **3** : promise of marriage **4** : handwriting **5** : assistance or participation **6** : applause **7** : cards held by a player **8** : worker ~ *vb* : lead, assist, give, or pass with the hand — **hand-clasp** *n* — **hand-craft** *vb* — **hand-ful** *n* — **hand-gun** *n* — **hand-less** *adj* — **hand-made** *adj* — **hand-rail** *n* — **hand-saw** *n* — **hand-wo-ven** *adj* — **hand-writ-ing** *n* — **hand-writ-ten** *adj*

hand-bag *n* : woman's purse

hand-ball *n* : game played by striking a ball with the hand

hand-bill *n* : printed advertisement or notice distributed by hand

hand-book *n* : concise reference book

hand-cuffs *n pl* : locking bracelets that bind the wrists together — **handcuff** *vb*

hand-i-cap \'handē,kap\ *n* **1** : advantage given or disadvantage imposed to equalize a competition **2** : disadvantage — **handicap** *vb* —

hand·i·capped *adj* — **hand·i·cap·per** *n*

hand·i·craft \'hande͟ˌkraft\ *n* **1** : manual skill **2** : article made by hand — **hand·i·craft·er** *n* — **hand·i·crafts·man** \-ˌkraftsmən\ *n*

hand·i·work \-ˌwərk\ *n* : work done personally or by the hands

hand·ker·chief \'haŋkərchəf, -ˌchēf\ *n, pl* **-chiefs** \-chəfs, -ˌchēfs\ : small piece of cloth carried for personal use

han·dle \'handᵊl\ *n* : part to be grasped ∼ *vb* **-dled; -dling 1** : touch, hold, or manage with the hands **2** : deal with **3** : deal or trade in — **han·dle·bar** *n* — **handled** \-dᵊld\ *adj* — **han·dler** \'handlər\ *n*

hand·maid·en *n* : female attendant

hand·out *n* : something given out

hand·pick *vb* : select personally

hand·shake *n* : clasping of hands (as in greeting)

hand·some \'hansəm\ *adj* **-somer; -est 1** : sizable **2** : generous **3** : nice-looking — **hand·some·ly** *adv* — **hand·some·ness** *n*

hand·spring *n* : somersault on the hands

hand·stand *n* : a balancing upside down on the hands

handy \'handē\ *adj* **hand·i·er; -est 1** : conveniently near **2** : easily used **3** : dexterous — **hand·i·ly** *adv* — **hand·i·ness** *n*

handy·man \-ˌman\ *n* : one who does odd jobs

◆ **hang** \'haŋ\ *vb* **hung** \'həŋ\; **hanging 1** : fasten or remain fastened to an elevated point without support from below **2** : suspend by the neck until dead — past tense often *hanged* **3** : droop ∼ *n* **1** : way a thing hangs **2** : an understanding of something — **hang·er** *n* — **hang·ing** *n*

han·gar \'haŋər\ *n* : airplane shelter

hang·dog \'haŋˌdȯg\ *adj* : ashamed or guilty

hang·man \-mən\ *n* : public executioner

hang·nail *n* : loose skin near a fingernail

hang·out *n* : place where one likes to spend time

hang·over *n* : sick feeling following heavy drinking

hank \'haŋk\ *n* : coil or loop

han·ker \'haŋkər\ *vb* : desire strongly — **han·ker·ing** *n*

han·ky-pan·ky \ˌhaŋkē'paŋkē\ *n* : questionable or underhanded activity

han·som \'hansəm\ *n* : 2-wheeled covered carriage

Ha·nuk·kah \'k̲änəkə, 'hän-\ *n* : 8-day Jewish holiday commemorating the rededication of the Temple of Jerusalem after its defilement by Antiochus of Syria

hap·haz·ard \hap'hazərd\ *adj* : having no plan or order — **hap·haz·ard·ly** *adv*

hap·less \'haplas\ *adj* : unfortunate — **hap·less·ly** *adv* — **hap·less·ness** *n*

hap·pen \'hapən\ *vb* **1** : take place **2** : be fortunate to encounter something unexpectedly — often used with infinitive

hap·pen·ing \-əniŋ\ *n* : occurrence

hap·py \'hapē\ *adj* **-pi·er; -est 1** : fortunate **2** : content, pleased, or joyous — **hap·pi·ly** \'hapəlē\ *adv* — **hap·pi·ness** *n*

ha·rangue \hə'raŋ\ *n* : ranting or scolding speech — **harangue** *vb* — **ha·rangu·er** \-'raŋər\ *n*

ha·rass \hə'ras, 'harəs\ *vb* **1** : disturb and impede by repeated raids

2 : annoy continually — **ha·rass·ment** n

har·bin·ger \'härbənjər\ n : one that announces or foreshadows what is coming

har·bor \-bər\ n : protected body of water suitable for anchorage ~ vb 1 : give refuge to 2 : hold as a thought or feeling

hard \'härd\ adj 1 : not easily penetrated 2 : firm or definite 3 : close or searching 4 : severe or unfeeling 5 : strenuous or difficult 6 : physically strong or intense — **hard** adv — **hard·ness** n

hard·en \'härdᵊn\ vb : make or become hard or harder — **hard·en·er** n

hard–head·ed \‚härd'hedəd\ adj 1 : stubborn 2 : realistic — **hard–head·ed·ly** adv — **hard–head·ed·ness** n

hard–heart·ed \-'härtəd\ adj : lacking sympathy — **hard–heart·ed·ly** adv — **hard–heart·ed·ness** n

hard·ly \'härdlē\ adv 1 : only just 2 : certainly not

hard–nosed \-‚nōzd\ adj : tough or uncompromising

hard·ship \-‚ship\ n : suffering or privation

hard·tack \-‚tak\ n : hard biscuit

hard·ware n 1 : cutlery or tools made of metal 2 : physical components of a vehicle or apparatus

hard·wood n : wood of a broad-leaved usu. deciduous tree — **hardwood** adj

har·dy \'härdē\ adj -di·er; -est : able to withstand adverse conditions — **har·di·ly** adv — **har·di·ness** n

hare \'har\ n, pl **hare** or **hares** : long-eared mammal related to the rabbit

hare·brained \-‚brānd\ adj : foolish

hare·lip n : deformity in which the upper lip is vertically split — **hare·lipped** \-‚lipt\ adj

ha·rem \'harəm\ n : house or part of a house allotted to women in a Muslim household or the women and servants occupying it

hark \'härk\ vb : listen

har·le·quin \'härlikən, -kwən\ n : clown

har·lot \'härlət\ n : prostitute

harm \'härm\ n 1 : physical or mental damage 2 : mischief ~ vb : cause harm — **harm·ful** \-fəl\ adj — **harm·ful·ly** adv — **harm·ful·ness** n — **harm·less** adj — **harm·less·ly** adv — **harm·less·ness** n

har·mon·ic \här'mänik\ adj 1 : of or relating to musical harmony 2 : pleasing to hear — **har·mon·i·cal·ly** \-iklē\ adv

har·mon·i·ca \här'mänikə\ n : small wind instrument with metallic reeds

har·mo·ny \'härmənē\ n, pl -nies 1 : musical combination of sounds 2 : pleasing arrangement of parts 3 : lack of conflict 4 : internal calm — **har·mo·ni·ous** \här'mōnēəs\ adj — **har·mo·ni·ous·ly** adv — **har·mo·ni·ous·ness** n — **har·mo·ni·za·tion** \‚härmənə'zāshən\ n — **har·mo·nize** \'härmə‚nīz\ vb

har·ness \'härnəs\ n : gear of a draft animal ~ vb 1 : put a harness on 2 : put to use

harp \'härp\ n : musical instrument with many strings plucked by the fingers ~ vb 1 : play on a harp 2 : dwell on a subject tiresomely — **harp·er** n — **harp·ist** n

har·poon \här'pün\ n : barbed spear used in hunting whales — **harpoon** vb — **har·poon·er** n

harp·si·chord \'härpsi‚kȯrd\ n : keyboard instrument with strings that are plucked

har·py \'härpē\ n, pl -pies : shrewish woman

har·row \'harō\ n : implement used to break up soil ~ vb 1 : cultivate with a harrow 2 : distress

har·ry \'harē\ vb -ried; -ry·ing : torment by or as if by constant attack

harsh \'härsh\ adj 1 : disagreeably rough 2 : severe — **harsh·ly** adv — **harsh·ness** n

har·um–scar·um \‚harəm'skarəm\ adv : recklessly

har·vest \'härvəst\ n 1 : act or time of gathering in a crop 2 : mature crop — **harvest** vb — **har·vest·er** n

has pres 3d sing of HAVE

hash \'hash\ vb : chop into small pieces ~ n : chopped meat mixed with potatoes and browned

hasp \'hasp\ n : hinged strap fastener esp. for a door

has·sle \'hasəl\ n 1 : quarrel 2 : struggle 3 : cause of annoyance — **hassle** vb

has·sock \'hasək\ *n* : cushion used as a seat or leg rest

haste \'hāst\ *n* 1 : rapidity of motion 2 : rash action 3 : excessive eagerness — **hast·i·ly** \'hāstəlē\ *adv* — **hast·i·ness** \-stēnəs\ *n* — **hasty** \-stē\ *adj*

has·ten \'hāsⁿn\ *vb* : hurry

hat \'hat\ *n* : covering for the head

¹**hatch** \'hach\ *n* : small door or opening — **hatch·way** *n*

²**hatch** *vb* : emerge from an egg — **hatch·ery** \-ərē\ *n*

hatch·et \'hachət\ *n* : short-handled ax

hate \'hāt\ *n* : intense hostility and aversion ∼ *vb* **hat·ed; hat·ing** 1 : express or feel hate 2 : dislike — **hate·ful** \-fəl\ *adj* — **hate·ful·ly** *adv* — **hate·ful·ness** *n* — **hat·er** *n*

ha·tred \'hātrəd\ *n* : hate

hat·ter \'hatər\ *n* : one that makes or sells hats

haugh·ty \'hotē\ *adj* **-ti·er; -est** : disdainfully proud — **haugh·ti·ly** *adv* — **haugh·ti·ness** *n*

haul \'hol\ *vb* 1 : draw or pull 2 : transport or carry ∼ *n* 1 : amount collected 2 : load or the distance it is transported — **haul·er** *n*

haunch \'honch\ *n* : hip or hindquarter — usu. pl.

haunt \'hont\ *vb* 1 : visit often 2 : visit or inhabit as a ghost ∼ *n* : place frequented — **haunt·er** *n* — **haunt·ing·ly** *adv*

have \'hav, *in sense 2 before "to" usu* ¹**haf**\ *vb* **had** \'had\; **hav·ing** \'haviŋ\; **has** \'haz, *in sense 2 before "to" usu* 'has\ 1 : hold in possession, service, or affection 2 : compelled or forced to 3 — used as an auxiliary with the past participle to form the present perfect, past perfect, or future perfect 4 : obtain or receive 5 : undergo 6 : cause to 7 : bear — **have to do with** : have in the way of connection or relation with or effect on

ha·ven \'hāvən\ *n* : place of safety

hav·oc \'havək\ *n* 1 : wide destruction 2 : great confusion

¹**hawk** \'hok\ *n* : bird of prey with a strong hooked bill and sharp talons

²**hawk** *vb* : offer for sale by calling out in the street — **hawk·er** *n*

haw·ser \'hozər\ *n* : large rope

haw·thorn \'ho,thorn\ *n* : spiny shrub or tree with pink or white fragrant flowers

hay \'hā\ *n* : herbs (as grass) cut and dried for use as fodder — **hay** *vb* — **hay·loft** *n* — **hay·mow** \-,maù\ *n* — **hay·stack** *n*

hay·cock \'hā,käk\ *n* : small pile of hay

hay·rick \-,rik\ *n* : large outdoor stack of hay

hay·seed \'hā,sēd\ *n* : bumpkin

hay·wire *adj* : being out of order

haz·ard \'hazərd\ *n* 1 : source of danger 2 : chance ∼ *vb* : venture or risk — **haz·ard·ous** *adj*

¹**haze** \'hāz\ *n* : fine dust, smoke, or light vapor in the air that reduces visibility

²**haze** *vb* **hazed; haz·ing** : harass by abusive and humiliating tricks

ha·zel \'hāzəl\ *n* 1 : shrub or small tree bearing edible nuts (**ha·zel·nuts**) 2 : light brown color

hazy \'hāzē\ *adj* **haz·i·er; -est** 1 : obscured by haze 2 : vague or indefinite — **haz·i·ly** *adv* — **haz·i·ness** *n*

he \'hē\ *pron* 1 : that male one 2 : a or the person

◆ **head** \'hed\ *n* 1 : front or upper part of the body 2 : mind 3 : upper or higher end 4 : director or leader 5 : place of leadership or honor ∼ *adj* : principal or chief ∼ *vb* 1

GIANT SCORPIONS!

THE WOLFMAN IS HEADED THIS WAY!

KING KONG HAS A HEAD COLD AND WANTS TO BORROW YOUR HANDKERCHIEF!

I'M NOT MOVING TILL I FINISH THIS SANDWICH

JIM DAVIS 7-31

: provide with or form a head **2** : put, stand, or be at the head **3** : point or proceed in a certain direction — **head·ache** n — **head·band** n — **head·dress** n — **head·ed** adj — **head·first** adv or adj — **head·gear** n — **head·less** adj — **head·rest** n — **head·ship** n — **head·wait·er** n

head·ing \-iŋ\ n **1** : direction in which a plane or ship heads **2** : something (as a title) standing at the top or beginning

head·land \'hedlənd, -ˌland\ n : promontory

head·light n : light on the front of a vehicle

head·line n : introductory line of a newspaper story printed in large type

head·long \-'lȯŋ\ adv **1** : head foremost **2** : in a rash or reckless manner — **head·long** \-ˌlȯŋ\ adj

head·mas·ter n : man who is head of a private school

head·mis·tress n : woman who is head of a private school

head–on adj : having the front facing in the direction of initial contact — **head–on** adv

head·phone n : an earphone held on by a band over the head — usu. pl.

head·quar·ters n sing or pl : command or administrative center

head·stone n : stone at the head of a grave

head·strong adj : stubborn or willful

head·wa·ters n pl : source of a stream

head·way n : forward motion

heady \'hedē\ adj **head·i·er; -est 1** : intoxicating **2** : shrewd

heal \'hēl\ vb : make or become sound or whole — **heal·er** n

health \'helth\ n : sound physical or mental condition

health·ful \-fəl\ adj : beneficial to health — **health·ful·ly** adv — **health·ful·ness** n

healthy \'helthē\ adj **health·i·er; -est** : enjoying or typical of good health — **health·i·ly** adv — **health·i·ness** n

heap \'hēp\ n : pile ~ vb : throw or lay in a heap

hear \'hir\ vb **heard** \'hərd\; **hearing** \'hiriŋ\ **1** : perceive by the ear **2** : heed **3** : learn

hear·ing n **1** : process or power of perceiving sound **2** : earshot **3** : session in which witnesses are heard

hear·ken \'härkən\ vb : give attention

hear·say n : rumor

hearse \'hərs\ n : vehicle for carrying the dead to the grave

heart \'härt\ n **1** : hollow muscular organ that keeps up the circulation of the blood **2** : playing card of a suit marked with a red heart **3** : whole personality or the emotional or moral part of it **4** : courage **5** : essential part — **heart·beat** n — **heart·ed** adj

heart·ache n : anguish of mind

heart·break n : crushing grief — **heart·break·er** n — **heart·breaking** adj — **heart·bro·ken** adj

heart·burn n : burning distress in the heart area after eating

heart·en \'härtᵊn\ vb : encourage

hearth \'härth\ n **1** : area in front of a fireplace **2** : home — **hearth·stone** n

heart·less \'härtləs\ adj : cruel

heart·rend·ing \-ˌrendiŋ\ adj : causing intense grief or anguish

heart·sick adj : very despondent — **heart·sick·ness** n

heart·strings n pl : deepest emotions

heart·throb n : sweetheart

heart·warm·ing *adj* : inspiring sympathetic feeling

heart·wood *n* : central portion of wood

hearty \'härtē\ *adj* **heart·i·er; -est 1** : vigorously healthy **2** : nourishing — **heart·i·ly** *adv* — **heart·i·ness** *n*

heat \'hēt\ *vb* : make or become warm or hot ~ *n* **1** : condition of being hot **2** : form of energy that causes a body to rise in temperature **3** : intensity of feeling — **heat·ed·ly** *adv* — **heat·er** *n*

heath \'hēth\ *n* **1** : often evergreen shrubby plant of wet acid soils **2** : tract of wasteland — **heathy** *adj*

hea·then \'hēthən\ *n, pl* **-thens** or **-then** : uncivilized or godless person — **heathen** *adj*

heath·er \'hethər\ *n* : evergreen heath with lavender flowers — **heath·ery** *adj*

heat·stroke *n* : disorder that follows prolonged exposure to excessive heat

heave \'hēv\ *vb* **heaved** or **hove** \'hōv\; **heav·ing 1** : rise or lift upward **2** : throw **3** : rise and fall ~ *n* **1** : an effort to lift or raise **2** : throw

◆ **heav·en** \'hevən\ *n* **1** *pl* : sky **2** : abode of the Deity and of the blessed dead **3** : place of supreme happiness — **heav·en·ly** *adj* — **heav·en·ward** *adv* or *adj*

heavy \'hevē\ *adj* **heavi·er; -est 1** : having great weight **2** : hard to bear **3** : greater than the average — **heav·i·ly** *adv* — **heavi·ness** *n* — **heavy·weight** *n*

heavy–du·ty *adj* : able to withstand unusual strain

heavy·set *adj* : stocky and compact in build

heck·le \'hekəl\ *vb* **-led; -ling** : harass with gibes — **heck·ler** \-'heklər\ *n*

hec·tic \'hektik\ *adj* : filled with excitement, activity, or confusion — **hec·ti·cal·ly** \-tiklē\ *adv*

hedge \'hej\ *n* **1** : fence or boundary of shrubs or small trees **2** : means of protection ~ *vb* **hedged; hedging 1** : protect oneself against loss **2** : evade the risk of commitment — **hedg·er** *n*

hedge·hog *n* : spiny mammal (as a porcupine)

he·do·nism \'hēdºn,izəm\ *n* : way of life devoted to pleasure — **he·do·nist** \-ºnist\ *n* — **he·do·nis·tic** \,hēdºnⁱistik\ *adj*

heed \'hēd\ *vb* : pay attention ~ *n* : attention — **heed·ful** \-fəl\ *adj* — **heed·ful·ly** *adv* — **heed·ful·ness** *n* — **heed·less** *adj* — **heed·less·ly** *adv* — **heed·less·ness** *n*

¹**heel** \'hēl\ *n* **1** : back of the foot **2** : crusty end of a loaf of bread **3** : solid piece forming the back of the sole of a shoe — **heel·less** \'hēlləs\ *adj*

²**heel** *vb* : tilt to one side

heft \'heft\ *n* : weight ~ *vb* : judge the weight of by lifting

hefty \'heftē\ *adj* **heft·i·er; -est** : big and bulky

he·ge·mo·ny \hⁱijemōnē\ *n* : preponderant influence over others

heif·er \'hefər\ *n* : young cow

height \'hīt, 'hītth\ *n* **1** : highest part or point **2** : distance from bottom to top **3** : altitude

height·en \'hītºn\ *vb* : increase in amount or degree

hei·nous \'hānəs\ *adj* : shockingly evil — **hei·nous·ly** *adv* — **hei·nous·ness** *n*

heir \'ar\ *n* : one who inherits or is entitled to inherit property

heir·ess \'arəs\ *n* : female heir esp. to great wealth

◆ **heir·loom** \'ar,lüm\ *n* : something

handed on from one generation to another

held *past of* HOLD

he·li·cal \'helikəl, 'hē-\ *adj* : spiral

he·li·cop·ter \'helə,käptər, 'hē-\ *n* : aircraft supported in the air by rotors

he·lio·trope \'hēlyə,trōp\ *n* : garden herb with small fragrant white or purple flowers

he·li·um \'hēlēəm\ *n* : very light nonflammable gaseous chemical element

he·lix \'hēliks\ *n, pl* **-li·ces** \'helə,sēz, 'hē-\ : something spiral

hell \'hel\ *n* **1** : nether world in which the dead continue to exist **2** : realm of the devil **3** : place or state of torment or destruction — **hell·ish** *adj*

hell-gram·mite \'helgrə,mīt\ *n* : aquatic insect larva

hel·lion \'helyən\ *n* : troublesome person

hel·lo \hə'lō, he-\ *n, pl* **-los** : expression of greeting

helm \'helm\ *n* : lever or wheel for steering a ship — **helms·man** \'helmzmən\ *n*

hel·met \'helmət\ *n* : protective covering for the head

help \'help\ *vb* **1** : supply what is needed **2** : be of use **3** : refrain from or prevent ∼ *n* **1** : something that helps or a source of help **2** : one who helps another — **help·er** *n* — **help·ful** \-fəl\ *adj* — **help·ful·ly** *adv* — **help·ful·ness** *n* — **help·less** *adj* — **help·less·ly** *adv* — **help·less·ness** *n*

help·ing \'helpiŋ\ *n* : portion of food

help·mate *n* **1** : helper **2** : wife

help·meet \-,mēt\ *n* : helpmate

hel·ter-skel·ter \,heltər'skeltər\ *adv* : in total disorder

hem \'hem\ *n* : border of an article of cloth doubled back and stitched down ∼ *vb* **-mm- 1** : sew a hem **2** : surround restrictively — **hem·line** *n*

he·ma·tol·o·gy \,hēmə'täləjē\ *n* : study of the blood and blood-forming organs — **hema·to·log·ic** \-mət'l'äjik\ *adj* — **he·ma·tol·o·gist** \-'täləjist\ *n*

hemi·sphere \'hemə,sfir\ *n* : one of the halves of the earth divided by the equator into northern and southern parts (**northern hemisphere, southern hemisphere**) or by a meridian into eastern and western parts (**eastern hemisphere, western hemisphere**) — **hemi·spher·ic** \,hemə'sfirik, -'sfer-\ **hemi·spher·i·cal** \-'sfirikəl, -'sfer-\ *adj*

hem·lock \'hem,läk\ *n* **1** : poisonous herb related to the carrot **2** : evergreen tree related to the pines

he·mo·glo·bin \'hēmə,glōbən\ *n* : iron-containing compound found in red blood cells

he·mo·phil·ia \,hēmə'filēə\ *n* : hereditary tendency to severe prolonged bleeding — **he·mo·phil·i·ac** \-ē,ak\ *adj or n*

hem·or·rhage \'hemərij\ *n* : large discharge of blood — **hemorrhage** *vb* — **hem·or·rhag·ic** \,hemə'rajik\ *adj*

hem·or·rhoids \'hemə,rȯidz\ *n pl* : swollen mass of dilated veins at or just within the anus

hemp \'hemp\ *n* : tall Asian herb grown for its tough fiber — **hemp·en** \'hempən\ *adj*

hen \'hen\ *n* : female domestic fowl

hence \'hens\ *adv* **1** : away **2** : therefore **3** : from this source or origin

hence·forth *adv* : from this point on

hence·for·ward *adv* : henceforth

hench·man \'henchmən\ *n* : trusted follower

hen·na \'henə\ *n* : reddish brown dye from a tropical shrub used esp. on hair

hen·peck \'hen,pek\ *vb* : subject (one's husband) to persistent nagging

he·pat·ic \hi'patik\ *adj* : relating to or resembling the liver

hep·a·ti·tis \,hepə'tītəs\ *n, pl* **-tit·i·des** \-'titə,dēz\ : disease in which the liver becomes inflamed

her \'hər\ *adj* : of or relating to her or herself ∼ \ər, (')hər\ *pron, objective case of* SHE

her·ald \'herəld\ *n* **1** : official crier or messenger **2** : harbinger ∼ *vb* : give notice

her·ald·ry \'herəldrē\ *n, pl* **-ries** : practice of devising and granting stylized emblems (as for a family) — **he·ral·dic** \he'raldik, hə-\ *adj*

herb \'ərb, 'hərb\ *n* **1** : seed plant that lacks woody tissue **2** : plant or plant part valued for medicinal or

savory qualities — **her·ba·ceous**
\ˌərˈbāshəs, ˌhər-\ adj — **herb·age**
\ˈərbij, ˈhər-\ n — **herb·al** \-bəl\ n
or adj — **herb·al·ist** \-bəlist\ n

her·bi·cide \ˈərbəˌsīd, ˈhər-\ n
: agent that destroys plants — **her·bi·cid·al** \ˌərbəˈsīdᵊl, ˌhər-\ adj

her·biv·o·rous \ˌərˈbivərəs, ˌhər-\
adj : feeding on plants — **her·bi·vore** \ˈərbəˌvōr, ˈhər-\ n

her·cu·le·an \ˌhərkyəˈlēən, ˌhər-kyüˈlēən\ adj : of extraordinary
power, size, or difficulty

herd \ˈhərd\ n : group of animals of
one kind ~ vb : assemble or move
in a herd — **herd·er** n — **herds·man** \ˈhərdzmən\ n

here \ˈhir\ adv 1 : in, at, or to this
place 2 : now 3 : at or in this point
or particular 4 : in the present life
or state ~ n : this place — **here·abouts** \ˈhirəˌbaůts\, **here·about**
\-ˌbaůt\ adv

here·af·ter adv : in some future
time or state ~ n : existence beyond earthly life

here·by adv : by means of this

he·red·i·tary \həˈredəˌterē\ adj 1
: genetically passed or passable
from parent to offspring 2 : passing by inheritance

he·red·i·ty \-ətē\ n : the passing of
characteristics from parent to offspring

here·in adv : in this

here·of adv : of this

here·on adv : on this

her·e·sy \ˈherəsē\ n, pl -sies : opinion or doctrine contrary to church
dogma — **her·e·tic** \-ˌtik\ n — **he·re·ti·cal** \həˈretikəl\ adj

here·to adv : to this document

here·to·fore \ˈhirtüˌfōr\ adv : up to
this time

here·un·der adv : under this

here·un·to adv : to this

here·upon adv : on this

here·with adv 1 : with this 2 : hereby
her·i·tage \ˈherətij\ n 1 : inheritance
2 : birthright

her·maph·ro·dite \hərˈmafrəˌdīt\ n : animal or plant having
both male and female reproduc-
tive organs — **hermaphrodite** adj
— **her·maph·ro·dit·ic** \-ˌmafrə-ˈditik\ adj

her·met·ic \hərˈmetik\ adj : sealed
airtight — **her·met·i·cal·ly** \-iklē\
adv

her·mit \ˈhərmət\ n : one who lives
in solitude

◆ **her·nia** \ˈhərnēə\ n, pl -ni·as or
-ni·ae \-nē̩ē, -nē̩ī\ : protrusion of
a bodily part through the weak-
ened wall of its enclosure — **her·ni·ate** \-nē̩āt\ vb

he·ro \ˈhērō, ˈhirō\ n, pl -roes : one
that is much admired or shows
great courage — **he·ro·ic** \hi-ˈrōik\ adj — **he·ro·i·cal·ly** \-iklē\
adv — **he·ro·ics** \-iks\ n pl — **her·o·ism** \ˈherəˌwizəm\ n

her·o·in \ˈherəwən\ n : strongly addictive narcotic

her·o·ine \ˈherəwən\ n : woman of
heroic achievements or qualities

her·on \ˈherən\ n : long-legged
long-billed wading bird

her·pes \ˈhərpēz\ n : virus disease
characterized by the formation of
blisters

her·pe·tol·o·gy \ˌhərpəˈtäləjē\ n
: study of reptiles and amphibians
— **her·pe·tol·o·gist** \-pəˈtäləjist\ n

her·ring \ˈheriŋ\ n, pl -ring or -rings
: narrow-bodied Atlantic food fish

hers \ˈhərz\ pron : one or the ones
belonging to her

her·self \hərˈself\ pron : she, her —
used reflexively or for emphasis

hertz \ˈherts, ˈhərts\ n, pl hertz
: unit of frequency equal to one
cycle per second

hes·i·tant \ˈhezətənt\ adj : tending

to hesitate — **hes·i·tance** \-tens\ *n* — **hes·i·tan·cy** \-tənsē\ *n* — **hes·i·tant·ly** *adv*

hes·i·tate \'hezə,tāt\ *vb* **-tat·ed; -tat·ing** 1 : hold back esp. in doubt 2 : pause — **hes·i·ta·tion** \,hezə-'tāshən\ *n*

het·er·o·ge·neous \,hetərə'jēnēəs, -nyəs\ *adj* : consisting of dissimilar ingredients or constituents — **het·er·o·ge·ne·ity** \-jə'nēətē\ *n* — **het·ero·ge·neous·ly** *adv*

het·ero·sex·u·al \,hetərō'sekshə-wəl\ *adj* : oriented toward the opposite sex — **heterosexual** *n* — **het·ero·sex·u·al·i·ty** \-,sekshə-'walətē\ *n*

hew \'hyü\ *vb* **hewed; hewed** *or* **hewn** \'hyün\; **hew·ing** 1 : cut or shape with or as if with an ax 2 : conform strictly — **hew·er** *n*

hex \'heks\ *vb* : put an evil spell on — **hex** *n*

hexa·gon \'hekə,gän\ *n* : 6-sided polygon — **hex·ag·o·nal** \hek-'sagənªl\ *adj*

hey·day \'hā,dā\ *n* : time of flourishing

hi·a·tus \hī'ātəs\ *n* : lapse in continuity

hi·ba·chi \hi'bächē\ *n* : brazier

hi·ber·nate \'hībər,nāt\ *vb* **-nat·ed; -nat·ing** : pass the winter in a torpid or resting state — **hi·ber·na·tion** \,hībər'nāshən\ *n* — **hi·ber·na·tor** \'hībər,nātər\ *n*

hic·cup \'hikəp\ *vb* **-cuped; -cup·ing** : to inhale spasmodically and make a peculiar sound — *n pl* : attack of hiccuping

hick \'hik\ *n* : awkward provincial person — **hick** *adj*

hick·o·ry \'hikərē\ *n, pl* **-ries** : No. American hardwood tree — **hick·ory** *adj*

¹**hide** \'hīd\ *vb* **hid** \'hid\; **hid·den** \'hidªn\ *or* **hid; hid·ing** : put or remain out of sight — **hid·er** *n*

²**hide** *n* : animal skin

hide·bound \'hīd,baund\ *adj* : inflexible or conservative

hid·eous \'hidēəs\ *adj* : very ugly — **hid·eous·ly** *adv* — **hid·eous·ness** *n*

hie \'hī\ *vb* **hied; hy·ing** *or* **hie·ing** : hurry

hi·er·ar·chy \'hīə,rärkē\ *n, pl* **-chies** : persons or things arranged in a graded series — **hi·er·ar·chi·cal** \,hīə'rärkikəl\ *adj*

hi·er·o·glyph·ic \,hīərə'glifik\ *n* : character in the picture writing of the ancient Egyptians

high \'hī\ *adj* 1 : having large extension upward 2 : elevated in pitch 3 : exalted in character 4 : of greater degree or amount than average 5 : expensive 6 : excited or stupefied by alcohol or a drug — *adv* : at or to a high place or degree — *n* 1 : elevated point or level 2 : automobile gear giving the highest speed — **high·ly** *adv*

high·boy *n* : high chest of drawers on legs

high·brow \-,brau\ *n* : person of superior learning or culture — **high·brow** *adj*

high–flown *adj* : pretentious

high–hand·ed *adj* : willful and arrogant — **high–hand·ed·ly** *adv* — **high–hand·ed·ness** *n*

high·land \'hīlənd\ *n* : hilly country — **high·land·er** \-ləndər\ *n*

high·light *n* : event or detail of major importance — *vb* 1 : emphasize 2 : be a highlight of

high·ness \-nəs\ *n* 1 : quality or degree of being high 2 — used as a title (as for kings)

high–rise *adj* : having several stories

high school *n* : school usu. including grades 9 to 12 or 10 to 12

high–spir·it·ed *adj* : lively

high–strung \,hī'strəŋ\ *adj* : very nervous or sensitive

high·way *n* : public road

high·way·man \-mən\ *n* : one who robs travelers on a road

hi·jack \'hī,jak\ *vb* : steal esp. by commandeering a vehicle — **hijack** *n* — **hi·jack·er** *n*

hike \'hīk\ *vb* **hiked; hik·ing** 1 : raise quickly 2 : take a long walk — *n* 1 : long walk 2 : increase — **hik·er** *n*

hi·lar·i·ous \hi'larēəs, hī'-\ *adj* : extremely funny — **hi·lar·i·ous·ly** *adv* — **hi·lar·i·ty** \-ətē\ *n*

hill \'hil\ *n* : place where the land rises — **hill·side** *n* — **hill·top** *n* — **hilly** *adj*

hill·bil·ly \'hil,bilē\ *n, pl* **-lies** : person from a backwoods area

hill·ock \'hilək\ *n* : small hill

hilt \'hilt\ *n* : handle of a sword

him \'him\ *pron, objective case of* HE

him·self \him'self\ *pron* : he, him

— used reflexively or for emphasis

¹**hind** \'hīnd\ *n* : female deer

²**hind** *adj* : back

hin·der \'hindər\ *vb* : obstruct or hold back

hind·most *adj* : farthest to the rear

hind·quar·ter *n* : back half of a complete side of a carcass

hin·drance \'hindrəns\ *n* : something that hinders

hind·sight *n* : understanding of an event after it has happened

Hin·du·ism \'hindü,izəm\ *n* : body of religious beliefs and practices native to India — **Hin·du** *n or adj*

hinge \'hinj\ *n* : jointed piece on which a swinging part (as a door) turns ~ *vb* **hinged; hing·ing 1** : attach by or furnish with hinges **2** : depend

hint \'hint\ *n* **1** : indirect suggestion **2** : clue **3** : very small amount — **hint** *vb*

hin·ter·land \'hintər,land\ *n* : remote region

hip \'hip\ *n* : part of the body on either side just below the waist — **hip·bone** *n*

hip·po·pot·a·mus \,hipə'pätəməs\ *n, pl* -**mus·es** *or* -**mi** \-,mī\ : large thick-skinned African river animal

hire \'hīr\ *n* **1** : payment for labor **2** : employment **3** : one who is hired ~ *vb* **hired; hir·ing** : employ for pay

hire·ling \-liŋ\ *n* : one who serves another only for gain

hir·sute \'hər,süt, 'hir-\ *adj* : hairy

his \'hiz\ *adj* : of or belonging to him ~ *pron* : ones belonging to him

hiss \'his\ *vb* **1** : make a sibilant sound **2** : show dislike by hissing — **hiss** *n*

his·to·ri·an \his'tōrēən\ *n* : writer of history

his·to·ry \'histərē\ *n, pl* -**ries 1** : chronological record of significant events **2** : study of past events **3** : an established record — **his·tor·ic** \his'tòrik\, **his·tor·i·cal** \-ikəl\ *adj* — **his·tor·i·cal·ly** \-klē\ *adv*

his·tri·on·ics \,histrē'äniks\ *n pl* : exaggerated display of emotion

hit \'hit\ *vb* **hit; hit·ting 1** : reach with a blow **2** : come or cause to come in contact **3** : affect detrimentally ~ *n* **1** : blow **2** : great success — **hit·ter** *n*

hitch \'hich\ *vb* **1** : move by jerks **2** : catch by a hook **3** : hitchhike ~ *n* **1** : jerk **2** : sudden halt

hitch·hike \'hich,hīk\ *vb* : travel by securing free rides from passing vehicles — **hitch·hik·er** *n*

hith·er \'hithər\ *adv* : to this place

hith·er·to \-,tü\ *adv* : up to this time

hive \'hīv\ *n* **1** : container housing honeybees **2** : colony of bees — **hive** *vb*

hives \'hīvz\ *n sing or pl* : allergic disorder with itchy skin patches

HMO \,āch,em'ō\ *n* : comprehensive health-care organization financed by clients

hoard \'hōrd\ *n* : hidden accumulation — **hoard** *vb* — **hoard·er** *n*

hoar·frost \'hōr,frost\ *n* : frost

hoarse \'hōrs\ *adj* **hoars·er;** -**est 1** : harsh in sound **2** : speaking in a harsh strained voice — **hoarse·ly** *adv* — **hoarse·ness** *n*

hoary \'hōrē\ *adj* **hoar·i·er;** -**est** : gray or white with age — **hoar·i·ness** *n*

hoax \'hōks\ *n* : act intended to trick or dupe — **hoax** *vb* — **hoax·er** *n*

hob·ble \'häbəl\ *vb* -**bled;** -**bling** : limp along ~ *n* : hobbling movement

hob·by \'häbē\ *n, pl* -**bies** : interest engaged in for relaxation — **hob·by·ist** \-ēist\ *n*

hob·gob·lin \'häb,gäblən\ *n* **1** : mischievous goblin **2** : bogey

hob·nail \-,nāl\ *n* : short nail for studding shoe soles — **hob·nailed** \-,nāld\ *adj*

hob·nob \-,näb\ *vb* -**bb-** : associate socially

ho·bo \'hōbō\ *n, pl* -**boes** : tramp

¹**hock** \'häk\ *n* : joint or region in the hind limb of a quadruped corresponding to the human ankle

²**hock** *n or vb* : pawn

hock·ey \'häkē\ *n* : game played on ice or a field by 2 teams

hod \'häd\ *n* : carrier for bricks or mortar

hodge·podge \'häj,päj\ *n* : heterogeneous mixture

hoe \'hō\ *n* : long-handled tool for cultivating or weeding — **hoe** *vb*

hog \'hòg, 'häg\ *n* **1** : domestic adult

swine 2 : glutton ∼ *vb* : take self-ishly — **hog·gish** *adj*
hogs·head \'hȯgz‚hed, 'hägz-\ *n* : large cask or barrel
hog·wash *n* : nonsense
hoist \'hȯist\ *vb* : lift ∼ *n* 1 : lift 2 : apparatus for hoisting
hok·ey \'hōkē\ *adj* **hok·i·er; -est** 1 : tiresomely simple or sentimental 2 : phony
¹**hold** \'hōld\ *vb* **held** \'held\; **holding** 1 : possess 2 : restrain 3 : have a grasp on 4 : remain or keep in a particular situation or position 5 : contain 6 : regard 7 : cause to occur 8 : occupy esp. by appointment or election ∼ *n* 1 : act or manner of holding 2 : restraining or controlling influence — **holder** *n* — **hold forth** : speak at length — **hold to** : adhere to — **hold with** : agree with
²**hold** *n* : cargo area of a ship
hold·ing \'hōldiŋ\ *n* : property owned — usu. pl.
hold·up *n* 1 : robbery at the point of a gun 2 : delay
hole \'hōl\ *n* 1 : opening into or through something 2 : hollow place (as a pit) 3 : den — **hole** *vb*
hol·i·day \'hälə‚dā\ *n* 1 : day of freedom from work 2 : vacation — **holiday** *vb*
ho·li·ness \'hōlēnəs\ *n* : quality or state of being holy — used as a title for a high religious official
ho·lis·tic \hō'listik\ *adj* : relating to a whole (as the body)
hol·ler \'hälər\ *vb* : cry out — **holler** *n*
hol·low \'hälō\ *adj* **-low·er** \-əwər\; **-est** 1 : sunken 2 : having a cavity within 3 : sounding like a noise made in an empty place 4 : empty of value or meaning ∼ *vb* : make or become hollow ∼ *n* 1 : surface

depression 2 : cavity — **hol·low·ness** *n*
hol·ly \'hälē\ *n, pl* **-lies** : evergreen tree or shrub with glossy leaves
hol·ly·hock \-‚häk, -‚hȯk\ *n* : tall perennial herb with showy flowers
ho·lo·caust \'hälə‚kȯst, 'hō-, 'hȯ-\ *n* : thorough destruction esp. by fire
hol·stein \'hōl‚stēn, -‚stīn\ *n* : large black-and-white dairy cow
hol·ster \'hōlstər\ *n* : case for a pistol
ho·ly \'hōlē\ *adj* **-li·er; -est** 1 : sacred 2 : spiritually pure
hom·age \'ämij, 'hä-\ *n* : reverent regard
home \'hōm\ *n* 1 : residence 2 : congenial environment 3 : place of origin or refuge ∼ *vb* **homed; homing** : go or return home — **home·bred** *adj* — **home·com·ing** *n* — **home·grown** *adj* — **home·land** \-‚land\ *n* — **home·less** *adj* — **home·made** \-'mād\ *adj*
home·ly \-lē\ *adj* **-li·er; -est** : plain or unattractive — **home·li·ness** *n*
home·mak·er *n* : one who manages a household — **home·mak·ing** *n*
home·sick *adj* : longing for home — **home·sick·ness** *n*
home·spun \-‚spən\ *adj* : simple
home·stead \-‚sted\ *n* : home and land occupied and worked by a family — **home·stead·er** \-ər\ *n*
home·stretch *n* 1 : last part of a racetrack 2 : final stage
home·ward \-wərd\, **home·wards** \-wərdz\ *adv* : toward home — **homeward** *adj*
◆ **home·work** *n* : school lessons to be done outside the classroom
hom·ey \'hōmē\ *adj* **hom·i·er; -est** : characteristic of home
ho·mi·cide \'hämə‚sīd, 'hō-\ *n* : the killing of one human being by another — **hom·i·cid·al** \‚hämə-'sīd°l, ‚hō-\ *adj*

hom·i·ly \'häməlē\ *n, pl* **-lies** : sermon

hom·i·ny \'hämənē\ *n* : type of processed hulled corn

ho·mo·ge·neous \ˌhōmə'jēnēəs, -nyəs\ *adj* : of the same or a similar kind — **ho·mo·ge·ne·i·ty** \-jə-'nēətē\ *n* — **ho·mo·ge·neous·ly** *adv*

ho·mog·e·nize \hō'mäjə,nīz, hə-\ *vb* **-nized; -niz·ing** : make the particles in (as milk) of uniform size and even distribution — **ho·mog·e·ni·za·tion** \-ˌmäjənə'zāshən\ *n* — **ho·mog·e·niz·er** *n*

ho·mo·graph \'hämə,graf, 'hō-\ *n* : one of 2 or more words (as the noun *conduct* and the verb *conduct*) spelled alike but different in origin or meaning or pronunciation

hom·onym \'hämə,nim, 'hō-\ *n* **1** : homophone **2** : homograph **3** : one of 2 or more words (as *pool* of water and *pool* the game) spelled and pronounced alike but different in meaning

ho·mo·phone \'hämə,fōn, 'hō-\ *n* : one of 2 or more words (as *to*, *too*, and *two*) pronounced alike but different in origin or meaning or spelling

Ho·mo sa·pi·ens \ˌhōmō'sapēənz, -'sä-\ *n* : humankind

ho·mo·sex·u·al \ˌhōmə'sekshəwəl\ *adj* : oriented toward one's own sex — **homosexual** *n* — **ho·mo·sex·u·al·i·ty** \-ˌseksha'walətē\ *n*

hone \'hōn\ *vb* : sharpen with or as if with an abrasive stone

hon·est \'änəst\ *adj* **1** : free from deception **2** : trustworthy **3** : frank — **hon·est·ly** *adv* — **hon·esty** \-əstē\ *n*

hon·ey \'hənē\ *n, pl* **-eys** : sweet sticky substance made by bees (**hon·ey·bees**) from the nectar of flowers

hon·ey·comb *n* : mass of 6-sided wax cells built by honeybees or something like it ~ *vb* : make or become full of holes like a honeycomb

hon·ey·moon *n* : holiday taken by a newly married couple — **honey·moon** *vb*

hon·ey·suck·le \-ˌsəkəl\ *n* : shrub or vine with flowers rich in nectar

honk \'häŋk, 'hȯŋk\ *n* : cry of a goose or a similar sound — **honk** *vb* — **honk·er** *n*

hon·or \'änər\ *n* **1** : good name **2** : outward respect or symbol of this **3** : privilege **4** : person of superior rank or position — used esp. as a title **5** : something or someone worthy of respect **6** : integrity ~ *vb* **1** : regard with honor **2** : confer honor on **3** : fulfill the terms of — **hon·or·able** \'änərəbəl\ *adj* — **hon·or·ably** \-blē\ *adv* — **hon·or·ari·ly** \ˌänə'rerəlē\ *adv* — **hon·or·ary** \'änəˌrerē\ *adj* — **hon·or·ee** \ˌänə-'rē\ *n*

hood \'hu̇d\ *n* **1** : part of a garment that covers the head **2** : covering over an automobile engine compartment — **hood·ed** *adj*

-hood \ˌhu̇d\ *n suffix* **1** : state, condition, or quality **2** : individuals sharing a state or character

hood·lum \'hu̇dləm, 'hüd-\ *n* : thug

hood·wink \'hu̇d,wiŋk\ *vb* : deceive

hoof \'hu̇f, 'hüf\ *n, pl* **hooves** \'hu̇vz, 'hüvz\ *or* **hoofs** : horny covering of the toes of some mammals (as horses or cattle) — **hoofed** \'hu̇ft, 'hüft\ *adj*

hook \'hu̇k\ *n* : curved or bent device for catching, holding, or pulling ~ *vb* : seize or make fast with a hook — **hook·er** *n*

hook·worm *n* : parasitic intestinal worm

hoo·li·gan \'hüligən\ *n* : thug

hoop \'hüp\ *n* : circular strip, figure, or object

hoot \'hüt\ *vb* **1** : shout in contempt **2** : make the cry of an owl — **hoot** *n* — **hoot·er** *n*

¹hop \'häp\ *vb* **-pp-** : move by quick springy leaps — **hop** *n*

²hop *n* : vine whose ripe dried flowers are used to flavor malt liquors

hope \'hōp\ *vb* **hoped; hop·ing** : desire with expectation of fulfillment ~ *n* **1** : act of hoping **2** : something hoped for — **hope·ful** \-fəl\ *adj* — **hope·ful·ly** *adv* — **hope·ful·ness** *n* — **hope·less** *adj* — **hope·less·ly** *adv* — **hope·less·ness** *n*

hop·per \'häpər\ *n* : container that releases its contents through the bottom

horde \'hōrd\ *n* : throng or swarm

ho·ri·zon \hə'rīz°n\ *n* : apparent junction of earth and sky

hor·i·zon·tal \ˌhòrə'zänt°l\ *adj* : parallel to the horizon — **hor·i·zon·tal·ly** *adv*

hor·mone \'hòrˌmōn\ *n* : cell product in body fluids that has a specific effect on other cells — **hor·mon·al** \hòr'mōn°l\ *adj*

horn \'hòrn\ *n* **1** : hard bony projection on the head of a hoofed animal **2** : brass wind instrument — **horned** *adj* — **horn·less** *adj*

hor·net \'hòrnət\ *n* : large social wasp

horny \'hòrnē\ *adj* **horn·i·er; -est 1** : made of horn **2** : hard or callous **3** : sexually aroused

◆ **horo·scope** \'hòrəˌskōp\ *n* : astrological forecast

hor·ren·dous \hò'rendəs\ *adj* : horrible

hor·ri·ble \'hòrəbəl\ *adj* **1** : having or causing horror **2** : highly disagreeable — **hor·ri·ble·ness** *n* — **hor·ri·bly** \-blē\ *adv*

hor·rid \'hòrəd\ *adj* : horrible — **hor·rid·ly** *adv*

hor·ri·fy \'hòrəˌfī\ *vb* **-fied; -fy·ing** : cause to feel horror

hor·ror \'hòrər\ *n* **1** : intense fear, dread, or dismay **2** : intense repugnance **3** : something horrible

hors d'oeuvre \òr'dərv\ *n*, *pl* **hors d'oeuvres** \-'dərvz\ : appetizer

horse \'hòrs\ *n* : large solid-hoofed domesticated mammal — **horse·back** *n or adv* — **horse·hair** *n* — **horse·hide** *n* — **horse·less** *adj* — **horse·man** \-mən\ *n* — **horse·man·ship** *n* — **horse·wom·an** *n* — **hors·ey, horsy** *adj*

horse·fly *n* : large fly with bloodsucking female

horse·play *n* : rough boisterous play

horse·pow·er *n* : unit of mechanical power

horse·rad·ish *n* : herb with a pungent root used as a condiment

horse·shoe *n* : U-shaped protective metal plate fitted to the rim of a horse's hoof

hor·ti·cul·ture \'hòrtəˌkəlchər\ *n* : science of growing fruits, vegetables, and flowers — **hor·ti·cul·tur·al** \ˌhòrtə'kəlchərəl\ *adj* — **hor·ti·cul·tur·ist** \-rist\ *n*

ho·san·na \hō'zanə, -'zän-\ *interj* — used as a cry of acclamation and adoration — **hosanna** *n*

hose \'hōz\ *n* **1** *pl* **hose** : stocking or sock **2** *pl* **hos·es** : flexible tube for conveying fluids ~ *vb* **hosed; hos·ing** : spray, water, or wash with a hose

ho·siery \'hōzhərē, 'hōzə-\ *n* : stockings or socks

hos·pice \'häspəs\ *n* **1** : lodging (as for travelers) maintained by a religious order **2** : facility or program for caring for dying persons

hos·pi·ta·ble \hä'spitəbəl, 'häsˌpit-\ *adj* : given to generous and cordial reception of guests — **hos·pi·ta·bly** \-blē\ *adv*

hos·pi·tal \'häsˌpit°l\ *n* : institution where the sick or injured receive medical care — **hos·pi·tal·i·za·tion** \ˌhäsˌpit°lə'zāshən\ *n* — **hos·pi·tal·ize** \'häsˌpit°lˌīz\ *vb*

hos·pi·tal·i·ty \ˌhäspə'talətē\ *n, pl* **-ties** : hospitable treatment, reception, or disposition

¹host \'hōst\ *n* **1** : army **2** : multitude

²host *n* : one who receives or entertains guests — **host** *vb*

³host *n* : eucharistic bread

hos·tage \'hästij\ *n* : person held to guarantee that promises be kept or demands met

hos·tel \'häst°l\ *n* : lodging for youth — **hos·tel·er** *n*

hos·tel·ry \-rē\ *n, pl* **-ries** : hotel

host·ess \'hōstəs\ *n* : woman who is host

hos·tile \'häst²l, -₁tīl\ *adj* : openly or actively unfriendly or opposed to someone or something — **hostile** *n* — **hos·tile·ly** *adv* — **hos·til·i·ty** \häs'tilətē\ *n*

hot \'hät\ *adj* -tt- 1 : having a high temperature 2 : giving a sensation of heat or burning 3 : ardent 4 : pungent — **hot** *adv* — **hot·ly** *adv* — **hot·ness** *n*

hot·bed *n* : environment that favors rapid growth

hot dog *n* : frankfurter

ho·tel \hō'tel\ *n* : building where lodging and personal services are provided

hot·head·ed *adj* : impetuous — **hot·head** *n* — **hot·head·ed·ly** *adv* — **hot·head·ed·ness** *n*

hot·house *n* : greenhouse

hound \'haůnd\ *n* : long-eared hunting dog ~ *vb* : pursue relentlessly

hour \'aůər\ *n* 1 : 24th part of a day 2 : time of day — **hour·ly** *adv* or *adj*

hour·glass *n* : glass vessel for measuring time

house \'haůs\ *n, pl* **hous·es** \'haůzəz\ 1 : building to live in 2 : household 3 : legislative body 4 : business firm ~ \'haůz\ *vb* **housed; hous·ing** : provide with or take shelter — **house·boat** \'haůs-₁bōt\ *n* — **house·clean** \'haůs-₁klēn\ *vb* — **house·clean·ing** *n* — **house·ful** \-₁fůl\ *n* — **house·maid** *n* — **house·wares** *n pl* — **house·work** *n*

house·bro·ken \-₁brōkən\ *adj* : trained in excretory habits acceptable in indoor living

house·fly *n* : two-winged fly common about human habitations

♦ **house·hold** \-₁hōld\ *n* : those who

dwell as a family under the same roof ~ *adj* 1 : domestic 2 : common or familiar — **house·hold·er** *n*

house·keep·ing \-₁kēpiŋ\ *n* : care and management of a house or institution — **house·keep·er** *n*

house·warm·ing *n* : party to celebrate moving into a house

house·wife \'haůs₁wīf\ *n* : married woman in charge of a household — **house·wife·ly** *adj* — **house·wif·ery** \-₁wīfərē\ *n*

hous·ing \'haůziŋ\ *n* 1 : dwellings for people 2 : protective covering

hove *past of* HEAVE

hov·el \'həvəl, 'häv-\ *n* : small wretched house

hov·er \'həvər, 'häv-\ *vb* 1 : remain suspended in the air 2 : move about in the vicinity

how \'haů\ *adv* 1 : in what way or condition 2 : for what reason 3 : to what extent ~ *conj* : the way or manner in which

how·ev·er \haů'evər\ *conj* : in whatever manner ~ *adv* 1 : to whatever degree or in whatever manner 2 : in spite of that

how·it·zer \'haůətsər\ *n* : short cannon

howl \'haůl\ *vb* : emit a loud long doleful sound like a dog — **howl** *n* — **howl·er** *n*

hoy·den \'hóid²n\ *n* : girl or woman of saucy or carefree behavior

hub \'həb\ *n* : central part of a circular object (as of a wheel) — **hub·cap** *n*

hub·bub \'həb₁əb\ *n* : uproar

hu·bris \'hyübrəs\ *n* : excessive pride

huck·le·ber·ry \'həkəl₁berē\ *n* 1 : shrub related to the blueberry or its berry 2 : blueberry

huck·ster \'həkstər\ *n* : peddler

hud·dle \'həd²l\ *vb* -dled; -dling 1

: crowd together **2** : confer — **huddle** *n*

hue \'hyü\ *n* : color or gradation of color — **hued** \'hyüd\ *adj*

huff \'həf\ *n* : fit of pique — **huffy** *adj*

hug \'həg\ *vb* **-gg- 1** : press tightly in the arms **2** : stay close to — **hug** *n*

huge \'hyüj\ *adj* **hug·er; hug·est** : very large or extensive — **huge·ly** *adv* — **huge·ness** *n*

hu·la \'hülə\ *n* : Polynesian dance

hulk \'həlk\ *n* **1** : bulky or unwieldy person or thing **2** : old ship unfit for service — **hulk·ing** *adj*

hull \'həl\ *n* **1** : outer covering of a fruit or seed **2** : frame or body of a ship or boat ~ *vb* : remove the hulls of — **hull·er** *n*

hul·la·ba·loo \'hələbə,lü\ *n, pl* **-loos** : uproar

hum \'həm\ *vb* **-mm- 1** : make a prolonged sound like that of the speech sound \m\ **2** : be busily active **3** : run smoothly **4** : sing with closed lips — **hum** *n* — **hum·mer** *n*

hu·man \'hyümən, 'yü-\ *adj* **1** : of or relating to the species people belong to **2** : by, for, or like people — **human** *n* — **hu·man·kind** *n* — **hu·man·ly** *adv* — **hu·man·ness** *n*

hu·mane \hyü'mān, ,yü-\ *adj* : showing compassion or consideration for others — **hu·mane·ly** *adv* — **hu·mane·ness** *n*

hu·man·ism \'hyümə,nizəm, 'yü-\ *n* : doctrine or way of life centered on human interests or values — **hu·man·ist** \-nist\ *n or adj* — **hu·man·is·tic** \,hyümə'nistik, ,yü-\ *adj*

hu·man·i·tar·i·an \hyü,manə'terēən, yü-\ *n* : person promoting human welfare — **humanitarian** *adj* — **hu·man·i·tari·an·ism** *n*

hu·man·i·ty \hyü'manətē, yü-\ *n, pl* **-ties 1** : human or humane quality or state **2** : the human race

hu·man·ize \'hyümə,nīz, 'yü-\ *vb* **-ized; -iz·ing** : make human or humane — **hu·man·iza·tion** \,hyümənə'zāshən, ,yü-\ *n* — **hu·man·iz·er** *n*

hu·man·oid \'hyümə,nȯid, 'yü-\ *adj* : having human form — **human·oid** *n*

hum·ble \'həmbəl\ *adj* **-bler; -blest 1** : not proud or haughty **2** : not pre-

tentious ~ *vb* **-bled; -bling** : make humble — **hum·ble·ness** *n* — **hum·bler** *n* — **hum·bly** \-blē\ *adv*

hum·bug \'həm,bəg\ *n* : nonsense

hum·drum \-,drəm\ *adj* : monotonous

hu·mid \'hyüməd, 'yü-\ *adj* : containing or characterized by moisture — **hu·mid·i·fi·ca·tion** \hyü,midəfə'kāshən\ *n* — **hu·mid·i·fi·er** \-'midə,fīər\ *n* — **hu·mid·i·fy** \-,fī\ *vb* — **hu·mid·ly** *adv*

hu·mid·i·ty \hyü'midətē, yü-\ *n, pl* **-ties** : atmospheric moisture

hu·mi·dor \'hyümə,dȯr, 'yü-\ *n* : humidified storage case (as for cigars)

hu·mil·i·ate \hyü'milē,āt, yü-\ *vb* **-at·ed; -at·ing** : injure the self-respect of — **hu·mil·i·at·ing·ly** *adv* — **hu·mil·i·ation** \-,milē'āshən\ *n*

hu·mil·i·ty \hyü'milətē, yü-\ *n* : humble quality or state

hum·ming·bird \'həmiŋ,bərd\ *n* : tiny American bird that can hover

hum·mock \'həmək\ *n* : mound or knoll — **hum·mocky** \-məkē\ *adj*

hu·mor \'hyümər, 'yü-\ *n* **1** : mood **2** : quality of being laughably ludicrous or incongruous **3** : appreciation of what is ludicrous or incongruous **4** : something intended to be funny ~ *vb* : comply with the wishes or mood of — **hu·mor·ist** \-ərist\ *n* — **hu·mor·less** *adj* — **hu·mor·less·ly** *adv* — **hu·mor·less·ness** *n* — **hu·mor·ous** \'hyümərəs, 'yü-\ *adj* — **hu·mor·ous·ly** *adv* — **hu·mor·ous·ness** *n*

hump \'həmp\ *n* : rounded protuberance — **humped** *adj*

hump·back *n* : hunchback — **hump·backed** *adj*

hu·mus \'hyüməs, 'yü-\ *n* : dark organic part of soil

hunch \'hənch\ *vb* : assume or cause to assume a bent or crooked posture ~ *n* : strong intuitive feeling

hunch·back *n* **1** : back with a hump **2** : person with a crooked back — **hunch·backed** *adj*

hun·dred \'həndrəd\ *n, pl* **-dreds or -dred** : 10 times 10 — **hundred** *adj* — **hun·dredth** \-drədth\ *adj or n*

¹hung *past of* HANG

²hung *adj* : unable to reach a verdict

hun·ger \'həŋgər\ *n* **1** : craving or urgent need for food **2** : strong de-

sire — **hunger** vb — **hun·gri·ly**
\-grəlē\ adv — **hun·gry** adj

hunk \'həŋk\ n : large piece

hun·ker \'həŋkər\ vb : settle in for a sustained period — used with *down*

hunt \'hənt\ vb **1** : pursue for food or sport **2** : try to find ∼ n : act or instance of hunting — **hunt·er** n

hur·dle \'hərd³l\ n **1** : barrier to leap over in a race **2** : obstacle — **hurdle** vb — **hur·dler** n

hurl \'hərl\ vb : throw with violence — **hurl** n — **hurl·er** n

hur·rah \hù'rä, -'rò\ interj — used to express joy or approval

hur·ri·cane \'hərə,kān\ n : tropical storm with winds of 74 miles per hour or greater

hur·ry \'hərē\ vb -ried; -ry·ing : go or cause to go with haste ∼ n : extreme haste — **hur·ried·ly** adv — **hur·ried·ness** n

hurt \'hərt\ vb hurt; hurt·ing **1** : feel or cause pain **2** : do harm to ∼ n **1** : bodily injury **2** : harm — **hurt·ful** \-fəl\ adj — **hurt·ful·ness** n

hur·tle \'hərt³l\ vb -tled; -tling : move rapidly or forcefully

hus·band \'həzbənd\ n : married man ∼ vb : manage prudently

hus·band·ry \-bəndrē\ n **1** : careful use **2** : agriculture

hush \'həsh\ vb : make or become quiet ∼ n : silence

husk \'həsk\ n : outer covering of a seed or fruit ∼ vb : strip the husk from — **husk·er** n

¹**hus·ky** \'həskē\ adj -ki·er; -est : hoarse — **hus·ki·ly** adv — **hus·ki·ness** n

²**husky** adj -ki·er; -est : burly — **husk·i·ness** n

³**husky** n, pl -kies : working dog of the arctic

hus·sy \'həsē, -zē\ n, pl -sies **1** : brazen woman **2** : mischievous girl

hus·tle \'həsəl\ vb -tled; -tling **1** : hurry **2** : work energetically — **hustle** n — **hus·tler** \'həslər\ n

hut \'hət\ n : small often temporary dwelling

hutch \'həch\ n **1** : cupboard with open shelves **2** : pen for an animal

hy·a·cinth \'hīə,sinth\ n : bulbous herb grown for bell-shaped flowers

hy·brid \'hībrəd\ n : offspring of genetically differing parents — **hybrid** adj — **hy·brid·iza·tion** \,hībrədə'zāshən\ n — **hy·brid·ize** \'hībrəd,īz\ vb — **hy·brid·iz·er** n

◆ **hy·drant** \'hīdrənt\ n : pipe from which water may be drawn to fight fires

hy·drau·lic \hī'dròlik\ adj : operated by liquid forced through a small hole — **hy·drau·lics** \-liks\ n

hy·dro·car·bon \,hīdrə'kärbən\ n : organic compound of carbon and hydrogen

hy·dro·elec·tric \,hīdrōi'lektrik\ adj : producing electricity by waterpower — **hy·dro·elec·tric·i·ty** \-,lek'trisətē\ n

hy·dro·gen \'hīdrəjən\ n : very light gaseous colorless odorless flammable chemical element

hydrogen bomb n : powerful bomb that derives its energy from the union of atomic nuclei

hy·dro·pho·bia \,hīdrə'fōbēə\ n : rabies

hy·dro·plane \'hīdrə,plān\ n : speedboat that skims the water

hy·drous \'hīdrəs\ adj : containing water

hy·e·na \hī'ēnə\ n : nocturnal carnivorous mammal of Asia and Africa

hy·giene \'hī,jēn\ n : conditions or practices conducive to health —

hy·gien·ic \hī'jenik, -'jēn-; ˌhījē-'enik\ *adj* — hy·gien·i·cal·ly \-iklē\ *adv* — hy·gien·ist \hī-'jēnist, -'jen-; 'hī͵jēn-\ *n*

hy·grom·e·ter \hī'grämətər\ *n* : instrument for measuring atmospheric humidity

hying *pres part of* HIE

hymn \'him\ *n* : song of praise esp. to God — hymn *vb*

hym·nal \'himnəl\ *n* : book of hymns

hype \'hīp\ *vb* hyped; hyp·ing : publicize extravagantly — hype *n*

hyper- *prefix* 1 : above or beyond 2 : excessively or excessive

hyperacid	hypernational-
hyperacidity	istic
hyperactive	hyperreactive
hyperacute	hyperrealistic
hyperaggres-	hyperromantic
sive	hypersensitive
hypercautious	hypersensitive-
hypercorrect	ness
hypercritical	hypersensitivi-
hyperemotional	ty
hyperenergetic	hypersexual
hyperexcitable	hypersuscepti-
hyperfastidious	ble
hyperintense	hypertense
hypermasculine	hypervigilant

hy·per·bo·le \hī'pərbəlē\ *n* : extravagant exaggeration

hy·per·ten·sion \'hīpər͵tenchən\ *n* : high blood pressure — hy·per·ten·sive \ˌhīpər'tensiv\ *adj or n*

hy·phen \'hīfən\ *n* : punctuation mark - used to divide or compound words — hyphen *vb*

hy·phen·ate \'hīfə͵nāt\ *vb* -at·ed; -at·ing : connect or divide with a hyphen — hy·phen·ation \ˌhīfə-'nāshən\ *n*

hyp·no·sis \hip'nōsəs\ *n, pl* -no·ses \-͵sēz\ : induced state like sleep in which the subject is responsive to suggestions of the inducer (hyp·no·tist \'hipnətist\) — hyp·no·tism \'hipnə͵tizəm\ *n* — hyp·no·tiz·able \ˌhipnə'tīzəbəl\ *adj* — hyp·no·tize \'hipnə͵tīz\ *vb*

hyp·not·ic \hip'nätik\ *adj* : relating to hypnosis — hypnotic *n* — hyp·not·i·cal·ly \-iklē\ *adv*

hy·po·chon·dria \ˌhīpə'kändrēə\ *n* : morbid concern for one's health — hy·po·chon·dri·ac \-drē͵ak\ *adj or n*

hy·poc·ri·sy \hip'äkrəsē\ *n, pl* -sies : a feigning to be what one is not — hyp·o·crite \'hipə͵krit\ *n* — hyp·o·crit·i·cal \ˌhipə'kritikəl\ *adj* — hyp·o·crit·i·cal·ly *adv*

hy·po·der·mic \ˌhīpə'dərmik\ *adj* : administered or used in making an injection beneath the skin ⁓ *n* : hypodermic syringe

hy·pot·e·nuse \hī'pätə͵nüs, -͵nüz, -͵nyüs, -͵nyüz\ *n* : side of a right-angled triangle opposite the right angle

hy·poth·e·sis \hī'päthəsəs\ *n, pl* -e·ses \-͵sēz\ : assumption made in order to test its consequences — hy·poth·e·size \-͵sīz\ *vb* — hy·po·thet·i·cal \ˌhīpə'thetikəl\ *adj* — hy·po·thet·i·cal·ly *adv*

hys·ter·ec·to·my \ˌhistə'rektəmē\ *n, pl* -mies : surgical removal of the uterus

hys·te·ria \his'terēə, -tir-\ *n* : uncontrollable fear or outburst of emotion — hys·ter·i·cal \-'terikəl\ *adj* — hys·ter·i·cal·ly *adv*

hys·ter·ics \-'teriks\ *n pl* : uncontrollable laughter or crying

I

i \ˈī\ *n, pl* **i's** *or* **is** \ˈīz\ : 9th letter of the alphabet

I \ˈī\ *pron* : the speaker

-ial *adj suffix* : of, relating to, or characterized by

-ian — see -AN

ibis \ˈībəs\ *n, pl* **ibis** *or* **ibis·es** : wading bird with a down-curved bill

-ible — see -ABLE

ibu·pro·fen \ˌībyüˈprōfən\ *n* : drug used to relieve inflammation, pain, and fever

-ic *adj suffix* **1** : of, relating to, or being **2** : containing **3** : characteristic of **4** : marked by **5** : caused by

-i·cal \ikəl\ *adj suffix* : -ic — **-i·cal·ly** \iklē, -kəlē\ *adv suffix*

ice \ˈīs\ *n* **1** : frozen water **2** : flavored frozen dessert ~ *vb* **iced; ic·ing 1** : freeze **2** : chill **3** : cover with icing

ice·berg \ˈīsˌbərg\ *n* : large floating mass of ice

ice·box *n* : refrigerator

ice·break·er *n* : ship equipped to cut through ice

ice cream *n* : sweet frozen food

ice-skate *vb* : skate on ice — **ice skater** *n*

ich·thy·ol·o·gy \ˌikthēˈäləjē\ *n* : study of fishes — **ich·thy·ol·o·gist** \-jist\ *n*

ici·cle \ˈīˌsikəl\ *n* : hanging mass of ice

ic·ing \ˈīsiŋ\ *n* : sweet usu. creamy coating for baked goods

icky \ˈikē\ *adj* **-i·er; -est** : offensive, distasteful

icon \ˈīˌkän\ *n* **1** : religious image **2** : small picture on a computer screen identified with an available function

icon·o·clast \ˈīˈkänəˌklast\ *n* : attacker of cherished beliefs or institutions — **icon·o·clasm** \-ˌklazəm\ *n*

icy \ˈīsē\ *adj* **ic·i·er; -est 1** : covered with or consisting of ice **2** : very cold — **ic·i·ly** *adv* — **ic·i·ness** *n*

id \ˈid\ *n* : unconscious instinctual part of the mind

idea \īˈdēə\ *n* **1** : something imagined in the mind **2** : purpose or plan

ide·al \īˈdēəl\ *adj* **1** : imaginary **2** : perfect ~ *n* **1** : standard of excellence **2** : model **3** : aim — **ide·al·ly** *adv*

ide·al·ism \īˈdēəˌlizəm\ *n* : adherence to ideals — **ide·al·ist** \-list\ *n* — **ide·al·is·tic** \ˌīˌdēəˈlistik\ *adj* — **ide·al·is·ti·cal·ly** \-tiklē\ *adv*

ide·al·ize \īˈdēəˌlīz\ *vb* **-ized; -iz·ing** : think of or represent as ideal — **ide·al·i·za·tion** \-ˌdēələˈzāshən\ *n*

iden·ti·cal \īˈdentikəl\ *adj* **1** : being the same **2** : exactly or essentially alike

iden·ti·fi·ca·tion \īˌdentəfəˈkāshən\ *n* **1** : act of identifying **2** : evidence of identity

iden·ti·fy \īˈdentəˌfī\ *vb* **-fied; -fy·ing 1** : associate **2** : establish the identity of — **iden·ti·fi·able** \īˌdentəˈfīəbəl\ *adj* — **iden·ti·fi·er** \īˈdentəˌfīər\ *n*

iden·ti·ty \īˈdentətē\ *n, pl* **-ties 1** : sameness of essential character **2** : individuality **3** : fact of being what is supposed

ide·ol·o·gy \ˌīdēˈäləjē, ˌid-\ *n, pl* **-gies** : body of beliefs — **ide·o·log·i·cal** \ˌīdēəˈläjikəl, ˌid-\ *adj*

id·i·om \ˈidēəm\ *n* **1** : language peculiar to a person or group **2** : expression with a special meaning — **id·i·om·at·ic** \ˌidēəˈmatik\ *adj* — **id·i·om·at·i·cal·ly** \-iklē\ *adv*

id·io·syn·cra·sy \ˌidēōˈsiŋkrəsē\ *n, pl* **-sies** : personal peculiarity — **id·io·syn·crat·ic** \-sinˈkratik\ *adj* — **id·io·syn·crat·i·cal·ly** \-ˈkrat-iklē\ *adv*

id·i·ot \ˈidēət\ *n* : mentally retarded or foolish person — **id·i·o·cy** \-əsē\ *n* — **id·i·ot·ic** \ˌidēˈätik\ *adj* — **id·i·ot·i·cal·ly** \-iklē\ *adv*

idle \ˈīdᵊl\ *adj* **idler; idlest 1** : worthless **2** : inactive **3** : lazy ~ *vb* **idled; idling** : spend time doing nothing — **idle·ness** *n* — **idler** *n* — **idly** \ˈīdlē\ *adv*

idol \ˈīdᵊl\ *n* **1** : image of a god **2** : object of devotion — **idol·iza-**

tion \ˌīdᵊlə'zāshən\ *n* — **idol·ize** \'īdᵊlīz\ *vb*

idol·a·ter, idol·a·tor \ī'dälətər\ *n* : worshiper of idols — **idol·a·trous** \-trəs\ *adj* — **idol·a·try** \-trē\ *n*

idyll \'īdᵊl\ *n* : period of peace and contentment — **idyl·lic** \ī'dilik\ *adj*

-ier — see -ER

if \'if\ *conj* 1 : in the event that 2 : whether 3 : even though

-i·fy \ə͵fī\ *vb suffix* : -fy

ig·loo \'iglü\ *n, pl* **-loos** : hut made of snow blocks

ig·nite \ig'nīt\ *vb* **-nit·ed; -nit·ing** : set afire or catch fire — **ig·nit·able** \-'nītəbəl\ *adj*

ig·ni·tion \ig'nishən\ *n* 1 : a setting on fire 2 : process or means of igniting fuel

ig·no·ble \ig'nōbəl\ *adj* : not honorable — **ig·no·bly** \-blē\ *adv*

ig·no·min·i·ous \ˌignə'minēəs\ *adj* 1 : dishonorable 2 : humiliating — **ig·no·min·i·ous·ly** *adv* — **ig·no·mi·ny** \'ignə͵minē, ig'nämənē\ *n*

ig·no·ra·mus \ˌignə'rāməs\ *n* : ignorant person

ig·no·rant \'ignərənt\ *adj* 1 : lacking knowledge 2 : showing a lack of knowledge or intelligence 3 : unaware — **ig·no·rance** \-rəns\ *n* — **ig·no·rant·ly** *adv*

◆ **ig·nore** \ig'nōr\ *vb* **-nored; -nor·ing** : refuse to notice

igua·na \i'gwänə\ *n* : large tropical American lizard

ilk \'ilk\ *n* : kind

ill \'il\ *adj* **worse** \'wərs\; **worst** \'wərst\ 1 : sick 2 : bad 3 : rude or unacceptable 4 : hostile ~ *adv* **worse; worst** 1 : with displeasure 2 : harshly 3 : scarcely 4 : badly ~ *n* 1 : evil 2 : misfortune 3 : sickness

il·le·gal \il'lēgəl\ *adj* : not lawful —

il·le·gal·i·ty \ˌili'galətē\ *n* — **il·le·gal·ly** \il'lēgəlē\ *adv*

il·leg·i·ble \il'lejəbəl\ *adj* : not legible — **il·leg·i·bil·i·ty** \il͵lejə'bilətē\ *n* — **il·leg·i·bly** \il'lejəblē\ *adv*

il·le·git·i·mate \ˌili'jitəmət\ *adj* 1 : born of unmarried parents 2 : illegal — **il·le·git·i·ma·cy** \-əməsē\ *n* — **il·le·git·i·mate·ly** *adv*

il·lic·it \il'lisət\ *adj* : not lawful — **il·lic·it·ly** *adv*

il·lim·it·able \il'limətəbəl\ *adj* : boundless — **il·lim·it·ably** \-blē\ *adv*

il·lit·er·ate \il'litərət\ *adj* : unable to read or write — **il·lit·er·a·cy** \-ərəsē\ *n* — **illiterate** *n*

ill-na·tured \-'nāchərd\ *adj* : cross — **ill-na·tured·ly** *adv*

ill·ness \'ilnəs\ *n* : sickness

il·log·i·cal \il'läjikəl\ *adj* : contrary to sound reasoning — **il·log·i·cal·ly** *adv*

ill-starred \'il'stärd\ *adj* : unlucky

il·lu·mi·nate \il'ümə͵nāt\ *vb* **-nat·ed; -nat·ing** 1 : light up 2 : make clear — **il·lu·mi·nat·ing·ly** \-͵nāt·iŋlē\ *adv* — **il·lu·mi·na·tion** \-͵ümə'nāshən\ *n*

ill-use \-'yüz\ *vb* : abuse — **ill-use** \-'yüs\ *n*

il·lu·sion \il'üzhən\ *n* 1 : mistaken idea 2 : misleading visual image

il·lu·so·ry \il'üsərē, -'üz-\ *adj* : based on or producing illusion

il·lus·trate \'iləs͵trāt\ *vb* **-trat·ed; -trat·ing** 1 : explain by example 2 : provide with pictures or figures — **il·lus·tra·tor** \-ər\ *n*

il·lus·tra·tion \ˌiləs'trāshən\ *n* 1 : example that explains 2 : pictorial explanation

il·lus·tra·tive \il'əstrətiv\ *adj* : designed to illustrate — **il·lus·tra·tive·ly** *adv*

il·lus·tri·ous \-trēəs\ *adj* : notably

or brilliantly outstanding — **il·lus·tri·ous·ness** n
ill will n : unfriendly feeling
im·age \'imij\ n 1 : likeness 2 : visual counterpart of an object formed by a lens or mirror 3 : mental picture ~ vb **-aged; -ag·ing** : create a representation of
im·ag·ery \'imijrē\ n 1 : images 2 : figurative language
imag·i·nary \im'ajə,nerē\ adj : existing only in the imagination
imag·i·na·tion \im,ajə'nāshən\ n 1 : act or power of forming a mental image 2 : creative ability — **imag·i·na·tive** \im'ajənətiv, -ə,nātiv\ adj — **imag·i·na·tive·ly** adv
imag·ine \im'ajən\ vb **-ined; -in·ing** : form a mental picture of something not present — **imag·in·able** \-'ajənəbəl\ adj — **imag·in·ably** \-blē\ adv
im·bal·ance \im'bəlans\ n : lack of balance
im·be·cile \'imbəsəl, -,sil\ n : idiot — **imbecile, im·be·cil·ic** \,imbə-'silik\ adj — **im·be·cil·i·ty** \-'silətē\ n
im·bibe \im'bīb\ vb **-bibed; -bib·ing** : drink — **im·bib·er** n
im·bro·glio \im'brōlyō\ n, pl **-glios** : complicated situation
im·bue \-'byü\ vb **-bued; -bu·ing** : fill (as with color or a feeling)
im·i·tate \'imə,tāt\ vb **-tat·ed; -tat·ing** 1 : follow as a model 2 : mimic — **im·i·ta·tive** \-,tātiv\ adj — **im·i·ta·tor** \-ər\ n
im·i·ta·tion \,imə'tāshən\ n 1 : act of imitating 2 : copy — **imitation** adj
im·mac·u·late \im'akyələt\ adj : without stain or blemish — **im·mac·u·late·ly** adv
im·ma·te·ri·al \,imə'tirēəl\ adj 1 : spiritual 2 : not relevant — **im·ma·te·ri·al·i·ty** \-,tirē'alətē\ n
im·ma·ture \,imə'tůr, -'tyůr\ adj : not yet mature — **im·ma·tu·ri·ty** \-ətē\ n
im·mea·sur·able \im'ezhərəbəl\ adj : indefinitely extensive — **im·mea·sur·ably** \-blē\ adv
im·me·di·a·cy \im'ēdēəsē\ n, pl **-cies** : quality or state of being urgent
im·me·di·ate \-ēət\ adj 1 : direct 2 : being next in line 3 : made or done at once 4 : not distant — **im·me·di·ate·ly** adv

im·me·mo·ri·al \,imə'mōrēəl\ adj : old beyond memory
im·mense \im'ens\ adj : vast — **im·mense·ly** adv — **im·men·si·ty** \-'ensətē\ n
im·merse \im'ərs\ vb **-mersed; -mers·ing** 1 : plunge or dip esp. into liquid 2 : engross — **im·mer·sion** \-'ərzhən\ n
im·mi·grant \'imigrənt\ n : one that immigrates
im·mi·grate \'imə,grāt\ vb **-grat·ed; -grat·ing** : come into a place and take up residence — **im·mi·gra·tion** \,imə'grāshən\ n
im·mi·nent \'imənənt\ adj : ready to take place — **im·mi·nence** \-nəns\ n — **im·mi·nent·ly** adv
im·mo·bile \im'ōbəl\ adj : incapable of being moved — **im·mo·bil·i·ty** \,imō'bilətē\ n — **im·mo·bi·lize** \im'ōbəlīz\ vb
im·mod·er·ate \im'ädərət\ adj : not moderate — **im·mod·er·a·cy** \-ərəsē\ n — **im·mod·er·ate·ly** adv
im·mod·est \im'ädəst\ adj : not modest — **im·mod·est·ly** adv — **im·mod·es·ty** \-əstē\ n
im·mo·late \'imə,lāt\ vb **-lat·ed; -lat·ing** : offer in sacrifice — **im·mo·la·tion** \,imə'lāshən\ n
im·mor·al \im'ȯrəl\ adj : not moral — **im·mo·ral·i·ty** \,imȯ'ralətē, ,imə-\ n — **im·mor·al·ly** adv
im·mor·tal \im'ȯrt°l\ adj 1 : not mortal 2 : having lasting fame ~ n : one exempt from death or oblivion — **im·mor·tal·i·ty** \,im,ȯr-'talətē\ n — **im·mor·tal·ize** \im-'ȯrt°l,īz\ vb
im·mov·able \im'üvəbəl\ adj 1 : stationary 2 : unyielding — **im·mov·abil·i·ty** \,im,üvə'bilətē\ n — **im·mov·ably** adv
im·mune \im'yün\ adj : not liable esp. to disease — **im·mu·ni·ty** \im'yünətē\ n — **im·mu·ni·za·tion** \,imyənə'zāshən\ n — **im·mu·nize** \'imyə,nīz\ vb
im·mu·nol·o·gy \,imyə'näləjē\ n : science of immunity to disease — **im·mu·no·log·ic** \-yən°l'äjik\, **im·mu·no·log·i·cal** \-ikəl\ adj — **im·mu·nol·o·gist** \,imyə'näləjist\ n
im·mu·ta·ble \im'yütəbəl\ adj : unchangeable — **im·mu·ta·bil·i·ty** \im,yütə'bilətē\ n — **im·mu·ta·bly** adv

imp \'imp\ *n* **1** : demon **2** : mischievous child

im·pact \im'pakt\ *vb* **1** : press close **2** : have an effect on ~ \'im,pakt\ *n* **1** : forceful contact **2** : influence

im·pact·ed \im'paktəd\ *adj* : wedged between the jawbone and another tooth

im·pair \im'par\ *vb* : diminish in quantity, value, or ability — **im·pair·ment** *n*

im·pa·la \im'palə\ *n, pl* **impalas** *or* **impala** : large African antelope

im·pale \im'pāl\ *vb* **-paled; -paling** : pierce with something pointed

im·pal·pa·ble \im'palpəbəl\ *adj* : incapable of being felt — **im·pal·pa·bly** *adv*

im·pan·el \im'pan°l\ *vb* : enter in or on a panel

im·part \-'pärt\ *vb* : give from or as if from a store

im·par·tial \im'pärshəl\ *adj* : not partial — **im·par·ti·al·i·ty** \im,pärshē'alətē\ *n* — **im·par·tial·ly** *adv*

im·pass·able \im'pasəbəl\ *adj* : not passable — **im·pass·ably** \-'pasəblē\ *adv*

im·passe \'im,pas\ *n* : inescapable predicament

im·pas·sioned \im'pashənd\ *adj* : filled with passion

im·pas·sive \im'pasiv\ *adj* : showing no feeling or interest — **im·pas·sive·ly** *adv* — **im·pas·siv·i·ty** \,im,pas'ivətē\ *n*

im·pa·tiens \im'pāshənz, -shəns\ *n* : annual herb with showy flowers

im·pa·tient \im'pāshənt\ *adj* : not patient — **im·pa·tience** \-shəns\ *n* — **im·pa·tient·ly** *adv*

im·peach \im'pēch\ *vb* **1** : charge (an official) with misconduct **2** : cast doubt on **3** : remove from office for misconduct — **im·peach·ment** *n*

im·pec·ca·ble \im'pekəbəl\ *adj* : faultless — **im·pec·ca·bly** *adv*

im·pe·cu·nious \,impi'kyünēəs\ *adj* : broke — **im·pe·cu·nious·ness** *n*

im·pede \im'pēd\ *vb* **-ped·ed; -ped·ing** : interfere with

im·ped·i·ment \-'pedəmənt\ *n* **1** : hindrance **2** : speech defect

im·pel \-'pel\ *vb* **-pelled; -pel·ling** : urge forward

im·pend \-'pend\ *vb* : be about to occur

im·pen·e·tra·ble \im'penətrəbəl\ *adj* : incapable of being penetrated or understood — **im·pen·e·tra·bil·i·ty** \im,penətrə'bilətē\ *n* — **im·pen·e·tra·bly** *adv*

im·pen·i·tent \im'penətənt\ *adj* : not penitent — **im·pen·i·tence** \-təns\ *n*

im·per·a·tive \im'perətiv\ *adj* **1** : expressing a command **2** : urgent ~ *n* **1** : imperative mood or verb form **2** : unavoidable fact, need, or obligation — **im·per·a·tive·ly** *adv*

im·per·cep·ti·ble \,impər'septəbəl\ *adj* : not perceptible — **im·per·cep·ti·bly** *adv*

im·per·fect \im'pərfikt\ *adj* : not perfect — **im·per·fec·tion** *n* — **im·per·fect·ly** *adv*

im·pe·ri·al \im'pirēəl\ *adj* **1** : relating to an empire or an emperor **2** : royal

im·pe·ri·al·ism \im'pirēə,lizəm\ *n* : policy of controlling other nations — **im·pe·ri·al·ist** \-list\ *n or adj* — **im·pe·ri·al·is·tic** \-,pirēə'listik\ *adj* — **im·pe·ri·al·is·ti·cal·ly** \-tiklē\ *adv*

im·per·il \im'perəl\ *vb* **-iled** *or* **-illed; -il·ing** *or* **-il·ling** : endanger

im·pe·ri·ous \im'pirēəs\ *adj* : arrogant or domineering — **im·pe·ri·ous·ly** *adv*

im·per·ish·able \im'perishəbəl\ *adj* : not perishable

im·per·ma·nent \-'pərmənənt\ *adj* : not permanent — **im·per·ma·nent·ly** *adv*

im·per·me·able \-'pərmēəbəl\ *adj* : not permeable

im·per·mis·si·ble \,impər'misəbəl\ *adj* : not permissible

im·per·son·al \im'pərs°nəl\ *adj* : not involving human personality or emotion — **im·per·son·al·i·ty** \im,pərs°n'alətē\ *n* — **im·per·son·al·ly** *adv*

im·per·son·ate \im'pərs°n,āt\ *vb* **-at·ed; -at·ing** : assume the character of — **im·per·son·a·tion** \-,pərs°n'āshən\ *n* — **im·per·son·a·tor** \-'pərs°n,ātər\ *n*

im·per·ti·nent \im'pərt°nənt\ *adj* **1** : irrelevant **2** : insolent — **im·per·ti·nence** \-°nəns\ *n* — **im·per·ti·nent·ly** *adv*

im·per·turb·able \,impər'tərbəbəl\ *adj* : calm and steady

im·per·vi·ous \im'pərvēəs\ *adj* : incapable of being penetrated or affected

im·pet·u·ous \im'pechəwəs\ *adj* : impulsive — **im·pet·u·os·i·ty** \im,pechə'wäsətē\ *n* — **im·pet·u·ous·ly** *adv*

im·pe·tus \'impətəs\ *n* : driving force

im·pi·ety \im'pīətē\ *n* : quality or state of being impious

im·pinge \im'pinj\ *vb* -pinged; -ping·ing : encroach — **im·pinge·ment** \-mənt\ *n*

im·pi·ous \'impēəs, im'pī-\ *adj* : not pious

imp·ish \'impish\ *adj* : mischievous — **imp·ish·ly** *adv* — **imp·ish·ness** *n*

im·pla·ca·ble \im'plakəbəl, -'plā-\ *adj* : not capable of being appeased or changed — **im·pla·ca·bil·i·ty** \im,plakə'bilətē, -,plā-\ *n* — **im·pla·ca·bly** \im'plakəblē\ *adv*

im·plant \im'plant\ *vb* 1 : set firmly or deeply 2 : fix in the mind or spirit ~ \'im,plant\ *n* : something implanted in tissue — **im·plan·ta·tion** \,im,plan'tāshən\ *n*

im·plau·si·ble \im'plòzəbəl\ *adj* : not plausible — **im·plau·si·bil·i·ty** \im,plòzə'bilətē\ *n*

im·ple·ment \'impləmənt\ *n* : tool, utensil ~ \-,ment\ *vb* : put into practice — **im·ple·men·ta·tion** \,impləmən'tāshən\ *n*

im·pli·cate \'implə,kāt\ *vb* -cat·ed; -cat·ing : involve

im·pli·ca·tion \,implə'kāshən\ *n* 1 : an implying 2 : something implied

im·plic·it \im'plisət\ *adj* 1 : understood though only implied 2 : complete and unquestioning — **im·plic·it·ly** *adv*

im·plode \im'plōd\ *vb* -plod·ed; -plod·ing : burst inward — **im·plo·sion** \-'plōzhən\ *n* — **im·plo·sive** \-'plōsiv\ *adj*

im·plore \im'plōr\ *vb* -plored; -plor·ing : entreat

im·ply \-'plī\ *vb* -plied; -ply·ing : express indirectly

im·po·lite \,impə'līt\ *adj* : not polite

im·pol·i·tic \im'pälə,tik\ *adj* : not politic

im·pon·der·a·ble \im'pändərəbəl\ *adj* : incapable of being precisely evaluated — **imponderable** *n*

im·port \im'pōrt\ *vb* 1 : mean 2 : bring in from an external source ~ \'im,pōrt\ *n* 1 : meaning 2 : importance 3 : something imported — **im·por·ta·tion** \,im,pór-'tāshən\ *n* — **im·port·er** *n*

im·por·tant \im'pórtənt\ *adj* : having great worth, significance, or influence — **im·por·tance** \-°ns\ *n* — **im·por·tant·ly** *adv*

im·por·tu·nate \im'pórchənət\ *adj* : troublesomely persistent or urgent

im·por·tune \,impər'tün, -'tyün; im'pórchən\ *vb* -tuned; -tun·ing : urge or beg persistently — **im·por·tu·ni·ty** \,impər'tünətē, -'tyü-\ *n*

im·pose \im'pōz\ *vb* -posed; -pos·ing 1 : establish as compulsory 2 : take unwarranted advantage of — **im·po·si·tion** \,impə'zishən\ *n*

im·pos·ing \im'pōziŋ\ *adj* : impressive — **im·pos·ing·ly** *adv*

im·pos·si·ble \im'päsəbəl\ *adj* 1 : incapable of occurring 2 : enormously difficult — **im·pos·si·bil·i·ty** \im,päsə'bilətē\ *n* — **im·pos·si·bly** \im'päsəblē\ *adv*

im·post \'im,pōst\ *n* : tax

im·pos·tor, im·pos·ter \im'pästər\ *n* : one who assumes an identity or title to deceive — **im·pos·ture** \-'päschər\ *n*

im·po·tent \'impətənt\ *adj* 1 : lacking power 2 : sterile — **im·po·tence** \-pətəns\ *n* — **im·po·ten·cy** \-ənsē\ *n* — **im·po·tent·ly** *adv*

im·pound \im'paùnd\ *vb* : seize and hold in legal custody — **im·pound·ment** *n*

im·pov·er·ish \im'pävərish\ *vb* : make poor — **im·pov·er·ish·ment** *n*

im·prac·ti·ca·ble \im'praktikəbəl\ *adj* : not practicable

im·prac·ti·cal \-'praktikəl\ *adj* : not practical

im·pre·cise \,impri'sīs\ *adj* : not precise — **im·pre·cise·ly** *adv* — **im·pre·cise·ness** *n* — **im·pre·ci·sion** \-'sizhən\ *n*

im·preg·na·ble \im'pregnəbəl\ *adj* : able to resist attack — **im·preg·na·bil·i·ty** \im,pregnə'bilətē\ *n*

im·preg·nate \im'preg,nāt\ *vb* -nat-

ed; -nat·ing 1 : make pregnant 2
: cause to be filled, permeated, or
saturated — im·preg·na·tion \,im-
,preg'nāshən\ n

im·pre·sa·rio \,imprə'särē,ō\ n, pl
-ri·os : one who sponsors an entertainment

♦ ¹im·press \im'pres\ vb 1 : apply
with or produce by pressure 2
: press, stamp, or print in or upon
3 : produce a vivid impression of 4
: affect (as the mind) forcibly

²im·press \im'pres\ vb : force into
naval service — im·press·ment n

im·pres·sion \im'preshən\ n 1
: mark made by impressing 2
: marked influence or effect 3
: printed copy 4 : vague notion or
recollection — im·pres·sion·able
\-'preshənəbəl\ adj

im·pres·sive \im'presiv\ adj : making a marked impression — im-
pres·sive·ly adv — im·pres·sive-
ness n

im·pri·ma·tur \,imprə'mä,tùr\ n
: official approval (as of a publication by a censor)

im·print \im'print, 'im,-\ vb : stamp
or mark by or as if by pressure ∼
\'im,-\ n : something imprinted or
printed

im·pris·on \im'priz°n\ vb : put in
prison — im·pris·on·ment
\-mənt\ n

im·prob·a·ble \im'präbəbəl\ adj
: unlikely to be true or to occur —
im·prob·a·bil·i·ty \im,präbə'bil-
ətē\ n — im·prob·a·bly adv

im·promp·tu \im'prämptü, -tyü\
adj : not planned beforehand —
impromptu adv or n

im·prop·er \im'präpər\ adj : not
proper — im·prop·er·ly adv

im·pro·pri·ety \,imprə'prīətē\ n, pl
-eties : state or instance of being
improper

im·prove \im'prüv\ vb -proved;
-proving : grow or make better —
im·prov·able \-'prüvəbəl\ adj —
im·prove·ment n

im·prov·i·dent \im'prävədənt\ adj
: not providing for the future —
im·prov·i·dence \-əns\ n

im·pro·vise \'imprə,vīz\ vb -vised;
-vis·ing : make, invent, or arrange
offhand — im·pro·vi·sa·tion \,im-
,prävə'zäshən, ,imprəvə-\ n — im-
pro·vis·er, im·pro·vi·sor \'imprə-
,vīzər\ n

im·pru·dent \im'prüd°nt\ adj : not
prudent — im·pru·dence \-°ns\ n

im·pu·dent \'impyədənt\ adj : insolent — im·pu·dence \-əns\ n —
im·pu·dent·ly adv

im·pugn \im'pyün\ vb : attack as
false

im·pulse \'im,pəls\ n 1 : moving
force 2 : sudden inclination

im·pul·sive \im'pəlsiv\ adj : acting
on impulse — im·pul·sive·ly adv
— im·pul·sive·ness n

im·pu·ni·ty \im'pyünətē\ n : exemption from punishment or
harm

im·pure \im'pyùr\ adj : not pure —
im·pu·ri·ty \-'pyùrətē\ n

im·pute \im'pyüt\ vb -put·ed; -put-
ing : credit to or blame on a person or cause — im·pu·ta·tion
\,impyə'tāshən\ n

in \'in\ prep 1 — used to indicate location, inclusion, situation, or
manner 2 : into 3 : during ∼ adv
: to or toward the inside ∼ adj
: located inside

in- \in\ prefix 1 : not 2 : lack of

inability	inadequacy
inaccessibility	inadequate
inaccessible	inadequately
inaccuracy	inadmissibility
inaccurate	inadmissible
inaction	inadvisability
inactive	inadvisable
inactivity	inapparent

inapplicable
inapposite
inappositely
inappositeness
inappreciative
inapproachable
inappropriate
inappropriately
inappropriate-
ness
inapt
inarguable
inartistic
inartistically
inattentive
inattentively
inattentiveness
inaudible
inaudibly
inauspicious
inauthentic
incapability
incapable
incautious
incoherence
incoherent
incoherently
incombustible
incommensu-
rate
incommodious
incommunica-
ble
incompatibility
incompatible
incomplete
incompletely
incompleteness
incomprehensi-
ble
inconclusive
incongruent
inconsecutive
inconsiderate
inconsiderately
inconsiderate-
ness
inconsistency
inconsistent
inconsistently
inconspicuous
inconspicuous-
ly
inconstancy
inconstant
inconstantly
inconsumable
incontestable
incontestably

incorporeal
incorporeally
incorrect
incorrectly
incorrectness
incorruptible
inculpable
incurable
incurious
indecency
indecent
indecently
indecipherable
indecisive
indecisively
indecisiveness
indecorous
indecorously
indecorousness
indefensible
indefinable
indefinably
indescribable
indescribably
indestructibili-
ty
indestructible
indigestible
indiscernible
indiscreet
indiscreetly
indiscretion
indisputable
indisputably
indistinct
indistinctly
indistinctness
indivisibility
indivisible
ineducable
ineffective
ineffectively
ineffectiveness
ineffectual
ineffectually
ineffectualness
inefficiency
inefficient
inefficiently
inelastic
inelasticity
inelegance
inelegant
ineligibility
ineligible
ineradicable
inessential
inexact
inexactly

inexpedient
inexpensive
inexperience
inexperienced
inexpert
inexpertly
inexpertness
inexplicable
inexplicably
inexplicit
inexpressible
inexpressibly
inextinguish-
able
inextricable
infeasibility
infeasible
infelicitous
infelicity
infertile
infertility
inflexibility
inflexible
inflexibly
infrequent
infrequently
inglorious
ingloriously
ingratitude
inhumane
inhumanely
injudicious
injudiciously
injudiciousness
inoffensive
inoperable

inoperative
insalubrious
insensitive
insensitivity
inseparable
insignificant
insincere
insincerely
insincerity
insolubility
insoluble
instability
insubstantial
insufficiency
insufficient
insufficiently
insupportable
intangibility
intangible
intangibly
intolerable
intolerably
intolerance
intolerant
intractable
invariable
invariably
inviable
invisibility
invisible
invisibly
involuntarily
involuntary
invulnerability
invulnerable
invulnerably

in·ad·ver·tent \ˌinəd'vərt°nt\ *adj*
: unintentional — **in·ad·ver·tence**
\-°ns\ *n* — **in·ad·ver·ten·cy**
\-°nsē\ *n* — **in·ad·ver·tent·ly** *adv*

in·alien·able \in'ālyənəbəl,
-'ālēənə-\ *adj* : incapable of being
transferred or given up — **in-
alien·abil·i·ty** \in‚ālyənə'bilətē,
-'ālēənə-\ *n* — **in·alien·ably** *adv*

inane \in'ān\ *adj* **inan·er; -est** : silly
or stupid — **inan·i·ty** \in'anətē\ *n*

in·an·i·mate \in'anəmət\ *adj* : not
animate or animated — **in·an·i-
mate·ly** *adv* — **in·an·i·mate·ness**
n

in·ap·pre·cia·ble \ˌinə'prēshəbəl\
adj : too small to be perceived —
in·ap·pre·cia·bly *adv*

in·ar·tic·u·late \ˌinär'tikyələt\ *adj*
: without the power of speech or
effective expression — **in·ar·tic-
u·late·ly** *adv*

in·as·much as \ˌinaz'məchaz\ *conj*
: because

in·at·ten·tion \ˌinə'tenchən\ *n* : failure to pay attention

in·au·gu·ral \in'ógyərəl, -gərəl\ *adj* : relating to an inauguration ～ *n* 1 : inaugural speech 2 : inauguration

in·au·gu·rate \in'ógyə₁rāt, -gə-\ *vb* -rat·ed; -rat·ing 1 : install in office 2 : start — **in·au·gu·ra·tion** \-₁ógyə'rāshən, -gə-\ *n*

in·board \'in₁bōrd\ *adv* : inside a vehicle or craft — **inboard** *adj*

in·born \'in₁bórn\ *adj* : present from birth

in·bred \'in₁bred\ *adj* : deeply ingrained in one's nature

in·breed·ing \'in₁brēdiŋ\ *n* : interbreeding of closely related individuals — **in·breed** \-₁brēd\ *vb*

in·cal·cu·la·ble \in'kalkyələbəl\ *adj* : too large to be calculated — **in·cal·cu·la·bly** *adv*

in·can·des·cent \ˌinkən'des°nt\ *adj* 1 : glowing with heat 2 : brilliant — **in·can·des·cence** \-°ns\ *n*

in·can·ta·tion \ˌin₁kan'tāshən\ *n* : use of spoken or sung charms or spells as a magic ritual

in·ca·pac·i·tate \ˌinkə'pasə₁tāt\ *vb* -tat·ed; -tat·ing : disable

in·ca·pac·i·ty \ˌinkə'pasətē\ *n, pl* -ties : quality or state of being incapable

in·car·cer·ate \in'kärsə₁rāt\ *vb* -at·ed; -at·ing : imprison — **in·car·cer·a·tion** \in₁kärsə'rāshən\ *n*

in·car·nate \in'kärnət, -₁nāt\ *adj* : having bodily form and substance — **in·car·nate** \-₁nāt\ *vb* — **in·car·na·tion** \-₁kär'nāshən\ *n*

in·cen·di·ary \in'sendē₁erē\ *adj* 1 : pertaining to or used to ignite fire 2 : tending to excite — **incendiary** *n*

in·cense \'in₁sens\ *n* : material burned to produce a fragrant odor or its smoke ～ \in'sens\ *vb* -censed; -cens·ing : make very angry

in·cen·tive \in'sentive\ *n* : inducement to do something

in·cep·tion \in'sepshən\ *n* : beginning

in·ces·sant \in'ses°nt\ *adj* : continuing without interruption — **in·ces·sant·ly** *adv*

in·cest \'in₁sest\ *n* : sexual intercourse between close relatives — **in·ces·tu·ous** \in'seschəwəs\ *adj*

inch \'inch\ *n* : unit of length equal to ¹⁄₁₂ foot ～ *vb* : move by small degrees

in·cho·ate \in'kōət, 'inkə₁wāt\ *adj* : new and not fully formed or ordered

in·ci·dent \'insədənt\ *n* : occurrence — **in·ci·dence** \-əns\ *n* — **incident** *adj*

in·ci·den·tal \ˌinsə'dent°l\ *adj* 1 : subordinate, nonessential, or attendant 2 : met by chance ～ *n* 1 : something incidental 2 *pl* : minor expenses that are not itemized — **in·ci·den·tal·ly** *adv*

in·cin·er·ate \in'sinə₁rāt\ *vb* -at·ed; -at·ing : burn to ashes — **in·cin·er·a·tor** \-₁rātər\ *n*

in·cip·i·ent \in'sipēənt\ *adj* : beginning to be or appear

in·cise \in'sīz\ *vb* -cised; -cis·ing : carve into

in·ci·sion \in'sizhən\ *n* : surgical cut

in·ci·sive \in'sīsiv\ *adj* : keen and discerning — **in·ci·sive·ly** *adv*

in·ci·sor \in'sīzər\ *n* : tooth for cutting

in·cite \in'sīt\ *vb* -cit·ed; -cit·ing : arouse to action — **in·cite·ment** *n*

in·ci·vil·i·ty \ˌinsə'vilətē\ *n* : rudeness

in·clem·ent \in'klemənt\ *adj* : stormy — **in·clem·en·cy** \-ənsē\ *n*

in·cline \in'klīn\ *vb* -clined; -clin·ing 1 : bow 2 : tend toward an opinion 3 : slope ～ *n* : slope — **in·cli·na·tion** \ˌinklə'nāshən\ *n* — **in·clin·er** *n*

inclose, inclosure *var of* ENCLOSE, ENCLOSURE

in·clude \in'klüd\ *vb* -clud·ed; -clud·ing : take in or comprise — **in·clu·sion** \in'klüzhən\ *n* — **in·clu·sive** \-'klüsiv\ *adj*

in·cog·ni·to \ˌin₁käg'nētō, in'kägnə₁tō\ *adv or adj* : with one's identity concealed

in·come \'in₁kəm\ *n* : money gained (as from work or investment)

in·com·ing \'in₁kəmiŋ\ *adj* : coming in

in·com·mu·ni·ca·do \ˌinkə₁myünə-'kädō\ *adv or adj* : without means of communication

in·com·pa·ra·ble \in'kämpərəbəl\ *adj* : eminent beyond comparison

♦ **in·com·pe·tent** \in'kämpətənt\ *adj* : lacking sufficient knowledge or skill — **in·com·pe·tence** \-pətəns\ *n* — **in·com·pe·ten·cy** \-ənsē\ *n* — **incompetent** *n*

in·con·ceiv·able \ˌinkən'sēvəbəl\ *adj* 1 : impossible to comprehend 2 : unbelievable — **in·con·ceiv·ably** \-blē\ *adv*

in·con·gru·ous \in'käŋgrəwəs\ *adj* : inappropriate or out of place — **in·con·gru·i·ty** \ˌinkən'grüətē, -ˌkän-\ *n* — **in·con·gru·ous·ly** *adv*

in·con·se·quen·tial \ˌin,känə-'kwenchəl\ *adj* : unimportant — **in·con·se·quence** \in'känə,kwens\ *n* — **in·con·se·quen·tial·ly** *adv*

in·con·sid·er·able \ˌinkən'sidər-əbəl\ *adj* : trivial

in·con·sol·able \ˌinkən'sōləbəl\ *adj* : incapable of being consoled — **in·con·sol·ably** *adv*

in·con·ve·nience \ˌinkən'vēnyəns\ *n* 1 : discomfort 2 : something that causes trouble or annoyance ~ *vb* : cause inconvenience to — **in·con·ve·nient** \ˌinkən'vēnyənt\ *adj* — **in·con·ve·nient·ly** *adv*

in·cor·po·rate \in'kórpə,rāt\ *vb* -rat·ed; -rat·ing 1 : blend 2 : form into a legal body — **in·cor·po·rat·ed** *adj* — **in·cor·po·ra·tion** \-ˌkórpə'rāshən\ *n*

in·cor·ri·gi·ble \in'kórəjəbəl\ *adj* : incapable of being corrected or reformed — **in·cor·ri·gi·bil·i·ty** \in,kórəjə'bilətē\ *n*

in·crease \in'krēs, 'in,krēs\ *vb* -creased; -creas·ing : make or become greater ~ \'in,-, in'-\ *n* 1 : enlargement in size 2 : something added — **in·creas·ing·ly** \-'krēs-iŋlē\ *adv*

in·cred·i·ble \in'kredəbəl\ *adj* : too extraordinary to be believed —

in·cred·ibil·i·ty \in,kredə'bilətē\ *n* — **in·cred·i·bly** \in'kredəblē\ *adv*

in·cred·u·lous \in'krejələs\ *adj* : skeptical — **in·cre·du·li·ty** \ˌinkri'dülətē, -'dyü-\ *n* — **in·cred·u·lous·ly** *adv*

in·cre·ment \'iŋkrəmənt, 'in-\ *n* : increase or amount of increase — **in·cre·men·tal** \ˌiŋkrə'mentᵊl, ˌin-\ *adj*

in·crim·i·nate \in'krimə,nāt\ *vb* -nat·ed; -nat·ing : show to be guilty of a crime — **in·crim·i·na·tion** \-,krimə'nāshən\ *n* — **in·crim·i·na·to·ry** \-'krimənə,tōrē\ *adj*

in·cu·bate \'iŋkyə,bāt, 'in-\ *vb* -bat·ed; -bat·ing : keep (as eggs) under conditions favorable for development — **in·cu·ba·tion** \ˌiŋkyə-'bāshən, ˌin-\ *n* — **in·cu·ba·tor** \'iŋkyə,bātər, 'in-\ *n*

in·cul·cate \in'kəl,kāt, 'in,kəl-\ *vb* -cat·ed; -cat·ing : instill by repeated teaching — **in·cul·ca·tion** \ˌin,kəl'kāshən\ *n*

in·cum·bent \in'kəmbənt\ *n* : holder of an office ~ *adj* : obligatory — **in·cum·ben·cy** \-bənsē\ *n*

in·cur \in'kər\ *vb* -rr- : become liable or subject to

in·cur·sion \in'kərzhən\ *n* : invasion

in·debt·ed \in'detəd\ *adj* : owing something — **in·debt·ed·ness** *n*

in·de·ci·sion \ˌindi'sizhən\ *n* : inability to decide

in·deed \in'dēd\ *adv* : without question

in·de·fat·i·ga·ble \ˌindi'fatigəbəl\ *adj* : not tiring — **in·de·fat·i·ga·bly** \-blē\ *adv*

in·def·i·nite \in'defənət\ *adj* 1 : not defining or identifying 2 : not precise 3 : having no fixed limit — **in·def·i·nite·ly** *adv*

in·del·i·ble \in'deləbəl\ *adj* : not capable of being removed or erased — **in·del·i·bly** *adv*

in·del·i·cate \in'delikət\ *adj* : improper — **in·del·i·ca·cy** \in-'deləkəsē\ *n*

in·dem·ni·fy \in'demnə,fī\ *vb* **-fied; -fy·ing** : repay for a loss — **in·dem·ni·fi·ca·tion** \-,demnəfə'kā-shən\ *n*

in·dem·ni·ty \in'demnətē\ *n, pl* **-ties** : security against loss or damage

¹**in·dent** \in'dent\ *vb* : leave a space at the beginning of a paragraph

²**indent** *vb* : force inward so as to form a depression or dent

in·den·ta·tion \,in,den'tashən\ *n* **1** : notch, recess, or dent **2** : action of indenting **3** : space at the beginning of a paragraph

in·den·ture \in'denchər\ *n* : contract binding one person to work for another for a given period — usu. in pl. ~ *vb* **-tured; -tur·ing** : bind by indentures

Independence Day *n* : July 4 observed as a legal holiday in commemoration of the adoption of the Declaration of Independence in 1776

in·de·pen·dent \,ində'pendənt\ *adj* **1** : not governed by another **2** : not requiring or relying on something or somebody else **3** : not easily influenced — **in·de·pen·dence** \-dəns\ *n* — **independent** *n* — **in·de·pen·dent·ly** *adv*

in·de·ter·mi·nate \,indi'tərmənət\ *adj* : not definitely determined — **in·de·ter·mi·na·cy** \-nəsē\ *n* — **in·de·ter·mi·nate·ly** *adv*

in·dex \'in,deks\ *n, pl* **-dex·es** *or* **-di·ces** \-də,sēz\ **1** : alphabetical list of items (as topics in a book) **2** : a number that serves as a measure or indicator of something ~ *vb* **1** : provide with an index **2** : serve as an index of

index finger *n* : forefinger

in·di·cate \'ində,kāt\ *vb* **-cat·ed; -cat·ing 1** : point out or to **2** : show indirectly **3** : state briefly — **in·di·ca·tion** \,ində'kāshən\ *n* — **in·di·ca·tor** \'ində,kātər\ *n*

in·dic·a·tive \in'dikətiv\ *adj* : serving to indicate

in·dict \in'dīt\ *vb* : charge with a crime — **in·dict·able** *adj* — **in·dict·ment** *n*

in·dif·fer·ent \in'difrənt\ *adj* **1** : having no preference **2** : showing neither interest nor dislike **3** : mediocre — **in·dif·fer·ence** \-'difrəns\ *n* — **in·dif·fer·ent·ly** *adv*

in·dig·e·nous \in'dijənəs\ *adj* : native to a particular region

in·di·gent \'indijənt\ *adj* : needy — **in·di·gence** \-jəns\ *n*

in·di·ges·tion \,indī'jeschən, -də-\ *n* : discomfort from inability to digest food

in·dig·na·tion \,indig'nāshən\ *n* : anger aroused by something unjust or unworthy — **in·dig·nant** \in'dignənt\ *adj* — **in·dig·nant·ly** *adv*

in·dig·ni·ty \in'dignətē\ *n, pl* **-ties 1** : offense against self-respect **2** : humiliating treatment

in·di·go \'indi,gō\ *n, pl* **-gos** *or* **-goes 1** : blue dye **2** : deep reddish blue color

in·di·rect \,ində'rekt, -dī-\ *adj* : not straight or straightforward — **in·di·rec·tion** \-'rekshən\ *n* — **in·di·rect·ly** *adv* — **in·di·rect·ness** *n*

in·dis·crim·i·nate \,indis'krimənət\ *adj* **1** : not careful or discriminating **2** : haphazard — **in·dis·crim·i·nate·ly** *adv*

in·dis·pens·able \,indis'penəbəl\ *adj* : absolutely essential — **in·dis·pens·abil·i·ty** \-,penə'bilətē\ *n* — **indispensable** *n* — **in·dis·pens·ably** \-'penəblē\ *adv*

in·dis·posed \-'pōzd\ *adj* : slightly ill — **in·dis·po·si·tion** \in,dispə-'zishən\ *n*

in·dis·sol·u·ble \,indis'älyəbəl\ *adj* : not capable of being dissolved or broken

in·di·vid·u·al \,ində'vijəwəl\ *n* **1** : single member of a category **2** : person — **individual** *adj* — **in·di·vid·u·al·ly** *adv*

in·di·vid·u·al·ist \-əwəlist\ *n* : person who is markedly independent in thought or action

in·di·vid·u·al·i·ty \-,vijə'walətē\ *n* : special quality that distinguishes an individual

in·di·vid·u·al·ize \-'vijəwə,līz\ *vb* **-ized; -iz·ing 1** : make individual **2** : treat individually

in·doc·tri·nate \in'däktrə,nāt\ *vb* **-nat·ed; -nat·ing** : instruct in fundamentals (as of a doctrine) —

in·doc·tri·na·tion \in,däktrə'nā-shən\ *n*

in·do·lent \'indələnt\ *adj* : lazy — **in·do·lence** \-ləns\ *n*

in·dom·i·ta·ble \in'dämətəbəl\ *adj* : invincible — **in·dom·i·ta·bly** \-blē\ *adv*

in·door \'in'dōr\ *adj* : relating to the inside of a building

in·doors \in'dōrz\ *adv* : in or into a building

in·du·bi·ta·ble \in'dübətəbəl, -'dyü-\ *adj* : being beyond question — **in·du·bi·ta·bly** \-blē\ *adv*

in·duce \in'düs, -'dyüs\ *vb* -**duced**; -**duc·ing 1** : persuade **2** : bring about — **in·duce·ment** *n* — **in·duc·er** *n*

in·duct \in'dəkt\ *vb* **1** : put in office **2** : admit as a member **3** : enroll (as for military service) — **in·duct·ee** \in,dək'tē\ *n*

in·duc·tion \in'dəkshən\ *n* **1** : act or instance of inducting **2** : reasoning from particular instances to a general conclusion

in·duc·tive \in'dəktiv\ *adj* : reasoning by induction

in·dulge \in'dəlj\ *vb* -**dulged**; -**dulg·ing** : yield to the desire of or for — **in·dul·gence** \-'dəljəns\ *n* — **in·dul·gent** \-jənt\ *adj* — **in·dul·gent·ly** *adv*

in·dus·tri·al \in'dəstrēəl\ *adj* **1** : relating to industry **2** : heavy-duty — **in·dus·tri·al·ist** \-əlist\ *n* — **in·dus·tri·al·iza·tion** \-,dəstrēələ-'zāshən\ *n* — **in·dus·tri·al·ize** \-'dəstrēə,līz\ *vb* — **in·dus·tri·al·ly** *adv*

in·dus·tri·ous \in'dəstrēəs\ *adj* : diligent or busy — **in·dus·tri·ous·ly** *adv* — **in·dus·tri·ous·ness** *n*

in·dus·try \'indəstrē\ *n, pl* -**tries 1** : diligence **2** : manufacturing enterprises or activity

in·ebri·at·ed \i'nēbrē,ātəd\ *adj* : drunk — **in·ebri·a·tion** \-,ēbrē-'āshən\ *n*

in·ef·fa·ble \in'efəbəl\ *adj* : incapable of being expressed in words — **in·ef·fa·bly** \-blē\ *adv*

in·ept \in'ept\ *adj* **1** : inappropriate or foolish **2** : generally incompetent — **in·ep·ti·tude** \in'eptə,tüd, -,tyüd\ *n* — **in·ept·ly** *adv* — **in·ept·ness** *n*

in·equal·i·ty \,ini'kwälətē\ *n* : quality of being unequal or uneven

in·ert \in'ərt\ *adj* **1** : powerless to move or act **2** : sluggish — **in·ert·ly** *adv* — **in·ert·ness** *n*

in·er·tia \in'ərshə\ *n* : tendency of matter to remain at rest or in motion — **in·er·tial** \-shəl\ *adj*

in·es·cap·able \,inə'skāpəbəl\ *adj* : inevitable — **in·es·cap·ably** \-blē\ *adv*

in·es·ti·ma·ble \in'estəməbəl\ *adj* : incapable of being estimated — **in·es·ti·ma·bly** \-blē\ *adv*

in·ev·i·ta·ble \in'evətəbəl\ *adj* : incapable of being avoided or escaped — **in·ev·i·ta·bil·i·ty** \in-,evətə'bilətē\ *n* — **in·ev·i·ta·bly** \in'evətəblē\ *adv*

in·ex·cus·able \,inik'skyüzəbəl\ *adj* : being without excuse or justification — **in·ex·cus·ably** \-blē\ *adv*

in·ex·haust·ible \,inig'zóstəbəl\ *adj* : incapable of being used up or tired out — **in·ex·haust·ibly** \-blē\ *adv*

in·ex·o·ra·ble \in'eksərəbəl\ *adj* : unyielding or relentless — **in·ex·o·ra·bly** *adv*

in·fal·li·ble \in'faləbəl\ *adj* : incapable of error — **in·fal·li·bil·i·ty** \in,falə'bilətē\ *n* — **in·fal·li·bly** *adv*

in·fa·mous \'infəməs\ *adj* : having the worst kind of reputation — **in·fa·mous·ly** *adv*

in·fa·my \-mē\ *n, pl* -**mies** : evil reputation

in·fan·cy \'infənsē\ *n, pl* -**cies 1** : early childhood **2** : early period of existence

in·fant \'infənt\ *n* : baby

in·fan·tile \'infən,tīl, -t⁰l, -,tēl\ *adj* **1** : relating to infants **2** : childish

in·fan·try \'infəntrē\ *n, pl* -**tries** : soldiers that fight on foot

in·fat·u·ate \in'fachə,wāt\ *vb* -**at·ed**; -**at·ing** : inspire with foolish love or admiration — **in·fat·u·a·tion** \-,fachə'wāshən\ *n*

in·fect \in'fekt\ *vb* : contaminate with disease-producing matter — **in·fec·tion** \-'fekshən\ *n* — **in·fec·tious** \-shəs\ *adj* — **in·fec·tive** \-'fektiv\ *adj*

in·fer \in'fər\ *vb* -**rr**- : deduce — **in·fer·ence** \'infərəns\ *n* — **in·fer·en·tial** \,infə'renchəl\ *adj*

in·fe·ri·or \in'firēər\ *adj* **1** : being lower in position, degree, rank, or merit **2** : of lesser quality — **infe-**

rior *n* — **in·fe·ri·or·i·ty** \in̩fire͞-
ˈȯrətē\ *n*

in·fer·nal \inˈfərnᵊl\ *adj* : of or like
hell — often used as a general expression of disapproval — **in·fer-
nal·ly** *adv*

in·fer·no \inˈfərnō\ *n, pl* **-nos** : place
or condition suggesting hell

in·fest \inˈfest\ *vb* : swarm or grow
in or over — **in·fes·ta·tion** \in̩-
̩fesˈtāshən\ *n*

in·fi·del \ˈinfədᵊl, -fə̩del\ *n* : one
who does not believe in a particular religion

in·fi·del·i·ty \in̩fəˈdelətē, -fī-\ *n, pl*
-ties : lack of faithfulness

in·field \ˈin̩fēld\ *n* : baseball field
inside the base lines — **in·field-
er** *n*

in·fil·trate \inˈfil̩trāt, ˈinfil-\ *vb*
-trat·ed; -trat·ing : enter or become established in without being
noticed — **in·fil·tra·tion** \in̩infil-
ˈtrāshən\ *n*

in·fi·nite \ˈinfənət\ *adj* 1 : having no
limit or extending indefinitely 2
: vast — **infinite** *n* — **in·fi·nite-
ly** *adv* — **in·fin·i·tude** \inˈfinə-
̩tüd, -ˈtyüd\ *n*

in·fin·i·tes·i·mal \in̩finəˈtesəməl\
adj : immeasurably small — **in-
fin·i·tes·i·mal·ly** *adv*

in·fin·i·tive \inˈfinətiv\ *n* : verb
form in English usu. used with *to*

in·fin·i·ty \inˈfinətē\ *n, pl* **-ties** 1
: quality or state of being infinite 2
: indefinitely great number or
amount

in·firm \inˈfərm\ *adj* : feeble from
age — **in·fir·mi·ty** \-ˈfərmətē\ *n*

in·fir·ma·ry \inˈfərmərē\ *n, pl* **-ries**
: place for the care of the sick

in·flame \inˈflām\ *vb* **-flamed;
-flam·ing** 1 : excite to intense action or feeling 2 : affect or become
affected with inflammation — **in-
flam·ma·to·ry** \-ˈflamə̩tōrē\ *adj*

in·flam·ma·ble \inˈflaməbəl\ *adj*
: flammable

in·flam·ma·tion \in̩infləˈmāshən\ *n*
: response to injury in which an affected area becomes red and painful and congested with blood

in·flate \inˈflāt\ *vb* **-flat·ed;
-flat·ing** 1 : swell or puff up (as
with gas) 2 : expand or increase
abnormally — **in·flat·able** *adj*

in·fla·tion \inˈflāshən\ *n* 1 : act of
inflating 2 : continual rise in pric-

es — **in·fla·tion·ary** \-shə̩nerē\
adj

in·flec·tion \inˈflekshən\ *n* 1
: change in pitch or loudness of
the voice 2 : change in form of a
word — **in·flect** \-ˈflekt\ *vb* — **in-
flec·tion·al** \-ˈflekshənəl\ *adj*

in·flict \inˈflikt\ *vb* : give by or as if
by hitting — **in·flic·tion**
\-ˈflikshən\ *n*

in·flu·ence \ˈin̩flüəns\ *n* 1 : power
or capacity of causing an effect in
indirect or intangible ways 2 : one
that exerts influence ∼ *vb* **-enced;
-enc·ing** : affect or alter by influence — **in·flu·en·tial** \in̩inflü-
ˈenchəl\ *adj*

in·flu·en·za \in̩inflüˈenzə\ *n* : acute
very contagious virus disease

in·flux \ˈin̩fləks\ *n* : a flowing in

in·form \inˈfȯrm\ *vb* : give information or knowledge to — **in·for-
mant** \-ənt\ *n* — **in·form·er** *n*

in·for·mal \inˈfȯrməl\ *adj* 1 : without formality or ceremony 2 : for
ordinary or familiar use — **in·for-
mal·i·ty** \in̩ifȯrˈmalətē, -fər-\ *n* —
in·for·mal·ly *adv*

in·for·ma·tion \in̩infərˈmāshən\ *n*
: knowledge obtained from investigation, study, or instruction —
in·for·ma·tion·al \-shənəl\ *adj*

in·for·ma·tive \inˈfȯrmətiv\ *adj*
: giving knowledge

in·frac·tion \inˈfrakshən\ *n* : violation

in·fra·red \in̩infrəˈred\ *adj* : being,
relating to, or using radiation of
wavelengths longer than those of
red light — **infrared** *n*

in·fra·struc·ture \ˈinfrə̩strəkchər\
n : foundation of a system or organization

in·fringe \inˈfrinj\ *vb* **-fringed;
-fring·ing** : violate another's right
or privilege — **in·fringe·ment** *n*

in·fu·ri·ate \inˈfyu̇rē̩āt\ *vb* **-at-
ed; -at·ing** : make furious — **in-
fu·ri·at·ing·ly** \-̩ātiŋlē\ *adv*

in·fuse \inˈfyüz\ *vb* **-fused; -fus-
ing** 1 : instill a principle or quality
in 2 : steep in liquid without boiling — **in·fu·sion** \-ˈfyüzhən\ *n*

¹-ing \iŋ\ *vb suffix or adj suffix* —
used to form the present participle
and sometimes an adjective resembling a present participle

²-ing *n suffix* 1 : action or process 2

: something connected with or resulting from an action or process

in·ge·nious \in'jēnyəs\ *adj* : very clever — **in·ge·nious·ly** *adv* — **in·ge·nious·ness** *n*

in·ge·nue, in·gé·nue \'anjə₁nü, 'än-; 'aⁿzhə-, 'äⁿ-\ *n* : naive young woman

in·ge·nu·ity \₁injə'nüətē, -'nyü-\ *n*, *pl* **-ities** : skill or cleverness in planning or inventing

in·gen·u·ous \in'jenyəwəs\ *adj* : innocent and candid — **in·gen·u·ous·ly** *adv* — **in·gen·u·ous·ness** *n*

in·gest \in'jest\ *vb* : eat — **in·ges·tion** \-'jeschən\ *n*

in·gle·nook \'iŋgəl₁nuk\ *n* : corner by the fireplace

in·got \'iŋgət\ *n* : block of metal

in·grained \in'grānd\ *adj* : deep-seated

in·grate \'in₁grāt\ *n* : ungrateful person

in·gra·ti·ate \in'grāshē₁āt\ *vb* **-ed; -at·ing** : gain favor for (oneself) — **in·gra·ti·at·ing** *adj*

in·gre·di·ent \in'grēdēənt\ *n* : one of the substances that make up a mixture

in·grown \'in₁grōn\ *adj* : grown in and esp. into the flesh

in·hab·it \in'habət\ *vb* : live or dwell in — **in·hab·it·able** *adj* — **in·hab·it·ant** \-ətənt\ *n*

◆ **in·hale** \in'hāl\ *vb* **-haled; -hal·ing** : breathe in — **in·hal·ant** \-ənt\ *n* — **in·ha·la·tion** \₁inhə-'lāshən, ₁inə-\ *n* — **in·hal·er** *n*

in·here \in'hir\ *vb* **-hered; -her·ing** : be inherent

in·her·ent \in'hirənt, -'her-\ *adj* : being an essential part of something — **in·her·ent·ly** *adv*

in·her·it \in'herət\ *vb* : receive from one's ancestors — **in·her·it·able** \-əbəl\ *adj* — **in·her·i·tance** \-ətəns\ *n* — **in·her·i·tor** \-ətər\ *n*

in·hib·it \in'hibət\ *vb* : hold in check — **in·hi·bi·tion** \₁inhə-'bishən, ₁inə-\ *n*

in·hu·man \in'hyümən, -'yü-\ *adj* : cruel or impersonal — **in·hu·man·i·ty** \-hyü'manətē, -yü-\ *n* — **in·hu·man·ly** *adv* — **in·hu·man·ness** *n*

in·im·i·cal \in'imikəl\ *adj* : hostile or harmful — **in·im·i·cal·ly** *adv*

in·im·i·ta·ble \in'imətəbəl\ *adj* : not capable of being imitated

in·iq·ui·ty \in'ikwətē\ *n*, *pl* **-ties** : wickedness — **in·iq·ui·tous** \-wətəs\ *adj*

ini·tial \in'ishəl\ *adj* **1** : of or relating to the beginning **2** : first ~ *n* : 1st letter of a word or name ~ *vb* **-tialed** *or* **-tialled; -tial·ing** *or* **-tial·ling** : put initials on — **ini·tial·ly** *adv*

ini·ti·ate \in'ishē₁āt\ *vb* **-at·ed; -at·ing 1** : start **2** : induct into membership **3** : instruct in the rudiments of something — **initiate** \-'ishēət\ *n* — **ini·ti·a·tion** \-₁ishē-'āshən\ *n* — **ini·tia·to·ry** \-'ishēə₁tōrē\ *adj*

ini·tia·tive \in'ishətiv\ *n* **1** : first step **2** : readiness to undertake something on one's own

in·ject \in'jekt\ *vb* : force or introduce into something — **in·jec·tion** \-'jekshən\ *n*

in·junc·tion \in'jəŋkshən\ *n* : court writ requiring one to do or to refrain from doing a specified act

in·jure \'injər\ *vb* **-jured; -jur·ing** : do damage, hurt, or a wrong to

in·ju·ry \'injərē\ *n*, *pl* **-ries 1** : act that injures **2** : hurt, damage, or loss sustained — **in·ju·ri·ous** \in-'jūrēəs\ *adj*

in·jus·tice \in'jəstəs\ *n* : unjust act

ink \'iŋk\ *n* : usu. liquid and colored material for writing and printing

~ *vb* : put ink on — **ink·well**
\-ˌwel\ *n* — **inky** *adj*
in·kling \'iŋkliŋ\ *n* : hint or idea
in·land \'inˌland, -lənd\ *n* : interior
of a country — **inland** *adj or adv*
in–law \'inˌló\ *n* : relative by marriage
in·lay \in'lā, 'inˌlā\ *vb* **-laid** \-'lād\;
-lay·ing : set into a surface for
decoration ~ \'inˌlā\ *n* **1** : inlaid
work **2** : shaped filling cemented
into a tooth
in·let \'inˌlet, -lət\ *n* : small bay
in·mate \'inˌmāt\ *n* : person confined to an asylum or prison
in me·mo·ri·am \ˌinməˈmōrēəm\
prep : in memory of
in·most \'inˌmōst\ *adj* : deepest
within
inn \'in\ *n* : hotel
in·nards \'inərdz\ *n pl* : internal
parts
in·nate \in'āt\ *adj* **1** : inborn **2** : inherent — **in·nate·ly** *adv*
in·ner \'inər\ *adj* : being on the inside
in·ner·most \'inərˌmōst\ *adj* : farthest inward
in·ner·sole \ˌinər'sōl\ *n* : insole
in·ning \'iniŋ\ *n* : baseball team's
turn at bat
inn·keep·er \'inˌkēpər\ *n* : owner of
an inn
in·no·cent \'inəsənt\ *adj* **1** : free
from guilt **2** : harmless **3** : not sophisticated — **in·no·cence** \-səns\
n — **innocent** *n* — **in·no·cent·ly**
adv
in·noc·u·ous \in'äkyəwəs\ *adj* **1**
: harmless **2** : inoffensive
in·no·va·tion \ˌinə'vāshən\ *n* : new
idea or method — **in·no·vate**
\'inəˌvāt\ *vb* — **in·no·va·tive** \'inə
ˌvātiv\ *adj* — **in·no·va·tor**
\-ˌvātər\ *n*
in·nu·en·do \ˌinyə'wendō\ *n, pl* **-dos**
or **-does** : insinuation
in·nu·mer·a·ble \in'ümərəbəl,
-'yüm-\ *adj* : countless
in·oc·u·late \in'äkyəˌlāt\ *vb* **-lat**
ed; **-lat·ing** : treat with something
esp. to establish immunity — **in**
oc·u·la·tion \-ˌäkyə'lāshən\ *n*
in·op·por·tune \inˌäpər'tün, -'tyün\
adj : inconvenient — **in·op·por·**
tune·ly *adv*
in·or·di·nate \in'órd°nət\ *adj* : unusual or excessive — **in·or·di·**
nate·ly *adv*

in·or·gan·ic \ˌinˌór'ganik\ *adj*
: made of mineral matter
in·pa·tient \'inˌpāshənt\ *n* : patient
who stays in a hospital
in·put \'inˌpùt\ *n* : something put in
— **input** *vb*
in·quest \'inˌkwest\ *n* : inquiry esp.
before a jury
in·quire \in'kwīr\ *vb* **-quired**; **-quir**
ing 1 : ask **2** : investigate — **in·**
quir·er *n* — **in·quir·ing·ly** *adv* —
in·qui·ry \'inˌkwīrē, in'kwīrē;
'inkwərē, 'iŋ-\ *n*
in·qui·si·tion \ˌinkwə'zishən, ˌiŋ-\ *n*
1 : official inquiry **2** : severe questioning — **in·quis·i·tor** \in
'kwizətər\ *n* — **in·quis·i·to·ri·al**
\-ˌkwizəˈtōrēəl\ *adj*
in·quis·i·tive \in'kwizətiv\ *adj* : curious — **in·quis·i·tive·ly** *adv* —
in·quis·i·tive·ness *n*
in·road \'inˌrōd\ *n* : encroachment
in·rush \'inˌrəsh\ *n* : influx
in·sane \in'sān\ *adj* **1** : not sane **2**
: absurd — **in·sane·ly** *adv* — **in·**
san·i·ty \in'sanətē\ *n*
in·sa·tia·ble \in'sāshəbəl\ *adj* : incapable of being satisfied — **in·**
sa·tia·bil·i·ty \-ˌsāshə'bilətē\ *n*
— **in·sa·tia·bly** *adv*
in·scribe \in'skrīb\ *vb* **1** : write **2**
: engrave **3** : dedicate (a book) to
someone — **in·scrip·tion**
\-'skripshən\ *n*
in·scru·ta·ble \in'skrütəbəl\ *adj*
: mysterious — **in·scru·ta·bly** *adv*
in·seam \'inˌsēm\ *n* : inner seam (of
a garment)
in·sect \'inˌsekt\ *n* : small usu.
winged animal with 6 legs
in·sec·ti·cide \in'sektəˌsīd\ *n* : insect poison — **in·sec·ti·cid·al** \in
ˌsektə'sīd°l\ *adj*
in·se·cure \ˌinsi'kyùr\ *adj* **1** : uncertain **2** : unsafe **3** : fearful — **in·**
se·cure·ly *adv* — **in·se·cu·ri·ty**
\-'kyùrətē\ *n*
in·sem·i·nate \in'seməˌnāt\ *vb* **-nat**
ed; **-nat·ing** : introduce semen
into — **in·sem·i·na·tion** \-ˌsemə
'nāshən\ *n*
in·sen·si·ble \in'sensəbəl\ *adj* **1** : unconscious **2** : unable to feel **3** : unaware — **in·sen·si·bil·i·ty** \in
ˌsensə'bilətē\ *n* — **in·sen·si·bly** *adv*
in·sen·tient \in'senchənt\ *adj* : lacking feeling — **in·sen·tience**
\-chəns\ *n*
in·sert \in'sərt\ *vb* : put in — **insert**

\\'in͵sərt\ *n* — **in·ser·tion** \in-'sərshən\ *n*

in·set \'in͵set\ *vb* **inset** *or* **in·set-ted; in·set·ting** : set in — **inset** *n*

in·shore \'in'shŏr\ *adj* **1** : situated near shore **2** : moving toward shore ~ *adv* : toward shore

in·side \in'sīd, 'in͵sīd\ *n* **1** : inner side **2** *pl* : innards ~ *prep* **1** : in or into the inside of **2** : within ~ *adv* **1** : on the inner side **2** : into the interior — **inside** *adj* — **in·sid·er** \in'sīdər\ *n*

inside of *prep* : inside

in·sid·i·ous \in'sīdēəs\ *adj* **1** : treacherous **2** : seductive — **in·sid·i·ous·ly** *adv* — **in·sid·i·ous·ness** *n*

in·sight \'in͵sīt\ *n* : understanding — **in·sight·ful** \in'sītfəl\ *adj*

in·sig·nia \in'signēə\; **in·sig·ne** \-͵nē\ *n, pl* **-nia** *or* **-ni·as** : badge of authority or office

in·sin·u·ate \in'sinyə͵wāt\ *vb* **-at-ed; -at·ing 1** : imply **2** : bring in artfully — **in·sin·u·a·tion** \-͵sinyə'wāshən\ *n*

in·sip·id \in'sipəd\ *adj* **1** : tasteless **2** : not stimulating — **in·si·pid·i-ty** \͵insə'pidətē\ *n*

in·sist \in'sist\ *vb* : be firmly demanding — **in·sis·tence** \in-'sistəns\ *n* — **in·sis·tent** \-tənt\ *adj* — **in·sis·tent·ly** *adv*

insofar as \͵insō'färaz\ *conj* : to the extent that

in·sole \'in͵sōl\ *n* : inside sole of a shoe

in·so·lent \'insələnt\ *adj* : contemptuously rude — **in·so·lence** \-ləns\ *n*

in·sol·vent \in'sälvənt\ *adj* : unable or insufficient to pay debts — **in·sol·ven·cy** \-vənsē\ *n*

in·som·nia \in'sämnēə\ *n* : inability to sleep

in·so·much as \͵insō'məchaz\ *conj* : inasmuch as

insomuch that *conj* : to such a degree that

in·sou·ci·ance \in'süsēəns, aⁿsü-'syäⁿs\ *n* : lighthearted indifference — **in·sou·ci·ant** \in'süsēənt, aⁿsü'syäⁿ\ *adj*

in·spect \in'spekt\ *vb* : view closely and critically — **in·spec·tion** \-'spekshən\ *n* — **in·spec·tor** \-tər\ *n*

in·spire \in'spīr\ *vb* **-spired; -spir-**ing **1** : inhale **2** : influence by example **3** : bring about **4** : stir to action — **in·spi·ra·tion** \͵inspə-'rāshən\ *n* — **in·spi·ra·tion·al** \-'rāshənəl\ *adj* — **in·spir·er** *n*

in·stall, in·stal \in'stŏl\ *vb* **-stalled; -stall·ing 1** : induct into office **2** : set up for use — **in·stal·la·tion** \͵instə'lāshən\ *n*

in·stall·ment \in'stŏlmənt\ *n* : partial payment

in·stance \'instəns\ *n* **1** : request or instigation **2** : example

in·stant \'instənt\ *n* : moment ~ *adj* **1** : immediate **2** : ready to mix — **in·stan·ta·neous** \͵instən-'tānēəs\ *adj* — **in·stan·ta·neous·ly** *adv* — **in·stant·ly** *adv*

in·stead \in'sted\ *adv* : as a substitute or alternative

instead of *prep* : as a substitute for or alternative to

in·step \'in͵step\ *n* : part of the foot in front of the ankle

in·sti·gate \'instə͵gāt\ *vb* **-gat·ed; -gat·ing** : incite — **in·sti·ga·tion** \͵instə'gāshən\ *n* — **in·sti·ga·tor** \'instə͵gātər\ *n*

in·still \in'stil\ *vb* **-stilled; -still-**ing : impart gradually

in·stinct \'in͵stiŋkt\ *n* **1** : natural talent **2** : natural inherited or subconsciously motivated behavior — **in·stinc·tive** \in'stiŋktiv\ *adj* — **in·stinc·tive·ly** *adv* — **in·stinc-tu·al** \in'stiŋkchəwəl\ *adj*

in·sti·tute \'instə͵tüt, -͵tyüt\ *vb* **-tut-ed; -tut·ing** : establish, start, or organize ~ *n* **1** : organization promoting a cause **2** : school

in·sti·tu·tion \͵instə'tüshən, -'tyü-\ *n* **1** : act of instituting **2** : custom **3** : corporation or society of a public character — **in·sti·tu·tion·al** \-shənəl\ *adj* — **in·sti·tu·tion·al-ize** \-͵īz\ *vb* — **in·sti·tu·tion·al·ly** *adv*

in·struct \in'strəkt\ *vb* **1** : teach **2** : give an order to — **in·struc·tion** \in'strəkshən\ *n* — **in·struc·tion·al** \-shənəl\ *adj* — **in·struc·tive** \in'strəktiv\ *adj* — **in·struc·tor** \in'strəktər\ *n* — **in·struc·tor-ship** *n*

in·stru·ment \'instrəmənt\ *n* **1** : something that produces music **2** : means **3** : device for doing work and esp. precision work **4** : legal document — **in·stru·men·tal**

\ˌinstrə'ment²l\ *adj* — **in·stru-men·tal·ist** \-ist\ *n* — **in·stru-men·tal·i·ty** \ˌinstrəmən'talətē, -ˌmen-\ *n* — **in·stru·men·ta·tion** \ˌinstrəmən'tāshən, -ˌmen-\ *n*

in·sub·or·di·nate \ˌinsə'bȯrd²nət\ *adj* : not obeying — **in·sub·or·di·na·tion** \-ˌbȯrd²n'āshən\ *n*

in·suf·fer·able \in'səfərəbəl\ *adj* : unbearable — **in·suf·fer·ably** \-blē\ *adv*

in·su·lar \'insülər, -syü-\ *adj* 1 : relating to or residing on an island 2 : narrow-minded — **in·su·lar·i·ty** \ˌinsü'larətē, -syü-\ *n*

in·su·late \'insə,lāt\ *vb* **-lat·ed; -lat·ing** : protect from heat loss or electricity — **in·su·la·tion** \ˌinsə-'lāshən\ *n* — **in·su·la·tor** \'insə-ˌlātər\ *n*

in·su·lin \'insələn\ *n* : hormone used by diabetics

in·sult \in'səlt\ *vb* : treat with contempt ∼ \'inˌsəlt\ *n* : insulting act or remark — **in·sult·ing·ly** \-iŋlē\ *adv*

in·su·per·a·ble \in'süpərəbəl\ *adj* : too difficult — **in·su·per·a·bly** \-blē\ *adv*

in·sure \in'shùr\ *vb* **-sured; -sur·ing** 1 : guarantee against loss 2 : make certain — **in·sur·able** \-əbəl\ *adj* — **in·sur·ance** \-əns\ *n* — **in·sured** \in'shùrd\ *n* — **in·sur·er** *n*

in·sur·gent \in'sərjənt\ *n* : rebel — **in·sur·gence** \-jəns\ *n* — **in·sur·gen·cy** \-jənsē\ *n* — **in·sur·gent** *adj*

in·sur·mount·able \ˌinsər'maùnt-əbəl\ *adj* : too great to be overcome — **in·sur·mount·ably** \-blē\ *adv*

in·sur·rec·tion \ˌinsə'rekshən\ *n* : revolution — **in·sur·rec·tion·ist** *n*

in·tact \in'takt\ *adj* : undamaged

in·take \'inˌtāk\ *n* 1 : opening through which something enters 2 : act of taking in 3 : amount taken in

in·te·ger \'intijər\ *n* : number that is not a fraction and does not include a fraction

in·te·gral \'intigrəl\ *adj* : essential

in·te·grate \'intəˌgrāt\ *vb* **-grat·ed; -grat·ing** 1 : unite 2 : end segregation of or at — **in·te·gra·tion** \ˌintə'grāshən\ *n*

in·teg·ri·ty \in'tegrətē\ *n* 1 : soundness 2 : adherence to a code of values 3 : completeness

in·tel·lect \'int²lˌekt\ *n* : power of knowing or thinking — **in·tel·lec·tu·al** \ˌint²l'ekchəwəl\ *adj or n* — **in·tel·lec·tu·al·ism** \-chəwə-ˌlizəm\ *n* — **in·tel·lec·tu·al·ly** *adv*

in·tel·li·gence \in'teləjəns\ *n* 1 : ability to learn and understand 2 : mental acuteness 3 : information

in·tel·li·gent \in'teləjənt\ *adj* : having or showing intelligence — **in·tel·li·gent·ly** *adv*

in·tel·li·gi·ble \in'teləjəbəl\ *adj* : understandable — **in·tel·li·gi·bil·i·ty** \-ˌteləjə'bilətē\ *n* — **in·tel·li·gi·bly** *adv*

in·tem·per·ance \in'tempərəns\ *n* : lack of moderation — **in·tem·per·ate** \-pərət\ *adj* — **in·tem·per·ate·ness** *n*

in·tend \in'tend\ *vb* : have as a purpose

in·tend·ed \-'tendəd\ *n* : engaged person — **intended** *adj*

in·tense \in'tens\ *adj* 1 : extreme 2 : deeply felt — **in·tense·ly** *adv* — **in·ten·si·fi·ca·tion** \-ˌtensəfə-'kāshən\ *n* — **in·ten·si·fy** \-'tensə-ˌfī\ *vb* — **in·ten·si·ty** \in'tensətē\ *n* — **in·ten·sive** \in'tensiv\ *adj* — **in·ten·sive·ly** *adv*

¹**in·tent** \in'tent\ *n* : purpose — **in·ten·tion** \-'tenchən\ *n* — **in·ten·tion·al** \-'tenchənəl\ *adj* — **in·ten·tion·al·ly** *adv*

²**intent** *adj* : concentrated — **in·tent·ly** *adv* — **in·tent·ness** *n*

in·ter \in'tər\ *vb* **-rr-** : bury

inter- *prefix* : between or among

interagency	intercultural
interatomic	interdenomina-
interbank	tional
interborough	interdepart-
intercampus	mental
interchurch	interdivisional
intercity	interelectronic
interclass	interethnic
intercoastal	interfaculty
intercollegiate	interfamily
intercolonial	interfiber
intercommunal	interfraternity
intercommuni-	intergalactic
ty	intergang
intercompany	intergovern-
intercontinen-	mental
tal	intergroup
intercounty	

interhemi-
spheric
interindustry
interinstitution-
al
interisland
interlibrary
intermolecular
intermountain
interoceanic
interoffice
interparticle
interparty
interpersonal
interplanetary
interpopulation
interprovincial
interracial
interregional

interreligious
interscholastic
intersectional
interstate
interstellar
intersystem
interterm
interterminal
intertribal
intertroop
intertropical
interuniversity
interurban
intervalley
intervillage
interwar
interzonal
interzone

in·ter·ac·tion \,intər'akshən\ *n* : mutual influence — **in·ter·act** \-'akt\ *vb* — **in·ter·ac·tive** *adj*

in·ter·breed \,intər'brēd\ *vb* -**bred** \-'bred\; -**breed·ing** : breed together

in·ter·ca·late \in'tərkə,lāt\ *vb* -**lat·ed**; -**lat·ing** : insert — **in·ter·ca·la·tion** \-,tərkə'lāshən\ *n*

in·ter·cede \,intər'sēd\ *vb* -**ced·ed**; -**ced·ing** : act to reconcile — **in·ter·ces·sion** \-'seshən\ *n* — **in·ter·ces·sor** \-'sesər\ *n*

in·ter·cept \,intər'sept\ *vb* : interrupt the progress of — **intercept** \'intər,sept\ *n* — **in·ter·cep·tion** \,intər'sepshən\ *n* — **in·ter·cep·tor** \-'septər\ *n*

in·ter·change \,intər'chānj\ *vb* 1 : exchange 2 : change places ~ \'intər,chānj\ *n* 1 : exchange 2 : junction of highways — **in·ter·change·able** \,intər'chānjəbəl\ *adj*

in·ter·course \'intər,kōrs\ *n* 1 : relations between persons or nations 2 : copulation

in·ter·de·pen·dent \,intərdi-'pendənt\ *adj* : mutually dependent — **in·ter·de·pen·dence** \-dəns\ *n*

in·ter·dict \,intər'dikt\ *vb* 1 : prohibit 2 : destroy or cut (an enemy supply line) — **in·ter·dic·tion** \-'dikshən\ *n*

in·ter·est \'intrəst, -tə,rest\ *n* 1 : right 2 : benefit 3 : charge for borrowed money 4 : readiness to pay special attention 5 : quality that causes interest ~ *vb* 1 : concern 2 : get the attention of — **in-**

ter·est·ing *adj* — **in·ter·est·ing·ly** *adv*

in·ter·face \'intər,fās\ *n* : common boundary — **in·ter·fa·cial** \,intər-'fāshəl\ *adj*

in·ter·fere \,intər'fir\ *vb* -**fered**; -**fer·ing** 1 : collide or be in opposition 2 : try to run the affairs of others — **in·ter·fer·ence** \-'firəns\ *n*

in·ter·im \'intərəm\ *n* : time between — **interim** *adj*

in·te·ri·or \in'tirēər\ *adj* : being on the inside ~ *n* 1 : inside 2 : inland area

in·ter·ject \,intər'jekt\ *vb* : stick in between

in·ter·jec·tion \-'jekshən\ *n* : an exclamatory word — **in·ter·jec·tion·al·ly** \-shənəlē\ *adv*

in·ter·lace \,intər'lās\ *vb* : cross or cause to cross one over another

in·ter·lin·ear \,intər'linēər\ *adj* : between written or printed lines

in·ter·lock \,intər'läk\ *vb* 1 : interlace 2 : connect for mutual effect — **interlock** \'intər,läk\ *n*

in·ter·lop·er \,intər'lōpər\ *n* : intruder or meddler

in·ter·lude \'intər,lüd\ *n* : intervening period

in·ter·mar·ry \,intər'marē\ *vb* 1 : marry each other 2 : marry within a group — **in·ter·mar·riage** \-'marij\ *n*

in·ter·me·di·ary \,intər'mēdē,erē\ *n, pl* -**ar·ies** : agent between individuals or groups — **intermediary** *adj*

in·ter·me·di·ate \,intər'mēdēət\ *adj* : between extremes — **intermediate** *n*

in·ter·ment \in'tərmənt\ *n* : burial

in·ter·min·a·ble \in'tərmənəbəl\ *adj* : endless — **in·ter·min·a·bly** *adv*

in·ter·min·gle \,intər'miŋgəl\ *vb* : mingle

in·ter·mis·sion \,intər'mishən\ *n* : break in a performance

in·ter·mit·tent \-'mit'nt\ *adj* : coming at intervals — **in·ter·mit·tent·ly** *adv*

in·ter·mix \,intər'miks\ *vb* : mix together — **in·ter·mix·ture** \-'mikschər\ *n*

¹in·tern \'in,tərn, in'tərn\ *vb* : confine esp. during a war — **in·tern·ee** \,in,tər'nē\ *n* — **in·tern·ment** *n*

²in·tern \'in,tərn\ n : advanced student (as in medicine) gaining supervised experience ~ vb : act as an intern — in·tern·ship n

in·ter·nal \in'tərn°l\ adj 1 : inward 2 : inside of the body 3 : relating to or existing in the mind — in·ter·nal·ly adv

in·ter·na·tion·al \,intər'nashənəl\ adj : affecting 2 or more nations ~ n : something having international scope — in·ter·na·tion·al·ism \-,izəm\ n — in·ter·na·tion·al·ize \-,īz\ vb — in·ter·na·tion·al·ly adv

in·ter·nist \'in,tərnist\ n : specialist in nonsurgical medicine

in·ter·play \'intər,plā\ n : interaction

in·ter·po·late \in'tərpə,lāt\ vb -lat·ed; -lat·ing : insert — in·ter·po·la·tion \-,tərpə'lāshən\ n

in·ter·pose \,intər'pōz\ vb -posed; -pos·ing 1 : place between 2 : intrude — in·ter·po·si·tion \-pə'zishən\ n

in·ter·pret \in'tərprət\ vb : explain the meaning of — in·ter·pre·ta·tion \in,tərprə'tāshən\ n — in·ter·pre·ta·tive \-'tərprə,tātiv\ adj — in·ter·pret·er n — in·ter·pre·tive \-'tərprətiv\ adj

in·ter·re·late \,intəri'lāt\ vb : have a mutual relationship — in·ter·re·lat·ed·ness \-'lātədnəs\ n — in·ter·re·la·tion \-'lāshən\ n — in·ter·re·la·tion·ship n

in·ter·ro·gate \in'terə,gāt\ vb -gat·ed; -gat·ing : question — in·ter·ro·ga·tion \-,terə'gāshən\ n — in·ter·rog·a·tive \,intə'rägətiv\ adj or n — in·ter·rog·a·tor \-'terə,gātər\ n — in·ter·rog·a·to·ry \,intə'rägə,tōrē\ adj

in·ter·rupt \,intə'rəpt\ vb : intrude so as to hinder or end continuity — in·ter·rupt·er n — in·ter·rup·tion \-'rəpshən\ n — in·ter·rup·tive \-'rəptiv\ adv

in·ter·sect \,intər'sekt\ vb 1 : cut across or divide 2 : cross — in·ter·sec·tion \-'sekshən\ n

in·ter·sperse \,intər'spərs\ vb -spersed; -spers·ing : insert at intervals — in·ter·sper·sion \-'spərzhən\ n

in·ter·stice \in'tərstəs\ n, pl -stic·es \-stə,sēz, -stəsəz\ : space between — in·ter·sti·tial \,intər'stishəl\ adj

in·ter·twine \,intər'twīn\ vb : twist together — in·ter·twine·ment n

in·ter·val \'intərvəl\ n 1 : time between 2 : space between

in·ter·vene \,intər'vēn\ vb -vened; -ven·ing 1 : happen between events 2 : intercede — in·ter·ven·tion \-'venchən\ n

in·ter·view \'intər,vyü\ n : a meeting to get information — interview vb — in·ter·view·er n

in·ter·weave \,intər'wēv\ vb -wove \-'wōv\; -wo·ven \-'wōvən\; -weav·ing : weave together — in·ter·wo·ven \-'wōvən\ adj

in·tes·tate \in'tes,tāt, -tət\ adj : not leaving a will

in·tes·tine \in'testən\ n : tubular part of the digestive system after the stomach including a long narrow upper part (small intestine) followed by a broader shorter lower part (large intestine) — in·tes·ti·nal \-tən°l\ adj

in·ti·mate \'intə,māt\ vb -mat·ed; -mat·ing : hint ~ \'intəmət\ adj 1 : very friendly 2 : suggesting privacy 3 : very personal ~ n : close friend — in·ti·ma·cy \'intəməsē\ n — in·ti·mate·ly adv — in·ti·ma·tion \,intə'māshən\ n

in·tim·i·date \in'timə,dāt\ vb -dat·ed; -dat·ing : make fearful — in·tim·i·da·tion \-,timə'dāshən\ n

in·to \'intü\ prep 1 : to the inside of 2 : to the condition of 3 : against

in·to·na·tion \,intō'nāshən\ n : way of singing or speaking

in·tone \in'tōn\ vb -toned; -ton·ing : chant

in·tox·i·cate \in'täkə,kāt\ vb -cat·ed; -cat·ing : make drunk — in·tox·i·cant \-sikənt\ n or adj — in·tox·i·ca·tion \-,täkə'kāshən\ n

in·tra·mu·ral \,intrə'myürəl\ adj : within a school

in·tran·si·gent \in'transəjənt\ adj : uncompromising — in·tran·si·gence \-jəns\ n — intransigent n

in·tra·ve·nous \,intrə'vēnəs\ adj : by way of the veins — in·tra·ve·nous·ly adv

in·trep·id \in'trepəd\ adj : fearless — in·tre·pid·i·ty \,intrə'pidətē\ n

in·tri·cate \'intrikət\ adj : very complex and delicate — in·tri-

ca·cy \-trikəsē\ *n* — **in·tri·cate·ly** *adv*

in·trigue \in'trēg\ *vb* **-trigued**; **-trigu·ing 1** : scheme **2** : arouse curiosity of ~ *n* : secret scheme — **in·trigu·ing·ly** \-iŋlē\ *adv*

in·trin·sic \in'trinzik, -sik\ *adj* : essential — **in·trin·si·cal·ly** \-ziklē, -si-\ *adv*

in·tro·duce \ˌintrə'düs, -'dyüs\ *vb* **-duced**; **-duc·ing 1** : bring in esp. for the 1st time **2** : cause to be acquainted **3** : bring to notice **4** : put in — **in·tro·duc·tion** \'dəkshən\ *n* — **in·tro·duc·to·ry** \-'dəktərē\ *adj*

in·tro·spec·tion \ˌintrə'spekshən\ *n* : examination of one's own thoughts or feelings — **in·tro·spec·tive** \-'spektiv\ *adj* — **in·tro·spec·tive·ly** *adv*

in·tro·vert \'intrəˌvərt\ *n* : shy or reserved person — **in·tro·ver·sion** \ˌintrə'vərzhən\ *n* — **introvert** *adj* — **in·tro·vert·ed** \'intrəˌvərtəd\ *adj*

in·trude \in'trüd\ *vb* **-trud·ed**; **-trud·ing 1** : thrust in **2** : encroach — **in·trud·er** *n* — **in·tru·sion** \-'trüzhən\ *n* — **in·tru·sive** \-'trüsiv\ *adj* — **in·tru·sive·ness** *n*

in·tu·i·tion \ˌintü'ishən, -tyü-\ *n* : quick and ready insight — **in·tu·it** \in'tüət, -'tyü-\ *vb* — **in·tu·i·tive** \-ətiv\ *adj* — **in·tu·i·tive·ly** *adv*

in·un·date \'inənˌdāt\ *vb* **-dat·ed**; **-dat·ing** : flood — **in·un·da·tion** \ˌinən'dāshən\ *n*

in·ure \in'ür, -'yùr\ *vb.* **-ured**; **-ur·ing** : accustom to accept something undesirable

in·vade \in'vād\ *vb* **-vad·ed**; **-vad·ing** : enter for conquest — **in·vad·er** *n* — **in·va·sion** \-'vāzhən\ *n*

¹**in·val·id** \in'valəd\ *adj* : not true or legal — **in·va·lid·i·ty** \ˌinvə-'lidətē\ *n* — **in·val·id·ly** *adv*

²**in·va·lid** \'invələd\ *adj* : sickly ~ *n* : one chronically ill

in·val·i·date \in'valəˌdāt\ *vb* : make invalid — **in·val·i·da·tion** \inˌvalə'dāshən\

in·valu·able \in'valyəwəbəl\ *adj* : extremely valuable

in·va·sive \in'vāsiv\ *adj* : involving entry into the body

in·vec·tive \in'vektiv\ *n* : abusive language — **invective** *adj*

in·veigh \in'vā\ *vb* : protest or complain forcefully

in·vei·gle \in'vāgəl, -'vē-\ *vb* **-gled**; **-gling** : win over or get by flattery

in·vent \in'vent\ *vb* **1** : think up **2** : create for the 1st time — **in·ven·tion** \-'venchən\ *n* — **in·ven·tive** \-'ventiv\ *adj* — **in·ven·tive·ness** *n* — **in·ven·tor** \-'ventər\ *n*

◆ **in·ven·to·ry** \'invənˌtōrē\ *n, pl* **-ries 1** : list of goods **2** : stock — **inventory** *vb*

in·verse \in'vərs, 'inˌvərs\ *adj or n* : opposite — **in·verse·ly** *adv*

in·vert \in'vərt\ *vb* **1** : turn upside down or inside out **2** : reverse — **in·ver·sion** \-'vərzhən\ *n*

in·ver·te·brate \in'vərtəbrət, -ˌbrāt\ *adj* : lacking a backbone ~ *n* : invertebrate animal

in·vest \in'vest\ *vb* **1** : give power or authority to **2** : endow with a quality **3** : commit money to someone else's use in hope of profit — **in·vest·ment** \-mənt\ *n* — **in·ves·tor** \-'vestər\ *n*

in·ves·ti·gate \in'vestəˌgāt\ *vb* **-gat·ed**; **-gat·ing** : study closely and systematically — **in·ves·ti·ga·tion** \-ˌvestə'gāshən\ *n* — **in·ves·ti·ga·tive** \-'vestəˌgātiv\ *adj* — **in·ves·ti·ga·tor** \-'vestəˌgātər\ *n*

in·ves·ti·ture \in'vestəˌchùr, -chər\ *n* : act of establishing in office

in·vet·er·ate \in'vetərət\ *adj* : acting out of habit

in·vid·i·ous \in'vidēəs\ *adj* : harmful or obnoxious — **in·vid·i·ous·ly** *adv*

in·vig·o·rate \in'vigə₁rāt\ *vb* -rat·ed; -rat·ing : give life and energy to — **in·vig·o·ra·tion** \-₁vigə'rāshən\ *n*

in·vin·ci·ble \in'vinsəbəl\ *adj* : incapable of being conquered — **in·vin·ci·bil·i·ty** \in₁vinsə'bilətē\ *n* — **in·vin·ci·bly** \in'vinsəblē\ *adv*

in·vi·o·la·ble \in'vīələbəl\ *adj* : safe from violation or desecration — **in·vi·o·la·bil·i·ty** \in₁vīələ'bilətē\ *n*

in·vi·o·late \in'vīələt\ *adj* : not violated or profaned

in·vite \in'vīt\ *vb* -vit·ed; -vit·ing 1 : entice 2 : increase the likelihood of 3 : request the presence or participation of 4 : encourage — **in·vi·ta·tion** \₁invə'tāshən\ *n* — **in·vit·ing** \in'vītiŋ\ *adj*

in·vo·ca·tion \₁invə'kāshən\ *n* 1 : prayer 2 : incantation

in·voice \'in₁vois\ *n* : itemized bill for goods shipped ∼ *vb* -voiced; -voic·ing : bill

in·voke \in'vōk\ *vb* -voked; -vok·ing 1 : call on for help 2 : cite as authority 3 : conjure 4 : carry out

in·volve \in'välv\ *vb* -volved; -volv·ing 1 : draw in as a participant 2 : relate closely 3 : require as a necessary part 4 : occupy fully — **in·volve·ment** *n*

in·volved \-'välvd\ *adj* : intricate

¹**in·ward** \'inwərd\ *adj* : inside

²**inward, in·wards** \-wərdz\ *adv* : toward the inside, center, or inner being

in·ward·ly *adv* 1 : mentally or spiritually 2 : internally 3 : to oneself

io·dide \'īə₁dīd\ *n* : compound of iodine

io·dine \'īə₁dīn, -ədⁿn\ *n* 1 : nonmetallic chemical element 2 : solution of iodine used as an antiseptic

io·dize \'īə₁dīz\ *vb* -dized; -diz·ing : treat with iodine or an iodide

ion \'īən, 'ī₁än\ *n* : electrically charged particle — **ion·ic** \ī'änik\ *adj* — **ion·iz·able** \'īə₁nīzəbəl\ *adj* — **ion·i·za·tion** \₁īənə'zāshən\ *n* — **ion·ize** \'īə₁nīz\ *vb* — **ion·iz·er** \'īə₁nīzər\ *n*

-ion *n suffix* 1 : act or process 2 : state or condition

ion·o·sphere \ī'änə₁sfir\ *n* : layer of the upper atmosphere containing ionized gases — **ion·o·spher·ic** \i₁änə'sfirik, -'sfer-\ *adj*

io·ta \ī'ōtə\ *n* : small quantity

IOU \₁ī₁ō'yü\ *n* : acknowledgment of a debt

iras·ci·ble \ir'asəbəl, ī'ras-\ *adj* : marked by hot temper — **iras·ci·bil·i·ty** \-₁asə'bilətē, -₁ras-\ *n*

irate \ī'rāt\ *adj* : roused to intense anger — **irate·ly** *adv*

ire \'īr\ *n* : anger

ir·i·des·cence \₁irə'desⁿns\ *n* : rainbowlike play of colors — **ir·i·des·cent** \-ⁿnt\ *adj*

iris \'īrəs\ *n, pl* **iris·es** *or* **iri·des** \'īrə₁dēz, 'ir-\ 1 : colored part around the pupil of the eye 2 : plant with long leaves and large showy flowers

irk \'ərk\ *vb* : annoy — **irk·some** \-əm\ *adj* — **irk·some·ly** *adv*

iron \'īərn\ *n* 1 : heavy metallic chemical element 2 : something made of iron 3 : heated device for pressing clothes 4 : hardness, determination ∼ *vb* : press or smooth out with an iron — **iron·ware** *n* — **iron·work** *n* — **iron·work·er** *n* — **iron·works** *n pl*

iron·clad \-'klad\ *adj* 1 : sheathed in iron armor 2 : strict or exacting

iron·ing \'īərniŋ\ *n* : clothes to be ironed

iron·wood \-₁wùd\ *n* : tree or shrub with very hard wood or this wood

◆ **iro·ny** \'īrənē\ *n, pl* -nies 1 : use of words to express the opposite of the literal meaning 2 : incongruity between the actual and expected result of events — **iron·ic** \ī'ränik\, **iron·i·cal** \-ikəl\ *adj* — **iron·i·cal·ly** \-iklē\ *adv*

ir·ra·di·ate \ir'ādē₁āt\ *vb* -at·ed; -at·ing : treat with radiation — **ir·ra·di·a·tion** \-₁ādē'āshən\ *n*

ir·ra·tio·nal \ir'ashənəl\ *adj* 1 : incapable of reasoning 2 : not based on reason — **ir·ra·tio·nal·i·ty** \ir₁ashə'nalətē\ *n* — **ir·ra·tio·nal·ly** *adv*

ir·rec·on·cil·able \ir₁ekən'sīləbəl\ *adj* : impossible to reconcile — **ir·rec·on·cil·abil·i·ty** \-₁sīlə'bilətē\ *n*

ir·re·cov·er·able \iri'kəvərəbəl\ *adj* : not capable of being recovered — **ir·re·cov·er·ably** \-blē\ *adv*

ir·re·deem·able \ˌiri'dēməbəl\ *adj* : not redeemable

ir·re·duc·ible \ˌiri'düsəbəl, -'dyü-\ *adj* : not reducible — **ir·re·duc·ibly** \-blē\ *adv*

ir·re·fut·able \ˌiri'fyütəbəl, ir-'refyət-\ *adj* : impossible to refute

ir·reg·u·lar \ir'egyələr\ *adj* : not regular or normal — **irregular** *n* — **ir·reg·u·lar·i·ty** \ir,egyə-'larətē\ *n* — **ir·reg·u·lar·ly** *adv*

ir·rel·e·vant \ir'eləvənt\ *adj* : not relevant — **ir·rel·e·vance** \-vəns\ *n*

ir·re·li·gious \ˌiri'lijəs\ *adj* : not following religious practices

ir·rep·a·ra·ble \ir'epərəbəl\ *adj* : impossible to make good, undo, or remedy

ir·re·place·able \ˌiri'plāsəbəl\ *adj* : not replaceable

ir·re·press·ible \-'presəbəl\ *adj* : impossible to repress or control

ir·re·proach·able \-'prōchəbəl\ *adj* : blameless

ir·re·sist·ible \-'zistəbəl\ *adj* : impossible to successfully resist — **ir·re·sist·ibly** \-blē\ *adv*

ir·res·o·lute \ir'ezəlüt\ *adj* : uncertain — **ir·res·o·lute·ly** *adv* — **ir·res·o·lu·tion** \-,ezə'lüshən\ *n*

ir·re·spec·tive of \ˌiri'spektiv-\ *prep* : without regard to

ir·re·spon·si·ble \ˌiri'spänsəbəl\ *adj* : not responsible — **ir·re·spon·si·bil·i·ty** \-ˌspänsə'bilətē\ *n* — **ir·re·spon·si·bly** *adv*

ir·re·triev·able \ˌiri'trēvəbəl\ *adj* : not retrievable

ir·rev·er·ence \ir'evərəns\ *n* **1** : lack of reverence **2** : irreverent act or utterance — **ir·rev·er·ent** \-rənt\ *adj*

ir·re·vers·ible \ˌiri'vərsəbəl\ *adj* : incapable of being reversed

ir·rev·o·ca·ble \ir'evəkəbəl\ *adj* : incapable of being revoked — **ir·rev·o·ca·bly** \-blē\ *adv*

ir·ri·gate \'irə,gāt\ *vb* **-gat·ed; -gat·ing** : supply with water by artificial means — **ir·ri·ga·tion** \ˌirə-'gāshən\ *n*

ir·ri·tate \'irə,tāt\ *vb* **-tat·ed; -tat·ing 1** : excite to anger **2** : make sore or inflamed — **ir·ri·ta·bil·i·ty** \ˌirətə'bilətē\ *n* — **ir·ri·ta·ble** \'irətəbəl\ *adj* — **ir·ri·ta·bly** \'irətəblē\ *adv* — **ir·ri·tant** \'irətənt\ *adj or n* — **ir·ri·tat·ing·ly** *adv* — **ir·ri·ta·tion** \ˌirə'tāshən\ *n*

is *pres 3d sing of* BE

-ish \ish\ *adj suffix* **1** : characteristic of **2** : somewhat

Is·lam \is'läm, iz-, -'lam\ *n* : religious faith of Muslims — **Is·lam·ic** \-ik\ *adj*

is·land \'īlənd\ *n* : body of land surrounded by water — **is·land·er** \'īləndər\ *n*

isle \'īl\ *n* : small island

is·let \'īlət\ *n* : small island

-ism \ˌizəm\ *n suffix* **1** : act or practice **2** : characteristic manner **3** : condition **4** : doctrine

iso·late \'īsə,lāt\ *vb* **-lat·ed; -lat·ing** : place or keep by itself — **iso·la·tion** \ˌīsə'lāshən\ *n*

iso·met·rics \ˌīsə'metriks\ *n sing or pl* : exercise against unmoving resistance — **isometric** *adj*

isos·ce·les \ī'säsə,lēz\ *adj* : having 2 equal sides

iso·tope \'īsə,tōp\ *n* : species of atom of a chemical element — **iso·to·pic** \ˌīsə'täpik, -'tō-\ *adj*

is·sue \'ishü\ *vb* **-sued; -su·ing 1** : go, come, or flow out **2** : descend from a specified ancestor **3** : emanate or result **4** : put forth or distribute officially ~ *n* **1** : action of issuing **2** : offspring **3** : result **4** : point of controversy **5** : act of

giving out or printing **6** : quantity given out or printed — **is·su·ance** \'ishəwəns\ *n* — **is·su·er** *n*

-ist \ist\ *n suffix* **1** : one that does **2** : one that plays **3** : one that specializes in **4** : follower of a doctrine

isth·mus \'isməs\ *n* : narrow strip of land connecting 2 larger portions

◆ **it** \'it\ *pron* **1** : that one — used of a lifeless thing or an abstract entity **2** — used as an anticipatory subject or object ∼ *n* : player who tries to catch others (as in a game of tag)

ital·ic \ə'talik, i-, ī-\ *n* : style of type with slanting letters — **italic** *adj* — **ital·i·ci·za·tion** \ə,taləsə-'zāshən, i-, ī-\ *n* — **ital·i·cize** \ə-'talə,sīz, i-, ī-\ *vb*

itch \'ich\ *n* **1** : uneasy irritating skin sensation **2** : skin disorder **3** : persistent desire — **itch** *vb* — **itchy** *adj*

item \'ītəm\ *n* **1** : particular in a list, account, or series **2** : piece of news — **item·iza·tion** \,ītəmə'zāshən\ *n* — **item·ize** \'ītə,mīz\ *vb*

itin·er·ant \ī'tinərənt, ə-\ *adj* : traveling from place to place

itin·er·ary \ī'tinə,rerē, ə-\ *n, pl* **-ar·ies** : route or outline of a journey

its \'its\ *adj* : relating to it

it·self \it'self\ *pron* : it — used reflexively or for emphasis

-ity \ətē\ *n suffix* : quality, state, or degree

-ive \iv\ *adj suffix* : that performs or tends toward an action

ivo·ry \'īvərē\ *n, pl* **-ries** **1** : hard creamy-white material of elephants' tusks **2** : pale yellow color

ivy \'īvē\ *n, pl* **ivies** : trailing woody vine with evergreen leaves

-ize \,īz\ *vb suffix* **1** : cause to be, become, or resemble **2** : subject to an action **3** : treat or combine with **4** : engage in an activity

J

j \'jā\ *n, pl* **j's** *or* **js** \'jāz\ : 10th letter of the alphabet

jab \'jab\ *vb* **-bb-** : thrust quickly or abruptly ∼ *n* : short straight punch

jab·ber \'jabər\ *vb* : talk rapidly or unintelligibly — **jabber** *n*

jack \'jak\ *n* **1** : mechanical device to raise a heavy body **2** : small flag **3** : small 6-pointed metal object used in a game (**jacks**) **4** : electrical socket ∼ *vb* **1** : raise with a jack **2** : increase

jack·al \'jakəl, -,ȯl\ *n* : wild dog

jack·ass *n* **1** : male ass **2** : stupid person

jack·et \'jakət\ *n* : garment for the upper body

jack·ham·mer \'jak,hamər\ *n* : pneumatic tool for drilling

jack·knife \'jak,nīf\ *n* : pocketknife ∼ *vb* : fold like a jackknife

jack-o'-lan·tern \'jakə,lantərn\ *n* : lantern made of a carved pumpkin

jack·pot \'jak,pät\ *n* : sum of money won

jack·rab·bit \-ˌrabət\ *n* : large hare of western No. America

jade \'jād\ *n* : usu. green gemstone

jad·ed \'jādəd\ *adj* : dulled or bored by having too much

jag·ged \'jagəd\ *adj* : sharply notched

jag·uar \'jag-ˌwär, 'jagyə-\ *n* : black-spotted tropical American cat

jai alai \'hī-ˌlī\ *n* : game with a ball propelled by a basket on the hand

jail \'jāl\ *n* : prison — **jail** *vb* — **jail·break** *n* — **jail·er, jail·or** *n*

ja·la·pe·ño \ˌhälə'pān-ˌyō, -ˌpēnō\ *n* : Mexican hot pepper

ja·lopy \jə'läpē\ *n, pl* **-lopies** : dilapidated vehicle

jal·ou·sie \'jaləsē\ *n* : door or window with louvers

jam \'jam\ *vb* **-mm- 1** : press into a tight position **2** : cause to become wedged and unworkable ~ *n* **1** : crowded mass that blocks or impedes **2** : difficult situation **3** : thick sweet food made of cooked fruit

jamb \'jam\ *n* : upright framing piece of a door

jam·bo·ree \ˌjambə'rē\ *n* : large festive gathering

jan·gle \'jaŋgəl\ *vb* **-gled; -gling** : make a harsh ringing sound — **jangle** *n*

jan·i·tor \'janətər\ *n* : person who has the care of a building — **jan·i·to·ri·al** \ˌjanə'tōrēəl\ *adj*

Jan·u·ary \'janyəˌwerē\ *n* : 1st month of the year having 31 days

¹jar \'jär\ *vb* **-rr- 1** : have a harsh or disagreeable effect **2** : vibrate or shake ~ *n* **1** : jolt **2** : painful effect

²jar *n* : wide-mouthed container

jar·gon \'järgən, -ˌgän\ *n* : special vocabulary of a group

jas·mine \'jazmən\ *n* : climbing shrub with fragrant flowers

jas·per \'jaspər\ *n* : red, yellow, or brown opaque quartz

jaun·dice \'jȯndəs\ *n* : yellowish discoloration of skin, tissues, and body fluids

jaun·diced \-dəst\ *adj* : exhibiting envy or hostility

jaunt \'jȯnt\ *n* : short pleasure trip

jaun·ty \'jȯntē\ *adj* **-ti·er; -est** : lively in manner or appearance — **jaun·ti·ly** \'jȯntʲlē\ *adv* — **jaun·ti·ness** *n*

jav·e·lin \'javələn\ *n* : light spear

jaw \'jȯ\ *n* **1** : either of the bony or cartilaginous structures that support the mouth **2** : one of 2 movable parts for holding or crushing ~ *vb* : talk indignantly or at length — **jaw·bone** \-ˌbōn\ *n* — **jawed** \'jȯd\ *adj*

jay \'jā\ *n* : noisy brightly colored bird

jay·bird *n* : jay

jay·walk *vb* : cross a street carelessly — **jay·walk·er** *n*

jazz \'jaz\ *vb* : enliven ~ *n* **1** : kind of American music involving improvisation **2** : empty talk — **jazzy** *adj*

jeal·ous \'jeləs\ *adj* : suspicious of a rival or of one believed to enjoy an advantage — **jeal·ous·ly** *adv* — **jeal·ou·sy** \-əsē\ *n*

jeans \'jēnz\ *n pl* : pants made of durable twilled cotton cloth

jeep \'jēp\ *n* : 4-wheel army vehicle

jeer \'jir\ *vb* **1** : speak or cry out in derision **2** : ridicule ~ *n* : taunt

Je·ho·vah \ji'hōvə\ *n* : God

je·june \ji'jün\ *adj* : dull or childish

jell \'jel\ *vb* **1** : come to the consistency of jelly **2** : take shape

jel·ly \'jelē\ *n, pl* **-lies** : a substance (as food) with a soft somewhat elastic consistency — **jelly** *vb*

jel·ly·fish *n* : sea animal with a saucer-shaped jellylike body

jen·ny \'jenē\ *n, pl* **-nies** : female bird or donkey

jeop·ar·dy \'jepərdē\ *n* : exposure to death, loss, or injury — **jeop·ar·dize** \-ərˌdīz\ *vb*

jerk \'jərk\ *vb* **1** : give a sharp quick push, pull, or twist **2** : move in short abrupt motions ~ *n* **1** : short quick pull or twist **2** : stupid or foolish person — **jerk·i·ly** *adv* — **jerky** *adj*

jer·kin \'jərkən\ *n* : close-fitting sleeveless jacket

jer·ry–built \'jerēˌbilt\ *adj* : built cheaply and flimsily

jer·sey \'jərzē\ *n, pl* **-seys 1** : plain knit fabric **2** : knitted shirt

jest \'jest\ *n* : witty remark — **jest** *vb*

jest·er \'jestər\ *n* : one employed to entertain a court

¹jet \'jet\ *n* : velvet-black coal used for jewelry

²jet *vb* **-tt- 1** : spout or emit in a stream **2** : travel by jet ~ *n* **1** : forceful rush of fluid through a narrow opening 2 : jet-propelled airplane

jet–propelled *adj* : driven by an engine (**jet engine**) that produces propulsion (**jet propulsion**) by the rearward discharge of a jet of fluid

jet·sam \'jetsəm\ *n* : jettisoned goods

jet·ti·son \'jetəsən\ *vb* 1 : throw (goods) overboard 2 : discard — **jettison** *n*

jet·ty \'jetē\ *n, pl* **-ties** : pier or wharf

Jew \'jü\ *n* : one whose religion is Judaism — **Jew·ish** *adj*

jew·el \'jüəl\ *n* 1 : ornament of precious metal 2 : gem ∼ *vb* **-eled** *or* **-elled**; **-el·ing** *or* **-el·ling** : adorn with jewels — **jew·el·er, jew·el·ler** \-ər\ *n* — **jew·el·ry** \-rē\ *n*

jib \'jib\ *n* : triangular sail

jibe \'jīb\ *vb* **jibed**; **jib·ing** : be in agreement

jif·fy \'jifē\ *n, pl* **-fies** : short time

jig \'jig\ *n* : lively dance ∼ *vb* **-gg-** : dance a jig

jig·ger \'jigər\ *n* : measure used in mixing drinks

jig·gle \'jigəl\ *vb* **-gled**; **-gling** : move with quick little jerks — **jiggle** *n*

jig·saw \'n : machine saw with a narrow blade that moves up and down

jilt \'jilt\ *vb* : drop (a lover) unfeelingly

jim·my \'jimē\ *n, pl* **-mies** : small crowbar ∼ *vb* **-mied**; **-my·ing** : pry open

jim·son·weed \'jimsən,wēd\ *n* : coarse poisonous weed

jin·gle \'jiŋgəl\ *vb* **-gled**; **-gling** : make a light tinkling sound ∼ *n* 1 : light tinkling sound 2 : short verse or song

jin·go·ism \'jiŋgō,izəm\ *n* : extreme chauvinism or nationalism — **jin·go·ist** \-ist\ *n* — **jin·go·is·tic** \,jiŋgō'istik\ *adj*

jinx \'jiŋks\ *n* : one that brings bad luck — **jinx** *vb*

jit·ney \'jitnē\ *n, pl* **-neys** : small bus

jit·ters \'jitərz\ *n pl* : extreme nervousness — **jit·tery** \-ərē\ *adj*

job \'jäb\ *n* 1 : something that has to be done 2 : regular employment — **job·hold·er** *n* — **job·less** *adj*

job·ber \'jäbər\ *n* : middleman

jock·ey \'jäkē\ *n, pl* **-eys** : one who rides a horse in a race ∼ *vb* **-eyed**; **-ey·ing** : manipulate or maneuver adroitly

jo·cose \jō'kōs\ *adj* : jocular

joc·u·lar \'jäkyələr\ *adj* : marked by jesting — **joc·u·lar·i·ty** \,jäkyə'larətē\ *n* — **joc·u·lar·ly** *adv*

jo·cund \'jäkənd\ *adj* : full of mirth or gaiety

jodh·purs \'jädpərz\ *n pl* : riding breeches

¹**jog** \'jäg\ *vb* **-gg-** 1 : give a slight shake or push to 2 : run or ride at a slow pace ∼ *n* 1 : slight shake 2 : slow pace — **jog·ger** *n*

²**jog** *n* : brief abrupt change in direction or line

join \'join\ *vb* 1 : come or bring together 2 : become a member of — **join·er** *n*

joint \'joint\ *n* 1 : point of contact between bones 2 : place where 2 parts connect 3 : often disreputable place ∼ *adj* : common to 2 or more — **joint·ed** *adj* — **joint·ly** *adv*

joist \'joist\ *n* : beam supporting a floor or ceiling

joke \'jōk\ *n* : something said or done to provoke laughter ∼ *vb* **joked**; **jok·ing** : make jokes — **jok·er** *n* — **jok·ing·ly** \'jōkiŋlē\ *adv*

jol·li·ty \'jälətē\ *n, pl* **-ties** : gaiety or merriment

jol·ly \'jälē\ *adj* **-li·er**; **-est** : full of high spirits

jolt \'jōlt\ *vb* 1 : move with a sudden jerky motion 2 : give a jolt to ∼ *n* 1 : abrupt jerky blow or movement 2 : sudden shock — **jolt·er** *n*

jon·quil \'jänkwəl\ *n* : narcissus with white or yellow flowers

josh \'jäsh\ *vb* : tease or joke

jos·tle \'jäsəl\ *vb* **-tled**; **-tling** : push or shove

jot \'jät\ *n* : least bit ∼ *vb* **-tt-** : write briefly and hurriedly

jounce \'jaůns\ *vb* **jounced**; **jounc·ing** : jolt — **jounce** *n*

jour·nal \'jərn³l\ *n* 1 : brief account of daily events 2 : periodical (as a newspaper)

jour·nal·ism \'jərn³l,izəm\ *n* : business of reporting or printing news — **jour·nal·ist** \-ist\ *n* — **jour·nal·is·tic** \,jərn³l'istik\ *adj*

jour·ney \'jərnē\ *n, pl* **-neys** : a going from one place to another ∼ *vb* **-neyed**; **-ney·ing** : make a journey

jour·ney·man \-mən\ *n* : worker

who has learned a trade and works
for another person

joust \'jaůst\ *n* : combat on horseback between 2 knights with lanc-
es — **joust** *vb*

jo·vi·al \'jōvēəl\ *adj* : marked by
good humor — **jo·vi·al·i·ty** \,jōvē-
'alətē\ *n* — **jo·vi·al·ly** \'jōvēəlē\
adv

♦ **¹jowl** \'jaůl\ *n* : loose flesh about
the lower jaw or throat

²jowl *n* **1** : lower jaw **2** : cheek

joy \'jói\ *n* **1** : feeling of happiness **2**
: source of happiness — **joy** *vb* —
joy·ful *adj* — **joy·ful·ly** *adv* — **joy-
less** *adj* — **joy·ous** \'jóiəs\ *adj* —
joy·ous·ly *adv* — **joy·ous·ness** *n*

joy·ride \-,rīd\ *n* : reckless ride for pleasure — **joy·rid·er** *n* — **joy·rid·
ing** *n*

ju·bi·lant \'jübələnt\ *adj* : expressing great joy — **ju·bi·lant·ly** *adv*
— **ju·bi·la·tion** \,jübə'lāshən\ *n*

ju·bi·lee \'jübə,lē\ *n* **1** : 50th anniversary **2** : season or occasion of
celebration

Ju·da·ism \'jüdə,izəm\ *n* : religion
developed among the ancient Hebrews — **Ju·da·ic** \jù'dāik\ *adj*

judge \'jəj\ *vb* **judged; judg·ing 1**
: form an opinion **2** : decide as a
judge ~ *n* **1** : public official authorized to decide questions
brought before a court **2** : one
who gives an authoritative opinion — **judge·ship** *n*

judg·ment, judge·ment \'jəjmənt\ *n*
1 : decision or opinion given after
judging **2** : capacity for judging —
judg·men·tal \,jəj'mentəl\ *adj* —
judg·men·tal·ly *adv*

ju·di·ca·ture \'jüdikə,chùr\ *n* : administration of justice

ju·di·cial \jù'dishəl\ *adj* : relating
to judicature or the judiciary —
ju·di·cial·ly *adv*

ju·di·cia·ry \jù'dishē,erē, -'dishərē\

n : system of courts of law or the
judges of them — **judiciary** *adj*

ju·di·cious \jù'dishəs\ *adj* : having
or characterized by sound judgment — **ju·di·cious·ly** *adv*

ju·do \'jüdō\ *n* : form of wrestling
— **judo·ist** *n*

jug \'jəg\ *n* : large deep container
with a narrow mouth and a handle

jug·ger·naut \'jəgər,nòt\ *n* : massive
inexorable force or object

jug·gle \'jəgəl\ *vb* **-gled; -gling 1**
: keep several objects in motion in
the air at the same time **2** : manipulate for an often tricky purpose
— **jug·gler** \'jəglər\ *n*

jug·u·lar \'jəgyələr\ *adj* : in or on
the throat or neck

juice \'jüs\ *n* **1** : extractable fluid
contents of cells or tissues **2** : electricity — **juic·er** *n* — **juic·i·ly**
\'jüsəlē\ *adv* — **juic·i·ness**
\-sēnəs\ *n* — **juicy** \'jüsē\ *adj*

ju·jube \'jü,jüb, 'jüjù,bē\ *n* : gummy
candy

juke·box \'jük,bäks\ *n* : coin-
operated machine for playing music recordings

ju·lep \'jüləp\ *n* : mint-flavored
bourbon drink

Ju·ly \jù'lī\ *n* : 7th month of the
year having 31 days

jum·ble \'jəmbəl\ *vb* **-bled; -bling**
: mix in a confused mass — **jum-
ble** *n*

jum·bo \'jəmbō\ *n, pl* **-bos** : very
large version — **jumbo** *adj*

jump \'jəmp\ *vb* **1** : rise into or
through the air esp. by muscular
effort **2** : pass over **3** : give a start
4 : rise or increase sharply ~ *n* **1**
: a jumping **2** : sharp sudden increase **3** : initial advantage

¹jump·er \'jəmpər\ *n* : one that
jumps

²jumper *n* : sleeveless one-piece dress

jumpy \\'jəmpē\\ *adj* **jump·i·er; -est**
: nervous or jittery

junc·tion \\'jəŋkshən\\ *n* **1** : a joining
2 : place or point of meeting

junc·ture \\'jəŋkchər\\ *n* **1** : joint or
connection **2** : critical time or
state of affairs

June \\'jün\\ *n* : 6th month of the
year having 30 days

jun·gle \\'jəŋgəl\\ *n* : thick tangled
mass of tropical vegetation

ju·nior \\'jünyər\\ *n* **1** : person who is
younger or of lower rank than an-
other **2** : student in the next-
to-last year ~ *adj* : younger or
lower in rank

ju·ni·per \\'jünəpər\\ *n* : evergreen
shrub or tree

¹junk \\'jəŋk\\ *n* **1** : discarded articles **2**
: shoddy product ~ *vb* : discard
or scrap — **junky** *adj*

²junk *n* : flat-bottomed ship of Chinese waters

jun·ket \\'jəŋkət\\ *n* : trip made by an
official at public expense

jun·ta \\'hùntə, 'jəntə, 'həntə\\ *n*
: group of persons controlling a
government

ju·ris·dic·tion \\,jùrəs'dikshən\\ *n* **1**
: right or authority to interpret
and apply the law **2** : limits within
which authority may be exercised
— **ju·ris·dic·tion·al** \\-shənəl\\ *adj*

ju·ris·pru·dence \\-'prüd³ns\\ *n* **1**
: system of laws **2** : science or philosophy of law

ju·rist \\'jùrist\\ *n* : judge

ju·ror \\'jùrər\\ *n* : member of a jury

ju·ry \\'jùrē\\ *n, pl* **-ries** : body of persons sworn to give a verdict on a
matter

just \\'jəst\\ *adj* **1** : reasonable **2** : correct or proper **3** : morally or legal-
ly right **4** : deserved ~ *adv* **1** : exactly **2** : very recently **3** : barely **4**
: only **5** : quite **6** : possibly — **justly** *adv* — **just·ness** *n*

jus·tice \\'jəstəs\\ *n* **1** : administration
of what is just **2** : judge **3** : administration of law **4** : fairness

♦ **jus·ti·fy** \\'jəstə,fī\\ *vb* **-fied; -fy-
ing** : prove to be just, right, or reasonable — **jus·ti·fi·able** *adj* —
jus·ti·fi·ca·tion \\,jəstəfə'kāshən\\
n

jut \\'jət\\ *vb* **-tt-** : stick out

jute \\'jüt\\ *n* : strong glossy fiber
from a tropical plant

ju·ve·nile \\'jüvə,nīl, -vən³l\\ *adj* : relating to children or young people
~ *n* : young person

jux·ta·pose \\'jəkstə,pōz\\ *vb* **-posed;
-pos·ing** : place side by side — **jux-
ta·po·si·tion** \\,jəkstəpə'zishən\\ *n*

K

k \\'kā\\ *n, pl* **k's** *or* **ks** \\'kāz\\ : 11th
letter of the alphabet

kai·ser \\'kīzər\\ *n* : German ruler

kale \\'kāl\\ *n* : curly cabbage

ka·lei·do·scope \\kə'līdə,skōp\\ *n*
: device containing loose bits of

colored material reflecting in
many patterns — **ka·lei·do·scop-
ic** \\-,līdə'skäpik\\ *adj* — **ka·lei·do-
scop·i·cal·ly** \\-iklē\\ *adv*

kan·ga·roo \\,kaŋgə'rü\\ *n, pl* **-roos**

: large leaping Australian mammal

ka·o·lin \'kāələn\ *n* : fine white clay

kar·at \'karət\ *n* : unit of gold content

ka·ra·te \kə'rätē\ *n* : art of self-defense by crippling kicks and punches

ka·ty·did \'kātē,did\ *n* : large American grasshopper

kay·ak \'kī,ak\ *n* : Eskimo canoe

ka·zoo \kə'zü\ *n, pl* **-zoos** : toy musical instrument

keel \'kēl\ *n* : central lengthwise strip on the bottom of a ship — **keeled** \'kēld\ *adj*

keen \'kēn\ *adj* 1 : sharp 2 : severe 3 : enthusiastic 4 : mentally alert — **keen·ly** *adv* — **keen·ness** *n*

keep \'kēp\ *vb* **kept** \'kept\; **keeping** 1 : perform 2 : guard 3 : maintain 4 : retain in one's possession 5 : detain 6 : continue in good condition 7 : refrain ～ *n* 1 : fortress 2 : means by which one is kept — **keep·er** *n*

keep·ing \'kēpiŋ\ *n* : conformity

keep·sake \'kēp,sāk\ *n* : souvenir

keg \'keg\ *n* : small cask or barrel

kelp \'kelp\ *n* : coarse brown seaweed

ken \'ken\ *n* : range of sight or understanding

ken·nel \'ken°l\ *n* : dog shelter — **ken·nel** *vb*

ker·chief \'kərchəf, -,chēf\ *n* : square of cloth worn as a head covering

ker·nel \'kərn°l\ *n* 1 : inner softer part of a seed or nut 2 : whole seed of a cereal 3 : central part

ker·o·sene, ker·o·sine \'kerə,sēn, ,kerə'-\ *n* : thin flammable oil from petroleum

ketch·up \'kechəp, 'ka-\ *n* : spicy tomato sauce

ket·tle \'ket°l\ *n* : vessel for boiling liquids

ket·tle·drum \-,drum\ *n* : brass or copper kettle-shaped drum

¹**key** \'kē\ *n* 1 : usu. metal piece to open a lock 2 : explanation 3 : lever pressed by a finger in playing an instrument or operating a machine 4 : leading individual or principle 5 : system of musical tones or pitch ～ *vb* : attune ～ *adj* : basic — **key·hole** *n* — **key up** *vb* : make nervous

²**key** *n* : low island or reef

key·board *n* : arrangement of keys

key·note \-,nōt\ *n* 1 : 1st note of a scale 2 : central fact, idea, or mood ～ *vb* 1 : set the keynote of 2 : deliver the major speech

key·stone *n* : wedge-shaped piece at the crown of an arch

key·word *n* : significant or most important word in a statement or document

kha·ki \'kakē, 'käk-\ *n* : light yellowish brown color

khan \'kän, 'kan\ *n* : Mongol leader

kib·butz \kib'üts, -'üts\ *n, pl* **-butzim** \-,üt'sēm, -,üt-\ : Israeli communal farm or settlement

ki·bitz·er \'kibətsər, kə'bit-\ *n* : one who offers unwanted advice — **kib·itz** \'kibəts\ *vb*

◆ **kick** \'kik\ *vb* 1 : strike out or hit with the foot 2 : object strongly 3 : recoil ～ *n* 1 : thrust with the foot 2 : recoil of a gun 3 : stimulating effect — **kick·er** *n*

kid \'kid\ *n* 1 : young goat 2 : child ～ *vb* **-dd-** 1 : deceive as a joke 2 : tease — **kid·der** *n* — **kid·ding·ly** *adv*

kid·nap \'kid,nap\ *vb* **-napped** *or* **-naped** \-,napt\; **-nap·ping** *or* **-naping** : carry a person away by illegal force — **kid·nap·per, kid·nap·er** *n*

kid·ney \'kidnē\ *n, pl* **-neys** : either of a pair of organs that excrete urine

kill \'kil\ *vb* **1** : deprive of life **2** : finish **3** : use up (time) ~ *n* : act of killing — **kill·er** *n*

kiln \'kil, 'kiln\ *n* : heated enclosure for burning, firing, or drying — **kiln** *vb*

ki·lo \'kēlō\ *n, pl* **-los** : kilogram

kilo·cy·cle \'kilə,sīkəl\ *n* : kilohertz

ki·lo·gram \'kēlə,gram, 'kilə-\ *n* : basic metric mass unit nearly equal to the mass of 1000 cubic centimeters of water at its maximum density

ki·lo·hertz \'kilə,hərts, 'kēlə-, -,herts\ *n* : 1000 hertz

ki·lo·me·ter \kil'ämətər, 'kilə,mēt-\ *n* : 1000 meters

ki·lo·volt \'kilə,vōlt\ *n* : 1000 volts

kilo·watt \'kilə,wät\ *n* : 1000 watts

kilt \'kilt\ *n* : knee-length pleated skirt

kil·ter \'kiltər\ *n* : proper condition

ki·mo·no \kə'mōnō\ *n, pl* **-nos** : loose robe

kin \'kin\ *n* **1** : one's relatives **2** : kinsman

kind \'kīnd\ *n* **1** : essential quality **2** : group with common traits **3** : variety ~ *adj* **1** : of a sympathetic nature **2** : arising from sympathy — **kind·heart·ed** *adj* — **kind·ness** *n*

kin·der·gar·ten \'kindər,gärt°n\ *n* : class for young children — **kin·der·gart·ner** \-,gärtnər\ *n*

kin·dle \'kind°l\ *vb* **-dled; -dling 1** : set on fire or start burning **2** : stir up

kin·dling \'kindliŋ, 'kinlən\ *n* : material for starting a fire

kind·ly \'kīndlē\ *adj* **-li·er; -est** : of a sympathetic nature ~ *adv* **1** : sympathetically **2** : courteously — **kind·li·ness** *n*

kin·dred \'kindrəd\ *n* **1** : related individuals **2** : kin ~ *adj* : of a like nature

kin·folk \'kin,fōk\; **kinfolks** *n pl* : kin

king \'kiŋ\ *n* : male sovereign — **king·dom** \-dəm\ *n* — **king·less** *adj* — **king·ly** *adj* — **king·ship** *n*

king·fish·er \-,fishər\ *n* : bright-colored crested bird

kink \'kiŋk\ *n* **1** : short tight twist or curl **2** : cramp — **kinky** *adj*

kin·ship *n* : relationship

kins·man \'kinzmən\ *n* : male relative

kins·wom·an \-,wùmən\ *n* : female relative

kip·per \'kipər\ *n* : dried or smoked fish — **kipper** *vb*

kiss \'kis\ *vb* : touch with the lips as a mark of affection — **kiss** *n*

kit \'kit\ *n* : set of articles (as tools or parts)

kitch·en \'kichən\ *n* : room with cooking facilities

kite \'kīt\ *n* **1** : small hawk **2** : covered framework flown at the end of a string

kith \'kith\ *n* : familiar friends

kit·ten \'kit°n\ *n* : young cat — **kit·ten·ish** *adj*

¹kit·ty \'kitē\ *n, pl* **-ties** : kitten

²kitty *n, pl* **-ties** : fund or pool (as in a card game)

kit·ty–cor·ner, kit·ty–cor·nered *var of* CATERCORNER

ki·wi \'kē,wē\ *n* : small flightless New Zealand bird

klep·to·ma·nia \,kleptə'mānēə\ *n* : neurotic impulse to steal — **klep·to·ma·ni·ac** \-nē,ak\ *adj*

knack \'nak\ *n* **1** : clever way of doing something **2** : natural aptitude

knap·sack \'nap,sak\ *n* : bag for carrying supplies on one's back

knave \'nāv\ *n* : rogue — **knav·ery** \'nāvərē\ *n* — **knav·ish** \'nāvish\ *adj*

knead \'nēd\ *vb* **1** : work and press with the hands **2** : massage — **knead·er** *n*

knee \'nē\ *n* : joint in the middle part of the leg — **kneed** \'nēd\ *adj*

knee·cap \'nē,kap\ *n* : bone forming the front of the knee

kneel \'nēl\ *vb* **knelt** \'nelt\ *or* **kneeled; kneel·ing** : rest on one's knees

knell \'nel\ *n* : stroke of a bell

knew *past of* KNOW

knick·ers \'nikərz\ *n pl* : pants gathered at the knee

knick·knack \'nik,nak\ *n* : small decorative object

knife \'nīf\ *n, pl* **knives** \'nīvz\ : sharp blade with a handle ~ *vb* **knifed; knif·ing** : stab or cut with a knife

knight \'nīt\ *n* **1** : mounted warrior of feudal times **2** : man honored by a sovereign ~ *vb* : make a

knight of — **knight·hood** *n* —
knight·ly *adv*
knit \'nit\ *vb* **knit** *or* **knit·ted; knit·ting 1** : link firmly or closely **2** : form a fabric by interlacing yarn or thread ∼ *n* : knitted garment — **knit·ter** *n*
knob \'näb\ *n* : rounded protuberance or handle — **knobbed** \'näbd\ *adj* — **knob·by** \'näbē\ *adj*
knock \'näk\ *vb* **1** : strike with a sharp blow **2** : collide **3** : find fault with ∼ *n* : sharp blow — **knock out** *vb* : make unconscious
knock·er *n* : device hinged to a door to knock with
knoll \'nōl\ *n* : small round hill
knot \'nät\ *n* **1** : interlacing (as of string) that forms a lump **2** : base of a woody branch in the stem **3** : group **4** : one nautical mile per hour ∼ *vb* -**tt**- : tie in or with a knot — **knot·ty** *adj*
know \'nō\ *vb* **knew** \'nü, 'nyü\; **known** \'nōn\; **know·ing 1** : perceive directly or understand **2** : be

familiar with — **know·able** *adj* — **know·er** *n*
know·ing \'nōin\ *adj* : shrewdly and keenly alert — **know·ing·ly** *adv*
knowl·edge \'nälij\ *n* **1** : understanding gained by experience **2** : range of information — **knowl·edge·able** *adj*
knuck·le \'nəkəl\ *n* : rounded knob at a finger joint
ko·ala \kō'älə\ *n* : gray furry Australian animal
kohl·ra·bi \kōl'rabē, -'räb-\ *n, pl* -**bies** : cabbage that forms no head
Ko·ran \kə'ran, -'rän\ *n* : book of Islam containing revelations made to Muhammad by Allah
ko·sher \'kōshər\ *adj* : ritually fit for use according to Jewish law
kow·tow \kau'tau, 'kau,tau\ *vb* : show excessive deference
kryp·ton \'krip,tän\ *n* : gaseous chemical element used in lamps
ku·dos \'kyü,däs, 'kü-, -,dōz\ *n* : fame and renown
kum·quat \'kəm,kwät\ *n* : small citrus fruit

L

l \'el\ *n, pl* **l's** *or* **ls** \'elz\ : 12th letter of the alphabet
lab \'lab\ *n* : laboratory
la·bel \'lābəl\ *n* **1** : identification slip **2** : identifying word or phrase ∼ *vb* -**beled** *or* -**belled;** -**bel·ing** *or* -**bel·ling** : put a label on
la·bi·al \'lābēəl\ *adj* : of or relating to the lips
la·bor \'lābər\ *n* **1** : physical or mental effort **2** : physical efforts of childbirth **3** : task **4** : people who work manually ∼ *vb* : work esp. with great effort — **la·bor·er** *n*
lab·o·ra·to·ry \'labrə,tōrē\ *n, pl* -**ries** : place for experimental testing
Labor Day *n* : 1st Monday in September observed as a legal holiday in recognition of working people
la·bo·ri·ous \lə'bōrēəs\ *adj* : requiring great effort — **la·bo·ri·ous·ly** *adv*

lab·y·rinth \'labə,rinth\ *n* : maze — **lab·y·rin·thine** \,labə'rinthən\ *adj*
lace \'lās\ *n* **1** : cord or string for tying **2** : fine net usu. figured fabric ∼ *vb* **laced; lac·ing 1** : tie **2** : adorn with lace — **lacy** \'lāsē\ *adj*
lac·er·ate \'lasə,rāt\ *vb* -**at·ed;** -**at·ing** : tear roughly — **lac·er·a·tion** \,lasə'rāshən\ *n*
lach·ry·mose \'lakrə,mōs\ *adj* : tearful
lack \'lak\ *vb* : be missing or deficient in ∼ *n* : deficiency
lack·a·dai·si·cal \,lakə'dāzikəl\ *adj* : lacking spirit — **lack·a·dai·si·cal·ly** \-klē\ *adv*
lack·ey \'lakē\ *n, pl* -**eys 1** : footman or servant **2** : toady
lack·lus·ter \'lak,ləstər\ *adj* : dull
la·con·ic \lə'känik\ *adj* : sparing of words — **la·con·i·cal·ly** \-iklē\ *adv*

lac·quer \'lakər\ *n* : glossy surface coating — **lacquer** *vb*

la·crosse \lə'krȯs\ *n* : ball game played with long-handled rackets

lac·tate \'lak,tāt\ *vb* **-tat·ed; -tat·ing** : secrete milk — **lac·ta·tion** \lak'tāshən\ *n*

lac·tic \'laktik\ *adj* : relating to milk

la·cu·na \lə'künə, -'kyü-\ *n, pl* **-nae** \-,nē\ *or* **-nas** : blank space or missing part

lad \'lad\ *n* : boy

lad·der \'ladər\ *n* : device with steps or rungs for climbing

lad·en \'lād³n\ *adj* : loaded

la·dle \'lād³l\ *n* : spoon with a deep bowl — **ladle** *vb*

la·dy \'lādē\ *n, pl* **-dies** **1** : woman of rank or authority **2** : woman

la·dy·bird \'lādē,bərd\ *n* : ladybug

la·dy·bug \-,bəg\ *n* : brightly colored beetle

lag \'lag\ *vb* **-gg-** : fail to keep up ~ *n* **1** : a falling behind **2** : interval

la·ger \'lägər\ *n* : beer

lag·gard \'lagərd\ *adj* : slow ~ *n* : one that lags — **lag·gard·ly** *adv or adj* — **lag·gard·ness** *n*

la·gniappe \'lan,yap\ *n* : bonus

la·goon \lə'gün\ *n* : shallow sound, channel, or pond near or connecting with a larger body of water

laid *past of* LAY

lain *past part of* LIE

lair \'lar\ *n* : den

lais·sez–faire \,les,ā'far\ *n* : doctrine opposing government interference in business

la·ity \'lāətē\ *n* : people of a religious faith who are not clergy members

lake \'lāk\ *n* : inland body of water

la·ma \'lämə\ *n* : Buddhist monk

lamb \'lam\ *n* : young sheep or its flesh used as food

lam·baste, lam·bast \lam'bāst, -'bast\ *vb* **1** : beat **2** : censure

lam·bent \'lambənt\ *adj* : light or bright — **lam·ben·cy** \-bənsē\ *n* — **lam·bent·ly** *adv*

lame \'lām\ *adj* **lam·er; lam·est** **1** : having a limb disabled **2** : weak ~ *vb* **lamed; lam·ing** : make lame — **lame·ly** *adv* — **lame·ness** *n*

la·mé \lä'mā, la-\ *n* : cloth with tinsel threads

lame·brain \'lām,brān\ *n* : fool

la·ment \lə'ment\ *vb* **1** : mourn **2** : express sorrow for ~ *n* **1**

: mourning **2** : complaint — **lam·en·ta·ble** \'laməntəbəl, lə'mentə-\ *adj* — **lam·en·ta·bly** \-blē\ *adv* — **lam·en·ta·tion** \,lamən'tāshən\ *n*

lam·i·nat·ed \'lamə,nātəd\ *adj* : made of thin layers of material — **lam·i·nate** \-,nāt\ *vb* — **lam·i·nate** \-nət\ *n or adj* — **lam·i·na·tion** \,lamə'nāshən\ *n*

lamp \'lamp\ *n* : device for producing light or heat

lam·poon \lam'pün\ *n* : satire — **lam·poon** *vb*

lam·prey \'lamprē\ *n, pl* **-preys** : sucking eellike fish

lance \'lans\ *n* : spear ~ *vb* **lanced; lanc·ing** : pierce or open with a lancet

lance corporal *n* : enlisted man in the marine corps ranking above a private first class and below a corporal

lan·cet \'lansət\ *n* : pointed surgical instrument

land \'land\ *n* **1** : solid part of the surface of the earth **2** : country ~ *vb* **1** : go ashore **2** : catch or gain **3** : touch the ground or a surface — **land·less** *adj* — **land·own·er** *n*

land·fill *n* : dump

land·ing \'landiŋ\ *n* **1** : action of one that lands **2** : place for loading passengers and cargo **3** : level part of a staircase

land·la·dy \'land,lādē\ *n* : woman landlord

land·locked *adj* : enclosed by land

land·lord *n* : owner of property

land·lub·ber \-,ləbər\ *n* : one with little sea experience

land·mark \-,märk\ *n* **1** : object that marks a boundary or serves as a guide **2** : event that marks a turning point

land·scape \-,skāp\ *n* : view of natural scenery ~ *vb* **-scaped; -scaping** : beautify a piece of land (as by decorative planting)

land·slide *n* **1** : slipping down of a mass of earth **2** : overwhelming victory

land·ward \'landwərd\ *adj* : toward the land — **landward** *adv*

lane \'lān\ *n* : narrow way

lan·guage \'laŋgwij\ *n* : words and the methods of combining them for communication

lan·guid \'laŋgwəd\ *adj* **1** : weak **2**

: sluggish — **lan·guid·ly** *adv* — **lan·guid·ness** *n*

lan·guish \ˈlaŋgwish\ *vb* : become languid or discouraged

lan·guor \ˈlaŋgər\ *n* : listless indolence — **lan·guor·ous** *adj* — **lan·guor·ous·ly** *adv*

lank \ˈlaŋk\ *adj* **1** : thin **2** : limp

lanky *adj* **lank·i·er; -est** : tall and thin

lan·o·lin \ˈlanᵊlən\ *n* : fatty wax from sheep's wool used in ointments

lan·tern \ˈlantərn\ *n* : enclosed portable light

¹lap \ˈlap\ *n* **1** : front part of the lower trunk and thighs of a seated person **2** : overlapping part **3** : one complete circuit completing a course (as around a track or pool) ∼ *vb* **-pp-** : fold over

²lap *vb* **-pp- 1** : scoop up with the tongue **2** : splash gently

lap·dog *n* : small dog

la·pel \ləˈpel\ *n* : fold of the front of a coat

lap·i·dary \ˈlapəˌderē\ *n* : one who cuts and polishes gems ∼ *adj* : relating to gems

lapse \ˈlaps\ *n* **1** : slight error **2** : termination of a right or privilege **3** : interval ∼ *vb* **lapsed; laps·ing 1** : slip **2** : subside **3** : cease

lap·top \ˈlapˌtäp\ *adj* : of a size that may be used on one's lap

lar·board \ˈlärbərd\ *n* : port side

lar·ce·ny \ˈlärsᵊnē\ *n, pl* **-nies** : theft — **lar·ce·nous** \ˈlärsᵊnəs\ *adj*

larch \ˈlärch\ *n* : tree like a pine that loses its needles

lard \ˈlärd\ *n* : pork fat

lar·der \ˈlärdər\ *n* : pantry

large \ˈlärj\ *adj* **larg·er; larg·est** : greater than average — **large·ly** *adv* — **large·ness** *n*

lar·gesse, lar·gess \lärˈzhes, -ˈjes; ˈlärˌ-\ *n* : liberal giving

lar·i·at \ˈlarēət\ *n* : lasso

¹lark \ˈlärk\ *n* : small songbird

²lark *vb or n* : romp

lar·va \ˈlärvə\ *n, pl* **-vae** \-ˌvē\ : wormlike form of an insect — **lar·val** \-vəl\ *adj*

lar·yn·gi·tis \ˌlarənˈjītəs\ *n* : inflammation of the larynx

lar·ynx \ˈlariŋks\ *n, pl* **-ryn·ges** \ləˈrinˌjēz\ *or* **-ynx·es** : upper part of the trachea — **la·ryn·ge·al** \ˌlarənˈjēəl, ləˈrinjēəl\ *adj*

◆ **la·sa·gna** \ləˈzänyə\ *n* : flat noodles baked usu. with tomato sauce, meat, and cheese

las·civ·i·ous \ləˈsivēəs\ *adj* : lewd — **las·civ·i·ous·ness** *n*

la·ser \ˈlāzər\ *n* : device that produces an intense light beam

¹lash \ˈlash\ *vb* : whip ∼ *n* **1** : stroke esp. of a whip **2** : eyelash

²lash *vb* : bind with a rope or cord

lass \ˈlas\ *n* : girl

lass·ie \ˈlasē\ *n* : girl

las·si·tude \ˈlasəˌtüd, -ˌtyüd\ *n* **1** : fatigue **2** : listlessness

las·so \ˈlasō, laˈsü\ *n, pl* **-sos** *or* **-soes** : rope with a noose for catching livestock — **lasso** *vb*

¹last \ˈlast\ *vb* : continue in existence or operation

²last *adj* **1** : final **2** : previous **3** : least likely ∼ *adv* **1** : at the end **2** : most recently **3** : in conclusion ∼ *n* : something that is last — **last·ly** *adv* — **at last** : finally

³last *n* : form on which a shoe is shaped

latch \ˈlach\ *vb* : catch or get hold ∼ *n* : catch that holds a door closed

late \ˈlāt\ *adj* **lat·er; lat·est 1** : coming or staying after the proper time **2** : advanced toward the end **3** : recently deceased **4** : recent — **late** *adv* — **late·com·er** \-ˌkəmər\ *n* — **late·ly** *adv* — **late·ness** *n*

la·tent \'lāt°nt\ *adj* : present but not visible or expressed — **la·ten·cy** \-°nsē\ *n*

lat·er·al \'latərəl\ *adj* : on or toward the side — **lat·er·al·ly** *adv*

la·tex \'lā,teks\ *n, pl* **-ti·ces** \'lātə,sēz, 'lat-\ *or* **-tex·es** : emulsion of synthetic rubber or plastic

lath \'lath, 'lath\ *n, pl* **laths** *or* **lath** : building material (as a thin strip of wood) used as a base for plaster — **lath** *vb* — **lath·ing** \-iŋ\ *n*

lathe \'lāth\ *n* : machine that rotates material for shaping

lath·er \'lathər\ *n* : foam ~ *vb* : form or spread lather

lat·i·tude \'latə,tüd, -,tyüd\ *n* 1 : distance north or south from the earth's equator 2 : freedom of action

la·trine \lə'trēn\ *n* : toilet

lat·ter \'latər\ *adj* 1 : more recent 2 : being the second of 2 — **lat·ter·ly** *adv*

lat·tice \'latəs\ *n* : framework of crossed strips

laud *vb or n* : praise — **laud·able** *adj* — **laud·ably** *adv*

laugh \'laf, 'laf\ *vb* : show mirth, joy, or scorn with a smile and explosive sound — **laugh** *n* — **laugh·able** *adj* — **laugh·ing·ly** \-iŋlē\ *adv*

laugh·ing·stock \'lafiŋ,stäk, 'laf-\ *n* : object of ridicule

laugh·ter \'laftər, 'laf-\ *n* : action or sound of laughing

¹**launch** \'lónch\ *vb* 1 : hurl or send off 2 : set afloat 3 : start — **launch** *n* — **launch·er** *n*

²**launch** *n* : small open boat

laun·der \'lóndər\ *vb* : wash or iron fabrics — **laun·der·er** *n* — **laun·dress** \-drəs\ *n* — **laun·dry** \-drē\ *n*

lau·re·ate \'lórēət\ *n* : recipient of honors — **laureate** *adj*

lau·rel \'lórəl\ *n* 1 : small evergreen tree 2 : honor

la·va \'lävə, 'lav-\ *n* : volcanic molten rock

lav·a·to·ry \'lavə,tōrē\ *n, pl* **-ries** : bathroom

lav·en·der \'lavəndər\ *n* 1 : aromatic plant used for perfume 2 : pale purple color

lav·ish \'lavish\ *adj* : expended profusely ~ *vb* : expend or give freely — **lav·ish·ly** *adv* — **lav·ish·ness** *n*

law \'ló\ *n* 1 : established rule of conduct 2 : body of such rules 3 : principle of construction or procedure 4 : rule stating uniform behavior under uniform conditions 5 : lawyer's profession — **law·break·er** *n* — **law·giv·er** *n* — **law·less** *adj* — **law·less·ly** *adv* — **law·less·ness** *n* — **law·mak·er** *n* — **law·man** \-mən\ *n* — **law·suit** *n*

law·ful \'lófəl\ *adj* : permitted by law — **law·ful·ly** *adv*

lawn \'lón\ *n* : grass-covered yard

law·yer \'lóyər\ *n* : legal practitioner

lax \'laks\ *adj* : not strict or tense — **lax·i·ty** \'laksətē\ *n* — **lax·ly** *adv*

lax·a·tive \'laksətiv\ *n* : drug relieving constipation

¹**lay** \'lā\ *vb* **laid** \'lād\; **lay·ing** 1 : put or set down 2 : produce eggs 3 : bet 4 : impose as a duty or burden 5 : put forward ~ *n* : way something lies or is laid

²**lay** *past of* LIE

³**lay** *n* : song

⁴**lay** *adj* : of the laity — **lay·man** \-mən\ *n* — **lay·wom·an** \-,wùmən\ *n*

lay·er \'lāər\ *n* 1 : one that lays 2 : one thickness over or under another

lay·off \'lā,óf\ *n* : temporary dismissal of a worker

lay·out \'lā,aút\ *n* : arrangement

la·zy \'lāzē\ *adj* **-zi·er; -est** : disliking activity or exertion — **la·zi·ly** \'lāzəlē\ *adv* — **la·zi·ness** *n*

lea \'lē, 'lā\ *n* : meadow

leach \'lēch\ *vb* : remove (a soluble part) with a solvent

¹**lead** \'lēd\ *vb* **led** \'led\; **lead·ing** 1 : guide on a way 2 : direct the activity of 3 : go at the head of 4 : tend to a definite result ~ *n* : position in front — **lead·er** *n* — **lead·er·less** *adj* — **lead·er·ship** *n*

²**lead** \'led\ *n* 1 : heavy bluish white chemical element 2 : marking substance in a pencil — **lead·en** \'led°n\ *adj*

leaf \'lēf\ *n, pl* **leaves** \'lēvz\ 1 : green outgrowth of a plant stem 2 : leaflike thing ~ *vb* 1 : produce leaves 2 : turn book pages — **leaf·age** \'lēfij\ *n* — **leafed** \'lēft\ *adj* — **leaf·less** *adj* — **leafy** *adj* — **leaved** \'lēfd\ *adj*

leaf·let \'lēflət\ *n* : pamphlet

¹league \\'lēg\ *n* : unit of distance equal to about 3 miles

²league *n* : association for a common purpose — **league** *vb* — **leaguer** *n*

leak \\'lēk\ *vb* **1** : enter or escape through a leak **2** : become or make known $\sim$ *n* : opening that accidentally admits or lets out a substance — **leak·age** \\'lēkij\ *n* — **leaky** *adj*

¹lean \\'lēn\ *vb* **1** : bend from a vertical position **2** : rely on for support **3** : incline in opinion — **lean** *n*

²lean *adj* **1** : lacking in flesh **2** : lacking richness — **lean·ness** \\'lēnnəs\ *n*

leap \\'lēp\ *vb* **leapt** *or* **leaped** \\'lēpt, 'lept\; **leap·ing** : jump — **leap** *n*

leap year *n* : 366-day year

learn \\'lərn\ *vb* **1** : gain understanding or skill by study or experience **2** : memorize **3** : find out — **learner** *n*

learn·ed \-əd\ *adj* : having great learning — **learn·ed·ness** *n*

learn·ing \-iŋ\ *n* : knowledge

lease \\'lēs\ *n* : contract transferring real estate for a term and usu. for rent $\sim$ *vb* **leased**; **leas·ing** : grant by or hold under a lease

leash \\'lēsh\ *n* : line to hold an animal — **leash** *vb*

least \\'lēst\ *adj* **1** : lowest in importance or position **2** : smallest **3** : scantiest $\sim$ *n* : one that is least $\sim$ *adv* : in the smallest or lowest degree

leath·er \\'lethər\ *n* : dressed animal skin — **leath·ern** \-ərn\ *adj* — **leath·ery** *adj*

¹leave \\'lēv\ *vb* **left** \\'left\; **leaving 1** : bequeath **2** : allow or cause to remain **3** : have as a remainder **4** : go away $\sim$ *n* **1** : permission **2** : authorized absence **3** : departure

²leave *vb* **leaved**; **leav·ing** : leaf

leav·en \\'levən\ *n* : substance for producing fermentation $\sim$ *vb* : raise dough with a leaven

leaves *pl of* LEAF

lech·ery \\'lechərē\ *n* : inordinate indulgence in sex — **lech·er** \\'lechər\ *n* — **lech·er·ous** \-chərəs\ *adj* — **lech·er·ous·ly** *adv* — **lech·er·ous·ness** *n*

lec·ture \\'lekchər\ *n* **1** : instructive talk **2** : reprimand — **lecture** *vb* — **lec·tur·er** *n* — **lec·ture·ship** *n*

led *past of* LEAD

ledge \\'lej\ *n* : shelflike projection

led·ger \\'lejər\ *n* : account book

lee \\'lē\ *n* : side sheltered from the wind — **lee** *adj*

leech \\'lēch\ *n* : segmented freshwater worm that feeds on blood

leek \\'lēk\ *n* : onionlike herb

leer \\'lir\ *n* : suggestive or malicious look — **leer** *vb*

leery \\'lirē\ *adj* : suspicious or wary

lees \\'lēz\ *n pl* : dregs

lee·ward \\'lēwərd, 'lüərd\ *adj* : situated away from the wind $\sim$ *n* : the lee side

lee·way \\'lē,wā\ *n* : allowable margin

¹left \\'left\ *adj* : on the same side of the body as the heart $\sim$ *n* : left hand — **left** *adv*

²left *past of* LEAVE

leg \\'leg\ *n* **1** : limb of an animal that supports the body **2** : something like a leg **3** : clothing to cover the leg $\sim$ *vb* **-gg-** : walk or run — **legged** \\'legəd\ *adj* — **leg·less** *adj*

leg·a·cy \\'legəsē\ *n, pl* **-cies** : inheritance

le·gal \\'lēgəl\ *adj* **1** : relating to law or lawyers **2** : lawful — **le·gal·is·tic** \,lēgə'listik\ *adj* — **le·gal·i·ty** \li'galətē\ *n* — **le·gal·ize** \\'lēgə,līz\ *vb* — **le·gal·ly** \-gəlē\ *adv*

leg·ate \\'legət\ *n* : official representative

le·ga·tion \li'gāshən\ *n* **1** : diplomatic mission **2** : official residence and office of a diplomat

leg·end \\'lejənd\ *n* **1** : story handed down from the past **2** : inscription **3** : explanation of map symbols — **leg·end·ary** \-ən,derē\ *adj*

leg·er·de·main \,lejərdə'mān\ *n* : sleight of hand

leg·ging, leg·gin \\'legən, -iŋ\ *n* : leg covering

leg·i·ble \\'lejəbəl\ *adj* : capable of being read — **leg·i·bil·i·ty** \,lejə-'bilətē\ *n* — **leg·i·bly** \\'lejəblē\ *adv*

le·gion \\'lējən\ *n* **1** : large army unit **2** : multitude **3** : association of former servicemen — **le·gion·ary** \-,erē\ *n* — **le·gion·naire** \,lējən-'ar\ *n*

leg·is·late \\'lejə,slāt\ *vb* **-lat·ed; -lat·ing** : enact or bring about with laws — **leg·is·la·tion** \,lejə-'slāshən\ *n* — **leg·is·la·tive** \\'lejə-

,slātiv\ *adj* — **leg·is·la·tor** \-ər\ *n*

leg·is·la·ture \'lejə,slāchər\ *n* : organization with authority to make laws

le·git·i·mate \li'jitəmət\ *adj* 1 : lawfully begotten 2 : genuine 3 : conforming with law or accepted standards — **le·git·i·ma·cy** \-məsē\ *n* — **le·git·i·mate·ly** *adv* — **le·git·i·mize** \-,mīz\ *vb*

le·gume \'leg,yüm, li'gyüm\ *n* : plant bearing pods — **le·gu·mi·nous** \li'gyümənəs\ *adj*

lei \'lā\ *n* : necklace of flowers

lei·sure \'lēzhər, 'lezh-, 'lāzh-\ *n* 1 : free time 2 : ease 3 : convenience — **lei·sure·ly** *adj or adv*

lem·ming \'lemiŋ\ *n* : short-tailed rodent

lem·on \'lemən\ *n* : yellow citrus fruit — **lem·ony** *adj*

◆ **lem·on·ade** \,lemə'nād\ *n* : sweetened lemon beverage

lend \'lend\ *vb* **lent** \'lent\; **lending** 1 : give for temporary use 2 : furnish — **lend·er** *n*

length \'leŋth\ *n* 1 : longest dimension 2 : duration in time 3 : piece to be joined to others — **length·en** \'leŋthən\ *vb* — **length·wise** *adv or adj* — **lengthy** *adj*

le·nient \'lēnēənt, -nyənt\ *adj* : of mild and tolerant disposition or effect — **le·ni·en·cy** \'lēnēənsē -nyənsē\ *n* — **le·ni·ent·ly** *adv*

len·i·ty \'lenətē\ *n* : leniency

lens \'lenz\ *n* 1 : curved piece for forming an image in an optical instrument 2 : transparent body in the eye that focuses light rays

Lent \'lent\ *n* : 40-day period of penitence and fasting from Ash Wednesday to Easter — **Lent·en** \-ᵊn\ *adj*

len·til \'lentᵊl\ *n* : legume with flat edible seeds

le·o·nine \'lēə,nīn\ *adj* : like a lion

leop·ard \'lepərd\ *n* : large tawny black-spotted cat

le·o·tard \'lēə,tärd\ *n* : close-fitting garment

lep·er \'lepər\ *n* : person with leprosy

lep·re·chaun \'leprə,kän\ *n* : mischievous Irish elf

lep·ro·sy \'leprəsē\ *n* : chronic bacterial disease — **lep·rous** \-rəs\ *adj*

les·bi·an \'lezbēən\ *n* : female homosexual — **lesbian** *adj* — **les·bi·an·ism** \-,izəm\ *n*

le·sion \'lēzhən\ *n* : abnormal area in the body due to injury or disease

less \'les\ *adj* 1 : fewer 2 : of lower rank, degree, or importance 3 : smaller ~ *adv* : to a lesser degree ~ *n pl* **less** : smaller portion ~ *prep* : minus — **less·en** \-ᵊn\ *vb*

-less \ləs\ *adj suffix* 1 : not having 2 : unable to act or be acted on

les·see \le'sē\ *n* : tenant under a lease

less·er \'lesər\ *adj* : of less size, quality, or significance

les·son \'lesᵊn\ *n* 1 : reading or exercise to be studied by a pupil 2 : something learned

les·sor \'les,ȯr, le'sȯr\ *n* : one who transfers property by a lease

lest \'lest\ *conj* : for fear that

¹**let** \'let\ *n* : hindrance or obstacle

²**let** *vb* **let**; **let·ting** 1 : cause to 2 : rent 3 : permit

-let \lət\ *n suffix* : small one

le·thal \'lēthəl\ *adj* : deadly — **le·thal·ly** *adv*

◆ **leth·ar·gy** \'lethərjē\ *n* 1 : drowsiness 2 : state of being lazy or indifferent — **le·thar·gic** \li'thärjik\ *adj*

let·ter \'letər\ *n* 1 : unit of an alphabet 2 : written or printed communication 3 *pl* : literature or learning 4 : literal meaning ~ *vb* : mark with letters — **let·ter·er** *n*

let·tuce \'letəs\ *n* : garden plant with crisp leaves

leu·ke·mia \lü'kēmēə\ *n* : cancerous blood disease — **leu·ke·mic** \-mik\ *adj or n*

lev·ee \'levē\ *n* : embankment to prevent flooding

lev·el \'levəl\ *n* 1 : device for establishing a flat surface 2 : horizontal surface 3 : position in a scale ~ *vb* **-eled** *or* **-elled; -el·ing** *or* **-el·ling** 1 : make flat or level 2 : aim 3 : raze ~ *adj* 1 : having an even surface 2 : of the same height or rank — **lev·el·er** *n* — **lev·el·ly** *adv* — **lev·el·ness** *n*

le·ver \'levər, 'lē-\ *n* : bar for prying or dislodging something — **le·ver·age** \'levərij, 'lēv-\ *n*

le·vi·a·than \li'vīəthən\ *n* 1 : large sea animal 2 : enormous thing

lev·i·ty \'levətē\ *n* : unseemly frivolity

levy \'levē\ *n, pl* **lev·ies** : imposition or collection of a tax ~ *vb* **lev·ied; levy·ing** 1 : impose or collect legally 2 : enlist for military service 3 : wage

lewd \'lüd\ *adj* 1 : sexually unchaste 2 : vulgar — **lewd·ly** *adv* — **lewd·ness** *n*

lex·i·cog·ra·phy \,leksə'kägrəfē\ *n* : dictionary making — **lex·i·cog·ra·pher** \-fər\ *n* — **lex·i·co·graph·i·cal** \-kō'grafikəl\ *or* **lex·i·co·graph·ic** \-ik\ *adj*

lex·i·con \'leksə,kän\ *n, pl* **-i·ca** \-sikə\ *or* **-icons** : dictionary

li·a·ble \'līəbəl\ *adj* 1 : legally obligated 2 : probable 3 : susceptible — **li·a·bil·i·ty** \,līə'bilətē\ *n*

li·ai·son \'lēə,zän, lē'ā-\ *n* 1 : close bond 2 : communication between groups

li·ar \'līər\ *n* : one who lies

li·bel \'lībəl\ *n* : action, crime, or an instance of injuring a person's reputation esp. by something written ~ *vb* **-beled** *or* **-belled; -bel·ing** *or* **-bel·ling** : make or publish a libel — **li·bel·er** *n* — **li·bel·ist** *n* — **li·bel·ous, li·bel·lous** \-bələs\ *adj*

lib·er·al \'librəl, 'libə-\ *adj* : not stingy, narrow, or conservative — **liberal** *n* — **lib·er·al·ism** \-,izəm\ *n* — **lib·er·al·i·ty** \,libə'ralətē\ *n* — **lib·er·al·ize** \'librə,līz, 'libə-\ *vb* — **lib·er·al·ly** \-rəlē\ *adv*

lib·er·ate \'libə,rāt\ *vb* **-at·ed; -at·ing** : set free — **lib·er·a·tion** \,libə-'rāshən\ *n* — **lib·er·a·tor** \'libə-,rātər\ *n*

lib·er·tine \'libər,tēn\ *n* : one who leads a dissolute life

lib·er·ty \'libərtē\ *n, pl* **-ties** 1 : quality or state of being free 2 : action going beyond normal limits

li·bi·do \lə'bēdō, -'bīd-\ *n, pl* **-dos** : sexual drive — **li·bid·i·nal** \lə-'bid²nəl\ *adj* — **li·bid·i·nous** \-əs\ *adj*

li·brary \'lī,brerē\ *n, pl* **-brar·ies** 1 : place where books are kept for use 2 : collection of books — **li·brar·i·an** \lī'brerēən\ *n*

li·bret·to \lə'bretō\ *n, pl* **-tos** *or* **-ti** \-ē\ : text of an opera — **li·bret·tist** \-ist\ *n*

lice *pl of* LOUSE

li·cense, li·cence \'līs²ns\ *n* 1 : legal permission to engage in some activity 2 : document or tag providing proof of a license 3 : irresponsible use of freedom — **license** *vb* — **li·cens·ee** \,līs²n'sē\ *n*

li·cen·tious \lī'senchəs\ *adj* : disregarding sexual restraints — **li·cen·tious·ly** *adv* — **li·cen·tious·ness** *n*

li·chen \'līkən\ *n* : complex lower plant made up of an alga and a fungus

lic·it \'lisət\ *adj* : lawful

lick \'lik\ *vb* **1** : draw the tongue over **2** : beat ~ *n* **1** : stroke of the tongue **2** : small amount

lic·o·rice \'likərish, -rəs\ *n* : dried root of a European legume or candy flavored by it

lid \'lid\ *n* **1** : movable cover **2** : eyelid

¹lie \'lī\ *vb* lay \'lā\; lain \'lān\; lying \'liiŋ\ **1** : be in, rest in, or assume a horizontal position **2** : occupy a certain relative position ~ *n* : position in which something lies

²lie *vb* lied; ly·ing \'liiŋ\ : tell a lie ~ *n* : untrue statement

liege \'lēj\ *n* : feudal superior or vassal

lien \'lēn, 'lēən\ *n* : legal claim on the property of another

lieu·ten·ant \lü'tenənt\ *n* **1** : representative **2** : first lieutenant or second lieutenant **3** : commissioned officer in the navy ranking next below a lieutenant commander — lieu·ten·an·cy \-ənsē\ *n*

lieutenant colonel *n* : commissioned officer (as in the army) ranking next below a colonel

lieutenant commander *n* : commissioned officer in the navy ranking next below a commander

lieutenant general *n* : commissioned officer (as in the army) ranking next below a general

lieutenant junior grade *n*, *pl* lieutenants junior grade : commissioned officer in the navy ranking next below a lieutenant

life \'līf\ *n*, *pl* lives \'līvz\ **1** : quality that distinguishes a vital and functional being from a dead body or inanimate matter **2** : physical and mental experiences of an individual **3** : biography **4** : period of existence **5** : way of living **6** : liveliness — life·less *adj* — life·like *adj*

life·blood *n* : basic source of strength and vitality

life·boat *n* : boat for saving lives at sea

life·guard *n* : one employed to safeguard bathers

life·long *adj* : continuing through life

life·sav·ing *n* : art or practice of saving lives — life·sav·er \-,sāvər\ *n*

life·style \'līf,stīl\ *n* : a way of life

life·time *n* : duration of an individual's existence

lift \'lift\ *vb* **1** : move upward or cause to move upward **2** : put an end to — lift *n* — lift·er *n*

lift·off \'lift,öf\ *n* : vertical takeoff by a rocket

lig·a·ment \'ligəmənt\ *n* : band of tough tissue that holds bones together

lig·a·ture \'ligə,chùr, -chər\ *n* : something that binds or ties

¹light \'līt\ *n* **1** : radiation that makes vision possible **2** : daylight **3** : source of light **4** : public knowledge **5** : aspect **6** : celebrity **7** : flame for lighting ~ *adj* **1** : bright **2** : weak in color ~ *vb* lit \'lit\ *or* light·ed; light·ing **1** : make or become light **2** : cause to burn — light·er *n* — light·ness *n* — light·proof *adj*

²light *adj* : not heavy, serious, or abundant — light *adv* — light·ly *adv* — light·ness *n* — light·weight *adj*

³light *vb* light·ed *or* lit \'lit\; light·ing : settle or dismount

¹light·en \'līt⁰n\ *vb* **1** : make light or bright **2** : give out flashes of lightning

²lighten *vb* **1** : relieve of a burden **2** : become lighter

light·heart·ed \-'härtəd\ *adj* : free from worry — light·heart·ed·ly *adv* — light·heart·ed·ness *n*

light·house *n* : structure with a powerful light for guiding sailors

light·ning \'lītniŋ\ *n* : flashing discharge of atmospheric electricity

light–year \'līt,yir\ *n* : distance traveled by light in one year equal to about 5.88 trillion miles

lig·nite \'lig,nīt\ *n* : brownish black soft coal

¹like \'līk\ *vb* liked; lik·ing **1** : enjoy **2** : desire ~ *n* : preference — lik·able, like·able \'līkəbəl\ *adj*

²like *adj* : similar ~ *prep* **1** : similar or similarly to **2** : typical of **3** : such as ~ *n* : counterpart ~ *conj* : as or as if — like·ness *n* — like·wise *adv*

-like \,līk\ *adj comb form* : resembling or characteristic of

like·li·hood \'līklē,hùd\ *n* : probability

like·ly \'līklē\ *adj* -li·er; -est **1**

: probable **2** : believable ~ *adv*
: in all probability

lik·en \\'līkən\\ *vb* : compare

lik·ing \\'līkiŋ\\ *n* : favorable regard

li·lac \\'līlək, -ˌlak, -ˌläk\\ *n* : shrub
with clusters of fragrant pink,
purple, or white flowers

lilt \\'lilt\\ *n* : rhythmical swing or
flow

lily \\'lilē\\ *n, pl* **lil·ies** : tall bulbous
herb with funnel-shaped flowers

lima bean \\'līmə-\\ *n* : flat edible seed
of a plant or the plant itself

limb \\'lim\\ *n* **1** : projecting appendage used in moving or grasping **2**
: tree branch — **limb·less** *adj*

lim·ber \\'limbər\\ *adj* : supple or agile ~ *vb* : make or become limber

lim·bo \\'limbō\\ *n, pl* **-bos** : place or
state of confinement or oblivion

¹lime \\'līm\\ *n* : caustic white oxide of
calcium

²lime *n* : small green lemonlike citrus
fruit — **lime·ade** \\-ˌād\\ *n*

lime·light *n* : center of public attention

lim·er·ick \\'limrik\\ *n* : light poem
of 5 lines

lime·stone *n* : rock that yields lime
when burned

lim·it \\'limət\\ *n* **1** : boundary **2**
: something that restrains or con-
fines ~ *vb* : set limits on — **lim·i·ta·tion** \\ˌliməˈtāshən\\ *n* — **lim·it·less** *adj*

lim·ou·sine \\'liməˌzēn, ˌliməˈ-\\ *n*
: large luxurious sedan

limp \\'limp\\ *vb* : walk lamely ~ *n*
: limping movement or gait ~ *adj*
: lacking firmness and body —
limp·ly *adv* — **limp·ness** *n*

lim·pid \\'limpəd\\ *adj* : clear or
transparent

lin·den \\'lindən\\ *n* : tree with large
heart-shaped leaves

¹line \\'līn\\ *vb* **lined; lin·ing** : cover
the inner surface of — **lin·ing** *n*

²line *n* **1** : cord, rope, or wire **2** : row
or something like a row **3** : note **4**
: course of action or thought **5**
: state of agreement **6** : occupation **7** : limit **8** : transportation system **9** : long narrow mark ~ *vb*
lined; lin·ing 1 : mark with a line **2**
: place in a line **3** : form a line

lin·e·age \\'linēij\\ *n* : descent from a
common ancestor

lin·e·al \\'linēəl\\ *adj* **1** : linear **2** : in a
direct line of ancestry

lin·e·a·ments \\'linēəmənts\\ *n pl*
: features or contours esp. of a
face

lin·e·ar \\'linēər\\ *adj* **1** : straight **2**
: long and narrow

◆ **lin·en** \\'linən\\ *n* **1** : cloth or
thread made of flax **2** : household
articles made of linen cloth

lin·er \\'līnər\\ *n* **1** : one that lines **2**
: ship or airplane belonging to a
line

line·up \\'līnˌəp\\ *n* **1** : line of persons
for inspection or identification **2**
: list of players in a game

-ling \\liŋ\\ *n suffix* **1** : one linked with
2 : young, small, or minor one

lin·ger \\'liŋgər\\ *vb* : be slow to leave
or act — **lin·ger·er** *n*

lin·ge·rie \\ˌlänjəˈrā, ˌlaⁿzhə-, -ˈrē\\ *n*
: women's underwear

lin·go \\'liŋgō\\ *n, pl* **-goes** : usu.
strange language

lin·guist \\'liŋgwist\\ *n* **1** : person
skilled in speech or languages **2**
: student of language — **lin·guis·tic** \\liŋˈgwistik\\ *adj* — **lin·guis·tics** *n pl*

lin·i·ment \\'linəmənt\\ *n* : liquid
medication rubbed on the skin

link \\'liŋk\\ *n* **1** : connecting structure (as a ring of a chain) **2** : bond
— **link** *vb* — **link·age** \\-ij\\ *n* —
link·er *n*

li·no·leum \\ləˈnōlēəm\\ *n* : floor covering with hard surface

PANEL 1: HERE WE SEE / A LION EATING / AN ANTELOPE

PANEL 3: PRETTY ICKY, / HUH? — I'LL SAY. / NO TABLE / LINEN!

lin·seed \'lin,sēd\ *n* : seeds of flax yielding an oil (**linseed oil**)

lint \'lint\ *n* : fine fluff or loose short fibers from fabric

lin·tel \'lint²l\ *n* : horizontal piece over a door or window

li·on \'līən\ *n* : large cat of Africa and Asia — **li·on·ess** \'līənəs\ *n*

li·on·ize \'līə,nīz\ *vb* **-ized; -iz·ing** : treat as very important — **li·on·iza·tion** \,līənə'zāshən\ *n*

lip \'lip\ *n* 1 : either of the 2 fleshy folds surrounding the mouth 2 : edge of something hollow — **lipped** \'lipt\ *adj* — **lip·read·ing** *n*

li·po·suc·tion \'lipə,səkshən, 'lī-\ *n* : surgical removal of fat deposits (as from the thighs)

lip·stick \'lip,stik\ *n* : stick of cosmetic to color lips

liq·ue·fy \'likwə,fī\ *vb* **-fied; -fy·ing** : make or become liquid — **liq·ue·fi·er** \'likwə,fīər\ *n*

li·queur \li'kər\ *n* : sweet or aromatic alcoholic liquor

liq·uid \'likwəd\ *adj* 1 : flowing freely like water 2 : neither solid nor gaseous 3 : of or convertible to cash — **liquid** *n* — **li·quid·i·ty** \lik'widətē\ *n*

liq·ui·date \'likwə,dāt\ *vb* **-dat·ed; -dat·ing** 1 : pay off 2 : dispose of — **liq·ui·da·tion** \,likwə'dāshən\ *n*

li·quor \'likər\ *n* : liquid substance and esp. a distilled alcoholic beverage

lisp \'lisp\ *vb* : pronounce *s* and *z* imperfectly — **lisp** *n*

lis·some \'lisəm\ *adj* : supple or agile

¹list \'list\ *n* 1 : series of names or items ~ *vb* 1 : make a list of 2 : put on a list

²list *vb* : tilt or lean over ~ *n* : slant

lis·ten \'lis²n\ *vb* 1 : pay attention in order to hear 2 : heed — **lis·ten·er** \'lis²nər\ *n*

list·less \'listləs\ *adj* : having no desire to act — **list·less·ly** *adv* — **list·less·ness** *n*

lit \'lit\ *past of* LIGHT

lit·a·ny \'lit²nē\ *n, pl* **-nies** 1 : prayer said as a series of responses to a leader 2 : long recitation

li·ter \'lētər\ *n* : unit of liquid measure equal to about 1.06 quarts

lit·er·al \'litərəl\ *adj* : being exactly as stated — **lit·er·al·ly** *adv*

lit·er·ary \'litə,rerē\ *adj* : relating to literature

lit·er·ate \'litərət\ *adj* : able to read and write — **lit·er·a·cy** \'litərəsē\ *n*

♦ **lit·er·a·ture** \'litərə,chùr, -chər\ *n* : writings of enduring interest

lithe \'līth, 'līth\ *adj* 1 : supple 2 : graceful — **lithe·some** \-səm\ *adj*

lith·o·graph \'lithə,graf\ *n* : print from a drawing on metal or stone — **li·thog·ra·pher** \lith'ägrəfər, 'lithə,grafər\ *n* — **lith·o·graph·ic** \,lithə'grafik\ *adj* — **li·thog·ra·phy** \lith'ägrəfē\ *n*

lit·i·gate \'litə,gāt\ *vb* **-gat·ed; -gat·ing** : carry on a lawsuit — **lit·i·gant** \'litigənt\ *n* — **lit·i·ga·tion** \,litə'gāshən\ *n* — **li·ti·gious** \lə'tijəs, li-\ *adj* — **li·ti·gious·ness** *n*

lit·mus \'litməs\ *n* : coloring matter that turns red in acid solutions and blue in alkaline

lit·ter \'litər\ *n* 1 : animal offspring of one birth 2 : stretcher 3 : rubbish 4 : material to absorb animal waste ~ *vb* 1 : give birth to young 2 : strew with litter

lit·tle \'lit²l\ *adj* **lit·tler** *or* **less** \'les\ *or* **less·er** \'lesər\; **lit·tlest** *or* **least** \'lēst\ 1 : not big 2 : not much 3 : not important — *adv* **less** \'les\; **least** \'lēst\ 1 : slightly 2 : not often ~ *n* : small amount — **lit·tle·ness** *n*

lit·ur·gy \'litərjē\ *n, pl* **-gies** : rite of

worship — **li·tur·gi·cal** \lə-'tərjikəl\ *adj* — **li·tur·gi·cal·ly** \-klē\ *adv* — **lit·ur·gist** \'litərjist\ *n*

liv·able \'livəbəl\ *adj* : suitable for living in or with — **liv·a·bil·i·ty** \,livə'bilətē\ *n*

¹live \'liv\ *vb* **lived; liv·ing 1** : be alive **2** : conduct one's life **3** : subsist **4** : reside

²live \'līv\ *adj* **1** : having life **2** : burning **3** : connected to electric power **4** : not exploded **5** : of continuing interest **6** : involving the actual presence of real people

live·li·hood \'līvlē,hùd\ *n* : means of subsistence

live·long \'liv'lòŋ\ *adj* : whole

live·ly \'līvlē\ *adj* **-li·er; -est** : full of life and vigor — **live·li·ness** *n*

liv·en \'līvən\ *vb* : enliven

liv·er \'livər\ *n* : organ that secretes bile

liv·ery \'livərē\ *n, pl* **-er·ies 1** : servant's uniform **2** : care of horses for pay — **liv·er·ied** \-rēd\ *adj* — **liv·ery·man** \-mən\ *n*

lives *pl of* LIFE

live·stock \'līv,stäk\ *n* : farm animals

liv·id \'livəd\ *adj* **1** : discolored by bruising **2** : pale **3** : enraged

liv·ing \'liviŋ\ *adj* : having life ∼ *n* : livelihood

liz·ard \'lizərd\ *n* : reptile with 4 legs and a long tapering tail

lla·ma \'lämə\ *n* : So. American mammal related to the camel

load \'lōd\ *n* **1** : cargo **2** : supported weight **3** : burden **4** : a large quantity — usu. pl. ∼ *vb* **1** : put a load on **2** : burden **3** : put ammunition in

¹loaf \'lōf\ *n, pl* **loaves** \'lōvz\ : mass of bread

²loaf *vb* : waste time — **loaf·er** *n*

loam \'lōm, 'lüm\ *n* : soil — **loamy** *adj*

loan \'lōn\ *n* **1** : money borrowed at interest **2** : something lent temporarily **3** : grant of use ∼ *vb* : lend

loath \'lōth, 'lòth\ *adj* : very reluctant

loathe \'lōth\ *vb* **loathed; loath·ing** : hate

loath·ing \'lōthiŋ\ *n* : extreme disgust

loath·some \'lōthsəm, 'lòth-\ *adj* : repulsive

lob \'läb\ *vb* **-bb-** : throw or hit in a high arc — **lob** *n*

lob·by \'läbē\ *n, pl* **-bies 1** : public waiting room at the entrance of a building **2** : persons lobbying ∼ *vb* **-bied; -by·ing** : try to influence legislators — **lob·by·ist** *n*

lobe \'lōb\ *n* : rounded part — **lo·bar** \'lōbər\ *adj* — **lobed** \'lōbd\ *adj*

lo·bot·o·my \lō'bätəmē\ *n, pl* **-mies** : surgical severance of nerve fibers in the brain

lob·ster \'läbstər\ *n* : marine crustacean with 2 large pincerlike claws

lo·cal \'lōkəl\ *adj* : confined to or serving a limited area — **local** *n* — **lo·cal·ly** *adv*

lo·cale \lō'kal\ *n* : setting for an event

lo·cal·i·ty \lō'kalətē\ *n, pl* **-ties** : particular place

lo·cal·ize \'lōkə,līz\ *vb* **-ized; -iz·ing** : confine to a definite place — **lo·cal·i·za·tion** \,lōkələ'zāshən\ *n*

lo·cate \'lō,kāt, lō'kāt\ *vb* **-cat·ed; -cat·ing 1** : settle **2** : find a site for **3** : discover the place of — **lo·ca·tion** \lō'kāshən\ *n*

¹lock \'läk\ *n* : tuft or strand of hair

²lock *n* **1** : fastener using a bolt **2** : enclosure in a canal to raise or lower boats ∼ *vb* **1** : make fast with a lock **2** : confine **3** : interlock

lock·er \'läkər\ *n* : storage compartment

lock·et \'läkət\ *n* : small case worn on a necklace

lock·jaw *n* : tetanus

lock·out *n* : closing of a plant by an employer during a labor dispute

lock·smith \-,smith\ *n* : one who makes or repairs locks

lo·co·mo·tion \,lōkə'mōshən\ *n* : power of moving — **lo·co·mo·tive** \-'mōtiv\ *adj*

lo·co·mo·tive \-'mōtiv\ *n* : vehicle that moves railroad cars

lo·co·weed \'lōkō,wēd\ *n* : western plant poisonous to livestock

lo·cust \'lōkəst\ *n* **1** : migratory grasshopper **2** : cicada **3** : tree with hard wood or this wood

lo·cu·tion \lō'kyüshən\ *n* : way of saying something

lode \'lōd\ *n* : ore deposit

lode·stone *n* : magnetic rock

lodge \'läj\ *vb* **lodged; lodg·ing 1** : provide quarters for **2** : come to rest 3 : file ~ *n* 1 : special house (as for hunters) 2 : animal's den 3 : branch of a fraternal organization — **lodg·er** \'läjər\ *n* — **lodg·ing** *n* — **lodge·ment, lodge·ment** \-mənt\ *n*

loft \'lóft\ *n* 1 : attic 2 : upper floor (as of a warehouse)

lofty \'lóftē\ *adj* **loft·i·er; -est** 1 : noble 2 : proud 3 : tall or high — **loft·i·ly** *adv* — **loft·i·ness** *n*

log \'lóg, 'läg\ *n* 1 : unshaped timber 2 : daily record of a ship's or plane's progress ~ *vb* **-gg-** 1 : cut (trees) for lumber 2 : enter in a log — **log·ger** \-ər\ *n*

log·a·rithm \'lógə,rithəm, 'läg-\ *n* : exponent to which a base number is raised to produce a given number

loge \'lōzh\ *n* : box in a theater

log·ger·head \'lógər,hed, 'läg-\ *n* : large Atlantic sea turtle — **at log-gerheads** : in disagreement

log·ic \'läjik\ *n* 1 : science of reasoning 2 : sound reasoning — **log·i·cal** \-ikəl\ *adj* — **log·i·cal·ly** *adv* — **lo·gi·cian** \lō'jishən\ *n*

lo·gis·tics \lō'jistiks\ *n sing or pl* : procurement and movement of people and supplies — **lo·gis·tic** *adj*

logo \'lōgō, 'lóg-, 'läg-\ *n, pl* **log·os** \-ōz\ : advertising symbol

loin \'lóin\ *n* 1 : part of the body on each side of the spine between the hip and lower ribs 2 *pl* : pubic regions

loi·ter \'lóitər\ *vb* : remain around a place idly — **loi·ter·er** *n*

loll \'läl\ *vb* : lounge

lol·li·pop, lol·ly·pop \'läli,päp\ *n* : hard candy on a stick

lone \'lōn\ *adj* 1 : alone or isolated 2 : only — **lone·li·ness** *n* — **lone·ly** *adj* — **lon·er** \'lōnər\ *n*

lone·some \-səm\ *adj* : sad from lack of company — **lone·some·ly** *adv* — **lone·some·ness** *n*

long \'lóŋ\ *adj* **lon·ger** \'lóŋgər\; **lon·gest** \'lóŋgəst\ 1 : extending far or for a considerable time 2 : having a specified length 3 : tedious 4 : well supplied — used with *on* ~ *adv* : for a long time ~ *n* : long period ~ *vb* : feel a strong desire — **long·ing** \lóŋiŋ\ *n* — **long·ing·ly** *adv*

lon·gev·i·ty \län'jevətē\ *n* : long life

long·hand *n* : handwriting

long·horn *n* : cattle with long horns

lon·gi·tude \'länjə,tüd, -,tyüd\ *n* : angular distance east or west from a meridian

lon·gi·tu·di·nal \,länjə'tüd°nəl, -'tyüd-\ *adj* : lengthwise — **lon·gi·tu·di·nal·ly** *adv*

long·shore·man \'lóŋ'shōrmən\ *n* : one who loads and unloads ships

look \'lùk\ *vb* 1 : see 2 : seem 3 : direct one's attention 4 : face ~ *n* 1 : action of looking 2 : appearance of the face 3 : aspect — **look after** : take care of — **look for** 1 : expect 2 : search for

look·out *n* 1 : one who watches 2 : careful watch

¹loom \'lüm\ *n* : frame or machine for weaving

²loom *vb* : appear large and indistinct or impressive

loon \'lün\ *n* : black-and-white diving bird

loo·ny, loo·ney \'lünē\ *adj* **-ni·er; -est** : crazy

loop \'lüp\ *n* 1 : doubling of a line that leaves an opening 2 : something like a loop — **loop** *vb*

loop·hole \'lüp,hōl\ *n* : means of evading

loose \'lüs\ *adj* **loos·er; -est** 1 : not fixed tight 2 : not restrained 3 : not dense 4 : slack 5 : not exact ~ *vb* **loosed; loos·ing** 1 : release 2 : untie or relax — **loose** *adv* — **loose·ly** *adv* — **loos·en** \'lüs°n\ *vb* — **loose·ness** *n*

loot \'lüt\ *n or vb* : plunder — **loot·er** *n*

lop \'läp\ *vb* **-pp-** : cut off

lope \'lōp\ *n* : bounding gait — **lope** *vb*

lop·sid·ed \'läp'sīdəd\ *adj* 1 : leaning to one side 2 : not symmetrical — **lop·sid·ed·ly** *adv* — **lop·sid·ed·ness** *n*

lo·qua·cious \lō'kwāshəs\ *adj* : very talkative — **lo·quac·i·ty** \-'kwas-ətē\ *n*

lord \'lórd\ *n* 1 : one with authority over others 2 : British nobleman

lord·ly \-lē\ *adj* **-li·er; -est** : haughty

lord·ship \-,ship\ *n* : rank of a lord

Lord's Supper *n* : Communion

lore \'lōr\ *n* : traditional knowledge

◆ **lose** \'lüz\ *vb* **lost** \'lóst\; **los·ing** \'lüziŋ\ 1 : have pass from one's possession 2 : be deprived of

3 : waste **4** : be defeated in **5** : fail to keep to or hold **6** : get rid of — **los·er** n

loss \'lòs\ n **1** : something lost **2** pl : killed, wounded, or captured soldiers **3** : failure to win

lost \'lòst\ adj **1** : not used, won, or claimed **2** : unable to find the way

lot \'lät\ n **1** : object used in deciding something by chance **2** : share **3** : fate **4** : plot of land **5** : much

loth \'lōth, 'lōth\ var of LOATH

lo·tion \'lōshən\ n : liquid to rub on the skin

lot·tery \'lätərē\ n, pl -ter·ies : drawing of lots with prizes going to winners

lo·tus \'lōtəs\ n **1** : legendary fruit that causes forgetfulness **2** : water lily

loud \'laùd\ adj **1** : high in volume of sound **2** : noisy **3** : obtrusive in color or pattern — **loud** adv — **loud·ly** adv — **loud·ness** n

loud·speak·er n : device that amplifies sound

lounge \'laùnj\ vb lounged; loung·ing : act or move lazily ∼ n : room with comfortable furniture

lour \'laùər\ var of LOWER

louse \'laùs\ n, pl lice \'līs\ : parasitic wingless usu. flat insect

lousy \'laùzē\ adj lous·i·er; -est **1** : infested with lice **2** : not good — **lous·i·ly** adv — **lous·i·ness** n

lout \'laùt\ n : stupid awkward person — **lout·ish** adj — **lout·ish·ly** adv

lou·ver, lou·vre \'lüvər\ n : opening having parallel slanted slats for ventilation or such a slat

love \'ləv\ n **1** : strong affection **2** : warm attachment **3** : beloved person ∼ vb loved; lov·ing **1** : feel affection for **2** : enjoy greatly — **lov·able** \-əbəl\ adj — **love·less** adj — **lov·er** n — **lov·ing·ly** adv

love·lorn \-‚lòrn\ adj : deprived of love or of a lover

love·ly \'ləvlē\ adj -li·er; -est : beautiful — **love·li·ness** n — **lovely** adv

¹low \'lō\ vb or n : moo

²low adj low·er; low·est **1** : not high or tall **2** : below normal level **3** : not loud **4** : humble **5** : sad **6** : less than usual **7** : falling short of a standard **8** : unfavorable ∼ n **1** : something low **2** : automobile gear giving the slowest speed — **low** adv — **low·ness** n

low·brow \'lō‚braù\ n : person with little taste or intellectual interest

¹low·er \'laùər\ vb **1** : scowl **2** : become dark and threatening

²low·er \'lōər\ adj : relatively low (as in rank)

³low·er \'lōər\ vb **1** : drop **2** : let descend **3** : reduce in amount

low·land \'lōlənd, -‚land\ n : low flat country

low·ly \'lōlē\ adj -li·er; -est **1** : humble **2** : low in rank — **low·li·ness** n

loy·al \'lòiəl\ adj : faithful to a country, cause, or friend — **loy·al·ist** n — **loy·al·ly** adv — **loy·al·ty** \'lòiəltē\ n

loz·enge \'läz°nj\ n : small medicated candy

lu·bri·cant \'lübrikənt\ n : material (as grease) to reduce friction

lu·bri·cate \-‚kāt\ vb -cat·ed; -cat·ing : apply a lubricant to — **lu·bri·ca·tion** \‚lübrə'kāshən\ n — **lu·bri·ca·tor** \'lübrə‚kātər\ n

lu·cid \'lüsəd\ adj **1** : mentally sound **2** : easily understood — **lu·cid·i·ty** \lü'sidətē\ n — **lu·cid·ly** adv — **lu·cid·ness** n

luck \'lək\ n **1** : chance **2** : good fortune — **luck·i·ly** adv — **luck·i·ness** n — **luck·less** adj — **lucky** adj

lu·cra·tive \'lükrətiv\ adj : profit-

able — **lu·cra·tive·ly** adv — **lu·cra·tive·ness** n

lu·di·crous \\'lüdəkrəs\\ adj : comically ridiculous — **lu·di·crous·ly** adv — **lu·di·crous·ness** n

lug \\'ləg\\ vb **-gg-** : drag or carry laboriously

lug·gage \\'ləgij\\ n : baggage

lu·gu·bri·ous \\lu̇'gübrēəs\\ adj : mournful often to an exaggerated degree — **lu·gu·bri·ous·ly** adv — **lu·gu·bri·ous·ness** n

luke·warm \\'lük'wȯrm\\ adj 1 : moderately warm 2 : not enthusiastic

lull \\'ləl\\ vb : make or become quiet or relaxed ~ n : temporary calm

lul·la·by \\'lələ̩bī\\ n, pl **-bies** : song to lull children to sleep

lum·ba·go \\̩ləm'bāgō\\ n : rheumatic back pain

lum·ber \\'ləmbər\\ n : timber dressed for use ~ vb : cut logs — **lum·ber·man** n — **lum·ber·yard** n

lum·ber·jack \\-̩jak\\ n : logger

lu·mi·nary \\'lümə̩nerē\\ n, pl **-nar·ies** : very famous person

lu·mi·nes·cence \\̩lümə'nes°ns\\ n : low-temperature emission of light — **lu·mi·nes·cent** \\-°nt\\ adj

lu·mi·nous \\'lümənəs\\ adj : emitting light — **lu·mi·nance** \\-nəns\\ n — **lu·mi·nos·i·ty** \\̩lümə'näsətē\\ n — **lu·mi·nous·ly** adv

lump \\'ləmp\\ n 1 : mass of irregular shape 2 : abnormal swelling ~ vb : heap together — **lump·ish** adj — **lumpy** adj

lu·na·cy \\'lünəsē\\ n, pl **-cies** : state of insanity

lu·nar \\'lünər\\ adj : of the moon

lu·na·tic \\'lünə̩tik\\ adj : insane — **lunatic** n

lunch \\'lənch\\ n : noon meal ~ vb : eat lunch

lun·cheon \\'lənchən\\ n : usu. formal lunch

lung \\'ləŋ\\ n : breathing organ in the chest — **lunged** \\'ləŋd\\ adj

lunge \\'lənj\\ n 1 : sudden thrust 2 : sudden move forward — **lunge** vb

lurch \\'lərch\\ n : sudden swaying — **lurch** vb

♦ **lure** \\'lu̇r\\ n 1 : something that attracts 2 : artificial fish bait ~ vb **lured; lur·ing** : attract

lu·rid \\'lu̇rəd\\ adj 1 : gruesome 2 : sensational — **lu·rid·ly** adv

lurk \\'lərk\\ vb : lie in wait

lus·cious \\'ləshəs\\ adj 1 : pleasingly sweet in taste or smell 2 : sensually appealing — **lus·cious·ly** adv — **lus·cious·ness** n

lush \\'ləsh\\ adj : covered with abundant growth

lust \\'ləst\\ n 1 : intense sexual desire 2 : intense longing — **lust** vb — **lust·ful** adj

lus·ter, lus·tre \\'ləstər\\ n 1 : brightness from reflected light 2 : magnificence — **lus·ter·less** adj — **lus·trous** \\-trəs\\ adj

lusty \\'ləstē\\ adj **lust·i·er; -est** : full of vitality — **lust·i·ly** adv — **lust·i·ness** n

lute \\'lüt\\ n : pear-shaped stringed instrument — **lute·nist, lu·ta·nist** \\'lüt°nist\\ n

lux·u·ri·ant \\̩ləg'zhu̇rēənt, ̩lək'shu̇r-\\ adj 1 : growing plentifully 2 : rich and varied — **lux·u·ri·ance** \\-ēəns\\ n — **lux·u·ri·ant·ly** adv

lux·u·ri·ate \\-ē̩āt\\ vb **-at·ed; -at·ing** : revel

lux·u·ry \\'ləkshərē, 'ləgzh-\\ n, pl **-ries** 1 : great comfort 2 : something adding to pleasure or comfort — **lux·u·ri·ous** \\̩ləg'zhu̇rēəs, ̩lək'shu̇r-\\ adj — **lux·u·ri·ous·ly** adv

-ly \\lē\\ adv suffix 1 : in a specified way 2 : from a specified point of view ly·ce·um \lī'sēəm, 'līsē-\ *n* : hall for public lectures

lye \'lī\ *n* : caustic alkaline substance

lying *pres part of* LIE

lymph \'limf\ *n* : bodily liquid consisting chiefly of blood plasma and white blood cells — lym·phat·ic \lim'fatik\ *adj*

lynch \'linch\ *vb* : put to death by mob action — lynch·er *n*

lynx \'liŋks\ *n*, *pl* lynx *or* lynx·es : wildcat

lyre \'līr\ *n* : ancient Greek stringed instrument

lyr·ic \'lirik\ *adj* 1 : suitable for singing 2 : expressing direct personal emotion ∼ *n* 1 : lyric poem 2 *pl* : words of a song — lyr·i·cal \-ikəl\ *adj*

M

m \'em\ *n*, *pl* m's *or* ms \'emz\ : 13th letter of the alphabet

ma'am \'mam\ *n* : madam

ma·ca·bre \mə'käb, -'käbər, -'käbrə\ *adj* : gruesome

mac·ad·am \mə'kadəm\ *n* : pavement of cemented broken stone — mac·ad·am·ize \-ˌīz\ *vb*

mac·a·ro·ni \ˌmakə'rōnē\ *n* : tube-shaped pasta

mac·a·roon \ˌmakə'rün\ *n* : cookie of ground almonds or coconut

ma·caw \mə'kò\ *n* : large long-tailed parrot

¹mace \'mās\ *n* 1 : heavy spiked club 2 : ornamental staff as a symbol of authority

²mace *n* : spice from the fibrous coating of the nutmeg

ma·chete \mə'shetē\ *n* : large heavy knife

mach·i·na·tion \ˌmakə'nāshən, ˌmashə-\ *n* : plot or scheme — mach·i·nate \'makə,nāt, 'mash-\ *vb*

ma·chine \mə'shēn\ *n* : combination of mechanical or electrical parts ∼ *vb* -chined; -chin·ing : modify by machine-operated tools — ma·chin·able *adj* — ma·chin·ery \-ərē\ *n* — ma·chin·ist *n*

mack·er·el \'makərəl\ *n*, *pl* -el *or* -els : No. Atlantic food fish

mack·i·naw \'makə,nò\ *n* : short heavy plaid coat

mac·ra·mé \ˌmakrə'mā\ *n* : coarse lace or fringe made by knotting

mac·ro \'makrō\ *adj* : very large

mac·ro·cosm \'makrə,käzəm\ *n* : universe

mad \'mad\ *adj* -dd- 1 : insane or rabid 2 : rash and foolish 3 : angry 4 : carried away by enthusiasm — mad·den \'madᵊn\ *vb* — mad·den·ing·ly \'madᵊniŋlē\ *adv* — mad·ly *adv* — mad·ness *n*

mad·am \'madəm\ *n*, *pl* mes·dames \mā'däm\ — used in polite address to a woman

ma·dame \mə'dam, *before a surname also* 'madəm\ *n*, *pl* mes·dames \mā'däm\ — used as a title for a woman not of English-speaking nationality

mad·cap \'mad,kap\ *adj* : wild or zany — madcap *n*

made *past of* MAKE

Ma·dei·ra \mə'dirə\ *n* : amber-colored dessert wine

ma·de·moi·selle \ˌmadmwə'zel, -mə'zel\ *n*, *pl* ma·de·moi·selles \-'zelz\ *or* mes·de·moi·selles \ˌmādmwə'zel\ : an unmarried girl or woman — used as a title for a woman esp. of French nationality

mad·house *n* 1 : insane asylum 2 : place of great uproar or confusion

mad·man \-,man, -mən\ *n* : lunatic

mad·ri·gal \'madrigəl\ *n* : elaborate song for several voice parts

mad·wom·an \'mad,wùmən\ *n* : woman who is insane

mael·strom \'mālstrəm\ *n* 1 : whirlpool 2 : tumult

♦ **mae·stro** \'mīstrō\ *n, pl* **-stros** *or* **-stri** \-,strē\ : eminent composer or conductor

Ma·fia \'mäfēə\ *n* : secret criminal organization

ma·fi·o·so \,mäfē'ōsō\ *n, pl* **-si** \-sē\ : member of the Mafia

mag·a·zine \'magə,zēn\ *n* **1** : storehouse **2** : publication issued at regular intervals **3** : cartridge container in a gun

ma·gen·ta \mə'jentə\ *n* : deep purplish red color

mag·got \'magət\ *n* : wormlike fly larva — **mag·goty** *adj*

mag·ic \'majik\ *n* **1** : art of using supernatural powers **2** : extraordinary power or influence **3** : sleight of hand — **magic, mag·i·cal** \-ikəl\ *adj* — **mag·i·cal·ly** *adv* — **ma·gi·cian** \mə'jishən\ *n*

mag·is·te·ri·al \,majə'stirēəl\ *adj* **1** : authoritative **2** : relating to a magistrate

mag·is·trate \'majə,strāt\ *n* : judge — **mag·is·tra·cy** \-strəsē\ *n*

mag·ma \'magmə\ *n* : molten rock

mag·nan·i·mous \mag'nanəməs\ *adj* : noble or generous — **mag·na·nim·i·ty** \,magnə'nimətē\ *n* — **mag·nan·i·mous·ly** *adv* — **mag·nan·i·mous·ness** *n*

mag·ne·sia \mag'nēzhə, -shə\ *n* : oxide of magnesium used as a laxative

mag·ne·sium \mag'nēzēəm, -zhəm\ *n* : silver-white metallic chemical element

mag·net \'magnət\ *n* **1** : body that attracts iron **2** : something that attracts — **mag·net·ic** \mag'netik\ *adj* — **mag·net·i·cal·ly** \-iklē\ *adv* — **mag·ne·tism** \'magnə,tizəm\ *n*

mag·ne·tite \'magnə,tīt\ *n* : black iron ore

mag·ne·tize \'magnə,tīz\ *vb* **-tized; -tiz·ing 1** : attract like a magnet **2**

: give magnetic properties to — **mag·ne·tiz·able** *adj* — **mag·ne·ti·za·tion** \,magnətə'zāshən\ *n* — **mag·ne·tiz·er** *n*

mag·nif·i·cent \mag'nifəsənt\ *adj* : splendid — **mag·nif·i·cence** \-əns\ *n* — **mag·nif·i·cent·ly** *adv*

mag·ni·fy \'magnə,fī\ *vb* **-fied; -fy·ing 1** : intensify **2** : enlarge — **mag·ni·fi·ca·tion** \,magnəfə'kāshən\ *n* — **mag·ni·fi·er** \'magnə,fīər\ *n*

mag·ni·tude \'magnə,tüd, -,tyüd\ *n* **1** : greatness of size or extent **2** : quantity

mag·no·lia \mag'nōlyə\ *n* : shrub with large fragrant flowers

mag·pie \'mag,pī\ *n* : long-tailed black-and-white bird

ma·hog·a·ny \mə'hägənē\ *n, pl* **-nies** : tropical evergreen tree or its reddish brown wood

maid \'mād\ *n* **1** : unmarried young woman **2** : female servant

maid·en \'mād⁰n\ *n* : unmarried young woman ∼ *adj* **1** : unmarried **2** : first — **maid·en·hood** \-,hůd\ *n* — **maid·en·ly** *adj*

maid·en·hair \-,har\ *n* : fern with delicate feathery fronds

¹mail \'māl\ *n* **1** : something sent or carried in the postal system **2** : postal system ∼ *vb* : send by mail — **mail·box** *n* — **mail·man** \-,man, -mən\ *n*

²mail *n* : armor of metal links or plates

maim \'mām\ *vb* : seriously wound or disfigure

main \'mān\ *n* **1** : force **2** : ocean **3** : principal pipe, duct, or circuit of a utility system ∼ *adj* : chief — **main·ly** *adv*

main·frame \'mān,frām\ *n* : large fast computer

main·land \'mān,land, -lənd\ *n* : part of a country on a continent

main·stay *n* : chief support

main·stream *n* : prevailing current or direction of activity or influence — **mainstream** *adj*

main·tain \mān'tān\ *vb* **1** : keep in an existing state (as of repair) **2** : sustain **3** : declare — **main·tain·abil·i·ty** \-ˌtānə'bilətē\ *n* — **main·tain·able** \-'tānəbəl\ *adj* — **main·te·nance** \'mānt°nəns\ *n*

mai·tre d'hô·tel \ˌmātrədō'tel, ˌme-\ *n* : head of a dining room staff

maize \'māz\ *n* : corn

maj·es·ty \'majəstē\ *n, pl* **-ties 1** : sovereign power or dignity — used as a title **2** : grandeur or splendor — **ma·jes·tic** \mə'jestik\ *adj* — **ma·jes·ti·cal·ly** \-tiklē\ *adv*

ma·jor \'mājər\ *adj* **1** : larger or greater **2** : noteworthy or conspicuous ~ *n* **1** : commissioned officer (as in the army) ranking next below a lieutenant colonel **2** : main field of study ~ *vb* **-jored; -jor·ing** : pursue an academic major

ma·jor·do·mo \ˌmājər'dōmō\ *n, pl* **-mos** : head steward

major general *n* : commissioned officer (as in the army) ranking next below a lieutenant general

ma·jor·i·ty \mə'jorətē\ *n, pl* **-ties 1** : age of full civil rights **2** : quantity more than half

make \'māk\ *vb* **made** \'mād\; **making 1** : cause to exist, occur, or appear **2** : fashion or manufacture **3** : formulate in the mind **4** : constitute **5** : prepare **6** : cause to be or become **7** : carry out or perform **8** : compel **9** : gain **10** : have an effect — used with *for* ~ *n* : brand — **mak·er** *n* — **make do** *vb* : get along with what is available — **make good** *vb* **1** : repay **2** : succeed — **make out** *vb* **1** : draw up or write **2** : discern or understand **3** : fare — **make up** *vb* **1** : invent **2** : become reconciled **3** : compensate for

make–be·lieve *n* : a pretending to believe ~ *adj* : imagined or pretended

make·shift *n* : temporary substitute — **makeshift** *adj*

make·up \-ˌəp\ *n* **1** : way in which something is constituted **2** : cosmetics

mal·ad·just·ed \ˌmalə'jəstəd\ *adj* : poorly adjusted (as to one's environment) — **mal·ad·just·ment** \-'jəstmənt\ *n*

mal·adroit \ˌmalə'droit\ *adj* : clumsy or inept

mal·a·dy \'malədē\ *n, pl* **-dies** : disease or disorder

mal·aise \mə'lāz, ma-\ *n* : sense of being unwell

mal·a·mute \'maləˌmyüt\ *n* : powerful heavy-coated dog

mal·a·prop·ism \'maləˌpräpˌizəm\ *n* : humorous misuse of a word

ma·lar·ia \mə'lerēə\ *n* : disease transmitted by a mosquito — **ma·lar·i·al** \-əl\ *adj*

ma·lar·key \mə'lärkē\ *n* : foolishness

mal·con·tent \ˌmalkən'tent\ *n* : discontented person — **malcontent** *adj*

male \'māl\ *adj* **1** : relating to the sex that performs a fertilizing function **2** : masculine ~ *n* : male individual — **male·ness** *n*

male·dic·tion \ˌmalə'dikshən\ *n* : curse

male·fac·tor \'maləˌfaktər\ *n* : one who commits an offense esp. against the law

ma·lef·i·cent \mə'lefəsənt\ *adj* : harmful

ma·lev·o·lent \mə'levələnt\ *adj* : malicious or spiteful — **ma·lev·o·lence** \-ləns\ *n*

mal·fea·sance \mal'fēz°ns\ *n* : misconduct by a public official

mal·for·ma·tion \ˌmalfor'māshən\ *n* : distortion or faulty formation — **mal·formed** \mal'formd\ *adj*

mal·func·tion \mal'fəŋkshən\ *vb* : fail to operate properly — **malfunction** *n*

mal·ice \'maləs\ *n* : desire to cause pain or injury to another — **ma·li·cious** \mə'lishəs\ *adj* — **ma·li·cious·ly** *adv*

ma·lign \mə'līn\ *adj* **1** : wicked **2** : malignant ~ *vb* : speak evil of

ma·lig·nant \mə'lignənt\ *adj* **1** : harmful **2** : likely to cause death — **ma·lig·nan·cy** \-nənsē\ *n* — **ma·lig·nant·ly** *adv* — **ma·lig·ni·ty** \-nətē\ *n*

ma·lin·ger \mə'liŋgər\ *vb* : pretend illness to avoid duty — **ma·lin·ger·er** *n*

mall \'mol\ *n* **1** : shaded promenade **2** : concourse providing access to rows of shops

mal·lard \\'malərd\\ *n, pl* **-lard** *or* **-lards** : common wild duck

mal·lea·ble \\'malēəbəl\\ *adj* **1** : easily shaped **2** : adaptable — **mal·lea·bil·i·ty** \\,malēə'bilətē\\ *n*

mal·let \\'malət\\ *n* : hammerlike tool

mal·nour·ished \\mal'nərisht\\ *adj* : poorly nourished

mal·nu·tri·tion \\,malnü'trishən, -nyü-\\ *n* : inadequate nutrition

mal·odor·ous \\mal'ōdərəs\\ *adj* : foul-smelling — **mal·odor·ous·ly** *adv* — **mal·odor·ous·ness** *n*

mal·prac·tice \\-'praktəs\\ *n* : failure of professional duty

malt \\'mȯlt\\ *n* : sprouted grain used in brewing

mal·treat \\mal'trēt\\ *vb* : treat badly — **mal·treat·ment** *n*

ma·ma, mam·ma \\'mämə\\ *n* : mother

mam·mal \\'maməl\\ *n* : warm= blooded vertebrate animal that nourishes its young with milk — **mam·ma·li·an** \\mə'mālēən, ma-\\ *adj or n*

mam·ma·ry \\'mamərē\\ *adj* : relating to the milk-secreting glands (**mammary glands**) of mammals

mam·mo·gram \\'mamə,gram\\ *n* : X= ray photograph of the breasts

mam·moth \\'maməth\\ *n* : large hairy extinct elephant ~ *adj* : enormous

man \\'man\\ *n, pl* **men** \\'men\\ **1** : human being **2** : adult male **3** : mankind ~ *vb* **-nn-** : supply with people for working — **man·hood** *n* — **man·hunt** *n* — **man·like** *adj* — **man·li·ness** *n* — **man·ly** *adj or adv* — **man–made** *adj* — **man·nish** *adj* — **man·nish·ly** *adv* — **man·nish·ness** *n* — **man–size, man–sized** *adj*

man·a·cle \\'manikəl\\ *n* : shackle for the hands or wrists — **manacle** *vb*

man·age \\'manij\\ *vb* **-aged; -aging 1** : control **2** : direct or carry on business or affairs **3** : cope — **man·age·abil·i·ty** \\,manijə'bilətē\\ *n* — **man·age·able** \\'manijəbəl\\ *adj* — **man·age·able·ness** *n* — **man·age·ably** \\-blē\\ *adv* — **management** \\'manijmənt\\ *n* — **manag·er** \\'manijər\\ *n* — **man·a·ge·ri·al** \\,manə'jirēəl\\ *adj*

man·da·rin \\'mandərən\\ *n* : Chinese imperial official

man·date \\'man,dāt\\ *n* : authoritative command

man·da·to·ry \\'mandə,tōrē\\ *adj* : obligatory

man·di·ble \\'mandəbəl\\ *n* : lower jaw — **man·dib·u·lar** \\man'dibyələr\\ *adj*

man·do·lin \\,mandə'lin, 'mand°lən\\ *n* : stringed musical instrument

man·drake \\'man,drāk\\ *n* : herb with a large forked root

mane \\'mān\\ *n* : animal's neck hair — **maned** \\'mānd\\ *adj*

ma·neu·ver \\mə'nüvər, -'nyü-\\ *n* **1** : planned movement of troops or ships **2** : military training exercise **3** : clever or skillful move or action — **maneuver** *vb* — **ma·neu·ver·abil·i·ty** \\-,nüvərə'bilətē, -,nyü-\\ *n*

man·ful \\'manfəl\\ *adj* : courageous — **man·ful·ly** *adv*

man·ga·nese \\'maŋgə,nēz, -,nēs\\ *n* : gray metallic chemical element

mange \\'mānj\\ *n* : skin disease of domestic animals — **mangy** \\'mānjē\\ *adj*

man·ger \\'mānjər\\ *n* : feeding trough for livestock

man·gle \\'maŋgəl\\ *vb* **-gled; -gling 1** : mutilate **2** : bungle — **man·gler** *n*

man·go \\'maŋgō\\ *n, pl* **-goes** : juicy yellowish red tropical fruit

man·grove \\'man,grōv, 'maŋ-\\ *n* : tropical tree growing in salt water

man·han·dle *vb* : handle roughly

man·hole *n* : entry to a sewer

ma·nia \\'mānēə, -nyə\\ *n* **1** : insanity marked by uncontrollable emotion or excitement **2** : excessive enthusiasm — **ma·ni·ac** \\-nē,ak\\ *n* — **ma·ni·a·cal** \\mə'nīəkəl\\ *adj* — **man·ic** \\'manik\\ *adj or n*

man·i·cure \\'manə,kyùr\\ *n* : treatment for the fingernails ~ *vb* **-cured; -cur·ing 1** : do manicure work on **2** : trim precisely — **man·i·cur·ist** \\-,kyùrist\\ *n*

¹man·i·fest \\'manə,fest\\ *adj* : clear to the senses or to the mind ~ *vb* : make evident — **man·i·fes·ta·tion** \\,manəfə'stāshən\\ *n* — **man·i·fest·ly** *adv*

²manifest *n* : invoice of cargo or list of passengers

man·i·fes·to \\,manə'festō\\ *n, pl* **-tos** *or* **-toes** : public declaration of policy or views

man·i·fold \'manə,fōld\ *adj* : marked by diversity or variety ~ *n* : pipe fitting with several outlets for connections

ma·nila paper \mə'nilə-\ *n* : durable brownish paper

ma·nip·u·late \mə'nipyə,lāt\ *vb* **-lat·ed; -lat·ing 1** : treat or operate manually or mechanically **2** : influence esp. by cunning — **ma·nip·u·la·tion** \mə,nipyə'lāshən\ *n* — **ma·nip·u·la·tive** \-'nipyə,lātiv, -lətiv\ *adj* — **ma·nip·u·la·tor** \-,lātər\ *n*

man·kind \'man'kīnd\ *n* : human race

man·na \'manə\ *n* : something valuable that comes unexpectedly

manned \'mand\ *adj* : carrying or performed by a man

man·ne·quin \'manikən\ *n* : dummy used to display clothes

man·ner \'manər\ *n* **1** : kind **2** : usual way of acting **3** : artistic method **4** *pl* : social conduct

man·nered \-ərd\ *adj* **1** : having manners of a specified kind **2** : artificial

man·ner·ism \'manə,rizəm\ *n* : individual peculiarity of action

man·ner·ly \-lē\ *adj* : polite — **man·ner·li·ness** *n* — **mannerly** *adv*

man–of–war \,manə'wȯr, -əv'wȯr\ *n, pl* **men–of–war** \,men-\ : warship

man·or \'manər\ *n* : country estate — **ma·no·ri·al** \mə'nȯrēəl\ *adj*

man·pow·er *n* : supply of people available for service

man·sard \'man,särd\ *n* : roof with two slopes on all sides and the lower slope the steeper

manse \'mans\ *n* : parsonage

man·ser·vant *n, pl* **men·ser·vants** : a male servant

man·sion \'manchən\ *n* : very big house

man·slaugh·ter *n* : unintentional killing of a person

man·tel \'mant³l\ *n* : shelf above a fireplace

man·tis \'mantəs\ *n, pl* **-tis·es** *or* **-tes** \'man,tēz\ : large green insect-eating insect with stout forelegs

man·tle \'mant³l\ *n* **1** : sleeveless cloak **2** : something that covers, enfolds, or envelops — **mantle** *vb*

man·tra \'mantrə\ *n* : mystical chant

♦ **man·u·al** \'manyəwəl\ *adj* : involving the hands or physical force ~ *n* : handbook — **man·u·al·ly** *adv*

man·u·fac·ture \,manyə'fakchər, ,manə-\ *n* : process of making wares by hand or by machinery ~ *vb* **-tured; -tur·ing** : make from raw materials — **man·u·fac·tur·er** *n*

ma·nure \mə'nu̇r, -'nyu̇r\ *n* : animal excrement used as fertilizer

manu·script \'manyə,skript\ *n* **1** : something written or typed **2** : document submitted for publication

many \'menē\ *adj* **more** \'mȯr\; **most** \'mōst\ : consisting of a large number — **many** *n or pron*

map \'map\ *n* : representation of a geographical area ~ *vb* **-pp- 1** : make a map of **2** : plan in detail — **map·pa·ble** \-əbəl\ *adj* — **map·per** *n*

ma·ple \'māpəl\ *n* : tree with hard light-colored wood

mar \'mär\ *vb* **-rr-** : damage

mar·a·schi·no \,marə'skēnō, -'shē-\ *n, pl* **-nos** : preserved cherry

mar·a·thon \'marə,thän\ *n* **1** : long-distance race **2** : test of endurance — **mar·a·thon·er** \-,thänər\ *n*

ma·raud \mə'rȯd\ *vb* : roam about in search of plunder — **ma·raud·er** *n*

mar·ble \'märbəl\ *n* 1 : crystallized limestone 2 : small glass ball used in a children's game (**marbles**)

mar·bling \-bəliŋ\ *n* : intermixture of fat and lean in meat

march \'märch\ *vb* : move with regular steps or in a purposeful manner ~ *n* 1 : distance covered in a march 2 : measured stride 3 : forward movement 4 : music for marching — **march·er** *n*

March *n* : 3d month of the year having 31 days

mar·chio·ness \'märshənəs\ *n* : woman holding the rank of a marquess

Mar·di Gras \'märdē,grä\ *n* : Tuesday before the beginning of Lent often observed with parades and merrymaking

mare \'mar\ *n* : female horse

mar·ga·rine \'märjərən\ *n* : butter substitute made usu. from vegetable oils

mar·gin \'märjən\ *n* 1 : edge 2 : spare amount, measure, or degree

mar·gin·al \-jənəl\ *adj* 1 : relating to or situated at a border or margin 2 : close to the lower limit of acceptability — **mar·gin·al·ly** *adv*

mari·gold \'marə,gōld\ *n* : garden plant with showy flower heads

mar·i·jua·na \,marə'wänə, -'hwä-\ *n* : intoxicating drug obtained from the hemp plant

ma·ri·na \mə'rēnə\ *n* : place for mooring pleasure boats

mar·i·nate \'marə,nāt\ *vb* **-nat·ed; -nat·ing** : soak in a savory sauce

ma·rine \mə'rēn\ *adj* 1 : relating to the sea 2 : relating to marines ~ *n* : infantry soldier associated with a navy

mar·i·ner \'marənər\ *n* : sailor

mar·i·o·nette \,marēə'net\ *n* : puppet

mar·i·tal \'marətᵊl\ *adj* : relating to marriage

mar·i·time \'marə,tīm\ *adj* : relating to the sea or commerce on the sea

mar·jo·ram \'märjərəm\ *n* : aromatic mint used as a seasoning

mark \'märk\ *n* 1 : something aimed at 2 : something (as a line) designed to record position 3 : visible sign 4 : written symbol 5 : grade 6 : lasting impression 7 : blemish ~ *vb* 1 : designate or set apart by a mark or make a mark on 2 : characterize 3 : remark — **mark·er** *n*

marked \'märkt\ *adj* : noticeable — **mark·ed·ly** \'märkədlē\ *adv*

mar·ket \'märkət\ *n* 1 : buying and selling of goods or the place this happens 2 : demand for commodities 3 : store ~ *vb* : sell — **mar·ket·able** *adj*

mar·ket·place *n* 1 : market 2 : world of trade or economic activity

marks·man \'märksmən\ *n* : good shooter — **marks·man·ship** *n*

mar·lin \'märlən\ *n* : large oceanic fish

mar·ma·lade \'märmə,lād\ *n* : jam with pieces of fruit and rind

mar·mo·set \'märmə,set\ *n* : small bushy-tailed monkey

mar·mot \'märmət\ *n* : burrowing rodent

¹**ma·roon** \mə'rün\ *vb* : isolate without hope of escape

²**maroon** *n* : dark red color

mar·quee \mär'kē\ *n* : canopy over an entrance

mar·quess \'märkwəs\; **mar·quis** \'märkwəs, mär'kē\ *n, pl* **-quess·es** *or* **-quis·es** *or* **-quis** : British noble ranking next below a duke

mar·quise \mär'kēz\ *n, pl* **mar·quises** \-'kēz, -'kēzəz\ : marchioness

marriage 243 master

mar·riage \'marij\ *n* **1** : state of being married **2** : wedding ceremony — **mar·riage·able** *adj*

mar·row \'marō\ *n* : soft tissue in the cavity of bone

mar·ry \'marē\ *vb* **-ried; -ry·ing 1** : join as husband and wife **2** : take or give in marriage — **mar·ried** *adj or n*

marsh \'märsh\ *n* : soft wet land — **marshy** *adj*

mar·shal \'märshəl\ *n* **1** : leader of ceremony **2** : usu. high military or administrative officer ∼ *vb* **-shaled** *or* **-shalled; -shal·ing** *or* **-shal·ling 1** : arrange in order, rank, or position **2** : lead with ceremony

♦ **marsh·mal·low** \'märsh,melō, -,malō\ *n* : spongy candy

mar·su·pi·al \mär'süpēəl\ *n* : mammal that nourishes young in an abdominal pouch — **marsupial** *adj*

mart \'märt\ *n* : market

mar·ten \'märt°n\ *n, pl* **-ten** *or* **-tens** : weasellike mammal with soft fur

mar·tial \'märshəl\ *adj* **1** : relating to war or an army **2** : warlike

mar·tin \'märt°n\ *n* : small swallow

mar·ti·net \,märt°n'et\ *n* : strict disciplinarian

mar·tyr \'märtər\ *n* : one who dies or makes a great sacrifice for a cause ∼ *vb* : make a martyr of — **mar·tyr·dom** \-dəm\ *n*

mar·vel \'märvəl\ *vb* **-veled** *or* **-velled; -vel·ing** *or* **-vel·ling** : feel surprise or wonder ∼ *n* : something amazing — **mar·vel·ous, mar·vel·lous** \'märvələs\ *adj* — **mar·vel·ous·ly** *adv* — **mar·vel·ous·ness** *n*

Marx·ism \'märk,sizəm\ *n* : political and social principles of Karl Marx — **Marx·ist** \-sist\ *n or adj*

mas·cara \mas'karə\ *n* : eye cosmetic

mas·cot \'mas,kät, -kət\ *n* : one believed to bring good luck

mas·cu·line \'maskyələn\ *adj* : relating to the male sex — **mas·cu·lin·i·ty** \,maskyə'linətē\ *n*

mash \'mash\ *n* **1** : crushed steeped grain for fermenting **2** : soft pulpy mass ∼ *vb* **1** : reduce to a pulpy mass **2** : smash — **mash·er** *n*

mask \'mask\ *n* : disguise for the face ∼ *vb* **1** : disguise **2** : cover to protect — **mask·er** *n*

mas·och·ism \'masə,kizəm, 'maz-\ *n* : pleasure in being abused — **mas·och·ist** \-kist\ *n* — **mas·och·is·tic** \,masə'kistik, ,maz-\ *adj*

ma·son \'mās°n\ *n* : workman who builds with stone or brick — **ma·son·ry** \-rē\ *n*

mas·quer·ade \,maskə'rād\ *n* **1** : costume party **2** : disguise ∼ *vb* **-ad·ed; -ad·ing 1** : disguise oneself **2** : take part in a costume party — **mas·quer·ad·er** *n*

mass \'mas\ *n* **1** : large amount of matter or number of things **2** : expanse or magnitude **3** : great body of people — usu. pl. ∼ *vb* : form into a mass — **mass·less** \-ləs\ *adj* — **massy** *adj*

Mass *n* : worship service of the Roman Catholic Church

mas·sa·cre \'masikər\ *n* : wholesale slaughter — **massacre** *vb*

mas·sage \mə'säzh, -'säj\ *n* : a rubbing of the body — **massage** *vb*

mas·seur \ma'sər\ *n* : man who massages

mas·seuse \-'sœz, -'süz\ *n* : woman who massages

mas·sive \'masiv\ *adj* **1** : being a large mass **2** : large in scope — **mas·sive·ly** *adv* — **mas·sive·ness** *n*

mast \'mast\ *n* : tall pole esp. for supporting sails — **mast·ed** *adj*

♦ **mas·ter** \'mastər\ *n* **1** : male teacher **2** : holder of an academic

degree between a bachelor's and a doctor's 3 : one highly skilled 4 : one in authority ~ *vb* 1 : subdue 2 : become proficient in — **mas·ter·ful** \-fəl\ *adj* — **mas·ter·ful·ly** *adv* — **mas·ter·ly** *adj* — **mas·tery** \'mastərē\ *n*

master chief petty officer *n* : petty officer of the highest rank in the navy

master gunnery sergeant *n* : noncommissioned officer in the marine corps ranking above a master sergeant

mas·ter·piece \'mastər,pēs\ *n* : great piece of work

master sergeant *n* 1 : noncommissioned officer in the army ranking next below a sergeant major 2 : noncommissioned officer in the air force ranking next below a senior master sergeant 3 : noncommissioned officer in the marine corps ranking next below a master gunnery sergeant

mas·ter·work *n* : masterpiece

mas·tic \'mastik\ *n* : pasty glue

mas·ti·cate \'mastə,kāt\ *vb* -cat·ed; -cat·ing : chew — **mas·ti·ca·tion** \,mastə'kāshən\ *n*

mas·tiff \'mastəf\ *n* : large dog

mast·odon \'mastə,dän\ *n* : extinct elephantlike animal

mas·toid \'mas,tȯid\ *n* : bone behind the ear — **mastoid** *adj*

mas·tur·ba·tion \,mastər'bāshən\ *n* : stimulation of sex organs by hand — **mas·tur·bate** \'mastər,bāt\ *vb*

¹**mat** \'mat\ *n* 1 : coarse woven or plaited fabric 2 : mass of tangled strands 3 : thick pad ~ *vb* -tt- : form into a mat

²**mat** *vb* -tt- 1 : make matte 2 : provide (a picture) with a mat ~ *or* **matt** *or* **matte** *n* : border around a picture

³**mat** *var of* MATTE

mat·a·dor \'matə,dȯr\ *n* : bullfighter

¹**match** \'mach\ *n* 1 : one equal to another 2 : one able to cope with another 3 : suitable pairing 4 : game 5 : marriage ~ *vb* 1 : set in competition 2 : marry 3 : be or provide the equal of 4 : fit or go together — **match·less** *adj* — **match·mak·er** *n*

²**match** *n* : piece of wood or paper material with a combustible tip

mate \'māt\ *n* 1 : companion 2 : subordinate officer on a ship 3 : one of a pair ~ *vb* **mat·ed; mat·ing** 1 : fit together 2 : come together as a pair 3 : copulate

ma·te·ri·al \mə'tirēəl\ *adj* 1 : natural 2 : relating to matter 3 : important 4 : of a physical or worldly nature ~ *n* : stuff something is made of — **ma·te·ri·al·ly** *adv*

ma·te·ri·al·ism \mə'tirēə,lizəm\ *n* 1 : theory that matter is the only reality 2 : preoccupation with material and not spiritual things — **ma·te·ri·al·ist** \-list\ *n or adj* — **ma·te·ri·al·is·tic** \-,tirēə'listik\ *adj*

ma·te·ri·al·ize \mə'tirēə,līz\ *vb* -ized; -iz·ing : take or cause to take bodily form — **ma·te·ri·al·i·za·tion** \mə,tirēələ'zāshən\ *n*

ma·té·ri·el, ma·te·ri·el \mə,tirē'el\ *n* : military supplies

ma·ter·nal \mə'tərn³l\ *adj* : motherly — **ma·ter·nal·ly** *adv*

ma·ter·ni·ty \mə'tərnətē\ *n, pl* -ties 1 : state of being a mother 2 : hospital's childbirth facility ~ *adj* 1 : worn during pregnancy 2 : relating to the period close to childbirth

math \'math\ *n* : mathematics

math·e·mat·ics \,mathə'matiks\ *n pl* : science of numbers and of shapes in space — **math·e·mat·i·cal** \-ikəl\ *adj* — **math·e·mat·i·cal·ly** *adv* — **math·e·ma·ti·cian** \,mathəmə'tishən\ *n*

mat·i·nee, mat·i·née \,mat³n'ā\ *n* : afternoon performance

mat·ins \'mat³nz\ *n* : morning prayers

ma·tri·arch \'mātrē,ärk\ *n* : woman who rules a family — **ma·tri·ar·chal** \,mātrē'ärkəl\ *adj* — **ma·tri·ar·chy** \'mātrē,ärkē\ *n*

ma·tri·cide \'matrə,sīd, 'mā-\ *n* : murder of one's mother — **ma·tri·cid·al** \,matrə'sīd³l, ,mā-\ *adj*

ma·tric·u·late \mə'trikyə,lāt\ *vb* -lat·ed; -lat·ing : enroll in school — **ma·tric·u·la·tion** \-,trikyə-'lāshən\ *n*

mat·ri·mo·ny \'matrə,mōnē\ *n* : marriage — **mat·ri·mo·ni·al** \,matrə'mōnēəl\ *adj* — **mat·ri·mo·ni·al·ly** *adv*

ma·trix \'mātriks\ *n, pl* -tri·ces

\\'mātrə,sēz, 'ma-\\ *or* -trix•es
\\'mātriksəz\\ : something (as a
mold) that gives form, foundation, or origin to something else
enclosed in it

ma•tron \\'mātrən\\ *n* 1 : dignified
mature woman 2 : woman supervisor — ma•tron•ly *adj*

matte \\'mat\\ *adj* : not shiny

mat•ter \\'matər\\ *n* 1 : subject of interest 2 *pl* : circumstances 3 : trouble 4 : physical substance ~ *vb*
: be important

mat•tock \\'matək\\ *n* : a digging tool

mat•tress \\'matrəs\\ *n* : pad to sleep
on

ma•ture \\mə'tùr, -'tyùr, -'chùr\\ *adj*
-tur•er; -est 1 : carefully considered 2 : fully grown or developed
3 : due for payment ~ *vb* -tured;
-tur•ing : become mature — mat-
u•ra•tion \\,machə'rāshən\\ *n* —
ma•ture•ly *adv* — ma•tu•ri•ty
\\-ətē\\ *n*

maud•lin \\'mòdlən\\ *adj* : excessively sentimental

♦ maul \\'mòl\\ *n* : heavy hammer ~
vb 1 : beat 2 : handle roughly

mau•so•le•um \\,mósə'lēəm, ,mòzə-\\
n, pl -leums *or* -lea \\-'lēə\\ : large
above-ground tomb

mauve \\'mōv, 'móv\\ *n* : lilac color

ma•ven, ma•vin \\'māvən\\ *n* : expert

mav•er•ick \\'mavrik\\ *n* 1 : unbranded range animal 2 : nonconformist

maw \\'mò\\ *n* 1 : stomach 2 : throat,
esophagus, or jaws

mawk•ish \\'mòkish\\ *adj* : sickly
sentimental — mawk•ish•ly *adv*
— mawk•ish•ness *n*

max•im \\'maksəm\\ *n* : proverb

max•i•mum \\'maksəməm\\ *n, pl* -ma
\\-əmə\\ *or* -mums 1 : greatest quantity 2 : upper limit 3 : largest
number — maximum *adj* — max-
i•mize \\-ə,mīz\\ *vb*

may \\'mā\\ *verbal auxiliary, past*

might \\'mīt\\; *pres sing & pl* may 1
: have permission 2 : be likely to 3
— used to express desire, purpose,
or contingency

May \\'mā\\ *n* : 5th month of the year
having 31 days

may•ap•ple *n* : woodland herb having edible fruit

may•be \\'mābē\\ *adv* : perhaps

may•flow•er *n* : spring-blooming
herb

may•fly *n* : fly with an aquatic larva

may•hem \\'mā,hem, 'māəm\\ *n*
: crippling or mutilation of a person 2 : needless damage

may•on•naise \\'māə,nāz\\ *n* : creamy
white sandwich spread

may•or \\'māər, 'mer\\ *n* : chief city
official — may•or•al \\-əl\\ *adj* —
may•or•al•ty \\-əltē\\ *n*

maze \\'māz\\ *n* : confusing network
of passages — mazy *adj*

ma•zur•ka \\mə'zərkə\\ *n* : Polish
dance

me \\'mē\\ *pron, objective case of* I

mead \\'mēd\\ *n* : alcoholic beverage
brewed from honey

mead•ow \\'medō\\ *n* : low-lying usu.
level grassland — mead•ow•land
\\-,land\\ *n*

mead•ow•lark *n* : songbird with a
yellow breast

mea•ger, mea•gre \\'mēgər\\ *adj* 1
: thin 2 : lacking richness or
strength — mea•ger•ly *adv* —
mea•ger•ness *n*

[1]meal \\'mēl\\ *n* 1 : food to be eaten at
one time 2 : act of eating — meal-
time *n*

[2]meal *n* : ground grain — mealy *adj*

[1]mean \\'mēn\\ *adj* 1 : humble 2 : worthy of or showing little regard 3
: stingy 4 : malicious — mean-
ly *adv* — mean•ness *n*

[2]mean \\'mēn\\ *vb* meant \\'ment\\;
mean•ing \\'mēniŋ\\ 1 : intend 2

GARFIELD, IF YOU'RE REEEEAL GOOD TODAY...

I'LL GIVE YOU A KITTY TREAT

HMMM

LOOKS LIKE I'LL HAVE TO MAUL HIM FOR THE BOX AGAIN

JIM DAVIS 5-20

: serve to convey, show, or indicate 3 : be important

³mean n 1 : middle point 2 pl : something that helps gain an end 3 pl : material resources 4 : sum of several quantities divided by the number of quantities ~ adj : being a mean

mean·der \mē'andər\ vb -dered; -der·ing 1 : follow a winding course 2 : wander aimlessly — meander n

mean·ing \'mēniŋ\ n 1 : idea conveyed or intended to be conveyed 2 : aim — mean·ing·ful \-fəl\ adj — mean·ing·ful·ly adv — mean·ing·less adj

mean·time \'mēn,tīm\ n : intervening time — meantime adv

mean·while \-,hwīl\ n : meantime ~ adv 1 : meantime 2 : at the same time

mea·sles \'mēzəlz\ n pl : disease that is marked by red spots on the skin

mea·sly \'mēzlē\ adj -sli·er; -est : contemptibly small in amount

mea·sure \'mezhər, 'māzh-\ n 1 : moderate amount 2 : dimensions or amount 3 : something to show amount 4 : unit or system of measurement 5 : act of measuring 6 : means to an end ~ vb -sured; -sur·ing 1 : find out or mark off size or amount of 2 : have a specified measurement — mea·sur·able \'mezhərəbəl, 'māzh-\ adj — mea·sur·ably \-blē\ adv — mea·sure·less adj — mea·sure·ment n — mea·sur·er n

meat \'mēt\ n 1 : food 2 : animal flesh used as food — meat·ball n — meaty adj

me·chan·ic \mi'kanik\ n : worker who repairs cars

me·chan·i·cal \mi'kanikəl\ adj 1 : relating to machines or mechanics 2 : involuntary — me·chan·i·cal·ly adv

me·chan·ics \-iks\ n sing or pl 1 : branch of physics dealing with energy and forces in relation to bodies 2 : mechanical details

mech·a·nism \'mekə,nizəm\ n 1 : piece of machinery 2 : technique for gaining a result 3 : basic processes producing a phenomenon — mech·a·nis·tic \,mekə'nistik\ adj — mech·a·ni·za·tion \,mekənə'zāshən\ n — mech·a-

nize \'mekə,nīz\ vb — mech·a-niz·er n

med·al \'med°l\ n 1 : religious pin or pendant 2 : coinlike commemorative metal piece

med·al·ist, med·al·list \'med°list\ n : person awarded a medal

me·dal·lion \mə'dalyən\ n : large medal

med·dle \'med°l\ vb -dled; -dling : interfere — med·dler \'med°lər\ n — med·dle·some \'med°lsəm\ adj

me·dia \'mēdēə\ n pl : communications organizations

me·di·an \'mēdēən\ n : middle value in a range — median adj

me·di·ate \'mēdē,āt\ vb -at·ed; -at·ing : help settle a dispute — me·di·a·tion \,mēdē'āshən\ n — me·di·a·tor \'mēdē,ātər\ n

med·ic \'medik\ n : medical worker esp. in the military

med·i·ca·ble \'medikəbəl\ adj : curable

med·ic·aid \'medi,kād\ n : government program of medical aid for the poor

med·i·cal \'medikəl\ adj : relating to medicine — med·i·cal·ly \-klē\ adv

medi·care \'medi,ker\ n : government program of medical care for the aged

med·i·cate \'medə,kāt\ vb -cat·ed; -cat·ing : treat with medicine

med·i·ca·tion \,medə'kāshən\ n 1 : act of medicating 2 : medicine

med·i·cine \'medəsən\ n 1 : preparation used to treat disease 2 : science dealing with the cure of disease — me·dic·i·nal \mə'dis°nəl\ adj — me·dic·i·nal·ly adv

me·di·e·val, me·di·ae·val \,mēdē-'ēval, ,med-, ,mid-; ,mē'dē-, ,me-, ,mi-\ adj : of or relating to the Middle Ages — me·di·e·val·ist \-ist\ n

me·di·o·cre \,mēdē'ōkər\ adj : not very good — me·di·oc·ri·ty \-'äkrətē\ n

med·i·tate \'medə,tāt\ vb -tat·ed; -tat·ing : contemplate — med·i·ta·tion \,medə'tāshən\ n — med·i·ta·tive \'medə,tātiv\ adj — med·i·ta·tive·ly adv

me·di·um \'mēdēəm\ n, pl -diums or -dia \-ēə\ 1 : middle position or degree 2 : means of effecting or conveying something **3** : surrounding substance **4** : means of communication **5** : mode of artistic expression — **medium** *adj*

med·ley \'medlē\ *n, pl* **-leys** : series of songs performed as one

meek \'mēk\ *adj* **1** : mild-mannered **2** : lacking spirit — **meek·ly** *adv* — **meek·ness** *n*

meer·schaum \'mirshəm, -ˌshȯm\ *n* : claylike tobacco pipe

¹meet \'mēt\ *vb* **met** \'met\; **meet·ing 1** : run into **2** : join **3** : oppose **4** : assemble **5** : satisfy **6** : be introduced to ~ *n* : sports team competition

²meet *adj* : proper

meet·ing \'mētiŋ\ *n* : a getting together — **meet·ing·house** *n*

mega·byte \'megəˌbīt\ *n* : unit of computer storage capacity

mega·hertz \-ˌhərts, -ˌherts\ *n* : one million hertz

mega·phone \'megəˌfōn\ *n* : cone-shaped device to intensify or direct the voice

mel·an·choly \'melənˌkälē\ *n* : depression — **mel·an·chol·ic** \ˌmelən'kälik\ *adj* — **melancholy** *adj*

mel·a·no·ma \ˌmelə'nōmə\ *n, pl* **-mas** : usu. malignant skin tumor

me·lee \'māˌlā, mā'lā\ *n* : brawl

me·lio·rate \'mēlyəˌrāt, 'mēlēə-\ *vb* **-rat·ed; -rat·ing** : improve — **me·lio·ra·tion** \ˌmēlyə'rāshən, ˌmēlēə-\ *n* — **me·lio·ra·tive** \'mēlyəˌrātiv, 'mēlēə-\ *adj*

mel·lif·lu·ous \me'lifləwəs, mə-\ *adj* : sweetly flowing — **mel·lif·lu·ous·ly** *adv* — **mel·lif·lu·ous·ness** *n*

mel·low \'melō\ *adj* **1** : grown gentle or mild **2** : rich and full — **mellow** *vb* — **mel·low·ness** *n*

melo·dra·ma \'meləˌdrämə, -ˌdram-\ *n* : overly theatrical play — **melo·dra·mat·ic** \ˌmelədrə'matik\ *adj* — **melo·dra·mat·i·cal·ly** \-tiklē\ *adv*

mel·o·dy \'melədē\ *n, pl* **-dies 1** : agreeable sound **2** : succession of musical notes — **me·lod·ic** \mə'lädik\ *adj* — **me·lod·i·cal·ly** \-iklē\ *adv* — **me·lo·di·ous** \mə'lōdēəs\ *adj* — **me·lo·di·ous·ly** *adv* — **me·lo·di·ous·ness** *n*

mel·on \'melən\ *n* : gourdlike fruit

♦ **melt** \'melt\ *vb* **1** : change from solid to liquid usu. by heat **2** : dissolve or disappear gradually **3** : move or be moved emotionally

mem·ber \'membər\ *n* **1** : part of a person, animal, or plant **2** : one of a group **3** : part of a whole — **mem·ber·ship** \-ˌship\ *n*

mem·brane \'memˌbrān\ *n* : thin layer esp. in an organism — **mem·bra·nous** \-brənəs\ *adj*

me·men·to \mi'mentō\ *n, pl* **-tos** *or* **-toes** : souvenir

memo \'memō\ *n, pl* **mem·os** : memorandum

mem·oirs \'memˌwärz\ *n pl* : autobiography

mem·o·ra·bil·ia \ˌmemərə'bilēə, -'bilyə\ *n pl* **1** : memorable things **2** : mementos

mem·o·ra·ble \'memərəbəl\ *adj* : worth remembering — **mem·o·ra·bil·i·ty** \ˌmemərə'bilətē\ *n* — **mem·o·ra·ble·ness** *n* — **mem·o·ra·bly** \-blē\ *adv*

mem·o·ran·dum \ˌmemə'randəm\ *n, pl* **-dums** *or* **-da** \-də\ : informal note

me·mo·ri·al \mə'mōrēəl\ *n* : something (as a monument) meant to keep remembrance alive — **memorial** *adj* — **me·mo·ri·al·ize** *vb*

Memorial Day *n* : last Monday in May or formerly May 30 observed as a legal holiday in commemoration of dead servicemen

mem·o·ry \'memrē, 'memə-\ *n, pl*

-ries 1 : power of remembering 2 : something remembered 3 : commemoration 4 : time within which past events are remembered — **mem·o·ri·za·tion** \ˌmemərə-ˈzāshən\ n — **mem·o·rize** \ˈmemə-ˌrīz\ vb — **mem·o·riz·er** n

men pl of MAN

men·ace \ˈmenəs\ n : threat of danger ∼ vb **-aced; -ac·ing** 1 : threaten 2 : endanger — **men·ac·ing·ly** adv

me·nag·er·ie \mə-ˈnajərē\ n : collection of wild animals

mend \ˈmend\ vb 1 : improve 2 : repair 3 : heal — **mend** n — **mend·er** n

men·da·cious \men-ˈdāshəs\ adj : dishonest — **men·da·cious·ly** adv — **men·dac·i·ty** \-ˈdasətē\ n

men·di·cant \ˈmendikənt\ n : beggar — **men·di·can·cy** \-kənsē\ n — **mendicant** adj

men·ha·den \men-ˈhād°n, mən-\ n, pl **-den** : fish related to the herring

me·nial \ˈmēnēəl, -nyəl\ adj 1 : relating to servants 2 : humble ∼ n : domestic servant — **me·ni·al·ly** adv

men·in·gi·tis \ˌmenən-ˈjītəs\ n, pl **-git·i·des** \-ˈjitəˌdēz\ : disease of the brain and spinal cord

meno·pause \ˈmenəˌpóz\ n : time when menstruation ends — **meno·paus·al** \ˌmenə-ˈpózəl\ adj

me·no·rah \mə-ˈnōrə\ n : candelabrum used in Jewish worship

men·stru·a·tion \ˌmenstrə-ˈwāshən, men-ˈstrā-\ n : monthly discharge of blood from the uterus — **men·stru·al** \ˈmenstrəwəl\ adj — **men·stru·ate** \ˈmenstrəˌwāt, -ˌstrāt\ vb

-ment \mənt\ n suffix 1 : result or means of an action 2 : action or process 3 : place of an action 4 : state or condition

men·tal \ˈment°l\ adj : relating to

the mind or its disorders — **men·tal·i·ty** \men-ˈtalətē\ n — **men·tal·ly** adv

men·thol \ˈmenˌthól, -ˌthōl\ n : soothing substance from oil of peppermint — **men·tho·lat·ed** \-thəˌlātəd\ adj

men·tion \ˈmenchən\ vb : refer to — **mention** n

men·tor \ˈmenˌtór, ˈmentər\ n : instructor

menu \ˈmenyü\ n 1 : restaurant's list of food 2 : list of offerings

me·ow \mē-ˈaú\ n : characteristic cry of a cat — **meow** vb

mer·can·tile \ˈmərkənˌtēl, -ˌtīl\ adj : relating to merchants or trade

mer·ce·nary \ˈmərs°nˌerē\ n, pl **-nar·ies** : hired soldier ∼ adj : serving only for money

mer·chan·dise \ˈmərchənˌdīz, -ˌdīs\ n : goods bought and sold ∼ vb **-dised; -dis·ing** : buy and sell — **mer·chan·dis·er** n

mer·chant \ˈmərchənt\ n : one who buys and sells

merchant marine n : commercial ships

mer·cu·ri·al \ˌmər-ˈkyúrēəl\ adj : unpredictable — **mer·cu·ri·al·ly** adv — **mer·cu·ri·al·ness** n

mer·cu·ry \ˈmərkyərē\ n : heavy liquid metallic chemical element

♦ **mer·cy** \ˈmərsē\ n, pl **-cies** 1 : show of pity or leniency 2 : divine blessing — **mer·ci·ful** \-sifəl\ adj — **mer·ci·ful·ly** adv — **mer·ci·less** \-siləs\ adj — **mer·ci·less·ly** adv — **mercy** adj

mere \ˈmir\ adj, superlative **mer·est** : nothing more than — **mere·ly** adv

merge \ˈmərj\ vb **merged; merg·ing** 1 : unite 2 : blend — **merg·er** \ˈmərjər\ n

me·rid·i·an \mə-ˈridēən\ n : imaginary circle on the earth's surface passing through the poles — **me·ridian** *adj*

me·ringue \mə'raŋ\ *n* : baked dessert topping of beaten egg whites

me·ri·no \mə'rēnō\ *n, pl* **-nos 1** : kind of sheep **2** : fine soft woolen yarn

mer·it \'merət\ *n* **1** : praiseworthy quality **2** *pl* : rights and wrongs of a legal case ~ *vb* : deserve — **mer·i·to·ri·ous** \ˌmerə'tōrēəs\ *adj* — **mer·i·to·ri·ous·ly** *adv* — **mer·i·to·ri·ous·ness** *n*

mer·maid \'mər͵mād\ *n* : legendary female sea creature

mer·ry \'merē\ *adj* **-ri·er; -est** : full of high spirits — **mer·ri·ly** *adv* — **mer·ri·ment** \'merimənt\ *n* — **mer·ry·mak·er** \'merē͵mākər\ *n* — **mer·ry·mak·ing** \'merē͵mākiŋ\ *n*

merry–go–round *n* : revolving amusement ride

me·sa \'māsə\ *n* : steep flat-topped hill

mesdames *pl of* MADAM *or of* MADAME *or of* MRS.

mesdemoiselles *pl of* MADEMOISELLE

mesh \'mesh\ *n* **1** : one of the openings in a net **2** : net fabric **3** : working contact ~ *vb* : fit together properly — **meshed** \'mesht\ *adj*

mes·mer·ize \'mezmə͵rīz\ *vb* **-ized; -iz·ing** : hypnotize

mess \'mes\ *n* **1** : meal eaten by a group **2** : confused, dirty, or offensive state ~ *vb* **1** : make dirty or untidy **2** : putter **3** : interfere — **messy** *adj*

mes·sage \'mesij\ *n* : news, information, or a command sent by one person to another

mes·sen·ger \'mesᵊnjər\ *n* : one who carries a message or does an errand

Mes·si·ah \mə'sīə\ *n* **1** : expected deliverer of the Jews **2** : Jesus Christ **3** *not cap* : great leader

messieurs *pl of* MONSIEUR

Messrs. *pl of* MR.

mes·ti·zo \me'stēzō\ *n, pl* **-zos** : person of mixed blood

met *past of* MEET

me·tab·o·lism \mə'tabə͵lizəm\ *n* : biochemical processes necessary to life — **met·a·bol·ic** \ˌmetə'bälik\ *adj* — **me·tab·o·lize** \mə'tabə͵līz\ *vb*

met·al \'metᵊl\ *n* : shiny substance that can be melted and shaped and conducts heat and electricity — **me·tal·lic** \mə'talik\ *adj* — **met·al·ware** *n* — **met·al·work** *n* — **met·al·work·er** *n* — **met·al·work·ing** *n*

met·al·lur·gy \'metᵊl͵ərjē\ *n* : science of metals — **met·al·lur·gi·cal** \ˌmetᵊl'ərjikəl\ *adj* — **met·al·lur·gist** \'metᵊl͵ərjist\ *n*

meta·mor·pho·sis \ˌmetə'mȯrfəsəs\ *n, pl* **-pho·ses** \-͵sēz\ : sudden and drastic change (as of form) — **meta·mor·phose** \-͵fōz, -͵fōs\ *vb*

met·a·phor \'metə͵fȯr, -fər\ *n* : use of a word denoting one kind of object or idea in place of another to suggest a likeness between them — **met·a·phor·i·cal** \ˌmetə'fȯrikəl\ *adj*

meta·phys·ics \ˌmetə'fiziks\ *n* : study of the causes and nature of things — **meta·phys·i·cal** \-'fizəkəl\ *adj*

mete \'mēt\ *vb* **met·ed; met·ing** : allot

me·te·or \'mētēər, -ē͵ȯr\ *n* : small body that produces a streak of light as it burns up in the atmosphere

me·te·or·ic \ˌmētē'ȯrik\ *adj* **1** : relating to a meteor **2** : sudden and spectacular — **me·te·or·i·cal·ly** \-iklē\ *adv*

me·te·or·ite \'mētēə͵rīt\ *n* : meteor that reaches the earth

me·te·o·rol·o·gy \ˌmētēə'räləjē\ *n* : science of weather — **me·te·o·ro·log·ic** \ˌmētē͵ȯrə'läjik\ **me·te·o·ro·log·i·cal** \-'läjikəl\ *adj* — **me·te·o·rol·o·gist** \-ē'räləjist\ *n*

¹**me·ter** \'mētər\ *n* : rhythm in verse or music

²**meter** *n* : unit of length equal to 39.37 inches

³**meter** *n* : measuring instrument

meth·a·done \'methə͵dōn\ *n* : synthetic addictive narcotic

meth·ane \'meth͵ān\ *n* : colorless odorless flammable gas

meth·a·nol \'methə͵nȯl, -͵nōl\ *n* : volatile flammable poisonous liquid

meth·od \'methəd\ *n* **1** : procedure for achieving an end **2** : orderly arrangement or plan — **me·thod·i·cal** \mə'thädikəl\ *adj* — **me·**

thod·i·cal·ly \-klē\ adv — me-
thod·i·cal·ness n

me·tic·u·lous \mə'tikyələs\ adj : extremely careful in attending to details — me·tic·u·lous·ly adv —
me·tic·u·lous·ness n

met·ric \'metrik\; met·ri·cal
\-trikəl\ adj : relating to meter or
the metric system — met·ri·cal·
ly adv

metric system n : system of weights
and measures using the meter and
kilogram

met·ro·nome \'metrə,nōm\ n : instrument that ticks regularly to
mark a beat in music

me·trop·o·lis \mə'träpələs\ n : major city — met·ro·pol·i·tan
\,metrə'pälətᵊn\ adj

met·tle \'metᵊl\ n : spirit or courage
— met·tle·some \-səm\ adj

mez·za·nine \'mezᵊn,ēn, ,mezᵊn'ēn\
n 1 : intermediate level between 2
main floors 2 : lowest balcony

mez·zo-so·pra·no \,metsōsə'pranō,
,medz-\ n : voice between soprano
and contralto

mi·as·ma \mī'azmə\ n 1 : noxious
vapor 2 : harmful influence — mi-
as·mic \-mik\ adj

mi·ca \'mīkə\ n : mineral separable
into thin transparent sheets

mice pl of MOUSE

mi·cro \'mīkrō\ adj : very small

mi·crobe \'mī,krōb\ n : disease-
causing microorganism — mi-
cro·bi·al \mī'krōbēəl\ adj

mi·cro·bi·ol·o·gy \,mīkrōbī'äləjē\ n
: biology dealing with microscopic
life — mi·cro·bi·o·log·i·cal
\'mīkrō,bīə'läjikəl\ adj — mi·cro·
bi·ol·o·gist \,mīkrōbī'äləjist\ n

mi·cro·com·put·er \'mīkrōkəm-
,pyütər\ n : small computer that
uses a microprocessor

mi·cro·cosm \'mīkrə,käzəm\ n
: one thought of as a miniature
universe

mi·cro·film \-,film\ n : small film recording printed matter — micro-
film vb

mi·crom·e·ter \mī'krämətər\ n : instrument for measuring minute
distances

mi·cro·min·i·a·tur·ized \,mīkrō-
'minēəchə,rīzd, -'minichə-\ adj
: reduced to a very small size
— mi·cro·min·i·a·tur·iza·tion

\-,minēə,chùrə'zāshən, -,mini,chùr-,
-chər-\ n

mi·cron \'mī,krän\ n : one millionth
of a meter

mi·cro·or·gan·ism \,mīkrō'òrgə-
,nizəm\ n : very tiny living thing

mi·cro·phone \'mīkrə,fōn\ n : instrument for changing sound
waves into variations of an electric current

mi·cro·pro·ces·sor \'mīkrō,prä-
sesər\ n : miniaturized computer
processing unit on a single chip

mi·cro·scope \-,skōp\ n : optical device for magnifying tiny objects
— mi·cro·scop·ic \,mīkrə'skäpik\
adj — mi·cro·scop·i·cal·ly adv —
mi·cros·co·py \mī'kräskəpē\ n

mi·cro·wave \'mīkrə,wāv\ n 1
: short radio wave 2 : oven that
cooks food using microwaves ~
vb : heat or cook in a microwave
oven — mi·cro·wav·able, mi·cro·
wave·able \,mīkrə'wāvəbəl\ adj

mid \'mid\ adj : middle — mid·
point n — mid·stream n — mid·
sum·mer n — mid·town n or adj
— mid·week n — mid·win·ter n
— mid·year n

mid·air n :˙a point in the air well
above the ground

mid·day n : noon

mid·dle \'midᵊl\ adj 1 : equally distant from the extremes 2 : being at
neither extreme ~ n : middle part
or point

Middle Ages n pl : period from
about A.D. 500 to about 1500

mid·dle·man \-,man\ n : dealer or
agent between the producer and
consumer

mid·dling \'midliŋ, -lən\ adj 1 : of
middle or medium size, degree, or
quality 2 : mediocre

midge \'mij\ n : very tiny fly

midg·et \'mijət\ n : very small person or thing

mid·land \'midlənd, -,land\ n : interior of a country

mid·most adj : being nearest the
middle — midmost adv

mid·night n : 12 o'clock at night

mid·riff \'mid,rif\ n : mid-region of
the torso

mid·ship·man \'mid,shipmən, ,mid-
'ship-\ n : student naval officer

midst \'midst\ n : position close to
or surrounded by others — midst
prep

mid·way \'mid,wā\ *n* : concessions and amusements at a carnival ~ *adv* : in the middle

mid·wife \'mid,wīf\ *n* : person who aids at childbirth — **mid·wife·ry** \mid'wifərē, -'wīf-\ *n*

mien \'mēn\ *n* : appearance

miff \'mif\ *vb* : upset or peeve

¹might \'mīt\ *past of* MAY — used to express permission or possibility or as a polite alternative to *may*

²might *n* : power or resources

mighty \'mītē\ *adj* **might·i·er; -est 1** : very strong **2** : great — **might·i·ly** *adv* — **might·i·ness** *n* — **mighty** *adv*

mi·graine \'mī,grān\ *n* : severe headache often with nausea

mi·grant \'mīgrənt\ *n* : one who moves frequently to find work

mi·grate \'mī,grāt\ *vb* **-grat·ed; -grat·ing 1** : move from one place to another **2** : pass periodically from one region or climate to another — **mi·gra·tion** \mī'grāshən\ *n* — **mi·gra·to·ry** \'mīgrə,tōrē\ *adj*

mild \'mīld\ *adj* **1** : gentle in nature or behavior **2** : moderate in action or effect — **mild·ly** *adv* — **mild·ness** *n*

mil·dew \'mil,dü, -,dyü\ *n* : whitish fungal growth — **mildew** *vb*

mile \'mīl\ *n* : unit of length equal to 5280 feet

mile·age \'mīlij\ *n* **1** : allowance per mile for traveling expenses **2** : amount or rate of use expressed in miles

mile·stone *n* : significant point in development

mi·lieu \mēl'yü, -'yœ̄\ *n, pl* **-lieus** *or* **-lieux** \-'yüz, -'yœ̄\ : surroundings or setting

mil·i·tant \'milətənt\ *adj* : aggressively active or hostile — **mil·i·tan·cy** \-tənsē\ *n* — **militant** *n* — **mil·i·tant·ly** *adv*

mil·i·tar·ism \'milətə,rizəm\ *n* : dominance of military ideals or of a policy of aggressive readiness for war — **mil·i·ta·rist** \-rist\ *n* — **mil·i·tar·is·tic** \,milətə'ristik\ *adj*

mil·i·tary \'milə,terē\ *adj* **1** : relating to soldiers, arms, or war **2** : relating to or performed by armed forces ~ *n* : armed forces or the people in them — **mil·i·tar·i·ly** \,milə'terəlē\ *adv*

mil·i·tate \-,tāt\ *vb* **-tat·ed; -tat·ing** : have an effect

mi·li·tia \mə'lishə\ *n* : civilian soldiers — **mi·li·tia·man** \-mən\ *n*

milk \'milk\ *n* : white nutritive fluid secreted by female mammals for feeding their young ~ *vb* **1** : draw off the milk of **2** : draw something from as if by milking — **milk·er** *n* — **milk·i·ness** \-ēnəs\ *n* — **milky** *adj*

milk·man \-,man, -mən\ *n* : man who sells or delivers milk

milk·weed *n* : herb with milky juice

¹mill \'mil\ *n* **1** : building in which grain is ground into flour **2** : manufacturing plant **3** : machine used esp. for forming or processing ~ *vb* **1** : subject to a process in a mill **2** : move in a circle — **mill·er** *n*

²mill *n* : ¹⁄₁₀ cent

♦ **mil·len·ni·um** \mə'lenēəm\ *n, pl* **-nia** \-ēə\ *or* **-niums** : a period of 1000 years

mil·let \'milət\ *n* : cereal and forage grass with small seeds

mil·li·gram \'milə,gram\ *n* : ¹⁄₁₀₀₀ gram

mil·li·li·ter \-,lētər\ *n* : ¹⁄₁₀₀₀ liter

mil·li·me·ter \-,mētər\ *n* : ¹⁄₁₀₀₀ meter

mil·li·ner \'milənər\ *n* : person who makes or sells women's hats — **mil·li·nery** \'milə,nerē\ *n*

mil·lion \'milyən\ *n, pl* **millions** *or* **million** : 1000 thousands — **million** *adj* — **mil·lionth** \-yənth\ *adj or n*

mil·lion·aire \ˌmilyəˈnar, ˈmilyəˌnar\ *n* : person worth a million or more (as of dollars)

mil·li·pede \'miləˌpēd\ *n* : long-bodied arthropod with 2 pairs of legs on most segments

mill·stone *n* : either of 2 round flat stones used for grinding grain

mime \'mīm\ *n* **1** : mimic **2** : pantomime — **mime** *vb*

mim·eo·graph \'mimēəˌgraf\ *n* : machine for making many stencil copies — **mimeograph** *vb*

mim·ic \'mimik\ *n* : one that mimics ~ *vb* **-icked; -ick·ing 1** : imitate closely **2** : ridicule by imitation — **mim·ic·ry** \'mimikrē\ *n*

min·a·ret \ˌminəˈret\ *n* : tower attached to a mosque

mince \'mins\ *vb* **minced; minc·ing 1** : cut into small pieces **2** : choose (one's words) carefully **3** : walk in a prim affected manner

mind \'mīnd\ *n* **1** : memory **2** : the part of an individual that feels, perceives, and esp. reasons **3** : intention **4** : normal mental condition **5** : opinion **6** : intellectual ability ~ *vb* **1** : attend to **2** : obey **3** : be concerned about **4** : be careful — **mind·ed** *adj* — **mind·less** \'mīndləs\ *adj* — **mind·less·ly** *adv* — **mind·less·ness** *n*

mind·ful \-fəl\ *adj* : aware or attentive — **mind·ful·ly** *adv* — **mind·ful·ness** *n*

¹mine \'mīn\ *pron* : that which belongs to me

²mine \'mīn\ *n* **1** : excavation from which minerals are taken **2** : explosive device placed in the ground or water for destroying enemy vehicles or vessels that later pass ~ *vb* **mined; min·ing 1** : get ore from **2** : place military mines in — **mine·field** *n* — **min·er** *n*

min·er·al \'minərəl\ *n* **1** : crystalline substance not of organic origin **2** : useful natural substance (as coal) obtained from the ground — **mineral** *adj*

min·er·al·o·gy \ˌminəˈräləjē, -ˈral-\ *n* : science dealing with minerals — **min·er·al·og·i·cal** \ˌminərə-ˈläjikəl\ *adj* — **min·er·al·o·gist** \ˌminəˈräləjist, -ˈral-\ *n*

min·gle \'miŋgəl\ *vb* **-gled; -gling** : bring together or mix

mini- *comb form* : miniature or of small dimensions

min·ia·ture \'minēəˌchùr, 'miniˌchùr, -chər\ *n* : tiny copy or very small version — **miniature** *adj* — **min·ia·tur·ist** \-ˌchùrist, -chər-\ *n* — **min·ia·tur·ize** \-ēəchəˌrīz, -ichə-\ *vb*

mini-bike \'minēˌbīk\ *n* : small motorcycle

mini-bus \-ˌbəs\ *n* : small bus

mini·com·put·er \-kəmˌpyütər\ *n* : computer intermediate between a mainframe and a microcomputer in size and speed

mini·course \-ˌkōrs\ *n* : short course of study

min·i·mal \'minəməl\ *adj* : relating to or being a minimum — **min·i·mal·ly** *adv*

min·i·mize \'minəˌmīz\ *vb* **-mized; -miz·ing 1** : reduce to a minimum **2** : underestimate intentionally

min·i·mum \'minəməm\ *n, pl* **-ma** \-mə\ *or* **-mums** : lowest quantity or amount — **minimum** *adj*

min·ion \'minyən\ *n* **1** : servile dependent **2** : subordinate official

mini·se·ries \'minēˌsirēz\ *n* : television story in several parts

mini·skirt \-ˌskərt\ *n* : very short skirt

min·is·ter \'minəstər\ *n* **1** : Protestant member of the clergy **2** : high officer of state **3** : diplomatic representative ~ *vb* : give aid or service — **min·is·te·ri·al** \ˌminə-ˈstirēəl\ *adj* — **min·is·tra·tion** *n*

min·is·try \'minəstrē\ *n, pl* **-tries 1** : office or duties of a minister **2** : body of ministers **3** : government department headed by a minister

mini·van \'minēˌvan\ *n* : small van

mink \'miŋk\ *n, pl* **mink** *or* **minks** : weasellike mammal or its soft brown fur

min·now \'minō\ *n, pl* **-nows** : small freshwater fish

mi·nor \'mīnər\ *adj* **1** : less in size, importance, or value **2** : not serious ~ *n* **1** : person not yet of legal age **2** : secondary field of academic specialization

mi·nor·i·ty \məˈnórətē, mī-\ *n, pl* **-ties 1** : time or state of being a minor **2** : smaller number (as of votes) **3** : part of a population differing from others (as in race or religion)

min·strel \'minstrəl\ *n* **1** : medieval singer of verses **2** : performer in a program usu. of black American songs and jokes — **min·strel·sy** \-sē\ *n*

¹mint \'mint\ *n* **1** : fragrant herb that yields a flavoring oil **2** : mint-flavored piece of candy — **minty** *adj*

²mint *n* **1** : place where coins are made **2** : vast sum ~ *adj* : unused — **mint** *vb* — **mint·er** *n*

min·u·et \ˌminyə'wet\ *n* : slow graceful dance

mi·nus \'mīnəs\ *prep* **1** : diminished by **2** : lacking ~ *n* : negative quantity or quality

mi·nus·cule \'minəs‚kyül, min'əs-\; **min·is·cule** \'minəs-\ *adj* : very small

¹min·ute \'minət\ *n* **1** : 60th part of an hour or of a degree **2** : short time **3** *pl* : official record of a meeting

²mi·nute \mī'nüt, mə-, -'nyüt\ *adj* **-nut·er**; **-est 1** : very small **2** : marked by close attention to details — **mi·nute·ly** *adv* — **mi·nute·ness** *n*

mir·a·cle \'mirikəl\ *n* **1** : extraordinary event taken as a sign of divine intervention in human affairs **2** : marvel — **mi·rac·u·lous** \mə-'rakyələs\ *adj* — **mi·rac·u·lous·ly** *adv*

mi·rage \mə'räzh\ *n* : distant illusion caused by atmospheric conditions (as in the desert)

mire \'mīr\ *n* : heavy deep mud ~ *vb* **mired; mir·ing** : stick or sink in mire — **miry** *adj*

mir·ror \'mirər\ *n* : smooth surface (as of glass) that reflects images ~ *vb* : reflect in or as if in a mirror

mirth \'mərth\ *n* : gladness and laughter — **mirth·ful** \-fəl\ *adj* — **mirth·ful·ly** *adv* — **mirth·ful·ness** *n* — **mirth·less** *adj*

mis·an·thrope \'mis°n‚thrōp\ *n* : one who hates mankind — **mis·an·throp·ic** \ˌmis°n'thräpik\ *adj* — **mis·an·thro·py** \mis'anthrəpē\ *n*

mis·ap·pre·hend \ˌmis‚aprə'hend\ *vb* : misunderstand — **mis·ap·pre·hen·sion** *n*

mis·ap·pro·pri·ate \ˌmisə'prōprē‚āt\ *vb* : take dishonestly for one's own use — **mis·ap·pro·pri·a·tion** *n*

mis·be·got·ten \-bi'gät°n\ *adj* **1** : illegitimate **2** : ill-conceived

mis·be·have \ˌmisbi'hāv\ *vb* : behave improperly — **mis·be·hav·er** *n* — **mis·be·hav·ior** *n*

mis·cal·cu·late \mis'kalkyə‚lāt\ *vb* : calculate wrongly — **mis·cal·cu·la·tion**

mis·car·ry \ˌmis'karē, 'mis‚karē\ *vb* **1** : give birth prematurely before the fetus can survive **2** : go wrong or be unsuccessful — **mis·car·riage** \-rij\ *n*

mis·ce·ge·na·tion \mis‚ejə'nāshən, ‚misijə'nā-\ *n* : marriage between persons of different races

mis·cel·la·neous \ˌmisə'lānēəs\ *adj* : consisting of many things of different kinds — **mis·cel·la·neous·ly** *adv* — **mis·cel·la·neous·ness** *n*

mis·cel·la·ny \'misə‚lānē\ *n, pl* **-nies** : collection of various things

mis·chance \mis'chans\ *n* : bad luck

mis·chief \'mischəf\ *n* : conduct esp. of a child that annoys or causes minor damage

mis·chie·vous \'mischəvəs\ *adj* **1** : causing annoyance or minor injury **2** : irresponsibly playful — **mis·chie·vous·ly** *adv* — **mis·chie·vous·ness** *n*

mis·con·ceive \ˌmiskən'sēv\ *vb* : interpret incorrectly — **mis·con·cep·tion** *n*

mis·con·duct \mis'kändəkt\ *n* **1** : mismanagement **2** : bad behavior

mis·con·strue \ˌmiskən'strü\ *vb* : misinterpret — **mis·con·struc·tion** *n*

mis·cre·ant \'miskrēənt\ *n* : one who behaves criminally or viciously — **miscreant** *adj*

mis·deed \mis'dēd\ *n* : wrong deed

mis·de·mean·or \ˌmisdi'mēnər\ *n* : crime less serious than a felony

mi·ser \'mīzər\ *n* : person who hoards and is stingy with money — **mi·ser·li·ness** \-lēnəs\ *n* — **mi·ser·ly** *adj*

mis·er·a·ble \'mizərəbəl\ *adj* **1** : wretchedly deficient **2** : causing extreme discomfort **3** : shameful — **mis·er·a·ble·ness** *n* — **mis·er·a·bly** \-blē\ *adv*

mis·ery \'mizərē\ *n, pl* **-er·ies** : suf-

fering and want caused by distress or poverty

mis·fire \mis'fīr\ *vb* **1** : fail to fire **2** : miss an intended effect — **misfire** \'mis,fīr\ *n*

mis·fit \'mis,fit, mis'fit\ *n* : person poorly adjusted to his environment

mis·for·tune \mis'fòrchən\ *n* **1** : bad luck **2** : unfortunate condition or event

mis·giv·ing \mis'givin\ *n* : doubt or concern

mis·guid·ed \mis'gīdəd\ *adj* : mistaken, uninformed, or deceived

mis·hap \'mis,hap\ *n* : accident

mis·in·form \,mis°n'fòrm\ *vb* : give wrong information to — **mis·in·for·ma·tion** \,mis,infər'māshən\ *n*

mis·in·ter·pret \,mis°n'tərprət\ *vb* : understand or explain wrongly — **mis·in·ter·pre·ta·tion** \-,tərprə'tāshən\ *n*

mis·judge \mis'jəj\ *vb* : judge incorrectly or unjustly — **mis·judgment** *n*

mis·lay \mis°'lā\ *vb* **-laid; -lay·ing** : misplace

mis·lead \mis'lēd\ *vb* **-led; -lead·ing** : lead in a wrong direction or into error — **mis·lead·ing·ly** *adv*

mis·man·age \mis'manij\ *vb* : manage badly — **mis·man·age·ment** *n*

mis·no·mer \mis'nōmər\ *n* : wrong name

mi·sog·y·nist \mə'säjənist\ *n* : one who hates or distrusts women — **mi·sog·y·nis·tic** \mə,säjə'nistik\ *adj* — **mi·sog·y·ny** \-nē\ *n*

mis·place \mis'plās\ *vb* : put in a wrong or unremembered place

◆ **mis·print** \'mis,print, mis'-\ *n* : error in printed matter

mis·pro·nounce \,misprə'naúns\ *vb* : pronounce incorrectly — **mis·pro·nun·ci·a·tion** *n*

mis·quote \mis'kwōt\ *vb* : quote incorrectly — **mis·quo·ta·tion** \,miskwō'tāshən\ *n*

mis·read \mis'rēd\ *vb* **-read; -read·ing** : read or interpret incorrectly

mis·rep·re·sent \,mis,repri'zent\ *vb* : represent falsely or unfairly — **mis·rep·re·sen·ta·tion** *n*

mis·rule \mis'rül\ *vb* : govern badly ~ *n* **1** : bad or corrupt government **2** : disorder

¹**miss** \'mis\ *vb* **1** : fail to hit, reach, or contact **2** : notice the absence of **3** : fail to obtain **4** : avoid **5** : omit — **miss** *n*

²**miss** *n* : young unmarried woman or girl — often used as a title

mis·sal \'misəl\ *n* : book containing what is said at mass during the year

mis·shap·en \mis'shāpən\ *adj* : distorted

mis·sile \'misəl\ *n* : object (as a stone or rocket) thrown or shot

miss·ing \'misin\ *adj* : absent or lost

mis·sion \'mishən\ *n* **1** : ministry sent by a church to spread its teaching **2** : group of diplomats sent to a foreign country **3** : task

mis·sion·ary \'mishə,nerē\ *adj* : relating to religious missions ~ *n pl* **-ar·ies** : person sent to spread religious faith

mis·sive \'misiv\ *n* : letter

mis·spell \mis'spel\ *vb* : spell incorrectly — **mis·spell·ing** *n*

mis·state \mis'stāt\ *vb* : state incorrectly — **mis·state·ment** *n*

mis·step \'mis,step\ *n* **1** : wrong step **2** : mistake

mist \'mist\ *n* : particles of water falling as fine rain

mis·take \mə'stāk\ *n* **1** : misunderstanding or wrong belief **2** : wrong action or statement — **mistake** *vb*

mis·tak·en \-'stākən\ *adj* : having a wrong opinion or incorrect information — **mis·tak·en·ly** *adv*

mis·ter \'mistər\ *n* : sir — used

without a name in addressing a man

mis·tle·toe \'misəl,tō\ *n* : parasitic green shrub with waxy white berries

mis·treat \mis'trēt\ *vb* : treat badly — **mis·treat·ment** *n*

mis·tress \'mistrəs\ *n* 1 : woman in control 2 : a woman not his wife with whom a married man has recurrent sexual relations

mis·tri·al \mis'trīəl\ *n* : trial that has no legal effect

mis·trust \-'trəst\ *n* : lack of confidence ~ *vb* : have no confidence in — **mis·trust·ful** \-fəl\ *adj* — **mis·trust·ful·ly** *adv* — **mis·trust·ful·ness** *n*

misty \'mistē\ *adj* **mist·i·er; -est** 1 : obscured by mist 2 : tearful — **mist·i·ly** *adv* — **mist·i·ness** *n*

mis·un·der·stand \,mis,əndər-'stand\ *vb* 1 : fail to understand 2 : interpret incorrectly

mis·un·der·stand·ing \-'standiŋ\ *n* 1 : wrong interpretation 2 : disagreement

mis·use \mis'yüz\ *vb* 1 : use incorrectly 2 : mistreat — **misuse** \-'yüs\ *n*

mite \'mīt\ *n* 1 : tiny spiderlike animal 2 : small amount

mi·ter, mi·tre \'mītər\ *n* 1 : bishop's headdress 2 : angular joint in wood ~ *vb* **-tered** *or* **-tred; -tering** *or* **-tring** \'mītəriŋ\ : bevel the ends of for a miter joint

mit·i·gate \'mitə,gāt\ *vb* **-gat·ed; -gat·ing** : make less severe — **mit·i·ga·tion** \,mitə'gāshən\ *n* — **mit·i·ga·tive** \'mitə,gātiv\ *adj*

mi·to·sis \mī'tōsəs\ *n, pl* **-to·ses** \-,sēz\ : process of forming 2 cell nuclei from one — **mi·tot·ic** \-'tätik\ *adj*

mitt \'mit\ *n* : mittenlike baseball glove

mit·ten \'mit³n\ *n* : hand covering without finger sections

mix \'miks\ *vb* : combine or join into one mass or group ~ *n* : commercially prepared food mixture — **mix·able** *adj* — **mix·er** *n* — **mix up** *vb* : confuse

mix·ture \'mikschər\ *n* : act or product of mixing

mix–up *n* : instance of confusion

mne·mon·ic \ni'mänik\ *adj* : relating to or assisting memory

moan \'mōn\ *n* : low prolonged sound of pain or grief — **moan** *vb*

moat \'mōt\ *n* : deep wide trench around a castle

mob \'mäb\ *n* 1 : large disorderly crowd 2 : criminal gang ~ *vb* **-bb-** : crowd around and attack or annoy

mo·bile \'mōbəl, -,bēl, -,bīl\ *adj* : capable of moving or being moved ~ \'mō,bēl\ *n* : suspended art construction with freely moving parts — **mo·bil·i·ty** \mō'bilətē\ *n*

mo·bi·lize \'mōbə,līz\ *vb* **-lized; -lizing** : assemble and make ready for war duty — **mo·bi·li·za·tion** \,mōbələ'zāshən\ *n*

moc·ca·sin \'mäkəsən\ *n* 1 : heelless shoe 2 : venomous U.S. snake

mo·cha \'mōkə\ *n* 1 : mixture of coffee and chocolate 2 : dark brown color

mock \'mäk, 'mok\ *vb* 1 : ridicule 2 : mimic in derision ~ *adj* 1 : simulated 2 : phony — **mock·er** *n* — **mock·ery** \-ərē\ *n* — **mock·ing·ly** *adv*

mock·ing·bird \'mäkiŋ,bərd, 'mok-\ *n* : songbird that mimics other birds

mode \'mōd\ *n* 1 : particular form or variety 2 : style — **mod·al** \-³l\ *adj* — **mod·ish** \'mōdish\ *adj*

mod·el \'mäd³l\ *n* 1 : structural design 2 : miniature representation 3 : something worthy of copying 4 : one who poses for an artist or displays clothes 5 : type or design ~ *vb* **-eled** *or* **-elled; -el·ing** *or* **-el·ling** 1 : shape 2 : work as a model ~ *adj* 1 : serving as a pattern 2 : being a miniature representation of

mo·dem \'mōdəm, -,dem\ *n* : device by which a computer communicates with another computer over telephone lines

mod·er·ate \'mädərət\ *adj* : avoiding extremes ~ \'mädə,rāt\ *vb* **-at·ed; -at·ing** 1 : lessen the intensity of 2 : act as a moderator — **moderate** *n* — **mod·er·ate·ly** *adv* — **mod·er·ate·ness** *n* — **mod·er·a·tion** \,mädə'rāshən\ *n*

mod·er·a·tor \'mädə,rātər\ *n* : one who presides

mod·ern \'mädərn\ *adj* : relating to or characteristic of the present — **modern** *n* — **mo·der·ni·ty** \mə-

'dərnətē\ *n* — **mod·ern·iza·tion** \,mädərnə'zāshən\ *n* — **mod·ern·ize** \'mädər,nīz\ *vb* — **mod·ern·iz·er** \'mädər,nīzər\ *n* — **mod·ern·ly** *adv* — **mod·ern·ness** *n*

mod·est \'mädəst\ *adj* **1** : having a moderate estimate of oneself **2** : reserved or decent in thoughts or actions **3** : limited in size, amount, or aim — **mod·est·ly** *adv* — **mod·es·ty** \-əstē\ *n*

mod·i·cum \'mädikəm\ *n* : small amount

mod·i·fy \'mädə,fī\ *vb* **-fied; -fy·ing 1** : limit the meaning of **2** : change — **mod·i·fi·ca·tion** \,mädəfə'kāshən\ *n* — **mod·i·fi·er** \'mädə,fīər\ *n*

mod·u·lar \'mäjələr\ *adj* : built with standardized units — **mod·u·lar·ized** \-lə,rīzd\ *adj*

mod·u·late \'mäjə,lāt\ *vb* **-lat·ed; -lat·ing 1** : keep in proper measure or proportion **2** : vary a radio wave — **mod·u·la·tion** \,mäjə-'lāshən\ *n* — **mod·u·la·tor** \'mäjə-,lātər\ *n* — **mod·u·la·to·ry** \-lə-,tōrē\ *adj*

mod·ule \'mäjül\ *n* : standardized unit

mo·gul \'mōgəl\ *n* : important person

mo·hair \'mō,har\ *n* : fabric made from the hair of the Angora goat

moist \'mȯist\ *adj* : slightly or moderately wet — **moist·en** \'mȯis²n\ *vb* — **moist·en·er** \'mȯis²nər\ *n* — **moist·ly** *adv* — **moist·ness** *n*

mois·ture \'mȯischər\ *n* : small amount of liquid that causes dampness — **mois·tur·ize** \-chə,rīz\ *vb* — **mois·tur·iz·er** *n*

mo·lar \'mōlər\ *n* : grinding tooth — **molar** *adj*

mo·las·ses \mə'lasəz\ *n* : thick brown syrup from raw sugar

¹**mold** \'mōld\ *n* : crumbly organic soil

²**mold** *n* : frame or cavity for forming ~ *vb* : shape in or as if in a mold — **mold·er** *n*

³**mold** *n* : surface growth of fungus ~ *vb* : become moldy — **mold·i·ness** \'mōldēnəs\ *n* — **moldy** *adj*

mold·er \'mōldər\ *vb* : crumble

mold·ing \'mōldiŋ\ *n* : decorative surface, plane, or strip

¹**mole** \'mōl\ *n* : spot on the skin

²**mole** *n* : small burrowing mammal — **mole·hill** *n*

mol·e·cule \'mäli,kyül\ *n* : small particle of matter — **mo·lec·u·lar** \mə'lekyələr\ *adj*

mole·skin \-,skin\ *n* : heavy cotton fabric

mo·lest \mə'lest\ *vb* **1** : annoy or disturb **2** : force physical and usu. sexual contact on — **mo·les·ta·tion** \,mōl,es'tāshən, ,māl-\ *n* — **mo·lest·er** *n*

mol·li·fy \'mälə,fī\ *vb* **-fied; -fy·ing** : soothe in temper — **mol·li·fi·ca·tion** \,mäləfə'kāshən\ *n*

mol·lusk, mol·lusc \'mäləsk\ *n* : shelled aquatic invertebrate — **mol·lus·can** \mə'ləskən\ *adj*

mol·ly·cod·dle \'mälē,käd²l\ *vb* **-dled; -dling** : pamper

molt \'mōlt\ *vb* : shed hair, feathers, outer skin, or horns periodically — **molt** *n* — **molt·er** *n*

mol·ten \'mōlt²n\ *adj* : fused or liquefied by heat

mom \'mäm, 'məm\ *n* : mother

mo·ment \'mōmənt\ *n* **1** : tiny portion of time **2** : time of excellence **3** : importance

mo·men·tari·ly \,mōmən'terəlē\ *adv* **1** : for a moment **2** : at any moment

mo·men·tary \'mōmən,terē\ *adj* : continuing only a moment — **mo·men·tar·i·ness** *n*

mo·men·tous \mō'mentəs\ *adj* : very important — **mo·men·tous·ly** *adv* — **mo·men·tous·ness** *n*

mo·men·tum \-əm\ *n, pl* **-ta** \-ə\ *or* **-tums** : force of a moving body

mon·arch \'mänərk, -,ärk\ *n* : ruler of a kingdom or empire — **mo·nar·chi·cal** \mə'närkikəl\ *adj*

mon·ar·chist \'mänərkist\ *n* : believer in monarchical government — **mon·ar·chism** \-,kizəm\ *n*

mon·ar·chy \'mänərkē\ *n, pl* **-chies** : realm of a monarch

mon·as·tery \'mänə,sterē\ *n, pl* **-ter·ies** : house for monks

mo·nas·tic \mə'nastik\ *adj* : relating to monasteries, monks, or nuns — **monastic** *n* — **mo·nas·ti·cal·ly** \-tiklē\ *adv* — **mo·nas·ti·cism** \-tə,sizəm\ *n*

Mon·day \'məndā, -dē\ *n* : 2d day of the week

mon·e·tary \'mänə,terē, 'mən-\ *adj* : relating to money

mon·ey \'mənē\ *n, pl* **-eys** *or* **-ies** \'mənēz\ **1** : something (as coins or paper currency) used in buying **2** : wealth — **mon·eyed** \-ēd\ *adj* — **mon·ey·lend·er** *n*

mon·ger \'məŋgər, 'mäŋ-\ *n* : dealer

mon·gol·ism \'mäŋgə,lizəm\ *n* : congenital mental retardation — **Mon·gol·oid** \-gə,lȯid\ *adj or n*

mon·goose \'män,güs, 'mäŋ-\ *n, pl* **-goos·es** : small agile mammal esp. of India

mon·grel \'mäŋgrəl, 'məŋ-\ *n* : offspring of mixed breed

mon·i·tor \'mänətər\ *n* **1** : student assistant **2** : television screen ~ *vb* : watch or observe esp. for quality

monk \'məŋk\ *n* : member of a religious order living in a monastery — **monk·ish** *adj*

mon·key \'məŋkē\ *n, pl* **-keys** : small long-tailed arboreal primate ~ *vb* **1** : fool **2** : tamper

mon·key·shines \-,shīnz\ *n pl* : pranks

monks·hood \'məŋks,hu̇d\ *n* : poisonous herb with showy flowers

mon·o·cle \'mänikəl\ *n* : eyeglass for one eye

mo·nog·a·my \mə'nägəmē\ *n* **1** : marriage with one person at a time **2** : practice of having a single mate for a period of time — **mo·nog·a·mist** \mə'nägəmist\ *n* — **mo·nog·a·mous** \-məs\ *adj*

mono·gram \'mänə,gram\ *n* : sign of identity made of initials — **monogram** *vb*

mono·graph \-,graf\ *n* : learned treatise

mono·lin·gual \,mänə'liŋgwəl\ *adj* : using only one language

mono·lith \'män°l,ith\ *n* **1** : single great stone **2** : single uniform massive whole — **mono·lith·ic** \,män°l'ithik\ *adj*

mono·logue \'män°l,ȯg\ *n* : long speech — **mono·logu·ist** \-,ȯgist\ **mo·nol·o·gist** \mə'näləjist, 'män°l,ȯgist\ *n*

mono·nu·cle·o·sis \,mänō,nüklē-'ōsəs, -,nyü-\ *n* : acute infectious disease

mo·nop·o·ly \mə'näpəlē\ *n, pl* **-lies** **1** : exclusive ownership or control of a commodity **2** : one controlling a monopoly — **mo·nop·o·list**

\-list\ *n* — **mo·nop·o·lis·tic** \mə-,näpə'listik\ *adj* — **mo·nop·o·li·za·tion** \-lə'zāshən\ *n* — **mo·nop·o·lize** \mə'näpə,līz\ *vb*

mono·rail \'mänə,rāl\ *n* : single rail for a vehicle or a vehicle or system using it

mono·syl·lab·ic \,mänəsə'labik\ *adj* : consisting of or using words of only one syllable — **mono·syl·la·ble** \'mänə,siləbəl\ *n*

mono·the·ism \'mänōthē,izəm\ *n* : doctrine or belief that there is only one deity — **mono·the·ist** \-,thēist\ *n* — **mono·the·is·tic** \,mänōthē'istik\ *adj*

mono·tone \'mänə,tōn\ *n* : succession of words in one unvarying tone

mo·not·o·nous \mə'nät°nəs\ *adj* **1** : sounded in one unvarying tone **2** : tediously uniform — **mo·not·o·nous·ly** *adv* — **mo·not·o·nous·ness** *n* — **mo·not·o·ny** \-°nē\ *n*

mon·ox·ide \mə'näk,sīd\ *n* : oxide containing one atom of oxygen in a molecule

mon·sieur \məs'yər, məsh-\ *n, pl* **mes·sieurs** \-yərz, mā'syərz\ : man of high rank or station — used as a title for a man esp. of French nationality

mon·si·gnor \män'sēnyər\ *n, pl* **mon·si·gnors** *or* **mon·si·gno·ri** \,män,sēn'yōrē\ : Roman Catholic prelate — used as a title

mon·soon \män'sün\ *n* : periodic rainy season

mon·ster \'mänstər\ *n* **1** : abnormal or terrifying animal **2** : ugly, wicked, or cruel person — **mon·stros·i·ty** \män'sträsətē\ *n* — **mon·strous** \'mänstrəs\ *adj* — **mon·strous·ly** *adv*

mon·tage \män'täzh\ *n* : artistic composition of several different elements

month \'mənth\ *n* : 12th part of a year — **month·ly** *adv or adj or n*

mon·u·ment \'mänyəmənt\ *n* : structure erected in remembrance

mon·u·men·tal \,mänyə'ment°l\ *adj* **1** : serving as a monument **2** : outstanding **3** : very great — **mon·u·men·tal·ly** *adv*

moo \'mü\ *vb* : make the noise of a cow — **moo** *n*

◆ **mood** \'müd\ *n* : state of mind or emotion

moody \'müdē\ *adj* **mood·i·er; -est 1** : sad **2** : subject to changing moods and esp. to bad moods — **mood·i·ly** \'müdᵊlē\ *adv* — **mood·i·ness** \-ēnəs\ *n*

moon \'mün\ *n* : natural satellite (as of earth) — **moon·beam** *n* — **moon·light** *n* — **moon·lit** *adj*

moon·light \-ˌlīt\ *vb* **-ed; -ing** : hold a 2d job — **moon·light·er** *n*

moon·shine *n* **1** : moonlight **2** : meaningless talk **3** : illegally distilled liquor

¹**moor** \'mùr\ *n* : open usu. swampy wasteland — **moor·land** \-lənd, -ˌland\ *n*

²**moor** *vb* : fasten with line or anchor

moor·ing \-iŋ\ *n* : place where boat can be moored

moose \'müs\ *n, pl* **moose** : large heavy-antlered deer

moot \'müt\ *adj* : open to question

mop \'mäp\ *n* : floor-cleaning implement ~ *vb* **-pp-** : use a mop on

mope \'mōp\ *vb* **moped; mop·ing** : be sad or listless

mo·ped \'mō,ped\ *n* : low-powered motorbike

mo·raine \mə'rān\ *n* : glacial deposit of earth and stones

mor·al \'mòrəl\ *adj* **1** : relating to principles of right and wrong **2** : conforming to a standard of right behavior **3** : relating to or acting on the mind, character, or will ~ *n* **1** : point of a story **2** *pl* : moral practices or teachings — **mor·al·ist** \'mòrəlist\ *n* — **mor·al·is·tic** \ˌmòrə'listik\ *adj* — **mor·al·i·ty** \mə'ralətē\ *n* — **mor·al·ize** \'mòrəˌlīz\ *vb* — **mor·al·ly** *adv*

mo·rale \mə'ral\ *n* : emotional attitude

mo·rass \mə'ras\ *n* : swamp

mor·a·to·ri·um \ˌmòrə'tōrēəm\ *n,* *pl* **-ri·ums** *or* **-ria** \-ēə\ : suspension of activity

mo·ray \'mòrˌā, mə'rā\ *n* : savage eel

mor·bid \'mòrbəd\ *adj* **1** : relating to disease **2** : gruesome — **mor·bid·i·ty** \mòr'bidətē\ *n* — **mor·bid·ly** *adv* — **mor·bid·ness** *n*

mor·dant \'mòrdᵊnt\ *adj* : sarcastic — **mor·dant·ly** *adv*

more \'mōr\ *adj* **1** : greater **2** : additional ~ *adv* **1** : in addition **2** : to a greater degree ~ *n* **1** : greater quantity **2** : additional amount ~ *pron* : additional ones

mo·rel \mə'rel\ *n* : pitted edible mushroom

more·over \mōr'ōvər\ *adv* : in addition

mo·res \'mòr,āz, -ēz\ *n pl* : customs

morgue \'mòrg\ *n* : temporary holding place for dead bodies

mor·i·bund \'mòrəˌbənd\ *adj* : dying

morn \'mòrn\ *n* : morning

morn·ing \'mòrniŋ\ *n* : time from sunrise to noon

mo·ron \'mòrˌän\ *n* **1** : mentally retarded person **2** : very stupid person — **mo·ron·ic** \mə'ränik\ *adj* — **mo·ron·i·cal·ly** *adv*

mo·rose \mə'rōs\ *adj* : sullen — **mo·rose·ly** *adv* — **mo·rose·ness** *n*

mor·phine \'mòrˌfēn\ *n* : addictive painkilling drug

mor·row \'märō\ *n* : next day

Morse code \'mòrs-\ *n* : code of dots and dashes or long and short sounds used for transmitting messages

mor·sel \'mòrsəl\ *n* : small piece or quantity

mor·tal \'mòrtᵊl\ *adj* **1** : causing or subject to death **2** : extreme — **mortal** *n* — **mor·tal·i·ty** \mòr'talətē\ *n* — **mor·tal·ly** \'mòrtᵊlē\ *adv*

mor·tar \'mòrtər\ *n* **1** : strong bowl

2 : short-barreled cannon 3 : masonry material used to cement bricks or stones in place — **mortar** *vb*

mort·gage \'mȯrgij\ *n* : transfer of property rights as security for a loan — **mortgage** *vb* — **mort·gag·ee** \ˌmȯrgi'jē\ *n* — **mort·ga·gor** \ˌmȯrgi'jȯr\ *n*

mor·ti·fy \'mȯrtəˌfī\ *vb* **-fied; -fy·ing 1** : subdue by abstinence or self-inflicted pain **2** : humiliate — **mor·ti·fi·ca·tion** \ˌmȯrtəfə'kāshən\ *n*

mor·tu·ary \'mȯrchəˌwerē\ *n, pl* **-ar·ies** : place where dead bodies are kept until burial

mo·sa·ic \mō'zāik\ *n* : inlaid stone decoration — **mosaic** *adj*

Mos·lem \'mäzləm\ *var of* MUSLIM

mosque \'mäsk\ *n* : building where Muslims worship

mos·qui·to \mə'skētō\ *n, pl* **-toes** : biting bloodsucking insect

moss \'mȯs\ *n* : green seedless plant — **mossy** *adj*

most \'mōst\ *adj* **1** : majority of **2** : greatest ~ *adv* : to the greatest or a very great degree ~ *n* : greatest amount ~ *pron* : greatest number or part

-most \ˌmōst\ *adj suffix* : most : most toward

most·ly \'mōstlē\ *adv* : mainly

mote \'mōt\ *n* : small particle

mo·tel \mō'tel\ *n* : hotel with rooms accessible from the parking lot

moth \'mȯth\ *n* : small pale insect related to the butterflies

moth·er \'məthər\ *n* **1** : female parent **2** : source ~ *vb* : give birth to or care for — **moth·er·hood** \-ˌhůd\ *n* — **moth·er·land** \-ˌland\ *n* — **moth·er·less** *adj* — **moth·er·ly** *adj*

moth·er-in-law *n, pl* **mothers-in-law** : spouse's mother

mo·tif \mō'tēf\ *n* : dominant theme

mo·tion \'mōshən\ *n* **1** : act or instance of moving **2** : proposal for action ~ *vb* : direct by a movement — **mo·tion·less** *adj* — **mo·tion·less·ly** *adv* — **mo·tion·less·ness** *n*

motion picture *n* : movie

♦ **mo·ti·vate** \'mōtəˌvāt\ *vb* **-vat·ed; -vat·ing** : provide with a motive — **mo·ti·va·tion** \ˌmōtə'vāshən\ *n* — **mo·ti·va·tor** \'mōtəˌvātər\ *n*

mo·tive \'mōtiv\ *n* : cause of a person's action ~ *adj* **1** : moving to action **2** : relating to motion — **mo·tive·less** *adj*

mot·ley \'mätlē\ *adj* : of diverse colors or elements

mo·tor \'mōtər\ *n* : unit that supplies power or motion ~ *vb* : travel by automobile — **mo·tor·ist** \-ist\ *n* — **mo·tor·ize** \'mōtəˌrīz\ *vb*

mo·tor·bike *n* : lightweight motorcycle

mo·tor·boat *n* : engine-driven boat

mo·tor·car *n* : automobile

mo·tor·cy·cle *n* : 2-wheeled automotive vehicle — **mo·tor·cy·clist** *n*

mo·tor·truck *n* : automotive truck

mot·tle \'mätᵊl\ *vb* **-tled; -tling** : mark with spots of different color

mot·to \'mätō\ *n, pl* **-toes** : brief guiding rule

mould \'mōld\ *var of* MOLD

mound \'maůnd\ *n* : pile (as of earth)

¹**mount** \'maůnt\ *n* : mountain

²**mount** *vb* **1** : increase in amount **2** : get up on **3** : put in position ~ *n* **1** : frame or support **2** : horse to ride — **mount·able** *adj* — **mount·er** *n*

moun·tain \'maůntᵊn\ *n* : elevated

land higher than a hill — **moun-tain·ous** \'maùnt°nəs\ *adj* — **moun·tain·top** *n*

moun·tain·eer \ˌmaùnt°n'ir\ *n* : mountain resident or climber

moun·te·bank \'maùntiˌbaŋk\ *n* : impostor

mourn \'mōrn\ *vb* : feel or express grief — **mourn·er** *n* — **mourn·ful** \-fəl\ *adj* — **mourn·ful·ly** *adv* — **mourn·ful·ness** *n* — **mourn·ing** *n*

mouse \'maùs\ *n, pl* **mice** \'mīs\ **1** : small rodent **2** : device for controlling cursor movement on a computer display — **mouse·trap** *n or vb* — **mousy, mous·ey** \'maùsė, -zė\ *adj*

mousse \'müs\ *n* **1** : light chilled dessert **2** : foamy hair-styling preparation

mous·tache \'məsˌtash, məs'tash\ *var of* MUSTACHE

mouth \'maùth\ *n* : opening through which an animal takes in food ∼ \'maùth\ *vb* **1** : speak **2** : repeat without comprehension or sincerity **3** : form soundlessly with the lips — **mouthed** \'maùthd, 'maùtht\ *adj* — **mouth·ful** \-ˌfül\ *n*

mouth·piece *n* **1** : part (as of a musical instrument) held in or to the mouth **2** : spokesman

mou·ton \'müˌtän\ *n* : processed sheepskin

move \'müv\ *vb* **moved; mov·ing 1** : go or cause to go to another point **2** : change residence **3** : change or cause to change position **4** : take or cause to take action **5** : make a formal request **6** : stir the emotions ∼ *n* **1** : act or instance of moving **2** : step taken to achieve a goal — **mov·able, move·able** \-əbəl\ *adj* — **move·ment** *n* — **mov·er** *n*

mov·ie \'müvē\ *n* : projected picture in which persons and objects seem to move

¹mow \'maù\ *n* : part of a barn where hay or straw is stored

²mow \'mō\ *vb* **mowed; mowed** *or* **mown** \'mōn\; **mow·ing** : cut with a machine — **mow·er** *n*

moz·za·rel·la \ˌmät-sə-'rel-ə\ *n* : a mild white rubbery cheese

Mr. \'mistər\ *n, pl* **Messrs.** \'mesərz\ — conventional title for a man

Mrs. \'misəz, -səs, *esp South* 'mizəz, -əs\ *n, pl* **Mes·dames** \mā'däm, -'dam\ — conventional title for a married woman

Ms. \'miz\ *n* — conventional title for a woman

much \'məch\ *adj* **more** \'mōr\; **most** \'mōst\ : great in quantity, extent, or degree ∼ *adv* **more; most** : to a great degree or extent ∼ *n* : great quantity, extent, or degree

mu·ci·lage \'myüsəlij\ *n* : weak glue

muck \'mək\ *n* : manure, dirt, or mud — **mucky** *adj*

mu·cus \'myükəs\ *n* : slippery protective secretion of membranes (**mucous membranes**) lining body cavities — **mu·cous** \-kəs\ *adj*

◆ **mud** \'məd\ *n* : soft wet earth — **mud·di·ly** \'məd°lē\ *adv* — **mud·di·ness** \-ēnəs\ *n* — **mud·dy** *adj or vb*

mud·dle \'məd°l\ *vb* **-dled; -dling 1** : make, be, or act confused **2** : make a mess of — **muddle** *n* — **mud·dle·head·ed** \ˌməd°l'hedəd\ *adj*

mu·ez·zin \mü'ez°n, myü-\ *n* : Muslim who calls the hour of daily prayer

¹muff \'məf\ *n* : tubular hand covering

²muff *vb* : bungle — **muff** *n*

muf·fin \\'məfən\\ *n* : soft cake baked in a cup-shaped container

muf·fle \\'məfəl\\ *vb* **-fled; -fling 1** : wrap up **2** : dull the sound of — **muf·fler** \\'məflər\\ *n*

muf·ti \\'məftē\\ *n* : civilian clothes

¹mug \\'məg\\ *n* : drinking cup ~ *vb* **-gg-** : make faces

²mug *vb* **-gg-** : assault with intent to rob — **mug·ger** *n*

mug·gy \\'məgē\\ *adj* **-gi·er; -est** : hot and humid — **mug·gi·ness** *n*

Mu·ham·mad·an \\mō'haməden, -'häm-; mü-\\ *n* : Muslim — **Muham·mad·an·ism** \\-,izəm\\ *n*

mu·lat·to \\mü'lätō, -'lat-\\ *n, pl* **-toes** *or* **-tos** : person of mixed black and white ancestry

mul·ber·ry \\'məl,berē\\ *n* : tree with small edible fruit

mulch \\'məlch\\ *n* : protective ground covering — **mulch** *vb*

mulct \\'məlkt\\ *n or vb* : fine

¹mule \\'myül\\ *n* **1** : offspring of a male ass and a female horse **2** : stubborn person — **mul·ish** \\'myülish\\ *adj* — **mul·ish·ly** *adv* — **mu·lish·ness** *n*

²mule *n* : backless shoe

mull \\'məl\\ *vb* : ponder

mul·let \\'məlet\\ *n, pl* **-let** *or* **-lets** : marine food fish

multi- *comb form* **1** : many or multiple **2** : many times over

multiarmed	**multigrade**
multibarreled	**multiheaded**
multibillion	**multihospital**
multibranched	**multihued**
multibuilding	**multilane**
multicenter	**multilevel**
multicham-	**multimedia**
bered	**multimember**
multichannel	**multimillion**
multicolored	**multimillion-**
multicounty	**aire**
multicultural	**multipart**
multidimen-	**multipartite**
sional	**multiparty**
multidirection-	**multiplant**
al	**multipolar**
multidisciplin-	**multiproblem**
ary	**multiproduct**
multidiscipline	**multipurpose**
multidivisional	**multiracial**
multifaceted	**multiroom**
multifamily	**multisense**
multifilament	**multiservice**
multifunction	**multisided**
multifunctional	**multispeed**

multistage	**multiunion**
multistep	**multiunit**
multistory	**multiuse**
multisyllabic	**multivitamin**
multitalented	**multiwarhead**
multitrack	**multiyear**

mul·ti·far·i·ous \\,məltə'farēəs\\ *adj* : diverse

mul·ti·lat·er·al \\,məlti'latərəl, -,tī-\\ *adj* : having many sides or participants

mul·ti·lin·gual \\-'liŋgwəl\\ *adj* : knowing or using several languages — **mul·ti·lin·gual·ism** \\-gwə,lizəm\\ *n*

mul·ti·na·tion·al \\-'nashənəl\\ *adj* **1** : relating to several nations or nationalities **2** : having divisions in several countries — **multinational** *n*

mul·ti·ple \\'məltəpəl\\ *adj* **1** : several or many **2** : various ~ *n* : product of one number by another

multiple sclerosis \\-sklə'rōsəs\\ *n* : brain or spinal disease affecting muscle control

mul·ti·pli·ca·tion \\,məltəplə'kāshən\\ *n* **1** : increase **2** : short method of repeated addition

mul·ti·plic·i·ty \\,məltə'plisətē\\ *n, pl* **-ties** : great number or variety

mul·ti·ply \\'məltə,plī\\ *vb* **-plied; -ply·ing 1** : increase in number **2** : perform multiplication — **mul·ti·pli·er** \\-,plīər\\ *n*

mul·ti·tude \\'məltə,tüd, -,tyüd\\ *n* : great number — **mul·ti·tu·di·nous** \\,məltə'tüd'nəs, -'tyü-\\ *adj*

¹mum \\'məm\\ *adj* : silent

²mum *n* : chrysanthemum

mum·ble \\'məmbəl\\ *vb* **-bled; -bling** : speak indistinctly — **mumble** *n* — **mum·bler** *n*

mum·mer \\'məmər\\ *n* **1** : actor esp. in a pantomime **2** : disguised merrymaker — **mum·mery** *n*

mum·my \\'məmē\\ *n, pl* **-mies** : embalmed body — **mum·mi·fi·ca·tion** \\,məmifə'kāshən\\ *n* — **mum·mi·fy** \\'məmi,fī\\ *vb*

mumps \\'məmps\\ *n sing or pl* : virus disease with swelling esp. of the salivary glands

munch \\'mənch\\ *vb* : chew

mun·dane \\,mən'dān, 'mən,-\\ *adj* **1** : relating to the world **2** : lacking concern for the ideal or spiritual — **mun·dane·ly** *adv*

mu·nic·i·pal \\myù'nisəpəl\\ *adj* : of

or relating to a town or city —
mu·nic·i·pal·i·ty \myu̇ˌnisə-ˈpalətē\ n

mu·nif·i·cent \myu̇ˈnifəsənt\ adj : generous — **mu·nif·i·cence** \-səns\ n

mu·ni·tion \myu̇ˈnishən\ n : armaments

mu·ral \ˈmyu̇rəl\ adj : relating to a wall ~ n : wall painting — **mu·ra·list** n

mur·der \ˈmərdər\ n : unlawful killing of a person ~ vb : commit a murder — **mur·der·er** n — **mur·der·ess** \-əs\ n — **mur·der·ous** \-əs\ adj — **mur·der·ous·ly** adv

murk \ˈmərk\ n : darkness — **murk·i·ly** \ˈmərkəlē\ adv — **murk·i·ness** \-kēnəs\ n — **murky** adj

mur·mur \ˈmərmər\ n 1 : muttered complaint 2 : low indistinct sound — murmur vb — **mur·mur·er** n — **mur·mur·ous** adj

mus·ca·tel \ˌməskəˈtel\ n : sweet wine

mus·cle \ˈməsəl\ n 1 : body tissue capable of contracting to produce motion 2 : strength ~ vb -cled; -cling : force one's way — **mus·cled** adj — **mus·cu·lar** \ˈməskyələr\ adj — **mus·cu·lar·i·ty** \ˌməskyəˈlarətē\ n

muscular dystrophy n : disease marked by progressive wasting of muscles

mus·cu·la·ture \ˈməskyələˌchu̇r\ n : bodily muscles

¹**muse** \ˈmyüz\ vb mused; mus·ing : ponder — **mus·ing·ly** adv

²**muse** n : source of inspiration

mu·se·um \myu̇ˈzēəm\ n : institution displaying objects of interest

mush \ˈməsh\ n 1 : corn meal boiled in water or something of similar consistency 2 : sentimental nonsense — **mushy** adj

mush·room \ˈməshˌru̇m, -ˌru̇m\ n : caplike organ of a fungus ~ vb : grow rapidly

mu·sic \ˈmyüzik\ n : vocal or instrumental sounds — **mu·si·cal** \-zikəl\ adj or n — **mu·si·cal·ly** adv

mu·si·cian \myu̇ˈzishən\ n : composer or performer of music — **mu·si·cian·ly** adj — **mu·si·cian·ship** n

musk \ˈməsk\ n : strong-smelling substance from an Asiatic deer

used in perfume — **musk·i·ness** \ˈməskēnəs\ n — **musky** adj

mus·kel·lunge \ˈməskəˌlənj\ n, pl -lunge : large No. American pike

mus·ket \ˈməskət\ n : former shoulder firearm — **mus·ke·teer** \ˌməskəˈtir\ n

musk·mel·on \ˈməskˌmelən\ n : small edible melon

musk–ox \ˈməskˌäks\ n : shaggy-coated wild ox of the arctic

musk·rat \-ˌrat\ n, pl -rat or -rats : No. American aquatic rodent

Mus·lim \ˈməzləm, ˈmu̇s-, ˈmu̇z-\ n : adherent of Islam — **Muslim** adj

mus·lin \ˈməzlən\ n : cotton fabric

muss \ˈməs\ n : untidy state ~ vb : disarrange — **muss·i·ly** \ˈməsəlē\ adv — **muss·i·ness** \-ēnəs\ n — **mussy** adj

mus·sel \ˈməsəl\ n : edible mollusk

must \ˈməst\ vb — used as an auxiliary esp. to express a command, obligation, or necessity ~ \ˈməst\ n : something necessary

mus·tache \ˈməsˌtash, məsˈ-\ n : hair of the human upper lip

mus·tang \ˈməsˌtaŋ\ n : wild horse of Western America

mus·tard \ˈməstərd\ n : pungent yellow seasoning

mus·ter \ˈməstər\ vb 1 : assemble 2 : rouse ~ n : assembled group

musty \ˈməstē\ adj mus·ti·er; -est : stale — **must·i·ly** adv — **must·i·ness** n

mu·ta·ble \ˈmyütəbəl\ adj : changeable — **mu·ta·bil·i·ty** \ˌmyütə-ˈbilətē\ n

mu·tant \ˈmyütᵊnt\ adj : relating to or produced by mutation — **mutant** n

mu·tate \ˈmyüˌtāt\ vb -tat·ed; -tat·ing : undergo mutation — **mu·ta·tive** \ˈmyüˌtätiv, ˈmyütət-\ adj

mu·ta·tion \myu̇ˈtāshən\ n : change in a hereditary character — **mu·ta·tion·al** adj

mute \ˈmyüt\ adj mut·er; mut·est 1 : unable to speak 2 : silent ~ n 1 : one who is mute 2 : muffling device ~ vb mut·ed; mut·ing : muffle — **mute·ly** adv — **mute·ness** n

mu·ti·late \ˈmyütᵊlˌāt\ vb -lat·ed; -lat·ing : damage seriously (as by cutting off or altering an essential part) — **mu·ti·la·tion** \ˌmyütᵊl-

'āshən\ *n* — **mu·ti·la·tor** \'myüt⁹l-
ˌātər\ *n*

mu·ti·ny \'myütənē\ *n, pl* **-nies** : rebellion — **mu·ti·neer** \ˌmyüt⁹n'ir\
n — **mu·ti·nous** \'myüt⁹nəs\ *adj*
— **mu·ti·nous·ly** *adv* — **mutiny** *vb*

mutt \'mət\ *n* : mongrel

mut·ter \'mətər\ *vb* **1** : speak indistinctly or softly **2** : grumble —
mutter *n*

mut·ton \'mət⁹n\ *n* : flesh of a mature sheep — **mut·tony** *adj*

◆ **mu·tu·al** \'myüchəwəl\ *adj* **1**
: given or felt by one another in
equal amount **2** : common — **mu-
tu·al·ly** *adv*

muz·zle \'məzəl\ *n* **1** : nose and jaws
of an animal **2** : muzzle covering
to immobilize an animal's jaws **3**
: discharge end of a gun ~ *vb*
-zled; -zling : restrain with or as if
with a muzzle

my \'mī\ *adj* **1** : relating to me or
myself **2** — used interjectionally
esp. to express surprise

my·nah, my·na \'mīnə\ *n* : dark
crested Asian bird

my·o·pia \mī'ōpēə\ *n* : nearsighted-
ness — **my·o·pic** \-'ōpik, -'äpik\
adj — **my·o·pi·cal·ly** *adv*

myr·i·ad \'mirēəd\ *n* : indefinitely
large number — **myriad** *adj*

myrrh \'mər\ *n* : aromatic plant
gum

myr·tle \'mərt⁹l\ *n* : shiny evergreen

my·self \mī'self\ *pron* : I, me —
used reflexively or for emphasis

mys·tery \'mistərē\ *n, pl* **-ter·ies 1**
: religious truth **2** : something not
understood **3** : puzzling or secret
quality or state — **mys·te·ri·ous**
\mis'tirēəs\ *adj* — **mys·te·ri·ous-
ly** *adv* — **mys·te·ri·ous·ness** *n*

mys·tic \'mistik\ *adj* : mystical or
mysterious ~ *n* : one who has
mystical experiences — **mys·ti-
cism** \-tə₁sizəm\ *n*

mys·ti·cal \'mistikəl\ *adj* **1** : spiritual **2** : relating to direct commu-
nion with God — **mys·ti·cal·ly** *adj*

mys·ti·fy \'mistə₁fī\ *vb* **-fied; -fy-
ing** : perplex — **mys·ti·fi·ca·tion**
\ˌmistəfə'kāshən\ *n*

mys·tique \mis'tēk\ *n* : aura of mystery surrounding something

myth \'mith\ *n* **1** : legendary narrative explaining a belief or phenomenon **2** : imaginary person or
thing — **myth·i·cal** \-ikəl\ *adj*

my·thol·o·gy \mith'äləjē\ *n, pl* **-gies**
: body of myths — **myth·o·log-
i·cal** \ˌmithə'läjikəl\ *adj* — **my-
thol·o·gist** \mith'äləjist\ *n*

N

n \'en\ *n, pl* **n's** *or* **ns** \'enz\ : 14th
letter of the alphabet

nab \'nab\ *vb* **-bb-** : seize or arrest

na·dir \'nā₁dir, 'nādər\ *n* : lowest
point

¹nag \'nag\ *n* : old or decrepit horse

²nag *vb* **-gg- 1** : complain **2** : scold or
urge continually **3** : be persistent-
ly annoying ~ *n* : one who nags
habitually

na·iad \'nāəd, 'nī-, -ₐad\ *n, pl* **-iads** *or* **-ia·des** \-ə,dēz\ : mythological water nymph

nail \'nāl\ *n* **1** : horny sheath at the end of each finger and toe **2** : pointed metal fastener ~ *vb* : fasten with a nail — **nail·er** *n*

na·ive, na·ïve \nä'ēv\ *adj* **-iv·er; -est 1** : innocent and unsophisticated **2** : easily deceived — **na·ive·ly** *adv* — **na·ive·ness** *n*

na·ïve·té \ₐnä,ēvə'tā, nä'ēvə,-\ *n* : quality or state of being naive

na·ked \'nākəd, 'nekəd\ *adj* **1** : having no clothes on **2** : uncovered **3** : plain or obvious **4** : unaided — **na·ked·ly** *adv* — **na·ked·ness** *n*

nam·by–pam·by \ₐnambē'pambē\ *adj* : weak or indecisive

name \'nām\ *n* **1** : word by which a person or thing is known **2** : disparaging word for someone **3** : distinguished reputation ~ *vb* **named; nam·ing 1** : give a name to **2** : mention or identify by name **3** : nominate or appoint ~ *adj* **1** : relating to a name **2** : prominent — **name·able** *adj* — **name·less** *adj* — **name·less·ly** *adv*

name·ly \'nāmlē\ *adv* : that is to say

name·sake \-ₐsāk\ *n* : one named after another

♦ **¹nap** \'nap\ *vb* **-pp- 1** : sleep briefly **2** : be off guard ~ *n* : short sleep

²nap *n* : soft downy surface — **nap·less** *adj* — **napped** \'napt\ *adj*

na·palm \'nä,pälm, -,päm\ *n* : gasoline in the form of a jelly

nape \'nāp, 'nap\ *n* : back of the neck

naph·tha \'nafthə\ *n* : flammable solvent

nap·kin \'napkən\ *n* : small cloth for use at the table

nar·cis·sism \'närsə,sizəm\ *n* : self= love — **nar·cis·sist** \-sist\ *n or adj*

— **nar·cis·sis·tic** \ₐnärsə'sistik\ *adj*

nar·cis·sus \när'sisəs\ *n, pl* **-cis·sus** *or* **-cis·sus·es** *or* **-cis·si** \-'sis,ī, -,ē\ : plant with flowers usu. borne separately

nar·cot·ic \när'kätik\ *n* : painkilling addictive drug — **narcotic** *adj*

nar·rate \'nar,āt\ *vb* **nar·rat·ed; nar·rat·ing** : tell (a story) — **nar·ra·tion** \na'rāshən\ *n* — **nar·ra·tive** \'narətiv\ *n or adj* — **nar·ra·tor** \'nar,ātər\ *n*

nar·row \'narō\ *adj* **1** : of less than standard width **2** : limited **3** : not liberal **4** : barely successful ~ *vb* : make narrow — **nar·row·ly** *adv* — **nar·row·ness** *n*

nar·row–mind·ed \ₐnarō'mīndəd\ *adj* : shallow, provincial, or bigoted

nar·rows \'narōz\ *n pl* : narrow passage

nar·whal \'när,hwäl, 'närwəl\ *n* : sea mammal with a tusk

na·sal \'nāzəl\ *adj* : relating to or uttered through the nose — **na·sal·ly** *adv*

nas·tur·tium \nə'stərshəm, na-\ *n* : herb with showy flowers

nas·ty \'nastē\ *adj* **nas·ti·er; -est 1** : filthy **2** : indecent **3** : malicious or spiteful **4** : difficult or disagreeable **5** : unfair — **nas·ti·ly** \'nastəlē\ *adv* — **nas·ti·ness** \-tēnəs\ *n*

na·tal \'nāt°l\ *adj* : relating to birth

na·tion \'nāshən\ *n* **1** : people of similar characteristics **2** : community with its own territory and government — **na·tion·al** \'nashənəl\ *adj or n* — **na·tion·al·ly** *adv* — **na·tion·hood** *n* — **na·tion·wide** *adj*

na·tion·al·ism \'nashənəl,izəm\ *n* : devotion to national interests, unity, and independence — **na-**

tion·al·ist \-ist\ *n or adj* — **na·tion·al·is·tic** \,nashənəl'istik\ *adj*

na·tion·al·i·ty \,nashə'nalətē\ *n, pl* **-ties 1** : national character **2** : membership in a nation **3** : political independence **4** : ethnic group

na·tion·al·ize \'nashənəl,īz\ *vb* **-ized; -iz·ing 1** : make national **2** : place under government control — **na·tion·al·i·za·tion** \,nashənələ'zāshən\ *n*

na·tive \'nātiv\ *adj* **1** : belonging to a person at or by way of birth **2** : born or produced in a particular place ~ *n* : one who belongs to a country by birth

Na·tiv·i·ty \nə'tivətē, nā-\ *n, pl* **-ties 1** : birth of Christ **2** *not cap* : birth

nat·ty \'natē\ *adj* **-ti·er; -est** : smartly dressed — **nat·ti·ly** \'nat'lē\ *adv* — **nat·ti·ness** \-ēnəs\ *n*

nat·u·ral \'nachərəl\ *adj* **1** : relating to or determined by nature **2** : not artificial **3** : simple and sincere **4** : lifelike ~ *n* : one having an innate talent — **nat·u·ral·ness** *n*

nat·u·ral·ism \'nachərə,lizəm\ *n* : realism in art and literature — **nat·u·ral·is·tic** \,nachərə'listik\ *adj*

nat·u·ral·ist \-list\ *n* **1** : one who practices naturalism **2** : student of animals or plants

nat·u·ral·ize \-,līz\ *vb* **-ized; -iz·ing 1** : become or cause to become established **2** : confer citizenship on — **nat·u·ral·i·za·tion** \,nachərələ'zāshən\ *n*

nat·u·ral·ly \'nachərəlē\ *adv* **1** : in a natural way **2** : as might be expected

na·ture \'nāchər\ *n* **1** : basic quality of something **2** : kind **3** : disposition **4** : physical universe **5** : natural environment

naught \'nȯt, 'nät\ *n* **1** : nothing **2** : zero

naugh·ty \'nȯtē, 'nät-\ *adj* **-ti·er; -est 1** : disobedient or misbehaving **2** : improper — **naught·i·ly** \'nȯt'lē, 'nät-\ *adv* — **naught·i·ness** \-ēnəs\ *n*

nau·sea \'nȯzēə, -shə\ *n* **1** : sickness of the stomach with a desire to vomit **2** : extreme disgust — **nau·seous** \-shəs, -zēəs\ *adj*

nau·se·ate \'nȯzē,āt, -zhē-, -sē-, -shē-\ *vb* **-ated; -at·ing** : affect or become affected with nausea — **nau·se·at·ing·ly** \-,ātiŋlē\ *adv*

nau·ti·cal \'nȯtikəl\ *adj* : relating to ships and sailing — **nau·ti·cal·ly** *adv*

nau·ti·lus \'nȯt'ləs\ *n, pl* **-lus·es** or **-li** \-'l,ī, -,ē\ : sea mollusk with a spiral shell

na·val \'nāvəl\ *adj* : relating to a navy

nave \'nāv\ *n* : central part of a church

na·vel \'nāvəl\ *n* : depression in the abdomen

nav·i·ga·ble \'navigəbəl\ *adj* : capable of being navigated — **nav·i·ga·bil·i·ty** \,navigə'bilətē\ *n*

nav·i·gate \'navə,gāt\ *vb* **-gat·ed; -gat·ing 1** : sail on or through **2** : direct the course of — **nav·i·ga·tion** \,navə'gāshən\ *n* — **nav·i·ga·tor** \'navə,gātər\ *n*

na·vy \'nāvē\ *n, pl* **-vies 1** : fleet **2** : nation's organization for sea warfare

nay \'nā\ *adv* : no — used in oral voting ~ *n* : negative vote

Na·zi \'nätsē, 'nat-\ *n* : member of a German fascist party from 1933 to 1945 — **Nazi** *adj* — **Na·zism** \'nät,sizəm, 'nat-\, **Na·zi·ism** \-sē-,izəm\ *n*

near \'nir\ *adv* : at or close to ~ *prep* : close to ~ *adj* **1** : not far away **2** : very much like ~ *vb* : approach — **near·ly** *adv* — **near·ness** *n*

near·by \nir'bī, 'nir,bī\ *adv or adj* : near

near·sight·ed \'nir'sītəd\ *adj* : seeing well at short distances only — **near·sight·ed·ly** *adv* — **near·sight·ed·ness** *n*

neat \'nēt\ *adj* **1** : not diluted **2** : tastefully simple **3** : orderly and clean — **neat** *adv* — **neat·ly** *adv* — **neat·ness** *n*

neb·u·la \'nebyələ\ *n, pl* **-lae** \-,lē, -,lī\ : large cloud of interstellar gas — **neb·u·lar** \-lər\ *adj*

neb·u·lous \-ləs\ *adj* : indistinct

nec·es·sary \'nesə,serē\ *n, pl* **-saries** : indispensable item ~ *adj* **1** : inevitable **2** : compulsory **3** : positively needed — **nec·es·sar·i·ly** \,nesə'serəlē\ *adv*

ne·ces·si·tate \ni'sesə,tāt\ *vb* **-tated; -tat·ing** : make necessary

ne·ces·si·ty \ni'sesətē\ *n, pl* **-ties 1**

: very great need **2** : something that is necessary **3** : poverty **4** : circumstances that cannot be changed

neck \'nek\ *n* **1** : body part connecting the head and trunk **2** : part of a garment at the neck **3** : narrow part ~ *vb* : kiss and caress — **necked** \'nekt\ *adj*

neck·er·chief \'nekərchəf, -ˌchēf\ *n, pl* **-chiefs** \-chəfs, -ˌchēfs\ : cloth worn tied about the neck

neck·lace \'nekləs\ *n* : ornament worn around the neck

neck·tie *n* : ornamental cloth tied under a collar

nec·ro·man·cy \'nekrəˌmansē\ *n* : art of conjuring up the spirits of the dead — **nec·ro·man·cer** \-sər\ *n*

ne·cro·sis \nə'krōsəs, ne-\ *n, pl* **-cro·ses** \-ˌsēz\ : death of body tissue

nec·tar \'nektər\ *n* : sweet plant secretion

nec·tar·ine \ˌnektə'rēn\ *n* : smooth-skinned peach

née, nee \'nā\ *adj* — used to identify a married woman by maiden name

need \'nēd\ *n* **1** : obligation **2** : lack of something or what is lacking **3** : poverty ~ *vb* **1** : be in want **2** : have cause for **3** : be under obligation — **need·ful** \-fəl\ *adj* — **need·less** *adj* — **need·less·ly** *adv* — **needy** *adj*

nee·dle \'nēdᵊl\ *n* **1** : pointed sewing implement or something like it **2** : movable bar in a compass **3** : hollow instrument for injecting or withdrawing material ~ *vb* **-dled; -dling** : incite to action by repeated gibes — **nee·dle·work** \-ˌwərk\ *n*

nee·dle·point \'nēdᵊlˌpȯint\ *n* **1** : lace fabric **2** : embroidery on canvas — **needlepoint** *adj*

ne·far·i·ous \ni'farēəs\ *adj* : very wicked — **ne·far·i·ous·ly** *adv*

ne·gate \ni'gāt\ *vb* **-gat·ed; -gat·ing 1** : deny **2** : nullify — **ne·ga·tion** \-'gāshən\ *n*

neg·a·tive \'negətiv\ *adj* **1** : marked by denial or refusal **2** : showing a lack of something suspected or desirable **3** : less than zero **4** : having more electrons than protons **5** : having light and shadow images reversed ~ *n* **1** : negative word or vote **2** : a negative number **3** : negative photographic image — **neg·a·tive·ly** *adv* — **neg·a·tive·ness** *n* — **neg·a·tiv·i·ty** \ˌnegə'tivətē\ *n*

ne·glect \ni'glekt\ *vb* **1** : disregard **2** : leave unattended to ~ *n* **1** : act of neglecting **2** : condition of being neglected — **ne·glect·ful** *adj*

neg·li·gee \ˌneglə'zhā\ *n* : woman's loose robe

neg·li·gent \'neglijənt\ *adj* : marked by neglect — **neg·li·gence** \-jəns\ *n* — **neg·li·gent·ly** *adv*

neg·li·gi·ble \'neglijəbəl\ *adj* : insignificant

ne·go·ti·ate \ni'gōshēˌāt\ *vb* **-at·ed; -at·ing 1** : confer with another to settle a matter **2** : obtain cash for **3** : get through successfully — **ne·go·tia·ble** \-shəbəl, -shēə-\ *adj* — **ne·go·ti·a·tion** \-ˌgōshē'āshən, -shē'ā-\ *n* — **ne·go·ti·a·tor** \-'gōshēˌātər\ *n*

Ne·gro \'nēgrō\ *n, pl* **-groes** : member of the black race — **Negro** *adj* — **Ne·groid** \'nēˌgrȯid\ *n or adj, often not cap*

neigh \'nā\ *n* : cry of a horse — **neigh** *vb*

◆ **neigh·bor** \'nābər\ *n* **1** : one living nearby **2** : fellowman ~ *vb* : be near or next to — **neigh·bor·hood** \-ˌhùd\ *n* — **neigh·bor·li·ness** *n* — **neigh·bor·ly** *adv*

nei·ther \'nēthər, 'nī-\ *pron or adj*

: not the one or the other ~ *conj* **1** : not either **2** : nor

nem·e·sis \'neməsəs\ *n, pl* **-e·ses** \-ə-ˌsēz\ **1** : old and usu. frustrating rival **2** : retaliation

ne·ol·o·gism \nē'äləˌjizəm\ *n* : new word

ne·on \'nēˌän\ *n* : gaseous colorless chemical element that emits a reddish glow in electric lamps — **neon** *adj*

neo·phyte \'nēəˌfīt\ *n* : beginner

neph·ew \'nefyü, *chiefly Brit* 'nev-\ *n* : a son of one's brother, sister, brother-in-law, or sister-in-law

nep·o·tism \'nepəˌtizəm\ *n* : favoritism shown in hiring a relative

nerd \'nərd\ *n* : one who is not stylish or socially at ease — **nerdy** *adj*

nerve \'nərv\ *n* **1** : strand of body tissue that connects the brain with other parts of the body **2** : self-control **3** : daring **4** *pl* : nervousness — **nerved** \'nərvd\ *adj* — **nerve·less** *adj*

ner·vous \'nərvəs\ *adj* **1** : relating to or made up of nerves **2** : easily excited **3** : timid or fearful — **ner·vous·ly** *adv* — **ner·vous·ness** *n*

nervy \'nərvē\ *adj* **nerv·i·er; -est** : insolent or presumptuous

-ness \nəs\ *n suffix* : condition or quality

nest \'nest\ *n* **1** : shelter prepared by a bird for its eggs **2** : place where eggs (as of insects or fish) are laid and hatched **3** : snug retreat **4** : set of objects fitting one inside or under another ~ *vb* : build or occupy a nest

nes·tle \'nesəl\ *vb* **-tled; -tling** : settle snugly (as in a nest)

¹net \'net\ *n* : fabric with spaces between strands or something made of this ~ *vb* **-tt-** : cover with or catch in a net

²net *adj* : remaining after deductions ~ *vb* **-tt-** : have as profit

neth·er \'netḥər\ *adj* : situated below

net·tle \'net°l\ *n* : coarse herb with stinging hairs ~ *vb* **-tled; -tling** : provoke or vex — **net·tle·some** *adj*

net·work *n* : system of crossing or connected elements

neu·ral \'nùrəl, 'nyùr-\ *adj* : relating to a nerve

neu·ral·gia \nù'raljə, nyù-\ *n* : pain

along a nerve — **neu·ral·gic** \-jik\ *adj*

neu·ri·tis \nù'rītəs, nyù-\ *n, pl* **-rit·i·des** \-'ritəˌdēz\ *or* **-ri·tis·es** : inflammation of a nerve

neu·rol·o·gy \nù'räləjē, nyù-\ *n* : study of the nervous system — **neu·ro·log·i·cal** \ˌnùrə'läjikəl, ˌnyùr-\ **neu·ro·log·ic** \-ik\ *adj* — **neu·rol·o·gist** \nù'räləjist, nyù-\ *n*

neu·ro·sis \nù'rōsəs, nyù-\ *n, pl* **-ro·ses** \-ˌsēz\ : nervous disorder

neu·rot·ic \nù'rätik, nyù-\ *adj* : relating to neurosis ~ *n* : unstable person — **neu·rot·i·cal·ly** *adv*

neu·ter \'nütər, 'nyü-\ *adj* : neither masculine nor feminine ~ *vb* : castrate or spay

neu·tral \-trəl\ *adj* **1** : not favoring either side **2** : being neither one thing nor the other **3** : not decided in color **4** : not electrically charged ~ *n* **1** : one that is neutral **2** : position of gears that are not engaged — **neu·tral·i·za·tion** \ˌnütrələ'zāshən, ˌnyü-\ *n* — **neu·tral·ize** \'nütrəˌlīz, 'nyü-\ *vb*

neu·tral·i·ty \nù'tralətē, nyù-\ *n* : state of being neutral

neu·tron \'nüˌträn, 'nyü-\ *n* : uncharged atomic particle

nev·er \'nevər\ *adv* **1** : not ever **2** : not in any degree, way, or condition

nev·er·more *adv* : never again

nev·er·the·less *adv* : in spite of that

new \'nü, 'nyü\ *adj* **1** : not old or familiar **2** : different from the former **3** : recently discovered or learned **4** : not accustomed **5** : refreshed or regenerated **6** : being such for the first time ~ *adv* : newly — **new·ish** *adj* — **new·ness** *n*

new·born *adj* **1** : recently born **2** : born anew ~ *n, pl* **-born** *or* **-borns** : newborn individual

new·ly \-lē\ *adv* : recently

news \'nüz, 'nyüz\ *n* : report of recent events — **news·let·ter** *n* — **news·mag·a·zine** *n* — **news·man** \-mən, -ˌman\ *n* — **news·pa·per** *n* — **news·pa·per·man** \-ˌman\ *n* — **news·stand** *n* — **news·wom·an** \-ˌwùmən\ *n* — **news·wor·thy** *adj*

news·cast \-ˌkast\ *n* : broadcast of news — **news·cast·er** \-ˌkastər\ *n*

news·print *n* : paper made from wood pulp

newsy \'nüzē, 'nyü-\ *adj* **news·i·er; -est** : filled with news

newt \'nüt, 'nyüt\ *n* : small salamander

New Year *n* : New Year's Day

New Year's Day *n* : January 1 observed as a legal holiday

next \'nekst\ *adj* : immediately preceding or following ~ *adv* **1** : in the time or place nearest **2** : at the first time yet to come ~ *prep* : nearest to

nex·us \'neksəs\ *n, pl* **-us·es** \-səsəz\ *or* **-us** \-səs, -ˌsüs\ : connection

nib \'nib\ *n* : pen point

nib·ble \'nibəl\ *vb* **-bled; -bling** : bite gently or bit by bit ~ *n* : small bite

nice \'nīs\ *adj* **nic·er; nic·est 1** : fastidious **2** : very precise or delicate **3** : pleasing **4** : respectable — **nice·ly** *adv* — **nice·ness** *n*

nice·ty \'nīsətē\ *n, pl* **-ties 1** : dainty or elegant thing **2** : fine detail **3** : exactness

niche \'nich\ *n* **1** : recess in a wall **2** : fitting place, work, or use

nick \'nik\ *n* **1** : small broken area or chip **2** : critical moment ~ *vb* : make a nick in

nick·el \'nikəl\ *n* **1** : hard silver-white metallic chemical element used in alloys **2** : U.S. 5-cent piece

nick·name \'nik,nām\ *n* : informal substitute name — **nickname** *vb*

nic·o·tine \'nikəˌtēn\ *n* : poisonous and addictive substance in tobacco

niece \'nēs\ *n* : a daughter of one's brother, sister, brother-in-law, or sister-in-law

nig·gard·ly \'nigərdlē\ *adj* : stingy — **nig·gard** *n* — **nig·gard·li·ness** *n*

nig·gling \'nigəliŋ\ *adj* : petty and annoying

nigh \'nī\ *adv or adj or prep* : near

night \'nīt\ *n* **1** : period between dusk and dawn **2** : the coming of night — **night** *adj* — **night·ly** *adj or adv* — **night·time** *n*

night·clothes *n pl* : garments worn in bed

night·club \-ˌkləb\ *n* : place for drinking and entertainment open at night

night crawler *n* : earthworm

night·fall *n* : the coming of night

night·gown *n* : gown worn for sleeping

night·in·gale \'nīt²nˌgāl, -iŋ-\ *n* : Old World thrush that sings at night

◆ **night·mare** \'nīt,mar\ *n* : frightening dream — **nightmare** *adj* — **night·mar·ish** \-ˌmarish\ *adj*

night·shade \'nīt,shād\ *n* : group of plants that include poisonous forms and food plants (as the potato and eggplant)

nil \'nil\ *n* : nothing

nim·ble \'nimbəl\ *adj* **-bler; -blest 1** : agile **2** : clever — **nim·ble·ness** *n* — **nim·bly** \-blē\ *adv*

nine \'nīn\ *n* **1** : one more than 8 **2** : 9th in a set or series — **nine** *adj or pron* — **ninth** \'nīnth\ *adj or adv or n*

nine·pins *n* : bowling game using 9 pins

nine·teen \nīn'tēn\ *n* : one more than 18 — **nineteen** *adj or pron* — **nine·teenth** \-'tēnth\ *adj or n*

nine·ty \'nīntē\ *n, pl* **-ties** : 9 times 10 — **nine·ti·eth** \-ēəth\ *adj or n* — **ninety** *adj or pron*

nin·ny \'ninē\ *n, pl* **nin·nies** : fool

¹**nip** \'nip\ *vb* **-pp- 1** : catch hold of and squeeze tightly **2** : pinch or bite off **3** : destroy the growth or fulfillment of ~ *n* **1** : biting cold **2** : tang **3** : pinch or bite

²**nip** *n* : small quantity of liquor ~ *vb* **-pp-** : take liquor in nips

nip·per \'nipər\ *n* **1** : one that nips **2** *pl* : pincers **3** : small boy

nip·ple \'nipəl\ *n* : tip of the breast or something resembling it

nip·py \'nipē\ *adj* **-pi·er; -est 1** : pungent **2** : chilly

nir·va·na \nir'vänə\ *n* : state of blissful oblivion

nit \'nit\ *n* : egg of a parasitic insect

ni·ter \'nītər\ *n* : potassium nitrate used in gunpowder or fertilizer or in curing meat

ni·trate \'nī,trāt, -trət\ *n* : chemical salt used esp. in curing meat

ni·tric acid \'nītrik-\ *n* : liquid acid used in making dyes, explosives, and fertilizers

ni·trite \-,trīt\ *n* : chemical salt used in curing meat

ni·tro·gen \'nītrəjən\ *n* : tasteless odorless gaseous chemical element

ni·tro·glyc·er·in, ni·tro·glyc·er·ine \,nītrō'glisərən\ *n* : heavy oily liquid used as an explosive and as a blood-vessel relaxer

nit·wit \'nit,wit\ *n* : stupid person

no \'nō\ *adv* **1** — used to express the negative **2** : in no respect or degree **3** : not so **4** — used as an interjection of surprise or doubt ~ *adj* **1** : not any **2** : not a ~ *n, pl* **noes** or **nos** \'nōz\ **1** : refusal **2** : negative vote

no·bil·i·ty \nō'bilətē\ *n* **1** : quality or state of being noble **2** : class of people of noble rank

no·ble \'nōbəl\ *adj* **-bler; -blest 1** : illustrious **2** : aristocratic **3** : stately **4** : of outstanding character ~ *n* : nobleman — **no·ble·ness** *n* — **no·bly** *adv*

no·ble·man \-mən\ *n* : member of the nobility

no·ble·wom·an \-,wùmən\ *n* : a woman of noble rank

no·body \'nōbədē, -,bädē\ *pron* : no person ~ *n, pl* **-bod·ies** : person of no influence or importance

noc·tur·nal \näk'tərn°l\ *adj* : relating to, occurring at, or active at night

noc·turne \'näk,tərn\ *n* : dreamy musical composition

nod \'näd\ *vb* **-dd- 1** : bend the head downward or forward (as in bowing or going to sleep or as a sign of assent) **2** : move up and down **3** : show by a nod of the head — **nod** *n*

node \'nōd\ *n* : stem part from which a leaf arises — **nod·al** \-°l\ *adj*

nod·ule \'näjül\ *n* : small lump or swelling — **nod·u·lar** \'näjələr\ *adj*

no·el \nō'el\ *n* **1** : Christmas carol **2** *cap* : Christmas season

noes *pl of* NO

nog·gin \'nägən\ *n* **1** : small mug **2** : person's head

no·how \'nō,haù\ *adv* : in no manner

noise \'nòiz\ *n* : loud or unpleasant sound ~ *vb* **noised; nois·ing** : spread by rumor — **noise·less** *adj* — **noise·less·ly** *adv* — **noise·mak·er** *n* — **nois·i·ly** \'nòizəlē\ *adv* — **nois·i·ness** \-zēnəs\ *n* — **noisy** \'nòizē\ *adj*

noi·some \'nòisəm\ *adj* : harmful or offensive

no·mad \'nō,mad\ *n* : one who has no permanent home — **nomad** *adj* — **no·mad·ic** \nō'madik\ *adj*

no·men·cla·ture \'nōmən,klāchər\ *n* : system of names

nom·i·nal \'nämən°l\ *adj* **1** : being something in name only **2** : small or negligible — **nom·i·nal·ly** *adv*

nom·i·nate \'nämə,nāt\ *vb* **-nat·ed; -nat·ing** : propose or choose as a candidate — **nom·i·na·tion** \,nämə-'nāshən\ *n*

nom·i·na·tive \'nämənətiv\ *adj* : relating to or being a grammatical case marking typically the subject of a verb — **nominative** *n*

nom·i·nee \,nämə'nē\ *n* : person nominated

non- \'nän, ,nän\ *prefix* **1** : not, reverse of, or absence of **2** : not important

nonabrasive	nonautomatic
nonabsorbent	nonbeliever
nonacademic	nonbinding
nonaccredited	nonbreakable
nonacid	noncancerous
nonaddictive	noncandidate
nonadhesive	non-Catholic
nonadjacent	non-Christian
nonadjustable	nonchurchgoer
nonaffiliated	noncitizen
nonaggression	nonclassical
nonalcoholic	nonclassified
nonaligned	noncombat
nonappearance	noncombatant

noncombustible
noncommercial
noncommunist
noncompliance
nonconflicting
nonconforming
nonconsecutive
nonconstructive
noncontagious
noncontrollable
noncontroversial
noncorrosive
noncriminal
noncritical
noncumulative
noncurrent
nondeductible
nondeferrable
nondegradable
nondelivery
nondemocratic
nondenominational
nondestructive
nondiscrimination
nondiscriminatory
noneducational
nonelastic
nonelected
nonelective
nonelectric
nonelectronic
nonemotional
nonenforcement
nonessential
nonexclusive
nonexistence
nonexistent
nonexplosive
nonfat
nonfatal
nonfattening
nonfictional
nonflammable
nonflowering
nonfunctional
nongovernmental
nongraded
nonhazardous
nonhereditary
nonindustrial
nonindustrialized

noninfectious
noninflationary
nonintegrated
nonintellectual
noninterference
nonintoxicating
noninvasive
non-Jewish
nonlegal
nonlethal
nonliterary
nonliving
nonmagnetic
nonmalignant
nonmedical
nonmember
nonmetal
nonmetallic
nonmilitary
nonmusical
nonnative
nonnegotiable
nonobjective
nonobservance
nonorthodox
nonparallel
nonparticipant
nonparticipating
nonpaying
nonpayment
nonperformance
nonperishable
nonphysical
nonpoisonous
nonpolitical
nonpolluting
nonporous
nonpregnant
nonproductive
nonprofessional
nonprofit
nonracial
nonradioactive
nonrated
nonrealistic
nonrecurring
nonrefillable
nonrefundable
nonreligious
nonrenewable
nonrepresentative
nonresident
nonresponsive
nonrestricted
nonreversible

nonsalable
nonscientific
nonscientist
nonsegregated
non-self-governing
nonsexist
nonsexual
nonsignificant
nonskier
nonsmoker
nonsmoking
nonspeaking
nonspecialist
nonspecific
nonstandard
nonstick
nonstop
nonstrategic
nonstudent

nonsugar
nonsurgical
nonswimmer
nontaxable
nonteaching
nontechnical
nontoxic
nontraditional
nontransferable
nontropical
nontypical
nonunion
nonuser
nonvenomous
nonverbal
nonvoter
nonwhite
nonworker

non·age \'nänij, 'nōnij\ *n* : period of youth and esp. legal minority

nonce \'näns\ *n* : present occasion ~ *adj* : occurring, used, or made only once

non·cha·lant \ˌnänshə'länt\ *adj* : showing indifference — **non·cha·lance** \-'läns\ *n* — **non·cha·lant·ly** *adv*

non·com·mis·sioned officer \ˌnänkə'mishənd-\ *n* : subordinate officer in the armed forces appointed from enlisted personnel

non·com·mit·tal \ˌnänkə'mit°l\ *adj* : indicating neither consent nor dissent

non·con·duc·tor *n* : substance that is a very poor conductor

non·con·form·ist *n* : one who does not conform to an established belief or mode of behavior — **non·con·for·mi·ty** *n*

non·de·script \ˌnändi'skript\ *adj* : lacking distinctive qualities

none \'nən\ *pron* : not any ~ *adv* : not at all

non·en·ti·ty *n* : one of no consequence

none·the·less \ˌnənthə'les\ *adv* : nevertheless

non·pa·reil \ˌnänpə'rel\ *adj* : having no equal ~ *n* **1** : one who has no equal **2** : chocolate candy disk

non·par·ti·san *adj* : not influenced by political party bias

non·per·son *n* : person without social or legal status

non·plus \ˌnän'pləs\ *vb* -ss- : perplex

non·pre·scrip·tion *adj* : available without a doctor's prescription

non·pro·lif·er·a·tion *adj* : aimed at ending increased use of nuclear arms

non·sched·uled *adj* : licensed to carry by air without a regular schedule

non·sense \'nän,sens, -səns\ *n* : foolish or meaningless words or actions — **non·sen·si·cal** \nän-'sensikəl\ *adj* — **non·sen·si·cal·ly** *adv*

non·sup·port *n* : failure in a legal obligation to provide for someone's needs

non·vi·o·lence *n* : avoidance of violence esp. in political demonstrations — **non·vi·o·lent** *adj*

noo·dle \'nüdᵊl\ *n* : ribbon-shaped food paste

nook \'nùk\ *n* **1** : inside corner **2** : private place

noon \'nün\ *n* : middle of the day — **noon** *adj*

noon·day \-,dā\ *n* : noon

no one *pron* : no person

noon·time *n* : noon

noose \'nüs\ *n* : rope loop that slips down tight

nor \nòr\ *conj* : and not — used esp. after *neither* to introduce and negate the 2d member of a series

norm \'nòrm\ *n* **1** : standard usu. derived from an average **2** : typical widespread practice or custom

nor·mal \'nòrməl\ *adj* : average, regular, or standard — **nor·mal·cy** \-sē\ *n* — **nor·mal·i·ty** \nòr-'malətē\ *n* — **nor·mal·i·za·tion** \,nòrmələ'zāshən\ *n* — **nor·mal·ize** \'nòrmə,līz\ *vb* — **nor·mal·ly** *adv*

north \'nòrth\ *adv* : to or toward the north — *adj* : situated toward, at, or coming from the north ~ *n* **1** : direction to the left of one facing east **2** *cap* : regions to the north — **north·er·ly** \'nòrthərlē\ *adv or adj* — **north·ern** \-ərn\ *adj* — **North·ern·er** *n* — **north·ern·most** \-,mōst\ *adj* — **north·ward** \-wərd\ *adv or adj* — **north·wards** \-wərdz\ *adv*

north·east \nòrth'ēst\ *n* **1** : direction between north and east **2** *cap* : regions to the northeast — **north·east** *adj or adv* — **north·east·er·ly** \-ərlē\ *adv or adj* — **north·east·ern** \-ərn\ *adj*

northern lights *n pl* : aurora borealis

north pole *n* : northernmost point of the earth

north·west \-'west\ *n* **1** : direction between north and west **2** *cap* : regions to the northwest — **north·west** *adj or adv* — **north·west·er·ly** \-ərlē\ *adv or adj* — **north·west·ern** \-ərn\ *adj*

nose \'nōz\ *n* **1** : part of the face containing the nostrils **2** : sense of smell **3** : front part ~ *vb* nosed; **nos·ing** **1** : detect by smell **2** : push aside with the nose **3** : pry **4** : inch ahead — **nose·bleed** *n* — **nosed** \'nōzd\ *adj* — **nose out** *vb* : narrowly defeat

nose·gay \-,gā\ *n* : small bunch of flowers

nos·tal·gia \nä'staljə, nə-\ *n* : wistful yearning for something past — **nos·tal·gic** \-jik\ *adj*

nos·tril \'nästrəl\ *n* : opening of the nose

nos·trum \-trəm\ *n* : questionable remedy

nosy, nos·ey \'nōzē\ *adj* **nos·i·er; -est** : tending to pry

not \'nät\ *adv* — used to make a statement negative

no·ta·ble \'nōtəbəl\ *adj* **1** : noteworthy **2** : distinguished ~ *n* : notable person — **no·ta·bil·i·ty** \nōtə-'bilətē\ *n* — **no·ta·bly** \'nōtəblē\ *adv*

no·ta·rize \'nōtə,rīz\ *vb* **-rized; -riz·ing** : attest as a notary public

no·ta·ry public \'nōtərē-\ *n, pl* **-ries public** *or* **-ry publics** : public official who attests writings to make them legally authentic

no·ta·tion \nō'tāshən\ *n* **1** : note **2** : act, process, or method of marking things down

notch \'näch\ *n* : V-shaped hollow — **notch** *vb*

note \'nōt\ *vb* **not·ed; not·ing** **1** : notice **2** : write down ~ *n* **1** : musical tone **2** : written comment or record **3** : short informal letter **4** : notice or heed — **note·book** *n*

not·ed \'nōtəd\ *adj* : famous

note·wor·thy \-,wərthē\ *adj* : worthy of special mention

noth·ing \'nəthiŋ\ *pron* **1** : no thing **2** : no part **3** : one of no value or importance ~ *adv* : not at all ~ *n* **1**

: something that does not exist **2**
: zero **3** : one of little or no importance — **noth·ing·ness** n

no·tice \'nōtəs\ n **1** : warning or announcement **2** : attention ~ vb **-ticed; -tic·ing** : take notice of — **no·tice·able** adj — **no·tice·ably** adv

no·ti·fy \'nōtə,fī\ vb **-fied; -fy·ing** : give notice of or to — **no·ti·fi·ca·tion** \,nōtəfə'kāshən\ n

no·tion \'nōshən\ n **1** : idea or opinion **2** : whim

no·to·ri·ous \nō'tōrēəs\ adj : widely and unfavorably known — **no·to·ri·e·ty** \,nōtə'rīətē\ n — **no·to·ri·ous·ly** adv

not·with·stand·ing \,nätwith-'standiŋ, -with-\ prep : in spite of ~ adv : nevertheless ~ conj : although

nou·gat \'nügət\ n : nuts or fruit pieces in a sugar paste

nought \'nȯt, 'nät\ var of NAUGHT

noun \'naún\ n : word that is the name of a person, place, or thing

nour·ish \'nərish\ vb : promote the growth of — **nour·ish·ing** adj — **nour·ish·ment** n

no·va \'nōvə\ n, pl **-vas** or **-vae** \-,vē, -,vī\ : star that suddenly brightens and then fades gradually

♦ **nov·el** \'nävəl\ adj : new or strange ~ n : long invented prose story — **nov·el·ist** \-əlist\ n

nov·el·ty \'nävəltē\ n, pl **-ties 1** : something new or unusual **2** : newness **3** : small manufactured article — usu. pl.

No·vem·ber \nō'vembər\ n : 11th month of the year having 30 days

nov·ice \'nävəs\ n **1** : one preparing to take vows in a religious order **2** : one who is inexperienced or untrained

no·vi·ti·ate \nō'vishət, nə-\ n : period or state of being a novice

now \'naú\ adv **1** : at the present

time or moment **2** : forthwith **3** : under these circumstances ~ conj : in view of the fact ~ n : present time

now·a·days \'naúə,dāz\ adv : now

no·where \-,hwer\ adv : not anywhere — **nowhere** n

nox·ious \'näkshəs\ adj : harmful

noz·zle \'näzəl\ n : device to direct or control a flow of fluid

nu·ance \'nü,äns, 'nyü-\ n : subtle distinction or variation

nub \'nəb\ n **1** : knob or lump **2** : gist

nu·bile \'nü,bīl, 'nyü-, -bəl\ adj **1** : of marriageable condition or age **2** : sexually attractive

nu·cle·ar \'nüklēər, 'nyü-\ adj **1** : relating to the atomic nucleus or atomic energy **2** : relating to a weapon whose power is from a nuclear reaction

nu·cle·us \'nüklēəs, 'nyü-\ n, pl **-clei** \-klē,ī\ : central mass or part (as of a cell or an atom)

nude \'nüd, 'nyüd\ adj **nud·er; nud·est** : naked ~ n : nude human figure — **nu·di·ty** \'nüdətē, 'nyü-\ n

nudge \'nəj\ vb **nudged; nudg·ing** : touch or push gently — **nudge** n

nud·ism \'nüd,izəm, 'nyü-\ n : practice of going nude — **nud·ist** \'nüdist, 'nyü-\ n

nug·get \'nəgət\ n : lump of gold

nui·sance \'nüs⁰ns, 'nyü-\ n : something annoying

null \'nəl\ adj : having no legal or binding force — **nul·li·ty** \'nələtē\ n

nul·li·fy \'nələ,fī\ vb **-fied; -fy·ing** : make null or valueless — **nul·li·fi·ca·tion** \,nələfə'kāshən\ n

numb \'nəm\ adj : lacking feeling — **numb** vb — **numb·ly** adv — **numb·ness** n

num·ber \'nəmbər\ n **1** : total of individuals taken together **2** : indefinite total **3** : unit of a mathematical system **4** : numeral **5** : one in a sequence ~ vb 1 : count 2 : assign a number to 3 : comprise in number — **num·ber·less** adj

nu·mer·al \'nümərəl, 'nyü-\ n : conventional symbol representing a number

nu·mer·a·tor \'nümə,rātər, 'nyü-\ n : part of a fraction above the line

nu·mer·i·cal \nü'merikəl, nyü-\; **nu·mer·ic** \-'merik\ adj 1 : relating to numbers 2 : expressed in or involving numbers — **nu·mer·i·cal·ly** adv

nu·mer·ol·o·gy \,nümə'räləjē, ,nyü-\ n : occult study of numbers — **nu·mer·ol·o·gist** \-jist\ n

nu·mer·ous \'nümərəs, 'nyü-\ adj : consisting of a great number

nu·mis·mat·ics \,nüməz'matiks, ,nyü-\ n : study or collection of monetary objects — **nu·mis·mat·ic** \-ik\ adj — **nu·mis·ma·tist** \nü-'mizmətist, nyü-\ n

num·skull \'nəm,skəl\ n : stupid person

nun \'nən\ n : woman belonging to a religious order — **nun·nery** \-ərē\ n

nup·tial \'nəpshəl\ adj : relating to marriage or a wedding ~ n : marriage or wedding — usu. pl.

nurse \'nərs\ n 1 : one hired to care for children 2 : person trained to care for sick people ~ vb **nursed**; **nurs·ing** 1 : suckle 2 : care for

nurs·ery \'nərsərē\ n, pl **-er·ies** 1 : place where children are cared for 2 : place where young plants are grown

nursing home n : private establishment providing care for persons who are unable to care for themselves

nur·ture \'nərchər\ n 1 : training or upbringing 2 : food or nourishment ~ vb **-tured**; **-tur·ing** 1 : care for or feed 2 : educate

nut \'nət\ n 1 : dry hard-shelled fruit or seed with a firm inner kernel 2 : metal block with a screw hole through it 3 : foolish, eccentric, or crazy person 4 : enthusiast — **nut·crack·er** n — **nut·shell** n — **nut·ty** adj

nut·hatch \'nət,hach\ n : small bird

nut·meg \'nət,meg, -,māg\ n : nutlike aromatic seed of a tropical tree

nu·tri·ent \'nütrēənt, 'nyü-\ n : something giving nourishment — **nutrient** adj

nu·tri·ment \-trəmənt\ n : nutrient

nu·tri·tion \nü'trishən, nyü-\ n : act or process of nourishing esp. with food — **nu·tri·tion·al** \-'trishənəl\ adj — **nu·tri·tious** \-'trishəs\ adj — **nu·tri·tive** \'nütrətiv, 'nyü-\ adj

nuts \'nəts\ adj 1 : enthusiastic 2 : crazy

nuz·zle \'nəzəl\ vb **-zled**; **-zling** 1 : touch with or as if with the nose 2 : snuggle

ny·lon \'nī,län\ n 1 : tough synthetic material used esp. in textiles 2 pl : stockings made of nylon

nymph \'nimf\ n 1 : lesser goddess in ancient mythology 2 : girl 3 : immature insect

O

o \'ō\ n, pl **o's** or **os** \'ōz\ 1 : 15th letter of the alphabet 2 : zero

O var of OH

oaf \'ōf\ n : stupid or awkward person — **oaf·ish** \'ōfish\ adj

oak \'ōk\ n, pl **oaks** or **oak** : tree bearing a thin-shelled nut or its wood — **oak·en** \'ōkən\ adj

oar \'ōr\ n : pole with a blade at the end used to propel a boat

oar·lock \-,läk\ n : u-shaped device for holding an oar

oa·sis \ō'āsəs\ n, pl **oa·ses** \-,sēz\ : fertile area in a desert

oat \'ōt\ n : cereal grass or its edible seed — **oat·cake** n — **oat·en** \-ᵊn\ adj — **oat·meal** n

oath \'ōth\ n, pl **oaths** \'ōthz, 'ōths\ 1 : solemn appeal to God as a pledge of sincerity 2 : profane utterance

ob·du·rate \'äbdùret, -dyù-\ *adj* : stubbornly resistant — **ob·du·ra·cy** \-rəsē\ *n*

obe·di·ent \ō'bēdēənt\ *adj* : willing to obey — **obe·di·ence** \-əns\ *n* — **obe·di·ent·ly** *adv*

obei·sance \ō'bēsəns, -'bās-\ *n* : bow of respect or submission

obe·lisk \'äbə,lisk\ *n* : 4-sided tapering pillar

obese \ō'bēs\ *adj* : extremely fat — **obe·si·ty** \-'bēsətē\ *n*

obey \ō'bā\ *vb* **obeyed; obey·ing 1** : follow the commands or guidance of **2** : behave in accordance with

ob·fus·cate \'äbfə,skāt\ *vb* **-cat·ed; -cat·ing** : confuse — **ob·fus·ca·tion** \,äbfəs'kāshən\ *n*

obit·u·ary \ə'bichə,werē\ *n, pl* **-ar·ies** : death notice

¹ob·ject \'äbjikt\ *n* **1** : something that may be seen or felt **2** : purpose **3** : noun or equivalent toward which the action of a verb is directed or which follows a preposition

²object \əb'jekt\ *vb* : offer opposition or disapproval — **ob·jec·tion** \-'jekshən\ *n* — **ob·jec·tion·able** \-shənəbəl\ *adj* — **ob·jec·tion·ably** \-blē\ *adv* — **ob·jec·tor** \-'jektər\ *n*

ob·jec·tive \əb'jektiv\ *adj* **1** : relating to an object or end **2** : existing outside an individual's thoughts or feelings **3** : treating facts without distortion **4** : relating to or being a grammatical case marking objects ~ *n* : aim or end of action — **ob·jec·tive·ly** *adv* — **ob·jec·tive·ness** *n* — **ob·jec·tiv·i·ty** \,äbjek'tivətē\ *n*

ob·li·gate \'äblə,gāt\ *vb* **-gat·ed; -gat·ing** : bind legally or morally — **ob·li·ga·tion** \,äblə'gāshən\ *n* — **oblig·a·to·ry** \ə'bligə,tōrē, 'äbligə-\ *adj*

oblige \ə'blīj\ *vb* **obliged; oblig·ing 1** : compel **2** : do a favor for — **oblig·ing** *adj* — **oblig·ing·ly** *adv*

oblique \ō'blēk, -'blīk\ *adj* **1** : lying at a slanting angle **2** : indirect — **oblique·ly** *adv* — **oblique·ness** *n* — **obliq·ui·ty** \-'blikwətē\ *n*

oblit·er·ate \ə'blitə,rāt\ *vb* **-at·ed; -at·ing** : completely remove or destroy — **oblit·er·a·tion** \-,blitə'rāshən\ *n*

obliv·i·on \ə'blivēən\ *n* **1** : state of having lost conscious awareness **2** : state of being forgotten

obliv·i·ous \-ēəs\ *adj* : not aware or mindful — with *to* or *of* — **obliv·i·ous·ly** *adv* — **obliv·i·ous·ness** *n*

ob·long \'äb,lȯŋ\ *adj* : longer in one direction than in the other with opposite sides parallel — **oblong** *n*

ob·lo·quy \'äbləkwē\ *n, pl* **-quies 1** : strongly condemning utterance **2** : bad repute

ob·nox·ious \äb'näkshəs, əb-\ *adj* : repugnant — **ob·nox·ious·ly** *adv* — **ob·nox·ious·ness** *n*

oboe \'ōbō\ *n* : slender woodwind instrument with a reed mouthpiece — **obo·ist** \'ō,bōist\ *n*

ob·scene \äb'sēn, əb-\ *adj* : repugnantly indecent — **ob·scene·ly** *adv* — **ob·scen·i·ty** \-'senətē\ *n*

ob·scure \äb'skyùr, əb-\ *adj* **1** : dim or hazy **2** : not well known **3** : vague ~ *vb* : make indistinct or unclear — **ob·scure·ly** *adv* — **ob·scu·ri·ty** \-'skyùrətē\ *n*

ob·se·quies \'äbsəkwēz\ *n pl* : funeral or burial rites

ob·se·qui·ous \əb'sēkwēəs\ *adj* : excessively attentive or flattering — **ob·se·qui·ous·ly** *adv* — **ob·se·qui·ous·ness** *n*

ob·ser·va·to·ry \əb'zərvə,tōrē\ *n, pl* **-ries** : place for observing astronomical phenomena

ob·serve \əb'zərv\ *vb* **-served; -serving 1** : conform to **2** : celebrate **3** : see, watch, or notice **4** : remark — **ob·serv·able** *adj* — **ob·ser·vance** \-'zərvəns\ *n* — **ob·ser·vant** \-vənt\ *adj* — **ob·ser·va·tion** \,äbsər'vāshən, -zər-\ *n*

ob·sess \əb'ses\ *vb* : preoccupy intensely or abnormally — **ob·ses·sion** \äb'seshən, əb-\ *n* — **ob·ses·sive** \-'sesiv\ *adj* — **ob·ses·sive·ly** *adv*

ob·so·les·cent \,äbsə'les³nt\ *adj* : going out of use — **ob·so·les·cence** \-³ns\ *n*

ob·so·lete \,äbsə'lēt, 'äbsə,-\ *adj* : no longer in use

ob·sta·cle \'äbstikəl\ *n* : something that stands in the way or opposes

ob·stet·rics \əb'stetriks\ *n sing or pl* : branch of medicine that deals with childbirth — **ob·stet·ric** \-rik\, **ob·stet·ri·cal** \-rikəl\ *adj* — **ob·ste·tri·cian** \,äbstə'trishən\ *n*

ob·sti·nate \'äbstənət\ *adj* : stubborn — **ob·sti·na·cy** \-nəsē\ *n* — **ob·sti·nate·ly** *adv*

ob·strep·er·ous \əb'strepərəs\ *adj* : uncontrollably noisy or defiant — **ob·strep·er·ous·ness** *n*

ob·struct \əb'strəkt\ *vb* : block or impede — **ob·struc·tion** \-'strəkshən\ *n* — **ob·struc·tive** \-'strəktiv\ *adj* — **ob·struc·tor** \-tər\ *n*

ob·tain \əb'tān\ *vb* 1 : gain by effort 2 : be generally recognized — **ob·tain·able** *adj*

ob·trude \əb'trüd\ *vb* **-trud·ed; -trud·ing** 1 : thrust out 2 : intrude — **ob·tru·sion** \-'trüzhən\ *n* — **ob·tru·sive** \-'trüsiv\ *adj* — **ob·tru·sive·ly** *adv* — **ob·tru·sive·ness** *n*

ob·tuse \äb'tüs, əb-, -'tyüs\ *adj* 1 : slow-witted 2 : exceeding 90 but less than 180 degrees — **ob·tuse·ly** *adv* — **ob·tuse·ness** *n*

ob·verse \'äb,vərs, äb'-\ *n* : principal side (as of a coin)

ob·vi·ate \'äbvē,āt\ *vb* **-at·ed; -at·ing** : make unnecessary — **ob·vi·a·tion** \,äbvē'āshən\ *n*

ob·vi·ous \'äbvēəs\ *adj* : plain or unmistakable — **ob·vi·ous·ly** *adv* — **ob·vi·ous·ness** *n*

oc·ca·sion \ə'kāzhən\ *n* 1 : favorable opportunity 2 : cause 3 : time of an event 4 : special event ∼ *vb* : cause — **oc·ca·sion·al** \-'kāzhənəl\ *adj* — **oc·ca·sion·al·ly** *adv*

oc·ci·den·tal \,äksə'dent³l\ *adj* : western — **Occidental** *n*

oc·cult \ə'kəlt, 'äk,əlt\ *adj* 1 : secret or mysterious 2 : relating to supernatural agencies — **oc·cult·ism** \-'kəl,tizəm\ *n* — **oc·cult·ist** \-tist\ *n*

oc·cu·pan·cy \'äkyəpənsē\ *n, pl* **-cies** : an occupying

oc·cu·pant \-pənt\ *n* : one who occupies

oc·cu·pa·tion \,äkyə'pāshən\ *n* 1 : vocation 2 : action or state of occupying — **oc·cu·pa·tion·al** \-shənəl\ *adj* — **oc·cu·pa·tion·al·ly** *adv*

oc·cu·py \'äkyə,pī\ *vb* **-pied; -py·ing** 1 : engage the attention of 2 : fill up 3 : take or hold possession of 4 : reside in — **oc·cu·pi·er** \-,pīər\ *n*

oc·cur \ə'kər\ *vb* **-rr-** 1 : be found or met with 2 : take place 3 : come to mind

oc·cur·rence \ə'kərəns\ *n* : something that takes place

ocean \'ōshən\ *n* 1 : whole body of salt water 2 : very large body of water — **ocean·front** *n* — **ocean·go·ing** *adj* — **oce·an·ic** \,ōshē-'anik\ *adj*

ocean·og·ra·phy \,ōshə'nägrəfē\ *n* : science dealing with the ocean — **ocean·og·ra·pher** \-fər\ *n* — **ocean·o·graph·ic** \-nə'grafik\ *adj*

oce·lot \'äsə,lät, 'ōsə-\ *n* : medium-sized American wildcat

ocher, ochre \'ōkər\ *n* : red or yellow pigment

o'·clock \ə'kläk\ *adv* : according to the clock

oc·ta·gon \'äktə,gän\ *n* : 8-sided polygon — **oc·tag·o·nal** \äk-'tagən³l\ *adj*

oc·tave \'äktiv\ *n* : musical interval of 8 steps or the notes within this interval

Oc·to·ber \äk'tōbər\ *n* : 10th month of the year having 31 days

♦ **oc·to·pus** \'äktəpəs\ *n, pl* **-pus·es** *or* **-pi** \-,pī\ : sea mollusk with 8 arms

oc·u·lar \'äkyələr\ *adj* : relating to the eye

oc·u·list \'äkyəlist\ *n* 1 : ophthalmologist 2 : optometrist

odd \'äd\ *adj* **1** : being only one of a pair or set **2** : not divisible by two without a remainder **3** : additional to what is usual or to the number mentioned **4** : queer — **odd·ly** *adv* — **odd·ness** *n*

odd·i·ty \'ädətē\ *n, pl* **-ties** : something odd

odds \'ädz\ *n pl* **1** : difference by which one thing is favored **2** : disagreement **3** : ratio between winnings and the amount of the bet

ode \'ōd\ *n* : solemn lyric poem

odi·ous \'ōdēəs\ *adj* : hated — **odi·ous·ly** *adv* — **odi·ous·ness** *n*

odi·um \'ōdēəm\ *n* **1** : merited loathing **2** : disgrace

odor \'ōdər\ *n* : quality that affects the sense of smell — **odor·less** *adj* — **odor·ous** *adj*

od·ys·sey \'ädəsē\ *n, pl* **-seys** : long wandering

o'er \'ōr\ *adv or prep* : OVER

of \'əv, 'äv\ *prep* **1** : from **2** : distinguished by **3** : because of **4** : made or written by **5** : made with, being, or containing **6** : belonging to or connected with **7** : about **8** : that is **9** : concerning **10** : before

off \'óf\ *adv* **1** : from a place **2** : unattached or removed **3** : to a state of being no longer in use **4** : away from work **5** : at a distance in time or space ～ *prep* **1** : away from **2** : at the expense of **3** : not engaged in or abstaining from **4** : below the usual level of ～ *adj* **1** : not operating, up to standard, or correct **2** : remote **3** : provided for

of·fal \'ófəl\ *n* **1** : waste **2** : viscera and trimmings of a butchered animal

of·fend \ə'fend\ *vb* **1** : sin or act in violation **2** : hurt, annoy, or insult — **of·fend·er** *n*

of·fense, of·fence \ə'fens, 'äf,ens\ *n* : attack, misdeed, or insult

of·fen·sive \ə'fensiv, 'äf,en-\ *adj* : causing offense ～ *n* : attack — **of·fen·sive·ly** *adv* — **of·fen·sive·ness** *n*

of·fer \'ófər\ *vb* **1** : present for acceptance **2** : propose **3** : put up (an effort) ～ *n* **1** : proposal **2** : bid — **of·fer·ing** *n*

of·fer·to·ry \'ófər,tōrē\ *n, pl* **-ries** : presentation of offerings or its musical accompaniment

off·hand *adv or adj* : without previous thought or preparation

of·fice \'ófəs\ *n* **1** : position of authority (as in government) **2** : rite **3** : place where a business is transacted — **of·fice·hold·er** *n*

of·fi·cer \'ófəsər\ *n* **1** : one charged with law enforcement **2** : one who holds an office of trust or authority **3** : one who holds a commission in the armed forces

of·fi·cial \ə'fishəl\ *n* : one in office ～ *adj* : authorized or authoritative — **of·fi·cial·dom** \-dəm\ *n* — **of·fi·cial·ly** *adv*

of·fi·ci·ant \ə'fishēənt\ *n* : clergy member who officiates at a religious rite

of·fi·ci·ate \ə'fishē,āt\ *vb* **-at·ed; -at·ing** : perform a ceremony or function

of·fi·cious \ə'fishəs\ *adj* : volunteering one's services unnecessarily — **of·fi·cious·ly** *adv* — **of·fi·cious·ness** *n*

off·ing \'ófiŋ\ *n* : future

off·set \'óf,set\ *vb* **-set; -set·ting** : provide an opposite or equaling effect to

off·shoot \'óf,shüt\ *n* : outgrowth

off·shore *adv* : at a distance from the shore ～ *adj* : moving away from or situated off the shore

off·spring \'óf,spriŋ\ *n, pl* **offspring** : one coming into being through animal or plant reproduction

of·ten \'ófən, 'óft-\ *adv* : many times — **of·ten·times, oft·times** *adv*

ogle \'ōgəl\ *vb* **ogled; ogling** : stare at lustily — **ogle** *n* — **ogler** \-ələr\ *n*

ogre \'ōgər\ *n* **1** : monster **2** : dreaded person

oh \'ō\ *interj* **1** — used to express an emotion **2** — used in direct address

ohm \'ōm\ *n* : unit of electrical resistance — **ohm·ic** \'ōmik\ *adj* — **ohm·me·ter** \'ōm,mētər\ *n*

oil \'óil\ *n* **1** : greasy liquid substance **2** : petroleum ～ *vb* : put oil in or on — **oil·er** *n* — **oil·i·ness** \'óilēnəs\ *n* — **oily** \'óilē\ *adj*

oil·cloth *n* : cloth treated with oil or paint and used for coverings

oil·skin *n* : oiled waterproof cloth

oink \'óiŋk\ *n* : natural noise of a hog — **oink** *vb*

oint·ment \\'óintmənt\ *n* : oily medicinal preparation

OK *or* **okay** \ō'kā\ *adv or adj* : all right ~ *vb* **OK'd** *or* **okayed; OK'-ing** *or* **okay·ing** : approve ~ *n* : approval

okra \'ōkrə, *South also* -krē\ *n* : leafy vegetable with edible green pods

old \'ōld\ *adj* 1 : of long standing 2 : of a specified age 3 : relating to a past era 4 : having existed a long time — **old·ish** \'ōldish\ *adj*

old·en \'ōldən\ *adj* : of or relating to a bygone era

old-fash·ioned \-'fashənd\ *adj* 1 : out-of-date 2 : conservative

old maid *n* : spinster

old-tim·er \ōld'tīmər\ *n* 1 : veteran 2 : one who is old

ole·an·der \'ōlē,andər\ *n* : poisonous evergreen shrub

oleo·mar·ga·rine \,ōlēō'märjərən\ *n* : margarine

ol·fac·to·ry \äl'faktərē, ōl-\ *adj* : relating to the sense of smell

oli·gar·chy \'älə,gärkē, 'ōlə-\ *n, pl* **-chies** 1 : government by a few people 2 : those holding power in an oligarchy — **oli·garch** \-,gärk\ *n* — **oli·gar·chic** \älə'gärkik, ,ōlə-\, **oli·gar·chi·cal** \-kikəl\ *adj*

ol·ive \'äliv, -əv\ *n* 1 : evergreen tree bearing small edible fruit or the fruit 2 : dull yellowish green color

om·buds·man \'äm,bùdzmən, äm'bùdz-\ *n, pl* **-men** \-mən\ : complaint investigator

om·e·let, om·e·lette \'ämələt\ *n* : beaten eggs lightly fried and folded

omen \'ōmən\ *n* : sign or warning of the future

om·i·nous \'ämənəs\ *adj* : presaging evil — **om·i·nous·ly** *adv* — **om·i·nous·ness** *n*

omit \ō'mit\ *vb* **-tt-** 1 : leave out 2 : fail to perform — **omis·si·ble** \ō'misəbəl\ *adj* — **omis·sion** \-'mishən\ *n*

om·nip·o·tent \äm'nipətənt\ *adj* : almighty — **om·nip·o·tence** \-əns\ *n* — **om·nip·o·tent·ly** *adv*

om·ni·pres·ent \,ämni'prez°nt\ *adj* : ever-present — **om·ni·pres·ence** \-°ns\ *n*

om·ni·scient \äm'nishənt\ *adj* : all-knowing — **om·ni·science** \-əns\ *n* — **om·ni·scient·ly** *adv*

om·niv·o·rous \äm'nivərəs\ *adj* 1 : eating both meat and vegetables 2 : avid — **om·niv·o·rous·ly** *adv*

on \'ón, 'än\ *prep* 1 : in or to a position over and in contact with 2 : at or to 3 : about 4 : from 5 : with regard to 6 : in a state or process 7 : during the time of ~ *adv* 1 : in or into contact with 2 : forward 3 : into operation

once \'wəns\ *adv* 1 : one time only 2 : at any one time 3 : formerly ~ *n* : one time ~ *conj* : as soon as ~ *adj* : former — **at once** 1 : simultaneously 2 : immediately

once-over *n* : swift examination

on·com·ing *adj* : approaching

one \'wən\ *adj* 1 : being a single thing 2 : being one in particular 3 : being the same in kind ~ *pron* 1 : certain indefinitely indicated person or thing 2 : a person in general ~ *n* 1 : 1st in a series 2 : single person or thing — **one·ness** *n*

oner·ous \'änərəs, 'ōnə-\ *adj* : imposing a burden

one·self \,wən'self\ *pron* : one's own self — usu. used reflexively or for emphasis

one-sid·ed \-'sīdəd\ *adj* 1 : occurring on one side only 2 : partial

one-time *adj* : former

one-way *adj* : made or for use in only one direction

on·go·ing *adj* : continuing

on·ion \'ənyən\ *n* : plant grown for its pungent edible bulb or this bulb

on·ly \'ōnlē\ *adj* : alone in its class ~ *adv* 1 : merely or exactly 2 : solely 3 : at the very least 4 : as a result ~ *conj* : but

on·set *n* : start

on·shore *adj* 1 : moving toward shore 2 : lying on or near the shore — **onshore** *adv*

on·slaught \'än,slòt, 'ón-\ *n* : attack

on·to \'óntü, 'än-\ *prep* : to a position or point on

onus \'ōnəs\ *n* : burden (as of obligation or blame)

on·ward \'ónwərd, 'än-\ *adv or adj* : forward

on·yx \'äniks\ *n* : quartz used as a gem

ooze \'üz\ *n* : soft mud ~ *vb* **oozed; ooz·ing** : flow or leak out slowly — **oozy** \'üzē\ *adj*

opac·i·ty \ō'pasətē\ *n* : quality or

state of being opaque or an opaque spot

opal \'ōpəl\ *n* : gem with delicate colors

opaque \ō'pāk\ *adj* **1** : blocking light **2** : not easily understood **3** : dull-witted — **opaque·ly** *adv*

open \'ōpən\ *adj* **1** : not shut or shut up **2** : not secret or hidden **3** : frank or generous **4** : extended **5** : free from controls **6** : not decided ~ *vb* **1** : make or become open **2** : make or become functional **3** : start — ~ *n* : outdoors — **open·er** \-ər\ *n* — **open·ly** *adv* — **open·ness** *n*

open·hand·ed \-'handəd\ *adj* : generous — **open·hand·ed·ly** *adv*

open·ing \'ōpəniŋ\ *n* **1** : act or instance of making open **2** : something that is open **3** : opportunity

op·era \'äpərə, 'äprə\ *n* : drama set to music — **op·er·at·ic** \,äpə-'ratik\ *adj*

op·er·a·ble \'äpərəbəl\ *adj* **1** : usable or in working condition **2** : suitable for surgical treatment

op·er·ate \'äpə,rāt\ *vb* **-at·ed; -at·ing 1** : perform work **2** : perform an operation **3** : manage — **op·er·a·tor** \-,rātər\ *n*

op·er·a·tion \,äpə'rāshən\ *n* **1** : act or process of operating **2** : surgical work on a living body **3** : military action or mission — **op·er·a·tion·al** \-shənəl\ *adj*

op·er·a·tive \'äpərətiv, -,rāt-\ *adj* : working or having an effect

op·er·et·ta \,äpə'retə\ *n* : light opera

oph·thal·mol·o·gy \,äf,thal'mäləjē\ *n* : branch of medicine dealing with the eye — **oph·thal·mol·o·gist** \-jist\ *n*

opi·ate \'ōpēət, -pē,āt\ *n* : preparation or derivative of opium

opine \ō'pīn\ *vb* **opined; opin·ing** : express an opinion

opin·ion \ə'pinyən\ *n* **1** : belief **2** : judgment **3** : formal statement by an expert

opin·ion·at·ed \-yə,nātəd\ *adj* : stubborn in one's opinions

opi·um \'ōpēəm\ *n* : addictive narcotic drug that is the dried juice of a poppy

opos·sum \ə'päsəm\ *n* : common tree-dwelling nocturnal mammal

op·po·nent \ə'pōnənt\ *n* : one that opposes

op·por·tune \,äpər'tün, -'tyün\ *adj* : suitable or timely — **op·por·tune·ly** *adv*

op·por·tun·ism \-'tü,nizəm, -'tyü-\ *n* : a taking advantage of opportunities — **op·por·tun·ist** \-nist\ *n* — **op·por·tu·nis·tic** \-tü'nistik, -tyü-\ *adj*

op·por·tu·ni·ty \-'tünətē, -'tyü-\ *n, pl* **-ties** : favorable time

op·pose \ə'pōz\ *vb* **-posed; -pos·ing 1** : place opposite or against something **2** : resist — **op·po·si·tion** \,äpə'zishən\ *n*

op·po·site \'äpəzət\ *n* : one that is opposed ~ *adj* **1** : set facing something that is at the other side or end **2** : opposed or contrary ~ *adv* : on opposite sides ~ *prep* : across from — **op·po·site·ly** *adv*

op·press \ə'pres\ *vb* **1** : persecute **2** : weigh down — **op·pres·sion** \-'preshən\ *n* — **op·pres·sive** \-'presiv\ *adj* — **op·pres·sive·ly** *adv* — **op·pres·sor** \-'presər\ *n*

op·pro·bri·ous \ə'prōbrēəs\ *adj* : expressing or deserving opprobrium — **op·pro·bri·ous·ly** *adv*

op·pro·bri·um \-brēəm\ *n* **1** : something that brings disgrace **2** : infamy

opt \'äpt\ *vb* : choose

op·tic \'äptik\ *adj* : relating to vision or the eye

op·ti·cal \'äptikəl\ *adj* : relating to optics, vision, or the eye

op·ti·cian \äp'tishən\ *n* : maker of or dealer in eyeglasses

op·tics \'äptiks\ *n pl* : science of light and vision

op·ti·mal \'äptəməl\ *adj* : most favorable — **op·ti·mal·ly** *adv*

op·ti·mism \'äptə,mizəm\ *n* : tendency to hope for the best — **op·ti·mist** \-mist\ *n* — **op·ti·mis·tic** \,äptə'mistik\ *adj* — **op·ti·mis·ti·cal·ly** *adv*

op·ti·mum \'äptəməm\ *n, pl* **-ma** \-mə\ : amount or degree of something most favorable to an end — **optimum** *adj*

op·tion \'äpshən\ *n* **1** : ability to choose **2** : right to buy or sell a stock **3** : alternative — **op·tion·al** \-shənəl\ *adj*

op·tom·e·try \äp'tämətrē\ *n* : profession of examining the eyes — **op·tom·e·trist** \-trist\ *n*

op·u·lent \'äpyələnt\ *adj* : lavish —

op·u·lence \-ləns\ *n* — **op·u·lent·ly** *adv*

opus \'ōpəs\ *n, pl* **opera** \'ōpərə, 'äpə-\ : work esp. of music

or \'ȯr\ *conj* — used to indicate an alternative

-or \ər\ *n suffix* : one that performs an action

or·a·cle \'ȯrəkəl\ *n* **1** : one held to give divinely inspired answers or revelations **2** : wise person or an utterance of such a person — **orac·u·lar** \ȯ'rakyələr\ *adj*

oral \'ōrəl\ *adj* **1** : spoken **2** : relating to the mouth — **oral·ly** *adv*

or·ange \'ȯrinj\ *n* **1** : reddish yellow citrus fruit **2** : color between red and yellow — **or·ange·ade** \ˌȯrinj-'ād\ *n*

orang·u·tan \ə'raŋəˌtaŋ, -ˌtan\ *n* : large reddish brown ape

ora·tion \ə'rāshən\ *n* : elaborate formal speech

or·a·tor \'ȯrətər\ *n* : one noted as a public speaker

or·a·to·rio \ˌȯrə'tōrē,ō\ *n, pl* **-rios** : major choral work

or·a·to·ry \'ȯrəˌtōrē\ *n* : art of public speaking — **or·a·tor·i·cal** \ˌȯrə'tȯrikəl\ *adj*

orb \'ȯrb\ *n* : spherical body

or·bit \'ȯrbət\ *n* : path made by one body revolving around another — *vb* : revolve around — **or·bit·al** \-ᵊl\ *adj* — **or·bit·er** *n*

or·chard \'ȯrchərd\ *n* : place where fruit or nut trees are grown — **or·chard·ist** \-ist\ *n*

◆ **or·ches·tra** \'ȯrkəstrə\ *n* **1** : group of musicians **2** : front seats of a theater's main floor — **or·ches·tral** \ȯr'kestrəl\ *adj* — **or·ches·tral·ly** *adv*

or·ches·trate \'ȯrkəˌstrāt\ *vb* **-trat·ed; -trat·ing** **1** : compose or arrange for an orchestra **2** : arrange or combine for best effect — **or·ches·tra·tion** \ˌȯrkə'strāshən\ *n*

or·chid \'ȯrkəd\ *n* : plant with showy 3-petal flowers or its flower

or·dain \ȯr'dān\ *vb* **1** : admit to the clergy **2** : decree

or·deal \ȯr'dēl, 'ȯrˌdēl\ *n* : severely trying experience

or·der \'ȯrdər\ *n* **1** : rank, class, or special group **2** : arrangement **3** : rule of law **4** : authoritative regulation or instruction **5** : working condition **6** : special request for a purchase or what is purchased ~ *vb* **1** : arrange **2** : give an order to **3** : place an order for

or·der·ly \-lē\ *adj* **1** : being in order or tidy **2** : well behaved ~ *n, pl* **-lies 1** : officer's attendant **2** : hospital attendant — **or·der·li·ness** *n*

or·di·nal \'ȯrdᵊnəl\ *n* : number indicating order in a series

or·di·nance \-ᵊnəns\ *n* : municipal law

or·di·nary \'ȯrdᵊnˌerē\ *adj* : of common occurrence, quality, or ability — **or·di·nar·i·ly** \ˌȯrdᵊn'erəlē\ *adv*

or·di·na·tion \ˌȯrdᵊn'āshən\ *n* : act of ordaining

ord·nance \'ȯrdnəns\ *n* : military supplies

ore \'ōr\ *n* : mineral containing a valuable constituent

oreg·a·no \ə'regəˌno\ *n* : mint used as a seasoning and source of oil

or·gan \'ȯrgən\ *n* **1** : air-powered or electronic keyboard instrument **2** : animal or plant structure with special function **3** : periodical

or·gan·ic \ȯr'ganik\ *adj* **1** : relating to a bodily organ **2** : relating to living things **3** : relating to or containing carbon or its compounds **4** : relating to foods produced without the use of laboratory-made products — **or·gan·i·cal·ly** *adv*

or·gan·ism \'ȯrgə,nizəm\ *n* : a living thing

or·gan·ist \'ȯrgənist\ *n* : organ player

or·ga·nize \'ȯrgə,nīz\ *vb* **-nized; -niz·ing** : form parts into a functioning whole — **or·ga·ni·za·tion** \,ȯrgənə'zāshən\ *n* — **or·ga·ni·za·tion·al** \-shənəl\ *adj* — **or·ga·niz·er** *n*

or·gasm \'ȯr,gazəm\ *n* : climax of sexual excitement — **or·gas·mic** \ȯr'gazmik\ *adj*

or·gy \'ȯrjē\ *n, pl* **-gies** : unrestrained indulgence (as in sexual activity)

ori·ent \'ȯrē,ent\ *vb* **1** : set in a definite position **2** : acquaint with a situation — **ori·en·ta·tion** \,ȯrēən'tāshən\ *n*

ori·en·tal \,ȯrē'ent°l\ *adj* : Eastern — **Oriental** *n*

or·i·fice \'ȯrəfəs\ *n* : opening

or·i·gin \'ȯrəjən\ *n* **1** : ancestry **2** : rise, beginning, or derivation from a source — **orig·i·nate** \ə'rijə,nāt\ *vb* — **orig·i·na·tor** \-ər\ *n*

orig·i·nal \ə'rijənəl\ *n* : something from which a copy is made ~ *adj* **1** : first **2** : not copied from something else **3** : inventive — **orig·i·nal·i·ty** *n* — **orig·i·nal·ly** *adv*

ori·ole \'ȯrē,ōl, -ēəl\ *n* : American songbird

or·na·ment \'ȯrnəmənt\ *n* : something that adorns ~ *vb* : provide with ornament — **or·na·men·tal** \,ȯrnə'ment°l\ *adj* — **or·na·men·ta·tion** \-mən'tāshən\ *n*

or·nate \ȯr'nāt\ *adj* : elaborately decorated — **or·nate·ly** *adv* — **or·nate·ness** *n*

or·nery \'ȯrnərē, 'än-\ *adj* : irritable

or·ni·thol·o·gy \,ȯrnə'thäləjē\ *n, pl* **-gies** : study of birds — **or·ni·tho·log·i·cal** \-thə'läjikəl\ *adj* — **or·ni·thol·o·gist** \-'thäləjist\ *n*

or·phan \'ȯrfən\ *n* : child whose parents are dead — **orphan** *vb* — **or·phan·age** \-ənij\ *n*

or·tho·don·tics \,ȯrthə'däntiks\ *n* : dentistry dealing with straightening teeth — **or·tho·don·tist** \-'däntist\ *n*

or·tho·dox \'ȯrthə,däks\ *adj* **1** : conforming to established doctrine **2** *cap* : of or relating to a Christian church originating in the Eastern Roman Empire — **or·tho·doxy** \-,däksē\ *n*

or·thog·ra·phy \ȯr'thägrəfē\ *n* : spelling — **or·tho·graph·ic** \,ȯrthə'grafik\ *adj*

or·tho·pe·dics \,ȯrthə'pēdiks\ *n sing or pl* : correction or prevention of skeletal deformities — **or·tho·pe·dic** \-ik\ *adj* — **or·tho·pe·dist** \-'pēdist\ *n*

-o·ry \,ȯrē, ,ȯrē, ərē\ *adj suffix* **1** : of, relating to, or characterized by **2** : serving for, producing, or maintaining

os·cil·late \'äsə,lāt\ *vb* **-lat·ed; -lat·ing** : swing back and forth — **os·cil·la·tion** \,äsə'lāshən\ *n*

os·mo·sis \äz'mōsəs, äs-\ *n* : diffusion esp. of water through a membrane — **os·mot·ic** \-'mätik\ *adj*

os·prey \'äsprē, -,prā\ *n, pl* **-preys** : large fish-eating hawk

os·si·fy \'äsə,fī\ *vb* **-fied; -fy·ing** : make or become hardened or set in one's ways

os·ten·si·ble \ä'stensəbəl\ *adj* : seeming — **os·ten·si·bly** \-blē\ *adv*

os·ten·ta·tion \,ästən'tāshən\ *n* : pretentious display — **os·ten·ta·tious** \-shəs\ *adj* — **os·ten·ta·tious·ly** *adv*

os·te·op·a·thy \,ästē'äpəthē\ *n* : system of healing that emphasizes manipulation (as of joints) — **os·te·o·path** \'ästēə,path\ *n* — **os·te·o·path·ic** \,ästēə'pathik\ *adj*

os·te·o·po·ro·sis \,ästēōpə'rōsəs\ *n, pl* **-ro·ses** \-,sēz\ : condition characterized by fragile and porous bones

os·tra·cize \'ästrə,sīz\ *vb* **-cized; -ciz·ing** : exclude by common consent — **os·tra·cism** \-,sizəm\ *n*

os·trich \'ästrich, 'ȯs-\ *n* : very large flightless bird

oth·er \'əthər\ *adj* **1** : being the one left **2** : alternate **3** : additional ~ *pron* **1** : remaining one **2** : different one

oth·er·wise *adv* **1** : in a different way **2** : in different circumstances **3** : in other respects — **otherwise** *adj*

ot·ter \'ätər\ *n* : fish-eating mammal with webbed feet

ot·to·man \'ätəmən\ *n* : upholstered footstool

ought \'ȯt\ *verbal auxiliary* — used

to express obligation, advisability, or expectation

ounce \'aůns\ *n* **1** : unit of weight equal to about 28.3 grams **2** : unit of capacity equal to about 29.6 milliliters

our \'är, 'aůr\ *adj* : of or relating to us

ours \'aůrz, 'ärz\ *pron* : that which belongs to us

our·selves \är'selvz, aůr-\ *pron* : we, us — used reflexively or for emphasis

-ous \əs\ *adj suffix* : having or having the qualities of

oust \'aůst\ *vb* : expel or eject

oust·er \'aůstər\ *n* : expulsion

out \'aůt\ *adv* **1** : away from the inside or center **2** : beyond control **3** : to extinction, exhaustion, or completion **4** : in or into the open ~ *vb* : become known ~ *adj* **1** : situated outside **2** : absent ~ *prep* **1** : out through **2** : outward on or along — **out·bound** *adj* — **out·build·ing** *n*

out·age \'aůtij\ *n* : period of no electricity

out·board \'aůt,bōrd\ *adv* : outside a boat or ship — **outboard** *adj*

out·break \'aůt,brāk\ *n* : sudden occurrence

out·burst \-,bərst\ *n* : violent expression of feeling

out·cast \-,kast\ *n* : person cast out by society

out·come \-,kəm\ *n* : result

out·crop \'aůt,kräp\ *n* : part of a rock stratum that appears above the ground — **outcrop** *vb*

out·cry \-,krī\ *n* : loud cry

out·dat·ed \aůt'dātəd\ *adj* : out-of-date

out·dis·tance *vb* : go far ahead of

out·do \aůt'dü\ *vb* **-did** \-'did\; **-done** \-'dən\; **-do·ing** \-'düiŋ\; **-does** \-'dəz\ : do better than

out·doors \aůt'dōrz\ *adv* : in or into the open air ~ *n* : open air — **out·door** *adj*

out·er \'aůtər\ *adj* **1** : external **2** : farther out — **out·er·most** *adj*

out·field \'aůt,fēld\ *n* : baseball field beyond the infield — **out·field·er** \-,fēldər\ *n*

out·fit \'aůt,fit\ *n* **1** : equipment for a special purpose **2** : group ~ *vb* **-tt-** : equip — **out·fit·ter** *n*

out·go \'aůt,gō\ *n, pl* **outgoes** : expenditure

out·go·ing \'aůt,gōiŋ\ *adj* **1** : retiring from a position **2** : friendly

out·grow \aůt'grō\ *vb* **-grew** \-'grü\; **-grown** \-'grōn\; **-grow·ing** **1** : grow faster than **2** : grow too large for

out·growth \'aůt,grōth\ *n* **1** : product of growing out **2** : consequence

out·ing \'aůtiŋ\ *n* : excursion

out·land·ish \aůt'landish\ *adj* : very strange — **out·land·ish·ly** *adv*

outlast *vb* : last longer than

out·law \'aůt,lò\ *n* **1** : lawless person ~ *vb* : make illegal

out·lay \'aůt,lā\ *n* : expenditure

out·let \'aůt,let, -lət\ *n* **1** : exit **2** : means of release **3** : market for goods **4** : electrical device that gives access to wiring

out·line \'aůt,līn\ *n* **1** : line marking the outer limits **2** : summary ~ *vb* **1** : draw the outline of **2** : indicate the chief parts of

out·live \aůt'liv\ *vb* : live longer than

out·look \'aůt,lůk\ *n* **1** : viewpoint **2** : prospect for the future

out·ly·ing \'aůt,līiŋ\ *adj* : far from a central point

out·ma·neu·ver \,aůtmə'nüvər, -'nyü,-\ *vb* : defeat by more skillful maneuvering

out·mod·ed \aůt'mōdəd\ *adj* : out-of-date

out·num·ber \-'nəmbər\ *vb* : exceed in number

out of *prep* **1** : out from within **2** : beyond the limits of **3** : among **4** — used to indicate absence or loss **5** : because of **6** : from or with

out–of–date *adj* : no longer in fashion or in use

out·pa·tient *n* : person treated at a hospital who does not stay overnight

out·post *n* : remote military post

out·put *n* : amount produced ~ *vb* **-put·ted** *or* **-put; -put·ting** : produce

out·rage \'aůt,rāj\ *n* **1** : violent or shameful act **2** : injury or insult **3** : extreme anger ~ *vb* **-raged; -rag·ing 1** : subject to violent injury **2** : make very angry

out·ra·geous \aůt'rājəs\ *adj* : extremely offensive or shameful —

out·ra·geous·ly *adv* — **out·ra·geous·ness** *n*

out·right *adv* 1 : completely 2 : instantly ~ *adj* 1 : complete 2 : given without reservation

out·set *n* : beginning

out·side \aùt'sīd, 'aùt,-\ *n* 1 : place beyond a boundary 2 : exterior 3 : utmost limit ~ *adj* 1 : outer 2 : coming from without 3 : remote ~ *adv* : on or to the outside ~ *prep* 1 : on or to the outside of 2 : beyond the limits of

outside of *prep* 1 : outside 2 : besides

out·sid·er \-'sīdər\ *n* : one who does not belong to a group

out·skirts *n pl* : outlying parts (as of a city)

out·smart \aùt'smärt\ *vb* : outwit

out·spo·ken *adj* : direct and open in speech — **out·spo·ken·ness** *n*

out·stand·ing *adj* 1 : unpaid 2 : very good — **out·stand·ing·ly** *adv*

out·strip \aùt'strip\ *vb* 1 : go faster than 2 : surpass

¹**out·ward** \'aùtwərd\ *adj* 1 : being toward the outside 2 : showing outwardly

²**outward, out·wards** \-wərdz\ *adv* : toward the outside — **out·ward·ly** *adv*

out·wit \aùt'wit\ *vb* : get the better of by superior cleverness

ova *pl of* OVUM

oval \'ōvəl\ *adj* : egg-shaped — **oval** *n*

ova·ry \'ōvərē\ *n, pl* **-ries** 1 : egg-producing organ 2 : seed-producing part of a flower — **ovar·i·an** \ō'varēən\ *adj*

ova·tion \ō'vāshən\ *n* : enthusiastic applause

ov·en \'əvən\ *n* : chamber (as in a stove) for baking

over \'ōvər\ *adv* 1 : across 2 : upside down 3 : in excess or addition 4 : above 5 : at an end 6 : again ~ *prep* 1 : above in position or authority 2 : more than 3 : along, through, or across 4 : because of ~ *adj* 1 : upper 2 : remaining 3 : ended

over- *prefix* 1 : so as to exceed or surpass 2 : excessive or excessively

overabundance
overabundant
overachiever
overactive
overaggressive
overambitious
overanalyze
overanxiety
overanxious
overarousal
overassertive
overbake
overbid
overbill
overbold
overborrow
overbright
overbroad
overbuild
overburden
overbusy
overbuy
overcapacity
overcapitalize
overcareful
overcautious
overcharge
overcivilized
overclean
overcommit
overcompensate
overcomplicate
overconcern
overconfidence
overconfident
overconscientious
overconsume
overconsumption
overcontrol
overcook
overcorrect
overcritical
overcrowd
overdecorate
overdependence
overdependent
overdevelop
overdose
overdramatic
overdramatize
overdress
overdrink
overdue
overeager
overeat
overeducated
overelaborate
overemotional
overemphasis
overemphasize
overenergetic
overenthusiastic
overestimate
overexaggerate
overexaggeration
overexcite
overexcited
overexercise
overexert
overexertion
overexpand
overexpansion
overexplain
overexploit
overexpose
overextend
overextension
overexuberant
overfamiliar
overfatigued
overfeed
overfertilize
overfill
overfond
overgeneralization
overgeneralize
overgenerous
overglamorize
overgraze
overharvest
overhasty
overheat
overidealize
overimaginative
overimpress
overindebtedness
overindulge
overindulgence
overindulgent
overinflate
overinsistent
overintense
overintensity
overinvestment
overladen
overlarge
overlend
overload
overlong
overloud
overmedicate
overmodest
overmuch
overobvious
overoptimistic
overorganize
overparticular

overpay
overpayment
overplay
overpopulated
overpraise
overprescribe
overpressure
overprice
overprivileged
overproduce
overproduction
overpromise
overprotect
overprotective
overqualified
overrate
overreact
overreaction
overrefined
overregulate
overregulation
overreliance
overrepresent-
ed
overrespond
overripe
oversaturate
oversell
oversensitive

overserious
oversexed
oversimple
oversimplify
oversolicitous
overspecialize
overspend
overstaff
overstimulation
overstock
overstrain
overstress
overstretch
oversubtle
oversupply
oversuspicious
oversweeten
overtax
overtighten
overtip
overtired
overtrain
overtreat
overuse
overutilize
overvalue
overweight
overwork
overzealous

¹over·age \ˌōvərˈāj\ *adj* : too old

²overage \ˈōvərij\ *n* : surplus

over·all \ˌōvərˈȯl\ *adj* : including everything

over·alls \ˈōvərˌȯlz\ *n pl* : pants with an extra piece covering the chest

over·awe *vb* : subdue by awe

over·bear·ing \-ˈbariŋ\ *adj* : arrogant

over·blown \-ˈblōn\ *adj* : pretentious

over·board *adv* : over the side into the water

over·cast *adj* : clouded over ∼ *n* : cloud covering

over·coat *n* : outer coat

over·come *vb* **-came** \-ˈkām\; **-come;**

-com·ing 1 : defeat **2** : make helpless or exhausted

over·do *vb* **-did; -done; -do·ing; -does** : do too much

over·draft *n* : overdrawn sum

over·draw *vb* **-drew; -drawn; -drawing** : write checks for more than one's bank balance

over·flow \ˌōvərˈflō\ *vb* **1** : flood **2** : flow over — **overflow** \ˈōvərˌflō\ *n*

over·grow *vb* **-grew; -grown; -growing** : grow over

over·hand *adj* : made with the hand brought down from above — **overhand** *adv* — **over·hand·ed** \-ˌhandəd\ *adv or adj*

over·hang *vb* **-hung; -hang·ing** : jut out over ∼ *n* : something that overhangs

over·haul *vb* **1** : repair **2** : overtake

over·head \ˌōvərˈhed\ *adv* : aloft ∼ \ˈōvərˌ-\ *adj* : situated above ∼ \ˈōvərˌ-\ *n* : general business expenses

over·hear *vb* **-heard; -hear·ing** : hear without the speaker's knowledge

over·joyed *adj* : filled with joy

over·kill \ˈōvərˌkil\ *n* : large excess

over·land \-ˌland, -lənd\ *adv or adj* : by, on, or across land

over·lap *vb* : lap over — **overlap** \ˈōvərˌlap\ *n*

over·lay \ˌōvərˈlā\ *vb* **-laid; -laying** : lay over or across — **overlay** \ˈōvərˌlā\ *n*

♦ **over·look** \ˌōvərˈlu̇k\ *vb* **1** : look down on **2** : fail to see **3** : ignore **4** : pardon **5** : supervise ∼ \ˈōvərˌ-\ *n* : observation point

over·ly \ˈōvərlē\ *adv* : excessively

over·night *adv* **1** : through the night **2** : suddenly — **overnight** *adj*

over·pass *n* : bridge over a road

over·pow·er *vb* : conquer

over·reach \ˌōvər'rēch\ *vb* : try or seek too much

over·ride *vb* **-rode; -rid·den; -rid·ing** : neutralize action of

over·rule *vb* : rule against or set aside

over·run *vb* **-ran; -run·ning 1** : swarm or flow over **2** : go beyond ∼ *n* : an exceeding of estimated costs

over·seas *adv or adj* : beyond or across the sea

over·see \ˌōvər'sē\ *vb* **-saw; -seen; -seeing** : supervise — **over·seer** \'ōvərˌsiər\ *n*

over·shad·ow *vb* : exceed in importance

over·shoe *n* : protective outer shoe

over·shoot *vb* **-shot; -shoot·ing** : shoot or pass beyond

over·sight *n* : inadvertent omission or error

over·sleep *vb* **-slept; -sleep·ing** : sleep longer than intended

over·spread *vb* **-spread; -spread·ing** : spread over or above

over·state *vb* : exaggerate — **over·state·ment** *n*

over·stay *vb* : stay too long

over·step *vb* : exceed

overt \ō'vərt, 'ō,vərt\ *adj* : not secret — **overt·ly** *adv*

over·take *vb* **-took; -tak·en; -tak·ing** : catch up with

over·throw \ˌōvər'thrō\ *vb* **-threw; -thrown; -throw·ing 1** : upset **2** : defeat — **overthrow** \'ōvərˌ-\ *n*

over·time *n* : extra working time — **overtime** *adv*

over·tone *n* **1** : higher tone in a complex musical tone **2** : suggestion

over·ture \'ōvərˌchür, -chər\ *n* **1** : opening offer **2** : musical introduction

over·turn *vb* **1** : turn over **2** : nullify

over·view *n* : brief survey

over·ween·ing \ˌōvər'wēniŋ\ *adj* **1** : arrogant **2** : excessive

over·whelm \ˌōvər'hwelm\ *vb* : overcome completely — **overwhelm·ing·ly** \-'hwelmiŋlē\ *adv*

over·wrought \ˌōvər'rȯt\ *adj* : extremely excited

ovoid \'ō,vȯid\; **ovoi·dal** \ō'vȯidᵊl\ *adj* : egg-shaped

ovu·late \'ävyəˌlāt, 'ōv-\ *vb* **-lated; -lat·ing** : produce eggs from an ovary — **ovu·la·tion** \ˌävyə-'lāshən, ˌōv-\ *n*

ovum \'ōvəm\ *n, pl* **ova** \-və\ : female germ cell

owe \'ō\ *vb* **owed; ow·ing 1** : have an obligation to pay **2** : be indebted to or for

owing to *prep* : because of

owl \'aül\ *n* : nocturnal bird of prey — **owl·ish** *adj* — **owl·ish·ly** *adv*

♦ **own** \'ōn\ *adj* : belonging to oneself ∼ *vb* **1** : have as property **2** : acknowledge ∼ *pron* : one or ones belonging to oneself — **own·er** *n* — **own·er·ship** *n*

ox \'äks\ *n, pl* **ox·en** \'äksən\ : bovine mammal and esp. a castrated bull

ox·ide \'äk,sīd\ *n* : compound of oxygen

ox·i·dize \'äksəˌdīz\ *vb* **-dized; -diz·ing** : combine with oxygen — **ox·i·da·tion** \ˌäksə'dāshən\ *n* — **ox·i·diz·er** *n*

ox·y·gen \'äksijən\ *n* : gaseous chemical element essential for life

oys·ter \'ȯistər\ *n* : bivalve mollusk — **oys·ter·ing** \-riŋ\ *n*

ozone \'ō,zōn\ *n* : very reactive bluish form of oxygen

P

p \'pē\ *n, pl* **p's** *or* **ps** \'pēz\ : 16th letter of the alphabet

pace \'pās\ *n* **1** : walking step **2** : rate of progress ~ *vb* **paced; pac·ing 1** : go at a pace **2** : cover with slow steps **3** : set the pace of

pace·mak·er *n* : electrical device to regulate heartbeat

pachy·derm \'paki,dərm\ *n* : elephant

pa·cif·ic \pə'sifik\ *adj* : calm or peaceful

pac·i·fism \'pasə,fizəm\ *n* : opposition to war or violence — **pac·i·fist** \-fist\ *n or adj* — **pac·i·fis·tic** \,pasə'fistik\ *adj*

pac·i·fy \'pasə,fī\ *vb* **-fied; -fy·ing** : make calm — **pac·i·fi·ca·tion** \,pasəfə'kāshən\ *n* — **pac·i·fi·er** \'pasə,fīər\ *n*

pack \'pak\ *n* **1** : compact bundle **2** : group of animals ~ *vb* **1** : put into a container **2** : fill tightly or completely **3** : send without ceremony — **pack·er** *n*

pack·age \'pakij\ *n* : items bundled together ~ *vb* **-aged; -ag·ing** : enclose in a package

pack·et \'pakət\ *n* : small package

pact \'pakt\ *n* : agreement

pad \'pad\ *n* **1** : cushioning part or thing **2** : floating leaf of a water plant **3** : tablet of paper ~ *vb* **-dd-** **1** : furnish with a pad **2** : expand with needless matter — **pad·ding** *n*

pad·dle \'pad°l\ *n* : implement with a flat blade ~ *vb* **-dled; -dling** : move, beat, or stir with a paddle

pad·dock \'padək\ *n* : enclosed area for racehorses

pad·dy \'padē\ *n, pl* **-dies** : wet land where rice is grown

pad·lock *n* : lock with a U-shaped catch — **padlock** *vb*

pae·an \'pēən\ *n* : song of praise

pa·gan \'pāgən\ *n or adj* : heathen — **pa·gan·ism** \-,izəm\ *n*

¹page \'pāj\ *n* : messenger ~ *vb* **paged; pag·ing** : summon by repeated calls — **pag·er** *n*

²page *n* : single leaf (as of a book) or one side of the leaf

pag·eant \'pajənt\ *n* : elaborate spectacle or procession — **pag·eant·ry** \-əntrē\ *n*

pa·go·da \pə'gōdə\ *n* : tower with roofs curving upward

paid *past of* PAY

pail \'pāl\ *n* : cylindrical container with a handle — **pail·ful** \-,fůl\ *n*

pain \'pān\ *n* **1** : punishment or penalty **2** : suffering of body or mind **3** *pl* : great care ~ *vb* : cause or experience pain — **pain·ful** \-fəl\ *adj* — **pain·ful·ly** *adv* — **pain·kill·er** *n* — **pain·kill·ing** *adj* — **pain·less** *adj* — **pain·less·ly** *adv*

pains·tak·ing \'pān,stākin\ *adj* : taking pains — **painstaking** *n* — **pains·tak·ing·ly** *adv*

paint \'pānt\ *vb* **1** : apply color or paint to **2** : portray esp. in color ~ *n* : mixture of pigment and liquid — **paint·brush** *n* — **paint·er** *n* — **paint·ing** *n*

pair \'par\ *n* : a set of two ~ *vb* : put or go together as a pair

pa·ja·mas \pə'jäməz, -'jam-\ *n pl* : loose suit for sleeping

pal \'pal\ *n* : close friend

pal·ace \'paləs\ *n* **1** : residence of a chief of state **2** : mansion — **pa·la·tial** \pə'lāshəl\ *adj*

pal·at·able \'palətəbəl\ *adj* : agreeable to the taste

pal·ate \'palət\ *n* **1** : roof of the mouth **2** : taste — **pal·a·tal** \-ət°l\ *adj*

pa·la·ver \pə'lavər, -'läv-\ *n* : talk — **palaver** *vb*

¹pale \'pāl\ *adj* **pal·er; pal·est 1** : lacking in color or brightness **2** : light in color or shade ~ *vb* **paled; pal·ing** : make or become pale — **pale·ness** *n*

²pale *n* **1** : fence stake **2** : enclosed place

pa·le·on·tol·o·gy \,pālē,än'täləjē\ *n* : branch of biology dealing with ancient forms of life known from fossils — **pa·le·on·tol·o·gist** \-,än'täləjist, -ən-\ *n*

pal·ette \'palət\ *n* : board on which paints are laid and mixed

pal·i·sade \,palə'sād\ *n* **1** : high fence **2** : line of cliffs

¹pall \'pȯl\ *n* **1** : cloth draped over a coffin **2** : something that produces gloom

²pall *vb* : lose in interest or attraction

pall·bear·er *n* : one who attends the coffin at a funeral

¹pal·let \'palət\ *n* : makeshift bed

²pallet *n* : portable storage platform

pal·li·ate \'palē̠āt\ *vb* **-at·ed; -at·ing 1** : ease without curing **2** : cover or conceal by excusing — **pal·li·a·tion** \͵palē'āshən\ *n* — **pal·li·a·tive** \'palē͵ātiv\ *adj or n*

pal·lid \'paləd\ *adj* : pale

pal·lor \'palər\ *n* : paleness

¹palm \'päm, 'pälm\ *n* **1** : tall tropical tree crowned with large leaves **2** : symbol of victory

²palm *n* : underside of the hand ~ *vb* **1** : conceal in the hand **2** : impose by fraud

palm·ist·ry \'päməstrē, 'pälmə-\ *n* : reading a person's character or future in his palms — **palm·ist** \'pämist, 'pälm-\ *n*

palmy \'pämē, 'pälmē\ *adj* **palm·i·er; -est** : flourishing

pal·o·mi·no \͵palə'mēnō\ *n, pl* **-nos** : light-colored horse

pal·pa·ble \'palpəbəl\ *adj* **1** : capable of being touched **2** : obvious — **pal·pa·bly** \-blē\ *adv*

pal·pi·tate \'palpə͵tāt\ *vb* **-tat·ed; -tat·ing** : beat rapidly — **pal·pi·ta·tion** \͵palpə'tāshən\ *n*

pal·sy \'pȯlzē\ *n, pl* **-sies 1** : paralysis **2** : condition marked by tremor — **pal·sied** \-zēd\ *adj*

pal·try \'pȯltrē\ *adj* **-tri·er; -est** : trivial

pam·per \'pampər\ *vb* : spoil or indulge

♦ **pam·phlet** \'pamflət\ *n* : unbound publication — **pam·phle·teer** \͵pamflə'tir\ *n*

pan \'pan\ *n* : broad, shallow, and open container ~ *vb* **1** : wash gravel in a pan to search for gold **2** : criticize severely

pan·a·cea \͵panə'sēə\ *n* : remedy for all ills or difficulties

pan·cake *n* : fried flat cake

pan·cre·as \'paŋkrēəs, 'pan-\ *n* : gland that produces insulin — **pan·cre·at·ic** \͵paŋkrē'atik, ͵pan-\ *adj*

pan·da \'pandə\ *n* : black-and-white bearlike animal

pan·de·mo·ni·um \͵pandə'mōnēəm\ *n* : wild uproar

pan·der \'pandər\ *n* **1** : pimp **2** : one who caters to others' desires or weaknesses ~ *vb* : act as a pander

pane \'pān\ *n* : sheet of glass

pan·e·gy·ric \͵panə'jirik\ *n* : eulogistic oration — **pan·e·gyr·ist** \-'jirist\ *n*

pan·el \'pan²l\ *n* **1** : list of persons (as jurors) **2** : discussion group **3** : flat piece of construction material **4** : board with instruments or controls ~ *vb* **-eled** *or* **-elled; -el·ing** *or* **-el·ling** : decorate with panels — **pan·el·ing** *n* — **pan·el·ist** \-ist\ *n*

pang \'paŋ\ *n* : sudden sharp pain

pan·han·dle \'pan͵hand²l\ *vb* **-dled; -dling** : ask for money on the street — **pan·han·dler** \-ər\ *n*

pan·ic \'panik\ *n* : sudden overpowering fright ~ *vb* **-icked; -ick·ing** : affect or be affected with panic — **pan·icky** \-ikē\ *adj*

pan·o·ply \'panəplē\ *n, pl* **-plies 1** : full suit of armor **2** : impressive array

pan·o·ra·ma \͵panə'ramə, -'räm-\ *n* : view in every direction — **pan·o·ram·ic** \-'ramik\ *adj*

pan·sy \'panzē\ *n, pl* **-sies** : low-growing garden herb with showy flowers

pant \'pant\ *vb* **1** : breathe with great effort **2** : yearn ~ *n* : panting sound

pan·ta·loons \ˌpantᵊlˈünz\ *n pl* : pants

pan·the·on \ˈpanthē₊än, -ən\ *n* 1 : the gods of a people 2 : group of famous people

pan·ther \ˈpanthər\ *n* : large wild cat

pant·ies \ˈpantēz\ *n pl* : woman's or child's short underpants

pan·to·mime \ˈpantə₊mīm\ *n* 1 : play without words 2 : expression by bodily or facial movements ~ *vb* : represent by pantomime

pan·try \ˈpantrē\ *n, pl* **-tries** : storage room for food and dishes

pants \ˈpants\ *n pl* 1 : 2-legged outer garment 2 : panties

pap \ˈpap\ *n* : soft food

pa·pa·cy \ˈpāpəsē\ *n, pl* **-cies** 1 : office of pope 2 : reign of a pope

pa·pal \ˈpāpəl\ *adj* : relating to the pope

pa·pa·ya \pəˈpīä\ *n* : tropical tree with large yellow edible fruit

pa·per \ˈpāpər\ *n* 1 : pliable substance used to write or print on, to wrap things in, or to cover walls 2 : printed or written document 3 : newspaper — **paper** *adj or vb* — **pa·per·hang·er** *n* — **pa·per-weight** *n* — **pa·pery** \ˈpāpərē\ *adj*

pa·per·board *n* : cardboard

pa·pier–mâ·ché \ˌpāpərməˈshā, ˌpap₊yämə-, -ma-\ *n* : molding material of waste paper

pa·poose \paˈpüs, pə-\ *n* : young child of American Indian parents

pa·pri·ka \pəˈprēkə, pa-\ *n* : mild red spice from sweet peppers

pa·py·rus \pəˈpīrəs\ *n, pl* **-rus·es** or **-ri** \-₊rē, -₊rī\ 1 : tall grasslike plant 2 : paper from papyrus

par \ˈpär\ *n* 1 : stated value 2 : common level 3 : accepted standard or normal condition — **par** *adj*

par·a·ble \ˈparəbəl\ *n* : simple story illustrating a moral truth

para·chute \ˈparə₊shüt\ *n* : large umbrella-shaped device for making a descent through air — **parachute** *vb* — **para·chut·ist** \-₊shütist\ *n*

pa·rade \pəˈrād\ *n* 1 : pompous display 2 : ceremonial formation and march ~ *vb* **-rad·ed; -rad·ing** 1 : march in a parade 2 : show off

par·a·digm \ˈparə₊dīm, -₊dim\ *n* : model

par·a·dise \ˈparə₊dīs, -₊dīz\ *n* : place of bliss

par·a·dox \ˈparə₊däks\ *n* : statement that seems contrary to common sense yet is perhaps true — **par·a·dox·i·cal** \ˌparəˈdäksikəl\ *adj* — **par·a·dox·i·cal·ly** *adv*

par·af·fin \ˈparəfən\ *n* : white waxy substance used esp. for making candles and sealing foods

par·a·gon \ˈparə₊gän, -gən\ *n* : model of perfection

para·graph \ˈparə₊graf\ *n* : unified division of a piece of writing ~ *vb* : divide into paragraphs

par·a·keet \ˈparə₊kēt\ *n* : small slender parrot

par·al·lel \ˈparə₊lel\ *adj* 1 : lying or moving in the same direction but always the same distance apart 2 : similar ~ *n* 1 : parallel line, curve, or surface 2 : line of latitude 3 : similarity ~ *vb* 1 : compare 2 : correspond to — **par·al·lel·ism** \-₊izəm\ *n*

par·al·lel·o·gram \ˌparəˈlelə₊gram\ *n* : 4-sided polygon with opposite sides equal and parallel

pa·ral·y·sis \pəˈraləsəs\ *n, pl* **-y·ses** \-₊sēz\ : loss of function and esp. of voluntary motion — **par·a·lyt·ic** \ˌparəˈlitik\ *adj or n*

par·a·lyze \ˈparə₊līz\ *vb* **-lyzed; -lyz·ing** : affect with paralysis — **par·a·lyz·ing·ly** *adv*

♦ **para·med·ic** \ˌparəˈmedik\ *n*

: person trained to provide initial emergency medical treatment

pa·ram·e·ter \pə'ramətər\ n : characteristic element — **para·met·ric** \₁parə'metrik\ adj

par·a·mount \'parə₁maùnt\ adj : superior to all others

par·amour \'parə₁mùr\ n : illicit lover

para·noia \₁parə'nóiə\ n : mental disorder marked by irrational suspicion — **para·noid** \'parə₁nóid\ adj or n

par·a·pet \'parəpət, -₁pet\ n : protecting rampart in a fort

par·a·pher·na·lia \₁parəfə'nālyə, -fər-\ n sing or pl : equipment

para·phrase \'parə₁frāz\ n : restatement of a text giving the meaning in different words — **paraphrase** vb

para·ple·gia \₁parə'plējə, -jēə\ n : paralysis of the lower trunk and legs — **para·ple·gic** \-jik\ adj or n

par·a·site \'parə₁sīt\ n : organism living on another — **par·a·sit·ic** \₁parə'sitik\ adj — **par·a·sit·ism** \'parəsə₁tizəm, -₁sīt₁iz-\ n

para·sol \'parə₁sòl\ n : umbrella used to keep off the sun

para·troops \-₁trüps\ n pl : troops trained to parachute from an airplane — **para·troop·er** \-₁trüpər\ n

par·boil \'pär₁bóil\ vb : boil briefly

par·cel \'pärsəl\ n 1 : lot 2 : package ~ vb -celed or -celled; -cel·ing or -cel·ling : divide into portions

parch \'pärch\ vb : toast or shrivel with dry heat

parch·ment \'pärchmənt\ n : animal skin prepared to write on

par·don \'pärd°n\ n : excusing of an offense ~ vb : free from penalty — **par·don·able** \'pärd°nəbəl\ adj — **par·don·er** \-°nər\ n

pare \'par\ vb **pared; par·ing** 1 : trim off an outside part 2 : reduce as if by paring — **par·er** n

par·e·gor·ic \₁parə'górik\ n : tincture of opium and camphor

par·ent \'parənt\ n : one that begets or brings up offspring — **par·ent·age** \-ij\ n — **pa·ren·tal** \pə'rent°l\ adj — **par·ent·hood** n

pa·ren·the·sis \pə'renthəsəs\ n, pl **-the·ses** \-₁sēz\ 1 : word or phrase inserted in a passage 2 : one of a pair of punctuation marks ( ) — **par·en·thet·ic** \₁parən'thetik,

par·en·thet·i·cal \-ikəl\ adj — **par·en·thet·i·cal·ly** adv

par·fait \pär'fā\ n : layered cold dessert

pa·ri·ah \pə'rīə\ n : outcast

par·ish \'parish\ n : local church community

pa·rish·io·ner \pə'rishənər\ n : member of a parish

par·i·ty \'parətē\ n, pl **-ties** : equality

park \'pärk\ n : land set aside for recreation or for its beauty ~ vb : leave a vehicle standing

par·ka \'pärkə\ n : usu. hooded heavy jacket

park·way \'pärk₁wā\ n : broad landscaped thoroughfare

par·lance \'pärləns\ n : manner of speaking

par·lay \'pär₁lā\ n : the risking of a stake plus its winnings — **parlay** vb

par·ley \'pärlē\ n, pl **-leys** : conference about a dispute — **parley** vb

par·lia·ment \'pärləmənt\ n : legislative assembly — **par·lia·men·tar·i·an** n — **par·lia·men·ta·ry** \₁pärlə'mentərē\ adj

par·lor \'pärlər\ n 1 : reception room 2 : place of business

pa·ro·chi·al \pə'rōkēəl\ adj 1 : relating to a church parish 2 : provincial — **pa·ro·chi·al·ism** \-ə-₁lizəm\ n

par·o·dy \'parədē\ n, pl **-dies** : humorous or satirical imitation — **parody** vb

pa·role \pə'rōl\ n : conditional release of a prisoner — **parole** vb — **pa·rol·ee** \-₁rō'lē, -'rō₁lē\ n

par·ox·ysm \'parək₁sizəm, pə-'räk-\ n : convulsion

par·quet \'pär₁kā, pär'kā\ n : flooring of patterned wood inlay

par·ra·keet var of PARAKEET

par·rot \'parət\ n : bright-colored tropical bird

par·ry \'parē\ vb **-ried; -ry·ing** 1 : ward off a blow 2 : evade adroitly — **parry** n

parse \'pärs\ vb **parsed; pars·ing** : analyze grammatically

par·si·mo·ny \'pärsə₁mōnē\ n : extreme frugality — **par·si·mo·ni·ous** \₁pärsə'mōnēəs\ adj — **par·si·mo·ni·ous·ly** adv

pars·ley \'pärslē\ n : garden plant used as a seasoning or garnish

pars·nip \'pärsnəp\ *n* : carrotlike vegetable with a white edible root

par·son \'pärs³n\ *n* : minister

par·son·age \'pärs³nij\ *n* : parson's house

part \'pärt\ *n* 1 : one of the units into which a larger whole is divided 2 : function or role ~ *vb* 1 : take leave 2 : separate 3 : go away 4 : give up

par·take \pär'tāk, pər-\ *vb* **-took; -tak·en -tak·ing** : have or take a share — **par·tak·er** *n*

par·tial \'pärshəl\ *adj* 1 : favoring one over another 2 : affecting a part only — **par·tial·i·ty** \ˌpärshē'alətē\ *n* — **par·tial·ly** \'pärshəlē\ *adv*

par·tic·i·pate \pər'tisə̩pāt, pär-\ *vb* **-pat·ed; -pat·ing** : take part in something — **par·tic·i·pant** \-pənt\ *adj or n* — **par·tic·i·pa·tion** \-ˌtisə'pāshən\ *n* — **par·tic·i·pa·to·ry** \-'tisəpə̩tōrē\ *adj*

par·ti·ci·ple \'pärtə̩sipēl\ *n* : verb form with functions of both verb and adjective — **par·ti·cip·i·al** \ˌpärtə'sipēəl\ *adj*

par·ti·cle \'pärtikəl\ *n* : small bit

par·tic·u·lar \pär'tikyələr\ *adj* 1 : relating to a specific person or thing 2 : individual 3 : hard to please ~ *n* : detail — **par·tic·u·lar·ly** *adv*

par·ti·san \'pärtəzən, -sən\ *n* 1 : adherent 2 : guerrilla — **partisan** *adj* — **par·ti·san·ship** *n*

par·tite \'pär̩tīt\ *adj* : divided into parts

par·ti·tion \pər'tishən, pär-\ *n* 1 : distribution 2 : something that divides — **partition** *vb*

part·ly \'pärtlē\ *adv* : in some degree

part·ner \'pärtnər\ *n* 1 : associate 2 : companion 3 : business associate — **part·ner·ship** *n*

part of speech : class of words distinguished esp. according to function

par·tridge \'pärtrij\ *n, pl* **-tridge** or **-tridg·es** : stout-bodied game bird

par·ty \'pärtē\ *n, pl* **-ties** 1 : political organization 2 : participant 3 : company of persons esp. with a purpose 4 : social gathering

par·ve·nu \'pärvə̩nü, -̩nyü\ *n* : social upstart

pass \'pas\ *vb* 1 : move past, over, or through 2 : go away or die 3 : allow to elapse 4 : go unchallenged 5 : transfer or undergo transfer 6 : render a judgment 7 : occur 8 : enact 9 : undergo testing successfully 10 : be regarded 11 : decline ~ *n* 1 : low place in a mountain range 2 : act of= passing 3 : accomplishment 4 : permission to leave, enter, or move about — **pass·able** *adj* — **pass·ably** *adv* — **pass·er** *n* — **pass·er·by** *n*

pas·sage \'pasij\ *n* 1 : process of passing 2 : means of passing 3 : voyage 4 : right to pass 5 : literary selection — **pas·sage·way** *n*

pass·book *n* : bankbook

pas·sé \pa'sā\ *adj* : out-of-date

pas·sen·ger \'pas³njər\ *n* 1 : traveler in a conveyance

pass·ing \'pasiŋ\ *n* : death

pas·sion \'pashən\ *n* 1 : strong feeling esp. of anger, love, or desire 2 : object of affection or enthusiasm — **pas·sion·ate** \'pashənət\ *adj* — **pas·sion·ate·ly** *adv* — **pas·sion·less** *adj*

pas·sive \'pasiv\ *adj* 1 : not active but acted upon 2 : submissive — **passive** *n* — **pas·sive·ly** *adv* — **pas·siv·i·ty** \pa'sivətē\ *n*

Pass·over \'pas̩ōvər\ *n* : Jewish holiday celebrated in March or April in commemoration of the Hebrews' liberation from slavery in Egypt

pass·port \'pas̩pōrt\ *n* : government document needed for travel abroad

pass·word *n* 1 : word or phrase spoken to pass a guard 2 : sequence of characters needed to get into a computer system

past \'past\ *adj* 1 : ago 2 : just gone by 3 : having existed before the present 4 : expressing past time ~ *prep or adv* : beyond ~ *n* 1 : time gone by 2 : verb tense expressing time gone by 3 : past life

pas·ta \'pästə\ *n* : fresh or dried shaped dough

paste \'pāst\ *n* 1 : smooth ground food 2 : moist adhesive ~ *vb* **past·ed; past·ing** : attach with paste — **pasty** *adj*

paste·board *n* : cardboard

pas·tel \pas'tel\ *n* : light color — **pastel** *adj*

pas·teur·ize \'paschə̩rīz, 'pastə-\ *vb*

-ized; -iz·ing : heat (as milk) so as to kill germs — pas·teur·i·za·tion \‚paschərə'zāshən, ‚pastə-\ n

pas·time \'pas‚tīm\ n : amusement

pas·tor \'pastər\ n : priest or minister serving a church or parish — pas·tor·ate \-tərət\ n

pas·to·ral \'pastərəl\ adj 1 : relating to rural life 2 : of or relating to spiritual guidance or a pastor ~ n : literary work dealing with rural life

past·ry \'pāstrē\ n, pl -ries : sweet baked goods

pas·ture \'paschər\ n : land used for grazing ~ vb -tured; -tur·ing : graze

pat \'pat\ n 1 : light tap 2 : small mass ~ vb -tt- : tap gently ~ adj or adv 1 : apt or glib 2 : unyielding

patch \'pach\ n 1 : piece used for mending 2 : small area distinct from surrounding area ~ vb 1 : mend with a patch 2 : make of fragments 3 : repair hastily — patchy \-ē\ adj

patch·work n : something made of pieces of different materials, shapes, or colors

pate \'pāt\ n : crown of the head

pa·tel·la \pə'telə\ n, pl -lae \-'tel‚ē, -‚ī\ or -las : kneecap

pa·tent adj 1 \'patᵊnt, 'pāt-\ : obvious 2 \'pat-\ : protected by a patent ~ \'pat-\ n : document conferring or securing a right ~ \'pat-\ vb : secure by patent — pat·ent·ly adv

pa·ter·nal \pə'tərnᵊl\ adj 1 : fatherly 2 : related through or inherited from a father — pa·ter·nal·ly adv

pa·ter·ni·ty \pə'tərnətē\ n : fatherhood

path \'path, 'pȧth\ n 1 : trodden way 2 : route or course — path·find·er n — path·way n — path·less adj

pa·thet·ic \pə'thetik\ adj : pitiful — pa·thet·i·cal·ly adv

pa·thol·o·gy \pə'thäləjē\ n, pl -gies 1 : study of disease 2 : physical abnormality — path·o·log·i·cal \‚pathə'läjikəl\ adj — pa·thol·o·gist \pə'thäləjist\ n

pa·thos \'pā‚thäs\ n : element evoking pity

pa·tience \'pāshəns\ n : habit or fact of being patient

pa·tient \'pāshənt\ adj : bearing pain or trials without complaint ~ n : one under medical care — pa·tient·ly adv

pa·ti·na \pə'tēnə, 'patənə\ n, pl -nas \-nəz\ or -nae \-‚nē, -‚nī\ : green film formed on copper and bronze

pa·tio \'patē‚ō, 'pät-\ n, pl -ti·os 1 : courtyard 2 : paved recreation area near a house

pa·tri·arch \'pātrē‚ärk\ n 1 : man revered as father or founder 2 : venerable old man — pa·tri·ar·chal \‚pātrē'ärkəl\ adj — pa·tri·ar·chy \-‚ärkē\ n

pa·tri·cian \pə'trishən\ n : person of high birth — patrician adj

pat·ri·mo·ny \'patrə‚mōnē\ n : something inherited — pat·ri·mo·ni·al \‚patrə'mōnēəl\ adj

pa·tri·ot \'pātrēət, -‚ät\ n : one who loves his or her country — pa·tri·ot·ic \‚pātrē'ätik\ adj — pa·tri·ot·i·cal·ly adv — pa·tri·o·tism \'pātrēə‚tizəm\ n

pa·trol \pə'trōl\ n 1 : a going around for observation or security 2 : group on patrol ~ vb -ll- : carry out a patrol

pa·trol·man \-mən\ n : police officer

pa·tron \'pātrən\ n 1 : special protector 2 : wealthy supporter 3 : customer

pa·tron·age \'patrənij, 'pā-\ n 1 : support or influence of a patron 2 : trade of customers 3 : control of government appointments

pa·tron·ess \'pātrənəs\ n : woman who is a patron

pa·tron·ize \'pātrə‚nīz, 'pa-\ vb -ized; -iz·ing 1 : be a customer of 2 : treat with condescension

¹pat·ter \'patər\ vb : talk glibly or mechanically ~ n : rapid talk

²patter vb : pat or tap rapidly ~ n : quick succession of pats or taps

pat·tern \'patərn\ n 1 : model for imitation or for making things 2 : artistic design 3 : noticeable formation or set of characteristics ~ vb : form according to a pattern

pat·ty \'patē\ n, pl -ties : small flat cake

pau·ci·ty \'pòsətē\ n : shortage

paunch \'pònch\ n : large belly — paunchy adj

pau·per \'pòpər\ n : poor person — pau·per·ism \-pə‚rizəm\ n — pau·per·ize \-pə‚rīz\ vb

pause \'pȯz\ *n* : temporary stop ~ *vb* paused; paus·ing : stop briefly

pave \'pāv\ *vb* paved; pav·ing : cover to smooth or firm the surface — **pave·ment** \-mənt\ *n* — **pav·ing** *n*

pa·vil·ion \pə'vilyən\ *n* 1 : large tent 2 : light structure used for entertainment or shelter

paw \'pȯ\ *n* : foot of a 4-legged clawed animal ~ *vb* 1 : handle clumsily or rudely 2 : touch or strike with a paw

pawn \'pȯn\ *n* 1 : goods deposited as security for a loan 2 : state of being pledged ~ *vb* : deposit as a pledge — **pawn·bro·ker** *n* — **pawn·shop** *n*

pay \'pā\ *vb* **paid** \'pād\; **pay·ing** 1 : make due return for goods or services 2 : discharge indebtedness for 3 : requite 4 : give freely or as fitting 5 : be profitable ~ *n* 1 : status of being paid 2 : something paid — **pay·able** *adj* — **pay·check** *n* — **pay·ee** \pā'ē\ *n* — **pay·er** *n* — **pay·ment** *n*

PC \pē'sē\ *n*, *pl* **PCs** *or* **PC's** : microcomputer

pea \'pē\ *n* : round edible seed of a leguminous vine

peace \'pēs\ *n* 1 : state of calm and quiet 2 : absence of war or strife — **peace·able** \-əbəl\ *adj* — **peace·ably** \-blē\ *adv* — **peace·ful** \-fəl\ *adj* — **peace·ful·ly** *adv* — **peace·keep·er** *n* — **peace·keep·ing** *n* — **peace·mak·er** *n* — **peace·time** *n*

peach \'pēch\ *n* : sweet juicy fruit of a flowering tree or this tree

pea·cock \'pē,käk\ *n* : brilliantly colored male pheasant

peak \'pēk\ *n* 1 : pointed or projecting part 2 : top of a hill 3 : highest level ~ *vb* : reach a maximum — **peak** *adj*

peak·ed \'pēkəd\ *adj* : sickly

peal \'pēl\ *n* : loud sound (as of ringing bells) ~ *vb* : give out peals

pea·nut \'pē,nət\ *n* : annual herb that bears underground pods or the pod or the edible seed inside

pear \'par\ *n* : fleshy fruit of a tree related to the apple

pearl \'pərl\ *n* : gem formed within an oyster — **pearly** \'pərlē\ *adj*

peas·ant \'pez°nt\ *n* : tiller of the soil — **peas·ant·ry** \-°ntrē\ *n*

peat \'pēt\ *n* : decayed organic deposit often dried for fuel — **peaty** *adj*

peb·ble \'pebəl\ *n* : small stone — **peb·bly** *adj*

pe·can \pi'kän, -'kan\ *n* : hickory tree bearing a smooth-shelled nut or the nut

pec·ca·dil·lo \,pekə'dilō\ *n*, *pl* **-loes** *or* **-los** : slight offense

¹**peck** \'pek\ *n* : unit of dry measure equal to 8 quarts

²**peck** *vb* : strike or pick up with the bill ~ *n* : quick sharp stroke

pec·tin \'pektən\ *n* : water-soluble plant substance that causes fruit jellies to set — **pec·tic** \-tik\ *adj*

pec·to·ral \'pektərəl\ *adj* : relating to the breast or chest

pe·cu·liar \pi'kyülyər\ *adj* 1 : characteristic of only one 2 : strange — **pe·cu·liar·i·ty** \-,kyül'yaratē, -ē'ar-\ *n* — **pe·cu·liar·ly** *adv*

pe·cu·ni·ary \pi'kyünē,erē\ *adj* : relating to money

ped·a·go·gy \'pedə,gōjē, -,gäj-\ *n* : art or profession of teaching — **ped·a·gog·ic** \,pedə'gäjik, -'gōj-,\ **ped·a·gog·i·cal** \-ikəl\ *adj* — **ped·a·gogue** \'pedə,gäg\ *n*

ped·al \'ped°l\ *n* : lever worked by the foot ~ *adj* : relating to the foot ~ *vb* : use a pedal

ped·ant \'ped°nt\ *n* : learned bore — **pe·dan·tic** \pi'dantik\ *adj* — **ped·ant·ry** \'ped°ntrē\ *n*

ped·dle \'ped°l\ *vb* **-dled; -dling** : offer for sale — **ped·dler** \'pedlər\ *n*

ped·es·tal \'pedəst°l\ *n* : support or foot of something upright

pe·des·tri·an \pə'destrēən\ *adj* 1 : ordinary 2 : walking ~ *n* : person who walks

pe·di·at·rics \,pēdē'atriks\ *n* : branch of medicine dealing with children — **pe·di·at·ric** \-trik\ *adj* — **pe·di·a·tri·cian** \,pēdēə-'trishən\ *n*

ped·i·gree \'pedə,grē\ *n* : line of ancestors or a record of it

ped·i·ment \'pedəmənt\ *n* : triangular gablelike decoration on a building

peek \'pēk\ *vb* 1 : look furtively 2 : glance — **peek** *n*

peel \'pēl\ *vb* 1 : strip the skin or rind from 2 : lose the outer layer ~ *n* : skin or rind — **peel·ing** *n*

¹**peep** \'pēp\ *vb or n* : cheep

²**peep** \'pēp\ vb **1** : look slyly **2** : begin to emerge ~ n : brief look — **peep·er** n — **peep·hole** n

¹**peer** \'pir\ n **1** : one's equal **2** : nobleman — **peer·age** \-ij\ n

²**peer** vb : look intently or curiously

peer·less \-ləs\ adj : having no equal

peeve \'pēv\ vb **peeved; peev·ing** : make resentful ~ n : complaint — **peev·ish** \-ish\ adj — **peev·ish·ly** adv — **peev·ish·ness** n

peg \'peg\ n : small pinlike piece ~ vb **-gg- 1** : put a peg into **2** : fix or mark with or as if with pegs

pei·gnoir \pān'wär, pen-\ n : negligee

pe·jo·ra·tive \pi'jôrətiv\ adj : having a negative or degrading effect ~ n : a degrading word or phrase — **pe·jo·ra·tive·ly** adv

pel·i·can \'pelikən\ n : large-billed seabird

pel·la·gra \pə'lagrə, -'läg-\ n : protein-deficiency disease

pel·let \'pelət\ n : little ball — **pel·let·al** \-⁰l\ adj — **pel·let·ize** \-ˌīz\ vb

pell-mell \'pel'mel\ adv : in confusion or haste

pel·lu·cid \pə'lüsəd\ adj : very clear

¹**pelt** \'pelt\ n : skin of a fur-bearing animal

²**pelt** vb : strike with blows or missiles

pel·vis \'pelvəs\ n, pl **-vis·es** \-vəsəz\ or **-ves** \-ˌvēz\ : cavity formed by the hip bones — **pel·vic** \-vik\ adj

¹**pen** \'pen\ n : enclosure for animals ~ vb **-nn-** : shut in a pen

²**pen** n : tool for writing with ink ~ vb **-nn-** : write

pe·nal \'pēn⁰l\ adj : relating to punishment

pe·nal·ize \'pēn⁰l,īz, 'pen-\ vb **-ized; -iz·ing** : put a penalty on

pen·al·ty \'pen⁰ltē\ n, pl **-ties 1** : punishment for crime **2** : disadvantage, loss, or hardship due to an action

pen·ance \'penəns\ n : act performed to show repentance

pence \'pens\ pl of PENNY

pen·chant \'penchənt\ n : strong inclination

pen·cil \'pensəl\ n : writing or drawing tool with a solid marking substance (as graphite) as its core ~ vb **-ciled** or **-cilled; -cil·ing** or **-cil·ling** : draw or write with a pencil

pen·dant \'pendənt\ n : hanging ornament

pen·dent, pen·dant \'pendənt\ adj : hanging

pend·ing \'pendiŋ\ prep : while awaiting ~ adj : not yet decided

pen·du·lous \'penjələs, -dyüləs\ adj : hanging loosely

pen·du·lum \-ləm\ n : a hanging weight that is free to swing

pen·e·trate \'penəˌtrāt\ vb **-trat·ed; -trat·ing 1** : enter into **2** : permeate **3** : see into — **pen·e·tra·ble** \-trəbəl\ adj — **pen·e·tra·tion** \ˌpenə'trāshən\ n — **pen·e·tra·tive** \'penəˌtrātiv\ adj

pen·guin \'peŋgwən, 'pen-\ n : short-legged flightless seabird

pen·i·cil·lin \ˌpenə'silən\ n : antibiotic usu. produced by a mold

pen·in·su·la \pə'ninsələ, -'ninchə-\ n : land extending out into the water — **pen·in·su·lar** \-lər\ adj

pe·nis \'pēnəs\ n, pl **-nes** \-ˌnēz\ or **-nis·es** : male organ of copulation

pen·i·tent \'penətənt\ adj : feeling sorrow for sins or offenses ~ n : penitent person — **pen·i·tence** \-təns\ n — **pen·i·ten·tial** \ˌpenə·'tenchəl\ adj

pen·i·ten·tia·ry \ˌpenə'tenchərē\ n, pl **-ries** : state or federal prison

pen·man·ship \'penmən,ship\ n : art or practice of penmanship

pen·nant \'penənt\ n : nautical or championship flag

pen·ny \'penē\ n, pl **-nies** \-ēz\ or **pence** \'pens\ **1** : monetary unit equal to ¹⁄₁₀₀ pound **2** pl **-nies** : cent — **pen·ni·less** \'peniləs\ adj

pen·sion \'penchən\ n : retirement income ~ vb : pay a pension to — **pen·sion·er** n

pen·sive \'pensiv\ adj : thoughtful — **pen·sive·ly** adv

pent \'pent\ adj : confined

pent·a·gon \'pentəˌgän\ n : 5-sided polygon — **pen·tag·o·nal** \pen'tagən⁰l\ adj

pen·tam·e·ter \pen'tamətər\ n : line of verse containing 5 metrical feet

pent·house \'pent,haùs\ n : rooftop apartment

pen·u·ry \'penyərē\ n **1** : poverty **2** : thrifty or stingy manner — **pe·nu·ri·ous** \pə'nùreəs, -'nyùr-\ adj

pe·on \'pē,än, -ən\ n, pl **-ons** or **-o·nes** \pā'ōnēz\ : landless laborer in

Spanish America — **pe·on·age** \-ənij\ *n*

pe·o·ny \'pēənē\ *n, pl* **-nies** : garden plant having large flowers

peo·ple \'pēpəl\ *n, pl* **people 1** *pl* : human beings in general **2** *pl* : human beings in a certain group (as a family) or community **3** *pl* **peoples** : tribe, nation, or race ~ *vb* **-pled; -pling** : constitute the population of

pep \'pep\ *n* : brisk energy ~ *vb* **pepped; pep·ping** : put pep into — **pep·py** *adj*

pep·per \'pepər\ *n* **1** : pungent seasoning from the berry (**peppercorn**) of a shrub **2** : vegetable grown for its hot or sweet fruit ~ *vb* : season with pepper — **pep·pery** \-ərē\ *adj*

pep·per·mint \-ˌmint, -mənt\ *n* : pungent aromatic mint

pep·per·o·ni \ˌpepə'rōnē\ *n* : spicy beef and pork sausage

pep·tic \'peptik\ *adj* : relating to digestion or the effect of digestive juices

per \'pər\ *prep* **1** : by means of **2** : for each **3** : according to

per·am·bu·late \pə'rambyəˌlāt\ *vb* **-lat·ed; -lat·ing** : walk — **per·am·bu·la·tion** \-ˌrambyə'lāshən\ *n*

per·cale \ˌpər'kāl, 'pər-ˌ; ˌpər'kal\ *n* : fine woven cotton cloth

per·ceive \pər'sēv\ *vb* **-ceived; -ceiving 1** : realize **2** : become aware of through the senses — **per·ceiv·able** *adj*

per·cent \pər'sent\ *adv* : in each hundred ~ *n pl* **-cent** *or* **-cents 1** : one part in a hundred **2** : percentage

per·cent·age \pər'sentij\ *n* : part expressed in hundredths

per·cen·tile \pər'senˌtīl\ *n* : a standing on a scale of 0–100

per·cep·ti·ble \pər'septəbəl\ *adj* : capable of being perceived — **per·cep·ti·bly** \-blē\ *adv*

per·cep·tion \pər'sepshən\ *n* **1** : act or result of perceiving **2** : ability to understand

per·cep·tive \pər'septiv\ *adj* : showing keen perception — **per·cep·tive·ly** *adv*

¹**perch** \'pərch\ *n* : roost for birds ~ *vb* : roost

²**perch** *n, pl* **perch** *or* **perch·es** : freshwater spiny-finned food fish

per·co·late \'pərkəˌlāt\ *vb* **-lat·ed; -lat·ing** : trickle or filter down through a substance — **per·co·la·tor** \-ˌlātər\ *n*

per·cus·sion \pər'kəshən\ *n* **1** : sharp blow **2** : musical instrument sounded by striking

pe·remp·to·ry \pə'remptərē\ *adj* **1** : imperative **2** : domineering — **pe·remp·to·ri·ly** \-tərəlē\ *adv*

pe·ren·ni·al \pə'renēəl\ *adj* **1** : present at all seasons **2** : continuing from year to year **3** : recurring regularly ~ *n* : perennial plant — **pe·ren·ni·al·ly** *adv*

per·fect \'pərfikt\ *adj* **1** : being without fault or defect **2** : exact **3** : complete ~ \pər'fekt\ *vb* : make perfect — **per·fect·ibil·i·ty** \pərˌfektə'bilətē\ *n* — **per·fect·ible** \pər'fektəbəl\ *adj* — **per·fect·ly** *adv* — **per·fect·ness** *n*

per·fec·tion \pər'fekshən\ *n* **1** : quality or state of being perfect **2** : highest degree of excellence — **per·fec·tion·ist** \-shənist\ *n*

per·fid·i·ous \pər'fidēəs\ *adj* : treacherous — **per·fid·i·ous·ly** *adv*

per·fo·rate \'pərfəˌrāt\ *vb* **-rat·ed; -rat·ing** : make a hole in — **per·fo·ra·tion** \ˌpərfə'rāshən\ *n*

per·force \pər'fōrs\ *adv* : of necessity

per·form \pər'fòrm\ *vb* **1** : carry out **2** : do in a set manner **3** : give a performance — **per·form·er** *n*

per·for·mance \pər'fòrˌməns\ *n* **1** : act or process of performing **2** : public presentation

per·fume \'pərˌfyüm, pər'-\ *n* **1** : pleasant odor **2** : something that gives a scent ~ \pər'-, 'pər-\ *vb* **-fumed; -fum·ing** : add scent to

per·func·to·ry \pər'fəŋktərē\ *adj* : done merely as a duty — **per·func·to·ri·ly** \-tərəlē\ *adv*

per·haps \pər'haps\ *adv* : possibly but not certainly

per·il \'perəl\ *n* : danger — **per·il·ous** *adj* — **per·il·ous·ly** *adv*

pe·rim·e·ter \pə'rimətər\ *n* : outer boundary of a body or figure

pe·ri·od \'pirēəd\ *n* **1** : punctuation mark . used esp. to mark the end of a declarative sentence or an abbreviation **2** : division of time **3** : stage in a process or development

pe·ri·od·ic \,pirē'ädik\ *adj* : occurring at regular intervals — **pe·ri·od·i·cal·ly** *adv*

pe·ri·od·i·cal \,pirē'ädikəl\ *n* : newspaper or magazine

pe·riph·ery \pə'rifərē\ *n, pl* **-er·ies** : outer boundary — **pe·riph·er·al** \-ərəl\ *adj*

peri·scope \'perə,skōp\ *n* : optical instrument for viewing from a submarine

per·ish \'perish\ *vb* : die or spoil — **per·ish·able** \-əbəl\ *adj or n*

per·ju·ry \'pərjərē\ *n* : lying under oath — **per·jure** \'pərjər\ *vb* — **per·jur·er** *n*

¹perk \'pərk\ *vb* **1** : thrust (as the head) up jauntily **2** : freshen **3** : gain vigor or spirit — **perky** *adj*

²perk *vb* : percolate

³perk *n* : privilege or benefit in addition to regular pay

per·ma·nent \'pərmənənt\ *adj* : lasting ~ *n* : hair wave — **per·ma·nence** \-nəns\ *n* — **per·ma·nent·ly** *adv*

per·me·able \'pərmēəbəl\ *adj* : permitting fluids to seep through — **per·me·a·bil·i·ty** \,pərmēə'bilətē\ *n*

per·me·ate \'pərmē,āt\ *vb* **-at·ed; -at·ing 1** : seep through **2** : pervade — **per·me·ation** \,pərmē'āshən\ *n*

per·mis·si·ble \pər'misəbəl\ *adj* : that may be permitted

per·mis·sion \pər'mishən\ *n* : formal consent

per·mis·sive \pər'misiv\ *adj* : granting freedom esp. to excess — **per·mis·sive·ly** *adv* — **per·mis·sive·ness** *n*

per·mit \pər'mit\ *vb* **-tt- 1** : approve **2** : make possible ~ \'pər,-, pər'-\ *n* : license

per·ni·cious \pər'nishəs\ *adj* : very harmful — **per·ni·cious·ly** *adv*

per·ox·ide \pə'räk,sīd\ *n* : compound (as hydrogen peroxide) in which oxygen is joined to oxygen

per·pen·dic·u·lar \,pərpən'dikyələr\ *adj* **1** : vertical **2** : meeting at a right angle — **perpendicular** *n* — **per·pen·dic·u·lar·i·ty** \-,dikyə'larətē\ *n* — **per·pen·dic·u·lar·ly** *adv*

per·pe·trate \'pərpə,trāt\ *vb* **-trat·ed; -trat·ing** : be guilty of doing — **per·pe·tra·tion** \,pərpə'trāshən\ *n* — **per·pe·tra·tor** \'pərpə,trātər\ *n*

per·pet·u·al \pər'pechəwəl\ *adj* **1** : continuing forever **2** : occurring continually — **per·pet·u·al·ly** *adv* — **per·pe·tu·ity** \,pərpə'tüətē, -'tyü-\ *n*

per·pet·u·ate \pər'pechə,wāt\ *vb* **-at·ed; -at·ing** : make perpetual — **per·pet·u·a·tion** \-,pechə'wāshən\ *n*

per·plex \pər'pleks\ *vb* : confuse — **per·plex·i·ty** \-ətē\ *n*

per·se·cute \'pərsi,kyüt\ *vb* **-cut·ed; -cut·ing** : harass, afflict — **per·se·cu·tion** \,pərsi'kyüshən\ *n* — **per·se·cu·tor** \'pərsi,kyütər\ *n*

per·se·vere \,pərsə'vir\ *vb* **-vered; -ver·ing** : persist — **per·se·ver·ance** \-'virəns\ *n*

per·sist \pər'sist, -'zist\ *vb* **1** : go on resolutely in spite of difficulties **2** : continue to exist — **per·sis·tence** \-'sistəns, -'zis-\ *n* — **per·sis·ten·cy** \-tənsē\ *n* — **per·sis·tent** \-tənt\ *adj* — **per·sis·tent·ly** *adv*

per·son \'pərsən\ *n* **1** : human being **2** : human being's body or individuality **3** : reference to the speaker, one spoken to, or one spoken of

per·son·able \'pərsənəbəl\ *adj* : having a pleasing personality

per·son·age \'pərsənij\ *n* : person of rank or distinction

per·son·al \'pərsənəl\ *adj* **1** : relating to a particular person **2** : done in person **3** : affecting one's body **4** : offensive to a certain individual — **per·son·al·ly** *adv*

◆ **per·son·al·i·ty** \,pərsən'alətē\ *n, pl* **-ties 1** : manner and disposition of an individual **2** : distinctive or well-known person

per·son·al·ize \'pərsənə,līz\ *vb* **-ized; -iz·ing** : mark as belonging to a particular person

per·son·i·fy \pər'sänə,fī\ *vb* **-fied; -fy·ing 1** : represent as a human being **2** : be the embodiment of — **per·son·i·fi·ca·tion** \-,sänəfə'kāshən\ *n*

per·son·nel \,pərsən'el\ *n* : body of persons employed

per·spec·tive \pər'spektiv\ *n* **1** : apparent depth and distance in painting **2** : view of things in their true relationship or importance

per·spi·ca·cious \,pərspə'kāshəs\ *adj* : showing keen understanding or discernment — **per·spi·cac·i·ty** \-'kasətē\ *n*

per·spire \pər'spīr\ *vb* **-spired; -spir·ing** : sweat — **per·spi·ra·tion** \ˌpərspə'rāshən\ *n*

per·suade \pər'swäd\ *vb* **-suad·ed; -suad·ing** : win over to a belief or course of action by argument or entreaty

per·sua·sion \pər'swäzhən\ *n* — **per·sua·sive** \-'swäsiv, -ziv\ *adj* — **per·sua·sive·ly** *adv* — **per·sua·sive·ness** *n*

pert \'pərt\ *adj* : flippant or irreverent

per·tain \pər'tān\ *vb* **1** : belong **2** : relate

per·ti·nent \'pərt°nənt\ *adj* : relevant — **per·ti·nence** \-əns\ *n*

per·turb \pər'tərb\ *vb* : make uneasy — **per·tur·ba·tion** \ˌpərtər-'bāshən\ *n*

pe·ruse \pə'rüz\ *vb* **-rused; -rus·ing** : read attentively — **pe·rus·al** \-'rüzəl\ *n*

per·vade \pər'vād\ *vb* **-vad·ed; -vad·ing** : spread through every part of — **per·va·sive** \-'vāsiv, -ziv\ *adj*

per·verse \pər'vərs\ *adj* **1** : corrupt **2** : unreasonably contrary — **per·verse·ly** *adv* — **per·verse·ness** *n* — **per·ver·sion** \pər'vərzhən\ *n* — **per·ver·si·ty** \-'vərsətē\ *n*

per·vert \pər'vərt\ *vb* : corrupt or distort ~ \'pər,-\ *n* : one that is perverted

pe·so \'pāsō\ *n, pl* **-sos** : monetary unit (as of Mexico)

pes·si·mism \'pesə,mizəm\ *n* : inclination to expect the worst — **pes·si·mist** \-mist\ *n* — **pes·si·mis·tic** \ˌpesə'mistik\ *adj*

pest \'pest\ *n* **1** : nuisance **2** : plant or animal detrimental to humans or their crops — **pes·ti·cide** \'pestə,sīd\ *n*

pes·ter \'pestər\ *vb* **-tered; -ter·ing** : harass with petty matters

pes·ti·lence \'pestələns\ *n* : plague — **pes·ti·lent** \-lənt\ *adj*

pes·tle \'pesəl, 'pest°l\ *n* : implement for grinding substances in a mortar

pet \'pet\ *n* **1** : domesticated animal kept for pleasure **2** : favorite ~ *vb* **-tt-** : stroke gently or lovingly

pet·al \'pet°l\ *n* : modified leaf of a flower head

pe·tite \pə'tēt\ *adj* : having a small trim figure

pe·ti·tion \pə'tishən\ *n* : formal written request ~ *vb* : make a request — **pe·ti·tion·er** *n*

pet·ri·fy \'petrə,fī\ *vb* **-fied; -fy·ing** **1** : change into stony material **2** : make rigid or inactive (as from fear) — **pet·ri·fac·tion** \ˌpetrə-'fakshən\ *n*

pe·tro·leum \pə'trōlēəm\ *n* : raw oil obtained from the ground

pet·ti·coat \'petē,kōt\ *n* : skirt worn under a dress

pet·ty \'petē\ *adj* **-ti·er; -est** **1** : minor **2** : of no importance **3** : narrow-minded or mean — **pet·ti·ly** \'pet°lē\ *adv* — **pet·ti·ness** *n*

petty officer *n* : subordinate officer in the navy or coast guard

pet·u·lant \'pechələnt\ *adj* : irritable — **pet·u·lance** \-ləns\ *n* — **pet·u·lant·ly** *adv*

pe·tu·nia \pi'tünyə, -'tyü-\ *n* : tropical herb with bright flowers

pew \'pyü\ *n* : bench with a back used in a church

pew·ter \'pyütər\ *n* : alloy of tin used for household utensils

pH \ˌpē'āch\ *n* : number expressing relative acidity and alkalinity

pha·lanx \'fā,laŋks\ *n, pl* **-lanx·es** *or* **-lan·ges** \fə'lan,jēz\ **1** : body (as of troops) in compact formation **2** *pl* **phalanges** : digital bone of the hand or foot

phal·a·rope \'falə,rōp\ n : a small shorebird

phal·lus \'faləs\ n, pl **-li** \'fal,ī\ or **-lus·es** : penis — **phal·lic** adj

phantasy var of FANTASY

phan·tom \'fantəm\ n : something that only appears to be real — **phantom** adj

pha·raoh \'ferō, 'fārō\ n : ruler of ancient Egypt

phar·ma·ceu·ti·cal \,färmə'sütikəl\ adj : relating to pharmacy or the making and selling of medicinal drugs — **pharmaceutical** n

phar·ma·col·o·gy \,färmə'käləjē\ n : science of drugs esp. as related to medicinal uses — **phar·ma·co·log·i·cal** \-ikəl\ adj — **phar·ma·col·o·gist** \-'käləjist\ n

phar·ma·cy \'färməsē\ n, pl **-cies** 1 : art or practice of preparing and dispensing medical drugs 2 : drugstore — **phar·ma·cist** \-sist\ n

phar·ynx \'fariŋks\ n, pl **pha·ryn·ges** \fə'rin,jēz\ : space behind the mouth into which the nostrils, esophagus, and windpipe open — **pha·ryn·ge·al** \fə'rinjəl, ,farən-'jēəl\ adj

phase \'fāz\ n 1 : particular appearance or stage in a series of changes 2 : stage in a process — **phase in** vb : introduce in stages — **phase out** vb : discontinue gradually

pheas·ant \'fez°nt\ n, pl **-ant** or **-ants** : long-tailed brilliantly colored game bird

phe·nom·e·non \fi'nämə,nän\ n, pl **-na** \-nə\ or **-nons** 1 : observable fact or event 2 pl **-nons** : prodigy — **phe·nom·e·nal** \-'nämən°l\ adj

phi·lan·der·er \fə'landərər\ n : one who makes love without serious intent

phi·lan·thro·py \fə'lanthrəpē\ n, pl **-pies** : charitable act or gift or an organization that distributes such gifts — **phil·an·throp·ic** \,filən-'thräpik\ adj — **phi·lan·thro·pist** \fə'lanthrəpist\ n

phi·lat·e·ly \fə'lat°lē\ n : collection and study of postage stamps — **phi·lat·e·list** \-°list\ n

phi·lis·tine \'filə,stēn, fə'listən\ n : one who is smugly indifferent to intellectual or artistic values — **philistine** adj

philo·den·dron \,filə'dendrən\ n, pl **-drons** or **-dra** \-drə\ : plant grown for its showy leaves

phi·los·o·pher \fə'läsəfər\ n 1 : reflective thinker 2 : student of philosophy

phi·los·o·phy \fə'läsəfē\ n, pl **-phies** 1 : critical study of fundamental beliefs 2 : sciences and liberal arts exclusive of medicine, law, and theology 3 : system of ideas 4 : sum of personal convictions — **phil·o·soph·ic** \,filə'säfik\, **phil·o·soph·i·cal** \-ikəl\ adj — **phil·o·soph·i·cal·ly** \-klē\ adv — **phi·los·o·phize** \fə'läsə,fīz\ vb

phle·bi·tis \fli'bītəs\ n : inflammation of a vein

phlegm \'flem\ n : thick mucus in the nose and throat

phlox \'fläks\ n, pl **phlox** or **phlox·es** : herb grown for its flower clusters

♦ **pho·bia** \'fōbēə\ n : irrational persistent fear

phoe·nix \'fēniks\ n : legendary bird held to burn itself to death and rise fresh and young from its ashes

phone \'fōn\ n : telephone — vb **phoned; phon·ing** : call on a telephone

pho·neme \'fō,nēm\ n : basic distinguishable unit of speech — **pho·ne·mic** \fō'nēmik\ adj

pho·net·ics \fə'netiks\ n : study of speech sounds — **pho·net·ic** \-ik\ adj — **pho·ne·ti·cian** \,fōnə-'tishən\ n

pho·nics \'fäniks\ n : method of

teaching reading by stressing sound values of syllables and words

pho·no·graph \'fōnə,graf\ *n* : instrument that reproduces sounds from a grooved disc

pho·ny, pho·ney \'fōnē\ *adj* -ni·er; -est : not sincere or genuine — **phony** *n*

phos·phate \'fäs,fāt\ *n* : chemical salt used in fertilizers — **phos·phat·ic** \fäs'fatik\ *adj*

phos·phor \'fäsfər\ *n* : phosphorescent substance

phos·pho·res·cence \,fäsfə'res°ns\ *n* : luminescence from absorbed radiation — **phos·pho·res·cent** \-°nt\ *adj* — **phos·pho·res·cent·ly** *adv*

phos·pho·rus \'fäsfərəs\ *n* : poisonous waxy chemical element — **phos·phor·ic** \fäs'förik, -'fär-\ *adj* — **phos·pho·rous** \'fäsfərəs, fäs-'förəs\ *adj*

pho·to \'fōtō\ *n, pl* -tos : photograph — **photo** *vb or adj*

pho·to·copy \'fōtə,käpē\ *n* : photographic copy (as of a printed page) — **photocopy** *vb*

pho·to·elec·tric \,fōtōi'lektrik\ *adj* : relating to an electrical effect due to the interaction of light with matter

pho·to·gen·ic \,fōtə'jenik\ *adj* : suitable for being photographed

pho·to·graph \'fōtə,graf\ *n* : picture taken by photography — **photograph** *vb* — **pho·tog·ra·pher** \fə-'tägrəfər\ *n*

pho·tog·ra·phy \fə'tägrəfē\ *n* : process of using light to produce images on a sensitized surface — **pho·to·graph·ic** \,fōtə'grafik\ *adj* — **pho·to·graph·i·cal·ly** *adv*

pho·to·syn·the·sis \,fōtō'sinthəsəs\ *n* : formation of carbohydrates by chlorophyll-containing plants exposed to sunlight — **pho·to·syn·the·size** \-,sīz\ *vb* — **pho·to·syn·thet·ic** \-sin'thetik\ *adj*

phrase \'frāz\ *n* **1** : brief expression **2** : group of related words that express a thought ~ *vb* **phrased;** **phras·ing** : express in a particular manner

phrase·ol·o·gy \,frāzē'äləjē\ *n, pl* -gies : manner of phrasing

phy·lum \'fīləm\ *n, pl* -la \-lə\ : ma-

jor division of the plant or animal kingdom

phys·i·cal \'fizikəl\ *adj* **1** : relating to nature **2** : material as opposed to mental or spiritual **3** : relating to the body ~ *n* : medical examination — **phys·i·cal·ly** \-klē\ *adv*

phy·si·cian \fə'zishən\ *n* : doctor of medicine

physician's assistant *n* : person certified to provide basic medical care under a physician's supervision

phys·i·cist \'fizəsist\ *n* : specialist in physics

phys·ics \'fiziks\ *n* : science that deals with matter and motion

phys·i·og·no·my \,fizē'ägnəmē\ *n, pl* -mies : facial appearance esp. as a reflection of inner character

phys·i·ol·o·gy \,fizē'äləjē\ *n* : functional processes in an organism — **phys·i·o·log·i·cal** \-ēə'läjikəl\, **phys·i·o·log·ic** \-ik\ *adj* — **phys·i·ol·o·gist** \-ē'äləjist\ *n*

phy·sique \fə'zēk\ *n* : build of a person's body

pi \'pī\ *n, pl* **pis** \'pīz\ : symbol π denoting the ratio of the circumference of a circle to its diameter or the ratio itself

pi·a·nist \pē'anist, 'pēənist\ *n* : one who plays the piano

pi·ano \pē'anō\ *n, pl* -anos : musical instrument with strings sounded by hammers operated from a keyboard

pi·az·za \pē'azə, -'äz-, -tsə\ *n, pl* -zas *or* -ze \-tsā\ : public square in a town

pic·a·yune \,pikē'yün\ *adj* : trivial or petty

pic·co·lo \'pikə,lō\ *n, pl* -los : small shrill flute

¹pick \'pik\ *vb* **1** : break up with a pointed instrument **2** : remove bit by bit **3** : gather by plucking **4** : select **5** : rob **6** : provoke **7** : unlock with a wire **8** : eat sparingly ~ *n* **1** : act of choosing **2** : choicest one — **pick·er** *n* — **pick up** *vb* **1** : improve **2** : put in order

²pick *n* : pointed digging tool

pick·ax *n* : pick

pick·er·el \'pikərəl\ *n, pl* -el *or* -els : small pike

pick·et \'pikət\ *n* **1** : pointed stake (as for a fence) **2** : worker demon-

strating on strike $\sim$ vb : demonstrate as a picket

◆ **pick·le** \'pikəl\ n 1 : brine or vinegar solution for preserving foods or a food preserved in a pickle 2 : bad state — **pickle** vb

pick·pock·et n : one who steals from pockets

pick·up \'pik,əp\ n 1 : revival or acceleration 2 : light truck with an open body

pic·nic \'pik,nik\ n : outing with food usu. eaten in the open $\sim$ vb -nicked; -nick·ing : go on a picnic

pic·to·ri·al \pik'tōrēəl\ adj : relating to pictures

pic·ture \'pikchər\ n 1 : representation by painting, drawing, or photography 2 : vivid description 3 : copy 4 : movie $\sim$ vb -tured; -tur·ing : form a mental image of

pic·tur·esque \,pikchə'resk\ adj : attractive or charming enough for a picture — **pic·tur·esque·ness** n

pie \'pī\ n : pastry crust and a filling

pie·bald \'pī,bȯld\ adj : blotched with white and black

piece \'pēs\ n 1 : part of a whole 2 : one of a group or set 3 : single item 4 : product of creative work $\sim$ vb pieced; piec·ing : join into a whole

piece·meal \'pēs,mēl\ adv or adj : gradually

pied \'pīd\ adj : colored in blotches

pier \'pir\ n 1 : support for a bridge span 2 : deck or wharf built out over water 3 : pillar

pierce \'pirs\ vb pierced; pierc·ing 1 : enter or thrust into or through 2 : penetrate 3 : see through

pi·ety \'pīətē\ n, pl -eties : devotion to religion

pig \'pig\ n 1 : young swine 2 : dirty or greedy individual 3 : iron cast-

ing — **pig·gish** \-ish\ adj — **pig·let** \-lət\ n — **pig·pen** n — **pig·sty** n

pi·geon \'pijən\ n : stout-bodied short-legged bird

pi·geon·hole n : small open compartment for letters or documents $\sim$ vb 1 : place in a pigeonhole 2 : classify

pig·gy·back \'pigē,bak\ adv or adj : up on the back and shoulders

pig·head·ed \-'hedəd\ adj : stubborn

pig·ment \'pigmənt\ n : coloring matter — **pig·men·ta·tion** n

pigmy var of PYGMY

pig·tail n : tight braid of hair

¹**pike** \'pīk\ n, pl pike or pikes : large freshwater fish

²**pike** n : former weapon consisting of a long wooden staff with a steel point

³**pike** n : turnpike

pi·laf, pi·laff \pi'läf, 'pē,läf\, **pi·lau** \pi'lō, -'lȯ; 'pēlō, -lȯ\ n : dish of seasoned rice

¹**pile** \'pīl\ n : supporting pillar driven into the ground

²**pile** n : quantity of things thrown on one another $\sim$ vb piled; pil·ing : heap up, accumulate

³**pile** n : surface of fine hairs or threads — **piled** adj

piles \'pīls\ n pl : hemorrhoids

pil·fer \'pilfər\ vb : steal in small quantities

pil·grim \'pilgrəm\ n 1 : one who travels to a shrine or holy place in devotion 2 cap : one of the English settlers in America in 1620

pil·grim·age \-grəmij\ n : pilgrim's journey

pill \'pil\ n : small rounded mass of medicine — **pill·box** n

pil·lage \'pilij\ vb -laged; -lag·ing : loot and plunder — **pillage** n

pil·lar \'pilər\ *n* : upright usu. supporting column — **pil·lared** *adj*

pil·lo·ry \'pilərē\ *n, pl* **-ries** : wooden frame for public punishment with holes for the head and hands ~ *vb* **-ried; -ry·ing 1** : set in a pillory **2** : expose to public scorn

pil·low \'pilō\ *n* : soft cushion for the head — **pil·low·case** *n*

pi·lot \'pīlət\ *n* **1** : helmsman **2** : person licensed to take ships into and out of a port **3** : guide **4** : one that flies an aircraft or spacecraft ~ *vb* : act as pilot of — **pi·lot·less** *adj*

pi·men·to \pə'mentō\ *n, pl* **-tos** or **-to 1** : allspice **2** : pimiento

pi·mien·to \pə'mentō, -'myen-\ *n, pl* **-tos** : mild red sweet pepper

pimp \'pimp\ *n* : man who solicits clients for a prostitute — **pimp** *vb*

pim·ple \'pimpəl\ *n* : small inflamed swelling on the skin — **pim·ply** \-pəlē\ *adj*

pin \'pin\ *n* **1** : fastener made of a small pointed piece of wire **2** : ornament or emblem fastened to clothing with a pin **3** : wooden object used as a target in bowling ~ *vb* **-nn- 1** : fasten with a pin **2** : hold fast or immobile — **pin·hole** *n*

pin·a·fore \'pinə,fōr\ *n* : sleeveless dress or apron fastened at the back

pin·cer \'pinsər\ *n* **1** *pl* : gripping tool with 2 jaws **2** : pincerlike claw

pinch \'pinch\ *vb* **1** : squeeze between the finger and thumb or between the jaws of a tool **2** : compress painfully **3** : restrict **4** : steal ~ *n* **1** : emergency **2** : painful effect **3** : act of pinching **4** : very small quantity

pin·cush·ion *n* : cushion for storing pins

¹pine \'pīn\ *n* : evergreen cone-bearing tree or its wood

²pine *vb* **pined; pin·ing 1** : lose health through distress **2** : yearn for intensely

pine·ap·ple *n* : tropical plant bearing an edible juicy fruit

pin·feath·er *n* : new feather just coming through the skin

¹pin·ion \'pinyən\ *vb* : restrain by binding the arms

²pinion *n* : small gear

¹pink \'piŋk\ *n* **1** : plant with narrow leaves and showy flowers **2** : highest degree

²pink *n* : light red color — **pink** *adj* — **pink·ish** *adj*

pink·eye *n* : contagious eye inflammation

pin·na·cle \'pinikəl\ *n* : highest point

pi·noch·le \'pē,nəkəl\ *n* : card game played with a 48-card deck

pin·point *vb* : locate, hit, or aim with great precision

pint \'pīnt\ *n* : 1/2 quart

pin·to \'pin,tō\ *n, pl* **pintos** : spotted horse or pony

pin·worm *n* : small parasitic intestinal worm

pi·o·neer \,pīə'nir\ *n* **1** : one that originates or helps open up a new line of thought or activity **2** : early settler ~ *vb* : act as a pioneer

pi·ous \'pīəs\ *adj* **1** : conscientious in religious practices **2** : affectedly religious — **pi·ous·ly** *adv*

pipe \'pīp\ *n* **1** : tube that produces music when air is forced through **2** : bagpipe **3** : long tube for conducting a fluid **4** : smoking tool ~ *vb* **piped; pip·ing 1** : play on a pipe **2** : speak in a high voice **3** : convey by pipes — **pip·er** *n*

pipe·line *n* **1** : line of pipe **2** : channel for information

pip·ing \'pīpiŋ\ *n* **1** : music of pipes **2** : narrow fold of material used to decorate edges or seams

pi·quant \'pēkənt\ *adj* **1** : tangy **2** : provocative or charming — **pi·quan·cy** \-kənsē\ *n*

pique \'pēk\ *n* : resentment ~ *vb* **piqued; piqu·ing 1** : offend **2** : arouse by provocation

pi·qué, pi·que \pi'kā\ *n* : durable ribbed clothing fabric

pi·ra·cy \'pīrəsē\ *n, pl* **-cies 1** : robbery on the seas **2** : unauthorized use of another's production or invention

pi·ra·nha \pə'ranyə, -'ränə\ *n* : small So. American fish with sharp teeth

pi·rate \'pīrət\ *n* : one who commits piracy — **pirate** *vb* — **pi·rat·i·cal** \pə'ratikəl, pī-\ *adj*

pir·ou·ette \,pirə'wet\ *n* : ballet turn on the toe or ball of one foot — **pirouette** *vb*

pis *pl of* PI

pis·ta·chio \pə'stashē,ō, -'stäsh-\ *n, pl* **-chios** : small tree bearing a greenish edible seed or its seed

pis·til \'pistᵊl\ *n* : female reproductive organ in a flower — **pis·til·late** \'pistə₁lāt\ *adj*

pis·tol \'pistᵊl\ *n* : firearm held with one hand

pis·ton \'pistən\ *n* : sliding piece that receives and transmits motion usu. inside a cylinder

¹**pit** \'pit\ *n* **1** : hole or shaft in the ground **2** : sunken or enclosed place for a special purpose **3** : hell **4** : hollow or indentation ∼ *vb* **-tt- 1** : form pits in **2** : become marred with pits

◆ ²**pit** *n* : stony seed of some fruits ∼ *vb* **-tt-** : remove the pit from

pit bull *n* : powerful compact dog bred for fighting

¹**pitch** \'pich\ *n* : resin from conifers — **pitchy** *adj*

²**pitch** *vb* **1** : erect and fix firmly in place **2** : throw **3** : set at a particular tone level **4** : fall headlong ∼ *n* **1** : action or manner of pitching **2** : degree of slope **3** : relative highness of a tone **4** : sales talk — **pitched** *adj*

¹**pitch·er** \'pichər\ *n* : container for liquids

²**pitcher** *n* : one that pitches (as in baseball)

pitch·fork *n* : long-handled fork for pitching hay

pit·e·ous \'pitēəs\ *adj* : arousing pity — **pit·e·ous·ly** *adv*

pit·fall \'pit₁fól\ *n* : hidden danger

pith \'pith\ *n* **1** : spongy plant tissue **2** : essential or meaningful part — **pithy** *adj*

piti·able \'pitēəbəl\ *adj* : pitiful

piti·ful \'pitifəl\ *adj* **1** : arousing or deserving pity **2** : contemptible — **piti·ful·ly** *adv*

pit·tance \'pitᵊns\ *n* : small portion or amount

pi·tu·i·tary \pə'tüə₁terē, -'tyü-\ *adj*

: relating to or being a small gland attached to the brain

pity \'pitē\ *n, pl* **pi·ties 1** : sympathetic sorrow **2** : something to be regretted ∼ *vb* **pit·ied; pity·ing** : feel pity for — **piti·less** *adj* — **piti·less·ly** *adv*

piv·ot \'pivət\ *n* : fixed pin on which something turns ∼ *vb* : turn on or as if on a pivot — **piv·ot·al** *adj*

pix·ie, pixy \'piksē\ *n, pl* **pix·ies** : mischievous sprite

piz·za \'pētsə\ *n* : thin pie of bread dough spread with a spiced mixture (as of tomatoes, cheese, and meat)

piz·zazz, pi·zazz \pə'zaz\ *n* : glamour

piz·ze·ria \₁pētsə'rēə\ *n* : pizza restaurant

plac·ard \'plakərd, -₁ärd\ *n* : poster ∼ *vb* : display placards in or on

pla·cate \'plā₁kāt, 'plak₁āt\ *vb* **-cat·ed; -cat·ing** : appease — **pla·ca·ble** \'plakəbəl, 'plāka-\ *adj*

place \'plās\ *n* **1** : space or room **2** : indefinite area **3** : a particular building, locality, area, or part **4** : relative position in a scale or sequence **5** : seat **6** : job ∼ *vb* **placed; plac·ing 1** : put in a place **2** : identify — **place·ment** *n*

pla·ce·bo \plə'sēbō\ *n, pl* **-bos** : something inactive prescribed as a remedy for its psychological effect

pla·cen·ta \plə'sentə\ *n, pl* **-tas** or **-tae** \-₁ē\ : structure in a uterus by which a fetus is nourished — **pla·cen·tal** \-'sentᵊl\ *adj*

plac·id \'plasəd\ *adj* : undisturbed or peaceful — **pla·cid·i·ty** \pla-'sidətē\ *n* — **plac·id·ly** *adv*

pla·gia·rize \'plājə₁rīz\ *vb* **-rized; -riz·ing** : use (words or ideas) of another as if your own — **pla·gia-**

rism \-ˌrizəm\ n — pla·gia·rist \-rist\ n

plague \'plāg\ n 1 : disastrous evil 2 : destructive contagious bacterial disease ~ vb **plagued; plaguing** 1 : afflict with disease or disaster 2 : harass

plaid \'plad\ n : woolen fabric with a pattern of crossing stripes or the pattern itself — **plaid** adj

plain \'plān\ n : expanse of relatively level treeless country ~ adj 1 : lacking ornament 2 : not concealed or disguised 3 : easily understood 4 : frank 5 : not fancy or pretty — **plain·ly** adv — **plain·ness** \'plānnəs\ n

plain·tiff \'plāntəf\ n : complaining party in a lawsuit

plain·tive \'plāntiv\ adj : expressive of suffering or woe — **plain·tive·ly** adv

plait \'plāt, 'plat\ n 1 : pleat 2 : braid of hair or straw — **plait** vb

plan \'plan\ n 1 : drawing or diagram 2 : method for accomplishing something ~ vb **-nn-** 1 : form a plan of 2 : intend — **plan·less** adj — **plan·ner** n

¹**plane** \'plān\ vb **planed; plan·ing** : smooth or level off with a plane ~ n : smoothing or shaping tool — **plan·er** n

²**plane** n 1 : level surface 2 : level of existence, consciousness, or development 3 : airplane ~ adj 1 : flat 2 : dealing with flat surfaces or figures

plan·et \'planət\ n : celestial body that revolves around the sun — **plan·e·tary** \-ə,terē\ adj

plan·e·tar·i·um \ˌplanə'terēəm\ n, pl **-iums** or **-ia** \-ēə\ : building or room housing a device to project images of celestial bodies

plank \'plaŋk\ n 1 : heavy thick board 2 : article in the platform of a political party — **plank·ing** n

plank·ton \'plaŋktən\ n : tiny aquatic animal and plant life — **plank·ton·ic** \plaŋk'tänik\ adj

plant \'plant\ vb 1 : set in the ground to grow 2 : place firmly or forcibly ~ n 1 : living thing without sense organs that cannot move about 2 : land, buildings, and machinery used esp. in manufacture

¹**plan·tain** \'plant⁵n\ n : short-stemmed herb with tiny greenish flowers

²**plantain** n : banana plant with starchy greenish fruit

plan·ta·tion \plan'tāshən\ n : agricultural estate usu. worked by resident laborers

plant·er \'plantər\ n 1 : plantation owner 2 : plant container

plaque \'plak\ n 1 : commemorative tablet 2 : film layer on a tooth

plas·ma \'plazmə\ n : watery part of blood — **plas·mat·ic** \plaz'matik\ adj

plas·ter \'plastər\ n 1 : medicated dressing 2 : hardening paste for coating walls and ceilings ~ vb : cover with plaster — **plas·ter·er** n

plas·tic \'plastik\ adj : capable of being molded ~ n : material that can be formed into rigid objects, films, or filaments — **plas·tic·i·ty** \plas'tisətē\ n

plate \'plāt\ n 1 : flat thin piece 2 : plated metalware 3 : shallow usu. circular dish 4 : denture or the part of it that fits to the mouth 5 : something printed from an engraving ~ vb **plat·ed; plat·ing** : overlay with metal — **plat·ing** n

pla·teau \pla'tō\ n, pl **-teaus** or **-teaux** \-'tōz\ : large level area of high land

plat·form \'plat,fórm\ n 1 : raised flooring or stage 2 : declaration of principles for a political party

plat·i·num \'plat⁵nəm\ n : heavy grayish-white metallic chemical element

plat·i·tude \'platə,tüd, -,tyüd\ n : trite remark — **plat·i·tu·di·nous** \ˌplatə'tüd⁵nəs, -'tyüd-\ adj

pla·toon \plə'tün\ n : small military unit

platoon sergeant n : noncommissioned officer in the army ranking below a first sergeant

plat·ter \'platər\ n : large serving plate

platy·pus \'platipəs\ n : small aquatic egg-laying mammal

plau·dit \'plódət\ n : act of applause

plau·si·ble \'plózəbəl\ adj : reasonable or believeable — **plau·si·bil·i·ty** \ˌplózə'bilətē\ n — **plau·si·bly** \-blē\ adv

play \'plā\ n 1 : action in a game 2 : recreational activity 3 : light or fitful movement **4** : free movement **5** : stage representation of a drama ∼ *vb* **1** : engage in recreation **2** : move or toy with aimlessly **3** : perform music **4** : act in a drama — **play·act·ing** *n* — **play·er** *n* — **play·ful** \-fəl\ *adj* — **play·ful·ly** *adv* — **play·ful·ness** *n* — **play·pen** *n* — **play·suit** *n* — **play·thing** *n*

play·ground *n* : place for children to play

play·house *n* **1** : theater **2** : small house for children to play in

playing card *n* : one of a set of 24 to 78 cards marked to show its rank and suit and used to play a game of cards

play·mate *n* : companion in play

play·off *n* : contest or series of contests to determine a champion

play·wright \-,rīt\ *n* : writer of plays

pla·za \'plazə, 'pläz-\ *n* **1** : public square **2** : shopping mall

plea \'plē\ *n* **1** : defendant's answer to charges **2** : urgent request

plead \'plēd\ *vb* **plead·ed** \'plēdəd\ *or* **pled** \'pled\; **plead·ing 1** : argue for or against in court **2** : answer to a charge or indictment **3** : appeal earnestly — **plead·er** *n*

pleas·ant \'plez²nt\ *adj* **1** : giving pleasure **2** : marked by pleasing behavior or appearance — **pleas·ant·ly** *adv* — **pleas·ant·ness** *n*

pleas·ant·ries \-²ntrēz\ *n pl* : pleasant and casual conversation

please \'plēz\ *vb* **pleased; pleas·ing 1** : give pleasure or satisfaction to **2** : desire or intend

pleas·ing \'plēzin\ *adj* : giving pleasure — **pleas·ing·ly** *adv*

plea·sur·able \'plezhərəbəl\ *adj* : pleasant — **plea·sur·ably** \-blē\ *adv*

plea·sure \'plezhər\ *n* **1** : desire or inclination **2** : enjoyment **3** : source of delight

pleat \'plēt\ *vb* : arrange in pleats ∼ *n* : fold in cloth

ple·be·ian \pli'bēən\ *n* : one of the common people ∼ *adj* : ordinary

pledge \'plej\ *n* **1** : something given as security **2** : promise or vow ∼ *vb* **pledged; pledg·ing 1** : offer as or bind by a pledge **2** : promise

ple·na·ry \'plēnərē, 'plen-\ *adj* : full

pleni·po·ten·tia·ry \,plenəpə-'tenchərē, -,tenchē,erē\ *n* : diplomatic agent having full authority — **plenipotentiary** *adj*

plen·i·tude \'plenə,tüd, -,tyüd\ *n* **1** : completeness **2** : abundance

plen·te·ous \'plentēəs\ *adj* : existing in plenty

plen·ty \'plentē\ *n* : more than adequate number or amount — **plen·ti·ful** \'plentifəl\ *adj* — **plen·ti·ful·ly** *adv*

pleth·o·ra \'plethərə\ *n* : excess

pleu·ri·sy \'plúrəsē\ *n* : inflammation of the chest membrane

pli·able \'plīəbəl\ *adj* : flexible

pli·ant \'plīənt\ *adj* : flexible — **pli·an·cy** \-ənsē\ *n*

pli·ers \'plīərz\ *n pl* : pinching or gripping tool

¹plight \'plīt\ *vb* : pledge

²plight *n* : bad state

plod \'pläd\ *vb* **-dd- 1** : walk heavily or slowly **2** : work laboriously and monotonously — **plod·der** *n* — **plod·ding·ly** \-inlē\ *adv*

◆ **plot** \'plät\ *n* **1** : small area of ground **2** : ground plan **3** : main story development (as of a book or movie) **4** : secret plan for doing something ∼ *vb* **-tt- 1** : make a plot or plan of **2** : plan or contrive — **plot·ter** *n*

plo·ver \'pləvər, 'plōvər\ *n, pl* **-ver** *or* **-vers** : shorebird related to the sandpiper

plow, plough \'plaů\ *n* **1** : tool used to turn soil **2** : device for pushing material aside ~ *vb* **1** : break up with a plow **2** : cleave or move through like a plow — **plow·man** \-mən, -ˌman\ *n*

plow·share \-ˌsher\ *n* : plow part that cuts the earth

ploy \'plói\ *n* : clever maneuver

pluck \'plək\ *vb* **1** : pull off or out **2** : tug or twitch ~ *n* **1** : act or instance of plucking **2** : spirit or courage

plucky \'pləkē\ *adj* **pluck·i·er; -est** : courageous or spirited

plug \'pləg\ *n* **1** : something for sealing an opening **2** : electrical connector at the end of a cord **3** : piece of favorable publicity ~ *vb* **-gg- 1** : stop or make tight or secure by inserting a plug **2** : publicize

plum \'pləm\ *n* **1** : smooth-skinned juicy fruit **2** : fine reward

plum·age \'plümij\ *n* : feathers of a bird — **plum·aged** \-mijd\ *adj*

plumb \'pləm\ *n* : weight on the end of a line (**plumb line**) to show vertical direction ~ *adv* **1** : vertically **2** : completely ~ *vb* : sound or test with a plumb ~ *adj* : vertical

plumb·er \'pləmər\ *n* : one who repairs usu. water pipes and fixtures

plumb·ing \'pləmiŋ\ *n* : system of water pipes in a building

plume \'plüm\ *n* : large, conspicuous, or showy feather ~ *vb* **plumed; plum·ing 1** : provide or deck with feathers **2** : indulge in pride — **plumed** \'plümd\ *adj*

plum·met \'pləmət\ *vb* : drop straight down

¹plump \'pləmp\ *vb* : drop suddenly or heavily ~ *adv* **1** : straight down **2** : in a direct manner

²plump *adj* : having a full rounded form — **plump·ness** *n*

plun·der \'pləndər\ *vb* : rob or take goods by force (as in war) ~ *n* : something taken in plundering — **plun·der·er** *n*

plunge \'plənj\ *vb* **plunged; plung·ing 1** : thrust or drive with force **2** : leap or dive into water **3** : begin an action suddenly **4** : dip or move suddenly forward or down ~ *n* : act or instance of plunging — **plung·er** *n*

plu·ral \'plůrəl\ *adj* : relating to a word form denoting more than one — **plural** *n*

plu·ral·i·ty \plů'ralətē\ *n, pl* **-ties** : greatest number of votes cast when not a majority

plu·ral·ize \'plůrəˌlīz\ *vb* **-ized; -iz·ing** : make plural — **plu·ral·i·za·tion** \ˌplůrələ'zāshən\ *n*

plus \'pləs\ *prep* : with the addition of ~ *n* **1** : sign + (**plus sign**) in mathematics to indicate addition **2** : added or positive quantity **3** : advantage ~ *adj* : being more or in addition ~ *conj* : and

plush \'pləsh\ *n* : fabric with a long pile ~ *adj* : luxurious — **plush·ly** *adv* — **plushy** *adj* — **plush·ness** *n*

plu·toc·ra·cy \plü'täkrəsē\ *n, pl* **-cies 1** : government by the wealthy **2** : a controlling class of the wealthy — **plu·to·crat** \'plütəˌkrat\ *n* — **plu·to·crat·ic** \ˌplütə'kratik\ *adj*

plu·to·ni·um \plü'tōnēəm\ *n* : radioactive chemical element

¹ply \'plī\ *n, pl* **plies** : fold, thickness, or strand of which something is made

²ply *vb* **plied; ply·ing 1** : use or work at **2** : keep supplying something to **3** : travel regularly usu. by sea

ply·wood *n* : sheets of wood glued and pressed together

pneu·mat·ic \nù'matik, nyù-\ *adj* **1** : moved by air pressure **2** : filled with compressed air — **pneu·mat·i·cal·ly** *adv*

pneu·mo·nia \nù'mōnyə, nyù-\ *n* : inflammatory lung disease

¹poach \'pōch\ *vb* : cook in simmering liquid

²poach *vb* : hunt or fish illegally — **poach·er** *n*

pock \'päk\ *n* : small swelling on the skin or its scar — **pock·mark** *n* — **pock·marked** *adj*

pock·et \'päkət\ *n* **1** : small open bag sewn into a garment **2** : container or receptacle **3** : isolated area or group ~ *vb* : put in a pocket — **pock·et·ful** \-ˌfúl\ *n*

pock·et·book *n* **1** : purse **2** : financial resources

pock·et·knife *n* : knife with a folding blade carried in the pocket

pod \'päd\ *n* **1** : dry fruit that splits open when ripe **2** : compartment on a ship or craft

po·di·a·try \pə'dīətrē, pō-\ *n* : branch of medicine dealing with the foot — **po·di·a·trist** \pə-'dīətrist, pō-\ *n*

po·di·um \'pōdēəm\ *n, pl* **-di·ums** *or* **-dia** \-ēə\ : dais

po·em \'pōəm\ *n* : composition in verse

po·et \'pōət\ *n* : writer of poetry

po·et·ry \'pōətrē\ *n* 1 : metrical writing 2 : poems — **po·et·ic** \pō'etik\, **po·et·i·cal** \-ikəl\ *adj*

po·grom \'pōgrəm, pə'gräm, 'pägrəm\ *n* : organized massacre

poi·gnant \'pöinyənt\ *adj* 1 : emotionally painful 2 : deeply moving — **poi·gnan·cy** \-nyənsē\ *n*

poin·set·tia \pöin'setēə, -'setə\ *n* : showy tropical American plant

point \'pöint\ *n* 1 : individual often essential detail 2 : purpose 3 : particular place, time, or stage 4 : sharp end 5 : projecting piece of land 6 : dot or period 7 : division of the compass 8 : unit of counting ~ *vb* 1 : sharpen 2 : indicate direction by extending a finger 3 : direct attention to 4 : aim — **point·ed·ly** \-ədlē\ *adv* — **point·less** *adj*

point–blank *adj* 1 : so close to a target that a missile fired goes straight to it 2 : direct — **point-blank** *adv*

point·er \'pöintər\ *n* 1 : one that points out 2 : large short-haired hunting dog 3 : hint or tip

◆ **poise** \'pöiz\ *vb* **poised; pois-ing** : balance ~ *n* : self-possessed calmness

poi·son \'pöiz°n\ *n* : chemical that can injure or kill ~ *vb* 1 : injure or kill with poison 2 : apply poison to 3 : affect destructively — **poi·son-er** *n* — **poi·son·ous** \'pöizºnəs\ *adj*

poke \'pōk\ *vb* **poked; pok·ing** 1 : prod 2 : dawdle ~ *n* : quick thrust

¹pok·er \'pōkər\ *n* : rod for stirring a fire

²poker *n* : card game for gambling

po·lar \'pōlər\ *adj* : relating to a geographical or magnetic pole

po·lar·ize \'pōlə͵rīz\ *vb* **-ized; -iz-ing** 1 : cause to have magnetic poles 2 : break up into opposing groups — **po·lar·i·za·tion** \͵pōlər-ə'zāshən\ *n*

¹pole \'pōl\ *n* : long slender piece of wood or metal

²pole *n* 1 : either end of the earth's axis 2 : battery terminal 3 : either end of a magnet

pole·cat \'pōl͵kat\ *n, pl* **polecats** *or* **polecat** 1 : European carnivorous mammal 2 : skunk

po·lem·ics \pə'lemiks\ *n sing or pl* : practice of disputation — **po·lem·i·cal** \-ikəl\ *adj* — **po·lem·i·cist** \-əsist\ *n*

po·lice \pə'lēs\ *n, pl* **police** 1 : department of government that keeps public order and enforces the laws 2 : members of the police ~ *vb* **-liced; -lic·ing** : regulate and keep in order — **po·lice-man** \-mən\ *n* — **po·lice·wom·an** *n*

police officer *n* : member of the police

¹pol·i·cy \'päləsē\ *n, pl* **-cies** : course of action selected to guide decisions

²policy *n, pl* **-cies** : insurance contract — **pol·i·cy·hold·er** *n*

po·lio \'pōlē͵ō\ *n* : poliomyelitis — **polio** *adj*

po·lio·my·eli·tis \-͵mīə'lītəs\ *n* : acute virus disease of the spinal cord

pol·ish \'pälish\ *vb* 1 : make smooth and glossy 2 : develop or refine ~ *n* 1 : shiny surface 2 : refinement

po·lite \pə'līt\ *adj* **-lit·er; -est** : marked by courteous social conduct — **po·lite·ly** *adv* — **po·lite·ness** *n*

pol·i·tic \\'päla,tik\\ *adj* : shrewdly tactful

politically correct *adj* : seeking to avoid offending members of a different group

pol·i·tics \\'päla,tiks\\ *n sing or pl* : practice of government and managing of public affairs — **po·lit·i·cal** \\pə'litikəl\\ *adj* — **po·lit·i·cal·ly** *adv* — **pol·i·ti·cian** \\,pälə-'tishən\\ *n*

pol·ka \\'pōlkə\\ *n* : lively couple dance — **polka** *vb*

pol·ka dot \\'pōkə,dät\\ *n* : one of a series of regular dots in a pattern

poll \\'pōl\\ *n* **1** : head **2** : place where votes are cast — usu. pl. **3** : a sampling of opinion ~ *vb* **1** : cut off **2** : receive or record votes **3** : question in a poll — **poll·ster** \\-stər\\ *n*

pol·len \\'pälən\\ *n* : spores of a seed plant

pol·li·na·tion \\,pälə'nāshən\\ *n* : the carrying of pollen to fertilize the seed — **pol·li·nate** \\'pälə,nāt\\ *vb* — **pol·li·na·tor** \\-ər\\ *n*

pol·lute \\pə'lüt\\ *vb* -lut·ed; -lut·ing : contaminating with waste products — **pol·lut·ant** \\-'lüt³nt\\ *n* — **pol·lut·er** *n* — **pol·lu·tion** \\-'lüshən\\ *n*

pol·ly·wog, pol·li·wog \\'pälē,wäg\\ *n* : tadpole

po·lo \\'pōlō\\ *n* : game played by 2 teams on horseback using long-handled mallets to drive a wooden ball

pol·ter·geist \\'pōltər,gīst\\ *n* : mischievous ghost

pol·troon \\päl'trün\\ *n* : coward

poly·es·ter \\'pälē,estər\\ *n* : synthetic fiber

po·lyg·a·my \\pə'ligəmē\\ *n* : marriage to several spouses at the same time — **po·lyg·a·mist** \\-mist\\ *n* — **po·lyg·a·mous** \\-məs\\ *adj*

poly·gon \\'päli,gän\\ *n* : closed plane figure with straight sides

poly·mer \\'päləmər\\ *n* : chemical compound of molecules joined in long strings — **po·lym·er·i·za·tion** \\pə,limərə'zāshən\\ *n* — **po·lym·er·ize** \\pə'limə,rīz\\ *vb*

poly·tech·nic \\,päli'teknik\\ *adj* : relating to many technical arts or applied sciences

poly·the·ism \\'pälithē,izəm\\ *n* : worship of many gods — **poly·the·ist** \\-,thēist\\ *adj or n*

poly·un·sat·u·rat·ed \\,pälē,ən-'sachə,rātəd\\ *adj* : having many double or triple bonds in a molecule

pome·gran·ate \\'päm,granət, 'pämə-\\ *n* : tropical reddish fruit with many seeds

pom·mel \\'pəməl, 'päm-\\ *n* **1** : knob on the hilt of a sword **2** : knob at the front of a saddle ~ \\'pəməl\\ *vb* -meled *or* -melled; -mel·ing *or* -mel·ling : pummel

pomp \\'pämp\\ *n* **1** : brilliant display **2** : ostentation

pomp·ous \\'pämpəs\\ *adj* : pretentiously dignified — **pom·pos·i·ty** \\päm'päsətē\\ *n* — **pomp·ous·ly** *adv*

pon·cho \\'pänchō\\ *n, pl* -chos : blanketlike cloak

pond \\'pänd\\ *n* : small body of water

pon·der \\'pändər\\ *vb* : consider

pon·der·ous \\'pändərəs\\ *adj* **1** : very heavy **2** : clumsy **3** : oppressively dull

pon·tiff \\'päntəf\\ *n* : pope — **pon·tif·i·cal** \\pän'tifikəl\\ *adj*

pon·tif·i·cate \\pän'tifə,kāt\\ *vb* -cat·ed; -cat·ing : talk pompously

pon·toon \\pän'tün\\ *n* : flat-bottomed boat or float

po·ny \\'pōnē\\ *n, pl* -nies : small horse

po·ny·tail \\-,tāl\\ *n* : hair arrangement like the tail of a pony

poo·dle \\'püd³l\\ *n* : dog with a curly coat

¹pool \\'pül\\ *n* **1** : small body of water **2** : puddle

²pool *n* **1** : amount contributed by participants in a joint venture **2** : game of pocket billiards ~ *vb* : combine in a common fund

poor \\'pu̇r, 'pōr\\ *adj* **1** : lacking material possessions **2** : less than adequate **3** : arousing pity **4** : unfavorable — **poor·ly** *adv*

¹pop \\'päp\\ *vb* -pp- **1** : move suddenly **2** : burst with or make a sharp sound **3** : protrude ~ *n* **1** : sharp explosive sound **2** : flavored soft drink

²pop *adj* : popular

♦ **pop·corn** \\'päp͵kȯrn\\ *n* : corn whose kernels burst open into a light mass when heated

pope \\'pōp\\ *n, often cap* : head of the Roman Catholic Church

pop·lar \\'päplər\\ *n* : slender quick=growing tree

pop·lin \\'päplən\\ *n* : strong plain=woven fabric with crosswise ribs

pop·over \\'päp͵ōvər\\ *n* : hollow muffin made from egg-rich batter

pop·py \\'päpē\\ *n, pl* **-pies** : herb with showy flowers

pop·u·lace \\'päpyələs\\ *n* **1** : common people **2** : population

pop·u·lar \\'päpyələr\\ *adj* **1** : relating to the general public **2** : widely accepted **3** : commonly liked — **pop·u·lar·i·ty** \\͵päpyə'larətē\\ *n* — **pop·u·lar·ize** \\'päpyələ͵rīz\\ *vb* — **pop·u·lar·ly** \\-lərlē\\ *adv*

pop·u·late \\'päpyə͵lāt\\ *vb* **-lat·ed**; **-lat·ing** : inhabit or occupy

pop·u·la·tion \\͵päpyə'lāshən\\ *n* : people or number of people in an area

pop·u·list \\'päpyəlist\\ *n* : advocate of the rights of the common people — **pop·u·lism** \\-͵lizəm\\ *n*

pop·u·lous \\'päpyələs\\ *adj* : densely populated — **pop·u·lous·ness** *n*

por·ce·lain \\'pȯrsələn\\ *n* : fine-grained ceramic ware

porch \\'pȯrch\\ *n* : covered entrance

por·cu·pine \\'pȯrkyə͵pīn\\ *n* : mammal with sharp quills

¹pore \\'pōr\\ *vb* **pored**; **por·ing** : read attentively

²pore *n* : tiny hole (as in the skin) — **pored** *adj*

pork \\'pōrk\\ *n* : pig meat

pork barrel *n* : government projects benefiting political patrons

por·nog·ra·phy \\pȯr'nägrəfē\\ *n* : depiction of erotic behavior intended to cause sexual excitement — **por·no·graph·ic** \\͵pȯrnə'grafik\\ *adj*

po·rous \\'pȯrəs\\ *adj* : permeable to fluids — **po·ros·i·ty** \\pə'räsətē\\ *n*

por·poise \\'pȯrpəs\\ *n* **1** : small whale with a blunt snout **2** : dolphin

por·ridge \\'pȯrij\\ *n* : soft boiled cereal

por·rin·ger \\'pȯrənjər\\ *n* : low one=handled metal bowl or cup

¹port \\'pōrt\\ *n* **1** : harbor **2** : city with a harbor

²port *n* **1** : inlet or outlet (as in an engine) for a fluid **2** : porthole

³port *n* : left side of a ship or airplane looking forward — **port** *adj*

⁴port *n* : sweet wine

por·ta·ble \\'pōrtəbəl\\ *adj* : capable of being carried — **portable** *n*

por·tage \\'pōrtij, pȯr'täzh\\ *n* : carrying of boats overland between navigable bodies of water or the route where this is done — **portage** *vb*

por·tal \\'pōrt²l\\ *n* : entrance

por·tend \\pȯr'tend\\ *vb* : give a warning of beforehand

por·tent \\'pȯr͵tent\\ *n* : something that foreshadows a coming event — **por·ten·tous** \\pȯr'tentəs\\ *adj*

por·ter \\'pōrtər\\ *n* : baggage carrier

por·ter·house \\-͵haús\\ *n* : choice cut of steak

port·fo·lio \\pōrt'fōlē͵ō\\ *n, pl* **-lios** **1** : portable case for papers **2** : office or function of a diplomat **3** : investor's securities

port·hole \\'pōrt͵hōl\\ *n* : window in the side of a ship or aircraft

por·ti·co \\'pōrti͵kō\\ *n, pl* **-coes** *or* **-cos** : colonnade forming a porch

por·tion \\'pōrshən\\ *n* : part or share of a whole ～ *vb* : divide into or allot portions

port·ly \\'pōrtlē\\ *adj* **-li·er**; **-est** : somewhat stout

por·trait \\'pōrtrət, -͵trāt\\ *n* : picture

of a person — **por·trait·ist** \-ist\ *n*
— **por·trai·ture** \'pōrtrə,chür\ *n*

por·tray \pōr'trā\ *vb* **1** : make a picture of **2** : describe in words **3** : play the role of — **por·tray·al** *n*

por·tu·la·ca \,pōrchə'lakə\ *n* : tropical herb with showy flowers

pose \'pōz\ *vb* **posed; pos·ing 1** : assume a posture or attitude **2** : propose **3** : pretend to be what one is not ~ *n* **1** : sustained posture **2** : pretense — **pos·er** *n*

posh \'päsh\ *adj* : elegant

po·si·tion \pə'zishən\ *n* **1** : stand taken on a question **2** : place or location **3** : status **4** : job — **position** *vb*

pos·i·tive \'päzətiv\ *adj* **1** : definite **2** : confident **3** : relating to or being an adjective or adverb form that denotes no increase **4** : greater than zero **5** : having a deficiency of electrons **6** : affirmative — **pos·i·tive·ly** *adv* — **pos·i·tive·ness** *n*

pos·se \'päsē\ *n* : emergency assistants of a sheriff

pos·sess \pə'zes\ *vb* **1** : have as property or as a quality **2** : control — **pos·ses·sion** \-'zeshən\ *n* — **pos·ses·sor** \-'zesər\ *n*

pos·ses·sive \pə'zesiv\ *adj* **1** : relating to a grammatical case denoting ownership **2** : jealous — **possessive** *n* — **pos·ses·sive·ness** *n*

pos·si·ble \'päsəbəl\ *adj* **1** : that can be done **2** : potential — **pos·si·bil·i·ty** \,päsə'bilətē\ *n* — **pos·si·bly** *adv*

pos·sum \'päsəm\ *n* : opossum

¹post \'pōst\ *n* : upright stake serving to support or mark ~ *vb* : put up or announce by a notice

²post *vb* **1** : mail **2** : inform

³post *n* **1** : sentry's station **2** : assigned task **3** : army camp ~ *vb* : station

post- *prefix* : after or subsequent to

postadolescent
postattack
postbaccalaureate
postbiblical
postcollege
postcolonial
postelection
postexercise
postflight
postgame
postgraduate
postgraduation
postharvest
posthospital
postimperial
postinaugural
postindustrial
postinoculation
postmarital
postmenopausal
postnatal
postnuptial
postproduction
postpuberty
postrecession
postretirement
postrevolutionary
postseason
postsecondary
postsurgical
posttreatment
posttrial
postvaccination
postwar

post·age \'pōstij\ *n* : fee for mail

post·al \'pōst°l\ *adj* : relating to the mail

♦ **post·card** *n* : card for mailing a message

post·date \,pōst'dāt\ *vb* : assign a date to that is later than the actual date of execution

post·er \'pōstər\ *n* : large usu. printed notice

pos·te·ri·or \pō'stirēər, pä-\ *adj* **1** : later **2** : situated behind ~ *n* : buttocks

pos·ter·i·ty \pä'sterətē\ *n* : all future generations

post·haste \'pōst'hāst\ *adv* : speedily

post·hu·mous \'päschəməs\ *adj* : occurring after one's death — **post·hu·mous·ly** *adv*

post·man \'pōstmən, -,man\ *n* : mail carrier

post·mark *n* : official mark on mail — **postmark** *vb*

post·mas·ter *n* : chief of a post office

post me·ri·di·em \'pōstmə'ridēəm, -ē,em\ *adj* : being after noon

JIM DAVIS 1-6-86

post·mor·tem \ˌpōst'mòrtəm\ adj : occurring or done after death ~ n 1 : medical examination of a corpse 2 : analysis after an event

post office n : agency or building for mail service

post·op·er·a·tive \ˌpōst'äpərətiv, -'äpəˌrāt-\ adj : following surgery

post·paid adv : with postage paid by the sender

post·par·tum \-'pärtəm\ adj : following childbirth — **postpartum** adv

post·pone \-'pōn\ vb -poned; -pon·ing : put off to a later time — **post·pone·ment** n

post·script \'pōst,skript\ n : added note

pos·tu·lant \'päschələnt\ n : candidate for a religious order

pos·tu·late \'päschəˌlāt\ vb -lat·ed; -lat·ing : assume as true ~ n : assumption

pos·ture \'päschər\ n : bearing of the body ~ vb -tured; -tur·ing : strike a pose

po·sy \'pōzē\ n, pl -sies : flower or bunch of flowers

pot \'pät\ n : rounded container ~ vb -tt- : place in a pot — **pot·ful** n

po·ta·ble \'pōtəbəl\ adj : drinkable

pot·ash \'pät,ash\ n : white chemical salt of potassium used esp. in agriculture

po·tas·si·um \pə'tasēəm\ n : silver-white metallic chemical element

po·ta·to \pə'tātō\ n, pl -toes : edible plant tuber

pot·bel·ly n : paunch — **pot·bel·lied** adj

po·tent \'pōt°nt\ adj : powerful or effective — **po·ten·cy** \-°nsē\ n

po·ten·tate \'pōt°n,tāt\ n : powerful ruler

po·ten·tial \pə'tenchəl\ adj : capable of becoming actual ~ n 1 : something that can become actu-

al 2 : degree of electrification with reference to a standard — **po·ten·ti·al·i·ty** \pə,tenchē'alətē\ n — **po·ten·tial·ly** adv

poth·er \'päthər\ n : fuss

pot·hole \'pät,hōl\ n : large hole in a road surface

po·tion \'pōshən\ n : liquid medicine or poison

pot·luck n : whatever food is available

pot·pour·ri \ˌpōpù'rē\ n 1 : mix of flowers, herbs, and spices used for scent 2 : miscellaneous collection

pot·shot n 1 : casual or easy shot 2 : random critical remark

pot·ter \'pätər\ n : pottery maker

pot·tery \'pätərē\ n, pl -ter·ies : objects (as dishes) made from clay

pouch \'pauch\ n 1 : small bag 2 : bodily sac

poul·tice \'pōltəs\ n : warm medicated dressing — **poultice** vb

poul·try \'pōltrē\ n : domestic fowl

pounce \'pauns\ vb pounced; pounc·ing : spring or swoop upon and seize

¹pound \'paund\ n 1 : unit of weight equal to 16 ounces 2 : monetary unit (as of the United Kingdom) — **pound·age** \-ij\ n

²pound n : shelter for stray animals

³pound vb 1 : crush by beating 2 : strike heavily 3 : drill 4 : move along heavily

pour \'pōr\ vb 1 : flow or supply esp. copiously 2 : rain hard

pout \'paut\ vb : look sullen — **pout** n

◆ **pov·er·ty** \'pävərtē\ n 1 : lack of money or possessions 2 : poor quality

pow·der \'paudər\ n : dry material of fine particles ~ vb : sprinkle or cover with powder — **pow·dery** adj

pow·er \'pauər\ n 1 : position of authority 2 : ability to act 3 : one that has power 4 : physical might 5 : force or energy used to do work ∼ *vb* : supply with power — **pow·er·ful** \-fəl\ *adj* — **pow·er·ful·ly** *adv* — **pow·er·less** *adj*

pow·er·house *n* : dynamic or energetic person

pow·wow \'pau̇ˌwau̇\ *n* : conference

pox \'päks\ *n, pl* **pox** *or* **pox·es** : disease marked by skin rash

prac·ti·ca·ble \'praktikəbəl\ *adj* : feasible — **prac·ti·ca·bil·i·ty** \ˌpraktikə'bilətē\ *n*

prac·ti·cal \'praktikəl\ *adj* 1 : relating to practice 2 : virtual 3 : capable of being put to use 4 : inclined to action as opposed to speculation — **prac·ti·cal·i·ty** \ˌprakti-'kalətē\ *n* — **prac·ti·cal·ly** \'praktiklē\ *adv*

prac·tice, **prac·tise** \'praktəs\ *vb* **-ticed** *or* **-tised; -tic·ing** *or* **-tis·ing** 1 : perform repeatedly to become proficient 2 : do or perform customarily 3 : be professionally engaged in ∼ *n* 1 : actual performance 2 : habit 3 : exercise for proficiency 4 : exercise of a profession

prac·ti·tio·ner \prak'tishənər\ *n* : one who practices a profession

prag·ma·tism \'pragmə,tizəm\ *n* : practical approach to problems — **prag·mat·ic** \prag'matik\ *adj* — **prag·mat·i·cal·ly** *adv*

prai·rie \'prerē\ *n* : broad grassy rolling tract of land

praise \'prāz\ *vb* **praised; prais·ing** 1 : express approval of 2 : glorify — **praise** *n* — **praise·wor·thy** *adj*

prance \'prans\ *vb* **pranced; pranc·ing** 1 : spring from the hind legs 2 : swagger — **prance** *n* — **pranc·er** *n*

prank \'praŋk\ *n* : playful or mischievous act — **prank·ster** \-stər\ *n*

prate \'prāt\ *vb* **prat·ed; prat·ing** : talk long and foolishly

prat·fall \'prat,fȯl\ *n* : fall on the buttocks

prat·tle \'pratᵊl\ *vb* **-tled; -tling** : babble — **prattle** *n*

prawn \'prȯn\ *n* : shrimplike crustacean

pray \'prā\ *vb* 1 : entreat 2 : ask earnestly for something 3 : address God or a god

prayer \'prer\ *n* 1 : earnest request 2 : an addressing of God or a god 3 : words used in praying — **prayer·ful** *adj* — **prayer·ful·ly** *adv*

praying mantis *n* : mantis

pre- *prefix* : before, prior to, or in advance

preadmission	preindustrial
preadolescence	preinterview
preadolescent	prejudge
preadult	prekindergar-
preanesthetic	ten
prearrange	prelaunch
prearrange-	prelife
ment	premarital
preassembled	premenopausal
preassign	premenstrual
prebattle	premix
prebiblical	premodern
prebreakfast	premodify
precalculus	premoisten
precancel	premold
precancellation	prenatal
preclear	prenotification
preclearance	prenotify
precollege	prenuptial
precolonial	preopening
precombustion	preoperational
precompute	preoperative
preconceive	preordain
preconception	prepackage
preconcert	prepay
precondition	preplan
preconstructed	preprocess
preconvention	preproduction
precook	preprofessional
precool	preprogram
precut	prepubertal
predawn	prepublication
predefine	prepunch
predeparture	prepurchase
predesignate	prerecorded
predetermine	preregister
predischarge	preregistration
predrill	prerehearsal
preelection	prerelease
preelectric	preretirement
preemployment	prerevolution-
preestablish	ary
preexist	prerinse
preexistence	presale
preexistent	preschool
prefight	preseason
preform	preselect
pregame	preset
preheat	preshrink
preinaugural	preshrunk

pre·soak pre·television
pre·sort pre·tournament
pre·stamp pre·treat
pre·sterilize pre·treatment
pre·strike pre·trial
pre·surgery pre·war
pre·sweeten pre·wash
pre·tape pre·wrap

preach \'prēch\ vb 1 : deliver a sermon 2 : advocate earnestly — **preach·er** n — **preach·ment** n

pre·am·ble \'prē,ambəl\ n : introduction

pre·can·cer·ous \,prē'kansərəs\ adj : likely to become cancerous

pre·car·i·ous \pri'karēəs\ adj : dangerously insecure — **pre·car·i·ous·ly** adv — **pre·car·i·ous·ness** n

pre·cau·tion \pri'kȯshən\ n : care taken beforehand — **pre·cau·tion·ary** \-shə,nerē\ adj

pre·cede \pri'sēd\ vb -ced·ed; -ced·ing : be, go, or come ahead of — **pre·ce·dence** \'presədəns, pri'sēd°ns\ n

prec·e·dent \'presədənt\ n : something said or done earlier that serves as an example

pre·cept \'prē,sept\ n : rule of action or conduct

pre·cinct \'prē,siŋkt\ n 1 : district of a city 2 pl : vicinity

pre·cious \'preshəs\ adj 1 : of great value 2 : greatly cherished 3 : affected

prec·i·pice \'presəpəs\ n : steep cliff

pre·cip·i·tate \pri'sipə,tāt\ vb -tat·ed; -tat·ing 1 : cause to happen quickly or abruptly 2 : cause to separate out of a liquid 3 : fall as rain, snow, or hail ~ n : solid matter precipitated from a liquid ~ \-'sipətət, -ə,tāt\ adj : unduly hasty — **pre·cip·i·tate·ly** adv — **pre·cip·i·tate·ness** n — **pre·cip·i·tous** \pri'sipətəs\ adj — **pre·cip·i·tous·ly** adv

pre·cip·i·ta·tion \pri,sipə'tāshən\ n 1 : rash haste 2 : rain, snow, or hail

pré·cis \prā'sē\ n, pl **pré·cis** \-'sēz\ : concise summary of essentials

pre·cise \pri'sīs\ adj 1 : definite 2 : highly accurate — **pre·cise·ly** adv — **pre·cise·ness** n

pre·ci·sion \pri'sizhən\ n : quality or state of being precise

pre·clude \pri'klüd\ vb -clud·ed; -clud·ing : make impossible

pre·co·cious \pri'kȯshəs\ adj : exceptionally advanced — **pre·co·cious·ly** adv — **pre·coc·i·ty** \pri'käsətē\ n

pre·cur·sor \pri'kərsər\ n : harbinger

pred·a·to·ry \'predə,tōrē\ adj : preying upon others — **pred·a·tor** \'predətər\ n

pre·de·ces·sor \'predə,sesər, 'prēd-\ n : a previous holder of a position

pre·des·tine \prē'destən\ vb : settle beforehand — **pre·des·ti·na·tion** \-,destə'nāshən\ n

pre·dic·a·ment \pri'dikəmənt\ n : difficult situation

pred·i·cate \'predikət\ n : part of a sentence that states something about the subject ~ \'predə,kāt\ vb -cat·ed; -cat·ing 1 : affirm 2 : establish — **pred·i·ca·tion** \,predə'kāshən\ n

pre·dict \pri'dikt\ vb : declare in advance — **pre·dict·abil·i·ty** \-,diktə'bilətē\ n — **pre·dict·able** \-'diktəbəl\ adj — **pre·dict·ably** \-blē\ adv — **pre·dic·tion** \-'dikshən\ n

pre·di·lec·tion \,pred°l'ekshən, ,prēd-\ n : established preference

pre·dis·pose \,prēdis'pōz\ vb : cause to be favorable or susceptible to something beforehand — **pre·dis·po·si·tion** \,prē,dispə'zishən\ n

pre·dom·i·nate \pri'dämə,nāt\ vb : be superior — **pre·dom·i·nance** \-nəns\ n — **pre·dom·i·nant** \-nənt\ adj — **pre·dom·i·nant·ly** adv

pre·em·i·nent \prē'emənənt\ adj : having highest rank — **pre·em·i·nence** \-nəns\ n — **pre·em·i·nent·ly** adv

♦ **pre·empt** \prē'empt\ vb 1 : seize for oneself 2 : take the place of — **pre·emp·tion** \-'empshən\ n — **pre·emp·tive** \-'emptiv\ adj

preen \'prēn\ vb : dress or smooth up (as feathers)

pre·fab·ri·cat·ed \'prē'fabrə,kātəd\ adj : manufactured for rapid assembly elsewhere — **pre·fab·ri·ca·tion** \,prē,fabri'kāshən\ n

pref·ace \'prefəs\ n : introductory comments ~ vb -aced; -ac·ing : introduce with a preface — **pref·a·to·ry** \'prefe,tōrē\ adj

pre·fect \'prē,fekt\ n : chief officer or judge — **pre·fec·ture** \-,fekchər\ n

pre·fer \pri'fər\ *vb* **-rr- 1** : like better **2** : bring (as a charge) against a person — **pref·er·a·ble** \'prefərəbəl\ *adj* — **pref·er·a·bly** *adv* — **pref·er·ence** \-ərəns\ *n* — **pref·er·en·tial** \,prefə'renchəl\ *adj*

pre·fer·ment \pri'fərmənt\ *n* : promotion

pre·fig·ure \prē'figyər\ *vb* : foreshadow

¹**pre·fix** \'prē,fiks, prē'fiks\ *vb* : place before

²**pre·fix** \'prē,fiks\ *n* : affix at the beginning of a word

preg·nant \'pregnənt\ *adj* **1** : containing unborn young **2** : meaningful — **preg·nan·cy** \-nənsē\ *n*

pre·hen·sile \prē'hensəl, -,sīl\ *adj* : adapted for grasping

pre·his·tor·ic \,prēhis'tórik\, **pre·his·tor·i·cal** \-ikəl\ *adj* : relating to the period before written history

prej·u·dice \'prejədəs\ *n* **1** : damage esp. to one's rights **2** : unreasonable attitude for or against something ~ *vb* **-diced; -dic·ing 1** : damage **2** : cause to have prejudice — **prej·u·di·cial** \,prejə'dishəl\ *adj*

prel·ate \'prelət\ *n* : clergy member of high rank — **prel·a·cy** \-əsē\ *n*

pre·lim·i·nary \pri'limə,nerē\ *n, pl* **-nar·ies** : something that precedes or introduces — **preliminary** *adj*

pre·lude \'prel,üd, -,yüd; 'prā,lüd\ *n* : introductory performance, event, or musical piece

pre·ma·ture \,prēmə'túər, -'tyùr, -'chùr\ *adj* : coming before the usual or proper time — **pre·ma·ture·ly** *adv*

pre·med·i·tate \pri'medə,tāt\ *vb* : plan beforehand — **pre·med·i·ta·tion** \-,medə'tāshən\ *n*

pre·mier \pri'mir, -'myir; 'prēmēər\ *adj* : first in rank or importance ~ *n* : prime minister — **pre·mier·ship** *n*

pre·miere \pri'myer, -'mir\ *n* : 1st performance ~ *vb* **-miered; -mier·ing** : give a 1st performance of

prem·ise \'preməs\ *n* **1** : statement made or implied as a basis of argument **2** *pl* : piece of land with the structures on it

pre·mi·um \'prēmēəm\ *n* **1** : bonus **2** : sum over the stated value **3** : sum paid for insurance **4** : high value

pre·mo·ni·tion \,prēmə'nishən, ,premə-\ *n* : feeling that something is about to happen — **pre·mon·i·to·ry** \pri'mänə,tōrē\ *adj*

pre·oc·cu·pied \prē'äkyə,pīd\ *adj* : lost in thought

pre·oc·cu·py \-,pī\ *vb* : occupy the attention of — **pre·oc·cu·pa·tion** \prē,äkyə'pāshən\ *n*

pre·pare \pri'par\ *vb* **-pared; -par·ing 1** : make or get ready often beforehand **2** : put together or compound — **prep·a·ra·tion** \,prepə-'rāshən\ *n* — **pre·pa·ra·to·ry** \pri-'parə,tōrē\ *adj* — **pre·pared·ness** \-'parədnəs\ *n*

pre·pon·der·ant \pri'pändərənt\ *adj* : having great weight, power, importance, or numbers — **pre·pon·der·ance** \-rəns\ *n* — **pre·pon·der·ant·ly** *adv*

prep·o·si·tion \,prepə'zishən\ *n* : word that combines with a noun or pronoun to form a phrase — **prep·o·si·tion·al** \-'zishənəl\ *adj*

pre·pos·sess·ing \,prēpə'zesiŋ\ *adj* : tending to create a favorable impression

pre·pos·ter·ous \pri'pästərəs\ *adj* : absurd

pre·req·ui·site \prē'rekwəzət\ *n* : something required beforehand — **prerequisite** *adj*

pre·rog·a·tive \pri'rägətiv\ *n* : special right or power

pre·sage \'presij, pri'sāj\ *vb* **-saged; -sag·ing 1** : give a warning of **2** : predict — **pres·age** \'presij\ *n*

pres·by·ter \'prezbətər\ *n* : priest or minister

pre·science \'prēshəns, 'presh-\ *n* : foreknowledge of events — **pre·scient** \-ənt\ *adj*

pre·scribe \pri'skrīb\ *vb* **-scribed; -scrib·ing 1** : lay down as a guide **2** : direct the use of as a remedy

pre·scrip·tion \pri'skripshən\ *n* : written direction for the preparation and use of a medicine or the medicine prescribed

pres·ence \'prez°ns\ *n* **1** : fact or condition of being present **2** : appearance or bearing

¹pres·ent \'prez°nt\ *n* : gift

²pre·sent \pri'zent\ *vb* **1** : introduce **2** : bring before the public **3** : make a gift to or of **4** : bring before a court for inquiry — **pre·sent·able** *adj* — **pre·sen·ta·tion** \ˌprē,zen-'tāshən, ˌprez°n-\ *n* — **pre·sent·ment** \pri'zentmənt\ *n*

³pres·ent \'prez°nt\ *adj* : now existing, in progress, or attending ~ *n* : present time

pre·sen·ti·ment \pri'zentəmənt\ *n* : premonition

pres·ent·ly \'prez°ntlē\ *adv* **1** : soon **2** : now

present participle *n* : participle that typically expresses present action

pre·serve \pri'zərv\ *vb* **-served; -serv·ing 1** : keep safe from danger or spoilage **2** : maintain ~ *n* **1** : preserved fruit — often in pl. **2** : area for protection of natural resources — **pres·er·va·tion** \ˌprezər'vāshən\ *n* — **pre·ser·va·tive** \pri'zərvətiv\ *adj or n* — **pre·serv·er** \-'zərvər\ *n*

pre·side \pri'zīd\ *vb* **-sid·ed; -sid·ing 1** : act as chairman **2** : exercise control

pres·i·dent \'prezədənt\ *n* **1** : one chosen to preside **2** : chief official (as of a company or nation) — **pres·i·den·cy** \-ənsē\ *n* — **pres·i·den·tial** \ˌprezə'denchəl\ *adj*

press \'pres\ *n* **1** : crowded condition **2** : machine or device for exerting pressure and esp. for printing **3** : pressure **4** : printing or publishing establishment **5** : news media and esp. newspapers ~ *vb* **1** : lie against and exert pressure on **2** : smooth with an iron or squeeze with something heavy **3** : urge **4** : crowd **5** : force one's way — **press·er** *n*

press·ing *adj* : urgent

pres·sure \'preshər\ *n* **1** : burden of distress or urgent business **2** : direct application of force — **pressure** *vb* — **pres·sur·i·za·tion** \ˌpreshərə'zāshən\ *n* — **pres·sur·ize** \-ˌīz\ *vb*

pres·ti·dig·i·ta·tion \ˌprestəˌdijə-'tāshən\ *n* : sleight of hand

pres·tige \pres'tēzh, -'tēj\ *n* : estimation in the eyes of people — **pres·ti·gious** \-'tijəs\ *adj*

pres·to \'prestō\ *adv or adj* : quickly

pre·sume \pri'züm\ *vb* **-sumed; -sum·ing 1** : assume authority without right to do so **2** : take for granted — **pre·sum·able** \-'züməbəl\ *adj* — **pre·sum·ably** \-blē\ *adv*

pre·sump·tion \pri'zəmpshən\ *n* **1** : presumptuous attitude or conduct **2** : belief supported by probability — **pre·sump·tive** \-tiv\ *adj*

pre·sump·tu·ous \pri'zəmpchəwəs\ *adj* : too bold or forward — **pre·sump·tu·ous·ly** *adv*

pre·sup·pose \ˌprēsə'pōz\ *vb* : take for granted — **pre·sup·po·si·tion** \ˌprēˌsəpə'zishən\ *n*

pre·tend \pri'tend\ *vb* **1** : act as if something is real or true when it is not **2** : act in a way that is false : lay claim — **pre·tend·er** *n*

pre·tense, pre·tence \'prē,tens, pri-'tens\ *n* **1** : insincere effort **2** : deception — **pre·ten·sion** \pri-'tenchən\ *n*

pre·ten·tious \pri'tenchəs\ *adj* : overly showy or self-important — **pre·ten·tious·ly** *adv* — **pre·ten·tious·ness** *n*

pre·ter·nat·u·ral \ˌprētər'nachərəl\ *adj* **1** : exceeding what is natural **2** : inexplicable by ordinary means — **pre·ter·nat·u·ral·ly** *adv*

pre·text \'prē,tekst\ *n* : falsely stated purpose

pret·ty \'pritē, 'pu̇rt-\ *adj* **-ti·er; -est** : pleasing by delicacy or attractiveness ~ *adv* : in some degree ~ *vb* **-tied; -ty·ing** : make pretty — **pret·ti·ly** \'prit°lē\ *adv* — **pret·ti·ness** *n*

pret·zel \'pretsəl\ *n* : twisted thin bread that is glazed and salted

pre·vail \pri'vāl\ *vb* 1 : triumph 2 : urge successfully 3 : be frequent, widespread, or dominant

prev·a·lent \'prevələnt\ *adj* : widespread — **prev·a·lence** \-ləns\ *n*

pre·var·i·cate \pri'varə₁kāt\ *vb* -cat·ed; -cat·ing : deviate from the truth — **pre·var·i·ca·tion** \-₁varə-'kāshən\ *n* — **pre·var·i·ca·tor** \-'varə₁kātər\ *n*

pre·vent \pri'vent\ *vb* : keep from happening or acting — **pre·vent·able** *adj* — **pre·ven·tion** \-'venchən\ *n* — **pre·ven·tive** \-'ventiv\ *adj or n* — **pre·ven·ta·tive** \-'ventətiv\ *adj or n*

pre·view \'prē₁vyü\ *vb* : view or show beforehand — **preview** *n*

pre·vi·ous \'prēvēəs\ *adj* : having gone, happened, or existed before — **pre·vi·ous·ly** *adv*

prey \'prā\ *n, pl* **preys** 1 : animal taken for food by another 2 : victim ~ *vb* 1 : seize and devour animals as prey 2 : have a harmful effect on

price \'prīs\ *n* : cost ~ *vb* **priced; pric·ing** : set a price on

price·less \-ləs\ *adj* : too precious to have a price

pric·ey \'prīsē\ *adj* **pric·i·er; -est** : expensive

prick \'prik\ *n* 1 : tear or small wound made by a point 2 : something sharp or pointed ~ *vb* : pierce slightly with a sharp point — **prick·er** *n*

prick·le \'prikəl\ *n* 1 : small sharp spine or thorn 2 : slight stinging pain ~ *vb* **-led; -ling** : tingle — **prick·ly** \'priklē\ *adj*

pride \'prīd\ *n* : quality or state of being proud ~ *vb* **prid·ed; prid·ing** : indulge in pride — **pride·ful** *adj*

priest \'prēst\ *n* : person having authority to perform the sacred rites of a religion — **priest·hood** *n* — **priest·li·ness** \-lēnəs\ *n* — **priest·ly** *adj*

priest·ess \'prēstəs\ *n* : woman who is a priest

prig \'prig\ *n* : one who irritates by rigid or pointed observance of proprieties — **prig·gish** \-ish\ *adj* — **prig·gish·ly** *adv*

prim \'prim\ *adj* **-mm-** : stiffly formal and proper — **prim·ly** *adv* — **prim·ness** *n*

pri·mal \'prīməl\ *adj* 1 : original or primitive 2 : most important

pri·ma·ry \'prī₁merē, 'prīmərē\ *adj* : first in order of time, rank, or importance ~ *n, pl* **-ries** : preliminary election — **pri·mar·i·ly** \prī-'merəlē\ *adv*

primary school *n* : elementary school

pri·mate *n* 1 \'prī₁māt, -mət\ : highest-ranking bishop 2 \-₁māt\ : mammal of the group that includes humans and monkeys

prime \'prīm\ *n* : earliest or best part or period ~ *adj* : standing first (as in significance or quality) ~ *vb* **primed; prim·ing** 1 : fill or load 2 : lay a preparatory coating on

prime minister *n* : chief executive of a parliamentary government

¹**prim·er** \'primər\ *n* : small introductory book

²**prim·er** \'prīmər\ *n* 1 : device for igniting an explosive 2 : material for priming a surface

pri·me·val \prī'mēvəl\ *adj* : relating to the earliest ages

prim·i·tive \'primətiv\ *adj* 1 : relating to or characteristic of an early stage of development 2 : of or relating to a tribal people or culture ~ *n* : one that is primitive — **prim·i·tive·ly** *adv* — **prim·i·tive·ness** *n*

pri·mor·di·al \prī'mòrdēəl\ *adj* : primeval

primp \'primp\ *vb* : dress or groom in a finicky manner

prim·rose \'prim₁rōz\ *n* : low herb with clusters of showy flowers

prince \'prins\ *n* 1 : ruler 2 : son of a king or queen — **prince·ly** *adj*

prin·cess \'prinsəs, -₁ses\ *n* 1 : daughter of a king or queen 2 : wife of a prince

prin·ci·pal \'prinsəpəl\ *adj* : most important ~ *n* 1 : leading person 2 : head of a school 3 : sum lent at interest — **prin·ci·pal·ly** *adv*

prin·ci·pal·i·ty \₁prinsə'palətē\ *n, pl* **-ties** : territory of a prince

prin·ci·ple \'prinsəpəl\ *n* 1 : general or fundamental law 2 : rule or code of conduct or devotion to such a code

print \'print\ *n* 1 : mark or impres-

sion made by pressure **2** : printed
state or form **3** : printed matter **4**
: copy made by printing **5** : cloth
with a figure stamped on it — *vb* **1**
: produce impressions of (as from
type) **2** : write in letters like those
of printer's type — **print·able** *adj*
— **print·er** *n*

print·ing \'printiŋ\ *n* : art or business of a printer

print·out \'print,aut\ *n* : printed
output produced by a computer
— **print out** *vb*

¹**pri·or** \'prīər\ *n* : head of a religious
house — **pri·o·ry** \'prīərē\ *n*

²**prior** *adj* : coming before in time,
order, or importance — **pri·or·**
i·ty \prī'ȯrətē\ *n*

pri·or·ess \'prīərəs\ *n* : nun who is
head of a religious house

prism \'prizəm\ *n* : transparent
3-sided object that separates light
into colors — **pris·mat·ic** \priz-
'matik\ *adj*

pris·on \'priz°n\ *n* : place where
criminals are confined

♦ **pris·on·er** \'priz°nər\ *n* : person
on trial or in prison

pris·sy \'prisē\ *adj* **-si·er; -est** : overly prim — **pris·si·ness** *n*

pris·tine \'pris,tēn, pris'-\ *adj* : pure

pri·va·cy \'prīvəsē\ *n, pl* **-cies** : quality or state of being apart from
others

pri·vate \'prīvət\ *adj* **1** : belonging
to a particular individual or group
2 : carried on independently **3**
: withdrawn from company or observation ~ *n* : enlisted person of
the lowest rank in the marine
corps or of one of the two lowest
ranks in the army — **pri·vate·ly**
adv

pri·va·teer \,prīvə'tir\ *n* : private
ship armed to attack enemy ships
and commerce

private first class *n* : enlisted person

ranking next below a corporal in
the army and next below a lance
corporal in the marine corps

pri·va·tion \prī'vāshən\ *n* : lack of
what is needed for existence

priv·i·lege \'privəlij\ *n* : right granted as an advantage or favor —
priv·i·leged *adj*

privy \'privē\ *adj* **1** : private or secret **2** : having access to private or
secret information ~ *n pl* **priv·**
ies : outdoor toilet — **priv·i·ly**
\'privəlē\ *adv*

¹**prize** \'prīz\ *n* **1** : something offered
or striven for in competition or in
contests of chance **2** : something
very desirable — **prize** *adj* —
prize·win·ner *n* — **prize·win·ning**
adj

²**prize** *vb* **prized; priz·ing** : value
highly

³**prize** *vb* **prized; priz·ing** : pry

prize·fight *n* : professional boxing
match — **prize·fight·er** *n* —
prize·fight·ing *n*

¹**pro** \'prō\ *n* : favorable argument or
person ~ *adv* : in favor

²**pro** *n or adj* : professional

prob·a·ble \'präbəbəl\ *adj* : seeming
true or real or to have a good
chance of happening — **prob·a·**
bil·i·ty \,präbə'bilətē\ *n* — **prob·**
a·bly \'präbəblē\ *adv*

pro·bate \'prō,bāt\ *n* : judicial determination of the validity of a
will ~ *vb* **-bat·ed; -bat·ing** : establish by probate

pro·ba·tion \prō'bāshən\ *n* **1** : period of testing and trial **2** : freedom
for a convict during good behavior under supervision — **pro·ba·**
tion·ary \-shə,nerē\ *adj* — **pro·**
ba·tion·er *n*

probe \'prōb\ *n* **1** : slender instrument for examining a cavity **2** : investigation ~ *vb* **probed; prob-**

ing 1 : examine with a probe 2 : investigate

pro·bi·ty \'prōbətē\ n : honest behavior

◆ **prob·lem** \'präbləm\ n 1 : question to be solved 2 : source of perplexity or vexation — **problem** adj — **prob·lem·at·ic** \ˌpräblə'matik\ adj — **prob·lem·at·i·cal** \-ikəl\ adj

pro·bos·cis \prə'bäsəs\ n, pl -cis·es also -ci·des \-ə‚dēz\ : long flexible snout

pro·ce·dure \prə'sējər\ n 1 : way of doing something 2 : series of steps in regular order — **pro·ce·dur·al** \-'sējərəl\ adj

pro·ceed \prō'sēd\ vb 1 : come forth 2 : go on in an orderly way 3 : begin and carry on an action 4 : advance

pro·ceed·ing n 1 : procedure 2 pl : something said or done or its official record

pro·ceeds \'prō‚sēdz\ n pl : total money taken in

pro·cess \'präs‚es, 'prōs-\ n, pl -cess·es \-‚esəz, -əsəz, -ə‚sēz\ 1 : something going on 2 : natural phenomenon marked by gradual changes 3 : series of actions or operations directed toward a result 4 : summons 5 : projecting part ~ vb : subject to a process — **pro·ces·sor** \-ər\ n

pro·ces·sion \prə'seshən\ n : group moving along in an orderly way

pro·ces·sion·al \-'seshənəl\ n : music for a procession

pro·claim \prō'klām\ vb : announce publicly or with conviction — **proc·la·ma·tion** \ˌpräklə'māshən\ n

pro·cliv·i·ty \prō'klivətē\ n, pl -ties : inclination

pro·cras·ti·nate \prə'krastə‚nāt\ vb -nat·ed; -nat·ing : put something

off until later — **pro·cras·ti·na·tion** \-ˌkrastə'nāshən\ n — **pro·cras·ti·na·tor** \-'krastə‚nātər\ n

pro·cre·ate \'prōkrē‚āt\ vb -at·ed; -at·ing : produce offspring — **pro·cre·ation** \ˌprōkrē'āshən\ n — **pro·cre·ative** \'prōkrē‚ātiv\ adj — **pro·cre·ator** \-‚ātər\ n

proc·tor \'präktər\ n : supervisor of students (as at an examination) — **proctor** vb

pro·cure \prə'kyùr\ vb -cured; -cur·ing : get possession of — **pro·cur·able** \-'kyùrəbəl\ adj — **pro·cure·ment** n — **pro·cur·er** n

prod \'präd\ vb -dd- : push with or as if with a pointed instrument — **prod** n

prod·i·gal \'prädigəl\ adj : recklessly extravagant or wasteful — **prodigal** n — **prod·i·gal·i·ty** \ˌprädə'galətē\ n

pro·di·gious \prə'dijəs\ adj : extraordinary in size or degree — **pro·di·gious·ly** adv

prod·i·gy \'prädəjē\ n, pl -gies : extraordinary person or thing

pro·duce \prə'düs, -'dyüs\ vb -duced; -duc·ing 1 : present to view 2 : give birth to 3 : bring into existence ~ \'präd‚üs, 'prōd-, -‚yüs\ n 1 : product 2 : agricultural products — **pro·duc·er** \prə'düsər, -'dyü-\ n

prod·uct \'präd‚əkt\ n 1 : number resulting from multiplication 2 : something produced

pro·duc·tion \prə'dəkshən\ n : act, process, or result of producing — **pro·duc·tive** \-'dəktiv\ adj — **pro·duc·tive·ness** n — **pro·duc·tiv·i·ty** \ˌprō‚dək'tivətē, ‚prä-\ n

pro·fane \prō'fān\ vb -faned; -fan·ing : treat with irreverence ~ adj 1 : not concerned with religion 2 : serving to debase what is holy —

THAT'S THE LAST TIME I HAND OUT PROGRAMS.

pro·fane·ly adv — pro·fane·ness n — pro·fan·i·ty \prō'fanətē\ n

pro·fess \prə'fes\ vb 1 : declare openly 2 : confess one's faith in — pro·fessed·ly \-ədlē\ adv

pro·fes·sion \prə'feshən\ n 1 : open declaration of belief 2 : occupation requiring specialized knowledge and academic training

pro·fes·sion·al \prə'feshənəl\ adj 1 : of, relating to, or engaged in a profession 2 : playing sport for pay — professional n — pro·fes·sion·al·ism n — pro·fes·sion·al·ize vb — pro·fes·sion·al·ly adv

pro·fes·sor \prə'fesər\ n : university or college teacher — pro·fes·so·ri·al \prōfə'sōrēəl, präfə-\ adj — pro·fes·sor·ship n

prof·fer \'präfər\ vb -fered; -fer·ing : offer — proffer n

pro·fi·cient \prə'fishənt\ adj : very good at something — pro·fi·cien·cy \-ənsē\ n — proficient n — pro·fi·cient·ly adv

pro·file \'prō,fīl\ n : picture in outline — profile vb

prof·it \'präfət\ n 1 : valuable return 2 : excess of the selling price of goods over cost ~ vb : gain a profit — prof·it·able \'präfətəbəl\ adj — prof·it·ably adv — prof·it·less adj

prof·i·teer \,präfə'tir\ n : one who makes an unreasonable profit — profiteer vb

prof·li·gate \'präfligət, -lə,gāt\ adj 1 : shamelessly immoral 2 : wildly extravagant — prof·li·ga·cy \-gəsē\ n — profligate n — prof·li·gate·ly adv

pro·found \prə'faùnd\ adj 1 : marked by intellectual depth or insight 2 : deeply felt — pro·found·ly adv — pro·fun·di·ty \-'fəndətē\ n

pro·fuse \prə'fyüs\ adj : pouring

forth liberally — pro·fuse·ly adv — pro·fu·sion \-'fyüzhən\ n

pro·gen·i·tor \prō'jenətər\ n : direct ancestor

prog·e·ny \'präjənē\ n, pl -nies : offspring

pro·ges·ter·one \prō'jestə,rōn\ n : female hormone

prog·no·sis \präg'nōsəs\ n, pl -no·ses \-,sēz\ : prospect of recovery from disease

prog·nos·ti·cate \präg'nästə,kāt\ vb -cat·ed; -cat·ing : predict from signs or symptoms — prog·nos·ti·ca·tion \-,nästə'kāshən\ n — prog·nos·ti·ca·tor \-'nästə,kātər\ n

◆ pro·gram \'prō,gram, -grəm\ n 1 : outline of the order to be pursued or the subjects included (as in a performance) 2 : plan of procedure 3 : coded instructions for a computer ~ vb -grammed or -gramed; -gram·ming or -gram·ing 1 : enter in a program 2 : provide a computer with a program — pro·gram·ma·bil·i·ty \,prō,gramə'bilətē\ n — pro·gram·ma·ble \'prō,gramələl\ adj — pro·gram·mer \'prō,gramər\ n

prog·ress \'prägrəs, -,res\ n : movement forward or to a better condition ~ \prə'gres\ vb 1 : move forward 2 : improve — pro·gres·sive \-'gresiv\ adj — pro·gres·sive·ly adv

pro·gres·sion \prə'greshən\ n 1 : act of progressing 2 : continuous connected series

pro·hib·it \prō'hibət\ vb : prevent by authority

pro·hi·bi·tion \,prōə'bishən\ n 1 : act of prohibiting 2 : legal restriction on sale or manufacture of alcoholic beverages — pro·hi·bi·tion·ist \-'bishənist\ n — pro·hib·i·tive \prō'hibətiv\ adj — prohib·i·tive·ly *adv* — **pro·hib·i·to·ry** \-'hibə,tōrē\ *adj*

proj·ect \'präj,ekt, -ikt\ *n* : planned undertaking ~ \prə'jekt\ *vb* 1 : design or plan 2 : protrude 3 : throw forward — **pro·jec·tion** \-'jekshən\ *n*

pro·jec·tile \prə'jekt°l\ *n* : missile hurled by external force

pro·jec·tor \-'jektər\ *n* : device for projecting pictures on a screen

pro·le·tar·i·an \,prōlə'terēən\ *n* : member of the proletariat — **proletarian** *adj*

pro·le·tar·i·at \-ēət\ *n* : laboring class

pro·lif·er·ate \prə'lifə,rāt\ *vb* **-at·ed; -at·ing** : grow or increase in number rapidly — **pro·lif·er·a·tion** \-,lifə'rāshən\ *n*

pro·lif·ic \prə'lifik\ *adj* : producing abundantly — **pro·lif·i·cal·ly** *adv*

pro·logue \'prō,lóg, -,läg\ *n* : preface

pro·long \prə'lóŋ\ *vb* : lengthen in time or extent — **pro·lon·ga·tion** \,prō,lóŋ'gāshən\ *n*

prom \'präm\ *n* : formal school dance

prom·e·nade \,prämə'nād, -'näd\ *n* 1 : leisurely walk 2 : place for strolling — **promenade** *vb*

prom·i·nence \'prämənəns\ *n* 1 : quality, state, or fact of being readily noticeable or distinguished 2 : something that stands out — **prom·i·nent** \-nənt\ *adj* — **prom·i·nent·ly** *adv*

pro·mis·cu·ous \prə'miskyəwəs\ *adj* : having a number of sexual partners — **prom·is·cu·ity** \,prämis'kyüətē, ,prō,mis-\ — **pro·mis·cu·ous·ly** *adv* — **pro·mis·cu·ous·ness** *n*

prom·ise \'präməs\ *n* 1 : statement that one will do or not do something 2 : basis for expectation — **promise** *vb* — **prom·is·so·ry** \-ə-,sōrē\ *adj*

prom·is·ing \'präməsiŋ\ *adj* : likely to succeed — **prom·is·ing·ly** *adv*

prom·on·to·ry \'prämən,tōrē\ *n, pl* **-ries** : point of land jutting into the sea

pro·mote \prə'mōt\ *vb* **-mot·ed; -mot·ing** 1 : advance in rank 2 : contribute to the growth, development, or prosperity of — **pro·mot·er** *n* — **pro·mo·tion**

\-'mōshən\ *n* — **pro·mo·tion·al** \-'mōshənəl\ *adj*

[1]**prompt** \'prämpt\ *vb* 1 : incite 2 : give a cue to (an actor or singer) — **prompt·er** *n*

[2]**prompt** *adj* : ready and quick — **prompt·ly** *adv* — **prompt·ness** *n*

prone \'prōn\ *adj* 1 : having a tendency 2 : lying face downward — **prone·ness** \'prōnnəs\ *n*

prong \'próŋ\ *n* : sharp point of a fork — **pronged** \'próŋd\ *adj*

pro·noun \'prō,naùn\ *n* : word used as a substitute for a noun

pro·nounce \prə'naùns\ *vb* **-nounced; -nounc·ing** 1 : utter officially or as an opinion 2 : say or speak esp. correctly — **pro·nounce·able** *adj* — **pro·nounce·ment** *n* — **pro·nun·ci·a·tion** \-,nənsē'āshən\ *n*

pro·nounced \-'naùnst\ *adj* : decided

[1]**proof** \'prüf\ *n* 1 : evidence of a truth or fact 2 : trial impression or print

[2]**proof** *adj* : designed for or successful in resisting or repelling

proof·read *vb* : read and mark corrections in — **proof·read·er** *n*

prop \'präp\ *vb* **-pp-** 1 : support 2 : sustain — **prop** *n*

pro·pa·gan·da \,präpə'gandə, ,prōpə-\ *n* : the spreading of ideas or information to further or damage a cause — **pro·pa·gan·dist** \-dist\ *n* — **pro·pa·gan·dize** \-,dīz\ *vb*

prop·a·gate \'präpə,gāt\ *vb* **-gat·ed; -gat·ing** 1 : reproduce biologically 2 : cause to spread — **prop·a·ga·tion** \,präpə'gāshən\ *n*

pro·pane \'prō,pān\ *n* : heavy flammable gaseous fuel

pro·pel \prə'pel\ *vb* **-ll-** : drive forward — **pro·pel·lant, pro·pel·lent** *n or adj*

pro·pel·ler \prə'pelər\ *n* : hub with revolving blades that propels a craft

pro·pen·si·ty \prə'pensətē\ *n, pl* **-ties** : particular interest or inclination

prop·er \'präpər\ *adj* 1 : suitable or right 2 : limited to a specified thing 3 : correct 4 : strictly adhering to standards of social manners, dignity, or good taste — **prop·er·ly** *adv*

prop·er·ty \'präpərtē\ *n, pl* **-ties 1**
: quality peculiar to an individual
2 : something owned **3** : piece of
real estate **4** : ownership

proph·e·cy \'präfəsē\ *n, pl* **-cies**
: prediction

proph·e·sy \-ₙsī\ *vb* **-sied; -sy·ing**
: predict — **proph·e·si·er** \-ₙsīər\
n

proph·et \'präfət\ *n* : one who utters
revelations or predicts events —
proph·et·ess \-əs\ *n* — **pro·phet·ic** \prə'fetik\, **pro·phet·i·cal**
\-ikəl\ *adj* — **pro·phet·i·cal·ly** *adv*

pro·pin·qui·ty \prə'piŋkwətē\ *n*
: nearness

pro·pi·ti·ate \prō'pishē₋ₐt\ *vb* **-at·ed; -at·ing** : gain or regain the favor of — **pro·pi·ti·a·tion** \-ₙpishē-
'āshən\ *n* — **pro·pi·ti·a·to·ry**
\-'pishēə₋tōrē\ *adj*

pro·pi·tious \prə'pishəs\ *adj* : favorable

pro·po·nent \prə'pōnənt\ *n* : one
who argues in favor of something

pro·por·tion \prə'pōrshən\ *n* **1** : relation of one part to another or to
the whole with respect to magnitude, quantity, or degree **2** : sym-
metry **3** : share ～ *vb* : adjust in
size in relation to others — **pro·por·tion·al** \-shənəl\ *adj* — **pro·por·tion·al·ly** *adv* — **pro·por·tion·ate** \-shənət\ *adj* — **pro·por·tion·ate·ly** *adv*

pro·pose \prə'pōz\ *vb* **-posed; -pos·ing 1** : plan or intend **2** : make an
offer of marriage **3** : present for
consideration — **pro·pos·al**
\-'pōzəl\ *n*

prop·o·si·tion \ₙpräpə'zishən\ *n*
: something proposed ～ *vb* : suggest sexual intercourse to

pro·pound \prə'paůnd\ *vb* : set
forth for consideration

pro·pri·etor \prə'prīətər\ *n* : owner
— **pro·pri·etary** \prə'prīə₋terē\

adj — **pro·pri·etor·ship** *n* — **pro·pri·etress** \-'prīətrəs\ *n*

pro·pri·ety \prə'prīətē\ *n, pl* **-eties**
: standard of acceptability in so-
cial conduct

pro·pul·sion \prə'pəlshən\ *n* **1** : action of propelling **2** : driving power — **pro·pul·sive** \-siv\ *adj*

pro·sa·ic \prō'zāik\ *adj* : dull

pro·scribe \prō'skrīb\ *vb* **-scribed; -scrib·ing** : prohibit — **pro·scrip·tion** \-'skripshən\ *n*

prose \'prōz\ *n* : ordinary language

pros·e·cute \'präsi₋kyūt\ *vb* **-cut·ed; -cut·ing 1** : follow to the end **2**
: seek legal punishment of —
pros·e·cu·tion \ₙpräsi'kyūshən\ *n*
— **pros·e·cu·tor** \'präsi₋kyūtər\ *n*

pros·e·lyte \'präsə₋līt\ *n* : new convert — **pros·e·ly·tize** \'präsələ-
₋tīz\ *vb*

◆ **pros·pect** \'präs₋pekt\ *n* **1** : extensive view **2** : something awaited **3**
: potential buyer ～ *vb* : look for
mineral deposits — **pro·spec·tive**
\prə'spektiv, 'präs₋pek-\ *adj* —
pro·spec·tive·ly *adv* — **pros·pec·tor** \-₋pektər, -'pek-\ *n*

pro·spec·tus \prə'spektəs\ *n* : introductory description of an enterprise

pros·per \'präspər\ *vb* : thrive or
succeed — **pros·per·ous** \-pərəs\
adj

pros·per·i·ty \präs'perətē\ *n* : economic well-being

pros·tate \'präs₋tāt\ *n* : glandular
body about the base of the male
urethra — **prostate** *adj*

pros·the·sis \präs'thēsəs, 'prästhə-\
n, pl **-the·ses** \-₋sēz\ : artificial replacement for a body part — **pros·thet·ic** \präs'thetik\ *adj*

pros·ti·tute \'prästə₋tüt, -₋tyüt\ *vb*
-tut·ed; -tut·ing 1 : offer sexual activity for money **2** : put to corrupt
or unworthy purposes ～ *n* : one

who engages in sexual activities for money — **pros·ti·tu·tion** \ˌprästəˈtüshən, -ˈtyü-\ *n*

pros·trate \ˈpräsˌträt\ *adj* : stretched out with face on the ground ~ *vb* **-trat·ed; -trat·ing 1** : fall or throw (oneself) into a prostrate position **2** : reduce to helplessness — **pros·tra·tion** \präsˈträshən\ *n*

pro·tag·o·nist \prōˈtagənist\ *n* : main character in a drama or story

pro·tect \prəˈtekt\ *vb* : shield from injury — **pro·tec·tor** \-tər\ *n*

pro·tec·tion \prəˈtekshən\ *n* **1** : act of protecting **2** : one that protects — **pro·tec·tive** \-ˈtektiv\ *adj*

pro·tec·tor·ate \-tərət\ *n* : state dependent upon the authority of another state

pro·té·gé \ˈprōtəˌzhā\ *n* : one under the care and protection of an influential person

pro·tein \ˈprōˌtēn\ *n* : complex combination of amino acids present in living matter

pro·test \ˈprōˌtest\ *n* **1** : organized public demonstration of disapproval **2** : strong objection ~ \prəˈtest\ *vb* **1** : assert positively **2** : object strongly — **pro·tes·ta·tion** \ˌprätəsˈtāshən\ *n* — **pro·test·er, pro·tes·tor** \ˈprōˌtestər\ *n*

Prot·es·tant \ˈprätəstənt\ *n* : Christian not of a Catholic or Orthodox church — **Prot·es·tant·ism** \ˈprätəstəntˌizəm\ *n*

pro·to·col \ˈprōtəˌkȯl\ *n* : diplomatic etiquette

pro·ton \ˈprōˌtän\ *n* : positively charged atomic particle

pro·to·plasm \ˈprōtəˌplazəm\ *n* : complex colloidal living substance of plant and animal cells — **pro·to·plas·mic** \ˌprōtəˈplazmik\ *adj*

pro·to·type \ˈprōtəˌtīp\ *n* : original model

pro·to·zo·an \ˌprōtəˈzōən\ *n* : single-celled lower invertebrate animal

pro·tract \prōˈtrakt\ *vb* : prolong

pro·trac·tor \-ˈtraktər\ *n* : instrument for drawing and measuring angles

pro·trude \prōˈtrüd\ *vb* **-trud·ed; -trud·ing** : stick out or cause to

stick out — **pro·tru·sion** \-ˈtrüzhən\ *n*

pro·tu·ber·ance \prōˈtübərəns, -ˈtyü-\ *n* : something that protrudes — **pro·tu·ber·ant** *adj*

proud \ˈpraud\ *adj* **1** : having or showing excessive self-esteem **2** : highly pleased **3** : having proper self-respect **4** : glorious — **proud·ly** *adv*

prove \ˈprüv\ *vb* **proved; proved** *or* **prov·en** \ˈprüvən\; **prov·ing 1** : test by experiment or by a standard **2** : establish the truth of by argument or evidence **3** : turn out esp. after trial or test — **prov·able** \ˈprüvəbəl\

prov·en·der \ˈprävəndər\ *n* : dry food for domestic animals

prov·erb \ˈprävˌərb\ *n* : short meaningful popular saying — **pro·ver·bi·al** \prəˈvərbēəl\ *adj*

pro·vide \prəˈvīd\ *vb* **-vid·ed; -vid·ing 1** : take measures beforehand **2** : make a stipulation **3** : supply what is needed — **pro·vid·er** *n*

pro·vid·ed *conj* : if

prov·i·dence \ˈprävədəns\ *n* **1** *often cap* : divine guidance **2** *cap* : God **3** : quality of being provident

prov·i·dent \-ədənt\ *adj* **1** : making provision for the future **2** : thrifty — **prov·i·dent·ly** *adv*

prov·i·den·tial \ˌprävəˈdenchəl\ *adj* **1** : relating to Providence **2** : opportune

pro·vid·ing *conj* : provided

prov·ince \ˈprävəns\ *n* **1** : administrative district **2** *pl* : all of a country outside the metropolis **3** : sphere

pro·vin·cial \prəˈvinchəl\ *adj* **1** : relating to a province **2** : limited in outlook — **pro·vin·cial·ism** \-ˌizəm\ *n*

pro·vi·sion \prəˈvizhən\ *n* **1** : act of providing **2** : stock of food — usu. in pl. **3** : stipulation ~ *vb* : supply with provisions

pro·vi·sion·al \-ˈvizhənəl\ *adj* : provided for a temporary need — **pro·vi·sion·al·ly** *adv*

pro·vi·so \prəˈvīzō\ *n, pl* **-sos** *or* **-soes** : stipulation

pro·voke \prəˈvōk\ *vb* **-voked; -vok·ing 1** : incite to anger **2** : stir up on purpose — **prov·o·ca·tion** \ˌprävəˈkāshən\ *n* — **pro·voc·a·tive** \prəˈväkətiv\ *adj*

prow \'praù\ *n* : bow of a ship

prow·ess \'praùəs\ *n* **1** : valor **2** : extraordinary ability

prowl \'praùl\ *vb* : roam about stealthily — **prowl** *n* — **prowl·er** *n*

prox·i·mate \'präksəmət\ *adj* : very near

prox·im·i·ty \präk'simətē\ *n* : nearness

proxy \'präksē\ *n, pl* **prox·ies** : authority to act for another — **proxy** *adj*

prude \'prüd\ *n* : one who shows extreme modesty — **prud·ery** \'prüdərē\ *n* — **prud·ish** \'prüdish\ *adj*

pru·dent \'prüdᵊnt\ *adj* **1** : shrewd **2** : cautious **3** : thrifty — **pru·dence** \-ᵊns\ *n* — **pru·den·tial** \prü-'denchəl\ *adj* — **pru·dent·ly** *adv*

¹**prune** \'prün\ *n* : dried plum

²**prune** *vb* **pruned; prun·ing** : cut off unwanted parts

pru·ri·ent \'prúrēənt\ *adj* : lewd — **pru·ri·ence** \-ēəns\ *n*

¹**pry** \'prī\ *vb* **pried; pry·ing** : look closely or inquisitively

♦ ²**pry** *vb* **pried; pry·ing** : raise, move, or pull apart with a lever

psalm \'säm, 'sälm\ *n* : sacred song or poem — **psalm·ist** *n*

pseu·do·nym \'südᵊn,im\ *n* : fictitious name — **pseu·don·y·mous** \sü'dänəməs\ *adj*

pso·ri·a·sis \sə'rīəsəs\ *n* : chronic skin disease

psy·che \'sīkē\ *n* : soul or mind

psy·chi·a·try \sə'kīətrē, sī-\ *n* : branch of medicine dealing with mental, emotional, and behavioral disorders — **psy·chi·at·ric** \,sīkē-'atrik\ *adj* — **psy·chi·a·trist** \sə-'kīətrist, sī-\ *n*

psy·chic \'sīkik\ *adj* **1** : relating to the psyche **2** : sensitive to supernatural forces ~ *n* : person sensitive to supernatural forces — **psy·chi·cal·ly** *adv*

psy·cho·anal·y·sis \,sīkōə'naləsəs\ *n* : study of the normally hidden content of the mind esp. to resolve conflicts — **psy·cho·an·a·lyst** \-'anᵊlist\ *n* — **psy·cho·an·al·yt·ic** \-,anᵊl'itik\ *adj* — **psy·cho·an·a·lyze** \-'anᵊl‚īz\ *vb*

psy·chol·o·gy \sī'käləjē\ *n, pl* **-gies 1** : science of mind and behavior **2** : mental and behavioral aspect (as of an individual) — **psy·cho·log·i·cal** \,sīkə'läjikəl\ *adj* — **psy·cho·log·i·cal·ly** *adv* — **psy·chol·o·gist** \sī'käləjist\ *n*

psy·cho·path \'sīkə,path\ *n* : mentally ill or unstable person — **psy·cho·path·ic** \,sīkə'pathik\ *adj*

psy·cho·sis \sī'kōsəs\ *n, pl* **-cho·ses** \-,sēz\ : mental derangement (as paranoia) — **psy·chot·ic** \-'kätik\ *adj or n*

psy·cho·so·mat·ic \,sīkəsə'matik\ *adj* : relating to bodily symptoms caused by mental or emotional disturbance

psy·cho·ther·a·py \,sīkō'therəpē\ *n* : treatment of mental disorder by psychological means — **psy·cho·ther·a·pist** \-pist\ *n*

pto·maine \'tō,mān\ *n* : bacterial decay product

pu·ber·ty \'pyübərtē\ *n* : time of sexual maturity

pu·bic \'pyübik\ *adj* : relating to the lower abdominal region

pub·lic \'pəblik\ *adj* **1** : relating to the people as a whole **2** : civic **3** : not private **4** : open to all **5** : well‑known ~ *n* : people as a whole — **pub·lic·ly** *adv*

pub·li·ca·tion \,pəblə'kāshən\ *n* **1** : process of publishing **2** : published work

pub·lic·i·ty \pə'blisətē\ *n* **1** : news information given out to gain public attention **2** : public attention

pub·li·cize \'pəblə,sīz\ vb -cized; -ciz·ing : bring to public attention — **pub·li·cist** \-sist\ n

pub·lish \'pəblish\ vb **1** : announce publicly **2** : reproduce for sale esp. by printing — **pub·lish·er** n

puck·er \'pəkər\ vb : pull together into folds or wrinkles ∼ n : wrinkle

pud·ding \'pùdiŋ\ n : creamy dessert

pud·dle \'pəd°l\ n : very small pool of water

pudgy \'pəjē\ adj **pudg·i·er; -est** : short and plump

pu·er·ile \'pyùrəl\ adj : childish

puff \'pəf\ vb **1** : blow in short gusts **2** : pant **3** : enlarge ∼ n **1** : short discharge (as of air) **2** : slight swelling **3** : something light and fluffy — **puffy** adj

pug \'pəg\ n : small stocky dog

pu·gi·lism \'pyüjə,lizəm\ n : boxing — **pu·gi·list** \-list\ n — **pu·gi·lis·tic** \,pyüjə'listik\ adj

pug·na·cious \,pəg'nāshəs\ adj : prone to fighting — **pug·nac·i·ty** \-'nasətē\ n

puke \'pyük\ vb **puked; puk·ing** : vomit — **puke** n

pul·chri·tude \'pəlkrə,tüd, -,tyüd\ n : beauty — **pul·chri·tu·di·nous** \,pəlkrə'tüd°nəs, -'tyüd-\ adj

pull \'pùl\ vb **1** : exert force so as to draw (something) toward or out **2** : move **3** : stretch or tear ∼ n **1** : act of pulling **2** : influence **3** : device for pulling something — **pull·er** n

pul·let \'pùlət\ n : young hen

pul·ley \'pùlē\ n, pl **-leys** : wheel with a grooved rim

Pull·man \'pùlmən\ n : railroad car with berths

pull·over \'pùl,ōvər\ adj : put on by being pulled over the head — **pull·over** n

pul·mo·nary \'pùlmə,nerē, 'pəl-\ adj : relating to the lungs

pulp \'pəlp\ n **1** : soft part of a fruit or vegetable **2** : soft moist mass (as of mashed wood) — **pulpy** adj

pul·pit \'pùl,pit\ n : raised desk used in preaching

pul·sate \'pəl,sāt\ vb **-sat·ed; -sat·ing** : expand and contract rhyth-

mically — **pul·sa·tion** \,pəl'sā-shən\ n

pulse \'pəls\ n : arterial throbbing caused by heart contractions — **pulse** vb

pul·ver·ize \'pəlvə,rīz\ vb **-ized; -iz·ing** : beat or grind into a powder

pu·ma \'pümə, 'pyü-\ n : cougar

pum·ice \'pəməs\ n : light porous volcanic glass used in polishing

pum·mel \'pəməl\ vb **-meled; -mel·ing** : beat

¹pump \'pəmp\ n : device for moving or compressing fluids ∼ vb **1** : raise (as water) with a pump **2** : fill by means of a pump — with *up* **3** : move like a pump — **pump·er** n

²pump n : woman's low shoe

pum·per·nick·el \'pəmpər,nikəl\ n : dark rye bread

pump·kin \'pəŋkən, 'pəmpkən\ n : large usu. orange fruit of a vine related to the gourd

pun \'pən\ n : humorous use of a word in a way that suggests two or more interpretations — **pun** vb

¹punch \'pənch\ vb **1** : strike with the fist **2** : perforate with a punch ∼ n : quick blow with the fist — **punch·er** n

²punch n : tool for piercing or stamping

³punch n : mixed beverage often including fruit juice

punc·til·i·ous \,pəŋk'tilēəs\ adj : marked by precise accordance with conventions

punc·tu·al \'pəŋkchəwəl\ adj : prompt — **punc·tu·al·i·ty** \,pəŋkchə'walətē\ n — **punc·tu·al·ly** adv

punc·tu·ate \'pəŋkchə,wāt\ vb **-at·ed; -at·ing** : mark with punctuation

punc·tu·a·tion \,pəŋkchə'wāshən\ n : standardized marks in written matter to clarify the meaning and separate parts

punc·ture \'pəŋkchər\ n : act or result of puncturing ∼ vb **-tured; -tur·ing** : make a hole in

pun·dit \'pəndət\ n **1** : learned person **2** : expert or critic

pun·gent \'pənjənt\ adj : having a sharp or stinging odor or taste — **pun·gen·cy** \-jənsē\ n — **pun·gent·ly** adv

pun·ish \'pənish\ vb : impose a penalty on or for — **pun·ish·able** *adj* — **pun·ish·ment** *n*

pu·ni·tive \'pyünətiv\ *adj* : inflicting punishment

pun·kin *var of* PUMPKIN

¹punt \'pənt\ *n* : long narrow flat-bottomed boat ~ *vb* : propel (a boat) by pushing with a pole

²punt *vb* : kick a ball dropped from the hands ~ *n* : act of punting a ball

pu·ny \'pyünē\ *adj* **-ni·er; -est** : slight in power or size

pup \'pəp\ *n* : young dog

pu·pa \'pyüpə\ *n, pl* **-pae** \-ˌpē, -ˌpī\ *or* **-pas** : insect (as a moth) when it is in a cocoon — **pu·pal** \-pəl\ *adj*

¹pu·pil \'pyüpəl\ *n* : young person in school

²pupil *n* : dark central opening of the iris of the eye

pup·pet \'pəpət\ *n* : small doll moved by hand or by strings — **pup·pe·teer** \ˌpəpə'tir\ *n*

pup·py \'pəpē\ *n, pl* **-pies** : young dog

pur·chase \'pərchəs\ *vb* **-chased; -chas·ing** : obtain in exchange for money ~ *n* **1** : act of purchasing **2** : something purchased **3** : secure grasp — **pur·chas·er** *n*

pure \'pyu̇r\ *adj* **pur·er; pur·est** : free of foreign matter, contamination, or corruption — **pure·ly** *adv*

pu·ree \pyu̇'rā, -'rē\ *n* : thick liquid mass of food — **puree** *vb*

pur·ga·to·ry \'pərgəˌtōrē\ *n, pl* **-ries** : intermediate state after death for purification by expiating sins — **pur·ga·to·ri·al** \ˌpərgə'tōrēəl\ *adj*

purge \'pərj\ *vb* **purged; purg·ing 1** : purify esp. from sin **2** : have or cause emptying of the bowels **3** : to get rid of ~ *n* **1** : act or result of purging **2** : something that purges — **pur·ga·tive** \'pərgətiv\ *adj or n*

pu·ri·fy \'pyu̇rəˌfī\ *vb* **-fied; -fy·ing** : make or become pure — **pu·ri·fi·ca·tion** \ˌpyu̇rəfə'kāshən\ *n* — **pu·ri·fi·er** \-ˌfīər\ *n*

Pu·rim \'pu̇rim\ *n* : Jewish holiday celebrated in February or March in commemoration of the deliverance of the Jews from the massacre plotted by Haman

pu·ri·tan \'pyu̇rət³n\ *n* : one who practices or preaches a very strict moral code — **pu·ri·tan·i·cal** \ˌpyu̇rə'tanikəl\ *adj* — **pu·ri·tan·i·cal·ly** *adv*

pu·ri·ty \'pyu̇rətē\ *n* : quality or state of being pure

purl \'pərl\ *n* : stitch in knitting ~ *vb* : knit in purl stitch

pur·loin \pər'lȯin, 'pərˌlȯin\ *vb* : steal

pur·ple \'pərpəl\ *n* : bluish red color — **pur·plish** \'pərpəlish\ *adj*

pur·port \pər'pōrt\ *vb* : convey outwardly as the meaning ~ \'pərˌpōrt\ *n* : meaning — **pur·port·ed·ly** \-ədlē\ *adv*

pur·pose \'pərpəs\ *n* **1** : something (as a result) aimed at **2** : resolution ~ *vb* **-posed; -pos·ing** : intend — **pur·pose·ful** \-fəl\ *adj* — **pur·pose·ful·ly** *adv* — **pur·pose·less** *adj* — **pur·pose·ly** *adv*

purr \'pər\ *n* : low murmur typical of a contented cat — **purr** *vb*

¹purse \'pərs\ *n* **1** : bag or pouch for money and small objects **2** : financial resource **3** : prize money

²purse *vb* **pursed; purs·ing** : pucker

pur·su·ance \pər'süəns\ *n* : act of carrying out or into effect

pursuant to \-'süənt-\ *prep* : according to

pur·sue \pər'sü\ *vb* **-sued; -su·ing 1** : follow in order to overtake **2** : seek to accomplish **3** : proceed along **4** : engage in — **pur·su·er** *n*

pur·suit \pər'süt\ *n* **1** : act of pursuing **2** : occupation

pur·vey \pər'vā\ *vb* **-veyed; -vey·ing** : supply (as provisions) usu. as a business — **pur·vey·or** \-ər\ *n*

pus \'pəs\ *n* : thick yellowish fluid (as in a boil)

push \'pu̇sh\ *vb* **1** : press against to move forward **2** : urge on or provoke ~ *n* **1** : vigorous effort **2** : act of pushing — **push·cart** *n* — **push·er** \'pu̇shər\ *n*

◆ **pushy** \'pu̇shē\ *adj* **push·i·er; -est** : objectionably aggressive

pu·sil·lan·i·mous \ˌpyüsə'lanəməs\ *adj* : cowardly

pussy \'pu̇sē\ *n, pl* **puss·ies** : cat

pus·tule \'pəschül\ *n* : pus-filled pimple

put \'pu̇t\ *vb* **put; put·ting 1** : bring to a specified position or condition **2** : subject to pain, suffering, or death **3** : impose or cause to exist **4** : express **5** : cause to be used

or employed — **put off** *vb* : postpone or delay — **put out** *vb* : bother or inconvenience — **put up** *vb* 1 : prepare for storage 2 : lodge 3 : contribute or pay — **put up with** : endure

pu·tre·fy \'pyütrə,fī\ *vb* **-fied; -fying** : make or become putrid — **pu·tre·fac·tion** \,pyütrə'fakshən\ *n*

pu·trid \'pyütrəd\ *adj* : rotten — **pu·trid·i·ty** \pyü'tridətē\ *n*

put·ty \'pətē\ *n, pl* **-ties** : doughlike cement — **putty** *vb*

puz·zle \'pəzəl\ *vb* **-zled; -zling** 1 : confuse 2 : attempt to solve — with *out* or *over* ∼ *n* : something that confuses or tests ingenuity — **puz·zle·ment** *n* — **puz·zler** \-ələr\ *n*

pyg·my \'pigmē\ *n, pl* **-mies** : dwarf — **pygmy** *adj*

py·lon \'pī,län, -lən\ *n* : tower or tall post

pyr·a·mid \'pirə,mid\ *n* : structure with a square base and 4 triangular sides meeting at a point

pyre \'pīr\ *n* : material heaped for a funeral fire

py·ro·ma·nia \,pīrō'mānēə\ *n* : irresistible impulse to start fires — **py·ro·ma·ni·ac** \-nē,ak\ *n*

py·ro·tech·nics \,pīrə'tekniks\ *n pl* : spectacular display (as of fireworks) — **py·ro·tech·nic** \-nik\ *adj*

Pyr·rhic \'pirik\ *adj* : achieved at excessive cost

py·thon \'pī,thän, -thən\ *n* : very large constricting snake

Q

q \'kyü\ *n, pl* **q's** *or* **qs** \'kyüz\ : 17th letter of the alphabet

¹**quack** \'kwak\ *vb* : make a cry like that of a duck — **quack** *n*

²**quack** *n* : one who pretends to have medical or healing skill — **quack** *adj* — **quack·ery** \-ərē\ *n* — **quack·ish** *adj*

quad·ran·gle \'kwäd,raŋgəl\ *n* : rectangular courtyard

quad·rant \'kwädrənt\ *n* : 1/4 of a circle

quad·ri·lat·er·al \,kwädrə'latərəl\ *n* : 4-sided polygon

qua·drille \kwä'dril, kə-\ *n* : square dance for 4 couples

quad·ru·ped \'kwädrə,ped\ *n* : animal having 4 feet

qua·dru·ple \kwä'drüpəl, -'drəp-; 'kwädrəp-\ *vb* **-pled; -pling** \-pliŋ\ : multiply by 4 ∼ *adj* : being 4 times as great or as many

qua·dru·plet \kwä'drəplət, -'drüp-; 'kwädrəp-\ *n* : one of 4 offspring born at one birth

quaff \'kwäf, 'kwaf\ *vb* : drink deeply or repeatedly — **quaff** *n*

quag·mire \'kwag,mīr, 'kwäg-\ *n* : soft land or bog

qua·hog \'kō,hóg, 'kwò-, 'kwō-, -,häg\ *n* : thick-shelled clam

¹**quail** \'kwāl\ *n, pl* **quail** *or* **quails** : short-winged plump game bird

²**quail** *vb* : cower in fear

quaint \'kwānt\ *adj* : pleasingly old-fashioned or odd — **quaint·ly** adv — **quaint·ness** n

quake \'kwāk\ vb **quaked; quaking** : shake or tremble ∼ n : earthquake

qual·i·fi·ca·tion \,kwäləfə'kāshən\ n 1 : limitation or stipulation 2 : special skill or experience for a job

qual·i·fy \'kwälə,fī\ vb **-fied; -fying** 1 : modify or limit 2 : fit by skill or training for some purpose 3 : become eligible — **qual·i·fied** adj — **qual·i·fi·er** \-,fīər\ n

qual·i·ty \'kwälətē\ n, pl **-ties** 1 : peculiar and essential character, nature, or feature 2 : excellence or distinction

qualm \'kwäm, 'kwälm, 'kwȯm\ n : sudden feeling of doubt or uneasiness

quan·da·ry \'kwändrē\ n, pl **-ries** : state of perplexity or doubt

quan·ti·ty \'kwäntətē\ n, pl **-ties** 1 : something that can be measured or numbered 2 : considerable amount

quan·tum theory \'kwäntəm-\ n : theory in physics that radiant energy (as light) is composed of separate packets of energy

quar·an·tine \'kwȯrən,tēn\ n 1 : restraint on the movements of persons or goods to prevent the spread of pests or disease 2 : place or period of quarantine — **quarantine** vb

quar·rel \'kwȯrəl\ n : basis of conflict — **quarrel** vb — **quar·rel·some** \-səm\ adj

¹**quar·ry** \'kwȯrē\ n, pl **-ries** : prey

²**quarry** n, pl **-ries** : excavation for obtaining stone — **quarry** vb

quart \'kwȯrt\ n : unit of liquid measure equal to .95 liter or of dry measure equal to 1.10 liters

quar·ter \'kwȯrtər\ n 1 : 1/4 part 2 : 1/4 of a dollar 3 : city district 4 pl : place to live esp. for a time 5 : mercy ∼ vb : divide into 4 equal parts

quar·ter·ly \'kwȯrtərlē\ adv or adj : at 3-month intervals ∼ n pl **-lies** : periodical published 4 times a year

quar·ter·mas·ter n 1 : ship's helmsman 2 : army supply officer

quar·tet \kwȯr'tet\ n 1 : music for 4 performers 2 : group of 4

quar·to \'kwȯrtō\ n, pl **-tos** : book printed on pages cut 4 from a sheet

quartz \'kwȯrts\ n : transparent crystalline mineral

quash \'kwäsh, 'kwȯsh\ vb 1 : set aside by judicial action 2 : suppress summarily and completely

qua·si \'kwā,zī, -sī; 'kwäzē, 'kwäs-; 'kwāzē\ adj : similar or nearly identical

qua·train \'kwä,trān\ n : unit of 4 lines of verse

qua·ver \'kwāvər\ vb : tremble or trill — **quaver** n

quay \'kē, 'kā, 'kwā\ n : wharf

quea·sy \'kwēzē\ adj **-si·er; -est** : nauseated — **quea·si·ly** \-zəlē\ adv — **quea·si·ness** \-zēnəs\ n

queen \'kwēn\ n 1 : wife or widow of a king 2 : female monarch 3 : woman of rank, power, or attractiveness 4 : fertile female of a social insect — **queen·ly** adj

queer \'kwir\ adj : differing from the usual or normal — **queer·ly** adv — **queer·ness** n

quell \'kwel\ vb : put down by force

quench \'kwench\ vb 1 : put out 2 : satisfy (a thirst) — **quench·able** adj — **quench·er** n

quer·u·lous \'kwerələs, -yələs\ adj : fretful or whining — **quer·u·lous·ly** adv — **quer·u·lous·ness** n

que·ry \'kwirē, 'kwer-\ n, pl **-ries** : question — **query** vb

quest \'kwest\ n or vb : search

ques·tion \'kweschən\ n 1 : something asked 2 : subject for debate 3 : dispute ∼ vb 1 : ask questions 2 : doubt or dispute 3 : subject to analysis — **ques·tion·er** n

ques·tion·able \'kweschənəbəl\ adj 1 : not certain 2 : of doubtful truth or morality — **ques·tion·ably** \-blē\ adv

question mark n : a punctuation mark ? used esp. at the end of a sentence to indicate a direct question

ques·tion·naire \,kweschə'nar\ n : set of questions

queue \'kyü\ n 1 : braid of hair 2 : a waiting line ∼ vb **queued; queuing** or **queue·ing** : line up

quib·ble \'kwibəl\ n : minor objection — **quibble** vb — **quib·bler** n

quick \'kwik\ *adj* **1** : rapid **2** : alert or perceptive ~ *n* : sensitive area of living flesh — **quick** *adv* — **quick·ly** *adv* — **quick·ness** *n*

quick·en \'kwikən\ *vb* **1** : come to life **2** : increase in speed

quick·sand *n* : deep mass of sand and water

quick·sil·ver *n* : mercury

qui·es·cent \kwī'esᵊnt\ *adj* : being at rest — **qui·es·cence** \-ᵊns\ *n*

◆ **qui·et** \'kwīət\ *adj* **1** : marked by little motion or activity **2** : gentle **3** : free from noise **4** : not showy **5** : secluded ~ *vb* : pacify — **quiet** *adv or n* — **qui·et·ly** *adv* — **qui·et·ness** *n*

qui·etude \'kwīə,tüd, -,tyüd\ *n* : quietness or repose

quill \'kwil\ *n* **1** : a large stiff feather **2** : porcupine's spine

quilt \'kwilt\ *n* : padded bedspread ~ *vb* : stitch or sew in layers with padding in between

quince \'kwins\ *n* : hard yellow applelike fruit

qui·nine \'kwī,nīn\ *n* : bitter drug used against malaria

quin·tes·sence \kwin'tesᵊns\ *n* **1** : purest essence of something **2** : most typical example — **quint·es·sen·tial** \,kwintə'senchəl\ *adj* — **quin·tes·sen·tial·ly** *adv*

quin·tet \kwin'tet\ *n* **1** : music for 5 performers **2** : group of 5

quin·tu·ple \kwin'tüpəl, -'tyüp-, -'təp-; 'kwintəp-\ *adj* **1** : having 5 units or members **2** : being 5 times as great or as many — **quintuple** *n or vb*

quin·tu·plet \-plət\ *n* : one of 5 offspring at one birth

quip \'kwip\ *vb* **-pp-** : make a clever remark — **quip** *n*

quire \'kwīr\ *n* : 24 or 25 sheets of paper of the same size and quality

quirk \'kwərk\ *n* : peculiarity of action or behavior — **quirky** *adj*

quit \'kwit\ *vb* **quit; quit·ting 1** : stop **2** : leave — **quit·ter** *n*

quite \'kwīt\ *adv* **1** : completely **2** : to a considerable extent

quits \'kwits\ *adj* : even or equal with another (as by repaying a debt)

¹**quiv·er** \'kwivər\ *n* : case for arrows

²**quiver** *vb* : shake or tremble — **quiver** *n*

quix·ot·ic \kwik'sätik\ *adj* : idealistic to an impractical degree — **quix·ot·i·cal·ly** \-tiklē\ *adv*

quiz \'kwiz\ *n, pl* **quiz·zes** : short test ~ *vb* **-zz-** : question closely

quiz·zi·cal \'kwizikəl\ *adj* **1** : teasing **2** : curious

quoit \'kóit, 'kwóit, 'kwät\ *n* : ring thrown at a peg in a game (**quoits**)

quon·dam \'kwändəm, -,dam\ *adj* : former

quo·rum \'kwórəm\ *n* : required number of members present

quo·ta \'kwōtə\ *n* : proportional part or share

quotation mark *n* : one of a pair of punctuation marks " " or ' ' used esp. to indicate the beginning and the end of a quotation

quote \'kwōt\ *vb* **quot·ed; quot·ing 1** : repeat (another's words) exactly **2** : state (a price) — **quot·able** *adj* — **quo·ta·tion** \kwō-'tāshən\ *n* — **quote** *n*

quo·tient \'kwōshənt\ *n* : number obtained from division

R

r \\'är\\ *n*, *pl* r's *or* rs \\'ärz\\ : 18th letter of the alphabet

rab•bet \\'rabət\\ *n* : groove in a board

rab•bi \\'rab,ī\\ *n* : Jewish religious leader — **rab•bin•ic** \\rə'binik\\ **rab•bin•i•cal** \\-ikəl\\ *adj*

rab•bin•ate \\'rabənət, -,nāt\\ *n* : office of a rabbi

rab•bit \\'rabət\\ *n*, *pl* -bit *or* -bits : long-eared burrowing mammal

rab•ble \\'rabəl\\ *n* : mob

ra•bid \\'rabəd\\ *adj* 1 : violent 2 : fanatical 3 : affected with rabies — **ra•bid•ly** *adv*

ra•bies \\'rābēz\\ *n*, *pl* rabies : acute deadly virus disease

rac•coon \\ra'kün\\ *n*, *pl* -coon *or* -coons : tree-dwelling mammal with a black mask and a bushy ringed tail

¹**race** \\'rās\\ *n* 1 : strong current of water 2 : contest of speed 3 : election campaign ∼ *vb* raced; rac•ing 1 : run in a race 2 : rush — **race•course** *n* — **rac•er** *n* — **race•track** *n*

²**race** *n* 1 : family, tribe, people, or nation of the same stock 2 : division of mankind based on hereditary traits — **ra•cial** \\'rāshəl\\ *adj* — **ra•cial•ly** *adv*

race•horse *n* : horse used for racing

rac•ism \\'rās,izəm\\ *n* : discrimination based on the belief that some races are by nature superior — **rac•ist** \\-ist\\ *n*

rack \\'rak\\ *n* 1 : framework for display or storage 2 : instrument that stretches the body for torture ∼ *vb* : torture with or as if with a rack

◆ ¹**rack•et** \\'rakət\\ *n* : bat with a tight netting across an open frame

²**racket** *n* 1 : confused noise 2 : fraudulent scheme — **rack•e•teer** \\,rakə'tir\\ *n* — **rack•e•teer•ing** *n*

ra•con•teur \\,rak,än'tər\\ *n* : storyteller

racy \\'rāsē\\ *adj* rac•i•er; -est : risqué — **rac•i•ly** *adv* — **rac•i•ness** *n*

ra•dar \\'rā,där\\ *n* : radio device for determining distance and direction of distant objects

ra•di•al \\'rādēəl\\ *adj* : having parts arranged like rays coming from a common center — **ra•di•al•ly** *adv*

ra•di•ant \\'rādēənt\\ *adj* 1 : glowing 2 : beaming with happiness 3 : transmitted by radiation — **ra•di•ance** \\-əns\\ *n* — **ra•di•ant•ly** *adv*

ra•di•ate \\'rādē,āt\\ *vb* -at•ed; -at•ing 1 : issue rays or in. rays 2 : spread from a center — **ra•di•a•tion** \\,rādē'āshən\\ *n*

ra•di•a•tor \\'rādē,ātər\\ *n* : cooling or heating device

rad•i•cal \\'radikəl\\ *adj* 1 : fundamental 2 : extreme ∼ *n* : person favoring extreme changes — **rad•i•cal•ism** \\-,izəm\\ *n* — **rad•i•cal•ly** *adv*

radii *pl of* RADIUS

ra•dio \\'rādē,ō\\ *n*, *pl* -di•os 1 : wireless transmission or reception of sound by means of electric waves 2 : radio receiving set ∼ *vb* : send a message to by radio — **radio** *adj*

ra•dio•ac•tiv•i•ty \\,rādēō,ak'tivətē\\ *n* : property of an element that emits energy through nuclear disintegration — **ra•dio•ac•tive** \\-'aktiv\\ *adj*

I FELL ASLEEP ON MY TENNIS RACKET, OKAY?!

OH

ra·di·ol·o·gy \‚rādē'älǝjē\ n : medical use of radiation — **ra·di·ol·o·gist** \-jist\ n

rad·ish \'radish\ n : pungent fleshy root usu. eaten raw

ra·di·um \'rādēǝm\ n : metallic radioactive chemical element

ra·di·us \'rādēǝs\ n, pl **-dii** \-ē‚ī\ 1 : line from the center of a circle or sphere to the circumference or surface 2 : area defined by a radius

ra·don \'rā‚dän\ n : gaseous radioactive chemical element

raff·ish \'rafish\ adj : flashily vulgar — **raff·ish·ly** adv — **raff·ish·ness** n

raf·fle \'rafǝl\ n : lottery among people who have bought tickets ~ vb **-fled**; **-fling** : offer in a raffle

¹**raft** \'raft\ n : flat floating platform ~ vb : travel or transport by raft

²**raft** n : large amount or number

raf·ter \'raftǝr\ n : beam supporting a roof

¹**rag** \'rag\ n : waste piece of cloth

²**rag** n : composition in ragtime

rag·a·muf·fin \'ragǝ‚mǝfǝn\ n : ragged dirty person

rage \'rāj\ n 1 : violent anger 2 : vogue ~ vb **raged**; **rag·ing** 1 : be extremely angry or violent 2 : be out of control

rag·ged \'ragǝd\ adj : torn — **rag·ged·ly** adv — **rag·ged·ness** n

ra·gout \ra'gü\ n : meat stew

rag·time n : syncopated music

rag·weed n : coarse weedy herb with allergenic pollen

raid \'rād\ n : sudden usu. surprise attack — **raid** vb — **raid·er** n

¹**rail** \'rāl\ n 1 : bar serving as a guard or barrier 2 : bar forming a track for wheeled vehicles 3 : railroad

²**rail** vb : scold someone vehemently — **rail·er** n

rail·ing \'rāliŋ\ n : rail or a barrier of rails

rail·lery \'rālǝrē\ n, pl **-ler·ies** : good-natured ridicule

rail·road \'rāl‚rōd\ n : road for a train laid with iron rails and wooden ties ~ vb : force something hastily — **rail·road·er** n — **rail·road·ing** n

rail·way \-‚wā\ n : railroad

rai·ment \'rāmǝnt\ n : clothing

rain \'rān\ n 1 : water falling in drops from the clouds 2 : shower of objects ~ vb : fall as or like rain — **rain·coat** n — **rain·drop** n — **rain·fall** n — **rain·mak·er** n — **rain·mak·ing** n — **rain·storm** n — **rain·water** n — **rainy** adj

rain·bow \-‚bō\ n : arc of colors formed by the sun shining through moisture

raise \'rāz\ vb **raised**; **rais·ing** 1 : lift 2 : arouse 3 : erect 4 : collect 5 : breed, grow, or bring up 6 : increase 7 : make light ~ n : increase esp. in pay — **rais·er** n

rai·sin \'rāz°n\ n : dried grape

ra·ja, ra·jah \'räjǝ\ n : Indian prince

¹**rake** \'rāk\ n : garden tool for smoothing or sweeping ~ vb **raked**; **rak·ing** 1 : gather, loosen, or smooth with or as if with a rake 2 : sweep with gunfire

²**rake** n : dissolute man

rak·ish \'rākish\ adj : smart or jaunty — **rak·ish·ly** adv — **rak·ish·ness** n

ral·ly \'ralē\ vb **-lied**; **-ly·ing** 1 : bring or come together 2 : revive or recover 3 : make a comeback ~ n pl **-lies** 1 : act of rallying 2 : mass meeting

ram \'ram\ n 1 : male sheep 2 : beam used in battering down walls or doors ~ vb **-mm-** 1 : force or drive in or through 2 : strike against violently

RAM \'ram\ n : main internal storage area in a computer

ram·ble \'rambǝl\ vb **-bled**; **-bling** : wander — **ramble** n — **ram·bler** \-blǝr\ n

ram·bunc·tious \ram'bǝŋkshǝs\ adj : unruly

ram·i·fi·ca·tion \‚ramǝfǝ'kāshǝn\ n : consequence

ram·i·fy \'ramǝ‚fī\ vb **-fied**; **-fy·ing** : branch out

ramp \'ramp\ n : sloping passage or connecting roadway

ram·page \'ram‚pāj, ram'pāj\ vb **-paged**; **-pag·ing** : rush about wildly ~ \'ram‚-\ n : violent or riotous action or behavior

ram·pant \'rampǝnt\ adj : widespread — **ram·pant·ly** adv

ram·part \'ram‚pärt\ n : embankment of a fortification

ram·rod n : rod used to load or clean a gun ~ adj : strict or inflexible

ram·shack·le \'ram₁shakəl\ *adj* : shaky

ran *past of* RUN

ranch \'ranch\ *n* 1 : establishment for the raising of cattle, sheep, or horses 2 : specialized farm ~ *vb* : operate a ranch — **ranch·er** *n*

ran·cid \'ransəd\ *adj* : smelling or tasting as if spoiled — **ran·cid·i·ty** \ran'sidətē\ *n*

ran·cor \'raŋkər\ *n* : bitter deep-seated ill will — **ran·cor·ous** *adj*

ran·dom \'randəm\ *adj* : occurring by chance — **ran·dom·ly** *adv* — **ran·dom·ness** *n* — **at random** : without definite aim or method

ran·dom·ize \'randə₁mīz\ *vb* -ized; -izing : select, assign, or arrange in a random way

rang *past of* RING

range \'rānj\ *n* 1 : series of things in a row 2 : open land for grazing 3 : cooking stove 4 : variation within limits 5 : place for target practice 6 : extent ~ *vb* ranged; rang·ing 1 : arrange 2 : roam at large, freely, or over 3 : vary within limits

rang·er \'rānjər\ *n* : officer who manages and protects public lands

rangy \'rānjē\ *adj* rang·i·er; -est : being slender with long limbs — **rang·i·ness** *n*

¹**rank** \'raŋk\ *adj* 1 : vigorous in growth 2 : unpleasantly strong-smelling — **rank·ly** *adv* — **rank·ness** *n*

²**rank** *n* 1 : line of soldiers 2 : orderly arrangement 3 : grade of official standing 4 : position within a group ~ *vb* 1 : arrange in formation or according to class 2 : take or have a relative position

rank and file *n* : general membership

ran·kle \'raŋkəl\ *vb* -kled; -kling : cause anger, irritation, or bitterness

ran·sack \'ran₁sak\ *vb* : search through and rob

ran·som \'ransəm\ *n* : something demanded for the freedom of a captive ~ *vb* : gain the freedom of by paying a price — **ran·som·er** *n*

rant \'rant\ *vb* : talk or scold violently — **rant·er** *n* — **rant·ing·ly** *adv*

¹**rap** \'rap\ *n* : sharp blow or rebuke

~ *vb* -pp- : strike or criticize sharply

²**rap** *vb* -pp- : talk freely

ra·pa·cious \rə'pāshəs\ *adj* 1 : excessively greedy 2 : ravenous — **ra·pa·cious·ly** *adv* — **ra·pa·cious·ness** *n* — **ra·pac·i·ty** \-'pasətē\ *n*

¹**rape** \'rāp\ *n* : herb grown as a forage crop and for its seeds (**rape·seed**)

²**rape** *vb* raped; rap·ing : force to have sexual intercourse — **rape** *n* — **rap·er** *n* — **rap·ist** \'rāpist\ *n*

rap·id \'rapəd\ *adj* : very fast — **ra·pid·i·ty** \rə'pidətē\ *n* — **rap·id·ly** *adv*

rap·ids \-ədz\ *n pl* : place in a stream where the current is swift

ra·pi·er \'rāpēər\ *n* : narrow 2-edged sword

rap·ine \'rapən, -₁īn\ *n* : plunder

rap·port \ra'pōr\ *n* : harmonious relationship

rapt \'rapt\ *adj* : engrossed — **rapt·ly** *adv* — **rapt·ness** *n*

rap·ture \'rapchər\ *n* : spiritual or emotional ecstasy — **rap·tur·ous** \-chərəs\ *adj* — **rap·tur·ous·ly** *adv*

¹**rare** \'rar\ *adj* rar·er; rar·est : having a portion relatively uncooked

²**rare** *adj* rar·er; rar·est 1 : not dense 2 : unusually fine 3 : seldom met with — **rare·ly** *adv* — **rare·ness** *n* — **rar·i·ty** \'rarətē\ *n*

rar·e·fy \'rarə₁fī\ *vb* -fied; -fy·ing : make or become rare, thin, or less dense — **rar·e·fac·tion** \₁rarə-'fakshən\ *n*

rar·ing \'rarən, -iŋ\ *adj* : full of enthusiasm

ras·cal \'raskəl\ *n* : mean, dishonest, or mischievous person — **ras·cal·i·ty** \ras'kalətē\ *n* — **ras·cal·ly** \'raskəlē\ *adj*

¹**rash** \'rash\ *adj* : too hasty in decision or action — **rash·ly** *adv* — **rash·ness** *n*

²**rash** *n* : a breaking out of the skin with red spots

rasp \'rasp\ *vb* 1 : rub with or as if with a rough file 2 : to speak in a grating tone ~ *n* : coarse file

rasp·ber·ry \'raz₁berē\ *n* : edible red or black berry

rat \'rat\ *n* : destructive rodent larger than the mouse ~ *vb* : betray or inform on

ratch·et \'rachət\ *n* : notched device

rate \\'rāt\\ *n* **1** : quantity, amount, or degree measured in relation to some other quantity **2** : rank ~ *vb* **rat·ed; rat·ing 1** : estimate or determine the rank or quality of **2** : deserve

rath·er \\'rath͟ər, 'rəth͟-, 'räth͟-\\ *adv* **1** : preferably **2** : on the other hand **3** : more properly **4** : somewhat

rat·i·fy \\'ratə,fī\\ *vb* **-fied; -fy·ing** : approve and accept formally — **rat·i·fi·ca·tion** \\,ratəfə'kāshən\\ *n*

rat·ing \\'rātiŋ\\ *n* : classification according to grade

ra·tio \\'rāshēō\\ *n, pl* **-tios** : relation in number, quantity, or degree between things

ra·tion \\'rashən, 'rāshən\\ *n* : share or allotment (as of food) ~ *vb* : use or allot sparingly

ra·tio·nal \\'rashənəl\\ *adj* **1** : having reason or sanity **2** : relating to reason — **ra·tio·nal·ly** *adv*

ra·tio·nale \\,rashə'nal\\ *n* **1** : explanation of principles of belief or practice **2** : underlying reason

ra·tio·nal·ize \\'rashənə,līz\\ *vb* **-ized; -iz·ing** : justify (as one's behavior or weaknesses) esp. to oneself — **ra·tio·nal·i·za·tion** \\,rashənələ-'zāshən\\ *n*

rat·tan \\ra'tan, rə-\\ *n* : palm with long stems used esp. for canes and wickerwork

rat·tle \\'ratᵊl\\ *vb* **-tled; -tling 1** : make a series of clattering sounds **2** : say briskly **3** : confuse or upset ~ *n* **1** : series of clattering sounds **2** : something (as a toy) that rattles

rat·tler \\'ratlər\\ *n* : rattlesnake

rat·tle·snake *n* : American venomous snake with a rattle at the end of the tail

rat·ty \\'ratē\\ *adj* **rat·ti·er; -est** : shabby

rau·cous \\'rókəs\\ *adj* : harsh or boisterous — **rau·cous·ly** *adv* — **rau·cous·ness** *n*

rav·age \\'ravij\\ *n* : destructive effect ~ *vb* **-aged; -ag·ing** : lay waste — **rav·ag·er** *n*

rave \\'rāv\\ *vb* **raved; rav·ing 1** : talk wildly in or as if in delirium **2** : talk with extreme enthusiasm ~ *n* **1** : act of raving **2** : enthusiastic praise

rav·el \\'ravəl\\ *vb* **-eled** *or* **-elled; -el·ing** *or* **-el·ling 1** : unravel **2** : tangle ~ *n* **1** : something tangled **2** : loose thread

ra·ven \\'rāvən\\ *n* : large black bird ~ *adj* : black and shiny

rav·en·ous \\'ravənəs\\ *adj* : very hungry — **rav·en·ous·ly** *adv* — **rav·en·ous·ness** *n*

ra·vine \\rə'vēn\\ *n* : narrow steep-sided valley

rav·ish \\'ravish\\ *vb* **1** : seize and take away by violence **2** : overcome with joy or delight **3** : rape — **rav·ish·er** *n* — **rav·ish·ment** *n*

raw \\'ró\\ *adj* **raw·er** \\'róər\\; **raw·est** \\'róəst\\ **1** : not cooked **2** : not processed **3** : not trained **4** : having the surface rubbed off **5** : cold and damp **6** : vulgar — **raw·ness** *n*

raw·hide \\'ró,hīd\\ *n* : untanned skin of cattle

ray \\'rā\\ *n* **1** : thin beam of radiant energy (as light) **2** : tiny bit

ray·on \\'rā,än\\ *n* : fabric made from cellulose fiber

raze \\'rāz\\ *vb* **razed; raz·ing** : destroy or tear down

ra·zor \\'rāzər\\ *n* : sharp cutting instrument used to shave off hair

re- \\rē, ,rē, 'rē\\ *prefix* **1** : again or anew **2** : back or backward

reaccelerate	reargue
reaccept	rearrange
reacclimatize	rearrest
reaccredit	reassemble
reacquaint	reassert
reacquire	reassess
reactivate	reassessment
reactivation	reassign
readdress	reassignment
readjust	reattach
readjustment	reattain
readmit	reawaken
readopt	rebalance
reaffirm	rebaptize
realign	rebid
realignment	rebind
reallocate	reborn
reanalysis	rebroadcast
reanalyze	rebuild
reappear	rebury
reappearance	recalculate
reapply	recapture
reappoint	recast
reapportion	recertification
reappraisal	recertify
reappraise	rechannel
reapprove	recharge

rechargeable
recheck
rechristen
recirculate
recirculation
reclassification
reclassify
recolonize
recombine
recompute
reconceive
reconnect
reconquer
reconquest
reconsider
reconsideration
reconsolidate
reconstruct
recontaminate
reconvene
reconvict
recopy
re-create
recross
redecorate
rededicate
rededication
redefine
redeposit
redesign
redevelop
rediscover
rediscovery
redissolve
redistribute
redraft
redraw
reemerge
reemergence
reemphasize
reenergize
reengage
reenlist
reenlistment
reenroll
reenter
reequip
reestablish
reestablishment
reestimate
reevaluate
reevaluation
reexamination
reexamine
refinance
refire
refloat
refocus
refold

reformulate
refreeze
refuel
regain
regrow
regrowth
rehear
reheat
rehire
rehospitaliza-
   tion
rehospitalize
reidentify
reignite
reimplant
reimpose
reincorporate
reindict
reinfection
reinflate
reinject
reinjection
reinoculate
reinsert
reinsertion
reinspect
reinstall
reinstitute
reintegrate
reintegration
reinter
reintroduce
reinvent
reinvestigate
reinvestigation
reinvigorate
rejudge
rekindle
reknit
relabel
relandscape
relaunch
relearn
relight
reline
reload
remarriage
remarry
rematch
remelt
remobilize
remoisten
remold
remotivate
rename
renegotiate
reoccupy
reoccur
reoccurrence

reoperate
reorchestrate
reorganization
reorganize
reorient
repack
repave
rephotograph
rephrase
replan
replaster
replay
replot
repolish
repopulate
repressurize
reprice
reprint
reprocess
reprogram
reread
rereading
rerecord
reregister
reroof
reroute
resalable
resale
reschedule
reseal
resegregate
resell
resentence
reset
resettle
resew
reshoot
reshow
resocialization
resod

resolidify
restage
restart
restate
restatement
restimulate
restock
restructure
restudy
restyle
resubmit
resupply
resurface
resurvey
resynthesis
resynthesize
retarget
reteach
retell
retest
rethink
retighten
retrain
retranslate
retransmit
retry
retune
retype
reupholster
reusable
reuse
reutilize
revaccinate
revaccination
revisit
rewash
reweave
rewind
rewire
rewrap

reach \'rēch\ *vb* 1 : stretch out 2 : touch or try to touch or grasp 3 : extend to or arrive at 4 : communicate with ~ *n* 1 : act of reaching 2 : distance one can reach 3 : ability to reach — **reach•able** *adj* — **reach•er** *n*

re•act \rē'akt\ *vb* 1 : act in response to some influence or stimulus 2 : undergo chemical change — **re•ac•tive** \-'aktiv\ *adj*

re•ac•tion \rē'akshən\ *n* 1 : action or emotion caused by and directly related to or counter to another action 2 : chemical change

re•ac•tion•ary \-shə,nerē\ *adj* : relating to or favoring return to an earlier political order or policy — **reactionary** *n*

re·ac·tor \rē'aktər\ *n* 1 : one that re- acts 2 : device for the controlled release of nuclear energy

read \'rēd\ *vb* **read** \'red\; **read- ing** \'rēdiŋ\ 1 : understand written language 2 : utter aloud printed words 3 : interpret 4 : study 5 : in- dicate ~ *adj* \'red\ : informed by reading — **read·a·bil·i·ty** \,rēdə- 'bilətē\ *n* — **read·able** *adj* — **read- ably** *adv* — **read·er** *n* — **read·er- ship** *n*

read·ing \'rēdiŋ\ *n* 1 : something read or for reading 2 : particular version, interpretation, or perfor- mance 3 : data indicated by an in- strument

♦ **ready** \'redē\ *adj* **read·i·er; -est** 1 : prepared or available for use or action 2 : willing to do something ~ *vb* **read·ied; ready·ing** : make ready — *n* : state of being ready — **read·i·ly** *adv* — **read·i·ness** *n*

re·al \'rēl\ *adj* 1 : relating to fixed or immovable things (as land) 2 : genuine 3 : not imaginary — *adv* : very — **re·al·ness** *n* — **for real** 1 : in earnest 2 : genuine

real estate *n* : property in houses and land

re·al·ism \'rēə,lizəm\ *n* 1 : disposi- tion to deal with facts practically 2 : faithful portrayal of reality — **re·al·ist** \-list\ *adj or n* — **re·al- is·tic** \,rēə'listik\ *adj* — **re·al·is- ti·cal·ly** \-tiklē\ *adv*

re·al·i·ty \rē'alətē\ *n, pl* **-ties** 1 : quality or state of being real 2 : something real

re·al·ize \'rēə,līz\ *vb* **-ized; -iz·ing** 1 : make actual 2 : obtain 3 : be aware of — **re·al·iz·able** *adj* — **re- al·i·za·tion** \,rēələ'zāshən\ *n*

re·al·ly \'rēlē, 'ril-\ *adv* : in truth

realm \'relm\ *n* 1 : kingdom 2 : sphere

¹ream \'rēm\ *n* : quantity of paper that is 480, 500, or 516 sheets

²ream *vb* : enlarge, shape, or clean with a specially shaped tool (**reamer**)

reap \'rēp\ *vb* : cut or clear (as a crop) with a scythe or machine — **reap·er** *n*

¹rear \'rir\ *vb* 1 : raise upright 2 : breed or bring up 3 : rise on the hind legs

²rear *n* 1 : back 2 : position at the back of something ~ *adj* : being at the back — **rear·ward** \-wərd\ *adj or adv*

rear admiral *n* : commissioned offi- cer in the navy or coast guard ranking next below a vice admiral

rea·son \'rēz°n\ *n* 1 : explanation or justification 2 : motive for action or belief 3 : power or process of thinking ~ *vb* 1 : use the faculty of reason 2 : try to persuade an- other — **rea·son·er** *n* — **rea·son- ing** \'rēz°niŋ\ *n*

rea·son·able \'rēz°nəbəl\ *adj* 1 : be- ing within the bounds of reason 2 : inexpensive — **rea·son·able·ness** *n* — **rea·son·ably** \-blē\ *adv*

re·as·sure \,rēə'shùr\ *vb* : restore one's confidence — **re·as·sur- ance** \-'shùrəns\ *n* — **re·as·sur- ing·ly** *adv*

re·bate \'rē,bāt\ *n* : return of part of a payment — **rebate** *vb*

reb·el \'rebəl\ *n* : one that resists au- thority ~ \ri'bel\ *vb* **-belled; -bel- ling** 1 : resist authority 2 : feel or exhibit anger — **rebel** \'rebəl\ *adj*

re·bel·lion \ri'belyən\ *n* : resistance to authority and esp. to one's gov- ernment

re·bel·lious \-yəs\ *adj* 1 : engaged in rebellion 2 : inclined to resist au- thority — **re·bel·lious·ly** *adv* — **re·bel·lious·ness** *n*

re·birth \'rē'bərth\ n 1 : new or second birth 2 : revival

re·bound \'rē'baund, ri-\ vb 1 : spring back on striking something 2 : recover from a reverse ~ \'rē,-\ n 1 : action of rebounding 2 : reaction to a reverse

re·buff \ri'bəf\ vb : refuse or repulse rudely — **rebuff** n

re·buke \-'byük\ vb -buked; -buking : reprimand sharply — **rebuke** n

re·bus \'rēbəs\ n : riddle representing syllables or words with pictures

re·but \ri'bət\ vb -but·ted; -but·ting : refute — **re·but·ter** n

re·but·tal \-'əl\ n : opposing argument

re·cal·ci·trant \ri'kalsətrənt\ adj 1 : stubbornly resisting authority 2 : resistant to handling or treatment — **re·cal·ci·trance** \-trəns\ n

re·call \ri'kȯl\ vb 1 : call back 2 : remember 3 : revoke ~ \ri'-, 'rē,-\ n 1 : a summons to return 2 : remembrance 3 : act of revoking

re·cant \ri'kant\ vb : take back (something said) publicly

re·ca·pit·u·late \,rēkə'pichə,lāt\ vb : summarize — **re·ca·pit·u·la·tion** \-,pichə'lāshən\ n

re·cede \ri'sēd\ vb -ced·ed; -ceding 1 : move back or away 2 : slant backward

re·ceipt \-'sēt\ n 1 : act of receiving 2 : something (as payment) received — usu. in pl. 3 : writing acknowledging something received

re·ceive \ri'sēv\ vb -ceived; -ceiving 1 : take in or accept 2 : greet or entertain (visitors) 3 : pick up radio waves and convert into sounds or pictures — **re·ceiv·able** adj

re·ceiv·er \ri'sēvər\ n 1 : one that receives 2 : one having charge of property or money involved in a lawsuit 3 : apparatus for receiving radio waves — **re·ceiv·er·ship** n

re·cent \'rēs°nt\ adj 1 : having lately come into existence 2 : of the present time or time just past — **re·cent·ly** adv — **re·cent·ness** n

re·cep·ta·cle \ri'septikəl\ n : container

re·cep·tion \ri'sepshən\ n 1 : act of receiving 2 : social gathering at which guests are formally welcomed

re·cep·tion·ist \-shənist\ n : person employed to greet callers

re·cep·tive \ri'septiv\ adj : open and responsive to ideas, impressions, or suggestions — **re·cep·tive·ly** adv — **re·cep·tive·ness** n — **re·cep·tiv·i·ty** \,rē,sep'tivətē\ n

re·cess \'rē,ses, ri'ses\ n 1 : indentation in a line or surface 2 : suspension of a session for rest ~ vb 1 : make a recess in or put into a recess 2 : interrupt a session for a recess

re·ces·sion \ri'seshən\ n 1 : departing procession 2 : period of reduced economic activity

rec·i·pe \'resə,pē\ n : instructions for making something

re·cip·i·ent \ri'sipēənt\ n : one that receives

re·cip·ro·cal \ri'siprəkəl\ adj 1 : affecting each in the same way 2 : so related that one is equivalent to the other — **re·cip·ro·cal·ly** adv — **re·ci·proc·i·ty** \,resə'präsətē\ n

re·cip·ro·cate \-,kāt\ vb : make a return for something done or given — **re·cip·ro·ca·tion** \-,siprə-'kāshən\ n

re·cit·al \ri'sīt°l\ n 1 : public reading or recitation 2 : music or dance concert or exhibition by pupils — **re·cit·al·ist** \-°list\ n

rec·i·ta·tion \,resə'tāshən\ n : a reciting or recital

re·cite \ri'sīt\ vb -cit·ed; -cit·ing 1 : repeat verbatim 2 : recount — **re·cit·er** n

reck·less \'rekləs\ adj : lacking caution — **reck·less·ly** adv — **reck·less·ness** n

reck·on \'rekən\ vb 1 : count or calculate 2 : consider

reck·on·ing n 1 : act or instance of reckoning 2 : settling of accounts

re·claim \ri'klām\ vb 1 : change to a desirable condition 2 : obtain from a waste product or by-product 3 : demand or obtain the return of — **re·claim·able** adj — **rec·la·ma·tion** \,reklə'māshən\ n

♦ **re·cline** \ri'klīn\ vb -clined; -clin-ing : lean backward or lie down

rec·luse \'rek,lüs, ri'klüs\ n : one who leads a secluded or solitary life

rec·og·ni·tion \,rekig'nishən\ n : act of recognizing or state of being recognized re·cog·ni·zance \ri'känəzəns, -'käg-\ *n* : promise recorded before a court

rec·og·nize \'rekig,nīz\ *vb* 1 : identify as previously known 2 : take notice of 3 : acknowledge esp. with appreciation — rec·og·niz·able \'rekəg,nīzəbəl\ *adj* — rec·og·niz·ably \-blē\ *adv*

re·coil \ri'kȯil\ *vb* : draw or spring back ~ \'rē,-, ri'-\ *n* : action of recoiling

rec·ol·lect \,rekə'lekt\ *vb* : remember

rec·ol·lec·tion \,rekə'lekshən\ *n* 1 : act or power of recollecting 2 : something recollected

rec·om·mend \,rekə'mend\ *vb* 1 : present as deserving of acceptance or trial 2 : advise — rec·om·mend·able \-'mendəbəl\ *adj*

rec·om·men·da·tion \,rekəmən'dāshən\ *n* 1 : act of recommending 2 : something recommended or that recommends

rec·om·pense \'rekəm,pens\ *n* : compensation — recompense *vb*

rec·on·cile \'rekən,sīl\ *vb* -ciled; -cil·ing 1 : cause to be friendly again 2 : adjust or settle 3 : bring to acceptance — rec·on·cil·able *adj* — rec·on·cile·ment *n* — rec·on·cil·er *n* — rec·on·cil·i·a·tion \,rekən,silē'āshən\ *n*

re·con·dite \'rekən,dīt, ri'kän-\ *adj* 1 : hard to understand 2 : little known

re·con·di·tion \,rēkən,dishən\ *vb* : restore to good condition

re·con·nais·sance \ri'känəzəns, -səns\ *n* : exploratory survey of enemy territory

re·con·noi·ter, re·con·noi·tre \,rēkə'nȯitər, ,rekə-\ *vb* -tered *or* -tred; -ter·ing *or* -tring : make a reconnaissance of

re·cord \ri'kȯrd\ *vb* 1 : set down in writing 2 : register permanently 3 : indicate 4 : preserve (as sound or images) for later reproduction ~ \'rekərd\ *n* 1 : something recorded 2 : best performance

re·cord·er \ri'kȯrdər\ *n* 1 : person or device that records 2 : wind instrument with finger holes

¹re·count \ri'kaunt\ *vb* : relate in detail

²re·count \,rē'-\ *vb* : count again — recount \'rē,-, ,rē'-\ *n*

re·coup \ri'küp\ *vb* : make up for (an expense or loss)

re·course \'rē,kȯrs, ri'-\ *n* : source of aid or a turning to such a source

re·cov·er \ri'kəvər\ *vb* 1 : regain position, poise, or health 2 : recoup — re·cov·er·able *adj* — re·cov·ery \-'kəvərē\ *n*

rec·re·a·tion \,rekrē'āshən\ *n* : a refreshing of strength or spirits as a change from work or study — rec·re·a·tion·al \-shənəl\ *adj*

re·crim·i·na·tion \ri,krimə'nāshən\ *n* : retaliatory accusation — re·crim·i·nate *vb*

re·cruit \ri'krüt\ *n* : newly enlisted member ~ *vb* : enlist the membership or services of — re·cruit·er *n* — re·cruit·ment *n*

rect·an·gle \'rek,taṅgəl\ *n* : 4-sided figure with 4 right angles — rect·an·gu·lar \rek'taṅgyələr\ *adj*

rec·ti·fy \'rektə,fī\ *vb* -fied; -fy·ing : make or set right — rec·ti·fi·ca·tion \,rektəfə'kāshən\ *n*

rec·ti·tude \'rektə,tüd, -,tyüd\ *n* : moral integrity

rec·tor \'rektər\ *n* : pastor

rec·to·ry \'rektərē\ *n, pl* -ries : rector's residence

rec·tum \'rektəm\ *n, pl* -tums *or* -ta \-tə\ : last part of the intestine joining the colon and anus — rec·tal \-t³l\ *adj*

re·cum·bent \ri'kəmbənt\ *adj* : lying down

re·cu·per·ate \ri'küpə,rāt, -'kyü-\ *vb* **-at·ed; -at·ing** : recover (as from illness) — **re·cu·per·a·tion** \-,küpə'rāshən, -,kyü-\ *n* — **re·cu·per·a·tive** \-'küpərātiv, -'kyü-\ *adj*

re·cur \ri'kər\ *vb* **-rr-** **1** : return in thought or talk **2** : occur again — **re·cur·rence** \-'kərəns\ *n* — **re·cur·rent** \-ənt\ *adj*

re·cy·cle \rē'sīkəl\ *vb* : process (as glass or cans) in order to regain a material for human use — **re·cy·cla·ble** \-kələbəl\ *adj*

red \'red\ *n* **1** : color of blood or of the ruby **2** *cap* : communist — **red** *adj* — **red·dish** *adj* — **red·ness** *n*

red·den \'red°n\ *vb* : make or become red or reddish

re·deem \ri'dēm\ *vb* **1** : regain, free, or rescue by paying a price **2** : atone for **3** : free from sin **4** : convert into something of value — **re·deem·able** *adj* — **re·deem·er** *n*

re·demp·tion \-'dempshən\ *n* : act of redeeming — **re·demp·tive** \-tiv\ *adj* — **re·demp·to·ry** \-tərē\ *adj*

red·head \-,hed\ *n* : one having red hair — **red·head·ed** \-'hedəd\ *adj*

red·o·lent \'red°lənt\ *adj* **1** : having a fragrance **2** : suggestive — **red·o·lence** \-əns\ *n* — **red·o·lent·ly** *adv*

re·dou·ble \rē'dəbəl\ *vb* **1** : make twice as great in size or amount **2** : intensify

re·doubt \ri'daut\ *n* : small fortification

re·doubt·able \-əbəl\ *adj* : arousing dread

re·dound \ri'daund\ *vb* : have an effect

re·dress \ri'dres\ *vb* : set right ∼ *n* **1** : relief or remedy **2** : compensation

red tape *n* : complex obstructive official routine

re·duce \ri'düs, -'dyüs\ *vb* **1** : lessen **2** : put in a lower rank **3** : lose weight — **re·duc·er** *n* — **re·duc·ible** \-'düsəbəl, -'dyü-\ *adj*

re·duc·tion \ri'dəkshən\ *n* **1** : act of reducing **2** : amount lost in reducing **3** : something made by reducing

re·dun·dant \ri'dəndənt\ *adj* : using more words than necessary — **re·dun·dan·cy** \-dənsē\ *n* — **re·dun·dant·ly** *adv*

red·wood *n* : tall coniferous timber tree

reed \'rēd\ *n* **1** : tall slender grass of wet areas **2** : elastic strip that vibrates to produce tones in certain wind instruments — **reedy** *adj*

reef \'rēf\ *n* : ridge of rocks or sand at or near the surface of the water

reek \'rēk\ *n* : strong or disagreeable fume or odor ∼ *vb* : give off a reek

¹reel \'rēl\ *n* : revolvable device on which something flexible is wound or a quantity of something wound on it ∼ *vb* **1** : wind on a reel **2** : pull in by reeling — **reel·able** *adj* — **reel·er** *n*

²reel *vb* **1** : whirl or waver as from a blow **2** : walk or move unsteadily ∼ *n* : reeling motion

³reel *n* : lively dance

re·fer \ri'fər\ *vb* **-rr-** **1** : direct or send to some person or place **2** : submit for consideration or action **3** : have connection **4** : mention or allude to something — **re·fer·able** \'refərəbəl, ri'fərə-\ *adj* — **re·fer·ral** \ri'fərəl\ *n*

ref·er·ee \,refə'rē\ *n* **1** : one to whom an issue is referred for settlement **2** : sports official ∼ *vb* **-eed; -ee·ing** : act as referee

ref·er·ence \'refərəns\ *n* **1** : act of referring **2** : a bearing on a matter **3** : consultation for information **4** : person who can speak for one's character or ability or a recommendation given by such a person

ref·er·en·dum \,refə'rendəm\ *n, pl* **-da** \-də\ *or* **-dums** : a submitting of legislative measures for voters' approval or rejection

re·fill \,rē'fil\ *vb* : fill again — **re·fill** \'rē,-\ *n* — **re·fill·able** *adj*

re·fine \ri'fīn\ *vb* **-fined; -fin·ing** **1** : free from impurities or waste matter **2** : improve or perfect **3** : free or become free of what is coarse or uncouth — **re·fine·ment** \-mənt\ *n* — **re·fin·er** *n*

re·fin·ery \ri'fīnərē\ *n, pl* **-er·ies** : place for refining (as oil or sugar)

re·flect \ri'flekt\ *vb* **1** : bend or cast back (as light or heat) **2** : bring as a result **3** : cast reproach or blame **4** : ponder — **re·flec·tion**

\-'flekshən\ *n* — re·flec·tive \-tiv\ *adj* — re·flec·tor \ri'flektər\ *n*

♦ re·flex \'rē‚fleks\ *n* : automatic response to a stimulus ∼ *adj* 1 : bent back 2 : relating to a reflex — re·flex·ly *adv*

re·flex·ive \ri'fleksiv\ *adj* : of or relating to an action directed back upon the doer or the grammatical subject — **reflexive** *n* — re·flex·ive·ly *adv* — re·flex·ive·ness *n*

re·form \ri'fȯrm\ *vb* : make or become better esp. by correcting bad habits — **reform** *n* — re·form·able *adj* — re·for·ma·tive \-'fȯrmətiv\ *adj* — re·form·er *n*

re·for·ma·to·ry \ri'fȯrmə‚tōrē\ *n, pl* -ries : penal institution for reforming young offenders

re·fract \ri'frakt\ *vb* : subject to refraction

re·frac·tion \-'frakshən\ *n* : the bending of a ray (as of light) when it passes from one medium into another — re·frac·tive \-tiv\ *adj*

re·frac·to·ry \ri'fraktərē\ *adj* : obstinate or unmanageable

re·frain \ri'frān\ *vb* : hold oneself back ∼ *n* : verse recurring regularly in a song — re·frain·ment *n*

re·fresh \ri'fresh\ *vb* 1 : make or become fresh or fresher 2 : supply or take refreshment — re·fresh·er *n* — re·fresh·ing·ly *adv*

re·fresh·ment \-mənt\ *n* 1 : act of refreshing 2 *pl* : light meal

re·frig·er·ate \ri'frijə‚rāt\ *vb* -ated; -ating : chill or freeze (food) for preservation — re·frig·er·ant \-ərənt\ *adj or n* — re·frig·er·a·tion \-‚frijə'rāshən\ *n* — re·frig·er·a·tor \-'frijə‚rātər\ *n*

ref·uge \'ref‚yüj\ *n* 1 : protection from danger 2 : place that provides protection

ref·u·gee \‚refyu'jē\ *n* : person who flees for safety

re·fund \ri'fənd, 'rē‚fənd\ *vb* : give or put back (money) ∼ \'rē‚-\ *n* 1 : act of refunding 2 : sum refunded — re·fund·able *adj*

re·fur·bish \ri'fərbish\ *vb* : renovate

¹re·fuse \ri'fyüz\ *vb* -fused; -fusing : decline to accept, do, or give — re·fus·al \-'fyüzəl\ *n*

²ref·use \'ref‚yüs, -‚yüz\ *n* : worthless matter

re·fute \ri'fyüt\ *vb* -fut·ed; -futing : prove to be false — ref·u·ta·tion \‚refyu'tāshən\ *n* — re·fut·er \ri'fyütər\ *n*

re·gal \'rēgəl\ *adj* 1 : befitting a king 2 : stately — re·gal·ly *adv*

re·gale \ri'gāl\ *vb* -galed; -gal·ing 1 : entertain richly or agreeably 2 : delight

re·ga·lia \ri'gālyə\ *n pl* 1 : symbols of royalty 2 : insignia of an office or order 3 : finery

re·gard \ri'gärd\ *n* 1 : consideration 2 : feeling of approval and liking 3 *pl* : friendly greetings 4 : relation ∼ *vb* 1 : pay attention to 2 : show respect for 3 : have an opinion of 4 : look at 5 : relate to — re·gard·ful *adj* — re·gard·less *adj*

re·gard·ing *prep* : concerning

regardless of \ri'gärdləs-\ *prep* : in spite of

re·gen·er·ate \ri'jenərət\ *adj* 1 : formed or created again 2 : spiritually reborn ∼ \-‚jenə‚rāt\ *vb* 1 : reform completely 2 : replace (a lost body part) by new tissue growth 3 : give new life to — re·gen·er·a·tion \-‚jenə'rāshən\ *n* — re·gen·er·a·tive \-'jenə‚rātiv\ *adj* — re·gen·er·a·tor \-‚rātər\ *n*

re·gent \'rējənt\ *n* 1 : person who rules during the childhood, absence, or incapacity of the sovereign 2 : member of a governing board — re·gen·cy \-jənsē\ *n*

re·gime \rā'zhēm, ri-\ *n* : government in power

reg·i·men \'rejəmən\ *n* : systematic course of treatment or training

reg·i·ment \'rejəmənt\ *n* : military unit ~ \-ˌment\ *vb* 1 : organize rigidly for control 2 : make orderly — **reg·i·men·tal** \ˌrejə'mentʲl\ *adj* — **reg·i·men·ta·tion** \-mən-'tāshən\ *n*

re·gion \'rējən\ *n* : indefinitely defined area — **re·gion·al** \'rējənəl\ *adj* — **re·gion·al·ly** *adv*

reg·is·ter \'rejəstər\ *n* 1 : record of items or details or a book for keeping such a record 2 : device to regulate ventilation 3 : counting or recording device 4 : range of a voice or instrument ~ *vb* 1 : enter in a register 2 : record automatically 3 : get special care for mail by paying more postage

reg·is·trar \-ˌsträr\ *n* : official keeper of records

reg·is·tra·tion \ˌrejə'strāshən\ *n* 1 : act of registering 2 : entry in a register

reg·is·try \'rejəstrē\ *n, pl* **-tries** 1 : enrollment 2 : place of registration 3 : official record book

re·gress \ri'gres\ *vb* : go or cause to go back or to a lower level — **re·gres·sion** \-'greshən\ *n* — **re·gres·sive** *adj*

re·gret \ri'gret\ *vb* **-tt-** 1 : mourn the loss or death of 2 : be very sorry for ~ *n* 1 : sorrow or the expression of sorrow 2 *pl* : message declining an invitation — **re·gret·ful** \-fəl\ *adj* — **re·gret·ful·ly** *adv* — **re·gret·ta·ble** \-əbəl\ *adj* — **re·gret·ta·bly** \-blē\ *adv* — **re·gret·ter** *n*

reg·u·lar \'regyələr\ *adj* 1 : conforming to what is usual, normal, or average 2 : steady, uniform, or unvarying — **regular** *n* — **reg·u·lar·i·ty** \ˌregyə'larətē\ *n* — **reg·u·lar·ize** \'regyələˌrīz\ *vb* — **reg·u·lar·ly** *adv*

reg·u·late \'regyəˌlāt\ *vb* **-lat·ed; -lat·ing** 1 : govern according to rule 2 : adjust to a standard — **reg·u·la·tive** \-ˌlātiv\ *adj* — **reg·u·la·tor** \-ˌlātər\ *n* — **reg·u·la·to·ry** \-lə·tōrē\ *adj*

reg·u·la·tion \ˌregyə'lāshən\ *n* 1 : act of regulating 2 : rule dealing with details of procedure

re·gur·gi·tate \rē'gərjəˌtāt\ *vb* **-tat·ed; -tat·ing** : vomit — **re·gur·gi·ta·tion** \-ˌgərjə'tāshən\ *n*

re·ha·bil·i·tate \ˌrēhə'biləˌtāt\ *vb* **-tat·ed; -tat·ing** 1 : reinstate 2 : make good or usable again — **re·ha·bil·i·ta·tion** \-ˌbilə'tāshən\ *n*

re·hears·al \ri'hərsəl\ *n* : practice session or performance

re·hearse \-'hərs\ *vb* **-hearsed; -hears·ing** 1 : repeat or recount 2 : engage in a rehearsal of — **re·hears·er** *n*

reign \'rān\ *n* : sovereign's authority or rule ~ *vb* : rule as a sovereign

re·im·burse \ˌrēəm'bərs\ *vb* **-bursed; -burs·ing** : repay — **re·im·burs·able** *adj* — **re·im·burse·ment** *n*

rein \'rān\ *n* 1 : strap fastened to a bit to control an animal 2 : restraining influence ~ *vb* : direct by reins

re·in·car·na·tion \ˌrē·inˌkär'nāshən\ *n* : rebirth of the soul — **re·in·car·nate** \ˌrēin'kärˌnāt\ *vb*

rein·deer \'rānˌdir\ *n* : caribou

re·in·force \ˌrēən'fōrs\ *vb* : strengthen or support — **re·in·force·ment** *n* — **re·in·forc·er** *n*

re·in·state \ˌrēən'stāt\ *vb* : restore to a former position — **re·in·state·ment** *n*

re·it·er·ate \rē'itəˌrāt\ *vb* : say again — **re·it·er·a·tion** \-ˌitə'rāshən\ *n*

re·ject \ri'jekt\ *vb* 1 : refuse to grant or consider 2 : refuse to admit, believe, or receive 3 : throw out as useless or unsatisfactory ~ \'rēˌ-\ *n* : rejected person or thing — **re·jec·tion** \-'jekshən\ *n*

re·joice \ri'jòis\ *vb* **-joiced; -joic·ing** : feel joy — **re·joic·er** *n*

re·join *vb* 1 \ˌrē'jòin\ : join again 2 \ri'-\ : say in answer

re·join·der \ri'jòindər\ *n* : answer

re·ju·ve·nate \ri'jüvəˌnāt\ *vb* **-nat·ed; -nat·ing** : make young again — **re·ju·ve·na·tion** \-ˌjüvə'nāshən\ *n*

re·lapse \ri'laps, 'rēˌlaps\ *n* : recurrence of illness after a period of improvement ~ \ri'-\ *vb* : suffer a relapse

re·late \ri'lāt\ *vb* **-lat·ed; -lat·ing** 1 : give a report of 2 : show a connection between 3 : have a relationship — **re·lat·able** *adj* — **re·lat·er, re·la·tor** *n*

re·la·tion \ri'lāshən\ *n* **1** : account **2** : connection **3** : relationship **4** : reference **5** *pl* : dealings

re·la·tion·ship \-,ship\ *n* : the state of being related or interrelated

rel·a·tive \'relətiv\ *n* : person connected with another by blood or marriage ∼ *adj* : considered in comparison with something else — **rel·a·tive·ly** *adv* — **rel·a·tive·ness** *n*

◆ **re·lax** \ri'laks\ *vb* **1** : make or become less tense or rigid **2** : make less severe **3** : seek rest or recreation — **re·lax·er** *n*

re·lax·a·tion \,rē,lak'sāshən\ *n* **1** : lessening of tension **2** : recreation

re·lay \'rē,lā\ *n* : fresh supply (as of horses or people) arranged to relieve others ∼ \'rē,-, ri'-\ *vb* **-layed; -lay·ing** : pass along in stages

re·lease \ri'lēs\ *vb* **-leased; -leas·ing 1** : free from confinement or oppression **2** : relinquish **3** : permit publication, performance, exhibition, or sale ∼ *n* **1** : relief from trouble **2** : discharge from an obligation **3** : act of releasing or what is released

rel·e·gate \'relə,gāt\ *vb* **-gat·ed; -gat·ing 1** : remove to some less prominent position **2** : assign to a particular class or sphere — **rel·e·ga·tion** \,relə'gāshən\ *n*

re·lent \ri'lent\ *vb* : become less severe

re·lent·less \-ləs\ *adj* : mercilessly severe or persistent — **re·lent·less·ly** *adv* — **re·lent·less·ness** *n*

rel·e·vance \'reləvəns\ *n* : relation to the matter at hand — **rel·e·vant** \-vənt\ *adj* — **rel·e·vant·ly** *adv*

re·li·able \ri'līəbəl\ *adj* : fit to be trusted — **re·li·abil·i·ty** \-,līə-**'bilətē\ *n* — **re·li·able·ness** *n* — **re·li·ably** \-'līəblē\ *adv*

re·li·ance \ri'līəns\ *n* : act or result of relying

re·li·ant \ri'līənt\ *adj* : dependent

rel·ic \'relik\ *n* **1** : object venerated because of its association with a saint or martyr **2** : remaining trace

re·lief \ri'lēf\ *n* **1** : lightening of something oppressive **2** : welfare

re·lieve \ri'lēv\ *vb* **-lieved; -liev·ing 1** : free from a burden or distress **2** : release from a post or duty **3** : break the monotony of — **re·liev·er** *n*

re·li·gion \ri'lijən\ *n* **1** : service and worship of God **2** : set or system of religious beliefs — **re·li·gion·ist** *n*

re·li·gious \-'lijəs\ *adj* **1** : relating or devoted to an ultimate reality or deity **2** : relating to religious beliefs or observances **3** : faithful, fervent, or zealous — **re·li·gious·ly** *adv*

re·lin·quish \-'liŋkwish, -'lin-\ *vb* **1** : renounce **2** : let go of — **re·lin·quish·ment** *n*

rel·ish \'relish\ *n* **1** : keen enjoyment **2** : highly seasoned sauce (as of pickles) ∼ *vb* : enjoy — **rel·ish·able** *adj*

re·live \,rē'liv\ *vb* : live over again (as in the imagination)

re·lo·cate \,rē'lō,kāt, ,rēlō'kāt\ *vb* : move to a new location — **re·lo·ca·tion** \,rēlō'kāshən\ *n*

re·luc·tant \ri'ləktənt\ *adj* : feeling or showing doubt or unwillingness — **re·luc·tance** \ri'ləktəns\ *n* — **re·luc·tant·ly** *adv*

re·ly \ri'lī\ *vb* **-lied; -ly·ing** : place faith or confidence — often with *on*

re·main \ri'mān\ *vb* **1** : be left after others have been removed **2** : be something yet to be done **3** : stay behind **4** : continue unchanged

WHERE'S ODIE? I HOPE HE'S OKAY

RELAX JON, HOW MUCH TROUBLE COULD HE GET INTO ON A PLANE?

re·main·der \-'māndər\ *n* : that which is left over

re·mains \-'mānz\ *n pl* **1** : remaining part or trace **2** : dead body

re·mark \ri'märk\ *vb* : express as an observation ~ *n* : passing comment

re·mark·able \-'märkəbəl\ *adj* : extraordinary — **re·mark·able·ness** *n* — **re·mark·ably** \-blē\ *adv*

re·me·di·al \ri'mēdēəl\ *adj* : intended to remedy or improve

rem·e·dy \'remədē\ *n, pl* **-dies** **1** : medicine that cures **2** : something that corrects an evil or compensates for a loss ~ *vb* **-died; -dy·ing** : provide or serve as a remedy for

re·mem·ber \ri'membər\ *vb* **1** : think of again **2** : keep from forgetting **3** : convey greetings from

re·mem·brance \-brəns\ *n* **1** : act of remembering **2** : something that serves to bring to mind

re·mind \ri'mīnd\ *vb* : cause to remember — **re·mind·er** *n*

rem·i·nisce \remə'nis\ *vb* **-nisced; -nisc·ing** : indulge in reminiscence

rem·i·nis·cence \-'nis°ns\ *n* **1** : recalling of a past experience **2** : account of a memorable experience

rem·i·nis·cent \-°nt\ *adj* **1** : relating to reminiscence **2** : serving to remind — **rem·i·nis·cent·ly** *adv*

re·miss \ri'mis\ *adj* : negligent or careless in performance of duty — **re·miss·ly** *adv* — **re·miss·ness** *n*

re·mis·sion \ri'mishən\ *n* **1** : act of forgiving **2** : a period of relief from or easing of symptoms of a disease

re·mit \ri'mit\ *vb* **-tt-** **1** : pardon **2** : send money in payment

re·mit·tance \ri'mit°ns\ *n* : sum of money remitted

rem·nant \'remnənt\ *n* : small part or trace remaining

re·mod·el \rē'mäd°l\ *vb* : alter the structure of

re·mon·strance \ri'mänstrəns\ *n* : act or instance of remonstrating

re·mon·strate \ri'män,strāt\ *vb* **-strat·ed; -strat·ing** : speak in protest, reproof, or opposition — **re·mon·stra·tion** \ri,män'strāshən, ,remən-\ *n*

re·morse \ri'mórs\ *n* : distress arising from a sense of guilt — **re·**morse·ful *adj* — **re·morse·less** *adj*

re·mote \ri'mōt\ *adj* **-mot·er; -est** **1** : far off in place or time **2** : hard to reach or find **3** : acting, acted on, or controlled indirectly or from afar **4** : slight **5** : distant in manner — **re·mote·ly** *adv* — **re·mote·ness** *n*

re·move \ri'müv\ *vb* **-moved; -moving** **1** : move by lifting or taking off or away **2** : get rid of — **re·mov·able** *adj* — **re·mov·al** \-vəl\ *n* — **re·mov·er** *n*

re·mu·ner·ate \ri'myünə,rāt\ *vb* **-at·ed; -at·ing** : pay — **re·mu·ner·a·tion** *n* — **re·mu·ner·a·tor** \-,rātər\ *n*

re·mu·ner·a·tive \ri'myünərətiv, -,rāt-\ *adj* : gainful

re·nais·sance \,renə'säns, -'zäns\ *n* : rebirth or revival

re·nal \'rēn°l\ *adj* : relating to the kidneys

rend \'rend\ *vb* **rent** \'rent\; **rending** : tear apart forcibly

ren·der \'rendər\ *vb* **1** : extract by heating **2** : hand over or give up **3** : do (a service) for another **4** : cause to be or become

ren·dez·vous \'rändi,vü, -dā-\ *n, pl* **ren·dez·vous** \-,vüz\ **1** : place appointed for a meeting **2** : meeting at an appointed place ~ *vb* **-voused; -vous·ing** : meet at a rendezvous

ren·di·tion \ren'dishən\ *n* : version

ren·e·gade \'reni,gād\ *n* : deserter of one faith or cause for another

re·nege \ri'nig, -'neg, -'nēg, -'nāg\ *vb* **-neged; -neg·ing** : go back on a promise — **re·neg·er** *n*

re·new \ri'nü, -'nyü\ *vb* **1** : make or become new, fresh, or strong again **2** : begin again **3** : grant or obtain an extension of — **re·new·able** *adj* — **re·new·al** *n* — **re·new·er** *n*

re·nounce \ri'naúns\ *vb* **-nounced; -nounc·ing** : give up, refuse, or resign — **re·nounce·ment** *n*

ren·o·vate \'renə,vāt\ *vb* **-vat·ed; -vating** : make like new again — **ren·o·va·tion** \,renə'vāshən\ *n* — **ren·o·va·tor** \'renə,vātər\ *n*

re·nown \ri'naún\ *n* : state of being widely known and honored — **re·nowned** \-'naúnd\ *adj*

¹rent \'rent\ *n* : money paid or due periodically for the use of another's property ~ vb : hold or give possession and use of for rent — **rent·al** n or adj — **rent·er** n

²**rent** n : a tear in cloth

re·nun·ci·a·tion \ri̯nənsē'āshən\ n : act of renouncing

¹**re·pair** \ri'par\ vb : go

²**repair** vb : restore to good condition ~ n 1 : act or instance of repairing 2 : condition — **re·pair·er** n — **re·pair·man** \-ˌman\ n

rep·a·ra·tion \ˌrepə'rāshən\ n : money paid for redress — usu. pl.

rep·ar·tee \ˌrepər'tē\ n : clever replies

re·past \ri'past, 'rēˌpast\ n : meal

re·pa·tri·ate \rē'pātrē̯āt\ vb -at·ed; -ating : send back to one's own country — **re·pa·tri·ate** \-trēət, -trē̯āt\ n — **re·pa·tri·a·tion** \-ˌpātrē'āshən\ n

re·pay \rē'pā\ vb -paid; -pay·ing : pay back — **re·pay·able** adj — **re·pay·ment** n

re·peal \ri'pēl\ vb : annul by legislative action — **repeal** n — **re·peal·er** n

re·peat \ri'pēt\ vb : say or do again ~ n 1 : act of repeating 2 : something repeated — **re·peat·able** adj — **re·peat·ed·ly** adv — **re·peat·er** n

re·pel \ri'pel\ vb -pelled; -pel·ling 1 : drive away 2 : disgust — **re·pel·lent** \-'pelənt\ adj or n

re·pent \ri'pent\ vb 1 : turn from sin 2 : regret — **re·pen·tance** \ri-'pent°ns\ n — **re·pen·tant** \-°nt\ adj

re·per·cus·sion \ˌrēpər'kəshən, ˌrep-\ n : effect of something done or said

rep·er·toire \'repərˌtwär\ n : pieces a company or performer can present

rep·er·to·ry \'repərˌtōrē\ n, pl -ries 1 : repertoire 2 : theater with a resident company doing several plays

rep·e·ti·tion \ˌrepə'tishən\ n : act or instance of repeating

rep·e·ti·tious \-'tishəs\ adj : tediously repeating — **rep·e·ti·tious·ly** adv — **rep·e·ti·tious·ness** n

re·pet·i·tive \ri'petətiv\ adj : repetitious — **re·pet·i·tive·ly** adv — **re·pet·i·tive·ness** n

re·pine \ri'pīn\ vb re·pined; re-

pin·ing : feel or express discontent

re·place \ri'plās\ vb 1 : restore to a former position 2 : take the place of 3 : put something new in the place of — **re·place·able** adj — **re·place·ment** n — **re·plac·er** n

re·plen·ish \ri'plenish\ vb : stock or supply anew — **re·plen·ish·ment** n

re·plete \ri'plēt\ adj : full — **re·plete·ness** n — **re·ple·tion** \-'plēshən\ n

rep·li·ca \'replikə\ n : exact copy

rep·li·cate \'replə̯kāt\ vb -cat·ed; -cating : duplicate or repeat — **rep·li·cate** \-likət\ n — **rep·li·ca·tion** \-lə'kāshən\ n

re·ply \ri'plī\ vb -plied; -ply·ing : say or do in answer ~ n pl -plies : answer

re·port \ri'pōrt\ n 1 : rumor 2 : statement of information (as events or causes) 3 : explosive noise ~ vb 1 : give an account of 2 : present an account of (an event) as news 3 : present oneself 4 : make known to authorities — **re·port·age** \ri'pōrtij, ˌrepər'täzh, ˌrepˌór'-\ n — **re·port·ed·ly** adv — **re·port·er** n — **re·por·to·ri·al** \ˌrepər'tōrēəl\ adj

re·pose \ri'pōz\ vb -posed; -pos·ing : lay or lie at rest ~ n 1 : state of resting 2 : calm or peace — **re·pose·ful** adj

re·pos·i·to·ry \ri'päzəˌtōrē\ n, pl -ries : place where something is stored

re·pos·sess \ˌrēpə'zes\ vb : regain possession and legal ownership of — **re·pos·ses·sion** \-'zeshən\ n

rep·re·hend \ˌrepri'hend\ vb : censure — **rep·re·hen·sion** \-'henchən\ n

rep·re·hen·si·ble \-'hensəbəl\ adj : deserving condemnation — **rep·re·hen·si·bly** adv

rep·re·sent \ˌrepri'zent\ vb 1 : serve as a sign or symbol of 2 : act or speak for 3 : describe as having a specified quality or character — **rep·re·sen·ta·tion** \ˌrepriˌzen'tā-hən\ n

rep·re·sen·ta·tive \ˌrepri'zentətiv\ adj 1 : standing or acting for another 2 : carried on by elected representatives ~ n 1 : typical example 2 : one that represents another 3 : member of usu. the lower house of a legislature — **rep·re·sen·ta·tive·ly** adv — **rep·re·sen·ta·tive·ness** n

re·press \ri'pres\ vb : restrain or suppress — **re·pres·sion** \-'preshən\ n — **re·pres·sive** \-'presiv\ adj

re·prieve \ri'prēv\ n 1 : a delay in punishment 2 : temporary respite — **reprieve** vb

rep·ri·mand \'reprə,mand\ n : formal or severe criticism — **reprimand** vb

re·pri·sal \ri'prīzəl\ n : act in retaliation

re·prise \ri'prēz\ n : musical repetition

re·proach \ri'prōch\ n 1 : disgrace 2 : rebuke ~ vb : express disapproval to — **re·proach·ful** adj — **re·proach·ful·ly** adv — **re·proach·ful·ness** n

rep·ro·bate \'reprə,bāt\ n : scoundrel — **reprobate** adj

rep·ro·ba·tion \,reprə'bāshən\ n : strong disapproval

re·pro·duce \,rēprə'düs, -'dyüs\ vb 1 : produce again or anew 2 : produce offspring — **re·pro·duc·ible** \-'düsəbəl, -'dyü-\ adj — **re·pro·duc·tion** \-'dəkshən\ n — **re·pro·duc·tive** \-'dəktiv\ adj

re·proof \ri'prüf\ n : blame or censure for a fault

re·prove \ri'prüv\ vb -proved; -prov·ing : express disapproval to or of

rep·tile \'rept°l, -,tīl\ n : air-breathing scaly vertebrate — **rep·til·ian** \rep'tilēən\ adj or n

re·pub·lic \ri'pəblik\ n : country with representative government

re·pub·li·can \-likən\ adj 1 : relating to or resembling a republic 2 : supporting a republic — **republican** n — **re·pub·li·can·ism** n

re·pu·di·ate \ri'pyüdē,āt\ vb -at·ed; -at·ing : refuse to have anything to do with — **re·pu·di·a·tion** \-,pyüdē'āshən\ n

re·pug·nant \ri'pəgnənt\ adj : contrary to one's tastes or principles — **re·pug·nance** \-nəns\ n — **re·pug·nant·ly** adv

re·pulse \ri'pəls\ vb -pulsed; -puls·ing 1 : drive or beat back 2 : rebuff 3 : be repugnant to — **repulse** n — **re·pul·sion** \-'pəlshən\ n

re·pul·sive \-siv\ adj : arousing

aversion or disgust — **re·pul·sive·ly** adv — **re·pul·sive·ness** n

rep·u·ta·ble \'repyətəbəl\ adj : having a good reputation — **rep·u·ta·bly** \-blē\ adv

rep·u·ta·tion \,repyə'tāshən\ n : one's character or public esteem

re·pute \ri'pyüt\ vb -put·ed; -put·ing : think of as being ~ n : reputation — **re·put·ed** adj — **re·put·ed·ly** adv

re·quest \ri'kwest\ n : act or instance of asking for something or a thing asked for ~ vb 1 : make a request of 2 : ask for — **re·quest·er** n

re·qui·em \'rekwēəm, 'räk-\ n : Mass for a dead person or a musical setting for this

re·quire \ri'kwīr\ vb -quired; -quir·ing 1 : insist on 2 : call for as essential — **re·quire·ment** n

req·ui·site \'rekwəzət\ adj : necessary — **requisite** n

req·ui·si·tion \,rekwə'zishən\ n : formal application or demand — **requisition** vb

re·quite \ri'kwīt\ vb -quit·ed; -quit·ing : make return for or to — **re·quit·al** \-'kwīt°l\ n

re·scind \ri'sind\ vb : repeal or cancel — **re·scis·sion** \-'sizhən\ n

res·cue \'reskyü\ vb -cued; -cu·ing : set free from danger or confinement — **rescue** n — **res·cu·er** n

re·search \ri'sərch, 'rē,sərch\ n : careful or diligent search esp. for new knowledge — **research** vb — **re·search·er** n

re·sem·ble \ri'zembəl\ vb -sem·bled; -sem·bling : be like or similar to — **re·sem·blance** \-'zembləns\ n

re·sent \ri'zent\ vb : feel or show annoyance at — **re·sent·ful** adj — **re·sent·ful·ly** adv — **re·sent·ment** n

res·er·va·tion \,rezər'vāshən\ n 1 : act of reserving or something reserved 2 : limiting condition

re·serve \ri'zərv\ vb -served; -serv·ing 1 : store for future use 2 : set aside for special use ~ n 1 : something reserved 2 : restraint in words or bearing 3 : military forces withheld from action or not part of the regular services — **reserved** adj

res·er·voir \'rezər,vwär, -,vwȯr, -,vȯr, -,vȯi\ *n* : place where something (as water) is kept in store

re·side \ri'zīd\ *vb* **-sid·ed; -sid·ing 1** : make one's home **2** : be present

res·i·dence \'rezədəns\ *n* **1** : act or fact of residing in a place **2** : place where one lives — **res·i·dent** \-ənt\ *adj or n* — **res·i·den·tial** \,rezə'denchəl\ *adj*

res·i·due \'rezə,dü, -,dyü\ *n* : part remaining — **re·sid·u·al** \ri-'zijəwəl\ *adj*

re·sign \ri'zīn\ *vb* **1** : give up deliberately **2** : give (oneself) over without resistance — **res·ig·na·tion** \,rezig'nāshən\ *n* — **re·sign·ed·ly** \-'zīnədlē\ *adv*

re·sil·ience \ri'zilyəns\ *n* : ability to recover or adjust easily

re·sil·ien·cy \-yənsē\ *n* : resilience

re·sil·ient \-yənt\ *adj* : elastic

res·in \'rez°n\ *n* : substance from the gum or sap of trees — **res·in·ous** *adj*

re·sist \ri'zist\ *vb* **1** : withstand the force or effect of **2** : fight against — **re·sist·ible** \-'zistəbəl\ *adj* — **re·sist·less** *adj*

re·sis·tance \ri'zistəns\ *n* **1** : act of resisting **2** : ability of an organism to resist disease **3** : opposition to electric current

re·sis·tant \-tənt\ *adj* : giving resistance

res·o·lute \'rezə,lüt\ *adj* : having a fixed purpose — **res·o·lute·ly** *adv* — **res·o·lute·ness** *n*

res·o·lu·tion \,rezə'lüshən\ *n* **1** : process of resolving **2** : firmness of purpose **3** : statement of the opinion, will, or intent of a body

re·solve \ri'zälv\ *vb* **-solved; -solv·ing 1** : find an answer to **2** : make a formal resolution ∼ *n* **1** : something resolved **2** : steadfast purpose — **re·solv·able** *adj*

res·o·nant \'rez°nənt\ *adj* **1** : continuing to sound **2** : relating to intensification or prolongation of sound (as by a vibrating body) — **res·o·nance** \-əns\ *n* — **res·o·nant·ly** *adv*

re·sort \ri'zȯrt\ *n* **1** : source of help **2** : place to go for vacation ∼ *vb* **1** : go often or habitually **2** : have recourse

re·sound \ri'zaund\ *vb* : become filled with sound

re·sound·ing \-iŋ\ *adj* : impressive — **re·sound·ing·ly** *adv*

re·source \'rē,sȯrs, ri'sȯrs\ *n* **1** : new or reserve source **2** *pl* : available funds **3** : ability to handle situations — **re·source·ful** *adj* — **re·source·ful·ness** *n*

re·spect \ri'spekt\ *n* **1** : relation to something **2** : high or special regard **3** : detail ∼ *vb* : consider deserving of high regard — **re·spect·er** *n* — **re·spect·ful** *adj* — **re·spect·ful·ly** *adv* — **re·spect·ful·ness** *n*

re·spect·able \ri'spektəbəl\ *adj* **1** : worthy of respect **2** : fair in size, quantity, or quality — **re·spect·abil·i·ty** \-,spektə'bilətē\ *n* — **re·spect·ably** \-'spektəblē\ *adv*

re·spec·tive \-tiv\ *adj* : individual and specific

re·spec·tive·ly \-lē\ *adv* **1** : as relating to each **2** : each in the order given

res·pi·ra·tion \,respə'rāshən\ *n* : act or process of breathing — **re·spi·ra·to·ry** \'respərə,tōrē, ri'spīrə-\ *adj* — **re·spire** \ri'spīr\ *vb*

res·pi·ra·tor \'respə,rātər\ *n* : device for artificial respiration

re·spite \'respət\ *n* : temporary delay or rest

re·splen·dent \ri'splendənt\ *adj* : shining brilliantly — **re·splen·dence** \-dəns\ *n* — **re·splen·dent·ly** *adv*

re·spond \ri'spänd\ *vb* **1** : answer **2** : react — **re·spon·dent** \-'spändənt\ *n or adj* — **re·spond·er** *n*

re·sponse \ri'späns\ *n* **1** : act of responding **2** : answer

re·spon·si·ble \ri'spänsəbəl\ *adj* **1** : answerable for acts or decisions **2** : able to fulfill obligations **3** : having important duties — **re·spon·si·bil·i·ty** \ri,spänsə'bilətē\ *n* — **re·spon·si·ble·ness** *n* — **re·spon·si·bly** \-blē\ *adv*

re·spon·sive \-siv\ *adj* : quick to respond — **re·spon·sive·ly** *adv* — **re·spon·sive·ness** *n*

¹**rest** \'rest\ *n* **1** : sleep **2** : freedom from work or activity **3** : state of inactivity **4** : something used as a support ∼ *vb* **1** : get rest **2** : cease action or motion **3** : give rest to **4** : sit or lie fixed or supported **5**

: depend — **rest·ful** *adj* — **rest·ful·ly** *adv*

²rest *n* : remainder

◆ **res·tau·rant** \'restərənt, -tə-ˌränt\ *n* : public eating place

res·ti·tu·tion \ˌrestə'tüshən, -'tyü-\ *n* : act or fact of restoring something or repaying someone

res·tive \'restiv\ *adj* : uneasy or fidgety — **res·tive·ly** *adv* — **res·tive·ness** *n*

rest·less \'restləs\ *adj* 1 : lacking or giving no rest 2 : always moving 3 : uneasy — **rest·less·ly** *adv* — **rest·less·ness** *n*

re·store \ri'stōr\ *vb* **-stored; -storing** 1 : give back 2 : put back into use or into a former state — **re·stor·able** *adj* — **res·to·ra·tion** \ˌrestə'rāshən\ *n* — **re·stor·ative** \ri'stōrətiv\ *n or adj* — **re·stor·er** *n*

re·strain \ri'strān\ *vb* : limit or keep under control — **re·strain·able** *adj* — **re·strained** \-'strānd\ *adj* — **re·strain·ed·ly** \-'strānədlē\ *adv* — **re·strain·er** *n*

restraining order *n* : legal order directing one person to stay away from another

re·straint \-'strānt\ *n* 1 : act of restraining 2 : restraining force 3 : control over feelings

re·strict \ri'strikt\ *vb* 1 : confine within bounds 2 : limit use of — **re·stric·tion** \-'strikshən\ *n* — **re·stric·tive** *adj* — **re·stric·tive·ly** *adv*

re·sult \ri'zəlt\ *vb* : come about because of something else ∼ *n* 1 : thing that results 2 : something obtained by calculation or investigation — **re·sul·tant** \-'zəlt°nt\ *adj or n*

re·sume \ri'züm\ *vb* **-sumed; -suming** : return to or take up again after interruption — **re·sump·tion** \-'zəmpshən\ *n*

ré·su·mé, re·su·me, re·su·mé \'rezəˌmā, ˌrezə'-\ *n* : summary of one's career and qualifications

re·sur·gence \ri'sərjəns\ *n* : a rising again — **re·sur·gent** \-jənt\ *adj*

res·ur·rect \ˌrezə'rekt\ *vb* 1 : raise from the dead 2 : bring to attention or use again — **res·ur·rec·tion** \-'rekshən\ *n*

re·sus·ci·tate \ri'səsəˌtāt\ *vb* **-tated; -tating** : bring back from apparent death — **re·sus·ci·ta·tion** \riˌsəsə'tāshən, ˌrē-\ *n* — **re·sus·ci·ta·tor** \-ˌtātər\ *n*

re·tail \'rēˌtāl\ *vb* : sell in small quantities directly to the consumer ∼ *n* : business of selling to consumers — **retail** *adj or adv* — **re·tail·er** *n*

re·tain \ri'tān\ *vb* 1 : keep or hold onto 2 : engage the services of

re·tain·er *n* 1 : household servant 2 : retaining fee

re·tal·i·ate \ri'talēˌāt\ *vb* **-at·ed; -ating** : return (as an injury) in kind — **re·tal·i·a·tion** \-ˌtalē'āshən\ *n* — **re·tal·ia·to·ry** \-'talyəˌtōrē\ *adj*

re·tard \ri'tärd\ *vb* : hold back — **re·tar·da·tion** \ˌrēˌtär'dāshən, ri-\ *n*

re·tard·ed \ri'tärdəd\ *adj* : slow or limited in intellectual development

retch \'rech\ *vb* : try to vomit

re·ten·tion \ri'tenchən\ *n* 1 : state of being retained 2 : ability to retain — **re·ten·tive** \-'tentiv\ *adj*

ret·i·cent \'retəsənt\ *adj* : tending not to talk — **ret·i·cence** \-səns\ *n* — **ret·i·cent·ly** *adv*

ret·i·na \'ret°nə\ *n, pl* **-nas** *or* **-nae** \-°nˌē\ : sensory membrane lining the eye — **ret·i·nal** \'ret°nəl\ *adj*

ret·i·nue \'ret°nˌü, -ˌyü\ *n* : attendants or followers of a distinguished person

re·tire \ri'tīr\ *vb* **-tired; -tir·ing** 1 : withdraw for privacy 2 : end a

career **3** : go to bed — **re·tir·ee**
\ri‚tī'rē\ *n* — **re·tire·ment** *n*

re·tir·ing \ri'tīriŋ\ *adj* : shy

re·tort \ri'tȯrt\ *vb* : say in reply ~ *n*
: quick, witty, or cutting answer

re·trace \‚rē'trās\ *vb* : go over again
or in reverse

re·tract \ri'trakt\ *vb* **1** : draw back
or in **2** : withdraw a charge or
promise — **re·tract·able** *adj* — **re·trac·tion** \-'trakshən\ *n*

re·treat \ri'trēt\ *n* **1** : act of withdrawing **2** : place of privacy or
safety or meditation and study ~
vb : make a retreat

re·trench \ri'trench\ *vb* : cut down
(as expenses) — **re·trench·ment** *n*

ret·ri·bu·tion \‚retrə'byushən\ *n*
: retaliation — **re·trib·u·tive** \ri-
'tribyətiv\ *adj* — **re·trib·u·to·ry**
\-yə‚tōrē\ *adj*

re·trieve \ri'trēv\ *vb* **-trieved**; **-triev-
ing 1** : search for and bring in
game **2** : recover — **re·triev·able**
adj — **re·triev·al** \-'trēvəl\ *n*

re·triev·er \-'trēvər\ *n* : dog for re-
trieving game

ret·ro·ac·tive \‚retrō'aktiv\ *adj*
: made effective as of a prior date
— **ret·ro·ac·tive·ly** *adv*

ret·ro·grade \'retrə‚grād\ *adj* **1**
: moving backward **2** : becoming
worse

ret·ro·gress \‚retrə'gres\ *vb* : move
backward — **ret·ro·gres·sion**
\-'greshən\ *n*

ret·ro·spect \'retrə‚spekt\ *n* : review
of past events — **ret·ro·spec·tion**
\‚retrə'spekshən\ *n* — **ret·ro·
spec·tive** \-'spektiv\ *adj* — **ret·ro·
spec·tive·ly** *adv*

re·turn \ri'tərn\ *vb* **1** : go or come
back **2** : pass, give, or send back to
an earlier possessor **3** : answer **4**
: bring in as a profit **5** : give or do
in return ~ *n* **1** : act of returning
or something returned **2** *pl* : report of balloting results **3** : statement of taxable income **4** : profit
— **return** *adj* — **re·turn·able** *adj*
or *n* — **re·turn·er** *n*

re·union \rē'yünyən\ *n* **1** : act of re-
uniting **2** : a meeting of persons after a separation

re·vamp \‚rē'vamp\ *vb* : renovate or
revise

re·veal \ri'vēl\ *vb* **1** : make known **2**
: show plainly

rev·eil·le \'revəlē\ *n* : military signal
sounded about sunrise

♦ **rev·el** \'revəl\ *vb* **-eled** *or* **-elled**;
-el·ing *or* **-el·ling 1** : take part in a
revel **2** : take great pleasure ~ *n*
: wild party or celebration — **rev-
el·er, rev·el·ler** \-ər\ *n* — **rev·el-
ry** \-rē\ *n*

rev·e·la·tion \‚revə'lāshən\ *n* **1** : act
of revealing **2** : something enlight-
ening or astonishing

re·venge \ri'venj\ *vb* : avenge ~ *n* **1**
: desire for retaliation **2** : act of retaliation — **re·venge·ful** *adj* — **re·
veng·er** *n*

rev·e·nue \'revə‚nü, -‚nyü\ *n* : money collected by a government

re·ver·ber·ate \ri'vərbə‚rāt\ *vb* **-at-
ed**; **-at·ing** : resound in a series of
echoes — **re·ver·ber·a·tion**
\-‚vərbə'rāshən\ *n*

re·vere \ri'vir\ *vb* **-vered**; **-ver-
ing** : show honor and devotion to
— **rev·er·ence** \'revərəns\ *n* —
rev·er·ent \-rənt\ *adj* — **rev·er-
ent·ly** *adv*

rev·er·end \'revərənd\ *adj* : worthy
of reverence ~ *n* : clergy member

rev·er·ie \'revərē\ *n, pl* **-er·ies** : daydream

re·verse \ri'vərs\ *adj* **1** : opposite to
a previous or normal condition **2**
: acting in an opposite way ~ *vb*
-versed; **-vers·ing 1** : turn upside
down or completely around **2**
: change to the contrary or in the

opposite direction $\sim$ *n* **1** : something contrary **2** : change for the worse **3** : back of something — **re·ver·sal** \-səl\ *n* — **re·verse·ly** *adv* — **re·vers·ible** \-'vərsəbəl\ *adj*

re·vert \ri'vərt\ *vb* : return to an original type or condition — **re·ver·sion** \-'vərzhⁿn\ *n*

re·view \ri'vyü\ *n* **1** : formal inspection **2** : general survey **3** : critical evaluation **4** : second or repeated study or examination $\sim$ *vb* **1** : examine or study again **2** : reexamine judicially **3** : look back over **4** : examine critically **5** : inspect — **re·view·er** *n*

re·vile \ri'vīl\ *vb* **-viled; -vil·ing** : abuse verbally — **re·vile·ment** *n* — **re·vil·er** *n*

re·vise \-'vīz\ *vb* **-vised; -vis·ing 1** : look over something written to correct or improve **2** : make a new version of — **re·vis·able** *adj* — **re·vise** *n* — **re·vis·er, re·vi·sor** \-'vīzər\ *n* — **re·vi·sion** \-'vizhən\ *n*

re·viv·al \-'vīvəl\ *n* **1** : act of reviving or state of being revived **2** : evangelistic meeting

re·vive \-'vīv\ *vb* **-vived; -viv·ing** : bring back to life or consciousness or into use — **re·viv·er** *n*

re·vo·ca·tion \ˌrevə'kāshən\ *n* : act or instance of revoking

re·voke \ri'vōk\ *vb* **-voked; -vok·ing** : annul by recalling — **re·vok·er** *n*

re·volt \-'vōlt\ *vb* **1** : throw off allegiance **2** : cause or experience disgust or shock $\sim$ *n* : rebellion or revolution — **re·volt·er** *n*

re·volt·ing \-iŋ\ *adj* : extremely offensive — **re·volt·ing·ly** *adv*

rev·o·lu·tion \ˌrevə'lüshən\ *n* **1** : rotation **2** : progress in an orbit **3** : sudden, radical, or complete change (as overthrow of a govern-

ment) — **rev·o·lu·tion·ary** \-shəˌnerē\ *adj* or *n*

rev·o·lu·tion·ize \-shəˌnīz\ *vb* **-ized; -iz·ing** : change radically — **rev·o·lu·tion·iz·er** *n*

re·volve \ri'välv\ *vb* **-volved; -volv·ing 1** : ponder **2** : move in an orbit **3** : rotate — **re·volv·able** *adj*

re·volv·er \ri'välvər\ *n* : pistol with a revolving cylinder

re·vue \ri'vyü\ *n* : theatrical production of brief numbers

re·vul·sion \ri'vəlshən\ *n* : complete dislike or repugnance

♦ **re·ward** \ri'wörd\ *vb* : give a reward to or for $\sim$ *n* : something offered for service or achievement

re·write \ˌrē'rīt\ *vb* **-wrote; -writ·ten; -writ·ing** : revise — **rewrite** *n*

rhap·so·dy \'rapsədē\ *n, pl* **-dies 1** : expression of extravagant praise **2** : flowing free-form musical composition — **rhap·sod·ic** \rap'sädik\ *adj* — **rhap·sod·i·cal·ly** \-iklē\ *adv* — **rhap·so·dize** \'rapsəˌdīz\ *vb*

rhet·o·ric \'retərik\ *n* : art of speaking or writing effectively — **rhe·tor·i·cal** \ri'tòrikəl\ *adj* — **rhet·o·ri·cian** \ˌretə'rishən\ *n*

rheu·ma·tism \'rüməˌtizəm, 'rùm-\ *n* : disorder marked by inflammation or pain in muscles or joints — **rheu·mat·ic** \rù'matik\ *adj*

rhine·stone \'rīnˌstōn\ *n* : a colorless imitation gem

rhi·no \'rīnō\ *n, pl* **-no** or **-nos** : rhinoceros

rhi·noc·er·os \rī'näsərəs\ *n, pl* **-noc·er·os·es** or **-noc·er·os** or **-noc·eri** \-'näsəˌrī\ : large thick-skinned mammal with 1 or 2 horns on the snout

rho·do·den·dron \ˌrōdə'dendrən\ *n* : flowering evergreen shrub

rhom·bus \'rämbəs\ *n, pl* **-bus·es** or **-bi** \-ˌbī\ : parallelogram with equal sides

rhu·barb \'rü₁bärb\ *n* : garden plant with edible stalks

rhyme \'rīm\ *n* 1 : correspondence in terminal sounds 2 : verse that rhymes ~ *vb* **rhymed; rhym·ing** : make or have rhymes

rhythm \'rithəm\ *n* : regular succession of sounds or motions — **rhyth·mic** \'rithmik \ **rhyth·mi·cal** \-mikəl\ *adj* — **rhyth·mi·cal·ly** *adv*

rhythm and blues *n* : popular music based on blues and black folk music

rib \'rib\ *n* 1 : curved bone joined to the spine 2 : riblike thing ~ *vb* **-bb-** 1 : furnish or mark with ribs 2 : tease — **rib·ber** *n*

rib·ald \'ribəld\ *adj* : coarse or vulgar — **rib·ald·ry** \-əldrē\ *n*

rib·bon \'ribən\ *n* 1 : narrow strip of fabric used esp. for decoration 2 : strip of inked cloth (as in a typewriter)

ri·bo·fla·vin \₁rībə'flāvən, 'rībə₁-\ *n* : growth-promoting vitamin

rice \'rīs\ *n, pl* **rice** : starchy edible seeds of an annual cereal grass

rich \'rich\ *adj* 1 : having a lot of money or possessions 2 : valuable 3 : containing much sugar, fat, or seasoning 4 : abundant 5 : deep and pleasing in color or tone 6 : fertile — **rich·ly** *adv* — **rich·ness** *n*

rich·es \'richəz\ *n pl* : wealth

rick·ets \'rikəts\ *n* : childhood bone disease

rick·ety \'rikətē\ *adj* : shaky

rick·sha, rick·shaw \'rik₁shó\ *n* : small covered 2-wheeled carriage pulled by one person

ric·o·chet \'rikə₁shā, *Brit also* -₁shet\ *vb* **-cheted** \-₁shād\ *or* **-chet·ted** \-₁shetəd\; **-chet·ing** \-₁shāiŋ\ *or* **-chet·ting** \-₁shetiŋ\ : bounce off at an angle — **ricochet** *n*

rid \'rid\ *vb* **rid; rid·ding** : make free of something unwanted — **rid·dance** \'ridᵊns\ *n*

rid·den \'ridᵊn\ *adj* : overburdened with — used in combination

¹**rid·dle** \'ridᵊl\ *n* : puzzling question ~ *vb* **-dled; -dling** : speak in riddles

²**riddle** *vb* **-dled; -dling** : fill full of holes

ride \'rīd\ *vb* **rode** \'rōd\; **rid·den** \'ridᵊn\; **rid·ing** \'rīdiŋ\ 1 : be carried along 2 : sit on and cause to move 3 : travel over a surface 4 : tease or nag ~ *n* 1 : trip on an animal or in a vehicle 2 : mechanical device ridden for amusement

rid·er *n* 1 : one that rides 2 : attached clause or document — **rid·er·less** *adj*

ridge \'rij\ *n* 1 : range of hills 2 : raised line or strip 3 : line of intersection of 2 sloping surfaces — **ridgy** *adj*

rid·i·cule \'ridə₁kyül\ *vb* : laugh at or make fun of — **ridicule** *n*

ri·dic·u·lous \rə'dikyələs\ *adj* : arousing ridicule — **ri·dic·u·lous·ly** *adv* — **ri·dic·u·lous·ness** *n*

rife \'rīf\ *adj* : abounding — **rife** *adv*

riff·raff \'rif₁raf\ *n* : mob

¹**ri·fle** \'rīfəl\ *vb* **-fled; -fling** : ransack esp. with intent to steal — **ri·fler** \-flər\ *n*

²**rifle** *n* : long shoulder weapon with spiral grooves in the bore — **ri·fle·man** \-mən\ *n* — **ri·fling** *n*

rift \'rift\ *n* : separation — **rift** *vb*

¹**rig** \'rig\ *vb* **-gg-** 1 : fit out with rigging 2 : set up esp. as a makeshift ~ *n* 1 : distinctive shape, number, and arrangement of sails and masts of a sailing ship 2 : equipment 3 : carriage with its horse

²**rig** *vb* **-gg-** : manipulate esp. by deceptive or dishonest means

rig·ging \'rigiŋ, -ən\ *n* : lines that hold and move the masts, sails, and spars of a sailing ship

right \'rīt\ *adj* 1 : meeting a standard of conduct 2 : correct 3 : genuine 4 : normal 5 : opposite of left ~ *n* 1 : something that is correct, just, proper, or honorable 2 : something to which one has a just claim 3 : something that is on the right side ~ *adv* 1 : according to what is right 2 : immediately 3 : completely 4 : on or to the right ~ *vb* 1 : restore to a proper state 2 : bring or become upright again — **right·er** *n* — **right·ness** *n* — **right·ward** \-wərd\ *adv*

right angle *n* : angle whose sides are perpendicular to each other — **right–an·gled** \'rīt'aŋgəld\ *or* **right–an·gle** \-gəl\ *adj*

righ·teous \'rīchəs\ *adj* : acting or being in accordance with what is just or moral — **righ·teous·ly** *adv* — **righ·teous·ness** *n*

right·ful \'rītfəl\ *adj* : lawful —

right·ful·ly \-ē\ *adv* — **right·ful·ness** *n*

right·ly \'rītlē\ *adv* 1 : justly 2 : properly 3 : correctly

rig·id \'rijəd\ *adj* : lacking flexibility — **ri·gid·i·ty** \rə'jidətē\ *n* — **rig·id·ly** *adv*

rig·ma·role \'rigmə,rōl, 'rigə-\ *n* 1 : meaningless talk 2 : complicated often unnecessary procedure

rig·or \'rigər\ *n* : severity — **rig·or·ous** *adj* — **rig·or·ous·ly** *adv*

rig·or mor·tis \,rigər'mòrtəs\ *n* : temporary stiffness of muscles occurring after death

rile \'rīl\ *vb* **riled; ril·ing** : anger

rill \'ril\ *n* : small brook

rim \'rim\ *n* : edge esp. of something curved ~ *vb* **-mm-** : border

¹rime \'rīm\ *n* : frost — **rimy** \'rīmē\ *adj*

²rime *var of* RHYME

rind \'rīnd\ *n* : usu. hard or tough outer layer

¹ring \'rin\ *n* 1 : circular band used as an ornament or for holding or fastening 2 : something circular 3 : place for contest or display 4 : group with a selfish or dishonest aim ~ *vb* : surround — **ringed** \'rind\ *adj* — **ring·like** *adj*

²ring *vb* **rang** \'ran\; **rung** \'rən\ **ring·ing** 1 : sound resonantly when struck 2 : cause to make a metallic sound by striking 3 : resound 4 : call esp. by a bell ~ *n* 1 : resonant sound or tone 2 : act or instance of ringing

ring·er \'rinər\ *n* 1 : one that sounds by ringing 2 : illegal substitute 3 : one that closely resembles another

ring·lead·er \'rin,lēdər\ *n* : leader esp. of troublemakers

ring·let *n* : long curl

ring·worm *n* : contagious skin disease caused by fungi

rink \'rink\ *n* : enclosed place for skating

rinse \'rins\ *vb* **rinsed; rins·ing** 1 : cleanse usu. with water only 2 : treat (hair) with a rinse ~ *n* : liquid used for rinsing — **rins·er** *n*

ri·ot \'rīət\ *n* 1 : violent public disorder 2 : random or disorderly profusion — **riot** *vb* — **ri·ot·er** *n* — **ri·ot·ous** *adj*

rip \'rip\ *vb* **-pp-** : cut or tear open ~ *n* : rent made by ripping — **rip·per** *n*

ripe \'rīp\ *adj* **rip·er; rip·est** : fully grown, developed, or prepared — **ripe·ly** *adv* — **rip·en** \'rīpən\ *vb* — **ripe·ness** *n*

rip-off *n* : theft — **rip off** *vb*

rip·ple \'ripəl\ *vb* **-pled; -pling** 1 : become lightly ruffled on the surface 2 : sound like rippling water — **ripple** *n*

rise \'rīz\ *vb* **rose** \'rōz\; **ris·en** \'riz³n\; **ris·ing** \'rīzin\ 1 : get up from sitting, kneeling, or lying 2 : take arms 3 : appear above the horizon 4 : ascend 5 : gain a higher position or rank 6 : increase ~ *n* 1 : act of rising 2 : origin 3 : elevation 4 : increase 5 : upward slope 6 : area of high ground — **ris·er** \'rīzər\ *n*

risk \'risk\ *n* : exposure to loss or injury — **risk** *vb* — **risk·i·ness** *n* — **risky** *adj*

ris·qué \ris'kā\ *adj* : nearly indecent

rite \'rīt\ *n* 1 : set form for conducting a ceremony 2 : liturgy of a church 3 : ceremonial action

rit·u·al \'richəwəl\ *n* : rite — **ritual** *adj* — **rit·u·al·ism** \-,izəm\ *n* — **rit·u·al·is·tic** \,richəwəl'istik\ *adj* — **rit·u·al·is·ti·cal·ly** \-tiklē\ *adv* — **rit·u·al·ly** \'richəwəlē\ *adv*

ri·val \'rīvəl\ *n* 1 : competitor 2 : peer ~ *vb* **-valed** *or* **-valled; -val·ing** *or* **-val·ling** 1 : be in competition with 2 : equal — **rival** *adj* — **ri·val·ry** \-rē\ *n*

riv·er \'rivər\ *n* : large natural stream of water — **riv·er·bank** *n* — **riv·er·bed** *n* — **riv·er·boat** *n* — **riv·er·side** *n*

riv·et \'rivət\ *n* : headed metal bolt ~ *vb* : fasten with a rivet — **riv·et·er** *n*

riv·u·let \'rivyələt\ *n* : small stream

roach \'rōch\ *n* : cockroach

road \'rōd\ *n* : open way for vehicles, persons, and animals — **road·bed** *n* — **road·side** *n or adj* — **road·way** *n*

road·block *n* : obstruction on a road

road·run·ner *n* : large fast-running bird

roam \'rōm\ *vb* : wander

roan \'rōn\ *adj* : of a dark color sprinkled with white ~ *n* : animal with a roan coat

roar \'rōr\ *vb* : utter a full loud prolonged sound — **roar** *n* — **roar·er** *n*

roast \'rōst\ *vb* **1** : cook by dry heat **2** : criticize severely ~ *n* : piece of meat suitable for roasting — **roast** *adj* — **roast·er** *n*

rob \'räb\ *vb* **-bb- 1** : steal from **2** : commit robbery — **rob·ber** *n*

rob·bery \'räbərē\ *n, pl* **-ber·ies** : theft of something from a person by use of violence or threat

robe \'rōb\ *n* **1** : long flowing outer garment **2** : covering for the lower body ~ *vb* **robed; rob·ing** : clothe with or as if with a robe

♦ **rob·in** \'räbən\ *n* : No. American thrush with a reddish breast

ro·bot \'rō,bät, -bət\ *n* **1** : machine that looks and acts like a human being **2** : efficient but insensitive person — **ro·bot·ic** \rō'bätik\ *adj*

ro·bust \rō'bəst, 'rō,bəst\ *adj* : strong and vigorously healthy — **ro·bust·ly** *adv* — **ro·bust·ness** *n*

¹**rock** \'räk\ *vb* : sway or cause to sway back and forth ~ *n* **1** : rock-

ing movement **2** : popular music marked by repetition and a strong beat

²**rock** *n* : mass of hard mineral material — **rock** *adj* — **rocky** *adj*

rock·er *n* **1** : curved piece on which a chair rocks **2** : chair that rocks

rock·et \'räkət\ *n* **1** : self-propelled firework or missile **2** : jet engine that carries its own oxygen ~ *vb* : rise abruptly and rapidly — **rock·et·ry** \-ətrē\ *n*

rod \'räd\ *n* **1** : straight slender stick **2** : unit of length equal to 5 yards

rode *past of* RIDE

ro·dent \'rōdᵊnt\ *n* : usu. small gnawing mammal

ro·deo \'rōdē,ō, rō'dāō\ *n, pl* **-de·os** : contest of cowboy skills

roe \'rō\ *n* : fish eggs

rogue \'rōg\ *n* : dishonest or mischievous person — **rogu·ery** \'rōgərē\ *n* — **rogu·ish** \'rōgish\ *adj* — **rogu·ish·ly** *adv* — **rogu·ish·ness** *n*

roil \'rȯil\ *vb* **1** : make cloudy or muddy by stirring up **2** : make angry

role \'rōl\ *n* **1** : part to play **2** : function

roll \'rōl\ *n* **1** : official record or list of names **2** : something rolled up or rounded **3** : bread baked in a small rounded mass **4** : sound of rapid drum strokes **5** : heavy reverberating sound **6** : rolling movement ~ *vb* **1** : move by turning over **2** : move on wheels **3** : flow in a continuous stream **4** : swing from side to side **5** : shape or be shaped in rounded form **6** : press with a roller

roll·er *n* **1** : revolving cylinder **2** : rod on which something is rolled up **3** : long heavy ocean wave

♦ **roller skate** *n* : a skate with

ODIE AND I ARE GOING TO PLAY ON THE ROOF

ROLLER SKATES?!

LOOK OUT BELOW!

JIM DAVIS 3-13

wheels instead of a runner — **roller–skate** vb

rol·lick·ing \'rälikiŋ\ adj : full of good spirits

Ro·man Catholic \'rōmən-\ n : member of a Christian church led by a pope — **Roman Catholic** adj — **Roman Catholicism** n

ro·mance \rō'mans, 'rō͵mans\ n 1 : medieval tale of knightly adventure 2 : love story 3 : love affair ∼ vb -manced; -manc·ing 1 : have romantic fancies 2 : have a love affair with — **ro·manc·er** n

ro·man·tic \rō'mantik\ adj 1 : visionary or imaginative 2 : appealing to one's emotions — **ro·man·ti·cal·ly** \-iklē\ adv

romp \'rämp\ vb : play actively and noisily — **romp** n

roof \'rüf, 'rúf\ n, pl **roofs** \'rüfs, 'rúfs; 'rüvz, 'rúvz\ : upper covering part of a building ∼ vb : cover with a roof — **roofed** \'rüft, 'rúft\ adj — **roof·ing** n — **roof·less** adj — **roof·top** n

¹**rook** \'rúk\ n : crowlike bird

²**rook** vb : cheat

rook·ie \'rúkē\ n : novice

room \'rüm, 'rúm\ n 1 : sufficient space 2 : partitioned part of a building ∼ vb : occupy lodgings — **room·er** n — **room·ful** n — **roomy** adj

room·mate n : one sharing the same lodgings

roost \'rüst\ n : support on which birds perch ∼ vb : settle on a roost

roost·er \'rüstər, 'rús-\ n : adult male domestic chicken

¹**root** \'rüt, 'rút\ n 1 : leafless underground part of a seed plant 2 : rootlike thing or part 3 : source 4 : essential core ∼ vb : form, fix, or become fixed by roots — **root·less** adj — **root·let** \-lət\ n — **root·like** adj

²**root** vb : turn up with the snout

³**root** \'rüt, 'rút\ vb : applaud or encourage noisily — **root·er** n

rope \'rōp\ n : large strong cord of strands of fiber ∼ vb **roped; rop·ing** 1 : tie with a rope 2 : lasso

ro·sa·ry \'rōzərē\ n, pl **-ries** 1 : string of beads used in praying 2 : Roman Catholic devotion

¹**rose** past of RISE

²**rose** \'rōz\ n 1 : prickly shrub with bright flowers 2 : purplish red — **rose** adj — **rose·bud** n — **rose·bush** n

rose·mary \'rōz͵merē\ n, pl **-mar·ies** : fragrant shrubby mint

ro·sette \rō'zet\ n : rose-shaped ornament

Rosh Ha·sha·nah \͵räshhä'shänə, ͵rōsh-\ n : Jewish New Year observed as a religious holiday in September or October

ros·in \'räz°n\ n : brittle resin

ros·ter \'rästər\ n : list of names

ros·trum \'rästrəm\ n, pl **-trums** or **-tra** \-trə\ : speaker's platform

rosy \'rōzē\ adj **ros·i·er; -est** 1 : of the color rose 2 : hopeful — **ros·i·ly** adv — **ros·i·ness** n

rot \'rät\ vb **-tt-** : undergo decomposition ∼ n 1 : decay 2 : disease in which tissue breaks down

ro·ta·ry \'rōtərē\ adj 1 : turning on an axis 2 : having a rotating part

ro·tate \'rō͵tāt\ vb **-tat·ed; -tat·ing** 1 : turn about an axis or a center 2 : alternate in a series — **ro·ta·tion** \rō'tāshən\ n — **ro·ta·tor** \'rō͵tātər\ n

rote \'rōt\ n : repetition from memory

ro·tor \'rōtər\ n 1 : part that rotates 2 : system of rotating horizontal blades for supporting a helicopter

rot·ten \'rät°n\ adj 1 : having rotted 2 : corrupt 3 : extremely unpleasant or inferior — **rot·ten·ness** n

ro·tund \rō'tənd\ adj : rounded — **ro·tun·di·ty** \-'təndətē\ n

ro·tun·da \rō'təndə\ n : building or room with a dome

roué \rù'ā\ n : man given to debauched living

rouge \'rüzh, 'rüj\ n : cosmetic for the cheeks — **rouge** vb

rough \'rəf\ adj 1 : not smooth 2 : not calm 3 : harsh, violent, or rugged 4 : crudely or hastily done ∼ n : rough state or something in that state ∼ vb 1 : roughen 2 : manhandle 3 : make roughly — **rough·ly** adv — **rough·ness** n

rough·age \'rəfij\ n : coarse bulky food

rough·en \'rəfən\ vb : make or become rough

rough·neck \'rəf͵nek\ n : rowdy

rou·lette \rü'let\ n : gambling game using a whirling numbered wheel

¹**round** \'raúnd\ adj 1 : having every

part the same distance from the center 2 : cylindrical 3 : complete 4 : approximate 5 : blunt 6 : moving in or forming a circle ~ n 1 : round or curved thing 2 : series of recurring actions or events 3 : period of time or a unit of action 4 : fired shot 5 : cut of beef ~ vb 1 : make or become round 2 : go around 3 : finish 4 : express as an approximation — **round·ish** adj — **round·ly** adv — **round·ness** n

²**round** prep or adv : around

round·about adj : indirect

round-up \'raund,əp\ n 1 : gathering together of range cattle 2 : summary — **round up** vb

rouse \'rauz\ vb **roused; rous·ing 1** : wake from sleep 2 : stir up

rout \'raut\ n 1 : state of wild confusion 2 : disastrous defeat ~ vb : defeat decisively

route \'rüt, 'raut\ n : line of travel ~ vb **rout·ed; rout·ing** : send by a selected route

rou·tine \rü'tēn\ n 1 : regular course of procedure 2 : an often repeated speech, formula, or part — **routine** adj — **rou·tine·ly** adv

rove \'rōv\ vb **roved; rov·ing** : wander or roam — **rov·er** n

¹**row** \'rō\ vb 1 : propel a boat with oars 2 : carry in a rowboat ~ n : act of rowing — **row·boat** n — **row·er** \'rōər\ n

²**row** n : number of objects in a line

³**row** \'rau\ n : noisy quarrel — **row** vb

row·dy \'raudē\ adj **-di·er; -est** : coarse or boisterous in behavior — **row·di·ness** n — **rowdy** n

roy·al \'roiəl\ adj : relating to or befitting a king ~ n : person of royal blood — **roy·al·ly** adv

roy·al·ty \'roiəltē\ n, pl **-ties 1** : state of being royal 2 : royal persons 3 : payment for use of property

rub \'rəb\ vb **-bb- 1** : use pressure and friction on a body 2 : scour, polish, erase, or smear by pressure and friction 3 : chafe with friction ~ n : difficulty

rub·ber \'rəbər\ n 1 : one that rubs 2 : waterproof elastic substance or something made of it — **rubber** adj — **rub·ber·ize** \-,īz\ vb — **rub·bery** adj

rub·bish \'rəbish\ n : waste or trash

rub·ble \'rəbəl\ n : broken fragments esp. of a destroyed building

ru·ble \'rübəl\ n : monetary unit of Russia

ru·by \'rübē\ n, pl **-bies** : precious red stone or its color — **ruby** adj

rud·der \'rədər\ n : steering device at the rear of a ship or aircraft

rud·dy \'rədē\ adj **-di·er; -est** : reddish — **rud·di·ness** n

♦ **rude** \'rüd\ adj **rud·er; rud·est 1** : roughly made 2 : impolite — **rude·ly** adv — **rude·ness** n

ru·di·ment \'rüdəmənt\ n 1 : something not fully developed 2 : elementary principle — **ru·di·men·ta·ry** \,rüdə'mentərē\ adj

rue \'rü\ vb **rued; ru·ing** : feel regret for ~ n : regret — **rue·ful** \-fəl\ adj — **rue·ful·ly** adv — **rue·ful·ness** n

ruf·fi·an \'rəfēən\ n : brutal person

ruf·fle \'rəfəl\ vb **-fled; -fling 1** : draw into or provide with pleats 2 : roughen the surface of 3 : irritate ~ n : strip of fabric pleated on one edge — **ruf·fly** \'rəfəlē, -flē\ adj

rug \'rəg\ n : piece of heavy fabric used as a floor covering

rug·ged \'rəgəd\ adj 1 : having a rough uneven surface 2 : severe 3 : strong — **rug·ged·ly** adv — **rug·ged·ness** n

ru·in \'rüən\ n 1 : complete collapse or destruction 2 : remains of

something destroyed — usu. in pl.
3 : cause of destruction ~ vb 1
: destroy 2 : damage beyond repair 3 : bankrupt

ru·in·ous \'rüənəs\ adj : causing
ruin — **ru·in·ous·ly** adv

rule \'rül\ n 1 : guide or principle for
governing action 2 : usual way of
doing something 3 : government 4
: straight strip (as of wood or metal) marked off in units for measuring ~ vb **ruled; rul·ing** 1 : govern
2 : give as a decision — **rul·er** n

rum \'rəm\ n : liquor made from
molasses or sugarcane

rum·ble \'rəmbəl\ vb **-bled; -bling**
: make a low heavy rolling sound
— **rumble** n

ru·mi·nant \'rümənənt\ n : hoofed
mammal (as a cow or deer) that
chews the cud — **ruminant** adj

ru·mi·nate \'rümə,nāt\ vb **-nat·ed; -nat·ing** : contemplate — **ru·min·na·tion** \,rümə'nāshən\ n

rum·mage \'rəmij\ vb **-maged; -maging** : search thoroughly

rum·my \'rəmē\ n : card game

ru·mor \'rümər\ n 1 : common talk
2 : widespread statement not authenticated — **rumor** vb

rump \'rəmp\ n : rear part of an animal

rum·ple \'rəmpəl\ vb **-pled; -pling**
: tousle or wrinkle — **rumple** n

rum·pus \'rəmpəs\ n : disturbance

run \'rən\ vb **ran** \'ran\; **run; running** 1 : go rapidly or hurriedly 2
: enter a race or election 3 : operate 4 : continue in force 5 : flow
rapidly 6 : take a certain direction
7 : manage 8 : incur ~ n 1 : act of
running 2 : brook 3 : continuous
series 4 : usual kind 5 : freedom of
movement 6 : lengthwise ravel

run·around n : evasive or delaying
action esp. in response to a request

run·away \'rənə,wā\ n : fugitive ~
adj 1 : fugitive 2 : out of control

run·down adj : being in poor condition

¹rung past part of RING

²rung \'rəŋ\ n : horizontal piece of a
chair or ladder

run·ner \'rənər\ n 1 : one that runs
2 : thin piece or part on which
something slides 3 : slender creeping branch of a plant

run·ner–up n, pl **run·ners–up** : competitor who finishes second

run·ning \'rəniŋ\ adj 1 : flowing 2
: continuous

runt \'rənt\ n : small person or animal — **runty** adj

run·way \'rən,wā\ n : strip on which
aircraft land and take off

ru·pee \rü'pē, 'rü,-\ n : monetary
unit (as of India)

rup·ture \'rəpchər\ n 1 : breaking or
tearing apart 2 : hernia ~ vb
-tured; -tur·ing : cause or undergo
rupture

ru·ral \'rúrəl\ adj : relating to the
country or agriculture

ruse \'rüs, 'rüz\ n : trick

¹rush \'rəsh\ n : grasslike marsh
plant

²rush vb 1 : move forward or act with
too great haste 2 : perform in a
short time ~ n : violent forward
motion ~ adj : requiring speed —
rush·er n

rus·set \'rəsət\ n 1 : reddish brown
color 2 : a baking potato — **russet**
adj

rust \'rəst\ n 1 : reddish coating on
exposed iron 2 : reddish brown
color — **rust** vb — **rusty** adj

rus·tic \'rəstik\ adj : relating to or
suitable for the country or country dwellers ~ n : rustic person —
rus·ti·cal·ly adv

rus·tle \'rəsəl\ vb **-tled; -tling** 1
: make or cause a rustle 2 : forage
food 3 : steal cattle from the range
~ n : series of small sounds —
rus·tler \-ələr\ n

rut \'rət\ n 1 : track worn by wheels
or feet 2 : set routine — **rut·ted**
adj

ruth·less \'rüthləs\ adj : having no
pity — **ruth·less·ly** adv — **ruth·less·ness** n

-ry \rē\ n suffix : -ery

rye \'rī\ n 1 : cereal grass grown for
grain 2 : whiskey from rye

S

s \'es\ *n, pl* **s's** *or* **ss** \'esəz\ : 19th letter of the alphabet

¹-s \s *after sounds* f, k, k̲, p, t, th; əz *after sounds* ch, j, s, sh, z, zh; z *after other sounds*\ — used to form the plural of most nouns

²-s *vb suffix* — used to form the 3d person singular present of most verbs

Sab·bath \'sabəth\ *n* **1** : Saturday observed as a day of worship by Jews and some Christians **2** : Sunday observed as a day of worship by Christians

sa·ber, sa·bre \'sābər\ *n* : curved cavalry sword

sa·ble \'sābəl\ *n* **1** : black **2** : dark brown mammal or its fur

sab·o·tage \'sabə,täzh\ *n* : deliberate destruction or hampering ~ *vb* **-taged; -tag·ing** : wreck through sabotage

sab·o·teur \,sabə'tər\ *n* : person who sabotages

sac \'sak\ *n* : anatomical pouch

sac·cha·rin \'sakərən\ *n* : low-calorie artificial sweetener

sac·cha·rine \-ərən\ *adj* : nauseatingly sweet

sa·chet \sa'shā\ *n* : small bag with perfumed powder (**sachet powder**)

¹sack \'sak\ *n* : bag ~ *vb* : fire

²sack *vb* : plunder a captured place

sack·cloth *n* : rough garment worn as a sign of penitence

sac·ra·ment \'sakrəmənt\ *n* : formal religious act or rite — **sac·ra·men·tal** \,sakrə'ment°l\ *adj*

sa·cred \'sākrəd\ *adj* **1** : set apart for or worthy of worship **2** : worthy of reverence **3** : relating to religion — **sa·cred·ly** *adv* — **sa·cred·ness** *n*

sac·ri·fice \'sakrə,fīs\ *n* **1** : the offering of something precious to a deity or the thing offered **2** : loss or deprivation ~ *vb* **-ficed; -fic·ing** : offer or give up as a sacrifice — **sac·ri·fi·cial** \,sakrə'fishəl\ *adj*

sac·ri·lege \'sakrəlij\ *n* : violation of something sacred — **sac·ri·le·gious** \,sakrə'lijəs, -'lējəs\ *adj*

sac·ro·sanct \'sakrō,saŋkt\ *adj* : sacred

sad \'sad\ *adj* **-dd-** **1** : affected with grief or sorrow **2** : causing sorrow — **sad·den** \'sad°n\ *vb* — **sad·ly** *adv* — **sad·ness** *n*

sad·dle \'sad°l\ *n* : seat for riding on horseback ~ *vb* **-dled; -dling** : put a saddle on

sa·dism \'sā,dizəm, 'sad,iz-\ *n* : delight in cruelty — **sa·dist** \'sādist, 'sad-\ *n* — **sa·dis·tic** \sə'distik\ *adj* — **sa·dis·ti·cal·ly** *adv*

sa·fa·ri \sə'färē, -'far-\ *n* : hunting expedition in Africa

safe \'sāf\ *adj* **saf·er; saf·est** **1** : free from harm **2** : providing safety ~ *n* : container to keep valuables safe — **safe·keep·ing** *n* — **safe·ly** *adv*

safe·guard *n* : measure or device for preventing accidents — **safeguard** *vb*

safe·ty \'sāftē\ *n, pl* **-ties** **1** : freedom from danger **2** : protective device

saf·flow·er \'saf,laůər\ *n* : herb with seeds rich in edible oil

saf·fron \'safrən\ *n* : orange powder from a crocus flower used in cooking

sag \'sag\ *vb* **-gg-** : droop, sink, or settle — **sag** *n*

sa·ga \'sägə\ *n* : story of heroic deeds

sa·ga·cious \sə'gāshəs\ *adj* : shrewd — **sa·gac·i·ty** \-'gasətē\ *n*

¹sage \'sāj\ *adj* : wise or prudent ~ *n* : wise man — **sage·ly** *adv*

²sage *n* : mint used in flavoring

sage·brush *n* : low shrub of the western U.S.

said *past of* SAY

sail \'sāl\ *n* **1** : fabric used to catch the wind and move a boat or ship **2** : trip on a sailboat ~ *vb* **1** : travel on a ship or sailboat **2** : move with ease or grace — **sail·boat** *n* — **sail·or** \'sālər\ *n*

sail·fish *n* : large fish with a very large dorsal fin

saint \'sānt, *before a name* ,sānt *or*

sənt\ n : holy or godly person — **saint·ed** \-əd\ adj — **saint·hood** \-ˌhu̇d\ n — **saint·li·ness** n — **saint·ly** adj

¹**sake** \'sāk\ n 1 : purpose or reason 2 : one's good or benefit

²**sa·ke, sa·ki** \'säkē\ n : Japanese rice wine

sa·la·cious \sə'lāshəs\ adj : sexually suggestive — **sa·la·cious·ly** adv

sal·ad \'saləd\ n : dish usu. of raw lettuce, vegetables, or fruit

sal·a·man·der \'saləˌmandər\ n : lizardlike amphibian

sa·la·mi \sə'lämē\ n : highly seasoned dried sausage

sal·a·ry \'salərē\ n, pl **-ries** : regular payment for services

sale \'sāl\ n 1 : transfer of ownership of property for money 2 : selling at bargain prices 3 **sales** pl : activities involved in selling — **sal·able, sale·able** \'sāləbəl\ adj — **sales·man** \-mən\ n — **sales·person** n — **sales·wom·an** n

sa·lient \'sālyənt\ adj : standing out conspicuously

sa·line \'sāˌlēn, -ˌlīn\ adj : containing salt — **sa·lin·i·ty** \sā'linətē, sə-\ n

sa·li·va \sə'līvə\ n : liquid secreted into the mouth — **sal·i·vary** \'saləˌverē\ adj — **sal·i·vate** \-ˌvāt\ vb — **sal·i·va·tion** \ˌsalə'vāshən\ n

sal·low \'salō\ adj : of a yellowish sickly color

sal·ly \'salē\ n, pl **-lies** 1 : quick attack on besiegers 2 : witty remark — **sally** vb

salm·on \'samən\ n, pl **salmon** 1 : food fish with pink or red flesh 2 : deep yellowish pink color

sa·lon \sə'län, 'salˌän, sa'lōⁿ\ n : elegant room or shop

◆ **sa·loon** \sə'lün\ n 1 : public cabin on a passenger ship 2 : barroom

sal·sa \'sȯlsə, 'säl-\ n : spicy sauce of tomatoes, onions, and hot peppers

salt \'sȯlt\ n 1 : white crystalline substance that consists of sodium and chlorine 2 : compound formed usu. from acid and metal — **salt** vb or adj — **salt·i·ness** n — **salty** adj

salt·wa·ter adj : relating to or living in salt water

sa·lu·bri·ous \sə'lübrēəs\ adj : good for health

sal·u·tary \'salyəˌterē\ adj : health-giving or beneficial

sal·u·ta·tion \ˌsalyə'tāshən\ n : greeting

sa·lute \sə'lüt\ vb **-lut·ed; -lut·ing** : honor by ceremony or formal movement — **salute** n

sal·vage \'salvij\ n : something saved from destruction ~ vb **-vaged; -vag·ing** : rescue or save

sal·va·tion \sal'vāshən\ n : saving of a person from sin or danger

salve \'sav, 'sȧv\ n : medicinal ointment ~ vb **salved; salv·ing** : soothe

sal·ver \'salvər\ n : small tray

sal·vo \'salvō\ n, pl **-vos** or **-voes** : simultaneous discharge of guns

same \'sām\ adj : being the one referred to ~ pron : the same one or ones ~ adv : in the same manner — **same·ness** n

sam·ple \'sampəl\ n : piece or part that shows the quality of a whole ~ vb **-pled; -pling** : judge by a sample

sam·pler \'samplər\ n : piece of needlework testing skill in embroidering

san·a·to·ri·um \ˌsanə'tōrēəm\ n, pl **-riums** or **-ria** \-ēə\ : hospital for the chronically ill

sanc·ti·fy \'saŋktəˌfī\ vb **-fied; -fy·ing** : make holy — **sanc·ti·fi·ca·tion** \ˌsaŋktəfə'kāshən\ n

sanc·ti·mo·nious \ˌsaŋktə'mōnēəs\

adj : hypocritically pious — **sanc-ti-mo-nious-ly** *adv*

sanc-tion \'saŋkshən\ *n* 1 : authoritative approval 2 : coercive measure — usu. pl ~ *vb* : approve

sanc-ti-ty \'saŋktətē\ *n, pl* **-ties** : quality or state of being holy or sacred

sanc-tu-ary \'saŋkchə,werē\ *n, pl* **-ar-ies** 1 : consecrated place 2 : place of refuge

sand \'sand\ *n* : loose granular particles of rock ~ *vb* : smooth with an abrasive — **sand-bank** *n* — **sand-er** *n* — **sand-storm** *n* — **sandy** *adj*

san-dal \'sand³l\ *n* : shoe consisting of a sole strapped to the foot

sand-pa-per *n* : abrasive paper — **sandpaper** *vb*

sand-pip-er \-,pīpər\ *n* : long-billed shorebird

sand-stone *n* : rock made of naturally cemented sand

sand-wich \'sand,wich\ *n* : 2 or more slices of bread with a filling between them ~ *vb* : squeeze or crowd in

sane \'sān\ *adj* **san-er; san-est** 1 : mentally healthy 2 : sensible — **sane-ly** *adv*

sang *past of* SING

san-gui-nary \'saŋgwə,nerē\ *adj* : bloody

san-guine \'saŋgwən\ *adj* 1 : reddish 2 : cheerful

san-i-tar-i-um \,sanə'tereəm\ *n, pl* **-i-ums** *or* **-ia** \-ēə\ : sanatorium

san-i-tary \'sanəterē\ *adj* 1 : relating to health 2 : free from filth or infective matter

san-i-ta-tion \,sanə'tāshən\ *n* : protection of health by maintenance of sanitary conditions

san-i-ty \'sanətē\ *n* : soundness of mind

sank *past of* SINK

---

¹**sap** \'sap\ *n* 1 : fluid that circulates through a plant 2 : gullible person

²**sap** *vb* **-pp-** 1 : undermine 2 : weaken or exhaust gradually

sa-pi-ent \'sāpēənt, 'sapē-\ *adj* : wise — **sa-pi-ence** \-əns\ *n*

sap-ling \'sapliŋ\ *n* : young tree

sap-phire \'saf,īr\ *n* : hard transparent blue gem

sap-py \'sapē\ *adj* **-pi-er; -est** 1 : full of sap 2 : overly sentimental

sap-suck-er \'sap,səkər\ *n* : small No. American woodpecker

sar-casm \'sär,kazəm\ *n* 1 : cutting remark 2 : ironical criticism or reproach — **sar-cas-tic** \sär'kastik\ *adj* — **sar-cas-ti-cal-ly** *adv*

sar-coph-a-gus \sär'käfəgəs\ *n, pl* **-gi** \-,gī, -,jī\ : large stone coffin

♦ **sar-dine** \sär'dēn\ *n* : small fish preserved for use as food

sar-don-ic \sär'dänik\ *adj* : disdainfully humorous — **sar-don-i-cal-ly** *adv*

sa-rong \sə'rȯŋ, -'räŋ\ *n* : loose garment worn esp. by Pacific islanders

sar-sa-pa-ril-la \,saspə'rilə, ,särs-\ *n* : dried roots of a tropical American plant used esp. for flavoring or a carbonated drink flavored with this

sar-to-ri-al \sär'tōrēəl\ *adj* : relating to a tailor or men's clothes

¹**sash** \'sash\ *n* : broad band worn around the waist or over the shoulder

²**sash** *n, pl* **sash** 1 : frame for a pane of glass in a door or window 2 : movable part of a window

sas-sa-fras \'sasə,fras\ *n* : No. American tree or its dried root bark

sassy \'sasē\ *adj* **sass-i-er; -est** : saucy

sat *past of* SIT

Sa-tan \'sāt³n\ *n* : devil — **sa-tan-**

ic \sə'tanik, sā-\ *adj* — **sa·tan·i·cal·ly** *adv*

satch·el \'sachəl\ *n* : small bag

sate \'sāt\ *vb* **sat·ed; sat·ing** : satisfy fully

sat·el·lite \'sat⁰l,īt\ *n* **1** : toady **2** : body or object that revolves around a larger celestial body

sa·ti·ate \'sāshē,āt\ *vb* **-at·ed; -at·ing** : sate — **sa·ti·ety** \sə'tīətē\ *n*

sat·in \'sat⁰n\ *n* : glossy fabric — **sat·iny** *adj*

sat·ire \'sa,tīr\ *n* : literary ridicule done with humor — **sa·tir·ic** \sə-'tirik\, **sa·tir·i·cal** \-ikəl\ *adj* — **sa·tir·i·cal·ly** *adv* — **sat·i·rist** \'satərist\ *n* — **sat·i·rize** \-ə,rīz\ *vb*

sat·is·fac·tion \,satəs'fakshən\ *n* : state of being satisfied — **sat·is·fac·to·ri·ly** \-'faktərəlē\ *adv* — **sat·is·fac·to·ry** \-'faktərē\ *adj*

sat·is·fy \'satəs,fī\ *vb* **-fied; -fy·ing 1** : make happy **2** : pay what is due to or on — **sat·is·fy·ing·ly** *adv*

sat·u·rate \'sachə,rāt\ *vb* **-rat·ed; -rat·ing** : soak or charge thoroughly — **sat·u·ra·tion** \,sachə-'rāshən\ *n*

Sat·ur·day \'satərdā, -dē\ *n* : 7th day of the week

sat·ur·nine \'satər,nīn\ *adj* : sullen

sa·tyr \'sātər, 'sat-\ *n* : pleasure-loving forest god of ancient Greece

sauce \'sȯs\ *n* : fluid dressing or topping for food — **sauce·pan** *n*

sau·cer \'sȯsər\ *n* : small shallow dish under a cup

saucy \'sasē, 'sȯsē\ *adj* **sauc·i·er; -est** : insolent — **sauc·i·ly** *adv* — **sauc·i·ness** *n*

sau·er·kraut \'saúər,kraút\ *n* : finely cut and fermented cabbage

sau·na \'saúnə\ *n* : steam or dry heat bath or a room or cabinet used for such a bath

saun·ter \'sȯntər, 'sänt-\ *vb* : stroll

sau·sage \'sȯsij\ *n* : minced and highly seasoned meat

sau·té \sȯ'tā, sō-\ *vb* **-téed** *or* **-téd; -té·ing** : fry in a little fat — **sauté** *n*

sav·age \'savij\ *adj* **1** : wild **2** : cruel ~ *n* : person belonging to a primitive society — **sav·age·ly** *adv* — **sav·age·ness** *n* — **sav·age·ry** *n*

¹save \'sāv\ *vb* **saved; sav·ing 1** : rescue from danger **2** : guard from destruction **3** : redeem from sin **4** : put aside as a reserve — **sav·er** *n*

²save *prep* : except

sav·ior, sav·iour \'sāvyər\ *n* **1** : one who saves **2** *cap* : Jesus Christ

sa·vor \'sāvər\ *n* : special flavor ~ *vb* : taste with pleasure — **sa·vory** *adj*

¹saw *past of* SEE

²saw \'sȯ\ *n* : cutting tool with teeth ~ *vb* **sawed; sawed** *or* **sawn; saw·ing** : cut with a saw — **saw·dust** \-,dəst\ *n* — **saw·mill** *n* — **saw·yer** \-yər\ *n*

saw·horse *n* : support for wood being sawed

sax·o·phone \'saksə,fōn\ *n* : wind instrument with a reed mouthpiece and usu. a bent metal body

say \'sā\ *vb* **said** \'sed\; **say·ing** \'sāiŋ\; **says** \'sez\ **1** : express in words **2** : state positively ~ *n, pl* **says** \'sāz\ **1** : expression of opinion **2** : power of decision

say·ing \'sāiŋ\ *n* : commonly repeated statement

scab \'skab\ *n* **1** : protective crust over a sore or wound **2** : worker taking a striker's job ~ *vb* **-bb- 1** : become covered with a scab **2** : work as a scab — **scab·by** *adj*

scab·bard \'skabərd\ *n* : sheath for the blade of a weapon

scaf·fold \'skafəld, -,ōld\ *n* **1** : raised platform for workmen **2** : platform on which a criminal is executed

scald \'skȯld\ *vb* **1** : burn with hot liquid or steam **2** : heat to the boiling point

¹scale \'skāl\ *n* : weighing device ~ *vb* **scaled; scal·ing** : weigh

²scale *n* **1** : thin plate esp. on the body of a fish or reptile **2** : thin coating or layer ~ *vb* **scaled; scal·ing** : strip of scales — **scaled** \'skāld\ *adj* — **scaleless** *adj* — **scaly** *adj*

³scale *n* **1** : graduated series **2** : size of a sample (as a model) in proportion to the size of the actual thing **3** : standard of estimation or judgment **4** : series of musical tones ~ *vb* **scaled; scal·ing 1** : climb by a ladder **2** : arrange in a graded series

scal·lion \'skalyən\ *n* : bulbless onion

scal·lop \'skäləp, 'skal-\ *n* **1** : marine

mollusk **2** : rounded projection on a border

scalp \'skalp\ *n* : skin and flesh of the head ~ *vb* **1** : remove the scalp from **2** : resell at a greatly increased price — **scalp·er** *n*

scal·pel \'skalpəl\ *n* : surgical knife

scamp \'skamp\ *n* : rascal

♦ **scam·per** \'skampər\ *vb* : run nimbly — **scamper** *n*

scan \'skan\ *vb* **-nn- 1** : read (verses) so as to show meter **2** : examine closely or hastily **3** : examine with a sensing device — **scan** *n* — **scan·ner** *n*

scan·dal \'skand²l\ *n* **1** : disgraceful situation **2** : malicious gossip — **scan·dal·ize** *vb* — **scan·dal·ous** *adj*

scant \'skant\ *adj* : barely sufficient ~ *vb* : stint — **scant·i·ly** *adv* — **scanty** *adj*

scape·goat \'skāp₁gōt\ *n* : one that bears the blame for others

scap·u·la \'skapyələ\ *n, pl* **-lae** \-₁lē\ *or* **-las** : shoulder blade

scar \'skär\ *n* : mark where a wound has healed — **scar** *vb*

scar·ab \'skarəb\ *n* : large dark beetle or an ornament representing one

scarce \'skers\ *adj* **scarc·er; scarc·est** : lacking in quantity or number — **scar·ci·ty** \'skersətē\ *n*

scarce·ly \'skerslē\ *adv* **1** : barely **2** : almost not

scare \'sker\ *vb* **scared; scar·ing** : frighten ~ *n* : fright — **scary** *adj*

scare·crow \'sker₁krō\ *n* : figure for scaring birds from crops

scarf \'skärf\ *n, pl* **scarves** \'skärvz\ *or* **scarfs** : cloth worn about the shoulders or the neck

scar·let \'skärlət\ *n* : bright red color — **scarlet** *adj*

scarlet fever *n* : acute contagious disease marked by fever, sore throat, and red rash

scath·ing \'skāthiŋ\ *adj* : bitterly severe

scat·ter \'skatər\ *vb* **1** : spread about irregularly **2** : disperse

scav·en·ger \'skavənjər\ *n* **1** : person that collects refuse or waste **2** : animal that feeds on decayed matter — **scav·enge** \'skavənj\ *vb*

sce·nar·io \sə'narē₁ō, -'när-\ *n, pl* **-i·os 1** : plot of a play or movie **2** : possible sequence of events

scene \'sēn\ *n* **1** : single situation in a play or movie **2** : stage setting **3** : view **4** : display of emotion — **sce·nic** \'sēnik\ *adj*

scen·ery \'sēnərē\ *n, pl* **-er·ies 1** : painted setting for a stage **2** : picturesque view

scent \'sent\ *vb* **1** : smell **2** : fill with odor ~ *n* **1** : odor **2** : sense of smell **3** : perfume — **scent·ed** \'sentəd\ *adj*

scep·ter \'septər\ *n* : staff signifying authority

scep·tic \'skeptik\ *var of* SKEPTIC

sched·ule \'skejül, *esp Brit* 'shedyül\ *n* : list showing sequence of events ~ *vb* **-uled; -ul·ing** : make a schedule of

scheme \'skēm\ *n* **1** : crafty plot **2** : systematic design ~ *vb* **schemed; schem·ing** : form a plot — **sche·mat·ic** \ski'matik\ *adj* — **schem·er** *n*

schism \'sizəm, 'skiz-\ *n* : split — **schis·mat·ic** \siz'matik, skiz-\ *n or adj*

schizo·phre·nia \₁skitsə'frēnēə\ *n* : severe mental illness — **schiz·oid** \'skit₁sȯid\ *adj or n* — **schizo·phren·ic** \₁skitsə'frenik\ *adj or n*

schol·ar \'skälər\ *n* : student or learned person — **schol·ar·ly** *adj*

schol·ar·ship \-₁ship\ *n* **1** : qualities or learning of a scholar **2** : money given to a student to pay for education

scho·las·tic \skə'lastik\ adj : relating to schools, scholars, or scholarship

¹school \'skül\ n 1 : institution for learning 2 : pupils in a school 3 : group with shared beliefs ~ vb : teach — school·boy n — school·girl n — school·house n — school·mate n — school·room n — school·teach·er n

²school n : large number of fish swimming together

schoo·ner \'skünər\ n : sailing ship

sci·ence \'sīəns\ n : branch of systematic study esp. of the physical world — sci·en·tif·ic \,sīən'tifik\ adj — sci·en·tif·i·cal·ly adv — sci·en·tist \'sīəntist\ n

scin·til·late \'sint³l,āt\ vb -lat·ed; -lat·ing : flash — scin·til·la·tion \,sint³l'āshən\ n

scin·til·lat·ing adj : brilliantly lively or witty

sci·on \'sīən\ n : descendant

scis·sors \'sizərz\ n pl : small shears

scoff \'skäf\ vb : mock — scoff·er n

scold \'skōld\ n : person who scolds ~ vb : criticize severely

scoop \'sküp\ n : shovellike utensil ~ vb 1 : take out with a scoop 2 : dig out

scoot \'sküt\ vb : move swiftly

scoot·er \'skütər\ n : child's foot-propelled vehicle

¹scope \'skōp\ n 1 : extent 2 : room for development

²scope n : viewing device (as a microscope)

scorch \'skȯrch\ vb : burn the surface of

score \'skȯr\ n, pl scores 1 or pl score : twenty 2 : cut 3 : record of points made (as in a game) 4 : debt 5 : music of a composition ~ vb scored; scor·ing 1 : record 2 : mark with lines 3 : gain in a game 4 : assign a grade to 5 : compose a score for — score·less adj — scor·er n

scorn \'skȯrn\ n : emotion involving both anger and disgust ~ vb : hold in contempt — scorn·er n — scorn·ful \-fəl\ adj — scorn·ful·ly adv

scor·pi·on \'skȯrpēən\ n : poisonous long-tailed animal

scoun·drel \'skaůndrəl\ n : villain

¹scour \'skaůər\ vb : examine thoroughly

²scour vb : rub in order to clean

scourge \'skərj\ n 1 : whip 2 : punishment ~ vb scourged; scourg·ing 1 : lash 2 : punish severely

scout \'skaůt\ vb : inspect or observe to get information ~ n : person sent out to get information

scow \'skaů\ n : large flat-bottomed boat with square ends

scowl \'skaůl\ vb : make a frowning expression of displeasure — scowl n

scrag·gly \'skraglē\ adj : irregular or unkempt

scram \'skram\ vb -mm- : go away at once

scram·ble \'skrambəl\ vb -bled; -bling 1 : clamber clumsily around 2 : struggle for possession of something 3 : mix together 4 : cook (eggs) by stirring during frying — scramble n

¹scrap \'skrap\ n 1 : fragment 2 : discarded material ~ vb -pp- : get rid of as useless

²scrap vb -pp- : fight — scrap n — scrap·per n

scrap·book n : blank book in which mementos are kept

scrape \'skrāp\ vb scraped; scrap·ing 1 : remove by drawing a knife over 2 : clean or smooth by rubbing 3 : draw across a surface with a grating sound 4 : damage by contact with a rough surface 5 : gather or proceed with difficulty ~ n 1 : act of scraping 2 : predicament — scrap·er n

scratch \'skrach\ vb 1 : scrape or dig with or as if with claws or nails 2 : cause to move gratingly 3 : delete by or as if by drawing a line through ~ n : mark or sound made in scratching — scratchy adj

scrawl \'skrȯl\ vb : write hastily and carelessly — scrawl n

scraw·ny \'skrȯnē\ adj -ni·er; -est : very thin

♦ scream \'skrēm\ vb : cry out loudly and shrilly ~ n : loud shrill cry

screech \'skrēch\ vb or n : shriek

screen \'skrēn\ n 1 : device or partition used to protect or decorate 2 : surface on which pictures appear (as in movies) ~ vb : shield or separate with or as if with a screen

screw \'skrü\ n 1 : grooved fastening device 2 : propeller ~ vb 1 : fasten by means of a screw 2 : move spirally

screw·driv·er \'skrü̱drīvər\ n : tool for turning screws

scrib·ble \'skribəl\ vb **-bled; -bling** : write hastily or carelessly — **scribble** n — **scrib·bler** \-ələr\ n

scribe \'skrīb\ n : one who writes or copies writing

scrimp \'skrimp\ vb : economize greatly

scrip \'skrip\ n 1 : paper money for less than a dollar 2 : certificate entitling one to something (as stock)

script \'skript\ n : text (as of a play)

scrip·ture \'skripchər\ n : sacred writings of a religion — **scrip·tur·al** \'skripchərəl\ adj

scroll \'skrōl\ n 1 : roll of paper for writing a document 2 : spiral or coiled design

scro·tum \'skrōtəm\ n, pl **-ta** \-ə\ or **-tums** : pouch containing the testes

scrounge \'skraùnj\ vb **scrounged; scroung·ing** : collect by or as if by foraging

¹**scrub** \'skrəb\ n : stunted tree or shrub or a growth of these — **scrub** adj — **scrub·by** adj

²**scrub** vb **-bb-** : clean or wash by rubbing — **scrub** n

scruff \'skrəf\ n : loose skin of the back of the neck

scrump·tious \'skrəmpshəs\ adj : delicious

scru·ple \'skrüpəl\ n : reluctance due to ethical considerations — **scruple** vb — **scru·pu·lous** \-pyələs\ adj — **scru·pu·lous·ly** adv

scru·ti·ny \'skrüt³nē\ n, pl **-nies**

: careful inspection — **scru·ti·nize** \-³n̲ız̲\

scud \'skəd\ vb **-dd-** : move speedily

scuff \'skəf\ vb : scratch, scrape, or wear away — **scuff** n

scuf·fle \'skəfəl\ vb **-fled; -fling** 1 : struggle at close quarters 2 : shuffle one's feet — **scuffle** n

scull \'skəl\ n 1 : oar 2 : racing shell propelled with sculls ~ vb : propel a boat by an oar over the stern

scul·lery \'skələrē\ n, pl **-ler·ies** : room for cleaning dishes and cookware

sculpt \'skəlpt\ vb : sculpture

sculp·ture \'skəlpchər\ n : work of art carved or molded ~ vb **-tured; -tur·ing** : form as sculpture — **sculp·tor** \-tər\ n — **sculp·tur·al** \-chərəl\ adj

scum \'skəm\ n : slimy film on a liquid

scur·ri·lous \'skərələs\ adj : vulgar or abusive

scur·ry \'skərē\ vb **-ried; -ry·ing** : scamper

scur·vy \'skərvē\ n : vitamin=deficiency disease

¹**scut·tle** \'skət³l\ n : pail for coal

²**scuttle** vb **-tled; -tling** : sink (a ship) by cutting holes in its bottom

³**scuttle** vb **-tled; -tling** : scamper

scythe \'sīth\ n : tool for mowing by hand — **scythe** vb

sea \'sē\ n 1 : large body of salt water 2 : ocean 3 : rough water — **sea** adj — **sea·coast** n — **sea·food** n — **sea·port** n — **sea·shore** n — **sea·wa·ter** n

sea·bird n : bird frequenting the open ocean

sea·board n : country's seacoast

sea·far·er \-ₐfarər\ n : seaman — **sea·far·ing** \-ₐfariŋ\ adj or n

sea horse n : small fish with a horse-like head

¹**seal** \'sēl\ *n* : large sea mammal of cold regions — **seal·skin** *n*

²**seal** *n* **1** : device for stamping a design **2** : something that closes ∼ *vb* **1** : affix a seal to **2** : close up securely **3** : determine finally — **seal·ant** \-ənt\ *n* — **seal·er** *n*

sea lion *n* : large Pacific seal with external ears

seam \'sēm\ *n* **1** : line of junction of 2 edges **2** : layer of a mineral ∼ *vb* : join by sewing — **seam·less** *adj*

sea·man \'sēmən\ *n* **1** : one who helps to handle a ship **2** : naval enlisted man ranking next below a petty officer third class — **sea·man·ship** *n*

seaman apprentice *n* : naval enlisted man ranking next below a seaman

seaman recruit *n* : naval enlisted man of the lowest rank

seam·stress \'sēmstrəs\ *n* : woman who sews

seamy \'sēmē\ *adj* **seam·i·er; -est** : unpleasant or sordid

sé·ance \'sā,äns\ *n* : meeting for communicating with spirits

sea·plane *n* : airplane that can take off from and land on the water

sear \'sir\ *vb* : scorch — **sear** *n*

search \'sərch\ *vb* **1** : look through **2** : seek — **search** *n* — **search·er** *n* — **search·light** *n*

sea·sick *adj* : nauseated by the motion of a ship — **sea·sick·ness** *n*

¹**sea·son** \'sēz°n\ *n* **1** : division of the year **2** : customary time for something — **sea·son·al** \'sēz°nəl\ *adj* — **sea·son·al·ly** *adv*

²**season** *vb* **1** : add spice to (food) **2** : make strong or fit for use — **sea·son·ing** \-°niŋ\ *n*

sea·son·able \'sēznəbəl\ *adj* : occurring at a suitable time — **sea·son·ably** \-blē\ *adv*

seat \'sēt\ *n* **1** : place to sit **2** : chair, bench, or stool for sitting on **3** : place that serves as a capital or center ∼ *vb* **1** : place in or on a seat **2** : provide seats for

sea·weed *n* : marine alga

sea·wor·thy *adj* : strong enough to hold up to a sea voyage

se·cede \si'sēd\ *vb* **-ced·ed; -ced·ing** : withdraw from a body (as a nation)

se·clude \si'klüd\ *vb* **-clud·ed; -clud·ing** : shut off alone — **se·clu·sion** \si'klüzhən\ *n*

¹**sec·ond** \'sekənd\ *adj* : next after the 1st ∼ *n* **1** : one that is second **2** : one who assists (as in a duel) — **second, se·cond·ly** *adv*

²**second** *n* **1** : 60th part of a minute **2** : moment

sec·ond·ary \'sekən,derē\ *adj* **1** : second in rank or importance **2** : coming after the primary or elementary

sec·ond·hand *adj* **1** : not original **2** : used before

second lieutenant *n* : lowest ranking commissioned officer of the army, air force, or marines

se·cret \'sēkrət\ *adj* **1** : hidden **2** : kept from general knowledge — **se·cre·cy** \-krəsē\ *n* — **secret** *n* — **se·cre·tive** \'sēkrətiv, si'krēt-\ *adj* — **se·cret·ly** *adv*

sec·re·tar·i·at \,sekrə'terēət\ *n* : administrative department

sec·re·tary \'sekrə,terē\ *n, pl* **-tar·ies 1** : one hired to handle correspondence and other tasks for a superior **2** : official in charge of correspondence or records **3** : head of a government department — **sec·re·tar·i·al** \,sekrə'terēəl\ *adj*

¹**se·crete** \si'krēt\ *vb* **-cret·ed; -cret·ing** : produce as a secretion

²**se·crete** \si'krēt, 'sēkrət\ *vb* **-cret·ed; -cret·ing** : hide

se·cre·tion \si'krēshən\ *n* **1** : process of secreting **2** : product of glandular activity

sect \'sekt\ *n* : religious group

sec·tar·i·an \sek'terēən\ *adj* **1** : relating to a sect **2** : limited in character or scope ∼ *n* : member of a sect

sec·tion \'sekshən\ *n* : distinct part — **sec·tion·al** \-shənəl\ *adj*

sec·tor \'sektər\ *n* **1** : part of a circle between 2 radii **2** : distinctive part

sec·u·lar \'sekyələr\ *adj* **1** : not sacred **2** : not monastic

se·cure \si'kyu̇r\ *adj* **-cur·er; -est** : free from danger or loss ∼ *vb* **1** : fasten safely **2** : get — **se·cure·ly** *adv*

se·cu·ri·ty \si'kyu̇rətē\ *n, pl* **-ties 1** : safety **2** : something given to guarantee payment **3** *pl* : bond or stock certificates

se·dan \si'dan\ *n* **1** : chair carried by 2 men **2** : enclosed automobile

¹**se·date** \si'dāt\ *adj* : quiet and dignified — **se·date·ly** *adv*

²**sedate** *vb* **-dat·ed; -dat·ing** : dose with sedatives — **se·da·tion** \si'dāshən\ *n*

sed·a·tive \'sedətiv\ *adj* : serving to relieve tension ~ *n* : sedative drug

sed·en·tary \'sed°n,terē\ *adj* : characterized by much sitting

sedge \'sej\ *n* : grasslike marsh plant

sed·i·ment \'sedəmənt\ *n* : material that settles to the bottom of a liquid or is deposited by water or a glacier — **sed·i·men·ta·ry** \,sedə-'mentərē\ *adj* — **sed·i·men·ta·tion** \-mən'tāshən, -,men-\ *n*

se·di·tion \si'dishən\ *n* : revolution against a government — **se·di·tious** \-əs\ *adj*

se·duce \si'düs, -'dyüs\ *vb* **-duced; -duc·ing** 1 : lead astray 2 : entice to sexual intercourse — **se·duc·er** *n* — **se·duc·tion** \-'dəkshən\ *n* — **se·duc·tive** \-tiv\ *adj*

sed·u·lous \'sejələs\ *adj* : diligent

¹**see** \'sē\ *vb* **saw** \'so\; **seen** \'sēn\; **see·ing** 1 : perceive by the eye 2 : have experience of 3 : understand 4 : make sure 5 : meet with or escort

²**see** *n* : jurisdiction of a bishop

seed \'sēd\ *n, pl* **seed** *or* **seeds** 1 : part by which a plant is propagated 2 : source ~ *vb* 1 : sow 2 : remove seeds from — **seed·less** *adj*

seed·ling \-liŋ\ *n* : young plant grown from seed

seedy \-ē\ *adj* **seed·i·er; -est** 1 : full of seeds 2 : shabby

seek \'sēk\ *vb* **sought** \'sot\; **seek·ing** 1 : search for 2 : try to reach or obtain — **seek·er** *n*

seem \'sēm\ *vb* : give the impression of being — **seem·ing·ly** *adv*

seem·ly \-lē\ *adj* **seem·li·er; -est** : proper or fit

seep \'sēp\ *vb* : leak through fine pores or cracks — **seep·age** \'sēpij\ *n*

seer \'sēər\ *n* : one who foresees or predicts events

seer·suck·er \'sir,səkər\ *n* : light puckered fabric

see·saw \'sē,so\ *n* : board balanced in the middle — **seesaw** *vb*

seethe \'sēth\ *vb* **seethed; seeth·ing** : become violently agitated

seg·ment \'segmənt\ *n* : division of a thing — **seg·ment·ed** \-,mentəd\ *adj*

seg·re·gate \'segri,gāt\ *vb* **-gat·ed; -gat·ing** 1 : cut off from others 2 : separate by races — **seg·re·ga·tion** \,segri'gāshən\ *n*

seine \'sān\ *n* : large weighted fishing net ~ *vb* : fish with a seine

seis·mic \'sīzmik, 'sīs-\ *adj* : relating to an earthquake

seis·mo·graph \-mə,graf\ *n* : apparatus for detecting earthquakes

seize \'sēz\ *vb* **seized; seiz·ing** : take by force — **sei·zure** \'sēzhər\ *n*

sel·dom \'seldəm\ *adv* : not often

se·lect \sə'lekt\ *adj* 1 : favored 2 : discriminating ~ *vb* : take by preference — **se·lec·tive** \-'lektiv\ *adj*

se·lec·tion \sə'lekshən\ *n* : act of selecting or thing selected

se·lect·man \si'lekt,man, -mən\ *n* : New England town official

self \'self\ *n, pl* **selves** \'selvz\ : essential person distinct from others

self- *comb form* 1 : oneself or itself 2 : of oneself or itself 3 : by oneself or automatic 4 : to, for, or toward oneself

self-addressed	self-destructive
self-adminis-	self-determina-
tered	tion
self-analysis	self-determined
self-appointed	self-discipline
self-assertive	self-doubt
self-assurance	self-educated
self-assured	self-employed
self-awareness	self-employ-
self-cleaning	ment
self-closing	self-esteem
self-complacent	self-evident
self-conceit	self-explanato-
self-confessed	ry
self-confidence	self-expression
self-confident	self-fulfilling
self-contained	self-fulfillment
self-contempt	self-governing
self-contradic-	self-govern-
tion	ment
self-contradic-	self-help
tory	self-image
self-control	self-importance
self-created	self-important
self-criticism	self-imposed
self-defeating	self-improve-
self-defense	ment
self-denial	self-indulgence
self-denying	self-indulgent
self-destruction	self-inflicted

self-interest
self-love
self-operating
self-pity
self-portrait
self-possessed
self-possession
self-preserva-
tion
self-proclaimed
self-propelled
self-propelling
self-protection
self-reliance
self-reliant

self-respect
self-respecting
self-restraint
self-sacrifice
self-satisfaction
self-satisfied
self-service
self-serving
self-starting
self-styled
self-sufficiency
self-sufficient
self-supporting
self-taught
self-winding

self–cen·tered *adj* : concerned only with one's own self

self–con·scious *adj* : uncomfortably aware of oneself as an object of observation — **self–con·scious·ly** *adv* — **self–con·scious·ness** *n*

self·ish \'selfish\ *adj* : excessively or exclusively concerned with one's own well-being — **self·ish·ly** *adv* — **self·ish·ness** *n*

self·less \'selfləs\ *adj* : unselfish — **self·less·ness** *n*

self–made *adj* : having succeeded by one's own efforts

self–righ·teous *adj* : strongly convinced of one's own righteousness

self·same \'self,sām\ *adj* : precisely the same

sell \'sel\ *vb* **sold** \'sōld\; **sell·ing 1** : transfer (property) esp. for money **2** : deal in as a business **3** : be sold — **sell·er** *n*

selves *pl of* SELF

se·man·tic \si'mantik\ *adj* : relating to meaning in language — **se·man·tics** \-iks\ *n sing or pl*

sem·a·phore \'semə,fōr\ *n* **1** : visual signaling apparatus **2** : signaling by flags

sem·blance \'sembləns\ *n* : appearance

se·men \'sēmən\ *n* : male reproductive fluid

se·mes·ter \sə'mestər\ *n* : half a school year

semi- \-,semi, 'sem-, -,ī\ *prefix* **1** : half **2** : partial

semi·co·lon \'semi,kōlən\ *n* : punctuation mark ;

semi·con·duc·tor *n* : substance between a conductor and a nonconductor in ability to conduct electricity — **semi·con·duct·ing** *adj*

semi·fi·nal *adj* : being next to the final — **semifinal** *n*

semi·for·mal *adj* : being or suitable for an occasion of moderate formality

sem·i·nal \'semən°l\ *adj* **1** : relating to seed or semen **2** : causing or influencing later development

sem·i·nar \'semə,när\ *n* : conference or conferencelike study

sem·i·nary \'semə,nerē\ *n, pl* **-nar·ies** : school and esp. a theological school — **sem·i·nar·i·an** \,semə'nerēən\ *n*

sen·ate \'senət\ *n* : upper branch of a legislature — **sen·a·tor** \-ər\ *n* — **sen·a·to·rial** \,senə'tōrēəl\ *adj*

send \'send\ *vb* **sent** \'sent\; **sending 1** : cause to go **2** : propel — **send·er** *n*

se·nile \'sēn,īl, 'sen-\ *adj* : mentally deficient through old age — **se·nil·i·ty** \si'nilətē\ *n*

se·nior \'sēnyər\ *adj* : older or higher ranking — **senior** *n* — **se·nior·i·ty** \,sēn'yórətē\ *n*

senior chief petty officer *n* : petty officer in the navy or coast guard ranking next below a master chief petty officer

senior master sergeant *n* : noncommissioned officer in the air force ranking next below a chief master sergeant

sen·sa·tion \sen'sāshən\ *n* **1** : bodily feeling **2** : condition of excitement or the cause of it — **sen·sa·tion·al** \-shənəl\ *adj*

sense \'sens\ *n* **1** : meaning **2** : faculty of perceiving something physical **3** : sound mental capacity ~ *vb* sensed; sens·ing 1 : perceive by the senses **2** : detect automatically — **sense·less** *adj* — **sense·less·ly** *adv*

sen·si·bil·i·ty \,sensə'bilətē\ *n, pl* **-ties** : delicacy of feeling

sen·si·ble \'sensəbəl\ *adj* **1** : capable of sensing or being sensed **2** : aware or conscious **3** : reasonable — **sen·si·bly** \-blē\ *adv*

sen·si·tive \'sensətiv\ *adj* **1** : subject to excitation by or responsive to stimuli **2** : having power of feeling **3** : easily affected — **sen·si·tive·ness** *n* — **sen·si·tiv·i·ty** \,sensə'tivətē\ *n*

sen·si·tize \'sensə,tīz\ *vb* **-tized; -tiz·ing** : make or become sensitive

sen·sor \'sen₁sȯr, -sər\ *n* : device that responds to a physical stimulus

sen·so·ry \'sensərē\ *adj* : relating to sensation or the senses

sen·su·al \'senchəwəl, -shəwəl\ *adj* 1 : pleasing the senses 2 : devoted to the pleasures of the senses — **sen·su·al·ist** *n* — **sen·su·al·i·ty** \₁senchə'walətē\ *n* — **sen·su·al·ly** *adv*

sen·su·ous \'senchəwəs\ *adj* : having strong appeal to the senses

sent *past of* SEND

sen·tence \'sent°ns, -°nz\ *n* 1 : judgment of a court 2 : grammatically self-contained speech unit ~ *vb* -tenced; -tenc·ing : impose a sentence on

sen·ten·tious \sen'tenchəs\ *adj* : using pompous language

sen·tient \'senchēənt\ *adj* : capable of feeling

sen·ti·ment \'sentəmənt\ *n* 1 : belief 2 : feeling

sen·ti·men·tal \₁sentə'ment°l\ *adj* : influenced by tender feelings — **sen·ti·men·tal·ism** *n* — **sen·ti·men·tal·ist** *n* — **sen·ti·men·tal·i·ty** \-₁men'talətē, -mən-\ *n* — **sen·ti·men·tal·ize** \-'ment°l₁īz\ *vb* — **sen·ti·men·tal·ly** *adv*

sen·ti·nel \'sent°nəl\ *n* : sentry

sen·try \'sentrē\ *n, pl* -tries : one who stands guard

se·pal \'sēpəl, 'sep-\ *n* : modified leaf in a flower calyx

sep·a·rate \'sepə₁rāt\ *vb* -rat·ed; -rat·ing 1 : set or keep apart 2 : become divided or detached ~ \'seprət, 'sepə-\ *adj* 1 : not connected or shared 2 : distinct from each other — **sep·a·ra·ble** \'sepərəbəl\ *adj* — **sep·a·rate·ly** *adv* — **sep·a·ra·tion** \₁sepə'rāshən\ *n* — **sep·a·ra·tor** \'sepə₁rātər\ *n*

se·pia \'sēpēə\ *n* : brownish gray

Sep·tem·ber \sep'tembər\ *n* : 9th month of the year having 30 days

sep·ul·chre, sep·ul·cher \'sepəlkər\ *n* : burial vault — **se·pul·chral** \sə'pəlkrəl\ *adj*

se·quel \'sēkwəl\ *n* 1 : consequence or result 2 : continuation of a story

se·quence \'sēkwəns\ *n* : continuous or connected series — **se·**quen·tial \si'kwenchəl\ *adj* — **se·quen·tial·ly** *adv*

se·ques·ter \si'kwestər\ *vb* : segregate

se·quin \'sēkwən\ *n* : spangle

se·quoia \si'kwȯiə\ *n* : huge California coniferous tree

sera *pl of* SERUM

ser·aph \'serəf\ *n, pl* -a·phim \-ə₁fim\ *or* -aphs : angel — **se·raph·ic** \sə'rafik\ *adj*

sere \'sir\ *adj* : dried up or withered

ser·e·nade \₁serə'nād\ *n* : music sung or played esp. to a woman being courted — **serenade** *vb*

ser·en·dip·i·ty \₁serən'dipətē\ *n* : good luck in finding things not sought for — **ser·en·dip·i·tous** \-əs\ *adj*

se·rene \sə'rēn\ *adj* : tranquil — **se·rene·ly** *adv* — **se·ren·i·ty** \sə-'renətē\ *n*

serf \'sərf\ *n* : peasant obligated to work the land — **serf·dom** \-dəm\ *n*

serge \'sərj\ *n* : twilled woolen cloth

ser·geant \'särjənt\ *n* : noncommissioned officer (as in the army) ranking next below a staff sergeant

sergeant first class *n* : noncommissioned officer in the army ranking next below a master sergeant

sergeant major *n, pl* **sergeants major** *or* **sergeant majors** 1 : noncommissioned officer serving as an enlisted adviser in a headquarters 2 : noncommissioned officer in the marine corps ranking above a first sergeant

se·ri·al \'sirēəl\ *adj* : being or relating to a series or sequence ~ *n* : story appearing in parts — **se·ri·al·ly** *adv*

se·ries \'sirēz\ *n, pl* **series** : number of things in order

se·ri·ous \'sirēəs\ *adj* 1 : subdued in appearance or manner 2 : sincere 3 : of great importance — **se·ri·ous·ly** *adv* — **se·ri·ous·ness** *n*

ser·mon \'sərmən\ *n* : lecture on religion or behavior

ser·pent \'sərpənt\ *n* : snake — **ser·pen·tine** \-pən₁tēn, -₁tīn\ *adj*

ser·rat·ed \'ser₁ātəd\ *adj* : saw-toothed

se·rum \'sirəm\ *n, pl* -rums *or* -ra \-ə\ : watery part of blood

ser·vant \'sərvənt\ *n* : person employed for domestic work

serve \'sərv\ *vb* **served; serv·ing** 1 : work through or perform a term of service 2 : be of use 3 : prove adequate 4 : hand out (food or drink) 5 : be of service to — **serv·er** *n*

ser·vice \'sərvəs\ *n* 1 : act or means of serving 2 : meeting for worship 3 : branch of public employment or the persons in it 4 : set of dishes or silverware 5 : benefit ∼ *vb* **-viced; -vic·ing** : repair — **ser·vice·able** *adj* — **ser·vice·man** \-,man, -mən\ *n* — **ser·vice·woman** *n*

ser·vile \'sərvəl, -,vīl\ *adj* : behaving like a slave — **ser·vil·i·ty** \sər-'vilətē\ *n*

serv·ing \'sərviŋ\ *n* : helping

ser·vi·tude \'sərvə,tüd, -,tyüd\ *n* : slavery

ses·a·me \'sesəmē\ *n* : annual herb or its seeds that are used in flavoring

ses·sion \'seshən\ *n* : meeting

set \'set\ *vb* **set; set·ting** 1 : cause to sit 2 : place 3 : settle, arrange, or adjust 4 : cause to be or do 5 : become fixed or solid 6 : sink below the horizon ∼ *adj* : settled ∼ *n* 1 : group classed together 2 : setting for the scene of a play or film 3 : electronic apparatus 4 : collection of mathematical elements — **set forth** : begin a trip — **set off** *vb* : set forth — **set out** *vb* : begin a trip or undertaking — **set up** *vb* 1 : assemble or erect 2 : cause

set·back *n* : reverse

set·tee \se'tē\ *n* : bench or sofa

set·ter \'setər\ *n* : large long-coated hunting dog

set·ting \'setiŋ\ *n* : the time, place, and circumstances in which something occurs

set·tle \'set²l\ *vb* **-tled; -tling** 1 : come to rest 2 : sink gradually 3 : establish in residence 4 : adjust or arrange 5 : calm 6 : dispose of (as by paying) 7 : decide or agree on — **set·tle·ment** \-mənt\ *n* — **set·tler** \'set²lər\ *n*

sev·en \'sevən\ *n* : one more than 6 — **seven** *adj or pron* — **sev·enth** \-ənth\ *adj or adv or n*

sev·en·teen \,sevən'tēn\ *n* : one more than 16 — **seventeen** *adj or pron* — **sev·en·teenth** \-'tēnth\ *adj or n*

sev·en·ty \'sevəntē\ *n, pl* **-ties** : 7 times 10 — **sev·en·ti·eth** \-tēəth\ *adj or n* — **seventy** *adj or pron*

sev·er \'sevər\ *vb* **-ered; -er·ing** : cut off or apart — **sev·er·ance** \'sevrəns, -vərəns\ *n*

sev·er·al \'sevrəl, 'sevə-\ *adj* 1 : distinct 2 : consisting of an indefinite but not large number — **sev·er·al·ly** *adv*

se·vere \sə'vir\ *adj* **-ver·er; -est** 1 : strict 2 : restrained or unadorned 3 : painful or distressing 4 : hard to endure — **se·vere·ly** *adv* — **se·ver·i·ty** \-'verətē\ *n*

sew \'sō\ *vb* **sewed; sewn** \'sōn\ *or* **sewed; sew·ing** : join or fasten by stitches — **sew·ing** *n*

sew·age \'süij\ *n* : liquid household waste

¹**sew·er** \'sōər\ *n* : one that sews

²**sew·er** \'süər\ *n* : pipe or channel to carry off waste matter

sex \'seks\ *n* 1 : either of 2 divisions into which organisms are grouped according to their reproductive roles or the qualities which differentiate them 2 : copulation — **sexed** \'sekst\ *adj* — **sex·less** *adj* — **sex·u·al** \'sekshəwəl\ *adj* — **sex·u·al·i·ty** \,seksho'walətē\ *n* — **sex·u·al·ly** *adv* — **sexy** *adj*

sex·ism \'sek,sizəm\ *n* : discrimination based on sex and esp. against women — **sex·ist** \'seksist\ *adj or n*

sex·tant \'sekstənt\ *n* : instrument for navigation

sex·tet \sek'stet\ *n* 1 : music for 6 performers 2 : group of 6

sex·ton \'sekstən\ *n* : church caretaker

shab·by \'shabē\ *adj* **-bi·er; -est** 1 : worn and faded 2 : dressed in worn clothes 3 : not generous or fair — **shab·bi·ly** *adv* — **shab·bi·ness** *n*

shack \'shak\ *n* : hut

shack·le \'shakəl\ *n* : metal device to bind legs or arms ∼ *vb* **-led; -ling** : bind or fasten with shackles

shad \'shad\ *n* : Atlantic food fish

shade \'shād\ *n* 1 : space sheltered from the light esp. of the sun 2 : gradation of color 3 : small difference 4 : something that shades ∼ *vb* **shad·ed; shad·ing** 1 : shelter from light and heat **2** : add shades of color to **3** : show slight differences esp. in color or meaning

shad·ow \'shadō\ *n* **1** : shade cast upon a surface by something blocking light **2** : trace **3** : gloomy influence ∼ *vb* **1** : cast a shadow **2** : follow closely — **shad·owy** *adj*

shady \'shādē\ *adj* **shad·i·er; -est 1** : giving shade **2** : of dubious honesty

shaft \'shaft\ *n* **1** : long slender cylindrical part **2** : deep vertical opening (as of a mine)

shag \'shag\ *n* : shaggy tangled mat

shag·gy \'shagē\ *adj* **-gi·er; -est 1** : covered with long hair or wool **2** : not neat and combed

shake \'shāk\ *vb* **shook** \'shu̇k\; **shak·en** \'shākən\; **shak·ing 1** : move or cause to move quickly back and forth **2** : distress **3** : clasp (hands) as friendly gesture — **shake** *n* — **shak·er** \-ər\ *n*

shake–up *n* : reorganization

shaky \'shākē\ *adj* **shak·i·er; -est** : not sound, stable, or reliable — **shak·i·ly** *adv* — **shak·i·ness** *n*

shale \'shāl\ *n* : stratified rock

shall \'shal\ *vb, past* **should** \'shu̇d\; *pres sing & pl* **shall** — used as an auxiliary to express a command, futurity, or determination

shal·low \'shalō\ *adj* **1** : not deep **2** : not intellectually profound

shal·lows \-ōz\ *n pl* : area of shallow water

sham \'sham\ *adj or n or vb* : fake

sham·ble \'shambəl\ *vb* **-bled; -bling** : shuffle along — **sham·ble** *n*

sham·bles \'shambəlz\ *n* : state of disorder

◆ **shame** \'shām\ *n* **1** : distress over guilt or disgrace **2** : cause of shame or regret ∼ *vb* **shamed; sham·ing 1** : make ashamed **2** : disgrace — **shame·ful** \-fəl\ *adj*

— **shame·ful·ly** \-ē\ *adv* — **shame·less** *adj* — **shame·less·ly** *adv*

shame·faced \'shām'fāst\ *adj* : ashamed

sham·poo \sham'pü\ *vb* : wash one's hair ∼ *n, pl* **-poos** : act of or preparation used in shampooing

sham·rock \'sham,räk\ *n* : plant of legend with 3-lobed leaves

shank \'shaŋk\ *n* : part of the leg between the knee and ankle

shan·ty \'shantē\ *n, pl* **-ties** : hut

shape \'shāp\ *vb* **shaped; shap·ing** : form esp. in a particular structure or appearance ∼ *n* **1** : distinctive appearance or arrangement of parts **2** : condition — **shape·less** \-ləs\ *adj* — **shape·li·ness** *n* — **shape·ly** *adj*

shard \'shärd\ *n* : broken piece

share \'sher\ *n* **1** : portion belonging to one **2** : interest in a company's stock ∼ *vb* **shared; shar·ing** : divide or use with others — **share·hold·er** *n* — **shar·er** *n*

share·crop·per \-,kräpər\ *n* : farmer who works another's land in return for a share of the crop — **share·crop** *vb*

shark \'shärk\ *n* : voracious sea fish

sharp \'shärp\ *adj* **1** : having a good point or cutting edge **2** : alert, clever, or sarcastic **3** : vigorous or fierce **4** : having prominent angles or a sudden change in direction **5** : distinct **6** : higher than the true pitch ∼ *adv* : exactly ∼ *n* : sharp note — **sharp·ly** *adv* — **sharp·ness** *n*

shar·pen \'shärpən\ *vb* : make sharp — **sharp·en·er** \-ənər\ *n*

sharp·shoot·er *n* : expert marksman — **sharp·shoot·ing** *n*

shat·ter \'shatər\ *vb* : smash or burst into fragments — **shat·ter·proof** \-,prüf\ *adj*

shave \'shāv\ *vb* **shaved; shaved** or **shav·en** \'shāvən\; **shav·ing 1** : cut off with a razor **2** : make bare by cutting the hair from **3** : slice very thin ～ *n* : act or instance of shaving — **shav·er** *n*

shawl \'shȯl\ *n* : loose covering for the head or shoulders

she \'shē\ *pron* : that female one

sheaf \'shēf\ *n, pl* **sheaves** \'shēvz\ : bundle esp. of grain stalks

shear \'shir\ *vb* **sheared; sheared** or **shorn** \'shȯrn\; **shear·ing 1** : trim wool from **2** : cut off with scissorlike action

shears \'shirz\ *n pl* : cutting tool with 2 blades fastened so that the edges slide by each other

sheath \'shēth\ *n, pl* **sheaths** \'shēthz, 'shēths\ : covering (as for a blade)

sheathe \'shēth\ *vb* **sheathed; sheath·ing** : put into a sheath

shed \'shed\ *vb* **shed; shed·ding 1** : give off (as tears or hair) **2** : cause to flow or diffuse ～ *n* : small storage building

sheen \'shēn\ *n* : subdued luster

sheep \'shēp\ *n, pl* **sheep** : domesticated mammal covered with wool — **sheep·skin** *n*

sheep·ish \'shēpish\ *adj* : embarrassed by awareness of a fault

sheer \'shir\ *adj* **1** : pure **2** : very steep **3** : very thin or transparent — **sheer** *adv*

sheet \'shēt\ *n* : broad flat piece (as of cloth or paper)

sheikh, sheik \'shēk, 'shāk\ *n* : Arab chief — **sheikh·dom, sheik·dom** \-dəm\ *n*

shelf \'shelf\ *n, pl* **shelves** \'shelvz\ **1** : flat narrow structure used for storage or display **2** : sandbank or rock ledge

shell \'shel\ *n* **1** : hard or tough outer covering **2** : case holding explosive powder and projectile for a weapon **3** : light racing boat with oars ～ *vb* **1** : remove the shell of **2** : bombard — **shelled** \'sheld\ *adj* — **shell·er** *n*

shel·lac \shə'lak\ *n* : varnish ～ *vb* **-lacked; -lack·ing 1** : coat with shellac **2** : defeat — **shel·lack·ing** *n*

shell·fish *n* : water animal with a shell

shel·ter \'sheltər\ *n* : something that gives protection ～ *vb* : give refuge to

shelve \'shelv\ *vb* **shelved; shelv·ing 1** : place or store on shelves **2** : dismiss or put aside

she·nan·i·gans \shə'nanigənz\ *n pl* : mischievous or deceitful conduct

shep·herd \'shepərd\ *n* : one that tends sheep ～ *vb* : act as a shepherd or guardian

shep·herd·ess \'shepərdəs\ *n* : woman who tends sheep

sher·bet \'shərbət\, **sher·bert** \-bərt\ *n* : fruit-flavored frozen dessert

sher·iff \'sherəf\ *n* : county law officer

sher·ry \'sherē\ *n, pl* **-ries** : type of wine

shield \'shēld\ *n* **1** : broad piece of armor carried on the arm **2** : something that protects — **shield** *vb*

shier *comparative of* SHY

shiest *superlative of* SHY

shift \'shift\ *vb* **1** : change place, position, or direction **2** : get by ～ *n* **1** : loose-fitting dress **2** : an act or instance of shifting **3** : scheduled work period

shift·less \-ləs\ *adj* : lazy

shifty \'shiftē\ *adj* **shift·i·er; -est** : tricky or untrustworthy

shil·le·lagh \shə'lālē\ *n* : club or stick

shil·ling \'shilin\ *n* : former British coin

shil·ly–shally \'shilē,shalē\ *vb* **-shallied; -shally·ing 1** : hesitate **2** : dawdle

shim·mer \'shimər\ *vb* or *n* : glimmer

shin \'shin\ *n* : front part of the leg below the knee ～ *vb* **-nn-** : climb by sliding the body close along

shine \'shīn\ *vb* **shone** \-shōn\ or **shined; shin·ing 1** : give off or cause to give off light **2** : be outstanding **3** : polish ～ *n* : brilliance

shin·gle \'shingəl\ *n* **1** : small thin piece used in covering roofs or exterior walls — **shingle** *vb*

shin·gles \'shingəlz\ *n pl* : acute inflammation of spinal nerves

shin·ny \'shinē\ *vb* **-nied; -ny·ing** : shin

shiny \'shīnē\ *adj* **shin·i·er; -est** : bright or polished

ship \'ship\ *n* **1** : large oceangoing vessel **2** : aircraft or spacecraft ~ *vb* **-pp-** **1** : put on a ship **2** : transport by carrier — **ship·board** *n* — **ship·build·er** *n* — **ship·per** *n* — **ship·wreck** *n or vb* — **ship·yard** *n*

-ship \ˌship\ *n suffix* **1** : state, condition, or quality **2** : rank or profession **3** : skill **4** : something showing a state or quality

ship·ment \-mənt\ *n* : an act of shipping or the goods shipped

ship·ping \'shipiŋ\ *n* **1** : ships **2** : transportation of goods

ship·shape *adj* : tidy

shire \'shīr, *in place-name compounds* ˌshir, shər\ *n* : British county

shirk \'shərk\ *vb* : evade — **shirk·er** *n*

shirr \'shər\ *vb* **1** : gather (cloth) by drawing up parallel lines of stitches **2** : bake (eggs) in a dish

shirt \'shərt\ *n* : garment for covering the torso — **shirt·less** *adj*

shiv·er \'shivər\ *vb* : tremble — **shiver** *n* — **shiv·ery** *adj*

shoal \'shōl\ *n* : shallow place (as in a river)

¹shock \'shäk\ *n* : pile of sheaves set up in a field

²shock *n* **1** : forceful impact **2** : violent mental or emotional disturbance **3** : effect of a charge of electricity **4** : depression of the vital bodily processes ~ *vb* **1** : strike with surprise, horror, or disgust **2** : subject to an electrical shock — **shock·proof** *adj*

³shock *n* : bushy mass (as of hair)

shod·dy \'shädē\ *adj* **-di·er; -est** : poorly made or done — **shod·di·ly** \'shädᵊlē\ *adv* — **shod·di·ness** *n*

shoe \'shü\ *n* **1** : covering for the human foot **2** : horseshoe ~ *vb* **shod** \'shäd\; **shoe·ing** : put horseshoes on — **shoe·lace** *n* — **shoe·ma·ker** *n*

shone *past of* SHINE

shook *past of* SHAKE

shoot \'shüt\ *vb* **shot** \'shät\; **shoot·ing 1** : propel (as an arrow or bullet) **2** : wound or kill with a missile **3** : discharge (a weapon) **4** : drive (as a ball) at a goal **5** : photograph **6** : move swiftly ~ *n* : new plant growth — **shoot·er** *n*

♦ **shop** \'shäp\ *n* : place where things are made or sold ~ *vb* **-pp-** : visit stores — **shop·keep·er** *n* — **shop·per** *n*

shop·lift *vb* : steal goods from a store — **shop·lift·er** \-ˌliftər\ *n*

¹shore \'shōr\ *n* : land along the edge of water — **shore·line** *n*

²shore *vb* **shored; shor·ing** : prop up ~ *n* : something that props

shore·bird *n* : bird of the seashore

shorn *past part of* SHEAR

short \'shȯrt\ *adj* **1** : not long or tall or extending far **2** : brief in time **3** : curt **4** : not having or being enough ~ *adv* : curtly ~ *n* **1** *pl* : short drawers or trousers **2** : short circuit — **short·en** \-ᵊn\ *vb* — **short·ly** *adv* — **short·ness** *n*

short·age \'shȯrtij\ *n* : deficiency

short·cake *n* : dessert of biscuit with sweetened fruit

short·change *vb* : cheat esp. by giving too little change

short circuit *n* : abnormal electric connection — **short–circuit** *vb*

short·com·ing *n* : fault or failing

short·cut \-ˌkət\ *n* **1** : more direct route than that usu. taken **2** : quicker way of doing something

short·hand *n* : method of speed writing

short–lived \'shȯrt'līvd, -ˌlivd\ *adj* : of short life or duration

short·sight·ed *adj* : lacking foresight

shot \'shät\ *n* **1** : act of shooting **2** : attempt (as at making a goal) **3** : small pellets forming a charge **4** : range or reach **5** : photograph **6** : injection of medicine **7** : small serving of liquor — **shot·gun** *n*

should \'shùd\ *past of* SHALL — used as an auxiliary to express condition, obligation, or probability

shoul·der \'shōldər\ *n* **1** : part of the body where the arm joins the trunk **2** : part that projects or lies to the side ~ *vb* : push with or bear on the shoulder

shoulder blade *n* : flat triangular bone at the back of the shoulder

shout \'shaùt\ *vb* : give voice loudly — **shout** *n*

shove \'shəv\ *vb* **shoved; shov·ing** : push along or away — **shove** *n*

shov·el \'shəvəl\ *n* : broad tool for digging or lifting ~ *vb* **-eled** *or* **-elled; -el·ing** *or* **-el·ling** : take up or dig with a shovel

show \'shō\ *vb* **showed** \'shōd\; **shown** \'shōn\ *or* **showed; show·ing 1** : present to view **2** : reveal or demonstrate **3** : teach **4** : prove **5** : conduct or escort **6** : appear or be noticeable ~ *n* **1** : demonstrative display **2** : spectacle **3** : theatrical, radio, or television program — **show·case** *n* — **show off** *vb* **1** : display proudly **2** : act so as to attract attention — **show up** *vb* : arrive

show·down *n* : decisive confrontation

show·er \'shaùər\ *n* **1** : brief fall of rain **2** : bath in which water sprinkles down on the person or a facility for such a bath **3** : party at which someone gets gifts ~ *vb* **1** : rain or fall in a shower **2** : bathe in a shower — **show·ery** *adj*

showy \'shōē\ *adj* **show·i·er; -est** : very noticeable or overly elaborate — **show·i·ly** *adv* — **show·i·ness** *n*

shrap·nel \'shrapnəl\ *n, pl* **shrapnel** : metal fragments of a bomb

shred \'shred\ *n* : narrow strip cut or torn off ~ *vb* **-dd-** : cut or tear into shreds

shrew \'shrü\ *n* **1** : scolding woman

2 : mouselike mammal — **shrew·ish** \-ish\ *adj*

shrewd \'shrüd\ *adj* : clever — **shrewd·ly** *adv* — **shrewd·ness** *n*

shriek \'shrēk\ *n* : shrill cry — **shriek** *vb*

shrill \'shril\ *adj* : piercing and high-pitched — **shril·ly** *adv*

shrimp \'shrimp\ *n* : small sea crustacean

shrine \'shrīn\ *n* **1** : tomb of a saint **2** : hallowed place

shrink \'shriŋk\ *vb* **shrank** \'shraŋk\; **shrunk** \'shrəŋk\ *or* **shrunk·en** \'shrəŋkən\; **shrink·ing 1** : draw back or away **2** : become smaller — **shrink·able** *adj*

shrink·age \'shriŋkij\ *n* : amount lost by shrinking

shriv·el \'shrivəl\ *vb* **-eled** *or* **-elled; -el·ing** *or* **-el·ling** : shrink or wither into wrinkles

shroud \'shraùd\ *n* **1** : cloth put over a corpse **2** : cover or screen ~ *vb* : veil or screen from view

shrub \'shrəb\ *n* : low woody plant — **shrub·by** *adj*

shrub·bery \'shrəbərē\ *n, pl* **-ber·ies** : growth of shrubs

shrug \'shrəg\ *vb* **-gg-** : hunch the shoulders up in doubt, indifference, or uncertainty — **shrug** *n*

shuck \'shək\ *vb* : strip of a shell or husk — **shuck** *n*

shud·der \'shədər\ *vb* : tremble — **shudder** *n*

shuf·fle \'shəfəl\ *vb* **-fled; -fling 1** : mix together **2** : walk with a sliding movement — **shuffle** *n*

shuf·fle·board \'shəfəl,bōrd\ *n* : game of sliding disks into a scoring area

shun \'shən\ *vb* **-nn-** : keep away from

shunt \'shənt\ *vb* : turn off to one side

shut \'shət\ *vb* **shut; shut·ting 1** : bar passage into or through (as by moving a lid or door) **2** : suspend activity — **shut out** *vb* : exclude — **shut up** *vb* : stop or cause to stop talking

shut–in *n* : invalid

shut·ter \'shətər\ *n* **1** : movable cover for a window **2** : camera part that exposes film

shut·tle \'shətəl\ *n* **1** : part of a weaving machine that carries thread back and forth **2** : vehicle traveling back and forth over a short route ~ *vb* **-tled; -tling** : move back and forth frequently

shut·tle·cock \'shət³l‚käk\ *n* : light conical object used in badminton

shy \'shī\ *adj* **shi·er** *or* **shy·er** \'shīər\; **shi·est** *or* **shy·est** \'shīəst\ **1** : sensitive and hesitant in dealing with others **2** : wary **3** : lacking ~ *vb* **shied; shy·ing** : draw back (as in fright) — **shy·ly** *adv* — **shy·ness** *n*

sib·i·lant \'sibələnt\ *adj* : having the sound of the *s* or the *sh* in *sash* — **sibilant** *n*

sib·ling \'sibliŋ\ *n* : brother or sister

sick \'sik\ *adj* **1** : not in good health **2** : nauseated **3** : relating to or meant for the sick — **sick·bed** *n* — **sick·en** \-ən\ *vb* — **sick·ly** *adj* — **sick·ness** *n*

sick·le \'sikəl\ *n* : curved short-handled blade

side \'sīd\ *n* **1** : part to left or right of an object or the torso **2** : edge or surface away from the center or at an angle to top and bottom or ends **3** : contrasting or opposing position or group — **sid·ed** *adj*

side·board *n* : piece of dining-room furniture for table service

side·burns \-‚bərnz\ *n pl* : whiskers in front of the ears

side·long \'sīd‚loŋ\ *adv or adj* : to or along the side

side·show *n* : minor show at a circus

side·step *vb* **1** : step aside **2** : avoid

side·swipe \-‚swīp\ *vb* : strike with a glancing blow — **sideswipe** *n*

side·track *vb* : lead aside or astray

side·walk *n* : paved walk at the side of a road

side·ways \-‚wāz\ *adv or adj* **1** : to or from the side **2** : with one side to the front

sid·ing \'sīdiŋ\ *n* **1** : short railroad track **2** : material for covering the outside of a building

si·dle \'sīd³l\ *vb* **-dled; -dling** : move sideways or unobtrusively

siege \'sēj\ *n* : persistent attack (as on a fortified place)

si·es·ta \sē'estə\ *n* : midday nap

sieve \'siv\ *n* : utensil with holes to separate particles

sift \'sift\ *vb* **1** : pass through a sieve **2** : examine carefully — **sift·er** *n*

sigh \'sī\ *n* : audible release of the

breath (as to express weariness) — **sigh** *vb*

sight \'sīt\ *n* **1** : something seen or worth seeing **2** : process, power, or range of seeing **3** : device used in aiming **4** : view or glimpse ~ *vb* : get sight of — **sight·ed** *adj* — **sight·less** *adj* — **sight–see·ing** *adj* — **sight·seer** \-‚sēər\ *n*

sign \'sīn\ *n* **1** : symbol **2** : gesture expressing a command or thought **3** : public notice to advertise or warn **4** : trace ~ *vb* **1** : mark with or make a sign **2** : write one's name on — **sign·er** *n*

sig·nal \'sign³l\ *n* **1** : sign of command or warning **2** : electronic transmission ~ *vb* **-naled** *or* **-nalled; -nal·ing** *or* **-nal·ling** : communicate or notify by signals ~ *adj* : distinguished

sig·na·to·ry \'signə‚tōrē\ *n, pl* **-ries** : person or government that signs jointly with others

sig·na·ture \'signə‚chùr\ *n* : one's name written by oneself

sig·net \'signət\ *n* : small seal

sig·nif·i·cance \sig'nifikəns\ *n* **1** : meaning **2** : importance — **sig·nif·i·cant** \-kənt\ *adj* — **sig·nif·i·cant·ly** *adv*

sig·ni·fy \'signə‚fī\ *vb* **-fied; -fy·ing 1** : show by a sign **2** : mean — **sig·ni·fi·ca·tion** \‚signəfə'kāshən\ *n*

si·lence \'sīləns\ *n* : state of being without sound ~ *vb* **-lenced; -lenc·ing** : keep from making noise or sound — **si·lenc·er** *n*

si·lent \'sīlənt\ *adj* : having or producing no sound — **si·lent·ly** *adv*

sil·hou·ette \‚silə'wet\ *n* : outline filled in usu. with black ~ *vb* **-etted; -ett·ing** : represent by a silhouette

sil·i·ca \'silikə\ *n* : mineral found as quartz and opal

sil·i·con \'silikən, -‚kän\ *n* : nonmetallic chemical element

silk \'silk\ *n* **1** : fine strong lustrous protein fiber from moth larvae (**silkworms** \-‚wərmz\) **2** : thread or cloth made from silk — **silk·en** \'silkən\ *adj* — **silky** *adj*

sill \'sil\ *n* : bottom part of a window frame or a doorway

sil·ly \'silē\ *adj* **sil·li·er; -est** : foolish or stupid — **sil·li·ness** *n*

FARM LIFE'S GREAT, ISN'T IT, GARFIELD? HOWEVER, I WILL ADMIT IT'S A LITTLE SLOW NOTHING MUCH TO DO BUT COUNT THE BRICKS IN THE OLD SILO

◆ **si·lo** \'sīlō\ *n, pl* **-los** : tall building for storing animal feed

silt \'silt\ *n* : fine earth carried by rivers — *vb* : obstruct or cover with silt

sil·ver \'silvər\ *n* **1** : white ductile metallic chemical element **2** : silverware — *adj* : having the color of silver — **sil·very** *adj*

sil·ver·ware \-,war\ *n* : eating and serving utensils esp. of silver

sim·i·lar \'simələr\ *adj* : resembling each other in some ways — **sim·i·lar·i·ty** \,simə'larətē\ *n* — **sim·i·lar·ly** \'simələrlē\ *adv*

sim·i·le \'simə,lē\ *n* : comparison of unlike things using *like* or *as*

sim·mer \'simər\ *vb* : stew gently

sim·per \'simpər\ *vb* : give a silly smile — **simper** *n*

sim·ple \'simpəl\ *adj* **-pler; -plest** **1** : free from dishonesty, vanity, or pretense **2** : of humble origin or modest position **3** : not complex **4** : lacking education, experience, or intelligence — **sim·ple·ness** *n* — **sim·ply** \-plē\ *adv*

sim·ple·ton \'simpəltən\ *n* : fool

sim·plic·i·ty \sim'plisətē\ *n* : state or fact of being simple

sim·pli·fy \'simplə,fī\ *vb* **-fied; -fy·ing** : make easier — **sim·pli·fi·ca·tion** \,simpləfə'kāshən\ *n*

sim·u·late \'simyə,lāt\ *vb* **-lat·ed; -lat·ing** : create the effect or appearance of — **sim·u·la·tion** \,simyə'lāshən\ *n* — **sim·u·la·tor** \'simyə,lātər\ *n*

si·mul·ta·ne·ous \,sīməl'tānēəs\ *adj* : occurring or operating at the same time — **si·mul·ta·ne·ous·ly** *adv* — **si·mul·ta·ne·ous·ness** *n*

sin \'sin\ *n* : offense against God — *vb* **-nn-** : commit a sin — **sin·ful** \-fəl\ *adj* — **sin·less** *adj* — **sin·ner** *n*

since \'sins\ *adv* **1** : from a past time until now **2** : backward in time — *prep* **1** : in the period after **2** : continuously from — *conj* **1** : from the time when **2** : because

sin·cere \sin'sir\ *adj* **-cer·er; -cer·est** : genuine or honest — **sin·cere·ly** *adv* — **sin·cer·i·ty** \-'serətē\ *n*

si·ne·cure \'sīni,kyúr, 'sini-\ *n* : well-paid job that requires little work

sin·ew \'sinyü\ *n* **1** : tendon **2** : physical strength — **sin·ewy** *adj*

sing \'siŋ\ *vb* **sang** \'saŋ\ *or* **sung** \'səŋ\; **sung; sing·ing** : produce musical tones with the voice — **sing·er** *n*

singe \'sinj\ *vb* **singed; singe·ing** : scorch lightly

sin·gle \'siŋgəl\ *adj* **1** : one only **2** : unmarried — *n* : separate one — **single·ness** *n* — **sin·gly** \-glē\ *adv* — **single out** *vb* : select or set aside

sin·gu·lar \'siŋgyələr\ *adj* **1** : relating to a word form denoting one **2** : outstanding or superior **3** : queer — **singular** *n* — **sin·gu·lar·i·ty** \,siŋgyə'larətē\ *n* — **sin·gu·lar·ly** \'siŋgyələrlē\ *adv*

sin·is·ter \'sinəstər\ *adj* : threatening evil

sink \'siŋk\ *vb* **sank** \'saŋk\ *or* **sunk** \'səŋk\; **sunk; sink·ing** **1** : submerge or descend **2** : grow worse **3** : make by digging or boring **4** : invest — *n* : basin with a drain

sink·er \'siŋkər\ *n* : weight to sink a fishing line

sin·u·ous \'sinyəwəs\ *adj* : winding in and out — **sin·u·os·i·ty** \,sinyə-'wäsətē\ *n* — **sin·u·ous·ly** *adv*

si·nus \'sīnəs\ *n* : skull cavity usu. connecting with the nostrils

sip \'sip\ *vb* **-pp-** : drink in small quantities — **sip** *n*

si·phon \'sīfən\ *n* : tube that draws liquid by suction — **siphon** *vb*

sir \'sər\ *n* **1** — used before the first name of a knight or baronet **2** —

used as a respectful form of address

sire \\'sīr\ *n* : father ∼ *vb* **sired; siring** : beget

si·ren \\'sīrən\ *n* **1** : seductive woman **2** : wailing warning whistle

sir·loin \\'sər,lȯin\ *n* : cut of beef

sirup *var of* SYRUP

si·sal \\'sīsəl, -zəl\ *n* : strong rope fiber

sis·sy \\'sisē\ *n, pl* **-sies** : timid or effeminate boy

sis·ter \\'sistər\ *n* : female sharing one or both parents with another person — **sis·ter·hood** \-,hüd\ *n* — **sis·ter·ly** *adj*

sis·ter–in–law *n, pl* **sis·ters–in–law** : sister of one's spouse or wife of one's brother

sit \\'sit\ *vb* **sat** \\'sat\; **sit·ting 1** : rest on the buttocks or haunches **2** : roost **3** : hold a session **4** : pose for a portrait **5** : have a location **6** : rest or fix in place — **sit·ter** *n*

site \\'sīt\ *n* : place

sit·u·at·ed \\'sichə,wātəd\ *adj* : located

sit·u·a·tion \,sichə'wāshən\ *n* **1** : location **2** : condition **3** : job

six \\'siks\ *n* : one more than 5 — **six** *adj or pron* — **sixth** \\'siksth\ *adj or adv or n*

six·teen \siks'tēn\ *n* : one more than 15 — **sixteen** *adj or pron* — **six·teenth** \-'tēnth\ *adj or n*

six·ty \\'sikstē\ *n, pl* **-ties** : 6 times 10 — **six·ti·eth** \-əth\ *adj or n* — **sixty** *adj or pron*

siz·able, size·able \\'sīzəbəl\ *adj* : quite large — **siz·ably** \-blē\ *adv*

size \\'sīz\ *n* : measurement of the amount of space something takes up ∼ *vb* : grade according to size

siz·zle \\'sizəl\ *vb* **-zled; -zling** : fry with a hissing sound — **sizzle** *n*

skate \\'skāt\ *n* **1** : metal runner on a shoe for gliding over ice **2** : roller skate — **skate** *vb* — **skat·er** *n*

skein \\'skān\ *n* : loosely twisted quantity of yarn or thread

skel·e·ton \\'skelətᵊn\ *n* : bony framework — **skel·e·tal** \-ətᵊl\ *adj*

skep·tic \\'skeptik\ *n* : one who is critical or doubting — **skep·ti·cal** \-tikəl\ *adj* — **skep·ti·cism** \-tə,sizəm\ *n*

sketch \\'skech\ *n* **1** : rough drawing

2 : short story or essay — **sketch** *vb* — **sketchy** *adj*

skew·er \\'skyüər\ *n* : long pin for holding roasting meat — **skewer** *vb*

ski \\'skē\ *n, pl* **skis** : long strip for gliding over snow or water — **ski** *vb* — **ski·er** *n*

skid \\'skid\ *n* **1** : plank for supporting something or on which it slides **2** : act of skidding ∼ *vb* **-dd-** : slide sideways

skiff \\'skif\ *n* : small boat

skill \\'skil\ *n* : developed or learned ability — **skilled** \\'skild\ *adj* — **skill·ful** \-fəl\ *adj* — **skill·ful·ly** *adv*

skil·let \\'skilət\ *n* : pan for frying

skim \\'skim\ *vb* **-mm- 1** : take off from the top of a liquid **2** : read or move over swiftly ∼ *adj* : having the cream removed — **skim·mer** *n*

skimp \\'skimp\ *vb* : give too little of something — **skimpy** *adj*

skin \\'skin\ *n* **1** : outer layer of an animal body **2** : rind ∼ *vb* **-nn-** : take the skin from — **skin·less** *adj* — **skinned** *adj* — **skin·tight** *adj*

skin diving *n* : sport of swimming under water with a face mask and flippers

skin·flint \\'skin,flint\ *n* : stingy person

skin·ny \\'skinē\ *adj* **-ni·er; -est** : very thin

skip \\'skip\ *vb* **-pp- 1** : move with leaps **2** : read past or ignore — **skip** *n*

skip·per \\'skipər\ *n* : ship's master — **skipper** *vb*

skir·mish \\'skərmish\ *n* : minor combat — **skirmish** *vb*

skirt \\'skərt\ *n* : garment or part of a garment that hangs below the waist ∼ *vb* : pass around the edge of

skit \\'skit\ *n* : brief usu. humorous play

skit·tish \\'skitish\ *adj* : easily frightened

skulk \\'skəlk\ *vb* : move furtively

skull \\'skəl\ *n* : bony case that protects the brain

skunk \\'skəŋk\ *n* : mammal that can forcibly eject an ill-smelling fluid

sky \\'skī\ *n, pl* **skies 1** : upper air **2**

: heaven — **sky·line** *n* — **sky·ward** \\-wərd\\ *adv or adj*

sky·lark \\'skī,lärk\\ *n* : European lark noted for its song

sky·light *n* : window in a roof or ceiling

sky·rock·et *n* : shooting firework ~ *vb* : rise suddenly

sky·scrap·er \\-,skrāpər\\ *n* : very tall building

slab \\'slab\\ *n* : thick slice

slack \\'slak\\ *adj* 1 : careless 2 : not taut 3 : not busy ~ *n* 1 : part hanging loose 2 *pl* : casual trousers — **slack·en** *vb* — **slack·ly** *adv* — **slack·ness** *n*

slag \\'slag\\ *n* : waste from melting of ores

slain *past part of* SLAY

slake \\'slāk\\ *vb* **slaked; slak·ing** : quench

slam \\'slam\\ *n* : heavy jarring impact ~ *vb* **-mm-** : shut, strike, or throw violently and loudly

slan·der \\'slandər\\ *n* : malicious gossip ~ *vb* : hurt (someone) with slander — **slan·der·er** *n* — **slan·der·ous** *adj*

slang \\'slaŋ\\ *n* : informal nonstandard vocabulary — **slangy** *adj*

slant \\'slant\\ *vb* 1 : slope 2 : present with a special viewpoint ~ *n* : sloping direction, line, or plane

slap \\'slap\\ *vb* **-pp-** : strike sharply with the open hand — **slap** *n*

slash \\'slash\\ *vb* 1 : cut with sweeping strokes 2 : reduce sharply ~ *n* : gash

slat \\'slat\\ *n* : thin narrow flat strip

slate \\'slāt\\ *n* 1 : dense fine-grained layered rock 2 : roofing tile or writing tablet of slate 3 : list of candidates ~ *vb* **slat·ed; slat·ing** : designate

slat·tern \\'slatərn\\ *n* : untidy woman — **slat·tern·ly** *adj*

slaugh·ter \\'slótər\\ *n* 1 : butchering of livestock for market 2 : great and cruel destruction of lives ~ *vb* : commit slaughter upon — **slaughter·house** *n*

slave \\'slāv\\ *n* : one owned and forced into service by another ~ *vb* **slaved; slav·ing** : work as or like a slave — **slave** *adj* — **slav·ery** \\'slāvərē\\ *n*

sla·ver \\'slavər, 'slāv-\\ *vb or n* : slobber

slav·ish \\'slāvish\\ *adj* : of or like a slave — **slav·ish·ly** *adv*

slay \\'slā\\ *vb* **slew** \\'slü\\; **slain** \\'slān\\; **slay·ing** : kill — **slay·er** *n*

slea·zy \\'slēzē, 'slā-\\ *adj* **-zi·er; -est** : shabby or shoddy

sled \\'sled\\ *n* : vehicle on runners — **sled** *vb*

¹**sledge** \\'slej\\ *n* : sledgehammer

²**sledge** *n* : heavy sled

sledge·ham·mer *n* : heavy longhandled hammer — **sledgeham·mer** *adj or vb*

sleek \\'slēk\\ *adj* : smooth or glossy — **sleek** *vb*

sleep \\'slēp\\ *n* : natural suspension of consciousness ~ *vb* **slept** \\'slept\\; **sleep·ing** : rest in a state of sleep — **sleep·er** *n* — **sleepless** *adj* — **sleep·walk·er** *n*

sleepy \\'slēpē\\ *adj* **sleep·i·er; -est** 1 : ready for sleep 2 : quietly inactive — **sleep·i·ly** \\'slēpəlē\\ *adv* — **sleep·i·ness** \\-pēnəs\\ *n*

sleet \\'slēt\\ *n* : frozen rain — **sleet** *vb* — **sleety** *adj*

sleeve \\'slēv\\ *n* : part of a garment for the arm — **sleeve·less** *adj*

sleigh \\'slā\\ *n* : horse-drawn sled with seats ~ *vb* : drive or ride in a sleigh

sleight of hand \\'slīt-\\ : skillful manual manipulation or a trick requiring it

slen·der \\'slendər\\ *adj* 1 : thin esp. in physique 2 : scanty

sleuth \\'slüth\\ *n* : detective

slew \\'slü\\ *past of* SLAY

slice \\'slīs\\ *n* : thin flat piece ~ *vb* **sliced; slic·ing** : cut a slice from

slick \\'slik\\ *adj* 1 : very smooth 2 : clever — **slick** *vb*

slick·er \\'slikər\\ *n* : raincoat

slide \\'slīd\\ *vb* **slid** \\'slid\\; **slid·ing** \\'slīdiŋ\\ : move smoothly along a surface ~ *n* 1 : act of sliding 2 : surface on which something slides 3 : transparent picture for projection

slier *comparative of* SLY

sliest *superlative of* SLY

slight \\'slīt\\ *adj* 1 : slender 2 : frail 3 : small in degree ~ *vb* 1 : ignore or treat as unimportant — **slight** *n* — **slight·ly** *adv*

slim \\'slim\\ *adj* **-mm-** 1 : slender 2 : scanty ~ *vb* **-mm-** : make or become slender

slime \'slīm\ *n* : dirty slippery film (as on water) — **slimy** *adj*

sling \'sliŋ\ *vb* **slung** \'sləŋ\; **sling-ing** : hurl with or as if with a sling ∼ *n* **1** : strap for swinging and hurling stones **2** : looped strap or bandage to lift or support

sling-shot *n* : forked stick with elastic bands for shooting pebbles

slink \'sliŋk\ *vb* **slunk** \'sləŋk\; **slink-ing** : move stealthily or sinuously — **slinky** *adj*

¹**slip** \'slip\ *vb* **-pp- 1** : escape quietly or secretly **2** : slide along smoothly **3** : make a mistake **4** : to pass without being noticed or done **5** : fall off from a standard ∼ *n* **1** : ship's berth **2** : sudden mishap **3** : mistake **4** : woman's undergarment

²**slip** *n* **1** : plant shoot **2** : small strip (as of paper)

slip-per \'slipər\ *n* : shoe that slips on easily

slip-pery \'slipərē\ *adj* **-peri-er; -est 1** : slick enough to slide on **2** : tricky — **slip-peri-ness** *n*

slip-shod \'slip,shäd\ *adj* : careless

slit \'slit\ *vb* **slit; slit-ting** : make a slit in ∼ *n* : long narrow cut

slith-er \'slithər\ *vb* : glide along like a snake — **slith-ery** *adj*

sliv-er \'slivər\ *n* : splinter

◆ **slob** \'släb\ *n* : untidy person

slob-ber \'släbər\ *vb* : dribble saliva — **slobber** *n*

slo-gan \'slōgən\ *n* : word or phrase expressing the aim of a cause

sloop \'slüp\ *n* : one-masted sailboat

slop \'släp\ *n* : food waste for animal feed ∼ *vb* **-pp-** : spill

slope \'slōp\ *vb* **sloped; slop-ing** : deviate from the vertical or horizontal ∼ *n* : upward or downward slant

slop-py \'släpē\ *adj* **-pi-er; -est** **1** : muddy **2** : untidy

slot \'slät\ *n* : narrow opening

sloth \'slóth, 'slōth\ *n, pl* **sloths** *with* ths *or* thz\ **1** : laziness **2** : slow-moving mammal — **sloth-ful** *adj*

slouch \'slaúch\ *n* **1** : drooping posture **2** : lazy or incompetent person ∼ *vb* : walk or stand with a slouch

¹**slough** \'slü, 'slaú\ *n* : swamp

²**slough** \'sləf\, **sluff** *vb* : cast off (old skin)

slov-en-ly \'sləvənlē\ *adj* : untidy

slow \'slō\ *adj* **1** : sluggish or stupid **2** : moving, working, or happening at less than the usual speed ∼ *vb* **1** : make slow **2** : go slower — **slow** *adv* — **slow-ly** *adv* — **slow-ness** *n*

sludge \'sləj\ *n* : slushy mass (as of treated sewage)

slug \'sləg\ *n* **1** : mollusk related to the snails **2** : bullet **3** : metal disk ∼ *vb* **-gg-** : strike forcibly — **slug-ger** *n*

slug-gish \'sləgish\ *adj* : slow in movement or flow — **slug-gish-ly** *adv* — **slug-gish-ness** *n*

sluice \'slüs\ *n* : channel for water ∼ *vb* **sluiced; sluic-ing** : wash in running water

slum \'sləm\ *n* : thickly populated area marked by poverty

slum-ber \'sləmbər\ *vb or n* : sleep

slump \'sləmp\ *vb* **1** : sink suddenly **2** : slouch — **slump** *n*

slung *past of* SLING

slunk *past of* SLINK

¹**slur** \'slər\ *vb* **-rr-** : run (words or notes) together — **slur** *n*

²**slur** *n* : malicious or insulting remark

slurp \'slərp\ *vb* : eat or drink noisily — **slurp** *n*

slush \'sləsh\ *n* : partly melted snow — **slushy** *adj*

slut \'slət\ *n* **1** : untidy woman **2** : lewd woman — **slut-tish** *adj*

sly \'slī\ *adj* **sli-er** \'slīər\; **sli-est** \'slīəst\ : given to or showing se-

crecy and deception — **sly·ly** *adv*
— **sly·ness** *n*

¹**smack** \'smak\ *n* : characteristic flavor ∼ *vb* : have a taste or hint

²**smack** *vb* **1** : move (the lips) so as to make a sharp noise **2** : kiss or slap with a loud noise ∼ *n* **1** : sharp noise made by the lips **2** : noisy slap

³**smack** *adv* : squarely and sharply

⁴**smack** *n* : fishing boat

small \'smol\ *adj* **1** : little in size or amount **2** : few in number **3** : trivial — **small·ish** *adj* — **small·ness** *n*

small·pox \'smol,päks\ *n* : contagious virus disease

smart \'smärt\ *vb* **1** : cause or feel stinging pain **2** : endure distress ∼ *adj* **1** : intelligent or resourceful **2** : stylish — **smart** *n* — **smart·ly** *adv* — **smart·ness** *n*

smash \'smash\ *vb* : break or be broken into pieces ∼ *n* **1** : smashing blow **2** : act or sound of smashing

smat·ter·ing \'smatərin\ *n* **1** : superficial knowledge **2** : small scattered number or amount

smear \'smir\ *n* : greasy stain ∼ *vb* **1** : spread (something sticky) **2** : smudge **3** : slander

smell \'smel\ *vb* **smelled** \'smeld\ *or* **smelt** \'smelt\; **smell·ing 1** : perceive the odor of **2** : have or give off an odor ∼ *n* **1** : sense by which one perceives odor **2** : odor — **smelly** *adj*

¹**smelt** \'smelt\ *n, pl* **smelts** *or* **smelt** : small food fish

²**smelt** *vb* : melt or fuse (ore) in order to separate the metal — **smelt·er** *n*

smile \'smīl\ *n* : facial expression with the mouth turned up usu. to show pleasure — **smile** *vb*

smirk \'smərk\ *vb* : wear a conceited smile — **smirk** *n*

smite \'smīt\ *vb* **smote** \'smōt\; **smitten** \'smit³n\ *or* **smote**; **smit·ing** \'smītin\ **1** : strike heavily or kill **2** : affect strongly

smith \'smith\ *n* : worker in metals and esp. a blacksmith

smithy \'smithē\ *n, pl* **smith·ies** : a smith's workshop

smock \'smäk\ *n* : loose dress or protective coat

smog \'smäg, 'smòg\ *n* : fog and smoke — **smog·gy** *adj*

smoke \'smōk\ *n* : sooty gas from burning ∼ *vb* **smoked; smok·ing 1** : give off smoke **2** : inhale the fumes of burning tobacco **3** : cure (as meat) with smoke — **smoke·less** *adj* — **smok·er** *n* — **smoky** *adj*

smoke·stack *n* : chimney through which smoke is discharged

smol·der, smoul·der \'smōldər\ *vb* **1** : burn and smoke without flame **2** : be suppressed but active — **smolder** *n*

smooth \'smüth\ *adj* **1** : having a surface without irregularities **2** : not jarring or jolting ∼ *vb* : make smooth — **smooth·ly** *adv* — **smooth·ness** *n*

smor·gas·bord \'smòrgəs,bòrd\ *n* : buffet consisting of many foods

smoth·er \'sməthər\ *vb* **1** : kill by depriving of air **2** : cover thickly

smudge \'sməj\ *vb* **smudged; smudg·ing** : soil or blur by rubbing ∼ *n* **1** : thick smoke **2** : dirty spot

smug \'sməg\ *adj* **-gg-** : content in one's own virtue or accomplishment — **smug·ly** *adv* — **smug·ness** *n*

smug·gle \'sməgəl\ *vb* **-gled; -gling** : import or export secretly or illegally — **smug·gler** \'sməglər\ *n*

smut \'smət\ *n* **1** : something that soils **2** : indecent language or matter **3** : disease of plants caused by fungi — **smut·ty** *adj*

snack \'snak\ *n* : light meal

snag \'snag\ *n* : unexpected difficulty ∼ *vb* **-gg-** : become caught on something that sticks out

snail \'snāl\ *n* : small mollusk with a spiral shell

snake \'snāk\ *n* : long-bodied limbless reptile — **snake·bite** *n*

snap \'snap\ *vb* **-pp- 1** : bite at something **2** : utter angry words **3** : break suddenly with a sharp sound ∼ *n* **1** : act or sound of snapping **2** : fastening that closes with a click **3** : something easy to do — **snap·per** *n* — **snap·pish** *adj*

snap·drag·on *n* : garden plant with spikes of showy flowers

snap·py \\'snap-ē\\ *adj* **-pi·er; -est 1**
: quickly made or done **2** : fashionable, stylish — **snap·pi·ly**
\\'snapəlē\\ *adv*

snap·shot \\'snap₁shät\\ *n* : casual
photograph

snare \\'snar\\ *n* : trap for catching
game ∼ *vb* : capture or hold with
or as if with a snare

¹**snarl** \\'snärl\\ *n* : tangle ∼ *vb* : cause
to become knotted

²**snarl** *vb or n* : growl

snatch \\'snach\\ *vb* **1** : try to grab
something suddenly **2** : seize or
take away suddenly ∼ *n* **1** : act of
snatching **2** : something brief or
fragmentary

sneak \\'snēk\\ *vb* : move or take in a
furtive manner ∼ *n* : one who
acts in a furtive manner — **sneak·
i·ly** \\'snēkəlē\\ *adv* — **sneak·ing·
ly** *adv* — **sneaky** *adj*

sneak·er \\'snēkər\\ *n* : sports shoe

sneer \\'snir\\ *vb* : smile scornfully —
sneer *n*

◆ **sneeze** \\'snēz\\ *vb* **sneezed; sneez·
ing** : force the breath out with
sudden and involuntary violence
— **sneeze** *n*

snick·er \\'snikər\\ *n* : partly suppressed laugh — **snicker** *vb*

snide \\'snīd\\ *adj* : subtly ridiculing

sniff \\'snif\\ *vb* **1** : draw air audibly
up the nose **2** : detect by smelling
— **sniff** *n*

snip \\'snip\\ *n* : fragment snipped off
∼ *vb* **-pp-** : cut off by bits

¹**snipe** \\'snīp\\ *n, pl* **snipes** *or* **snipe**
: game bird of marshy areas

²**snipe** *vb* **sniped; snip·ing** : shoot at
an enemy from a concealed posi-
tion — **snip·er** *n*

snips \\'snips\\ *n pl* : scissorslike tool

sniv·el \\'snivəl\\ *vb* **-eled** *or* **-elled;
-el·ing** *or* **-el·ling 1** : have a running nose **2** : whine

snob \\'snäb\\ *n* : one who acts supe-

rior to others — **snob·bery** \\-ərē\\
n — **snob·bish** *adj* — **snob·bish·
ly** *adv* — **snob·bish·ness** *n*

snoop \\'snüp\\ *vb* : pry in a furtive
way ∼ *n* : prying person

snooze \\'snüz\\ *vb* **snoozed; snooz·
ing** : take a nap — **snooze** *n*

snore \\'snōr\\ *vb* **snored; snor·ing**
: breathe with a hoarse noise while
sleeping — **snore** *n*

snort \\'snȯrt\\ *vb* : force air noisily
through the nose — **snort** *n*

snout \\'snaȯt\\ *n* : long projecting
muzzle (as of a swine)

snow \\'snō\\ *n* : crystals formed from
water vapor ∼ *vb* : fall as snow —
snow·ball *n* — **snow·bank** *n* —
snow·drift *n* — **snow·fall** *n* —
snow·plow *n* — **snow·storm** *n* —
snowy *adj*

snow·shoe *n* : frame of wood strung
with thongs for walking on snow

snub \\'snəb\\ *vb* **-bb-** : ignore or
avoid through disdain — **snub** *n*

¹**snuff** \\'snəf\\ *vb* : put out (a candle)
— **snuff·er** *n*

²**snuff** *vb* : draw forcibly into the
nose ∼ *n* : pulverized tobacco

snug \\'snəg\\ *adj* **-gg- 1** : warm, secure, and comfortable **2** : fitting
closely — **snug·ly** *adv* — **snug·
ness** *n*

snug·gle \\'snəgəl\\ *vb* **-gled; -gling**
: curl up comfortably

so \\'sō\\ *adv* **1** : in the manner or to
the extent indicated **2** : in the
same way **3** : therefore **4** : finally **5**
: thus ∼ *conj* : for that reason

soak \\'sōk\\ *vb* **1** : lie in a liquid **2**
: absorb ∼ *n* : act of soaking

soap \\'sōp\\ *n* : cleaning substance
— **soap** *vb* — **soapy** *adj*

soar \\'sōr\\ *vb* : fly upward on or as
if on wings

sob \\'säb\\ *vb* **-bb-** : weep with convulsive heavings of the chest —
sob *n*

so·ber \'sōbər\ *adj* 1 : not drunk 2 : serious or solemn — **so·ber·ly** *adv*

so·bri·ety \sə'brīətē, sō-\ *n* : quality or state of being sober

soc·cer \'säkər\ *n* : game played by kicking a ball

so·cia·ble \'sōshəbəl\ *adj* : friendly — **so·cia·bil·i·ty** \,sōshə'bilətē\ *n* — **so·cia·bly** \'sōshəblē\ *adv*

so·cial \'sōshəl\ *adj* 1 : relating to pleasant companionship 2 : naturally living or growing in groups 3 : relating to human society ~ *n* : social gathering — **so·cial·ly** *adv*

so·cial·ism \'sōshə,lizəm\ *n* : social system based on government control of the production and distribution of goods — **so·cial·ist** \'sōshəlist\ *n or adj* — **so·cial·is·tic** \,sōshə'listik\ *adj*

so·cial·ize \'sōshə,līz\ *vb* **-ized; -iz·ing** 1 : regulate by socialism 2 : adapt to social needs 3 : participate in a social gathering — **so·cial·i·za·tion** \,sōshələ'zāshən\ *n*

social work *n* : services concerned with aiding the poor and socially maladjusted — **social worker** *n*

so·ci·ety \sə'sīətē\ *n, pl* **-et·ies** 1 : companionship 2 : community life 3 : rich or fashionable class 4 : voluntary group

so·ci·ol·o·gy \,sōsē'äləjē\ *n* : study of social relationships — **so·ci·o·log·i·cal** \-ə'läjikəl\ *adj* — **so·ci·ol·o·gist** \-'äləjist\ *n*

¹**sock** \'säk\ *n, pl* **socks** *or* **sox** : short stocking

²**sock** *vb or n* : punch

sock·et \'säkət\ *n* : hollow part that holds something

sod \'säd\ *n* : turf ~ *vb* **-dd-** : cover with sod

so·da \'sōdə\ *n* 1 : carbonated water or a soft drink 2 : ice cream drink made with soda

sod·den \'säd²n\ *adj* 1 : lacking spirit 2 : soaked or soggy

so·di·um \'sōdēəm\ *n* : soft waxy silver white metallic chemical element

♦ **so·fa** \'sōfə\ *n* : wide padded chair

soft \'soft\ *adj* 1 : not hard, rough, or harsh 2 : nonalcoholic — **soft·en** \'sofən\ *vb* — **soft·en·er** \-ənər\ *n* — **soft·ly** *adv* — **soft·ness** *n*

soft·ball *n* : game like baseball

soft·ware \'soft,war\ *n* : computer programs

sog·gy \'sägē\ *adj* **-gi·er; -est** : heavy with moisture — **sog·gi·ness** \-ēnəs\ *n*

¹**soil** \'soil\ *vb* : make or become dirty ~ *n* : embedded dirt

²**soil** *n* : loose surface material of the earth

so·journ \'sō,jərn, sō'jərn\ *n* : temporary stay ~ *vb* : reside temporarily

so·lace \'säləs\ *n or vb* : comfort

so·lar \'sōlər\ *adj* : relating to the sun or the energy in sunlight

sold *past of* SELL

sol·der \'sädər, 'sód-\ *n* : metallic alloy melted to join metallic surfaces ~ *vb* : cement with solder

sol·dier \'sōljər\ *n* : person in military service ~ *vb* : serve as a soldier — **sol·dier·ly** *adj or adv*

¹**sole** \'sōl\ *n* : bottom of the foot or a shoe — **soled** *adj*

²**sole** *n* : flatfish caught for food

³**sole** *adj* : single or only — **sole·ly** *adv*

sol·emn \'säləm\ *adj* 1 : dignified and ceremonial 2 : highly serious — **so·lem·ni·ty** \sə'lemnətē\ *n* — **sol·emn·ly** *adv*

so·lic·it \sə'lisət\ *vb* : ask for — **so·lic·i·ta·tion** \-,lisə'tāshən\ *n*

so·lic·i·tor \sə'lisətər\ *n* 1 : one that solicits 2 : lawyer

so·lic·i·tous \sə'lisətəs\ *adj* : showing or expressing concern — **so·lic·i·tous·ly** adv — **so·lic·i·tude** \sə'lisə,tüd, -,tyüd\ n

sol·id \'säləd\ adj 1 : not hollow 2 : having 3 dimensions 3 : hard 4 : of good quality 5 : of one character ~ n 1 : 3-dimensional figure 2 : substance in solid form — **solid** adv — **so·lid·i·ty** \sə'lidətē\ n — **sol·id·ly** adv — **sol·id·ness** n

sol·i·dar·i·ty \,sälə'darətē\ n : unity of purpose

so·lid·i·fy \sə'lidə,fī\ vb **-fied; -fy·ing** : make or become solid — **so·lid·i·fi·ca·tion** \-,lidəfə'käshən\ n

so·lil·o·quy \sə'liləkwē\ n, pl **-quies** : dramatic monologue — **so·lil·o·quize** \-,kwīz\ vb

sol·i·taire \'sälə,tar\ n 1 : solitary gem 2 : card game for one person

sol·i·tary \-,terē\ adj 1 : alone 2 : secluded 3 : single

sol·i·tude \-,tüd, -,tyüd\ n : state of being alone

so·lo \'sōlō\ n, pl **-los** : performance by only one person ~ adv : alone — **solo** adj or vb — **so·lo·ist** n

sol·stice \'sälstəs\ n : time of the year when the sun is farthest north or south of the equator

sol·u·ble \'sälyəbəl\ adj 1 : capable of being dissolved 2 : capable of being solved — **sol·u·bil·i·ty** \,sälyə'bilətē\ n

so·lu·tion \sə'lüshən\ n 1 : answer to a problem 2 : homogeneous liquid mixture

solve \'sälv\ vb **solved; solv·ing** : find a solution for — **solv·able** adj

◆ **sol·vent** \'sälvənt\ adj 1 : able to pay all debts 2 : dissolving or able to dissolve ~ n : substance that dissolves or disperses another substance — **sol·ven·cy** \-vənsē\ n

som·ber, som·bre \'sämbər\ adj 1 : dark 2 : grave — **som·ber·ly** adv

som·bre·ro \səm'brerō\ n, pl **-ros** : broad-brimmed hat

some \'səm\ adj 1 : one unspecified 2 : unspecified or indefinite number of 3 : at least a few or a little ~ pron : a certain number or amount

-some \səm\ adj suffix : characterized by a thing, quality, state, or action

some·body \'səmbədē, -,bäd-\ pron : some person

some·day \'səm,dā\ adv : at some future time

some·how \-,haů\ adv : by some means

some·one \-,wən\ pron : some person

som·er·sault \'səmər,sölt\ n : body flip — **somersault** vb

some·thing \'səmthiŋ\ pron : some undetermined or unspecified thing

some·time \'səm,tīm\ adv : at a future, unknown, or unnamed time

some·times \-,tīmz\ adv : occasionally

some·what \-,hwət, -,hwät\ adv : in some degree

some·where \-,hwer\ adv : in, at, or to an unknown or unnamed place

som·no·lent \'sämnələnt\ adj : sleepy — **som·no·lence** \-ləns\ n

son \'sən\ n : male offspring

so·nar \'sō,när\ n : device that detects and locates underwater objects using sound waves

so·na·ta \sə'nätə\ n : instrumental composition

song \'söŋ\ n : music and words to be sung

song·bird n : bird with musical tones

son·ic \'sänik\ adj : relating to sound waves or the speed of sound

son-in-law *n, pl* **sons-in-law** : husband of one's daughter

son·net \'sänət\ *n* : poem of 14 lines

so·no·rous \sə'nōrəs, 'sänərəs\ *adj* 1 : loud, deep, or rich in sound 2 : impressive — **so·nor·i·ty** \sə-'nórətē\ *n*

soon \'sün\ *adv* 1 : before long 2 : promptly.3 : early

soot \'sut, 'sət, 'süt\ *n* : fine black substance formed by combustion — **sooty** *adj*

soothe \'süth\ *vb* **soothed; soothing** : calm or comfort — **soother** *n*

sooth·say·er \'süth,sāər\ *n* : prophet — **sooth·say·ing** \-iŋ\ *n*

sop \'säp\ *n* : conciliatory bribe, gift, or concession ∼ *vb* **-pp-** 1 : dip in a liquid 2 : soak 3 : mop up

so·phis·ti·cat·ed \sə'fistə,kātəd\ *adj* 1 : complex 2 : wise, cultured, or shrewd in human affairs — **so·phis·ti·ca·tion** \-,fistə'kāshən\ *n*

soph·ist·ry \'säfəstrē\ *n* : subtly fallacious reasoning or argument — **sophist** \'säfist\ *n*

soph·o·more \'säf°m,ōr, 'säf,mōr\ *n* : 2d-year student

so·po·rif·ic \,säpə'rifik, ,sōp-\ *adj* : causing sleep or drowsiness

so·pra·no \sə'pranō\ *n, pl* **-nos** : highest singing voice

sor·cery \'sòrsərē\ *n* : witchcraft — **sor·cer·er** \-rər\ *n* — **sor·cer·ess** \-rəs\ *n*

sor·did \'sòrdəd\ *adj* : filthy or vile — **sor·did·ly** *adv* — **sor·did·ness** *n*

sore \'sōr\ *adj* **sor·er; sor·est** 1 : causing pain or distress 2 : severe or intense 3 : angry ∼ *n* : sore usu. infected spot on the body — **sore·ly** *adv* — **sore·ness** *n*

sor·ghum \'sòrgəm\ *n* : forage grass

so·ror·i·ty \sə'rórətē\ *n, pl* **-ties** : women's student social group

¹**sor·rel** \'sórəl\ *n* : brownish orange to light brown color or an animal of this color

²**sorrel** *n* : herb with sour juice

sor·row \'särō\ *n* : deep distress, sadness, or regret or a cause of this — **sor·row·ful** \-fəl\ *adj* — **sor·row·ful·ly** *adv*

sor·ry \'särē\ *adj* **-ri·er; -est** 1 : feeling sorrow, regret, or penitence 2 : dismal

sort \'sòrt\ *n* 1 : kind 2 : nature ∼ *vb* : classify — **out of sorts** : grouchy

sor·tie \'sòrtē, sòr'tē\ *n* : military attack esp. against besiegers

SOS \,es,ō'es\ *n* : call for help

so-so \'sō'sō\ *adj or adv* : barely acceptable

sot \'sät\ *n* : drunkard — **sot·tish** *adj*

souf·flé \sü'flā\ *n* : baked dish made light with beaten egg whites

sought *past of* SEEK

soul \'sōl\ *n* 1 : immaterial essence of an individual life 2 : essential part 3 : person

soul·ful \'sōlfəl\ *adj* : full of or expressing deep feeling — **soul·ful·ly** *adv*

¹**sound** \'saund\ *adj* 1 : free from fault, error, or illness 2 : firm or hard 3 : showing good judgment — **sound·ly** *adv* — **sound·ness** *n*

²**sound** *n* 1 : sensation of hearing 2 : energy of vibration sensed in hearing 3 : something heard ∼ *vb* 1 : make or cause to make a sound 2 : seem — **sound·less** *adj* — **sound·less·ly** *adv* — **sound·proof** *adj or vb*

³**sound** *n* : wide strait ∼ *vb* 1 : measure the depth of (water) 2 : investigate

soup \'süp\ *n* : broth usu. containing pieces of solid food — **soupy** *adj*

sour \'saùər\ *adj* 1 : having an acid or tart taste 2 : disagreeable ∼ *vb* : become or make sour — **sourish** *adj* — **sour·ly** *adv* — **sourness** *n*

source \'sōrs\ *n* 1 : point of origin 2 : one that provides something needed

souse \'saus\ *vb* **soused; sous·ing** 1 : pickle 2 : immerse 3 : intoxicate ∼ *n* 1 : something pickled 2 : drunkard

south \'saùth\ *adv* : to or toward the south ∼ *adj* : situated toward, at, or coming from the south ∼ *n* 1 : direction to the right of sunrise 2 *cap* : regions to the south — **south·er·ly** \'səthərlē\ *adv or adj* — **south·ern** \'səthərn\ *adj* — **South·ern·er** *n* — **south·ern·most** \-,mōst\ *adj* — **southward** \'saùthwərd\ *adv or adj* — **southwards** \-wərdz\ *adv*

south·east \saùth'ēst, *naut* saù'ēst\ *n* 1 : direction between south and east 2 *cap* : regions to the south-

east — **southeast** *adj or adv* —
south·east·er·ly *adv or adj* —
south·east·ern \-ərn\ *adj*

south pole *n* : the southernmost
point of the earth

south·west \saûth'west, *naut* saû-
'west\ *n* **1** : direction between
south and west **2** *cap* : regions to
the southwest — **southwest** *adj or
adv* — **south·west·er·ly** *adv or adj*
— **south·west·ern** \-ərn\ *adj*

sou·ve·nir \'süvə,nir\ *n* : something
that is a reminder of a place or event

sov·er·eign \'sävərən\ *n* **1** : supreme
ruler **2** : gold coin of the United
Kingdom *~ adj* **1** : supreme **2** : independent — **sov·er·eign·ty** \-tē\ *n*

¹sow \'saû\ *n* : female swine

²sow \'sō\ *vb* **sowed; sown** \'sōn\ *or*
sowed; sow·ing **1** : plant or strew
with seed **2** : scatter abroad —
sow·er \'sōər\ *n*

sox *pl of* SOCK

soy·bean \'sòi,bēn\ *n* : legume with
edible seeds

spa \'spä\ *n* : resort at a mineral
spring

space \'spās\ *n* **1** : period of time **2**
: area in, around, or between **3** : region beyond earth's atmosphere **4**
: accommodations *~ vb* **spaced;**
spac·ing : place at intervals —
space·craft *n* — **space·flight** *n* —
space·man *n* — **space·ship** *n*

spa·cious \'spāshəs\ *adj* : large or
roomy — **spa·cious·ly** *adv* — **spa-
cious·ness** *n*

¹spade \'spād\ *n or vb* : shovel —
spade·ful *n*

²spade *n* : playing card marked with
a black figure like an inverted
heart

spa·ghet·ti \spə'getē\ *n* : pasta
strings

span \'span\ *n* **1** : amount of time **2**
: distance between supports *~ vb*
-nn- : extend across

span·gle \'spaŋgəl\ *n* : small disk of
shining metal or plastic — **spangle**
vb

span·iel \'spanyəl\ *n* : small or
medium-sized dog with drooping
ears and long wavy hair

spank \'spaŋk\ *vb* : hit on the buttocks with an open hand

¹spar \'spär\ *n* : pole or boom

²spar *vb* **-rr-** : practice boxing

spare \'spar\ *adj* **1** : held in reserve
2 : thin or scanty *~ vb* **spared;**
spar·ing **1** : reserve or avoid using
2 : avoid punishing or killing —
spare *n*

spar·ing \'spariŋ\ *adj* : thrifty —
spar·ing·ly *adv*

spark \'spärk\ *n* **1** : tiny hot and
glowing particle **2** : smallest beginning or germ **3** : visible electrical
discharge *~ vb* **1** : emit or produce sparks **2** : stir to activity

spar·kle \'spärkəl\ *vb* **-kled; -kling** **1**
: flash **2** : effervesce *~ n* : gleam
— **spark·ler** \-klər\ *n*

spar·row \'sparō\ *n* : small singing
bird

sparse \'spärs\ *adj* **spars·er; spars-
est** : thinly scattered — **sparsely** *adv*

spasm \'spazəm\ *n* **1** : involuntary
muscular contraction **2** : sudden, violent, and temporary effort or feeling — **spas·mod·ic** \spaz'mädik\
adj — **spas·mod·i·cal·ly** *adv*

spas·tic \'spastik\ *adj* : relating to,
marked by, or affected with muscular spasm — **spastic** *n*

¹spat \'spat\ *past of* SPIT

²spat *n* : petty dispute

spa·tial \'spāshəl\ *adj* : relating to
space — **spa·tial·ly** *adv*

spat·ter \'spatər\ *vb* : splash with
drops of liquid — **spatter** *n*

spat·u·la \'spachələ\ *n* : flexible
knifelike utensil

♦ **spawn** \'spón\ *vb* **1** : produce eggs

or offspring **2** : bring forth ∼ *n*
: egg cluster — **spawn·er** *n*

spay \\'spā\\ *vb* : remove the ovaries
of (a female)

speak \\'spēk\\ *vb* **spoke** \\'spōk\\; **spo·ken** \\'spōkən\\; **speak·ing 1** : utter
words **2** : express orally **3** : address
an audience **4** : use (a language) in
talking — **speak·er** *n*

spear \\'spir\\ *n* : long pointed weapon
∼ *vb* : strike or pierce with a spear

spear·head *n* : leading force, element, or influence — **spearhead** *vb*

spear·mint *n* : aromatic garden mint

spe·cial \\'speshəl\\ *adj* **1** : unusual or
unique **2** : particularly favored **3**
: set aside for a particular use —
special *n* — **spe·cial·ly** *adv*

spe·cial·ist \\'speshəlist\\ *n* **1** : person
who specializes in a particular
branch of learning or activity **2**
: any of four enlisted ranks in the
army corresponding to the grades
of corporal through sergeant first
class

spe·cial·ize \\'speshə₁līz\\ *vb* **-ized;
-iz·ing** : concentrate one's efforts
— **spe·cial·i·za·tion** \\₁speshələ-
'zāshən\\ *n*

spe·cial·ty \\'speshəltē\\ *n, pl* **-ties**
: area or field in which one specializes

spe·cie \\'spēshē, -sē\\ *n* : money in
coin

spe·cies \\'spēshēz, -sēz\\ *n, pl* **species** : biological grouping of closely related organisms

spe·cif·ic \\spi'sifik\\ *adj* : definite or
exact — **spe·cif·i·cal·ly** *adv*

spec·i·fi·ca·tion \\₁spesəfə'kāshən\\ *n*
1 : act or process of specifying **2**
: detailed description of work to
be done — usu. pl.

spec·i·fy \\'spesə₁fī\\ *vb* **-fied; -fy·ing** : mention precisely or by
name

spec·i·men \\-əmən\\ *n* : typical example

spe·cious \\'spēshəs\\ *adj* : apparently
but not really genuine or correct

speck \\'spek\\ *n* : tiny particle or
blemish — **speck** *vb*

speck·led \\'spekəld\\ *adj* : marked
with spots

spec·ta·cle \\'spektikəl\\ *n* **1** : impressive public display **2** *pl* : eyeglasses

spec·tac·u·lar \\spek'takyələr\\ *adj*
: sensational or showy

spec·ta·tor \\'spek₁tātər\\ *n* : person
who looks on

spec·ter, spec·tre \\'spektər\\ *n* **1**
: ghost **2** : haunting vision

spec·tral \\'spektrəl\\ *adj* : relating to
or resembling a specter or spectrum

spec·trum \\'spektrəm\\ *n, pl* **-tra**
\\-trə\\ *or* **-trums** : series of colors
formed when white light is dispersed into its components

spec·u·late \\'spekyə₁lāt\\ *vb* **-lat·ed; -lat·ing 1** : think about things
yet unknown **2** : risk money in a
business deal in hope of high profit — **spec·u·la·tion** \\₁spekyə-
'lāshən\\ *n* — **spec·u·la·tive**
\\'spekyə₁lātiv\\ *adj* — **spec·u·la·tor** \\-₁lātər\\ *n*

speech \\'spēch\\ *n* **1** : power, act, or
manner of speaking **2** : talk given
to an audience — **speech·less**
adj

speed \\'spēd\\ *n* **1** : quality of being
fast **2** : rate of motion or performance ∼ *vb* **sped** \\'sped\\ *or*
speed·ed; speed·ing : go at a great
or excessive rate of speed —
speed·boat *n* — **speed·er** *n* —
speed·i·ly \\'spēd°lē\\ *adv* — **speed-up** \\-₁əp\\ *n* — **speedy** *adj*

speed·om·e·ter \\spi'dämətər\\ *n* : instrument for indicating speed

¹**spell** \\'spel\\ *n* : influence of or like
magic

²**spell** *vb* **1** : name, write, or print the
letters of **2** : mean — **spell·er** *n*

³**spell** *vb* : substitute for or relieve
(someone) ∼ *n* **1** : turn at work **2**
: period of time

spell·bound *adj* : held by a spell

spend \\'spend\\ *vb* **spent** \\'spent\\;
spend·ing 1 : pay out **2** : cause or
allow to pass — **spend·er** *n*

spend·thrift \\'spend₁thrift\\ *n*
: wasteful person

sperm \\'spərm\\ *n, pl* **sperm** *or*
sperms : semen or a germ cell in it

spew \\'spyü\\ *vb* : gush out in a
stream

sphere \\'sfir\\ *n* **1** : figure with every
point on its surface at an equal
distance from the center **2** : round
body **3** : range of action or influence — **spher·i·cal** \\'sfirikəl,
'sfer-\\ *adj*

spher·oid \\'sfir-\\ *n* : spherelike figure

spice \\'spīs\\ *n* **1** : aromatic plant

product for seasoning food **2** : interesting quality — **spice** *vb* — **spicy** *adj*

spi·der \'spīdər\ *n* : small insectlike animal with 8 legs — **spi·dery** *adj*

spig·ot \'spigət, 'spikət\ *n* : faucet

spike \'spīk\ *n* : very large nail ~ *vb* **spiked; spik·ing** : fasten or pierce with a spike — **spiked** \'spīkt\ *adj*

spill \'spil\ *vb* **1** : fall, flow, or run out unintentionally **2** : divulge ~ *n* **1** : act of spilling **2** : something spilled — **spill·able** *adj*

spill·way *n* : passage for surplus water

spin \'spin\ *vb* **spun** \'spən\; **spin·ning 1** : draw out fiber and twist into thread **2** : form thread from a sticky body fluid **3** : revolve or cause to revolve extremely fast ~ *n* : rapid rotating motion — **spin·ner** *n*

◆ **spin·ach** \'spinich\ *n* : garden herb with edible leaves

spi·nal \'spīn°l\ *adj* : relating to the backbone — **spi·nal·ly** *adv*

spinal cord *n* : thick strand of nervous tissue that extends from the brain along the back within the backbone

spin·dle \'spind°l\ *n* **1** : stick used for spinning thread **2** : shaft around which something turns

spin·dly \'spindlē\ *adj* : tall and slender

spine \'spīn\ *n* **1** : backbone **2** : stiff sharp projection on a plant or animal — **spine·less** *adj* — **spiny** *adj*

spin·et \'spinət\ *n* : small piano

spin·ster \'spinstər\ *n* : woman who has never married

spi·ral \'spīrəl\ *adj* : circling or winding around a single point or line — **spiral** *n or vb* — **spi·ral·ly** *adv*

spire \'spīr\ *n* : steeple — **spiry** *adj*

spir·it \'spirət\ *n* **1** : life-giving force

2 *cap* : presence of God **3** : ghost **4** : mood **5** : vivacity or enthusiasm **6** *pl* : alcoholic liquor ~ *vb* : carry off secretly — **spir·it·ed** *adj* — **spir·it·less** *adj*

spir·i·tu·al \'spirichəwəl\ *adj* **1** : relating to the spirit or sacred matters **2** : deeply religious ~ *n* : religious folk song — **spir·i·tu·al·i·ty** \,spirichə'walətē\ *n* — **spir·i·tu·al·ly** *adv*

spir·i·tu·al·ism \'spirichəwə,lizəm\ *n* : belief that spirits communicate with the living — **spir·i·tu·al·ist** \-list\ *n or adj*

¹**spit** \'spit\ *n* **1** : rod for holding and turning meat over a fire **2** : point of land that runs into the water

²**spit** *vb* **spit** *or* **spat** \'spat\; **spit·ting** : eject saliva from the mouth ~ *n* **1** : saliva **2** : perfect likeness

spite \'spīt\ *n* : petty ill will ~ *vb* **spit·ed; spit·ing** : annoy or offend — **spite·ful** \-fəl\ *adj* — **spite·ful·ly** *adv* — **in spite of** : in defiance or contempt of

spit·tle \'spit°l\ *n* : saliva

spit·toon \spi'tün\ *n* : receptacle for spit

splash \'splash\ *vb* : scatter a liquid on — **splash** *n*

splat·ter \'splatər\ *vb* : spatter — **splatter** *n*

splay \'splā\ *vb* : spread out or apart — **splay** *n or adj*

spleen \'splēn\ *n* **1** : organ for maintenance of the blood **2** : spite or anger

splen·did \'splendəd\ *adj* **1** : impressive in beauty or brilliance **2** : outstanding — **splen·did·ly** *adv*

splen·dor \'splendər\ *n* **1** : brilliance **2** : magnificence

splice \'splīs\ *vb* **spliced; splic·ing** : join (2 things) end to end — **splice** *n*

splint \'splint\ *n* **1** : thin strip of

wood **2** : something that keeps an injured body part in place

splin·ter \'splintər\ *n* : thin needle-like piece ~ *vb* : break into splinters

split \'split\ *vb* **split; split·ting** : divide lengthwise or along a grain — **split** *n*

splotch \'spläch\ *n* : blotch

splurge \'splərj\ *vb* **splurged; splurg·ing** : indulge oneself — **splurge** *n*

splut·ter \'splətər\ *n* : sputter — **splutter** *vb*

spoil \'spȯil\ *n* : plunder ~ *vb* **spoiled** \'spȯild, 'spȯilt\ *or* **spoilt** \'spȯilt\; **spoil·ing 1** : pillage **2** : ruin **3** : rot — **spoil·age** \'spȯilij\ *n* — **spoil·er** *n*

¹spoke \'spōk\ *past of* SPEAK

²spoke *n* : rod from the hub to the rim of a wheel

spo·ken \'spōkən\ *past part of* SPEAK

spokes·man \'spōksmən\ *n* : person who speaks for others

spokes·wom·an \-ˌwumən\ *n* : woman who speaks for others

sponge \'spənj\ *n* **1** : porous water-absorbing mass that forms the skeleton of some marine animals **2** : spongelike material used for wiping ~ *vb* **sponged; spong·ing 1** : wipe with a sponge **2** : live at another's expense — **spongy** \'spənjē\ *adj*

◆ **spon·sor** \'spänsər\ *n* : one who assumes responsibility for another or who provides financial support — **sponsor** *vb* — **spon·sor·ship** *n*

spon·ta·ne·ous \spän'tānēəs\ *adj* : done, produced, or occurring naturally or without planning — **spon·ta·ne·i·ty** \ˌspäntən'ēətē\ *n* — **spon·ta·ne·ous·ly** \spän-'tānēəslē\ *adv*

spoof \'spüf\ *vb* : make good-natured fun of — **spoof** *n*

spook \'spük\ *n* : ghost ~ *vb* : frighten — **spooky** *adj*

spool \'spül\ *n* : cylinder on which something is wound

spoon \'spün\ *n* : utensil consisting of a small shallow bowl with a handle — **spoon** *vb* — **spoon·ful** \-ˌful\ *n*

spoor \'spur, 'spōr\ *n* : track or trail esp. of a wild animal

spo·rad·ic \spə'radik\ *adj* : occasional — **spo·rad·i·cal·ly** *adv*

spore \spōr\ *n* : primitive usu. one-celled reproductive body

sport \'spōrt\ *vb* **1** : frolic **2** : show off ~ *n* **1** : physical activity engaged in for pleasure **2** : jest **3** : person who shows good sportsmanship — **sport·ive** \-iv\ *adj* — **sporty** *adj*

sports·cast \'spōrtsˌkast\ *n* : broadcast of a sports event — **sports·cast·er** \-ˌkastər\ *n*

sports·man \-mən\ *n* : one who enjoys hunting and fishing

sports·man·ship \-mənˌship\ *n* : ability to be gracious in winning or losing

spot \'spät\ *n* **1** : blemish **2** : distinctive small part **3** : location ~ *vb* -**tt- 1** : mark with spots **2** : see or recognize ~ *adj* : made at random or in limited numbers — **spot·less** *adj* — **spot·less·ly** *adv*

spot·light *n* **1** : intense beam of light **2** : center of public interest — **spotlight** *vb*

spot·ty \'spätē\ *adj* -**ti·er; -est** : uneven in quality

spouse \'spaus\ *n* : one's husband or wife

spout \'spaut\ *vb* **1** : shoot forth in a stream **2** : say pompously ~ *n* **1** : opening through which liquid spouts **2** : jet of liquid

sprain \'sprān\ *n* : twisting injury to a joint ~ *vb* : injure with a sprain

sprat \'sprat\ *n* : small or young herring

sprawl \'spról\ *vb* : lie or sit with limbs spread out — **sprawl** *n*

¹**spray** \'sprā\ *n* : branch or arrangement of flowers

²**spray** *n* **1** : mist **2** : device that discharges liquid as a mist — **spray** *vb* — **spray•er** *n*

spread \'spred\ *vb* **spread; spreading 1** : open up or unfold **2** : scatter or smear over a surface **3** : cause to be known or to exist over a wide area ~ *n* **1** : extent to which something is spread **2** : cloth cover **3** : something intended to be spread — **spread•er** *n*

spread•sheet \'spred͵shēt\ *n* : accounting program for a computer

spree \'sprē\ *n* : burst of indulging in something

sprig \'sprig\ *n* : small shoot or twig

spright•ly \'sprītlē\ *adj* **-li•er; -est** : lively — **spright•li•ness** *n*

♦ **spring** \'sprin\ *vb* **sprang** \'spran\ *or* **sprung** \'spran\; **sprung; spring•ing 1** : move or grow quickly or by elastic force **2** : come from by descent **3** : make known suddenly ~ *n* **1** : source **2** : flow of water from underground **3** : season between winter and summer **4** : elastic body or device (as a coil of wire) **5** : leap **6** : elastic power — **springy** *adj*

sprin•kle \'sprinkəl\ *vb* **-kled; -kling** : scatter in small drops or particles ~ *n* : light rainfall — **sprin•kler** *n*

sprint \'sprint\ *n* : short run at top speed — **sprint** *vb* — **sprint•er** *n*

sprite \'sprīt\ *n* : elf or elfish person

sprock•et \'spräkət\ *n* : toothed wheel whose teeth engage the links of a chain

sprout \'spraut\ *vb* : send out new growth ~ *n* : plant shoot

¹**spruce** \'sprüs\ *n* : conical evergreen tree

²**spruce** *adj* **spruc•er; spruc•est** : neat and stylish in appearance ~ *vb* **spruced; spruc•ing** : make or become neat

spry \'sprī\ *adj* **spri•er** *or* **spry•er** \'sprīər\; **spri•est** *or* **spry•est** \'sprīəst\ : agile and active

spume \'spyüm\ *n* : froth

spun *past of* SPIN

spunk \'spənk\ *n* : courage — **spunky** *adj*

spur \'spər\ *n* **1** : pointed device used to urge on a horse **2** : something that urges to action **3** : projecting part ~ *vb* **-rr-** : urge on — **spurred** *adj*

spu•ri•ous \'spyurēəs\ *adj* : not genuine

spurn \'spərn\ *vb* : reject

¹**spurt** \'spərt\ *n* : burst of effort, speed, or activity ~ *vb* : make a spurt

²**spurt** *vb* : gush out ~ *n* : sudden gush

sput•ter \'spətər\ *vb* **1** : talk hastily and indistinctly in excitement **2** : make popping sounds — **sputter** *n*

spy \'spī\ *vb* **spied; spy•ing** : watch or try to gather information secretly — **spy** *n*

squab \'skwäb\ *n, pl* **squabs** *or* **squab** : young pigeon

squab•ble \'skwäbəl\ *n or vb* : dispute

squad \'skwäd\ *n* : small group

squad•ron \'skwädrən\ *n* : small military unit

squal•id \'skwäləd\ *adj* : filthy or wretched

squall \'skwól\ *n* : sudden violent brief storm — **squally** *adj*

squa•lor \'skwälər\ *n* : quality or state of being squalid

squan•der \'skwändər\ *vb* : waste

AH! THE FIRST FLOWER OF SPRING!

GULP!

NOW LET'S FIND THAT FIRST ROBIN

square \\'skwar\ *n* **1** : instrument for measuring right angles **2** : flat figure that has 4 equal sides and 4 right angles **3** : open area in a city **4** : product of number multiplied by itself ～ *adj* **squar·er; squar·est 1** : being a square in form **2** : having sides meet at right angles **3** : multiplied by itself **4** : being a square unit of area **5** : honest ～ *vb* **squared; squar·ing 1** : form into a square **2** : multiply (a number) by itself **3** : conform **4** : settle — **square·ly** *adv*

¹**squash** \\'skwäsh, 'skwȯsh\ *vb* **1** : press flat **2** : suppress

²**squash** *n, pl* **squash·es** *or* **squash** : garden vegetable

squat \\'skwät\ *vb* **-tt- 1** : stoop or sit on one's heels **2** : settle on land one does not own ～ *n* : act or posture of squatting ～ *adj* **squat·ter; squat·test** : short and thick — **squat·ter** *n*

squaw \\'skwȯ\ *n* : American Indian woman

squawk \\'skwȯk\ *n* : harsh loud cry — **squawk** *vb*

squeak \\'skwēk\ *vb* : make a thin high-pitched sound — **squeak** *n* — **squeaky** *adj*

squeal \\'skwēl\ *vb* **1** : make a shrill sound or cry **2** : protest — **squeal** *n*

squea·mish \\'skwēmish\ *adj* : easily nauseated or disgusted

squeeze \\'skwēz\ *vb* **squeezed; squeez·ing 1** : apply pressure to **2** : extract by pressure — **squeeze** *n* — **squeez·er** *n*

squelch \\'skwelch\ *vb* : suppress (as with a retort) — **squelch** *n*

squid \\'skwid\ *n, pl* **squid** *or* **squids** : 10-armed long-bodied sea mollusk

squint \\'skwint\ *vb* : look with the eyes partly closed — **squint** *n or adj*

squire \\'skwīr\ *n* **1** : knight's aide **2** : country landholder **3** : lady's devoted escort ～ *vb* **squired; squir·ing** : escort

squirm \\'skwərm\ *vb* : wriggle

squir·rel \\'skwərəl\ *n* : rodent with a long bushy tail

squirt \\'skwərt\ *vb* : eject liquid in a spurt — **squirt** *n*

stab \stab\ *n* **1** : wound made by a pointed weapon **2** : quick thrust

3 : attempt ～ *vb* **-bb-** : pierce or wound with or as if with a pointed weapon

¹**sta·ble** \\'stābəl\ *n* : building for domestic animals ～ *vb* **-bled; -bling** : keep in a stable

²**stable** *adj* **sta·bler; sta·blest 1** : firmly established **2** : mentally and emotionally healthy **3** : steady — **sta·bil·i·ty** \stə'bilətē\ *n* — **sta·bil·iza·tion** \ˌstābələ'zāshən\ *n* — **sta·bi·lize** \\'stābəˌlīz\ *vb* — **sta·bi·liz·er** *n*

stac·ca·to \stə'kätō\ *adj* : disconnected

stack \\'stak\ *n* : large pile ～ *vb* : pile up

sta·di·um \\'stādēəm\ *n* : outdoor sports arena

staff \\'staf\ *n, pl* **staffs** \\'stafs, stavz\ *or* **staves** \\'stavz, 'stāvz\ **1** : rod or supporting cane **2** : people assisting a leader **3** : 5 horizontal lines on which music is written ～ *vb* : supply with workers — **staff·er** *n*

staff sergeant *n* : noncommissioned officer ranking next above a sergeant in the army, air force, or marine corps

stag \\'stag\ *n, pl* **stags** *or* **stag** : male deer ～ *adj* : only for men ～ *adv* : without a date

stage \\'stāj\ *n* **1** : raised platform for a speaker or performers **2** : theater **3** : step in a process ～ *vb* **staged; stag·ing** : produce (a play)

stage·coach *n* : passenger coach

stag·ger \\'stagər\ *vb* **1** : reel or cause to reel from side to side **2** : overlap or alternate — **stagger** *n* — **stag·ger·ing·ly** *adv*

stag·nant \\'stagnənt\ *adj* : not moving or active — **stag·nate** \-ˌnāt\ *vb* — **stag·na·tion** \stag'nāshən\ *n*

¹**staid** \\'stād\ *adj* : sedate

²**staid** *past of* STAY

stain \\'stān\ *vb* **1** : discolor **2** : dye (as wood) **3** : disgrace ～ *n* **1** : discolored area **2** : mark of guilt **3** : coloring preparation — **stain·less** *adj*

stair \\'star\ *n* **1** : step in a series for going from one level to another **2** *pl* : flight of steps — **stair·way** *n*

stair·case *n* : series of steps with their framework

stake \\'stāk\ *n* **1** : usu. small post driven into the ground **2** : bet **3**

: prize in a contest ~ *vb* **staked;**
stak·ing 1 : mark or secure with a
stake **2** : bet

sta·lac·tite \stə'lak,tīt\ *n* : icicle-
shaped deposit hanging in a cav-
ern

sta·lag·mite \stə'lag,mīt\ *n* : icicle-
shaped deposit on a cavern floor

stale \'stāl\ *adj* **stal·er; stal·est 1**
: having lost good taste and qual-
ity from age **2** : no longer new,
strong, or effective — **stale·ness** *n*

stale·mate \'stāl,māt\ *n* : deadlock
— **stalemate** *vb*

¹stalk \'stok\ *vb* **1** : walk stiffly or
proudly **2** : pursue stealthily

²stalk *n* : plant stem — **stalked**
\'stokt\ *adj*

¹stall \'stol\ *n* **1** : compartment in a
stable **2** : booth where articles are
sold

²stall *vb* : bring or come to a stand-
still unintentionally

³stall *vb* : delay, evade, or keep a situation going to gain advantage or
time

stal·lion \'stalyən\ *n* : male horse

stal·wart \'stolwərt\ *adj* : strong or
brave

sta·men \'stāmən\ *n* : flower organ
that produces pollen

stam·i·na \'stamənə\ *n* : endurance

stam·mer \'stamər\ *vb* : hesitate in
speaking — **stammer** *n*

stamp \'stamp\ *vb* **1** : pound with
the sole of the foot or a heavy implement **2** : impress or imprint **3**
: cut out with a die **4** : attach a
postage stamp to ~ *n* **1** : device
for stamping **2** : act of stamping **3**
: government seal showing a tax
or fee has been paid

stam·pede \stam'pēd\ *n* : headlong
rush of frightened animals ~ *vb*
-ped·ed; -ped·ing : flee in panic

stance \'stans\ *n* : way of standing

¹stanch \'stonch, 'stänch\ *vb* : stop
the flow of (as blood)

²stanch *var of* STAUNCH

stan·chion \'stanchən\ *n* : upright
support

♦ **stand** \'stand\ *vb* **stood** \'stud\;
stand·ing 1 : be at rest in or assume an upright position **2** : remain unchanged **3** : be steadfast **4**
: maintain a relative position or
rank **5** : set upright **6** : undergo or
endure ~ *n* **1** : act or place of
standing, staying, or resisting **2**
: sales booth **3** : structure for holding something upright **4** : group of
plants growing together **5** *pl* : ti-
ered seats **6** : opinion or viewpoint

stan·dard \'standərd\ *n* **1** : symbolic
figure or flag **2** : model, rule, or
guide **3** : upright support — **stan-**
dard *adj* — **stan·dard·i·za·tion**
\,standərdə'zāshən\ *n* — **stan-**
dard·ize \'standərd,īz\ *vb*

standard time *n* : time established
over a region or country

stand·ing \'standiŋ\ *n* **1** : relative position or rank **2** : duration

stand·still *n* : state of rest

stank *past of* STINK

stan·za \'stanzə\ *n* : division of a
poem

¹sta·ple \'stāpəl\ *n* : U-shaped wire
fastener — **staple** *vb* — **sta·pler**
\-plər\ *n*

²staple *n* : chief commodity or item
— **staple** *adj*

star \'stär\ *n* **1** : celestial body visible as a point of light **2** : 5- or
6-pointed figure representing a
star **3** : leading performer ~ *vb*
-rr- 1 : mark with a star **2** : play the
leading role — **stardom**
\'stärdəm\ *n* — **star·less** *adj* —
star·light *n* — **star·ry** *adj*

star·board \'stärbərd\ *n* : right side
of a ship or airplane looking forward — **starboard** *adj*

starch \'stärch\ *n* : nourishing carbohydrate from plants also used in adhesives and laundering ～ *vb* : stiffen with starch — **starchy** *adj*

stare \'star\ *vb* **stared; star·ing** : look intently with wide-open eyes — **stare** *n* — **star·er** *n*

stark \'stärk\ *adj* **1** : absolute **2** : severe or bleak ～ *adv* : completely — **stark·ly** *adv*

star·ling \'stärliŋ\ *n* : bird related to the crows

start \'stärt\ *vb* **1** : twitch or jerk (as from surprise) **2** : perform or show performance of the first part of an action or process ～ *n* **1** : sudden involuntary motion **2** : beginning — **start·er** *n*

star·tle \'stärt°l\ *vb* **-tled; -tling** : frighten or surprise suddenly

starve \'stärv\ *vb* **starved; starv·ing 1** : suffer or die from hunger **2** : kill with hunger — **star·va·tion** \stär'vāshən\ *n*

stash \'stash\ *vb* : store in a secret place for future use — **stash** *n*

state \'stāt\ *n* **1** : condition of being **2** : condition of mind **3** : nation or a political unit within it ～ *vb* **stated; stat·ing 1** : express in words **2** : establish — **state·hood** \-,hu̇d\ *n*

state·ly \'stātlē\ *adj* **-li·er; -est** : having impressive dignity — **state·li·ness** *n*

state·ment \'stātmənt\ *n* **1** : something stated **2** : financial summary

state·room *n* : private room on a ship

states·man \'stātsmən\ *n* : one skilled in government or diplomacy — **states·man·like** *adj* — **states·man·ship** *n*

stat·ic \'statik\ *adj* **1** : relating to bodies at rest or forces in equilibrium **2** : not moving **3** : relating to stationary charges of electricity ～ *n* : noise on radio or television from electrical disturbances

sta·tion \'stāshən\ *n* **1** : place of duty **2** : regular stop on a bus or train route **3** : social standing **4** : place where radio or television programs originate ～ *vb* : assign to a station

sta·tion·ary \'stāshə,nerē\ *adj* **1** : not moving or not movable **2** : not changing

sta·tio·nery \'stāshə,nerē\ *n* : letter paper with envelopes

sta·tis·tic \stə'tistik\ *n* : single item of statistics

sta·tis·tics \-tiks\ *n pl* : numerical facts collected for study — **sta·tis·ti·cal** \-tikəl\ *adj* — **sta·tis·ti·cal·ly** *adv* — **stat·is·ti·cian** \,statə'stishən\ *n*

stat·u·ary \'stachə,werē\ *n, pl* **-ar·ies** : collection of statues

stat·ue \'stachü\ *n* : solid 3-dimensional likeness — **stat·u·ette** \,stachə'wet\ *n*

stat·u·esque \,stachə'wesk\ *adj* : tall and shapely

stat·ure \'stachər\ *n* **1** : height **2** : status gained by achievement

sta·tus \'stātəs, 'stat-\ *n* : relative situation or condition

sta·tus quo \-'kwō\ *n* : existing state of affairs

stat·ute \'stachüt\ *n* : law — **stat·u·to·ry** \'stachə,tōrē\ *adj*

staunch \'stȯnch\ *adj* : steadfast — **staunch·ly** *adv*

stave \'stāv\ *n* : narrow strip of wood ～ *vb* **staved** *or* **stove** \'stōv\; **stav·ing 1** : break a hole in **2** : drive away

staves *pl of* STAFF

¹**stay** \'stā\ *n* : support ～ *vb* **stayed; stay·ing** : prop up

²**stay** *vb* **stayed** *or* **staid** \'stād\; **stay·ing 1** : pause **2** : remain **3** : reside **4** : stop or postpone **5** : satisfy for a time ～ *n* : a staying

stead \'sted\ *n* : one's place, job, or function — **in good stead** : to advantage

stead·fast \-,fast\ *adj* : faithful or determined — **stead·fast·ly** *adv*

steady \'stedē\ *adj* **steadi·er; -est 1** : firm in position or sure in movement **2** : calm or reliable **3** : constant **4** : regular ～ *vb* **stead·ied; steady·ing** : make or become steady — **steadi·ly** \'sted°lē\ *adv* — **steadi·ness** *n* — **steady** *adv*

steak \'stāk\ *n* : thick slice of meat

♦ **steal** \'stēl\ *vb* **stole** \'stōl\; **sto·len** \'stōlən\; **steal·ing 1** : take and carry away wrongfully and with intent to keep **2** : move secretly or slowly

stealth \'stelth\ *n* : secret or unobtrusive procedure — **stealth·i·ly** \-thəlē\ *adv* — **stealthy** *adj*

steam \'stēm\ *n* : vapor of boiling water ～ *vb* : give off steam —

steam·boat *n* — **steam·ship** *n* — **steamy** *adj*

steed \'stēd\ *n* : horse

steel \'stēl\ *n* : tough carbon-containing iron ~ *vb* : fill with courage — **steel** *adj* — **steely** *adj*

¹**steep** \'stēp\ *adj* : having a very sharp slope or great elevation — **steep·ly** *adv* — **steep·ness** *n*

²**steep** *vb* : soak in a liquid

stee·ple \'stēpəl\ *n* : usu. tapering church tower

stee·ple·chase *n* : race over hurdles

¹**steer** \'stir\ *n* : castrated ox

²**steer** *vb* **1** : direct the course of (as a ship or car) **2** : guide

steer·age \'stirij\ *n* : section in a ship for people paying the lowest fares

stein \'stīn\ *n* : mug

stel·lar \'stelər\ *adj* : relating to stars or resembling a star

¹**stem** \'stem\ *n* : main upright part of a plant ~ *vb* **-mm- 1** : derive **2** : make progress against — **stem·less** *adj* — **stemmed** *adj*

²**stem** *vb* **-mm-** : stop the flow of

stench \'stench\ *n* : stink

sten·cil \'stensəl\ *n* : printing sheet cut with letters to let ink pass through — **stencil** *vb*

ste·nog·ra·phy \stə'nägrəfē\ *n* : art or process of writing in shorthand — **ste·nog·ra·pher** \-fər\ *n* — **steno·graph·ic** \ˌstenə'grafik\ *adj*

sten·to·ri·an \sten'tōrēən\ *adj* : extremely loud and powerful

step \'step\ *n* **1** : single action of a leg in walking or running **2** : rest for the foot in going up or down **3** : degree, rank, or stage **4** : way of walking ~ *vb* **-pp- 1** : move by steps **2** : press with the foot

step- \'step-\ *comb form* : related by a remarriage and not by blood

step·lad·der *n* : light portable set of steps in a hinged frame

steppe \'step\ *n* : dry grassy treeless land esp. of Asia

-ster \stər\ *n suffix* **1** : one that does, makes, or uses **2** : one that is associated with or takes part in **3** : one that is

ste·reo \'sterē̱ˌō, 'stir-\ *n, pl* **-reos** : stereophonic sound system — **stereo** *adj*

ste·reo·phon·ic \ˌsterēə'fänik, ˌstir-\ *adj* : relating to a 3-dimensional effect of reproduced sound

ste·reo·type \'sterēəˌtīp, 'stir-\ *n* : gross often mistaken generalization — **stereotype** *vb* — **ste·reo·typ·i·cal** \ˌsterēə'tipikəl\ *adj* — **ste·reo·typi·cal·ly** *adv*

ste·reo·typed \'sterēəˌtīpt, 'stir-\ *adj* : lacking originality or individuality

ster·ile \'sterəl\ *adj* **1** : unable to bear fruit, crops, or offspring **2** : free from disease germs — **ste·ril·i·ty** \stə'rilətē\ *n* — **ster·il·i·za·tion** \ˌsterələ'zāshən\ *n* — **ster·il·ize** \-əˌlīz\ *vb* — **ster·il·iz·er** *n*

ster·ling \'stərliŋ\ *adj* **1** : being or made of an alloy of 925 parts of silver with 75 parts of copper **2** : excellent

¹**stern** \'stərn\ *adj* : severe — **stern·ly** *adv* — **stern·ness** *n*

²**stern** *n* : back end of a boat

ster·num \'stərnəm\ *n, pl* **-nums** or **-na** \-nə\ : long flat chest bone joining the 2 sets of ribs

stetho·scope \'stethəˌskōp\ *n* : instrument used for listening to sounds in the chest

ste·ve·dore \'stēvəˌdōr\ *n* : worker who loads and unloads ships

stew \'stü, 'styü\ *n* **1** : dish of boiled meat and vegetables **2** : state of worry or agitation — **stew** *vb*

stew·ard \'stüərd, 'styü-\ *n* **1** : manager of an estate or an organization **2** : person on a ship or airliner

who looks after passenger comfort — **stew·ard·ship** n

stew·ard·ess \-əs\ n : woman who is a steward (as on an airplane)

◆ ¹**stick** \'stik\ n 1 : cut or broken branch 2 : long thin piece of wood or something resembling it

◆ ²**stick** vb **stuck** \'stək\; **stick·ing 1** : stab 2 : thrust or project 3 : hold fast to something 4 : attach 5 : become jammed or fixed

stick·er \'stikər\ n : adhesive label

stick·ler \'stiklər\ n : one who insists on exactness or completeness

sticky \'stikē\ adj **stick·i·er; -est 1** : adhesive or gluey 2 : muggy 3 : difficult

stiff \'stif\ adj **1** : not bending easily 2 : tense 3 : formal 4 : strong 5 : severe — **stiff·en** \'stifən\ vb — **stiff·en·er** \-ənər\ n — **stiff·ly** adv — **stiff·ness** n

sti·fle \'stīfəl\ vb **-fled; -fling 1** : smother or suffocate 2 : suppress

stig·ma \'stigmə\ n, pl **-ma·ta** \stig-'mätə, 'stigmətə\ or **-mas** : mark of disgrace — **stig·ma·tize** \'stigmə-ˌtīz\ vb

stile \'stīl\ n : steps for crossing a fence

sti·let·to \stə'letō\ n, pl **-tos** or **-toes** : slender dagger

¹**still** \'stil\ adj **1** : motionless 2 : silent ~ vb : make or become still ~ adv **1** : without motion 2 : up to and during this time 3 : in spite of that ~ n : silence — **still·ness** n

²**still** n : apparatus used in distillation

still·born adj : born dead — **still·birth** n

stilt \'stilt\ n : one of a pair of poles for walking

stilt·ed \'stiltəd\ adj : not easy and natural

stim·u·lant \'stimyələnt\ n : substance that temporarily increases

the activity of an organism — **stimulant** adj

stim·u·late \-ˌlāt\ vb **-lat·ed; -lat·ing** : make active — **stim·u·la·tion** \ˌstimyə'lāshən\ n

stim·u·lus \'stimyələs\ n, pl **-li** \-ˌlī\ : something that stimulates

sting \'stiŋ\ vb **stung** \'stəŋ\; **sting·ing 1** : prick painfully 2 : cause to suffer acutely ~ n : act of stinging or a resulting wound — **sting·er** n

stin·gy \'stinjē\ adj **stin·gi·er; -est** : not generous — **stin·gi·ness** n

stink \'stiŋk\ vb **stank** \'staŋk\ or **stunk** \'stəŋk\; **stunk; stink·ing** : have a strong offensive odor — **stink** n — **stink·er** n

stint \'stint\ vb : be sparing or stingy ~ n **1** : restraint 2 : quantity or period of work

sti·pend \'stī,pend, -pənd\ n : money paid periodically

stip·ple \'stipəl\ vb **-pled; -pling** : engrave, paint, or draw with dots instead of lines — **stipple** n

stip·u·late \'stipyə,lāt\ vb **-lat·ed; -lat·ing** : demand as a condition — **stip·u·la·tion** \ˌstipyə'lāshən\ n

stir \'stər\ vb **-rr- 1** : move slightly 2 : prod or push into activity 3 : mix by continued circular movement ~ n : act or result of stirring

stir·rup \'stərəp\ n : saddle loop for the foot

stitch \'stich\ n **1** : loop formed by a needle in sewing 2 : sudden sharp pain ~ vb **1** : fasten or decorate with stitches 2 : sew

stock \'stäk\ n **1** : block or part of wood 2 : original from which others derive 3 : farm animals 4 : supply of goods 5 : money invested in a large business 6 pl : instrument of punishment like a pillory with holes for the feet or feet and hands ~ vb : provide with stock

stock•ade \stä'kād\ *n* : defensive or confining enclosure

stock•ing \'stäkin\ *n* : close-fitting covering for the foot and leg

stock•pile *n* : reserve supply — **stockpile** *vb*

stocky \'stäkē\ *adj* **stock•i•er; -est** : short and relatively thick

stock•yard *n* : yard for livestock to be slaughtered or shipped

stodgy \'stäjē\ *adj* **stodg•i•er; -est 1** : dull **2** : old-fashioned

sto•ic \'stōik\, **sto•i•cal** \-ikəl\ *adj* : showing indifference to pain — **stoic** *n* — **sto•ical•ly** *adv* — **sto•i•cism** \'stōə₁sizəm\ *n*

stoke \'stōk\ *vb* **stoked; stok•ing** : stir up a fire or supply fuel to a furnace — **stok•er** *n*

¹stole \'stōl\ *past of* STEAL

²stole *n* : long wide scarf

stolen *past part of* STEAL

stol•id \'stäləd\ *adj* : having or showing little or no emotion — **stol•id•ly** \'stälədlē\ *adv*

stom•ach \'stəmək, -ik\ *n* **1** : saclike digestive organ **2** : abdomen **3** : appetite or desire ∼ *vb* : put up with — **stom•ach•ache** *n*

stomp \'stämp, 'stómp\ *vb* : stamp

stone \'stōn\ *n* **1** : hardened earth or mineral matter **2** : small piece of rock **3** : seed that is hard or has a hard covering ∼ *vb* **stoned; ston•ing** : pelt or kill with stones — **stony** *adj*

stood *past of* STAND

stool \'stül\ *n* **1** : seat usu. without back or arms **2** : footstool **3** : discharge of feces

¹stoop \'stüp\ *vb* **1** : bend over **2** : lower oneself ∼ *n* **1** : act of bending over **2** : bent position of shoulders

²stoop *n* : small porch at a house door

stop \'stäp\ *vb* **-pp- 1** : block an opening **2** : end or cause to end **3** : pause for rest or a visit in a journey ∼ *n* **1** : plug **2** : act or place of stopping **3** : delay in a journey — **stop•light** *n* — **stop•page** \-ij\ *n* — **stop•per** *n*

stop•gap *n* : temporary measure or thing

stor•age \'stōrij\ *n* : safekeeping of goods (as in a warehouse)

store \'stōr\ *vb* **stored; stor•ing** : put aside for future use ∼ *n* **1** : some-

thing stored **2** : retail business establishment — **store•house** *n* — **store•keep•er** *n* — **store•room** *n*

stork \'stórk\ *n* : large wading bird

storm \'stórm\ *n* **1** : heavy fall of rain or snow **2** : violent outbreak ∼ *vb* **1** : rain or snow heavily **2** : rage **3** : make an attack against — **stormy** *adj*

¹sto•ry \'stōrē\ *n, pl* **-ries 1** : narrative **2** : report — **sto•ry•tell•er** *n*

²story *n, pl* **-ries** : floor of a building

stout \'staút\ *adj* **1** : firm or strong **2** : thick or bulky — **stout•ly** *adv* — **stout•ness** *n*

¹stove \'stōv\ *n* : apparatus for providing heat (as for cooking or heating)

²stove *past of* STAVE

stow \'stō\ *vb* **1** : pack in a compact mass **2** : put or hide away

strad•dle \'strad⁰l\ *vb* **-dled; -dling** : stand over or sit on with legs on opposite sides — **straddle** *n*

strafe \'sträf\ *vb* **strafed; strafing** : fire upon with machine guns from a low-flying airplane

strag•gle \'stragəl\ *vb* **-gled; -gling** : wander or become separated from others — **strag•gler** \-ələr\ *n*

straight \'strāt\ *adj* **1** : having no bends, turns, or twists **2** : just, proper, or honest **3** : neat and orderly ∼ *adv* : in a straight manner — **straight•en** \'strāt⁰n\ *vb*

straight•for•ward \strāt'fórwərd\ *adj* : frank or honest

straight•way *adv* : immediately

¹strain \'strān\ *n* **1** : lineage **2** : trace

²strain *vb* **1** : exert to the utmost **2** : filter or remove by filtering **3** : injure by improper use ∼ *n* **1** : excessive tension or exertion **2** : bodily injury from excessive effort — **strain•er** *n*

strait \'strāt\ *n* **1** : narrow channel connecting 2 bodies of water **2** *pl* : distress

strait•en \'strāt⁰n\ *vb* **1** : hem in **2** : make distressing or difficult

¹strand \'strand\ *vb* **1** : drive or cast upon the shore **2** : leave helpless

²strand *n* **1** : twisted fiber of a rope **2** : length of something ropelike

strange \'strānj\ *adj* **strang•er; strang•est 1** : unusual or queer **2** : new — **strange•ly** *adv* — **strange•ness** *n*

strang·er \'strānjər\ *n* : person with whom one is not acquainted

stran·gle \'straŋgəl\ *vb* **-gled; -gling** : choke to death — **stran·gler** \-glər\ *n*

stran·gu·la·tion \ˌstraŋgyə'lāshən\ *n* : act or process of strangling

strap \'strap\ *n* : narrow strip of flexible material used esp. for fastening ~ *vb* **1** : secure with a strap **2** : beat with a strap — **strap·less** *n*

strap·ping \'strapiŋ\ *adj* : robust

strat·a·gem \'stratəjəm, -ˌjem\ *n* : deceptive scheme or maneuver

strat·e·gy \'stratəjē\ *n*, *pl* **-gies** : carefully worked out plan of action — **stra·te·gic** \strə'tējik\ *adj* — **strat·e·gist** \'stratəjist\ *n*

strat·i·fy \'stratəˌfī\ *vb* **-fied; -fying** : form or arrange in layers — **strat·i·fi·ca·tion** \ˌstratəfə'kāshən\ *n*

strato·sphere \'stratəˌsfir\ *n* : earth's atmosphere from about 7 to 31 miles above the surface

stra·tum \'strātəm, 'strat-\ *n*, *pl* **-ta** \'strātə, 'strat-\ : layer

straw \'stró\ *n* **1** : grass stems after grain is removed **2** : tube for drinking ~ *adj* : made of straw

straw·ber·ry \'stró.berē\ *n* : juicy red pulpy fruit

stray \'strā\ *vb* : wander or deviate ~ *n* : person or animal that strays ~ *adj* : separated from or not related to anything close by

streak \'strēk\ *n* **1** : mark of a different color **2** : narrow band of light **3** : trace **4** : run (as of luck) or series ~ *vb* **1** : form streaks in or on **2** : move fast

stream \'strēm\ *n* **1** : flow of water on land **2** : steady flow (as of water or air) ~ *vb* **1** : flow in a stream **2** : pour out streams

stream·er \'strēmər\ *n* : long ribbon or ribbonlike flag

stream·lined \-ˌlīnd, -'līnd\ *adj* **1** : made with contours to reduce air or water resistance **2** : simplified **3** : modernized — **streamline** *vb*

street \'strēt\ *n* : thoroughfare esp. in a city or town

street·car *n* : passenger vehicle running on rails in the streets

strength \'streŋth\ *n* **1** : quality of being strong **2** : toughness **3** : intensity

strength·en \'streŋthən\ *vb* : make, grow, or become stronger — **strength·en·er** \'streŋthənər\ *n*

stren·u·ous \'strenyəwəs\ *adj* **1** : vigorous **2** : requiring or showing energy — **stren·u·ous·ly** *adv*

stress \'stres\ *n* **1** : pressure or strain that tends to distort a body **2** : relative prominence given to one thing among others **3** : state of physical or mental tension or something inducing it ~ *vb* : put stress on — **stress·ful** \'stresfəl\ *adj*

stretch \'strech\ *vb* **1** : spread or reach out **2** : draw out in length or breadth **3** : make taut **4** : exaggerate **5** : become extended without breaking ~ *n* : act of extending beyond normal limits

stretch·er \'strechər\ *n* : device for carrying a sick or injured person

strew \'strü\ *vb* **strewed; strewed** *or* **strewn** \'strün\; **strew·ing 1** : scatter **2** : cover by scattering something over

strick·en \'strikən\ *adj* : afflicted with disease

strict \'strikt\ *adj* **1** : allowing no escape or evasion **2** : precise — **strict·ly** *adv* — **strict·ness** *n*

stric·ture \'strikchər\ *n* : hostile criticism

stride \'strīd\ *vb* **strode** \'strōd\; **strid·den** \'stridⁿn\; **strid·ing** : walk or run with long steps ~ *n* **1** : long step **2** : manner of striding

stri·dent \'strīdⁿnt\ *adj* : loud and harsh

strife \'strīf\ *n* : conflict

strike \'strīk\ *vb* **struck** \'strək\; **struck; strik·ing** \'strīkiŋ\ **1** : hit sharply **2** : delete **3** : produce by impressing **4** : cause to sound **5** : afflict **6** : occur to or impress **7** : cause (a match) to ignite by rubbing **8** : refrain from working **9** : find **10** : take on (as a pose) ~ *n* **1** : act or instance of striking **2** : work stoppage **3** : military attack — **strik·er** *n* — **strike out** *vb* : start out vigorously — **strike up** *vb* : start

strik·ing \'strīkiŋ\ *adj* : very noticeable — **strik·ing·ly** *adv*

string \'striŋ\ *n* **1** : line usu. of twisted threads **2** : series **3** *pl* : stringed instruments ~ *vb* **strung** \'strəŋ\; **string·ing 1** : thread on or with a string **2** : hang or fasten by a string

stringed \'striṇd\ *adj* : having strings

strin·gent \'strinjənt\ *adj* : severe

stringy \'striṇē\ *adj* **string·i·er; -est** : tough or fibrous

¹**strip** \'strip\ *vb* **-pp- 1** : take the covering or clothing from **2** : undress — **strip·per** *n*

²**strip** *n* : long narrow flat piece

stripe \'strīp\ *n* : distinctive line or long narrow section ~ *vb* **striped** \'strīpt\; **strip·ing** : make stripes on — **striped** \'strīpt, 'strīpəd\ *adj*

strive \'strīv\ *vb* **strove** \'strōv\; **stri·ven** \'strivən\ *or* **strived**; **striv·ing** \'strīviṇ\ **1** : struggle **2** : try hard

strode *past of* STRIDE

stroke \'strōk\ *vb* **stroked; strok·ing** : rub gently ~ *n* **1** : act of swinging or striking **2** : sudden action

stroll \'strōl\ *vb* : walk leisurely — **stroll** *n* — **stroll·er** *n*

strong \'stroṇ\ *adj* **1** : capable of exerting great force or of withstanding stress or violence **2** : healthy **3** : zealous — **strong·ly** *adv*

strong·hold *n* : fortified place

struck *past of* STRIKE

struc·ture \'strəkchər\ *n* **1** : building **2** : arrangement of elements ~ *vb* **-tured; -tur·ing** : make into a structure — **struc·tur·al** \-chərəl\ *adj*

strug·gle \'strəgəl\ *vb* **-gled; -gling 1** : make strenuous efforts to overcome an adversary **2** : proceed with great effort ~ *n* **1** : strenuous effort **2** : intense competition for superiority

strum \'strəm\ *vb* **-mm-** : play (a musical instrument) by brushing the strings with the fingers

strum·pet \'strəmpət\ *n* : prostitute

strung *past of* STRING

strut \'strət\ *vb* **-tt-** : walk in a proud or showy manner ~ *n* **1** : proud walk **2** : supporting bar or rod

strych·nine \'strik,nīn, -nən, -,nēn\ *n* : bitter poisonous substance

stub \'stəb\ *n* : short end or section ~ *vb* **-bb-** : strike against something

stub·ble \'stəbəl\ *n* : short growth left after cutting — **stub·bly** *adj*

stub·born \'stəbərn\ *adj* **1** : determined not to yield **2** : hard to control — **stub·born·ly** *adv* — **stub·born·ness** *n*

stub·by \'stəbē\ *adj* : short, blunt, and thick

stuc·co \'stəkō\ *n, pl* **-cos** *or* **-coes** : plaster for coating outside walls — **stuc·coed** \'stəkōd\ *adj*

stuck *past of* STICK

stuck-up \'stək'əp\ *adj* : conceited

¹**stud** \'stəd\ *n* : male horse kept for breeding

²**stud** *n* **1** : upright beam for holding wall material **2** : projecting nail, pin, or rod ~ *vb* **-dd-** : supply or dot with studs

stu·dent \'stüd°nt, 'styü-\ *n* : one who studies

stud·ied \'stədēd\ *adj* : premeditated

stu·dio \'stüdē,ō, 'styü-\ *n, pl* **-dios 1** : artist's workroom **2** : place where movies are made or television or radio shows are broadcast

stu·di·ous \'stüdēəs, 'styü-\ *adj* : devoted to study — **stu·di·ous·ly** *adv*

study \'stədē\ *n, pl* **stud·ies 1** : act or process of learning about something **2** : branch of learning **3** : careful examination **4** : room for reading or studying ~ *vb* **stud·ied; study·ing** : apply the attention and mind to a subject

◆ **stuff** \'stəf\ *n* **1** : personal property **2** : raw or fundamental material

ARE YOU GOING TO EAT THAT HAMBURGER, POOKY?

I LOVE EATING WITH TEDDY BEARS

THEY'RE ALWAYS STUFFED

JIM DAVIS

3 : unspecified material or things ~ *vb* : fill by packing things in — **stuff·ing** *n*

stuffy \'stəfē\ *adj* **stuff·i·er; -est 1** : lacking fresh air **2** : unimaginative or pompous

stul·ti·fy \'stəltə‚fī\ *vb* **-fied; -fy·ing 1** : cause to appear foolish **2** : impair or make ineffective **3** : have a dulling effect on

stum·ble \'stəmbəl\ *vb* **-bled; -bling 1** : lose one's balance or fall in walking or running **2** : speak or act clumsily **3** : happen by chance — **stumble** *n*

stump \'stəmp\ *n* : part left when something is cut off ~ *vb* : confuse — **stumpy** *adj*

stun \'stən\ *vb* **-nn- 1** : make senseless or dizzy by or as if by a blow **2** : bewilder

stung *past of* STING

stunk *past of* STINK

stun·ning \'stənin\ *adj* **1** : astonishing or incredible **2** : strikingly beautiful — **stun·ning·ly** *adv*

¹**stunt** \'stənt\ *vb* : hinder the normal growth or progress of

²**stunt** *n* : spectacular feat

stu·pe·fy \'stüpə‚fī, 'styü-\ *vb* **-fied; -fy·ing 1** : make insensible by or as if by drugs **2** : amaze

stu·pen·dous \stü'pendəs, styü-\ *adj* : very big or impressive — **stupendous·ly** *adv*

stu·pid \'stüpəd, 'styü-\ *adj* : not sensible or intelligent — **stu·pid·i·ty** \stü'pidətē, styü-\ *n* — **stupid·ly** *adv*

stu·por \'stüpər, 'styü-\ *n* : state of being conscious but not aware or sensible

stur·dy \'stərdē\ *adj* **-di·er; -est** : strong — **stur·di·ly** \'stərd°lē\ *adv* — **stur·di·ness** *n*

stur·geon \'stərjən\ *n* : fish whose roe is caviar

stut·ter \'stətər\ *vb or n* : stammer

¹**sty** \'stī\ *n, pl* **sties** : pig pen

²**sty, stye** \'stī\ *n, pl* **sties** *or* **styes** : inflamed swelling on the edge of an eyelid

style \'stīl\ *n* **1** : distinctive way of speaking, writing, or acting **2** : elegant or fashionable way of living ~ *vb* **styled; styl·ing 1** : name **2** : give a particular design or style to — **stylish** \'stīlish\ *adj* — **styl·ish·ly** *adv* — **styl·ish·ness** *n* —

styl·ist \-ist\ *n* — **styl·ize** \'stīəl‚īz\ *vb*

sty·lus \'stīləs\ *n, pl* **-li** \'stīl‚ī\ **1** : pointed writing tool **2** : phonograph needle

sty·mie \'stīmē\ *vb* **-mied; -mie·ing** : block or frustrate

suave \'swäv\ *adj* : well-mannered and gracious — **suave·ly** *adv*

¹**sub** \'səb\ *n or vb* : substitute

²**sub** *n* : submarine

sub- \‚səb, 'səb\ *prefix* **1** : under or beneath **2** : subordinate or secondary **3** : subordinate portion of **4** : with repetition of a process so as to form, stress, or deal with subordinate parts or relations **5** : somewhat **6** : nearly

subacute	subindustry
subagency	sublease
subagent	sublethal
subarctic	sublevel
subarea	subliterate
subatmospheric	subnetwork
subaverage	suboceanic
subbase	suborder
subbasement	subpar
subbranch	subpart
subcabinet	subplot
subcategory	subpolar
subclass	subprincipal
subclassifica-	subprocess
tion	subprogram
subclassify	subproject
subcommission	subregion
subcommittee	subsea
subcommunity	subsection
subcomponent	subsense
subcontract	subspecialty
subcontractor	subspecies
subculture	substage
subdean	subsurface
subdepartment	subsystem
subdistrict	subtemperate
subentry	subtheme
subfamily	subtopic
subfreezing	subtotal
subgroup	subtreasury
subhead	subtype
subheading	subunit
subhuman	subvariety
subindex	

sub·con·scious \‚səb'känchəs\ *adj* : existing without conscious awareness ~ *n* : part of the mind concerned with subconscious activities — **sub·con·scious·ly** *adv*

sub·di·vide \‚səbdə'vīd, 'səbdə-

ˌvīd\ *vb* **1** : divide into several parts **2** : divide (land) into building lots — **sub·di·vi·sion** \-'vizhən, -ˌvizh-\ *n*

sub·due \səb'dü, -'dyü\ *vb* **-dued; -du·ing 1** : bring under control **2** : reduce the intensity of

sub·ject \'səbjikt\ *n* **1** : person under the authority of another **2** : something being discussed or studied **3** : word or word group about which something is said in a sentence ~ *adj* **1** : being under one's authority **2** : prone **3** : dependent on some condition or act ~ \səb'jekt\ *vb* **1** : bring under control **2** : cause to undergo — **sub·jec·tion** \-'jek-shən\ *n*

sub·jec·tive \ˌsəb'jektiv\ *adj* : deriving from an individual viewpoint or bias — **sub·jec·tive·ly** *adv* — **sub·jec·tiv·i·ty** \-ˌjek'tivətē\ *n*

sub·ju·gate \'səbjiˌgāt\ *vb* **-gat·ed; -gat·ing** : bring under one's control — **sub·ju·ga·tion** \ˌsəbji-'gāshən\ *n*

sub·junc·tive \səb'jənktiv\ *adj* : relating to a verb form which expresses possibility or contingency — **subjunctive** *n*

sub·let \'səbˌlet\ *vb* **-let; -let·ting** : rent (a property) from a lessee

sub·lime \sə'blīm\ *adj* : splendid — **sub·lime·ly** *adv*

sub·ma·rine \'səbməˌrēn, ˌsəb-mə'-\ *adj* : existing, acting, or growing under the sea ~ *n* : underwater boat

sub·merge \səb'mərj\ *vb* **-merged; -merg·ing** : put or plunge under the surface of water — **sub·mer·gence** \-'mərjəns\ *n* — **sub·mers·ible** \səb'mərsəbəl\ *adj or n* — **sub·mer·sion** \-'mərzhən\ *n*

sub·mit \səb'mit\ *vb* **-tt- 1** : yield **2** : give or offer ~ **sub·mis·sion** \-'mishən\ *n* — **sub·mis·sive** \-'misiv\ *adj*

sub·nor·mal \ˌsəb'nórməl\ *adj* : falling below what is normal

sub·or·di·nate \sə'bórdᵊnət\ *adj* : lower in rank ~ *n* : one that is subordinate ~ \sə'bórdᵊnˌāt\ *vb* **-nat·ed; -nat·ing** : place in a lower rank or class — **sub·or·di·na·tion** \-ˌbórdᵊn'āshən\ *n*

sub·poe·na \sə'pēnə\ *n* : summons to appear in court ~ *vb* **-naed;**

-na·ing : summon with a subpoena

sub·scribe \səb'skrīb\ *vb* **-scribed; -scrib·ing 1** : give consent or approval **2** : agree to support or to receive and pay for — **sub·scrib·er** *n*

sub·scrip·tion \səb'skripshən\ *n* : order for regular receipt of a publication

sub·se·quent \'səbsikwənt, -səˌkwent\ *adj* : following after — **sub·se·quent·ly** \-ˌkwentlē, -kwənt-\ *adv*

sub·ser·vi·ence \səb'sərvēəns\ *n* : obsequious submission — **sub·ser·vi·en·cy** \-ənsē\ *n* — **sub·ser·vi·ent** \-ənt\ *adj*

sub·side \səb'sīd\ *vb* **-sid·ed; -sid·ing** : die down in intensity

sub·sid·iary \səb'sidēˌerē\ *adj* **1** : furnishing support **2** : of secondary importance ~ *n* : company controlled by another company

sub·si·dize \'səbsəˌdīz\ *vb* **-dized; -diz·ing** : aid with a subsidy

sub·si·dy \'səbsədē\ *n, pl* **-dies** : gift of supporting funds

sub·sist \səb'sist\ *vb* : acquire the necessities of life — **sub·sis·tence** \-'sistəns\ *n*

sub·stance \'səbstəns\ *n* **1** : essence or essential part **2** : physical material **3** : wealth

sub·stan·dard \ˌsəb'standərd\ *adj* : falling short of a standard or norm

sub·stan·tial \səb'stanchəl\ *adj* **1** : plentiful **2** : considerable — **sub·stan·tial·ly** *adv*

sub·stan·ti·ate \səb'stanchēˌāt\ *vb* **-at·ed; -at·ing** : verify — **sub·stan·ti·a·tion** \-ˌstanchē'āshən\ *n*

sub·sti·tute \'səbstəˌtüt, -ˌtyüt\ *n* : replacement ~ *vb* **-tut·ed; -tut·ing** : put or serve in place of another — **substitute** *adj* — **sub·sti·tu·tion** \ˌsəbstə'tüshən, -'tyü-\ *n*

sub·ter·fuge \'səbtərˌfyüj\ *n* : deceptive trick

sub·ter·ra·nean \ˌsəbtə'rānēən\ *adj* : lying or being underground

sub·ti·tle \'səbˌtītᵊl\ *n* : movie caption

sub·tle \'sətᵊl\ *adj* **-tler** \-ər\; **-tlest** \-ist\ **1** : hardly noticeable **2** : clever — **sub·tle·ty** \-tē\ *n* — **sub·tly** \-ᵊlē\ *adv*

sub·tract \səb'trakt\ vb : take away (as one number from another) — **sub·trac·tion** \-'trakshən\ n

sub·urb \'səb,ərb\ n : residential area adjacent to a city — **sub·ur·ban** \sə'bərbən\ adj or n — **sub·ur·ban·ite** \-bə,nīt\ n

sub·vert \səb'vərt\ vb : overthrow or ruin — **sub·ver·sion** \-'vər-zhən\ n — **sub·ver·sive** \-'vər-siv\ adj

sub·way \'səb,wā\ n : underground electric railway

suc·ceed \sək'sēd\ vb 1 : follow (someone) in a job, role, or title 2 : attain a desired object or end

suc·cess \-'ses\ n 1 : favorable outcome 2 : gaining of wealth and fame 3 : one that succeeds — **suc·cess·ful** \-fəl\ adj — **suc·cess·ful·ly** adv

suc·ces·sion \sək'seshən\ n 1 : order, act, or right of succeeding 2 : series

suc·ces·sive \-'sesiv\ adj : following in order — **suc·ces·sive·ly** adv

suc·ces·sor \-'sesər\ n : one that succeeds another

suc·cinct \sək'siŋkt, sə'siŋkt\ adj : brief — **suc·cinct·ly** adv — **suc·cinct·ness** n

suc·cor \'səkər\ n or vb : help

suc·co·tash \'səkə,tash\ n : beans and corn cooked together

suc·cu·lent \'səkyələnt\ adj : juicy — **suc·cu·lence** \-ləns\ n — **succulent** n

suc·cumb \sə'kəm\ vb 1 : yield 2 : die

such \'səch\ adj 1 : of this or that kind 2 : having a specified quality — **such** pron or adv

suck \'sək\ vb 1 : draw in liquid with the mouth 2 : draw liquid from by or as if by mouth — **suck** n

♦ **suck·er** \'səkər\ n 1 : one that sucks or clings 2 : easily deceived person

suck·le \'səkəl\ vb -led; -ling : give or draw milk from the breast or udder

suck·ling \'səkliŋ\ n : young unweaned mammal

su·crose \'sü,krōs, -,krōz\ n : cane or beet sugar

suc·tion \'səkshən\ n 1 : act of sucking 2 : act or process of drawing in by partially exhausting the air

sud·den \'səd²n\ adj 1 : happening unexpectedly 2 : steep 3 : hasty — **sud·den·ly** adv — **sud·den·ness** n

suds \'sədz\ n pl : soapy water esp. when frothy — **sudsy** \'sədzē\ adj

sue \'sü\ vb sued; su·ing 1 : petition 2 : bring legal action against

suede, suède \'swād\ n : leather with a napped surface

su·et \'süət\ n : hard beef fat

suf·fer \'səfər\ vb 1 : experience pain, loss, or hardship 2 : permit — **suf·fer·er** n

suf·fer·ing \-əriŋ\ n : pain or hardship

suf·fice \sə'fīs\ vb -ficed; -fic·ing : be sufficient

suf·fi·cient \sə'fishənt\ adj : adequate — **suf·fi·cien·cy** \-ənsē\ n — **suf·fi·cient·ly** adv

suf·fix \'səf,iks\ n : letters added at the end of a word — **suffix** \'səfiks, sə'fiks\ vb — **suf·fix·a·tion** \,səf,ik'sāshən\ n

suf·fo·cate \'səfə,kāt\ vb -cat·ed; -cat·ing : suffer or die or cause to die from lack of air — **suf·fo·cat·ing·ly** adv — **suf·fo·ca·tion** \,səfə-'kāshən\ n

suf·frage \'səfrij\ n : right to vote

suf·fuse \sə'fyüz\ vb -fused; -fus·ing : spread over or through

sug·ar \'shùgər\ n : sweet substance ~ vb : mix, cover, or sprinkle with sugar — **sug·ar·cane** n — **sug·ary** adj

sug·gest \sə'jest, səg-\ vb 1 : put into

someone's mind **2** : remind one by association of ideas — **sug·gest·ible** \-'jestəbəl\ *adj* — **sug·ges·tion** \'jeschən\ *n*

sug·ges·tive \-'jestiv\ *adj* : suggesting something improper — **sug·ges·tive·ly** *adv* — **sug·ges·tive·ness** *n*

sui·cide \'süə,sīd\ *n* **1** : act of killing oneself purposely **2** : one who commits suicide — **sui·cid·al** \,süə'sīd°l\ *adj*

suit \'süt\ *n* **1** : action in court to recover a right or claim **2** : number of things used or worn together **3** : one of the 4 sets of playing cards ∼ *vb* **1** : be appropriate or becoming to **2** : meet the needs of — **suit·abil·i·ty** \,sütə'bilətē\ *n* — **suit·able** \'sütəbəl\ *adj* — **suit·ably** *adv*

suit·case *n* : case for a traveler's clothing

suite \'swēt, *for 2 also* 'süt\ *n* **1** : group of rooms **2** : set of matched furniture

suit·or \'sütər\ *n* : one who seeks to marry a woman

sul·fur \'səlfər\ *n* : nonmetallic yellow chemical element — **sul·fu·ric** \,səl'fyurik\ *adj* — **sul·fu·rous** \-'fyurəs, 'səlfərəs, 'səlfyə-\ *adj*

sulk \'səlk\ *vb* : be moodily silent or irritable — **sulk** *n*

sulky \'səlkē\ *adj* : inclined to sulk ∼ *n* : light 2-wheeled horse-drawn cart — **sulk·i·ly** \'səlkəlē\ *adv* — **sulk·i·ness** \-kēnəs\ *n*

sul·len \'sələn\ *adj* **1** : gloomily silent **2** : dismal — **sul·len·ly** *adv* — **sul·len·ness** *n*

sul·ly \'səlē\ *vb* **-lied; -ly·ing** : cast doubt or disgrace on

sul·tan \'səlt°n\ *n* : sovereign of a Muslim state — **sul·tan·ate** \-,āt\ *n*

sul·try \'səltrē\ *adj* **-tri·er; -est 1** : very hot and moist **2** : sexually arousing

sum \'səm\ *n* **1** : amount **2** : gist **3** : result of addition ∼ *vb* **-mm-** : find the sum of

su·mac \'shü,mak, 'sü-\ *n* : shrub with spikes of berries

sum·ma·ry \'səmərē\ *adj* **1** : concise **2** : done without delay or formality ∼ *n, pl* **-ries** : concise statement — **summar·i·ly** \sə'merəlē,

'səmərəlē\ *adv* — **sum·ma·rize** \'səmə,rīz\ *vb*

sum·ma·tion \sə'māshən\ *n* : a summing up esp. in court

sum·mer \'səmər\ *n* : season in which the sun shines most directly — **summery** *adj*

sum·mit \'səmət\ *n* **1** : highest point **2** : high-level conference

sum·mon \'səmən\ *vb* **1** : send for or call together **2** : order to appear in court — **sum·mon·er** *n*

sum·mons \'səmənz\ *n, pl* **sum·mons·es** : an order to answer charges in court

sump·tu·ous \'səmpchəwəs\ *adj* : lavish

sun \'sən\ *n* **1** : shining celestial body around which the planets revolve **2** : light of the sun ∼ *vb* **-nn-** : expose to the sun — **sun·beam** *n* — **sun·block** *n* — **sun·burn** *n or vb* — **sun·glass·es** *n pl* — **sun·light** *n* — **sun·ny** *adj* — **sun·rise** *n* — **sun·set** *n* — **sun·shine** *n* — **sun·dae** \'səndē\ *n* : ice cream with topping

Sun·day \'səndā, -dē\ *n* : 1st day of the week

sun·di·al \-,dīəl\ *n* : device for showing time by the sun's shadow

sun·dries \'səndrēz\ *n, pl* : various small articles

sun·dry \-drē\ *adj* : several

sun·fish *n* : perchlike freshwater fish

sun·flow·er *n* : tall plant grown for its oil-rich seeds

sung *past of* SING

sunk *past of* SINK

sunk·en \'səŋkən\ *adj* **1** : submerged **2** : fallen in

sun·spot *n* : dark spot on the sun

sun·stroke *n* : heatstroke from the sun

sup \'səp\ *vb* **-pp-** : eat the evening meal

super \'süpər\ *adj* : very fine

super- \,süpər, 'sü-\ *prefix* **1** : higher in quantity, quality, or degree than **2** : in addition **3** : exceeding a norm **4** : in excessive degree or intensity **5** : surpassing others of its kind **6** : situated above, on, or at the top of **7** : more inclusive than **8** : superior in status or position

superabun-dance	superabundant
	superambitious

superathlete
superbomb
superclean
supercolossal
superconvenient
supercop
superdense
supereffective
superefficiency
superefficient
superfast
supergood
supergovernment
supergroup
superhero
superheroine
superhuman
superintellectual
superintelligence
superintelligent
superman
supermodern
superpatriot
superpatriotic
superpatriotism

superplane
superpolite
superport
superpowerful
superrich
supersalesman
superscout
supersecrecy
supersecret
supersensitive
supersize
supersized
superslick
supersmooth
supersoft
superspecial
superspecialist
superspy
superstar
superstate
superstrength
superstrong
supersystem
supertanker
superthick
superthin
supertight
superweapon
superwoman

su·perb \sù'pərb\ *adj* : outstanding — su·perb·ly *adv*

su·per·cil·ious \ˌsüpər'silēəs\ *adj* : haughtily contemptuous

su·per·fi·cial \ˌsüpər'fishəl\ *adj* : relating to what is only apparent — su·per·fi·ci·al·i·ty \-ˌfishē'alətē\ *n* — su·per·fi·cial·ly *adv*

su·per·flu·ous \sù'pərflowəs\ *adj* : more than necessary — su·per·flu·i·ty \ˌsüpər'flüətē\ *n*

su·per·im·pose \ˌsüpərim'pōz\ *vb* : lay over or above something

su·per·in·tend \ˌsüpərin'tend\ *vb* : have charge and oversight of — su·per·in·ten·dence \-'tendəns\ *n* — su·per·in·ten·den·cy \-dənsē\ *n* — su·per·in·ten·dent \-dənt\ *n*

♦ su·pe·ri·or \sù'pirēər\ *adj* 1 : higher, better, or more important 2 : haughty — superior *n* — su·pe·ri·or·i·ty \-ˌpirē'órətē\ *n*

su·per·la·tive \sù'pərlətiv\ *adj* 1 : relating to or being an adjective or adverb form that denotes an extreme level 2 : surpassing others — superlative *n* — su·per·la·tive·ly *adv*

su·per·mar·ket \'süpərˌmärkət\ *n* : self-service grocery store

su·per·nat·u·ral \ˌsüpər'nachərəl\ *adj* : beyond the observable physical world — su·per·nat·u·ral·ly *adv*

su·per·pow·er \'süpərˌpaùər\ *n* : politically and militarily dominant nation

su·per·sede \ˌsüpər'sēd\ *vb* -sed·ed; -sed·ing : take the place of

su·per·son·ic \-'sänik\ *adj* : faster than the speed of sound

su·per·sti·tion \ˌsüpər'stishən\ *n* : beliefs based on ignorance, fear of the unknown, or trust in magic — su·per·sti·tious \-əs\ *adj*

su·per·struc·ture \'süpərˌstrəkchər\ *n* : something built on a base or as a vertical extension

su·per·vise \'süpərˌvīz\ *vb* -vised; -vis·ing : have charge of — su·per·vi·sion \ˌsüpər'vizhən\ *n* — su·per·vi·sor \'süpərˌvīzər\ *n* — su·per·vi·so·ry \ˌsüpər'vīzərē\ *adj*

su·pine \sù'pīn\ *adj* 1 : lying on the back 2 : indifferent or abject

sup·per \'səpər\ *n* : evening meal

sup·plant \sə'plant\ *vb* : take the place of

sup·ple \'səpəl\ *adj* -pler; -plest : able to bend easily

sup·ple·ment \'səpləmənt\ *n* : something that adds to or makes up for a lack — supplement *vb* — sup·ple·men·tal \ˌsəplə'ment°l\ *adj* — sup·ple·men·ta·ry \-'mentərē\ *adj*

sup·pli·ant \'səplēənt\ *n* : one who supplicates

sup·pli·cate \'səplə‚kāt\ *vb* -cat·ed; -cat·ing 1 : pray to God 2 : ask earnestly and humbly — **sup·pli·cant** \-likənt\ *n* — **sup·pli·ca·tion** \‚səplə'kāshən\ *n*

sup·ply \sə'plī\ *vb* -plied; -ply·ing : furnish ~ *n, pl* -plies 1 : amount needed or available 2 *pl* : provisions — **sup·pli·er** \-'plīər\ *n*

sup·port \sə'pōrt\ *vb* 1 : take sides with 2 : provide with food, clothing, and shelter 3 : hold up or serve as a foundation for — **support** *n* — **sup·port·able** *adj* — **sup·port·er** *n*

sup·pose \sə'pōz\ *vb* -posed; -pos·ing 1 : assume to be true 2 : expect 3 : think probable — **sup·po·si·tion** \‚səpə'zishən\ *n*

sup·pos·i·to·ry \sə'päzə‚tōrē\ *n, pl* -ries : medicated material for insertion (as into the rectum)

sup·press \sə'pres\ *vb* 1 : put an end to by authority 2 : keep from being known 3 : hold back — **sup·pres·sant** \sə'pres³nt\ *n* — **sup·pres·sion** \-'preshən\ *n*

su·prem·a·cy \sủ'preməsē\ *n, pl* -cies : supreme power or authority

su·preme \sủ'prēm\ *adj* 1 : highest in rank or authority 2 : greatest possible — **su·preme·ly** *adv*

Supreme Being *n* : God

sur·charge \'sər‚chärj\ *n* 1 : excessive load or burden 2 : extra fee or cost

sure \'shủr\ *adj* **sur·er; sur·est** 1 : confident 2 : reliable 3 : not to be disputed 4 : bound to happen ~ *adv* : surely — **sure·ness** *n*

sure·ly \'shủrlē\ *adv* 1 : in a sure manner 2 : without doubt 3 : indeed

sure·ty \'shủrətē\ *n, pl* -ties 1 : guarantee 2 : one who gives a guarantee for another person

surf \'sərf\ *n* : waves that break on the shore ~ *vb* : ride the surf — **surf·board** *n* — **surf·er** *n* — **surf·ing** *n*

sur·face \'sərfəs\ *n* 1 : the outside of an object 2 : outward aspect ~ *vb* -faced; -fac·ing : rise to the surface

sur·feit \'sərfət\ *n* 1 : excess 2 : excessive indulgence (as in food or drink) 3 : disgust caused by excess ~ *vb* : feed, supply, or indulge to the point of surfeit

surge \'sərj\ *vb* **surged; surg·ing** : rise and fall in or as if in waves ~ *n* : sudden increase

sur·geon \'sərjən\ *n* : physician who specializes in surgery

sur·gery \'sərjərē\ *n, pl* -ger·ies : medical treatment involving cutting open the body

sur·gi·cal \'sərjikəl\ *adj* : relating to surgeons or surgery — **sur·gi·cal·ly** *adv*

sur·ly \'sərlē\ *adj* -li·er; -est : having a rude nature — **sur·li·ness** *n*

sur·mise \sər'mīz\ *vb* -mised; -mis·ing : guess — **surmise** *n*

sur·mount \-'maůnt\ *vb* 1 : prevail over 2 : get to or be the top of

sur·name \'sər‚nām\ *n* : family name

sur·pass \sər'pas\ *vb* : go beyond or exceed — **sur·pass·ing·ly** *adv*

sur·plice \'sərpləs\ *n* : loose white outer ecclesiastical vestment

sur·plus \'sər‚pləs\ *n* : quantity left over

sur·prise \sə'prīz, sər-\ *vb* -prised; -pris·ing 1 : come upon or affect unexpectedly 2 : amaze — **surprise** *n* — **sur·pris·ing** *adj* — **sur·pris·ing·ly** *adv*

sur·ren·der \sə'rendər\ *vb* : give up oneself or a possession to another ~ *n* : act of surrendering

sur·rep·ti·tious \‚sərəp'tishəs\ *adj* : done, made, or acquired by stealth — **sur·rep·ti·tious·ly** *adv*

sur·rey \'sərē\ *n, pl* -reys : horse-drawn carriage

sur·ro·gate \'sərəgāt, -gət\ *n* : substitute

sur·round \sə'raůnd\ *vb* : enclose on all sides

sur·round·ings \sə'raůndiɲz\ *n pl* : objects, conditions, or area around something

sur·veil·lance \sər'vāləns, -'vālyəns, -'vāəns\ *n* : careful watch

sur·vey \sər'vā\ *vb* -veyed; -vey·ing 1 : look over and examine closely 2 : make a survey of (as a tract of land) ~ \'sər‚-\ *n, pl* -veys 1 : inspection 2 : process of measuring (as land) — **sur·vey·or** \-ər\ *n*

sur·vive \sər'vīv\ *vb* -vived; -viv·ing 1 : remain alive or in existence

2 : outlive or outlast — **sur·viv·al** *n* — **sur·vi·vor** \-'vīvər\ *n*

sus·cep·ti·ble \sə'septəbəl\ *adj* : likely to allow or be affected by something — **sus·cep·ti·bil·i·ty** \-ˌseptə'bilətē\ *n*

sus·pect \'səsˌpekt, sə'spekt\ *adj* 1 : regarded with suspicion 2 : questionable ~ \'səsˌpekt\ *n* : one who is suspected (as of a crime) \sə-'spekt\ *vb* 1 : have doubts of 2 : believe guilty without proof 3 : guess

sus·pend \sə'spend\ *vb* 1 : temporarily stop or keep from a function or job 2 : withhold (judgment) temporarily 3 : hang

sus·pend·er \sə'spendər\ *n* : one of 2 supporting straps holding up trousers and passing over the shoulders

sus·pense \sə'spens\ *n* : excitement and uncertainty as to outcome — **suspense·ful** *adj*

sus·pen·sion \sə'spenchən\ *n* : act of suspending or the state or period of being suspended

sus·pi·cion \sə'spishən\ *n* 1 : act of suspecting something 2 : trace

sus·pi·cious \-əs\ *adj* 1 : arousing suspicion 2 : inclined to suspect — **sus·pi·cious·ly** *adv*

sus·tain \sə'stān\ *vb* 1 : provide with nourishment 2 : keep going 3 : hold up 4 : suffer 5 : support or prove

sus·te·nance \'səstənəns\ *n* 1 : nourishment 2 : something that sustains or supports

svelte \'sfelt\ *adj* : slender and graceful

swab \'swäb\ *n* 1 : mop 2 : wad of absorbent material for applying medicine ~ *vb* **-bb-** : use a swab on

swad·dle \'swäd°l\ *vb* **-dled; -dling** \'swäd°liŋ\ : bind (an infant) in bands of cloth

swag·ger \'swagər\ *vb* **-gered; -gering** 1 : walk with a conceited swing 2 : boast — **swagger** *n*

¹**swal·low** \'swälō\ *n* : small migratory bird

♦ ²**swallow** *vb* 1 : take into the stomach through the throat 2 : envelop or take in 3 : accept too easily — **swallow** *n*

swam *past of* SWIM

swamp \'swämp\ *n* : wet spongy land ~ *vb* : deluge (as with water) — **swampy** *adj*

swan \'swän\ *n* : white long-necked swimming bird

swap \'swäp\ *vb* **-pp-** : trade — **swap** *n*

swarm \'swórm\ *n* 1 : mass of honeybees leaving a hive to start a new colony 2 : large crowd ~ *vb* : gather in a swarm

swar·thy \'swórthē, -thē\ *adj* **-thier; -est** : dark in complexion

swash·buck·ler \'swäsh‚bəklər\ *n* : swaggering or daring soldier or adventurer — **swash·buck·ling** \-ˌbəkliŋ\ *adj*

swat \'swät\ *vb* **-tt-** : hit sharply — **swat** *n* — **swat·ter** *n*

swatch \'swäch\ *n* : sample piece (as of fabric)

swath \'swäth, 'swóth\, **swathe** \'swäth, 'swóth, 'swäth\ *n* : row or path cut (as through grass)

swathe \'swäth, 'swóth, 'swäth\ *vb* **swathed; swath·ing** : wrap with or as if with a bandage

sway \'swā\ *vb* 1 : swing gently from side to side 2 : influence ~ *n* 1 : gentle swinging from side to side 2 : controlling power or influence

swear \'swar\ *vb* **swore** \'swór\; **sworn** \'swórn\; **swear·ing** 1 : make or cause to make a solemn statement under oath 2 : use profane language — **swear·er** *n* — **swear·ing** *n*

sweat \'swet\ *vb* **sweat** *or* **sweat-ed**; **sweat·ing 1** : excrete salty moisture from skin glands **2** : form drops of moisture on the surface **3** : work or cause to work hard — **sweat** *n* — **sweaty** *adj*

sweat·er \'swetər\ *n* : knitted jacket or pullover

sweat·shirt \'swet,shərt\ *n* : loose collarless heavy cotton jersey pullover

sweep \'swēp\ *vb* **swept** \'swept\; **sweep·ing 1** : remove or clean by a brush or a single forceful wipe (as of the hand) **2** : move over with speed and force (as of the hand) **3** : move or extend in a wide curve ∼ *n* **1** : a clearing off or away **2** : single forceful wipe or swinging movement **3** : scope — **sweep·er** *n* — **sweep·ing** *adj*

sweep·stakes \'swēp,stāks\ *n, pl* **sweep·stakes** : contest in which the entire prize may go to the winner

sweet \'swēt\ *adj* **1** : being or causing the pleasing taste typical of sugar **2** : not stale or spoiled **3** : not salted **4** : pleasant **5** : much loved ∼ *n* : something sweet — **sweet·en** \'swēt^?n\ *vb* — **sweet·ly** *adv* — **sweet·ness** *n* — **sweet·en·er** \-^?nər\ *n*

sweet·heart *n* : person one loves

sweet potato *n* : sweet yellow edible root of a tropical vine

swell \'swel\ *vb* **swelled**; **swelled** *or* **swol·len** \'swōlən\; **swell·ing 1** : enlarge **2** : bulge **3** : fill or be filled with emotion ∼ *n* **1** : long rolling ocean wave **2** : condition of bulging — **swell·ing** *n*

swel·ter \'sweltər\ *vb* : be uncomfortable from excessive heat

swept *past of* SWEEP

swerve \'swərv\ *vb* **swerved**; **swerv·ing** : move abruptly aside from a course — **swerve** *n*

¹**swift** \'swift\ *adj* **1** : moving with great speed **2** : occurring suddenly — **swift·ly** *adv* — **swift·ness** *n*

²**swift** *n* : small insect-eating bird

swig \'swig\ *vb* **-gg-** : drink in gulps — **swig** *n*

swill \'swil\ *vb* : swallow greedily ∼ *n* **1** : animal food of refuse and liquid **2** : garbage

swim \'swim\ *vb* **swam** \'swam\; **swum** \'swəm\; **swim·ming 1** : pro-pel oneself in water **2** : float in or be surrounded with a liquid **3** : be dizzy ∼ *n* : act or period of swimming — **swim·mer** *n*

swin·dle \'swind^?l\ *vb* **-dled**; **-dling** \-iŋ\ : cheat (someone) of money or property — **swindle** *n* — **swin-dler** \-^?r\ *n*

swine \'swīn\ *n, pl* **swine** : short-legged hoofed mammal with a snout — **swinish** \'swīnish\ *adj*

swing \'swiŋ\ *vb* **swung** \'swəŋ\; **swing·ing 1** : move or cause to move rapidly in an arc **2** : sway or cause to sway back and forth **3** : hang so as to sway or sag **4** : turn on a hinge or pivot **5** : manage or handle successfully ∼ *n* **1** : act or instance of swinging **2** : swinging movement (as in trying to hit something) **3** : suspended seat for swinging — **swing** *adj* — **swing-er** *n*

swipe \'swīp\ *n* : strong sweeping blow ∼ *vb* **swip·ing 1** : strike or wipe with a sweeping motion **2** : steal esp. with a quick movement

swirl \'swərl\ *vb* : move or cause to move in a circle — **swirl** *n*

swish \'swish\ *n* : hissing, sweeping, or brushing sound — **swish** *vb*

switch \'swich\ *n* **1** : slender flexible whip or twig **2** : blow with a switch **3** : shift, change, or reversal **4** : device that opens or closes an electrical circuit ∼ *vb* **1** : punish or urge on with a switch **2** : change or reverse roles, positions, or subjects **3** : operate a switch

switch·board *n* : panel of switches to make and break telephone connections

swiv·el \'swivəl\ *vb* **-eled** *or* **-elled**; **-eling** *or* **-el·ling** : swing or turn on a pivot — **swivel** *n*

swollen *past part of* SWELL

swoon \'swün\ *n* : faint — **swoon** *vb*

swoop \'swüp\ *vb* : make a swift diving attack — **swoop** *n*

sword \'sord\ *n* : thrusting or cutting weapon with a long blade

sword·fish *n* : large ocean fish with a long swordlike projection

swore *past of* SWEAR

sworn *past part of* SWEAR

swum *past part of* SWIM

swung *past of* SWING

sycamore 398 syringe

syc·a·more \'sikə₁mōr\ *n* : shade tree

sy·co·phant \'sikəfənt\ *n* : servile flatterer — **syc·o·phan·tic** \₁sikə-'fantik\ *adj*

syl·la·ble \'siləbəl\ *n* : unit of a spoken word — **syl·lab·ic** \sə'labik\ *adj*

syl·la·bus \'siləbəs\ *n, pl* **-bi** \-₁bī\ *or* **-bus·es** : summary of main topics (as of a course of study)

syl·van \'silvən\ *adj* 1 : living or located in a wooded area 2 : abounding in woods

sym·bol \'simbəl\ *n* : something that represents or suggests another thing — **sym·bol·ic** \sim'bälik\ *adj* — **sym·bol·i·cal·ly** *adv*

sym·bol·ism \'simbə₁lizəm\ *n* : representation of meanings with symbols

sym·bol·ize \'simbə₁līz\ *vb* **-ized; -izing** : serve as a symbol of — **sym·bol·i·za·tion** \₁simbələ'zā-shən\ *n*

sym·me·try \'simətrē\ *n, pl* **-tries** : regularity and balance in the arrangement of parts — **sym·met·ri·cal** \sə'metrikəl\ *adj* — **sym·met·ri·cal·ly** *adv*

sym·pa·thize \'simpə₁thīz\ *vb* **-thized; -thiz·ing** : feel or show sympathy — **sym·pa·thiz·er** *n*

sym·pa·thy \'simpəthē\ *n, pl* **-thies** 1 : ability to understand or share the feelings of another 2 : expression of sorrow for another's misfortune — **sym·pa·thet·ic** \₁simpə-'thetik\ *adj* — **sym·pa·thet·i·cal·ly** *adv*

sym·pho·ny \'simfənē\ *n, pl* **-nies** : composition for an orchestra or the orchestra itself — **sym·phon·ic** \sim'fänik\ *adj*

sym·po·sium \sim'pōzēəm\ *n, pl* **-sia** \-zēə\ *or* **-siums** : conference at which a topic is discussed

symp·tom \'simptəm\ *n* : unusual feeling or reaction that is a sign of disease — **symp·tom·at·ic** \₁simp-tə'matik\ *adj*

syn·a·gogue, syn·a·gog \'sinə-₁gäg, -₁góg\ *n* : Jewish house of worship

♦ **syn·chro·nize** \'siŋkrə₁nīz, 'sin-\ *vb* **-nized; -niz·ing** 1 : occur or cause to occur at the same instant 2 : cause to agree in time — **syn·chro·ni·za·tion** \₁siŋkrənə'zāshən, ₁sin-\ *n*

syn·co·pa·tion \₁siŋkə'pāshən, ₁sin-\ *n* : shifting of the regular musical accent to the weak beat — **syn·co·pate** \'siŋkə₁pāt, 'sin-\ *vb*

syn·di·cate \'sindikət\ *n* : business association ~ \-də₁kāt\ *vb* **-cated; -cat·ing** 1 : form a syndicate 2 : publish through a syndicate — **syn·di·ca·tion** \₁sində'kā-shən\ *n*

syn·drome \'sin₁drōm\ *n* : particular group of symptoms

syn·onym \'sinə₁nim\ *n* : word with the same meaning as another — **syn·on·y·mous** \sə'nänəməs\ *adj* — **syn·on·y·my** \-mē\ *n*

syn·op·sis \sə'näpsəs\ *n, pl* **-op·ses** \-₁sēz\ : condensed statement or outline

syn·tax \'sin₁taks\ *n* : way in which words are put together — **syn·tac·tic** \sin'taktik\ *or* **syn·tac·ti·cal** \-tikəl\ *adj*

syn·the·sis \'sinthəsəs\ *n, pl* **-the·ses** \-₁sēz\ : combination of parts or elements into a whole — **syn·the·size** \-₁sīz\ *vb*

syn·thet·ic \sin'thetik\ *adj* : artificially made — **synthetic** *n* — **syn·thet·i·cal·ly** *adv*

syph·i·lis \'sifələs\ *n* : venereal disease

sy·ringe \sə'rinj, 'sirinj\ *n* : plunger device for injecting or withdrawing liquids

syr·up \'sərəp, 'sirəp\ *n* : thick sticky sweet liquid — **syr·upy** *adj*

sys·tem \'sistəm\ *n* 1 : arrangement of units that function together 2 : regular order — **sys·tem·at·ic** \,sistə'matik\ *adj* — **sys·tem·at·i·cal·ly** *adv* — **sys·tem·a·tize** \'sistəmə,tīz\ *vb*

sys·tem·ic \sis'temik\ *adj* : relating to the whole body

T

t \'tē\ *n*, *pl* **t's** *or* **ts** \'tēz\ : 20th letter of the alphabet

tab \'tab\ *n* 1 : short projecting flap 2 *pl* : careful watch

tab·by \'tabē\ *n*, *pl* **-bies** : domestic cat

tab·er·na·cle \'tabər,nakəl\ *n* : house of worship

ta·ble \'tābəl\ *n* 1 : piece of furniture having a smooth slab fixed on legs 2 : supply of food 3 : arrangement of data in columns 4 : short list — **ta·ble·cloth** *n* — **ta·ble·top** *n* — **ta·ble·ware** *n* — **tab·u·lar** \'tabyələr\ *adj*

tab·leau \'tab,lō\ *n*, *pl* **-leaux** \-,lōz\ 1 : graphic description 2 : depiction of a scene by people in costume

ta·ble·spoon *n* 1 : large serving spoon 2 : measuring spoon holding ½ fluid ounce — **ta·ble·spoon·ful** \-,fúl\ *n*

tab·let \'tablət\ *n* 1 : flat slab suited for an inscription 2 : collection of sheets of paper glued together at one edge 3 : disk-shaped pill

tab·loid \'tab,lóid\ *n* : newspaper of small page size

ta·boo \tə'bü, ta-\ *adj* : banned esp. as immoral or dangerous — **taboo** *n or vb*

tab·u·late \'tabyə,lāt\ *vb* **-lat·ed; -lat·ing** : put in the form of a table — **tab·u·la·tion** \,tabyə'lāshən\ *n* — **tab·u·la·tor** \'tabyə,lātər\ *n*

tac·it \'tasət\ *adj* : implied but not expressed — **tac·it·ly** *adv* — **tac·it·ness** *n*

tac·i·turn \'tasə,tərn\ *adj* : not inclined to talk

tack \'tak\ *n* 1 : small sharp nail 2 : course of action ～ *vb* 1 : fasten with tacks 2 : add on

tack·le \'takəl, *naut often* 'tāk-\ *n* 1 : equipment 2 : arrangement of ropes and pulleys 3 : act of tackling ～ *vb* **-led; -ling** 1 : seize or throw down 2 : start dealing with

¹**tacky** \'takē\ *adj* **tack·i·er; -est** : sticky to the touch

²**tacky** *adj* **tack·i·er; -est** : cheap or gaudy

tact \'takt\ *n* : sense of the proper thing to say or do — **tact·ful** \-fəl\ *adj* — **tact·ful·ly** *adv* — **tact·less** *adj* — **tact·less·ly** *adv*

tac·tic \'taktik\ *n* : action as part of a plan

tac·tics \'taktiks\ *n sing or pl* 1 : science of maneuvering forces in combat 2 : skill of using available means to reach an end — **tac·ti·cal** \-tikəl\ *adj* — **tac·ti·cian** \tak'tishən\ *n*

tac·tile \'takt³l, -,tīl\ *adj* : relating to or perceptible through the sense of touch

tad·pole \'tad,pōl\ *n* : larval frog or toad with tail and gills

taf·fe·ta \'tafətə\ *n* : crisp lustrous fabric (as of silk)

taf·fy \'tafē\ *n*, *pl* **-fies** : candy stretched until porous

¹**tag** \'tag\ *n* : piece of hanging or attached material ～ *vb* **-gg-** 1 : provide or mark with a tag 2 : follow closely

²**tag** *n* : children's game of trying to catch one another ～ *vb* : touch a person in tag

tail \'tāl\ *n* 1 : rear end or a growth extending from the rear end of an animal 2 : back or last part 3 : the reverse of a coin ～ *vb* : follow — **tailed** \'tāld\ *adj* — **tail·less** *adj*

tail·gate \-,gāt\ *n* : hinged gate on the back of a vehicle that can be lowered for loading ～ *vb* **-gat-**

ed; -gat·ing : drive too close behind another vehicle

tail·light *n* : red warning light at the back of a vehicle

tai·lor \'tālər\ *n* : one who makes or alters garments ∼ *vb* **1 :** fashion or alter (clothes) **2 :** make or adapt for a special purpose

tail·spin *n* : spiral dive by an airplane

taint \'tānt\ *vb* : affect or become affected with something bad and esp. decay ∼ *n* : trace of decay or corruption

take \'tāk\ *vb* **took** \'tùk\; **tak·en** \'tākən\; **tak·ing 1 :** get into one's possession **2 :** become affected by **3 :** receive into one's body (as by eating) **4 :** pick out or remove **5 :** use for transportation **6 :** need or make use of **7 :** lead, carry, or cause to go to another place **8 :** undertake and do, make, or perform ∼ *n* : amount taken — **take·over** *n* — **tak·er** *n* — **take advantage of :** profit by — **take exception :** object — **take off** *vb* **1 :** remove **2 :** go away **3 :** mimic **4 :** begin flight — **take over** *vb* : assume control or possession of or responsibility for — **take place :** happen

take·off *n* : act or instance of taking off

talc \'talk\ *n* : soft mineral used in making toilet powder (**tal·cum powder** \'talkəm-\)

tale \'tāl\ *n* **1 :** story or anecdote **2 :** falsehood

tal·ent \'talənt\ *n* : natural mental or creative ability — **tal·ent·ed** *adj*

tal·is·man \'taləsmən, -əz-\ *n, pl* **-mans :** object thought to act as a charm

talk \'tòk\ *vb* **1 :** express one's thoughts in speech **2 :** discuss **3 :** influence to a position or course of action by talking ∼ *n* **1 :** act of talking **2 :** formal discussion **3 :** rumor **4 :** informal lecture — **talk·a·tive** \-ətiv\ *adj* — **talk·er** *n*

tall \'tòl\ *adj* : extending to a great or specified height — **tall·ness** *n*

tal·low \'talō\ *n* : hard white animal fat used esp. in candles

tal·ly \'talē\ *n, pl* **-lies :** recorded amount ∼ *vb* **-lied; -ly·ing 1 :** add or count up **2 :** match

tal·on \'talən\ *n* : bird's claw

tam \'tam\ *n* : tam-o'-shanter

tam·bou·rine \,tambə'rēn\ *n* : small drum with loose disks at the sides

tame \'tām\ *adj* **tam·er; tam·est 1 :** changed from being wild to being controllable by man **2 :** docile **3 :** dull ∼ *vb* **tamed; tam·ing :** make or become tame — **tam·able, tame·able** *adj* — **tame·ly** *adv* — **tam·er** *n*

tam-o'-shan·ter \'tamə,shantər\ *n* : Scottish woolen cap with a wide flat circular crown

tamp \'tamp\ *vb* : drive down or in by a series of light blows

tam·per \'tampər\ *vb* : interfere so as to change for the worse

tan \'tan\ *vb* **-nn- 1 :** change (hide) into leather esp. by soaking in a liquid containing tannin **2 :** make or become brown (as by exposure to the sun) ∼ *n* **1 :** brown skin color induced by the sun **2 :** light yellowish brown — **tan·ner** *n* — **tan·nery** \'tanərē\ *n*

tan·dem \'tandəm\ *adv* : one behind another

tang \'taŋ\ *n* : sharp distinctive flavor — **tangy** *adj*

tan·gent \'tanjənt\ *adj* : touching a curve or surface at only one point ∼ *n* **1 :** tangent line, curve, or surface **2 :** abrupt change of course — **tan·gen·tial** \tan'jenchəl\ *adj*

tan·ger·ine \'tanjə,rēn, ,tanjə'-\ *n* : deep orange citrus fruit

tan·gi·ble \'tanjəbəl\ *adj* **1 :** able to be touched **2 :** substantially real — **tan·gi·bly** *adv*

tan·gle \'taŋgəl\ *vb* **-gled; -gling :** unite in intricate confusion ∼ *n* : tangled twisted mass

tan·go \'taŋgō\ *n, pl* **-gos :** dance of Latin-American origin — **tango** *vb*

tank \'taŋk\ *n* **1 :** large artificial receptacle for liquids **2 :** armored military vehicle — **tank·ful** *n*

tan·kard \'taŋkərd\ *n* : tall one-handled drinking vessel

tank·er \'taŋkər\ *n* : vehicle or vessel with tanks for transporting a liquid

tan·nin \'tanən\ *n* : substance of plant origin used in tanning and dyeing

tan·ta·lize \'tant°l,īz\ *vb* **-lized; -liz·ing :** tease or torment by keeping something desirable just out of reach — **tan·ta·liz·er** *n* — **tan·ta·liz·ing·ly** *adv*

tan·ta·mount \'tantə,maunt\ *adj* : equivalent in value or meaning

♦ **tan·trum** \'tantrəm\ *n* : fit of bad temper

¹**tap** \'tap\ *n* 1 : faucet 2 : act of tapping ~ *vb* **-pp-** 1 : pierce so as to draw off fluid 2 : connect into — **tap·per** *n*

²**tap** *vb* **-pp-** : rap lightly ~ *n* : light stroke or its sound

tape \'tāp\ *n* 1 : narrow flexible strip (as of cloth, plastic, or metal) 2 : tape measure ~ *vb* **taped; tap·ing** 1 : fasten with tape 2 : record on tape

tape measure *n* : strip of tape marked in units for use in measuring

ta·per \'tāpər\ *n* 1 : slender wax candle 2 : gradual lessening of width in a long object ~ *vb* 1 : make or become smaller toward one end 2 : diminish gradually

tap·es·try \'tapəstrē\ *n, pl* **-tries** : heavy handwoven ruglike wall hanging

tape·worm *n* : long flat intestinal worm

tap·i·o·ca \,tapē'ōkə\ *n* : a granular starch used esp. in puddings

tar \'tär\ *n* : thick dark sticky liquid distilled (as from coal) ~ *vb* **-rr-** : treat or smear with tar

ta·ran·tu·la \tə'ranchələ, -'rant°lə\ *n* : large hairy usu. harmless spider

tar·dy \'tärdē\ *adj* **-di·er; -est** : late — **tar·di·ly** \'tärd°lē\ *adv* — **tar·di·ness** *n*

tar·get \'tärgət\ *n* 1 : mark to shoot at 2 : goal to be achieved ~ *vb* 1 : make a target of 2 : establish as a goal

tar·iff \'tarəf\ *n* 1 : duty or rate of duty imposed on imported goods 2 : schedule of tariffs, rates, or charges

tar·nish \'tärnish\ *vb* : make or become dull or discolored — **tarnish** *n*

tar·pau·lin \tär'póɫən, 'tärpə-\ *n* : waterproof protective covering

¹**tar·ry** \'tarē\ *vb* **-ried; -ry·ing** : be slow in leaving

²**tar·ry** \'tärē\ *adj* : resembling or covered with tar

¹**tart** \'tärt\ *adj* 1 : pleasantly sharp to the taste 2 : caustic — **tart·ly** *adv* — **tart·ness** *n*

²**tart** *n* : small pie

tar·tan \'tärt°n\ *n* : woolen fabric with a plaid design

tar·tar \'tärtər\ *n* : hard crust on the teeth

task \'task\ *n* : assigned work

task·mas·ter *n* : one that burdens another with labor

tas·sel \'tasəl, 'täs-\ *n* : hanging ornament made of a bunch of cords fastened at one end

taste \'tāst\ *vb* **tast·ed; tast·ing** 1 : test or determine the flavor of 2 : eat or drink in small quantities 3 : have a specific flavor ~ *n* 1 : small amount tasted 2 : bit 3 : special sense that identifies sweet, sour, bitter, or salty qualities 4 : individual preference 5 : critical appreciation of quality — **taste·ful** \-fəl\ *adj* — **taste·ful·ly** *adv* — **taste·less** *adj* — **taste·less·ly** *adv* — **tast·er** *n*

tasty \'tāstē\ *adj* **tast·i·er; -est** : pleasing to the sense of taste — **tast·i·ness** *n*

tat·ter \'tatər\ *n* 1 : part torn and left hanging 2 *pl* : tattered clothing ~ *vb* : make or become ragged

tat·tle \'tat°l\ *vb* **-tled; -tling** : inform on someone — **tat·tler** *n*

tat·tle·tale *n* : one that tattles

tat·too \ta'tü\ *vb* : mark the skin with indelible designs or figures — **tattoo** *n*

taught *past of* TEACH

taunt \'tȯnt\ *n* : sarcastic challenge or insult — **taunt** *vb* — **taunt·er** *n*

taut \'tȯt\ *adj* : tightly drawn — **taut·ly** *adv* — **taut·ness** *n*

tav·ern \'tavərn\ *n* : establishment where liquors are sold to be drunk on the premises

taw·dry \'tȯdrē\ *adj* **-dri·er; -est** : cheap and gaudy — **taw·dri·ly** \'tȯdrəlē\ *adv*

taw·ny \'tȯnē\ *adj* **-ni·er; -est** : brownish orange

tax \'taks\ *vb* **1** : impose a tax on **2** : charge **3** : put under stress ~ *n* **1** : charge by authority for public purposes **2** : strain — **tax·able** *adj* — **tax·a·tion** \tak'sāshən\ *n* — **tax·pay·er** *n* — **tax·pay·ing** *adj*

taxi \'taksē\ *n, pl* **tax·is** \-sēz\ : automobile transporting passengers for a fare ~ *vb* **tax·ied; taxi·ing** *or* **taxy·ing; tax·is** *or* **tax·ies 1** : transport or go by taxi **2** : move along the ground before takeoff or after landing

taxi·cab \'taksē,kab\ *n* : taxi

taxi·der·my \'taksə,dərmē\ *n* : skill or job of stuffing and mounting animal skins — **taxi·der·mist** \-mist\ *n*

tea \'tē\ *n* : cured leaves of an oriental shrub or a drink made from these — **tea·cup** *n* — **tea·pot** *n*

teach \'tēch\ *vb* **taught** \'tȯt\; **teaching 1** : tell or show the fundamentals or skills of something **2** : cause to know the consequences **3** : impart knowledge of — **teach·able** *adj* — **teach·er** *n* — **teach·ing** *n*

teak \'tēk\ *n* : East Indian timber tree or its wood

tea·ket·tle \'tē,ket°l\ *n* : covered kettle with a handle and spout for boiling water

teal \'tēl\ *n, pl* **teal** *or* **teals** : small short-necked wild duck

team \'tēm\ *n* **1** : draft animals harnessed together **2** : number of people organized for a game or work ~ *vb* : form or work together as a team — **team** *adj* — **team·mate** *n* — **team·work** *n*

team·ster \'tēmstər\ *n* **1** : one that

drives a team of animals **2** : one that drives a truck

¹tear \'tir\ *n* : drop of salty liquid that moistens the eye — **tear·ful** \-fəl\ *adj* — **tear·ful·ly** *adv*

²tear \'tar\ *vb* **tore** \'tōr\; **torn** \'tōrn\; **tear·ing 1** : separate or pull apart by force **2** : move or act with violence or haste ~ *n* : act or result of tearing

tease \'tēz\ *vb* **teased; teas·ing** : annoy by goading, coaxing, or tantalizing ~ *n* **1** : act of teasing or state of being teased **2** : one that teases

tea·spoon \'tē,spün\ *n* **1** : small spoon for stirring or sipping **2** : measuring spoon holding ⅙ fluid ounce — **tea·spoon·ful** \-,fůl\ *n*

teat \'tēt\ *n* : protuberance through which milk is drawn from an udder or breast

tech·ni·cal \'teknikəl\ *adj* **1** : having or relating to special mechanical or scientific knowledge **2** : by strict interpretation of rules — **tech·ni·cal·ly** *adv*

tech·ni·cal·i·ty \,teknə'kalətē\ *n, pl* **-ties** : detail meaningful only to a specialist

technical sergeant *n* : noncommissioned officer in the air force ranking next below a master sergeant

tech·ni·cian \tek'nishən\ *n* : person with the technique of a specialized skill

tech·nique \tek'nēk\ *n* : manner of accomplishing something

tech·nol·o·gy \tek'näləjē\ *n, pl* **-gies** : applied science — **tech·no·log·i·cal** \,teknə'läjikəl\ *adj*

te·dious \'tēdēəs\ *adj* : wearisome from length or dullness — **te·dious·ly** *adv* — **te·dious·ness** *n*

te·di·um \'tēdēəm\ *n* : tedious state or quality

tee \'tē\ *n* : mound or peg on which a golf ball is placed before beginning play — **tee** *vb*

teem \'tēm\ *vb* : become filled to overflowing

teen·age \'tēn,āj\ *or* **teen·aged** \-,ājd\ *adj* : relating to people in their teens — **teen·ag·er** \-,ājər\ *n*

teens \'tēnz\ *n pl* : years 13 to 19 in a person's life

tee·pee *var of* TEPEE

tee·ter \'tētər\ *vb* 1 : move unsteadily 2 : seesaw — **teeter** *n*

teeth *pl of* TOOTH

teethe \'tēth\ *vb* **teethed; teething** : grow teeth

tele·cast \'teli,kast\ *vb* **-cast; -casting** : broadcast by television — **telecast** *n* — **tele·cast·er** *n*

tele·com·mu·ni·ca·tion \'teləkə-myünə'kāshən\ *n* : communication at a distance (as by radio or telephone)

tele·gram \'telə,gram\ *n* : message sent by telegraph

tele·graph \-,graf \ *n* : system for communication by electrical transmission of coded signals ~ *vb* : send by telegraph — **te·leg·ra·pher** \tə'legrəfər\ *n* — **telegraph·ic** \,telə'grafik\ *adj*

te·lep·a·thy \tə'lepəthē\ *n* : apparent communication without known sensory means — **tele·path·ic** \,telə'pathik\ *adj* — **tele·path·i·cal·ly** *adv*

◆ **tele·phone** \'telə,fōn\ *n* : instrument or system for electrical transmission of spoken words ~ *vb* **-phoned; -phon·ing** : communicate with by telephone — **tele·phon·er** *n*

tele·scope \-,skōp\ *n* : tube-shaped optical instrument for viewing distant objects ~ *vb* **-scoped; -scop·ing** : slide or cause to slide inside another similar section — **tele·scop·ic** \,telə'skäpik\ *adj*

tele·vise \'telə,vīz\ *vb* **-vised; -vis·ing** : broadcast by television

tele·vi·sion \-,vizhən\ *n* : transmission and reproduction of images by radio waves

tell \'tel\ *vb* **told** \'tōld\; **tell·ing** 1 : count 2 : relate in detail 3 : reveal 4 : give information or an order to 5 : find out by observing

tell·er \'telər\ *n* 1 : one that relates or counts 2 : bank employee handling money

te·mer·i·ty \tə'merətē\ *n, pl* **-ties** : boldness

temp \'temp\ *n* 1 : temperature 2 : temporary worker

tem·per \'tempər\ *vb* 1 : dilute or soften 2 : toughen ~ *n* 1 : characteristic attitude or feeling 2 : toughness 3 : disposition or control over one's emotions

tem·per·a·ment \'tempərəmənt\ *n* : characteristic frame of mind — **tem·per·a·men·tal** \,temprə-'ment²l\ *adj*

tem·per·ance \'temprəns\ *n* : moderation in or abstinence from indulgence and esp. the use of intoxicating drink

tem·per·ate \'tempərət\ *adj* : moderate

tem·per·a·ture \'tempər,chùr, -prə-,chùr, -chər\ *n* 1 : degree of hotness or coldness 2 : fever

tem·pest \'tempəst\ *n* : violent storm — **tem·pes·tu·ous** \tem-'peschəwəs\ *adj*

¹**tem·ple** \'tempəl\ *n* : place of worship

²**temple** *n* : flattened space on each side of the forehead

tem·po \'tempō\ *n, pl* **-pi** \-,pē\ *or* **-pos** : rate of speed

tem·po·ral \'tempərəl\ *adj* : relating to time or to secular concerns

tem·po·rary \'tempə,rerē\ *adj* : lasting for a short time only — **tem·po·rar·i·ly** \,tempə'rerəlē\ *adv*

tempt \'tempt\ *vb* 1 : coax or persuade to do wrong 2 : attract or provoke — **tempt·er** *n* — **tempt·ing·ly** *adv* — **tempt·ress** \'temptrəs\ *n*

temp·ta·tion \temp'tāshən\ *n* 1 : act of tempting 2 : something that tempts

ten \'ten\ *n* 1 : one more than 9 2

: 10th in a set or series **3** : thing having 10 units — **ten** *adj or pron* — **tenth** \'tenth\ *adj or adv or n*

ten·a·ble \'tenəbəl\ *adj* : capable of being held or defended — **ten·a·bil·i·ty** \ˌtenə'bilətē\ *n*

te·na·cious \tə'nāshəs\ *adj* **1** : holding fast **2** : retentive — **te·na·cious·ly** *adv* — **te·nac·i·ty** \tə-'nasətē\ *n*

ten·ant \'tenənt\ *n* : one who occupies a rented dwelling — **ten·an·cy** \-ənsē\ *n*

¹tend \'tend\ *vb* : take care of or supervise something

²tend *vb* **1** : move in a particular direction **2** : show a tendency

ten·den·cy \'tendənsē\ *n, pl* **-cies** : likelihood to move, think, or act in a particular way

¹ten·der \'tendər\ *adj* **1** : soft or delicate **2** : expressing or responsive to love or sympathy **3** : sensitive (as to touch) — **ten·der·ly** *adv* — **ten·der·ness** *n*

²tend·er \'tendər\ *n* **1** : one that tends **2** : boat providing transport to a larger ship **3** : vehicle attached to a steam locomotive for carrying fuel and water

³ten·der *n* **1** : offer of a bid for a contract **2** : something that may be offered in payment — **tender** *vb*

ten·der·ize \'tendəˌrīz\ *vb* **-ized; -izing** : make (meat) tender — **ten·der·iz·er** \'tendəˌrīzər\ *n*

ten·der·loin \'tendərˌlȯin\ *n* : tender beef or pork strip from near the backbone

ten·don \'tendən\ *n* : cord of tissue attaching muscle to bone — **ten·di·nous** \-dənəs\ *adj*

ten·dril \'tendrəl\ *n* : slender coiling growth of some climbing plants

ten·e·ment \'tenəmənt\ *n* **1** : house divided into apartments **2** : shabby dwelling

te·net \'tenət\ *n* : principle of belief

ten·nis \'tenəs\ *n* : racket-and-ball game played across a net

ten·or \'tenər\ *n* **1** : general drift or meaning **2** : highest natural adult male voice

ten·pin \'tenˌpin\ *n* : bottle-shaped pin bowled at in a game (**tenpins**)

¹tense \'tens\ *n* : distinct verb form that indicates time

²tense *adj* **tens·er; tens·est** **1** : stretched tight **2** : marked by

nervous tension — **tense** *vb* — **tense·ly** *adv* — **tense·ness** *n* — **ten·si·ty** \'tensətē\ *n*

ten·sile \'tensəl, -ˌsīl\ *adj* : relating to tension

ten·sion \'tenchən\ *n* **1** : tense condition **2** : state of mental unrest or of potential hostility or opposition

tent \'tent\ *n* : collapsible shelter

ten·ta·cle \'tentikəl\ *n* : long flexible projection of an insect or mollusk — **ten·ta·cled** \-kəld\ *adj* — **ten·tac·u·lar** \ten'takyələr\ *adj*

ten·ta·tive \'tentətiv\ *adj* : subject to change or discussion — **ten·ta·tive·ly** *adv*

ten·u·ous \'tenyəwəs\ *adj* **1** : not dense or thick **2** : flimsy or weak — **ten·u·ous·ly** *adv* — **ten·u·ous·ness** *n*

ten·ure \'tenyər\ *n* : act, right, manner, or period of holding something — **ten·ured** \-yərd\ *adj*

te·pee \'tēˌpē\ *n* : conical tent

tep·id \'tepəd\ *adj* : moderately warm

term \'tərm\ *n* **1** : period of time **2** : mathematical expression **3** : special word or phrase **4** *pl* : conditions **5** *pl* : relations ∼ *vb* : name

ter·mi·nal \'tərmənᵊl\ *n* **1** : end **2** : device for making an electrical connection **3** : station at end of a transportation line — **terminal** *adj*

ter·mi·nate \'tərməˌnāt\ *vb* **-nat·ed; -nat·ing** : bring or come to an end — **ter·mi·na·ble** \-nəbəl\ *adj* — **ter·mi·na·tion** \ˌtərmə'nāshən\ *n*

ter·mi·nol·o·gy \ˌtərmə'näləjē\ *n* : terms used in a particular subject

ter·mi·nus \'tərmənəs\ *n, pl* **-ni** \-ˌnī\ *or* **-nus·es 1** : end **2** : end of a transportation line

ter·mite \'tərˌmīt\ *n* : wood-eating insect

tern \'tərn\ *n* : small sea bird

ter·race \'terəs\ *n* **1** : balcony or patio **2** : bank with a flat top ∼ *vb* **-raced; -rac·ing** : landscape in a series of banks

ter·ra-cot·ta \ˌterə'kätə\ *n* : reddish brown earthenware

ter·rain \tə'rān\ *n* : features of the land

ter·ra·pin \'terəpən\ *n* : No. American turtle

ter·rar·i·um \tə'rareəm\ *n, pl* **-ia**

\-ēə\ *or* -i·ums : container for keeping plants or animals

ter·res·tri·al \tə'restrēəl\ *adj* 1 : relating to the earth or its inhabitants 2 : living or growing on land

ter·ri·ble \'terəbəl\ *adj* 1 : exciting terror 2 : distressing 3 : intense 4 : of very poor quality — ter·ri·bly \-blē\ *adv*

ter·ri·er \'terēər\ *n* : small dog

ter·rif·ic \tə'rifik\ *adj* 1 : exciting terror 2 : extraordinary

ter·ri·fy \'terə,fī\ *vb* -fied; -fy·ing : fill with terror — ter·ri·fy·ing·ly *adv*

ter·ri·to·ry \'terə,tōrē\ *n, pl* -ries : particular geographical region — ter·ri·to·ri·al \,terə'tōrēəl\ *adj*

ter·ror \'terər\ *n* : intense fear and panic or a cause of it

ter·ror·ism \-,izəm\ *n* : systematic covert warfare to produce terror for political coercion — ter·ror·ist \-ist\ *adj or n*

ter·ror·ize \-,īz\ *vb* -ized; -iz·ing 1 : fill with terror 2 : coerce by threat or violence

ter·ry \'terē\ *n, pl* -ries : absorbent fabric with a loose pile

terse \'tərs\ *adj* ters·er; ters·est : concise — terse·ly *adv* — terse·ness *n*

ter·tia·ry \'tərshē,erē\ *adj* : of 3d rank, importance, or value

test \'test\ *n* : examination or evaluation ~ *vb* : examine by a test — test·er *n*

tes·ta·ment \'testəmənt\ *n* 1 *cap* : division of the Bible 2 : will — tes·ta·men·ta·ry \,testə'mentərē\ *adj*

tes·ti·cle \'testikəl\ *n* : testis

tes·ti·fy \'testə,fī\ *vb* -fied; -fy·ing 1 : give testimony 2 : serve as evidence

tes·ti·mo·ni·al \,testə'mōnēəl\ *n* 1 : favorable recommendation 2 : tribute — testimonial *adj*

tes·ti·mo·ny \'testə,mōnē\ *n, pl* -nies : statement given as evidence in court

tes·tis \'testəs\ *n, pl* -tes \-,tēz\ : male reproductive gland

tes·ty \'testē\ *adj* -ti·er; -est : easily annoyed

tet·a·nus \'tet³nəs\ *n* : bacterial disease producing violent spasms

tête–à–tête \,tātə'tāt\ *adv* : privately ~ *n* : private conversation ~ *adj* : private

teth·er \'tethər\ *n* : leash ~ *vb* : restrain with a leash

text \'tekst\ *n* 1 : author's words 2 : main body of printed or written matter on a page 3 : textbook 4 : scriptural passage used as the theme of a sermon 5 : topic — tex·tu·al \'tekschəwəl\ *adj*

text·book \-,bůk\ *n* : book on a school subject

tex·tile \'tek,stīl, 'tekst³l\ *n* : fabric

tex·ture \'tekschər\ *n* 1 : feel and appearance of something 2 : structure

than \'than\ *conj or prep* — used in comparisons

thank \'thaŋk\ *vb* : express gratitude to

♦ thank·ful \-fəl\ *adj* : giving thanks — thank·ful·ly *adv* — thank·ful·ness *n*

thank·less *adj* : not appreciated

thanks \'thaŋks\ *n pl* : expression of gratitude

Thanks·giv·ing \thaŋks'giviŋ\ *n* : 4th Thursday in November observed as a legal holiday for giving thanks for divine goodness

that \'that\ *pron, pl* those \'thōz\ 1 : something indicated or understood 2 : the one farther away ~ *adj, pl* those : being the one mentioned or understood or farther away ~ *conj or pron* — used to in-

troduce a clause ~ *adv* : to such an extent

thatch \'thach\ *vb* : cover with thatch ~ *n* : covering of matted straw

thaw \'thȯ\ *vb* : melt or cause to melt — **thaw** *n*

the \thə, *before vowel sounds usu* thē\ *definite article* : that particular one ~ *adv* — used before a comparative or superlative

the·ater, the·atre \'thēətər\ *n* **1** : building or room for viewing a play or movie **2** : dramatic arts

the·at·ri·cal \thē'atrikəl\ *adj* **1** : relating to the theater **2** : involving exaggerated emotion

thee \'thē\ *pron, archaic objective case of* THOU

theft \'theft\ *n* : act of stealing

their \'ther\ *adj* : relating to them

theirs \'theərz\ *pron* : their one or ones

the·ism \'thē,izəm\ *n* : belief in the existence of a god or gods — **the·ist** \-ist\ *n or adj* — **the·is·tic** \thē-'istik\ *adj*

them \'them\ *pron, objective case of* THEY

theme \'thēm\ *n* **1** : subject matter **2** : essay **3** : melody developed in a piece of music — **the·mat·ic** \thi-'matik\ *adj*

them·selves \thəm'selvz, them-\ *pron pl* : they, them — used reflexively or for emphasis

then \'then\ *adv* **1** : at that time **2** : soon after that **3** : in addition **4** : in that case **5** : consequently ~ *n* : that time ~ *adj* : existing at that time

thence \'thens, 'thens\ *adv* : from that place or fact

the·oc·ra·cy \thē'äkrəsē\ *n, pl* -cies : government by officials regarded as divinely inspired — **the·o·crat·ic** \,thēə'kratik\ *adj*

the·ol·o·gy \thē'äləjē\ *n, pl* -gies : study of religion — **the·o·lo·gian** \,thēə'lōjən\ *n* — **the·o·log·i·cal** \-'läjikəl\ *adj*

the·o·rem \'thēərəm, 'thirəm\ *n* : provable statement of truth

the·o·ret·i·cal \,thēə'retikəl\ *adj* : relating to or being theory — **the·o·ret·i·cal·ly** *adv*

the·o·rize \'thēə,rīz\ *vb* -rized; -riz-

ing : put forth theories — **the·o·rist** *n*

the·o·ry \'thēərē, 'thirē\ *n, pl* -ries **1** : general principles of a subject **2** : plausible or scientifically acceptable explanation **3** : judgment, guess, or opinion

ther·a·peu·tic \,therə'pyütik\ *adj* : offering or relating to remedy — **ther·a·peu·ti·cal·ly** *adv*

ther·a·py \'therəpē\ *n, pl* -pies : treatment for mental or physical disorder — **ther·a·pist** \-pist\ *n*

there \'thar\ *adv* **1** : in, at, or to that place **2** : in that respect ~ *pron* — used to introduce a sentence or clause ~ *n* : that place or point

there·abouts, there·about \,thara-'bauts, 'thara,-, -'baut\ *adv* : near that place, time, number, or quantity

there·af·ter \thar'aftər\ *adv* : after that

there·by \thar'bī, 'thar,bī\ *adv* **1** : by that **2** : connected with or with reference to that

there·fore \'thar,fōr\ *adv* : for that reason

there·in \thar'in\ *adv* **1** : in or into that place, time, or thing **2** : in that respect

there·of \-'əv, -'äv\ *adv* **1** : of that or it **2** : from that

there·upon \'thara,pȯn, -,pän; ,thara'pȯn, -'pän\ *adv* **1** : on that matter **2** : therefore **3** : immediately after that

there·with \thar'with, -'with\ *adv* : with that

ther·mal \'thərməl\ *adj* : relating to, caused by, or conserving heat — **ther·mal·ly** *adv*

ther·mo·dy·nam·ics \,thərmədī-'namiks\ *n* : physics of heat

ther·mom·e·ter \thər'mämətər\ *n* : instrument for measuring temperature — **ther·mo·met·ric** \,thərmə'metrik\ *adj* — **ther·mo·met·ri·cal·ly** *adv*

ther·mos \'thərməs\ *n* : double-walled bottle used to keep liquids hot or cold

ther·mo·stat \'thərmə,stat\ *n* : automatic temperature control — **ther·mo·stat·ic** \,thərmə'statik\ *adj* — **ther·mo·stat·i·cal·ly** *adv*

the·sau·rus \thi'sȯrəs\ *n, pl* -sau·ri \-'sȯr,ī\ *or* -sau·rus·es

\-'sȯrəsəz\ : book of words and esp. synonyms

these pl of THIS

the·sis \'thēsəs\ n, pl **the·ses** \'thē-ˌsēz\ **1** : proposition to be argued for **2** : essay embodying results of original research

thes·pi·an \'thespēən\ adj : dramatic ~ n : actor

they \'thā\ pron **1** : those ones **2** : people in general

thi·a·mine \'thīəmən, -ˌmēn\ n : essential vitamin

thick \'thik\ adj **1** : having relatively great mass from front to back or top to bottom **2** : viscous ~ n : most crowded or thickest part — **thick·ly** adv — **thick·ness** n

thick·en \'thikən\ vb : make or become thick — **thick·en·er** \-ənər\ n

thick·et \'thikət\ n : dense growth of bushes or small trees

thick–skinned \-'skind\ adj : insensitive to criticism

thief \'thēf\ n, pl **thieves** \'thēvz\ : one that steals

thieve \'thēv\ vb **thieved; thieving** : steal — **thiev·ery** n

thigh \'thī\ n : upper part of the leg

thigh·bone \'thīˌbōn\ n : femur

thim·ble \'thimbəl\ n : protective cap for the finger in sewing — **thim·ble·ful** n

thin \'thin\ adj **-nn- 1** : having relatively little mass from front to back or top to bottom **2** : not closely set or placed **3** : relatively free flowing **4** : lacking substance, fullness, or strength ~ vb **-nn-** : make or become thin — **thin·ly** adv — **thin·ness** n

thing \'thiŋ\ n **1** : matter of concern **2** : event or act **3** : object **4** pl : possessions

think \'thiŋk\ vb **thought** \'thȯt\; **think·ing 1** : form or have in the mind **2** : have as an opinion **3** : ponder **4** : devise by thinking **5** : imagine — **think·er** n

thin–skinned adj : extremely sensitive to criticism

third \'thərd\ adj : being number 3 in a countable series ~ n **1** : one that is third **2** : one of 3 equal parts — **third, third·ly** adv

third dimension n : thickness or depth — **third–dimensional** adj

third world n : less developed nations of the world

thirst \'thərst\ n **1** : dryness in mouth and throat **2** : intense desire ~ vb : feel thirst — **thirsty** adj

thir·teen \ˌthər'tēn\ n : one more than 12 — **thirteen** adj or pron — **thir·teenth** \-'tēnth\ adj or n

thir·ty \'thərtē\ n, pl **thirties** : 3 times 10 — **thir·ti·eth** \-ēəth\ adj or n — **thirty** adj or pron

this \'this\ pron, pl **these** \'thēz\ : something close or under immediate discussion ~ adj, pl **these** : being the one near, present, just mentioned, or more immediately under observation ~ adv : to such an extent or degree

this·tle \'thisəl\ n : tall prickly herb

thith·er \'thithər\ adv : to that place

thong \'thȯŋ\ n : strip of leather or hide

tho·rax \'thōrˌaks\ n, pl **-rax·es** or **-races** \'thōrəˌsēz\ **1** : part of the body between neck and abdomen **2** : middle of 3 divisions of an insect body — **tho·rac·ic** \thə-'rasik\ adj

thorn \'thȯrn\ n : sharp spike on a plant or a plant bearing these — **thorny** adj

thor·ough \'thərō\ adj : omitting or overlooking nothing — **thor·ough·ly** adv — **thor·ough·ness** n

thor·ough·bred \'thərəˌbred\ n **1** cap : light speedy racing horse **2** : one of excellent quality — **thoroughbred** adj

thor·ough·fare \'thərəˌfar\ n : public road

those pl of THAT

thou \'thau̇\ pron, archaic : you

though \'thō\ adv : however ~ conj **1** : despite the fact that **2** : granting that

thought \'thȯt\ past of THINK ~ n **1** : process of thinking **2** : serious consideration **3** : idea

thought·ful \-fəl\ adj **1** : absorbed in or showing thought **2** : considerate of others — **thought·ful·ly** adv — **thought·ful·ness** n

thought·less \-ləs\ adj **1** : careless or reckless **2** : lacking concern for others — **thought·less·ly** adv

thou·sand \'thau̇zənd\ n, pl **-sands** or **-sand** : 10 times 100 — **thousand** adj — **thou·sandth** \-ᵊnth\ adj or n

thrash \'thrash\ *vb* **1** : thresh **2** : beat **3** : move about violently — **thrash·er** *n*

thread \'thred\ *n* **1** : fine line of fibers **2** : train of thought **3** : ridge around a screw ∼ *vb* **1** : pass thread through **2** : put together on a thread **3** : make one's way through or between

thread·bare *adj* **1** : worn so that the thread shows **2** : trite

threat \'thret\ *n* **1** : expression of intention to harm **2** : thing that threatens

threat·en \'thretᵊn\ *vb* **1** : utter threats **2** : show signs of being near or impending — **threat·en·ing·ly** *adv*

three \'thrē\ *n* **1** : one more than 2 **2** : 3d in a set or series — **three** *adj or pron*

three·fold \'thrē,fōld\ *adj* : triple — **three·fold** \-'fōld\ *adv*

three·score *adj* : being 3 times 20

thresh \'thresh, 'thrash\ *vb* : beat to separate grain — **thresh·er** *n*

thresh·old \'thresh,ōld\ *n* **1** : sill of a door **2** : beginning stage

threw *past of* THROW

thrice \'thrīs\ *adv* : 3 times

thrift \'thrift\ *n* : careful management or saving of money — **thrift·i·ly** \'thriftəlē\ *adv* — **thrift·less** *adj* — **thrifty** *adj*

thrill \'thril\ *vb* **1** : have or cause to have a sudden sharp feeling of excitement **2** : tremble — **thrill** *n* — **thrill·er** *n* — **thrill·ing·ly** *adv*

thrive \'thrīv\ *vb* **throve** \'thrōv\ **thrived**; **thriv·en** \'thrivən\ **1** : grow vigorously **2** : prosper

throat \'thrōt\ *n* **1** : front part of the neck **2** : passage to the stomach — **throat·ed** *adj* — **throaty** *adj*

throb \'thräb\ *vb* **-bb-** : pulsate — **throb** *n*

throe \'thrō\ *n* **1** : pang or spasm **2** *pl* : hard or painful struggle

throne \'thrōn\ *n* : chair representing power or sovereignty

throng \'thröŋ\ *n or vb* : crowd

throt·tle \'thrätᵊl\ *vb* **-tled; -tling** : choke ∼ *n* : valve regulating volume of fuel and air delivered to engine cylinders

through \'thrü\ *prep* **1** : into at one side and out at the other side of **2** : by way of **3** : among, between, or all around **4** : because of **5** : throughout the time of ∼ \'thrü\ *adv* **1** : from one end or side to the other **2** : from beginning to end **3** : to the core **4** : into the open ∼ *adj* **1** : going directly from origin to destination **2** : finished

through·out \thrü'aut\ *adv* **1** : everywhere **2** : from beginning to end ∼ *prep* **1** : in or to every part of **2** : during the whole of

throve *past of* THRIVE

throw \'thrō\ *vb* **threw** \'thrü\; **thrown** \'thrōn\; **throw·ing 1** : propel through the air **2** : cause to fall or fall off **3** : put suddenly in a certain position or condition **4** : move quickly as if throwing **5** : put on or off hastily — **throw** *n* — **throw·er** \'thrōər\ *n* — **throw up** *vb* : vomit

thrush \'thrəsh\ *n* : songbird

thrust \'thrəst\ *vb* **thrust; thrusting 1** : shove forward **2** : stab or pierce — **thrust** *n*

thud \'thəd\ *n* : dull sound of something falling — **thud** *vb*

thug \'thəg\ *n* : ruffian or gangster

thumb \'thəm\ *n* **1** : short thick division of the hand opposing the fingers **2** : glove part for the thumb ∼ *vb* : leaf through with the thumb — **thumb·nail** *n*

thump \'thəmp\ *vb* : strike with something thick or heavy causing a dull sound — **thump** *n*

thun·der \'thəndər\ *n* : sound following lightning — **thunder** *vb* — **thun·der·clap** *n* — **thun·der·ous** \'thəndərəs\ *adj* — **thun·der·ous·ly** *adv*

thun·der·bolt \-,bōlt\ *n* : discharge of lightning with thunder

thun·der·show·er \'thəndər,shaüər\ *n* : shower with thunder and lightning

thun·der·storm *n* : storm with thunder and lightning

Thurs·day \'thərzdā, -dē\ *n* : 5th day of the week

thus \'thəs\ *adv* **1** : in this or that way **2** : to this degree or extent **3** : because of this or that

thwart \'thwórt\ *vb* : block or defeat

thy \'thī\ *adj, archaic* : your

thyme \'tīm, 'thīm\ *n* : cooking herb

thy·roid \'thī,róid\ *adj* : relating to a large endocrine gland (**thyroid gland**)

thy·self \thī'self\ *pron, archaic* : yourself

ti·ara \tē'arə, -'är-\ *n* : decorative formal headband

tib·ia \'tibēə\ *n, pl* **-i·ae** \-ē,ē\ : bone between the knee and ankle

tic \'tik\ *n* : twitching of facial muscles

♦ **¹tick** \'tik\ *n* : small 8-legged blood-sucking animal

²tick *n* **1** : light rhythmic tap or beat **2** : check mark ~ *vb* **1** : make ticks **2** : mark with a tick **3** : operate

tick·er \'tikər\ *n* **1** : something (as a watch) that ticks **2** : telegraph instrument that prints on paper tape

tick·et \'tikət\ *n* **1** : tag showing price, payment of a fee or fare, or a traffic offense **2** : list of candidates ~ *vb* : put a ticket on

tick·ing \'tikiŋ\ *n* : fabric covering of a mattress

tick·le \'tikəl\ *vb* **-led; -ling 1** : please or amuse **2** : touch lightly causing uneasiness, laughter, or spasmodic movements — **tickle** *n*

tick·lish \'tiklish\ *adj* **1** : sensitive to tickling **2** : requiring delicate handling — **tick·lish·ly** *adv* — **tick·lish·ness** *n*

tid·al wave \'tīdᵊl-\ *n* : high sea wave following an earthquake

tid·bit \'tid,bit\ *n* : choice morsel

tide \'tīd\ *n* : alternate rising and falling of the sea ~ *vb* **tid·ed; tid·ing** : be enough to allow (one) to get by for a time — **tid·al** \'tīdᵊl\ *adj* — **tide·wa·ter** *n*

tid·ings \'tīdiŋz\ *n pl* : news or message

ti·dy \'tīdē\ *adj* **-di·er; -est 1** : well ordered and cared for **2** : large or substantial — **ti·di·ness** *n* — **tidy** *vb*

tie \'tī\ *n* **1** : line or ribbon for fastening, uniting, or closing **2** : cross support to which railroad rails are fastened **3** : uniting force **4** : equality in score or tally or a deadlocked contest **5** : necktie ~ *vb* **tied; ty·ing** *or* **tie·ing 1** : fasten or close by wrapping and knotting a tie **2** : form a knot in **3** : gain the same score or tally as an opponent

tier \'tir\ *n* : one of a steplike series of rows

tiff \'tif\ *n* : petty quarrel — **tiff** *vb*

ti·ger \'tīgər\ *n* : very large black-striped cat — **ti·ger·ish** \-gərish\ *adj* — **ti·gress** \-grəs\ *n*

tight \'tīt\ *adj* **1** : fitting close together esp. so as not to allow air or water in **2** : held very firmly **3** : taut **4** : fitting too snugly **5** : difficult **6** : stingy **7** : evenly contested **8** : low in supply — **tight** *adv* — **tight·en** \-ᵊn\ *vb* — **tight·ly** *adv* — **tight·ness** *n*

tights \'tīts\ *n pl* : skintight garments

tight·wad \'tīt,wäd\ *n* : stingy person

tile \'tīl\ *n* : thin piece of stone or fired clay used on roofs, floors, or walls ~ *vb* : cover with tiles

¹till \'til\ *prep or conj* : until

²till *vb* : cultivate (soil) — **till·able** *adj*

³till *n* : money drawer

¹till·er \'tilər\ *n* : one that cultivates soil

²til·ler \'tilər\ *n* : lever for turning a boat's rudder

tilt \'tilt\ *vb* : cause to incline ~ *n* : slant

tim·ber \'timbər\ *n* **1** : cut wood for building **2** : large squared piece of wood **3** : wooded land or trees for timber ~ *vb* : cover, frame, or support with timbers — **tim·bered** *adj* — **tim·ber·land** \-,land\ *n*

tim·bre \'tambər, 'tim-\ *n* : sound quality

time \'tīm\ n 1 : period during which something exists or continues or can be accomplished 2 : point at which something happens 3 : customary hour 4 : age 5 : tempo 6 : moment, hour, day, or year as indicated by a clock or calendar 7 : one's experience during a particular period ~ vb timed; tim·ing 1 : arrange or set the time of 2 : determine or record the time, duration, or rate of — time·keep·er n — time·less adj — time·less·ness n — time·li·ness n — time·ly adv — tim·er n

time·piece n : device to show time

times \'tīmz\ prep : multiplied by

time·ta·ble \'tīm,tābəl\ n : table of departure and arrival times

tim·id \'timəd\ adj : lacking in courage or self-confidence — ti·mid·i·ty \tə'midətē\ n — tim·id·ly adv

tim·o·rous \'timərəs\ adj : fearful — tim·o·rous·ly adv — tim·o·rous·ness n

tim·pa·ni \'timpənē\ n pl : set of kettledrums — tim·pa·nist \-nist\ n

tin \'tin\ n 1 : soft white metallic chemical element 2 : metal food can

tinc·ture \'tiŋkchər\ n : alcoholic solution of a medicine

tin·der \'tindər\ n : substance used to kindle a fire

tine \'tīn\ n : one of the points of a fork

tin·foil \'tin,fȯil\ n : thin metal sheeting

tinge \'tinj\ vb tinged; tinge·ing or ting·ing \'tinjiŋ\ 1 : color slightly 2 : affect with a slight odor ~ n : slight coloring or flavor

tin·gle \'tiŋgəl\ vb -gled; -gling : feel a ringing, stinging, or thrilling sensation — tingle n

tin·ker \'tiŋkər\ vb : experiment in repairing something — tin·ker·er n

tin·kle \'tiŋkəl\ vb -kled; -kling : make or cause to make a high ringing sound — tinkle n

tin·sel \'tinsəl\ n : decorative thread or strip of glittering metal or paper

tint \'tint\ n 1 : slight or pale coloration 2 : color shade ~ vb : give a tint to

ti·ny \'tīnē\ adj -ni·er; -est : very small

¹tip \'tip\ vb -pp- 1 : overturn 2 : lean ~ n : act or state of tipping

²tip n : pointed end of something ~ vb -pp- 1 : furnish with a tip 2 : cover the tip of

³tip n : small sum given for a service performed ~ vb : give a tip to

⁴tip n : piece of confidential information ~ vb -pp- : give confidential information to

tip-off \'tip,ȯf\ n : indication

tip·ple \'tipəl\ vb -pled; -pling : drink intoxicating liquor esp. habitually or excessively — tip·pler n

tip·sy \'tipsē\ adj -si·er; -est : unsteady or foolish from alcohol

tip·toe \'tip,tō\ n : the toes of the feet ~ adv or adj : supported on tiptoe ~ vb -toed; -toe·ing : walk quietly or on tiptoe

tip-top n : highest point ~ adj : excellent

ti·rade \tī'rād, 'tī,-\ n : prolonged speech of abuse

¹tire \'tīr\ vb tired; tir·ing 1 : make or become weary 2 : wear out the patience of — tire·less adj — tire·less·ly adv — tire·less·ness n — tire·some \-səm\ adj — tire·some·ly adv — tire·some·ness n

²tire n : rubber cushion encircling a car wheel

tired \'tīrd\ adj : weary

◆ **tis·sue** \'tishü\ *n* **1** : soft absorbent paper **2** : layer of cells forming a basic structural element of an animal or plant body

ti·tan·ic \tī'tanik, tə-\ *adj* : gigantic

ti·ta·ni·um \tī'tānēəm, tə-\ *n* : gray light strong metallic chemical element

tithe \'tīth\ *n* : tenth part paid or given esp. for the support of a church — **tithe** *vb* — **tith·er** *n*

tit·il·late \'tit²l,āt\ *vb* -**lat·ed**; -**lat·ing** : excite pleasurably — **tit·il·la·tion** \,tit²l'āshən\ *n*

ti·tle \'tīt²l\ *n* **1** : legal ownership **2** : distinguishing name **3** : designation of honor, rank, or office **4** : championship — **ti·tled** *adj*

tit·ter \'titər\ *n* : nervous or affected laugh — **titter** *vb*

tit·u·lar \'tichələr\ *adj* **1** : existing in title only **2** : relating to or bearing a title

tiz·zy \'tizē\ *n, pl* **tizzies** : state of agitation or worry

TNT \,tē,en'tē\ *n* : high explosive

to \'tü\ *prep* **1** : in the direction of **2** : at, on, or near **3** : resulting in **4** : before or until **5** — used to show a relationship or object of a verb **6** — used with an infinitive ∼ *adv* **1** : forward **2** : to a state of consciousness

toad \'tōd\ *n* : tailless leaping amphibian

toad·stool \-,stül\ *n* : mushroom esp. when inedible or poisonous

toady \'tōdē\ *n, pl* **toad·ies** : one who flatters to gain favors — **toady** *vb*

toast \'tōst\ *vb* **1** : make (as a slice of bread) crisp and brown **2** : drink in honor of someone or something **3** : warm ∼ *n* **1** : toasted sliced bread **2** : act of drinking in honor of someone — **toast·er** *n*

to·bac·co \tə'bakō\ *n, pl* -**cos** : broad-leaved herb or its leaves prepared for smoking or chewing

to·bog·gan \tə'bägən\ *n* : long flat-bottomed light sled ∼ *vb* : coast on a toboggan

to·day \tə'dā\ *adv* **1** : on or for this day **2** : at the present time ∼ *n* : present day or time

tod·dle \'täd²l\ *vb* -**dled**; -**dling** : walk with tottering steps like a young child — **toddle** *n* — **tod·dler** \'täd²lər\ *n*

to–do \tə'dü\ *n, pl* **to–dos** \-'düz\ : disturbance or fuss

toe \'tō\ *n* : one of the 5 end divisions of the foot — **toe·nail** *n*

tof·fee, tof·fy \'tòfē, 'tä-\ *n, pl* **tof·fees** *or* **toffies** : candy made of boiled sugar and butter

to·ga \'tōgə\ *n* : loose outer garment of ancient Rome

to·geth·er \tə'gethər\ *adv* **1** : in or into one place or group **2** : in or into contact or association **3** : at one time **4** : as a group — **to·geth·er·ness** *n*

togs \'tägz, 'tògz\ *n pl* : clothing

toil \'tòil\ *vb* : work hard and long — **toil** *n* — **toil·er** *n* — **toil·some** *adj*

toi·let \'tòilət\ *n* **1** : dressing and grooming oneself **2** : bathroom **3** : water basin to urinate and defecate in

to·ken \'tōkən\ *n* **1** : outward sign or expression of something **2** : small part representing the whole **3** : piece resembling a coin

told *past of* TELL

tol·er·a·ble \'tälərəbəl\ *adj* **1** : capable of being endured **2** : moderately good — **tol·er·a·bly** \-blē\ *adv*

tol·er·ance \'tälərəns\ *n* **1** : lack of opposition for beliefs or practices differing from one's own **2** : capacity for enduring **3** : allowable deviation — **tol·er·ant** *adj* — **tol·er·ant·ly** *adv*

tol·er·ate \'tälə,rāt\ *vb* -**at·ed**; -**at·ing** **1** : allow to be or to be done without opposition **2** : endure or resist the action of — **tol·er·a·tion** \,tälə'rāshən\ *n*

¹**toll** \'tōl\ *n* **1** : fee paid for a privilege or service **2** : cost of achievement in loss or suffering — **toll·booth** *n* — **toll·gate** *n*

²**toll** *vb* **1** : cause the sounding of (a bell) **2** : sound with slow measured strokes ∼ *n* : sound of a tolling bell

tom·a·hawk \'tämə,hòk\ *n* : light ax used as a weapon by American Indians

to·ma·to \tə'mātō, -'mät-\ *n, pl* -**toes** : tropical American herb or its fruit

tomb \'tüm\ *n* : house, vault, or grave for burial

tom·boy \'täm,bòi\ *n* : girl who be-

haves in a manner usu. considered boyish

tomb·stone *n* : stone marking a grave

tom·cat \'täm,kat\ *n* : male cat

tome \'tōm\ *n* : large or weighty book

to·mor·row \tə'märō\ *adv* : on or for the day after today — **tomorrow** *n*

tom—tom \'täm,täm\ *n* : small-headed drum beaten with the hands

ton \'tən\ *n* : unit of weight equal to 2000 pounds

tone \'tōn\ *n* **1** : vocal or musical sound **2** : sound of definite pitch **3** : manner of speaking that expresses an emotion or attitude **4** : color quality **5** : healthy condition **6** : general character or quality ~ *vb* : soften or muffle — often used with *down* — **ton·al** \-ºl\ *adj* — **to·nal·i·ty** \tō'nalətē\ *n*

tongs \'tänz, 'tȯnz\ *n pl* : grasping device of 2 joined or hinged pieces

◆ **tongue** \'təŋ\ *n* **1** : fleshy movable organ of the mouth **2** : language **3** : something long and flat and fastened at one end — **tongued** \'təŋd\ *adj* — **tongue·less** *adj*

ton·ic \'tänik\ *n* : something (as a drug) that invigorates or restores health — **tonic** *adj*

to·night \tə'nīt\ *adv* : on this night ~ *n* : present or coming night

ton·sil \'tänsəl\ *n* : either of a pair of oval masses in the throat — **ton·sil·lec·to·my** \,tänsə'lektəmē\ *n* — **ton·sil·li·tis** \-'lītəs\ *n*

too \'tü\ *adv* **1** : in addition **2** : excessively

took *past of* TAKE

tool \'tül\ *n* : device worked by hand ~ *vb* : shape or finish with a tool

toot \'tüt\ *vb* : sound or cause to sound esp. in short blasts — **toot** *n*

tooth \'tüth\ *n, pl* **teeth** \'tēth\ **1** : one of the hard structures in the jaws for chewing **2** : one of the projections on the edge of a gear wheel — **tooth·ache** *n* — **tooth·brush** *n* — **toothed** \'tütht\ *adj* — **tooth·less** *adj* — **tooth·paste** *n* — **tooth·pick** *n*

tooth·some \'tüthsəm\ *adj* **1** : delicious **2** : attractive

¹top \'täp\ *n* **1** : highest part or level of something **2** : lid or covering ~ *vb* **-pp-** **1** : cover with a top **2** : surpass **3** : go over the top of ~ *adj* : being at the top — **topped** *adj*

²top *n* : spinning toy

to·paz \'tō,paz\ *n* : hard gem

top·coat *n* : lightweight overcoat

top·ic \'täpik\ *n* : subject for discussion or study

top·i·cal \-ikəl\ *adj* **1** : relating to or arranged by topics **2** : relating to current or local events — **top·i·cal·ly** *adv*

top·most \'täp,mōst\ *adj* : highest of all

top-notch \-'näch\ *adj* : of the highest quality

to·pog·ra·phy \tə'pägrəfē\ *n* **1** : art of mapping the physical features of a place **2** : outline of the form of a place — **to·pog·ra·pher** \-fər\ *n* — **top·o·graph·ic** \,täpə'grafik\, **top·o·graph·i·cal** \-ikəl\ *adj*

top·ple \'täpəl\ *vb* **-pled; -pling** : fall or cause to fall

top·sy-tur·vy \,täpsē'tərvē\ *adv or adj* **1** : upside down **2** : in utter confusion

torch \'tȯrch\ *n* : flaming light — **torch·bear·er** *n* — **torch·light** *n*

tore *past of* TEAR

tor·ment \'tȯr,ment\ *n* : extreme pain or anguish or a source of this ~ *vb* **1** : cause severe anguish to **2** : harass — **tor·men·tor** \-ər\ *n*

torn *past part of* TEAR

tor·na·do \tȯr'nādō\ *n, pl* **-does or**

-dos : violent destructive whirling wind

tor·pe·do \tȯr'pēdō\ *n, pl* **-does** : self-propelled explosive submarine missile ~ *vb* : hit with a torpedo

tor·pid \'tȯrpəd\ *adj* 1 : having lost motion or the power of exertion 2 : lacking vigor — **tor·pid·i·ty** \tȯr'pidətē\ *n*

tor·por \'tȯrpər\ *n* : extreme sluggishness or lethargy

torque \'tȯrk\ *n* : turning force

tor·rent \'tȯrənt\ *n* 1 : rushing stream 2 : tumultuous outburst — **tor·ren·tial** \tȯ'renchəl, tə-\ *adj*

tor·rid \'tȯrəd\ *adj* 1 : parched with heat 2 : impassioned

tor·sion \'tȯrshən\ *n* : a twisting or being twisted — **tor·sion·al** \'tȯrshənəl\ *adj* — **tor·sion·al·ly** *adv*

tor·so \'tȯrsō\ *n, pl* **-sos** *or* **-si** \-ˌsē\ : trunk of the human body

tor·ti·lla \tȯr'tēyə\ *n* : round flat cornmeal or wheat flour bread

tor·toise \'tȯrtəs\ *n* : land turtle

tor·tu·ous \'tȯrchəwəs\ *adj* 1 : winding 2 : tricky

tor·ture \'tȯrchər\ *n* 1 : use of pain to punish or force 2 : agony ~ *vb* **-tured; -tur·ing** : inflict torture on — **tor·tur·er** *n*

toss \'tȯs, 'täs\ *vb* 1 : move to and fro or up and down violently 2 : throw with a quick light motion 3 : move restlessly — **toss** *n*

toss–up *n* 1 : a deciding by flipping a coin 2 : even chance

tot \'tät\ *n* : small child

to·tal \'tōt'l\ *n* : entire amount ~ *vb* **-taled** *or* **-talled; -tal·ing** *or* **-tal·ling** 1 : add up 2 : amount to — **to·tal** *adj* — **to·tal·ly** *adv*

to·tal·i·tar·i·an \tō̱ˌtalə'terēən\ *adj* : relating to a political system in which the government has complete control over the people — **totalitarian** *n* — **to·tal·i·tar·i·an·ism** \-ē̱əˌnizəm\ *n*

to·tal·i·ty \tō'talətē\ *n, pl* **-ties** : whole amount or entirety

tote \'tōt\ *vb* **tot·ed; tot·ing** : carry

to·tem \'tōtəm\ *n* : often carved figure used as a family or tribe emblem

tot·ter \'tätər\ *vb* 1 : sway as if about to fall 2 : stagger

touch \'təch\ *vb* 1 : make contact with so as to feel 2 : be or cause to be in contact 3 : take into the hands or mouth 4 : treat or mention a subject 5 : relate or concern 6 : move to sympathetic feeling ~ *n* 1 : light stroke 2 : act or fact of touching or being touched 3 : sense of feeling 4 : trace 5 : state of being in contact — **touch up** *vb* : improve with minor changes

touch·down \'təchˌdaȯn\ *n* : scoring of 6 points in football

touch·stone *n* : test or criterion of genuineness or quality

touchy \'təchē\ *adj* **touch·i·er; -est** 1 : easily offended 2 : requiring tact

tough \'təf\ *adj* 1 : strong but elastic 2 : not easily chewed 3 : severe or disciplined 4 : stubborn ~ *n* : rowdy — **tough·ly** *adv* — **tough·ness** *n*

tough·en \'təfən\ *vb* : make or become tough

tou·pee \tü'pā\ *n* : small wig for a bald spot

tour \'tȯr\ *n* 1 : period of time spent at work or on an assignment 2 : journey with a return to the starting point ~ *vb* : travel over to see the sights — **tour·ist** \'tȯrist\ *n*

tour·na·ment \'tȯrnəmənt, 'tər-\ *n* 1 : medieval jousting competition 2 : championship series of games

tour·ney \-nē\ *n, pl* **-neys** : tournament

tour·ni·quet \'tȯrnikət, 'tər-\ *n* : tight bandage for stopping blood flow

tou·sle \'taȯzəl\ *vb* **-sled; -sling** : dishevel (as someone's hair)

tout \'taȯt, 'tüt\ *vb* : praise or publicize loudly

tow \'tō\ *vb* : pull along behind — **tow** *n*

to·ward, to·wards \'tōrd, tə'wȯrd, 'tȯrdz, tə'wȯrdz\ *prep* 1 : in the direction of 2 : with respect to 3 : in part payment on

tow·el \'taȯəl\ *n* : absorbent cloth or paper for wiping or drying

tow·er \'taȯər\ *n* : tall structure ~ *vb* : rise to a great height — **tow·ered** \'taȯərd\ *adj* — **tow·er·ing** *adj*

tow·head \'tōˌhed\ *n* : person having whitish blond hair — **tow·head·ed** \-ˌhedəd\ *adj*

town \'taȯn\ *n* 1 : small residential

area **2** : city — **towns·peo·ple** \'taůnz‚pēpəl\ *n pl*

town·ship \'taůn‚ship\ *n* **1** : unit of local government **2** : 36 square miles of U.S. public land

tox·ic \'täksik\ *adj* : poisonous — **tox·ic·i·ty** \täk'sisətē\ *n*

tox·in \'täksən\ *n* : poison produced by an organism

toy \'tȯi\ *n* : something for a child to play with ~ *vb* : amuse oneself or play with something ~ *adj* **1** : designed as a toy **2** : very small

¹trace \'trās\ *vb* **traced; trac·ing** **1** : mark over the lines of (a drawing) **2** : follow the trail or the development of ~ *n* **1** : track **2** : tiny amount or residue — **trace·able** *adj* — **trac·er** *n*

²trace *n* : line of a harness

tra·chea \'trākēə\ *n, pl* **-che·ae** \-kē‚ē\ : windpipe — **tra·che·al** \-kēəl\ *adj*

♦ **track** \'trak\ *n* **1** : trail left by wheels or footprints **2** : racing course **3** : train rails **4** : awareness of a progression **5** : looped belts propelling a vehicle ~ *vb* **1** : follow the trail of **2** : make tracks on — **track·er** *n*

track–and–field *adj* : relating to athletic contests of running, jumping, and throwing events

¹tract \'trakt\ *n* **1** : stretch of land **2** : system of body organs

²tract *n* : pamphlet of propaganda

trac·ta·ble \'traktəbəl\ *adj* : easily controlled

trac·tion \'trakshən\ *n* : gripping power to permit movement — **trac·tion·al** \-shənəl\ *adj* — **trac·tive** \'traktiv\ *adj*

trac·tor \'traktər\ *n* **1** : farm vehicle used esp. for pulling **2** : truck for hauling a trailer

trade \'trād\ *n* **1** : one's regular business **2** : occupation requiring skill

3 : the buying and selling of goods **4** : act of trading ~ *vb* **trad·ed; trad·ing** **1** : give in exchange for something **2** : buy and sell goods **3** : be a regular customer — **trades·peo·ple** \'trādz‚pēpəl\ *n pl*

trade-in \'trād‚in\ *n* : an item traded to a merchant at the time of a purchase

trade·mark \'trād‚märk\ *n* : word or mark identifying a manufacturer — **trademark** *vb*

trades·man \'trādzmən\ *n* : shopkeeper

tra·di·tion \trə'dishən\ *n* : belief or custom passed from generation to generation — **tra·di·tion·al** \-'dishənəl\ *adj* — **tra·di·tion·al·ly** *adv*

tra·duce \trə'düs, -'dyüs\ *vb* **-duced; -duc·ing** : lower the reputation of — **tra·duc·er** *n*

traf·fic \'trafik\ *n* **1** : business dealings **2** : movement along a route ~ *vb* : do business — **traf·fick·er** *n* — **traffic light** *n*

trag·e·dy \'trajədē\ *n, pl* **-dies** **1** : serious drama describing a conflict and having a sad end **2** : disastrous event

trag·ic \'trajik\ *adj* : being a tragedy — **trag·i·cal·ly** *adv*

trail \'trāl\ *vb* **1** : hang down and drag along the ground **2** : draw along behind **3** : follow the track of **4** : dwindle ~ *n* **1** : something that trails **2** : path or evidence left by something

trail·er \'trālər\ *n* **1** : vehicle intended to be hauled **2** : dwelling designed to be towed to a site

train \'trān\ *n* **1** : trailing part of a gown **2** : retinue or procession **3** : connected series **4** : group of linked railroad cars ~ *vb* **1** : cause to grow as desired **2** : make or become prepared or skilled **3** : point

— **train·ee** n — **train·er** n — **train·load** n

trai·pse \'trāps\ *vb* **traipsed; traips·ing** : walk

trait \'trāt\ n : distinguishing quality

trai·tor \'trātər\ n : one who betrays a trust or commits treason — **trai·tor·ous** *adj*

tra·jec·to·ry \trə'jektərē\ n, *pl* **-ries** : path of something moving through air or space

tram·mel \'traməl\ *vb* **-meled** *or* **-melled; -mel·ing** *or* **-mel·ling** : impede — **trammel** n

tramp \'tramp\ *vb* **1** : walk or hike **2** : tread on ~ n : beggar or vagrant

tram·ple \'trampəl\ *vb* **-pled; -pling** : walk or step on so as to bruise or crush — **trample** n — **tram·pler** \-plər\ n

tram·po·line \,trampə'lēn, 'trampə,-\ n : resilient sheet or web supported by springs and used for bouncing — **tram·po·lin·ist** \-'ist\ n

trance \'trans\ n **1** : sleeplike condition **2** : state of mystical absorption

tran·quil \'traŋkwəl, 'tran-\ *adj* : quiet and undisturbed — **tran·quil·ize** \-kwə,līz\ *vb* — **tran·quil·iz·er** n — **tran·quil·li·ty** *or* **tran·quil·i·ty** \traŋ'kwilətē, tran-\ n — **tran·quil·ly** *adv*

trans·act \trans'akt, tranz-\ *vb* : conduct (business)

trans·ac·tion \-'akshən\ n **1** : business deal **2** *pl* : records of proceedings

tran·scend \trans'end\ *vb* : rise above or surpass — **tran·scen·dent** \-'endənt\ *adj* — **tran·scen·den·tal** \,trans,en'dent³l, -ən-\ *adj*

tran·scribe \trans'krīb\ *vb* **-scribed; -scrib·ing** : make a copy, arrangement, or recording of — **tran·scrip·tion** \trans'kripshən\ n

tran·script \'trans,kript\ n : official copy

tran·sept \'trans,ept\ n : part of a church that crosses the nave at right angles

trans·fer \trans'fər, 'trans,fər\ *vb* **-rr-** **1** : move from one person, place, or situation to another **2** : convey ownership of **3** : print or copy by contact **4** : change to another vehicle or transportation line ~ \'trans,fər\ n **1** : act or process of transferring **2** : one that transfers or is transferred **3** : ticket permitting one to transfer — **trans·fer·able** \trans'fərəbəl\ *adj* — **trans·fer·al** \-əl\ n — **trans·fer·ence** \-əns\ n

trans·fig·ure \trans'figyər\ *vb* **-ured; -ur·ing** **1** : change the form or appearance of **2** : glorify — **trans·fig·u·ra·tion** \,trans,figyə-'rāshən\ n

trans·fix \trans'fiks\ *vb* **1** : pierce through **2** : hold motionless

trans·form \-'fórm\ *vb* **1** : change in structure, appearance, or character **2** : change (an electric current) in potential or type — **trans·for·ma·tion** \,transfər'māshən\ n — **trans·form·er** \trans'fórmər\ n

trans·fuse \trans'fyüz\ *vb* **-fused; -fus·ing** **1** : diffuse into or through **2** : transfer (as blood) into a vein — **trans·fu·sion** \-'fyüzhən\ n

trans·gress \trans'gres, tranz-\ *vb* : sin — **trans·gres·sion** \-'greshən\ n — **trans·gres·sor** \-'gresər\ n

tran·sient \'tranchənt\ *adj* : not lasting or staying long — **transient** n — **tran·sient·ly** *adv*

tran·sis·tor \tranz'istər, trans-\ n : small electronic device used in electronic equipment — **tran·sis·tor·ize** \-tə,rīz\ *vb*

tran·sit \'transət, 'tranz-\ n **1** : movement over, across, or through **2** : local and esp. public transportation **3** : surveyor's instrument

tran·si·tion \trans'ishən, tranz-\ n : passage from one state, stage, or subject to another — **tran·si·tion·al** \-'ishənəl\ *adj*

tran·si·to·ry \'transə,tōrē, 'tranz-\ *adj* : of brief duration

trans·late \trans'lāt, tranz-\ *vb* **-lat·ed; -lat·ing** : change into another language — **trans·lat·able** *adj* — **trans·la·tion** \-'lāshən\ n — **trans·la·tor** \-'lātər\ n

trans·lu·cent \trans'lüs³nt, tranz-\ *adj* : not transparent but clear enough to allow light to pass through — **trans·lu·cence** \-³ns\ n — **trans·lu·cen·cy** \-³nsē\ n — **trans·lu·cent·ly** *adv*

trans·mis·sion \-'mishən\ n **1** : act or process of transmitting **2** : system of gears between a car engine and drive wheels

trans·mit \-'mit\ *vb* **-tt-** 1 : transfer from one person or place to another 2 : pass on by inheritance 3 : broadcast — **trans·mis·si·ble** \-'misəbəl\ *adj* — **trans·mit·ta·ble** \-'mitəbəl\ *adj* — **trans·mit·tal** \-'mit³l\ *n* — **trans·mit·ter** *n*

tran·som \'transəm\ *n* : often hinged window above a door

trans·par·ent \trans'parənt\ *adj* 1 : clear enough to see through 2 : obvious — **trans·par·en·cy** \-ənsē\ *n* — **trans·par·ent·ly** *adv*

tran·spire \trans'pīr\ *vb* **-spired**; **-spir·ing** : take place — **tran·spi·ra·tion** \,transpə'rāshən\ *n*

trans·plant \trans'plant\ *vb* 1 : dig up and move to another place 2 : transfer from one body part or person to another — **transplant** \'trans,-\ *n* — **trans·plan·ta·tion** \,trans,plan'tāshən\ *n*

trans·port \trans'pōrt\ *vb* 1 : carry or deliver to another place 2 : carry away by emotion ∼ \'trans,-\ *n* 1 : act of transporting 2 : rapture 3 : ship or plane for carrying troops or supplies — **trans·por·ta·tion** \,transpər'tāshən\ *n* — **trans·port·er** *n*

trans·pose \trans'pōz\ *vb* **-posed**; **-pos·ing** : change the position, sequence, or key — **trans·po·si·tion** \,transpə'zishən\ *n*

trans·ship \tran'ship, trans-\ *vb* : transfer from one mode of transportation to another — **trans·ship·ment** *n*

trans·verse \trans'vərs, tranz-\ *adj* : lying across — **trans·verse** \'trans,vərs, 'tranz-\ *n* — **trans·verse·ly** *adv*

trap \'trap\ *n* 1 : device for catching animals 2 : something by which one is caught unawares 3 : device to allow one thing to pass through while keeping other things out ∼ *vb* **-pp-** : catch in a trap — **trap·per** *n*

trap·door *n* : door in a floor or roof

tra·peze \tra'pēz\ *n* : suspended bar used by acrobats

trap·e·zoid \'trapə,zòid\ *n* : plane 4-sided figure with 2 parallel sides — **trap·e·zoi·dal** \,trapə'zòid³l\ *adj*

trap·pings \'trapiŋz\ *n pl* 1 : orna-

mental covering 2 : outward decoration or dress

trash \'trash\ *n* : something that is no good — **trashy** *adj*

trau·ma \'traùmə, 'trȯ-\ *n* : bodily or mental injury — **trau·mat·ic** \trə'matik, trȯ-, traù-\ *adj*

tra·vail \trə'vāl, 'trav,āl\ *n* : painful work or exertion ∼ *vb* : labor hard

trav·el \'travəl\ *vb* **-eled** *or* **-elled**; **-el·ing** *or* **-el·ling** 1 : take a trip or tour 2 : move or be carried from point to point ∼ *n* : journey — often pl. — **trav·el·er**, **trav·el·ler** *n*

tra·verse \trə'vərs, tra'vərs, 'travərs\ *vb* **-versed**; **-vers·ing** : go or extend across — **tra·verse** \'travərs\ *n*

trav·es·ty \'travəstē\ *n*, *pl* **-ties** : imitation that makes crude fun of something — **travesty** *vb*

trawl \'trȯl\ *vb* : fish or catch with a trawl ∼ *n* : large cone-shaped net — **trawl·er** *n*

tray \'trā\ *n* : shallow flat-bottomed receptacle for holding or carrying something

treach·er·ous \'trechərəs\ *adj* : disloyal or dangerous — **treach·er·ous·ly** *adv*

treach·ery \'trechərē\ *n*, *pl* **-er·ies** : betrayal of a trust

tread \'tred\ *vb* **trod** \'träd\; **trod·den** \'träd°n\ *or* **trod**; **tread·ing** 1 : step on or over 2 : walk 3 : press or crush with the feet ∼ *n* 1 : way of walking 2 : sound made in walking 3 : part on which a thing runs

trea·dle \'tred°l\ *n* : foot pedal operating a machine — **treadle** *vb*

tread·mill *n* 1 : mill worked by walking persons or animals 2 : wearisome routine

trea·son \'trēz°n\ *n* : attempt to overthrow the government — **trea·son·able** \'trēz°nəbəl\ *adj* — **trea·son·ous** \-°nəs\ *adj*

trea·sure \'trezhər, 'trāzh-\ *n* 1 : wealth stored up 2 : something of great value ∼ *vb* **-sured**; **-sur·ing** : keep as precious

trea·sur·er \'trezhərər, 'trāzh-\ *n* : officer who handles funds

trea·sury \'trezhərē, 'trāzh-\ *n*, *pl* **-sur·ies** : place or office for keeping and distributing funds

♦ **treat** \'trēt\ *vb* 1 : have as a topic

2 : pay for the food or entertainment of **3 :** act toward or regard in a certain way **4 :** give medical care to ~ *n* **1 :** food or entertainment paid for by another **2 :** something special and enjoyable — **treatment** \-mənt\ *n*

trea·tise \'trētəs\ *n* : systematic written exposition or argument

trea·ty \'trētē\ *n, pl* **-ties** : agreement between governments

tre·ble \'trebəl\ *n* **1 :** highest part in music **2 :** upper half of the musical range ~ *adj* : triple in number or amount ~ *vb* **-bled; -bling** : make triple — **tre·bly** *adv*

tree \'trē\ *n* : tall woody plant ~ *vb* **treed; tree·ing** : force up a tree — **tree·less** *adj*

trek \'trek\ *n* : difficult trip ~ *vb* **-kk-** : make a trek

trel·lis \'treləs\ *n* : structure of crossed strips

trem·ble \'trembəl\ *vb* **-bled; -bling** **1 :** shake from fear or cold **2 :** move or sound as if shaken

tre·men·dous \tri'mendəs\ *adj* : amazingly large, powerful, or excellent — **tre·men·dous·ly** *adv*

trem·or \'tremər\ *n* : a trembling

trem·u·lous \'tremyələs\ *adj* : trembling or quaking

trench \'trench\ *n* : long narrow cut in land

tren·chant \'trenchənt\ *adj* : sharply perceptive

trend \'trend\ *n* : prevailing tendency, direction, or style ~ *vb* : move in a particular direction — **trendy** \'trendē\ *adj*

trep·i·da·tion \ˌtrepə'dāshən\ *n* : nervous apprehension

tres·pass \'trespəs, -ˌpas\ *n* **1 :** sin **2 :** unauthorized entry onto someone's property ~ *vb* **1 :** sin **2 :** enter illegally — **tres·pass·er** *n*

tress \'tres\ *n* : long lock of hair

tres·tle \'tresəl\ *n* **1 :** support with a horizontal piece and spreading legs **2 :** framework bridge

tri·ad \'trī,ad, -əd\ *n* : union of 3

tri·age \trē'äzh, 'trē,äzh\ *n* : system of dealing with cases (as patients) according to priority guidelines intended to maximize success

tri·al \'trīəl\ *n* **1 :** hearing and judgment of a matter in court **2 :** source of great annoyance **3 :** test use or experimental effort — **trial** *adj*

tri·an·gle \'trī,aŋgəl\ *n* : plane figure with 3 sides and 3 angles — **tri·an·gu·lar** \trī'aŋgyələr\ *adj*

tribe \'trīb\ *n* : social group of numerous families — **trib·al** \'trībəl\ *adj* — **tribes·man** \'trībzmən\ *n*

trib·u·la·tion \ˌtribyə'lāshən\ *n* : suffering from oppression

tri·bu·nal \trī'byün³l, tri-\ *n* **1 :** court **2 :** something that decides

trib·u·tary \'tribyəˌterē\ *n, pl* **-tar·ies** : stream that flows into a river or lake

trib·ute \'trib,yüt\ *n* **1 :** payment to acknowledge submission **2 :** tax **3 :** gift or act showing respect

trick \'trik\ *n* **1 :** scheme to deceive **2 :** prank **3 :** deceptive or ingenious feat **4 :** mannerism **5 :** knack **6 :** tour of duty ~ *vb* : deceive by cunning — **trick·ery** \-ərē\ *n* — **trick·ster** \-stər\ *n*

trick·le \'trikəl\ *vb* **-led; -ling** : run in drops or a thin stream — **trickle** *n*

tricky \'trikē\ *adj* **trick·i·er; -est** **1 :** inclined to trickery **2 :** requiring skill or caution

tri·cy·cle \'trī,sikəl\ *n* : 3-wheeled bicycle

tri·dent \'trīd³nt\ *n* : 3-pronged spear

tri·en·ni·al \'trī'enēəl\ *adj* : lasting,

OH, GARFIELD!

YOU'VE DONE SO WELL ON YOUR DIET I'M GIVING YOU A TREAT

OH MY GOSH! I'VE FORGOTTEN HOW TO EAT!

JIM DAVIS 5-21

occurring, or done every 3 years
— **tri·en·nial** n
tri·fle \'trīfəl\ n : something of little
value or importance ~ vb **-fled;**
-fling 1 : speak or act in a playful
or flirting way **2** : toy — **tri·fler** n
tri·fling \'trīfliṇ\ adj : trivial
trig·ger \ n : finger-piece of a
firearm lock that fires the gun ~
vb : set into motion — **trigger** adj
— **trig·gered** \-ərd\ adj
trig·o·nom·e·try \ˌtrigə'nämətrē\ n
: mathematics dealing with triangular measurement — **trig·o·no·**
met·ric \-nə'metrik\ adj
trill \'tril\ n **1** : rapid alternation between 2 adjacent tones **2** : rapid vibration in speaking ~ vb : utter in
or with a trill
tril·lion \'trilyən\ n : 1000 billions
— **trillion** adj — **tril·lionth**
\-yənth\ adj or n
tril·o·gy \'triləjē\ n, pl **-gies** : 3-part
literary or musical composition
trim \'trim\ vb **-mm- 1** : decorate **2**
: make neat or reduce by cutting
~ adj **-mm- :** neat and compact
~ n **1** : state or condition **2** : ornaments — **trim·ly** adv — **trim-**
mer n
trim·ming \'trimiṇ\ n : something
that ornaments or completes
Trin·i·ty \'trinətē\ n : divine unity
of Father, Son, and Holy Spirit
trin·ket \'triṇkət\ n : small ornament
trio \'trēō\ n, pl **tri·os 1** : music for 3
performers **2** : group of 3
trip \'trip\ vb **-pp- 1** : step lightly **2**
: stumble or cause to stumble **3**
: make or cause to make a mistake
4 : release (as a spring or switch)
~ n **1** : journey **2** : stumble **3**
: drug-induced experience
tri·par·tite \trī'pärˌtīt\ adj : having
3 parts or parties
tripe \'trīp\ n **1** : animal's stomach
used as food **2** : trash
tri·ple \'tripəl\ vb **-pled; -pling**
: make 3 times as great ~ n
: group of 3 ~ adj **1** : having 3
units **2** : being 3 times as great or
as many
trip·let \'triplət\ n **1** : group of 3 **2**
: one of 3 offspring born together
trip·li·cate \'triplikət\ adj : made in
3 identical copies ~ n : one of 3
copies
tri·pod \'trīˌpäd\ n : a stand with 3

legs — **tripod, tri·po·dal** \'trī-
pəd°l, 'trīˌpäd-\ adj
tri·sect \'trīˌsekt, trī'-\ vb : divide
into 3 usu. equal parts — **tri·sec-**
tion \'trīˌsekshən\ n
trite \'trīt\ adj **trit·er; trit·est** : com-
monplace
tri·umph \'trīəmf\ n, pl **-umphs**
: victory or great success ~ vb
: obtain or celebrate victory —
tri·um·phal \trī'əmfəl\ adj — **tri·**
um·phant \-fənt\ adj — **tri·um-**
phant·ly adv
tri·um·vi·rate \trī'əmvərət\ n : ruling body of 3 persons
triv·et \'trivət\ n : 3-legged stand **2**
: stand to hold a hot dish
triv·ia \'trivēə\ n sing or pl : unimportant details
triv·i·al \'trivēəl\ adj : of little importance — **triv·i·al·i·ty** \ˌtrivē-
'alətē\ n
trod past of TREAD
trod·den past part of TREAD
troll \'trōl\ n : dwarf or giant of
folklore inhabiting caves or hills
trol·ley \'trälē\ n, pl **-leys** : streetcar
run by overhead electric wires
trol·lop \'träləp\ n : untidy or immoral woman
trom·bone \träm'bōn, 'trämˌ-\ n
: musical instrument with a long
sliding tube — **trom·bon·ist**
\-'bōnist, -ˌbō-\ n
troop \'trüp\ n **1** : cavalry unit **2** pl
: soldiers **3** : collection of people
or things ~ vb : move or gather in
crowds
troop·er \'trüpər\ n **1** : cavalry soldier **2** : police officer on horseback or state police officer
tro·phy \'trōfē\ n, pl **-phies** : prize
gained by a victory
trop·ic \'träpik\ n **1** : either of the 2
parallels of latitude one 23½ de-
grees north of the equator (**tropic
of Cancer** \-'kansər\) and one 23½
degrees south of the equator
(**tropic of Cap·ri·corn** \-'kaprə-
ˌkȯrn\) **2** pl : region lying between
the tropics — **tropic, trop·i·cal**
\-ikəl\ adj
trot \'trät\ n : moderately fast gait
esp. of a horse with diagonally
paired legs moving together ~ vb
-tt- : go at a trot — **trot·ter** n
troth \'träth, 'trȯth, 'trōth\ n **1**
: pledged faithfulness **2** : betrothal

trou·ba·dour \'trübə,dōr\ *n* : medieval lyric poet

trou·ble \'trəbəl\ *vb* **-bled; -bling 1** : disturb **2** : afflict **3** : make an effort ~ *n* **1** : cause of mental or physical distress **2** : effort — **trou·ble·mak·er** *n* — **trou·ble·some** *adj* — **trou·ble·some·ly** *adv*

trough \'tróf\ *n, pl* **troughs** \'trófs, 'tróvz\ **1** : narrow container for animal feed or water **2** : long channel or depression (as between waves)

trounce \'traúns\ *vb* **trounced; trounc·ing** : thrash, punish, or defeat severely

troupe \'trüp\ *n* : group of stage performers — **troup·er** *n*

trou·sers \'traúzərz\ *n pl* : long pants — **trouser** *adj*

trous·seau \'trüsō, trü'sō\ *n, pl* **-seaux** \-sōz, -'sōz\ *or* **-seaus** : bride's collection of clothing and personal items

trout \'traút\ *n, pl* **trout** : freshwater food and game fish

trow·el \'traúəl\ *n* **1** : tool for spreading or smoothing **2** : garden scoop — **trowel** *vb*

troy \'trói\ *n* : system of weights based on a pound of 12 ounces

tru·ant \'trüənt\ *n* : student absent from school without permission — **tru·an·cy** \-ənsē\ *n* — **truant** *adj*

truce \'trüs\ *n* : agreement to halt fighting

truck \'trək\ *n* **1** : wheeled frame for moving heavy objects **2** : automotive vehicle for transporting heavy loads ~ *vb* : transport on a truck — **truck·er** *n* — **truck·load** *n*

truck·le \'trəkəl\ *vb* **-led; -ling** : yield slavishly to another

tru·cu·lent \'trəkyələnt\ *adj* : aggressively self-assertive — **truc·u·lence** \-ləns\ *n* — **truc·u·len-**cy \-lənsē\ *n* — **tru·cu·lent·ly** *adv*

trudge \'trəj\ *vb* **trudged; trudg·ing** : walk or march steadily and with difficulty

true \'trü\ *adj* **tru·er; tru·est 1** : loyal **2** : in agreement with fact or reality **3** : genuine ~ *adv* **1** : truthfully **2** : accurately ~ *vb* **trued; tru·ing** : make balanced or even — **tru·ly** *adv*

true–blue *adj* : loyal

♦ **truf·fle** \'trəfəl\ *n* **1** : edible fruit of an underground fungus **2** : ball=shaped chocolate candy

tru·ism \'trü,izəm\ *n* : obvious truth

trump \'trəmp\ *n* : card of a designated suit any of whose cards will win over other cards ~ *vb* : take with a trump

trumped–up \'trəmpt'əp\ *adj* : made-up

trum·pet \'trəmpət\ *n* : tubular brass wind instrument with a flaring end ~ *vb* **1** : blow a trumpet **2** : proclaim loudly — **trum·pet·er** *n*

trun·cate \'trəŋ,kāt, 'trən-\ *vb* **-cat·ed; -cat·ing** : cut short — **trun·ca·tion** \,trəŋ'kāshən\ *n*

trun·dle \'trənd⁹l\ *vb* **-dled; -dling** : roll along

trunk \'trəŋk\ *n* **1** : main part (as of a body or tree) **2** : long muscular nose of an elephant **3** : storage chest **4** : storage space in a car **5** *pl* : shorts

truss \'trəs\ *vb* : bind tightly ~ *n* **1** : set of structural parts forming a framework **2** : appliance worn to hold a hernia in place

trust \'trəst\ *n* **1** : reliance on another **2** : assured hope **3** : credit **4** : property held or managed in behalf of another **5** : combination of firms that reduces competition **6** : something entrusted to another's care **7** : custody ~ *vb* **1** : depend **2** : hope **3** : entrust **4** : have faith in

— **trust·ful** \-fəl\ *adj* — **trust·ful·ly** *adv* — **trust·ful·ness** *n* — **trust·worth·i·ness** *n* — **trust·wor·thy** *adj*

trust·ee \ˌtrəs'tē\ *n* : person holding property in trust — **trust·ee·ship** *n*

trusty \'trəstē\ *adj* **trust·i·er; -est** : dependable

truth \'trüth\ *n, pl* **truths** \'trüthz, 'trüths\ **1** : real state of things **2** : true or accepted statement **3** : agreement with fact or reality — **truth·ful** \-fəl\ *adj* — **truth·ful·ly** *adv* — **truth·ful·ness** *n*

try \'trī\ *vb* **tried; try·ing 1** : conduct the trial of **2** : put to a test **3** : strain **4** : make an effort at ∼ *n pl* **tries** : act of trying

try·out *n* : competitive test of performance esp. for athletes or actors — **try out** *vb*

tryst \'trist, 'trīst\ *n* : secret rendezvous of lovers

tsar \'zär, 'tsär, 'sär\ *var of* CZAR

T–shirt \'tē,shərt\ *n* : collarless pullover shirt with short sleeves

tub \'təb\ *n* **1** : wide bucketlike vessel **2** : bathtub

tu·ba \'tübə, 'tyüb-\ *n* : large low-pitched brass wind instument

tube \'tüb, 'tyüb\ *n* **1** : hollow cylinder **2** : round container from which a substance can be squeezed **3** : airtight circular tube of rubber inside a tire **4** : electronic device consisting of a sealed usu. glass container with electrodes inside — **tubed** \'tübd, 'tyübd\ *adj* — **tube·less** *adj*

tu·ber \'tübər, 'tyü-\ *n* : fleshy underground growth (as of a potato) — **tu·ber·ous** \-rəs\ *adj*

tu·ber·cu·lo·sis \tuˌbərkyə'lōsəs, tyü-\ *n, pl* **-lo·ses** \-ˌsēz\ : bacterial disease esp. of the lungs — **tu·ber·cu·lar** \-'bərkyələr\ *adj* — **tu·ber·cu·lous** \-ləs\ *adj*

tub·ing \'tübiŋ, 'tyü-\ *n* : series or arrangement of tubes

tu·bu·lar \'tübyələr, 'tyü-\ *adj* : of or like a tube

tuck \'tək\ *vb* **1** : pull up into a fold **2** : put into a snug often concealing place **3** : make snug in bed — with in ∼ *n* : fold in a cloth

tuck·er \'təkər\ *vb* : fatigue

Tues·day \'tüzdā, 'tyüz-, -dē\ *n* : 3d day of the week

tuft \'təft\ *n* : clump (as of hair or feathers) — **tuft·ed** \'təftəd\ *adj*

tug \'təg\ *vb* **-gg- 1** : pull hard **2** : move by pulling ∼ *n* **1** : act of tugging **2** : tugboat

tug·boat *n* : boat for towing or pushing ships through a harbor

tug–of–war \ˌtəgə'wör\ *n, pl* **tugs-of–war** : pulling contest between 2 teams

tu·ition \tù'ishən, 'tyü-\ *n* : cost of instruction

tu·lip \'tüləp, 'tyü-\ *n* : herb with cup-shaped flowers

tum·ble \'təmbəl\ *vb* **-bled; -bling 1** : perform gymnastic feats of rolling and turning **2** : fall or cause to fall suddenly **3** : toss ∼ *n* : act of tumbling

tum·bler \'təmblər\ *n* **1** : acrobat **2** : drinking glass **3** : obstruction in a lock that can be moved (as by a key)

tu·mid \'tüməd, 'tyü-\ *adj* : turgid

tum·my \'təmē\ *n, pl* **-mies** : belly

tu·mor \'tümər, 'tyü-\ *n* : abnormal and useless growth of tissue — **tu·mor·ous** *adj*

tu·mult \'tü,məlt, 'tyü-\ *n* **1** : uproar **2** : violent agitation of mind or feelings — **tu·mul·tu·ous** \tù-'məlchəwəs, tyü-\ *adj*

tun \'tən\ *n* : large cask

tu·na \'tünə, 'tyü-\ *n, pl* **-na** *or* **-nas** : large sea food fish

tun·dra \'təndrə\ *n* : treeless arctic plain

tune \'tün, 'tyün\ *n* **1** : melody **2** : correct musical pitch **3** : harmonious relationship ∼ *vb* **tuned; tun·ing 1** : bring or come into harmony **2** : adjust in musical pitch **3** : adjust a receiver so as to receive a broadcast **4** : put in first-class working order — **tun·able** *adj* — **tune·ful** \-fəl\ *adj* — **tun·er** *n*

tung·sten \'təŋstən\ *n* : metallic element used for electrical purposes and in hardening alloys (as steel)

tu·nic \'tünik, 'tyü-\ *n* **1** : ancient knee-length garment **2** : hip-length blouse or jacket

tun·nel \'tənᵊl\ *n* : underground passageway ∼ *vb* **-neled** *or* **-nelled; -nel·ing** *or* **-nel·ling** : make a tunnel through or under something

tur·ban \'tərbən\ *n* : wound headdress worn esp. by Muslims

tur·bid \'tərbəd\ *adj* **1** : dark with stirred-up sediment **2** : confused — **tur·bid·i·ty** \ˌtər'bidətē\ *n*

tur·bine \'tərbən, -ˌbīn\ *n* : engine turned by the force of gas or water on fan blades

tur·bo·jet \'tərbōˌjet\ *n* : airplane powered by a jet engine having a turbine-driven air compressor or the engine itself

tur·bo·prop \'tərbōˌpräp\ *n* : airplane powered by a propeller turned by a jet engine-driven turbine

tur·bu·lent \'tərbyələnt\ *adj* **1** : causing violence or disturbance **2** : marked by agitation or tumult — **tur·bu·lence** \-ləns\ *n* — **tur·bu·lent·ly** *adv*

tu·reen \tə'rēn, tyu̇-\ *n* : deep bowl for serving soup

turf \'tərf\ *n* : upper layer of soil bound by grass and roots

tur·gid \'tərjəd\ *adj* **1** : swollen **2** : too highly embellished in style — **tur·gid·i·ty** \ˌtər'jidətē\ *n*

tur·key \'tərkē\ *n, pl* **-keys** : large American bird raised for food

tur·moil \'tərˌmȯil\ *n* : extremely agitated condition

turn \'tərn\ *vb* **1** : move or cause to move around an axis **2** : twist (a mechanical part) to operate **3** : wrench **4** : cause to face or move in a different direction **5** : reverse the sides or surfaces of **6** : upset **7** : go around **8** : become or cause to become **9** : seek aid from a source ∼ *n* **1** : act or instance of turning **2** : change **3** : place at which something turns **4** : place, time, or opportunity to do something in order — **turn·er** *n* — **turn down** *vb* : decline to accept — **turn in** *vb* **1** : deliver or report to authorities **2** : go to bed — **turn off** *vb* : stop the functioning of — **turn out** *vb*

1 : expel **2** : produce **3** : come together **4** : prove to be in the end — **turn up** *vb* **1** : discover or appear **2** : happen unexpectedly

turn·coat *n* : traitor

tur·nip \'tərnəp\ *n* : edible root of an herb

turn·out \'tərnˌau̇t\ *n* **1** : gathering of people for a special purpose **2** : size of a gathering

turn·over *n* **1** : upset or reversal **2** : filled pastry **3** : volume of business **4** : movement (as of goods or people) into, through, and out of a place

turn·pike \'tərnˌpīk\ *n* : expressway on which tolls are charged

turn·stile \-ˌstīl\ *n* : post with arms pivoted on the top that allows people to pass one by one

turn·ta·ble *n* : platform that turns a phonograph record

◆ **tur·pen·tine** \'tərpənˌtīn\ *n* : oil distilled from pine-tree resin and used as a solvent

tur·pi·tude \'tərpəˌtüd, -ˌtyüd\ *n* : inherent baseness

tur·quoise \'tərˌkȯiz, -ˌkwȯiz\ *n* : blue or greenish gray gemstone

tur·ret \'tərət\ *n* **1** : little tower on a building **2** : revolving tool holder or gun housing

tur·tle \'tərt°l\ *n* : reptile with the trunk enclosed in a bony shell

tur·tle·dove *n* : wild pigeon

tur·tle·neck *n* : high close-fitting collar that can be turned over or a sweater or shirt with this collar

tusk \'təsk\ *n* : long protruding tooth (as of an elephant) — **tusked** \'təskt\ *adj*

tus·sle \'təsəl\ *n or vb* : struggle

tu·te·lage \'tüt°lij, 'tyüt-\ *n* **1** : act of protecting **2** : instruction esp. of an individual

tu·tor \'tütər, 'tyü-\ *n* : private

teacher ~ vb : teach usu. individually

tux·e·do \ˌtəkˈsēdō\ n, pl -dos or -does : semiformal evening clothes for a man

TV \ˌtēˈvē, ˈtēˌvē\ n : television

twain \ˈtwān\ n : two

twang \ˈtwaŋ\ n 1 : harsh sound like that of a plucked bowstring 2 : nasal speech or resonance ~ vb : sound or speak with a twang

tweak \ˈtwēk\ vb : pinch and pull playfully — tweak n

tweed \ˈtwēd\ n 1 : rough woolen fabric 2 pl : tweed clothing — tweedy adj

tweet \ˈtwēt\ n : chirping note — tweet vb

twee·zers \ˈtwēzərz\ n pl : small pincerlike tool

twelve \ˈtwelv\ n 1 : one more than 11 2 : 12th in a set or series 3 : something having 12 units — twelfth \ˈtwelfth\ adj or n — twelve adj or pron

twen·ty \ˈtwentē\ n, pl -ties : 2 times 10 — twen·ti·eth \-ēəth\ adj or n — twenty adj or pron

twen·ty–twen·ty, 20–20 adj : being vision of normal sharpness

twice \ˈtwīs\ adv 1 : on 2 occasions 2 : 2 times

twig \ˈtwig\ n : small branch — twig·gy adj

twi·light \ˈtwīˌlīt\ n : light from the sky at dusk or dawn — twilight adj

twill \ˈtwil\ n : fabric with a weave that gives an appearance of diagonal lines in the fabric

twilled \ˈtwild\ adj : made with a twill weave

twin \ˈtwin\ n : either of 2 offspring born together ~ adj 1 : born with one another or as a pair at one birth 2 : made up of 2 similar parts

twine \ˈtwīn\ n : strong twisted thread ~ vb twined; twin·ing 1 : twist together 2 : coil about a support — twin·er n — twiny adj

twinge \ˈtwinj\ vb twinged; twinging or twinge·ing : affect with or feel a sudden sharp pain ~ n : sudden sharp stab (as of pain)

twin·kle \ˈtwiŋkəl\ vb -kled; -kling : shine with a flickering light ~ n 1 : wink 2 : intermittent shining — twin·kler \-klər\ n

twirl \ˈtwərl\ vb : whirl round ~ n 1 : act of twirling 2 : coil — twirler n

twist \ˈtwist\ vb 1 : unite by winding (threads) together 2 : wrench 3 : move in or have a spiral shape 4 : follow a winding course ~ n 1 : act or result of twisting 2 : unexpected development

twist·er \ˈtwistər\ n : tornado

¹twit \ˈtwit\ n : fool

²twit vb -tt- : taunt

twitch \ˈtwich\ vb : move or pull with a sudden motion ~ n : act of twitching

twit·ter \ˈtwitər\ vb : make chirping noises ~ n : small intermittent noise

two \ˈtü\ n, pl twos 1 : one more than one 2 : the 2d in a set or series 3 : something having 2 units — two adj or pron

two·fold \ˈtüˌfōld\ adj : double — two·fold \-ˈfōld\ adv

two·some \ˈtüsəm\ n : couple

-ty n suffix : quality, condition, or degree

ty·coon \tīˈkün\ n : powerful and successful businessman

tying pres part of TIE

tyke \ˈtīk\ n : small child

tym·pa·num \ˈtimpənəm\ n, pl -na \-nə\ : eardrum or the cavity which it closes externally — tympan·ic \timˈpanik\ adj

type \ˈtīp\ n 1 : class, kind, or group set apart by common characteristics 2 : special design of printed letters ~ vb typed; typ·ing 1 : write with a typewriter 2 : identify or classify as a particular type

type·writ·er n : keyboard machine that produces printed material by striking a ribbon with raised letters — type·write vb

ty·phoid \ˈtīˌfȯid, tīˈ-\ adj : relating to or being a communicable bacterial disease (typhoid fever)

ty·phoon \tīˈfün\ n : hurricane of the western Pacific ocean

ty·phus \ˈtīfəs\ n : severe disease with fever, delirium, and rash

typ·i·cal \ˈtipikəl\ adj : having the essential characteristics of a group — typ·i·cal·i·ty \ˌtipəˈkalətē\ n — typ·i·cal·ly adv — typ·i·cal·ness n

typ·i·fy \ˈtipəˌfī\ vb -fied; -fy·ing : be typical of

typ·ist \'tīpist\ *n* : one who operates a typewriter

ty·pog·ra·phy \tī'pägrəfē\ *n* **1** : art of printing with type **2** : style, arrangement, or appearance of printed matter — **ty·po·graph·ic** \ˌtīpə'grafik,\ **ty·po·graph·i·cal** \-ikəl\ *adj* — **ty·po·graph·i·cal·ly** *adv*

ty·ran·ni·cal \tə'ranikəl, tī-\ *adj* : relating to a tyrant — **ty·ran·ni·cal·ly** *adv*

tyr·an·nize \'tirəˌnīz\ *vb* **-nized; -niz·ing** : rule or deal with in the manner of a tyrant — **tyr·an·niz·er** *n*

tyr·an·ny \'tirənē\ *n, pl* **-nies** : unjust use of absolute governmental power

ty·rant \'tīrənt\ *n* : harsh ruler having absolute power

ty·ro \'tīrō\ *n, pl* **-ros** : beginner

tzar \'zär, 'tsär, 'sär\ *var of* CZAR

U

u \'yü\ *n, pl* **u's** *or* **us** \'yüz\ : 21st letter of the alphabet

ubiq·ui·tous \yü'bikwətəs\ *adj* : omnipresent — **ubiq·ui·tous·ly** *adv* — **ubiq·ui·ty** \-wətē\ *n*

◆ **ud·der** \'ədər\ *n* : animal sac containing milk glands and nipples

ug·ly \'əglē\ *adj* **ug·li·er; -est 1** : offensive to look at **2** : mean or quarrelsome — **ug·li·ness** *n*

uku·le·le \ˌyükə'lālē\ *n* : small 4-string guitar

ul·cer \'əlsər\ *n* : eroded sore — **ul·cer·ous** *adj*

ul·cer·ate \'əlsəˌrāt\ *vb* **-at·ed; -at·ing** : become affected with an ulcer — **ul·cer·a·tion** \ˌəlsə'rāshən\ *n* — **ul·cer·a·tive** \'əlsəˌrātiv\ *adj*

ul·na \'əlnə\ *n* : bone of the forearm opposite the thumb

ul·te·ri·or \ˌəl'tirēər\ *adj* : not revealed

ul·ti·mate \'əltəmət\ *adj* : final, maximum, or extreme — **ultimate** *n* — **ul·ti·mate·ly** *adv*

ul·ti·ma·tum \ˌəltə'mātəm, -'mät-\ *n, pl* **-tums** *or* **-ta** \-ə\ : final proposition or demand carrying or implying a threat

ul·tra·vi·o·let \ˌəltrə'vīələt\ *adj* : having a wavelength shorter than visible light

um·bi·li·cus \ˌəmbə'līkəs, ˌəm'bili-\ *n, pl* **-li·ci** \-bə'līˌkī, -ˌsī; -'bilə-ˌkī, -ˌkē\ *or* **-li·cus·es** : small depression on the abdominal wall marking the site of the cord (**umbilical cord**) that joins the unborn fetus to its mother — **um·bil·i·cal** \ˌəm'bilikəl\ *adj*

um·brage \'əmbrij\ *n* : resentment

um·brel·la \ˌəm'brelə\ *n* : collapsible fabric device to protect from sun or rain

um·pire \'əmˌpīr\ *n* **1** : arbitrator **2** : sport official — **umpire** *vb*

ump·teen \'əmp'tēn\ *adj* : very numerous — **ump·teenth** \-'tēnth\ *adj*

un- \ˌən, 'ən\ *prefix* **1** : not **2** : opposite of

unable
unabridged
unacceptable
unaccompanied
unaccounted
unacquainted
unaddressed
unadorned
unadulterated
unafraid
unaided
unalike
unambiguous
unambitious
unannounced
unanswered
unanticipated
unappetizing
unappreciated
unapproved
unarguable
unarguably
unassisted
unattended
unattractive
unauthorized
unavailable
unavoidable
unbearable
unbiased
unbranded
unbreakable
uncensored
unchallenged
unchangeable
unchanged
unchanging
uncharacteris-
tic
uncharged
unchaste
uncivilized
unclaimed
unclear
uncleared
unclothed
uncluttered
uncombed
uncomfortable
uncomfortably
uncomplimen-
tary
unconfirmed
unconsummat-
ed
uncontested
uncontrolled
uncontroversial
unconventional

unconvention-
ally
unconverted
uncooked
uncooperative
uncoordinated
uncovered
uncultivated
undamaged
undated
undecided
undeclared
undefeated
undemocratic
undependable
undeserving
undesirable
undetected
undetermined
undeveloped
undeviating
undignified
undisturbed
undivided
undomesticated
undrinkable
unearned
uneducated
unemotional
unending
unendurable
unenforceable
unenlightened
unethical
unexcitable
unexciting
unexplainable
unexplored
unfair
unfairly
unfairness
unfavorable
unfavorably
unfeigned
unfilled
unfinished
unflattering
unforeseeable
unforeseen
unforgivable
unforgiving
unfulfilled
unfurnished
ungenerous
ungentlemanly
ungraceful
ungrammatical
unharmed
unhealthful

unheated
unhurt
unidentified
unimaginable
unimaginative
unimportant
unimpressed
uninformed
uninhabited
uninjured
uninsured
unintelligent
unintelligible
unintelligibly
unintended
unintentional
unintentionally
uninterested
uninteresting
uninterrupted
uninvited
unjust
unjustifiable
unjustified
unjustly
unknowing
unknowingly
unknown
unleavened
unlicensed
unlikable
unlimited
unlovable
unmanageable
unmarked
unmarried
unmerciful
unmercifully
unmerited
unmolested
unmotivated
unmoving
unnamed
unnecessarily
unnecessary
unneeded
unnoticeable
unnoticed
unobjectionable
unobservable
unobservant
unobtainable
unobtrusive
unobtrusively
unofficial
unopened
unopposed
unorganized
unoriginal

unorthodox
unorthodoxy
unpaid
unpardonable
unpatriotic
unpaved
unpleasant
unpleasantly
unpleasantness
unpopular
unpopularity
unposed
unpredictabili-
ty
unpredictable
unpredictably
unprejudiced
unprepared
unpretentious
unproductive
unprofitable
unprotected
unproved
unproven
unprovoked
unpunished
unqualified
unquenchable
unquestioning
unreachable
unreadable
unready
unrealistic
unreasonable
unreasonably
unrefined
unrelated
unreliable
unremembered
unrepentant
unrepresented
unrequited
unresolved
unresponsive
unrestrained
unrestricted
unrewarding
unripe
unsafe
unsalted
unsanitary
unsatisfactory
unsatisfied
unscented
unscheduled
unseasoned
unseen
unselfish
unselfishly

unselfishness
unshaped
unshaven
unskillful
unskillfully
unsolicited
unsolved
unsophisticated
unsound
unsoundly
unsoundness
unspecified
unspoiled
unsteadily
unsteadiness
unsteady
unstructured
unsubstantiat-
ed
unsuccessful
unsuitable
unsuitably
unsuited
unsupervised
unsupported
unsure
unsurprising
unsuspecting
unsweetened
unsympathetic
untamed

untanned
untidy
untouched
untrained
untreated
untrue
untrustworthy
untruthful
unusable
unusual
unvarying
unverified
unwanted
unwarranted
unwary
unwavering
unweaned
unwed
unwelcome
unwholesome
unwilling
unwillingly
unwillingness
unwise
unwisely
unworkable
unworthily
unworthiness
unworthy
unyielding

un·ac·cus·tomed *adj* 1 : not customary 2 : not accustomed

un·af·fect·ed *adj* 1 : not influenced
or changed by something 2 : natural and sincere — **un·af·fect·ed·
ly** *adv*

unan·i·mous \yu̇'nanəməs\ *adj* 1
: showing no disagreement 2
: formed with the agreement of all
— **una·nim·i·ty** \ˌyünə'nimətē\ *n*
— **unan·i·mous·ly** *adv*

un·armed *adj* : not armed or armored

un·as·sum·ing *adj* : not bold or arrogant

un·at·tached *adj* 1 : not attached 2
: not married or engaged

un·aware *adv* : unawares ∼ *adj*
: not aware

un·awares \ˌənə'warz\ *adv* 1 : without warning 2 : unintentionally

un·bal·anced *adj* 1 : not balanced 2
: mentally unstable

un·beat·en *adj* : not beaten

un·be·com·ing *adj* : not proper or
suitable — **un·be·com·ing·ly** *adv*

un·be·liev·able *adj* 1 : improbable 2

: superlative — **un·be·liev·ably**
adv

un·bend *vb* -**bent**; -**bend·ing** : make
or become more relaxed and
friendly

un·bend·ing *adj* : formal and inflexible

un·bind *vb* -**bound**; -**bind·ing** 1 : remove bindings from 2 : release

un·bolt *vb* : open or unfasten by
withdrawing a bolt

un·born *adj* : not yet born

un·bo·som *vb* : disclose thoughts or
feelings

un·bowed \ˌən'bau̇d\ *adj* : not defeated or subdued

un·bri·dled \ˌən'brīdᵊld\ *adj* : unrestrained

un·bro·ken *adj* 1 : not damaged 2
: not interrupted

un·buck·le *vb* : undo the buckle of

un·bur·den *vb* : relieve (oneself) of
anxieties

un·but·ton *vb* : undo the buttons of

un·called-for *adj* : too harsh or
rude for the occasion

un·can·ny \ən'kanē\ *adj* 1 : weird 2
: suggesting superhuman powers
— **un·can·ni·ly** \-'kanᵊlē\ *adv*

un·ceas·ing *adj* : never ceasing —
un·ceas·ing·ly *adv*

un·cer·e·mo·ni·ous *adj* : acting
without ordinary courtesy — **un·
cer·e·mo·ni·ous·ly** *adv*

un·cer·tain *adj* 1 : not determined,
sure, or definitely known 2 : subject to chance or change — **un·
cer·tain·ly** *adv* — **un·cer·tain·ty** *n*

un·chris·tian *adj* : not consistent
with Christian teachings

un·cle \'əŋkəl\ *n* 1 : brother of one's
father or mother 2 : husband of
one's aunt

un·clean *adj* : not clean or pure —
un·clean·ness *n*

un·clog *vb* : remove an obstruction
from

un·coil *vb* : release or become released from a coiled state

un·com·mit·ted *adj* : not pledged to
a particular allegiance or course
of action

un·com·mon *adj* 1 : rare 2 : superior
— **un·com·mon·ly** *adv*

un·com·pro·mis·ing *adj* : not making or accepting a compromise

un·con·cerned *adj* 1 : disinterested 2
: not anxious or upset — **un·con·
cerned·ly** *adv*

un·con·di·tion·al *adj* : not limited in any way — **un·con·di·tion·al·ly** *adv*

un·con·scio·na·ble *adj* : shockingly unjust or unscrupulous — **un·con·scio·na·bly** *adv*

un·con·scious *adj* **1** : not awake or aware of one's surroundings **2** : not consciously done ~ *n* : part of one's mental life that one is not aware of — **un·con·scious·ly** *adv* — **un·con·scious·ness** *n*

un·con·sti·tu·tion·al *adj* : not according to or consistent with a constitution

un·con·trol·la·ble *adj* : incapable of being controlled — **un·con·trol·la·bly** *adv*

un·count·ed *adj* : countless

un·couth \ˌən'küth\ *adj* : rude and vulgar

un·cov·er *vb* **1** : reveal **2** : expose by removing a covering

unc·tion \'əŋkshən\ *n* **1** : rite of anointing **2** : exaggerated or insincere earnestness

unc·tu·ous \'əŋkchəwəs\ *adj* **1** : oily **2** : insincerely smooth in speech or manner — **unc·tu·ous·ly** *adv*

un·cut *adj* **1** : not cut down, into, off, or apart **2** : not shaped by cutting **3** : not abridged

un·daunt·ed *adj* : not discouraged — **un·daunt·ed·ly** *adv*

un·de·ni·able *adj* : plainly true — **un·de·ni·ably** *adv*

un·der \'əndər\ *adv* : below or beneath something ~ *prep* **1** : lower than and sheltered by **2** : below the surface of **3** : covered or concealed by **4** : subject to the authority of **5** : less than ~ *adj* **1** : lying below or beneath **2** : subordinate **3** : less than usual, proper, or desired

un·der·age \ˌəndər'āj\ *adj* : of less than legal age

un·der·brush \'əndər,brəsh\ *n* : shrubs and small trees growing beneath large trees

un·der·clothes \'əndər,klōz, -ˌklōthz\ *n pl* : underwear

un·der·cloth·ing \-ˌklōthiŋ\ *n* : underwear

un·der·cov·er \ˌəndər'kəvər\ *adj* : employed or engaged in secret investigation

un·der·cur·rent \'əndər,kərənt\ *n* : hidden tendency or opinion

un·der·cut \ˌəndər'kət\ *vb* **-cut; -cut·ting** : offer to sell or to work at a lower rate than

un·der·de·vel·oped \ˌəndərdi'veləpt\ *adj* : not normally or adequately developed esp. economically

un·der·dog \'əndər,dog\ *n* : contestant given least chance of winning

un·der·done \ˌəndər'dən\ *adj* : not thoroughly done or cooked

un·der·es·ti·mate \ˌəndər'estə,māt\ *vb* : estimate too low

un·der·ex·pose \ˌəndərik'spōz\ *vb* : give less than normal exposure to — **un·der·ex·po·sure** *n*

un·der·feed \ˌəndər'fēd\ *vb* **-fed; -feed·ing** : feed inadequately

un·der·foot \ˌəndər'füt\ *adv* **1** : under the feet **2** : in the way of another

un·der·gar·ment \'əndər,gärmənt\ *n* : garment to be worn under another

un·der·go \ˌəndər'gō\ *vb* **-went** \-'went\; **-gone; -go·ing 1** : endure **2** : go through (as an experience)

un·der·grad·u·ate \ˌəndər'grajəwət\ *n* : university or college student

un·der·ground \ˌəndər'graund\ *adv* **1** : beneath the surface of the earth **2** : in secret ~ \'əndər,-\ *adj* **1** : being or growing under the surface of the ground **2** : secret ~ \'əndər,-\ *n* : secret political movement or group

un·der·growth \'əndər'grōth\ *n* : low growth on the floor of a forest

un·der·hand \'əndər,hand\ *adv or adj* **1** : with secrecy and deception **2** : with the hand kept below the waist

un·der·hand·ed \ˌəndər'handəd\ *adj or adv* : underhand — **un·der·hand·ed·ly** *adv* — **un·der·hand·ed·ness** *n*

un·der·line \'əndər,līn\ *vb* **1** : draw a line under **2** : stress — **underline** *n*

un·der·ling \'əndərliŋ\ *n* : inferior

un·der·ly·ing \ˌəndər,līiŋ\ *adj* : basic

un·der·mine \ˌəndər'mīn\ *vb* **1** : excavate beneath **2** : weaken or wear away secretly or gradually

un·der·neath \ˌəndər'nēth\ *prep* : directly under ~ *adv* **1** : below a surface or object **2** : on the lower side

un·der·nour·ished \ˌəndər'nərisht\ *adj* : insufficiently nourished — **un·der·nour·ish·ment** *n*

un·der·pants \'əndərˌpants\ *n pl* : short undergarment for the lower trunk

un·der·pass \-ˌpas\ *n* : passageway crossing underneath another

un·der·pin·ning \'əndərˌpiniŋ\ *n* : support

un·der·priv·i·leged *adj* : poor

un·der·rate \ˌəndər'rāt\ *vb* : rate or value too low

un·der·score \'əndərˌskōr\ *vb* **1** : underline **2** : emphasize — **under·score** *n*

un·der·sea \ˌəndər'sē\ *adj* : being, carried on, or used beneath the surface of the sea ~ \ˌəndər'sē,\; **un·der·seas** \-'sēz\ *adv* : beneath the surface of the sea

un·der sec·re·tary *n* : deputy secretary

un·der·sell \ˌəndər'sel\ *vb* **-sold; -sell·ing** : sell articles cheaper than

un·der·shirt \'əndərˌshərt\ *n* : shirt worn as underwear

un·der·shorts \'əndərˌshòrts\ *n pl* : short underpants

◆ **un·der·side** \'əndərˌsīd, ˌəndər'sīd\ *n* : side or surface lying underneath

un·der·sized \ˌəndər'sīzd\ *adj* : unusually small

un·der·stand \ˌəndər'stand\ *vb* **-stood** \-'stùd\; **-stand·ing 1** : be aware of the meaning of **2** : deduce **3** : have a sympathetic attitude — **un·der·stand·able** \-'standəbəl\ *adj* — **un·der·stand·ably** \-blē\ *adv*

un·der·stand·ing \ˌəndər'standiŋ\ *n* **1** : intelligence **2** : ability to comprehend and judge **3** : mutual agreement ~ *adj* : sympathetic

un·der·state \ˌəndər'stāt\ *vb* **1** : represent as less than is the case **2** : state with restraint — **un·der·state·ment** *n*

un·der·stood \ˌəndər'stùd\ *adj* **1** : agreed upon **2** : implicit

un·der·study \'əndərˌstədē, ˌəndər'-\ *vb* : study another actor's part in order to substitute — **understudy** \'əndər,-\ *n*

un·der·take \ˌəndər'tāk\ *vb* **-took; -tak·en; -tak·ing 1** : attempt (a task) or assume (a responsibility) **2** : guarantee

un·der·tak·er \'əndərˌtākər\ *n* : one in the funeral business

un·der·tak·ing \'əndərˌtākiŋ, ˌəndər'-\ *n* **1** : something (as work) that is undertaken **2** : promise

under–the–counter *adj* : illicit

un·der·tone \'əndərˌtōn\ *n* : low or subdued tone or utterance

un·der·tow \-ˌtō\ *n* : current beneath the waves that flows seaward

un·der·val·ue \ˌəndər'valyü\ *vb* : value too low

un·der·wa·ter \-'wòtər, -'wät-\ *adj* : being or used below the surface of the water — **underwater** *adv*

under way *adv* : in motion or in progress

un·der·wear \'əndərˌwar\ *n* : clothing worn next to the skin and under ordinary clothes

un·der·world \'əndərˌwərld\ *n* **1** : place of departed souls **2** : world of organized crime

un·der·write \'əndərˌrīt, ˌəndərˌ-\ *vb* **-wrote; -writ·ten; -writ·ing 1** : provide insurance for **2** : guarantee financial support of — **un·der·writ·er** *n*

un·dies \'əndēz\ *n pl* : underwear

un·do *vb* **-did; -done; -do·ing 1** : un-

LIFE IS UGLY

THOUGH NOT AS UGLY AS THE UNDERSIDE OF A DOG'S TONGUE

fasten **2** : reverse **3** : ruin — **un-do-ing** *n*

un-doubt-ed *adj* : certain — **un-doubt-ed-ly** *adv*

un-dress *vb* : remove one's clothes ~ *n* : state of being naked

un-due *adj* : excessive — **un-du-ly** *adv*

un-du-late \'ənjə,lāt\ *vb* **-lat-ed; -lat-ing** : rise and fall regularly — **un-du-la-tion** \ənjə'lāshən\ *n*

un-dy-ing *adj* : immortal or perpetual

un-earth *vb* : dig up or discover

un-earth-ly *adj* : supernatural

un-easy *adj* **1** : awkward or embarrassed **2** : disturbed or worried — **un-eas-i-ly** *adv* — **un-eas-i-ness** *n*

un-em-ployed *adj* : not having a job — **un-em-ploy-ment** *n*

un-equal *adj* : not equal or uniform — **un-equal-ly** *adv*

un-equaled, un-equalled *adj* : having no equal

un-equiv-o-cal *adj* : leaving no doubt — **un-equiv-o-cal-ly** *adv*

un-err-ing *adj* : infallible — **un-err-ing-ly** *adv*

un-even *adj* **1** : not smooth **2** : not regular or consistent — **un-even-ly** *adv* — **un-even-ness** *n*

◆ **un-event-ful** *adj* : lacking interesting or noteworthy incidents — **un-event-ful-ly** *adv*

un-ex-pect-ed \ənik'spektəd\ *adj* : not expected — **un-ex-pect-ed-ly** *adv*

un-fail-ing *adj* : steadfast — **un-fail-ing-ly** *adv*

un-faith-ful *adj* : not loyal — **un-faith-ful-ly** *adv* — **un-faith-ful-ness** *n*

un-fa-mil-iar *adj* **1** : not well known **2** : not acquainted — **un-fa-mil-iar-i-ty** *n*

un-fas-ten *vb* : release a catch or lock

un-feel-ing *adj* : lacking feeling or compassion — **un-feel-ing-ly** *adv*

un-fit *adj* : not suitable — **un-fit-ness** *n*

un-flap-pa-ble \ən'flapəbəl\ *adj* : not easily upset or panicked — **un-flap-pa-bly** *adv*

un-fold *vb* **1** : open the folds of **2** : reveal **3** : develop

un-for-get-ta-ble *adj* : memorable — **un-for-get-ta-bly** *adv*

un-for-tu-nate *adj* **1** : not lucky or successful **2** : deplorable — **unfortunate** *n* — **un-for-tu-nate-ly** *adv*

un-found-ed *adj* : lacking a sound basis

un-freeze *vb* **-froze; -fro-zen; -freezing** : thaw

un-friend-ly *adj* : not friendly or kind — **un-friend-li-ness** *n*

un-furl *vb* : unfold or unroll

un-gain-ly *adj* : clumsy — **un-gain-li-ness** *n*

un-god-ly *adj* : wicked — **un-god-li-ness** *n*

un-grate-ful *adj* : not thankful for favors — **un-grate-ful-ly** *adv* — **un-grate-ful-ness** *n*

un-guent \'əngwənt, 'ən-\ *n* : ointment

un-hand *vb* : let go

un-hap-py *adj* **1** : unfortunate **2** : sad — **un-hap-pi-ly** *adv* — **un-hap-pi-ness** *n*

un-healthy *adj* **1** : not wholesome **2** : not well

un-heard-of \ən'hərdəv, -ˌäv\ *adj* : unprecedented

un-hinge \ən'hinj\ *vb* **1** : take from the hinges **2** : make unstable esp. mentally

un-hitch *vb* : unfasten

un-ho-ly *adj* : sinister or shocking — **un-ho-li-ness** *n*

un-hook *vb* : release from a hook

uni-cel-lu-lar \ˌyüni'selyələr\ *adj*

: having or consisting of a single cell

uni·corn \'yünə,kȯrn\ *n* : legendary animal with one horn in the middle of the forehead

uni·cy·cle \'yüni,sīkəl\ *n* : pedal-powered vehicle with only a single wheel

uni·di·rec·tion·al \,yünidə'rek-shənəl, -dī-\ *adj* : working in only a single direction

uni·form \'yünə,fȯrm\ *adj* : not changing or showing any variation ~ *n* : distinctive dress worn by members of a particular group — **uni·for·mi·ty** \,yünə'fȯrmətē\ *n* — **uni·form·ly** *adv*

uni·fy \'yünə,fī\ *vb* **-fied; -fy·ing** : make into a coherent whole — **uni·fi·ca·tion** \,yünəfə'kāshən\ *n*

uni·lat·er·al \,yünə'latərəl\ *adj* : having, affecting, or done by one side only — **uni·lat·er·al·ly** *adv*

un·im·peach·able *adj* : blameless

un·in·hib·it·ed *adj* : free of restraint — **un·in·hib·it·ed·ly** *adv*

union \'yünyən\ *n* 1 : act or instance of joining 2 or more things into one or the state of being so joined 2 : confederation of nations or states 3 : organization of workers (labor union, trade union)

union·ize \'yünyə,nīz\ *vb* **-ized; -iz·ing** : form into a labor union — **union·i·za·tion** \,yünyənə'zā-shən\ *n*

unique \yu'nēk\ *adj* 1 : being the only one of its kind 2 : very unusual — **unique·ly** *adv* — **unique·ness** *n*

uni·son \'yünəsən, -nəzən\ *n* 1 : sameness in pitch 2 : exact agreement

unit \'yünət\ *n* 1 : smallest whole number 2 : definite amount or quantity used as a standard of measurement 3 : single part of a whole — **unit** *adj*

unite \yu'nīt\ *vb* **unit·ed; unit·ing** : put or join together

uni·ty \'yünətē\ *n, pl* **-ties** 1 : quality or state of being united or a unit 2 : harmony

uni·ver·sal \,yünə'vərsəl\ *adj* 1 : relating to or affecting everyone or everything 2 : present or occurring everywhere — **uni·ver·sal·ly** *adv*

uni·verse \'yünə,vərs\ *n* : the complete system of all things that exist

uni·ver·si·ty \,yünə'vərsətē\ *n, pl* **-ties** : institution of higher learning

un·kempt \,ən'kempt\ *adj* : not neat or combed

un·kind *adj* : not kind or sympathetic — **un·kind·li·ness** *n* — **un·kind·ly** *adv* — **un·kind·ness** *n*

un·law·ful *adj* : illegal — **un·law·ful·ly** *adv*

un·leash *vb* : free from control or restraint

un·less \ən'les\ *conj* : except on condition that

◆ **un·like** \ən'līk, 'ən,līk\ *adj* 1 : not similar 2 : not equal ~ *prep* : different from — **un·like·ly** \ən-'līklē\ *adv* — **un·like·ness** \-nəs\ *n* — **un·like·li·hood** \-lēhůd\ *n*

un·load *vb* 1 : take (cargo) from a vehicle, vessel, or plane 2 : take a load from 3 : discard

un·lock *vb* 1 : unfasten through release of a lock 2 : release or reveal

un·lucky *adj* 1 : experiencing bad luck 2 : likely to bring misfortune — **un·luck·i·ly** *adv*

un·mis·tak·able *adj* : not capable of being mistaken or misunderstood — **un·mis·tak·ably** *adv*

un·moved *adj* 1 : not emotionally affected 2 : remaining in the same place or position

un·nat·u·ral *adj* **1** : not natural or spontaneous **2** : abnormal — **un·nat·u·ral·ly** *adv* — **un·nat·u·ral·ness** *n*

un·nerve *vb* : deprive of courage, strength, or steadiness

un·oc·cu·pied *adj* **1** : not busy **2** : not occupied

un·pack *vb* **1** : remove (things packed) from a container **2** : remove the contents of (a package)

un·par·al·leled *adj* : having no equal

un·plug *vb* **1** : unclog **2** : disconnect from an electric circuit by removing a plug

un·prec·e·dent·ed *adj* : unlike or superior to anything known before

un·prin·ci·pled *adj* : unscrupulous

un·ques·tion·able *adj* : acknowledged as beyond doubt — **un·ques·tion·ably** *adv*

un·rav·el *vb* **1** : separate the threads of **2** : solve

un·re·al *adj* : not real or genuine — **un·re·al·i·ty** *n*

un·rea·son·ing *adj* : not using or being guided by reason

un·re·lent·ing *adj* : not yielding or easing — **un·re·lent·ing·ly** *adv*

un·rest *n* : turmoil

un·ri·valed, un·ri·valled *adj* : having no rival

un·roll *vb* **1** : unwind a roll of **2** : become unrolled

un·ruf·fled *adj* : not agitated or upset

un·ru·ly \ˌən'rülē\ *adj* : not readily controlled or disciplined — **un·rul·i·ness** *n*

un·scathed \ˌən'skāthd\ *adj* : unharmed

un·sci·en·tif·ic *adj* : not in accord with the principles and methods of science

un·screw *vb* : loosen or remove by withdrawing screws or by turning

un·scru·pu·lous *adj* : being or acting in total disregard of conscience, ethical principles, or rights of others — **un·scru·pu·lous·ly** *adv* — **un·scru·pu·lous·ness** *n*

un·seal *vb* : break or remove the seal of

un·sea·son·able *adj* : not appropriate or usual for the season — **un·sea·son·ably** *adv*

un·seem·ly \ˌən'sēmlē\ *adj* : not polite or in good taste — **un·seem·li·ness** *n*

un·set·tle *vb* : disturb — **un·set·tled** *adj*

un·sight·ly \ˌən'sītlē\ *adj* : not attractive

un·skilled *adj* : not having or requiring a particular skill

un·snap *vb* : loosen by undoing a snap

un·speak·able \ˌən'spēkəbəl\ *adj* : extremely bad — **un·speak·ably** \-blē\ *adv*

un·sta·ble *adj* **1** : not mentally or physically balanced **2** : tending to change

un·stop *vb* **1** : unclog **2** : remove a stopper from

un·stop·pa·ble \ˌən'stäpəbəl\ *adj* : not capable of being stopped

un·strung \ˌən'strəŋ\ *adj* : nervously tired or anxious

un·sung \ˌən'səŋ\ *adj* : not celebrated in song or verse

un·tan·gle *vb* **1** : free from a state of being tangled **2** : find a solution to

un·think·able \ˌən'thiŋkəbəl\ *adj* : not to be thought of or considered possible

un·think·ing *adj* : careless — **un·think·ing·ly** *adv*

un·tie *vb* **-tied; -ty·ing** *or* **-tie·ing** : open by releasing ties

un·til \ˌən'til\ *prep* : up to the time of ~ *conj* : to the time that

un·time·ly *adj* **1** : premature **2** : coming at an unfortunate time

un·to \ˌən'tü, 'ən-\ *prep* : to

un·told *adj* **1** : not told **2** : too numerous to count

un·to·ward \ˌən'tōrd\ *adj* **1** : difficult to manage **2** : inconvenient

un·truth *n* **1** : lack of truthfulness **2** : lie

un·used *adj* **1** \ˌən'yüst, -'yüzd\ : not accustomed **2** \-'yüzd\ : not used

un·well *adj* : sick

un·wieldy \ˌən'wēldē\ *adj* : too big or awkward to manage easily

un·wind *vb* **-wound; -wind·ing 1** : undo something that is wound **2** : become unwound **3** : relax

un·wit·ting *adj* **1** : not knowing **2** : not intended — **un·wit·ting·ly** *adv*

un·wont·ed *adj* **1** : unusual **2** : not accustomed by experience

un·wrap *vb* : remove the wrappings from

un·writ·ten *adj* : made or passed on only in speech or through tradition

un·zip *vb* : zip open

up \'əp\ *adv* **1** : in or to a higher position or level **2** : from beneath a surface or level **3** : in or into an upright position **4** : out of bed **5** : to or with greater intensity **6** : into existence, evidence, or knowledge **7** : away **8** — used to indicate a degree of success, completion, or finality **9** : in or into parts ~ *adj* **1** : in the state of having risen **2** : raised to or at a higher level **3** : moving, inclining, or directed upward **4** : in a state of greater intensity **5** : at an end ~ *vb* **upped** *or* in *1* **up; upped; up·ping; ups** *or* in *1* **up 1** : act abruptly **2** : move or cause to move upward ~ *prep* **1** : to, toward, or at a higher point of **2** : along or toward the beginning of

up·braid \,əp'brād\ *vb* : criticize or scold

up·bring·ing \'əp,briniŋ\ *n* : process of bringing up and training

up·com·ing \,əp'kəmiŋ\ *adj* : approaching

up·date \,əp'dāt\ *vb* : bring up to date — **update** \'əp,dāt\ *n*

up·end \,əp'end\ *vb* **1** : stand or rise on end **2** : overturn

up·grade \'əp,grād\ *n* **1** : upward slope **2** : increase ~ \'əp,-, ,əp'-\ *vb* : raise to a higher position

up·heav·al \,əp'hēvəl\ *n* **1** : a heaving up (as of part of the earth's crust) **2** : violent change

up·hill \,əp'hil\ *adv* : upward on a hill or incline ~ \'əp,-\ *adj* **1** : going up **2** : difficult

up·hold \,əp'hōld\ *vb* **-held; -holding** : support or defend — **up·hold·er** *n*

up·hol·ster \,əp'hōlstər\ *vb* : cover (furniture) with padding and fabric (**up·hol·stery** \-stərē\) — **up·hol·ster·er** *n*

up·keep \'əp,kēp\ *n* : act or cost of keeping up or maintaining

up·land \'əplənd, -,land\ *n* : high land — **upland** *adj*

up·lift \,əp'lift\ *vb* **1** : lift up **2** : improve the condition or spirits of — **up·lift** \'əp,-\ *n*

up·on \ə'pón, -'pän\ *prep* : on

up·per \'əpər\ *adj* : higher in position, rank, or order ~ *n* : top part of a shoe

upper·hand *n* : advantage

up·per·most \'əpər,mōst\ *adv* : in or into the highest or most prominent position — **uppermost** *adj*

up·pi·ty \'əpətē\ *adj* : acting with a manner of undue importance

up·right \'əp,rīt\ *adj* **1** : vertical **2** : erect in posture **3** : morally correct ~ *n* : something that stands upright — **up·right** *adv* — **up·right·ly** *adv* — **up·right·ness** *n*

up·ris·ing \'əp,rīziŋ\ *n* : revolt

up·roar \'əp,rōr\ *n* : state of commotion or violent disturbance

up·roar·i·ous \,əp'rōrēəs\ *adj* **1** : marked by uproar **2** : extremely funny — **up·roar·i·ous·ly** *adv*

up·root \,əp'rüt, -'rùt\ *vb* : remove by or as if by pulling up by the roots

up·set \,əp'set\ *vb* **-set; -set·ting 1** : force or be forced out of the usual position **2** : disturb emotionally or physically ~ \'əp,-\ *n* **1** : act of throwing into disorder **2** : minor physical disorder ~ *adj* : emotionally disturbed or agitated

up·shot \'əp,shät\ *n* : final result

up·side down \,əp,sīd'daùn\ *adv* **1** : turned so that the upper and lower parts are reversed **2** : in or into confusion or disorder — **upside-down** *adj*

up·stairs \'əp,starz, ,əp'-\ *adv* : up the stairs or to the next floor ~ *adj* : situated on the floor above ~ *n sing or pl* : part of a building above the ground floor

up·stand·ing \,əp'standiŋ, 'əp,-\ *adj* : honest

up·start \'əp,stärt\ *n* : one who claims more personal importance than is warranted — **up·start** *adj*

up·swing \'əp,swiŋ\ *n* : marked increase (as in activity)

up·tight \,əp'tīt\ *adj* **1** : tense **2** : angry **3** : rigidly conventional

up-to-date *adj* : current — **up-to-date·ness** *n*

up·town \'əp,taùn\ *n* : upper part of a town or city — **uptown** *adj or adv*

up·turn \'əp,tərn\ *n* : improvement or increase

up·ward \'əpwərd\, **up·wards** \-wərdz\ *adv* **1** : in a direction from lower to higher **2** : toward a higher or greater state or number ~ *adj* : directed toward or situated in a higher place — **up·ward·ly** *adv*

up·wind \\,əp'wind\\ *adv or adj* : in the direction from which the wind is blowing

ura·ni·um \\yu̇'rānēəm\\ *n* : metallic radioactive chemical element

ur·ban \\'ərbən\\ *adj* : characteristic of a city

ur·bane \\,ər'bān\\ *adj* : polished in manner — **ur·ban·i·ty** \\,ər'banətē\\ *n*

ur·ban·ite \\'ərbə,nīt\\ *n* : city dweller

ur·chin \\'ərchən\\ *n* : mischievous youngster

-ure *n suffix* : act or process

ure·thra \\yu̇'rēthrə\\ *n, pl* **-thras** *or* **-thrae** \\-,thrē\\ : canal that carries off urine from the bladder — **ure·thral** \\-thrəl\\ *adj*

urge \\'ərj\\ *vb* **urged; urging 1** : earnestly plead for or insist on (an action) **2** : try to persuade **3** : impel to a course of activity ~ *n* : force or impulse that moves one to action

ur·gent \\'ərjənt\\ *adj* **1** : calling for immediate attention **2** : urging insistently — **ur·gen·cy** \\-jənsē\\ *n* — **ur·gent·ly** *adv*

uri·nal \\'yu̇rən°l\\ *n* : receptacle to urinate in

uri·nate \\'yu̇rə,nāt\\ *vb* **-nat·ed; -nating** : discharge urine — **uri·na·tion** \\,yu̇rə'nāshən\\ *n*

urine \\'yu̇rən\\ *n* : liquid waste material from the kidneys — **uri·nary** \\-ə,nerē\\ *adj*

urn \\'ərn\\ *n* **1** : vaselike or cuplike vessel on a pedestal **2** : large coffee pot

us \\'əs\\ *pron, objective case of* WE

us·able \\'yüzəbəl\\ *adj* : suitable or fit for use — **us·abil·i·ty** \\,yüzə'bilətē\\ *n*

us·age \\'yüsij, -zij\\ *n* **1** : customary practice **2** : way of doing or of using something

use \\'yüs\\ *n* **1** : act or practice of putting something into action **2** : state of being used **3** : way of using **4** : privilege, ability, or power to use something **5** : utility or function **6** : occasion or need to

use ~ \\'yüz\\ *vb* **used** \\'yüzd\\; *"used to" usu* \\'yüstə\\; **us·ing** \\'yüziŋ\\ **1** : put into action or service **2** : consume **3** : behave toward **4** : to make use of **5** — used in the past tense with *to* to indicate a former practice — **use·ful** \\'yüsfəl\\ *adj* — **use·ful·ly** *adv* — **use·ful·ness** *n* — **use·less** \\'yüsləs\\ *adj* — **use·less·ly** *adv* — **use·less·ness** *n* — **us·er** *n*

used \\'yüzd\\ *adj* : not new

ush·er \\'əshər\\ *n* : one who escorts people to their seats ~ *vb* : conduct to a place

ush·er·ette \\,əshə'ret\\ *n* : woman or girl who is an usher

usu·al \\'yüzhəwəl\\ *adj* : being what is expected according to custom or habit — **usu·al·ly** \\'yüzhəwəlē\\ *adv*

usurp \\yu̇'sərp, -'zərp\\ *vb* : seize and hold by force or without right — **usur·pa·tion** \\,yüsər'pāshən, -zər-\\ *n* — **usurp·er** *n*

usu·ry \\'yüzhərē\\ *n, pl* **-ries 1** : lending of money at excessive interest or the rate or amount of such interest — **usu·rer** \\-zhərər\\ *n* — **usu·ri·ous** \\yu̇'zhu̇rēəs\\ *adj*

uten·sil \\yu̇'tensəl\\ *n* **1** : eating or cooking tool **2** : useful tool

uter·us \\'yütərəs\\ *n, pl* **uteri** \\-,rī\\ : organ for containing and nourishing an unborn offspring — **uter·ine** \\-,rīn, -rən\\ *adj*

util·i·tar·i·an \\,yü,tilə'terēən\\ *adj* : being or meant to be useful rather than beautiful

util·i·ty \\yü'tilətē\\ *n, pl* **-ties 1** : usefulness **2** : regulated business providing a public service (as electricity)

uti·lize \\'yüt°l,īz\\ *vb* **-lized; -lizing** : make use of — **uti·li·za·tion** \\,yüt°lə'zāshən\\ *n*

ut·most \\'ət,mōst\\ *adj* **1** : most distant **2** : of the greatest or highest degree or amount — **utmost** *n*

uto·pia \\yu̇'tōpēə\\ *n* : place of ideal perfection — **uto·pi·an** \\-pēən\\ *adj or n*

ut·ter \\'ətər\\ *adj* : absolute ~ *vb* : express with the voice — **ut·ter·er** \\-ərər\\ *n* — **ut·ter·ly** *adv*

ut·ter·ance \\'ətərəns\\ *n* : what one says

V

v \'vē\ *n, pl* **v's** *or* **vs** \'vēz\ : 22d letter of the alphabet

va·can·cy \'vākənsē\ *n, pl* **-cies 1** : state of being vacant **2** : unused or unoccupied place or office

va·cant \-kənt\ *adj* **1** : not occupied, filled, or in use **2** : devoid of thought or expression — **va·cant·ly** *adv*

va·cate \-ˌkāt\ *vb* **-cat·ed; -cat·ing 1** : annul **2** : leave unfilled or unoccupied

va·ca·tion \vā'kāshən, və-\ *n* : period of rest from routine — **vacation** *vb* — **va·ca·tion·er** *n*

vac·ci·nate \'vaksə,nāt\ *vb* **-nat·ed; -nat·ing** : administer a vaccine usu. by injection

vac·ci·na·tion \ˌvaksə'nāshən\ *n* : act of or the scar left by vaccinating

vac·cine \vak'sēn, 'vakˌ-\ *n* : substance to induce immunity to a disease

vac·il·late \'vasə,lāt\ *vb* **-lat·ed; -lat·ing** : waver between courses or opinions — **vac·il·la·tion** \ˌvasə-'lāshən\ *n*

vac·u·ous \'vakyəwəs\ *adj* **1** : empty **2** : dull or inane — **va·cu·ity** \va-'kyüətē, və-\ *n* — **vac·u·ous·ly** *adv* — **vac·u·ous·ness** *n*

vac·u·um \'vak,yüm, -yəm\ *n, pl* **vac·u·ums** *or* **vac·ua** \-yəwə\ : empty space with no air ∼ *vb* : clean with a vacuum cleaner

vacuum cleaner *n* : appliance that cleans by suction

vag·a·bond \'vagə,bänd\ *n* : wanderer with no home — **vagabond** *adj*

va·ga·ry \'vāgərē, və'gerē\ *n, pl* **-ries** : whim

va·gi·na \və'jīnə\ *n, pl* **-nae** \-ˌnē\ *or* **-nas** : canal that leads out from the uterus — **vag·i·nal** \'vajən°l\ *adj*

va·grant \'vāgrənt\ *n* : person with no home and no job — **va·gran·cy** \-grənsē\ *n* — **vagrant** *adj*

vague \'vāg\ *adj* **vagu·er; vagu·est** : not clear, definite, or distinct — **vague·ly** *adv* — **vague·ness** *n*

◆ **vain** \'vān\ *adj* **1** : of no value **2** : unsuccessful **3** : conceited — **vain·ly** *adv*

va·lance \'valəns, 'vāl-\ *n* : border drapery

vale \'vāl\ *n* : valley

vale·dic·to·ri·an \ˌvalə,dik'tōrēən\ *n* : student giving the farewell address at commencement

vale·dic·to·ry \-'diktərē\ *adj* : bidding farewell — **valedictory** *n*

va·lence \'vāləns\ *n* : degree of combining power of a chemical element

val·en·tine \'valən,tīn\ *n* : sweetheart or a card sent to a sweetheart or friend on St. Valentine's Day

va·let \'valət, 'val,ā, va'lā\ *n* : male personal servant

val·iant \'valyənt\ *adj* : brave or heroic — **val·iant·ly** *adv*

val·id \'valəd\ *adj* **1** : proper and legally binding **2** : founded on truth or fact — **va·lid·i·ty** \və'lidətē, va-\ *n* — **val·id·ly** *adv*

val·i·date \'valə,dāt\ *vb* **-dat·ed; -dat·ing** : establish as valid — **val·i·da·tion** \ˌvalə'dāshən\ *n*

va·lise \və'lēs\ *n* : suitcase

val·ley \'valē\ *n, pl* **-leys** : long depression between ranges of hills

val·or \'valər\ *n* : bravery or heroism — **val·or·ous** \'valərəs\ *adj*

valu·able \'valyəwəbəl\ *adj* **1** : worth a lot of money **2** : being of great importance or use — **valuable** *n*

val·u·a·tion \ˌvalyə'wāshən\ *n* **1** : act or process of valuing **2** : market value of a thing

val·ue \'valyü\ *n* **1** : fair return or equivalent for something exchanged **2** : how much something is worth **3** : distinctive quality (as of a color or sound) **4** : guiding principle or ideal — usu. pl. ~ *vb* **val·ued; valu·ing 1** : estimate the worth of **2** : appreciate the importance of — **val·ue·less** *adj* — **val·u·er** *n*

valve \'valv\ *n* : structure or device to control flow of a liquid or gas — **valved** \'valvd\ *adj* — **valveless** *adj*

◆ **vam·pire** \'vam,pīr\ *n* **1** : legendary night-wandering dead body that sucks human blood **2** : bat that feeds on the blood of animals

¹van \'van\ *n* : vanguard

²van *n* : enclosed truck

va·na·di·um \və'nādēəm\ *n* : soft ductile metallic chemical element

van·dal \'vand⁊l\ *n* : person who willfully defaces or destroys property — **van·dal·ism** \-ˌizəm\ *n* — **van·dal·ize** \-ˌīz\ *vb*

vane \'vān\ *n* : bladelike device designed to be moved by force of the air or water

van·guard \'van,gärd\ *n* **1** : troops moving at the front of an army **2** : forefront of an action or movement

va·nil·la \və'nilə\ *n* : a flavoring made from the pods of a tropical orchid or this orchid

van·ish \'vanish\ *vb* : disappear suddenly

van·i·ty \'vanətē\ *n, pl* **-ties 1** : futility or something that is futile **2** : undue pride in oneself **3** : makeup case or table

van·quish \'vaŋkwish, 'van-\ *vb* **1** : overcome in battle or in a contest **2** : gain mastery over

van·tage \'vantij\ *n* : position of advantage or perspective

va·pid \'vapəd, 'vāpəd\ *adj* : lacking spirit, liveliness, or zest — **va·pid·i·ty** \va'pidətē\ *n* — **vap·id·ly** \'vapədlē\ *adv* — **vap·id·ness** *n*

va·por \'vāpər\ *n* **1** : fine separated particles floating in and clouding the air **2** : gaseous form of an ordinarily liquid substance — **va·por·ous** \-pərəs\ *adj*

va·por·ize \'vāpə,rīz\ *vb* **-ized; -iz·ing** : convert into vapor — **va·por·i·za·tion** \ˌvāpərə'zāshən\ *n* — **va·por·iz·er** *n*

var·i·able \'verēəbəl\ *adj* : apt to vary — **var·i·abil·i·ty** \ˌverēə'bilətē\ *n* — **var·i·able** *n* — **var·i·ably** *adv*

var·i·ance \'verēəns\ *n* **1** : instance or degree of variation **2** : disagreement or dispute **3** : legal permission to build contrary to a zoning law

var·i·ant \-ənt\ *n* : something that differs from others of its kind — **variant** *adj*

vari·a·tion \ˌverē'āshən\ *n* : instance or extent of varying

var·i·cose \'varə,kōs\ *adj* : abnormally swollen and dilated

var·ied \'verēd\ *adj* : showing variety — **var·ied·ly** *adv*

var·ie·gat·ed \'verēə,gāted\ *adj* : having patches, stripes, or marks of different colors — **var·ie·gate** \-ˌgāt\ *vb* — **var·ie·ga·tion** \ˌverēə'gāshən\ *n*

va·ri·ety \və'rīətē\ *n, pl* **-et·ies 1**

var·i·ous \'verēəs\ *adj* : being many and unlike — **var·i·ous·ly** *adv*

var·nish \'värnish\ *n* : liquid that dries to a hard glossy protective coating ~ *vb* : cover with varnish

var·si·ty \'värsətē\ *n, pl* **-ties** : principal team representing a school

vary \'verē\ *vb* **var·ied; vary·ing 1** : alter **2** : make or be of different kinds

vas·cu·lar \'vaskyələr\ *adj* : relating to a channel for the conveyance of a body fluid (as blood or sap)

vase \'vās, 'vāz\ *n* : tall usu. ornamental container to hold flowers

vas·sal \'vasəl\ *n* **1** : one acknowledging another as feudal lord **2** : one in a dependent position — **vas·sal·age** \-əlij\ *n*

vast \'vast\ *adj* : very great in size, extent, or amount — **vast·ly** *adv* — **vast·ness** *n*

vat \'vat\ *n* : large tub- or barrel-shaped container

vaude·ville \'vódvəl, 'vád-, 'vōd-, -₁vil, -əvəl, -ə₁vil\ *n* : stage entertainment of unrelated acts

¹vault \'vólt\ *n* **1** : masonry arch **2** : usu. underground storage or burial room ~ *vb* : form or cover with a vault — **vault·ed** *adj* — **vaulty** *adj*

²vault *vb* : spring over esp. with the help of the hands or a pole ~ *n* : act of vaulting — **vault·er** *n*

vaunt \'vónt\ *vb* : boast — **vaunt** *n*

veal \'vēl\ *n* : flesh of a young calf

veer \'vir\ *vb* : change course esp. gradually — **veer** *n*

veg·e·ta·ble \'vejtəbəl, 'vejə-\ *adj* **1** : relating to or obtained from plants **2** : like that of a plant ~ *n* **1** : plant **2** : plant grown for food

veg·e·tar·i·an \₁vejə'terēən\ *n* : person who eats no meat — **vegetarian** *adj* — **veg·e·tar·i·an·ism** \-ēə-₁nizəm\ *n*

veg·e·tate \'vejə₁tāt\ *vb* **-tat·ed; -tat·ing** : lead a dull inert life

veg·e·ta·tion \₁vejə'tāshən\ *n* : plant life — **veg·e·ta·tion·al** \-shənəl\ *adj* — **veg·e·ta·tive** \'vejə₁tātiv\ *adj*

ve·he·ment \'vēəmənt\ *adj* : showing strong esp. violent feeling —

ve·he·mence \-məns\ *n* — **ve·he·ment·ly** *adv*

ve·hi·cle \'vē₁hikəl, 'vēəkəl\ *n* **1** : medium through which something is expressed, applied, or administered **2** : structure for transporting something esp. on wheels — **ve·hic·u·lar** \vē'hikyələr\ *adj*

veil \'vāl\ *n* **1** : sheer material to hide something or to cover the face and head **2** : something that hides ~ *vb* : cover with a veil

vein \'vān\ *n* **1** : rock fissure filled with deposited mineral matter **2** : vessel that carries blood toward the heart **3** : sap-carrying tube in a leaf **4** : distinctive element or style of expression — **veined** \'vānd\ *adj*

ve·loc·i·ty \və'läsətē\ *n, pl* **-ties** : speed

ve·lour, ve·lours \və'lûr\ *n, pl* **ve·lours** \-'lúrz\ : fabric with a velvetlike pile

vel·vet \'velvət\ *n* : fabric with a short soft pile — **velvet** *adj* — **vel·vety** *adj*

ve·nal \'vēn°l\ *adj* : capable of being corrupted esp. by money — **ve·nal·i·ty** \vi'nalətē\ *n* — **ve·nal·ly** *adv*

vend \'vend\ *vb* : sell — **vend·ible** *adj* — **ven·dor** \'vendər\ *n*

ven·det·ta \ven'detə\ *n* : feud marked by acts of revenge

ve·neer \və'nir\ *n* **1** : thin layer of fine wood glued over a cheaper wood **2** : superficial display ~ *vb* : overlay with a veneer

ven·er·a·ble \'venərəbəl\ *adj* : deserving of respect

ven·er·ate \'venə₁rāt\ *vb* **-at·ed; -at·ing** : respect esp. with reverence — **ven·er·a·tion** \₁venə'rāshən\ *n*

venereal disease \və'nirēəl-\ *n* : contagious disease spread through copulation

ven·geance \'venjəns\ *n* : punishment in retaliation for an injury or offense

venge·ful \'venjfəl\ *adj* : filled with a desire for revenge — **venge·ful·ly** *adv*

ve·nial \'vēnēəl\ *adj* : capable of being forgiven

ven·i·son \'venəsən, -əzən\ *n* : deer meat

ven·om \'venəm\ *n* **1** : poison secret-

ed by certain animals **2** : ill will — **ven·om·ous** \-əməs\ *adj*

vent \'vent\ *vb* **1** : provide with or let out at a vent **2** : give expression to ~ *n* : opening for passage or for relieving pressure

ven·ti·late \'vent³l‚āt\ *vb* **-lat·ed; -lat·ing** : allow fresh air to circulate through — **ven·ti·la·tion** \‚vent³l'āshən\ *n* — **ven·ti·la·tor** \'vent³l‚ātər\ *n*

ven·tri·cle \'ventrikəl\ *n* : heart chamber that pumps blood into the arteries

ven·tril·o·quist \ven'trilə‚kwist\ *n* : one who can make the voice appear to come from another source — **ven·tril·o·quism** \-‚kwizəm\ *n* — **ven·tril·o·quy** \-kwē\ *n*

ven·ture \'venchər\ *vb* **-tured; -tur·ing 1** : risk or take a chance on **2** : put forward (an opinion) ~ *n* : speculative business enterprise

ven·ture·some \-səm\ *adj* : brave or daring — **ven·ture·some·ly** *adv* — **ven·ture·some·ness** *n*

ven·ue \'venyü\ *n* : scene of an action or event

ve·rac·i·ty \və'rasətē\ *n, pl* **-ties** : truthfulness or accuracy — **ve·ra·cious** \və'rāshəs\ *adj*

ve·ran·da, ve·ran·dah \və'randə\ *n* : large open porch

verb \'vərb\ *n* : word that expresses action or existence

ver·bal \'vərbəl\ *adj* **1** : having to do with or expressed in words **2** : oral **3** : relating to or formed from a verb — **ver·bal·i·za·tion** \‚vərbələ'zāshən\ *n* — **ver·bal·ize** \'vərbə‚līz\ *vb* — **ver·bal·ly** \-ē\ *adv*

verbal auxiliary *n* : auxiliary verb

ver·ba·tim \vər'bātəm\ *adv or adj* : using the same words

ver·biage \'vərbēij\ *n* : excess of words

ver·bose \vər'bōs\ *adj* : using more words than are needed — **ver·bos·i·ty** \-'bäsətē\ *n*

ver·dant \'vərd³nt\ *adj* : green with growing plants — **ver·dant·ly** *adv*

ver·dict \'vərdikt\ *n* : decision of a jury

ver·dure \'vərjər\ *n* : green growing vegetation or its color

verge \'vərj\ *vb* **verged; verg·ing** : be almost on the point of happening or doing something ~ *n* **1** : edge **2** : threshold

ver·i·fy \'verə‚fī\ *vb* **-fied; -fy·ing** : establish the truth, accuracy, or reality of — **ver·i·fi·able** *adj* — **ver·i·fi·ca·tion** \‚verəfə'kāshən\ *n*

ver·i·ly \'verəlē\ *adv* : truly or confidently

veri·si·mil·i·tude \‚verəsə'milə‚tüd\ *n* : appearance of being true

ver·i·ta·ble \'verətəbəl\ *adj* : actual or true — **ver·i·ta·bly** *adv*

ver·i·ty \'verətē\ *n, pl* **-ties** : truth

ver·mi·cel·li \‚vərmə'chelē, -'sel-\ *n* : thin spaghetti

◆ **ver·min** \'vərmən\ *n, pl* **vermin** : small animal pest

ver·mouth \vər'müth\ *n* : dry or sweet wine flavored with herbs

ver·nac·u·lar \vər'nakyələr\ *adj* : relating to a native language or dialect and esp. its normal spoken form ~ *n* : vernacular language

ver·nal \'vərn³l\ *adj* : relating to spring

ver·sa·tile \'vərsət³l\ *adj* : having many abilities or uses — **ver·sa·til·i·ty** \‚vərsə'tilətē\ *n*

¹**verse** \'vərs\ *n* **1** : line or stanza of poetry **2** : poetry **3** : short division of a chapter in the Bible

²**verse** *vb* **versed; versing** : make familiar by experience, study, or practice

ver·sion \'vərzhən\ *n* **1** : translation of the Bible **2** : account or description from a particular point of view

ver·sus \'vərsəs\ *prep* : opposed to or against

ver·te·bra \'vərtəbrə\ *n, pl* **-brae** \-ˌbrā, -ˌbrē\ *or* **-bras** : segment of the backbone — **ver·te·bral** \vər-'tēbrəl, 'vərtə-\ *adj*

ver·te·brate \'vərtəbrət, -ˌbrāt\ : animal with a backbone — **verte·brate** *adj*

ver·tex \'vərˌteks\ *n, pl* **ver·ti·ces** \'vərtəˌsēz\ **1** : point of intersection of lines or surfaces **2** : highest point

ver·ti·cal \'vərtikəl\ *adj* : rising straight up from a level surface — **vertical** *n* — **ver·ti·cal·i·ty** \ˌvərtə'kalətē\ *n* — **ver·ti·cal·ly** *adv*

ver·ti·go \'vərtiˌgō\ *n, pl* **-goes** *or* **-gos** : dizziness

verve \'vərv\ *n* : liveliness or vividness

very \'verē\ *adj* **veri·er; -est 1** : exact **2** : exactly suitable **3** : mere or bare **4** : precisely the same ~ *adv* **1** : to a high degree **2** : in actual fact

ves·i·cle \'vesikəl\ *n* : membranous cavity — **ve·sic·u·lar** \və-'sikyələr\ *adj*

ves·pers \'vespərz\ *n pl* : late afternoon or evening worship service

ves·sel \'vesəl\ *n* **1** : a container (as a barrel, bottle, bowl, or cup) for a liquid **2** : craft for navigation esp. on water **3** : tube in which a body fluid is circulated

¹vest \'vest\ *vb* **1** : give a particular authority, right, or property to **2** : clothe with or as if with a garment

²vest *n* : sleeveless garment usu. worn beneath a suit coat

ves·ti·bule \'vestəˌbyül\ *n* : enclosed entrance — **ves·tib·u·lar** \ve-'stibyələr\ *adj*

ves·tige \'vestij\ *n* : visible trace or remains — **ves·ti·gial** \ve'stijēəl\ *adj* — **ves·ti·gial·ly** *adv*

vest·ment \'vestmənt\ *n* : clergy member's garment

ves·try \'vestrē\ *n, pl* **-tries** : church storage room for garments and articles

vet·er·an \'vetərən\ *n* **1** : former member of the armed forces **2** : person with long experience — **veteran** *adj*

Veterans Day *n* : 4th Monday in October or formerly November 11 observed as a legal holiday in commemoration of the end of war in 1918 and 1945

vet·er·i·nar·i·an \ˌvetərən'erēən\ *n* : doctor of animals — **vet·er·i·nary** \'vetərənˌerē\ *adj*

ve·to \'vētō\ *n, pl* **-toes 1** : power to forbid and esp. the power of a chief executive to prevent a bill from becoming law **2** : exercise of the veto ~ *vb* **1** : forbid **2** : reject a legislative bill

vex \'veks\ *vb* **vexed; vex·ing** : trouble, distress, or annoy — **vex·a·tion** \vek'sāshən\ *n* — **vex·a·tious** \-shəs\ *adj*

via \'vīə, 'vēə\ *prep* : by way of

vi·a·ble \'vīəbəl\ *adj* **1** : capable of surviving or growing **2** : practical or workable — **vi·a·bil·i·ty** \ˌvīə-'bilətē\ *n* — **vi·a·bly** \'vīəblē\ *adv*

via·duct \'vīəˌdəkt\ *n* : elevated roadway or railway bridge

vi·al \'vīəl\ *n* : small bottle

vi·brant \'vībrənt\ *adj* **1** : vibrating **2** : pulsing with vigor or activity **3** : sounding from vibration — **vi·bran·cy** \-brənsē\ *n*

vi·brate \'vīˌbrāt\ *vb* **-brat·ed; -brat·ing 1** : move or cause to move quickly back and forth or side to side **2** : respond sympathetically — **vi·bra·tion** \vī'brāshən\ *n* — **vi·bra·tor** \'vīˌbrātər\ *n* — **vi·bra·tory** \'vībrəˌtórē\ *adj*

vic·ar \'vikər\ *n* : parish clergy member — **vi·car·i·ate** \-ēət\ *n*

vi·car·i·ous \vī'karēəs\ *adj* : sharing in someone else's experience through imagination or sympathetic feelings — **vi·car·i·ous·ly** *adv* — **vi·car·i·ous·ness** *n*

vice \'vīs\ *n* **1** : immoral habit **2** : depravity

vice- \ˌvīs\ *prefix* : one that takes the place of

  vice-chancellor   **vice presiden-**
  vice-consul   **tial**
  vice presidency   **vice-regent**
  vice president

vice admiral *n* : commissioned officer in the navy or coast guard ranking above a rear admiral

vice·roy \'vīsˌrói\ *n* : provincial governor who represents the sovereign

vice ver·sa \ˌvīsiˈvərsə, ˌvīsˈvər-\ adv : with the order reversed

vi·cin·i·ty \vəˈsinətē\ n, pl -ties : surrounding area

vi·cious \ˈvishəs\ adj 1 : wicked 2 : savage 3 : malicious — vi·cious·ly adv — vi·cious·ness n

vi·cis·si·tude \vəˈsisəˌtüd, vī-, -ˌtyüd\ n : irregular, unexpected, or surprising change — usu. used in pl.

vic·tim \ˈviktəm\ n : person killed, hurt, or abused

vic·tim·ize \ˈviktəˌmīz\ vb -ized; -iz·ing : make a victim of — vic·tim·i·za·tion \ˌviktəməˈzāshən\ n — vic·tim·iz·er \ˈviktəˌmīzər\ n

vic·tor \ˈviktər\ n : winner

Vic·to·ri·an \vikˈtōrēən\ adj : relating to the reign of Queen Victoria of England or the art, taste, or standards of her time ∼ n : one of the Victorian period

vic·to·ri·ous \vikˈtōrēəs\ adj : having won a victory — vic·to·ri·ous·ly adv

vic·to·ry \ˈviktərē\ n, pl -ries : success in defeating an enemy or opponent or in overcoming difficulties

vict·uals \ˈvitᵊlz\ n pl : food

vid·eo \ˈvidēˌō\ adj : relating to the television image

vid·eo·cas·sette \ˌvidēˌōkəˈset\ n : cassette containing videotape

vid·eo·tape \ˈvidēōˌtāp\ vb : make a recording of (a television production) on special tape — videotape n

vie \ˈvī\ vb vied; vy·ing : contend — vi·er \ˈvīər\ n

view \ˈvyü\ n 1 : process of seeing or examining 2 : opinion 3 : area of landscape that can be seen 4 : range of vision 5 : purpose or object ∼ vb 1 : look at 2 : think about or consider — view·er n

view·point n : position from which something is considered

vig·il \ˈvijəl\ n 1 : day of devotion before a religious feast 2 : act or time of keeping awake 3 : long period of keeping watch (as over a sick or dying person)

vig·i·lant \ˈvijələnt\ adj : alert esp. to avoid danger — vig·i·lance \-ləns\ n — vig·i·lant·ly adv

vig·i·lan·te \ˌvijəˈlantē\ n : one of a group independent of the law working to suppress crime

vi·gnette \vinˈyet\ n : short descriptive literary piece

vig·or \ˈvigər\ n 1 : energy or strength 2 : intensity or force — vig·or·ous \ˈvigərəs\ adj — vig·or·ous·ly adv — vig·or·ous·ness n

vile \ˈvīl\ adj vil·er; vil·est : thoroughly bad or contemptible — vile·ly adv — vile·ness n

vil·i·fy \ˈviləˌfī\ vb -fied; -fy·ing : speak evil of — vil·i·fi·ca·tion \ˌviləfəˈkāshən\ n — vil·i·fi·er \ˈviləˌfīər\ n

◆ vil·la \ˈvilə\ n : country estate

vil·lage \ˈvilij\ n : small country town — vil·lag·er n

vil·lain \ˈvilən\ n : bad person — vil·lain·ess \-ənəs\ n — vil·lainy n

vil·lain·ous \-ənəs\ adj : evil or corrupt — vil·lain·ous·ly adv — vil·lain·ous·ness n

vim \ˈvim\ n : energy

vin·di·cate \ˈvindəˌkāt\ vb -cat·ed; -cat·ing 1 : avenge 2 : exonerate 3 : justify — vin·di·ca·tion \ˌvindəˈkāshən\ n — vin·di·ca·tor \ˈvindəˌkātər\ n

vin·dic·tive \vinˈdiktiv\ adj : seeking or meant for revenge — vin·dic·tive·ly adv — vin·dic·tive·ness n

vine \ˈvīn\ n : climbing or trailing plant

vin·e·gar \ˈvinigər\ n : acidic liquid

obtained by fermentation — **vine·gary** \-gərē\ *adj*

vine·yard \'vinyərd\ *n* : plantation of grapevines

vin·tage \'vintij\ *n* **1** : season's yield of grapes or wine **2** : period of origin ~ *adj* : of enduring interest

vi·nyl \'vīn°l\ *n* : strong plastic

vi·o·la \vē'ōlə\ *n* : instrument of the violin family tuned lower than the violin — **vi·o·list** \-list\ *n*

vi·o·late \'vīə₁lāt\ *vb* **-lat·ed; -lating 1** : act with disrespect or disregard of **2** : rape **3** : desecrate — **vi·o·la·tion** \₁vīə'lāshən\ *n* — **vi·o·la·tor** \'vīə₁lātər\ *n*

vi·o·lence \'vīələns\ *n* : intense physical force that causes or is intended to cause injury or destruction — **vi·o·lent** \-lənt\ *adj* — **vi·o·lent·ly** *adv*

vi·o·let \'vīələt\ *n* **1** : small flowering plant **2** : reddish blue

vi·o·lin \₁vīə'lin\ *n* : bowed stringed instrument — **vi·o·lin·ist** \-nist\ *n*

VIP \₁vē₁ī'pē\ *n, pl* **VIPs** \-'pēz\ : very important person

vi·per \'vīpər\ *n* **1** : venomous snake **2** : treacherous or malignant person

vi·ra·go \və'rägō, -'rā-; 'virə₁gō\ *n, pl* **-goes** *or* **-gos** : shrew

vi·ral \'vīrəl\ *adj* : relating to or caused by a virus

vir·gin \'vərjən\ *n* **1** : unmarried woman **2** : a person who has never had sexual intercourse ~ *adj* **1** : chaste **2** : natural and unspoiled — **vir·gin·al** \-əl\ *adj* — **vir·gin·al·ly** *adv* — **vir·gin·i·ty** \vər'jinətē\ *n*

vir·gule \'vərgyül\ *n* : mark / used esp. to denote "or" or "per"

vir·ile \'virəl\ *adj* : masculine — **vi·ril·i·ty** \və'rilətē\ *n*

vir·tu·al \'vərchəwəl\ *adj* : being in effect but not in fact or name — **vir·tu·al·ly** *adv*

vir·tue \'vərchü\ *n* **1** : moral excellence **2** : effective or commendable quality **3** : chastity

vir·tu·os·i·ty \₁vərchə'wäsətē\ *n, pl* **-ties** : great skill (as in music)

vir·tu·o·so \₁vərchə'wōsō, -zō\ *n, pl* **-sos** *or* **-si** \-₁sē, -₁zē\ : highly skilled performer esp. of music — **virtuoso** *adj*

vir·tu·ous \'vərchəwəs\ *adj* **1** : morally good **2** : chaste — **vir·tu·ous·ly** *adv*

vir·u·lent \'virələnt, -yələnt\ *adj* **1** : extremely severe or infectious **2** : full of malice — **vir·u·lence** \-ləns\ *n* — **vir·u·lent·ly** *adv*

vi·rus \'vīrəs\ *n* **1** : tiny disease-causing agent **2** : a computer program that performs a malicious action (as destroying data)

vi·sa \'vēzə, -sə\ *n* : authorization to enter a foreign country

vis·age \'vizij\ *n* : face

vis·cera \'visərə\ *n pl* : internal bodily organs esp. of the trunk

vis·cer·al \'visərəl\ *adj* **1** : bodily **2** : instinctive **3** : deeply or crudely emotional — **vis·cer·al·ly** *adv*

vis·cid \'visəd\ *adj* : viscous — **vis·cid·i·ty** \vis'idətē\ *n*

vis·count \'vī₁kaùnt\ *n* : British nobleman ranking below an earl and above a baron

vis·count·ess \-əs\ *n* **1** : wife of a viscount **2** : woman with rank of a viscount

vis·cous \'viskəs\ *adj* : having a thick or sticky consistency — **vis·cos·i·ty** \vis'käsətē\ *n*

vise \'vīs\ *n* : device for clamping something being worked on

vis·i·bil·i·ty \₁vizə'bilətē\ *n, pl* **-ties** : degree or range to which something can be seen

vis·i·ble \'vizəbəl\ *adj* **1** : capable of being seen **2** : manifest or apparent — **vis·i·bly** *adv*

vi·sion \'vizhən\ *n* **1** : vivid picture seen in a dream or trance or in the imagination **2** : foresight **3** : power of seeing ~ *vb* : imagine

vi·sion·ary \'vizhə₁nerē\ *adj* **1** : given to dreaming or imagining **2** : illusory **3** : not practical ~ *n* : one with great dreams or projects

vis·it \'vizət\ *vb* **1** : go or come to see **2** : stay with for a time as a guest **3** : cause or be a reward, affliction, or punishment ~ *n* : short stay as a guest — **vis·it·able** *adj* — **vis·i·tor** \-ər\ *n*

vis·i·ta·tion \₁vizə'tāshən\ *n* **1** : official visit **2** : divine punishment or favor **3** : severe trial

vi·sor \'vīzər\ *n* **1** : front piece of a helmet **2** : part (as on a cap or car windshield) that shades the eyes

vis·ta \'vistə\ *n* : distant view

vi·su·al \'vizhəwəl\ *adj* **1** : relating

to sight **2** : visible — **vi·su·al·ly** adv

vi·su·al·ize \'vizhəwə,līz\ vb **-ized; -iz·ing** : form a mental image of — **vi·su·al·i·za·tion** \,vizhəwələ-'zāshən\ n — **vi·su·al·iz·er** \'vizhəwə,līzər\ n

vi·tal \'vīt°l\ adj **1** : relating to, necessary for, or characteristic of life **2** : full of life and vigor **3** : fatal **4** : very important — **vi·tal·ly** adv

vi·tal·i·ty \vī'talətē\ n, pl **-ties 1** : life force **2** : energy

vital signs n pl : body's pulse rate, respiration, temperature, and usu. blood pressure

vi·ta·min \'vītəmən\ n : natural organic substance essential to health

vi·ti·ate \'vishē,āt\ vb **-at·ed; -at·ing 1** : spoil or impair **2** : invalidate — **vi·ti·a·tion** \,vishē'āshən\ n — **vi·ti·a·tor** \'vishē,ātər\ n

vit·re·ous \'vitrēəs\ adj : relating to or resembling glass

vit·ri·ol \'vitrēəl\ n : something caustic, corrosive, or biting — **vit·ri·ol·ic** \,vitrē'älik\ adj

vi·tu·per·ate \vī'tüpə,rāt, və-, -'tyü-\ vb **-at·ed; -at·ing** : abuse in words — **vi·tu·per·a·tion** \-,tüpə'rāshən, -,tyü-\ n — **vi·tu·per·a·tive** \-'tüpərətiv, -'tyü-, -pə,rāt-\ adj — **vi·tu·per·a·tive·ly** adv

vi·va·cious \və'vāshəs, vī-\ adj : lively — **vi·va·cious·ly** adv — **vi·va·cious·ness** n — **vi·vac·i·ty** \-'vasətē\ n

viv·id \'vivəd\ adj **1** : lively **2** : brilliant **3** : intense or sharp — **viv·id·ly** adv — **viv·id·ness** n

viv·i·fy \'vivə,fī\ vb **-fied; -fy·ing** : give life or vividness to

vivi·sec·tion \,vivə'sekshən, 'vivə,-\ n : experimental operation on a living animal

vix·en \'viksən\ n **1** : scolding woman **2** : female fox

vo·cab·u·lary \vō'kabyə,lerē\ n, pl **-lar·ies 1** : list or collection of words **2** : stock of words used by a person or about a subject

vo·cal \'vōkəl\ adj **1** : relating to or produced by or for the voice **2** : speaking out freely and usu. emphatically

vocal cords n pl : membranous folds in the larynx that are important in making vocal sounds

vo·cal·ist \'vōkəlist\ n : singer

vo·cal·ize \-,līz\ vb **-ized; -iz·ing** : give vocal expression to

vo·ca·tion \vō'kāshən\ n : regular employment — **vo·ca·tion·al** \-shənəl\ adj

vo·cif·er·ous \vō'sifərəs\ adj : noisy and insistent — **vo·cif·er·ous·ly** adv

vod·ka \'vädkə\ n : colorless distilled grain liquor

vogue \'vōg\ n : brief but intense popularity — **vogu·ish** \'vōgish\ adj

voice \'vȯis\ n **1** : sound produced through the mouth by humans and many animals **2** : power of speaking **3** : right of choice or opinion ~ vb **voiced; voic·ing** : express in words — **voiced** \'vȯist\ adj

void \'vȯid\ adj **1** : containing nothing **2** : lacking — with of **3** : not legally binding ~ n **1** : empty space **2** : feeling of hollowness ~ vb **1** : discharge (as body waste) **2** : make (as a contract) void — **void·able** adj — **void·er** n

vol·a·tile \'välət°l\ adj **1** : readily vaporizing at a relatively low temperature **2** : likely to change suddenly — **vol·a·til·i·ty** \,välə'tilətē\ n — **vol·a·til·ize** \'välət°l,īz\ vb

vol·ca·no \väl'kānō\ n, pl **-noes** or **-nos** : opening in the earth's crust from which molten rock and steam come out — **vol·ca·nic** \-'kanik\ adj

vo·li·tion \vō'lishən\ n : free will — **vo·li·tion·al** \-'lishənəl\ adj

vol·ley \'välē\ n, pl **-leys 1** : flight of missiles (as arrows) **2** : simultaneous shooting of many weapons

vol·ley·ball n : game of batting a large ball over a net

volt \'vōlt\ n : unit for measuring the force that moves an electric current

volt·age \'vōltij\ n : quantity of volts

vol·u·ble \'välyəbəl\ adj : fluent and smooth in speech — **vol·u·bil·i·ty** \,välyə'bilətē\ n — **vol·u·bly** \'välyəblē\ adv

vol·ume \'välyəm\ n **1** : book **2** : space occupied as measured by cubic units **3** : amount **4** : loudness of a sound

vo·lu·mi·nous \və'lümənəs\ adj : large or bulky

vol·un·tary \'välən,terē\ *adj* **1**
: done, made, or given freely and
without expecting compensation
2 : relating to or controlled by the
will — **vol·un·tar·i·ly** *adv*

vol·un·teer \,välən'tir\ *n* : person
who offers to help or work without expecting payment or reward
~ *vb* **1** : offer or give voluntarily **2**
: offer oneself as a volunteer

vo·lup·tuous \və'ləpchəwəs\ *adj* **1**
: luxurious **2** : having a full and
sexually attractive figure — **vo-
lup·tuous·ly** *adv* — **vo·lup·tuous-
ness** *n*

vom·it \'vämət\ *vb* : throw up the
contents of the stomach — **vomit**
n

voo·doo \'vüdü\ *n, pl* **voodoos 1** : religion derived from African poly-
theism and involving sorcery **2**
: one who practices voodoo **3**
: charm or fetish used in voodoo
— **voodoo** *adj* — **voo·doo·ism**
\-,izəm\ *n*

vo·ra·cious \vȯ'rāshəs, və-\ *adj*
: greedy or exceedingly hungry —
vo·ra·cious·ly *adv* — **vo·ra·cious-
ness** *n* — **vo·rac·i·ty** \-'rasətē\ *n*

vor·tex \'vȯr,teks\ *n, pl* **vor·ti·ces**
\'vȯrtə,sēz\ : whirling liquid

vo·ta·ry \'vōtərē\ *n, pl* **-ries 1** : devoted participant, adherent, ad-
mirer, or worshiper

vote \'vōt\ *n* **1** : individual expression of preference in choosing or
reaching a decision **2** : right to indicate one's preference or the
preference expressed ~ *vb* **voted; vot·ing 1** : cast a vote **2**
: choose or defeat by vote — **vote-
less** *adj* — **vot·er** *n*

vo·tive \'vōtiv\ *adj* : consisting of or
expressing a vow, wish, or desire

vouch \'vauch\ *vb* : give a guarantee
or personal assurance

vouch·er \'vauchər\ *n* : written record or receipt that serves as
proof of a transaction

vouch·safe \vauch'sāf\ *vb* **-safed;
-saf·ing** : grant as a special favor

vow \vau\ *n* : solemn promise to do
something or to live or act a certain way — **vow** *vb*

vow·el \'vauəl\ *n* **1** : speech sound
produced without obstruction or
friction in the mouth **2** : letter representing such a sound

voy·age \'vȯiij\ *n* : long journey esp.
by water or through space ~ *vb*
-aged; -ag·ing : make a voyage —
voy·ag·er *n*

vul·ca·nize \'vəlkə,nīz\ *vb* **-nized;
-niz·ing** : treat (as rubber) to
make more elastic or stronger

vul·gar \'vəlgər\ *adj* **1** : relating to
the common people **2** : lacking refinement **3** : offensive in manner
or language — **vul·gar·ism**
\-,rizəm\ *n* — **vul·gar·ize** \-,rīz\
vb — **vul·gar·ly** *adv*

vul·gar·i·ty \,vəl'garətē\ *n, pl* **-ties 1**
: state of being vulgar **2** : vulgar
language or act

vul·ner·a·ble \'vəlnərəbəl\ *adj* : susceptible to attack or damage —
vul·ner·a·bil·i·ty \,vəlnərə'bilətē\
n — **vul·ner·a·bly** *adv*

vul·ture \'vəlchər\ *n* : large flesh-
eating bird

vul·va \'vəlvə\ *n, pl* **-vae** \-,vē, -,vī\
: external genital parts of the fe-
male

vying *pres part of* VIE

W

w \'dəbəl,yü\ *n, pl* **w's** *or* **ws** \-,yüz\
: 23d letter of the alphabet

wad \'wäd\ *n* **1** : little mass **2** : soft
mass of fibrous material **3** : pliable
plug to retain a powder charge **4**
: considerable amount ~ *vb* **1**
: form into a wad **2** : stuff with a
wad

wad·dle \'wäd°l\ *vb* **-dled; -dling**
: walk with short steps swaying
from side to side — **waddle** *n*

wade \'wād\ *vb* **wad·ed; wad·ing 1**
: step in or through (as water) **2**
: move with difficulty — **wade** *n*
— **wad·er** *n*

wa·fer \'wāfər\ *n* **1** : thin crisp cake or cracker **2** : waferlike thing

waf·fle \'wäfəl\ *n* : crisped cake of batter cooked in a hinged utensil **(waffle iron)** ~ *vb* : vacillate

waft \'wäft, 'waft\ *vb* : cause to move lightly by wind or waves — **waft** *n*

¹wag \'wag\ *vb* **-gg-** : sway or swing from side to side or to and fro — **wag** *n*

²wag *n* : wit — **wag·gish** *adj*

wage \'wāj\ *vb* **waged; wag·ing** : engage in ~ *n* **1** : payment for labor or services **2** : compensation

wa·ger \'wājər\ *n or vb* : bet

wag·gle \'wagəl\ *vb* **-gled; -gling** : wag — **waggle** *n*

wag·on \'wagən\ *n* **1** : 4-wheeled vehicle drawn by animals **2** : child's 4-wheeled cart

waif \'wāf\ *n* : homeless child

wail \'wāl\ *vb* **1** : mourn **2** : make a sound like a mournful cry — **wail** *n*

wain·scot \'wānskət, -ˌskōt, -ˌskät\ *n* : usu. paneled wooden lining of an interior wall — **wainscot** *vb*

waist \'wāst\ *n* **1** : narrowed part of the body between chest and hips **2** : waistlike part — **waist·line** *n*

◆ **wait** \'wāt\ *vb* **1** : remain in readiness or expectation **2** : delay **3** : attend as a waiter ~ *n* **1** : concealment **2** : act or period of waiting

wait·er \'wātər\ *n* : person who serves others at tables

wait·per·son \'wātˌpərsən\ *n* : a waiter or waitress

wait·ress \'wātrəs\ *n* : woman who serves others at tables

waive \'wāv\ *vb* **waived; waiv·ing** : give up claim to

waiv·er \'wāvər\ *n* : act of waiving right, claim, or privilege

¹wake \'wāk\ *vb* **woke** \'wōk\; **wo·ken** \'wōkən\; **wak·ing 1** : keep watch **2** : bring or come back to consciousness after sleep ~ *n* **1** : state of being awake **2** : watch held over a dead body

²wake *n* : track left by a ship

wake·ful \'wākfəl\ *adj* : not sleeping or able to sleep — **wake·ful·ness** *n*

wak·en \'wākən\ *vb* : wake

wale \'wāl\ *n* : ridge on cloth

walk \'wȯk\ *vb* **1** : move or cause to move on foot **2** : pass over, through, or along by walking ~ *n* **1** : a going on foot **2** : place or path for walking **3** : distance to be walked **4** : way of living **5** : way of walking **6** : slow 4-beat gait of a horse — **walk·er** *n*

wall \'wȯl\ *n* **1** : structure for defense or for enclosing something **2** : upright enclosing part of a building or room **3** : something like a wall ~ *vb* : provide, separate, surround, or close with a wall — **walled** \'wȯld\ *adj*

wal·la·by \'wäləbē\ *n, pl* **-bies** : small or medium-sized kangaroo

wal·let \'wälət\ *n* : pocketbook with compartments

wall·flow·er *n* **1** : mustardlike plant with showy fragrant flowers **2** : one who remains on the sidelines of social activity

wal·lop \'wäləp\ *n* **1** : powerful blow **2** : ability to hit hard ~ *vb* **1** : beat soundly **2** : hit hard

wal·low \'wälō\ *vb* **1** : roll about in deep mud **2** : indulge oneself excessively ~ *n* : place for wallowing

wall·pa·per *n* : decorative paper for walls — **wallpaper** *vb*

wal·nut \'wȯlˌnət\ *n* **1** : nut with a furrowed shell and adherent husk **2** : tree on which this nut grows or its brown wood

◆ **wal·rus** \'wȯlrəs, 'wäl-\ *n, pl* **-rus**

or **-rus·es** : large seallike mammal of northern seas having ivory tusks

waltz \'wȯlts\ *n* : gliding dance to music having 3 beats to the measure or the music — **waltz** *vb*

wam·pum \'wämpəm\ *n* : strung shell beads used by No. American Indians as money

wan \'wän\ *adj* **-nn-** : sickly or pale — **wan·ly** *adv* — **wan·ness** *n*

wand \'wänd\ *n* : slender staff

wan·der \'wändər\ *vb* **1** : move about aimlessly **2** : stray **3** : become delirious — **wan·der·er** *n*

wan·der·lust \'wändər,ləst\ *n* : strong urge to wander

wane \'wän\ *vb* **waned; wan·ing 1** : grow smaller or less **2** : lose power, prosperity, or influence — **wane** *n*

wan·gle \'waŋgəl\ *vb* **-gled; -gling** : obtain by sly or devious means

want \'wȯnt\ *vb* **1** : lack **2** : need **3** : desire earnestly ∼ *n* **1** : deficiency **2** : dire need **3** : something wanted

want·ing \-iŋ\ *adj* **1** : not present or in evidence **2** : falling below standards **3** : lacking in ability ∼ *prep* **1** : less or minus **2** : without

wan·ton \'wȯntᵊn\ *adj* **1** : lewd **2** : having no regard for justice or for others' feelings, rights, or safety ∼ *n* **:** lewd or immoral person ∼ *vb* : be wanton — **wan·ton·ly** *adv* — **wan·ton·ness** *n*

wa·pi·ti \'wäpətē\ *n, pl* **-ti** *or* **-tis** : elk

war \'wȯr\ *n* **1** : armed fighting between nations **2** : state of hostility or conflict **3** : struggle between opposing forces or for a particular end ∼ *vb* **-rr-** : engage in warfare — **war·less** \-ləs\ *adj* — **war·time** *n*

war·ble \'wȯrbəl\ *n* **1** : melodious succession of low pleasing sounds **2** : musical trill ∼ *vb* **-bled; -bling** : sing or utter in a trilling way

war·bler \'wȯrblər\ *n* **1** : small thrushlike singing bird **2** : small bright-colored insect-eating bird

ward \'wȯrd\ *n* **1** : a guarding or being under guard or guardianship **2** : division of a prison or hospital **3** : electoral or administrative division of a city **4** : person under protection of a guardian or a law court ∼ *vb* : turn aside — **ward·ship** *n*

¹-ward \wərd\ *adj suffix* **1** : that moves, tends, faces, or is directed toward **2** : that occurs or is situated in the direction of

²-ward, -wards *adv suffix* **1** : in a (specified) direction **2** : toward a (specified) point, position, or area

war·den \'wȯrdᵊn\ *n* **1** : guardian **2** : official charged with supervisory duties or enforcement of laws **3** : official in charge of a prison

ward·er \'wȯrdər\ *n* : watchman or warden

ward·robe \'wȯrd,rōb\ *n* **1** : clothes closet **2** : collection of wearing apparel

ware \'war\ *n* **1** : articles for sale — often pl. **2** : items of fired clay

ware·house \-,haüs\ *n* : place for storage of merchandise — **warehouse** *vb* — **ware·house·man** \-mən\ *n* — **ware·hous·er** \-,haüzər, -sər\ *n*

war·fare \'wȯr,far\ *n* **1** : military operations between enemies **2** : struggle

war·head \-,hed\ *n* : part of a missile holding the explosive material

war·like *adj* : fond of, relating to, or used in war

warm \'wȯrm\ *adj* **1** : having or giving out moderate or adequate heat

2 : serving to retain heat 3 : showing strong feeling 4 : giving a pleasant impression of warmth, cheerfulness, or friendliness ∼ vb 1 : make or become warm 2 : give warmth or energy to 3 : experience feelings of affection 4 : become increasingly ardent, interested, or competent — **warm·er** n — **warm·ly** adv — **warm up** vb : make ready by preliminary activity

war·mon·ger \'wȯr‚məŋgər, -‚mäŋ-\ n : one who attempts to stir up war

warmth \'wȯrmth\ n 1 : quality or state of being warm 2 : enthusiasm

warn \'wȯrn\ vb 1 : put on guard 2 : notify in advance — **warn·ing** \-iŋ\ n or adj

warp \'wȯrp\ n 1 : lengthwise threads in a woven fabric 2 : twist ∼ vb 1 : twist out of shape 2 : lead astray 3 : distort

war·rant \'wȯrənt, 'wär-\ n 1 : authorization 2 : legal writ authorizing action ∼ vb 1 : declare or maintain positively 2 : guarantee 3 : approve 4 : justify

warrant officer n 1 : officer in the armed forces ranking next below a commissioned officer 2 : commissioned officer in the navy or coast guard ranking below an ensign

war·ran·ty \'wȯrəntē, 'wär-\ n, pl -ties : guarantee of the integrity of a product

war·ren \'wȯrən, 'wär-\ n : area where rabbits are bred and kept

war·rior \'wȯryər, 'wȯrēər; 'wärē-, 'wäryər\ n : man engaged or experienced in warfare

war·ship \'wȯr‚ship\ n : naval vessel

wart \'wȯrt\ n 1 : small projection on the skin caused by a virus 2 : wartlike protuberance — **warty** adj

wary \'warē\ adj **war·i·er; -est** : careful in guarding against danger or deception

was past 1st & 3d sing of BE

◆ **wash** \'wȯsh, 'wäsh\ vb 1 : cleanse with or as if with a liquid (as water) 2 : wet thoroughly with liquid 3 : flow along the border of 4 : flow in a stream 5 : move or remove by or as if by the action of water 6 : cover or daub lightly with a liquid 7 : undergo laundering ∼ n 1 : act of washing or being washed 2 : articles to be washed 3 : surging action of water or disturbed air — **wash·able** \-əbəl\ adj

wash·board n : grooved board to scrub clothes on

wash·bowl n : large bowl for water for washing hands and face

wash·cloth n : cloth used for washing one's face and body

washed–up \'wȯsht'əp, 'wäsht-\ adj : no longer capable or usable

wash·er \'wȯshər, 'wäsh-\ n 1 : machine for washing 2 : ring used around a bolt or screw to ensure tightness or relieve friction

wash·ing \'wȯshiŋ, 'wäsh-\ n : articles to be washed

Washington's Birthday n : the 3d Monday in February or formerly February 22 observed as a legal holiday

wash·out n 1 : washing out or away of earth 2 : failure

wash·room n : bathroom

wasp \'wäsp, 'wȯsp\ n : slender‚ bodied winged insect related to the bees and having a formidable sting

wasp·ish \'wäspish, 'wȯs-\ adj : irritable

was·sail \'wäsəl, wä'säl\ n 1 : toast to someone's health 2 : liquor drunk on festive occasions 3 : riotous drinking — **wassail** vb

waste \'wāst\ n 1 : sparsely settled or

barren region **2** : act or an instance of wasting **3** : refuse (as garbage or rubbish) **4** : material (as feces) produced but not used by a living body ~ *vb* **wast·ed**; **wast·ing 1** : ruin **2** : spend or use carelessly **3** : lose substance or energy ~ *adj* **1** : wild and uninhabited **2** : being of no further use — **wast·er** *n* — **waste·ful** \-fəl\ *adj* — **waste·ful·ly** *adv* — **waste·ful·ness** *n*

waste·bas·ket \-ˌbaskət\ *n* : receptacle for refuse

waste·land \-ˌland, -lənd\ *n* : barren uncultivated land

wast·rel \'wāstrəl, 'wästrəl\ *n* : one who wastes

watch \'wäch, 'wóch\ *vb* **1** : be or stay awake intentionally **2** : be on the lookout for danger **3** : observe **4** : keep oneself informed about ~ *n* **1** : act of keeping awake to guard **2** : close observation **3** : one that watches **4** : period of duty on a ship or those on duty during this period **5** : timepiece carried on the person — **watch·er** *n*

watch·dog *n* **1** : dog kept to guard property **2** : one that protects

watch·ful \-fəl\ *adj* : steadily attentive — **watch·ful·ly** *adv* — **watch·ful·ness** *n*

watch·man \-mən\ *n* : person assigned to watch

watch·word *n* **1** : secret word used as a signal **2** : slogan

wa·ter \'wótər, 'wät-\ *n* **1** : liquid that descends as rain and forms rivers, lakes, and seas **2** : liquid containing or resembling water ~ *vb* **1** : supply with or get water **2** : dilute with or as if with water **3** : form or secrete watery matter

water buffalo *n* : common oxlike often domesticated Asian buffalo

wa·ter·col·or *n* **1** : paint whose liquid part is water **2** : picture made with watercolors

wa·ter·course *n* : stream of water

wa·ter·cress \-ˌkres\ *n* : perennial salad plant with white flowers

wa·ter·fall *n* : steep descent of the water of a stream

wa·ter·fowl *n* **1** : bird that frequents the water **2** **waterfowl** *pl* : swimming game birds

wa·ter·front *n* : land fronting a body of water

water lily *n* : aquatic plant with floating leaves and showy flowers

wa·ter·logged \-ˌlógd, -ˌlägd\ *adj* : filled or soaked with water

wa·ter·mark *n* **1** : mark showing how high water has risen **2** : a marking in paper visible under light ~ *vb* : mark (paper) with a watermark

◆ **wa·ter·mel·on** *n* : large fruit with sweet juicy usu. red pulp

water moccasin *n* : venomous snake of the southeastern U.S.

wa·ter·pow·er *n* : power of moving water used to run machinery

wa·ter·proof *adj* : not letting water through ~ *vb* : make waterproof — **wa·ter·proof·ing** *n*

wa·ter·shed \-ˌshed\ *n* : dividing ridge between two drainage areas or one of these areas

water ski *n* : ski used on water when the wearer is towed — **wa·ter–ski** *vb* — **wa·ter–ski·er** *n*

wa·ter·spout *n* **1** : pipe from which water is spouted **2** : tornado over a body of water

wa·ter·tight *adj* **1** : so tight as not to let water in **2** : allowing no possibility for doubt or uncertainty

wa·ter·way *n* : navigable body of water

wa·ter·works *n pl* : system by which water is supplied (as to a city)

wa·tery \'wótərē, 'wät-\ *adj* **1** : con-

taining, full of, or giving out water **2** : being like water **3** : soft and soggy

watt \'wät\ *n* : unit of electric power — **watt·age** \'wätij\ *n*

wat·tle \'wät°l\ *n* **1** : framework of flexible branches used in building **2** : fleshy process hanging usu. about the head or neck (as of a bird) — **wat·tled** \-°ld\ *adj*

wave \'wāv\ *vb* **waved; wav·ing 1** : flutter **2** : signal with the hands **3** : wave to and fro with the hand **4** : curve up and down like a wave ~ *n* **1** : moving swell on the surface of water **2** : wave-like shape **3** : waving motion **4** : surge **5** : disturbance that transfers energy from point to point — **wave·let** \-lət\ *n* — **wave·like** *adj* — **wavy** *adj*

wave·length \'wāv,leŋth\ *n* **1** : distance from crest to crest in the line of advance of a wave **2** : line of thought that reveals a common understanding

wa·ver \'wāvər\ *vb* **1** : fluctuate in opinion, allegiance, or direction **2** : flicker **3** : falter — **waver** *n* — **wa·ver·er** *n* — **wa·ver·ing·ly** *adv*

¹wax \'waks\ *n* **1** : yellowish plastic substance secreted by bees **2** : substance like beeswax ~ *vb* : treat or rub with wax esp. for polishing

²wax *vb* **1** : grow larger **2** : become

wax·en \'waksən\ *adj* : made of or resembling wax

waxy \'waksē\ *adj* **wax·i·er; -est** : made of, full of, or resembling wax

way \'wā\ *n* **1** : thoroughfare for travel or passage **2** : route **3** : course of action **4** : method **5** : detail **6** : usual or characteristic state of affairs **7** : condition **8** : distance **9** : progress along a course — **by the way** : in a digression —

by way of 1 : for the purpose of **2** : by the route through — **out of the way** : remote

way·bill *n* : paper that accompanies a shipment and gives details of goods, route, and charges

way·far·er \'wā,farər\ *n* : traveler esp. on foot — **way·far·ing** \-,fariŋ\ *adj*

way·lay \'wā,lā\ *vb* **-laid** \-,lād\; **-lay·ing** : lie in wait for

way·side *n* : side of a road

way·ward \'wāwərd\ *adj* **1** : following one's own capricious inclinations **2** : unpredictable

we \'wē\ *pron* — used of a group that includes the speaker or writer

♦ **weak** \'wēk\ *adj* **1** : lacking strength or vigor **2** : deficient in vigor of mind or character **3** : of less than usual strength **4** : not having or exerting authority — **weak·en** \'wēkən\ *vb* — **weak·ly** *adv*

weak·ling \-liŋ\ *n* : person who is physically, mentally, or morally weak

weak·ly \'wēklē\ *adj* : feeble

weak·ness \-nəs\ *n* **1** : quality or state of being weak **2** : fault **3** : object of special liking

wealth \'welth\ *n* **1** : abundant possessions or resources **2** : profusion

wealthy \'welthē\ *adj* **wealth·i·er; -est** : having wealth

wean \'wēn\ *vb* **1** : accustom (a young mammal) to take food by means other than nursing **2** : free from dependence

weap·on \'wepən\ *n* **1** : something (as a gun) that may be used to fight with **2** : means by which one contends against another — **weap·on·less** *adj*

wear \'war\ *vb* **wore** \'wōr\; **worn** \'wōrn\; **wear·ing 1** : use as an article of clothing or adornment **2**

: carry on the person **3** : show an appearance of **4** : decay by use or by scraping **5** : lessen the strength of **6** : endure use — ~ *n* **1** : act of wearing **2** : clothing **3** : lasting quality **4** : result of use — **wear-able** \'warəbəl\ *adj* — **wear-er** *n* — **wear out** *vb* **1** : make or become useless by wear **2** : tire

wea-ri-some \'wirēsəm\ *adj* : causing weariness — **wea-ri-some-ly** *adv* — **wea-ri-some-ness** *n*

wea-ry \'wirē\ *adj* **-ri-er; -est 1** : worn out in strength, freshness, or patience **2** : expressing or characteristic of weariness ~ *vb* **-ried; -ry-ing** : make or become weary — **wea-ri-ly** *adv* — **wea-ri-ness** *n*

◆ **wea-sel** \'wēzəl\ *n* : small slender flesh-eating mammal

weath-er \'wethər\ *n* : state of the atmosphere ~ *vb* **1** : expose to or endure the action of weather **2** : endure

weath-er-beat-en *adj* : worn or damaged by exposure to the weather

weath-er-man \-,man\ *n* : one who forecasts and reports the weather

weath-er-proof *adj* : able to withstand exposure to weather — **weatherproof** *vb*

weather vane *n* : movable device that shows the way the wind blows

weave \'wēv\ *vb* **wove** \'wōv\ *or* **weaved; wo-ven** \'wōvən\ *or* **weaved; weav-ing 1** : form by interlacing strands of material **2** : to make as if by weaving together parts **3** : follow a winding course ~ *n* : pattern or method of weaving — **weav-er** *n*

web \'web\ *n* **1** : cobweb **2** : animal or plant membrane **3** : network ~ *vb* **-bb-** : cover or provide with a web — **webbed** \'webd\ *adj*

web-bing \'webiŋ\ *n* : strong closely woven tape

wed \'wed\ *vb* **-dd- 1** : marry **2** : unite

wed-ding \'wediŋ\ *n* : marriage ceremony and celebration

wedge \'wej\ *n* : V-shaped object used for splitting, raising, forcing open, or tightening ~ *vb* **wedged; wedg-ing 1** : tighten or split with a wedge **2** : force into a narrow space

wed-lock \'wed,läk\ *n* : marriage

Wednes-day \'wenzdā, -dē\ *n* : 4th day of the week

wee \'wē\ *adj* : very small

weed \'wēd\ *n* : unwanted plant ~ *vb* **1** : remove weeds **2** : get rid of — **weed-er** *n* — **weedy** *adj*

weeds *n pl* : mourning clothes

week \'wēk\ *n* **1** : 7 successive days **2** : calendar period of 7 days beginning with Sunday and ending with Saturday **3** : the working or school days of the calendar week

week-day \'wēk,dā\ *n* : any day except Sunday and often Saturday

week-end \-,end\ *n* : Saturday and Sunday ~ *vb* : spend the weekend

week-ly \'wēklē\ *adj* : occurring, appearing, or done every week ~ *n, pl* **-lies** : weekly publication — **weekly** *adv*

weep \'wēp\ *vb* **wept** \'wept\; **weep-ing** : shed tears — **weep-er** *n* — **weepy** *adj*

wee-vil \'wēvəl\ *n* : small injurious beetle with a long head usu. curved into a snout — **wee-vily, wee-vil-ly** \'wēvəlē\ *adj*

weft \'weft\ *n* : crosswise threads or yarn in weaving

weigh \'wā\ *vb* **1** : determine the heaviness of **2** : have a specified weight **3** : consider carefully **4** : raise (an anchor) off the sea floor **5** : press down or burden

weight \\'wāt\ *n* **1** : amount that something weighs **2** : relative heaviness **3** : heavy object **4** : burden or pressure **5** : importance ~ *vb* **1** : load with a weight **2** : oppress — **weight·less** \-ləs\ — **weight·less·ness** *n* — **weighty** \\'wātē\ *adj*

weird \\'wird\ *adj* **1** : unearthly or mysterious **2** : strange — **weird·ly** *adv* — **weird·ness** *n*

wel·come \\'welkəm\ *vb* **-comed; -com·ing** : accept or greet cordially ~ *adj* : received or permitted gladly ~ *n* : cordial greeting or reception

weld \\'weld\ *vb* : unite by heating, hammering, or pressing ~ *n* : union by welding — **weld·er** *n*

wel·fare \\'wel,far\ *n* **1** : prosperity **2** : government aid for those in need

¹**well** \\'wel\ *n* **1** : spring **2** : hole sunk in the earth to obtain a natural deposit (as of oil) **3** : source of supply **4** : open space extending vertically through floors ~ *vb* : flow forth

²**well** *adv* **bet·ter** \\'betər\; **best** \\'best\ **1** : in a good or proper manner **2** : satisfactorily **3** : fully **4** : intimately **5** : considerably ~ *adj* **1** : satisfactory **2** : prosperous **3** : desirable **4** : healthy

well–adjusted \,welə'jəstəd\ *adj* : well-balanced

well–ad·vised \,weləd'vīzd\ *adj* : prudent

well–balanced \\'wel'balənst\ *adj* **1** : evenly balanced **2** : emotionally or psychologically sound

well–be·ing \\'wel'bēiŋ\ *n* : state of being happy, healthy, or prosperous

well–bred \-'bred\ *adj* : having good manners

well–done *adj* **1** : properly performed **2** : cooked thoroughly

well–heeled \-'hēld\ *adj* : financially well-off

well–mean·ing *adj* : having good intentions

well–nigh *adv* : nearly

well–off *adj* : being in good condition esp. financially

well–read \-'red\ *adj* : well informed through reading

well–round·ed \-'raŭndəd\ *adj* : broadly developed

well·spring *n* : source

well–to–do \,weltə'dü\ *adj* : prosperous

welsh \\'welsh, 'welch\ *vb* **1** : avoid payment **2** : break one's word

Welsh rabbit *n* : melted often seasoned cheese poured over toast or crackers

Welsh rare·bit \-'rarbət\ *n* : Welsh rabbit

welt \\'welt\ *n* **1** : narrow strip of leather between a shoe upper and sole **2** : ridge raised on the skin usu. by a blow ~ *vb* : hit hard

wel·ter \\'weltər\ *vb* **1** : toss about **2** : wallow ~ *n* : confused jumble

wen \\'wen\ *n* : abnormal growth or cyst

wench \\'wench\ *n* : young woman

wend \\'wend\ *vb* : direct one's course

went *past of* GO

wept *past of* WEEP

were *past 2d sing, past pl, or past subjunctive of* BE

were·wolf \\'wer,wůlf, 'wir-, 'wər-\ *n*, *pl* **-wolves** \-,wůlvz\ : person held to be able to change into a wolf

west \\'west\ *adv* : to or toward the west ~ *adj* : situated toward or at or coming from the west ~ *n* **1** : direction of sunset **2** *cap* : regions to the west — **west·er·ly** \\'westərlē\ *adv or adj* — **west·ward** \-wərd\ *adv or adj* — **west·wards** \-wərdz\ *adv*

west·ern \\'western\ *adj* **1** *cap* : of a region designated West **2** : lying toward or coming from the west — **West·ern·er** *n*

wet \\'wet\ *adj* **-tt- 1** : consisting of or covered or soaked with liquid **2** : not dry ~ *n* : moisture ~ *vb* **-tt-** : make or become moist — **wet·ly** *adv* — **wet·ness** *n*

whack \\'hwak\ *vb* : strike sharply ~ *n* **1** : sharp blow **2** : proper working order **3** : chance **4** : try

¹**whale** \\'hwāl\ *n*, *pl* **whales** *or* **whale** : large marine mammal ~ *vb* **whaled; whal·ing** : hunt for whales — **whale·boat** *n* — **whal·er** *n*

²**whale** *vb* **whaled; whal·ing** : strike or hit vigorously

whale·bone *n* : horny substance attached to the upper jaw of some large whales (**whalebone whales**)

wharf \\'hwȯrf\ *n*, *pl* **wharves**

\'hwȯrvz\ : structure alongside which boats lie to load or unload

what \'hwät\ *pron* **1** — used to inquire the identity or nature of something **2** : that which **3** : whatever ~ *adv* : in what respect ~ *adj* **1** — used to inquire about the identity or nature of something **2** : how remarkable or surprising **3** : whatever

what·ev·er \hwät'evər\ *pron* **1** : anything or everything that **2** : no matter what ~ *adj* : of any kind at all

what·not \'hwät,nät\ *pron* : any of various other things that might be mentioned

what·so·ev·er \,hwätsō'evər\ *pron or adj* : whatever

wheal \'hwēl\ *n* : a welt on the skin

wheat \'hwēt\ *n* : cereal grain that yields flour — **wheat·en** *adj*

whee·dle \'hwēd³l\ *vb* -**dled; -dling** : coax or tempt by flattery

wheel \'hwēl\ *n* **1** : disk or circular frame capable of turning on a central axis **2** : device of which the main part is a wheel ~ *vb* **1** : convey or move on wheels or a wheeled vehicle **2** : rotate **3** : turn so as to change direction — **wheeled** *adj* — **wheel·er** *n* — **wheel·less** *adj*

wheel·bar·row \-,barō\ *n* : one=wheeled vehicle for carrying small loads

wheel·base *n* : distance in inches between the front and rear axles of an automotive vehicle

wheel·chair *n* : chair mounted on wheels esp. for the use of disabled persons

◆ **wheeze** \'hwēz\ *vb* **wheezed; wheez·ing** : breathe with difficulty and with a whistling sound — **wheeze** *n* — **wheezy** *adj*

whelk \'hwelk\ *n* : large sea snail

whelp \'hwelp\ *n* : one of the young of various carnivorous mammals (as a dog) ~ *vb* : bring forth whelps

when \'hwen\ *adv* — used to inquire about or designate a particular time ~ *conj* **1** : at or during the time that **2** : every time that **3** : if **4** : although ~ *pron* : what time

whence \'hwens\ *adv or conj* : from what place, source, or cause

when·ev·er \hwen'evər\ *conj or adv* : at whatever time

where \'hwer\ *adv* **1** : at, in, or to what place **2** : at, in, or to what situation, position, direction, circumstances, or respect ~ *conj* **1** : at, in, or to what place, position, or circumstance **2** : at, in, or to which place ~ *n* : place

where·abouts \-ə,baủts\ *adv* : about where ~ *n sing or pl* : place where a person or thing is

where·as \hwer'az\ *conj* **1** : while on the contrary **2** : since

where·by *conj* : by, through, or in accordance with which

where·fore \'hwer,fōr\ *adv* **1** : why **2** : therefore ~ *n* : reason

where·in \hwer'in\ *adv* : in what respect

where·of \-'əv, -'äv\ *conj* : of what, which, or whom

where·up·on \'hwerə,pȯn, -,pän\ *conj* **1** : on which **2** : and then

wher·ev·er \hwer'evər\ *adv* : where ~ *conj* : at, in, or to whatever place or circumstance

where·with·al \'hwerwith,ȯl, -with-\ *n* : resources and esp. money

whet \'hwet\ *vb* -**tt-** **1** : sharpen by rubbing (as with a stone) **2** : stimulate — **whet·stone** *n*

whether \'hwethər\ *conj* **1** : if it is or

was true that **2** : if it is or was better **3** : whichever is the case

whey \'hwā\ *n* : watery part of sour milk

which \'hwich\ *adj* **1** : being what one or ones out of a group **2** : whichever ~ *pron* **1** : which one or ones **2** : whichever

which·ev·er \hwich'evər\ *pron or adj* : no matter what one

whiff \'hwif\ *n* **1** : slight gust **2** : inhalation of odor, gas, or smoke **3** : slight trace ~ *vb* : inhale an odor

while \'hwīl\ *n* **1** : period of time **2** : time and effort used ~ *conj* **1** : during the time that **2** : as long as **3** : although ~ *vb* **whiled; whil·ing** : cause to pass esp. pleasantly

whim \'hwim\ *n* : sudden wish, desire, or change of mind

whim·per \'hwimpər\ *vb* : cry softly — **whimper** *n*

whim·si·cal \'hwimzikəl\ *adj* **1** : full of whims **2** : erratic — **whim·si·cal·i·ty** \,hwimzə'kalətē\ *n* — **whim·si·cal·ly** *adv*

whim·sy, whim·sey \'hwimzē\ *n, pl* **-sies** *or* **-seys 1** : whim **2** : fanciful creation

whine \'hwīn\ *vb* **whined; whin·ing 1** : utter a usu. high-pitched plaintive cry **2** : complain — **whine** *n* — **whin·er** *n* — **whiny** *adj*

whin·ny \'hwinē\ *vb* **-nied; -ny·ing** : neigh — **whinny** *n*

whip \'hwip\ *vb* **-pp- 1** : move quickly **2** : strike with something slender and flexible **3** : defeat **4** : incite **5** : beat into a froth ~ *n* **1** : flexible device used for whipping **2** : party leader responsible for discipline **3** : thrashing motion — **whip·per** *n*

whip·cord *n* **1** : thin tough cord **2** : cloth made of hard-twisted yarns

whip·lash *n* : injury from a sudden sharp movement of the neck and head

whip·per·snap·per \'hwipər,snapər\ *n* : small, insignificant, or presumptuous person

whip·pet \'hwipət\ *n* : small swift dog often used for racing

whip·poor·will \'hwipər,wil\ *n* : American nocturnal bird

whir \'hwər\ *vb* **-rr-** : move, fly, or revolve with a whir ~ *n* : continuous fluttering or vibratory sound

whirl \'hwərl\ *vb* **1** : move or drive in a circle **2** : spin **3** : move or turn quickly **4** : reel ~ *n* **1** : rapid circular movement **2** : state of commotion or confusion **3** : try

whirl·pool *n* : whirling mass of water having a depression in the center

whirl·wind *n* : whirling wind storm

whisk \'hwisk\ *n* **1** : quick light sweeping or brushing motion **2** : usu. wire kitchen implement for beating ~ *vb* **1** : move or convey briskly **2** : beat **3** : brush lightly

whisk broom *n* : small broom

whis·ker \'hwiskər\ *n* **1** *pl* : beard **2** : long bristle or hair near an animal's mouth — **whis·kered** \-kərd\ *adj*

whis·key, whis·ky \'hwiskē\ *n, pl* **-keys** *or* **-kies** : liquor distilled from a fermented mash of grain

whis·per \'hwispər\ *vb* **1** : speak softly **2** : tell by whispering ~ *n* **1** : soft low sound **2** : rumor

whist \'hwist\ *n* : card game

whis·tle \'hwisəl\ *n* **1** : device by which a shrill sound is produced **2** : shrill clear sound made by a whistle or through the lips ~ *vb* **-tled; -tling 1** : make or utter a whistle **2** : signal or call by a whistle **3** : produce by whistling — **whis·tler** *n*

whis·tle–blow·er \'hwisəl,blōər\ *n* : informer

whis·tle–stop *n* : brief political appearance

whit \'hwit\ *n* : bit

white \'hwīt\ *adj* **whit·er; -est 1** : free from color **2** : of the color of new snow or milk **3** : having light skin ~ *n* **1** : color of maximum lightness **2** : white part or thing **3** : person who is light-skinned — **white·ness** *n* — **whit·ish** *adj*

white blood cell *n* : blood cell that does not contain hemoglobin

white·cap \'hwīt,kap\ *n* : wave crest breaking into white foam

white–col·lar *adj* : relating to salaried employees with duties not requiring protective or work clothing

white elephant *n* : something costly but of little use or value

white·fish \'hwīt,fish\ *n* : freshwater food fish

whit·en \'hwīt°n\ *vb* : make or become white — **whit·en·er** \'hwīt͞'nər\ *n*

white slave *n* : woman or girl held unwillingly for purposes of prostitution — **white slavery** *n*

white·tail \'hwīt,tāl\ *n* : No. American deer

white·wash *vb* **1** : whiten with a composition (as of lime and water) **2** : gloss over or cover up faults or wrongdoing — **whitewash** *n*

whith·er \'hwithər\ *adv* **1** : to what place **2** : to what situation, position, degree, or end

¹**whit·ing** \'hwītiŋ\ *n* : usu. light or silvery food fish

²**whiting** *n* : pulverized chalk or limestone

whit·tle \'hwit͞'l\ *vb* **-tled; -tling 1** : pare **2** : shape by paring **3** : reduce gradually

whiz, whizz \'hwiz\ *vb* **-zz-** : make a sound like a speeding object — **whiz, whizz** *n*

◆ **who** \'hü\ *pron* **1** : what or which person or persons **2** : person or persons that **3** — used to introduce a relative clause

who·dun·it \hü'dənət\ *n* : detective or mystery story

who·ev·er \hü'evər\ *pron* : no matter who

whole \'hōl\ *adj* **1** : being in healthy or sound condition **2** : having all its parts or elements **3** : constituting the total sum of ~ *n* **1** : complete amount or sum **2** : something whole or entire — **on the whole 1** : considering all circumstances **2** : in general — **wholeness** *n*

whole·heart·ed \'hōl'härtəd\ *adj* : sincere

whole number *n* : integer

whole·sale *n* : sale of goods in quan-

tity usu. for resale by a retail merchant ~ *adj* **1** : of or relating to wholesaling **2** : performed on a large scale ~ *vb* **-saled; -sal·ing** : sell at wholesale — **wholesale** *adv* — **whole·sal·er** *n*

whole·some \-səm\ *adj* **1** : promoting mental, spiritual, or bodily health **2** : healthy — **whole·some·ness** *n*

whole wheat *adj* : made of ground entire wheat kernels

whol·ly \'hōlē\ *adv* **1** : totally **2** : solely

whom \'hüm\ *pron, objective case of* WHO

whom·ev·er \hüm'evər\ *pron, objective case of* WHOEVER

whoop \'hwùp, 'hwüp, 'hüp, 'hùp\ *vb* : shout loudly ~ *n* : shout

whooping cough *n* : infectious disease marked by convulsive coughing fits

whop·per \'hwäpər\ *n* **1** : something unusually large or extreme of its kind **2** : monstrous lie

whop·ping \'hwäpiŋ\ *adj* : extremely large

whore \'hōr\ *n* : prostitute

whorl \'hwòrl, 'hwərl\ *n* : spiral — **whorled** *adj*

whose \'hüz\ *adj* : of or relating to whom or which ~ *pron* : whose one or ones

who·so·ev·er \,hüsō'evər\ *pron* : whoever

why \'hwī\ *adv* : for what reason, cause, or purpose ~ *conj* **1** : reason for which **2** : for which ~ *n, pl* **whys** : reason ~ *interj* — used esp. to express surprise

wick \'wik\ *n* : cord that draws up oil, tallow, or wax to be burned

wick·ed \'wikəd\ *adj* **1** : morally bad **2** : harmful or troublesome **3** : very unpleasant **4** : very impres-

sive — **wick·ed·ly** *adv* — **wick·ed·ness** *n*

wick·er \'wikər\ *n* **1** : small pliant branch **2** : wickerwork — **wicker** *adj*

wick·er·work *n* : work made of wickers

wick·et \'wikət\ *n* **1** : small gate, door, or window **2** : frame in cricket or arch in croquet

wide \'wīd\ *adj* **wid·er; wid·est 1** : covering a vast area **2** : measured at right angles to the length **3** : having a great measure across **4** : opened fully **5** : far from the thing in question ∼ *adv* **wid·er; wid·est 1** : over a great distance **2** : so as to leave considerable space between **3** : fully — **wide·ly** *adv* — **wid·en** \'wīd°n\ *vb*

wide–awake *adj* : alert

wide–eyed *adj* **1** : having the eyes wide open **2** : amazed **3** : naive

wide·spread *adj* : widely extended

wid·ow \'widō\ *n* : woman who has lost her husband by death and has not married again ∼ *vb* : cause to become a widow — **wid·ow·hood** *n*

wid·ow·er \'widəwər\ *n* : man who has lost his wife by death and has not married again

width \'width\ *n* **1** : distance from side to side **2** : largeness of extent **3** : measured and cut piece of material

wield \'wēld\ *vb* **1** : use or handle esp. effectively **2** : exert — **wield·er** *n*

wie·ner \'wēnər\ *n* : frankfurter

wife \'wīf\ *n, pl* **wives** \'wīvz\ : married woman — **wife·hood** *n* — **wife·less** *adj* — **wife·ly** *adj*

wig \'wig\ *n* : manufactured covering of hair for the head

wig·gle \'wigəl\ *vb* **-gled; -gling 1** : move with quick jerky or shaking movements **2** : wriggle — **wig·gle** *n* — **wig·gler** *n*

wig·gly \-əlē\ *adj* **1** : tending to wiggle **2** : wavy

wig·wag \'wig,wag\ *vb* : signal by a flag or light waved according to a code

wig·wam \'wig,wäm\ *n* : American Indian hut consisting of a framework of poles overlaid with bark, rush mats, or hides

wild \'wīld\ *adj* **1** : living or being in a state of nature and not domesticated or cultivated **2** : unrestrained **3** : turbulent **4** : crazy **5** : uncivilized **6** : erratic ∼ *n* **1** : wilderness **2** : undomesticated state ∼ *adv* : without control — **wild·ly** *adv* — **wild·ness** *n*

wild·cat \-,kat\ *n* : any of various undomesticated cats (as a lynx) ∼ *adj* **1** : not sound or safe **2** : unauthorized

wil·der·ness \'wildərnəs\ *n* : uncultivated and uninhabited region

wild·fire \'wīld,fir\ *n* : sweeping and destructive fire

wild·fowl *n* : game waterfowl

wild·life \'wīld,līf\ *n* : undomesticated animals

wile \'wīl\ *n* : trick to snare or deceive ∼ *vb* **wiled; wil·ing** : lure

will \'wil\ *vb, past* **would** \'wüd\; *pres sing & pl* **will 1** : wish **2** — used as an auxiliary verb to express (1) desire or willingness (2) customary action (3) simple future time (4) capability (5) determination (6) probability (7) inevitability or (8) a command **3** : dispose of by a will ∼ *n* **1** : often determined wish **2** : act, process, or experience of willing **3** : power of controlling one's actions or emotions **4** : legal document disposing of property after death

will·ful, wil·ful \'wilfəl\ *adj* **1** : governed by will without regard to reason **2** : intentional — **will·ful·ly** *adv*

will·ing \'wiliŋ\ *adj* **1** : inclined or favorably disposed in mind **2** : prompt to act **3** : done, borne, or accepted voluntarily or without reluctance — **will·ing·ly** *adv* — **will·ing·ness** *n*

will–o'–the–wisp \,wiləthə'wisp\ *n* **1** : light that appears at night over marshy grounds **2** : misleading or elusive goal or hope

wil·low \'wilō\ *n* : quick-growing shrub or tree with flexible shoots

wil·lowy \'wiləwē\ *adj* : gracefully tall and slender

will·pow·er \'wil,paůər\ *n* : energetic determination

wil·ly–nil·ly \,wilē'nilē\ *adv or adj* : without regard for one's choice

wilt \'wilt\ *vb* **1** : lose or cause to lose freshness and become limp esp. from lack of water **2** : grow weak

wily \'wīlē\ *adj* **wil·i·er; -est** : full of craftiness — **wil·i·ness** *n*

win \'win\ *vb* **won** \'wən\; **win·ning 1** : get possession of esp. by effort **2** : gain victory in battle or a contest **3** : make friendly or favorable ∼ *n* : victory

wince \'wins\ *vb* **winced; winc·ing** : shrink back involuntarily — **wince** *n*

winch \'winch\ *n* : machine for hoisting or pulling with a drum around which rope is wound — **winch** *vb*

¹**wind** \'wind\ *n* **1** : movement of the air **2** : breath **3** : gas in the stomach or intestines **4** : air carrying a scent **5** : intimation ∼ *vb* **1** : get a scent of **2** : cause to be out of breath

²**wind** \'wīnd\ *vb* **wound** \'waůnd\; **wind·ing 1** : have or follow a curving course **2** : move or lie to encircle **3** : encircle or cover with something pliable **4** : tighten the spring of ∼ *n* : turn or coil — **wind·er** *n*

wind·break \-,brāk\ *n* : trees and shrubs to break the force of the wind

wind·break·er \-,brākər\ *n* : light wind-resistant jacket

wind·fall \'wind,fól\ *n* **1** : thing blown down by wind **2** : unexpected benefit

wind instrument *n* : musical instrument (as a flute or horn) sounded by wind and esp. by the breath

wind·lass \'windləs\ *n* : winch esp. for hoisting anchor

wind·mill \'wind,mil\ *n* : machine worked by the wind turning vanes

win·dow \'windō\ *n* **1** : opening in the wall of a building to let in light and air **2** : pane in a window **3** : span of time for something **4** : area of a computer display — **win·dow·less** *adj*

win·dow–shop *vb* : look at the displays in store windows — **win·dow–shop·per** *n*

wind·pipe \'wind,pīp\ *n* : passage for the breath from the larynx to the lungs

wind·shield \'-,shēld\ *n* : transparent screen in front of the occupants of a vehicle

wind·up \'wīnd,əp\ *n* : end — **wind up** *vb*

wind·ward \'windwərd\ *adj* : being in or facing the direction from which the wind is blowing ∼ *n* : direction from which the wind is blowing

windy \'windē\ *adj* **wind·i·er; -est** : having wind **2** : indulging in useless talk

wine \'wīn\ *n* **1** : fermented grape juice **2** : usu. fermented juice of a plant product (as fruit) used as a beverage ∼ *vb* : treat to or drink wine

wing \'win\ *n* **1** : movable paired appendage for flying **2** : winglike thing **3** *pl* : area at the side of the stage out of sight **4** : faction ∼ *vb* **1** : fly **2** : propel through the air — **winged** *adj* — **wing·less** *adj* — **on the wing** : in flight — **under one's wing** : in one's charge or care

wink \'wink\ *vb* **1** : close and open the eyes quickly **2** : avoid seeing or noticing something **3** : twinkle **4** : close and open one eye quickly as a signal or hint ∼ *n* **1** : brief sleep **2** : act of winking **3** : instant — **wink·er** *n*

win·ner \'winər\ *n* : one that wins

win·ning \-in\ *n* **1** : victory **2** : money won at gambling ∼ *adj* **1** : victorious **2** : charming

win·now \'winō\ *vb* **1** : remove (as chaff) by a current of air **2** : sort or separate something

win·some \'winsəm\ *adj* **1** : causing joy **2** : cheerful or gay — **win·some·ly** *adv* — **win·some·ness** *n*

win·ter \'wintər\ *n* : season between autumn and spring ∼ *adj* : sown in autumn for harvest the next spring or summer — **win·ter·time** *n*

win·ter·green \'wintər,grēn\ *n* : low heathlike evergreen plant with red berries

win·try \'wintrē\ *adj* **win·tri·er; -est 1** : characteristic of winter **2** : cold in feeling

wipe \'wīp\ *vb* **wiped; wip·ing 1** : clean or dry by rubbing **2** : remove by rubbing **3** : erase completely **4** : destroy **5** : pass over a surface ∼ *n* : act or instance of wiping — **wip·er** *n*

wire \'wīr\ *n* **1** : thread of metal **2** : work made of wire **3** : telegram or cablegram ∼ *vb* **1** : provide with wire **2** : bind or mount with

wire 3 : telegraph — **wire•less** *adj*
wire•less \-ləs\ *n, chiefly Brit* : radio
wire•tap *vb* : connect into a telephone or telegraph wire to get information — **wiretap** *n* — **wire-
tap•per** *n*
wir•ing \'wīriŋ\ *n* : system of wires
wiry \'wīrē\ *adj* **wir•i•er** \'wīrēər\;
-est 1 : resembling wire **2** : slender
yet strong and sinewy — **wir•i-
ness** *n*
wis•dom \'wizdəm\ *n* **1** : accumulated learning **2** : good sense
wisdom tooth *n* : last tooth on each
half of each human jaw
¹wise \'wīz\ *n* : manner
²wise *adj* **wis•er**; **wis•est 1** : having or
showing wisdom, good sense, or
good judgment **2** : aware of what
is going on — **wise•ly** *adv*
wise•crack *n* : clever, smart, or flippant remark ~ *vb* : make a wise-
crack
wish \'wish\ *vb* **1** : have a desire **2**
: express a wish concerning **3** : request ~ *n* **1** : a wishing or desire **2**
: expressed will or desire
wish•bone *n* : forked bone in front
of the breastbone in most birds
wish•ful \-fəl\ *adj* **1** : expressive of a
wish **2** : according with wishes
rather than fact
wishy–washy \'wishē,wȯshē,
-,wäsh-\ *adj* : weak or insipid
wisp \'wisp\ *n* **1** : small bunch of hay
or straw **2** : thin strand, strip, fragment, or streak **3** : something frail,
slight, or fleeting — **wispy** *adj*
wis•te•ria \wis'tirēə\ *n* : pealike
woody vine with long clusters of
flowers
wist•ful \'wistfəl\ *adj* : full of longing — **wist•ful•ly** *adv* — **wist•ful-
ness** *n*
◆ **wit** \'wit\ *n* **1** : reasoning power **2**
: mental soundness — usu. pl. **3**
: quickness and cleverness in han-

dling words and ideas **4** : talent for
clever remarks or one noted for
witty remarks — **wit•less** *adj* —
wit•less•ly *adv* — **wit•less•ness** *n*
— **wit•ted** *adj*
witch \'wich\ *n* **1** : person believed
to have magic power **2** : ugly old
woman ~ *vb* : bewitch
witch•craft \'wich,kraft\ *n* : power
or practices of a witch
witch•ery \'wichərē\ *n, pl* **-er•ies 1**
: witchcraft **2** : charm
witch ha•zel \'wich,hāzəl\ *n* **1**
: shrub having small yellow flowers in fall **2** : alcoholic lotion made
from witch hazel bark
witch–hunt *n* **1** : searching out and
persecution of supposed witches **2**
: harassment esp. of political opponents
with \'with, 'with\ *prep* **1** : against,
to, or toward **2** : in support of **3**
: because of **4** : in the company of
5 : having **6** : despite **7** : containing
8 : by means of
with•draw \with'drȯ, with-\ *vb*
-drew \-'drü\; **-drawn** \-'drȯn\;
-draw•ing \-'drȯiŋ\ **1** : take back
or away **2** : call back or retract **3**
: go away **4** : terminate one's participation in or use of — **with-
draw•al** \-'drȯəl\ *n*
with•drawn \with'drȯn\ *adj* : socially detached and unresponsive
with•er \'withər\ *vb* **1** : shrivel **2**
: lose or cause to lose energy,
force, or freshness
with•ers \'withərz\ *n pl* : ridge between the shoulder bones of a
horse
with•hold \with'hōld, with-\ *vb*
-held \-'held\; **-hold•ing 1** : hold
back **2** : refrain from giving
with•in \with'in, with-\ *adv* **1** : in or
into the interior **2** : inside oneself
~ *prep* **1** : in or to the inner part of
2 : in the limits or compass of

with·out \with'aùt, with-\ *prep* **1** : outside **2** : lacking **3** : unaccompanied or unmarked by — **without** *adv*

with·stand \with'stand, with-\ *vb* **-stood** \-'stùd\; **-stand·ing** : oppose successfully

wit·ness \'witnəs\ *n* **1** : testimony **2** : one who testifies **3** : one present at a transaction to testify that it has taken place **4** : one who has personal knowledge or experience **5** : something serving as proof ~ *vb* **1** : bear witness to **2** : act as legal witness of **3** : furnish proof of **4** : be a witness of **5** : be the scene of

wit·ti·cism \'witə,sizəm\ *n* : witty saying or phrase

wit·ting \'witiŋ\ *adj* : intentional — **wit·ting·ly** *adv*

wit·ty \'witē\ *adj* **-ti·er; -est** : marked by or full of wit — **wit·ti·ly** \'wit°lē\ *adv* — **wit·ti·ness** *n*

wives *pl of* WIFE

wiz·ard \'wizərd\ *n* **1** : magician **2** : very clever person — **wiz·ard·ry** \-ərdrē\ *n*

wiz·ened \'wiz°nd\ *adj* : dried up

wob·ble \'wäbəl\ *vb* **-bled; -bling** **1** : move or cause to move with an irregular rocking motion **2** : tremble **3** : waver — **wobble** *n* — **wob·bly** \'wäbəlē\ *adj*

woe \'wō\ *n* **1** : deep suffering **2** : misfortune

woe·be·gone \'wōbi,gòn\ *adj* : exhibiting woe, sorrow, or misery

woe·ful \'wōfəl\ *adj* **1** : full of woe **2** : bringing woe — **woe·ful·ly** *adv*

woke *past of* WAKE

woken *past part of* WAKE

wolf \'wùlf\ *n, pl* **wolves** \'wùlvz\ : large doglike predatory mammal ~ *vb* : eat greedily — **wolf·ish** *adj*

wol·fram \'wùlfrəm\ *n* : tungsten

wol·ver·ine \ˌwùlvə'rēn\ *n, pl* **-ines** : flesh-eating mammal related to the weasels

wom·an \'wùmən\ *n, pl* **wom·en** \'wimən\ **1** : adult female person **2** : womankind **3** : feminine nature — **wom·an·hood** \-ˌhùd\ *n* — **wom·an·ish** *adj*

wom·an·kind \-ˌkīnd\ *n* : females of the human race

wom·an·ly \-lē\ *adj* : having qualities characteristic of a woman — **wom·an·li·ness** \-lēnəs\ *n*

womb \'wüm\ *n* : uterus

won *past of* WIN

♦ **won·der** \'wəndər\ *n* **1** : cause of astonishment or surprise **2** : feeling (as of astonishment) aroused by something extraordinary ~ *vb* **1** : feel surprise **2** : feel curiosity or doubt

won·der·ful \'wəndərfəl\ *adj* **1** : exciting wonder **2** : unusually good — **won·der·ful·ly** *adv* — **won·der·ful·ness** *n*

won·der·land \-ˌland, -lənd\ *n* **1** : fairylike imaginary realm **2** : place that excites admiration or wonder

won·der·ment \-mənt\ *n* : wonder

won·drous \'wəndrəs\ *adj* : wonderful — **won·drous·ly** *adv* — **won·drous·ness** *n*

wont \'wònt, 'wōnt\ *adj* : accustomed ~ *n* : habit — **wont·ed** *adj*

woo \'wü\ *vb* : try to gain the love or favor of — **woo·er** *n*

wood \'wùd\ *n* **1** : dense growth of trees usu. smaller than a forest — often *pl.* **2** : hard fibrous substance of trees and shrubs beneath the bark **3** : wood prepared for some use (as burning) ~ *adj* **1** : wooden **2** : suitable for working with wood **3** *or* **woods** \'wùdz\ : living or growing in woods — **wood·chop·per** *n* — **wood·pile** *n* — **wood·shed** *n*

wood·bine \'wùd‚bīn\ n : climbing vine

wood·chuck \-‚chək\ n : thick-bodied grizzled animal of No. America

wood·craft n 1 : skill and practice in matters relating to the woods 2 : skill in making articles from wood

wood·cut \-‚kət\ n 1 : relief printing surface engraved on wood 2 : print from a woodcut

wood·ed \'wùdəd\ adj : covered with woods

wood·en \'wùd²n\ adj 1 : made of wood 2 : lacking resilience 3 : lacking ease, liveliness or interest — **wood·en·ly** adv — **wood·en·ness** n

wood·land \-lənd, -‚land\ n : land covered with trees

wood·peck·er \'wùd‚pekər\ n : brightly marked bird with a hard bill for drilling into trees

woods·man \'wùdzmən\ n : person who works in the woods

wood·wind \'wùd‚wind\ n : one of a group of wind instruments (as a flute or oboe)

wood·work n : work (as interior house fittings) made of wood

woody \'wùdē\ adj **wood·i·er; -est** 1 : abounding with woods 2 : of, containing, or like wood fibers — **wood·i·ness** n

woof \'wùf \ n : weft

wool \'wùl\ n 1 : soft hair of some mammals and esp. the sheep 2 : something (as a textile) made of wool — **wooled** \'wùld\ adj

wool·en, wool·len \'wùlən\ adj 1 : made of wool 2 : relating to the manufacture of woolen products ~ n 1 : woolen fabric 2 : woolen garments — usu. pl.

wool·gath·er·ing n : idle daydreaming

wool·ly \'wùlē\ adj **-li·er; -est** 1 : of, relating to, or bearing wool 2 : consisting of or resembling wool 3 : confused or turbulent

woo·zy \'wüzē\ adj **-zi·er; -est** 1 : confused 2 : somewhat dizzy, nauseated, or weak — **woo·zi·ness** n

word \'wərd\ n 1 : brief remark 2 : speech sound or series of speech sounds that communicates a

meaning 3 : written representation of a word 4 : order 5 : news 6 : promise 7 pl : dispute ~ vb : express in words — **word·less** adj

word·ing \'wərdiŋ\ n : verbal expression

word processing n : production of structured and printed documents through a computer program (**word processor**) — **word process** vb

wordy \'wərdē\ adj **word·i·er; -est** : using many words — **word·i·ness** n

wore past of WEAR

work \'wərk\ n 1 : labor 2 : employment 3 : task 4 : something (as an artistic production) produced by mental effort or physical labor 5 pl : place where industrial labor is done 6 pl : moving parts of a mechanism 7 : workmanship ~ adj 1 : suitable for wear while working 2 : used for work ~ vb **worked** \'wərkt\ or **wrought** \'ròt\; **work·ing** 1 : bring to pass 2 : create by expending labor upon 3 : bring or get into a form or condition 4 : set or keep in operation 5 : solve 6 : cause to labor 7 : arrange 8 : excite 9 : labor 10 : perform work regularly for wages 11 : function according to plan or design 12 : produce a desired effect — **work·bench** n — **work·man** \-mən\ n — **work·room** n — **in the works** : in preparation

work·able \'wərkəbəl\ adj 1 : capable of being worked 2 : feasible — **work·able·ness** n

work·a·day \'wərkə‚dā\ adj 1 : relating to or suited for working days 2 : ordinary

work·a·hol·ic \‚wərkə'hòlik, -'häl-\ n : compulsive worker

work·day \'wərk‚dā\ n 1 : day on which work is done 2 : period of time during which one is working

work·er \'wərkər\ n : person who works esp. for wages

work·horse n 1 : horse used for hard work 2 : person who does most of the work of a group task

work·house n : place of confinement for persons who have committed minor offenses

work·ing \'wərkiŋ\ adj 1 : adequate to allow work to be done 2 : adopted or assumed to help further work or activity ~ *n* : operation — usu. used in pl.

work·ing·man \'wərkiŋ,man\ *n* : worker

work·man·like \-,līk\ *adj* : worthy of a good workman

work·man·ship \-,ship\ *n* **1** : art or skill of a workman **2** : quality of a piece of work

♦ **work·out** \'wərk,aut\ *n* : exercise to improve one's fitness

work out *vb* **1** : bring about by effort **2** : solve **3** : develop **4** : to be successful **5** : perform exercises

work·shop *n* **1** : small establishment for manufacturing or handicrafts **2** : seminar emphasizing exchange of ideas and practical methods

world \'wərld\ *n* **1** : universe **2** : earth with its inhabitants and all things upon it **3** : people in general **4** : great number or quantity **5** : class of persons or their sphere of interest

world·ly \'wərldlē\ *adj* **1** : devoted to this world and its pursuits rather than to religion **2** : sophisticated — **world·li·ness** *n*

world·ly-wise *adj* : possessing understanding of human affairs

world·wide *adj* : extended throughout the entire world — **worldwide** *adv*

worm \'wərm\ *n* **1** : earthworm or a similar animal **2** *pl* : disorder caused by parasitic worms ~ *vb* **1** : move or cause to move in a slow and indirect way **2** : to free from worms — **wormy** *adj*

worm·wood \'wərm,wud\ *n* **1** : aromatic woody herb (as sagebrush) **2** : something bitter or grievous

worn *past part of* WEAR

worn-out \'wōrn,aut\ *adj* : exhausted or used up by or as if by wear

wor·ri·some \'wərēsəm\ *adj* **1** : causing worry **2** : inclined to worry

wor·ry \'wərē\ *vb* **-ried; -ry·ing 1** : shake and mangle with the teeth **2** : disturb **3** : feel or express anxiety ~ *n, pl* **-ries 1** : anxiety **2** : cause of anxiety — **wor·ri·er** *n*

worse \'wərs\ *adj, comparative of* BAD *or of* ILL **1** : bad or evil in a greater degree **2** : more unwell ~ *n* **1** : one that is worse **2** : greater degree of badness ~ *adv, comparative of* BAD *or of* ILL : in a worse manner

wors·en \'wərs°n\ *vb* : make or become worse

wor·ship \'wərshəp\ *n* **1** : reverence toward a divine being or supernatural power **2** : expression of reverence **3** : extravagant respect or devotion ~ *vb* **-shiped** *or* **-shipped; -ship·ing** *or* **-ship·ping 1** : honor or reverence **2** : perform or take part in worship — **wor·ship·er, wor·ship·per** *n*

worst \'wərst\ *adj, superlative of* BAD *or of* ILL **1** : most bad, evil, ill, or corrupt **2** : most unfavorable, unpleasant, or painful ~ *n* : one that is worst ~ *adv, superlative of* ILL *or of* BAD *or* BADLY : to the extreme degree of badness ~ *vb* : defeat

wor·sted \'wustəd, 'wərstəd\ *n* : smooth compact wool yarn or fabric made from such yarn

worth \'wərth\ *prep* **1** : equal in value to **2** : deserving of ~ *n* **1** : monetary value **2** : value of something measured by its qualities **3** : moral or personal merit

worth·less \-ləs\ *adj* **1** : lacking worth **2** : useless — **worth·less·ness** *n*

worth·while \-'hwīl\ *adj* : being worth the time or effort spent

wor·thy \'wərthē\ *adj* **-thi·er; -est 1** : having worth or value **2** : having sufficient worth ~ *n, pl* **-thies** : worthy person — **wor·thi·ly** *adv* — **wor·thi·ness** *n*

would \'wŭd\ *past of* WILL — used to express (1) preference (2) intent (3) habitual action (4) contingency (5) probability or (6) a request

would–be \'wŭd'bē\ *adj* : desiring or pretending to be

¹**wound** \'wünd\ *n* 1 : injury in which the skin is broken 2 : mental hurt ~ *vb* : inflict a wound to or in

²**wound** \'waůnd\ *past of* WIND

wove *past of* WEAVE

woven *past part of* WEAVE

wrack \'rak\ *n* : ruin

wraith \'rāth\ *n, pl* **wraiths** \'rāths, 'rāthz\ 1 : ghost 2 : insubstantial appearance

wran·gle \'raŋgəl\ *vb or n* : quarrel — **wran·gler** *n*

wrap \'rap\ *vb* -**pp**- 1 : cover esp. by winding or folding 2 : envelop and secure for transportation or storage 3 : enclose, surround, or conceal wholly 4 : coil, fold, draw, or twine about something ~ *n* 1 : wrapper or wrapping 2 : outer garment (as a shawl)

wrap·per \'rapər\ *n* 1 : that in which something is wrapped 2 : one that wraps

wrap·ping *n* : something used to wrap an object

wrath \'rath\ *n* : violent anger — **wrath·ful** \-fəl\ *adj*

wreak \'rēk\ *vb* 1 : inflict 2 : bring about

wreath \'rēth\ *n, pl* **wreaths** \'rēthz, 'rēths\ : something (as boughs) intertwined into a circular shape

wreathe \'rēth\ *vb* **wreathed**; **wreath·ing** 1 : shape into or take on the shape of a wreath 2 : decorate or cover with a wreath

wreck \'rek\ *n* 1 : broken remains (as of a ship or vehicle) after heavy damage 2 : something disabled or in a state of ruin 3 : an individual who has become weak or infirm 4 : action of breaking up or destroying something ~ *vb* : ruin or damage by breaking up

wreck·age \'rekij\ *n* 1 : act of wrecking 2 : remains of a wreck

wreck·er \-ər\ *n* 1 : automotive vehicle for removing disabled cars 2 : one that wrecks or tears down and removes buildings

wren \'ren\ *n* : small mostly brown singing bird

wrench \'rench\ *vb* 1 : pull with violent twisting or force 2 : injure or disable by a violent twisting or straining ~ *n* 1 : forcible twisting 2 : tool for exerting a twisting force

wrest \'rest\ *vb* 1 : pull or move by a forcible twisting movement 2 : gain with difficulty ~ *n* : forcible twist

wres·tle \'resəl, 'ras-\ *vb* -**tled**; -**tling** 1 : scuffle with and attempt to throw and pin an opponent 2 : compete against in wrestling 3 : struggle (as with a problem) ~ *n* : action or an instance of wrestling — **wres·tler** \'reslər, 'ras-\ *n*

wres·tling \'resliŋ\ *n* : sport in which 2 opponents try to throw and pin each other

wretch \'rech\ *n* 1 : miserable unhappy person 2 : vile person

wretch·ed \'rechəd\ *adj* 1 : deeply afflicted, dejected, or distressed 2 : grievous 3 : inferior — **wretch·ed·ly** *adv* — **wretch·ed·ness** *n*

wrig·gle \'rigəl\ *vb* -**gled**; -**gling** 1 : twist and turn restlessly 2 : move along by twisting and turning — **wrig·gle** *n* — **wrig·gler** \'rigələr\ *n*

wring \'riŋ\ *vb* **wrung** \'rəŋ\; **wring·ing** 1 : squeeze or twist out moisture 2 : get by or as if by twisting or pressing 3 : twist together in anguish 4 : pain — **wring·er** *n*

◆ **wrin·kle** \'riŋkəl\ *n* : crease or small fold on a surface (as in the skin or in cloth) ~ *vb* **-kled; -kling** : develop or cause to develop wrinkles — **wrin·kly** \-kəlē\ *adj*

wrist \'rist\ *n* **1** : joint or region between the hand and the arm

writ \'rit\ *n* **1** : something written **2** : legal order in writing

write \'rīt\ *vb* **wrote** \'rōt;\; **written** \'rit²n\; **writ·ing** \'rītiŋ\ **1** : form letters or words on a surface **2** : form the letters or the words of (as on paper) **3** : make up and set down for others to read **4** : write a letter to — **write off** *vb* : cancel

writ·er \'rītər\ *n* : one that writes esp. as a business or occupation

writhe \'rīth\ *vb* **writhed; writh·ing** : twist and turn this way and that

writ·ing \'rītiŋ\ *n* **1** : act of one that writes **2** : handwriting **3** : something written or printed

wrong \'ròŋ\ *n* **1** : unfair or unjust act **2** : something that is contrary to justice to **3** : state of being or doing wrong ~ *adj* **wrong·er** \'ròŋər\; **wrong·est** \'ròŋəst\ **1** : sinful **2** : not right according to a standard **3** : unsuitable **4** : incorrect ~ *adv* **1** : in a wrong direction or manner **2** : incorrectly ~ *vb* **wronged; wrong·ing 1** : do wrong to **2** : treat unjustly — **wrong·ly** *adv*

wrong·do·er \-'düər\ *n* : one who does wrong — **wrong·do·ing** \-'düiŋ\ *n*

wrong·ful \-fəl\ *adj* **1** : wrong **2** : illegal — **wrong·ful·ly** *adv* — **wrong·ful·ness** *n*

wrong·head·ed \'ròŋ'hedəd\ *adj* : stubborn in clinging to wrong opinion or principles — **wrong·head·ed·ly** *adv* — **wrong·head·ed·ness** *n*

wrote *past of* WRITE

wrought \'ròt\ *adj* **1** : formed **2** : hammered into shape **3** : deeply stirred

wrung *past of* WRING

wry \'rī\ *adj* **wri·er** \'rīər\; **wri·est** \'rīəst\ **1** : turned abnormally to one side **2** : twisted **3** : cleverly and often ironically humorous — **wry·ly** *adv* — **wry·ness** *n*

X

x \'eks\ *n, pl* **x's** *or* **xs** \'eksəz\ **1** : 24th letter of the alphabet **2** : unknown quantity ~ *vb* **x-ed; x-ing** *or* **x'ing** : cancel with a series of *x*'s — usu. with *out*

xe·non \'zē,nän, 'zen,än\ *n* : heavy gaseous chemical element

xe·no·pho·bia \,zenə'fōbēə, ,zēn-\ *n* : fear and hatred of foreign people and things — **xe·no·phobe** \'zenə-,fōb, 'zēn-\ *n*

Xmas \'krisməs\ *n* : Christmas

x–ra·di·a·tion *n* **1** : exposure to X rays **2** : radiation consisting of X rays

x–ray \'eks,rā\ *vb* : examine, treat, or photograph with X rays

X ray *n* **1** : radiation of short wavelength that is able to penetrate solids **2** : photograph taken with X rays — **X–ray** *adj*

xy·lo·phone \'zīlə,fōn\ *n* : musical instrument with wooden bars that are struck — **xy·lo·phon·ist** \-,fōnist\ *n*

Y

y \\'wī\ *n, pl* **y's** *or* **ys** \\'wīz\ : 25th letter of the alphabet

¹-y \ē\ *adj suffix* **1** : composed or full of **2** : like **3** : performing or apt to perform an action

²-y \ē\ *n suffix, pl* **-ies 1** : state, condition, or quality **2** : activity, place of business, or goods dealt with **3** : whole group

yacht \\'yät\ *n* : luxurious pleasure boat ~ *vb* : race or cruise in a yacht

ya·hoo \\'yähü, 'yä-\ *n, pl* **-hoos** : uncouth or stupid person

◆ **yak** \\'yak\ *n* : big hairy Asian ox

yam \\'yam\ *n* **1** : edible root of a tropical vine **2** : deep orange sweet potato

yam·mer \\'yamər\ *vb* **1** : whimper **2** : chatter — **yammer** *n*

yank \\'yaŋk\ *n* : strong sudden pull — **yank** *vb*

Yank \\'yaŋk\ *n* : Yankee

Yan·kee \\'yaŋkē\ *n* : native or inhabitant of New England, the northern U.S., or the U.S.

yap \\'yap\ *vb* **-pp- 1** : yelp **2** : chatter — **yap** *n*

¹yard \\'yärd\ *n* **1** : 3 feet **2** : long spar for supporting and spreading a sail — **yard·age** \-ij\ *n*

²yard *n* **1** : enclosed roofless area **2** : grounds of a building **3** : work area

yard·arm \\'yärd,ärm\ *n* : end of the yard of a square-rigged ship

yard·stick *n* **1** : measuring stick 3 feet long **2** : standard for judging

yar·mul·ke \\'yäməkə, 'yär-, -məl-\ *n* : a small brimless cap worn by Jewish males in a synagogue

yarn \\'yärn\ *n* **1** : spun fiber for weaving or knitting **2** : tale

yaw \\'yo\ *vb* : deviate erratically from a course — **yaw** *n*

yawl \\'yol\ *n* : sailboat with 2 masts

◆ **yawn** \\'yon\ *vb* : open the mouth wide ~ *n* : deep breath through a wide-open mouth — **yawn·er** *n*

ye \\'yē\ *pron* : you

yea \\'yā\ *adv* **1** : yes **2** : truly ~ *n* : affirmative vote

year \\'yir\ *n* **1** : period of about 365 days **2** *pl* : age

year·book *n* : annual report of the year's events

year·ling \\'yirliŋ, 'yərlən\ *n* : one that is or is rated as a year old

year·ly \\'yirlē\ *adj* : annual — **yearly** *adv*

yearn \\'yərn\ *vb* **1** : feel desire esp. for what one cannot have **2** : feel tenderness or compassion

yearn·ing \-iŋ\ *n* : tender or urgent desire

yeast \\'yēst\ *n* : froth or sediment in sugary liquids containing a tiny fungus and used in making alcoholic liquors and as a leaven in baking — **yeasty** *adj*

yell \\'yel\ *vb* : utter a loud cry — **yell** *n*

yel·low \\'yelō\ *adj* **1** : of the color yellow **2** : sensational **3** : cowardly ~ *vb* : make or turn yellow ~ *n* **1** : color of lemons **2** : yolk of an egg — **yel·low·ish** \\'yeləwish\ *adj*

yellow fever *n* : virus disease marked by prostration, jaundice, fever, and often hemorrhage

yellow jacket *n* : wasp with yellow stripes

yelp \'yelp\ *vb* : utter a sharp quick shrill cry — **yelp** *n*

yen \'yen\ *n* : strong desire

yeo·man \'yōmən\ *n* 1 : attendant or officer in a royal or noble household 2 : small farmer 3 : naval petty officer with clerical duties — **yeo·man·ry** \-rē\ *n*

-yer — see -ER

yes \'yes\ *adv* — used to express consent or agreement ~ *n* : affirmative answer

ye·shi·va, ye·shi·vah \yə'shēvə\ *n*, *pl* **yeshivas** *or* **ye·shi·voth** \-ˌshē-'vōt, -'vōth\ : Jewish school

yes–man \'yes.man\ *n* : person who agrees with every opinion or suggestion of a boss

yes·ter·day \'yestərdē\ *adv* 1 : on the day preceding today 2 : only a short time ago ~ *n* 1 : day last past 2 : time not long past

yet \'yet\ *adv* 1 : in addition 2 : up to now 3 : so soon as now 4 : nevertheless ~ *conj* : but

yew \'yü\ *n* : evergreen tree or shrubs with dark stiff poisonous needles

yield \'yēld\ *vb* 1 : surrender 2 : grant 3 : bear as a crop 4 : produce 5 : cease opposition or resistance ~ *n* : quantity produced or returned

yo·del \'yōd°l\ *vb* **-deled** *or* **-delled**; **-del·ing** *or* **-del·ling** : sing by abruptly alternating between chest voice and falsetto — **yodel** *n* — **yo·del·er** \'yōd°lər\ *n*

yo·ga \'yōgə\ *n* : system of exercises for attaining bodily or mental control and well-being

yo·gi \'yōgē\ : person who practices yoga

yo·gurt \'yōgərt\ *n* : fermented slightly acid soft food made from milk

yoke \'yōk\ *n* 1 : neck frame for coupling draft animals or for carrying loads 2 : clamp 3 : slavery 4 : tie or link 5 : piece of a garment esp. at the shoulder ~ *vb* **yoked**; **yok·ing** 1 : couple with a yoke 2 : join

yo·kel \'yōkəl\ *n* : naive and gullible country person

yolk \'yōk\ *n* : yellow part of an egg — **yolked** \'yōkt\ *adj*

Yom Kip·pur \ˌyōmki'pùr, ˌyäm-, -'kipər\ *n* : Jewish holiday observed in September or October with fasting and prayer as a day of atonement

yon \'yän\ *adj or adv* : yonder

yon·der \'yändər\ *adv* : at or to that place ~ *adj* : distant

yore \'yōr\ *n* : time long past

you \'yü\ *pron* 1 : person or persons addressed 2 : person in general

young \'yəŋ\ *adj* **youn·ger** \'yəŋgər\; **youn·gest** \'yəŋgəst\ 1 : being in the first or an early stage of life, growth, or development 2 : recently come into being 3 : youthful ~ *n, pl* **young** : persons or animals that are young — **young·ish** \-ish\ *adj*

young·ster \-stər\ *n* 1 : young person 2 : child

your \yər, 'yùr, 'yōr\ *adj* : relating to you or yourself

yours \'yùrz, 'yōrz\ *pron* : the ones belonging to you

your·self \yər'self\ *pron, pl* **your·selves** \-'selvz\ : you — used reflexively or for emphasis

youth \'yüth\ *n, pl* **youths** \'yüthz, 'yüths\ 1 : period between childhood and maturity 2 : young man 3 : young persons 4 : state or quality of being young, fresh, or vigorous

youth·ful \'yüthfəl\ *adj* 1 : relating to or appropriate to youth 2

: young **3** : vigorous and fresh —
youth·ful·ly *adv* — **youth·ful·ness**
n

yowl \'yaùl\ *vb* : utter a loud long
mournful cry — **yowl** *n*

yo-yo \'yō₋yō\ *n, pl* **-yos** : toy that
falls from or rises to the hand as it
unwinds and rewinds on a string

yuc·ca \'yəkə\ *n* : any of several
plants related to the lilies that
grow in dry regions

yule \'yül\ *n* : Christmas — **yule-
tide** \-₋tīd\ *n*

yum·my \'yəmē\ *adj* **-mi·er; -est**
: highly attractive or pleasing

Z

z \'zē\ *n, pl* **z's** *or* **zs** : 26th letter of
the alphabet

za·ny \'zānē\ *n, pl* **-nies 1** : clown **2**
: silly person ~ *adj* **-ni·er; -est**
: crazy or foolish — **za·ni·ly** *adv*
— **za·ni·ness** *n*

zeal \'zēl\ *n* : enthusiasm

zeal·ot \'zelət\ *n* : fanatical partisan

zeal·ous \'zeləs\ *adj* : filled with zeal
— **zeal·ous·ly** *adv* — **zeal·ous-
ness** *n*

ze·bra \'zēbrə\ *n* : horselike African
mammal marked with light and
dark stripes

zeit·geist \'tsīt₋gīst, 'zīt-\ *n* : general
spirit of an era

ze·nith \'zēnəth\ *n* : highest point

zeph·yr \'zefər\ *n* : gentle breeze

zep·pe·lin \'zepələn\ *n* : rigid airship like a blimp

ze·ro \'zērō\ *n, pl* **-ros 1** : number
represented by the symbol 0 or the
symbol itself **2** : starting point **3**
: lowest point ~ *adj* : having no
size or quantity

zest \'zest\ *n* **1** : quality of enhanc-
ing enjoyment **2** : keen enjoyment
— **zest·ful** \-fəl\ *adj* — **zest·ful-
ly** *adv* — **zest·ful·ness** *n*

zig·zag \'zig₋zag\ *n* : one of a series

of short sharp turns or angles ~
adj : having zigzags ~ *adv* : in or
by a zigzag path ~ *vb* **-gg-** : proceed along a zigzag path

◆ **zil·lion** \'zilyən\ *n* : large indeter-
minate number

zinc \'ziŋk\ *n* : bluish white
crystaline metallic chemical element

zing \'ziŋ\ *n* **1** : shrill humming noise
2 : energy — **zing** *vb*

zin·nia \'zinēə, 'zēnyə\ *n* : American
herb widely grown for its showy
flowers

¹zip \'zip\ *vb* **-pp-** : move or act with
speed ~ *n* : energy

²zip *vb* **-pp-** : close or open with a zip-
per

zip code *n* : number that identifies a
U.S. postal delivery area

zip·per \'zipər\ *n* : fastener consisting of 2 rows of interlocking teeth

zip·py \'zipē\ *adj* **-pi·er; -est** : brisk

zir·con \'zər₋kän\ *n* : zirconium-
containing mineral sometimes
used in jewelry

zir·co·ni·um \₋zər'kōnēəm\ *n*
: corrosion-resistant gray metallic
element

zit \'zit\ *n, slang* : pimple

zith·er \\'zithər, 'zith-\ *n* : stringed musical instrument played by plucking

zi·ti \\'zētē\ *n, pl* **ziti** : short tubular pasta

zo·di·ac \\'zōdē,ak\ *n* : imaginary belt in the heavens encompassing the paths of the planets and divided into 12 signs used in astrology — **zo·di·a·cal** \zō'dīəkəl\ *adj*

◆ **zom·bie** \\'zämbē\ *n* : person thought to have died and been brought back to life without free will

zon·al \\'zōn°l\ *adj* : of, relating to, or having the form of a zone — **zon·al·ly** *adv*

zone \\'zōn\ *n* **1** : division of the earth's surface based on latitude and climate **2** : distinctive area ~ *vb* **zoned; zon·ing 1** : mark off into zones **2** : reserve for special purposes — **zo·na·tion** \zō'nāshən\ *n*

zoo \\'zü\ *n, pl* **zoos** : collection of living animals usu. for public display — **zoo·keep·er** *n*

zo·ol·o·gy \zō'äləjē\ *n* : science of animals — **zo·o·log·i·cal** \,zōə-'läjikəl\ *adj* — **zo·ol·o·gist** \zō-'äləjist\ *n*

zoom \\'züm\ *vb* **1** : move with a loud hum or buzz **2** : move or increase with great speed — **zoom** *n*

zuc·chi·ni \zú'kēnē\ *n, pl* **-ni** *or* **-nis** : summer squash with smooth cylindrical dark green fruits

zwie·back \\'swēbak, 'swī-, 'zwē-, 'zwī-\ *n* : biscuit of baked, sliced, and toasted bread

zy·gote \\'zī,gōt\ *n* : cell formed by the union of 2 sexual cells — **zy·got·ic** \zī'gätik\ *adj*

Abbreviations

Most of these abbreviations have been given in one form. Variation in use of periods, in type, and in capitalization is frequent and widespread (as *mph, MPH, m.p.h., Mph*).

abbr	abbreviation	*Aug*	August
AC	alternating current	*auth*	authentic, author, authorized
acad	academic, academy		
AD	in the year of our Lord	*aux,*	
adj	adjective	*auxil*	auxiliary
adv	adverb, advertisement	*av*	avoirdupois
advt	advertisement	*AV*	audiovisual
AF	air force, audio frequency	*ave*	avenue
		avg	average
agric	agricultural, agriculture	*AZ*	Arizona
AK	Alaska	*BA*	bachelor of arts
aka	also known as	*bal*	balance
AL, Ala	Alabama	*bar*	barometer, barrel
alg	algebra	*bbl*	barrel, barrels
Alta	Alberta	*BC*	before Christ, British Columbia
a.m., AM	before noon		
Am,		*BCE*	before Christian Era, before Common Era
Amer	America, American		
amp	ampere	*bet*	between
amt	amount	*biog*	biographer, biographical, biography
anc	ancient		
anon	anonymous	*biol*	biologic, biological, biologist, biology
ans	answer		
ant	antonym	*bldg*	building
APO	army post office	*blvd*	boulevard
approx	approximate, approximately	*BO*	backorder, best offer, body odor, box office, branch office
Apr	April		
apt	apartment, aptitude	*Brit*	Britain, British
AR	Arkansas	*bro*	brother, brothers
arith	arithmetic	*bros*	brothers
Ariz	Arizona	*BS*	bachelor of science
Ark	Arkansas	*Btu*	British thermal unit
art	article, artificial	*bu*	bureau, bushel
assn	association	*c*	carat, cent, centimeter, century, chapter, circa, cup
assoc	associate, associated, association		
asst	assistant	*C*	Celsius, centigrade
ATM	automated teller machine	*ca*	circa
		CA, Cal, Calif	California
att	attached, attention, attorney		
		cal	calendar, caliber, calorie
attn	attention		
atty	attorney		

Can,	
Canad	Canada, Canadian
cap	capacity, capital, capitalize, capitalized
Capt	captain
CB	citizens band
CDT	central daylight time
cen	central
cert	certificate, certification, certified, certify
cf	compare
chap	chapter
chem	chemistry
cir	circle, circuit, circular, circumference
civ	civil, civilian
cm	centimeter
co	company, county
CO	Colorado
c/o	care of
COD	cash on delivery, collect on delivery
col	colonial, colony, color, colored, column, counsel
Col	colonel, Colorado
Colo	Colorado
comp	comparative, compensation, compiled, compiler, composition, compound, comprehensive, comptroller
cong	congress, congressional
conj	conjunction
Conn	Connecticut
cont	continued
contr	contract, contraction
corp	corporal, corporation
corr	corrected, correction
cp	compare, coupon
CPR	cardiopulmonary resuscitation
cr	credit, creditor
CSA	Confederate States of America
CST	central standard time
ct	carat, cent, count, court
CT	central time, certified teacher, Connecticut
cu	cubic
cur	currency, current
CZ	Canal Zone
d	penny
DA	district attorney
dag	dekagram
dal	dekaliter
dam	dekameter
dbl	double
DC	direct current, District of Columbia
DDS	doctor of dental science, doctor of dental surgery
DE	Delaware
dec	deceased, decrease
Dec	December
deg	degree
Del	Delaware
Dem	Democrat, Democratic
dept	department
det	detached, detachment, detail, determine
dg	decigram
dia,	
diam	diameter
diag	diagonal, diagram
dict	dictionary
dif, diff	difference
dim	dimension, diminished
dir	director
disc	discount
dist	distance, district
div	divided, dividend, division, divorced
dl	deciliter
dm	decimeter
DMD	doctor of dental medicine
DOB	date of birth
doz	dozen
DP	data processing
dr	dram, drive, drum
Dr	doctor
DST	daylight saving time
DUI	driving under the influence
DWI	driving while intoxicated
dz	dozen
e	east, eastern, excellent
ea	each
ecol	ecological, ecology
econ	economics, economist, economy
EDT	eastern daylight time
e.g.	for example

EKG	electrocardiogram, electrocardiograph	*hgt*	height
		hgwy	highway
elec	electric, electrical, electricity	*HI*	Hawaii
		hist	historian, historical, history
elem	elementary		
eng	engine, engineer, engineering	*hon*	honor, honorable, honorary
Eng	England, English	*hr*	here, hour
esp	especially	*HS*	high school
EST	eastern standard time	*ht*	height
ET	eastern time	*HT*	Hawaii time
et al	and others	*hwy*	highway
etc	et cetera	*i*	intransitive, island, isle
ex	example, express, extra	*Ia, IA*	Iowa
exec	executive	*ICU*	intensive care unit
f	false, female, feminine	*ID*	Idaho, identification
F, Fah, Fahr	Fahrenheit	*i.e.*	that is
		IL, Ill	Illinois
Feb	February	*imp*	imperative, imperfect
fed	federal, federation	*in*	inch
fem	female, feminine	*IN*	Indiana
FL, Fla	Florida	*inc*	incomplete, incorporated
fl oz	fluid ounce		
FPO	fleet post office	*ind*	independent
fr	father, friar, from	*Ind*	Indian, Indiana
Fri	Friday	*inf*	infinitive
ft	feet, foot, fort	*int*	interest
fut	future	*interj*	interjection
FYI	for your information	*intl, intnl*	international
g	gram	*ital*	italic, italicized
Ga, GA	Georgia	*Jan*	January
gal	gallery, gallon	*JD*	juvenile delinquent
gen	general	*jour*	journal, journeyman
geog	geographic, geographical, geography	*JP*	justice of the peace
		jr, jun	junior
geol	geologic, geological, geology	*JV*	junior varsity
		Kan, Kans	Kansas
geom	geometric, geometrical, geometry	*kg*	kilogram
		km	kilometer
gm	gram	*KS*	Kansas
GMT	Greenwich mean time	*kW*	kilowatt
GOP	Grand Old Party (Republican)	*Ky, KY*	Kentucky
		l	late, left, liter, long
gov	government, governor	*L*	large
govt	government	*La*	Louisiana
GP	general practice, general practitioner	*LA*	Los Angeles, Louisiana
		lat	latitude
gr	grade, grain, gram	*lb*	pound
gram	grammar, grammatical	*lg*	large, long
gt	great	*lib*	liberal, librarian, library
GU	Guam	*long*	longitude
hd	head		
hf	half		

m	male, masculine, meter, mile	*NE, Neb,*	
M	medium	*Nebr*	Nebraska
MA	Massachusetts	*neg*	negative
Man	Manitoba	*neut*	neuter
Mar	March	*Nev*	Nevada
masc	masculine	*Nfld*	Newfoundland
Mass	Massachusetts	*NH*	New Hampshire
math	mathematical, mathematician	*NJ*	New Jersey
		NM,	
max	maximum	*N Mex*	New Mexico
Md	Maryland	*no*	north, number
MD	doctor of medicine, Maryland	*Nov*	November
		NR	not rated
MDT	mountain daylight time	*NS*	Nova Scotia
Me, ME	Maine	*NV*	Nevada
med	medium	*NWT*	Northwest Territories
mg	milligram	*NY*	New York
mgr	manager	*NYC*	New York City
MI, Mich	Michigan	*O*	Ohio
mid	middle	*obj*	object, objective
min	minimum, minor, minute	*occas*	occasionally
		Oct	October
Minn	Minnesota	*off*	office, officer, official
misc	miscellaneous	*OH*	Ohio
Miss	Mississippi	*OJ*	orange juice
ml	milliliter	*OK, Okla*	Oklahoma
mm	millimeter	*ON, Ont*	Ontario
MN	Minnesota	*opp*	opposite
mo	month	*OR, Ore,*	
Mo, MO	Missouri	*Oreg*	Oregon
Mon	Monday	*orig*	original, originally
Mont	Montana	*oz*	ounce, ounces
mpg	miles per gallon	*p*	page
mph	miles per hour	*Pa*	Pennsylvania
MRI	magnetic resonance imaging	*PA*	Pennsylvania, public address
MS	Mississippi	*PAC*	political action committee
MST	mountain standard time		
mt	mount, mountain	*par*	paragraph, parallel
MT	Montana, mountain time	*part*	participle, particular
		pass	passenger, passive
n	neuter, north, northern, noun	*pat*	patent
NA	North America, not applicable	*PC*	percent, politically correct, postcard
nat	national, native, natural	*pd*	paid
natl	national	*PD*	police department
naut	nautical	*PDT*	Pacific daylight time
NB	New Brunswick	*PE*	physical education
NC	North Carolina	*PEI*	Prince Edward Island
ND,		*Penn,*	
N Dak	North Dakota	*Penna*	Pennsylvania
		pg	page

PIN	personal identification number	*RI*	Rhode Island
pk	park, peak, peck	*rm*	room
pkg	package	*RPM*	revolutions per minute
pl	place, plural	*RR*	railroad, rural route
p.m., PM	afternoon	*RSVP*	please reply
PMS	premenstrual syndrome	*rt*	right
PO	post office	*rte*	route
Port	Portugal, Portuguese	*s*	small, south, southern
pos	position, positive	*SA*	South America
poss	possessive	*SASE*	self-addressed stamped envelope
pp	pages		
PQ	Province of Quebec	*Sask*	Saskatchewan
pr	pair, price, printed	*Sat*	Saturday
PR	public relations, Puerto Rico	*SC*	South Carolina
		sci	science, scientific
prep	preposition	*SD, S Dak*	South Dakota
pres	present, president	*secy*	secretary
prob	probable, probably, problem	*sen*	senate, senator, senior
		Sept, Sep	September
prof	professor	*sing*	singular
pron	pronoun	*sm*	small
prov	province	*so*	south, southern
PS	postscript, public school	*soph*	sophomore
PST	Pacific standard time	*sp*	spelling
psych	psychology	*spec*	special, specifically
pt	part, payment, pint, point	*specif*	specific, specifically
		SPF	sun protection factor
PT	Pacific time, physical therapy	*sq*	square
		sr	senior
pvt	private	*Sr*	sister
qr	quarter	*SSN*	Social Security number
qt	quantity, quart	*SSR*	Soviet Socialist Republic
Que	Quebec		
quot	quotation	*st*	street
r	right, river	*St*	saint
rd	road, rod, round	*std*	standard
RDA	recommended daily allowance, recommended dietary allowance	*subj*	subject
		Sun	Sunday
		supt	superintendent
recd	received	*SWAT*	Special Weapons and Tactics
reg	region, register, registered, regular		
		syn	synonym
rel	relating, relative, religion	*t*	teaspoon, temperature, ton, transitive, troy, true
rep	report, reporter, representative, republic		
		T	tablespoon
Rep	Republican	*tbs, tbsp*	tablespoon
res	residence	*TD*	touchdown
rev	reverse, review, revised, revision, revolution	*tech*	technical, technician, technology
Rev	reverend	*Tenn*	Tennessee
RFD	rural free delivery	*terr*	territory

Tex	Texas	*var*	variant, variety
Th, Thu,		*vb*	verb
Thur,		*VG*	very good
Thurs	Thursday	*VI*	Virgin Islands
TN	Tennessee	*vol*	volume, volunteer
trans	translated, translation, translator	*VP*	vice president
		vs	versus
tsp	teaspoon	*Vt, VT*	Vermont
Tu, Tue,		*w*	west, western
Tues	Tuesday	*WA,*	
TX	Texas	*Wash*	Washington
UK	United Kingdom	*Wed*	Wednesday
UN	United Nations	*WI, Wis,*	
univ	universal, university	*Wisc*	Wisconsin
US	United States	*wk*	week, work
USA	United States of America	*wt*	weight
		WV,	
USSR	Union of Soviet Socialist Republics	*W Va*	West Virginia
usu	usual, usually	*WY, Wyo*	Wyoming
UT	Utah	*XL*	extra large, extra long
UV	ultraviolet	*yd*	yard
v	verb, versus	*yr*	year, younger, your
Va, VA	Virginia	*YT*	Yukon Territory

Confused, Misused, and Misspelled Words

a/an *A* is used before a word beginning with a consonant or consonant sound ("a door", "a one-time deal"). *An* is usually used before a word beginning with a vowel or vowel sound ("an operation"). *A* is used before *h* when the *h* is pronounced ("a headache"); *an* is used if the *h* is not pronounced ("an honor").

accept/except The verb *accept* means "to agree to, receive" ("accept a gift"). *Except* most often means "not including" ("will visit all national parks except the Grand Canyon").

adapt/adopt The verb *adapt* means "to change or modify" ("adapt to the warmer climate"); the verb *adopt* means "to take as one's own" ("adopt a child").

affect/effect The verb *affect* means to "cause a change in something" ("rain affects plant growth"); the noun *effect* means "the result" ("the effect of rain on plant growth").

ain't *Ain't* is used by some people in informal speech to mean "are not," "is not," or "am not," among other things. Because *aint* is considered very informal, it is not generally used in schoolwork, or in formal speech and writing.

aisle/isle *Aisle* means "a walkway between seats"; *isle* is a poetic word meaning "island".

a lot, allot *A lot*, meaning "a great number", is spelled as two words; it is sometimes written incorrectly as *alot*. *Allot* is a verb meaning "to give out in portions or set aside" ("alloted one hour for homework").

an See *a/an*.

apt See *liable/likely/apt*.

as . . . as Is it more correct to say "she is as smart as I" or "she is as smart as me"? Actually, both ways are correct. In comparisons with "as . . . as", it is okay to use either subject pronouns (like *I*, *you*, *he*, *she*, *it*, *we*, and *they*) or object pronouns (like *me*, *you*, *him*, *her*, *it*, *us*, and *them*) after the second *as*. However, subject pronouns sound more formal. So you may want to use subject pronouns in your comparisons when you are doing schoolwork.

as/like Sometimes *as* is used with the same meaning as *like* ("do as I do"), ("do like I do"). At other times, *as* means "in the role of" ("acted as a substitute teacher").

as well as When *as well as* is used in a comparison, the pronoun following the second *as* is usually in the subject form ("she can spell as well as I [can]", not "she can spell as well as me"). (For a list of subject pronouns, see *as . . . as*.)

aural/oral *Aural* and *oral* are sometimes pronounced the same, but they have different meanings. *Aural* means "of or relating to the ear or sense of hearing." It comes from the Latin word for "ear". *Oral* means "of, relating to, given by, or near the mouth," and comes from a Latin word for "mouth." (See also *verbal/oral*.)

bare/bear *Bare* means "without clothes or a covering" ("bare feet"); *bear* means "to carry".

bazaar/bizarre *Bazaar* is a fair; *bizarre* means "weird."

beside/besides *Beside* generally means "next to or at the side of" something; *besides* means "in addition to".

born/borne *Born* is having come into life; *borne* means "carried".

bring/take *Bring* usually means "to carry to a closer place"; *take*, "to carry to a farther place".

can/may *Can* usually means "to be able to or know how to" ("they can read and write"); *may* means "to have permission to" ("may I go?"). In casual conversation, *can* also is used to mean "to have permission to" ("can I go?"), but *may* is used instead in more formal speech or in writing.

canvas/canvass *Canvas* is a cloth; *canvass* is a means of asking people's opinions.

capital/capitol *Capital* is the place or city of government; *capitol* is the building of government.

cereal/serial *Cereal* is a breakfast food; *serial* is a story presented in parts.

colonel/kernel *Colonel* is a military rank; *kernel* is a part of a seed.

compliment/complement A *compliment* is a nice thing to say; a *complement* is something that completes.

council/counsel A *council* is a group of people meeting; *counsel* is advice.

country/county *Country* is a nation; *county* is a small, local government area.

data This was originally a plural form, but today it is used as both a singular and a plural noun.

desert/dessert *Desert* (with one *s*) is a dry, barren place; *dessert* (with two *s*'s) is a sweet eaten after a meal.

die/dye To *die* is to cease to live; to *dye* is to change the color of.

dived/dove Both spellings are common as a past tense of the verb *dive* ("she dived into the pool", "she dove into the pool").

effect See *affect/effect*.

except See *accept/except*.

farther/further *Farther* usually refers to distance ("he ran farther than I did"). *Further* refers to degree or extent ("she further explained the situation")

flammable/inflammable Both words mean "capable of catching fire", but *inflammable* is also sometimes used to mean "excitable".

forth/fourth *Forth* means "forward"; *fourth* means "number four in a sequence".

further See *farther/further*.

good/well To feel *good* generally means "to be in good health and good spirits." *To feel well* usually means "to be healthy".

half/half a/a half a *Half* is often used with the word *a*, which can either come before *half* or after it ("ate a half sandwich", "ate half a sandwich"). In casual speech, *a half a* is sometimes used ("ate a half a sandwich"), but it is avoided in more formal speech and in writing.

hanged/hung Both *hanged* and *hung* are used as the past tense of the verb *hang*. *Hanged* is used when referring to execution by hanging; *hung* is used in all other senses.

hardy/hearty *Hardy* (suggestive of *hard*) means "strong"; *hearty* (suggestive of *heart*) means "friendly, enthusiastic".

isle See *aisle/isle*.

its/it's *Its* means "of or relating to it or itself" ("the dog wagged its tail"). *It's* is a contraction of *it is* ("it's polite to say thank you").

kernel See *colonel/kernel*.

later/latter *Later* is the comparative form of *late*; it means "after a given time" ("they started later than they had intended"). *Latter* is an adjective that refers to the second of two things mentioned, or the last one of a sequence ("of the two choices, the latter is preferred").

lay/lie *Lay* means "to put (something) down"; *lie* means "to put one's body in a flat position".

lead/led These two words are pronounced the same, but have different meanings. *Lead* is a metal; *led* is the past tense of the verb *lead*.

less/fewer *Less* is usually used with things that cannot be counted ("there is less sunshine today") and *fewer* with things that can be counted ("there are fewer people today").

liable/likely/apt All three words mean the same thing, but *likely* and *apt* are more often used in situations that could have a positive or neutral outcome ("she's apt to burst out laughing", "they'll likely visit today"). *Liable* is usually used where there is a possibility of a negative outcome ("you're liable to get hurt if you play with knives").

lie See *lay/lie*.

like See *as/like*.

liter/litter A *liter* is a unit of measurement; *litter* is a messy collection of things.

loose/lose *Loose* means "not tight"; *lose* means "to misplace or fail to win".

marital/martial *Marital* has to do with marriage; *martial* has to do with the military.

may See *can/may*.

moral/morale *Moral* has to do with high ideals; *morale* is the state of feelings of a person or group ("after the victory, morale was high").

naval/navel *Naval* has to do with the Navy; a *navel* is a belly button.

no way *No way* is an expression meaning "no" or "not at all." It is used in everyday speech, but is usually considered too casual for formal speech and writing.

oral See *verbal/oral* and *aural/oral*.

peace See *piece/peace*.

pedal/peddle *Pedal* means "to use or work the pedals of something" ("pedal a bicycle"). *Peddle* means "to sell from house to house".

piece/peace A *piece* is a portion of something ("a piece of cake"); *peace* is the freedom from war or fighting.

precede/proceed *Precede* means "to go ahead of or come before"; *proceed* means "to start or move forward".

principal/principle A *principal* is the head of a school; a *principle* is a rule or guiding truth. It may help you to remember that *principal* ends with the letters *pal*, and that *principle* and *rule* end with the same two letters.

serial See *cereal/serial*.

set/sit The verb *set* means "to rest on eggs to hatch them"; *sit* means "to rest on the part of the body where the hips and legs join".

stationary/stationery Something that is *stationary* stands still; *stationery* is paper that is used for writing letters. Its easy to tell these two words apart if you remember that *stationery* and *letter* both contain "er".

take See *bring/take*.

than/then *Than* is a conjunction used to indicate a comparison ("better than that"); *then* means "at that time" ("then we went home").

there/their *There* points to a place ("there it is"); *their* refers to "what belongs to them" ("that is their house").

to/too/two *To* implies a direction ("went to the store"). *Too* means "also", "very", or "excessively" ("brought a pen and pencil too", "not too difficult", "too much"). *Two* is the number 2.

used to/use to The phrases *used to* and *use to* are often confused since they have the same pronunciation. *Used to* is correct in most instances ("we used to go to the lake every summer", "I used to know that"). But when it follows *did* or *didn't*, the correct spelling is *use to* ("that didn't use to be a problem").

verbal/oral Both *verbal* and *oral* are sometimes used to mean "spoken rather than written" ("a verbal agreement", "an oral agreement"). *Verbal* can also mean "of, relating to, or formed by a verb," or "of, relating to, or consisting of words." (For more about *oral,* see *aural/oral.*)

want See *won't/want*.

were/we're *Were* is a past tense verb form of *be* ("they were very young"); *we're* is a contraction of *we are* ("we're glad to see you").

who's/whose The word *who's* is a contraction of *who is* ("who's there?"); *whose* is an adjective indicating ownership or quality ("whose book is this?")

who/whom *Who* is used as the subject of a clause (where one would use *he, she,* or *they*). *Whom* is used as the object of a clause (where one would use *him*, *her*, or *them*), and often follows prepositions like *to*, *for*, *from*, or *with*. Subject: "Who is coming to the party?" "He is coming to the party." Object: "John is coming with whom?" "John is coming with them."

won't/want *Won't* is a contraction of *will not* ("I won't go"); *want* is a verb meaning "to need or desire" ("do you want some milk?").

Xmas *Xmas* is a shortened form of the word *Christmas*; the *X* comes from a Greek letter which is the first letter of the Greek word for *Christ*. *Xmas* is used in very casual writing, but is inappropriate for formal writing or schoolwork.

your/you're *Your* is an adjective meaning "that which belongs to you" ("is that your sister?"). *You're* is a contraction of *you are* ("you're going, aren't you?").

Frequently Misspelled Words

about	bought	data	foreign
accept	boys	debt	forth
accidental	bring	definite	forty
accidentally	brother	dependent	fourth
accommodate	brought	describe	freight
ache	build	description	Friday
acquire	built	desert	friend
across	bureau	dessert	fulfill
adapt	business	develop	further
address	busy	diction	getting
adopt	buy	dictionary	goes
affect	calendar	didn't	going
afternoon	can	die	good-by
again	cannot	different	good-bye
aisle	can't	dived	government
all right	canvas	divine	grammar
along	canvass	doctor	guess
already	capital	does	half
always	capitol	done	handkerchiefs
among	ceiling	don't	hanged
answer	cellar	dove	hardy
antarctic	cemetery	down	haven't
anything	cereal	dye	having
anyway	changeable	early	hear
apparent	chief	easily	heard
appear	children	easy	hearty
appearance	choose	effect	height
April	chose	eight	hello
apt	close	eighth	hoarse
arctic	cocoa	eligible	hospital
attendance	colonel	embarrass	hour
aunt	column	encyclopedia	house
awhile	coming	enough	how's
balloon	commit	envelop (verb)	hung
bare	commitment	envelope	hygiene
bargain	committee	(noun)	illegal
bazaar	complement	environment	imagine
bear	compliment	every	independence
because	concede	everybody	inflammable
before	conceive	everything	instead
beginning	conscience	exceed	isle
believable	conscious	except	isn't
believe	cough	existence	it's
beside	could	familiar	January
besides	couldn't	farther	judgment
between	council	father	kernel
bicycle	counsel	February	knew
birthday	country	fewer	know
bizarre	county	fine	knowledge
born	cousin	first	laboratory
borne	cylinder	flammable	laid

later	niece	scissors	tying
latter	ninety	secretary	unique
laugh	ninth	separate	until
lay	none	serial	usable
lead	noticeable	set	used to
league	nowadays	sheriff	use to
led	occur	similar	usual
leisure	occurrence	sincerely	usually
less	o'clock	sit	vacation
letter	offense	somebody	vacuum
liable	often	something	vegetable
library	once	sometime	verbal
license	oral	speech	villain
lie	ought	squirrel	visible
like	parallel	stationary	volume
likely	parliament	stationery	want
liter	peace	straight	weak
litter	pedal	strength	wear
little	peddle	studying	weather
loose	people	succeed	Wednesday
lose	piece	sugar	week
lovely	please	superintendent	weird
loving	pneumonia	supersede	were
lying	prairie	suppose	when
maintenance	precede	sure	whether
management	principal	surely	which
manual	principle	surprise	who
marital	probably	synagogue	whole
marshal	proceed	take	wholly
martial	quiet	tear	whom
mathematics	quit	than	who's
may	quite	their	whose
maybe	raise	them	witch
meant	raspberry	then	women
minute	ready	there	won't
mischief	receipt	though	would
misspell	receive	thought	wouldn't
moral	recommend	thoughtful	write
morale	remember	through	writing
morning	rhyme	Thursday	wrote
mosquito	rhythm	to	X-ray
mosquitoes	right	together	yacht
mother	said	tomorrow	yeast
movable	sandwich	tonight	yield
naval	satellite	too	your
navel	Saturday	trouble	you're
neighbor	says	truly	youthful
nice	schedule	Tuesday	zenith
nickel	school	two	zodiac

STATES OF THE U.S.

NAME and (abbr.)	AREA[1] sq. mi. (sq. km.) and rank	POPULATION (2000 census) and rank	CAPITAL
Alabama (AL)	51,705 (133,916) 29th	4,447,100 23d	Montgomery
Alaska (AK)	591,004 (1,530,700) 1st	626,932 48th	Juneau
Arizona (AZ)	114,000 (295,260) 6th	5,130,632 20th	Phoenix
Arkansas (AR)	53,187 (137,754) 27th	2,673,400 33d	Little Rock
California (CA)	158,706 (411,048) 3d	33,871,648 1st	Sacramento
Colorado (CO)	104,247 (270,000) 8th	4,301,261 24th	Denver
Connecticut (CT)	5,018 (12,997) 48th	3,405,565 29th	Hartford
Delaware (DE)	2,057 (5,328) 49th	783,600 45th	Dover
Florida (FL)	58,664 (151,940) 22d	15,982,378 4th	Tallahassee
Georgia (GA)	58,910 (152,577) 21st	8,186,453 10th	Atlanta
Hawaii (HI)	6,471 (16,760) 47th	1,211,537 42d	Honolulu
Idaho (ID)	83,557 (216,413) 13th	1,293,953 39th	Boise
Illinois (IL)	56,400 (146,076) 24th	12,419,293 5th	Springfield

NAME and (abbr.)	AREA[1] sq. mi. (sq. km.) and rank	POPULATION (2000 census) and rank	CAPITAL
Indiana (IN)	36,291 (93,994) 38th	6,080,485 14th	Indianapolis
Iowa (IA)	56,275 (145,752) 25th	2,926,324 30th	Des Moines
Kansas (KS)	82,277 (213,097) 14th	2,688,418 32d	Topeka
Kentucky (KY)	40,395 (104,623) 37th	4,041,769 25th	Frankfort
Louisiana (LA)	48,523 (125,674) 31st	4,468,976 22d	Baton Rouge
Maine (ME)	33,265 (86,156) 39th	1,274,923 40th	Augusta
Maryland (MD)	10,460 (27,091) 42d	5,296,486 19th	Annapolis
Massachusetts (MA)	8,284 (21,456) 45th	6,349,097 13th	Boston
Michigan (MI)	58,216[2] (150,779) 23d	9,938,444 8th	Lansing
Minnesota (MN)	84,068 (217,736) 12th	4,919,479 21st	St. Paul
Mississippi (MS)	47,689 (123,514) 32d	2,844,658 31st	Jackson
Missouri (MO)	69,697 (180,515) 19th	5,595,211 17th	Jefferson City
Montana (MT)	147,046 (380,849) 4th	902,195 44th	Helena
Nebraska (NE)	77,355 (200,349) 15th	1,711,263 38th	Lincoln

NAME and (abbr.)	AREA[1] sq. mi. (sq. km.) and rank	POPULATION (2000 census) and rank	CAPITAL
Nevada (NV)	110,561 (286,353) 7th	1,998,257 35th	Carson City
New Hampshire (NH)	9,279 (24,033) 44th	1,235,786 41st	Concord
New Jersey (NJ)	7,787 (20,168) 46th	8,414,350 9th	Trenton
New Mexico (NM)	121,593 (314,926) 5th	1,819,046 36th	Sante Fe
New York (NY)	49,576 (128,402) 30th	18,976,457 3d	Albany
North Carolina (NC)	52,669 (136,413) 28th	8,049,313 11th	Raleigh
North Dakota (ND)	70,665 (183,022) 17th	642,200 47th	Bismarck
Ohio (OH)	41,222 (106,765) 35th	11,353,140 7th	Columbus
Oklahoma (OK)	69,956 (181,186) 18th	3,450,654 27th	Oklahoma City
Oregon (OR)	97,073 (251,419) 10th	3,421,399 28th	Salem
Pennsylvania (PA)	45,333 (117,412) 33d	12,281,054 6th	Harrisburg
Rhode Island (RI)	1,212 (3,139) 50th	1,048,319 43d	Providence
South Carolina (SC)	31,113 (80,583) 40th	4,012,012 26th	Columbia
South Dakota (SD)	77,116 (199,730) 16th	754,844 46th	Pierre

NAME and (abbr.)	AREA[1] sq. mi. (sq. km.) and rank	POPULATION (2000 census) and rank	CAPITAL
Tennessee (TN)	42,144 (109,153) 34th	5,689,283 16th	Nashville
Texas (TX)	266,807 (691,030) 2d	20,851,820 2d	Austin
Utah (UT)	84,899 (219,888) 11th	2,233,169 34th	Salt Lake City
Vermont (VT)	9,609 (24,887) 43d	608,827 49th	Montpelier
Virginia (VA)	40,767 (105,586) 36th	7,078,515 12th	Richmond
Washington (WA)	68,192 (176,617) 20th	5,894,121 15th	Olympia
West Virginia (WV)	24,181 (62,629) 41st	1,808,344 37th	Charleston
Wisconsin (WI)	56,154 (145,439) 26th	5,363,675 18th	Madison
Wyoming (WY)	97,914 (253,597) 9th	493,782 50th	Cheyenne
District of Columbia[3] (DC)	69 (179)	572,059	Washington

Total:
281,421,906

[1] Total land and inland water.
[2] Total land and inland water, does not include 74,364 sq. mi. (192,603 sq. km.) of Great Lakes and other primary bodies of water, of which total the state of Michigan has 38,575 sq. mi. (99,909 sq. km.).
[3] Coextensive with the city of Washington.

Branches of U.S. Government

EXECUTIVE

President, elected (by vote of the Electoral College after a popular vote) for a four-year term; serves as chief executive, head of state, and commander-in-chief of the armed forces; responsible for administering the laws, proposing new legislation to Congress, and for meeting with foreign heads of state and making treaties.

Vice President, elected with the President; serves as a stand-in for the President; presides over the Senate but does not vote as a member except when a tie-breaking vote is needed.

Cabinet, appointed by the President with approval of the Senate; acts as advisors to the President; includes the secretaries of State, the Treasury, Defense, Interior, Agriculture, Commerce, Labor, Health and Human Services, Housing and Urban Development, Transportation, Energy, Education, Veterans Affairs, and the Attorney General.

Principal agencies under authority of the Executive Branch include the Office of Budget and Management, the National Security Council, and the Council of Economic Advisors.

LEGISLATIVE

Congress, made up of the Senate and the House of Representatives, has the power to levy taxes, borrow money, declare war, and regulate commerce between states. Bills must be approved by both houses and signed by the President to become law.

Senate, consists of 100 members (two members elected at large from each state) with each elected for a term of six years; presided over by the Vice President; special responsibility for approving or rejecting Cabinet and Supreme Court appointees and treaties made by the President.

House of Representatives, consists of 435 members (the number of representatives for each state based on population) with each elected for a term of two years; presided over by the Speaker of the House chosen by the majority vote in the House; special responsibility for initiating all bills involving taxation.

Principal agencies under authority of the Legislative Branch include the General Accounting Office, the Government Printing Office, and the Library of Congress.

JUDICIAL

Supreme Court, consists of a Chief Justice and eight Associate Justices, each appointed for life terms after nomination by the President and approval by the Senate; has original jurisdiction for all cases affecting ambassadors to the United States and public ministers (including the President), and all matters between individual states; has responsibility for hearing appeals of cases from the federal and state court system.

Other courts in the federal Judicial Branch include the U.S. Tax Court, the U.S. Court of Customs and Patent Appeals, and the twelve circuit Courts of Appeals.

Presents of the United States

No.	Name	Life Dates	Term Dates
1	George Washington	1732–1799	1789–1797
2	John Adams	1735–1826	1797–1801
3	Thomas Jefferson	1743–1826	1801–1809
4	James Madison	1751–1836	1809–1817
5	James Monroe	1758–1831	1817–1825
6	John Quincy Adams	1767–1848	1825–1829
7	Andrew Jackson	1767–1845	1829–1837
8	Martin Van Buren	1782–1862	1837–1841
9	William Henry Harrison	1773–1841	1841
10	John Tyler	1790–1862	1841–1845
11	James Knox Polk	1795–1849	1845–1849
12	Zachary Taylor	1784–1850	1849–1850
13	Millard Fillmore	1800–1874	1850–1853
14	Franklin Pierce	1804–1869	1853–1857
15	James Buchanan	1791–1868	1857–1861
16	Abraham Lincoln	1809–1865	1861-1865
17	Andrew Johnson	1808–1875	1865–1869
18	Ulysses Simpson Grant	1822–1885	1869-1877
19	Rutherford Birchard Hayes	1822–1893	1877–1881
20	James Abram Garfield	1831–1881	1881
21	Chester Alan Arthur	1830–1886	1881–1885
22	Grover Cleveland	1837–1908	1885-1889
23	Benjamin Harrison	1833–1901	1889–1893
24	Grover Cleveland	1837–1908	1893–1897
25	William McKinley	1843–1901	1897–1901
26	Theodore Roosevelt	1858–1919	1901–1909
27	William Howard Taft	1857–1930	1909–1913
28	Woodrow Wilson	1856–1924	1913–1921
29	William Gamaliel Harding	1865–1923	1921–1923
30	Calvin Coolidge	1872–1933	1923–1929
31	Herbert Clark Hoover	1874–1964	1929–1933
32	Franklin Delano Roosevelt	1882–1945	1933–1945
33	Harry S. Truman	1884–1972	1945–1953
34	Dwight David Eisenhower	1890–1969	1953–1961
35	John Fitzgerald Kennedy	1917–1963	1961–1963
36	Lyndon Baines Johnson	1908–1973	1963–1969
37	Richard Milhous Nixon	1913–1994	1969–1974
38	Gerald Rudolph Ford	1913–	1974–1977
39	Jimmy Carter	1924–	1977–1981
40	Ronald Wilson Reagan	1911–	1981–1989
41	George H. W. Bush	1924–	1989–1993
42	William Jefferson Clinton	1946–	1993–2001
43	George W. Bush	1946–	2001–

Vice Presidents of the United States

No.	Name	Life Dates	Term Dates
1	John Adams	1735–1826	1789–1797
2	Thomas Jefferson	1743–1826	1797–1801
3	Aaron Burr	1756–1836	1801–1805
4	George Clinton	1739–1812	1805–1812
5	Elbridge Gerry	1744–1814	1813–1814
6	Daniel D. Tompkins	1774–1825	1817–1825
7	John C. Calhoun	1782–1850	1825–1832
8	Martin Van Buren	1782–1862	1833–1837
9	Richard M. Johnson	1780–1850	1837–1841
10	John Tyler	1790–1862	1841
11	George M. Dallas	1792–1864	1845–1849
12	Millard Fillmore	1800–1874	1849–1850
13	William R. King	1786–1853	1853
14	John C. Breckinridge	1821–1875	1857–1861
15	Hannibal Hamlin	1809–1891	1861–1865
16	Andrew Johnson	1808–1875	1865
17	Schuyler Colfax	1823–1885	1869–1873
18	Henry Wilson	1812–1875	1873–1875
19	William A. Wheeler	1819–1887	1877–1881
20	Chester A. Arthur	1830–1886	1881
21	Thomas A. Hendricks	1819–1885	1885
22	Levi P. Morton	1824–1920	1889–1893
23	Adlai E. Stevenson	1835–1914	1893–1897
24	Garret A. Hobart	1844–1899	1897–1899
25	Theodore Roosevelt	1858–1919	1901
26	Charles W. Fairbanks	1852–1918	1905–1909
27	James S. Sherman	1855–1912	1909–1912
28	Thomas R. Marshall	1854–1925	1913–1921
29	Calvin Coolidge	1872–1933	1921–1923
30	Charles G. Dawes	1865–1951	1925–1929
31	Charles Curtis	1860–1936	1929–1933
32	John N. Garner	1868–1967	1933–1941
33	Henry A. Wallace	1888–1965	1941–1945
34	Harry S. Truman	1884–1972	1945
35	Alben W. Barkley	1877–1956	1949–1953
36	Richard M. Nixon	1913–1994	1953–1961
37	Lyndon B. Johnson	1908–1973	1961–1963
38	Hubert H. Humphrey	1911–1978	1965–1969
39	Spiro T. Agnew	1918–1996	1969–1973
40	Gerald R. Ford	1913–	1973–1974
41	Nelson A. Rockefeller	1908–1979	1974–1977
42	Walter F. Mondale	1928–	1977–1981
43	George H. W. Bush	1924–	1981–1989
44	James Danforth Quayle	1947–	1989–1993
45	Albert Gore, Jr.	1948–	1993–2001
46	Richard B. Cheney	1941–	2001–

Important Events in U.S. History

1565 · First permanent European settlement in what is now the United States established by the Spanish at St. Augustine (Fla.).

1598 · Spanish begin settlements in what is now New Mexico.

1607 · First permanent English settlement established at Jamestown (Va.).

1620 · Pilgrims land Mayflower and establish a colony at Plymouth (Mass.).

1626 · Dutch establish settlement on what is now Manhattan Island (N.Y.).

1629–36 · Colonies established in Massachusetts, Maryland, Connecticut, and Rhode Island.

1643 · New England Confederation, a union of colonies, is governed by the first written constitution in America.

1660 · Parliament introduces Navigation Acts that restrict the shipment of goods to and from the colonies.

1663 · Carolina colony established.

1664 · Duke of York acquires land between the Connecticut and Delaware rivers, naming it New York; later separates a portion for New Jersey colony.

1679–81 · New Hampshire and Pennsylvania colonies established.

1682 · French from Canada explore Mississippi River, claiming entire valley for France and naming the area Louisiana.

1692–3 · Salem witchcraft trials held in Massachusetts.

1704 · Delaware becomes a colony.

1729 · North and South Carolina become colonies.

1732 · Charter granted for Georgia colony.

1749 · Ohio Company organized for colonizing Ohio River Valley, west of the Appalachian Mountains, challenging French dominance in the area.

1754 · Georgia becomes a royal colony.

1763 · After a seven-year war in Europe, France gives to Great Britain all of Canada and Louisiana east of the Mississippi River.

1764 · Parliament passes Sugar Act to raise money in the colonies to pay off war debt; limits much of colonies' independent trade.

1765 · Parliament passes Stamp Act, which is first direct tax on the colonies.

1767 · Townshend Acts: duties imposed on imports to colonies from Britain; colonies resist by boycotting British goods.

1769 · Spanish begin settlements in California.

1770 · Boston Massacre: several colonists shot in clash with British troops at the Customs House.

1773 · Tea Act gives British East India Company a virtual monopoly on tea sales to colonies; Bostonians rebel with Boston Tea Party.

1774 · First Continental Congress meets in Philadelphia to outline grievances with Britain.

1775 · Parliament declares Massachusetts in rebellion; troops sent to restore order. · Minutemen repel British troops at Concord (Mass.); the clash begins the American Revolution. · Second Continental Congress meets in Philadelphia, and serves as the first federal government. · George Washington assumes command of Continental Army. · Kentucky settlements established.

1776 · Continental Congress adopts Declaration of Independence (on July 4th).

1777 · Continental Congress adopts Articles of Confederation; ratified by the states by 1781. · Continental Congress adopts "Stars and Stripes" as national flag.

1781 · Continental Army, with help from French fleet, defeats British at Yorktown (Va.).

1783 · Revolutionary War ends with Treaty of Paris; America given unlimited independence.

1784 · Russians establish settlements in Alaska.

1787 · Constitutional Convention in Philadelphia drafts a federal Constitution. · Delaware becomes first of the original 13 states to ratify new Constitution.

1789 · George Washington unanimously elected first President.

1789 · Congress submits to the states 12 Amendments to the Constitution for ratification; 10 of the 12 are ratified and become the "Bill of Rights" in 1791.

1790 · First United States census taken.

1791 · Vermont becomes 14th state.

1792 · Kentucky becomes 15th state.

1796 · Tennessee becomes 16th state.

1798 · Mississippi organized as a Territory.

1800 · Washington (D.C.) becomes the seat of government.

1803 · Ohio becomes 17th state. · Louisiana Purchase: President Thomas Jefferson purchases from France all of Louisiana Territory (most of the land between the Mississippi River and Rocky Mountains) for $11,250,000 plus the payment of debts of U.S. citizens to France; U.S. claims western part of Florida as part of purchase.

1804–1806 · Lewis and Clark expedition explores Louisiana Territory.

1805 · Michigan organized as a Territory.

1808 · Congress outlaws African slave trade.

1809 · Illinois organized as a Territory.

1812 · Louisiana becomes 18th state.

1814 · "Star Spangled Banner" written by Francis Scott Key during "War of 1812".

1816 · Indiana becomes 19th state.

1817 · Alabama organized as a Territory. · Mississippi becomes 20th state. · Work begins on Erie Canal, 584 km. waterway from Hudson River (in N.Y.) to Lake Erie.

1818 · Illinois becomes 21st state.

1819 · U.S. purchases eastern part of Florida from Spain for $5,000,000. · Arkansas

organized as a Territory.
· Alabama becomes 22nd state.

1820 · Missouri Compromise: Congressional compromise between the forces for and against slavery to balance the number of free and slave states admitted to the Union. · Maine (a free state) and Missouri (a slave state) become 23rd and 24th states.

1821–80 · Santa Fe Trail, from Missouri to New Mexico, becomes a major route to the Southwest.

1822 · U.S. colony established in Texas (part of Mexico).

1823 · Monroe Doctrine advanced by President James Monroe; sets out policy of discouraging more European colonization of New World.

1830s · Underground Railroad begins and operates for some 30 years as a clandestine route by which fugitive slaves escape from the South.

1836 · Texas declares independence from Mexico after battles, including siege of the Alamo; recognized by U. S. as an independent nation. · Wisconsin organized as a Territory. · Arkansas becomes 25th state.

1837 · Michigan becomes 26th state.

1838 · Trail of Tears: government removes Indians from homelands in Georgia, Tennessee, Arkansas, and Missouri and forces them to march overland to reservations in Oklahoma and Kansas. · Iowa organized as a Territory.

1842–60 · Oregon Trail, a 2000-mile trail from Missouri to Oregon, becomes a major set-

tlement route to the West.

1845 · Florida becomes 27th state. · Texas annexed by U.S. and becomes 28th state.

1846 · Iowa becomes 29th state. · Treaty establishes the northwestern border between U.S. and Canada.

1846–8 · War with Mexico, over annexation of Texas; Treaty of Guadalupe Hidalgo in 1848 gives U.S. rights to New Mexico Territory and California; Mexico gives up all claim to Texas in exchange for $15 million.

1847 · Mormons migrate from Iowa to Utah, arriving at the Great Salt Lake Valley.

1848 · Wisconsin becomes 30th state. · Oregon organized as a Territory. · Gold discovered in California. · Women's Rights Convention in Seneca Falls (N.Y.).

1849 · California gold rush. · Minnesota organized as a Territory.

1850 · Compromise of 1850 between forces for and against slavery, admits California as a free state (31st state), establishes Texas boundaries, establishes New Mexico and Utah as Territories, and abolishes slave trade in District of Columbia.

1853 · Gadsden Purchase: U.S. pays Mexico $10 million for 300,000 square miles, now part of Arizona and New Mexico. · Washington organized as a Territory.

1854 · Kansas and Nebraska organized as Territories. · Chinese immigrants begin arriving in large numbers on the West Coast.

1858 · Minnesota becomes 32nd state.

1859 · Oregon becomes 33rd state. · Abolitionist John Brown attacks government arsenal at Harper's Ferry (Va.); becomes symbol for antislavery cause.

1860 · South Carolina secedes from Union after Abraham Lincoln is elected President. · Pony Express begins overland mail service from Missouri to California.

1861 · Transcontinental telegraph line completed. · Mississippi, Florida, Alabama, Georgia, Louisiana, and Texas secede from Union and with South Carolina form Confederate States of America. · Kansas becomes 34th state. · Civil War begins. Virginia, Arkansas, Tennessee, and North Carolina secede and join Confederacy. · Western counties of Virginia separate from Virginia and form West Virginia, loyal to the Union. · Dakota, Colorado, and Nevada organized as Territories.

1863 · Emancipation Proclamation grants freedom to all slaves in the states joining the Confederacy. · Arizona organized as a Territory. · Battle of Gettysburg; casualties for both sides numbered more than 40,000 in three days; Abraham Lincoln's Gettysburg Address given later at the dedication of a cemetery at the battlefield.

1864 · Montana organized as a Territory. · Nevada becomes 36th state.

1865 · Confederate General Lee surrenders to General Grant, ending Civil War. · President Abraham Lincoln is assassinated. · Thirteenth Amendment ratified, abolishing slavery.

1867 · Reconstruction of the former Confederate states begins. · Nebraska becomes 37th state. · Alaska bought from Russia for $7.2 million.

1868 · Wyoming organized as a Territory and grants women the right to vote. · President Andrew Johnson is impeached and later acquitted in a Senate trial.

1869 · Union Pacific and Central Pacific Railroad lines join at Promontory (Utah), establishing first transcontinental railroad.

1872 · Yellowstone established as first national park.

1876 · Colorado becomes 38th state. · Alexander Graham Bell demonstrates the telephone.

1878 · Congress establishes local government for the District of Columbia.

1879 · Thomas Edison introduces the modern electric lightbulb.

1881 · President James Garfield is assassinated.

1883 · Four standard time zones adopted by U.S. and Canadian railroads.

1886 · Statue of Liberty dedicated.

1889 · North Dakota, South Dakota, Montana, and Washington become 39th, 40th, 41st, and 42nd states. · Johnstown (Pa.) and 4 other towns destroyed by flood after dam breaks. · Oklahoma Land rush.

1890 · Oklahoma organized as a Territory. · Idaho and Wyoming become 43rd and 44th states. · Wounded Knee (S. Dak.): Some 200 Sioux

Indians massacred by U.S. Cavalry forces; this site later becomes a focal point of Native American protests against the government.

1893 · Colorado gives women the right to vote.

1893 · Hawaii Republic established when Queen Liliuokalani is overthrown with American intervention.

1896 · Utah becomes 45th state.

1897 · First subway in North America opens in Boston (Mass.).

1898 · Annexation of Hawaii by U.S. · Spanish-American War: U.S. invades Cuba to ensure Cuban independence from Spain; U.S. declares war on Spain, conquers Puerto Rico, Guam, Philippines; by Treaty of Paris, Spain abandons Cuba, gives Puerto Rico and Guam to U.S.; U.S. gives Spain $20 million for Philippines.

1900 · Orville and Wilbur Wright fly glider at Kitty Hawk (N.C.).

1901 · Oil found in Texas · President William McKinley is assassinated.

1903 · Panama revolts, seeking independence from Colombia; U.S. supports Panama and in treaty gives Panama $10 million plus $250,000 annually for a 10-mile-wide strip for a canal zone. · Orville Wright flies powered airplane.

1904 · Work begins on Panama Canal.

1906 · Earthquake destroys most of San Francisco.

1907 · Oklahoma becomes 46th state.

1908 · Henry Ford introduces the Model T automobile.

1909 · NAACP formed.

1912 · New Mexico and Arizona become 47th and 48th states. · Alaska organized as a Territory.

1913 · Sixteenth Amendment ratified, establishing a federal income tax.

1914 · In treaty, U.S. agrees to give Colombia $25 million compensation for taking Panama; treaty not ratified until 1921. · Panama Canal opens.

1917 · U.S. declares war on Germany and enters World War I. · Puerto Rico established as a U.S. Territory. · U.S. buys Virgin Islands (Danish West Indies) from Denmark for $25 million.

1918 · Daylight saving time goes into effect. · Armistice signed, ending WWI.

1920 · Nineteenth Amendment ratified, giving women the right to vote. · Eighteenth Amendment, prohibition, goes into effect.

1925 · Nellie Tayloe Ross becomes governor of Wyoming—first woman governor. · "Monkey trial": John Scopes convicted of teaching the theory of evolution in Tennessee in defiance of state law. · Demonstration of television.

1926 · Robert Goddard successfully tests a liquid-fuel rocket.

1929 · Stock market crash leads to an economic depression.

1931 · "Star-Spangled Banner" officially made the national anthem.

1933 · Prohibition ends with ratification of the Twenty-first Amendment.

1934 · U.S. grants independence to Cuba.

1935 · Social Security is established. · Philippines begins United States Commonwealth status.

1941 · U.S. enters World War II after Japan attacks Pearl Harbor Naval Base in Hawaii.

1942–45 · Federal government moves more than 100,000 Japanese immigrants and American citizens of Japanese ancestry from the West Coast into inland relocation camps for the duration of the war. · First American jet airplane test flown.

1945 · Germany surrenders. · First use of atomic bombs: Bombs dropped by U.S. on Japanese cities of Hiroshima and Nagasaki. · Japan surrenders.

1946 · Philippines granted independence. · First general-purpose electronic digital computer introduced.

1947 · Marshall Plan: Secretary of State George Marshall proposes a plan by which the U.S. contributes to the economic recovery of European countries after World War II. · Transistor is invented.

1948-49 · U.S. and Britain airlift supplies into West Berlin (East Germany) after the Soviet Union blockades surface transport.

1949 · North Atlantic Treaty Organization (NATO) established.

1950–53 · Korean War: U.S. troops are sent to support South Korea after North Korea invades; fighting ends with an armistice. · Guam becomes a U.S. Territory.

1954 · McCarthy hearings: Senate Permanent Subcommittee on Investigations, chaired by Senator Joseph McCarthy, holds televised hearings after McCarthy makes unsubstantiated charges of Communist activity in the U.S. Army and accuses the Democratic party of treason. · Brown v. Board of Education of Topeka (Kan.): Supreme Court holds that racial segregation violates the Constitution.

1954–9 · St. Lawrence Seaway is constructed.

1956 · Interstate highway system begins.

1958 · U.S. launches first space satellites; begins "space race" with Soviet Union.

1959 · Alaska and Hawaii become 49th and 50th states.

1961 · Astronaut Alan Shepard becomes first American in space.

1962 · Astronaut John Glenn is first American to orbit the earth. · Cuban Missile Crisis: Confrontation between U.S. and Soviet Union over the presence of Soviet nuclear missiles in Cuba.

1963 · President John Kennedy is assassinated.

1965-73 · Vietnam War: U.S. troops become directly involved in fighting between North and South Vietnam.

1967 · Thurgood Marshall becomes first African-American Supreme Court justice.

1968 · Civil Rights leader Rev. Martin Luther King, Jr. and presidential candidate Robert Kennedy (brother of John) are assassinated.

1969 · U.S. mission lands on the Moon; American astronaut Neil Armstrong becomes first person to walk on the Moon.

1970 · Members of Ohio

National Guard fire into a crowd of students protesting the Vietnam War at Kent State University, killing four.

1971 · Twenty-sixth Amendment ratified, giving 18 year olds the right to vote in national elections.

1974 · President Richard Nixon resigns from office after Watergate scandal.

1977 · Treaty (approved by Senate in 1978) gives complete control of Panama Canal to Panama by the year 2000.

1979 · Iranian militants seize the U.S. embassy in Tehran and hold 90 hostages (63 Americans) for more than a year. · Nuclear reactor at Three Mile Island (Pa.) undergoes a partial meltdown.

1981 · Sandra Day O'Connor becomes first woman Supreme Court justice. · Space shuttle *Columbia* completes maiden voyage becoming the first reusable spacecraft.

1986 · Space shuttle *Challenger* explodes after liftoff killing all 7 astronauts aboard, including Christa McAuliffe, a schoolteacher, to be the first private citizen in space.

1991 · Persian Gulf War: U.S. Armed Forces, supported by a coalition of nations, help liberate Kuwait after an earlier invasion by Iraq.

1992 · L.A. Riots: Riots break out in Los Angeles (Calif.) after four white police officers are acquitted of charges of beating a black man.

1993 · Author Toni Morrison becomes the first African-American to win a Nobel Prize.

1995 · A truck bomb explodes outside a federal office building in Oklahoma City (Okla.), killing 168 persons.

1996 · Shannon Lucid sets an American space endurance record by spending 188 days aboard the Mir space station.

1998 · President William Jefferson Clinton becomes the second sitting president to be impeached. He is later acquitted in a Senate trial.

1999 · Two high school students go on a shooting rampage at Columbine High School in Colorado, killing 15 people before killing themselves.

2001 · Four U.S. airliners are hijacked by Islamic militants. Two are flown into the twin towers of the World Trade Center in New York City, one into the Pentagon outside Washington, and one crashes in rural Pa. after passengers try to retake the plane.

PROVINCES AND TERRITORIES OF CANADA

NAME (abbr.)	AREA sq km. (sq. mi.) and rank	POPULATION (2001 census) and rank	CAPITAL
Alberta (AB)	661,190 sq. km. (255,285 sq. mi.) 6th	2,974,807 4th	Edmonton
British Columbia (BC)	947,800 sq. km. (365,946 sq. mi.) 5th	3,907,738 3d	Victoria
Manitoba (MB)	649,950 sq. km. (250,946 sq. mi.) 8th	1,119,583 5th	Winnipeg
New Brunswick (NB)	73,440 sq. km. (28,355 sq. mi.) 11th	729,498 8th	Fredericton
Newfoundland (NF)	405,720 sq. km. (156,648 sq. mi.) 10th	512,930 9th	St. John's
Northwest Territories (NT)	1,432,320 sq. km. (553,019 sq. mi.) 3d	37,360 11th	Yellowknife
Nova Scotia (NS)	55,490 sq. km. (21,425 sq. mi.) 12th	908,007 7th	Halifax
Nunavut* (NU)	1,994,000 sq. km. (769,883 sq. mi.) 1st	26,745 13th	Iqaluit

NAME (abbr.)	AREA sq km. (sq. mi.) and rank	POPULATION (2001 census) and rank	CAPITAL
Ontario (ON)	1,068,580 sq. km. (412,579 sq. mi.) 4th	11,410,046 1st	Toronto
Prince Edward Island (PE)	5,660 sq. km. (2,185 sq. mi.) 13th	135,294 10th	Charlotte-town
Quebec (PQ)	1,540,680 sq. km. (594,857 sq. mi.) 2d	7,237,479 2d	Quebec
Saskatchewan (SK)	652,330 sq. km. (251,864 sq. mi.) 7th	978,933 6th	Regina
Yukon Territory (YT)	483,450 sq. km. (186,660 sq. mi.) 9th	28,674 12th	Whitehorse

* Nunavut became a separate territory in 1999, comprising land that was formerly part of Northwest Territories.

Prime Ministers of Canada

No.	Name	Life Dates	Term Dates
1	John A. Macdonald	1815–1891	1867–1873
2	Alexander Mackenzie	1822–1892	1873–1878
3	John A. Macdonald	1815–1891	1878–1891
4	John J. C. Abbott	1821–1893	1891–1892
5	John S. D. Thompson	1844–1894	1892–1894
6	Mackenzie Bowell	1823–1917	1894–1896
7	Charles Tupper	1821–1915	1896
8	Wilfrid Laurier	1841–1919	1896–1911
9	Robert L. Borden	1854–1937	1911–1920
10	Arthur Meighen	1874–1960	1920–1921
11	W. L. Mackenzie King	1874–1950	1921–1926
12	Arthur Meighen	1874–1960	1926
13	W. L. Mackenzie King	1874–1950	1926–1930
14	Richard B. Bennett	1870–1947	1930–1935
15	W. L. Mackenzie King	1874–1950	1935–1948
16	Louis Stephen St. Laurent	1882–1973	1948–1957
17	John George Diefenbaker	1895–1979	1957–1963
18	Lester B. Pearson	1897–1972	1963–1968
19	Pierre Elliott Trudeau	1919–2000	1968–1979
20	Joe Clark	1939–	1979–1980
21	Pierre Elliott Trudeau	1919–2000	1980–1984
22	John Turner	1929–	1984
23	Brian Mulroney	1939–	1984–1993
24	Kim Campbell	1947–	1993
25	Jean Chrétien	1934–	1993–

Weights and Measures

UNIT (abbreviation)	EQUIVALENTS (in same system)	METRIC EQUIVALENT
WEIGHT		
Avoirdupois		
ton		
short ton	20 short hundred-weight, 2000 lbs	0.907 metric ton
long ton	20 long hundre-weight, 2240 lbs	1.016 metric tons
hundredweight (cwt)		
short cwt	100 pounds	45.359 kilograms
long cwt	112 pounds	50.802 kilograms
pound (lb, #)	16 ounces, 7000 grains	0.454 kilogram
ounce (oz)	16 drams, 437.5 grains	28.350 grams
dram (dr)	27.344 grains	1.772 grams
grain (gr)		0.0648 gram
Troy		
pound (lb t)	12 ounces, 5760 grains	0.373 kilogram
ounce (oz t)	20 pennyweight, 480 grains	31.103 grams
pennyweight (dwt *also* pwt)	24 grains, 0.05 ounce	1.555 grams
grain (gr)		0.0648 gram
Apothecaries'		
pound (lb ap)	12 ounces, 5760 grains	0.373 kilogram
ounce (oz ap *or* ℥)	8 drams, 480 grains	31.103 grams
dram (dr ap *or* ℨ)	3 scruples, 60 grains	3.888 grams
scruple (s ap *or* ℈)	20 grains	1.296 grams
grain (gr)		0.0648 gram

LENGTH

UNIT (abbreviation)	EQUIVALENTS (in same system)	METRIC EQUIVALENT
mile (mi)	5280 feet, 1760 yards	1.609 kilometers
yard (yd)	3 feet, 36 inches	0.9144 meter
foot (ft *or* ′)	12 inches,	30.48 centimeters
inch (in *or* ″)	1/12 foot	2.54 centimeters

CAPACITY

U.S. liquid measure

gallon (gal)	4 quarts (231 cu inches)	3.785 liters
quart (qt)	2 pints (57.75 cu inches)	0.946 liter
pint (pt)	4 gills (28.875 cu inches)	473.176 milliliters
fluid ounce (fl oz)	8 fluid drams (1.805) cu inches)	29.573 milliliters
fluid dram (fl dr)	60 minims (0.226 cu inch)	3.697 milliliters
minim (min *or* ♏)	1/60 fluid dram (0.003760 cu inch)	0.061610 milliliter<

U.S. dry measure

bushel (bu)	4 pecks (2150.42 cu inches)	35.239 liters
peck (pk)	8 quarts (537.605 cu inches)	8.810 liters
quart (qt)	2 pints (67.201 cu inches)	1.101 liters
pint (pt)	1/2 quart (33.600 cu inches)	0.551 liter

Volume

cubic yard (cu yd)	27 cubic feet (46,656 cu inches)	0.765 cu meter
cubic foot (cu ft)	1728 cubic inches	0.028 cu meter
cubic inch (cu in)		16.387 cu centi- meters

AREA

UNIT (abbreviation)	EQUIVALENTS (in same system)	METRIC EQUIVALENT
square mile (sq mi)	640 acres	2.590 sq kilometers
acre	4840 sq yards, 43,560 sq feet	4047 sq meters
square yard (sq yd)	9 sq feet, 1296 sq inches	0.836 sq meter
square foot (sq ft)	144 sq inches	0.093 sq meter
square inch (sq in)		6.452 sq centi- meters

Metric System

LENGTH

UNIT (abbreviation)	METERS	APPROXIMATE U.S. EQUIVALENT
kilometer (km)	1,000 m	0.62 mile
meter (m)	1.0 m	39.37 inches
centimeter (cm)	0.01m	0.39 inch
millimeter (mm)	0.001m	0.039 inch

AREA

UNIT (abbreviation)	SQUARE METERS	APPROXIMATE U.S. EQUIVALENT
square kilometer (sq km)	1,000,000 sq m	0.3861 sq miles
are (a)	100 sq m	119.60 sq yards
square centimeter (sq cm)	0.0001 sq m	0.155 sq inch

VOLUME

UNIT (abbreviation)	CUBIC CENTIMETERS	APPROXIMATE U.S. EQUIVALENT
cubic meter (cu m)	1,000,000 cu cm	1.308 cu yards
cubic centimeter (cu cm)	1 cu cm	0.061 cu inch

CAPACITY

UNIT (abbreviation)	LITERS	APPROXIMATE U.S. EQUIVALENT	
		dry	liquid
kiloliter (kl)	1,000 liters		
liter (l)	1 liter	0.908 quart	1.057 quarts
deciliter (dl)	0.1 liter	0.18 pint	0.21 pint
centiliter (cl)	0.01 liter		0.338 fluid ounce
milliliter (ml)	0.001 liter		0.27 fluid dram

MASS AND WEIGHT

UNIT (abbreviation)	GRAMS	APPROXIMATE U.S. EQUIVALENT
metric ton	1,000,000 g	1.102 short tons
kilogram (kg)	1,000 g	2.2046 pounds
dekagram (dag)	10 g	0.353 oz
gram (g)	1 g	0.035 oz
decigram(dg)	0.1 g	1.543 grains
centigram (cg)	0.01 g	0.154 grain
milligram (mg)	0.001 g	0.015 grain

Roman Numerals

1	I	16	XVI	55	LV	97	XCVII	192	CXCII
2	II	17	XVII	56	LVI	98	XCVIII	199	CXCIX
3	III	18	XVIII	57	LVII	99	XCIX	200	CC
4	IV	19	XIX	58	LVIII	100	C	300	CCC
5	V	20	XX	59	LIX	101	CI	400	CD
6	VI	21	XXI	60	LX	102	CII	500	D
7	VII	22	XXII	61	LXI	etc.		600	DC
8	VIII	etc.		etc.		110	CX	900	CM
9	IX	30	XXX	90	XC	120	CXX	901	CMI
10	X	40	XL	91	XCI	149	CXLIX	etc.	
11	XI	50	L	92	XCII	150	CL	999	CMXCIX
12	XII	51	LI	93	XCIII	151	CLI	1000	M
13	XIII	52	LII	94	XCIV	etc.		1001	MI
14	XIV	53	LIII	95	XCV	190	CXC	1002	MII
15	XV	54	LIV	96	XCVI	191	CXCI	etc.	

Garfield's Daffy Definitions

alarm clock: A device for waking people who don't have kids or pets.

Arbuckle: From the Latin *arbuculus,* "wiener-chested"; a geek; a nerd; a geeky nerd; you get the picture.

bed: Furniture piece designed for that most exciting of all activities—sleep.

bird: A feathered, flying cat snack.

brother: A common household pest; synonymous with "bother."

calories: The best-tasting bits of any food. Take thousands, they're small.

car: An automotive machine that almost any doofus is allowed to operate; but can a cat get a license? Noooooooo!

cat: A highly intelligent and attractive animal of the feline persuasion; nature's most perfect pet.

chocolate: A sweet, highly fattening substance; one of the four basic food groups.

Christmas: December holiday that promotes the spirit of getting; also has some religious significance.

claw: A cat's best friend; a drape's worst nightmare.

diet: Like "die" with a "t"; an eating program that removes excess pounds and your will to live.

dog: A brainless, four-legged flea magnet whose breath could stun a moose.

dream: A fantasy, like no-cal lasagna, or a woman who thinks Jon is cool.

eat: What one does between naps.

exercise: Any completely unnecessary physical activity, such as jogging or rolling over.

fat: Overweight; obese; Santa-waisted; in other words, just right.

french fries: Slivers of potato cooked in hot oil; best when eaten or stuck in your nose.

Halloween: Ancient Celtic celebration of the dead that has evolved quite nicely into an excuse to eat candy until you explode.

homework: Cruel and unusual punishment best suffered in front of the TV.

kitten: A small, cuddly animal used to trick people into buying cats.

lasagna: Nature's most perfect food.

lazy: Indolent, slothful; in extreme cases, comatose.

mailman: One who delivers the mail; see also scratching post.

mouse: Furry, germ-infested, cheese-licking rodent. This is suitable cat cuisine? I don't think so.

morning: The bad end to a good night; would be much better if it started later.

Nermal: The world's cutest kitten; soon to become extinct.

Odie: A type of dog or fungus; it's hard to tell.

parent: An adult keeper of children; not easily understood, but at least they provide snacks and TV.

party: A type of fun assembly guaranteed by the Constitution; see also soiree, wingding, riot.

pet: A domestic animal who provides love and companionship in exchange for blind obedience and twelve square meals a day.

pizza: Delicious tomato and cheese plant that scientists have trained to grow in flat, cardboard boxes. It's true!

Pooky: A huggable "beddy" bear who never says a harsh word . . . or anything else.

school: An educational institution designed to train your brain, assuming they can find it.

sister: An annoying female sibling usually found in the bathroom.

sleep: A state of unconsciousness best experienced in large quantities; also the perfect exercise.

snoring: The loud, irritating breathing of a sleeper; easily remedied with a pair of cymbals.

spider: Web-spinning, eight-legged insect; generally harmless, especially if bludgeoned with a sledgehammer.

teacher: One who instructs; comes in "good," "bad," and "ogre" models.

telephone: A communication device permanently attached to an adolescent's ear.

television: Device that receives mind-numbing video signals; don't grow up without it.

tomorrow: The best time for starting anything unpleasant, like homework or a diet.

veterinarian: A doctor who treats animals, whether they like it or not; synonymous with "needles as long as your arm."

Garfield's Favorite Dictionary

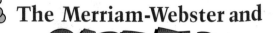

IT'S FUN... AND FUNCTIONAL!

The Merriam-Webster and GARFIELD Mini Dictionary

Merriam-Webster®

- **CLEAR DEFINITIONS HELP YOU COMMUNICATE WELL.**

  Includes more than 65,000 concise meanings that are easy to understand.

- **EXPERT GUIDANCE ON WORD USAGE HELPS YOU CHOOSE YOUR WORDS WISELY.**

  Filled with usage examples within dictionary entries and in Garfield strips.

- **PRACTICAL INFORMATION COMBINED WITH POPULAR COMICS.**

  Garfield and his friends make discovering new words tons of fun!

GARFIELD © PAWS

Merriam-Webster Inc.

Springfield, MA 01102

www.WordCentral.com • www.Merriam-Webster.com

AOL keyword: MERRIAM • www.garfield.com

ISBN 0-87779-922-9